The

WATERLOO
COMPANION

By Mark Adkin

Urgent Fury
The Last Eleven?
Goose Green
The Bear Trap (with Mohammad Yousaf)
The Quiet Operator (with John Simpson)
Prisoner of the Turnip Heads (with George Wright-Nooth)
The Charge
The Sharpe Companion

THE
WATERLOO
COMPANION

Mark Adkin

AURUM PRESS

First published 2001 by
Aurum Press Limited, 25 Bedford Avenue, London WC1B 3AT

Text copyright © 2001 by Mark Adkin

Mark Adkin has asserted his right to be identified as the author of this work under the
Copyright, Designs and Patents Act 1988.

A catalogue record for this book is available from the British Library.

ISBN 1 85410 764 X

Book design by Robert Updegraff

Production management by Geoff Barlow

Plates by Clive Farmer, who also drew the illustrations on
pages 177, 187, 208, 239, 251, 269 and 299 copyright © 2001 by Aurum Press Ltd

Maps and plans copyright © 2001 by Aurum Press Ltd. Produced by GEOprojects (UK) Ltd
(telephone: 0118 939 3567; e-mail: enquiries@geoprojects.demon.co.uk)

Orders of Battle and other diagrams by Robert Updegraff copyright © 2001 by Aurum Press Ltd

Colour photographs by Mark Adkin copyright © 2001 by Mark Adkin

Portraits of Blücher, Bülow, Drouot, Gneisenau, Ney, Reille and Soult by courtesy of Hulton Getty
Picture Library. Illustrations on pages 198, 214 and 216 by Bryan Fosten, reproduced by courtesy of
the artist. Illustrations on pages 235, 237, 260, 261, 266 and 291 reproduced by courtesy of Osprey
Publishing. Illustrations on pages 258 and 318 from *Weapons and Equipment of the Napoleonic Wars* by
Philip Haythornthwaite, published by Blandford Press; the publisher's attempts to trace the owner's of
the copyright of this work were unsuccessful.

3 5 7 9 10 8 6 4

2003 2005 2004

Printed and bound in Singapore by Imago

A note on the cover painting

While this dramatic painting gives an excellent impression of how a British square fought
off massed cavalry assaults in four ranks and of how Anglo-Allied guns were temporarily
abandoned, it cannot be identified with a particular regimental square. It is shown as a
combined square, with highlanders wearing kilts and bonnets along the front face but line
infantry wearing shakos on the left face. The only Highland battalion that formed a mixed
square to see off the cuirassiers was the 2/73 with the 2/30 – but they did not wear kilts.
The kilted regiments were the 42nd, 79th and 92nd, all of which deployed and fought east
of the Brussels–Genappe road. None of these three battalions formed a square with
another unit or faced sustained cuirassier attacks.

Contents

Illustrations of uniforms can be found between pages 208 and 209

ACKNOWLEDGEMENTS

I owe a considerable debt of gratitude to a number of individuals who have assisted and encouraged me during the last two years in my efforts to assemble the huge diversity of information needed to complete this book. First and foremost, I must thank Philip Haythornthwaite, the distinguished military author of a considerable number of books on the Napoleonic period. He is an acknowledged expert in this field and was unfailingly generous in sharing his expertise with me. On countless occasions I telephoned Philip when I was stuck for information, or when I just wanted to discuss an aspect of the battle. Nothing was too much trouble. Invariably, by return of post, he would send me copies of any documents he had on the subject, together with his views on their contents.

At the start of this book my knowledge of the detailed organization of Napoleonic infantry battalions and cavalry regiments, and how they drilled and manoeuvred, was sketchy. John Cook came to my rescue. He was able to consult the relevant eighteenth-century drill manuals and answer all my queries, usually by sending beautifully produced colour diagrams – many thanks for this essential help.

Ken Rowley, a fellow member of the Association of Friends of the Waterloo Committee, made available publications that I had difficulty in obtaining. He also carried out research for me on the battlefield, took photographs and kept me up to date with what was happening on the ground.

Michael Crumplin MB, FRCS, a consultant surgeon and specialist in Napoleonic medical history, very kindly agreed to check the medical aspects of my manuscript and to make appropriate comments. This was most helpful.

No publication or document that I have seen during my research was able to give me the names of the French and Prussian battalion commanders at Waterloo. No English language work that I know of gives the names of officers of these armies below regimental commander. Therefore, I am particularly pleased that the *Companion* provides this information (probably for the first time) in the 'Orders of Battle' section. With the French battalion commanders this is due to the efficient and helpful response I received from General A. Bach, Head of the Historical Branch of the French Army at Vincennes. He was able to supply a complete list – despite my writing to him in French! The names of almost all the Prussian commanders were supplied by Oliver Schmidt who, residing in Germany, had access to the relevant nineteenth-century publications that were impossible for me to consult. He went to considerable length to extract the information I needed and I am most grateful for his efforts.

My final thanks must go to Alastair White, who resides in Belgium, quite close to the battlefield. He has a comprehensive knowledge of the ground and was kind enough to smooth the way for my week's visit to the battlefield in 1997. He showed considerable kindness in delivering me to, and collecting me from, the battlefield every day. He also went out of his way to explain events and relate them to the ground. His assistance was invaluable.

INTRODUCTION

WATERLOO WAS FOUGHT almost two hundred years ago to bring about the end to what was arguably the first true World War. For twenty years men from every nation in continental Europe had marched and fought, from Copenhagen in the north to Cadiz and Cairo in the south. Not even tiny, mountainous Switzerland, now so renowned for its neutrality, could avoid the bloodshed. French invaders and their allies had reached Moscow. Had it not been for the British naval victory at Trafalgar in 1805, England would have been attacked by the huge invasion force camped on the coast across the Channel. During these momentous years Britain's soldiers fought on the subcontinent of India, captured Java (the seat of Dutch power in the Far East), and battled to wrest today's Caribbean tourist islands, such as St Lucia, St Kitts and Guadeloupe, from French control. In 1812 Britain was also at war with America. In Europe British troops battled in Holland, Denmark, Italy, Sicily, Spain and Portugal (as well as Egypt), before the final confrontation at Waterloo on 18 June 1815.

Navies too played a critical role (for Britain, the key role) in the Napoleonic Wars. The Royal Navy, after Trafalgar, literally did 'rule the waves'. Her warships blockaded French-controlled Europe, escorted convoys, transported troops, and patrolled the Mediterranean, the Atlantic, the North Sea and the Channel. In addition, her guns opened fire in the West Indies and along the eastern seaboard of America.

Waterloo finally put an end to all this. For nine hours on an unseasonably wet and overcast Sunday in June, 200,000 men with 537 guns fought one of the most intense, bitter battles in military history. The two foremost generals of the age – indeed of any age – faced each other for the first time. The Emperor Napoleon, the artilleryman, the man who had won his empire by taking the offensive, was to attack the Duke of Wellington, the infantryman, who had gained so many of his victories defending a position. At the end of the day some 54,000 men lay dead, dying or injured within an area of only six square kilometres. Put another way, if the casualties had been equally spread there would have been a dead or wounded soldier in every ten square metres of the battlefield. Compare this with the opening day of the Battle of the Somme on 1 July 1916 (almost exactly 100 years later). There eleven British divisions attacked over a 20-kilometre front, sustaining 60,000 casualties – an appalling price but lacking the gory, gruesome concentration of death and disablement that the Waterloo battlefield presented.

Waterloo has been the irresistible subject of hundreds of authors for almost two centuries. Countless books in English, French and German are stacked on thousands of personal bookcases and library shelves. They continue to be published. Arguments as to why the French lost, who was to blame, could they have won, what happened, proliferate. Many questions can never be answered, even with the benefit of hindsight. Societies and re-enactment groups devoted to the study of the battle exist across Europe and the United States. The editor of the ever-popular *Waterloo Journal* is an Australian living in Victoria. So why another book?

As anyone who picks up this publication will quickly discover, it is not another rehash of the battle. It is a 'companion' to the battle. A companion is a friend, a helper, an associate – someone who accompanies you, who shares your interest, explains, guides and comments. *The Waterloo Companion* is such a book. It is does not provide a blow by blow account of the action but rather looks at ten different aspects of the battle in considerable detail with the aid of maps, uniform plates, photographs, panoramic views of the ground and numerous diagrams – virtually all in colour. It is a unique, comprehensive gathering together of information on Waterloo that can be dipped into for facts, comments or accounts of the experiences of soldiers of all three armies – or read from start to finish.

There are separate sections on the campaign, orders of battle, command and control, the battlefield today, the infantry, the cavalry, the artillery, other arms and services, the highlights of the battle, and some of the myths and controversies that have arisen over the intervening years. Every section has a number of 'boxes' containing additional interesting facts, figures or anecdotal information to enhance and enliven the main text. Further comment on the way the *Companion* has been compiled and some of these sections may be helpful.

Text and 'boxes'

The text is not always primarily descriptive. A deliberate emphasis has been placed on assessing and commenting on decisions, plans, actions and events. These comments are, of course, mine, but they are made after a careful study of the evidence, by trying to view the situation without using the benefit of hindsight, an examination of the ground itself and by using my own experience as a soldier. The 'boxes' take up about a third of the text. They are there to provide additional interesting information. Many of them are anecdotal and contain the comments of soldiers who fought at Waterloo. Hopefully, they add flavour to the main meal.

Maps

No battle can be fully understood without the aid of detailed maps. The *Companion* has over forty – all in full colour. Use has been made of modern maps to show the contours on which the topographical detail of 1815 has been superimposed. These details (roads, tracks, buildings, woods, orchards and hedges) have been taken from the map drawn up by the Dutch surveyor W.B. Craan in 1816. This is generally acknowledged to be the most topographically accurate map of the battlefield ever produced; its only failing was the lack of proper contour lines. While it is impossible to position every unit or to show all movements with complete certainty, considerable effort has been made with troop dispositions to depict events as accurately as possible. Unit symbols, at least with regard to their frontage, cover approximately the same ground as they did in reality. The symbols are roughly proportional in size to the units they represent. This helps to give a reasonable approximation to a bird's-eye view of events.

The deployment of Wellington's and Napoleon's armies at the outset of the battle have also been shown on a modern map to facilitate the orientation of today's visitor.

Photographs

There are a substantial number of coloured photographs of the present battlefield. The great majority were taken by me in the course of a fascinating week spent walking the ground. They include views of all the locations where important events took place, together with most of the memorials that have been erected to commemorate a particular action or person. I believe the panoramic shots, which have some of the troops' dispositions superimposed on them, are of special value in helping both readers and visitors understand what happened and, crucially, where it happened. A number were taken from the summit of the Lion Mound – which is an essential viewpoint (if you have the energy) for those wishing to get a quick overview of the battle or, indeed, for those about to embark on a more adventurous exploration.

Orders of Battle

A problem that defies a really accurate solution is that of numbers, not only of troops present, but of casualties – this is particularly so of French losses during the actual battle. It is, however, possible to make informed estimates. In the *Companion* the main sources used have been Scott Bowden's *Armies at Waterloo* supplemented by Lieutenant-Colonel John Waters' *The Morning State* and W. Siborne's *History of the Waterloo Campaign*. Needless to say, they cannot always be reconciled. A factor that few historians have taken into account is that a number of soldiers who are recorded as sick or wounded on parade states were actually present at a battle (this is usual for any battle of any age). Undoubtedly, men of all three armies who were lightly wounded at Ligny or Quatre-Bras had their wound roughly dressed and were sent to fight again at Waterloo. I have taken this into account so the numbers present, particularly in the Anglo-Allied and French armies, are slightly larger than in some other accounts. The orders of battle themselves take the form of diagrams for ease of reference.

A word of explanation on the French ranks is necessary. The French words for their ranks have been used, most of which present no difficulty in translating. Those that do, include a 'Maréchal de Camp' (a royalist rank that continued to be used during the Waterloo campaign) who acted as a brigade commander. A 'Chef de Bataillon' commanded an infantry battalion and was equivalent to a major in other armies. A French major was one rank higher. Majors in Napoleon's army either commanded Imperial Guard battalions or were staff officers. Other differences are explained in the text.

Command and Control

As its title implies, this section sets out how each army was commanded, although most of it is devoted to detailed biographical notes and comments on all divisional commanders and above. As such, it is primarily a reference section.

The Battlefield

With the aid of maps and numerous recent photographs, this section examines the tactical features of the ground over which the armies fought. The advantages and disadvantages that particular features presented are discussed and commented on from the point of view of both attackers and defenders. The deployment of the Anglo-Allied and French armies is shown down to battalion/squadron/battery level. About half of the section is devoted to describing the numerous memorials scattered over the field and in various buildings. They are all marked on a special modern map.

Infantry, cavalry, artillery, other arms and services

These four sections discuss the organization, weapons, drills and tactics used by all arms of each army at Waterloo. Emphasis is placed on analysis of statistics and detailed comparisons between the armies. This includes a close look at casualties, together with some hitherto neglected aspects of the battle, such as the composition, ammunition expenditure and effectiveness of the French 'Grand Battery'. Only a brief mention is made of uniforms. Readers who have a particular interest in this aspect of the subject are referred to the magnificent colour uniform plates by Clive Farmer.

Highlights of the battle

Rather than attempt to write yet another account of the battle, six highlights have been selected for close study. These highlights are: the struggle for Hougoumont; d'Erlon's I Corps attack and Wellington's response; the French massed cavalry attacks; the struggle for La Haie Sainte; the struggle for Plancenoit and the Imperial Guard's final assault. All are assessed and commented on in depth with the aid of maps and panoramic photographs.

Myths and Controversies

There is no aspect of Waterloo that has not thrown up argument and controversy. They must number in the hundreds. Most will never be definitively resolved. Many concern the question 'what if?' What if the Prussians had not arrived? What if Napoleon had attacked one of Wellington's flanks? What if Hougoumont had been ignored by Napoleon? What if the battle had started earlier? What if Ney had not frittered away the French cavalry? The list is endless. In this section three myths and ten controversies have been selected at random for a close inspection. They are commented on, the arguments and counter-arguments discussed, after which I have ventured to put forward some tentative, personal conclusions on each.

ABBREVIATIONS AND SYMBOLS

(-)	Under strength formation/unit	Capt.	Captain	Engr.	Engineer	m	Metres
(k)	Killed	Car	Carabineer	Fus	Fusiliers	Maj.	Major
(mw)	Mortally wounded	Cav.	Cavalry	FA	Foot Artillery	Maj-Gen.	Major-General
(w&c)	Wounded and captured	Ch. à C	Châsseurs à Cheval	Fd	Field	Mil.	Militia
(w)	Wounded	Chas.	Châsseurs	F-M	Field Marshal	N	Nassau/Napoleon
2/C	2nd (Coldstream) Guards	CO	Commanding Officer	G de D	Général de Division	NCO	Non-commissioned officer
2IC	Second-in-command	Co.	Column	Gen. d'Elite	Gendarmerie d'Elite	Neth.	Netherlands
AAG	Assistant Adjutant General	Col	Colonel	Gen.	General	Neu.	Neumärk
ACG	Assistant-Commissary-General	Comd.	Commander	GOC	General Officer Commanding	O/Nassau	Orange/Nassau
		Comdt	Commandant			Old Gd	Old Guard
ADC	Aide de Camp	Cont	Contingent	Gren. à C	Grenadiers à Cheval	Pdrs	Pounders
Adjt	Adjutant	COS	Chief of Staff	Gren. Or G	Grenadiers	Pol.	Polish
Adjt-Comdt	Adjutant-Commandant	Coy	Company	H	Hussars	Pom.	Pomeranian
Admin.	Administrative/Administration	CRA	Commander Royal Artillery	HA	Horse Artillery	Q. Bras	Quatre-Bras
				Han.	Hanoverian	QMG	Quartermaster General
AG	Adjutant General	CRHA	Commander Royal Horse Artillery	Hosp.	Hospital	RA	Royal Artillery
Ammo.	Ammunition			How.	Howitzers	RAP	Regimental Aid Post
approx.	Approximate	Cuir.	Cuirassier	HQ	Headquarters	RE	Royal Engineers
AQMG	Assistant Quartermaster General	Cum.	Cumberland	Hy	Heavy	Regt	Regiment
		D	Dragoons	Imp. Gd(s)	Imperial Guards	Res.	Reserve
Arty	Artillery	DAAG	Deputy Assistant Adjutant General	Inf.	Infantry	RFA	Royal Foot Artillery
Asst	Assistant			KGL	King's German Legion	RHA	Royal Horse Artillery
Att.	Attached	DACG	Deputy-Assistant-Commissary-General	L of C	Line of Communication	RHG	Royal Horse Guards
Bde	Brigade			L	Lancers	RSM	Regimental Sergeant Major
BM	Brigade Major	DAG	Deputy Adjutant General	LD	Light Dragoons	Sgt(s)	Sergeants
Bn	Battalions	DAQMG	Deputy Assistant Quartermaster General	Ldr	Landwehr	Sgt-Maj.	Sergeant-Major
Br.	British			Leg.	Légère (Light)	Sil.	Silesian
Brig.	Brigadier	DCG	Deputy-Commissary-General	LG	Life Guards	Sous-Lieut	Sous-Lieutenant
Brun.	Brunswick			Lieut	Lieutenant	Sqn	Squadron
Bty	Battery	Det	Detachment	Lt	Light	T	Tirailleurs
C de B	Chef de Bataillon	DG	Dragoon Guards	Lt-Col	Lieutenant-Colonel	Tp	Troop
C in C	Commander-in-Chief	Div.	Division	Lt-Gen.	Lieutenant-General	U	Uhlans
C. Gds	Coldstream Guards	DQMG	Deputy Quartermaster General	M de C	Maréchal de Camp	V	Voltigeurs
				M de L	Maréchal de Logis	West.	Westphalian
		E. Ldr	Elbe Landwehr	M de LC	Maréchal de Logis Chef	Y Gd	Young Guard

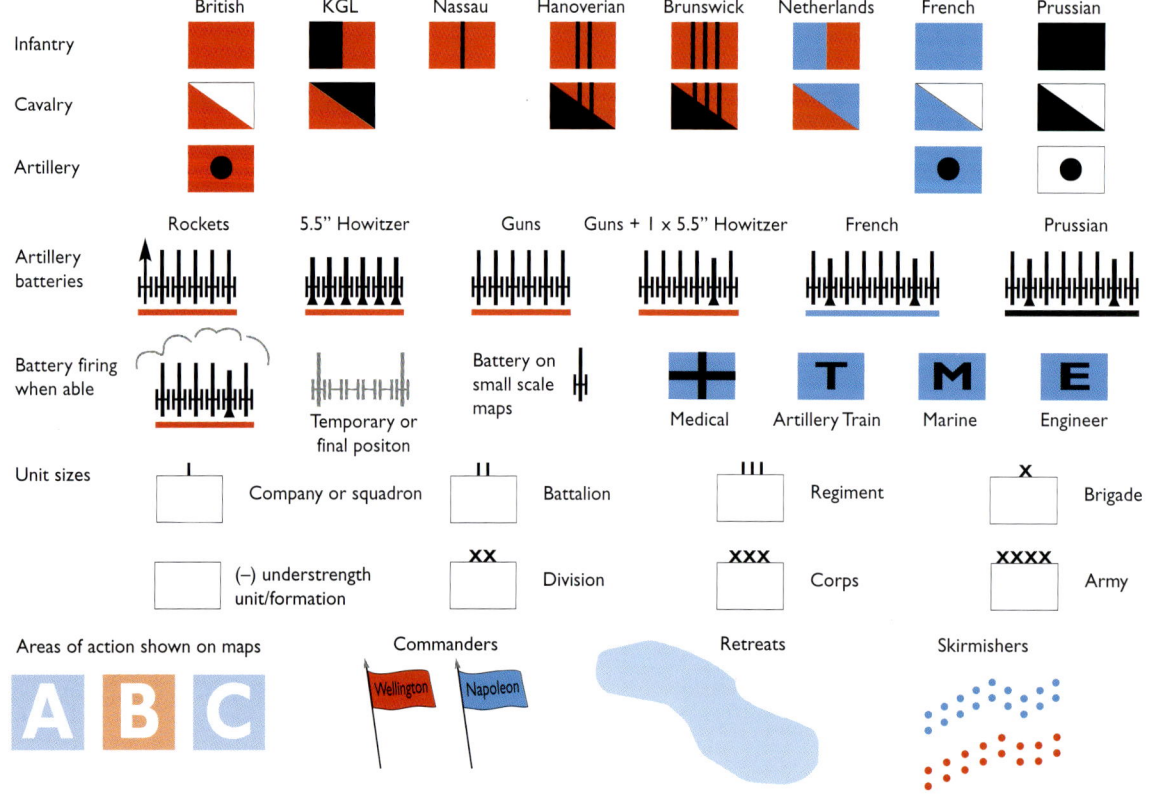

Prologue

THE EAGLE'S RETURN

*'Victory will advance at the charge; the eagle, with the national colours,
will fly from steeple to steeple all the way to the towers of Notre Dame...'*

Napoleon's proclamation, 9 March 1815.

SHORTLY BEFORE MIDDAY on 29 April 1815, artillerymen paraded on the walls of all the main fortresses in France. As noon approached the gunnery officers stared at their watches. Precisely on the hour, at the shout of '*Tirez!*' non-commissioned officers (NCOs) touched the vents with glowing port-fires. From Brest overlooking the Atlantic, eastward to Belfort guarding the gap between the Jura and the Vosges mountains; from Lille on the Belgian border, southward to Toulon on the Mediterranean coast, the cannons crashed out. The officers carefully counted each shot. The steady thump of the guns rolled across towns, villages, farms and fields. At about two shots a minute, the 100-gun salute seemed to last an eternity. It announced, unmistakably, that imperial authority had been re-established everywhere.

For ten months Napoleon had been Emperor of Elba. It was hardly a rewarding experience for a man whose recent mainland empire had exceeded that of the Romans. For a general with some fifty battlefield victories to his credit, and whose military conquests at their height rivalled those of Alexander the Great and Genghis Khan, ten months on an island of 140 square miles with 12,000 inhabitants was an insufferable humiliation. The flight of the eagle to Notre Dame began on Sunday 26 February, on a calm, moonlit evening in the tiny capital, Portoferraio.

Napoleon was the last to board the 300-ton 16-gun (18 pounders) brigantine *Inconstant* under the command of Captain Chautard that was to take him the 190 kilometres to France. Apart from the brig, the tiny flotilla consisted of four other small vessels – *Etoile, Caroline, Saint-Joseph, Saint-Esprit* – plus two feluccas, the *Bee* and the *Fly*. Crammed into the larger ships was one of the smallest invasion forces in history. About 1,100 men, mostly devoted grenadiers of the Imperial Guard (who had formed the Napoleon Battalion), plus a handful of lancers, some artillerymen with two cannons, three generals (Bertrand, Cambronne and Drouot), a treasure chest stuffed with gold coins, and a small carriage, constituted the instrument with which the Emperor intended to win back his throne.

The date selected for the venture was 26 February, as Colonel Sir Neil Campbell, the British officer who had escorted Napoleon to Elba and been invited to stay on by the Emperor, was away visiting Florence in the British brigantine HMS *Partridge*. As soon as he had left on February 16, Napoleon had given orders for his tiny fleet and even smaller 'army' to prepare – which included having the *Inconstant* painted to resemble a British ship. All was almost ruined when the *Partridge* returned unexpectedly, having dropped Campbell in Florence. A frantic scramble got the *Inconstant* to sea and out of sight. Captain Adye on the *Partridge* noticed nothing untoward, so within a day sailed back to pick up Colonel Campbell.

The entire populace of the tiny port had assembled on the quayside to see Napoleon go. His soldiers had sung the 'Marseillaise' when he arrived in the small pony trap that had belonged to his sister Pauline, wearing his legendary grey overcoat and black cocked hat. However, for several hours after he had clambered aboard, the whole enterprise faltered – there was no wind. Not until midnight did a light breeze fill the sails sufficiently for the flotilla to glide slowly, very slowly, out to sea. A solemn silence enveloped the lantern swinging well-wishers ashore. It was not an encouraging start, particularly as most of the watchers knew Campbell was preparing to sail that same day only 80 kilometres away at Livorno.

By dawn they were still in sight of Elba. It took all of Monday for the sails to finally slip over the horizon. The short journey to France was eventually to take over sixty hours instead of the anticipated fifteen. Two islands, Capraia and Gorgona, guarded the 65-kilometre channel between northern Corsica and the Italian mainland. The French royalist government had despatched two frigates, the *Fleur de Lys* and the *Melpomène*, whose duty it was to patrol the channels between Corsica and these small islands. Throughout most of Monday, in clear weather, all onboard the

The Elba Generals

In keeping with his officially recognized authority over his miniature kingdom, Napoleon was permitted some of the trappings of power on the island. These included the services of three senior generals who had particularly strong bonds with their Emperor. First, Général de Division Comte Henri Bertrand (1773–1847), who was an engineer by training and a longstanding imperial aid. Although immensely loyal, he had limitations as a senior commander. His great success in the field was the construction of the pontoon bridges across the Danube in front of Aspern-Essling during the Austrian campaign in 1809. Realizing he was out of his depth as a corps commander, in Germany in 1813 Napoleon appointed him Grand Master of the Palace. It was in this capacity that he accompanied the Emperor to Elba. He was present at Waterloo and was at Napoleon's bedside when he died on St Helena in 1821, having remained with him throughout his exile.

Second, Général de Division Comte Antoine Drouot (1774–1847), who was an artillerymen first and imperial aide second. Unique among Napoleon's generals, he had fought as a major with the French troops serving as marines onboard the *Indomitable* during the Battle of Trafalgar in 1805 – thus becoming probably the only French senior officer to have fought at both Trafalgar and Waterloo. He was a man of considerable courage, integrity and endurance who acquired the nickname 'Sage de la Grande Armée'. During the appalling conditions of the retreat from Moscow it was said that he was the only man in the army to shave in the open daily with a mirror propped up on a gun carriage. A bachelor, who limped as a result of a foot wound (his only injury) received at Wagram, he had been fighting almost continuously since 1793. In 1814 he renounced his French citizenship and insisted on accompanying Napoleon to Elba as a private citizen. With reluctance he was persuaded to become governor of the island – he wanted to devote himself to reflection and the study of theology and philosophy. At Waterloo

he was both chief of staff to, and acting commander of, the Imperial Guard. He successfully defended himself at his court martial in 1816 and finally retired from the Army in 1825. He devoted many years to improving the lot of former Imperial guardsmen. Highly regarded as a fine, honest soldier and gentleman, he died, blind, in 1847.

Third, Maréchal de Camp Vicomte Pierre Cambronne (1770–1842). A tough, hard swearing, brash and outspoken soldier who had been almost continuously under fire since 1792. He had been wounded so many times that his body was said to be tattooed with scars. Like his two fellow generals, he had originally enlisted as a private soldier. As a lieutenant he had sworn at and accused a senior officer of cowardice – for which he was almost court-martialled. For two years he fought in the vicious guerrilla war in Spain. He was in action at Austerlitz, Aspern-Essling, Wagram, Lutzen, Dresden, Leipzig, Hanau, Craonne and the defence of Paris. Selected as an outstanding regimental officer, he joined the Imperial Guard Tirailleur Châsseur Regiments on their formation in early 1809. On Elba he was the island's military commander and responsible for law and order. He led the vanguard of Napoleon's march from Antibes to Paris where he refused promotion to général de division as it would mean leaving his troops. Instead he was made colonel-major of the 1st Châsseurs à Pied of the Imperial Guard. He fought at Ligny. At Waterloo his battalions, formed in square, helped protect the Emperor and cover the retreat at the end of the battle. He was wounded by a ball in the forehead and taken prisoner (see Section 10 'Myths and Controversies'). He later faced a court martial, but was acquitted due to the brilliance of his lawyer, thus remaining in the army to become, to most observers' amazement, as staunch a monarchist as he had been a rabid Bonapartist. Like Drouot, in retirement, he devoted much time to the welfare of his Old Guard comrades.

Inconstant could see the *Melpomène*, and presumably vice versa. But from the royalist ship there was no reaction – perhaps her captain's loyalty to the King was not as strong as had been supposed. It is also highly unlikely that the *Fleur de Lys* failed to spot this suspect fleet sailing slowly north-west towards France. Even the log of the *Partridge*, timed 11.00 a.m. on 27 February, noted sighting 'three sail' to the south-west – but no alarm was raised.

At about 6.00 p.m., off the northern tip of Corsica (Napoleon's birthplace), there was real concern as another armed French ship approached – the *Zephyr*, under Captain Andrieux. Orders were given to fight if necessary; but the grenadiers removed their bearskins and lay on the decks while the captains shouted at each other through trumpets. 'How is the Great Man?' enquired an obviously sympathetic Andrieux. 'Extraordinarily well', replied Chautard, adding that they were bound for Genoa. It was

Napoleon Escapes from Elba 26 February to 1 March 1815 — Map 1

Key

1 'Inconstant' with Napoleon onboard sails with his small flotilla very late on 26 February (Sunday).

2 11.00 a.m. 27th HMS 'Partridge' with Campbell on board sights three sails to SW.

3 Both 'Melpoméne' and 'Fleur de Lys' sight 'Inconstant' during 27th but do nothing.

4 The captains of the 'Zephyr' and 'Inconstant' hail each other about 6.00 p.m. on 27th.

5 The 'Partridge', having discovered Napoleon's escape, gives chase on 28th and meets the 'Fleur de Lys' whose captain denies seeing the 'Inconstant'.

6 The Royal Artillery rocket demonstration is delayed while the tiny flotilla sails through the target area at about noon on 28th.

7 About 1.00 p.m. on 1 March 'Inconstant' anchors off Golfe Juan.

enough. Again, it is hard to conceive that Andrieux had no inkling of what was going on. Whatever the truth, Napoleon made sure he was promoted a few weeks later.

Meanwhile Campbell had arrived back at Portoferraio. He had to be rowed ashore, as the *Partridge* was becalmed a mile or so outside the harbour. Within minutes of arrival Campbell was told the 'eagle' had flown. The embarrassed colonel was hastily rowed back out to his ship and set off, frustratingly slowly, in pursuit. Early on 28 February he closed with the *Fleur de Lys*, from whose deck a flustered Captain Garat claimed to have seen nothing due to poor visibility – an obvious lie. At that moment the Emperor was 88 kilometres away, sailing south-west along the Riviera coast.

Even then the whole enterprise still came within a whisker of discovery as the flotilla sailed passed Cap Noli at about midday on 28 February. By an incredible coincidence, it was at that moment that ashore the British Royal Artillery was about to start a live firing demonstration of artillery rockets, recently invented by Sir William Congreve. They were to be fired out to sea, watched by the King of Sardinia together with a large gaggle of courtiers and ladies. Shortly before launching the first salvo, the officer in charge spotted the group of small ships sailing sedately through the target area. Firing was postponed while the King and his court had a picnic lunch. Napoleon, whose symbols on the standards of his Elba units were golden bees, would have been amused to know that the picnic ashore was plagued by numerous hostile wasps.

Not until early afternoon on 1 March did the little ships drop anchor off Golfe Juan, about two kilometres from the small town of Antibes. Captain Lamouret (who was to fight with the 2nd Battalion of the Châsseurs à Pied of the Imperial Guard at Waterloo) was the first ashore, accompanied by twenty grenadiers. He was greeted by a customs official who thrust health

The Elba Garrison

Commander-in-Chief – Napoleon • *Garrison commander* – Maréchal de Camp Cambronne

Units Brought to the Island with Napoleon

INFANTRY – The Napoleon Battalion under Major Malet (as a maréchal de camp he commanded the 3rd Regiment of Châsseurs à Pied at Waterloo) – 607 veteran grenadiers and châsseurs à pied of the former Imperial Guard in six companies. Its standard was a white flag with, on one side, a crowned red 'N', and on the other a red diagonal stripe embroidered with three gold bees.

CAVALRY – A squadron of Polish Lancers under Chef d'Escadron Jerzmanowski and Major Roul – 125 men divided into a mounted company of twenty-two under Capitaine Schultz (a giant of over 2.13 metres who was present at Waterloo); a dismounted company of ninety-six under Capitaine Balinski (who also fought at Waterloo as a major commanding a squadron). There was also a group of seven châsseurs and mamelukes commanded by Lieutenant Seraphin (a mameluke officer attached to the châsseurs à cheval at Waterloo). The lancers had a white standard emblazoned in crimson with the words, 'Polish Light-Horse, Napoleon Squadron' with a crowned 'N' on the reverse.

ARTILLERY – 100 gunners under Capitaines Cornuel and Raoul.

MARINES – Twenty-one marines under Adjutant-Chef Benigni, who were attached to the Elban Navy commanded by the captain of the 18-gun brig *Inconstant*, Lieutenant Taillade.

Existing Garrison and Locally Raised Units

INFANTRY
* The 35th Légère Regiment.
* A battalion of the Italian Colonial Regiment.
* A three company Corsican Châsseur Battalion, raised by Napoleon.
* A battalion of Corsican militia, raised by Napoleon.
* Twenty-five engineers who were employed as the local fire brigade.
  In all, around 2,500 troops, the locally raised units of questionable military value, were stationed on Elba during Napoleon's sojourn there.

regulations in his face. 'But it's the Emperor!' said Lamouret. 'He can issue permits…'. Sentries were posted on the roads while the captain with a dozen soldiers marched to the local fort at Antibes. They were allowed in but the gates were slammed behind them. Confronting them was the fully armed garrison under Colonel Cuneo d'Ornano. Scuffles broke out, the grenadiers were disarmed and Lamouret temporarily arrested – he escaped by jumping off the wall, although he broke his leg in the process. It was not a promising start. Napoleon, however, did not hold this incident against d'Ornano as he later approved his promotion to general. Shortly afterwards, he was shot through the lungs by General Bonnet in a duel, after being accused of prejudicing the Emperor against Bonnet.

Meanwhile, throughout the afternoon the rest of the troops, the handful of horses, the guns and the treasure chest under the watchful supervision of the Emperor's faithful paymaster, Inspector Peyrusse, were offloaded. It was early evening before Napoleon was rowed from the *Inconstant*. Marines standing waist deep in the water held a gangplank steady as he stepped ashore. He rejected a commandeered cottage as too smoky, electing instead to have his bed and campaign chair set up under some olive trees. He slept for a few hours. The spot was close to Cannes, near a fishermen's church appropriately named Notre Dame du Bon Voyage. It is now the sacristy of the modern church at the western end of La Croisette – Cannes' seafront. The scenery familiar to Napoleon has long since been engulfed by the town's expansion, although there is a street named the Rue de Bivouac to remind the visitor that France's most famous son encamped nearby.

Confronted by over a thousand troops, the fort commander at Antibes capitulated, releasing the imprisoned soldiers. At 5.00 a.m. on 2 March, the Mayor of Cannes was persuaded to bring 1,700 rations of bread and meat to enliven the grenadiers' soup. By then Napoleon had gone, preceded by fifty grenadiers under the personal command of Maréchal de Camp Pierre Cambronne. He was heading north-west over 225 kilometres of rough tracks across the southern tip of the Alps, for a town called Grenoble. It contained among its garrison the La Fère Artillery Regiment, into which the young Napoleon had been commissioned thirty years before. The Emperor's orders were short and simple: 'Cambronne, you will go ahead, always ahead, but remember, I forbid you to shed one drop of French blood in the recovery of my crown.' Trudging behind came the remainder of the column, swollen slightly by some soldiers of the Antibes garrison, a staff captain, a lieutenant and three half-pay officers of the 11th Cuirassiers. These additional men became the nucleus of the so-called

The Emperor's Return: Napoleon's Route from Elba to Paris, 26 February to 20 March 1815   **Map 2**

Louis XVIII's flight from Paris on 19 March. In Ghent his gluttony, which often brought him out in a sweat, became well known prompting yet another derogatory nickname - 'Louis di zweet' (Louis who sweats) which is pronounced much like 'Louis dix-huit'.

20 March
Napoleon, with an army of two divisions, arrives in triumph at the Tuileries.

17 March
Napoleon arrives at Auxerre and is joined by Ney.

10–13 March
Napoleon in Lyon. Comte d'Artois and Maréchal Macdonald flee and more troops defect. The 100-day clock starts as Napoleon issues Imperial Decrees.

6 March
Major Lansard's battalion of 5th Ligne meets Napoleon's vanguard at La Mure, then retires to Laffrey.

5 March
King Louis is informed of landing. Ney ordered south to stop Napoleon. Ordinance is published declaring Napoleon a traitor. Napoleon reaches Gap.

4 March
Napoleon arrives in Digne.

11 March
Ney announces he is joining Napoleon.

10 March
Ney arrives at Besançon and receives Napoleon's letter requesting that he rejoin the Emperor.

7 March
Napoleon confronts Lansard's battalion at Laffrey. Troops refuse to fire and go over to the Emperor. That evening Colonel de la Bédoyère defects to Napoleon with 7th Ligne. Congress of Vienna is informed of Napoleon's escape.

3 March
More rations, wine and mules are supplied at Castellane. Guns are abandoned en route.

1 March
Napoleon arrives at Golfe Juan – rations supplied by Cannes.

26 February
Napoleon leaves Elba with 1,100 men on the brig 'Inconstant'.

Napoleon's Orderlies

Napoleon had always had two personal orderlies throughout most of his campaigns. The first deserted him in 1814, but the second went with him to Elba. The one who eventually abandoned his master was Raza Roustam, a mameluke and former slave, who was given to Napoleon – together with a black stallion – by Sheik El Bekri of Egypt in 1799. Thereafter he became his personal bodyguard and valet, always dressed in his exotic mameluke robes. In the field Roustam carried a flask of brandy, the Emperor's cloak and spare coat in a bundle across his saddle. He made a fortune selling favours, deserted Napoleon before his first abdication, and in later years ran a state lottery, wrote some colourful memoirs and lived, for a time, in London. He died in 1845. The other, more faithful follower was Napoleon's second valet de chambre Louis Saint-Denis who carried in his saddlebag his master's pens, pencils, paper, ink, sealing wax, dividers and telescope. He joined the Emperor's service at the age of eighteen as an under-groom. He accompanied Napoleon to Spain, Germany and Holland, after which he was promoted to 2nd Mameluke (under Roustam) and given the name Ali. He was at Napoleon's side in Russia, at Ligny and Waterloo. On Elba he was a copyist and librarian. He eventually followed Napoleon into exile on St Helena.

'sacred battalions', composed of individual volunteers who were numbered in their thousands three weeks later in Paris. It was cold; some light snow fell.

The first village was Grasse, centre of the world-renowned perfume industry. Napoleon rested not in the village, but in the hills above at a place now called the Plâteau de Napoléon. It was long after dark when the column reached the next halting place at Seranon. Here the Emperor was presented with a bottle of local lavender water. When they marched out on 3 March it was supposedly accidentally left behind. Since then this toiletry has sold well under the name 'L'Oubli Napoléon' – 'Napoleon's Forgetfulness'. They did not, however, forget to take along a Monsieur Blaise Rebuffel as a reluctant guide – his wife gave birth three days later. Nowadays his descendants, who still live in Seranon, are the proud owners of a table and chair used by the Emperor.

As they headed for the next small town of Castellane, deep mud and steep slopes slowed progress. It was hard on the light cavalrymen, stumbling along carrying their lances and sabres with their saddles on their heads and their *czapksas* (square lancer caps) slung round their necks. After a while the cannons were abandoned in the darkness. At Castellane more supplies and transport were demanded of the sub-prefect:

Sir,
I beg of you to give orders to have furnished at once 5000 rations of bread, 5000 of meat and 5000 of wine; 40 carts or 200 pack-mules. His Majesty will be at Castellane by ten o'clock.
Cambronne, Général of Brigade, Commanding the Imperial Guard.

The paymaster's heavy coffers could not be dragged any further.

Next, on 4 March, came Digne 95 kilometres from the sea and later made famous by Victor Hugo in *Les Misérables* as the place where Jean Valjean stole the bishop's candles. It was a Saturday – market day – so the soldiers went shopping, the officers had proclamations printed and purchased horses for themselves and half the lancers. More carts were hired.

At around noon on 6 March all were delighted to find the bridge over the Durance at Malijai intact. Napoleon was so relieved that this crucial crossing place had been secured so easily that he exclaimed: 'Now I am in Paris.' Then on through Volonne and Sisteron to Gap, which was reached late on the same day. There is a delightful story and plaque to prove it at Volonne. Napoleon stopped to address a curious crowd in the village centre but while doing so one of his stirrup straps broke. The story has it that while it was being repaired the Emperor nipped behind a nearby wall to attend an urgent call of nature. Today, a small stone house by the roadside has a plaque on the wall that reads, in the local Provençal dialect, '*Eishi lou Napoleon P.P.*' – 'Here Napoleon had a pee.'

It was not until 5 March, the day before Napoleon made his historical visit behind the wall at Volonne, that King Louis was informed of the landing. The war minister, Maréchal Soult, was quick to formulate a plan to destroy the traitorous intruder. Comte d'Artois, the brother of the executed King Louis XVI, was to command an army of 30,000 men already in the south, while Maréchal Ney (another marshal who had found no problem switching from revolutionary to royalist) assembled another 30,000 around Bésancon. At odds, as they thought, of sixty-to-one in their favour there should be little difficulty in seizing Napoleon and putting him up against the nearest wall. On the day the Emperor reached Gap, a royal ordinance was published declaring him a traitor, a rebel and calling on all good Frenchmen 'to apprehend and convey him forthwith before a military tribunal'.

The first real test of loyalties came on 7 March, not at the gates of Grenoble as many accounts suggest, but at the narrow defile at Laffrey lake guarding the southern approach to the town. General Marchand was the royalist district commander with a formidable force of six infantry battalions – three each of the 5th and 7th Ligne Regiments plus the 4th Hussars and the 3rd Engineer Regiment. He selected Major Lansard's battalion of the 5th Infantry, with some engineers, for the actual confrontation. Lansard, whose task involved blowing bridges and blocking roads, went as far south as La Mure, some 30 kilometres from Grenoble, arriving there on 6 March. There he met Napoleon's small vanguard force under Capitaine Raoul of the Guard Artillery. Raoul tried in vain to get the soldiers from both sides to fraternize, to drink together. Lansard withdrew hurriedly to the Laffrey lake defile without blowing any bridges.

On the same day, over 800 kilometres away on the other side of the Alps, the Allied delegates at the Congress of Vienna (who included the Duke of Wellington) were at last informed of Napoleon's escape. However, there was no official confirmation that he had landed in France until 12 March.

Napoleon arrived for the showdown at about 1.00 p.m. He was mounted on his horse Taurus, and had dressed appropriately for what he knew was the real test of loyalties ahead. He wore what he had worn at his most splendid of victories nine years before at Austerlitz. His uniform was that of a colonel of the Châsseurs of the Imperial Guard, but over the green jacket was the old, familiar grey greatcoat, on his head the battered, black bicorne hat and around his waist the sword of Austerlitz. He rode forward at the head of his Guard.

Lansard had his battalion, with shouldered muskets and bayonets fixed, drawn up on an open space astride the road at the northern end of the lake, in front of the village of Laffrey. There was only a narrow, 100-metre gap between the lake on one side and the mountainside on the other – today it is called 'La Prairie de la Rencontre' – 'The Meadow of the Meeting'. A fine equestrian statue of Napoleon now stands in the centre of this defile. Nineteen-year-old Capitaine Randon (who became a Marshal of France under Napoleon III) commanded the company deployed in line facing down the road. When the advancing column, headed by lancers, halted there was an exchange of shouts: 'We are all Frenchmen', 'If you fire on the Emperor you will be responsible to all of France.' Napoleon rode to the front, ordered his grenadiers to reverse their arms, dismounted and walked calmly, slowly forward to within a pistol shot of the company. As he came closer the young officer gave a command that he would remember to his deathbed – he shouted 'Fire!' Had anybody obeyed it would have been finished; just one shot at that range would not have missed, the 'hundred day' clock would never have started, Waterloo would never have been fought. But not a single soldier dared shoot. Napoleon halted and unbuttoned his greatcoat. 'If there is any man among you who wants to kill his Emperor, here I am.' There was a stunned silence for a few moments. Then a solitary voice

Lieutenant Noisot

This officer of the 1st Grenadiers à Pied – the senior Imperial Guard Regiment that was to carry the Eagle at Waterloo – was selected from a host of applicants as one of the junior officers to go to Elba with the Napoleon Battalion. He was probably one of Napoleon's most fanatical followers, a zealot whose devotion to his Emperor he took with him to his grave. Years later in retirement Noisot, who lived near Dijon, had an elaborate bronze monument to Napoleon erected at his own expense. At the December 1845 reunion dinner of former officers of the Imperial Guard the president, General Schramm, congratulated Noisot for his loyalty and generosity. When Noisot died he arranged to be buried standing up a few yards away so that he could continue to stand guard for eternity.

from the ranks yelled '*Vive l'Empereur!*' The troops cheered, broke ranks and ran forward to touch him. Randon galloped off; Lansard, overcome with emotion and with tears on his cheeks, surrendered his sword. It had been a coolly calculated act of courage, of bluff – a classic personal demonstration of his own principle that he had applied so often on the battlefield, that moral factors are to physical as three are to one.

That evening at the gates of Grenoble, the 7th Regiment was paraded to formally surrender by their commander, Colonel Comte de la Bédoyère, under an Imperial Eagle that he had brought out of hiding for the occasion. He was promoted maréchal de camp (general of brigade), and appointed a personal ADC (aide-de-camp) on the spot (he was given several vital messages to deliver at Waterloo). The garrison of the town looked on impassively as the townsfolk, wild with enthusiasm, smashed open the gates. Later, as a prisoner on St Helena, Napoleon would say: 'Before Grenoble I was an adventurer, at Grenoble I was a ruling prince.' By then he had covered 320 kilometres in six days – no mean marching rate. Before leaving on the afternoon of the 9 March, he issued his famous proclamation addressed to his 'Soldiers' throughout France, which ended with the quotation at the start of this prologue.

What was fast becoming a triumphal progress continued the following day towards Lyon. The advance guard, still under Cambronne, deliberately carried no ammunition. Inside the city walls were the Comte d'Artois and Maréchal Macdonald with a mere 3000 troops out of the 30,000 with which they had hoped to block the march. Napoleon, arriving late on 10 March, then had six regiments numbering about 8000 men, including the 7th and 11th Ligne, 4th Hussars, 3rd Engineers and 25th Artillery (in which the Emperor had served twenty-five years earlier), thirty cannons, the Elba troops, and over 1000 'sacred battalion' volunteer officers and NCOs. As the crowds yelled 'Death to Artois!', 'Death to priests!' and '*Vive l'Empereur!*', the Count's courage faltered and he fled to Paris. As the 4th Hussars advanced on the bridge Maréchal Macdonald dropped an unfired musket, leaped into his saddle and spurred away, saving his life but losing his hat to an exultant sergeant named Lecourbe.

Napoleon stayed in the city, in the Palace of the Archbishop, until 13 March. While there he began issuing Imperial Decrees as Emperor of France and it is from this time that the so called 'hundred days' should perhaps be counted – until he abdicated for the second time on 22 June. These famous 'Lyon Decrees' included appointing the chief officers of state, such as the reappointment of the dreaded Fouché as Minister of Police. He effectively cancelled the Treaty of Fontainebleau and set up a puppet assembly called the 'Champs de Mai'. When he left, his force had more than doubled and included fifty guns. The day before in Paris, some wag had posted a notice in the Place Vendome that read, ' From Napoleon to Louis XVIII, My good brother, there is no need to send me any more soldiers – I have enough.' It was also on the 13th that the Congress of Vienna published a document declaring Napoleon an outlaw, which empowered the

---

The 100 Days Campaign?

Napoleon's dramatic but unsuccessful campaign to win back his throne is frequently referred to as 'The 100 Days'. The problem with this is that no writer seems actually to define with any accuracy how this 100 days has been calculated. When does the 100 days start or finish? Did the 100 day clock start ticking as Napoleon left Elba (late on 26 February), or when he landed in France (1 March), or when he started issuing Imperial Decrees (13 March), or when he arrived in Paris (20 March)? And when did the clock stop? Was it at Waterloo (18 June), or when Napoleon abdicated for the second time (22 June), or when

King Louis returned to Paris (8 July), or when Napoleon finally surrendered on board HMS *Bellerophon* (15 July)?

The nearest one can get to fitting 100 days to actual events of importance is to assume it started on 13 March when Napoleon's march on Paris was obviously succeeding and he began to issue decrees at Lyon. One hundred days from then is 20 June – two days after Waterloo. Nothing else remotely fits. A more obvious starting point is 1 March, the day he landed back on mainland France, with the end being his defeat at Waterloo but, alas, there are 110 days in between.

Napoleon's Horses on Elba

If the 'Emperor of Elba' commanded a less than lavish military establishment the same was not true of his stable, which included the following horses:

• 'Wagram', a grey Arab which had carried the Emperor at that great victory. A favourite of Napoleon's. When he gave Wagram sugar he used to say, '*Te voila mon cousin*' ('There you are my cousin').

• Montevideo', a large bay from South America that had seen service in Spain.

• 'Emin', a chestnut from Turkey that Napoleon had ridden into Madrid.

• 'Gonslavo', a big bay that he had ridden in Spain, Russia and France. At Brienne the left bridle had been cut in two by a musket ball.

• 'Roitelet', an English-Limoisine cross. At Schoenbrunn in 1809 he bolted during a review and nearly threw the Emperor.

This did not deter him from riding him in Russia. At Lutzen a cannon ball that nearly killed them both came so close that it tore a piece of skin and hair from Roitelet's hock. At Arcis-sur-Aube this horse threw the Emperor when yet another near miss made him rear up.

• 'Taurus' was a silvery grey, slightly dappled Persian gifted to the Emperor by the Tsar of Russia during their meeting at Erfurt in 1808. A veteran of the march on Moscow, she was one of two horses referred to as 'The White Charger'. Napoleon rode her at the battles of Vitepsk, Smolensk, and Borodino and then throughout much of that awful retreat from Moscow.

• 'Intendant', a pure white Norman, was ridden on parades and ceremonial occasions. The other 'White Charger' Intendant was a favourite of the soldiers who nicknamed him 'Coco'. They would often shout in unison, '*Voila Coco!*' whenever they saw their Emperor riding him.

military to arrest, summarily try and execute him with no questions asked. Wellington signed reluctantly under considerable political pressure. Parliament in Britain later repudiated it.

News of 'His' return spread rapidly throughout France. Anti-Bourbon sentiment became rampant, insurrections broke out, National Guard units attacked several royalist strongholds, and a royalist mayor was shot while trying to prevent the raising of the tricolour. Tax officials were beaten, their homes ransacked. All this was done with mounting enthusiasm. With the country declaring for the Emperor all round him, Maréchal Ney arrived at Bésancon on 10 March, having rashly promised the King to bring back Napoleon in an iron cage. Awaiting him were few loyal troops but a letter from the Emperor suggesting that Ney switch sides yet again and join him at Chalon saying, 'I will receive you as I did after the Battle of Moscow.' On that occasion Ney had received the title Prince de la Moskowa. On 14 March Ney switched allegiance once more. When he addressed the assembled troops and people at the small village of Lons-le Saunier some 75 kilometres north-east of Lyon, he proclaimed that the rightful ruler of France had returned and that the Bourbon cause was dead, lost forever. Before he could finish, the crowd became hysterical with delight. With Ney changing sides the King's last chance had gone.

The march continued northwards. Through Chalon and Autun to Auxerre on 17 March, by which time the head of the procession had taken on a truly imperial appearance. In front was the coach of the local prefect, followed by that of Général de Division Drouot – until a few days before, Governor of Elba. The Emperor, riding in a carriage with his Grand Master of the Palace, Général de Division Bertrand, and escorted by the Elba squadron of Polish Lancers, was wearing the sword of Austerlitz on a belt with a diamond buckle. On either side rode the Lancers' commander Major Jerzmanowski and the artillery commander Major Duchand, who was to command a horse artillery battery in the Imperial Guard's last attack at Waterloo. Behind, a trooper led Taurus, his dapple-grey Persian charger. Two coaches with his personal household and servants followed. Behind, stretched over many kilometres of road, with some straggling and frequent gaps, came an army of three divisions. They were commanded by Generals Brayer, Girard (who joined him at Auxerre and was to receive the title Duc de Ligny on his deathbed after that battle) and Jeanin – who was to command the 20th Infantry Division at Waterloo.

At Auxerre Ney joined his Emperor who reviewed the 14th Ligne (that had just marched in from Lons-le Saunier). Ney offered Napoleon a written explanation of his conduct over the last

King Louis XVIII (1755–1824)

He was fortunate to escape the fate of his brother (Louis XVI), whose dripping head tumbled into the basket after being kissed by 'Madame Guillotine', by fleeing to Belgium during the Revolution. He was regarded as regent-in-exile for the ten-year old Louis XVII, who later died in gaol of ill-treatment. He spent much of his exile in England before returning to France to assume the throne in April 1814. Bourbons called him 'Louis the yearned for', which soon changed to 'Louis the unloved', and, with his second restoration after Waterloo, 'Louis the unavoidable'. At sixty he was physically decrepit – short winded, bloated, gouty, and barely able to stand unaided, let alone mount a horse. Wellington described him as, 'A perfect walking sore, not a part of his body sound, even his head let out a sort of humour (unwholesome discharge)'. Surprisingly, Louis lasted another nine uncomfortable years after Waterloo. The 'new' royalist army consisted mainly of former Bonapartist soldiers, most of whom boasted of their service under the Eagles. They openly spoke of Louis XVIII as *'le cochon'* and when playing cards referred to the king of spades or hearts as the 'pig'.

year, which his Emperor did not bother to read. Although welcoming Ney warmly, Napoleon sidelined him to raising troops in Dijon. Ney was disappointed to miss the coming triumphal return to Paris, but even more worrying was the lack of a specific command. A far happier soldier was Capitaine Coignet. Napoleon appointed this former grenadier who had risen from the ranks, Chief Wagon-Master of the Palace. Although he later wrote, 'I laughed myself silly', the old soldier was immensely pleased. From there to Sens, Fontainebleau and finally, on 20 March, to Paris from which the King had fled the night before. At the Tuileries the escort brandished their sabres, while the crush all but overwhelmed the Emperor as he was lifted bodily through the doors. Pale, exhausted, his eyes shut and with arms outstretched, he was carried up the great staircase.

In three weeks, without firing a shot, without shedding a drop of blood (discounting thirty-three soldiers of the 76th Ligne who drowned when their boat overturned at night in the river at Pont-sur-Yonne near Sens) Napoleon had won back his crown. It had been deceptively easy. Starting with a battalion he had marched nearly 800 kilometres (averaging around 38 kilometres a day) and ended up with an army. Unbeknownst to him he was just a week into his hundred days, and three months from Waterloo. Later, in exile on St Helena, he had this to say about his extraordinary comeback:

> I owed my restoration to the inhabitants of the towns and villages, to the soldiers and junior company officers. I could only rely on them. All the generals I met on my journey hesitated, or received me badly, even if they were not hostile, but they were obliged to give way before the excitement of their soldiers.

The Emperor Presents New Eagles

The finale to the Convocation of the Champs de Mai, held on 1 June 1815, was the presentation of Eagles to the new Army. The Emperor, dressed in imperial robes rather than uniform, rose from his throne to address the assembled Regiments. What followed were several hours of pure theatre – his troops loved it.

'Soldiers of the National Guard of the Empire! Soldiers of the land and sea forces! To your hands I confide the Imperial Eagle with the National Colours. Swear to defend it with the sacrifice of your blood, against the enemies of France, and of this throne. Swear that it shall always be your rallying signal.' The response was immediate and unequivocal – 'We swear it.' Napoleon then left for the Champs de Mars to mount another gilded throne. The massed squadrons and battalions followed.

Napoleon then handed over the Eagles saying, 'Soldiers of the National Guard of Paris! Soldiers of the Imperial Guard! I confide to you the National Eagles, and the National Colours. You swear to perish, if necessary, in defending them against the enemies of the country and the throne.' From the assembled troops came back repeated roars of, 'We swear it! We swear it!' The drums rolled for silence. The Emperor continued, 'You swear never to acknowledge any other rallying sign. You soldiers of the National Guard of Paris swear never to suffer foreigners again to pollute by their presence the capitol of this great nation!' Again and again the soldiers repeated their oath. For two more hours the battalions and squadrons marched past their Emperor. Within less than three weeks the dream was shattered.

The Campaign

And there was mounting in hot haste: the steed,
The mustering squadron, and the clattering car,
Went pouring forward with impetuous speed,
And swiftly forming in the ranks of war;
And deep thunder peal on peal afar;
And near, the beat of the alarming drum
Roused up the soldier ere the morning star;
While throng'd the citizen with terror dumb,
Or whispering, with white lips – 'The foe! They come! They come!'

Lord Byron

General Situation in Europe – March 1815

When Napoleon abdicated on 6 April 1814 and was shipped off to Elba on a British warship, he left the disposition of his empire to those who had overthrown him – Austria, Prussia, Russia and Britain. They were the 'big four'. Other countries, of whom Spain, Portugal and Sweden were the most important, had also contributed to his downfall and were also, therefore, signatories to the Treaty of Paris, 30 May 1814. However, the 'big four' had previously bound themselves to prosecute the war against Napoleon to a successful conclusion by the Treaty of Chaumont (1 March 1814). In Paris it had been decided that some of the details of carving up France's imperial empire should be given to a special Congress set up in Vienna. It was a glittering gathering of kings, princes, diplomats and statesmen (mostly foreign ministers). Accompanied by hordes of courtiers, ladies, secretaries and servants, it assembled in November 1814, intent on enjoying the lavish hospitality of the almost bankrupt Austrian court.

It had the outward appearance of an extravagant, social bonanza. Inwardly, the serious business of settling European territorial boundaries was anything but amicable. The 'big four', determined to be the principal decision-makers, were soon at loggerheads over the fate of Poland and Saxony. The restored King Louis XVIII of France was represented at the Congress by a former bishop, probably the most astute statesman of the time, the sixty-year-old Prince Charles Maurice Talleyrand. For many years he had served the revolution and Napoleon as foreign minister and international diplomat. As such, he had accumulated an impressive list of titles – Grand Chamberlain of the Empire, Duke of Benavente, Arch-Chancellor and Grand Elector. However, like many of his military colleagues, he had found few problems in changing from royalist to revolutionary to imperialist, and then back to royalist. His ability as a diplomat in Vienna was soon in evidence, and he successfully insisted on France joining the 'big four', which thus became the 'big five'.

It was Talleyrand who stood up to announce to the Congress that Napoleon had escaped. It was greeted with hoots of loud laughter. It was no joke, and it soon concentrated minds. Napoleon was declared an outlaw, a common enemy and disturber of the peace. On 25 March a Treaty of Alliance was concluded by the signatories of Chaumont to settle the unfinished business. It was a declaration of war, not against a country (France), but against a man. Each of the four countries (Austria, Prussia, Russia and Britain) pledged to provide armies of 150,000 men, one-tenth to be cavalry, with a fair proportion of artillery. It was acknowledged that this figure was impossible for Britain, so she was permitted to meet the shortfall by substituting money for men. In the event, Britain became the reluctant paymaster for the whole enterprise as the other countries were verging on bankruptcy; to get their armies moving required some £6 million in British subsidies, with the bulk of the actual coinage coming from the Rothschild Bank.

Situation Facing Napoleon – March/April 1815

Napoleon faced an array of pressing problems, all of which had to be overcome in a matter of weeks if he was to secure the leadership of France that he had so audaciously snatched back from the Bourbons. They were, firstly, the establishment of his power in France itself; secondly, the organization of diplomatic relations and consolidation of the civil administration; thirdly, the overhaul of public finances; fourthly, the creation of armies; fifthly, the equipping of these men for war; and finally, the appointment of competent senior commanders. All of these had to be tackled simultaneously. The validity of one of his own better-known sayings, 'Ask of me anything but time', had never been more compelling.

RE-ESTABLISHMENT OF POWER IN FRANCE

Napoleon acted immediately to assert his authority in France. Before he had reached Paris, royalist uprisings had occurred in the departments of Bordeaux, Guienne, Languedoc and Provence. Troops were despatched from Lyon to 'put an end to the civil war at whatever the cost'. These operations were energetically carried out. On 29 April their success was signalled by the firing of the 100-gun salute (as described in the prologue). It was, however, slightly premature, as two days later the Marquis de la Rochejaquelain landed on the coast of La Vendée to stir up a rebellion that soon had 20,000 followers. Napoleon was forced to send 17,000 troops, including Imperial Guard units, to what became a prolonged struggle. These men would be missed at Waterloo.

DIPLOMATIC RELATIONS

Napoleon did not want to go to war in 1815. Nevertheless, he realized its inevitability and desperately prepared for it while attaching the highest importance to diplomatic and political efforts to avoid, or at least postpone, it. He wrote personally to all Allied sovereigns in conciliatory, even humble, terms stressing that France wanted peace with its neighbours, that the days of French aggression had gone, and that he renounced all claims to Belgium, Holland, Italy, Germany and Poland. His letters were ignored. The one to the Prince Regent in London was returned unopened on the instructions of the foreign minister (Castlereagh). French diplomats were turned back at the borders. Europe was determined to rid itself of this menace. Much safer a feeble French king in Paris than such a formidable general with republican political ideas.

PUBLIC FINANCES

The financial difficulties confronting Napoleon seemed little short of insurmountable – way beyond anything contained in the treasure chests that Inspector Peyrusse had guarded so diligently all the way from Elba. The Fr.40 million left by Louis in the treasury were quickly exhausted (just to pay the Armée du Nord would cost Fr.5 million a month), and arrears of taxes proved impossible to collect. Numerous short-term measures were implemented to raise money. Supplies were secured by requisitioning or the issue of receipts dated well into the future; the government 'sinking fund' was sold to an association of reluctant bankers for Fr.32 million, and the revenues of future years abandoned in various ways in favour of cash up front. By these and other means, some Fr.80 million were raised during April and May. It was sufficient for Napoleon's most urgent needs. After Waterloo others would have to unscramble the financial mess and pay the bills.

THE RAISING OF ARMIES (Map 3, p. 23)

It was with the creation of armies and the means of waging war that Napoleon demonstrated most convincingly that he had lost little of his former vigour or drive. Within twelve weeks he had nearly 500,000 men under arms with many more en route to the depots. Of these, nearly 40 per cent (some 200,000) were actually with the field armies deployed in a 'watch and ward' role around the French frontiers, or part of the central reserve force (L'Armée du Nord comprising 123,000 soldiers and 358 guns) with which he could take the offensive. The remainder were largely National Guard units called up to garrison fortresses and key points. The barrel had undoubtedly been scraped and his methods were by no means universally popular, but had he won at Waterloo there is little doubt that he would have been able to double the number to face a depleted and seriously demoralized opposition. The quality of the troops Napoleon led to Waterloo was first class, with a very high proportion of experienced, battle-hardened veterans whose morale at 'His' return was excellent.

His 500,000 under arms were assembled by the following methods:

1. 200,000 men already under arms in the Royalist Army – mostly experienced campaigners.

Baron (Inspector) Peyrusse

Napoleon's paymaster was another devoted follower who showed courage and initiative in securing a considerable amount of money for Napoleon after his first abdication. The Emperor had amassed a huge hoard of wealth, much of which went missing in those desperate days of April 1814. One of the first acts of the new Bourbon government had been to order commissioners to find and seize Napoleon's treasure. The Attorney-General, Dudon (a former officer cashiered for deserting his post in Spain), with an escort of Gendarmes d'Elite was sent to find it. On 11 April they rode to Orleans where the Empress was on her way to join Napoleon. Also riding to the same city was Peyrusse. He carried a letter authorizing Napoleon's Treasurer-General, de la Bouillerie, to send the funds with Peyrusse to Briare, 65 kilometres south-east of Orleans. Later the same day Napoleon despatched an escort of Polish cavalry and grenadiers in case Peyrusse needed more muscle in arguments over ownership. Dudon arrived first. Waving his piece of paper he demanded custody of the treasure, but de la Bouillerie refused to hand it over. There was a great deal at stake. The wagons and carriages parked in the courtyard of the town hall contained Fr.23 million in gold plus over Fr.4 million in portraits encrusted with diamonds, gold and silver services, and jewels. Soldiers of the Imperial Guard protected it.

Peyrusse had a difficult journey. He had left Fontainebleau with one servant and a guide, and had been compelled to make many detours. At one point he hid from a band of Cossacks in a forest; then he lost his way. It was not until noon on 12 April that the exhausted paymaster reached Orleans, only to find he was too late. De la Bouillerie had, after protracted arguments, handed the fortune to Dudon. The wagons were on their way to Paris. But not quite all the loot had gone. Fr.6 million had been secretly 'withdrawn' from the coffers before they departed from the Place de la Cathédrale. From these Peyrusse managed to salvage over Fr.2.5 million in gold, which he packed into eight boxes that he hid, with commendable initiative, under a pile of manure in the cathedral stables. All next day he waited anxiously in the loft, having sent his servant and guide back to Fontainebleau for help. Towards evening he was found by Capitaine Laborde, who commanded the escort Napoleon had sent to help him. This money went with the Emperor to Elba, as did Peyrusse.

Army Deployments in May and Intended Allied Advances in June/July 1815   Map 3

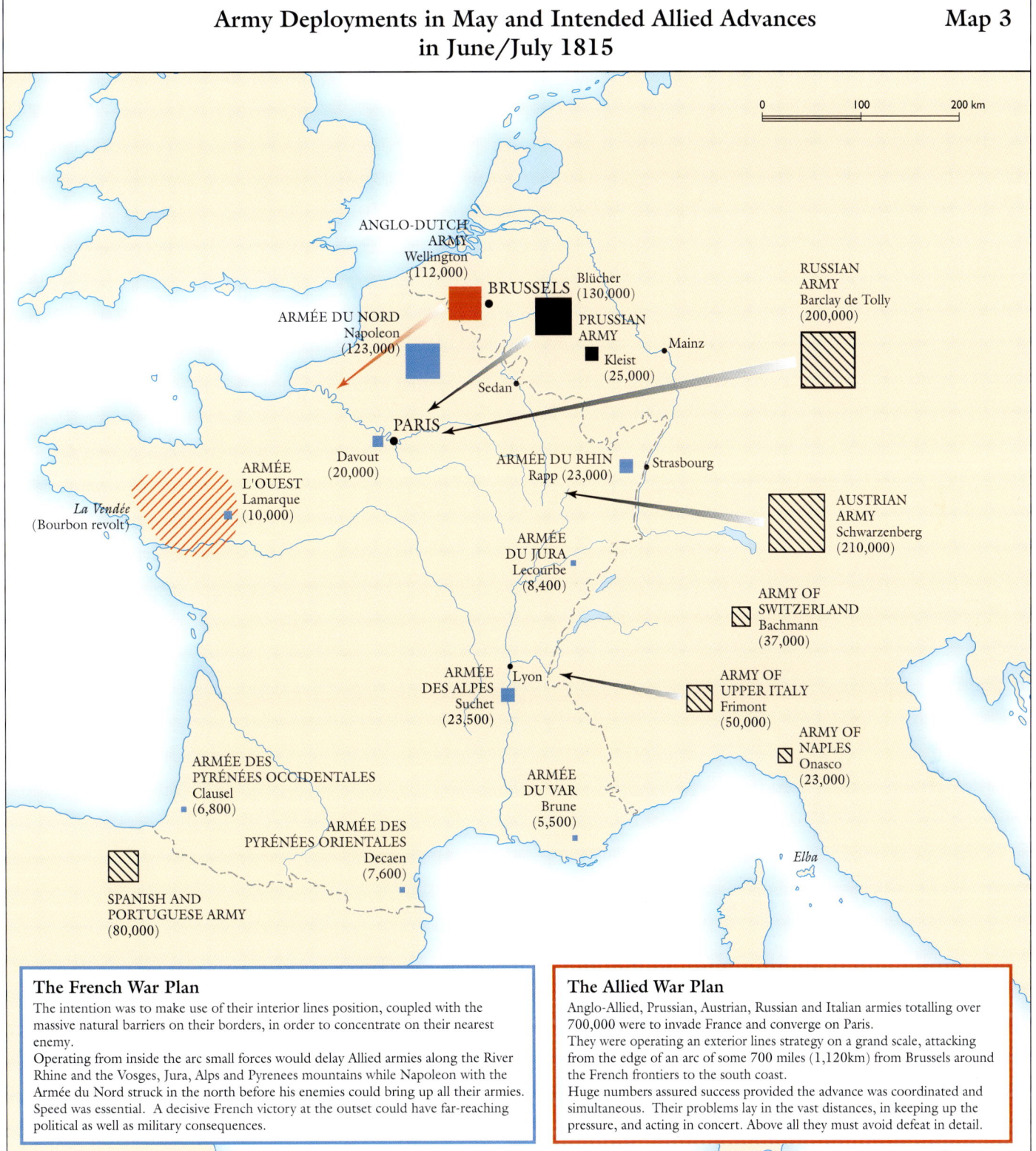

0   100   200 km

ANGLO-DUTCH
ARMY
Wellington
(112,000)

BRUSSELS   Blücher
             (130,000)

RUSSIAN
ARMY
Barclay de Tolly
(200,000)

ARMÉE DU NORD
Napoleon
(123,000)

PRUSSIAN
ARMY

Kleist
(25,000)   Mainz

Sedan

PARIS

Davout
(20,000)

ARMÉE
L'OUEST
Lamarque
(10,000)

ARMÉE DU RHIN
Rapp (23,000)   Strasbourg

La Vendée
(Bourbon revolt)

AUSTRIAN
ARMY
Schwarzenberg
(210,000)

ARMÉE
DU JURA
Lecourbe
(8,400)

ARMY OF
SWITZERLAND
Bachmann
(37,000)

ARMÉE
DES ALPES   Lyon
Suchet
(23,500)

ARMY OF
UPPER ITALY
Frimont
(50,000)

ARMÉE DES
PYRÉNÉES OCCIDENTALES
Clausel
(6,800)

ARMÉE
DU VAR
Brune
(5,500)

ARMY OF
NAPLES
Onasco
(23,000)

ARMÉE DES
PYRÉNÉES ORIENTALES
Decaen
(7,600)

Elba

SPANISH AND
PORTUGUESE ARMY
(80,000)

The French War Plan

The intention was to make use of their interior lines position, coupled with the massive natural barriers on their borders, in order to concentrate on their nearest enemy.

Operating from inside the arc small forces would delay Allied armies along the River Rhine and the Vosges, Jura, Alps and Pyrenees mountains while Napoleon with the Armée du Nord struck in the north before his enemies could bring up all their armies. Speed was essential. A decisive French victory at the outset could have far-reaching political as well as military consequences.

The Allied War Plan

Anglo-Allied, Prussian, Austrian, Russian and Italian armies totalling over 700,000 were to invade France and converge on Paris.

They were operating an exterior lines strategy on a grand scale, attacking from the edge of an arc of some 700 miles (1,120km) from Brussels around the French frontiers to the south coast.

Huge numbers assured success provided the advance was coordinated and simultaneous. Their problems lay in the vast distances, in keeping up the pressure, and acting in concert. Above all they must avoid defeat in detail.

---

2. The recall of men on leave and the rounding up of the thousands who were absent without leave. According to the records, there were about 32,800 of the former and 85,000 of the latter, of whom the great majority could not be traced in time and were unlikely to make reliable soldiers.

3. A call for volunteers produced some 15,000.

4. The raising of several foreign regiments.

5. Although he desperately wanted to avoid outright conscription (recently abolished by King Louis), which would prove immensely unpopular, he agreed in early June to recall the reserves of 1815. By 11 June over 46,000 had assembled at the depots, but none would be ready for the Waterloo campaign.

6. There was little work for a navy, reduced to a handful of seaworthy ships with two-thirds of its seamen on leave, so thousands of sailors were converted into soldiers. By June some twenty battalions had been formed on paper, but with only one on duty – at Calais.

The response to 10 April Decree calling out the National Guard, whose main duty it was to man fixed defences and release regulars for the field armies, was patchy. In around twenty Departments the call out went well, but in others there was considerable vocal and 'passive' resistance. In half the country only one-quarter of the expected units was formed. Probably the worst example was the Department of the Orne that produced a measly 107 men out of the anticipated 2,160. At Amiens a placard was displayed that read – 'Who recalled Buonaparte? The Army. Well, let the Army defend him. It is not for us to carry arms in the defence of a man cast up by hell itself.' Nevertheless, by mid-June some 150,000 had assembled, to which were added 'stationary' National Guards (reservists confined to the defence of major cities such as Paris), gendarmes, customs personnel, forest rangers and some battalions of 'sharpshooters'.

EQUIPPING THE ARMIES

When Napoleon arrived in Paris he took over a military organization that had been neglected for almost a year. Although most regular regiments had weapons and equipment of some sort, virtually nothing had been spent on repair or replacement. Coupled with the need to double, even treble, the numbers under arms quickly, the scale of the problem was daunting. There was an insatiable appetite for all types of military equipment – in particular for muskets, cartridges, shoes (twenty regiments had none) and horses. Despite galvanizing factories, workshops, armouries, magazines and depots; despite the recall of hundreds of discharged armourers; despite the virtual abolition of unemployment, men reported for duty faster than muskets or uniforms could be provided.

Orders were issued for 235,000 muskets and 15,000 brace of pistols. In most main towns special workshops were formed of gunsmiths, armourers, brass-workers and cabinet-makers; in Paris there were six of them employing over 6000 workers. Some muskets were even purchased from England, and any person handing in a firearm was paid twelve francs. Despite these efforts 40,000 muskets (new and repaired) was the maximum monthly output. By early June only half the National Guard had been properly armed.

There were few bayonets to go with the muskets so the manufacture of sabres was postponed in order that workers could concentrate on what was considered the more important weapon – even then the issue of bayonets was initially confined to grenadier companies. As for cuirasses, Napoleon wrote, 'Never mind

cuirasses, send the men off; cuirasses are not indispensable in warfare.' The 11th Cuirassiers fought without them at Waterloo. The production of cartridges – to give each man fifty in his pouches and another fifty in the wagons – was more successful. At the factory at Vincennes twelve million were made in two months.

The procurement of horses for the cavalry, artillery and transport proved equally taxing. The army had never really recovered from the crippling loss of animals in Russia three years earlier. Nevertheless, by the time the campaign started 40,000 had been acquired for the cavalry (half of France's gendarmes were compelled to hand over their horse for 600 francs), and 16,000 for the gunners and transport services.

APPOINTMENT OF SENIOR COMMANDERS

The commanders who served directly under Napoleon at Waterloo are discussed in more detail in Section Three 'Command and Control'. Here it will be sufficient to note who he appointed at the outset to key commands for the defence of France, and the opening of the offensive into Belgium. He had a limited choice. There were few marshals available and several of these were suspect, having proclaimed steadfast loyalty to the king only a matter of days before. The most difficult problem was deciding who to trust for the top posts – War Minister, chief of staff, and the independent commands that must hold the frontiers against invasion. Then, as he built up his field army (the Armée du Nord) and devised an offensive campaign plan, there was the need to appoint capable, hopefully trustworthy, subordinate generals and corps commanders. The appointments he made were:

- Minister of War (whose role in Paris was crucial): Maréchal Louis Nicholas Davout Duc de Auerstadt and Prince d'Eckmuhl.
- Chief of Staff: Maréchal Nicolas Jean de Dieu Soult Duc de Dalmatia.
- Independent commands guarding the borders (see Map 3): Armée du Rhin, Général de Division Comte Jean Rapp; Armée du Jura, Général de Division Lecourbe; Armée des Alpes, Maréchal Louis Suchet Duc d'Albufera; Armée du Var, Maréchal Guillaume Brune; Armée de Pyrénées Orientales, Général de Division Decaen; Armée de Pyrénées Occidentales, Général de Division Comte Bertrand Clausel; Armée de l'Ouest, Général de Division Lamarque.
- Armée du Nord (under Napoleon's personal command): Imperial Guard, Napoleon; Reserve Cavalry Corps (I, II, III and IV Corps), initially Maréchal Emmanuel Grouchy (the last marshal appointed by Napoleon); I Corps, Général de Division Jean Baptiste Drouet,

---

The Emperor's Foreign Regiments

Louis had kept three foreign regiments – the first, the Latour d'Auvergne; the second, the Isenberg; and third, the Irish. Napoleon disbanded the first but retained the other two. He was unable to keep four Swiss Regiments, as the officers could not be trusted and refused to wear the tricolour cockade. He did, however, raise five new regiments. They were Polish (many from the old Vistula Legion), Swiss (from the more loyal soldiers of the four disbanded units), Italian, German and one made up of Dutch and Belgians. The latter three were composed largely of deserters from Blücher and the Prince of Orange. Finally, a battalion of coloured troops was formed in the Department of Gironde, and a few companies of Spanish soldiers. In total some 3,500 men were raised to fight, none of whom participated at Waterloo.

Horses Lost in Russia

Of the 187,600 horses that crossed the River Niemen in 1812, only 1,600 came back. Of these catastrophic losses, just a tiny fraction was due to enemy action, the great bulk dying of starvation. These animals had once been well fed, strong and trained for war – losses of this magnitude could not be replaced. During the retreat, officers who still owned horses were formed into special squadrons 150 strong, commanded by generals with colonels acting as sergeants. The 4th Lancers, who fought under Colonel Bro at Waterloo, went into Russia 600 strong but returned with only one officer and sixteen lancers. Three years later they had only recovered sufficiently to field two squadrons of 150 men each.

Comte d'Erlon; II Corps, Général de Division Comte Honore Charles Reille; III Corps, Général de Division Comte Dominique Joseph Vandamme; IV Corps, Général de Division Comte Maurice Etienne Gérard; VI Corps, Général de Division Georges Mouton, Comte de Lobau.

Situation Facing Wellington – April 1815

Wellington arrived in Brussels on 5 April to take over command of the forces then stationed in Belgium, from the Prince of Orange. He was far from pleased with what he found. The Napoleonic Wars had ended a year before, the American War had finished on Christmas Eve 1814, so for months the armies of Europe had been deliberately, and understandably, run down. There was a huge expectation of a 'peace dividend' after so many long years of war. In England the Prime Minister, Lord Liverpool, wrote in February 1815, 'The country at the moment is peace-mad'. The last thing anybody had anticipated was Napoleon's triumphal reappearance in Paris.

Wellington's problems were not so complex or on the same scale as Napoleon's. He had to reinforce and train one army, not nine; he was not, as was the Emperor, trying to exert political, economic and diplomatic leadership over an entire nation. His difficulties were more narrowly military. In simple terms, they revolved around the quantity and quality of the officers and soldiers being made available to him in Belgium.

THE QUANTITY

Wellington initially had at his disposal in Belgium twenty-five battalions of infantry and six regiments of cavalry (some 15,000 men). Fifteen of these battalions were weak units (500 men or less) that had recently been with General Graham at the unsuccessful storming of Bergen-op-Zoom. Other units promised had a high proportion of half-trained boys. Three more were battalions destined for America but turned around at sea, while others would march straight from garrison duties on the south coast of England. More would come from America, but there was no knowing when they might arrive. A brigade of heavy cavalry, four battalions from Ireland, another Guards battalion and some Household Cavalry

squadrons represented the final effort of a government who could find cash to finance a war more quickly than soldiers to fight it.

Immediately following Napoleon's first abdication, Britain had shipped veteran battalions to America where there was still a war going on. She then proceeded to discharge 47,000 soldiers, including eleven veteran battalions, twenty-four second battalions and 7000 artillerymen. Cavalry regiments were cut to four squadrons of 120 men. Many of the remaining troops were later committed to a troublesome Ireland or to suppress rioters protesting the Corn Laws and income tax. Until a way round the legal nicety of Britain not being at war with France could be found – only the man, Napoleon – calling out the militia was not an option. The government dithered on this issue until four days before Waterloo.

To the British contingents must be added those of the King's German Legion (five cavalry regiments, eight weak battalions and three batteries of guns) that were actually part of the British Army, plus the Hanoverians, Nassauers, Brunswickers, Dutch and Belgian units. These latter formations formed the 'Allied' part of the Anglo-Allied Army that fought at Waterloo. At the start of the campaign in mid-June Wellington commanded a polyglot army, where English was spoken by a minority of his soldiers, totalling some 112,000 men with 203 guns.

THE QUALITY

Within six days of his arrival in Brussels Wellington had ordered the total regrouping of his army. He had formed a poor opinion of the quality of the majority of his force (including a few of his British units) so he determined, as far as he was allowed by national sensitivities, to adopt his highly successful practice from the Peninsular War. He would mix formations, combine the good with the indifferent, the reliable with the doubtful (particularly within infantry formations), down to divisional level. Within each of his three corps there would be divisions of differing nationality and experience. The same would hold true within infantry divisions, except for the 1st British (Guards) Division.

I Corps, under the youthful and impetuous Prince of Orange, and II Corps, under the hugely experienced Lord Hill, would each have two British and the equivalent of two Dutch-Belgian divisions.

3/14 Foot (Buckinghamshire)

A good account of just how raw some of the troops sent to Belgium were is given in the memoirs of the 6th Earl of Albemarle (at the time Ensign the Honourable George Keppel). He was commissioned into the 14th Foot while still only fifteen-years-old, and fought at Waterloo five days after his sixteenth birthday. He described the situation thus:

The 3rd battalion of the 14th Foot … was one which in ordinary times would not have been considered fit to be sent on foreign service at all, much less against an enemy in the field. Fourteen of the officers and 300 of the men were under twenty years of age. These last, consisting principally of Buckinghamshire lads straight from the plough, were called at home 'the Bucks', but their un-buckish appearance procured for them the appellation of 'the Peasants'. On reaching Brussels … the battalion was inspected by an old general … who called out, 'Well, I

never saw such a set of boys, both officers and men.' The general could not reconcile it with his conscience to declare the raw striplings fit for active service, and ordered the Colonel to march them off the ground, and to join a brigade about to proceed to garrison Antwerp. Tidy [the officer commanding] would not budge a step.

Tidy protested vigorously to Lord Hill who happened to be passing, and he in turn brought Wellington to a window overlooking the parade. The Duke inspected the battalion and reversed the decision. They fought in the 4th British Brigade (4th British Division) under Colonel Mitchell and were deployed as brigade reserve, posted well back on the extreme right of Wellington's line. This battalion had the lowest number of casualties of any British battalion in the battle – seven soldiers killed, and one officer and twenty-one soldiers wounded out of some 640 men present.

Lieutenant-General Sir Thomas Picton
(1758–1815)

The General Officer Commanding (GOC) 5th British Division in Wellington's Reserve Corps at Waterloo. One of the best known fighting generals of Wellington's Peninsular army who, nevertheless, had the courage to admit he had had enough of battle by early 1814. The Duke later recalled Picton telling him, 'My lord I must give up. I am grown so nervous, that when there is any service to be done it works upon my mind so that it is impossible for me to sleep at nights. I cannot possibly stand it, and I shall be forced to retire.' Retire he did, and was only persuaded with great difficulty to take the field again. He was convinced (rightly as it happened) that he would be killed. Just before leaving Wales to take up his command he jumped into an open grave, lay down and exclaimed, 'Why, I think this would do for me!' He was wounded at Quatre-Bras, but concealed his injury, only to be shot dead by a musket ball through his top hat at the height of d'Erlon's attack at Waterloo.

The Reserve, in effect III Corps, under Wellington's personal control would eventually have two British divisions, the Brunswick Contingent and a brigade of just under 3000 Nassauers. But it was within the divisions that the skill of the mixing was most apparent. The British Army's historian, J.W. Fortescue, described it thus:

> In every British Division except the First foreigners were blended with red-coats. Alten's and Clinton's had each one brigade of British, one of the Legion [KGL] and one of Hanoverians; Picton's and Colville's had each two brigades of British and one of Hanoverians. Even so, however, the subtlety of the mixture is not yet wholly expressed. In Cooke's division of Guards the three young battalions were stiffened by one old one from the Peninsula. In Alten's, where all the British were young, the battalions of the Legion were veterans and the Hanoverians were regulars; in Colville's, where the British were both old and young, the Hanoverians were both regulars and militia; in Clinton's where the British as well as the troops of the Legion were old, the Hanoverians were all militia.

In the event this mixing of the hotchpotch of nationalities, languages, experience and training was one of the factors that ensured the Anglo-Allied Army withstood the sustained assaults and bombardment of Waterloo.

APPOINTMENT OF SENIOR COMMANDERS
Like Napoleon, Wellington had his difficulties in selecting who should fill key appointments. Potentially, perhaps the most serious problem stemmed from having to accept two unqualified senior commanders on the basis of their royal birth and nationality. The first was Prince William of Orange, nicknamed 'Slender Billy' on account of his long neck (or 'the Young Frog' to distinguish him from his father, King William I, who was 'the Old Frog'). Although he had seen service in the Peninsular as an ADC, at the tender age of twenty-three he had no experience of high command, yet still had, for purely diplomatic reasons, to keep a meaningful, prestigious appointment befitting his status. He got I Corps, which contained the British Guards Division. He was to make a costly blunder at both Quatre-Bras and Waterloo. The

second was the need to accept as the commander of a small Netherlands Corps the eighteen-year-old Prince Frederick of the Netherlands. Perhaps fortunately (or intentionally), this force was not present at Waterloo. Wellington was also compelled to accept, as his overall cavalry commander, the comparatively inexperienced Earl of Uxbridge who had the patronage of both the Prince Regent and Duke of York. That he had also run off with Wellington's younger brother's wife perhaps contributed to the coolness of his reception – although in the field any antagonism was not apparent.

Wellington also expressed dissatisfaction – although with far less justification – with his staff. He replaced the quartermaster-general (his *de facto* chief of staff) Major-General Sir Hudson Lowe, with Colonel Sir William De Lancey who had served with him in a similar capacity in the Peninsular. The man he really wanted, Colonel Sir George Murray, had been sent to Canada. Despite his grumbling, however, Wellington was to be well served by his thirty-three immediate staff officers at Waterloo, only two of whom had not seen service in Spain. Many would be killed or wounded in the battle.

With his divisional and brigade commanders there was always, until they proved otherwise in the field, a question mark over the reliability of those who had once served the French. These included Generals Chassé, Collaert, Dornberg, Ghigny, Merlen and Trip, some of whom continued to wear French decorations. However, they were more than balanced by the old Peninsular hands of proven reliability: Alten, Barnes, Byng, Clinton, Colville, Halkett, Hill, Kempt, Lambert, Maitland, Pack, Picton, Ponsonby, Somerset, Vandeleur and Vivian.

Major-General Hudson Lowe (1769–1844)

An experienced staff officer who was unfortunate enough to alienate Wellington within a few days of his arrival. This resulted in his removal from the key post of quartermaster-general, in which capacity he had been serving the Prince of Orange. Lowe had accompanied Wellington on a tour of troop cantonments. At one point the Duke snapped, 'Where does that road lead to?' Lowe was uncertain and started to fumble with his map, whereupon his commander-in-chief called him a 'damned old fool' and rode on. It was one of Wellington's quirks that he insisted on his officers giving an instant reply to his questions. Those that did not have an answer or became flustered were instantly labelled incompetent. Had Lowe served with Wellington before, he would no doubt have given some immediate response – any response. More astute staff would not have been caught out. One general when asked how many rounds of ammunition were available, immediately replied, 'Four hundred and twenty', telling another officer afterwards that the number 'could always be adjusted later'.

Ironically, Lowe was to be Napoleon's custodian on St Helena, where he soon antagonized the former Emperor by insisting (on instructions) on calling him General Bonaparte. A long running dispute developed over Napoleon's famous list of grievances about his restrictions on the island and Lowe's allegedly obstructive attitude (see Epilogue p. 423). Lowe was knighted in 1817. He was made Governor of Antigua in 1823 and a lieutenant-general in 1830. His papers formed the basis of an early account of Napoleon's captivity.

The Earl of Uxbridge (1768–1854)

Henry Paget, Earl of Uxbridge and later the Marquis of Anglesey, was a cavalry officer of immense stamina, courage and dashing good looks. He first wife, Lady Caroline Villiers (known as 'Car'), bore him eight children. Then in 1809 he took more than a passing fancy to Lady Charlotte Wellesley, the wife of Wellington's younger brother, herself the mother of four children. They scandalized London society by eloping, driven off together in a hackney coach. Lady Charlotte's brother, Colonel Henry Cadogan, challenged Paget to a duel on Wimbledon Common. Cadogan fired first and missed, whereupon Paget chivalrously declined to fire back. Paget later married Lady Charlotte (called 'Char'), and fathered another ten children despite the loss of a leg at Waterloo!

Situation Facing Blücher – April/May 1815

Like the rest of Europe, Prussia had more than its fill of war by 1814. As with other countries, other people, the Germans longed for peace. Napoleon's return caught the armies of Prussia in the midst of a massive demobilization. Militia and volunteer units had been disbanded, while regulars were dispersed and depleted. There were many complications hindering a rapid reinforcement and regrouping of a field army.

Perhaps the most serious handicap was the virtual bankruptcy of the country and its population. The state had been impoverished by long years of French occupation, loss of territory and the massive costs of the war in 1813–14. The lack of cash was to be felt most prominently in the field, when the enormous daily burden of feeding an army became acute. Food and fodder needed to be requisitioned and paid for. Whereas the British usually had the money, the Prussians often did not, which made them particularly unwelcome guests in Belgium.

Nevertheless, undeterred by the problems ahead and only three days after Napoleon's arrival at the Tuileries, the King of Prussia ordered full-scale mobilization. The entire militia was recalled. The aim was to create an 'Army of the Lower Rhine' under the eventual command of Field-Marshal Gebhard von Blücher, an uncouth, illiterate soldier's soldier with an implacable hatred of all things French, who had fought Napoleon with some success in the 1813–14 campaigns. It was to consist of four army corps, each a small army in itself, complete with staff, infantry, cavalry, guns, supply and service units. By June the commanders were: I Corps, Major-General Hans Joachim von Ziethen; II Corps, Major-General Georg von Pirch I; III Corps, Lieutenant-General Johann von Thielemann; IV Corps, General Graf Bülow von Dennewitz. At the start of the campaign the army's strength totalled around 130,000 men with 304 guns. The chief of staff of this army, the man who organized its formation and was the second-in-command to, and strategic brain behind, Blücher, was Lieutenant-General Graf Neidhardt von Gneisenau. Gneisenau was the planner, the strategist, the administrator and the experienced, painstaking staff officer; Blücher the popular, courageous, seventy-two-year-old 'Papa Blücher', 'Old Forwards', the fighting general loved by his troops. The two men worked well together, making a formidable military combination.

However, a serious challenge to the Prussians came as late as May 1815, and it came from the Saxon element within their army – mutiny. Some of Prussia's newly acquired territories came from Saxony and thus the Saxon Army was required to join the Army of the Lower Rhine. Many Saxons took strong objection. Saxon soldiers at Blücher's headquarters at Liège mutinied, refused to fight, threw stones and shouted threats. Blücher's reaction was instantaneous – seven officers were executed and the Saxon units sent home. It was an effective warning to troops in other newly acquired provinces, but it deprived the army of 14,000 well-equipped soldiers before a shot had been fired.

Overall Campaign Strategies

To understand the Battle of Waterloo it is necessary to read it strategically. The final struggle on Sunday 18 June was the climax, the endgame of three days of complex manoeuvres by both sides, each striving to gain an advantage of position that would bring tactical benefits on the battlefield. Often superior tactics can negate sound strategy, but with Waterloo this was not so. Napoleon's defeat was not so much due to faulty tactics on the battlefield (although there were several questionable examples), but what happened between the French advance across the border in the early hours of Thursday morning (15th) and late on the Saturday night (17th).

The armies of France operated on what, in strategic terms, is called 'interior lines'. They held the central position while the Allies, threatening invasion from Belgium to the Mediterranean, were on 'exterior lines', hoping to converge in overwhelming numbers on Paris from the rim of the arc. Armies on exterior lines can normally march to ultimate victory provided they advance simultaneously, co-operate and co-ordinate their movements – not an easy task when separated by hundreds of miles, and without modern communications technology. If they fail to combine and are unable to bring their superior strength to bear in combination on the battlefield, they risk being defeated in detail – that is, one after another – before they can join forces.

To operate on interior lines gives an army of inferior numbers faced by several opponents the chance of delaying more distant enemies while concentrating all, or most, of its strength against smaller forces or detachments. Success always requires skilful generalship. Napoleon was a master of making use of a central position, of striking swiftly at detachments of a scattered enemy, of defeating them one at a time. He was to adopt this strategy again during the three days leading to Waterloo. But this time he failed.

THE FRENCH STRATEGIC PLAN (Map 4)

The Emperor chose to attack into Belgium for a number of good reasons. The alternative was to wait for the Allies' advance and to use the time for defensive preparations, the continued enlistment of more men and the strengthening of fortifications. This would inevitably have led to a repeat of the 1814 campaigns: considerable loss of French territory with the consequent shrinking pool of manpower and resources, the alienation of the people and, ultimately, a last ditch defence of Paris. Time, as usual, was on the side of the big battalions.

To strike at the Allies in Belgium, however, would give Napoleon the initiative. With the initiative he could choose the time and place of attack, he could concentrate at a selected point and, with careful preparation, hopefully achieve surprise – arguably the most precious advantage in war. If, on the other hand, the

The French Treatment of the Belgians

An anonymous French eyewitness, writing in 1815, was unusually frank about the behaviour of the French troops towards the Belgians. Campaign habits acquired in Europe, Russia and Spain had not been forgotten. Describing the French advance into Belgium, he wrote:

> ... we saw a few groups of peasants waiting for us at the entrances of villages we passed through, and who came out with shouts of 'Vive l'Empereur!'; but they did not appear to be animated by sincere enthusiasm; and, to be quite frank, they looked more like paid criers than citizens wanting to vent their true sentiments.
>
> ... in the end they were only friends of the strongest, and their exclamations only meant that: 'We only want to be French if your bayonets bring us law; for pity's sake do not pillage, do not destroy our countryside, treat us as your compatriots.'
>
> ... [however] destruction and banditry marked the passage of the army. No sooner were troops billeted temporarily around a village, than they burst like a torrent on the unfortunate dwellings left to their rapacity: beverages, food, furniture, linen goods, clothes, in a word everything, disappeared instantly. A village where an encampment was established was, on leaving it in the morning, nothing but vast ruins; one would say rubble, around which was strewn all that had been the dwellings' furniture. The surrounding area, usually covered with the richest of crops, looked like it had been hit by a deluge of hail... .
>
> At the moment of departure, the dumbstruck inhabitants, tearful women, half-naked and frightened children, came out of their abodes in droves to criss-cross the devastated fields in the hope of finding furniture, vases and all manner of objects... .

The French Concentration on the Border (situation on the evening of Wednesday, 14 June 1815) **Map 4**

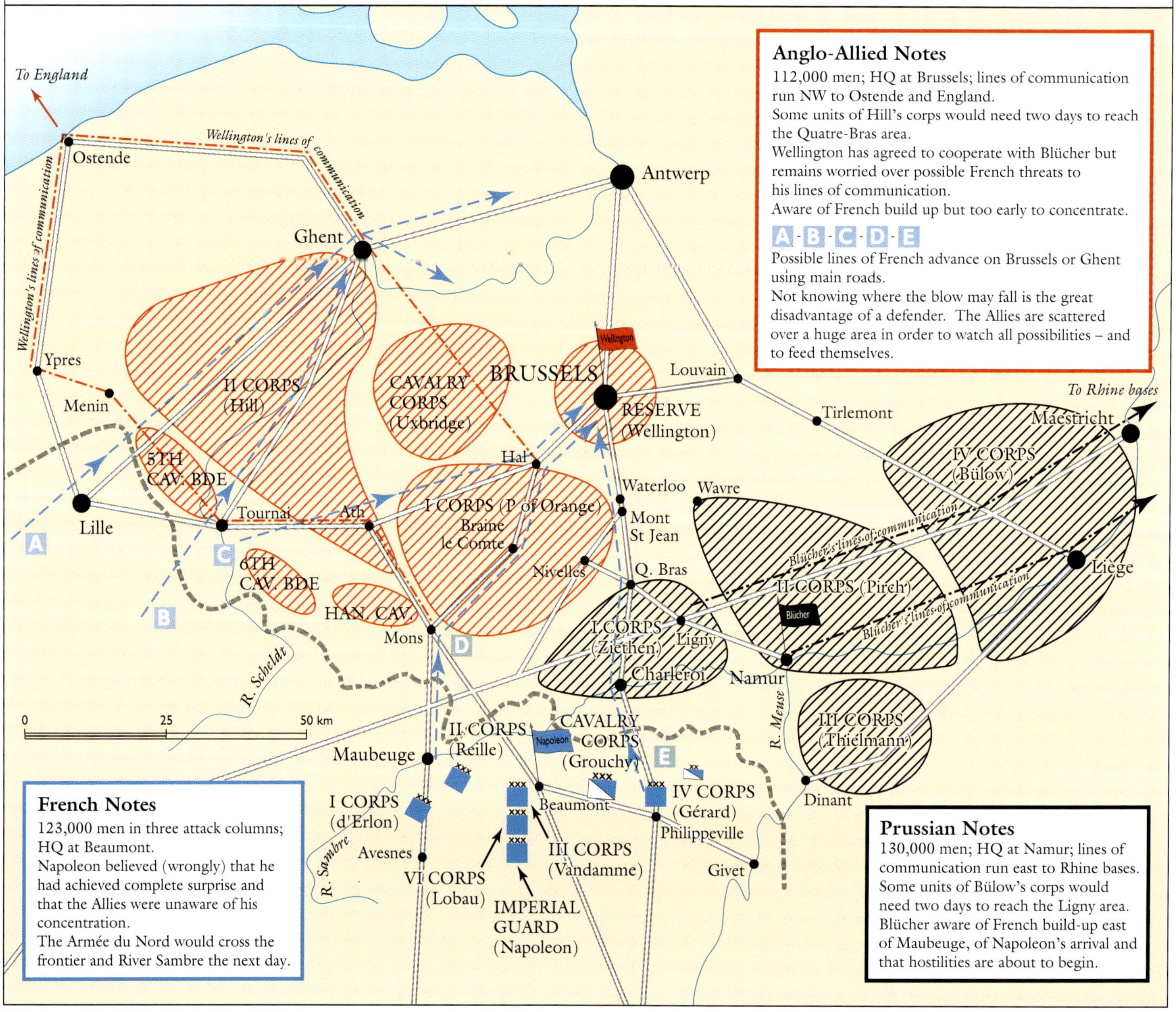

To England
Wellington's lines of communication
Ostende
Antwerp
Ghent
Ypres
Menin
Lille
Tournai
Ath
Hal
BRUSSELS
Wellington
RESERVE (Wellington)
Louvain
Tirlemont
Maestricht
To Rhine bases
Liège
II CORPS (Hill)
CAVALRY CORPS (Uxbridge)
5TH CAV. BDE
6TH CAV. BDE
HAN. CAV
I CORPS (P of Orange)
Braine le Comte
Nivelles
Mons
Waterloo
Wavre
Mont St Jean
Q. Bras
Ligny
Charleroi
Namur
Blücher
I CORPS (Ziethen)
II CORPS (Pirch)
IV CORPS (Bülow)
III CORPS (Thielmann)
Blücher's lines of communication
R. Scheldt
R. Meuse
R. Sambre
Maubeuge
Avesnes
Beaumont
Philippeville
Givet
Dinant
Napoleon
I CORPS (d'Erlon)
II CORPS (Reille)
CAVALRY CORPS (Grouchy)
III CORPS (Vandamme)
IV CORPS (Gérard)
VI CORPS (Lobau)
IMPERIAL GUARD (Napoleon)
A B C D E
0 25 50 km
Anglo-Allied Notes
112,000 men; HQ at Brussels; lines of communication run NW to Ostende and England.
Some units of Hill's corps would need two days to reach the Quatre-Bras area.
Wellington has agreed to cooperate with Blücher but remains worried over possible French threats to his lines of communication.
Aware of French build up but too early to concentrate.
A-B-C-D-E
Possible lines of French advance on Brussels or Ghent using main roads.
Not knowing where the blow may fall is the great disadvantage of a defender. The Allies are scattered over a huge area in order to watch all possibilities – and to feed themselves.
French Notes
123,000 men in three attack columns; HQ at Beaumont.
Napoleon believed (wrongly) that he had achieved complete surprise and that the Allies were unaware of his concentration.
The Armée du Nord would cross the frontier and River Sambre the next day.
Prussian Notes
130,000 men; HQ at Namur; lines of communication run east to Rhine bases.
Some units of Bülow's corps would need two days to reach the Ligny area.
Blücher aware of French build-up east of Maubeuge, of Napoleon's arrival and that hostilities are about to begin.

Allies attacked first it was the enemy in Belgium that had the shortest march to Paris. Other advantages of a pre-emptive strike into Belgium came to mind. It had a French speaking population; it was a country that had recently been French territory, with elements that still supported the Emperor and the revolutionary ideal; and the nearest Allied armies were located there, which included the Anglo-Allied force under Wellington. Defeat Wellington, and England – the paymaster of the alliance – might be out of the contest. The political fallout of such a victory would be enormous, his personal hold on France would be assured, and the possibility of opening up negotiations for a suitable peace deal hugely improved. A quick victory in Belgium was probably the only hope Napoleon had of keeping his throne.

The French campaign plan was simple. To concentrate the Armée du Nord (123,000 men) secretly just south of the junction point of Wellington's Anglo-Allied army (112,000 men) and Blücher's Prussians (130,000 men) a few miles from the Belgian border. Next, to burst through their widely scattered cantonments at Charleroi, with the aim of defeating his two enemies separately and taking Brussels. Napoleon would be like a man coming up unexpectedly to attack two, hoping to kill one before the other could intervene. If he surprised them; if one was closer than the other or stood his ground; if the second man hesitated or was prevented from rushing up to help, then the attacker had a fair chance of killing, disabling or chasing away his first adversary before turning on the second.

In the event, Napoleon penetrated between his two opponents and attacked one (Blücher) at Ligny while keeping the second (Wellington), who was initially slow to appreciate what was happening, at arm's length at Quatre-Bras. Unfortunately for Napoleon, he only wounded Blücher at Ligny, failed to finish him off and then neglected to chase him away. When Napoleon turned to deal with Wellington he found he had disappeared. He pursued him until he turned to fight at Mont St Jean (Waterloo). Napoleon hurled himself at Wellington, only to find the injured Blücher had not sat nursing his wounds in hiding or gone home, but limped up later to join the fight. As Napoleon grappled with Wellington, Blücher arrived and stabbed the Emperor (mortally) in the right side. In oversimplified terms that is the essence of the French plan and its failure in execution during the four days of the campaign. The concept was fine, it came within a whisker of success, but the errors in implementation were frequent and accumulative.

After penetrating the Allies' front (which was essentially a column attacking a line on a vast strategic scale), Napoleon planned to revert to the interior lines strategy for the conduct of opera-

tions. For this purpose, on 15 June he divided his army into three parts – two wings and a reserve. The left wing under Maréchal Ney consisted of d'Erlon's I Corps, Reille's II Corps and the Imperial Guard light cavalry, totalling about 47,000 men plus 100 guns. The right wing, under the newly promoted Maréchal Grouchy, consisted of Vandamme's III Corps, Gérard's IV Corps plus the I and II Cavalry Corps. These amounted to about another 46,000 men and almost 100 guns. The Emperor controlled the reserve directly. In it were the Imperial Guard infantry divisions, Lobau's VI Corps and the III and IV Cavalry Corps – altogether around 30,000 men with about 150 guns. A finely balanced force. He intended to maintain complete flexibility and to switch forces from wings to the reserve, or to use the reserve to reinforce either wing. He made the principles under which he intended to conduct the campaign abundantly clear to Ney when he wrote: 'I have adopted for this campaign the following general principle, to divide my army into two wings and a reserve... . The Guard will form the Reserve, and I shall bring it into action on either Wing just as the actual circumstances may dictate... . Also, according to circumstances, I shall draw troops from one Wing to strengthen my Reserve...'.

THE ALLIES' AND PRUSSIANS' STRATEGIC PLAN
(Maps 3 & 4, pp. 23 & 28)

Ultimately the Allies wanted to attack. Unfortunately, they were forced to remain on the defensive while they waited for the Austrians and Russians to come up and make their presence felt on the frontiers. The overall strategic plan was one mighty push for Paris by all the armies simultaneously. Until everybody was ready it was a case of waiting and watching, hoping that Napoleon would not be able to take the offensive first and, if he did so, to ensure the maximum co-operation between Allies so they did not fight alone. In Belgium this waiting was particularly galling for Blücher who had little money to pay for the huge tonnage of food and fodder that his men and animals consumed daily, and whose soldiers angrily bemoaned the delay that prevented them from marching into France.

The strategic difficulties of the Allies in Belgium were those of defensive warfare since man first decided he could not live with man. In essence, a defender, be he one man or an army, has surrendered the initiative to his opponent; he does not know for certain when or where the enemy will strike. The defender is vulnerable to being caught by surprise. He must guard against many possibilities so he cannot be strong everywhere. He is forced to spread his troops in the knowledge that when the attack comes he will be outnumbered at the point of contact, and he must gain time to

---

Ney Receives Command of the Left Wing

When Ney reached Avesnes on 13 June he was invited to dinner by Napoleon. Expecting to be given his task, he was bewildered when the Emperor made no mention of his plan of campaign or the role he expected his marshal to play. Ney had been made welcome, the atmosphere was convivial, but he hesitated to press for more information. The next day the imperial headquarters moved to Beaumont, leaving Ney without a command, or even a horse. He followed, trailing behind in a requisitioned peasant's cart. On the morning of the 15 June he purchased two chargers from Maréchal Mortier (commander of the Imperial Guard, whose

acute sciatica was to prevent him exercising his command in the days ahead). That afternoon he caught up with the Emperor again in Charleroi. Napoleon was sitting on his chair outside La Belle Vue inn watching the Young Guard march past. Seemingly on the spur of the moment Napoleon exclaimed, 'How are you Ney? I am very pleased to see you. You will take command of the I and II Army Corps. I will give you, besides, the light cavalry of my Guard, but do not make use of it. Tomorrow you will be joined by Kellerman's cuirassiers. Now you can go; drive the enemy onto the Brussels road, and take up your position at Quatre-Bras.'

bring up reinforcements. Then, even when an attack comes, how can he be certain it is not a feint?

The Anglo-Allied and Prussian armies, with a combined total of some 242,000 troops and 500 guns, were spread over a 190-kilometre line from Liège in the east to Ypres in the west. In places this 'line' was over 50 kilometres deep. At best, if hit in the centre, units on the extremities would be unable to join the battle for thirty-six to forty-eight hours. If the line was struck on a flank, say from the Lille area, these timings would be further prolonged. Wherever the blow came, in the first engagement the French would almost certainly seriously outnumber the Allies.

In early May Wellington and Blücher met to discuss plans at Tirlemont. They parted with an agreement that if the French invaded Belgium then the Prussians would march to Wellington's assistance as quickly as possible (the consensus being that Wellington's army would be attacked first). It was appreciated that to stand alone was to invite defeat. In practice such battlefield co-operation was made more difficult by both generals having differing defensive objectives and lines of communication running in opposite directions. In the event of a French invasion, Wellington's aim would be to protect Brussels and his lines of communications that ran west to the sea at Ostend. There were five possible routes for a French march on Brussels and they are marked as A, B, C, D and E on Map 4. The four westerly routes, for which Wellington was responsible for watching, not only ended up at Brussels, Ghent and Antwerp but, in the process, cut his lines of communication. Worrying about these routes was to condition Wellington's thoughts, planning and deployment up to, and including, the battle at Waterloo. The fifth road ran direct from the Beaumont-Philippeville area, via Quatre-Bras and Waterloo, to Brussels – in Blücher's operational area.

If the French marched north or north-east, Blücher's primary aim was to prevent an attack reaching German soil, so his lines of communication ran east to the Rhine. There was every reason for Napoleon to hope that if the Allies could be pushed apart, one or both of them defeated, then they would retire in haste in opposite directions along their lines of communications. This thinking was a key element in the Emperor's use of an interior lines strategy.

THURSDAY 15 JUNE 1815 (Map 5, p. 31)

At half-past three in the morning the leading French patrols crossed the frontier into Belgium. They belonged to thirty-two squadrons of light cavalry from three cavalry divisions. The châsseurs à cheval, lancers and hussars trotted forward across 16 kilometres of front, probing for the first enemy positions between the border and the Sambre. The massive infantry and artillery columns forming behind had received their marching orders from the Emperor via his chief of staff, Soult. They were complex, detailed and had been delivered by hard riding ADCs. Formations were to move off at half-hour intervals with the first on the road by 3.00 a.m., the last five hours later. The instructions stressed that engineers should be positioned immediately behind advance guard units; three pontoon companies were to follow Vandammes' Corps; all baggage wagons were banned from the roads and were grouped at the rear of the army to move together under the personal control of the wagon-master-general. Any unauthorized vehicle found in the marching columns was to be burnt.

Despite the elaborate orders, the march did not start smoothly. Sloppy staff work earlier had placed Lobau's VI Corps in the centre column when it should have been on the right. Consequently, the congestion became acute as the entire force (except for Reille's and d'Erlon's corps) converged on Charleroi. D'Erlon, for reasons known only to himself, started at 4.30 a.m. instead of 3.00 a.m. as ordered. Vandamme, who should also have been moving at 3.00 a.m., never received his movement orders as the ADC delivering them had been riding too hard, fallen from his horse and broken his leg. Then, in addition to breaking camp late, Gérard's leading divisional commander (Général de Division Comte Louis Bourmont, who had been Ney's second-in-command when he promised to bring Napoleon to Paris in an iron cage) chose this moment to desert to the Prussians, together with his senior staff. This caused further delay and consternation, and the corps was re-routed to cross the river at Chatelet instead of Charleroi.

The first clash came near Thuin shortly after 3.30 a.m. Here the leading elements of Jérôme Bonaparte's 6th Division opened fire on the 2nd Battalion of the 1st Westphalian Landwehr Regiment. They

---

Bourmont's Betrayal

Bourmont had received the command of the 14th Infantry Division in Gérard's IV Corps only after repeated entreaties from Ney and Gérard. He had served under Gérard in 1814 when he received his promotion to général de division, and he had been Ney's second-in-command when the marshal was sent to confront the Emperor on his march from Elba to Paris, three months earlier.

At around 5.00 a.m. on 15 June Bourmont, whose division was the leading one in the corps' order of march, rode forward accompanied by five staff officers plus an escort of five lancers. Once through the French outposts he dismissed his escort, giving the corporal a letter for Gérard before replacing the Tricolour on his coat with the white cockade, and cantering towards the Prussian lines with his staff. He took with him a copy of Napoleon's operation order. He told the Prussians the Emperor would attack Charleroi that afternoon and informed Ziethen's chief of staff, Lieutenant-Colonel von Reiche, that the French had 120,000 men. At 3.00 p.m. he was taken to Blücher's headquarters expecting to be closely questioned.

Blücher was not impressed by Bourmont's behaviour or the conspicuous Bourbon cockade. He spoke to him brusquely, showing no inclination to listen to Bourmont, ending with the remark that, 'A cur must always be a cur!'

The Allies barely reacted to Bourmont's desertion, but Gérard's formations were delayed while the confusion was sorted out, and Maréchal de Camp Baron Hulot from the 1st Brigade assumed command of Bourmont's division. Gérard, the corps commander, had to personally ride up and down columns of angry, distrustful soldiers assuring them of the loyalty of the officer corps and promising to lead them to victory. The corps was re-routed from Charleroi to Chatelet. Bourmont was later a key prosecution witness at Ney's trial for treason. His evidence was the primary reason for the guilty verdict and Ney's execution. He subsequently served the Bourbons for many years, becoming Minister of War briefly in 1829 before leading an expedition to Algeria the following year – which earned him a marshal's baton. He died in 1846.

15 June: The French Invade Belgium (situation around 9.00 p.m.)   Map 5

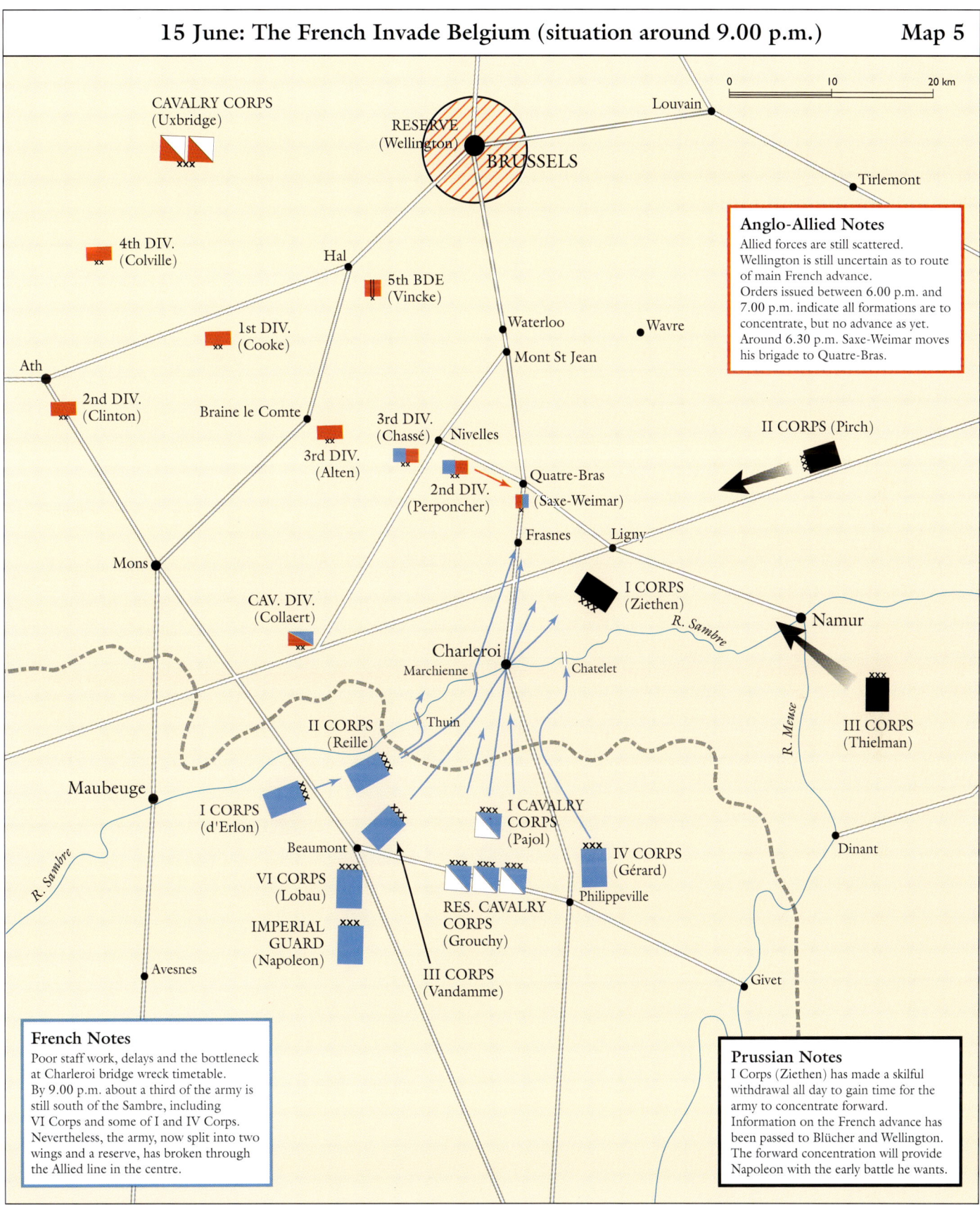

CAVALRY CORPS
(Uxbridge)

RESERVE
(Wellington)
BRUSSELS

Louvain

Tirlemont

4th DIV.
(Colville)

Hal

5th BDE
(Vincke)

Anglo-Allied Notes
Allied forces are still scattered.
Wellington is still uncertain as to route
of main French advance.
Orders issued between 6.00 p.m. and
7.00 p.m. indicate all formations are to
concentrate, but no advance as yet.
Around 6.30 p.m. Saxe-Weimar moves
his brigade to Quatre-Bras.

1st DIV.
(Cooke)

Waterloo

Wavre

Mont St Jean

Ath

2nd DIV.
(Clinton)

Braine le Comte

3rd DIV.
(Chassé)

Nivelles

II CORPS (Pirch)

3rd DIV.
(Alten)

2nd DIV.
(Perponcher)

Quatre-Bras
(Saxe-Weimar)

Mons

Frasnes

Ligny

CAV. DIV.
(Collaert)

I CORPS
(Ziethen)

R. Sambre

Namur

Charleroi

Marchienne

Chatelet

R. Meuse

III CORPS
(Thielman)

Maubeuge

II CORPS
(Reille)

Thuin

I CAVALRY
CORPS
(Pajol)

Dinant

I CORPS
(d'Erlon)

Beaumont

IV CORPS
(Gérard)

R. Sambre

VI CORPS
(Lobau)

RES. CAVALRY
CORPS
(Grouchy)

Philippeville

IMPERIAL
GUARD
(Napoleon)

Avesnes

III CORPS
(Vandamme)

Givet

French Notes
Poor staff work, delays and the bottleneck
at Charleroi bridge wreck timetable.
By 9.00 p.m. about a third of the army is
still south of the Sambre, including
VI Corps and some of I and IV Corps.
Nevertheless, the army, now split into two
wings and a reserve, has broken through
the Allied line in the centre.

Prussian Notes
I Corps (Ziethen) has made a skilful
withdrawal all day to gain time for the
army to concentrate forward.
Information on the French advance has
been passed to Blücher and Wellington.
The forward concentration will provide
Napoleon with the early battle he wants.

were part of the 2nd Brigade in Lieutenant-General von Ziethen's I Corps. As the French increased the pressure across the whole front, the Prussians fired and retired under it. By mid-morning Maréchal de Camp Clary's 1st Hussars faced infantry across the barricaded bridge at Charleroi. A spirited attempt to charge failed, so the cavalry were compelled to await infantry support. To their surprise, at around 11.00 a.m., the next troops to appear were engineers and marines of the Imperial Guard accompanied by the Emperor in person. On his orders the sappers and marines rushed the bridge and swept away the opposition. By midday Charleroi was once again

16 June: The Battles of Ligny and Quatre-Bras   Map 6

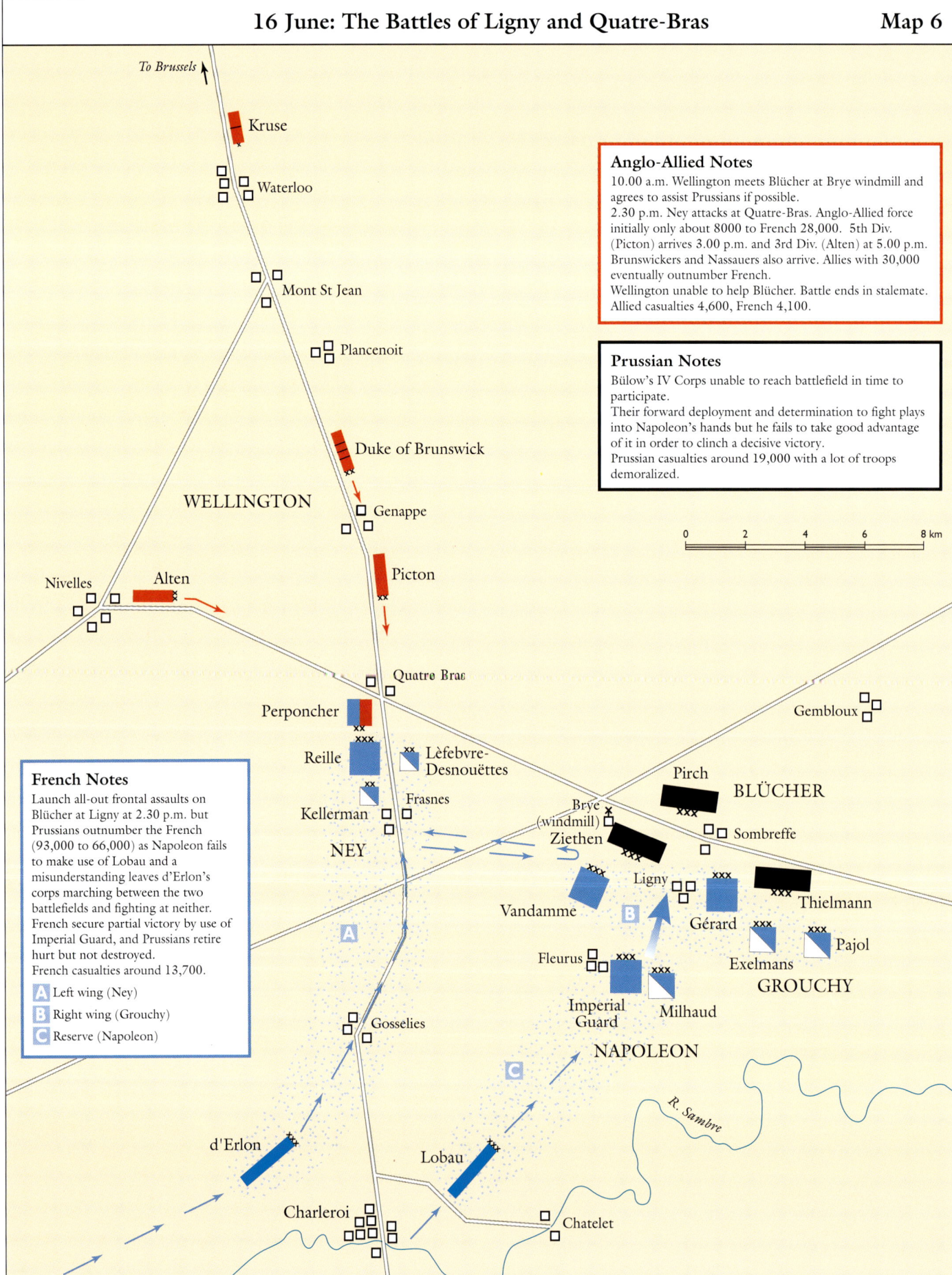

To Brussels

Kruse

Waterloo

Mont St Jean

Plancenoit

Duke of Brunswick

WELLINGTON

Genappe

Nivelles

Alten

Picton

Quatre Bras

Perponcher

Gembloux

Reille

Lèfebvre-
Desnouëttes

Pirch

BLÜCHER

Kellerman

Frasnes

Brye
(windmill)

Sombreffe

NEY

Ziethen

Vandamme

Ligny

Thielmann

Gérard

Fleurus

Pajol

Exelmans

GROUCHY

Imperial
Guard

Milhaud

NAPOLEON

Gosselies

R. Sambre

d'Erlon

Lobau

Charleroi

Chatelet

Anglo-Allied Notes

10.00 a.m. Wellington meets Blücher at Brye windmill and agrees to assist Prussians if possible.
2.30 p.m. Ney attacks at Quatre-Bras. Anglo-Allied force initially only about 8000 to French 28,000. 5th Div. (Picton) arrives 3.00 p.m. and 3rd Div. (Alten) at 5.00 p.m. Brunswickers and Nassauers also arrive. Allies with 30,000 eventually outnumber French.
Wellington unable to help Blücher. Battle ends in stalemate. Allied casualties 4,600, French 4,100.

Prussian Notes

Bülow's IV Corps unable to reach battlefield in time to participate.
Their forward deployment and determination to fight plays into Napoleon's hands but he fails to take good advantage of it in order to clinch a decisive victory.
Prussian casualties around 19,000 with a lot of troops demoralized.

0   2   4   6   8 km

French Notes

Launch all-out frontal assaults on Blücher at Ligny at 2.30 p.m. but Prussians outnumber the French (93,000 to 66,000) as Napoleon fails to make use of Lobau and a misunderstanding leaves d'Erlon's corps marching between the two battlefields and fighting at neither. French secure partial victory by use of Imperial Guard, and Prussians retire hurt but not destroyed.
French casualties around 13,700.

A Left wing (Ney)
B Right wing (Grouchy)
C Reserve (Napoleon)

British Rockets Open Fire – 17 June

Captain Mercer of the Royal Horse Artillery described in his journal how he watched the rockets open fire for the first time at Genappe during Wellington's withdrawal on the afternoon of 17 June.

… the rocketeers had placed a little iron triangle in the road with a rocket lying on it. The order to fire is given – port-fire applied – the fidgety missile begins to sputter out sparks and wiggle its tail for a second or so, and then darts forth straight up the chaussée. A gun stands right in its way, between the wheels of which the shell in the head of the rocket bursts, the gunners fall right and left, and, those of the other guns taking to their heels, the battery is deserted in an instant. Strange: but so it was. I saw them run, and for some minutes afterwards I saw the guns standing mute and unmanned, whilst our rocketeers kept shooting off rockets, none of which ever followed the course of the first: most of them, on arriving about the middle of the ascent, took a vertical direction, whilst some actually turned back upon ourselves – and one of these, following me like a squib until its shell exploded putting me in more danger than all the fire of the enemy throughout the day… .

French territory, with Napoleon seated on a chair by the roadside near an inn called La Belle Vue, watching his regiments tramp past. There was much cheering, drums rolled and his horse was kissed. After a while the Emperor dozed.

By dusk on 15 June the French had broken through the Allies' line at their junction point; Ney had arrived and received (enthusiastically) command of the left wing, and Grouchy (reluctantly) the right. Lancers of the Guard had reached Frasne on the Brussels road but found the route north blocked by Nassauers. No serious attempt was made to dislodge them. As the French troops bivouacked for the night, about a third were still south of the Sambre, while the vital link between Wellington and Blücher, the Nivelles to Namur road, still belonged to the enemy.

FRIDAY 16 JUNE 1815 (Map 6, p. 32)

Wellington had been slow to accept that the French would not advance via Mons, or that the push from Charleroi was their main effort. Consequently, the widely scattered Anglo-Allied contingents received their marching orders late and would be a long time arriving at Quatre-Bras on 16 June – many would not make it at all. Wellington rode over to meet Blücher in order to discuss co-operation by the windmill at Brye. The Prussians were concentrating forward around Sombreffe/Ligny, and Wellington agreed to come to their aid if he could.

With Blücher coming forward, determined to fight around Ligny, and Wellington being kept busy and at arm's length by Ney at Quatre-Bras, Napoleon had an excellent opportunity to concentrate against, and crush, the Prussians. In the event, his successful strategy was negated by a communications failure that had d'Erlon's corps marching uselessly to and fro between the battlefields of Quatre-Bras and Ligny, and not firing a shot at either. Similarly, Napoleon failed to ensure the timely arrival of Lobau's VI Corps on the battlefield. The result was that the French were outnumbered at Ligny, forced to make costly frontal attacks and, although eventually defeating the Prussians, failed to do so decisively. At Quatre-Bras Ney attacked late while his piecemeal assaults allowed the Anglo-Allied reinforcements, that trickled in all day, to keep them at bay. By evening the French were outnumbered, the battle a stalemate.

SATURDAY 17 JUNE 1815

Early on the morning of 17 June Napoleon still had the opportunity of reaping the rewards of his interior lines strategy. It depended on two things, neither of which happened. First, he

The Night Before Waterloo

The weather never respects nationality, rank, recruit or veteran, man or animal. Most soldiers in all three armies would start the fight cold, hungry and in sodden uniforms caked in mud after a sleepless night. Thomas Hardy's poem 'The Dynasts' puts it well:

The young sleep sound; but the weather awakes
In the veterans, pains from the past that numb;
Old stabs of Ind, old Peninsular aches,
Old Friedland chills, haunt their moist mud bed,
Cramps from Austerlitz; till their slumber breaks.

Captain Mercer recalled:

We set up a small tent into which … we crept, and rolling ourselves into wet blankets, huddled close together, in hope, wet as we were, and wet as the ground was, of keeping each other warm. … the tent proved no shelter, the water pouring through the canvas in streams; so up I got, and to my infinite joy, found that some of the men had managed to make a couple of fires, round which they were sitting smoking their short pipes in something like comfort.

Assistant-Surgeon William Gibney of the 15th Light Dragoons tells the same sad story of their attempts to bivouac not far from Mont St Jean:

A wretched bivouac it was, far worse than on the previous night [16/17 June].

Officers, men and horses were completely done up with the long march of the day before … We were up to our knees in mud and stinking water, but not a drop of drinking water or a particle of food was to be found in the villages. … there was no choice; we had to settle down in the mud and filth as best we could … we got some straw and boughs of trees, and with these tried to lessen the mud and to make a rough shelter against the torrents of rain which fell all night. …Very early on the morning of the 18th June we were ordered to bridle up and prepare for action. We did this in darkness … we stood round a watch fire giving out more smoke than heat … both horses and men were shaking with cold.

The Strategic Situation: Night of 17/18 June   Map 7

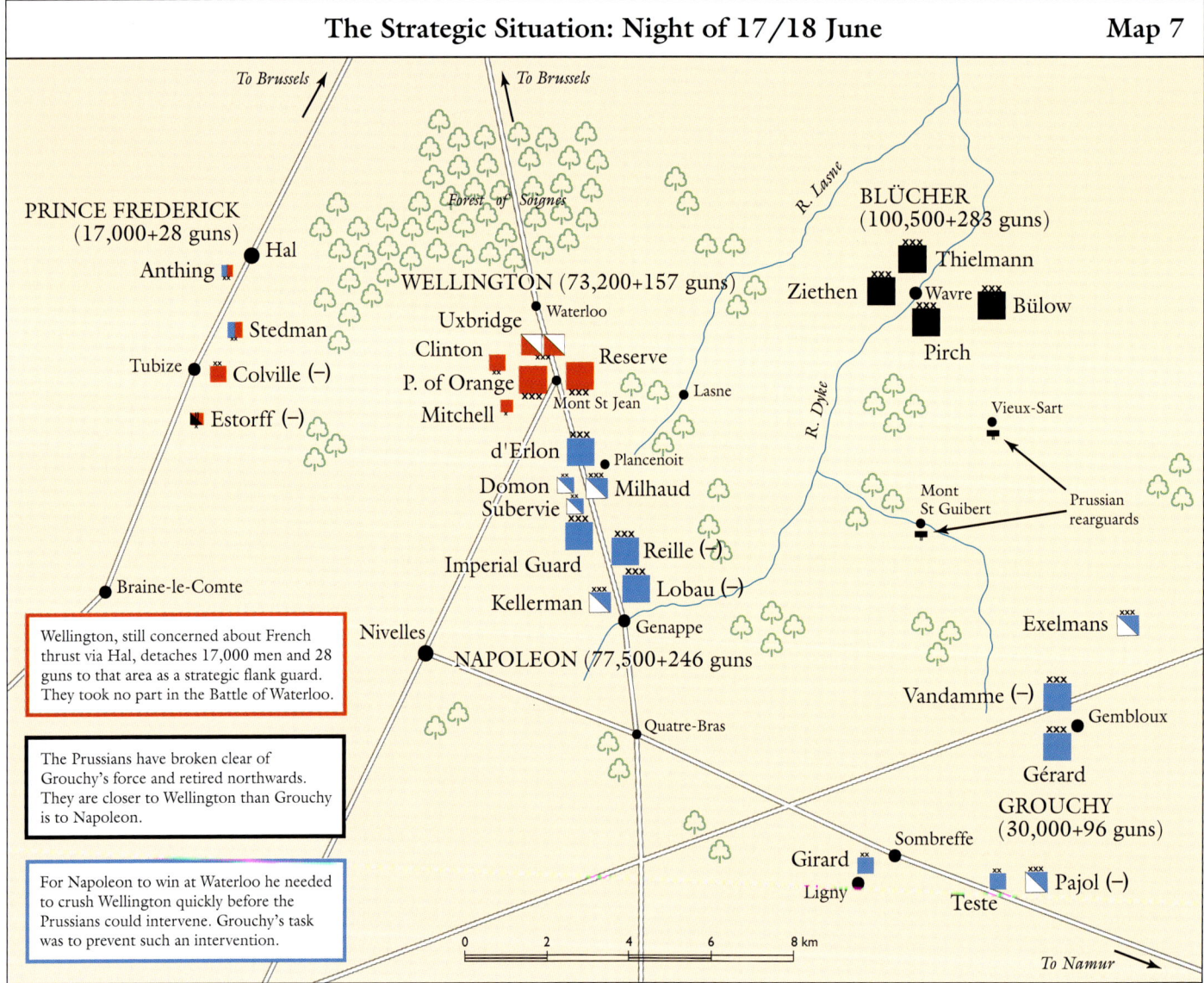

To Brussels

To Brussels

Forest of Soignes

R. Lasne

PRINCE FREDERICK
(17,000+28 guns)

BLÜCHER
(100,500+283 guns)

Hal

Thielmann

Anthing

Ziethen   Wavre   Bülow

WELLINGTON (73,200+157 guns)

Pirch

Uxbridge   Waterloo

Stedman

Clinton

Tubize   Colville (−)

P. of Orange   Reserve

R. Dyke

Mont St Jean

Estorff (−)

Mitchell   Lasne

Vieux-Sart

d'Erlon   Plancenoit

Domon   Milhaud   Mont
Subervie   St Guibert   Prussian
rearguards

Reille (−)

Braine-le-Comte

Imperial Guard   Lobau (−)

Exelmans

Kellerman

Nivelles   Genappe

Vandamme (−)   Gembloux

NAPOLEON (77,500+246 guns)

Gérard

GROUCHY
(30,000+96 guns)

Quatre-Bras

Sombreffe

Girard

Ligny   Teste   Pajol (−)

To Namur

0   2   4   6   8 km

> Wellington, still concerned about French thrust via Hal, detaches 17,000 men and 28 guns to that area as a strategic flank guard. They took no part in the Battle of Waterloo.

> The Prussians have broken clear of Grouchy's force and retired northwards. They are closer to Wellington than Grouchy is to Napoleon.

> For Napoleon to win at Waterloo he needed to crush Wellington quickly before the Prussians could intervene. Grouchy's task was to prevent such an intervention.

needed to turn at once on Wellington, who was still at Quatre-Bras, and at the same time ensure a close follow up of Blücher to keep him moving away from the action. Second, he had to ensure Ney held onto Wellington at the crossroads. If the marshal, now with d'Erlon firmly back under command, attacked the Anglo-Allied army with vigour, Wellington would not be able to withdraw. With Wellington firmly held in front Napoleon could swing in against his left (eastern) flank, with a crushing victory the almost certain result – and Brussels the prize.

Fortunately for the Allies the Emperor did not see the chance until it was too late, while Ney, seldom a man to demonstrate strategic insight, allowed his enemy to slip away northwards. Napoleon spent the morning riding round the Ligny battlefield talking to his soldiers and the wounded. He seemed lethargic, content with ensuring medical aid and brandy were available to Prussians as well as French casualties. He stopped to congratulate units, to receive their acclaim and to chat with Grouchy on the political situation in Paris. Not until after 11.00 a.m., with the

receipt of further information on both the Prussian and Anglo-Allied movements, did Napoleon grasp what was left of the opportunity. It was just too late. Wellington, on hearing of the Prussian withdrawal northwards, pulled back from Quatre-Bras while Ney remained inactive as he did so.

The remainder of the day, and on through thunderstorms and drenching rain into the late evening, the French desperately struggled to catch up with Wellington. Skilful rearguard actions by cavalry and horse artillery units coupled with the foul weather, frustrated their efforts. That night, after retiring some 13 kilomteres, Wellington turned to fight on the Mont St Jean ridge. On the eastern wing Grouchy had grouped around Gembloux, still uncertain as to whether the bulk of the Prussian Army was retreating east, as expected, along their line of communication towards Namur and Liège, or north to Wavre. As the sodden soldiers in each army sank exhausted into the mud for a miserable night in the field, Wellington and Blücher were closer to each other than Grouchy was to Napoleon. The strategic situation was as depicted on Map 7.

Orders of Battle

'Hark! I hear the tramp of thousands,
And of armed men the hum;
Lo! a nation's hosts have gathered
Round the quick alarming drum, –
Saying 'Come,
Freeman, come,
Ere your heritage be wasted,' said the quick alarming drum.

Brete Harte

General

An order of battle sets out in detail exactly how a military formation or unit is organized, how strong it is, and its composition in terms of the troop types within it. Those in this section are depicted in diagrammatic form with a picture of all army and corps commanders. They show the three armies early on the morning of 18 June 1815 before a shot was fired at Waterloo. Considerable detail is provided for those forces that actually fought at Waterloo. Those detached elsewhere are shown in outline.

They cover all formations (corps, divisions and brigades) down to unit (regiment or battalion) level. With the cavalry and artillery the orders of battle also include sub-units (squadrons, or batteries with the type of ordnance used). The estimated strength of the formation or unit is shown in brackets after the appropriate symbol. If it is known for certain that a commander was a casualty at Waterloo it is indicated thus – (k), killed; (w), wounded; (mw), mortally wounded; or (w&c), wounded and captured, is placed after his name. Brief notes on points of interest, the role of the formation prior to Waterloo, its tasks in the battle or its losses, are given alongside the order of battle diagram.

All three armies at Waterloo were organized on similar lines under their commanders-in-chief. However, there were some signif-

A Corps on the Line of March

A corps is a very large formation. It took a considerable length of time to move from A to B and deploy for battle, and it could be several hours after the leading units moved off before the tail began to march. Once on the road there would be continual stopping, starting and bunching up. Infantry in column of fours on the march took up about 270 metres per thousand men; a thousand cavalry 750 metres; a battery of six or eight guns with all its ammunition and supply wagons between 550–750 metres. D'Erlon's corps of almost 20,000 men (17,000 infantry, 1,500 cavalry, 48 guns plus staff engineers, etc.) would have stretched for up to 12 kilometres if all its units marched along a single road. This endless snake would have been even longer if supply wagons were included, which they were not during the march to Waterloo on 17–18 June. The distance from Quatre-Bras to La Belle Alliance is over 10 kilometres.

icant national differences that require explanation if the orders of battle are to be fully understood. The armies were organized into:

CORPS

In practice a small army, usually commanded by a general or a lieutenant-general. In the French Army it was a senior général de division. An infantry corps was a formation of all arms, services and staff. It could move and fight independently if required. Infantry corps varied in strength at Waterloo from over 31,000 (I British Corps) to around 10,600 (French VI Corps). Wellington and Napoleon both employed cavalry corps which were always much smaller in numbers – 10,000 (Anglo-Allied Cavalry Corps) down to just over 3000 (French IV Reserve Cavalry Corps). This huge difference in size between cavalry and infantry formations was due to the fact that cavalry regiments had sometimes only 400 men, whereas infantry battalions could be double that number. Also there were always more infantry battalions in an infantry corps than cavalry units in a cavalry corps. At Waterloo Wellington deployed four corps (three infantry and one cavalry), Napoleon mustered six (four infantry and two cavalry), including the Imperial Guard, and late in the battle Blücher brought one complete infantry corps and part of two others onto the field. The Prussians did not have separate cavalry corps.

DIVISIONS

A division comprised of two or more brigades of infantry or cavalry. It would also have some artillery (foot or horse) permanently attached and under command. As with a corps, cavalry divisions were much smaller than infantry ones for the same reasons. A division was a semi-independent formation with some staff and administrative units attached. It was normally a major-general's command, but at Waterloo the system was different. The Prussian Army did not have divisions at all. Instead they had big brigades. A Prussian brigade was the equivalent strength of an Allied or French division and was under a major-general. A British division at Waterloo was a lieutenant-general's command, leaving only the French to comply with normal military custom and give the command to a général de division. The number of divisions engaged during the battle was as follows:

	Infantry	Cavalry	Total
Anglo-Allied	8.5	4.5*	13
Prussian	8	5	13
French	12	10	22
Totals	**28.5**	**19.5**	**48**

* This is an equivalent figure as British cavalry brigades were not grouped into divisions.

BRIGADES

The smallest military formations, usually commanded by a brigadier-general. It consisted of two or more infantry regiments or battalions or cavalry regiments. The strength of an infantry brigade varied from 2000 to nearly 4000, with cavalry brigades being between 1000 and 2000. As noted above, the Prussian brigade was equal in size to a division in the other armies. A British brigade at Waterloo usually had three or four battalions while the 1st Hanoverian Brigade had five-and-a-half, and the 1st and 2nd Netherlands Brigades had six each. The French had up to seven. Cavalry brigades had two or three regiments.

REGIMENTS

The largest military units. Only in the British Army did the infantry regiment have no tactical purpose. British infantry deployed on the battlefield in battalions, with the regiment to which they belonged being an administrative and recruiting organization based at home. In the French and Prussian Armies the infantry regiment was a tactical unit consisting of several battalions, usually three, commanded by a colonel. Cavalry regiments, however, were basically the same in all armies, having between two and four squadrons each. A lieutenant-colonel or major normally commanded.

French Artillery Distribution

Despite having many more guns than Wellington, the number was less than intended. The French Army artillery establishment would, in normal circumstances, have meant each corps having twice the number of guns under command than was the case at Waterloo. A corps order of battle should have shown two 12-pounder companies as a reserve, plus two 6-pounder companies (one horse and one foot) in each division. In 1815 this arrangement had only been possible in the Imperial Guard. The problem was not lack of manpower or ordnance, but lack of horses.

Variable Number of Companies in a Battalion

The internal organization of infantry battalions at Waterloo varied considerably, particularly within Wellington's army. Battalions of about the same strength, say 600, could be composed of ten companies of 60 or four of 150, depending on nationality. The table below gives the approximate situation at the battle:

Nationality	Companies per battalion	All ranks per company
British	10	60–75 (Guards 100)
KGL	6	80–100
Nassau	6	80–100
Dutch-Belgian	6	70–100
Hanoverian	4	130–150
Brunswick	4	150–170
Prussian	4	150
French Imperial Guard	4	150
French line battalion	6	100

BATTALIONS

The infantry battalion was the unit by which an army's main fighting strength was measured. 'God', as Napoleon once said, 'was on the side of the big battalions' – although at Waterloo the French battalions were the smallest, averaging only 520 all ranks. A quick way of assessing an army's strength was to total up the number of infantry battalions (plus cavalry squadrons and artillery batteries). On 18 June they varied in size from over 1,100 to under 350 and were commanded, at the start of the battle, by lieutenant-colonels or majors. The position at Waterloo was as given below:

	Battalions	Cavalry Squadrons	Artillery Batteries
Anglo-Allied	84	93	24.5
Prussian	62	61	15.75
French	103	113.5	34
Total	**249**	**267.5**	**74**

Average battalion strengths were (to the nearest five) – Anglo-Allied 640, Prussian 615 and French 520.

SQUADRONS, COMPANIES, BATTERIES, TROOPS AND PLATOONS

These were the sub-units into which cavalry, infantry and artillery units were divided, commanded by junior officers. These sub-units are dealt with in greater detail in the Cavalry, Infantry and Artillery Sections.

OVERALL STRENGTHS AT WATERLOO

The orders of battle show an estimated strength for all ranks present and under arms with the formations or units on the morning of 18 June. The figures show the Anglo-Allied Army having 73,200 men with 157 guns at Mont St Jean, plus another 17,000 men and 22 guns detached near Hal. The French, deployed on either side of La Belle Alliance, mustered around 77,500 men with 246 guns, with another 30,000 men and 96 guns away to the east with Grouchy. Blücher eventually managed to bring about 49,000 men and 134 guns onto the Waterloo battlefield. Some 26,300 Prussians saw no action that day, as they were still marching from Wavre to Waterloo when the battle ended. Most of the remaining 25,000 Prussians faced Grouchy at Wavre. A brief explanation as to how these figures were arrived at is given below, as for both Wellington's and Napoleon's armies the totals are about 6000 higher than many writers have suggested.

Anglo-Allied Strengths

GENERAL

Using the parade states in Wellington's despatches and including officers, senior NCOs and bandsmen (which W. Siborne in his *History of War in France and Belgium 1815* did not) and all garrison troops, a grand total of 112,000 men was available to Wellington throughout Belgium in mid-June. Deduct from this figure the garrisons, the troops left around Brussels, the 4,600 casualties lost at Quatre-Bras and on the retreat to Waterloo on the 17 June, plus the 17,000 at Hal, and Wellington had some 72,400 at the start of the battle. The final total of 73,200 includes an estimated 600–800 soldiers who were only slightly wounded or sick, never left their units, and thus fought again at Waterloo. Sir Thomas Picton is an example of such a man.

The 17,000 men Wellington kept posted around Hal and Tublize (Map 7) throughout the battle represented some 23 per cent of his force assembled to confront Napoleon that day, with the twenty-two guns being 14 per cent of his artillery. This force was two-thirds of Hill's II Corps, with the young (eighteen-year-old) Prince Frederick of the Netherlands in command of the 1st Netherlands Division and the Indonesian Brigade.

STRENGTHS BY NATIONALITY

British
Infantry: 25.5 battalions (30% of all infantry battalions).
Cavalry: 16 regiments, 45 squadrons (49% of cavalry squadrons).
Artillery: 8 Troops RHA and 5 Brigades RFA (77 guns, 49% of total).

King's German Legion (KGL)
Infantry: 8 battalions (9.5% of total infantry).
Cavalry: 4 regiments, 16 squadrons (17% of cavalry squadrons).
Artillery: 2 horse batteries, 1 foot battery (18 guns, 11.5% of total artillery).

Nassau
Infantry: 8.5 battalions (10% of total infantry).
Cavalry: nil.
Artillery: nil.

Brunswick
Infantry: 8 battalions (9.5% of total infantry).
Cavalry: 1 regiment, plus a squadron, total 5 squadrons (5% of cavalry squadrons).
Artillery: 1 horse, 1 foot battery (16 guns, 10% of artillery).

Hanoverian
Infantry: 17 battalions (21% of total infantry).
Cavalry: 1 regiment, 4 squadrons (4% of cavalry squadrons).
Artillery: 1 horse, 1 foot battery (12 guns, 7.5% of artillery).

Dutch
Infantry: 13 battalions (15% of total infantry).
Cavalry: 4 regiments, 14 squadrons (15% of cavalry squadrons).
Artillery: 2 horse batteries (16 guns, 10% of artillery).

Belgian
Infantry: 4 battalions (5% of total infantry).
Cavalry: 3 regiments, 9 squadrons (10% of cavalry squadrons).
Artillery: 1 horse battery, 1.25 foot batteries (18 guns, 12% of artillery).

Overall percentages by nationality
British 36%, King's German Legion 10%, Nassau 10%, Brunswick 8%, Hanoverian 17%, Dutch 13%, and Belgian 6%. In total some 45% of the army spoke German as a first language.

SUMMARY

Infantry: 84 battalions	53,850
Cavalry: 29 regiments, 93 squadrons	13,350
Artillery: 24.25 batteries, 157 guns + 1 rocket section	5,000
Others (staff, sappers, medical, engineers, etc.)	1,000
Grand total at Waterloo (estimated):	**73,200**

ADDITIONAL STATISTICS – INFANTRY

- There were four infantrymen to every cavalryman.
- The strongest battalion was the 1/52 Foot (Oxfordshire) with 1,130 all ranks.
- The smallest battalion was the 1/42 Foot (Black Watch) with only 338 all ranks. It had suffered nearly 300 casualties in severe fighting at Quatre-Bras.
- The average strength of an Anglo-Allied battalion at Waterloo was about 640 all ranks.
- The strongest battalions were those from Nassau with an average of 855 all ranks while the weakest were those of the King's German Legion with 525.

ADDITIONAL STATISTICS – CAVALRY

- Within the Anglo-Allied Army only the three Netherlands cavalry brigades were grouped as a division under a divisional commander (Collaert). The remaining seven brigades and one regiment (Cumberland Hussars) were controlled by the cavalry corps commander, Uxbridge. The only other exception was the Brunswick Hussar Regiment and Uhlan squadron that formed part of the Brunswick Contingent.
- There were three heavy cavalry brigades and the equivalent of eight light brigades present at the battle. Several of the British heavy regiments were particularly small numerically at the outset and were to suffer considerably during the battle.
- The largest regiment was the 3rd Hussars KGL with 712.
- The smallest regiment was the 2nd Life Guards with a mere 235 men in two squadrons, although the Royal Horse Guards at 246 and the 1st Life Guards with 255 came close.
- The average strength of a regiment of Anglo-Allied cavalry was 460.
- All British light cavalry regiments had three squadrons; King's German Legion cavalry and some others had four. The average strength of a squadron was 144 all ranks.

ADDITIONAL STATISTICS – ARTILLERY

- Wellington deployed 157 guns and howitzers at Waterloo in just over twenty-four batteries (or equivalent) – that is one gun for every 466 soldiers on the battlefield or just under two guns for every battalion on the battlefield.
- Of the twenty-four batteries, fifteen were horse artillery – although in the event, with the exception of a single battery, all were used as stationary guns of position from the outset.
- The British provided the bulk of the cannons (seventy-seven), together with some rockets, with the Hanoverians fielding the least (twelve), although the Nassauers had none at all.

Wellington had mixed together
nationalities, regulars, militia,
experienced and inexperienced units
at both corps and divisional level
(see detailed orders of battle).

The detached force at Hal was part
of II Corps but with the young
Prince Frederick of the Netherlands
in nominal command of his national
element (10,000 plus troops).

THE ANGLO-ALLIED ARMY
a.m. 18 June 1815

**C in C Field Marshal
the Duke of Wellington**

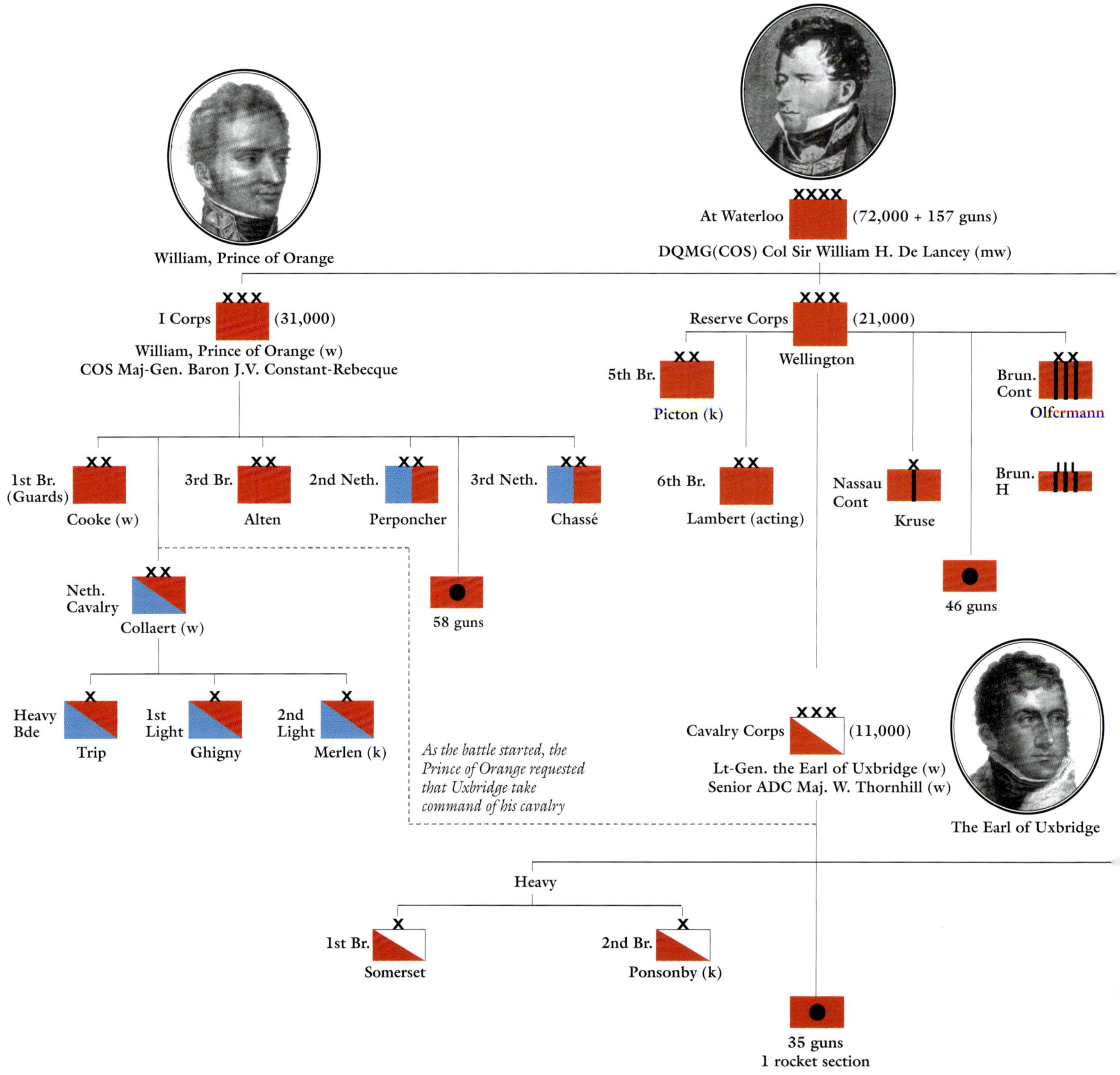

At Waterloo   **XXXX**   (72,000 + 157 guns)

DQMG(COS) Col Sir William H. De Lancey (mw)

William, Prince of Orange

I Corps   **XXX**   (31,000)

William, Prince of Orange (w)
COS Maj-Gen. Baron J.V. Constant-Rebecque

Reserve Corps   **XXX**   (21,000)

Wellington

5th Br.   **XX**

Picton (k)

Brun.
Cont   **XX**

Olfermann

1st Br.
(Guards)   **XX**

Cooke (w)

3rd Br.   **XX**

Alten

2nd Neth.   **XX**

Perponcher

3rd Neth.   **XX**

Chassé

6th Br.   **XX**

Lambert (acting)

Nassau
Cont   **X**

Kruse

Brun.
H   **X**

Neth.
Cavalry   **XX**

Collaert (w)

58 guns

46 guns

Heavy
Bde   **X**

Trip

1st
Light   **X**

Ghigny

2nd
Light   **X**

Merlen (k)

*As the battle started, the
Prince of Orange requested
that Uxbridge take
command of his cavalry*

Cavalry Corps   **XXX**   (11,000)

Lt-Gen. the Earl of Uxbridge (w)
Senior ADC Maj. W. Thornhill (w)

The Earl of Uxbridge

Heavy

1st Br.   **X**

Somerset

2nd Br.   **X**

Ponsonby (k)

35 guns
1 rocket section

Overall Strength Summary

	At Waterloo	At Hal	Total
Infantry	53,850	15,000	68,850
Cavalry	13,350	1,200	14,550
Artillery	5,000	700	5,700
Others*	1,000	100	1,100
Totals	73,200	17,000	90,200
Guns	157		
Rockets	1 section		

*Includes - RE, Sappers, Miners, Staff Corps, Medical Wagon Train and HQ Staff.

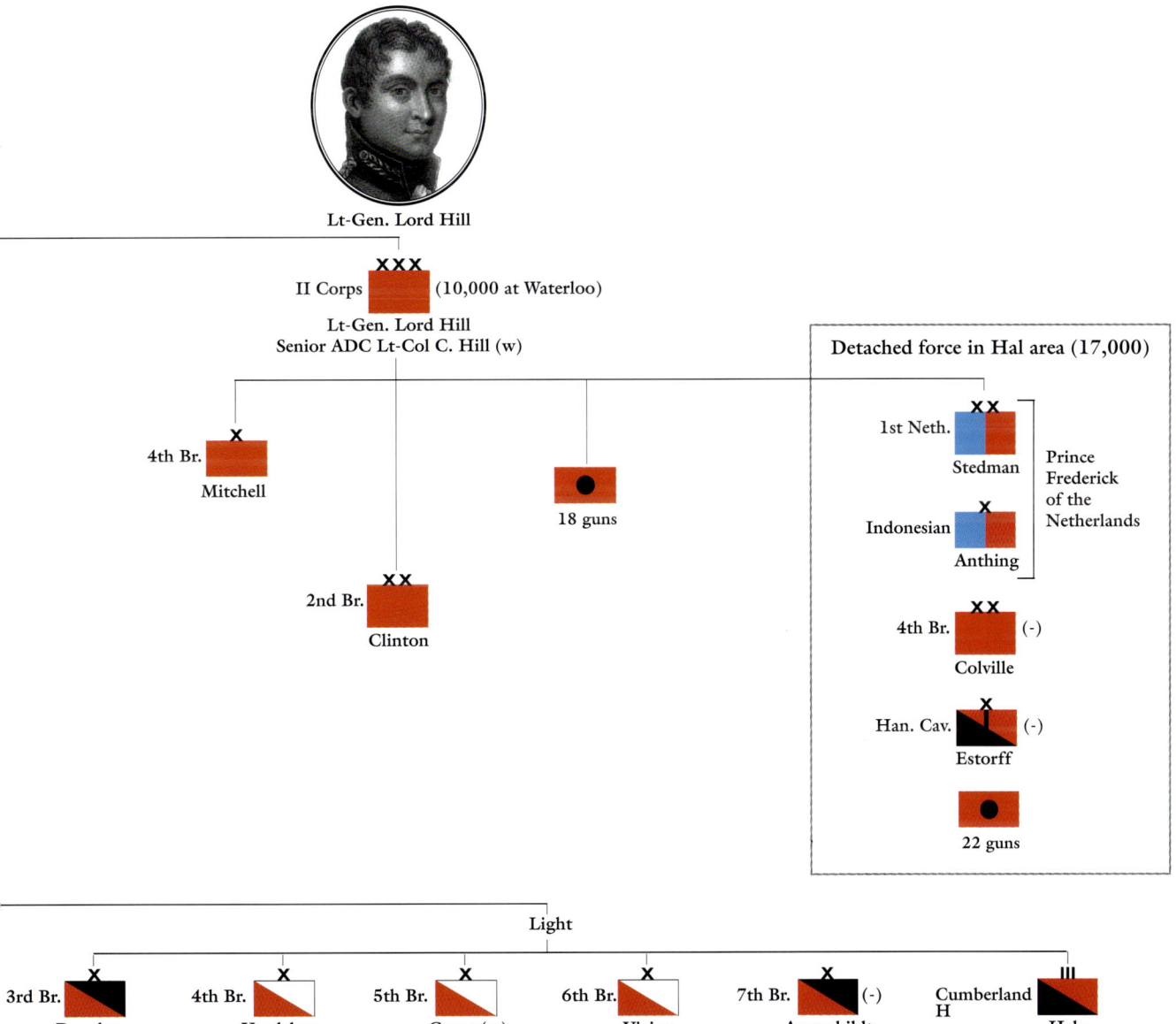

Lt-Gen. Lord Hill

II Corps (10,000 at Waterloo)
Lt-Gen. Lord Hill
Senior ADC Lt-Col C. Hill (w)

Detached force in Hal area (17,000)

4th Br.
Mitchell

18 guns

2nd Br.
Clinton

1st Neth.
Stedman

Indonesian
Anthing

Prince Frederick of the Netherlands

4th Br. (-)
Colville

Han. Cav. (-)
Estorff

22 guns

Light

3rd Br.
Dornberg

4th Br.
Vandeleur

5th Br.
Grant (w)

6th Br.
Vivian

7th Br. (-)
Arenschildt

Cumberland H

Hake

THE 1ST BRITISH INFANTRY (GUARDS) DIVISION (4,266)

GOC Major General George Cooke (w)

Guards division not mixed. Commanders, staff and troops all guardsmen. The only British Division commanded by a Major-General.

With four battalions plus twelve guns it was the smallest British Division although the battalions were initially 1000 strong, almost twice the strength of other British units.

Casualties at Waterloo about 1,350 (30%).

Deployed on the right of Wellington's line, close to Hougoumont.

2nd Brigade and Light Coys of 1st Brigade committed to defence of Hougoumont. 1st Brigade involved in repulse of Imperial Guard attack around 7.30 p.m. for which 1st Foot Guards given title 'Grenadiers', although they repulsed the Châsseurs not the Grenadiers of the Imperial Guard.

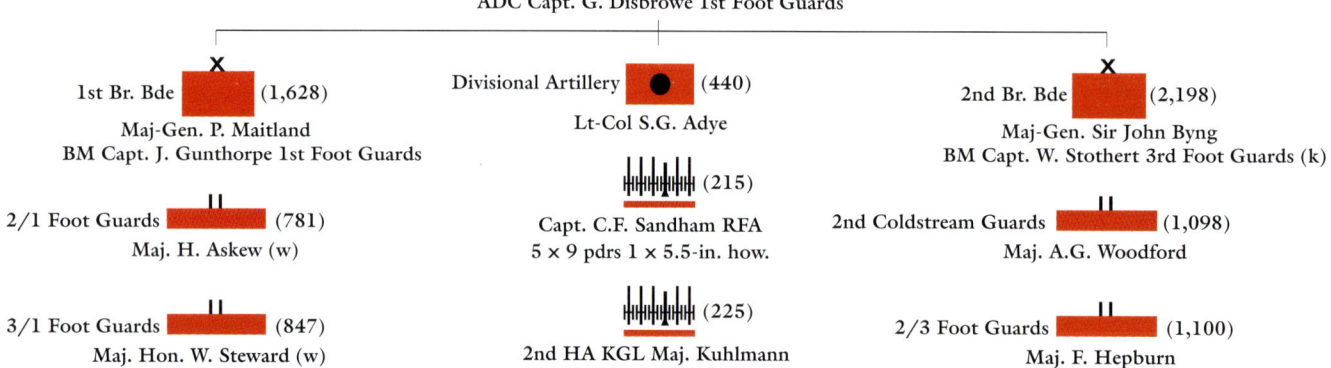

ADC Capt. G. Disbrowe 1st Foot Guards

1st Br. Bde (1,628)
Maj-Gen. P. Maitland
BM Capt. J. Gunthorpe 1st Foot Guards

Divisional Artillery (440)
Lt-Col S.G. Adye

2nd Br. Bde (2,198)
Maj-Gen. Sir John Byng
BM Capt. W. Stothert 3rd Foot Guards (k)

2/1 Foot Guards (781)
Maj. H. Askew (w)

(215)
Capt. C.F. Sandham RFA
5 × 9 pdrs 1 × 5.5-in. how.

2nd Coldstream Guards (1,098)
Maj. A.G. Woodford

3/1 Foot Guards (847)
Maj. Hon. W. Steward (w)

(225)
2nd HA KGL Maj. Kuhlmann
5 × 9 pdrs 1 × 5.5-in. how.

2/3 Foot Guards (1,100)
Maj. F. Hepburn

THE 3RD BRITISH INFANTRY DIVISION (8,091)

GOC Lt-Gen. Charles, Count Alten

With the thirteen and a half battalions plus twelve guns it was, at the outset, the strongest British division, although it subsequently lost 3,725 casualties (47%).

2/69 lost King's Colour at Quatre-Bras.

At Waterloo the 1st Hanoverian Brigade lost 1,532 men, of whom 45% were missing. Three out of four unit commanders in the brigade were killed or wounded at either Quatre-Bras or Waterloo.

Deployed on the right/centre of Wellington's line after a 30-mile march via Quatre-Bras.

Suffered severely from artillery fire. Spent much time in squares resisting cavalry attacks.

5th Line (KGL) suffered losses of 93% after being caught in wrong formation by cuirassiers after Allied loss of La Haie Sainte.

ADCs
Maj. A. Heise 2nd Light Bn KGL
Lt W. Havelock 43rd Foot (w)

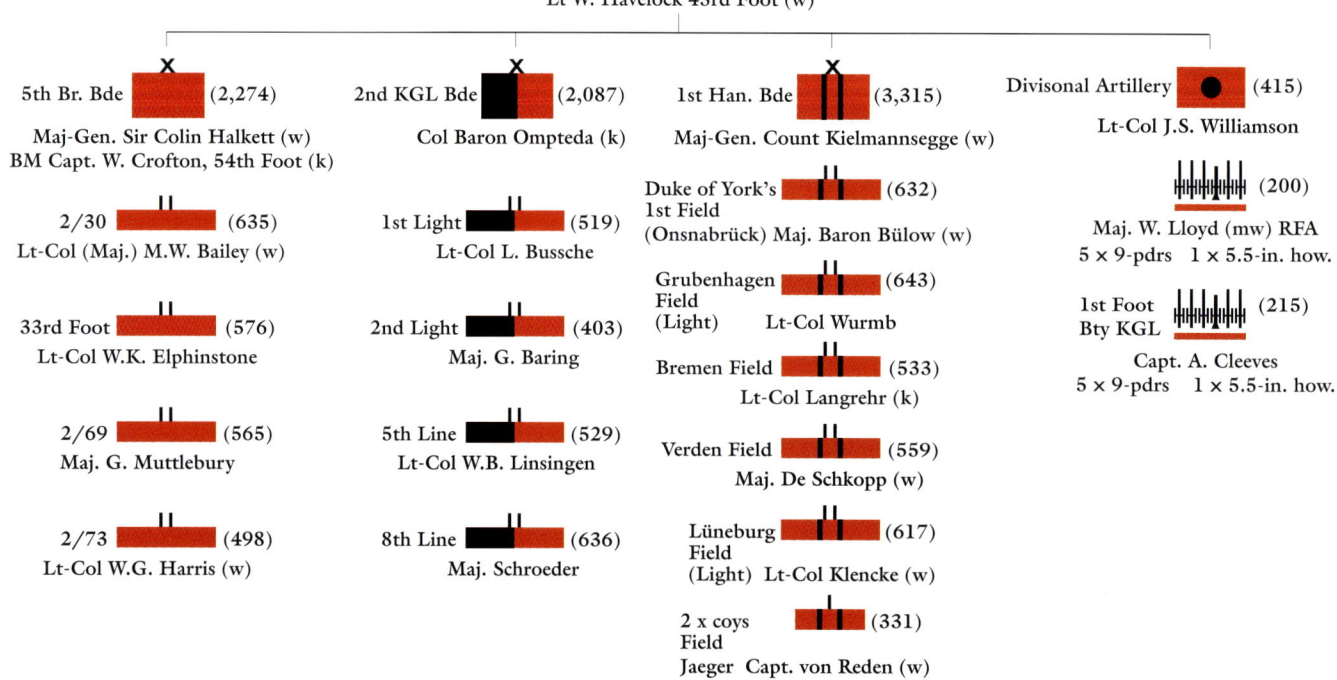

5th Br. Bde (2,274)
Maj-Gen. Sir Colin Halkett (w)
BM Capt. W. Crofton, 54th Foot (k)

2nd KGL Bde (2,087)
Col Baron Ompteda (k)

1st Han. Bde (3,315)
Maj-Gen. Count Kielmannsegge (w)

Divisonal Artillery (415)
Lt-Col J.S. Williamson

2/30 (635)
Lt-Col (Maj.) M.W. Bailey (w)

1st Light (519)
Lt-Col L. Bussche

Duke of York's 1st Field (632)
(Onsnabrück) Maj. Baron Bülow (w)

(200)
Maj. W. Lloyd (mw) RFA
5 × 9-pdrs 1 × 5.5-in. how.

33rd Foot (576)
Lt-Col W.K. Elphinstone

2nd Light (403)
Maj. G. Baring

Grubenhagen Field (643)
(Light) Lt-Col Wurmb

1st Foot Bty KGL (215)
Capt. A. Cleeves
5 × 9-pdrs 1 × 5.5-in. how.

2/69 (565)
Maj. G. Muttlebury

5th Line (529)
Lt-Col W.B. Linsingen

Bremen Field (533)
Lt-Col Langrehr (k)

2/73 (498)
Lt-Col W.G. Harris (w)

8th Line (636)
Maj. Schroeder

Verden Field (559)
Maj. De Schkopp (w)

Lüneburg Field (617)
(Light) Lt-Col Klencke (w)

2 x coys Field (331)
Jaeger Capt. von Reden (w)

THE 2ND NETHERLANDS INFANTRY DIVISION (7,620)

GOC Lt-Gen. Baron Henri-Georges Perponcher-Sedlnitzky

A division with three languages – French, Dutch and German.

It was the first Allied formation deployed at Quatre-Bras and bore the brunt of Ney's initial assaults, holding the line until more troops arrived. Losses were around 1,100 on the 16th.

Casualties at Waterloo amounted to just over 2000 (24%), with the 1st Brigade sustaining twice those of the 2nd Brigade.

The division was split with 1st Brigade on the left centre, initially in a line in front of Picton's division with the 2nd on the east (left) defending Papelotte and La Haie. The 1/2 Nassau was sent to Hougoumont.

1st Brigade almost entirely Dutch with 2nd Brigade all German (Nassau) except for the artillery. 2nd Nassau battalions having nearly 900 all ranks.

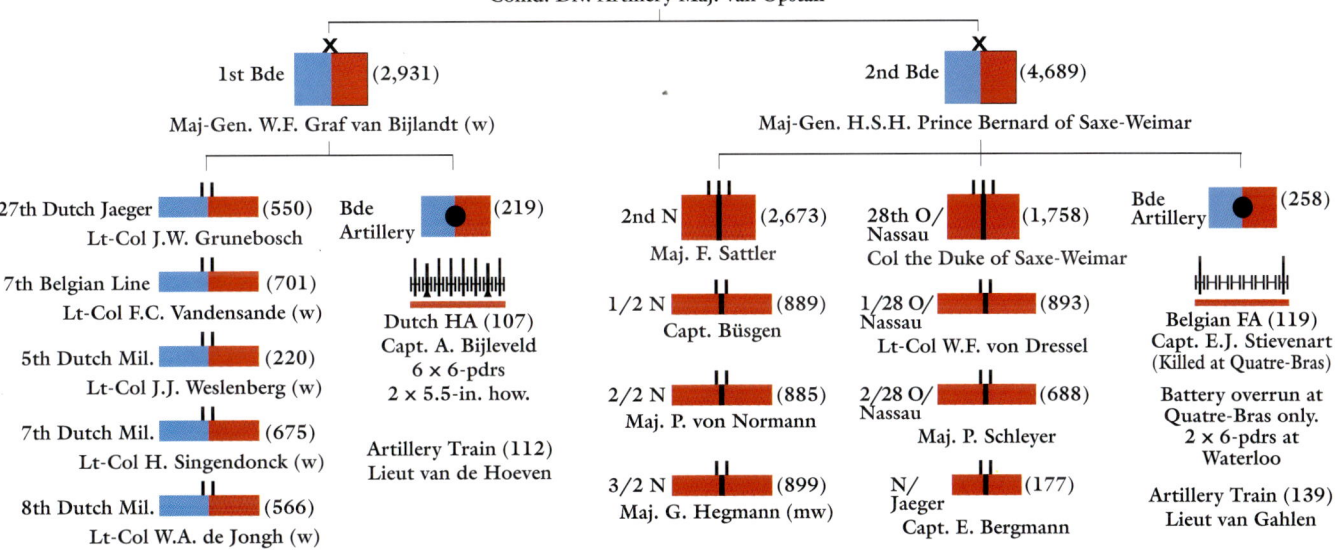

COS Col P.H. Baron van Zuylen van Nyevelt (w)
Comd. Div. Artillery Maj. van Opstall

1st Bde (2,931)
Maj-Gen. W.F. Graf van Bijlandt (w)

- 27th Dutch Jaeger (550) — Lt-Col J.W. Grunebosch
- 7th Belgian Line (701) — Lt-Col F.C. Vandensande (w)
- 5th Dutch Mil. (220) — Lt-Col J.J. Weslenberg (w)
- 7th Dutch Mil. (675) — Lt-Col H. Singendonck (w)
- 8th Dutch Mil. (566) — Lt-Col W.A. de Jongh (w)

Bde Artillery (219)
Dutch HA (107) — Capt. A. Bijleveld — 6 × 6-pdrs — 2 × 5.5-in. how.
Artillery Train (112) — Lieut van de Hoeven

2nd Bde (4,689)
Maj-Gen. H.S.H. Prince Bernard of Saxe-Weimar

- 2nd N (2,673) — Maj. F. Sattler
- 1/2 N (889) — Capt. Büsgen
- 2/2 N (885) — Maj. P. von Normann
- 3/2 N (899) — Maj. G. Hegmann (mw)
- 28th O/Nassau (1,758) — Col the Duke of Saxe-Weimar
- 1/28 O/Nassau (893) — Lt-Col W.F. von Dressel
- 2/28 O/Nassau (688) — Maj. P. Schleyer
- N/Jaeger (177) — Capt. E. Bergmann

Bde Artillery (258)
Belgian FA (119) — Capt. E.J. Stievenart (Killed at Quatre-Bras) — Battery overrun at Quatre-Bras only. 2 × 6-pdrs at Waterloo
Artillery Train (139) — Lieut van Gahlen

THE 3RD NETHERLANDS INFANTRY DIVISION (7,146)

GOC Lt-Gen. Baron David-Hendrik Chassé

A mixed Dutch-Belgian formation with the Dutch units predominating – 9 out of 12 battalions being Dutch.

Some doubts initially as to the commitment of these troops. An inexperienced formation with 50% of its units being militia.

When called upon to fight late on in the battle, the 1st Brigade performed satisfactorily.

Losses 743 (10%)

Because of the uncertainty of its quality this division was posted on the extreme west of the Allied line around the village of Braine l'Alleud. It remained in reserve for much of the day.

In the evening the division moved behind the right centre of the line and was committed to the action to repulse the final Imperial Guard attack. The 1st Brigade charged the Grenadiers of the Middle Guard.

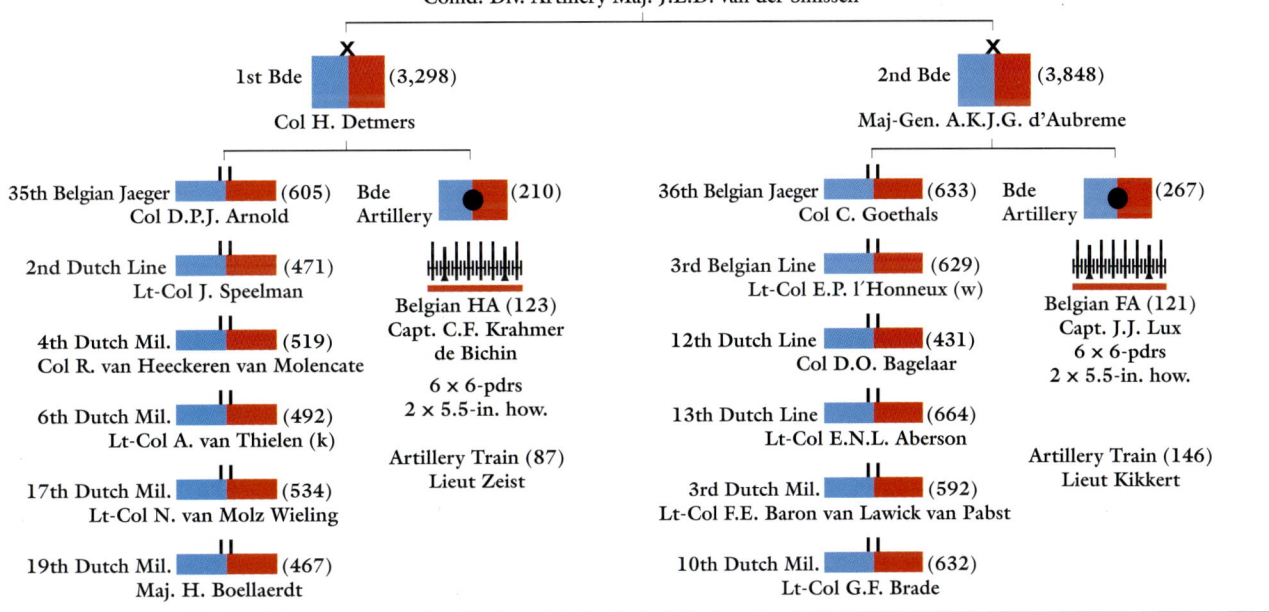

COS Maj. L.A.C. Baron van Delen
Comd. Div. Artillery Maj. J.L.D. van der Smissen

1st Bde (3,298)
Col H. Detmers

- 35th Belgian Jaeger (605) — Col D.P.J. Arnold
- 2nd Dutch Line (471) — Lt-Col J. Speelman
- 4th Dutch Mil. (519) — Col R. van Heeckeren van Molencate
- 6th Dutch Mil. (492) — Lt-Col A. van Thielen (k)
- 17th Dutch Mil. (534) — Lt-Col N. van Molz Wieling
- 19th Dutch Mil. (467) — Maj. H. Boellaerdt

Bde Artillery (210)
Belgian HA (123) — Capt. C.F. Krahmer de Bichin — 6 × 6-pdrs — 2 × 5.5-in. how.
Artillery Train (87) — Lieut Zeist

2nd Bde (3,848)
Maj-Gen. A.K.J.G. d'Aubreme

- 36th Belgian Jaeger (633) — Col C. Goethals
- 3rd Belgian Line (629) — Lt-Col E.P. l'Honneux (w)
- 12th Dutch Line (431) — Col D.O. Bagelaar
- 13th Dutch Line (664) — Lt-Col E.N.L. Aberson
- 3rd Dutch Mil. (592) — Lt-Col F.E. Baron van Lawick van Pabst
- 10th Dutch Mil. (632) — Lt-Col G.F. Brade

Bde Artillery (267)
Belgian FA (121) — Capt. J.J. Lux — 6 × 6-pdrs — 2 × 5.5-in. how.
Artillery Train (146) — Lieut Kikkert

THE NETHERLANDS CAVALRY DIVISION (3,305)

GOC Lt-Gen. Baron J.A. de Collaert (w)

This division was initially deployed well back in reserve behind the centre, on either side of the Brussels road close to Mont St Jean farm.

All brigade commanders had at one time fought for the French but performed creditably against them at Waterloo with the possible exception of Trip.

The division was heavily engaged, especially against French cavalry in the afternoon.

Losses were high – 1,225 (37%) with the dragoons and hussars of the 1st Light Brigade losing 49%.

COS Lt-Col A.J. Hoynek van Papendrecht

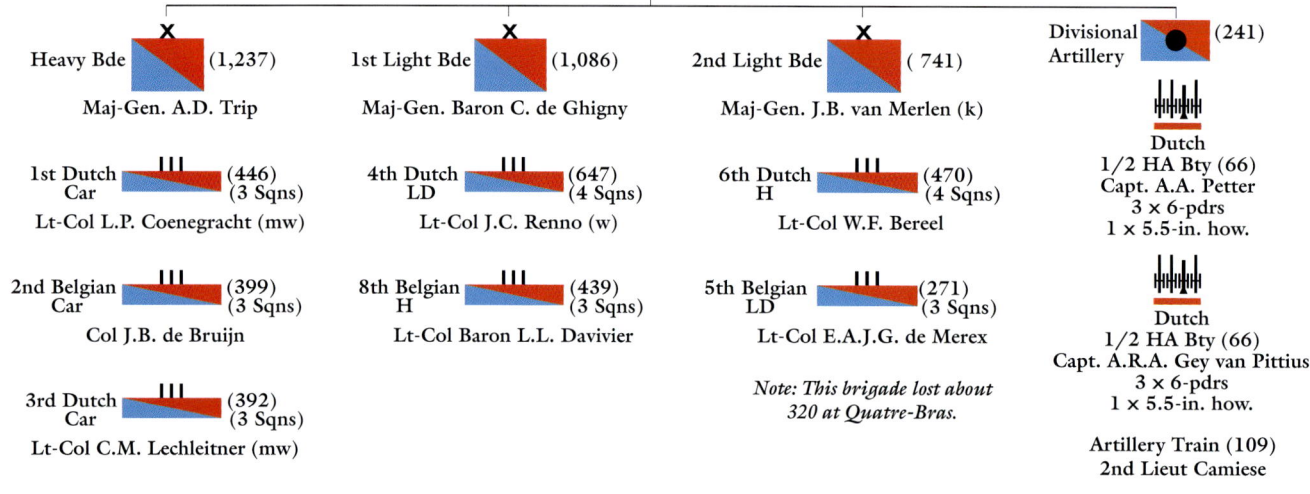

Heavy Bde (1,237)	1st Light Bde (1,086)	2nd Light Bde (741)	Divisional Artillery (241)
Maj-Gen. A.D. Trip	Maj-Gen. Baron C. de Ghigny	Maj-Gen. J.B. van Merlen (k)	

1st Dutch Car (446) (3 Sqns)	4th Dutch LD (647) (4 Sqns)	6th Dutch H (470) (4 Sqns)	Dutch 1/2 HA Bty (66) Capt. A.A. Petter 3 × 6-pdrs 1 × 5.5-in. how.
Lt-Col L.P. Coenegracht (mw)	Lt-Col J.C. Renno (w)	Lt-Col W.F. Bereel	

2nd Belgian Car (399) (3 Sqns)	8th Belgian H (439) (3 Sqns)	5th Belgian LD (271) (3 Sqns)	Dutch 1/2 HA Bty (66) Capt. A.R.A. Gey van Pittius 3 × 6-pdrs 1 × 5.5-in. how.
Col J.B. de Bruijn	Lt-Col Baron L.L. Davivier	Lt-Col E.A.J.G. de Merex	

3rd Dutch Car (392) (3 Sqns)
Lt-Col C.M. Lechleitner (mw)

Note: This brigade lost about 320 at Quatre-Bras.

Artillery Train (109)
2nd Lieut Camiese

BRITISH RESERVE ARTILLERY (360)

These two troops of the RHA had not been attached to a cavalry brigade but rather kept in reserve.

They were both deployed in the front line from the outset. Ross (with the 'Chestnut' Troop) was close to the crossroads in the centre and Beane further to the right in front of the Guards.

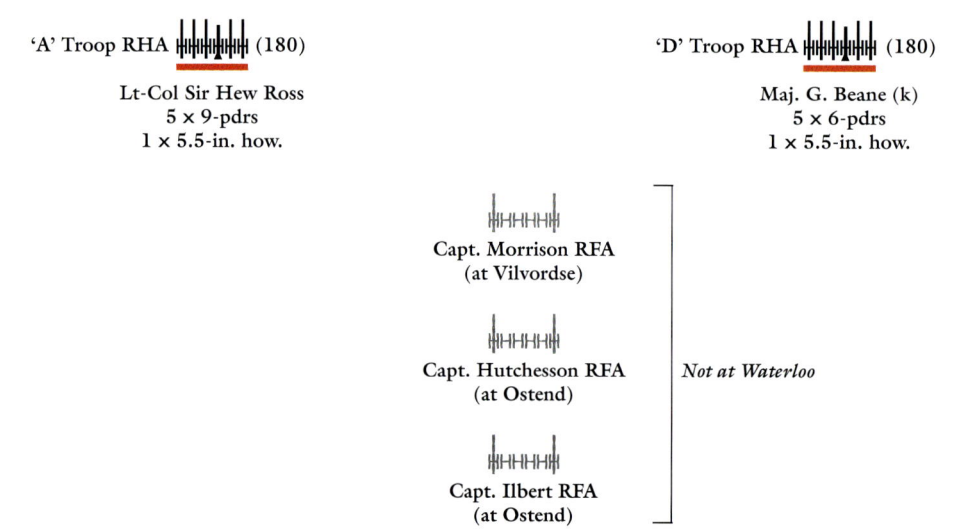

'A' Troop RHA (180)
Lt-Col Sir Hew Ross
5 × 9-pdrs
1 × 5.5-in. how.

'D' Troop RHA (180)
Maj. G. Beane (k)
5 × 6-pdrs
1 × 5.5-in. how.

Capt. Morrison RFA
(at Vilvordse)

Capt. Hutchesson RFA
(at Ostend)

Not at Waterloo

Capt. Ilbert RFA
(at Ostend)

THE 2ND BRITISH INFANTRY DIVISION (7,992)

GOC Lt-Gen. Sir Henry Clinton

A strong division, with two of its three brigades German speaking. A good example of how an inexperienced Han. Landwehr brigade was stiffened by serving alongside British and KGL regular units.

Not involved at Quatre-Bras. Casualties at Waterloo amounted to around 1,540 (19%).

Initially deployed in reserve behind the right of the Allied line and north of the Nivelles road.

Moved forward to the front line in the early evening. The 1/52, which was probably the strongest battalion in the army, played a major role in defeating the Imperial Guard by attacking them in flank.

ADCs
Capt. F. Dawkins 1st Foot Guards
Capt. J. Gurwood 10th H (w)

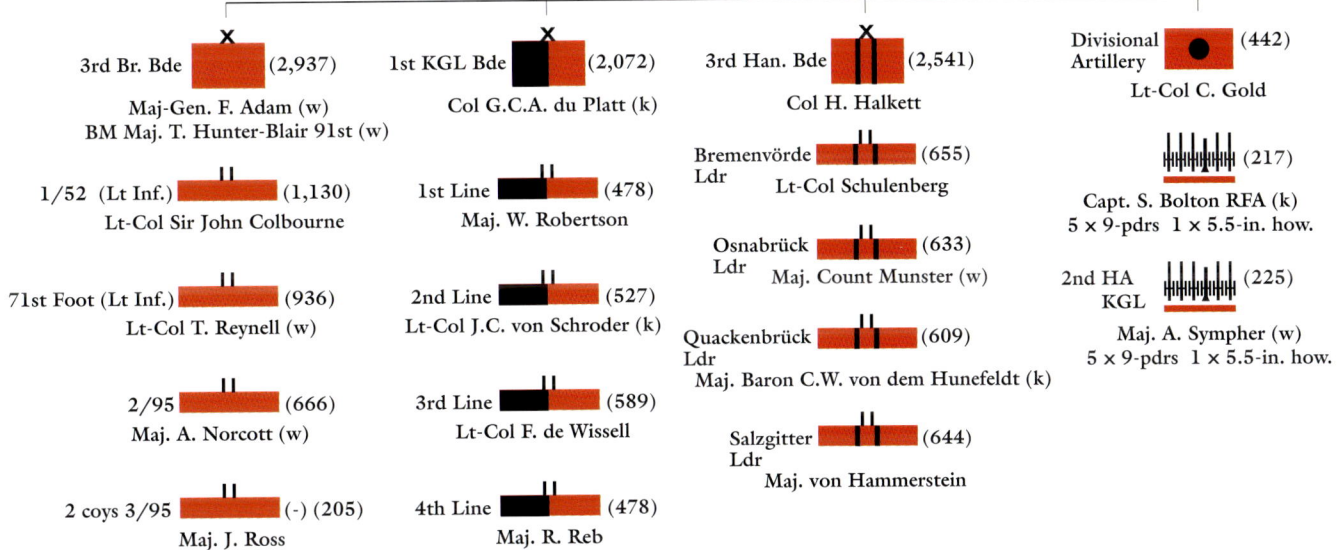

3rd Br. Bde (2,937)
Maj-Gen. F. Adam (w)
BM Maj. T. Hunter-Blair 91st (w)

1/52 (Lt Inf.) (1,130)
Lt-Col Sir John Colbourne

71st Foot (Lt Inf.) (936)
Lt-Col T. Reynell (w)

2/95 (666)
Maj. A. Norcott (w)

2 coys 3/95 (-) (205)
Maj. J. Ross

1st KGL Bde (2,072)
Col G.C.A. du Platt (k)

1st Line (478)
Maj. W. Robertson

2nd Line (527)
Lt-Col J.C. von Schroder (k)

3rd Line (589)
Lt-Col F. de Wissell

4th Line (478)
Maj. R. Reb

3rd Han. Bde (2,541)
Col H. Halkett

Bremenvörde Ldr (655)
Lt-Col Schulenberg

Osnabrück Ldr (633)
Maj. Count Munster (w)

Quackenbrück Ldr (609)
Maj. Baron C.W. von dem Hunefeldt (k)

Salzgitter Ldr (644)
Maj. von Hammerstein

Divisional Artillery (442)
Lt-Col C. Gold

(217)
Capt. S. Bolton RFA (k)
5 × 9-pdrs 1 × 5.5-in. how.

2nd HA KGL (225)
Maj. A. Sympher (w)
5 × 9-pdrs 1 × 5.5-in. how.

THE 4TH BRITISH INFANTRY DIVISION (2,245)

GGOC Lt-Gen. Hon. Sir Charles Colville
(not present at Waterloo)

Mixed Br./Han. brigade. Only the 4th Br. Brigade and Capt. Rettberg's guns fought at Waterloo. The remainder deployed near Hal to the west.

Not involved at Quatre-Bras. Losses to 4th Br. Brigade at Waterloo were about 182 (9%).

Although absent from the battle, members of the 2/34, 1/54, 2/59 and 1/91 were granted the Waterloo Medal and two years extra service, but 'Waterloo' is not a battle honour on their Colours.

4th Br. Brigade deployed on right (west) of line with raw 3/14 north of Nivelles road.

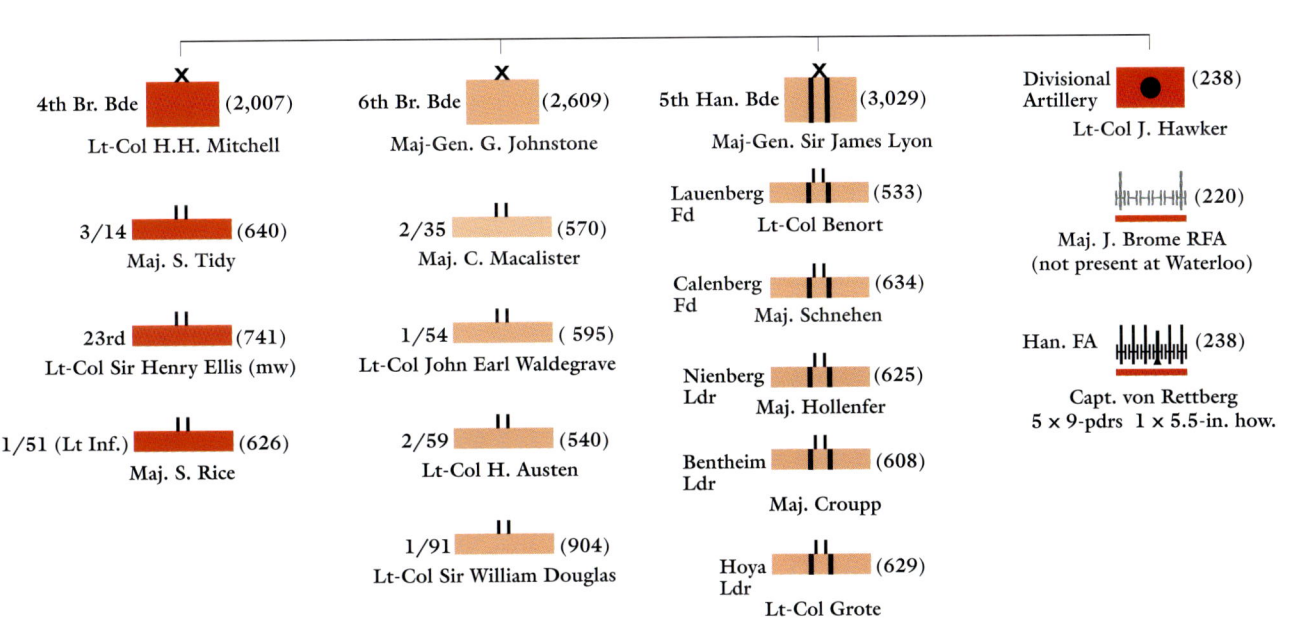

4th Br. Bde (2,007)
Lt-Col H.H. Mitchell

3/14 (640)
Maj. S. Tidy

23rd (741)
Lt-Col Sir Henry Ellis (mw)

1/51 (Lt Inf.) (626)
Maj. S. Rice

6th Br. Bde (2,609)
Maj-Gen. G. Johnstone

2/35 (570)
Maj. C. Macalister

1/54 (595)
Lt-Col John Earl Waldegrave

2/59 (540)
Lt-Col H. Austen

1/91 (904)
Lt-Col Sir William Douglas

5th Han. Bde (3,029)
Maj-Gen. Sir James Lyon

Lauenberg Fd (533)
Lt-Col Benort

Calenberg Fd (634)
Maj. Schnehen

Nienberg Ldr (625)
Maj. Hollenfer

Bentheim Ldr (608)
Maj. Croupp

Hoya Ldr (629)
Lt-Col Grote

Divisional Artillery (238)
Lt-Col J. Hawker

(220)
Maj. J. Brome RFA
(not present at Waterloo)

Han. FA (238)
Capt. von Rettberg
5 × 9-pdrs 1 × 5.5-in. how.

THE 5TH BRITISH INFANTRY DIVISION (6,724)

GOC Lt-Gen. Sir Thomas Picton (k)

A mixed Br./Han. formation, the Br. brigades of which were heavily engaged at Quatre-Bras.

Part of Wellington's Reserve Corps, it marched from Brussels to Quatre-Bras on the 16th where it lost the equivalent of two battalions.

Picton was wounded at Quatre-Bras and killed at Waterloo. Kempt assumed command. Division lost 2,943 (43%) at Waterloo.

ADCs
Capt. A. Langton 61st Foot (w)
Capt. J. Tyler 93rd Foot (w)
Capt. N. Chambers 1st Foot Guards (k)

Deployed on the left and centre of the Allied line and suffered heavily from the fire of the French 'Grand Battery'. Faced d'Erlon's attack at 2.00 p.m. Picton shot dead after ordering bayonet charge.

The division was spread thinly over nearly a mile of front along and behind the ridge. Initially Picton had Best's brigade of Han. attached as the other brigade of 6th Division was late arriving.

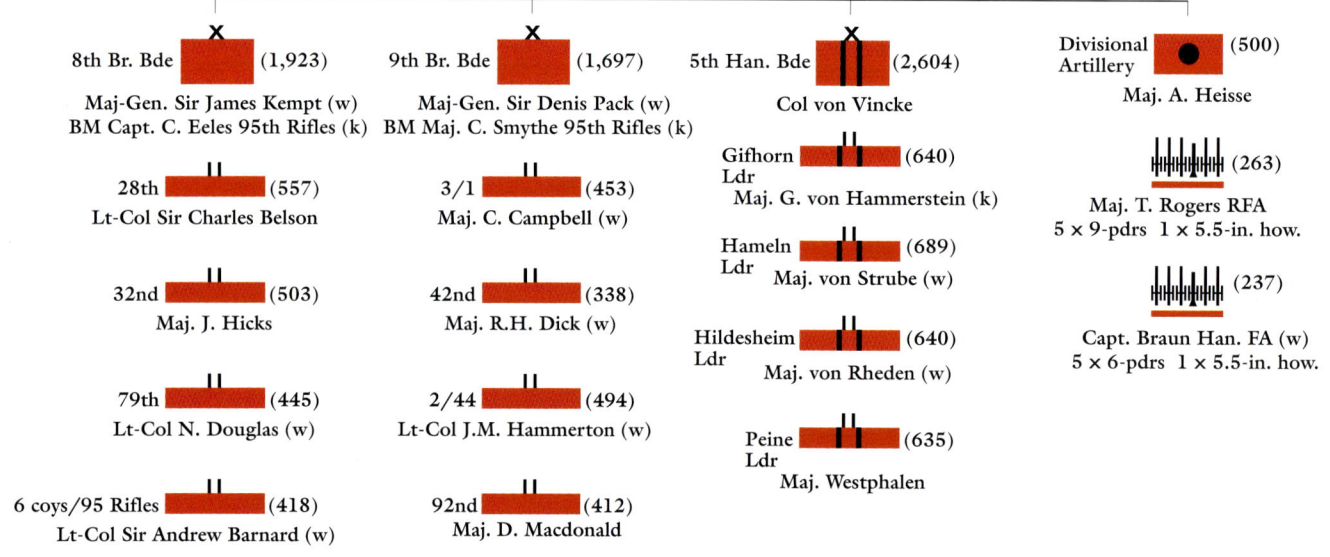

8th Br. Bde (1,923)
Maj-Gen. Sir James Kempt (w)
BM Capt. C. Eeles 95th Rifles (k)

28th (557) Lt-Col Sir Charles Belson
32nd (503) Maj. J. Hicks
79th (445) Lt-Col N. Douglas (w)
6 coys/95 Rifles (418) Lt-Col Sir Andrew Barnard (w)

9th Br. Bde (1,697)
Maj-Gen. Sir Denis Pack (w)
BM Maj. C. Smythe 95th Rifles (k)

3/1 (453) Maj. C. Campbell (w)
42nd (338) Maj. R.H. Dick (w)
2/44 (494) Lt-Col J.M. Hammerton (w)
92nd (412) Maj. D. Macdonald

5th Han. Bde (2,604)
Col von Vincke

Gifhorn Ldr (640) Maj. G. von Hammerstein (k)
Hameln Ldr (689) Maj. von Strube (w)
Hildesheim Ldr (640) Maj. von Rheden (w)
Peine Ldr (635) Maj. Westphalen

Divisional Artillery (500) Maj. A. Heisse

(263) Maj. T. Rogers RFA 5 × 9-pdrs 1 × 5.5-in. how.
(237) Capt. Braun Han. FA (w) 5 × 6-pdrs 1 × 5.5-in. how.

THE 6TH BRITISH INFANTRY DIVISION (5,158)

GOC Lt-Gen. Sir Lowry Cole
(not present at Waterloo)

A mixed division of only two brigades, one Br. one Han. militia. Initially it was split, with 4th Han. Brigade attached to 5th Division until Lambert's brigade arrived.

All battalions well up to strength as 10th Brigade not engaged at Quatre-Bras. Casualties at Waterloo 1,325 (25%).

Formed part of Wellington's Reserve Corps. Br. battalions just returned from America. 1/4 had only 4 capts.

ADC Lieut T. Baynes 39th Foot

4th Han. Brigade deployed with 5th Division on left centre of position. Lambert's 10th Br. Brigade arrived at 10.30 a.m. and was held initially in reserve near Mont St Jean.

Lambert assumed command of division in absence of Cole on his honeymoon. His brigade had marched 50 miles from Ghent. During afternoon 1/27 were pounded to pieces near crossroads with sgts commanding coys after 66% loss.

10th Br. Bde (2,289)
Maj-Gen. Sir John Lambert (acting Div. Comd. on arrival)
BM Maj. H.G.W. Smith (w)

1/4 (677) Lt-Col F. Brooke
1/27 (750) Capt. J. Hare (w)
1/40 (862) Maj. A.R. Hayland (k)
2/81 (498) Left in Brussels

Divisional Artillery (200) Lt-Col Bruckmann

(200) Capt. J. Sinclair RFA 5 × 9-pdrs 1 × 5.5-in. how.
Maj. G.W. Unett RFA (not present at Waterloo)

4th Han. Bde (2,669)
Col C. Best
(This brigade initially attached to 5th Division until arrival of Lambert's brigade)

Verden Ldr (642) Maj. de Decken
Lüneberg Ldr (647) Lt-Col de Ramdohr
Munden Ldr (680) Maj. de Schmidt
Osterode Ldr (700) Maj. Baron Reden (w)

THE BRUNSWICK CONTINGENT (DIVISION) (6,244)

Acting GOC Col Olfermann

Formed by the 'Black' Duke of Brunswick and wore black uniforms, hence the nickname 'Black Brunswickers'.

Mixed force of 8 bns of infantry, 5 sqns of cavalry plus 16 guns. Men mostly recruits.

Part of Wellington's reserve. Heavily engaged at Quatre-Bras with losses of 846, including Duke of Brunswick who was killed.

Initially deployed in reserve at Waterloo about half a mile behind the right/centre, close to the hamlet of Merbraine.

Later bns moved to front line. All involved in resisting French cavalry attacks and the Hussars were used in counterattacks.

Losses at Waterloo 600 (10%).

QMG Lt-Col von Heinemann (k)
COS Maj. von Wachholtz
Comd. Artillery Maj. von Lubecq

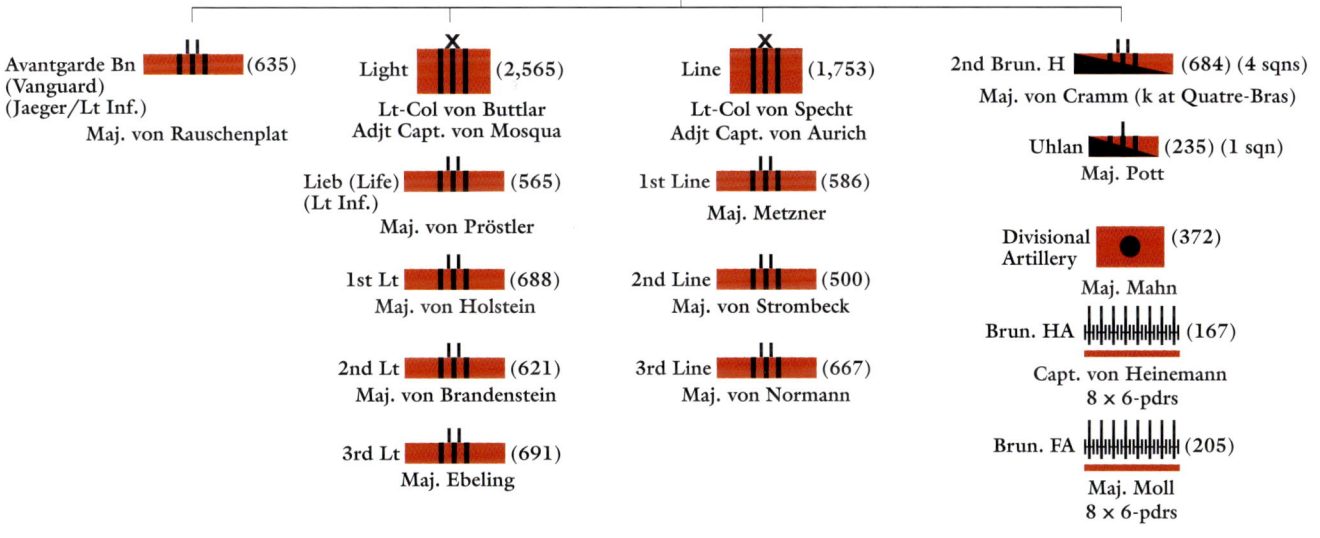

Avantgarde Bn (635)
(Vanguard)
(Jaeger/Lt Inf.)
Maj. von Rauschenplat

Light (2,565)
Lt-Col von Buttlar
Adjt Capt. von Mosqua

Lieb (Life) (565)
(Lt Inf.)
Maj. von Pröstler

1st Lt (688)
Maj. von Holstein

2nd Lt (621)
Maj. von Brandenstein

3rd Lt (691)
Maj. Ebeling

Line (1,753)
Lt-Col von Specht
Adjt Capt. von Aurich

1st Line (586)
Maj. Metzner

2nd Line (500)
Maj. von Strombeck

3rd Line (667)
Maj. von Normann

2nd Brun. H (684) (4 sqns)
Maj. von Cramm (k at Quatre-Bras)

Uhlan (235) (1 sqn)
Maj. Pott

Divisional (372)
Artillery
Maj. Mahn

Brun. HA (167)
Capt. von Heinemann
8 × 6-pdrs

Brun. FA (205)
Maj. Moll
8 × 6-pdrs

THE NASSAU RESERVE CONTINGENT (BRIGADE) (2,841)

GOC Maj-Gen. A.H.E. von Kruse

A brigade-strength force that operated independently under Wellington.

The great majority of the soldiers were inexperienced but many officers were veterans.

Not involved at Quatre-Bras.

Deployed initially immediately behind the right centre of the Allied line.

Later involved with the repulse of the French cavalry and in the fighting to prevent the loss of La Haie Sainte.

Casualties 643 (23%), of which a high proportion were killed (40%).

2IC Lt-Col von Haven
COS Capt. von Morrenhoffen

1st Nassau (2,841)
Col E. von Steuben

1/1 N (951)
Maj. J. von Weyhers

2/1 N (943)
Maj. A. von Nauendorf

Ldr (947)
Maj. F. von Preen

THE 1ST BRITISH (HOUSEHOLD) CAVALRY BRIGADE (1,319)

GOC Maj-Gen. Lord Edward Somerset

A Guards heavy cavalry brigade. With only two squadrons in three of its regiments it was barely 50% of war strength. Like most cavalry units it should have had four squadrons of 150 men each.

Losses at Waterloo were severe – 632 (48%).

Deployed initially in reserve behind the centre west of the Brussels road.

Charged (with Union Brigade) to defeat French cuirassiers and d'Erlon's infantry, it reached the French 'Grand Battery' where it was attacked by cavalry and badly mauled.

BM Maj. H.G. Smith 25th Foot (k)
ADC Lt H. Somerset 18th H

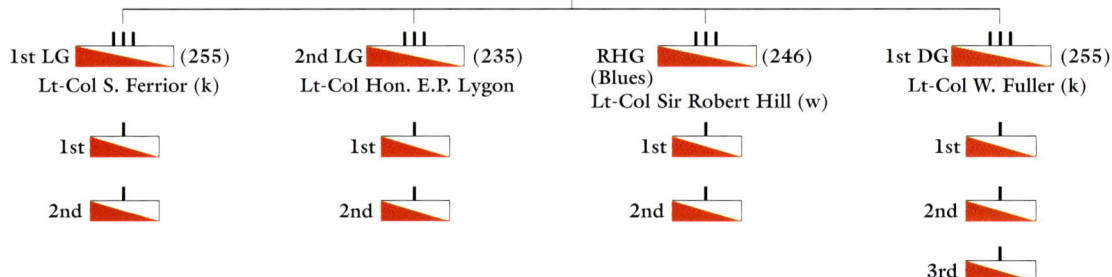

1st LG (255)	2nd LG (235)	RHG (Blues) (246)	1st DG (255)
Lt-Col S. Ferrior (k)	Lt-Col Hon. E.P. Lygon	Lt-Col Sir Robert Hill (w)	Lt-Col W. Fuller (k)
1st	1st	1st	1st
2nd	2nd	2nd	2nd
			3rd

THE 2ND BRITISH (UNION) CAVALRY BRIGADE (1,332)

GOC Maj-Gen. Hon. Sir William Ponsonby (k)

A heavy cavalry unit called the 'Union' Brigade, on account of its having a regiment each from England, Scotland and Ireland.

Although it had only three regiments they each had three squadrons giving it about equal strength to the Household Brigade.

Deployed initially behind the centre east of the Brussels road.

Charged d'Erlon's infantry and reached 'Grand Battery' where Ponsonby was killed. Lt-Col Clifton took over command.

Losses heavy – 616 (46%).

BM Maj. T. Reignolds 2nd D (k)
ADC Lt B. Christie 5th DG

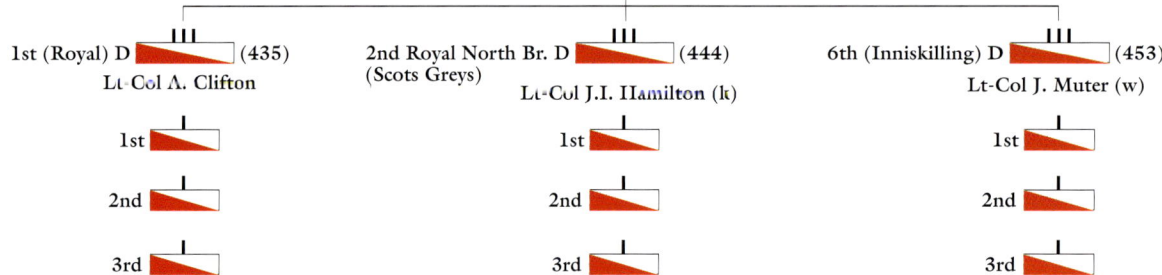

1st (Royal) D (435)	2nd Royal North Br. D (Scots Greys) (444)	6th (Inniskilling) D (453)
Lt-Col A. Clifton	Lt-Col J.I. Hamilton (k)	Lt-Col J. Muter (w)
1st	1st	1st
2nd	2nd	2nd
3rd	3rd	3rd

THE 3RD BRITISH CAVALRY BRIGADE (1,401)

GOC Maj-Gen. Sir William Dornberg (w)

A predominantly German speaking brigade, with the two KGL regiments almost at full strength.

The CO of 23rd LD, Lord Portalington, missed the start of the battle, as he was late back from Brussels. Maj. Cutcliffe commanded at Waterloo and Portalington never recovered from the disgrace, eventually dying in penury.

Initially deployed behind the Allied right centre with Colin Halkett's infantry in front. Were involved in counterattacking the French cavalry that penetrated between Allies' squares. Joined in the general Allied advance that pushed the French back after the repulse of the Imperial Guard.

Casualties 310 (2%) which were the lowest for any British cavalry brigade.

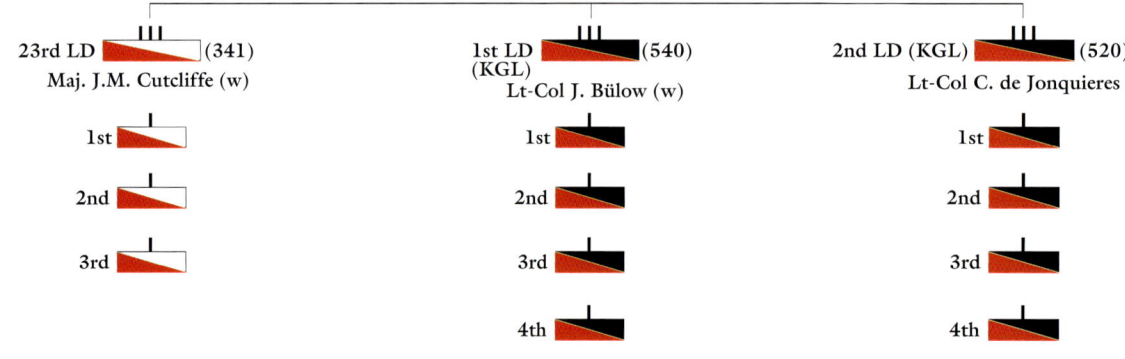

23rd LD (341)	1st LD (KGL) (540)	2nd LD (KGL) (520)
Maj. J.M. Cutcliffe (w)	Lt-Col J. Bülow (w)	Lt-Col C. de Jonquieres
1st	1st	1st
2nd	2nd	2nd
3rd	3rd	3rd
	4th	4th

THE 4TH BRITISH CAVALRY BRIGADE (1,315)

GOC Maj-Gen. Sir John Vandeleur

A typical British light cavalry brigade of average strength with three squadrons per regiment.

Was used to cover the withdrawal of the remnants of the Union Brigade. During this action charged Pégot's brigade of Durutte's division.

As the next senior cavalry general Vandeleur took over command of the whole of the Allied cavalry when Uxbridge was wounded in the evening. Lt-Col Sleigh assumed command of the brigade.

Losses of 319 (23%) occurred mostly during the brigade's advance against French rearguards after the Imperial Guard's repulse.

BM Maj. M. Childers 11th LD
ADC Capt. W. Armstrong 19th LD

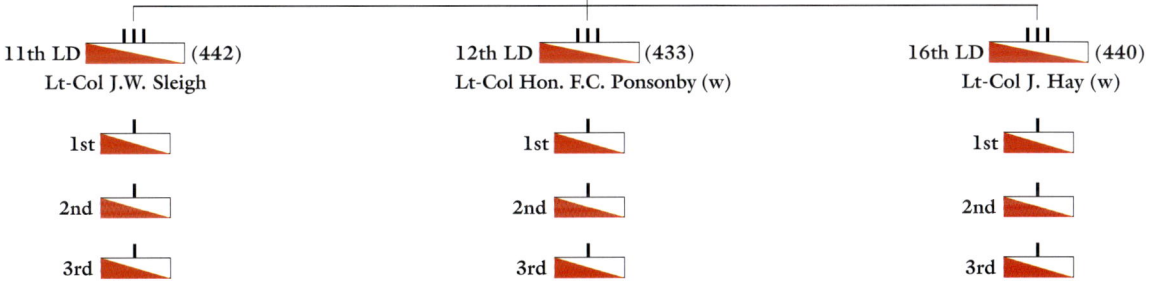

THE 5TH BRITISH CAVALRY BRIGADE (1,267)

GOC Maj-Gen. Sir Colquhoun Grant (w)

A light cavalry brigade with one regiment still away on the frontier that was replaced for the battle by the 13th LD.

Grant was wounded and had five horses shot under him.

Losses 392 (31%) – many during encounters with French cavalry.

Deployed from the start behind the 1st (Guards) Division on the Allied right this brigade was heavily engaged.

Took part in numerous cavalry charges throughout the afternoon against French cavalry attacking Allied squares.

BM Capt. C. Jones 15th H
ADC Lieut R. Mansfield 15th H (w)

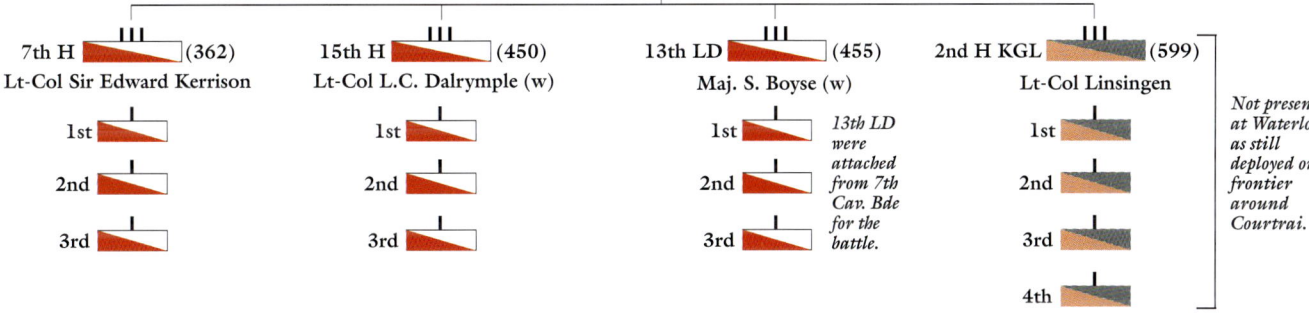

THE 6TH BRITISH CAVALRY BRIGADE (1,504)

Maj-Gen. Sir Hussey Vivian

The light cavalry brigade holding the extreme left (east) of the Allied line. It was the only British cavalry brigade to retain its RHA troop under command for the battle.

It saw little action until evening when it was moved (with 4th Cavalry Brigade) behind the centre.

The brigade was involved in several actions against the retiring French cavalry at the end of the battle.

Casualties amounted to 208 (13%). The 1st Hussars (KGL) only suffered one man killed out of ten casualties. At 1.6% this was the least of any Allied unit in the battle.

BM Capt. T.N. Harris (w)
ADC Capt. E. Keane 7th H

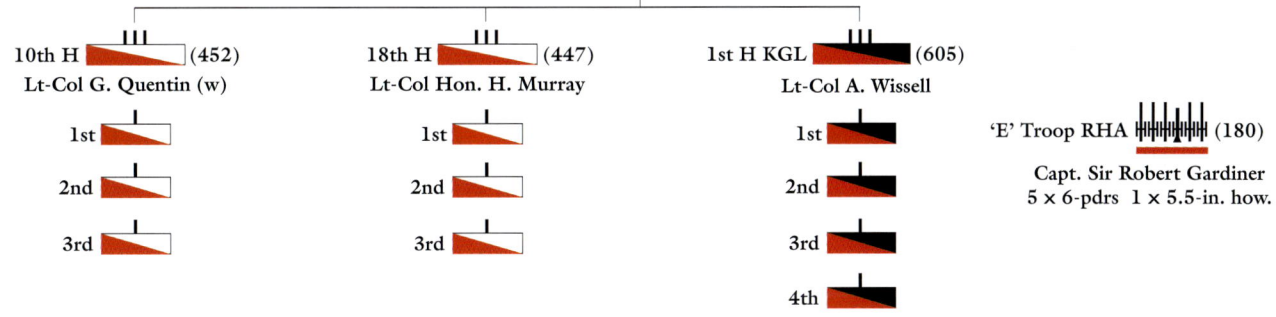

THE 7TH BRITISH CAVALRY BRIGADE (712)

Comd. Col Sir Frederick Arenschildt

This brigade fought as a single (strong) regiment under the supervision of Arenschildt who personally led it forward against French cuirassiers.

Deployed initially behind right centre. Losses 136 (19%).

13th LD (455)
Maj. S. Boyse (w)

See 5th British Cavalry Brigade to which they were attached.

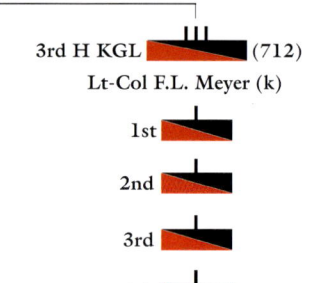

3rd H KGL (712)
Lt-Col F.L. Meyer (k)

1st
2nd
3rd
4th

THE HANOVERIAN CAVALRY BRIGADE (516 at Waterloo)

Comd. Col Baron Estorff
(not present at Waterloo)

Two of the three regiments were posted near Hal under Col Estorff and saw no action.

The Cumberland Hussars consisted of young wealthy Hanoverian gentlemen who provided their own horses and equipment.

During the French cavalry attacks the Cumberland Hussars came under fire, refused to advance and broke ranks to flee back to Brussels. Col Hake spurned all pleas to rally his regiment and was later court-martialled.

Losses 61 (12%).

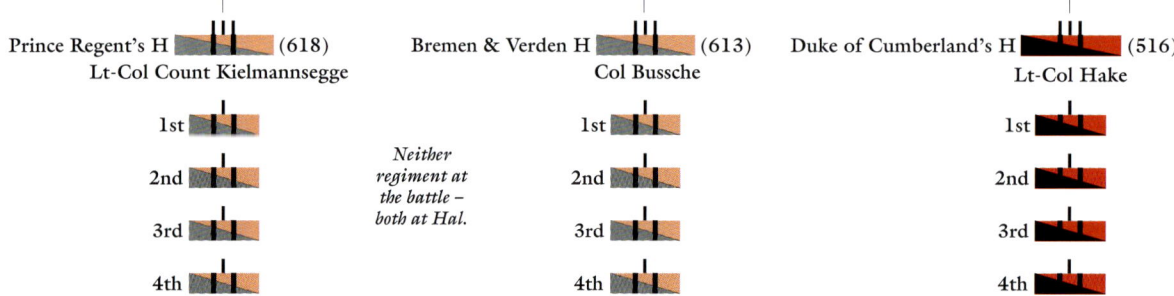

Prince Regent's H (618)
Lt-Col Count Kielmannsegge
1st 2nd 3rd 4th

Neither regiment at the battle – both at Hal.

Bremen & Verden H (613)
Col Bussche
1st 2nd 3rd 4th

Duke of Cumberland's H (516)
Lt-Col Hake
1st 2nd 3rd 4th

ROYAL HORSE ARTILLERY ATTACHED CAVALRY CORPS (1,020)

Comd. Lt-Col A. Macdonald

These RHA Troops were normally under command of, and attached to, the cavalry brigades. With the exception of 'E' Troop, this did not happen at Waterloo where these Troops fought as guns of position away from their brigades and controlled by senior artillery commanders.

Summary:
6 x troops (1,020 men)
15 x 6-pounders
10 x 9-pounders
10 x 5.5-inch howitzers
1 x rocket section
total 35 guns/howitzers

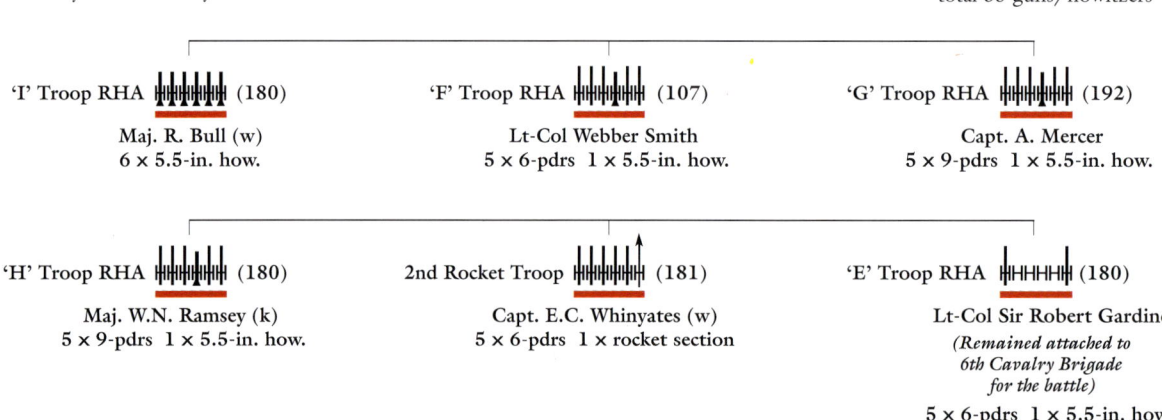

'I' Troop RHA (180)
Maj. R. Bull (w)
6 x 5.5-in. how.

'F' Troop RHA (107)
Lt-Col Webber Smith
5 x 6-pdrs 1 x 5.5-in. how.

'G' Troop RHA (192)
Capt. A. Mercer
5 x 9-pdrs 1 x 5.5-in. how.

'H' Troop RHA (180)
Maj. W.N. Ramsey (k)
5 x 9-pdrs 1 x 5.5-in. how.

2nd Rocket Troop (181)
Capt. E.C. Whinyates (w)
5 x 6-pdrs 1 x rocket section

'E' Troop RHA (180)
Lt-Col Sir Robert Gardiner
(Remained attached to 6th Cavalry Brigade for the battle)
5 x 6-pdrs 1 x 5.5-in. how.

DETACHED ANGLO-ALLIED FORCES – HAL AND TUBIZE AREA (17,559)

Wellington, still worried about a possible French thrust up the Mons–Hal–Brussels route despite no reports of such a movement, posted 17,000 troops around Hal to check such an advance.

Many were unenthusiastic Dutch and Belgian units, stiffened by one British brigade. They saw no action and could hear nothing of the battle raging only 13 kilometres away.

Had Wellington lost at Waterloo he would have had great difficulty justifying leaving so many men idle only 2–3 hours march away.

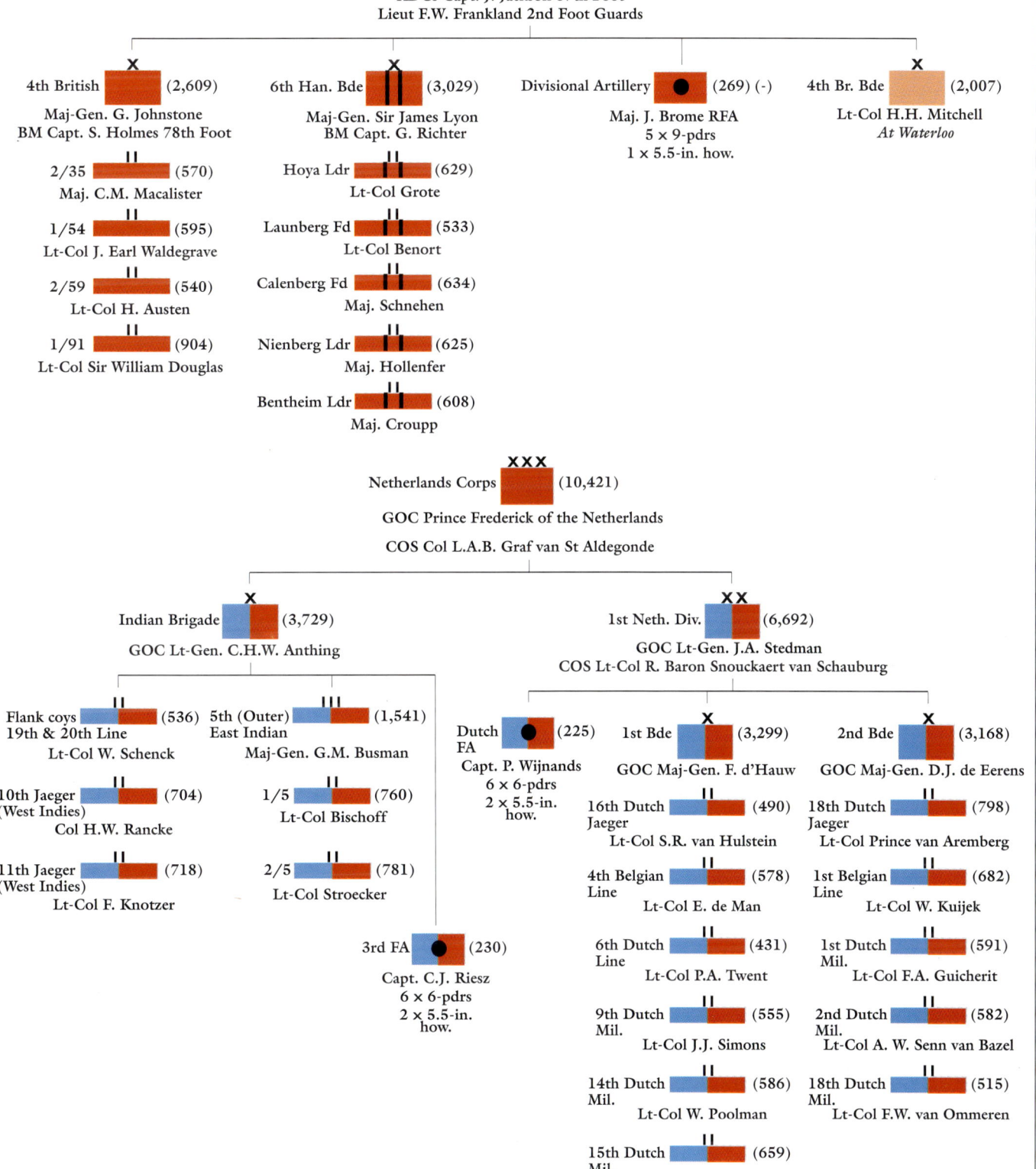

Under overall command of Lt-Gen. Lord Hill, II Corps

4th British (5,907) (-)
Lt-Gen. Hon. Sir Charles Colville

ADCs Capt. J. Jackson 37th Foot
Lieut F.W. Frankland 2nd Foot Guards

4th British (2,609)
Maj-Gen. G. Johnstone
BM Capt. S. Holmes 78th Foot

2/35 (570)
Maj. C.M. Macalister

1/54 (595)
Lt-Col J. Earl Waldegrave

2/59 (540)
Lt-Col H. Austen

1/91 (904)
Lt-Col Sir William Douglas

6th Han. Bde (3,029)
Maj-Gen. Sir James Lyon
BM Capt. G. Richter

Hoya Ldr (629)
Lt-Col Grote

Launberg Fd (533)
Lt-Col Benort

Calenberg Fd (634)
Maj. Schnehen

Nienberg Ldr (625)
Maj. Hollenfer

Bentheim Ldr (608)
Maj. Croupp

Divisional Artillery (269) (-)
Maj. J. Brome RFA
5 × 9-pdrs
1 × 5.5-in. how.

4th Br. Bde (2,007)
Lt-Col H.H. Mitchell
At Waterloo

Netherlands Corps (10,421)
GOC Prince Frederick of the Netherlands

COS Col L.A.B. Graf van St Aldegonde

Indian Brigade (3,729)
GOC Lt-Gen. C.H.W. Anthing

Flank coys (536)
19th & 20th Line
Lt-Col W. Schenck

5th (Outer) (1,541)
East Indian
Maj-Gen. G.M. Busman

10th Jaeger (704)
(West Indies)
Col H.W. Rancke

11th Jaeger (718)
(West Indies)
Lt-Col F. Knotzer

1/5 (760)
Lt-Col Bischoff

2/5 (781)
Lt-Col Stroecker

3rd FA (230)
Capt. C.J. Riesz
6 × 6-pdrs
2 × 5.5-in. how.

1st Neth. Div. (6,692)
GOC Lt-Gen. J.A. Stedman
COS Lt-Col R. Baron Snouckaert van Schauburg

Dutch FA (225)
Capt. P. Wijnands
6 × 6-pdrs
2 × 5.5-in. how.

1st Bde (3,299)
GOC Maj-Gen. F. d'Hauw

16th Dutch Jaeger (490)
Lt-Col S.R. van Hulstein

4th Belgian Line (578)
Lt-Col E. de Man

6th Dutch Line (431)
Lt-Col P.A. Twent

9th Dutch Mil. (555)
Lt-Col J.J. Simons

14th Dutch Mil. (586)
Lt-Col W. Poolman

15th Dutch Mil. (659)
Lt-Col P.C. Colthoff

2nd Bde (3,168)
GOC Maj-Gen. D.J. de Eerens

18th Dutch Jaeger (798)
Lt-Col Prince van Aremberg

1st Belgian Line (682)
Lt-Col W. Kuijek

1st Dutch Mil. (591)
Lt-Col F.A. Guicherit

2nd Dutch Mil. (582)
Lt-Col A. W. Senn van Bazel

18th Dutch Mil. (515)
Lt-Col F.W. van Ommeren

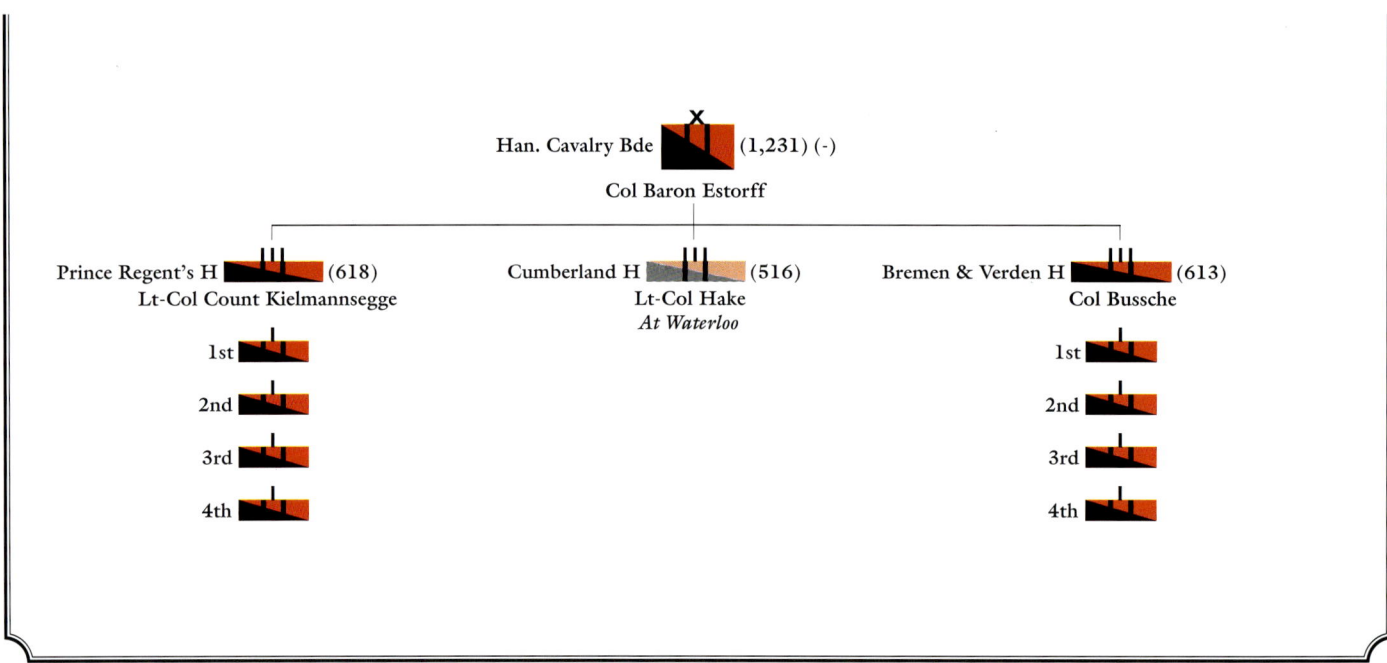

Han. Cavalry Bde (1,231) (-)
Col Baron Estorff

Prince Regent's H (618)
Lt-Col Count Kielmannsegge

1st
2nd
3rd
4th

Cumberland H (516)
Lt-Col Hake
At Waterloo

Bremen & Verden H (613)
Col Bussche

1st
2nd
3rd
4th

French Strengths

GENERAL

French Army returns taken on 9, 10 and 16 June show almost 123,000 men available to invade Belgium. From this must be deducted the losses sustained on 15 June, the casualties at Ligny and Quatre-Bras on 16 June totalling some 17,500. This meant the Armée du Nord had around 105,500 men available on 18 June. Grouchy took 30,000 towards Wavre, leaving Napoleon with 75,500 at La Belle Alliance. Adding in 2000 lightly wounded who would have stayed with the Eagles, the figure of 77,500 is reached.

The French orders of battle indicate a well-balanced force. At Waterloo Napoleon had three primarily infantry corps (I, II and the Imperial Guard) each of a similar strength (around 20,000), and each with its own cavalry division(s) and artillery, which included 12-pounder guns, under command. VI Corps was part of the reserve, small in numbers (10,600) but comprising two infantry and two cavalry divisions. Finally, also in reserve, were two heavy cavalry corps, each over 3000 strong.

STRENGTHS BY CORPS

Imperial Guard
Infantry: 22 battalions (21% of all French infantry battalions).
Cavalry: 4 regiments, 18.5 squadrons (16% of all cavalry squadrons).
Artillery: 3 x 12-pounder companies (batteries), 6 foot artillery companies and 4 horse artillery companies (96 guns, 39% of the total).

I Corps
Infantry: 33 battalions (32% of the total).
Cavalry: 4 regiments, 15 squadrons (12% of cavalry squadrons).
Artillery: 1 x 12-pounder company, 4 foot artillery companies, 1 horse artillery company (46 guns, 19% of the total).

II Corps
Infantry: 33 battalions (32% of the total).
Cavalry: 4 regiments, 15 squadrons (12% of cavalry squadrons).
Artillery: 1 x 12-pounder company, 3 foot artillery companies, 1 horse artillery company (38 guns, 15% of the total).

VI Corps
Infantry: 15 battalions (15% of the total).
Cavalry: 6 regiments, 20 squadrons (17% of cavalry squadrons).
Artillery: 1 x 12-pounder company, 2 foot artillery companies, 3 horse artillery companies (42 guns, 17% of total).

III Reserve Cavalry Corps
Infantry: nil.
Cavalry: 8 regiments, 25 squadrons (22% of cavalry squadrons).
Artillery: 2 horse artillery companies (12 guns, 5% of the total).

IV Reserve Cavalry Corps
Infantry: nil.
Cavalry: 8 regiments, 24 squadrons (21% of cavalry squadrons).
Artillery: 2 horse artillery companies (12 guns, 5% of the total).

Summary

Infantry: 103 battalions	53,400
Cavalry: 34 regiments, 113.5 squadrons	15,600
Artillery: 34 companies (batteries), 246 guns	6,500
Others: Staff, engineers, equipment train, medical, etc.	2,000
Grand total at Waterloo (estimated)	**77,500**

ADDITIONAL STATISTICS – INFANTRY

• There were approximately 3.4 infantrymen to every cavalryman.
• The strongest battalion was the 1/10 Ligne with 718 all ranks.
• The weakest battalion was the 3/108 Ligne with 251 all ranks.
• The average strength of a French battalion was about 520 all ranks.

ADDITIONAL STATISTICS – CAVALRY

• All cavalry were grouped into divisions, with a division attached to I and II Corps, two to VI Corps and the remaining six held in reserve.
• The cavalry was approximately equally divided between the ten divisions, five each of light and heavy cavalry.
• The strongest regiment was the Châsseurs à Cheval of the Imperial Guard with 1,197 in five squadrons.
• The weakest was the 7th Cuirassiers with a mere 180 in two squadrons.
• The average strength of a French cavalry regiment was about 460.

ADDITIONAL STATISTICS – ARTILLERY

• Napoleon deployed 246 guns and howitzers in thirty-four companies, giving a ratio of about one gun to every 315 soldiers.
• Of the thirty-four companies, six were 12-pounders, fifteen were foot artillery and thirteen horse artillery companies. Early in the battle Napoleon grouped eighty guns into a 'Grand Battery' in a co-ordinated attempt to smash Wellington's line before the first main attack.

OUTLINE ORGANIZATION OF THE ARMÉE DU NORD
a.m. 18 June 1815
C in C The Emperor Napoleon Bonaparte

Napoleon had a well-balanced force at Waterloo consisting of Ney's left wing and the central reserve. However, almost a third of his army was with Grouchy committed to keeping the Prussians away – which he failed to do.

In terms of overall numbers the French army was only slightly larger that Wellington's but was appreciably stronger in artillery.

At Waterloo **XXXX** (77,500 + 246 guns)

COS Maréchal Jean de Dieu Soult, Duc de Dalmatia

Comte d'Erlon (Drouet)

XXX
I Corps (19,800)

G de D Comte d'Erlon (Drouet)
COS M de C Baron Delcambre

XX	**XX**	**XX**	**XX**
1st	2nd	3rd	4th
Quiot	Donzelot	Marcognet	Durutte (w)

XX
1st
Jacquinot

Desales
46 guns

Comte Drouot

XXX
Garde Impériale (20,200)

G de D Comte Drouot

XX	**XX**	**XX**
Grenadiers	Châsseurs	Jeune (Young) Garde
Friant (w)	Morand	Duhesme (mw)

XX
Light Cavalry
Lefèbvre-Desnoüettes (w)

XX
Heavy Cavalry
Guyot (w)

Saint Maurice (k)
96 guns

Grand Artillery Park
At Quatre-Bras

G de D Baron Neigre

Reserve | Cavalry (-)

XXX
III Corps (3,600)

G de D Kellerman Comte de Valmy (w)
COS Adjt-Comdt Tancarville

XXX
IV Corps (3,100)

G de D Comte Milhaud
COS Adjt-Comdt Baron Chasseriau (mw)

XX	**XX**	**XX**	**XX**
11th	12th	13th	14th
L'Héritier (w)	D'Hurbal (w)	Wathier	Delort (w)

12 guns

12 guns

Overall Strength Summary (Approximate)

	At Waterloo	At Wavre	Total
Infantry	53,400	24,000	77,400
Cavalry	15,600	3,500	19,100
Artillery & Train	6,500	2,000	8,500
Others*	2,000	500	2,500
Totals	77,500	30,000	107,500
Guns	246	96	342

+8 at Ligny

*Includes Imperial but not regimental staffs that are included in the infantry and cavalry figures.

Comte Reille

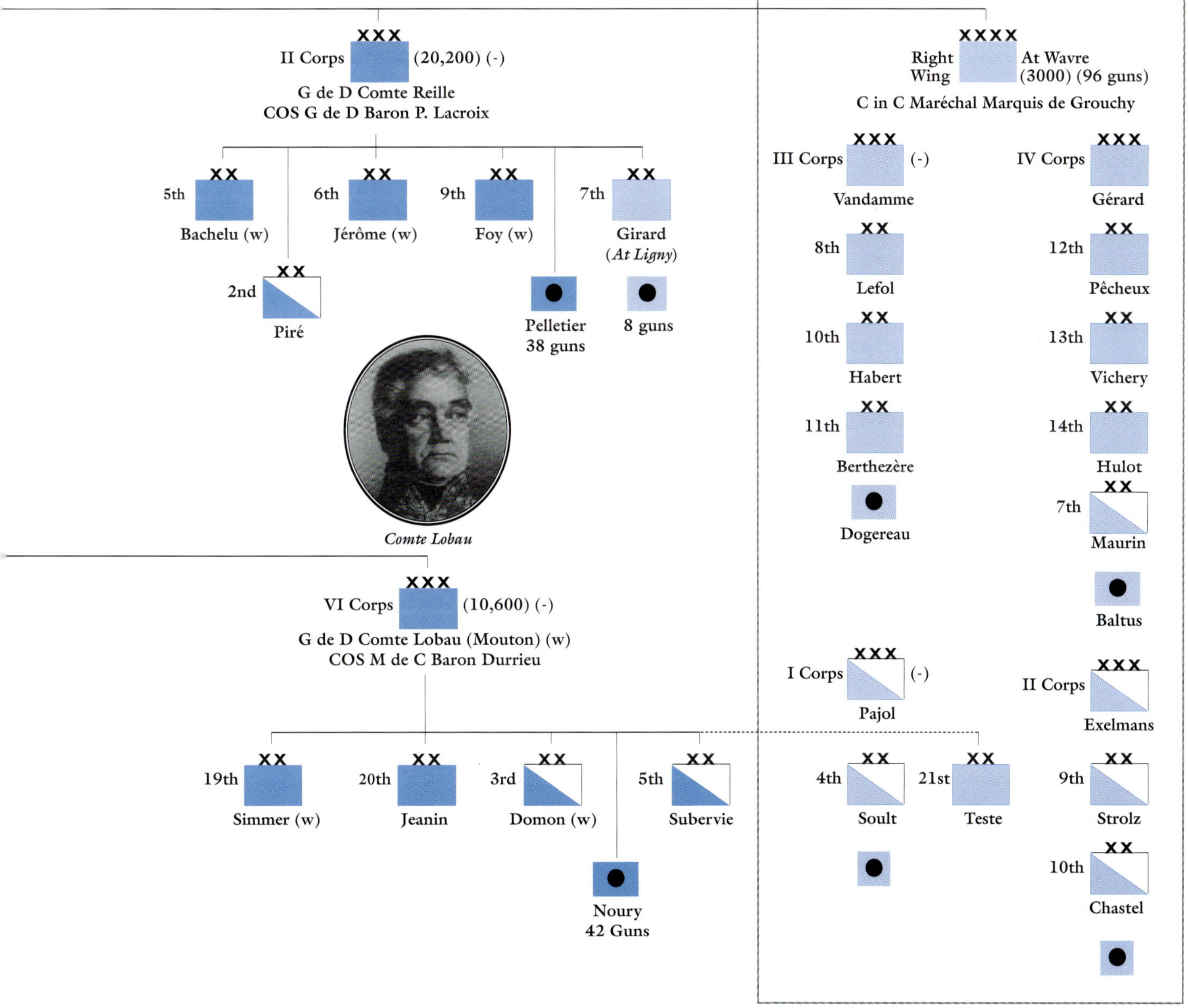

XXX
II Corps (20,200) (-)
G de D Comte Reille
COS G de D Baron P. Lacroix

XX 5th Bachelu (w) — XX 6th Jérôme (w) — XX 9th Foy (w) — XX 7th Girard (*At Ligny*)

XX 2nd Piré

Pelletier 38 guns • 8 guns •

Comte Lobau

XXX
VI Corps (10,600) (-)
G de D Comte Lobau (Mouton) (w)
COS M de C Baron Durrieu

XX 19th Simmer (w) — XX 20th Jeanin — XX 3rd Domon (w) — XX 5th Subervie

Noury 42 Guns •

XXXX
Right Wing At Wavre (3000) (96 guns)
C in C Maréchal Marquis de Grouchy

XXX **III Corps** (-) Vandamme — XXX **IV Corps** Gérard

XX 8th Lefol — XX 12th Pêcheux
XX 10th Habert — XX 13th Vichery
XX 11th Berthezère — XX 14th Hulot
XX 7th Maurin
Dogereau • Baltus •

XXX **I Corps** (-) Pajol — XXX **II Corps** Exelmans
XX 4th Soult — XX 21st Teste — XX 9th Strolz
XX 10th Chastel

STRUCTURAL ORGANIZATION OF THE IMPERIAL GUARD

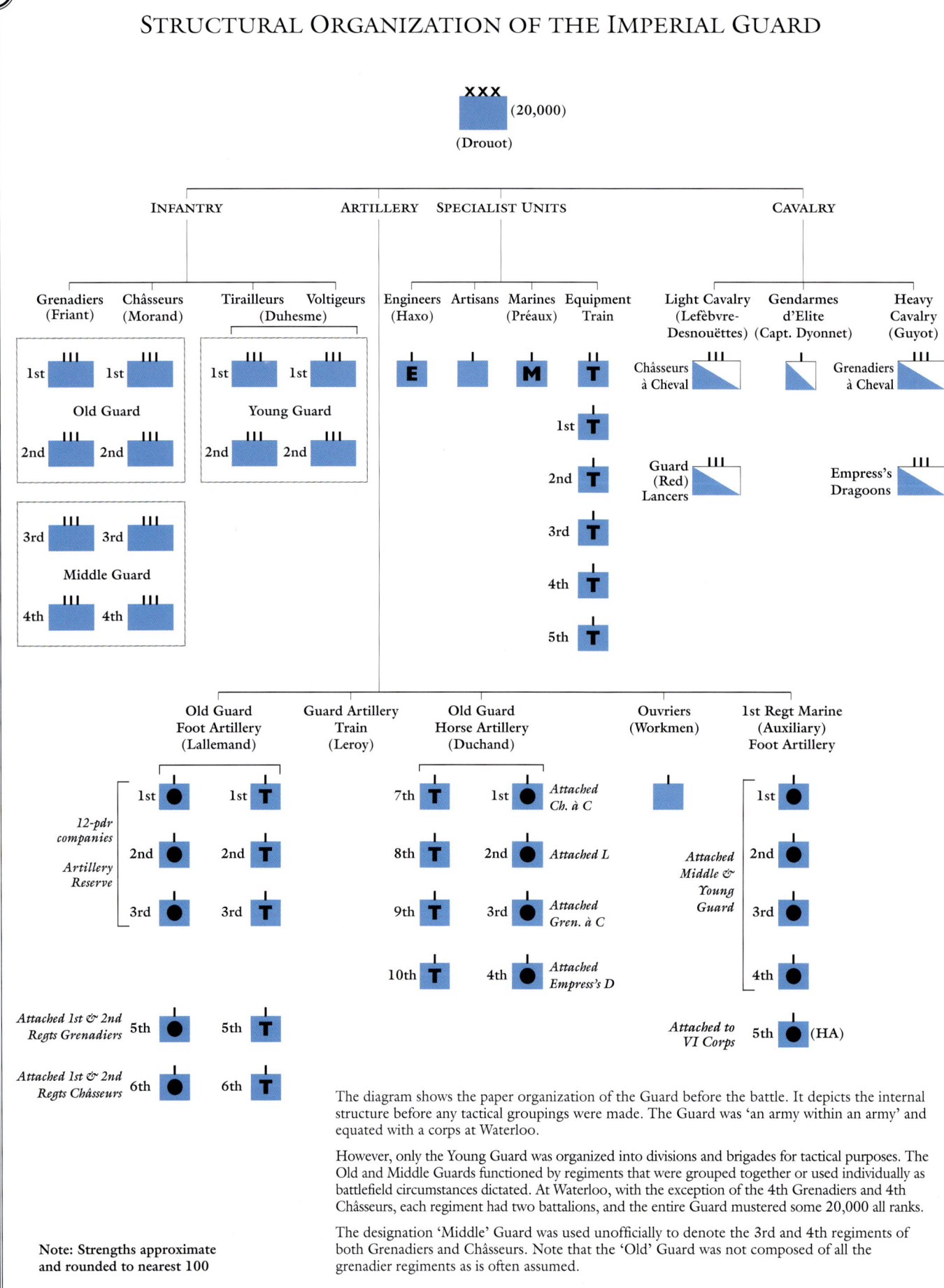

The diagram shows the paper organization of the Guard before the battle. It depicts the internal structure before any tactical groupings were made. The Guard was 'an army within an army' and equated with a corps at Waterloo.

However, only the Young Guard was organized into divisions and brigades for tactical purposes. The Old and Middle Guards functioned by regiments that were grouped together or used individually as battlefield circumstances dictated. At Waterloo, with the exception of the 4th Grenadiers and 4th Châsseurs, each regiment had two battalions, and the entire Guard mustered some 20,000 all ranks.

The designation 'Middle' Guard was used unofficially to denote the 3rd and 4th regiments of both Grenadiers and Châsseurs. Note that the 'Old' Guard was not composed of all the grenadier regiments as is often assumed.

Note: Strengths approximate and rounded to nearest 100

IMPERIAL GUARD HEADQUARTERS

Acting GOC G de D Comte Antoine Drouot

Maréchal Mortier's sciatica prevented his commanding the Guard during this short campaign so his Chief of Staff Drouot took over and performed both duties admirably. However, the Guard was never committed to battle without the authority of the Emperor.

The HQ had immediate close control over the specialist units – engineers, equipment train, medical personnel, marine company and, at the outset, the artillery reserve.

The 24 heavy guns and howitzers were the Guards' artillery reserve.

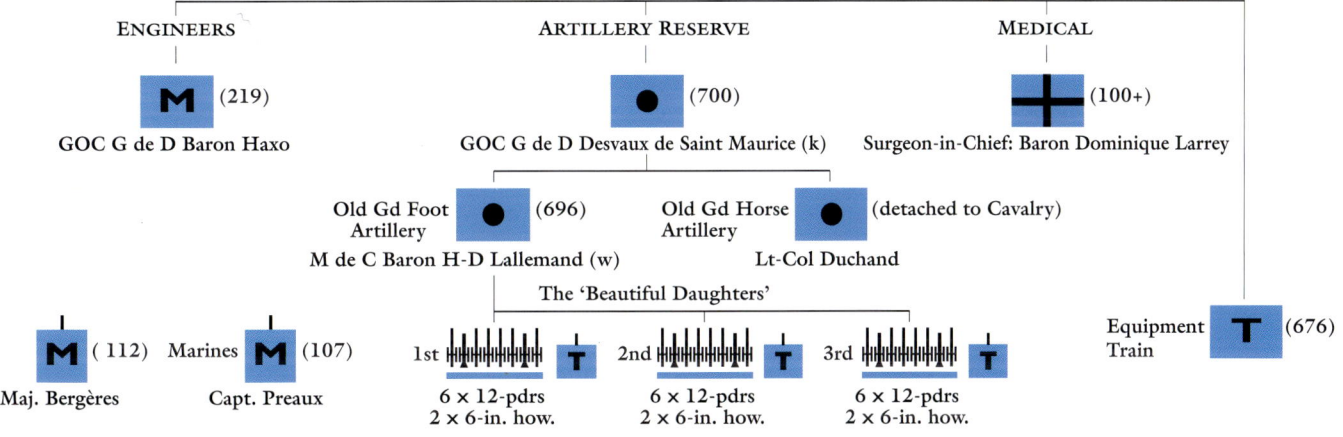

Garde HQ

COS G de D Comte Antoine Drouot

ENGINEERS

M (219)

GOC G de D Baron Haxo

ARTILLERY RESERVE

● (700)

GOC G de D Desvaux de Saint Maurice (k)

MEDICAL

✚ (100+)

Surgeon-in-Chief: Baron Dominique Larrey

Old Gd Foot Artillery ● (696)

M de C Baron H-D Lallemand (w)

Old Gd Horse Artillery ● (detached to Cavalry)

Lt-Col Duchand

The 'Beautiful Daughters'

M (112)   Marines   M (107)

Maj. Bergères   **Capt. Preaux**

1st T   2nd T   3rd T

6 × 12-pdrs   6 × 12-pdrs   6 × 12-pdrs
2 × 6-in. how.   2 × 6-in. how.   2 × 6-in. how.

Equipment Train   T (676)

THE DIVISION OF GRENADIERS À PIED (4,489)

GOC G de D Comte Louis Friant (w)

Administratively the grenadier regiments were grouped as a division but they did not fight as such at Waterloo. Like the other Guard infantry units they fought by regiments grouped as necessary to meet the tactical situation.

21C:
G de D Comte
François Roguet

Like the rest of the Guard, the grenadier regiments were initially grouped well back in reserve north of Rossomme. The 1st Grenadiers (the 'Oldest of the Old') remained uncommitted to the very end. Other battalions were involved in the fight for Plancenoit and the final evening attack.

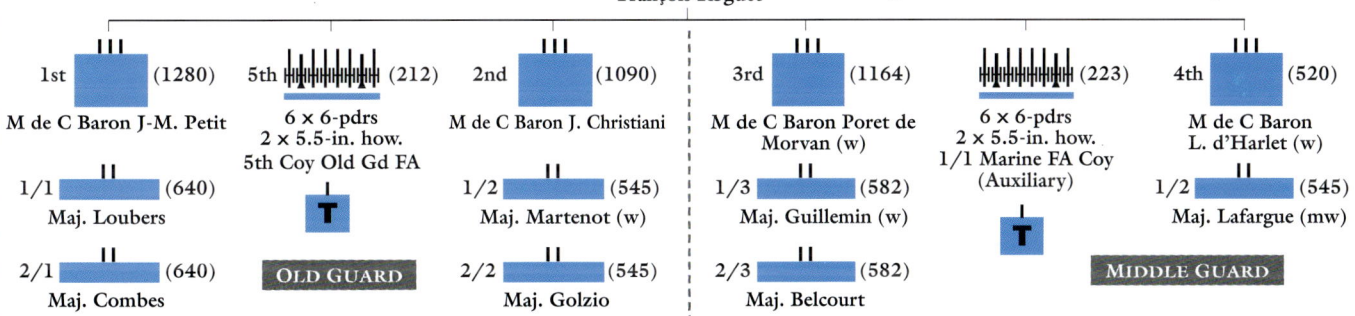

1st (1280)

M de C Baron J-M. Petit

5th (212)
6 × 6-pdrs
2 × 5.5-in. how.
5th Coy Old Gd FA

2nd (1090)

M de C Baron J. Christiani

3rd (1164)

M de C Baron Poret de Morvan (w)

(223)
6 × 6-pdrs
2 × 5.5-in. how.
1/1 Marine FA Coy (Auxiliary)

4th (520)

M de C Baron L. d'Harlet (w)

1/1 (640)

Maj. Loubers

1/2 (545)

Maj. Martenot (w)

1/3 (582)

Maj. Guillemin (w)

1/2 (545)

Maj. Lafargue (mw)

2/1 (640)

Maj. Combes

OLD GUARD

2/2 (545)

Maj. Golzio

2/3 (582)

Maj. Belcourt

MIDDLE GUARD

THE DIVISION OF CHÂSSEURS À PIED (4,789)

GOC G de D Comte Charles Antoine Morand

The two senior regiments formed half of the Old Guard and the two junior half of the Middle Guard. There were eight battalions at Waterloo, although the 4th Châsseurs had suffered severely at Ligny and so were combined to participate in the final assault at Waterloo.

21C
G de D Comte
Claude Michel (k)

Initially held in reserve but were later committed in Plancenoit where the 1/2 Grenadiers and 1/2 Châsseurs had some intense close quarter street fighting. Three battalions took part in the final desperate assault on the Allied right centre. The 1/1 Châsseurs were retained at Le Caillou.

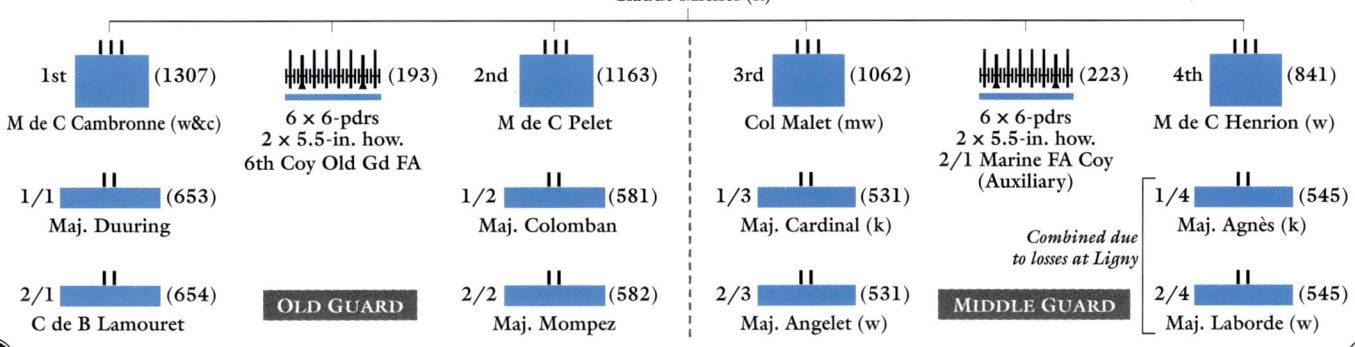

1st (1307)

M de C Cambronne (w&c)

(193)
6 × 6-pdrs
2 × 5.5-in. how.
6th Coy Old Gd FA

2nd (1163)

M de C Pelet

3rd (1062)

Col Malet (mw)

(223)
6 × 6-pdrs
2 × 5.5-in. how.
2/1 Marine FA Coy (Auxiliary)

4th (841)

M de C Henrion (w)

1/1 (653)

Maj. Duuring

1/2 (581)

Maj. Colomban

1/3 (531)

Maj. Cardinal (k)

1/4 (545)

Maj. Agnès (k)

2/1 (654)

C de B Lamouret

OLD GUARD

2/2 (582)

Maj. Mompez

2/3 (531)

Maj. Angelet (w)

Combined due to losses at Ligny

MIDDLE GUARD

2/4 (545)

Maj. Laborde (w)

THE YOUNG GUARD DIVISION (4,774)

GOC G de D Comte Philibert Duhesme (mw)

Unlike the Old and Middle Guards, the Young Guard was organized into two divisions each of two brigades. The 1st was present at Waterloo, the 2nd, under G de D Bruyer, was deployed in the Vendée suppressing a monarchist uprising.

Deployed initially with the rest of the Guard in the reserve north of Rossomme, the Young Guard were the first Guard units to be committed to battle. They were drawn into the defence of Plancenoit with the task of holding back the Prussians.

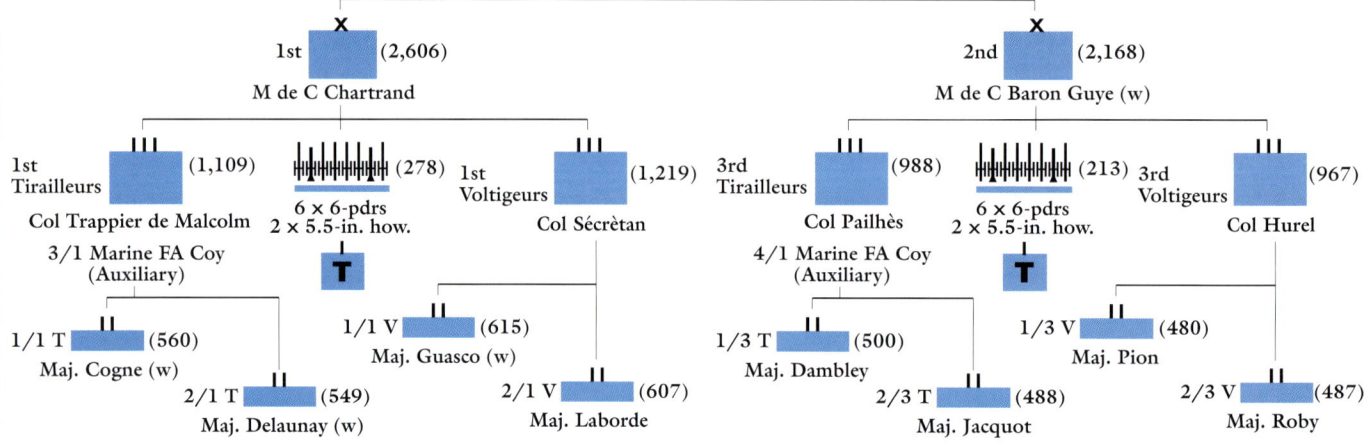

2IC G de D Comte Pierre Barrois (w)

1st (2,606)
M de C Chartrand

2nd (2,168)
M de C Baron Guye (w)

1st Tirailleurs (1,109)
Col Trappier de Malcolm

(278) 6 × 6-pdrs 2 × 5.5-in. how.

1st Voltigeurs (1,219)
Col Sécrétan

3rd Tirailleurs (988)
Col Pailhès

(213) 6 × 6-pdrs 2 × 5.5-in. how.

3rd Voltigeurs (967)
Col Hurel

3/1 Marine FA Coy (Auxiliary)

4/1 Marine FA Coy (Auxiliary)

1/1 T (560)
Maj. Cogne (w)

1/1 V (615)
Maj. Guasco (w)

1/3 T (500)
Maj. Dambley

1/3 V (480)
Maj. Pion

2/1 T (549)
Maj. Delaunay (w)

2/1 V (607)
Maj. Laborde

2/3 T (488)
Maj. Jacquot

2/3 V (487)
Maj. Roby

THE IMPERIAL GUARD LIGHT CAVALRY DIVISION (2,439)

GOC G de D Comte Charles Lefèbvre-Desnouëttes (w)

Part of Napoleon's left wing under Ney, they had just led the advance on Quatre-Bras, halting just south of the crossroads on the evening of the 15th. They were not heavily involved at Quatre-Bras and thus were up to strength at Waterloo.

They were deployed as part of the cavalry reserve in the third line, behind the right centre, at Waterloo.

Became heavily involved in the series of cavalry attacks during the afternoon.

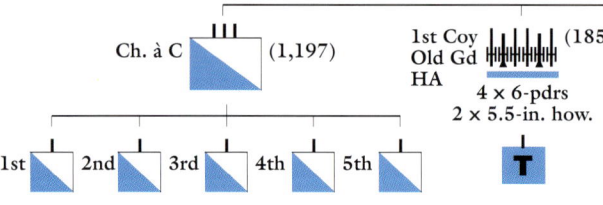

G de D Baron Francois Lallemand (w)

Ch. à C (1,197)

1st Coy Old Gd HA (185)
4 × 6-pdrs 2 × 5.5-in. how.

1st 2nd 3rd 4th 5th

G de D Comte Pierre Colbert Chabanais (w)

2nd Chevaux-Légers Lanciers ('Red' Lancers) (880)
Lt-Col Jerzmanowski

2nd Coy Old Gd HA (177)
4 × 6-pdrs 2 × 5.5-in. how.

1st 2nd 3rd 4th 5th
Maj. Balinski
Polish (Elba) Squadron

THE IMPERIAL GUARD HEAVY CAVALRY DIVISION (2,068)

GOC G de D Comte Charles Etienne Guyot (w)

The Empress's Dragoons lost their gallant commander in a skirmish at Gilly on the 15th and so Col Hoffmayer commanded at Waterloo.

Present at Ligny but not engaged.

These heavy cavalrymen, arguably the best in Europe, were deployed in the third line, in reserve, on the left of the French line at Waterloo.

Like the rest of the cavalry they were sucked into the futile massed cavalry assaults on the Allied right centre.

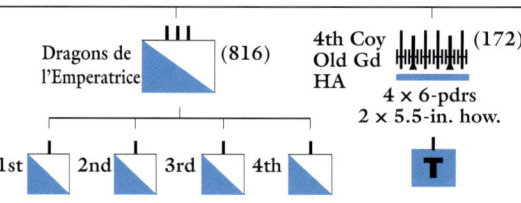
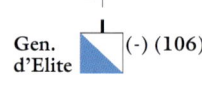

M de C Jamin, Marquis de Bermuy (k)

Gren. à C (796)

3rd Coy Old Gd HA (178)
4 × 6-pdrs 2 × 5.5-in. how.

1st 2nd 3rd 4th

Col Hoffmayer

Dragons de l'Emperatrice (816)

4th Coy Old Gd HA (172)
4 × 6-pdrs 2 × 5.5-in. how.

1st 2nd 3rd 4th

Capt. Dyonnet

Gen. d'Elite (-) (106)

THE I ARMY CORPS (19,900)

GOC Jean Baptiste Drouet, Comte d'Erlon

CORPS ARTILLERY RESERVE
Artillery Comd. M de C Desales
Artillery COS Col Bernard
Comd. Artillery Park Maj. Monchel

COS M de C Baron Delcambre
Asst COS Col Viala

CORPS ENGINEERS
Engineer Comd. M de C Baron Garbé
Engineer COS Col Baraillon

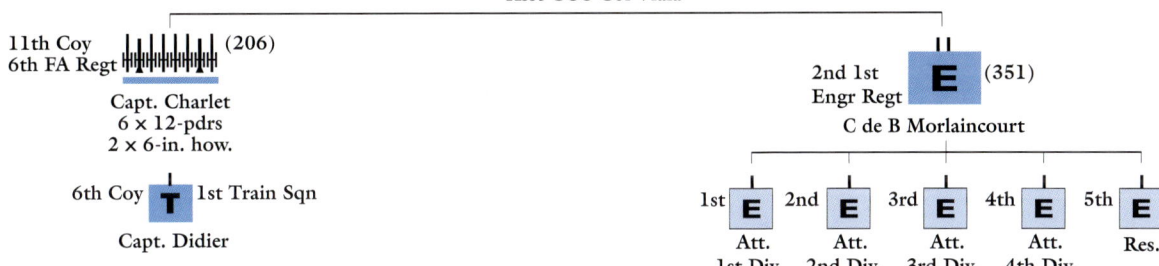

11th Coy (206)
6th FA Regt
Capt. Charlet
6 × 12-pdrs
2 × 6-in. how.

6th Coy — 1st Train Sqn
Capt. Didier

2nd 1st Engr Regt (351)
C de B Morlaincourt

1st Att. 1st Div. | 2nd Att. 2nd Div. | 3rd Att. 3rd Div. | 4th Att. 4th Div. | 5th Res.

THE 1ST INFANTRY DIVISION (4,183)

GOC M de C Baron Quiot du Passage

GOC was Quiot who had replaced Allix de Vaux who is often wrongly shown as commanding this division at Waterloo. The senior colonel, Charlet from 54th Ligne, took over 1st Brigade. Interestingly his son commanded the 12-pounder guns in the corps reserve.

1st Brigade was a very experienced formation whose regiments had served at Austerlitz, Jena, Friedland, Ulm and in the Peninsula.

Part of Ney's left wing of the Army. Due to confused orders it had spent 16 June marching to and fro between the battlefields of Quatre-Bras and Ligny without being engaged at either.

Deployed on the left of the corps in the front line just east of the Charleroi road. Heavily involved in the attacks on La Haie Sainte and suffered severely from Allied heavy cavalry attacks. The 105th Regiment lost its Eagle.

COS Col Giraut de Coehorn

1st (2,111)
Col Charlet

20th Coy (191)
6th FA Regt
Capt. Hamelin
6 × 6-pdrs
2 × 5.5-in. how.

2nd (1,881)
M de C Baron Bourgeois (w)

54th Ligne (962)
Col Charlet

55th Ligne (1,149)
Col Morin

5th Coy — 1st Train Sqn
Capt. Paleprat

28th Ligne (898)
C de B Senac (acting)

105th Ligne (983)
Col Gentry (w)

1/54 (480)
C de B Guyot

1/55 (580)
C de B Durand

1st Coy 2/1 Engr Regt
Capt. Emon

1/28 (449)
C de B Senac

1/105 (488)
C de B Coste

2/54 (482)
C de B Prieur

2/55 (569)
C de B Delamoussay

2/28 (449)
C de B Marrens (mw)

2/105 (495)
C de B Bonnet (k)

THE 2ND INFANTRY DIVISION (5,262)

GOC G de D Baron Francois Donzelot

Another experienced 1st Brigade. The 13th Légère had a particularly illustrious history, being present at Austerlitz, Auerstadt, Eylau, Eckmuhl, Wagram and Borodino.

The 13th Légère was a powerful regiment with three battalions, each over 600 strong. It was the 13th Légère that finally captured La Haie Sainte.

Like the 1st Division, it had spent the 16th marching aimlessly between the two battlefields.

Deployed on the right of 1st Division. Heavily involved with the corps attack in the early afternoon on the Allied left centre. Badly cut up by the Union Brigade. Charge. Later involved in the capture of La Haie Sainte.

COS Col Devienne (w)

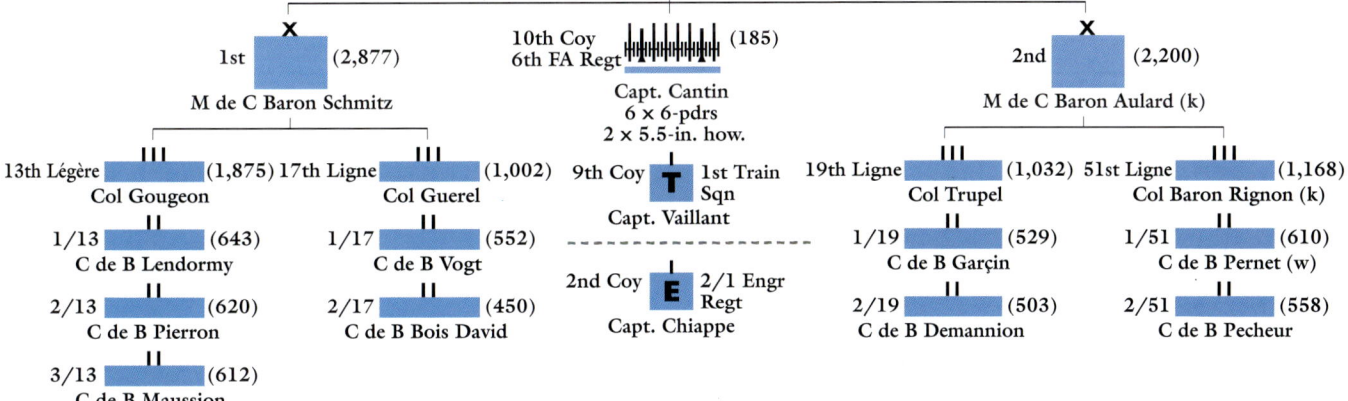

1st (2,877)
M de C Baron Schmitz

10th Coy (185)
6th FA Regt
Capt. Cantin
6 × 6-pdrs
2 × 5.5-in. how.

2nd (2,200)
M de C Baron Aulard (k)

13th Légère (1,875)
Col Gougeon

17th Ligne (1,002)
Col Guerel

9th Coy — 1st Train Sqn
Capt. Vaillant

19th Ligne (1,032)
Col Trupel

51st Ligne (1,168)
Col Baron Rignon (k)

1/13 (643)
C de B Lendormy

1/17 (552)
C de B Vogt

2nd Coy 2/1 Engr Regt
Capt. Chiappe

1/19 (529)
C de B Garçin

1/51 (610)
C de B Pernet (w)

2/13 (620)
C de B Pierron

2/17 (450)
C de B Bois David

2/19 (503)
C de B Demannion

2/51 (558)
C de B Pecheur

3/13 (612)
C de B Maussion

THE 3RD INFANTRY DIVISION (4,181)

GOC G de D Baron Pierre Louis Binet de Marcognet

Part of Ney's left wing of the army. An orthodox infantry division whose regiments had extensive battlefield experience in Germany, Russia and France. Not particularly strong numerically as its eight battalions were mostly slightly below average strength.

Not engaged at either Quatre-Bras or Ligny.

Of the eight battalion commanders seven, and one regimental commander, were wounded at Waterloo. Posted in the front line between the 2nd and 4th Divisions on the right (east) of the Charleroi–Brussels road. Took part in d'Erlon's frontal attack and confronted Pack's Brigade on the ridge. Badly mauled by the Union Brigade charge with the 45th Regiment losing its eagle.

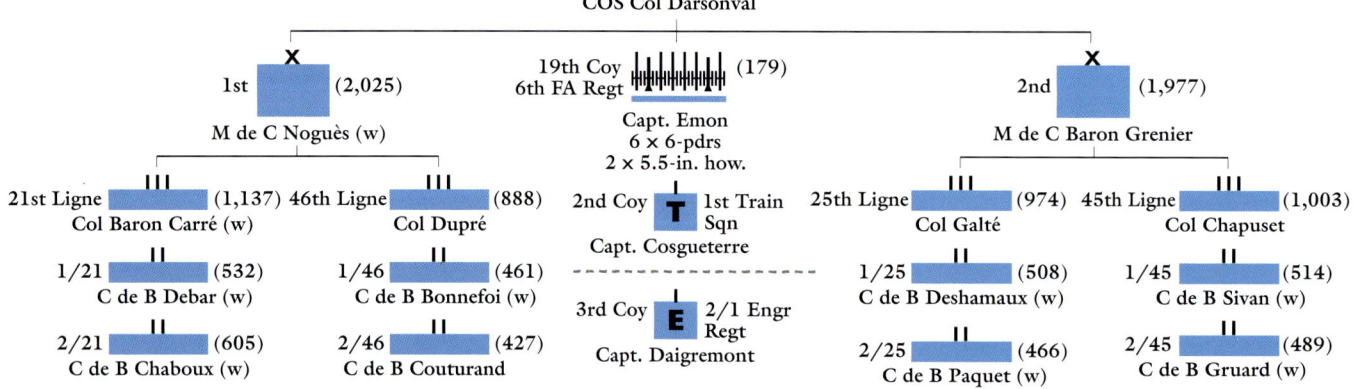

COS Col Darsonval

1st (2,025) — M de C Noguès (w)

19th Coy 6th FA Regt (179) — Capt. Emon — 6 × 6-pdrs — 2 × 5.5-in. how.

2nd (1,977) — M de C Baron Grenier

21st Ligne (1,137) — Col Baron Carré (w)
46th Ligne (888) — Col Dupré

2nd Coy 1st Train Sqn — Capt. Cosgueterre

25th Ligne (974) — Col Galté
45th Ligne (1,003) — Col Chapuset

1/21 (532) — C de B Debar (w)
1/46 (461) — C de B Bonnefoi (w)

3rd Coy 2/1 Engr Regt — Capt. Daigremont

1/25 (508) — C de B Deshamaux (w)
1/45 (514) — C de B Sivan (w)

2/21 (605) — C de B Chaboux (w)
2/46 (427) — C de B Couturand

2/25 (466) — C de B Paquet (w)
2/45 (489) — C de B Gruard (w)

THE 4TH INFANTRY DIVISION (4,037)

GOC G de D Comte Pierre Francois Joseph Durutte (w)

Another solid, experienced line division that was the leading infantry formation of the corps as it approached Quatre-Bras and was switched to Ligny on the 16th. Left at Ligny when the rest of the corps returned to Quatre-Bras. Due to d'Erlon's 'be prudent' orders the division's cautious advance achieved nothing at Ligny.

Deployed on the right of the French front line at Waterloo. Involved in the fighting in and around Papelotte.

Badly cut up by Vandeleur's cavalry during the French retreat. Durutte lost his right hand and was badly disfigured by a sword slash to the head.

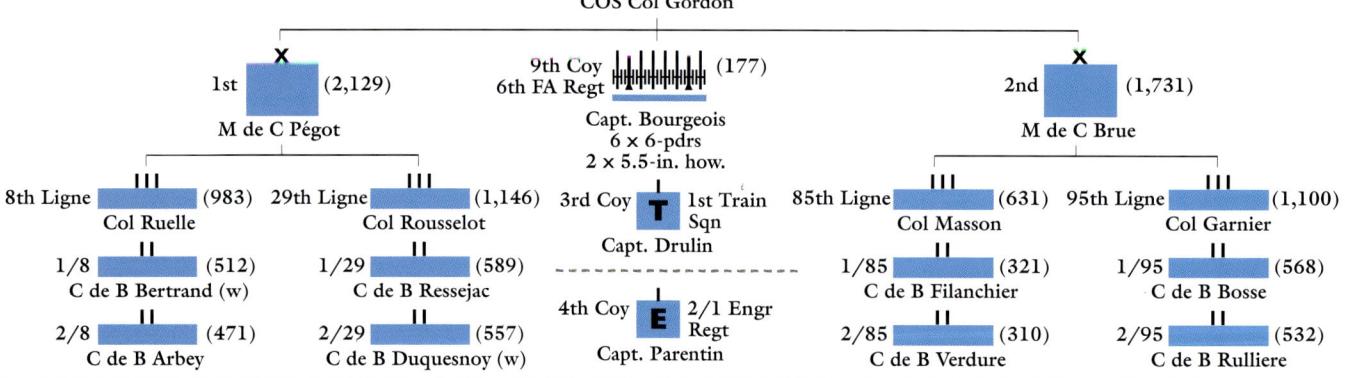

COS Col Gordon

1st (2,129) — M de C Pégot

9th Coy 6th FA Regt (177) — Capt. Bourgeois — 6 × 6-pdrs — 2 × 5.5-in. how.

2nd (1,731) — M de C Brue

8th Ligne (983) — Col Ruelle
29th Ligne (1,146) — Col Rousselot

3rd Coy 1st Train Sqn — Capt. Drulin

85th Ligne (631) — Col Masson
95th Ligne (1,100) — Col Garnier

1/8 (512) — C de B Bertrand (w)
1/29 (589) — C de B Ressejac

4th Coy 2/1 Engr Regt — Capt. Parentin

1/85 (321) — C de B Filanchier
1/95 (568) — C de B Bosse

2/8 (471) — C de B Arbey
2/29 (557) — C de B Duquesnoy (w)

2/85 (310) — C de B Verdure
2/95 (532) — C de B Rulliere

THE 1ST CAVALRY DIVISION (1,664)

GOC G de D Baron Charles Claude Jacquinot

A mixed light cavalry division with hussars, châsseurs and lancers. The 7th Hussars were an exceptionally experienced regiment having been almost continuously on active service since 1805 throughout Germany, Russia and France.

Present at Ligny, staying to support the 4th Division's limited push to Wagnelee village. On the 17th this division was fully committed in the pursuit of Wellington from Quatre-Bras to Waterloo. Deployed on the extreme right of the French line, the division successfully counter-attacked the Allied Household and Union Brigades when they over-reached themselves.

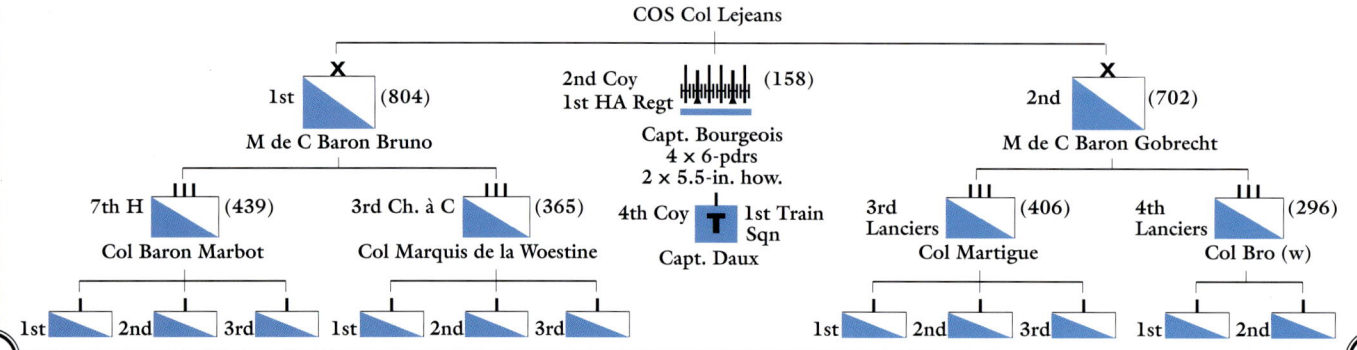

COS Col Lejeans

1st (804) — M de C Baron Bruno

2nd Coy 1st HA Regt (158) — Capt. Bourgeois — 4 × 6-pdrs — 2 × 5.5-in. how.

2nd (702) — M de C Baron Gobrecht

7th H (439) — Col Baron Marbot
3rd Ch. à C (365) — Col Marquis de la Woestine

4th Coy 1st Train Sqn — Capt. Daux

3rd Lanciers (406) — Col Martigue
4th Lanciers (296) — Col Bro (w)

1st 2nd 3rd   1st 2nd 3rd   1st 2nd 3rd   1st 2nd

THE II ARMY CORPS (20,000)

GOC G de D Comte Honoré Charles Reille

CORPS ARTILLERY RESERVE
Artillery Comd. M de C Baron Le Pelletier
Artillery COS C de B Bobillier
Comd. Artillery Park Maj. Poivel

CORPS ENGINEERS
Engineer Comd. M de C Baron de Richemont
Engineer COS Col Daullé

COS G de D Baron Pamphile Lacroix
Asst COS Col Lecouturier

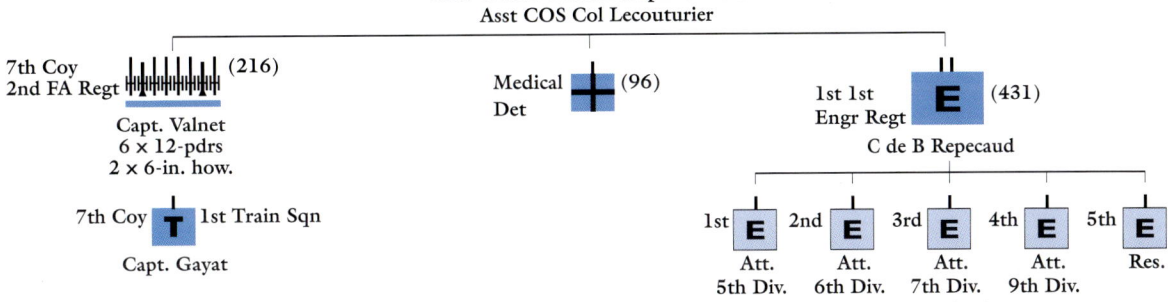

7th Coy
2nd FA Regt (216)
Capt. Valnet
6 × 12-pdrs
2 × 6-in. how.

7th Coy **T** 1st Train Sqn
Capt. Gayat

Medical Det (96)

1st 1st Engr Regt **E** (431)
C de B Repecaud

1st **E** Att. 5th Div. | 2nd **E** Att. 6th Div. | 3rd **E** Att. 7th Div. *(at Ligny)* | 4th **E** Att. 9th Div. | 5th **E** Res.

THE 5TH INFANTRY DIVISION (4,177)

GOC G de D Baron Gilbert Desiré Bachelu (w)

On 10 June it had transferred its 2nd Légère Regt to the 6th Division and received in its place the 3rd Ligne.

A division of average strength but with nine battalions the weakest in the corps. It was heavily engaged at Quatre-Bras where II Corps provided Ney's infantry for the attacks on the crossroads. It suffered significant losses there (about 1,500).

This division was composed of experienced regiments with numerous battle honours from campaigns in Germany and Russia.

Formed on the right of the corps at Waterloo, immediately left (west) of the Charleroi road. Some of its troops attempted to advance on the orchard at Hougoumont later in the day but were driven off by heavy artillery fire.

COS Col Trefcon

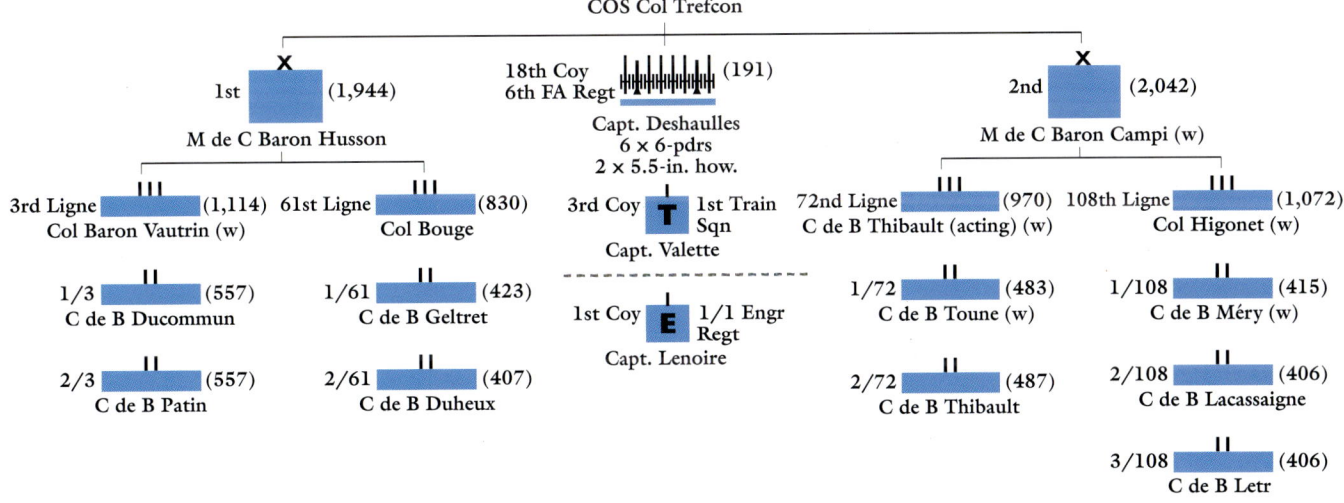

1st ✕ (1,944)
M de C Baron Husson

18th Coy
6th FA Regt (191)
Capt. Deshaulles
6 × 6-pdrs
2 × 5.5-in. how.

3rd Coy **T** 1st Train Sqn
Capt. Valette

1st Coy **E** 1/1 Engr Regt
Capt. Lenoire

2nd ✕ (2,042)
M de C Baron Campi (w)

3rd Ligne (1,114) Col Baron Vautrin (w) | 61st Ligne (830) Col Bouge
1/3 (557) C de B Ducommun | 1/61 (423) C de B Geltret
2/3 (557) C de B Patin | 2/61 (407) C de B Duheux

72nd Ligne (970) C de B Thibault (acting) (w) | 108th Ligne (1,072) Col Higonet (w)
1/72 (483) C de B Toune (w) | 1/108 (415) C de B Méry (w)
2/72 (487) C de B Thibault | 2/108 (406) C de B Lacassaigne
3/108 (406) C de B Letr

THE 6TH INFANTRY DIVISION (7,877)

With thirteen battalions, by far the largest infantry division in the army, probably reflecting the status of its commander – the Emperor's brother. Heavily engaged at Quatre-Bras where it suffered some 1000 casualties. The 2nd Ligne fought as marines at Trafalgar.

GOC
G de D
Prince Jérôme Bonaparte (w)

21C G de D Count Guilleminot
COS Col Hortode

Deployed on the left of the French line at Waterloo, where it opened the battle with what was supposed to be a diversionary attack on the wood and château of Hougoumont. The entire division quickly became embroiled in the struggle that lasted all day. Only once did a handful of soldiers force an entrance to the château compound through the north gate.

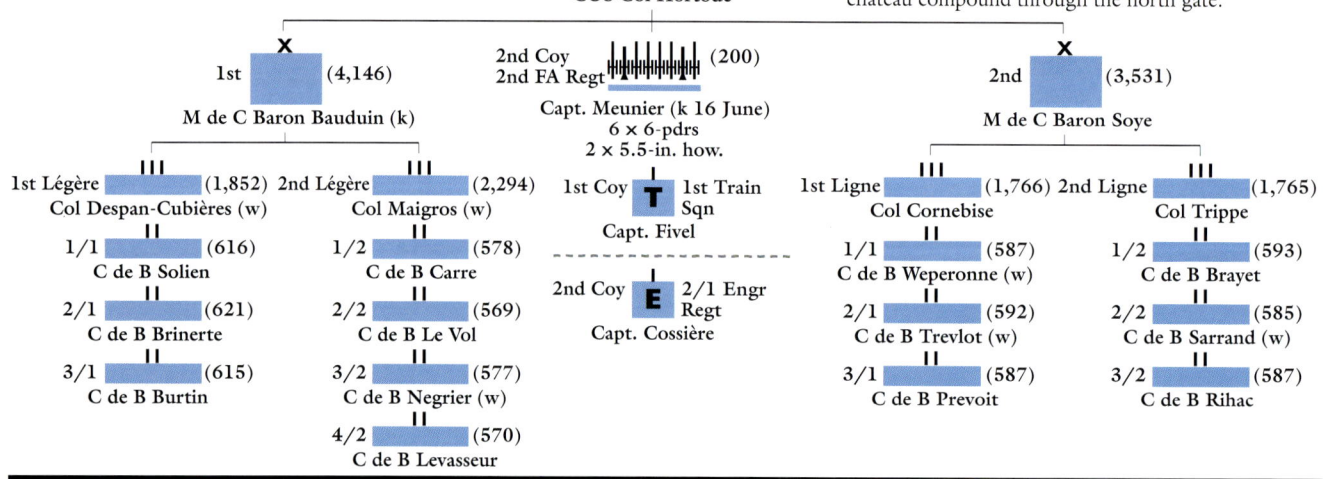

THE 9TH INFANTRY DIVISION (5,363)

A comparatively strong, experienced division that was fully committed at Quatre-Bras on 16 June. It lost some 800 men, including the commander of the 1st Brigade, Baron Gauthier.

Like the other divisions, it needed that 17th to recover and reorganize.

GOC
G de D Comte
Maximilien
Sebastien Foy (w)

COS Col Hudry (w)

The division moved forward slowly on the 17th, spending the night well south of the Waterloo battlefield at the village of Genappe. It deployed west of the Charleroi road between the 5th and 6th Divisions after 9.00 a.m. It joined the fruitless assaults on Hougoumont and later supported the Imperial Guard's final attack. The 93rd Ligne fought as marines at Trafalgar.

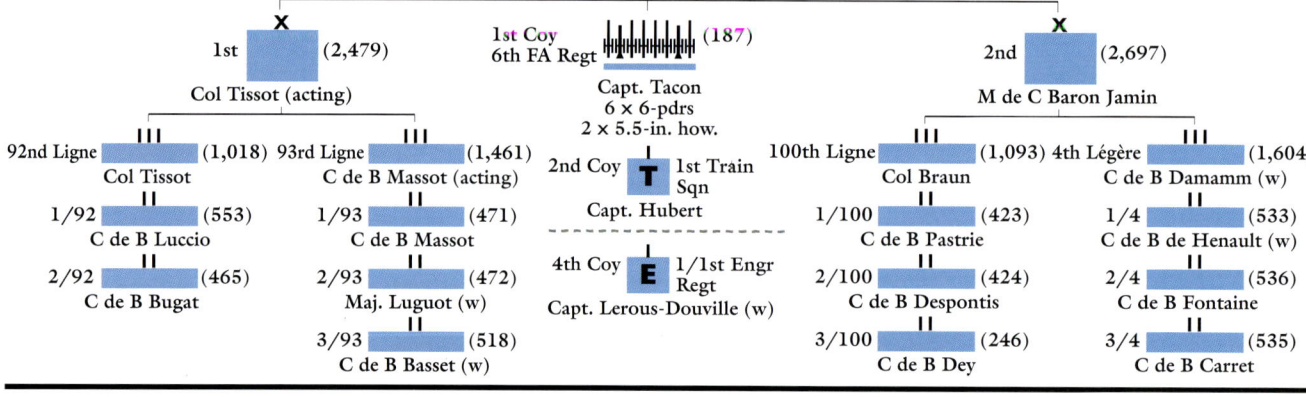

THE 2ND CAVALRY DIVISION (2,025)

GOC G de D Comte Hippolyte Marie Guillame Piré

The division advanced to Quatre-Bras early on the 16th and the 1st Brigade supported Bachelu's attack. It routed two Dutch cavalry regiments and became involved in furious attacks on British infantry squares.

At Waterloo it was posted on the extreme left of the line to cover that flank and support attacks on Hougoumont.

A light cavalry division with one regiment each of chasseurs and lancers. Both types wore predominantly dark green uniforms.

With fifteen squadrons and over 2000 horsemen it was the strongest cavalry division at Waterloo except for the Guard Light Cavalry Division.

COS Col Baron Rippert

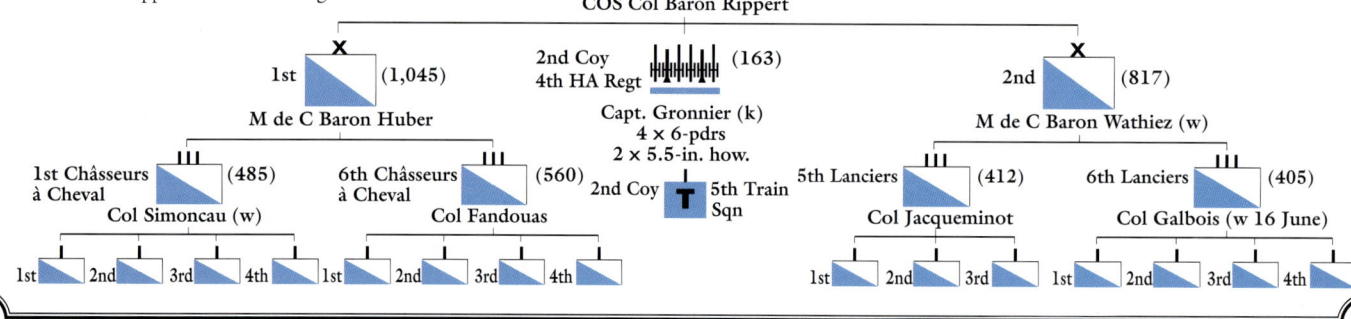

THE VI ARMY CORPS (10,600)

GOC G de D Georges Mouton, Comte de Lobau (w)

CORPS ARTILLERY RESERVE
Artillery Comd. G de D Baron Noury
Artillery COS Maj. Chaudon (w)

CORPS ENGINEERS
Engineer Comd. M de C Sabatier
Engineer COS Col Constantin

COS M de C Baron Durrieu (w)
Asst COS Col Janin (w)

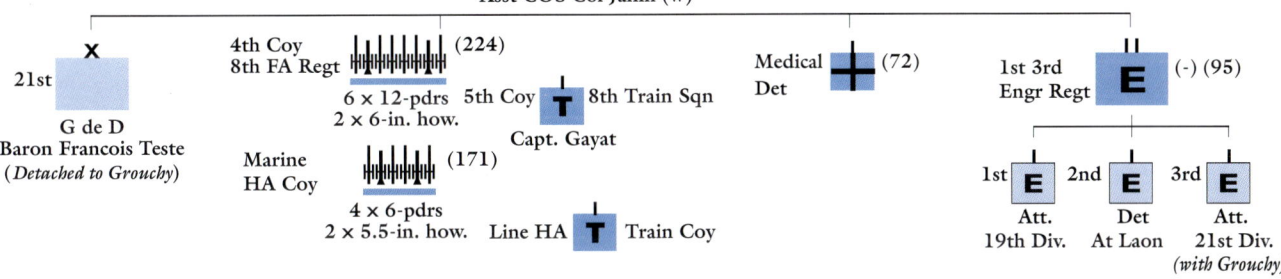

21st — G de D Baron Francois Teste (*Detached to Grouchy*)

4th Coy 8th FA Regt (224)
6 × 12-pdrs
2 × 6-in. how.

Marine HA Coy (171)
4 × 6-pdrs
2 × 5.5-in. how.

5th Coy 8th Train Sqn — Capt. Gayat

Line HA Train Coy

Medical Det (72)

1st 3rd Engr Regt E (-) (95)
1st E Att. 19th Div.
2nd E Det At Laon
3rd E Att. 21st Div. (*with Grouchy*)

THE 19TH INFANTRY DIVISION (4,122)

A weak corps having only about half of the strength of other infantry corps. This was due to the 21st Division (Teste) being detached to Grouchy's force, and the 47th Ligne being in the Vendée.

The 19th Division was formed from the Paris garrison. It was the last to pass through Charleroi and arrived at Ligny too late to be used effectively.

GOC G de D Baron Francois Martin Simmer (w)

At Waterloo it was held back in reserve until the Prussians were sighted on the right flank. It was deployed to delay them and participated in a fighting withdrawal to Plancenoit where it was engaged in heavy street fighting.

Reinforced by the Young Guard, it initially helped hold the village and thus keep the jaws of the Allied vice from closing completely.

COS M de C Col Juchereau de Saint-Denis (w)

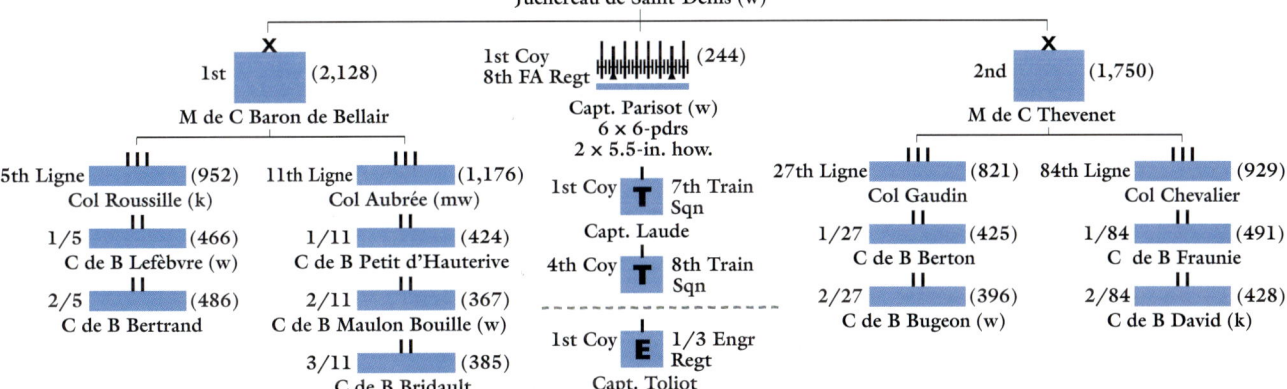

1st (2,128) — M de C Baron de Bellair

5th Ligne (952) — Col Roussille (k)
1/5 (466) — C de B Lefèbvre (w)
2/5 (486) — C de B Bertrand

11th Ligne (1,176) — Col Aubrée (mw)
1/11 (424) — C de B Petit d'Hauterive
2/11 (367) — C de B Maulon Bouille (w)
3/11 (385) — C de B Bridault

1st Coy 8th FA Regt (244) — Capt. Parisot (w)
6 × 6-pdrs
2 × 5.5-in. how.

1st Coy 7th Train Sqn — Capt. Laude
4th Coy 8th Train Sqn

1st Coy 1/3 Engr Regt — Capt. Toliot

2nd (1,750) — M de C Thevenet

27th Ligne (821) — Col Gaudin
1/27 (425) — C de B Berton
2/27 (396) — C de B Bugeon (w)

84th Ligne (929) — Col Chevalier
1/84 (491) — C de B Fraunie
2/84 (428) — C de B David (k)

THE 20TH INFANTRY DIVISION (3,311)

This division was the weakest in the army with only 3,300 all ranks in one and a half brigades. Over 1000 men of the 47th Ligne were deployed with the Army of the Loire. This was partially compensated for by the 10th Ligne being the largest regiment in the army with over 1,400 men.

Like the 19th Division it arrived late at Ligny.

GOC G de D Baron Jean Baptiste Jeanin

At Waterloo it was initially in reserve behind the centre of the French line with the rest of Lobau's Corps. At around 1.30 p.m. it was moved to the right flank to block the approaching Prussians in front of the Bois de Paris.

With the 19th Division it fought a skilful delaying action back to Plancenoit where it held the line to the north of the village.

COS Col Laflèche

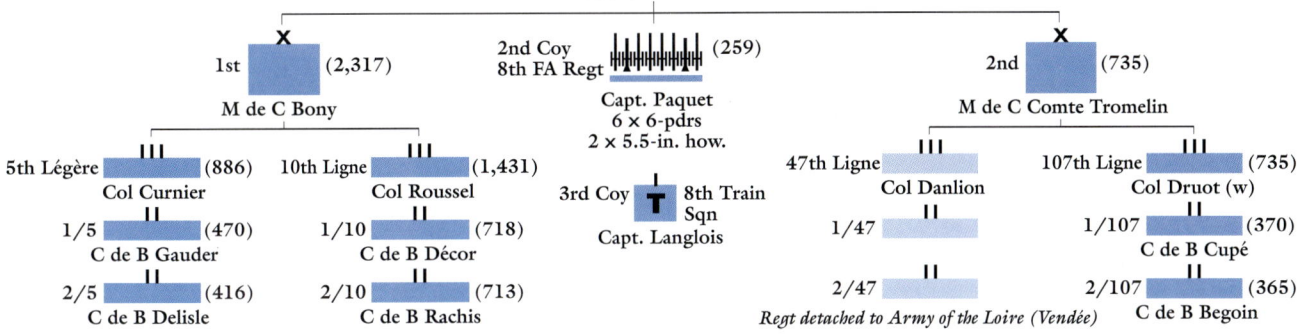

1st (2,317) — M de C Bony

5th Légère (886) — Col Curnier
1/5 (470) — C de B Gauder
2/5 (416) — C de B Delisle

10th Ligne (1,431) — Col Roussel
1/10 (718) — C de B Décor
2/10 (713) — C de B Rachis

2nd Coy 8th FA Regt (259) — Capt. Paquet
6 × 6-pdrs
2 × 5.5-in. how.

3rd Coy 8th Train Sqn — Capt. Langlois

2nd (735) — M de C Comte Tromelin

47th Ligne — Col Danlion
1/47
2/47
Regt detached to Army of the Loire (Vendée)

107th Ligne (735) — Col Druot (w)
1/107 (370) — C de B Cupé
2/107 (365) — C de B Begoin

THE 3RD CAVALRY DIVISION (1,197) – Attached from III Army Corps

GOC G de D Baron Jean Simon Domon (w)

Attached from the III Army Corps as Lobau had no cavalry. A weak division of châsseurs with only nine squadrons – barely 1000 horsemen.

It had led the advance into Belgium and tried, unsuccessfully, to charge the dyke leading to the bridge at Charleroi. Initially on the extreme left at Ligny, where it routed two Prussian cavalry brigades at the close of the battle.

Switched from Vandamme, on 17 June it harried Wellington back to Mont St Jean. Riding boldly up to La Belle Alliance it forced the Allies to open up a cannonade that revealed the extent of their position.

During the battle it was deployed in the east against the advancing Prussians where it conducted a skilful withdrawal that included scattering enemy Uhlan and Hussar regiments.

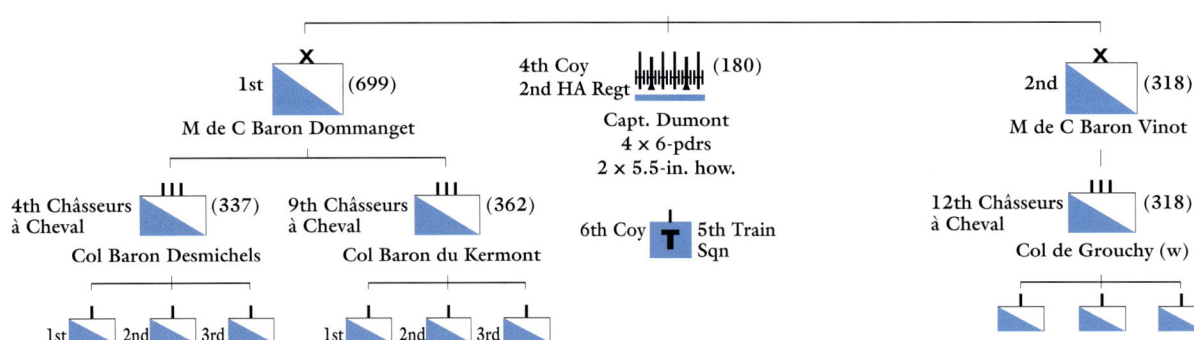

COS Col Maurin

1st (699) — M de C Baron Dommanget
4th Châsseurs à Cheval (337) — Col Baron Desmichels — 1st 2nd 3rd
9th Châsseurs à Cheval (362) — Col Baron du Kermont — 1st 2nd 3rd

4th Coy 2nd HA Regt (180) — Capt. Dumont — 4 × 6-pdrs, 2 × 5.5-in. how.
6th Coy 5th Train Sqn

2nd (318) — M de C Baron Vinot
12th Châsseurs à Cheval (318) — Col de Grouchy (w)

THE 5TH CAVALRY DIVISION (1,487) – Attached from I Reserve Cavalry Corps

GOC G de D Baron Jacques Gervais Subervie

Another weak division (under 1,500) with only eleven squadrons in three regiments – two of lancers and one of châsseurs. It was attached from Pajol's I Reserve Cavalry Corps.

Deployed on the French left at Ligny it spent much of the day in inconclusive feints and artillery duels with the Prussian right wing.

Involved in the follow up of Wellington's Army as it withdrew from Quatre-Bras on 17 June. It tried to charge an Allied rearguard in a thunderstorm at Genappe.

Participated, along with the rest of VI Corps, in the holding back of the Prussian advance on Plancenoit. Charged and checked the cavalry of Bülow's corps.

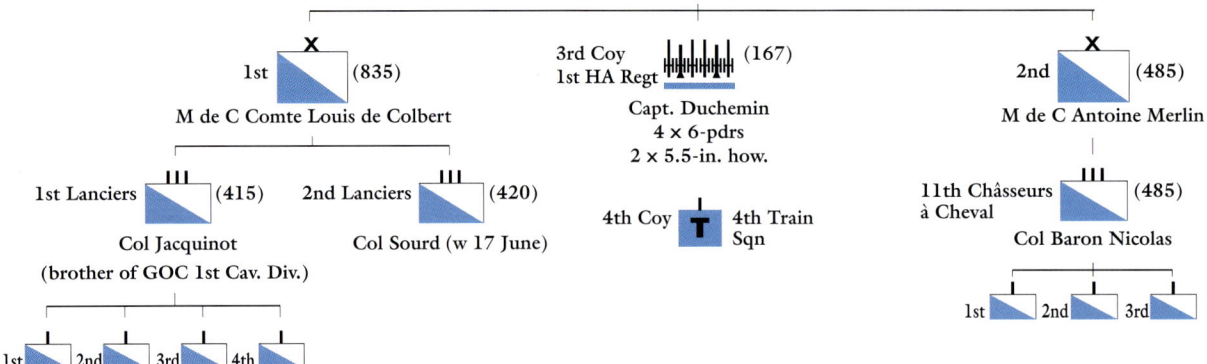

1st (835) — M de C Comte Louis de Colbert
1st Lanciers (415) — Col Jacquinot (brother of GOC 1st Cav. Div.) — 1st 2nd 3rd 4th
2nd Lanciers (420) — Col Sourd (w 17 June)

3rd Coy 1st HA Regt (167) — Capt. Duchemin — 4 × 6-pdrs, 2 × 5.5-in. how.
4th Coy 4th Train Sqn

2nd (485) — M de C Antoine Merlin
11th Châsseurs à Cheval (485) — Col Baron Nicolas — 1st 2nd 3rd

THE III RESERVE CAVALRY CORPS (3,600)

GOC G de D Comte Francois Etienne Kellerman (w)

COS Col Tancarville

THE 11TH CAVALRY DIVISION (1,812)

GOC G de D Baron Samuel Francois L'Héritier (w)

A heavy cavalry division having one brigade each of dragoons and cuirassiers (the 11th Cuirassiers did not wear cuirasses).

Saw no action on the 15th. Kellerman, ordered to join Ney's force, took the cuirassier brigade forward to Quatre-Bras on the 16th where he carried out an almost successful charge on the Allied-held crossroads. The remaining brigade arrived just too late to participate.

At Waterloo posted on the west of the Charleroi–Brussels road. Spent the first four hours watching the two leading infantry corps attack Hougoumont and the Allied left centre – both unsuccessfully.

Also observed the IV Reserve Cavalry Corps launch fruitless assaults on Allied right centre. At 5.00 p.m. this division also joined the onslaught, only to lose 800 men.

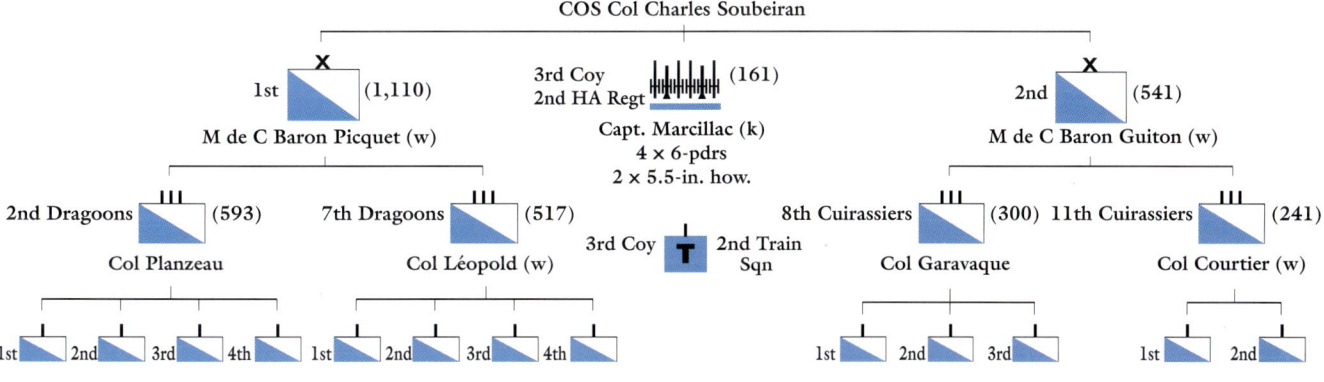

THE 12TH CAVALRY DIVISION (1,796)

GOC G de D Baron Nicolas Francois Roussel d'Hurbal (w)

A heavy cavalry division with a brigade each of carabineers and cuirassiers, each with six squadrons.

It had been seriously delayed crossing the Sambre so did not arrive at Quatre-Bras in time to take part in the action. Had this division been present when Kellerman led his one brigade charge, the battle might have ended differently.

At Waterloo deployed on the left (west) of the Charleroi road with the rest of Kellerman's corps.

Inactive until late afternoon when this division followed l'Héritier's into the desperate efforts to crush the Allied infantry squares. It lost nearly 1000 men. The divisional, both brigade, and three out of four regimental commanders were wounded (one mortally).

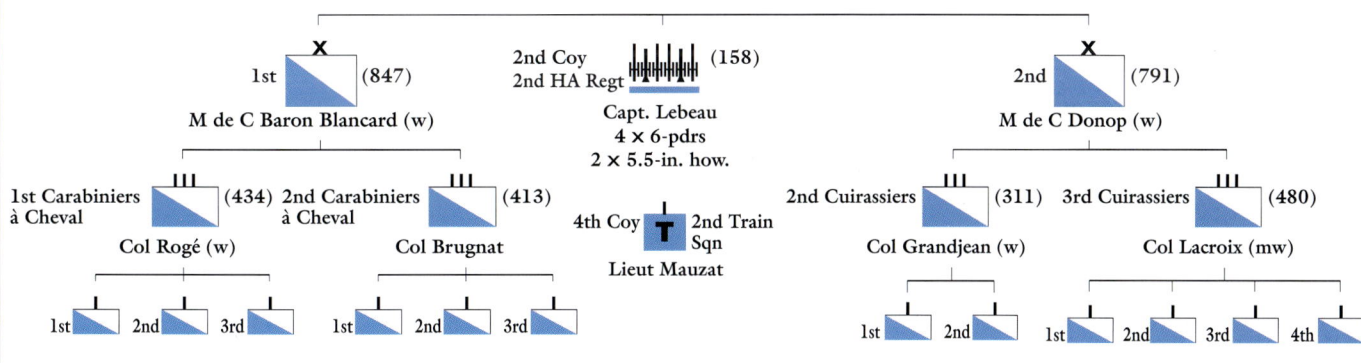

THE IV RESERVE CAVALRY CORPS (3,100)

GOC G de D Comte Edouard Jean Baptiste Milhaud

COS Col Baron Chasseriau (mw)

THE 13TH CAVALRY DIVISION (1,376)

GOC G de D Comte Pierre Watier

An entirely cuirassier division but not well balanced numerically as the 2nd Brigade had only four squadrons due to it being unable to procure sufficient suitable horses.

Held in reserve all day at Ligny but advanced at the end of the battle to join a limited pursuit.

At Waterloo initially in reserve in the second line to right (east) of the Charleroi road. From there it had a magnificent view of the 'Grand Battery' bombarding the Allied line and d'Erlon's corps' unsuccessful assault on the enemy centre and left.

At 3.30 p.m. it supported 14th Cavalry Division in the massed cavalry attacks.

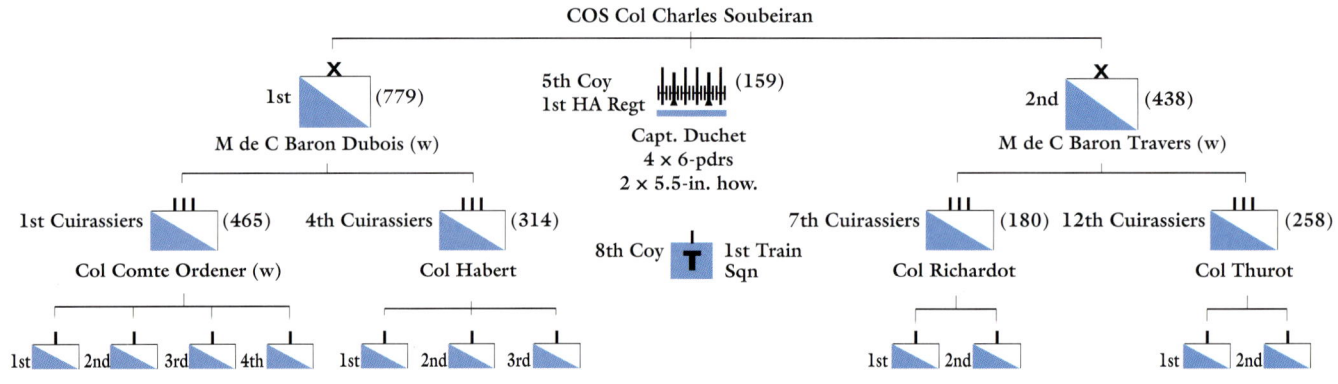

THE 14TH CAVALRY DIVISION (1,739)

GOC G de D Baron Jacques Antoine Adrien Delort (w)

Probably the best equipped and motivated cuirassier formation in the army. With only thirteen squadrons (1,700 sabres) it was only slightly smaller than l'Héritier's division.

Initially in reserve at Ligny. Later it charged and routed some Prussian cavalry and unhorsed Blücher – although they failed to recognize him.

At Waterloo initially in reserve to the right (east) of the Charleroi road. In the early afternoon the 5th and 10th Cuirassiers supported Jacquinot's lancers in a successful counterattack against the Allied heavy cavalry that had penetrated to the 'Grand Battery'.

At 3.30 Delort reluctantly joined the massive cavalry assault on the Allied line.

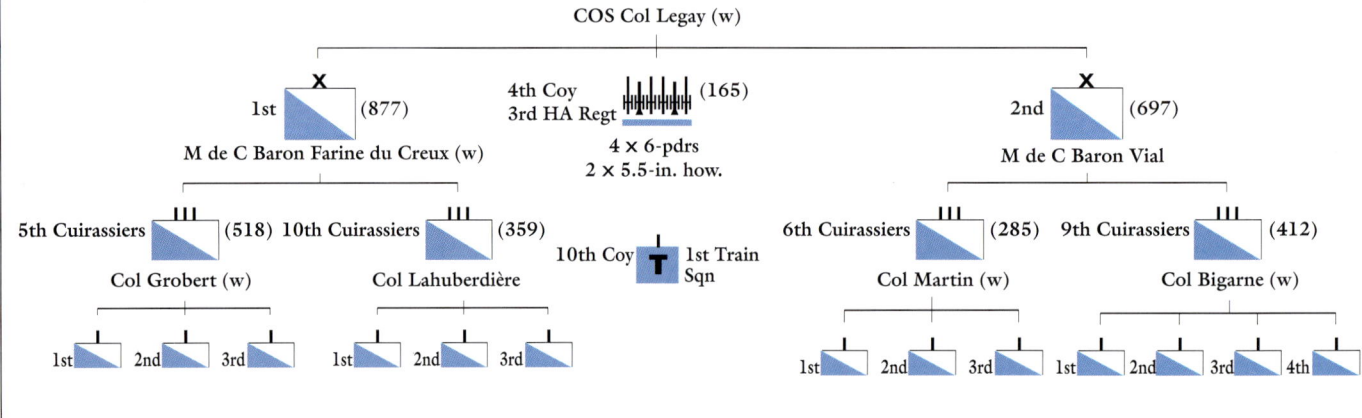

Prussian Strengths

The Prussian returns of 14 June show slightly over 130,000 men with 304 guns under Blücher's command. Although IV Corps was not engaged at all during the period 15–17 June, the other corps were defeated at Ligny after very heavy casualties in I and II Corps. Then some 8000–10,000 men 'disappeared' during the retreat from Ligny to Wavre on 17 June. By 18 June Blücher had 100,000 men and 283 guns available for operations.

The IV Corps under Bülow was the only Prussian corps to fight in its entirety at Waterloo. However, its leading units did not arrive on the edge of the battlefield until 4.30 p.m. As this corps did not receive a battering at Ligny and was not involved in opposing the Sambre crossings, it went into action at virtually full strength. It provided 31,000 men and 86 guns out of the total Prussian involvement of 49,000 and 134 guns. II Corps provided 12,800 at around 6.30 p.m. and I Corps (the last to arrive at about 7.30 p.m.) a total of 5000.

STRENGTHS BY CORPS

I Corps
Infantry: 7 battalions (11% of all Prussian infantry battalions).
Cavalry: 4 regiments, 13 squadrons (21% of all cavalry squadrons).
Artillery: 1 battery of foot artillery, 2 batteries of horse artillery (24 guns, 18% of the total).

II Corps
Infantry: 21 battalions (34% of all battalions).
Cavalry: 3.5 regiments, 14 squadrons (23% of all cavalry squadrons).
Artillery: 2 batteries of foot artillery, 1 battery of horse artillery (24 guns, 18% of the total).

IV Corps
Infantry: 34 battalions (55% of the total).
Cavalry: 10 regiments, 34 squadrons (56% of all cavalry squadrons).
Artillery: 8 batteries of foot artillery, 3 batteries of horse artillery (86 guns, 64% of the total).

Summary

Infantry: 62 battalions	38,000
Cavalry: 17.5 regiments, 61 squadrons	7,000
Artillery: 17 batteries, 134 guns	2,500
Others: staff, munitions columns, engineers, medical personnel, etc.	1,500
Grand total:	**49,000**

The average strength of a Prussian battalion was about 615 all ranks.

THE PRUSSIAN ARMY OF THE LOWER RHINE

p.m. 18 June 1815

**C in C Field-Marshal
Gebhard Leberecht von Blücher**

By 18 June the Prussians had fought the French along the Sambre and been defeated at a major battle at Ligny. In three days they had lost almost 30,000 men, a third of whom had deserted.

This order of battle shows how Blücher's army was split into three parts with only about half of the total able to participate on the battlefield at Waterloo.

Overall Strength Summary (Approximate)

	At Waterloo	En route	At Wavre	Total
Infantry	38,000	20,300	20,000	78,300
Cavalry	7,000	3,000	3,000	13,000
Artillery	2,500	2,000	1,250	5,750
Others*	1,500	1,000	750	3,250
Totals	49,000	26,300	25,000	100,300
Guns	134	106	41 + 2	283

* Includes staff, engineers, munitions, medical, etc.

At Waterloo **XXXX** **(49,000 + 134 guns)**

COS Lt-Gen. Count August von Gneisenau

IV Corps **XXX** **(31,000)**

Gen. Count Bülow von Dennewitz
COS Maj-Gen. von Valentini

Arrived between about
4.30 p.m. – 5.30 p.m.

13th X — Hake

14th X (-) — Ryssel

15th X — Losthin

16th X — Hiller

Prince William of Prussia

1st X (-) — Schwerin

Braun
86 guns

2nd X — Watzdorff

3rd X — Sydow

2nd Sil. Ldr — Schallern

3rd Sil. Ldr — Falckenhäusen

II Corps **XXX** **(12,800) (-)**

Maj-Gen. von Pirch I
COS Col von Aster

Arrived between about
6.30 p.m. – 7.30 p.m.

5th X — Tippelskirch

6th X — Krafft

7th X (-) — Brause

2nd X (-) — Sohr

Röhl
(acting commander
of Army Artillery)
24 guns

En route to
battlefield

II Corps (10,700)

8th X — Bose

14th III
22nd III 7th Brigade

1st X — Lt-Col von Schmiedeberg

3rd X (-) — Col Graf von Schulenburg

11th H | (-)

48 guns

1st Corps **XXX** **(5000) (-)**

Lt-Gen. von Ziethen
COS Lt-Col von Reiche

Arrived between about
7.00 p.m. – 8.00 p.m.

1st X (-) — Steinmetz

1st X — Treskow II

von Lehmann
24 guns

En route to
battlefield

I Corps (15,600)

2nd X — Pirch II

3rd X — Jagow

4th X (-) — Schütter

2nd X (-)
(Lützow – taken prisoner at Ligny)

1st West. Ldr III

58 guns

At
Wavre

III Corps **XXX** **(25,000)**

Lt-Gen. Baron von Thielmann
COS Col von Clausewitz

9th X — Borcke

10th X — Krauseneck

11th X — Luck

12th X — Stülpnagel

1st X — Marwitz

2nd X — Lottum

3rd Kurmärk Ldr III

6th Kurmärk Ldr III

Monhaupt
41 guns

IV Corps
2 guns on
detachment

THE I ARMY CORPS (4,600)

GOC Lt-Gen. Count Hans von Ziethen

COS Lt-Col von Reiche
Asst COS Maj. von Dedenroth
Comd. Corps Artillery Lt-Col von Lehmann
Comd. Corps Reserve Cavalry Lt-Gen. von Roeder
COS Maj. Count Gröben

This corps started the campaign with around 33,000 men. From the 15th–17th it had borne the brunt of the fighting along the Sambre as it fell back before the French invasion to cover the Prussian concentration at Sombreffe/Ligny. By the 18th it had lost over 13,500 (41%) as it was heavily engaged at Ligny, mainly in the bitter struggle for the village of St Amand.

It was the last Prussian corps to make an appearance on the battlefield at Waterloo. It arrived at around 7.00 p.m. on Wellington's extreme left (eastern) flank.

Only some 25% (4,600 men) were involved in the battle in the closing stages around the village of Papelotte/La Haie as they linked up with Wellington's forces.

THE 1ST INFANTRY BRIGADE (DIVISION) (3,230) (-)

GOC Maj-Gen. Karl von Steinmetz

This brigade had suffered severely in the days preceding Waterloo. By the time its leading units reached the battlefield it had shrunk from nearly 8000 to under 5000, but it remained an effective force.

At Ligny this brigade had lost 46 officers and 2,300 men in the fighting around St Amand.

It is not possible to put exact figures to regimental losses prior to Waterloo but battalions marched from Ligny with strengths between 420–460. The 1st Westphalian Landwehr did not arrive in time to participate at Waterloo.

It was the first infantry formation of the corps to arrive on Wellington's left flank around 7.00 p.m. It attacked 30 minutes later in the Papelotte area.

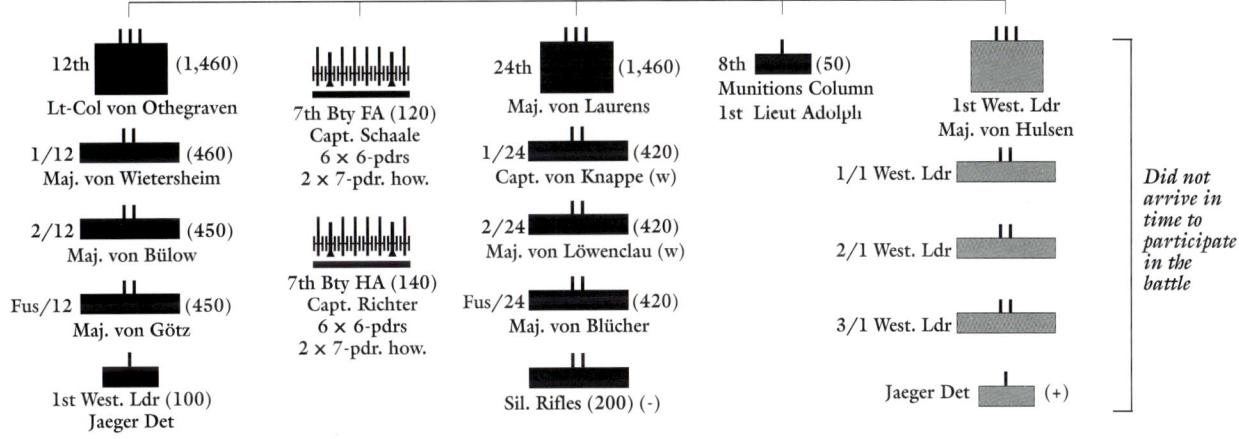

THE 1ST CAVALRY BRIGADE (DIVISION) (1,370)

GOC Maj-Gen. von Treskow II

This brigade had been involved in the fighting withdrawal from the line of the Sambre and around Charleroi when the French invaded Belgium on the 15th.

The 2nd Dragoons had clashed with dragoons of the Imperial Guard near the Bois de Fleurus. At Ligny the brigade suffered from artillery fire in an exposed position.

The brigade was involved in holding off the French in the final stages at Ligny. The 2nd Dragoons was one of the regiments led by Blücher in a charge in which he was unhorsed in an attempt to rally the army.

By the time it arrived at Waterloo the brigade was down to 1,370 men (a loss of 32%). The 5th Dragoons charged Durutte's disorganized battalions in the late evening.

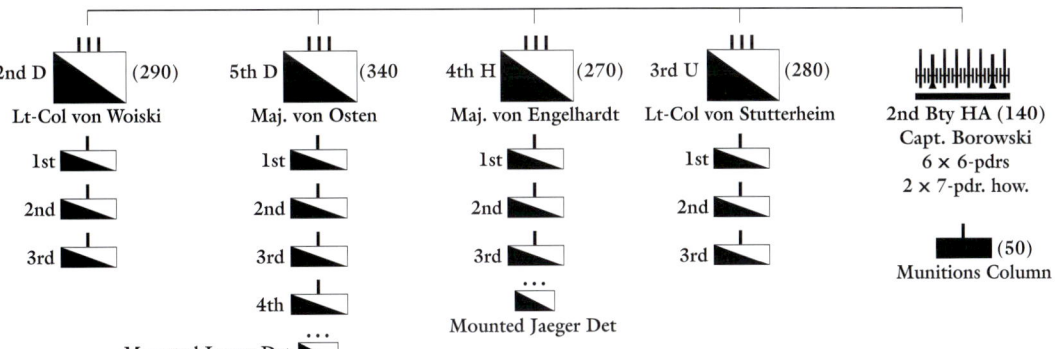

THE II ARMY CORPS (13,000)

GOC Maj-Gen. von Pirch I

COS Col von Aster
Asst COS Maj. von Clausewitz
Comd. Corps Reserve Cavalry Maj-Gen. von Wahlen-Jürgass
Comd. Corps Artillery Lt-Col von Röhl

At the start of the campaign it was the strongest corps with some 35,000 all ranks. Not involved in delaying the French advance over the Sambre.

At Ligny it was fully committed and suffered accordingly. It was embroiled in the ferocious fighting for the village of Ligny itself and losses amounted to almost 6000 with as many again deserting in the retreat to Wavre.

From Wavre this corps followed Bülow's IV Corps in the line of march through Lasne to the eastern edge of the battlefield.

The 5th Brigade, leading the column, arrived around 6.30 p.m. and was almost immediately thrown into the fight for Plancenoit. However, it was the only formation that reached the field to be heavily engaged.

THE 5TH INFANTRY BRIGADE (DIVISION) (5,300)

GOC Maj-Gen. Count Von Tippelskirch

A typical Prussian infantry brigade, with two regular and one landwehr regiment, each with attached jaeger detachments plus two cavalry squadrons and a munitions column.

Involved in prolonged and bitter street fighting at Ligny. Battalions originally 800 strong were reduced on average to about 500 with many commanded by captains.

Arrived at Waterloo just in time to spearhead the final attack on Plancenoit village. Again, it was thrown into desperate close quarter combat, particularly around the church and cemetery. The bulk of the corps' losses (about 350) occurred here.

The brigade also participated in the immediate pursuit of the French at the close of the battle.

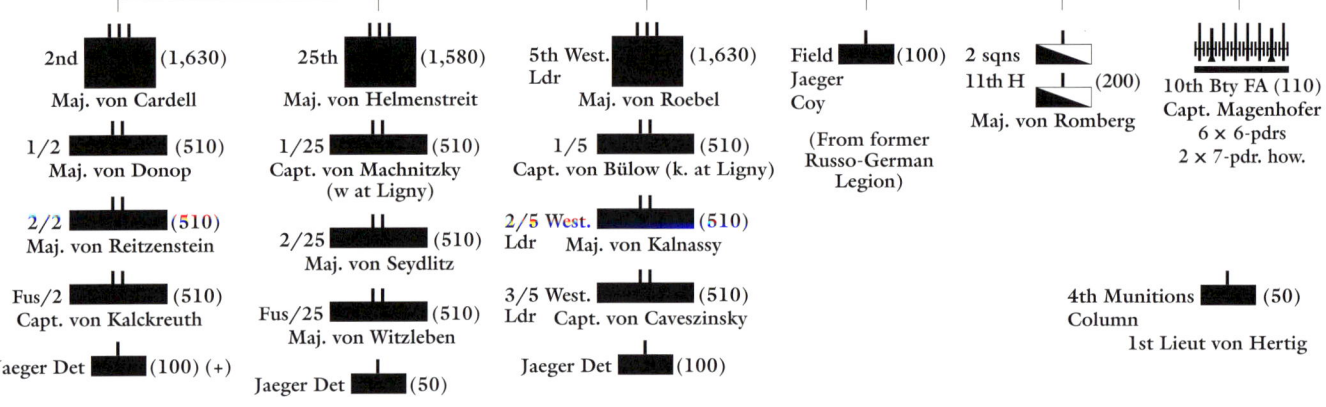

THE 6TH INFANTRY BRIGADE (DIVISION) (4,480)

GOC Maj-Gen. Von Krafft

Another typical Prussian brigade with two regular and one landwehr regiment.

Like the 5th Brigade, it had been very severely mauled in the horrific struggle for the village of Ligny. Its strength fell from over 7000 to about 4,200 infantry – a loss of 40%. Particularly badly hit was the 26th whose battalions at Waterloo were less than 350 strong with junior officers in command.

This brigade did not arrive on the edge of the battlefield until after 7.00 p.m. It was just in time to be the reserve brigade for the final corps attack on Plancenoit. It was not involved in the fighting and suffered negligible losses from artillery fire.

Two days later it went into action at Namur against the French rearguard when Col Bismarck, the uncle of the future Chancellor of Germany, was killed.

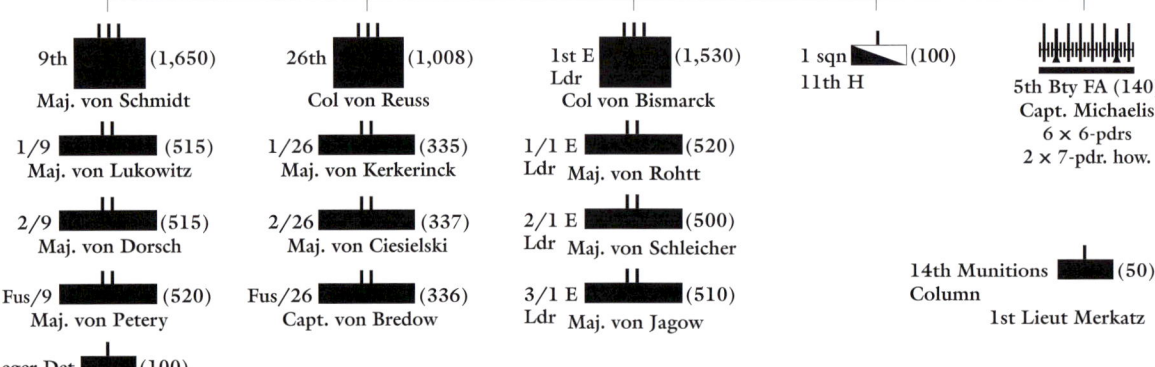

THE 7TH INFANTRY BRIGADE (DIVISION) (1,950)

GOC Maj-Gen. von Brause

Another strong brigade, but one which although involved at Ligny, did not suffer so severely as the other two.

On reaching Chapelle St Lambert en route to Waterloo, this brigade was diverted southwards onto the left flank with orders to march on the village of Maransart.

Only the 2nd Elbe Landwehr Regiment saw action at Waterloo and that on the Prussian's extreme southern flank. Less than 2000 troops from this formation fought in the battle, as the remainder did not arrive in time. Casualties were very light.

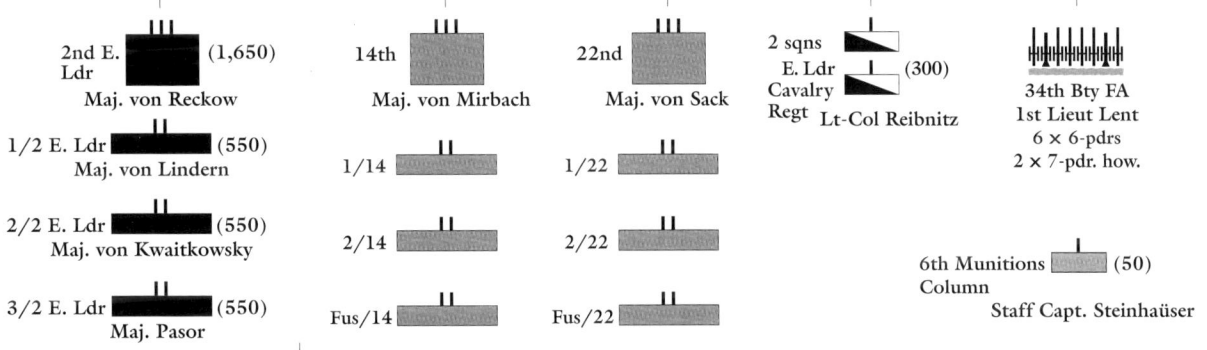

Except for the cavalry these units did not arrive in time to actively participate in the battle

THE 2ND CAVALRY BRIGADE (DIVISION) (1,250)

Acting Comd. Lt-Col von Sohr

A smaller than usual light cavalry brigade with only two regiments, each of four squadrons.

At Ligny it was involved in the fighting and made a charge against French skirmishers.

This brigade was present at Waterloo but was not committed to action until the pursuit.

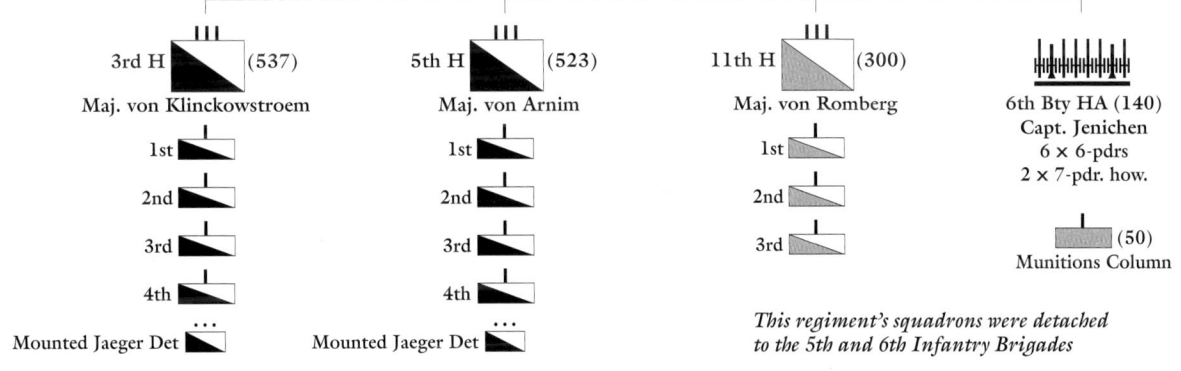

This regiment's squadrons were detached to the 5th and 6th Infantry Brigades

THE IV ARMY CORPS (30,500)

GOC General Count Freidrich Wilhelm Bülow von Dennewitz

This corps, apart from one detachment, was the only Prussian corps to fight in its entirety at Waterloo. Its units were at full strength as it was not engaged at Ligny. It arrived too late for that battle with some units having to march over 80 kilometres from Maastricht.

It was the leading corps in the march from Wavre. It faced serious delays and had the furthest to march so its brigades did not arrive until between 4.30 - 5.30 p.m.

At Waterloo its task was to attack Napoleon's right flank, pushing for the village of Plancenoit with the church spire acting as marker for most of the advance.

It made slow progress, first against Lobau's VI Corps, then against the Imperial Guard in the village where the fighting was intense and prolonged. Total losses were over 6,200 or about 20%.

COS Maj-Gen. von Valentini
Asst COS Maj. von Rüts
Comd. Corps Artillery Maj-Gen. von Braun
Comd. Corps Reserve Cavalry Gen. Prince William of Prussia
COS Maj. von Hedemann

THE 13TH INFANTRY BRIGADE (DIVISION) (7,221)

GOC Lt-Gen. von Hake

A strong brigade with the normal complement of two squadrons of cavalry and a battery of guns under command.

It was the third brigade in the order of march to Waterloo and thus did not deploy until late afternoon.

At around 5.30 p.m. it deployed in support of the 15th Brigade on the northern half of the Prussian line of advance. It became heavily involved with driving Lobau's troops back eastwards across the very exposed ground NE of Plancenoit. Losses were just under 1000.

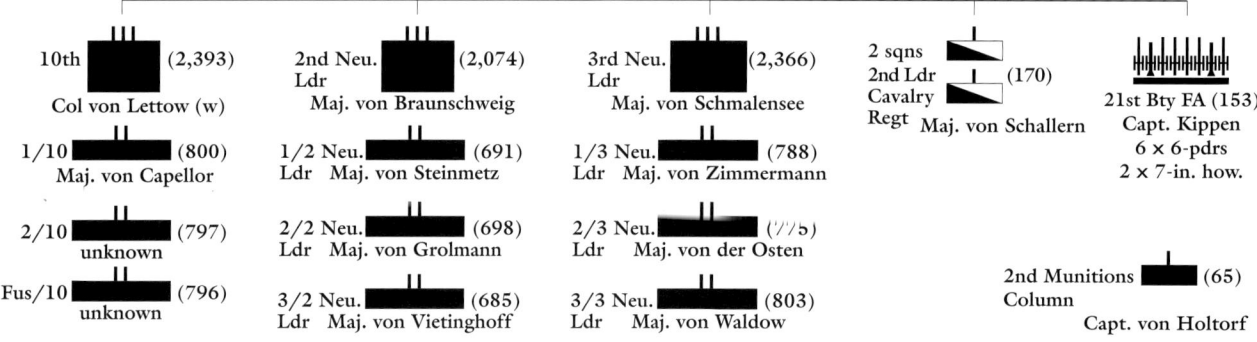

THE 14TH INFANTRY BRIGADE (DIVISION) (5,863)

GOC Maj-Gen. von Ryssel

This formation was well below its full strength due to two battalions being on detachment at Mont St Guibert south of Wavre. It was entirely a landwehr formation that fought with great tenacity and courage mainly against French guardsmen.

It was the last infantry formation in the corps' order of march to Waterloo, only arriving at Chapelle St Lambert at 3.00 p.m.

It was initially tasked with trying to get round the southern flank of Lobau's Corps as it withdrew slowly westwards towards Plancenoit.

Later it was committed to the assault on the village and it fought in the desperate struggle with the Young Guard around the church and cemetery. It was repulsed by Old Guard reinforcements. Losses almost 1,400 - with the 2nd Pomeranian Landwehr suffering 571.

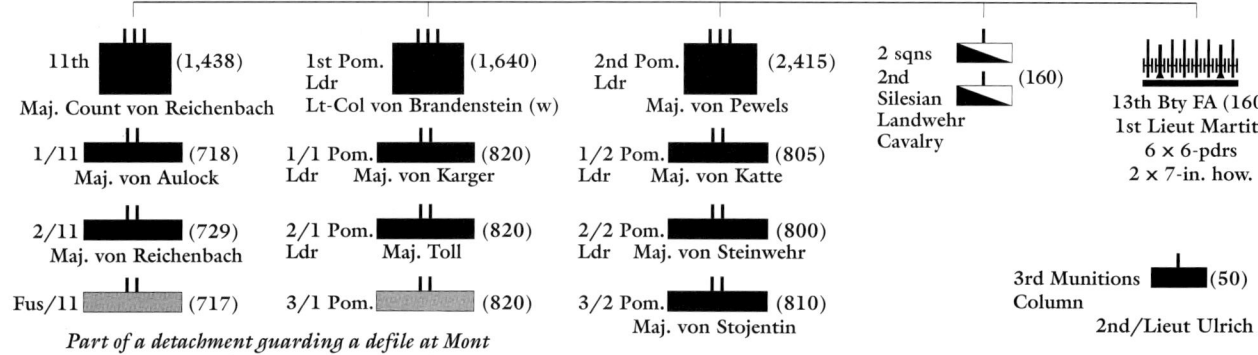

Part of a detachment guarding a defile at Mont St Guibert south of Wavre. Not at Waterloo.

THE 15TH INFANTRY BRIGADE (DIVISION) (6,500)

GOC Maj-Gen. von Losthin

A comparatively strong brigade. It set off around 4.00 a.m. to lead the march of the corps from Wavre. It was delayed for two hours in that town by a fire before continuing – led by a local shepherd. It was a hard march and the 18th Infantry Regiment threw away their stiff collars. Thereafter the regiment wore pink collars to commemorate this incident.

The first brigade to emerge from the Bois de Paris to confront the French behind a screen of the 6th Hussars.

Heavily involved in the fighting against Lobau's corps. Deployed on the north (right) flank of the advance. Some units moved on Frichermont and Smohain where they inadvertently fired on Nassau troops. Casualties heavy – 1,800.

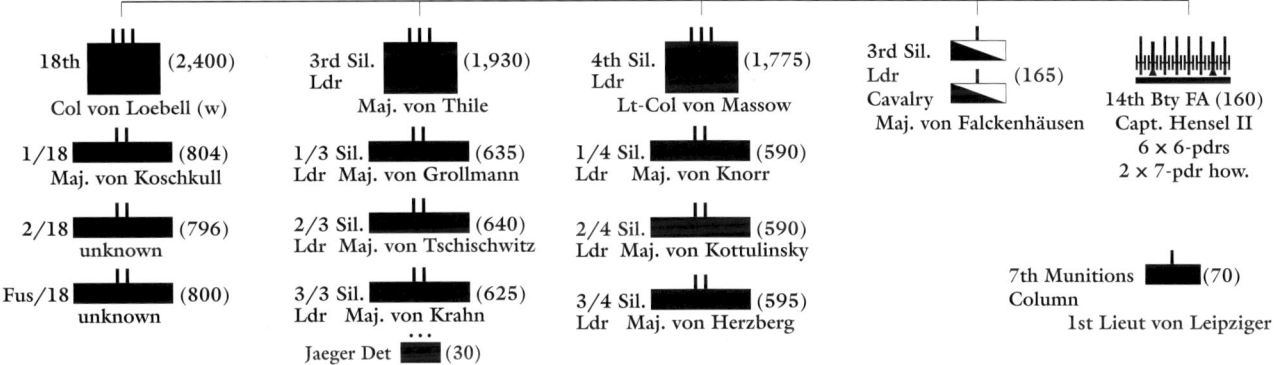

THE 16TH INFANTRY BRIGADE (DIVISION) (6,285)

Acting GOC Col Hiller von Gartringen

A comparatively weak brigade with under 6000 infantry – six of the nine Silesian battalions having only 600 or less men.

It was second in the order of march from Wavre.

At Waterloo it deployed south of the 15th Brigade in the push for Plancenoit. Later it was fully committed to the struggle for the village with its units fighting hand-to-hand with the Young and then the Old Guard. It attacked, was repulsed, and attacked again. Its losses were very high – over 1,800 – but it fought extremely well.

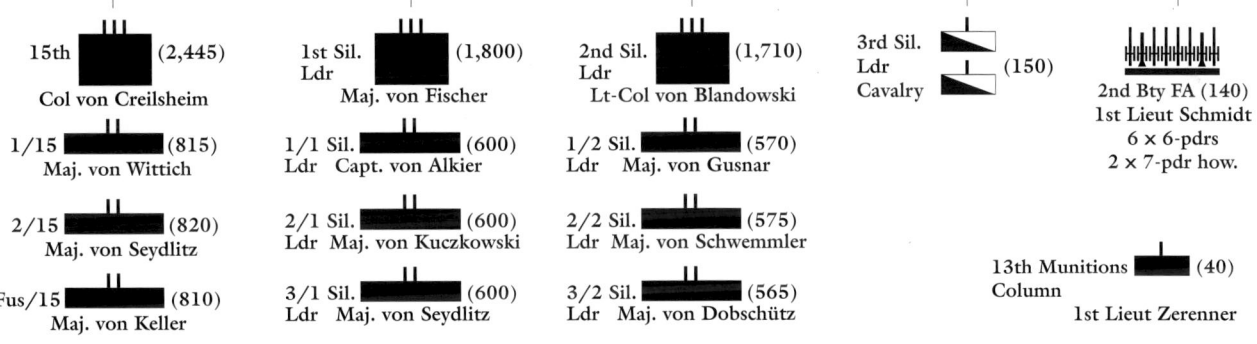

THE 1ST CAVALRY BRIGADE (DIVISION) (1,360)

Comd Col Count von Schwerin (k)

This brigade was only two-thirds of its normal strength at Waterloo as the 10th Hussars were on detachment with two infantry battalions and two guns south of Wavre under Col Ledebur.

The 6th Hussars led the advance from Wavre, screening the infantry. During a clash with French cavalry and guns on the edge of the Bois de Paris, Col Schwerin was killed.

In the battle it supported 15th Brigade and lost some 50 men.

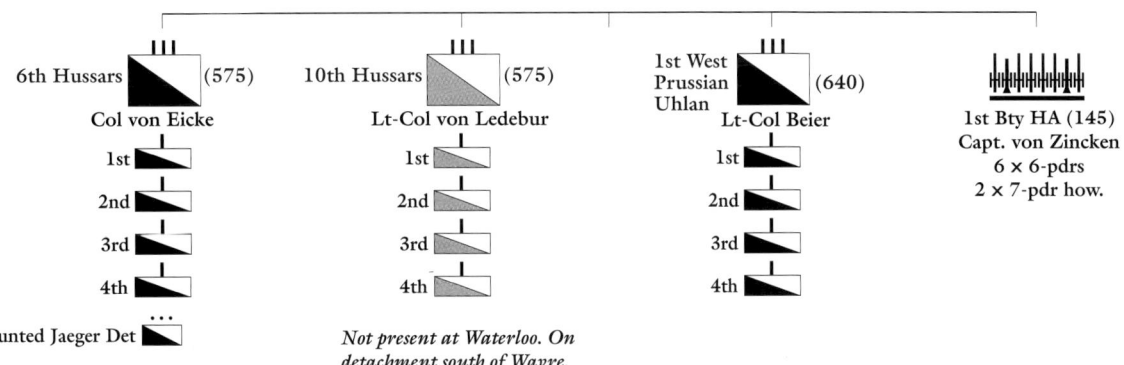

THE 2ND CAVALRY BRIGADE (DIVISION) (560)

Comd Lt-Col von Watzdorff (k)

A very weak brigade that only consisted of three squadrons of the 8th Hussars totalling some 450 men. Its second regiment, the 8th Dragoons, did not manage to join the army until the end of the month.

The 8th Hussars were involved in the advance towards Plancenoit and at one stage were called on to charge French skirmishers that strayed too far east of the village. The regiment had 68 casualties in the battle, the second highest of all cavalry regiments in the corps.

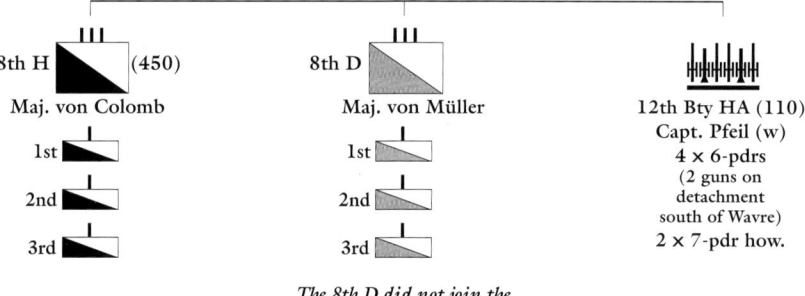

8th H (450)
Maj. von Colomb
1st
2nd
3rd

8th D
Maj. von Müller
1st
2nd
3rd

12th Bty HA (110)
Capt. Pfeil (w)
4 × 6-pdrs
(2 guns on detachment south of Wavre)
2 × 7-pdr how.

The 8th D did not join the army until late June.

THE 3RD CAVALRY BRIGADE (DIVISION) (1,836)

GOC Maj-Gen. von Sydow

By far the strongest cavalry formation in the corps with five small landwehr regiments each of three squadrons.
Apart from the 2nd Neumärk Landwehr Cavalry Regiment, which saw action, this brigade was not heavily committed at Waterloo.

The 1st Silesians scouted south of the Lasne River and lost 5 men. The 1st Pomeranians supported the 15th Brigade and lost three. The 2nd Neumärk covered the corps advance from the Bois de Paris and suffered losses of 122 (28%). The other two were barely engaged losing only one man between them.

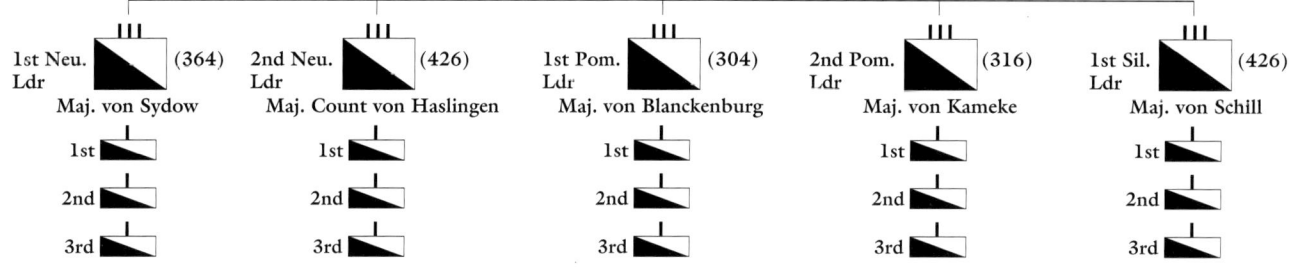

1st Neu. Ldr (364)
Maj. von Sydow
1st
2nd
3rd

2nd Neu. Ldr (426)
Maj. Count von Haslingen
1st
2nd
3rd

1st Pom. Ldr (304)
Maj. von Blanckenburg
1st
2nd
3rd

2nd Pom. Ldr (316)
Maj. von Kameke
1st
2nd
3rd

1st Sil. Ldr (426)
Maj. von Schill
1st
2nd
3rd

THE 4TH ARTILLERY RESERVE (873)

Comd Maj-Gen. von Braun

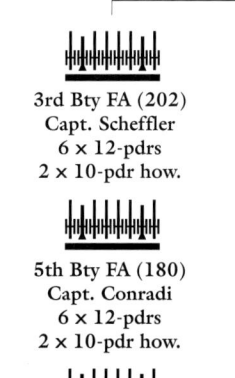

3rd Bty FA (202)
Capt. Scheffler
6 × 12-pdrs
2 × 10-pdr how.

11th Bty FA (161)
Capt. von Mengden
6 × 12-pdrs
2 × 10-pdr how.

11th Bty HA (143)
Capt. Borchard
6 × 12-pdrs
2 × 10-pdr how.

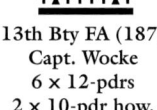

5th Bty FA (180)
Capt. Conradi
6 × 12-pdrs
2 × 10-pdr how.

13th Bty FA (187)
Capt. Wocke
6 × 12-pdrs
2 × 10-pdr how.

Casualties at Waterloo

ANGLO-ALLIED CASUALTIES

Wellington's Army lost just over 17,000 men of all ranks at Waterloo. This figure includes killed, wounded and missing. They represent 23 per cent of those engaged. In round numbers there were 3,500 killed, 10,200 wounded and the balance, 3,300, went missing. Of the latter almost half were Dutch or Belgian troops, and of the remainder about 500 were from the Hanoverian Duke of Cumberland's Hussars who decamped en masse during the afternoon.

Again in round figures, officer casualties amounted to 950 out of 3,300 that took the field. This means some 29 per cent of officers became casualties. With the other ranks there were about 16,200 killed, wounded or missing out of 69,700 – or 23 per cent. Put another way, seventeen soldiers fell for every officer casualty. Officer losses amounted to 5.5 per cent of all casualties.

FRENCH CASUALTIES

After their defeat at Waterloo followed by the long retreat south, French commanders assembled and took parade states of the men that remained with them. This regrouping took place between 23 and 26 June. It follows that it is impossible to isolate the losses at Waterloo from the losses in the retreat afterwards, many of which were absentees rather than battlefield casualties. French Army archives contain most of these returns, and the figures used below are based on those extracted from these archives by Scott Bowden and included in his book *Armies at Waterloo*.

An estimate of the numbers lost by each army corps during the period 18–26 June can be made by comparing the strengths at the start of the battle at Waterloo with the numbers parading at the final musters about a week later.

The French Losses at Waterloo

Napoleon's battlefield casualties (killed or wounded) are difficult to estimate, as it is impossible to be certain how many were lost during the fighting and how many absented themselves during the following week before musters were held. The likelihood is that the battlefield losses were considerably higher than Wellington's, as the French were continuously attacking over exposed ground and were subjected to sustained gunfire at short ranges. The strength of the Armée du Nord at the start of the battle is known – 77,000 in round figures – and the losses during the battle and shortly afterwards amounted to about 46,500, of which 2,400 were lost at Wavre.

There are two ways of estimating the French battlefield losses. Firstly, of those engaged at Waterloo Wellington lost 17,000 men or 23 per cent, and the Prussians 7000 or 14 per cent. If one assumes that the French casualties were almost twice those of the Anglo-Allied Army, say 40 per cent, then that would give a figure of 30,800. Secondly, the Prussians had about 10,000 deserters on 17 June on their retreat from Ligny to Wavre. The French would have had at least as many after Waterloo, say 25 per cent of the total losses. This would indicate some 11,000 went missing after the battle, giving a figure of 30,600 lost on the battlefield. Both these attempts give a figure of almost 31,000 Frenchmen killed or wounded at Waterloo – with several thousand more captured.

With reference to officer losses, the returns seem to show some 1,677 out of about 3,200 (52 per cent) remained with their units a week after the battle. Officer losses amounted to 3.6 per cent of the total. Their battlefield casualties were high but their desertion rate after the rout would be expected to be much less than that of the soldiers.

PRUSSIAN CASUALTIES

By 18 June the Prussians had lost a lot of men. I Corps had fought a withdrawing action back from the Sambre to cover Blücher's concentration around Ligny. I Corps, plus II and III Corps, were defeated at Ligny with substantial casualties. Shortly afterwards, up to 10,000 deserted during the retreat to Wavre. In total over 31,000 men had been lost in three days. It says a lot for Prussian morale and leadership that they fought again with such vigour and courage in the closing stages at Waterloo.

The Prussians lost 7000 in the battle, the great majority (over 6000) occurring in IV Corps during its struggle for Plancenoit. Of these casualties 223 (3 per cent) were officers.

Comparisons

COMPARISON OF STRENGTHS AT WATERLOO

There is a striking similarity in the numbers deployed by Wellington and Napoleon at the start of the battle. Normally an attacker would hope to outnumber a defender by three to one, but in this instance the French only outnumbered the Anglo-Allied force by a few thousand men. Their superiority lay in artillery. Napoleon intended to attack an army of 73,500 with 77,300. As the figures below illustrate, he had no advantage with infantry, 3000 with cavalry and 89 more guns.

	Wellington	Napoleon
Infantry:	53,850 (84 battalions)	53,400 (103 battalions)
Cavalry:	13,350 (93 squadrons)	15,600 (113.5 squadrons)
Artillery:	157 guns + rocket section	246 guns

Although the Prussians did not appear on the battlefield until 4.30 p.m. they were sighted in the distance at about 1.00 p.m.. Half an hour later Napoleon, whose main attack on Wellington's line was just starting, had been compelled to send Lobau's corps of 10,600 men to protect his eastern flank. This corps was thus unavailable to him to reinforce his assaults on Wellington.

	Strength at Waterloo	Strength on 26 June	Losses (%)
Imperial Guard	20,200	7,580	12,620 (62)
I Army Corps	19,800	5,573	14,227 (72)
II Army Corps	20,200	6,813	13,387 (66)
VI Army Corps	10,600	5,600	5,000 (47)
III Res. Cavalry Corps	3,600	1,628	1,972 (55)
IV Res. Cavalry Corps	3,100	3,650*	+ 550
Totals	**77,500**	**30,844**	**46,656 (60)**

* This corps appears to have received drafts in the week following the battle that more than compensated for its losses.

Consequently, the Emperor was forced to attack with an overall inferiority against his primary enemy – 66,900 against 73,200. However, this comparison of numbers takes no account of concentration at the point of attack, training, leadership, morale and the other factors that make up the overall effectiveness of an army.

COMPARISON OF LOSSES

As noted above, it is difficult to isolate with any degree of accuracy the numbers of French casualties at the battle from those they lost during the retreat afterwards. This being so it is more infor-mative to compare the losses of all three armies over the period 15–26 June.

This table indicates (approximately) that during June, Wellington lost 19.5 per cent of the 112,000 men available to him, out of 130,000 Blücher lost 31 per cent, and out of 123,000 Napoleon lost 55 per cent. Looked at another way the combined Allies' losses were only about 5000 lower than that of the French – 62,100 to 67,400. An informed guess at the French battlefield casualties (killed and wounded) at Waterloo would be around 31,000 (see box on previous page).

Date and battle	Anglo-Allied	Prussian	French
15 June – Gilly	nil	2,000	600
16 June – Quatre-Bras	4,600	nil	4,100
– Ligny	nil	18,800	13,700
17 June – Prussian retreat	nil	10,000	nil
– Allies' retreat	250	nil	120
18 June – Waterloo/French retreat	17,000	7,000	46,500
18/19 June – Wavre and retreat	nil	2,450	2,400
Totals	21,850	40,250	67,420

Command and Control

*The relationship between a general and his troops is
very much like that between the rider and his horse.
The horse must be controlled and disciplined, and yet
encouraged: he should be cared for in the stables as if
he was worth £500 and ridden in the field as if he
were not worth half-a-crown*

Field-Marshal Earl Wavell

General

In all armies at Waterloo, officers, both senior and junior, can be cat-egorized broadly as either commanders or staff officers (including ADCs, supply officers and medical officers). The former com-manded, made plans, received instructions and gave orders to achieve their mission. They took responsibility for success or failure of their army, formation, unit or sub-unit. Commanders ranged in rank from the emperor or a field-marshal commanding an army, down to a lieutenant or sergeant in charge of a picquet. Staff officers existed to facilitate control, to ensure the commander's instructions were issued, delivered and understood. They were the channels through which the commander controlled and administered his army. Again, their rank could range from the very highest (Maréchal Soult, chief of staff to Napoleon) to the lowest (Lieutenant Mansfield, ADC to Major-General Sir Colquhoun Grant).

At Waterloo the French staff officers were more numerous than those of the Allies. This was due, firstly, to Napoleon need-ing not only to directly command the Armée du Nord, but also to keep in touch with, and if necessary give instructions to, the other armies on the frontiers, the war ministry in Paris and the national government. These responsibilities virtually doubled the throngs of staff, both military and civil, at his headquarters. Secondly, like the Prussians, the French had several staff officers at every regi-mental headquarters. An approximate comparison for the number of military staff officers at various levels, including ADCs at army headquarters (but not elsewhere) is shown below.

Nationality	Army	Corps	Division	Brigade	Regiment
French	85	6–8	2	2	5–8
British	73	6–8	3	2–3	–
Dutch-Belgian	–	9	5	3-4	2–3
Prussian	58	20	–	2	5–8

Discounting the commanders-in-chief, for the Battle of Waterloo the French fielded 2.8 times as many generals (staff, brigade commanders and upwards) as the Anglo-Allied force – 114 to 41. They were undoubtedly top-heavy with generals. However, if one includes the Prussian generals who eventually arrived on the battlefield, the difference is slightly less startling – 114 to 67. A particular disparity occurred with the ranks of artillery and engineer commanders. Napoleon mustered ten sup-porting arms generals, while Blücher had only four and Wellington none at all. The ratios of generals to troops of all other ranks are equally revealing. With the French it was 1:680, the Anglo-Allied 1:1,785 and the Prussians 1:1,885. Put another way, Napoleon had eleven more generals than infantry battalions (114 to 103). If the Emperor's army was over officered in the higher echelons of command, the reverse was true within its infantry battalions. Discounting regimental staffs, a French battal-ion averaged (on paper) about eighteen officers, while a British had thirty. A comparative table is given below of brigade com-manders and upwards on the battlefield

A Comparison of General Officers and Casualties at Waterloo

It is of interest to compare the ratio of generals to troops on the battlefield. The figures given below exclude Army HQ staff and more junior officers who were acting up temporarily, but they do include senior staff officers who were with their formation in the field at corps or divisional headquarters, for example.

	Infantry	Cavalry	Artillery/ Engineer	Total	Ratio
French	51	31	8	90	1: 861
Anglo-Allied	22	6	0	28	1: 2,607
Prussians	12	4	3	19	1: 2,579

Note: Napoleon had over three times as many generals in the field with the troops as Wellington. Wellington's artillery and engineers were commanded by many more junior officers than the Emperor's. Of the above general officers the French lost 38 (6 killed and 32 wounded) out of 90, or 42 per cent. The Anglo-Allied Army lost 13 out of 28 (3 killed and 10 wounded) or 46 per cent. The casualty rate among generals in these two armies was roughly even therefore. If the number of French generals seems excessive, a comparison with the modern U.S. military is revealing. In an American Army division (about 12,000 men) there are 30 generals (brigadier-general and higher), the Air Force boasts a general for every 23 planes and the Navy an admiral for every 1.6 ships!

	GHQ Staff	Infantry	Cavalry	Artillery/ engineers	Totals
French	27	45	32	10	114
Anglo-Allied	4	26	11	0	41
Prussian	3	12	7	4	26

The percentage of general officer casualties also makes for an interesting comparison. Overall percentage levels were:

	Killed (%)	Wounded (%)	Total (%)
French	6 (5.25)	37 (32.45)	43 (37.71)
Anglo-Allied	5 (12)	9 (22)	14 (34)
Prussian	2 (7.7)	1 (3.8)	3 (11.5)

Generals led from the front at Waterloo and were exposed to cannon shot, musket ball, sword and bayonet just as much as their soldiers. From the figures perhaps the Prussian senior commanders were not always as far forward as in the other armies. The level of casualties among the generals in both the main attacking army and defending army is very high and remarkably similar: French 37.7 per cent, Anglo-Allied 34 per cent.

The French Commander-in-Chief
EMPEROR NAPOLEON BONAPARTE

They will talk of his glory
Under the thatch for a long time.
For fifty years, the humble cottage
Will know no other story.

Jean de Beranger

APPEARANCE AND HEALTH

Napoleon was forty-six years old at Waterloo, the same age as Wellington. He had been a soldier for thirty years, had fought in nearly fifty battles, winning most of them. Debatably the greatest general the world has yet seen. Wellington remarked that on a battlefield Napoleon was worth 40,000 men. Certainly Waterloo was a contest between the two greatest commanders, the two military giants, of the age. For well over twenty years the Napoleonic Wars had ravaged Europe. Yet these two men had never, until that Sunday morning, faced each other across a battlefield. It can be said, with some degree of accuracy, that the supreme strategist, Napoleon, was at last confronting the consummate tactician, Wellington. Or perhaps, that the general who had won his crown by attacking was about to take the offensive against one whose reputation was built primarily as a successful defender.

The Emperor wore his favourite uniform, the one he would be buried in six years later, the green, white and gold undress uniform of a colonel of the Châsseurs à Cheval of the Imperial Guard, with white breeches and high, black riding boots. All these were partially concealed by his well-worn, shabby grey greatcoat. Napoleon liked comfortable clothes, ones he had worn for a long time – his melancholy tailor, Bastide, being expected to keep them in repair. Inevitably that day he put on his battered, black, half-moon shaped hat that was lined with white satin. Worn sideways across his head it was the most famous part of his profile. Pictures of Napoleon at Waterloo always depict him on a white or grey horse. Several mounts would have been available and it is known that he rode three at Waterloo: Marie, and the greys Desirée and Marengo.

If his soldiers instantly recognized him at a distance from his familiar coat and hat, some of those who saw him closer were shocked at the recent change in his physical appearance. He did not look well and was unhealthily overweight. An officer commenting after seeing him at Ligny said, '... He had grown much stouter than when he was at Leipzig, and looked yellow. If it had not been for his grey coat and his hat, I should hardly have recognized him. His cheeks were sunken and he looked much older...'. According to another officer, since his stay on Elba:

> Napoleon's stoutness had increased rapidly. His head had become enlarged and more deeply set between his shoulders. His pot-belly was unusually pronounced for a man of forty-five [*sic*]. Furthermore, it was noticeable that during this campaign that he remained on horseback much less than in the past. ... his dull white complexion, his heavy walk made him appear very different... .

Undoubtedly, Napoleon was not a fit man at Waterloo. But neither was he incapacitated. He had suffered from a variety of ailments for several years, yet still he had worked unstintingly, with all his old decisiveness and determination, in the weeks prior to Waterloo. His strategic planning had been masterly. However, the last three days had been exhausting and he had slept little at night. Bouts of weariness caused him to doze off, as he had in his roadside chair in Charleroi. Nevertheless, he was capable of commanding. He had certainly not reached the stage described by his chamberlain, Las Cases, on St Helena that, 'all his strength is in his mind'.

Plans and orders

When Napoleon discovered, shortly after dawn on 18 June, that Wellington was still in position along the Mont St Jean ridge, he exclaimed, '*Ah! Je les tiens donc, ces Anglais*', ('Ah! I have them, these English'). He wanted them to stand and fight. His intention was to smash his way through to the Mont St Jean crossroads and then march to Brussels. He was confident, almost recklessly so, dismissing any suggestion that some caution, some manoeuvring, might be wise. He was also convinced that he had nothing to worry about as far as the Prussians were concerned. Napoleon was

Imperial Magic

Napoleon believed that a general must love his soldiers to understand them, and understand them to lead them. He had been a soldier all his life, climbing from sous-lieutenant to emperor, so the professional bond with his troops was profound. To his *grognards* (veterans) 'emperor' was a military rank above 'general' or 'marshal'. Soldiers never addressed him as 'Your Majesty' or 'Sire' but always '*Mon Empereur*'. He seldom forgot a face, never a kindness.

At a review in 1809 he recognized a grenadier who had risked his life to save his hat at the Siege of Acre nine years earlier. Napoleon demanded to know why he was still a grenadier. The man replied that he could not write and gestured that he was something of a drunkard. His Emperor gave him 50 francs. After Austerlitz he adopted all the children of soldiers killed in the battle. The boys would be brought up at the Imperial Palace of Rambouillet (at the time of writing being used for international negotiations to try to bring peace to Kosovo) and the girls at Sainte Germaine. All could add 'Napoleon' to their names. Such acts, such calculated use of emotion would have been unthinkable for the austere, reserved 'Iron Duke'.

---

totally in command at this stage and, crucially, he contemplated an early attack. His orders, decisions and plans prior to the battle are summarized below. They provide a fascinating insight into how the French plan evolved, the certainty of Napoleon as to a favourable result, and the way in which events eroded the substance of the main French attack before a single soldier had crossed the start line.

• Between 10.00 p.m. and 11.00 p.m. the previous night Napoleon had given precise orders as to how the army was to deploy for battle on either side of the Charleroi–Brussels road, with La Belle Alliance in the centre (Map 8, p. 119). Details of the actual assault, however, were not given. At that stage Napoleon wanted an early attack, probably around 6.00 a.m. or a little later. Unlike other important orders, there is no record of this one, but its existence is implicit for several reasons. First, all the various corps knew where to go on the ground without any instructions on the 18th. Second, General Foy's troops were ordered to parade at Genappe ready to move at 3.30 a.m. – far too early for a battle planned for after midday. Thirdly, Soult's written order of around 5.00 a.m. refers to 'positions indicated overnight'.

• At around 4.00 a.m. Napoleon realized that the rain, the sodden ground, the widely scattered bivouacs, and the fact that the entire army had only one good road for its final approach march, meant an early morning attack was impossible. He postponed it for over two hours. Soult issued the written order that changed the timing, not the deployment – details of which commanders already knew. Napoleon required his army to be ready on the start line at 9.00 a.m., but there were still no instructions as to how the battle was to be fought.

• Exactly how to attack Wellington was debated over breakfast at Le Caillou where the Emperor had spent the night. At about 8.00 a.m. maps were spread out and Napoleon considered his plan of attack with Generals Soult, Drouot and several others of his staff. He was in an unshakeably positive mood. Despite thinking (erroneously) that his enemy seriously outnumbered him, he declared that there were, 'ninety chances in our favour, and not ten against us.' Ney, who arrived in time to hear this remark, stated that Wellington was retiring and that an immediate attack was required to catch him. Napoleon brusquely dismissed this as nonsense: 'You have seen wrong…'.

Soult broached the subject of getting Grouchy to bring part of his force to Mont St Jean. He had mentioned it the night before. An exasperated Emperor slapped him down, 'Because you have been beaten by Wellington, you consider him a great general. And now I tell you that Wellington is a bad general, that the English are bad troops, and that this affair is nothing more serious than eating one's breakfast.' It was not the most tactful way of putting his chief of staff in his place in front of senior officers. Soult responded quietly, 'I earnestly hope so.'

Prince Jérôme (Napoleon's younger brother, of whose military skills he had scant regard) and General Reille joined the group. The Emperor asked Reille, who had fought against Wellington's army many times in Spain, his opinion of it. 'Well posted,' answered this experienced general, 'as Wellington knows how to post it, and attacked from the front, I consider the English infantry to be impregnable …'. Napoleon did not bother to reply. Jérôme then warned the Emperor that a waiter at the Roi d'Espagne who had attended him the previous evening had earlier also attended on Wellington at breakfast. The waiter had told the Prince that he had overheard an ADC commenting that the Allies intended to concentrate in front of the Forest of Soignes, and that the Prussians were at Wavre. Napoleon ridiculed the idea, believing that after their defeat at Ligny a junction between the Allies was impossible for at least two days.

• The meeting broke up and Napoleon rode forward to assess the situation. It was nearly 9.00 a.m. and his troops should have been fully deployed, ready to receive his plan of attack. They were not. The ground was extremely sticky and many formations were still on the line of march. Time passed; the Emperor stood with a telescope to his eye, scanning the ground ahead. However, he could see little of the enemy, the great majority of

Napoleon's 9.00 a.m. Attack Order

The following order was addressed to Ney, copied to Drouot of the Imperial Guard and signed by Soult:

The Emperor commands that the army will be formed up ready to attack the enemy by 9.00 a.m. General Officers Commanding Army Corps will concentrate their troops, they will arrange that the arms are put in serviceable condition, they will permit the soldiers to prepare their soup, also they will cause the men to complete their meal so that by 9.00 a.m. to the minute the whole force will be ready and formed up in battle array, and in the positions indicated in the Emperor's overnight order. The Lieutenant-Generals commanding both Infantry and Cavalry Corps will despatch officers at once to report to the Chief of the General Staff the positions now occupied by their corps, and these officers will also act as bearers of further orders.

Discipline Sometimes Suspect

While the great majority of the French soldiery was passionately devoted to the Emperor and longed for the return of their past glory, the control over many units, including the Imperial Guard, by their officers off the battlefield was sometimes shaky. The soldiers doubted the loyalty and competence of many senior officers. They resented officers being promoted merely for going over to the Emperor while they received nothing for doing the same. Six officers of the 1st Cuirassiers who had been rewarded in this way were greeted with groans and shouts on parade. The 12th Dragoons petitioned the Emperor requesting, '... the dismissal of our colonel, whose ardour in the cause of your Majesty is by no means equal to our own'.

Units that scattered to find loot, food, and shelter in Belgium prior to the battle were out of the control of their officers. This was a factor in the late arrival of some formations at Waterloo and the consequent delayed start of the French assault. The quest for plunder and resultant indiscipline compelled the resignation of the army's Provost-Marshal, Général de Division Radet. On 17 June he wrote to Soult, 'Marauding and pillage are rampant in the Army now, the Guard itself sets the example. ... plunder has been going on all night in the homes of Belgians ... the men flatly defy the authority of the gendarmerie. I beg to tender my resignation ...'. Despite this Radet stayed to fight at Waterloo, where he was wounded in the knee and hip. At Genappe, in great pain, he attempted to rally the fugitives. He was swept aside by the mob.

whom were in dead ground behind the ridge. The general commanding the Engineers of the Imperial Guard, Haxo, was sent further forward to report on any entrenchments. His report was negative.

• By now it was close to 11.00 a.m. and Napoleon had returned to near Rossomme. Yet still the army was not ready, although by now the rain had long since stopped and the ground was, perhaps, marginally less soggy. Napoleon dictated his attack orders. Soult wrote them down, timing them as 11.00 a.m. exactly. They were addressed to corps commanders:

Directly the army has formed up, and soon after 1 p.m. the Emperor will give the order to Marshal Ney and the attack will be delivered on Mt. St. Jean village in order to seize the crossroads at that place. To this end the 12-pounder batteries of II and VI Corps will mass with that of I Corps. These 24 guns will bombard the troops holding Mont St Jean, and Count D'Erlon will commence the attack by first launching the left division, and, when necessary, supporting it by the other divisions of I Corps.

II Corps also will advance keeping abreast of I Corps. The company of engineers belonging to I Corps will hold themselves in readiness to barricade and fortify Mt. St. Jean directly it is taken.

• Napoleon's plan was brutally simple: a preliminary artillery bombardment followed by a massive frontal assault by Ney's two infantry corps, one on either side of the main road that was to be the axis of advance. The attack was to be led by the left-hand division of I Corps (Quiot's 1st Division). The main assault would be followed by the advance of the reserve formations (VI Corps, the cavalry and the Imperial Guard), who were to punch through to the crossroads

some 2,300 metres away, when the opportunity arose. There was no intention to manoeuvre, no outflanking and, interestingly, no mention of Hougoumont, the Anglo-Allied outpost that was to absorb so many of Reille's infantrymen.

• On Soult's original order Ney scribbled in pencil – 'Count d'Erlon will understand that the action is to commence on the left, not the right. Communicate this new arrangement to Général Reille.' It was quite clear from the 11.00 a.m. orders that Napoleon had instructed d'Erlon to start the main attack with his corps on the right of the Brussels road. 'The action is to commence on the left' was almost certainly a reference to Reille's diversionary assault on Hougoumont which was opposite the left of the French line.

• Events proved that the Emperor started to tinker with the details of his plan within minutes of the 11.00 a.m. orders being despatched. At about 11.30 a.m. Reille's guns opened up on the left while Jérôme's men advanced on Hougoumont Wood. Reille would never have opened fire an hour and a half early without fresh instructions – Ney's pencilled note. Napoleon also set about strengthening the preparatory artillery bombardment by ordering the number of guns to be increased from twenty-four to eighty – to form what became known as the 'Grand Battery'.

• An attack, originally scheduled for 6.00 a.m., was postponed to 9.00 a.m. and again to after 1.00 p.m. Even then it went off at 'half-cock'. Napoleon's brother succeeded in dragging most of Reille's corps into a pointless and bloody struggle for Hougoumont that was to last all day. So, by the time 1.00 p.m. came and the 'Grand Battery' was ready to open fire, only d'Erlon's four divisions were poised to advance on Mont St Jean. Just twenty minutes before they stepped off, the Prussians were sighted in the east!

Late Arrival of Some French Formations

Several witnesses at the battle have testified that the main reason for an early start being impossible was the late arrival of key formations, and that even by 11.00 a.m. the front line was incomplete. The son of the owner of Le Caillou stated that at 9.00 a.m. many troops were marching past the farm from Genappe. By this time it is likely that Reille's corps was the only one approaching its deployment area. Maréchal de Camp Petit stated that the Imperial Guard did not break camp until ten. Général de Division Durutte later wrote that when his division formed up on the right of the front line, artillery had been firing for some while – it was then probably around midday, possibly even later.

Sergeant Hippolyte de Mauduit makes it clear that there was considerable chaos and confusion during the night and the morning before the battle: 'During all the marches of that frightful night there was real helter-skelter. Regiments, battalions, even companies became muddled; and in complete darkness and drenching rain people were hunting vainly for their generals and officers.' There really never was much of a chance of an early start to the action.

METHOD OF COMMAND

The Emperor, even at Waterloo, was still the overall commander-in-chief of all armies within the frontiers of France, while also retaining ultimate responsibility for the civil and political affairs of the country. The size of his imperial headquarters reflected the range of his responsibilities. He commanded through his chief of staff and subordinate army or corps commanders. Napoleon used the chain of command – he delegated. At Waterloo Ney was the commander of the left wing of the Armée du Nord. It was his two infantry corps that made up the entire French front line. He had been given the task of overseeing a frontal assault on Wellington's position. Napoleon retained personal control of the reserves – Lobau's VI Corps and the Imperial Guard. The Emperor had handed Ney the initial task of smashing a hole in the enemy line, and had provided him with a massive weight of supporting artillery. The detailed control and co-ordination of this attack was left to the marshal. Napoleon, however, retained control of the battle as a whole. As will be shown below, he had not abrogated his responsibility as commander-in-chief to Ney: he continued to make important decisions affecting the outcome, though at times it was a positive decision to do nothing.

MOVEMENT ON THE BATTLEFIELD

Unlike Wellington, Napoleon spent most of his time at his forward tactical headquarters rather than riding around directly supervising what was happening. Health problems and lack of fitness may be part of the reason for this. Only rarely did he intervene in the minor tactics of the battle – such as when he personally ordered up howitzers to shell Hougoumont. He gave his orders and expected his subordinates to carry them out. His movements took place largely before the battle. A possible reconstruction of the approximate timings and journeys are summarized below:

Night 17/18 June	At Le Caillou
8.00–8.30 a.m.	Breakfast at Le Caillou. Discussed plans with Soult, Ney and others.
8.30–9.00 a.m.	Rode to the front for reconnaissance, accompanied by local guide (Decoster).
9.00–9.30 a.m.	At the front. Sent General Haxo forward to check on fortifications.
9.30–10.00 a.m.	Moved back to near Rossomme Farm.
10.00–10.45 a.m.	Sent message to Grouchy. Sent 7th Hussars under Marbot to probe the eastern flank. Dictated attack orders.
10.45–11.30 a.m.	Rode to front to review his troops.
11.30–noon	Reviewed troops as they moved into final positions.
Noon–12.30 p.m.	Moved back to Rossomme area. Ordered the assembly of the 'Grand Battery'.
1.00–1.15 p.m.	Sent another letter to Grouchy. The Prussians were seen near St Lambert/ St Robert, and Prussian prisoner brought in. Ordered VI Corps to move to eastern flank.
2.00 p.m. (estimated)	Moved forward to tactical command post on some rising ground south of La Belle Alliance, not far from Decoster's house.

BATTLEFIELD DECISIONS

Although Napoleon allowed Ney to continue in command of the many frontal assaults by both infantry and cavalry, he remained in command of the Armée du Nord throughout, taking a series of crucial decisions that influenced the outcome. The more important positive ones were:

• The battle plan was Napoleon's and he brooked no argument on its merits.
• He gave detailed instructions as to the formation, composition, location and task of the 'Grand Battery'.
• He reacted immediately to the appearance of the Prussians on his right flank by despatching part of his reserve to counter it.
• It was he who decided to employ the Young Guard first and then some of the Old Guard in the fight for Plancenoit.
• He finally launched the Middle Guard, late in the evening, in an effort to snatch victory at the last moment.

The Emperor also made several negative decisions by deciding to do nothing at a critical juncture, or by allowing events to develop without interfering when he could (or should) have done so. It is assumed these were conscious decisions on his part as commander-in-chief. They were:

• He did not stop Ney or Reille from allowing most of II Corps to be frittered away in fruitless assaults on Hougoumont. This draining away of infantry manpower continued throughout the day. The capture of the Château never featured in his initial plan which was seriously weakened by this error of judgement, initiated by his brother, Prince Jérôme, but perpetuated by Reille, Ney and Napoleon. As it so often is, doing nothing was a poor decision.
• Later, for some two hours, he watched as Ney committed the army's entire cavalry reserves to a series of poorly supported assaults on infantry squares under close range artillery fire. He did

Decoster – Napoleon's Reluctant Guide

As maps were often inaccurate, or lacked detail, it was usual for the Emperor to enlist the services of local guides. On this occasion a man named Decoster was reluctantly pressed into service. He owned a small inn on the roadside just south of La Belle Alliance. When Napoleon's headquarters moved from Le Caillou, Decoster was mounted on a horse that was attached by a long strap to the saddle-bow of a châsseur of the escort. He cut a sorry sight, repeatedly bowing and bending over his horse's neck during the battle, provoking Napoleon to remark, 'Now, my friend, do not be so restless. A musket shot may kill you just as well from behind as from the front, and will make a much worse wound.' After the Emperor had taken up his position not far from La Belle Alliance, and had his map table placed before him on a small wooden table, Decoster described how he continually paced up and down, sometimes with arms crossed, but more often with arms behind his back, thumbs hooked into his greatcoat pockets. He watched the battle constantly, every so often consulting his watch or taking a pinch of snuff. Decoster survived to claim he gave false information to the French and to write a colourful account of the day, which was in its fourth edition by 1816. Général de Division Foy confirmed Decoster's observations. He wrote, 'I saw him through my glass, walking up and down, wearing his grey greatcoat, and frequently leaning over the little table on which his map was placed.'

nothing to stop them. This decision to allow his subordinate to reinforce failure for so long is difficult to understand.

• At around 6.00 p.m. d'Erlon's men at last captured La Haie Sainte, close to the centre of Wellington's line. A gap, a weakness, appeared that needed exploitation, and Ney asked for fresh infantry to do so. Napoleon refused, claiming he had none. This was untrue, as the Middle Guard was still uncommitted. The opportunity passed. When the Middle Guard was eventually launched well over an hour later it was too little, too late. This decision of the Emperor's almost certainly cost him his last chance of victory.

THE IMPERIAL HEADQUARTERS AND THE STAFF

The staff that accompanied the Emperor for the Waterloo campaign (a comparatively small undertaking) was on a far grander scale, including a large civilian element, than that at either the Anglo-Allied or Prussian headquarters. Nevertheless, it was a bare bones affair compared to the old Grand Quartier-Général Imperial (Imperial Headquarters) that Napoleon had taken on his great campaigns across Europe and into Russia. A headquarters' staff frees the general to command. Its function is to facilitate command and decision making, to ensure the general receives timely information, that his orders are disseminated, and that administration and supply services operate smoothly. The staff is to an army as oil is to an engine – without it the machine quickly grinds expensively to a halt. There were three distinct groupings of personnel at Napoleon's headquarters on 18 June. First, the Maison Militaire or the Emperor's Military Household; second, the Etat-Major Général or Army Staff and third, the various supporting arms commanders, each with their own staff. It is impossible to be certain of the total number of personnel at the French headquarters at Waterloo, but it would not have been less than 300 and could have been as high as 600 if all the multitude of grooms and servants are included. Several hundred horses were needed to keep the officers mobile, as each had one or two spares. In simplified outline form the headquarters is set out below, with notes on the duties of the branches given in the appropriate boxes.

LA MAISON MILITAIRE
Personal staff of the Emperor
Grand Marshal of the Palace: Général de Division Comte Henri-Gatien Bertrand

Master of the Horse
Général de Division Comte Fouler

'General Officers near His Majesty' (General Officer ADCs)
Général de Division Lebrun, Duc de Plaisance
Général de Division Comte Drouot
Général de Division Comte Corbineau
Général de Division Comte Flahaut de la Billarderie
Général de Division Comte Dejean
Maréchal de Camp Baron Bernard
Maréchal de Camp Comte de la Bédoyère
Maréchal de Camp Baron Bussy
Each of the above officers would have had two or three assistant ADCs (captains or lieutenants) that the Emperor 'borrowed' if things got hectic.

Officiers d'Ordnnance (Orderly Officers/Junior ADCs)
Colonel Gourgaud
Capitaine Regnault, Capitaine Moline, Capitaine Saint-Yon, Capitaine de Resigny, Capitaine de Lannoy, Capitaine Amilhet, Capitaine Chiappe, Capitaine de Lariboisiere, Capitaine Planat, Capitaine Saint-Jacques, Capitaine Autric

War Cabinet
Secretary of State – Hughes-Bernard Maret, Duc de Bassano
Head of Secretariat – Baron Agathon Fian

Chamberlain to His Majesty
Vicomte Turenne

Surgeon to the Maison Militaire
Docteur Baron Yvan

'General Officers near His Majesty'
They were hand-picked senior officers capable of commanding a force of all arms. Highly respected throughout the army, they spoke in the Emperor's name. Theirs was not the job of taking straightforward messages or passing on orders. Rather they could be given a variety of responsible tasks on or off the battlefield. Examples would be commanding a special task force, conducting an important reconnaissance, grouping together a large number of guns for a massive bombardment, sorting out major supply problems, carrying out inspections on behalf of the Emperor or, sometimes, diplomatic missions. It was an extremely prestigious appointment, the most recent being Maréchal de Camp de la Bédoyère who had received his promotion outside Grenoble just three months earlier. Each of these generals had two or three personal ADCs called 'les petits aides-de-camp'. The best example of a senior officer, who had spent much of his service as such an aide, was Général de Division Mouton Comte de Lobau, VI Corps commander at Waterloo.

Officiers d'Ordnnance
These young officers were Napoleon's eyes and ears. Twelve in number, they carried orders, inspected units, gathered information and reported back to the Emperor. They were usually captains from different combat arms. As they had always to be in attendance on the Emperor in the field, they were required to have eight horses and sufficient 'domestics' to look after them. They received the pay of a cavalry captain, but were supposed to also have the support of their families to the tune of 6000 francs a year. Their uniforms were sky-blue and silver. At Waterloo it is likely that some of these old regulations had lapsed, but the job was much sought after as it was a stepping stone to promotion, ensuring an officer was 'noticed'. Interestingly, during World War II Field-Marshal Montgomery made use of a similar group of young ADCs who reported to him personally.

ETAT-MAJOR GÉNÉRAL (ARMY GENERAL STAFF)

The Major-General (Chief of the General Staff)
Maréchal Jean de Dieu Soult, Duc de Dalmatia

Deputy Chief of the General Staff
Général de Division Comte Bailly de Monthion

Assistant Chiefs of the General Staff
Maréchal de Camp Baron Gressot
Maréchal de Camp Baron Couture
Maréchal de Camp Lebel

Prisoners of War
Maréchal de Camp Baron Dentzel

Adjutant-Commandants (Senior Staff Officers)
Colonel Baron Michel, Colonel Baron Stoffel, Colonel Babut
Colonel d'Hincourt, Colonel Petiet

Assistant Staff Officers
Colonels: Comte Gramont, Raoul, Forbin de Janson, Hugo,
Zenowicz, Duzaire
Majors: Desaix, Tessier de Marguerittes
Chefs de Bataillon: Dalbenas, Girard, Rollin, Grondal, Laplace,
Lefebure, Gentet, Waleski, Desmarquet de Cire, Bernard, Arnaud,
Favelas, Fourchy, Hirne, Deschamps
Capitaines: Clavet Gaubert, Descrivieux, de Joly, Noaillon,
Coignet (wagonmaster), Dulnas de Saint-Leon, Baudisson,
Guettard, Favier, Ramorino
Sous-Lieutenant: Garda

Note: Majors commanded Imperial Guard battalions, held staff appointments or commanded
regimental depots. They outranked chefs de bataillon who normally commanded infantry line
battalions.

SUPPORTING ARMS AND SERVICES

Artillery
Army Artillery Commander – Général de Division Comte Ruty

Artillery Parks
Director　Général de Division Baron Neigre
Deputy Director　Colonel Triquenot

Etat-Major-General (Army General Staff)

Soult, as chief of staff, worked closely with a small group of
general officers. One was his deputy, Bailly de Monthion, who
had for years been deputy to Maréchal Berthier and so was well
versed in how an efficient headquarters should function. He
resented Soult's appointment over himself, as Soult was not a
particularly experienced staff officer. There were a number of
examples of sloppy staff work during the campaign, such as orders
not going out in triplicate, d'Erlon's marching and counter-
marching between Quatre-Bras and Ligny, and Lobau's late
arrival at Ligny. Of the other three senior assistant chiefs of staff
Gressot supervised staff procedures and maintained
correspondence with the army corps; Couture was responsible for
camps, cantonments and marches; and Lebel, in co-operation
with Colonel Bonne, controlled the topographical section.
Directly under the generals came the adjutant-commandants who
were in turn assisted by a large group of staff officers and ADCs.

Assistants　Chef d'Escadron Lechesne, Chef de Bataillon Sesilly,
Director　Colonel Renaud
Deputy Director　Chef de Bataillon Barre
Assistants　Lieutenant Marion (Security) plus twelve junior officers

Engineers
Commander Army Engineers – Général de Division Baron
Rogniat

Engineer Staff
Chief of Staff – Colonel Baudrand
Director, Engineer Park – Major Legentil
Assistants – Chef de Bataillon Lesecq, Capitaine Coffinal,
Capitaine Bellonnet, Capitaine Robert Saint-Vincent

Topographical Services
Colonel Bonne

Gendarmerie
Général de Division Baron Radet

Logistics/Administration
Intendant Général – M. Daru

When the army was on the move the Imperial Headquarters normally split into two echelons. Command was exercised by
Napoleon and Soult riding ahead with what today would be
termed a tactical headquarters – a small group of key staff officers
and ADCs. They travelled just behind the advance guard formations. It was for this reason that on 15 June the Emperor was to
be found co-ordinating the stalled attack on the Charleroi bridge
with engineers and marines of the Guard, well before the line
infantry arrived. The rear echelon of the headquarters followed
much further back.

On the battlefield the headquarters personnel around the
Emperor became more numerous. With Napoleon for the most
part static after 2.00 p.m., between 80 and 100 officers were
required in the vicinity of the Emperor and chief of staff. They
were usually dismounted and grouped within calling distance,
their horses being held a short distance further in rear. The whole

area was protected by mounted picquets from the duty squadron
of the Imperial Guard Cavalry, with another from the Gendarmes
d'Elite close to hand.

Staff were also employed at corps, division and brigade level
by all the armies at Waterloo. At each French corps headquarters
there were at least six officers, including those commanding the
artillery and engineers. For example, at I Corps headquarters
d'Erlon had the assistance of a chief of staff (Maréchal de Camp
Baron Delcambre), a deputy chief of staff (Adjutant-Commandant
or Colonel Viala), a commander of artillery (Maréchal de Camp
Baron Desales), an artillery chief of staff (Colonel Bernard), a
commander of engineers (Maréchal de Camp Baron Garbe), and a
chief of staff for the engineers (Colonel Baraillon). Each had more
junior assistants or ADCs. In addition there were medical and
supply staff. The numbers were correspondingly less with the
lower formations.

French senior commanders at Waterloo

The generals that rode into Belgium with Napoleon in 1815 were vastly experienced soldiers, most of whom had been fighting for France and the Empire for well over twenty years. In 1814, after the first abdication, a few die-hard Bonapartists had gone with Napoleon to Elba, others had retired on half-pay, while some had accepted to serve in the King's army. Those generals that rejoined Napoleon to fight at Waterloo did so voluntarily – they had a choice. Most undoubtedly felt it was their duty to serve France when she was threatened with invasion. The top commanders, including Marshals Soult, Ney and Grouchy, together with all the corps commanders, were offered their commands by the Emperor personally. The divisional commanders were selected and appointed by the Minister of War, Marshal Davout, for Napoleon's approval. All could have refused their positions. They accepted for a variety of motives and with varying enthusiasm. When Napoleon first landed in southern France some had actively opposed him, the most notable being Ney, who had vowed to bring him to Paris in an iron cage. At the other extreme were those who instantly rallied to his side, longing for a return of the glorious days of empire; men such as Lefèbvre-Desnouëttes, the Lallemand brothers and d'Erlon. Whatever their motives for joining, all the generals bar one, Bourmont, eventually did their duty on the battlefield.

This does not mean that they were a contented bunch – far from it. There was a deep feeling of mistrust, jealousy and bitterness over appointments and promotion among the general officer corps. They denounced each other as being 'lukewarm patriots', 'ardent royalists', or being 'without energy'. Those who had first rallied to the Emperor were openly critical of the appointment of men like Soult, Ney, Durutte and Bourmont. Even as they were about to cross the Sambre, a disgruntled and disloyal general was interrupted by an irate major who declared, ' It is not for you to express such feelings. Our bed is made, we must lie on it. Do not try to demoralize us.'

The corps and divisional commanders were, for the most part, surprisingly fit men. Despite wounds, arduous years in the field and the crude medical facilities of the day, most of those who died natural deaths did so at a fairly ripe old age. Their average age at Waterloo being 43.6 and their age at death 72. Marcognet at eighty-nine lived the longest of the French generals (the British General Kempt lived to be ninety). The oldest French divisional commander on the battlefield was Friant at fifty-seven, the youngest Prince Jérôme at thirty-one with Piré next at thirty-seven. The youngest general present at Waterloo was de la Bédoyère at twenty-nine (this is ignoring the Prince of Orange who was twenty-three, but received his rank for purely diplomatic reasons). Short biographical details are given below.

CHIEF OF STAFF

Soult, Maréchal Nicolas Jean de Dieu Duc de Dalmatia (1769–1851)

Napoleon's chief of staff was the same age as the Emperor, had no education, and was short, bow-legged, physically hard and inordinately ambitious. But his predominant vice was avarice. In twenty years of high command he had amassed a vast fortune by systematically plundering furniture and art treasures from virtually every country in Europe except his own. Three months before, Soult had been King Louis' Minister of War; now he was responsible for the efficient functioning in the field of the Emperor's military machine. He had been a marshal for eleven years but had, exceptionally, reached that pinnacle in 1804 without ever having served directly under Napoleon. He managed, like many of his contemporaries, to switch allegiance from Emperor to King, back to Emperor and then, after Waterloo, revert to being a royalist without too many serious qualms. If asked his loyalties, his response would surely have been France, the Army and himself.

A soldier since he was sixteen, Soult had been a corporal, sergeant and drill instructor, before rising rapidly to command a brigade in 1794 when he was only twenty-five. In 1805, as a corps commander with three divisions at the Battle of Austerlitz, Soult earned the Emperor's lasting respect by his storming of the Pratzen Heights – an action that, at the critical moment, gave Napoleon one of his finest victories. Afterwards he referred to Soult as 'the first tactician in Europe'. Soult had fought in Germany, Switzerland, Italy, Austria, Poland, Spain, Portugal, France and now Belgium (he missed Russia). He had made his name, however, as a commander rather than as a staff officer. Wellington rated him an able general.

The blame for faulty staff work in the Waterloo campaign has been laid at his door. The fact that messages no longer went out in triplicate (as in Berthier's time) caused delays and problems. But his deputy Bailly de Monthion, who was responsible for the detailed staff routine and supervision, and had considerable experience under Berthier, must shoulder most of the blame for this procedural shortcoming. Napoleon was later to say Soult 'made an excellent Major-General [chief of staff]'.

When Napoleon left for Paris after Waterloo, Soult took command and succeeded in stemming the rout and joining up with Grouchy. Initially banished, he was pardoned in 1819 and his marshal's baton restored. For ten years he lived on his wealth (much of it acquired during his years in Spain) before returning to politics and the role of elder statesman. He was Minister of War from 1830–34 and yet again in 1840. He was appointed President of the Council and, in 1847, made Maréchal-Général: a rank only previously held by Turenne, Villars and Saxe. Soult travelled to England for Queen Victoria's coronation in 1838 where he had a cordial meeting with Wellington. He was one of the four surviving marshals present when Napoleon's body was laid to rest in Les Invalides in 1840 – the others were Moncey, Oudinot and Grouchy. He died in 1851, aged eighty-two.

COMMANDER OF THE LEFT WING OF THE ARMÉE DU NORD

Ney, Maréchal Michel Duc d'Elchingen, Prince de la Moskowa (1769–1815)

Ney had five horses shot under him at Waterloo but escaped unscathed, despite 'leading his corps like a captain of grenadiers'. A tall, redheaded man with a foul temper to match and a life-long fondness for a four-letter word meaning sexual intercourse, Ney displayed all the virtues and vices that had characterized his long years of soldiering. If there is one word that perhaps summed up his tenure of high command, it was 'erratic' – frequently impetuous, sometimes lethargic, always heroic. At Quatre-Bras he had first hesitated, then attacked, then lost his temper and acted rashly, and finally, the following morning, failed to understand the overriding strategic urgency for action. At Waterloo his was the task of breaking through Wellington's line, creating the hole through which the

Emperor would pour his reserves. Until 6.00 p.m., when his men took La Haie Sainte, he had frittered away first infantry and then cavalry by reinforcing failure. He had proved unable to properly co-ordinate a combined arms assault. Then, when La Haie Sainte fell and he screamed for infantry support, Napoleon refused to release the only infantry he had left – the Middle Guard.

Ney, of German descent, had enlisted into the cavalry in 1788, and within four years was a sergeant-major. Seven years later he was a général de division, six years after that, a marshal. Perhaps his finest hour was in 1812 at Borodino when he led the assault on the Grand Redoubt to earn himself his second title. But he is probably most remembered for his brilliant command of the rearguard during the endless winter retreat from Russia. Reputedly he was the last man to leave Russian soil – unshaven in a tattered fur coat and clutching a musket. 'I'm damnably tired,' he told an inn-keeper, 'bring me some soup.' Ney's talents were best employed commanding a division or corps on the battlefield and much less well utilized when given an army in a semi-independent strategic role.

After Waterloo he was a marked man. He was given passports to Switzerland but declined to use them, thus clinching his arrest. He was charged with treason. He could have got off on a technicality – he was born a German – but refused to use this ploy. There was difficulty in assembling a military tribunal of his peers to try him. One marshal (Moncey) was jailed for three months for refusing to serve on the court. Eventually the proceedings dissolved in uproar when Ney, unwisely, demanded to be tried by the Chamber of Peers instead of his fellow officers. The Royalist Chamber condemned him by 107 votes to 47. He was shot by a firing squad on 7 December 1815 in the Luxembourg Gardens dressed in civilian clothes.

Ney's Execution

Ney was not present when his peers pronounced his condemnation, so the Secretary was charged with notifying him. After reading out the long rigmarole of his titles and the sentence the Secretary asked if the marshal wanted a priest. He replied that he would think about it, adding, 'I want no priest to teach me how to die.' He fell asleep on his bed, to be awakened at 4.00 a.m. by the arrival of his wife and children, the oldest being about eleven. Ney spoke softly to them for a long time. As they left, wife and children broke down. One of his guards then suggested he should see a priest and Ney agreed to see the Rector of Saint Sulpice, who remained with him for nearly an hour. At 8.30 a.m. Ney left for the execution ground dressed in a waistcoat, black breeches and stockings, blue frock coat and a round hat, and accompanied by the priest. The party left by carriage for the Luxembourg Gardens. There some sixty veterans had been waiting since 6.00 a.m. The carriage stopped some thirty paces from a wall. Ney embraced the priest, who remained by the coach praying fervently, and walked to within eight paces of the wall. He then took charge of the proceedings and, refusing a blindfold, he addressed the firing party: 'Soldiers, when I give the command to fire, fire straight at the heart. Wait for the order, it will be my last to you.' As he shouted, 'Fire!' he removed his hat and held it over his chest. He fell, hit by eleven of the twelve shots fired – aged forty-six.

under him at Austerlitz and was wounded twice at Borodino. Held in high regard by Napoleon, he was appointed colonel-in-chief of the Foot Grenadiers of the Imperial Guard in 1812, having never served with them previously. However, he blatantly collaborated with the Bourbons after Napoleon's first abdication in order to keep his position as commander of the newly named Foot Grenadiers of France. That he was one of the finest of the old divisional commanders is borne out by Napoleon's summoning him and re-appointing him as commander of the Old Guard Grenadiers, the most prestigious divisional command in the army, in March 1815.

He led his men forward in the final assault by the Imperial Guard at Waterloo, taking refuge, along with other senior officers, in the square of the 1st Foot Grenadiers during the rout. As he had not volunteered to serve the Emperor, he escaped the wholesale dismissals after the second restoration. This embarrassed Friant and he resigned from the Army and retired, dying peacefully aged seventy-one.

Morand, Général de Division Comte Charles Antoine Louis (1771–1835)

Commanded the Châsseurs à Pied of the Imperial Guard at Waterloo. From a middle-class background, he qualified as a lawyer in 1791 but enlisted a month later. Quickly elected captain, he rose to maréchal de camp in 1800 and général de division five years later. He saw active service in Egypt, Austria, East Prussia, Poland, Germany, Russia and Italy. He was a member of the triumvirate of generals (the others being Friant and Gudin) that earned Davout's III Corps the title 'Napoleon's X Legion'. Badly wounded by a shell splinter that smashed his jaw and disfigured his face at Borodino, he nevertheless was given the task of escorting the treasures looted from Moscow during the retreat.

Kept in reserve at Waterloo until late afternoon, Morand was involved in the intense fighting for Plancenoit and the desperate stand in the village churchyard. With only 250 men he cut his way to the Quatre-Bras road during the rout. Initially he fled to Poland. Tried and condemned to death in absentia, he was pardoned in 1820 and his rank restored. A competent tactician and divisional commander who probably deserved a corps at Waterloo. He died of a stroke aged sixty-four.

Duhesme, Général de Division Comte Philibert Guillaume (1766–1815)

Commanded the Young Guard Division at Waterloo. A thoroughly unpleasant individual who, as a military administrator in both Italy and Spain, had been guilty of corruption, wanton looting and personal participation in torture and murder. He was dismissed in 1810, the Emperor banishing him from Paris. A labourer's son, it

IMPERIAL GUARD

Drouot, Général de Division Comte Antoine (1774–1847)
Drouot commanded the Imperial Guard at Waterloo in the absence of Maréchal Mortier. For further details see box on p. 12.

Friant, Général de Division Comte Louis (1758–1829)
Commanded the Old Guard Grenadier Division at Waterloo where he was wounded. The son of a wax polisher, he enlisted at the age of twenty-three. After failing to get promoted to sergeant he left the army for five years. He re-enlisted in 1789 and within three years was a sergeant-major in the National Guard. Within months his men had elected him their commanding officer (lieutenant-colonel). By 1794, two years later, he was an acting brigade commander. Promoted général de division at forty-one, Friant saw continuous service in Austria, Prussia, Poland, Russia and France. He had four horses shot

was his natural flair for rabble rousing that had secured him a meteoric rise during the Revolution. However, he always regarded Napoleon as an upstart who had betrayed true revolutionary principles. Desperately short of competent generals, he was given command of a division in 1814 and handled it well, particularly at the Battle of La Rothière. On the battlefield he was a tenacious leader, an expert on light infantry tactics on which he wrote a training manual that was to become a standard work in military colleges.

In 1815 Duhesme waited until two days before Napoleon entered Paris before abandoning his royalist command. The Emperor, overcoming his qualms, gave him command of the Young Guard Division. He led the Young Guard with admirable dash and courage in the struggle for Plancenoit where he was severely wounded in the head. During the French rout he was carried to the Auberge du Roi d'Espagne in Genappe and abandoned. The inn became Blücher's headquarters on the night after the battle and Duhesme died there in the care of Blücher's staff on 20 June, aged forty-nine.

Lefèbvre-Desnouëttes, Général de Division Comte Charles (1773–1822)

Commanded the Imperial Guard Light Cavalry Division at Waterloo. One of the most gallant soldiers in the army who was to benefit under Napoleon's will. He joined the army as a châsseur in 1792, first serving along the Rhine. As a captain, he was one of Napoleon's ADCs for a while. He fought as a cavalry leader at Marengo, was promoted to command a brigade in 1802 and a division in 1808. He fought in Spain where he was captured by the British and taken to live, on parole, in Chelmsford where his good looks caused a stir among society ladies. Early in 1812 his wife joined him and, with her help, disguised as a Russian count he broke his parole and escaped to France. He fought at Smolensk and Borodino before being wounded at Vinkovo. He recovered sufficiently to join the Emperor on 6 December 1812 for the journey by fast sleigh back to Paris. Thereafter he fought in Germany and France in 1814, commanding the Young Guard Cavalry Division.

Immediately on hearing of Napoleon's return from Elba, Lefèbvre-Desnouëttes unsuccessfully tried to get his troops to go over to the Emperor. For a short period he was forced into hiding. In June 1815 he led the advance of Ney's left wing on Quatre-Bras, but was not committed to the battle. At Waterloo he joined the second wave of massed cavalry attacks on Wellington's centre, although he was wounded in the latter stages. After the battle he shaved off his moustache and, disguised as a commercial traveller, caught a ship to America where he settled down to a frontier life in Alabama. A court in France sentenced him to death *in absentia* in 1816 but he was pardoned after Napoleon's death. He had the misfortune to drown in a shipwreck off the coast of Ireland on his way home in 1822, aged forty-nine.

Guyot, Général de Division Comte Claude Etienne (1768–1837)

Commanded the Imperial Guard Heavy Cavalry Division at Waterloo. He enlisted at as trooper in 1791 and served with the Army of the Rhine. Within two years he was a maréchal de logis (sergeant). While serving in Germany and Bavaria he became a captain and in 1802 was able to transfer into the expanded Guard Châsseurs à Cheval.

He distinguished himself at Austerlitz, then in 1805 led his Châsseurs across Prussia and into Poland, fighting with great dash and determination at Eylau where his regiment suffered some 250 casualties, including the colonel – Guyot took command. He fought

in Spain in the race to catch General Moore in his retreat to Corunna, narrowly escaping capture when Lefèbvre-Desnouëttes was taken prisoner. Yet again he stepped into his commander's shoes. In 1811 he was promoted général de division. Lefèbvre-Desnouëttes escaped from England in time to resume his command of the Guard Châsseurs for the Russian campaign, so Guyot took command of the Emperor's personal escort. In December 1813 he was switched from light to heavy cavalry when he took charge of the élite Grenadiers à Cheval. The campaign of 1814 in France did not go well with him, as twice he was accused of allowing French guns to fall into enemy hands. On the second occasion Napoleon stripped him of his divisional command, only to relent when the full circumstances were clear. Guyot once more took over Napoleon's escort.

Guyot's Waterloo, like the rest of his cavalry companions, was largely taken up by two hours of fruitless, uphill charges against infantry squares supported by cannons. He lost two horses and was wounded twice. Guyot retired at his own request in 1816, having served in the Guard Cavalry for fourteen years – undoubted proof of his ability and leadership. He accepted recall in 1830 for three years as commandant of the 10th Military Division in Toulouse, dying in Paris in 1837.

I CORPS

Drouet, Général de Division Jean Baptiste Comte d'Erlon (1765–1844)

D'Erlon, as he is most commonly referred to, commanded I Corps at Waterloo. A staunch Bonapartist, his military reputation was ruined for posterity by the incident on 16 June 1815 when he marched his divisions to and fro between the battlefields of Quatre-Bras and Ligny without firing a shot at either. He was not, however, entirely to blame for this confusion. Prior to this episode his career can be judged as successful. Before the Revolution he had served five years as a soldier and then obtained a discharge due to ill-health – in fact he was disillusioned by his lack of promotion. He re-enlisted and rose rapidly after being elected captain by his men. He was commanding a brigade in 1799 and a division four years later. He had served with credit in Switzerland, Germany, Austria, Prussia and Poland, before being sent to Portugal and Spain in 1810. He was to remain there for the rest of the Peninsular War, mostly as a corps commander. There he had faced Wellington in major battles at Fuentes de Onoro (1811), Vitoria (1813) and then in southern France at the Nive (1813), Orthez (1814) and Toulouse (1814).

King Louis made d'Erlon commander of the Lille Military District after the Restoration. However, as early as 8 March, a week after Napoleon's landing near Cannes, d'Erlon called out the Lille garrison to march on Paris. This attempt to return to the Eagles was thwarted by the arrival of Maréchal Mortier who persuaded the troops to return to barracks. D'Erlon was locked in the citadel. His jailers released him on 21 March, the day following Napoleon's arrival in Paris.

D'Erlon's corps had the task of smashing a hole in Wellington's line at Waterloo. His divisions were almost continuously in action from 1.30 p.m. until the final rout in the late evening. His only real success was the capture of La Haie Sainte around 6.30 p.m. but this was not exploited by Ney or the Emperor. He was one of the last commanders to quit the field. As he did so, Ney shouted at him, 'If they catch us, you and I will be shot.' D'Erlon took this sound advice and fled, first to Munich, then to Bayreuth. A court martial condemned him to death for treason *in absentia* in 1816. Granted an amnesty in 1825, d'Erlon took a military post in Nantes in 1832 and was briefly a not very successful Governor of Algeria in 1834–5. He was made a Marshal of France in 1843 and died less than a year later in Paris.

Quiot du Passage, Maréchal de Camp Baron Joachim (1775–1849)

Quiot was initially commander of a brigade (54th and 55th Ligne) but when the divisional commander (Allix) did not appear he was promoted to command the 1st Infantry Division. He was not only a loyal Bonapartist but also an experienced soldier who had won promotion after years of service, which included the Russian campaign, the Battle of Leipzig and the desperate struggle to defend France in 1814.

At Waterloo Quiot had probably the most difficult task of any divisional commander. He spearheaded the assault on the enemy centre, a vital part of which entailed the taking of La Haie Sainte. It would take him five hours, the assistance of the 2nd Division and the personal example of Ney. It was a vain triumph as his success was not exploited – the reinforcements Ney demanded were not forthcoming.

Quiot was proscribed after the second Restoration but later pardoned.

Donzelot, Général de Divison Baron François (1764–1844)

Commanded the 2nd Infantry Division. Donzelot's qualifications to command an infantry division in the field were not impressive. His previous experience in command of troops in a major campaign had been sixteen years earlier, when he commanded about 1000 men in Egypt at the Battle of the Pyramids. Since then he had earned his promotion in staff posts and as a military governor of the Ionian Islands where he had spent the seven years from 1807–14, while his contemporaries were campaigning from Madrid to Moscow. Prior to that he had proved a competent chief of staff to Generals Desaix, Augereau and Massena. He was decidedly out of practice at Waterloo. His division advanced in an unsuitable formation and was badly mauled in I Corps' main frontal attack, and then routed by the British heavy cavalry counterattack. It took him until after 4.00 p.m. to rally his men. They, along with the 1st Division, managed to take La Haie Sainte in the evening, although lack of support nullified this small victory. Quickly forgiven after Waterloo, Donzelot's undoubted talents as an administrator were put to good use for eight years (1818–26) as Governor of Martinique. He died quietly in retirement, aged seventy-nine.

Marcognet, Général de Division Baron Pierre Louis (1765–1854)

A mediocre general in command of the 3rd Infantry Division. Marcognet was of noble birth and started his military career as an officer cadet – a distinct liability during the Revolution. As a young lieutenant he spent two years in America fighting in the War of Independence. He rose steadily in rank and took part in most of the momentous campaigns of the Empire, being present at the Ulm, Jena and Friedland as a brigade commander. Three years in Spain, however, did not enhance his reputation. At the battle of Tamames in 1809 against Spanish forces Marcognet's brigade was heavily repulsed. The 76th Ligne lost its Eagle. While in Paris in 1811 he was unexpectedly promoted to divisional command but was not required for Napoleon's Russian venture. Instead he got the mundane post of commander of the 14th

Military Division at Caen in Normandy. During the period 1813–14 he saw some action in Italy against the Austrians.

He readily accepted Napoleon's return, but at Waterloo, although courageous and tenacious, his division advanced in an inappropriate formation and received a hammering as part of I Corps' frontal attack, during which another regiment under his command lost its Eagle (45th Ligne). In the years that followed he played no active role and died aged eighty-nine, the greatest age reached by any of his fellow generals who fought at Waterloo.

Durutte, Général de Division Comte Pierre François Joseph (1767–1827)

A competent commander of the 4th Infantry Division. He enlisted in 1792 and was soon commissioned as a sous-lieutenant. He was conspicuously brave at the Battle of Hondschoote when the Duke of York was defeated in 1793. Durutte fought with the Army of the Rhine from 1799–1801, and in 1803 became a général de division and was posted to Dunkirk as commander of the huge camp preparing for the invasion of England. However, as an ardent revolutionary he was openly critical of the First Consul's (Napoleon's) ambitions. He was briefly imprisoned, tried and lost his command. Soon recalled, he was given the ultimate in dead-end jobs for the next four years – Governor of Elba. Not until 1809 were his services required again, this time in the Austrian and then the Russian campaigns. In 1813 he was in Germany and fought well at Leipzig. As Governor of Metz in 1814, his small garrison held down over 40,000 enemy troops before he broke out to join Napoleon. With the restoration of Louis, Durutte was sent back to Metz where he sat on the fence waiting to see if the Emperor from Elba would retrieve his throne.

In the Waterloo campaign it was his division that led the march of d'Erlon's Corps from Quatre-Bras to Ligny on 16 June. He, with three of Jacquinot's cavalry regiments, was left on the edge of the Ligny battlefield when d'Erlon turned back to rejoin Ney. Unfortunately for the French cause, he followed his corps commander's last order to be 'prudent' literally, thus achieving little on the open Prussian right flank.

He handled his division well at Waterloo, deployed on the right flank opposite Papelotte. He was forced to retire when the remainder of his corps was driven back after the initial advance but succeeded in taking Papelotte in the evening. With the Imperial Guard's final assault defeated and the Prussians threatening his right, Durutte's division gave way. In the mêlée he had his right hand lopped off by one of Vandeleur's troopers; defenceless, his head was then split open by another sword blow. He recovered slowly in Paris but was maimed and blind in the right eye. He left France and settled in Ypres, Belgium, dying peacefully in 1827 aged sixty. His family had a magnificent mausoleum built in the Ypres cemetery. The inscription reads: 'His military career started at Valmy and ended at Waterloo. Under the Republic, under the Consulate, under the Empire, under the Monarchy he served only France. R.I.P.' At the Belgian Army Museum in Brussels the bloodstained saddlecloth he used at Waterloo is on display.

Jacquinot, Général de Division Baron Charles Claude (1772–1848)

Commanded the 1st Cavalry Division. A sound professional cavalryman, he was not really an ardent Bonapartist – as shown by his hesitation before taking up a command after Napoleon's return from Elba. Educated at a military academy, he was first an infantry officer for a year before transferring to the cavalry. He was wounded in 1792 by a shell splinter and again by a sabre cut at the Battle of Hohenlinden in 1800. Jacquinot fought in Austria, Prussia, Poland, on the Danube and in Russia. He was present at Austerlitz, Eylau and Wagram, receiving promotion to colonel and command of the 11th Châsseurs à Cheval in 1806. He was a brigade commander in Russia and was given his division in 1814 for the bitter fighting in France.

He at first declined to take up a command under Napoleon in March 1815 but accepted when he saw war as inevitable. He supported Durutte's division on the fringes of the Ligny battlefield but did little other than briefly follow up some retreating Prussians. He played a prominent role in the pursuit of Wellington's army as it withdrew from Quatre-Bras on 17 June. At Waterloo Jacquinot was posted on the extreme right of the French front. His lancers played a critical part in the counterattack that routed the Union Brigade after it had charged, out of control, up to the French 'Grand Battery'. They killed Major-General Ponsonby, the brigade commander, as he struggled to retire on a blown horse. Jacquinot's division, together with that of Subervie's, were deployed to confront the Prussians as they emerged from the Bois de Paris on the right flank. They were slowly pushed back towards Plancenoit.

In the years following Waterloo Jacquinot had a successful if uneventful career, mostly in the cavalry inspectorate. His final reward came in 1844 when he was given the Grand Cross of the Legion of Honour. He retired from the army on 12 April 1848 and died twelve days later, aged seventy-six.

II CORPS

Reille, Général de Division Comte Honore Charles Michel (1775–1860)

Commanded II Corps at Waterloo. Reille enlisted as a grenadier in 1791 but gained his commission within a year and fought in the Italy campaign of 1796 as an aide to the future marshal, André Massena. He was present at Montenotte and the crossing of the Lodi. He remained in Italy until 1804, mainly as a senior staff officer. Then came a posting as second-in-command of the troops with the Toulon squadron preparing for the invasion of England. He sailed with the fleet in early 1805 and, after a voyage that took in Spain and the West Indies, was present at the naval battle off Cape Finisterre in July 1805. He was sent to Paris to report on events, thus missing the Battle of Trafalgar.

Reille fought with the Grand Armée in Austria and was present at Jena, receiving promotion to divisional command in late 1806. After a brief period in Spain, in 1808 Reille served as one of Napoleon's aides in Germany and was present at the Battle of Aspern-Essling and then led the Guard Tirailleurs at Wagram. From 1810 to the end of the Peninsular War Reille was fighting Wellington (and Spanish guerrillas) in Spain and southern France. His troops put up particularly strong resistance at Vitoria. However, his relationship with his commander, Soult, was strained to the extent that Reille abandoned his post for a brief period in 1814.

In the Waterloo campaign it was his corps that did the bulk of the fighting under Ney on 16 June, belatedly trying to take the crossroads at Quatre-Bras. His three divisions formed the left half of the French front line at Waterloo, where he allowed the bulk of his command to get sucked into the unnecessary struggle for Hougoumont which lasted on and off for the entire day.

He was created a marshal by Louis Philippe in 1847 and died thirteen years later, aged eighty-five.

Bachelu, Général de Division Baron Gilbert Desire Joseph (1777–1849)

Commanded the 5th Infantry Division. A respected, competent general but an outspoken, unrepentant republican, Bachelu was an engineer by training, having been commissioned into the engineers from the Metz Military Academy at seventeen. The first ten years of his service were as an engineer, first with the Army of the Rhine in 1795, then in Egypt, then in San Domingo, and finally as chief of staff of engineers at Camp Boulogne in 1803, by which time he had the equivalent rank to a brigade commander. In 1805, at his request, he secured a transfer to the infantry at the expense of dropping a rank, and was given command of the 11th Ligne as a colonel. He served in Dalmatia and Austria and was promoted to maréchal de camp in 1809. He distinguished himself at Wagram where his men spearheaded the attack by XI Corps that broke the Austrian line. He played an important role in the retreat from Russia. Making good use of his engineering skills, he successfully defended Danzig for a year (1813–14) against the Russians and thus earned his promotion to divisional general.

He rallied to Napoleon after he reached Paris, but divisional command was only offered to Bachelu after the death of the then commander of the 5th Division. His division bore the brunt of the attacks on the Allies' line at Quatre-Bras, ending the day with 1,500 casualties. At Waterloo his division was posted immediately left (west) of the Charleroi road. His was the only division of II Corps not to get dragged into the wasteful struggle for Hougoumont. He was severely wounded in the head by a shell splinter. After a brief period in exile Bachelu entered politics at the start of a lengthy but unsuccessful second career. In 1849 he died quietly in Paris, aged seventy-two.

Bonaparte, Général de Division Prince Jérôme (1784–1860)

Commanded the 6th Infantry Division, by far the strongest division in the army with almost 8000 men. Jérôme was Napoleon's youngest brother, an outrageously extravagant wastrel who, although not lacking in courage, was first and foremost a socialite rather than a sailor or soldier. He served as a naval officer from 1800 for two years when, disgruntled and bored, he jumped ship in Martinique and sailed for America where he stayed for another two years and married a Miss Elizabeth Patterson. The couple tried to return to France in 1805 but Jérôme was forced to abandon his pregnant wife in Lisbon, as Napoleon refused to allow them into France. The marriage was later annulled by imperial decree while the unfortunate Elizabeth gave birth to a son in London. Promoted to command the 74-gun

Prince Jérôme Bonaparte's American Descendants

After bearing Prince Jérôme's son (another Jérôme, 1805–1870) Elizabeth Patterson returned to Maryland, America. It was the start of the American branch of the Bonaparte family. In 1905 their grandson, Charles Joseph Bonaparte (1851–1921), became the United States Naval Secretary in President Theodore Roosevelt's administration. Another prominent member was Charles Francis Bonaparte who founded the FBI. The male line endured until the death of Jérôme Napoleon Charles Bonaparte in 1945.

Veteran, the squadron to which his ship belonged spent fifteen months zigzagging across the Atlantic hunting merchantmen. In 1806 Jérôme had seen enough of the sea and, abandoning his squadron, sailed for France. En route he was fortunate to capture eleven English merchantmen, thus arriving home a hero. He was promoted rear-admiral.

Jérôme then switched from seafaring to soldiering, commanding (with the aid of experienced seconds-in-command) a Bavarian division and then a corps in the Jena-Auerstadt campaign of 1806. The year 1807 was a good one for the twenty-three-year-old – he was promoted général de division, proclaimed King of Westphalia and married to a German princess. However, his wildly extravagant court impoverished his kingdom and brought a string of rebukes from Napoleon. In 1812 he was given command of the entire right wing during the Russian campaign. Inevitably, his bungling incurred his brother's wrath, to which he responded by abandoning the army and returning to his kingdom, which was overrun by the Allies in 1813. He remained unemployed until Napoleon's return from Elba.

Jérôme, who was given Général de Division Comte Guilleminot as his deputy (an infantry tactics expert), managed to lose 1000 men at Quatre-Bras and spend the entire day at Waterloo (ignoring Guilleminot's advice) in an endless series of bloody attempts to take Hougoumont. Afterwards he spent thirty-two years of dissolute wandering around Europe, only returning to France in 1847. During the Second Empire (1852–70) his nephew, Napoleon III, made him Governor of Les Invalides (which included an annual stipend of 45,000 francs) and a Marshal of France! He died of a stroke while gambling at cards, aged seventy-six.

Foy, Général de Division Comte Maximilien Sebastien (1775–1825)

Commanded the 9th Infantry Division. A competent commander and staff officer whose reputation, unlike many of his peers, remained high despite some six years campaigning in Spain and Portugal. Commissioned at seventeen as an artillery officer, Foy was summoned before a Revolutionary Tribunal in 1794 on trumped up charges of selling army rations. He was stripped of his rank and sentenced to prison but released soon afterwards when Robespierre's government fell. He served with the artillery on the Rhine, and with the armies of Germany and Italy from 1800–01. In 1803 he organized coastal defences and mobile batteries to protect the Calais and Boulogne areas. The next year he moved to become corps artillery chief of staff to Marmont, and thence as the artillery commander in Dalmatia. In 1807 Foy was transferred to Lisbon as the Army of Portugal's Director of Fortifications. He was wounded at the Battle of Vimeiro – his first brush with Wellington – in 1808, the year he was promoted to maréchal de camp. For the next six years he remained in Spain except for a brief trip to Paris in 1810 with Massena's report on the situation in the Peninsular. Napoleon was so impressed with his comments that he promoted him on the spot to général de division. In the final battle at Orthez in early 1814 he was captured after being hit in the shoulder by a shell splinter. He was deeply moved when Wellington took the time to visit him, shake his hand and discuss the war.

Foy declared for Napoleon only after he had reached Paris. His division lost some 800 men in the fruitless struggle for the crossroads at Quatre-Bras. At Waterloo he was quickly drawn into the fight for Hougoumont and, while encouraging his men in the

orchard east of the Château, he was hit yet again in the shoulder and carried from the field. Foy was elected to the Chamber of Deputies in 1819 and wrote a celebrated account of the Peninsular War. He died of a heart attack in 1825, aged fifty. Over 100,000 people joined his funeral procession, while a public appeal for his penniless young family raised a million francs in a few weeks. His tomb in the Père Lachaise cemetery in Paris (Victor Hugo's 'City of Sepulchres'), where many of his fellow generals lie, is 30-feet high and includes his statue.

Piré, Général de Division Comte Hippolyte Marie Guillaume (1778–1850)

A fine cavalry leader and able tactician, Piré commanded the 2nd Cavalry Division at Waterloo. There were not many senior officers present that day who had seen more action than the thirty-seven-year-old Piré. Of noble birth, at fourteen he had joined his father, a colonel in the old *émigré* 'Army of the Princes', as an aide. He first saw action fighting the revolutionary forces with the *émigré* Rohan Regiment that fought alongside the English under the Duke of Cumberland in 1794. The following year he landed at Quiberon Bay as part of the force supporting the Royalist insurrection in the Vendée. He was shot in the chest (while still only seventeen) but evacuated before the rebellion was crushed. Piré was on the losing side but his fortunes changed in 1800 when Napoleon offered an amnesty to all *émigrés*.

It was not until 1805 that Capitaine Piré secured a worthwhile posting on Berthier's staff with the Grande Armée. From then on he was almost continuously in the field. He was present at the Ulm, Austerlitz, Jena-Auerstadt, Eylau, Aspern-Essling, Wagram, Friedland, Borodino (where he was wounded), Dresden (after which he was promoted général de division) and Leipzig. In 1814 his division was switched from corps to corps, as the fighting to defend, first France and then Paris, became increasingly desperate. As if all this was not enough, as a colonel Piré had managed to squeeze in a few months in Spain as an aide to Berthier during Napoleon's invasion of that country in late 1808.

Piré handled his division brilliantly at Quatre-Bras, where one of his regiments broke through to the Namur road and virtually destroyed a Brunswick battalion that had not formed square. At Waterloo he was deployed on the extreme left of the line tasked with guarding the exposed flank and supporting the assault on Hougoumont. He performed these duties admirably, making good use of his horse gunners as well as his mounted regiments. As an *émigré* who had joined Napoleon, Piré was forced to flee to Russia after Waterloo but was allowed to return in 1819. After the overthrow of Charles X, he held several divisional posts before retiring in 1848. He died in Paris two years later, aged seventy-two.

VI CORPS

Mouton, Général de Division Georges, Comte de Lobau (1770–1838)

Mouton, usually referred to as Lobau in most histories, commanded VI Corps at Waterloo. As one of his baker father's fourteen children there was little prospect for him in the family business, so he began work as an iron merchant in 1790. Soon bored, he welcomed the opportunity to enlist on the outbreak of war two years later. His tough, commanding personality quickly won him promotion to lieutenant. From 1795–1800 he served in Italy, where his forceful leadership ensured a continued rapid rise to maréchal de camp. He particularly distinguished himself at the Siege of Genoa, falling at the head of his brigade with a musket ball in the chest while trying to recapture Fort Quezzi.

In 1805 he was persuaded, reluctantly, to become, 'A General Officer near His Majesty', in other words, one of the Emperor's senior military aides. It was the making of him. He was at Marengo, Jena-Auerstadt, Eylau and Friedland, where he was again badly wounded. Awards and promotion to général de division followed. It was in the Austrian campaign of 1809, however, that he achieved his greatest success as an imperial aide. At Landshut he was given the task of taking a key bridge over the Isar River that had been set ablaze and was furiously defended. Sword in hand, Mouton put himself in front of the grenadiers of the 17th Ligne, bellowed the command, 'No firing – march!' and strode across. It was after this action that Napoleon coined the phrase, '*Mon Mouton est un lion*' ('My sheep is a lion'). A month later at Aspern-Essling Napoleon selected him for another critical mission. At the head of two battalions of tirailleurs of the Young Guard, he was ordered to retake the village of Essling and thus save another division that was in danger of being cut off. Mouton swept into the village, counterattacked when his force was later ordered to withdraw and saved the day. His reward was the title Comte de Lobau, the name of the island on the Danube from which the battle was launched. Lobau was an imperial aide in Russia and chief of staff of the Imperial Guard and a corps commander in Germany in 1813.

Untypically, his corps was too late arriving at Ligny to be of real use. At Waterloo the criticism that he failed to deploy his men far enough east, thus forcing the Prussians to fight for the Bois de Paris, is discussed in Section 10 'Myths and Controversies'. The Prussians took long enough to reach the battlefield without resistance; with it they might never have arrived at all. His fighting withdrawal towards Plancenoit was heroic, and kept open the jaws of the Allied pincers long enough to prevent a real catastrophe. After the restoration of the monarchy he became an elected member of the Chamber of Deputies, commander of the Paris National Guard and, finally, Marshal of France in 1831. Seven years later the old chest wound received at Genoa (thirty-eight years before) opened, and he died the same day, aged sixty-eight.

Simmer, Général de Division Baron François Martin Valenti (1776–1847)

Commanded the 19th Infantry Division. Simmer was a steady, reliable, professional soldier whose courage was beyond doubt (he was wounded nine times), but whose career suffered by spending too long as a staff officer – he only secured promotion to divisional commander after declaring for Napoleon on his return from Elba.

Simmer enlisted in 1791 into the infantry at the age of sixteen, but quickly transferred to the 7th Cavalry in which he was promoted sous-lieutenant. From 1805 onwards he was primarily a staff officer with only a few brief periods of command. Nevertheless, he managed to see continuous active service for the next nine years, being present at almost all of the important battles (he missed Borodino because of a wound). Had he been awarded campaign medals throughout his career they would have made an impressive sight: Belgium/Holland 1793, Germany 1796, Germany 1800, Austria 1805, Prussia 1806, Poland 1807, Spain/Portugal 1808–09, Austria 1809, Spain/Portugal 1812, Russia, 1812, Germany 1813 and France 1814. Not many officers could better that record.

His division was formed from the Paris garrison and, as part of VI Corps, arrived late at Ligny – too late to see action. At Waterloo he was initially held in reserve behind La Belle Alliance. Around 1.30 p.m. his division, along with the 20th, marched to the extreme eastern flank and deployed in front of the Bois de Paris to await the Prussians. From about 4.30 he was in action fighting a slow but skilful withdrawal westwards towards Plancenoit against Bülow's corps. He was fighting continuously until the end of the battle.

For the rest of his life he was more a politician than a soldier, being elected to the Chamber of Deputies several times. His military service ended with retirement in 1841. He died quietly six years later, aged seventy-one.

Jeanin, Général de Division Baron Jean Baptiste (1769–1830)

Commanded the 20th Infantry Division. He enlisted in 1791 in the 10th Jura Volunteers and rose quickly through the ranks to lieutenant in 1792. He saw service in the first Italian campaign in 1796 and later in Egypt, taking part in the capture of Alexandria, the Battle of the Pyramids and the Siege of Acre, where his jaw was smashed by a shell splinter leaving him disfigured for life. In 1802 he joined the Foot Châsseurs of the Consular Guard and after two years was promoted chef de bataillon. In 1805 he accepted the colonelcy of the 12th Légère but his regiment missed the main battles of the Prussian campaign and he was wounded in the leg at Heilsberg in 1807. Three years in Spain saw his promotion to brigade commander and appointment as commander of the Astorga Province. This proved a poisoned chalice as he had insufficient men to hold down the region against the numerous guerrillas and the Spanish Army of Galicia. He was compelled to evacuate the city. Although it was retaken, a disillusioned Jeanin requested a recall. For two years he was on half-pay, his career in tatters. He was not even recalled for the great Russian adventure of 1812. He did, however, manage to get some further active service in Illyria and Italy during 1813–14. When Napoleon abdicated in 1814 Jeanin had missed virtually all the great events of the past ten years.

As luck would have it, when Napoleon marched on Grenoble in March 1815, the deputy commander of the 7th Military Division based at that town was Jeanin. When he saw his troops' enthusiasm for the returning Emperor he too offered him his sword. His reward was a divisional command. Like the rest of VI Corps he did not play any part in the victory at Ligny. At Waterloo, however, he handled his division with skill and tenacity during the slow withdrawal in the face of the ever-strengthening Prussian advance on Plancenoit. Forced to yield the village, he rallied his men and, with the support of the Young Guard, Plancenoit was recaptured.

Recalled in 1820, he never again held an active command, retiring five years later on an annual pension of 6000 francs. He died in 1830, aged sixty-one, probably regretting that in all those eventful years in Europe he had never really been in the right place at the right time.

Domon, Général de Division Baron Jean Simon (1774–1830)

Commanded the 3rd Cavalry Division. Domon was elected sous-lieutenant on the day he enlisted into the infantry in 1791. For three years from 1792 he was in and out of action serving with the Army of the North in Holland and Belgium. He fought at Courtrai, the Siege of Lille, Jemappes, Tourcoing, and the Siege of Nijmegen. He was wounded at the assault on Nechin. Transferred to Germany, he marched with the Army of the Sambre and Meuse, receiving a commendation for bravery at the crossing of the Rhine. After a year (1798) with the Army of England he was posted to the Army of the Danube where, at Liptingen, he was wounded in the leg.

Domon then switched to the cavalry and was confirmed as chef d'escadron. He served with the Grand Armée against Austria and Prussia, was wounded in the neck at Elchingen and fought at Jena, Eylau and Friedland. In 1809 he commanded the 7th Hussars at Eckmuhl and Wagram. In 1812 Domon served in Murat's I Cavalry Corps, taking over from his brigade commander, Piré, when he was wounded at Borodino. He then transferred to the Neapolitan Army with the rank of lieutenant-general, and was with Murat during the retreat from Moscow before returning with him to Naples. He raised a brigade of Neapolitan cavalry, taking it to Germany in 1813, but was wounded in a skirmish and returned to Naples. In 1814 he resigned from the Neapolitan Army on the defection of Naples to the Allies and returned to France but was not employed again.

In the Waterloo campaign it was Domon's cavalry that led the advance into Belgium and tried unsuccessfully to rush the bridge at Charleroi on 15 June. At Ligny his division routed two Prussian cavalry brigades as they tried to cover Blücher's retreat. At Waterloo Domon was attached to Lobau's VI Corps, initially held in reserve. Moved to the eastern flank in early afternoon Domon, with Subervie's division, fought a skilful delaying action against the Prussians as they pressed towards Plancenoit. He was wounded for the fifth time in the fighting near the village.

Although initially exiled from Paris, the Bourbons recalled him as an Inspector-General of Cavalry in 1820. He commanded a dragoon division when the French intervened in Spain to restore Ferdinand VII to his throne, fighting successfully at Compillo and El Castillo in July 1823. He continued his various inspectorate duties until he died in Paris in 1830, aged fifty-six.

Subervie, Général de Division Baron Jacques Gervais (1776–1856)

Commanded the 5th Cavalry Division. Subervie was elected lieutenant in the Gers Volunteers in 1792 and served in the Army of the Pyrenees until the following year. In 1795, as an aide to the future Maréchal Lannes, he took part in the capture of Malta. He was with Lannes at the Ulm and Austerlitz, but then took command of the 10th Châsseurs à Cheval in late 1805. He led his regiment at Jena, was reprimanded for his part in the confusion before Eylau, but redeemed himself at Friedland. The years 1808–12 were spent in Spain, mainly operating against Spanish armies. His worst moment came in 1809 when the Spanish General Cuesta set an ambush for the 10th Châsseurs as they pursued the Spanish over the Santa Cruz pass in the Sierra Guadaloupe. Subervie, pushing ahead of the rest of the division, charged a small body of Spanish cavalry in a village called Miajades. He was suddenly surrounded by infantry on either side and lost 150 men before he could cut his way out. Subervie had his revenge at the Battle of Medellin where the Spanish lost some 10,000 men, many of them put to the sword by the 10th Châsseurs. He fought at Ocana in 1809 and as a brigade commander at Sarguntum in 1811.

Subervie was badly wounded in the thigh at Borodino and had to be evacuated, thus fortunately missing the dreadful winter retreat. It took almost a year for the wound to heal. He returned to duty in August 1813 and was present at the Battle of Leipzig. During the campaign in France he served in Piré's division. Wounded by three lance thrusts during the defence of Paris, one of Napoleon's last acts before his first abdication was to promote Subervie to général de division.

Subervie's division was initially part of Pajol's I Cavalry Corps during the Waterloo campaign. At Ligny he was only engaged in artillery duels and cavalry feints against the Prussian right, but the next day was to the fore in the pursuit of Wellington through the drenching rain to Mont St Jean. At Genappe he tried unsuccessfully to charge a battery of horse artillery in a thunderstorm. At Waterloo he was sent with Domon's division to delay the Prussians as they debouched from the Bois de Paris. As the Prussian cavalry under Prince William advanced, Subervie charged and scattered them. It was an excellent start to the skilful withdrawal towards Plancenoit.

Subervie's career after Waterloo was long and illustrious. He served many times in the Chamber of Deputies and for years in the military inspectorate. He was made Grand Chancellor of the Legion of Honour, received the Grand Cross of the Legion of Honour and was, with Flahaut, the only divisional general to serve in the First and Second Empires. He died in 1856, aged eighty.

Kellerman, Général de Division Comte François Etienne (1770–1835)

The son of Maréchal Kellerman, he commanded the III Reserve Cavalry Corps. A brilliant linguist but of fragile physique, the young Kellerman was initially destined for a diplomatic rather than a military career. Although his father got him a commission as acting sous-lieutenant in his own regiment, the Colonel General Hussars, he was posted to the French Embassy staff in Philadelphia. Diplomatic duties did not stop further military promotion. Due to his father's patronage he rose steadily in rank. By October 1792 he was an acting lieutenant-colonel in the Kellerman Legion. He was recalled to France in 1792 and joined his father who was commander of the Army of the Alps. The older Kellerman, however, fell foul of the Revolutionaries for showing lack of zeal after taking Lyons and was imprisoned in Paris. Young Kellerman was later arrested and gaoled in Metz.

After his release he served for a year as a trooper of châsseurs. They were difficult days for the former officer. Small of stature, with frizzy hair and pallid skin, the young Kellerman was nicknamed the 'ugliest man in the army'. This unpleasant situation did not last long, as when his father was recalled to command the army François Etienne was quickly able to don a colonel's uniform in which to confront his former tormentors.

He served in the Army of Italy and fought at Arcola, Rivoli, and at the crossing of the Tagliamento where he was wounded. Promoted to brigade command in 1797 he led a celebrated charge at Marengo in 1800 but when he was not immediately promoted incurred Napoleon's displeasure by boasting that he had saved the day. Surprisingly, he got his promotion some three weeks later. Commands in Italy and Germany led to service in the Ulm and Austerlitz campaigns in 1805. He was in Portugal in 1808 and in action at Vimiero against Wellington where he was commanding Junot's reserve. Long service in Spain followed, including the pursuit of Moore to Corunna and inflicting some 4000 Spanish casualties in a wild cavalry action at Alba des Tormes in 1809. The absence of Bessieres in 1810 put Kellerman in acting command of an army in Castile. The power went to his head and he spent much of his energies plundering. When confronted with these excesses years later, he replied, 'I did not cross the Pyrenees merely for my health.' At the time he avoided dismissal by requesting sick leave on Bessieres' return.

Although recalled to serve in Russia, his poor health prevented it (he suffered from depression and bouts of neuralgia) and he retired at his own request in early 1813. The retirement was short as he rejoined the army in April to command the cavalry under Ney in Germany, fighting at Lutzen, Bautzen, Dresden and, although ill again, at the great cavalry action at Wachau. He recovered sufficiently to take part in the campaign defending France in 1814. As soon as he heard of Napoleon's abdication he declared for the King and was able to sufficiently ingratiate himself with the Bourbons to secure a post on the Council of War for the Royal Guard.

His great success in the Waterloo campaign occurred at Quatre-Bras when with only a brigade available (Ney insisted he act with what troops were immediately to hand) he led a charge up to the crossroads. His cuirassiers captured the Colours of the 69th Foot and chased the 33rd Foot (Wellington's old regiment) into the Bois de Bossu. Kellerman careered on up to the crossroads only to be beaten back by point blank gunfire from a KGL battery. His horse was killed as the disorganized rout began and Kellerman only escaped by hanging on to the bits of two trooper's horses. At Waterloo his was the last cavalry reserve thrown into the reckless and futile mounted attacks during the afternoon.

Various administrative posts came his way in the years following, before he died of a stroke in Paris in 1835, aged sixty-five.

L'Héritier, Général de Division Baron Samuel François (1772–1829)

Commanded the 11th Cavalry (Heavy) Division. Another baker's son who, in 1792, started his military career in the ranks – as a grenadier and corporal in the Indre-Loire Regiment. After commissioning he served on the staff, assisting in the topographical section of the Army of the Rhine. As a captain he was shot in the thigh at Marengo in 1800. On recovery he was attached to the cavalry and served in Switzerland and Northern Italy where he gained another promotion. He fought well at Austerlitz and in 1806 was given command of the 10th Cuirassiers as a colonel. He led his regiment in Murat's great charge at Jena and was wounded by a sabre cut to his hand at Eylau. In the Danube campaign of 1809 L'Héritier led his cuirassiers at Eckmuhl and Aspern-Essling where he was severely wounded in the shoulder. Within two months he was hit again, this time in the head by a shell splinter, but his leadership gained him promotion to brigade command. A long leave and administrative posts occupied L'Héritier for the next two years.

It was not until 1812 that he was recalled for active duty in the Russian campaign to command a brigade of cuirassiers. Much of his time was spent in keeping open the endless supply lines for the Army or in flank protection, although he was involved in some heavy fighting around the city of Polotsk. By the end of the infamous retreat his brigade had virtually ceased to exist. In early 1813 he got his promotion to général de division and the command of an ad hoc heavy cavalry division for the campaign in Germany, where he saw action at Leipzig as an acting corps com-

mander after Pajol was wounded. In 1814 during the defence of France, while in command of the 4th Dragoon Division, he was severely admonished for failing to charge the exposed flank of a Bavarian division around Valjouan.

After Napoleon's first abdication L'Héritier was made Commander of the Legion of Honour and took up the appointment of Inspector-General of Cavalry for the 16th Military Division at Lille. There he sat out the events of March 1815 until after Napoleon arrived in Paris. At the request of Kellerman he was given command of the 11th Cavalry Division, one of the finest heavy cavalry formations in the Army, consisting of a brigade each of dragoons and cuirassiers. On the approach march to Quatre-Bras his division became strung out and arrived too late to support the corps commander in his furious charge on the crossroads. At Waterloo it was not until around 5.00 p.m. that L'Héritier's division, along with 12th Cavalry Division, was flung forward to reinforce failure as part of the last attempt to break Wellington's line with cavalry alone. By evening, wounded for the fifth time by a musket ball in the shoulder, his magnificent division in tatters, L'Héritier could do nothing but watch the Imperial Guard's recoil and the rout begin.

Placed on half pay, L'Héritier was not recalled until December 1818. For the next ten years his employment in the military inspectorate was intermittent until he died in 1829 at the comparatively young age of fifty-one.

Roussel D'Hurbal, Général de Division Vicomte Nicolas François (1763–1849)

Commanded the 12th (Heavy) Cavalry Division. Roussel had an unusual career prior to Waterloo. Only Friant at fifty-seven was older among the generals present that morning. Of noble birth, at fifty-two Roussel had already been a soldier for thirty-four years, and for fifteen of them he had been actively fighting the French, although he had been born in France (at Neuf Château in the Vosges). It was his family's German origins that led to his entering the Austrian service as an officer cadet in 1782. He was an accomplished horseman and although originally an infantryman, quickly transferred to the cavalry. From 1799–1801 he served in Germany against the French. Despite the war, promotion was slow and not until 1804 did he become a lieutenant-colonel. The following year he was present at the capture of Munich and narrowly escaped the great French encircling manoeuvre at Ulm. Promoted colonel and given command of a cuirassier regiment, he fought well at Aspern-Essling in 1809 despite a wound to his hand. Within four months he was a major-general. At Wagram he was again noted for fine leadership in trying to halt the French advance.

In accordance with the peace treaty between France and Austria, the Austrian Army was drastically reduced in size and Roussel found himself out of a command. As an admirer of Napoleon, as a professional soldier and from a wish to return to the country of his birth, he resigned from the Austrian Army. In July 1811 the French made him a maréchal de camp and gave him, as a fluent German speaker, command of the 9th and then the 10th Polish Lancers at Hamburg. For the Russian campaign he commanded the 5th Light Cavalry Brigade composed of Polish Uhlans and Prussian Hussars. Roussel did particularly well at Smolensk, routing a Russian battery that was causing much damage. At Borodino he took part in the great cavalry clash for the Bagration Fleches but was shot in the leg. In December 1812 he was promoted général de division. The year 1813 was not a good one for Roussel, as his division of light cavalry under Maréchal Macdonald was among the French swamped by Prussian cavalry at the Katzbach. A sabre blow to the head ended his participation in the campaign. In 1814 he commanded the 6th Heavy Cavalry Division with mixed success. At Craonne he successfully charged the Russians but at Fère Champenoise he failed to cover Marmont's retirement, which resulted in a division being destroyed.

The Bourbons made him Inspector-General of Cavalry for the 6th and 19th Military Divisions. On 11 March he marched his troops out of Bésancon to oppose Napoleon. When he saw the mood of his men he quietly slipped away to await events at home. His command at Waterloo was a magnificent one – nearly 1,800 carabiniers and cuirassiers – and it caused some ill feeling in view of his less than enthusiastic welcome to the Emperor and performance the previous year. Roussel missed Quatre-Bras as he arrived too late to participate. At Waterloo he joined the second wave of massed cavalry assaults on the Allies' line. Having watched the destruction of so many superb regiments, he attempted on orders from Kellerman to hold back his carabiniers in a dip, but unfortunately Ney detected this hesitation and ordered them forward.

Within a year of Waterloo Roussel was recalled by the Bourbons and began a long and distinguished third career that included the award of the Order of Saint Louis, the Spanish Grand Cross of Saint Ferdinand and the Governorship of Corsica. He retired in 1832 but, old and doddering, was summoned to become a Grand Officer of the Legion of Honour in 1846. He died in Paris three years later, aged eighty-six.

Milhaud, Général de Division Comte Edouard Jean Baptiste (1766–1833)

Commanded the IV Reserve Cavalry Corps. A rabid revolutionary and political soldier, Milhaud combined politics and the army to ensure his own advancement, but for all that he was a courageous, resourceful cavalry commander and convincing orator. The son of a farmer, he secured an appointment as a junior officer in a colonial regiment at the start of the Revolution. In 1792 he began his political career by being elected as a deputy in the National Convention, serving on various missions as an extreme republican, ruthlessly weeding out officers who did not prosecute the war with sufficient vigour. In October 1792 he had supported every move to have King Louis XVI executed, to the extent of wanting to expel all deputies from the Convention who had opposed the King's death. His role as a regicide would not be forgotten.

Temporarily tiring of politics, Milhaud resumed a military career, serving in Italy in 1796. Three years later he did himself a good turn by playing a leading role in the success of Napoleon's *coup d'état* in Paris when he took over the Chamber of Deputies by force. Within weeks Milhaud was a brigade commander. He commanded light cavalry formations in Italy, at Austerlitz and later at Eylau as a général de division. Transferred to Spain in 1808, he fought at Talavera and at Ocana. The latter battle was perhaps the most sensational of the Peninsular War. A Spanish Army lost some 27,000 men, including 14,000 prisoners, after being attacked frontally and then from the flank and rear by a massed cavalry onslaught. Milhaud's command was in the thick of it. He was on the staff for the Russian campaign, commanded a cavalry corps in Germany the following year, and played a promi-

nent role in the battles around Leipzig in 1813. He was continuously in action in the defence of France in 1813–14, being present at the last battle of the campaign at Saint Dizier.

He had the gall to accept service as a Cavalry Inspector-General under the Bourbons, until the outcry at appointing a regicide forced his retirement. He quickly rallied to Napoleon on his return from Elba. His command at Waterloo presented a truly awesome sight when paraded en masse. His corps consisted entirely of cuirassiers: eight regiments, twenty-four squadrons, over 3000 men. At Ligny his command performed well in exploiting the breach in the Prussian centre made by the Imperial Guard at the end of the day. At Waterloo, however, through no fault of Milhaud's (he received the order personally from Ney), his magnificent command smashed itself to pieces in endless assaults on infantry in square supported by cannons.

Yet again, after Waterloo Milhaud managed to get appointed a cavalry inspector-general, but yet again his past forced his retirement within a month. He narrowly escaped exile and died in 1833, aged sixty-seven.

Watier, Général de Division Comte Pierre (1770–1846)

Commanded the 13th (Cuirassier) Division. A competent, reliable divisional general, who like many others owed his loyalty primarily to France and the army rather than an individual, be he emperor or king. Watier was always a cavalryman since he first joined an independent squadron as a sous-lieutenant in 1792. He saw intermittent active service in Belgium and Holland until 1799, by which time he had risen steadily to command the 4th Dragoons. He served in Germany in the campaign of 1800 and with the Grande Armée in Austria in 1805. After the capitulation of the enemy at Ulm he had the misfortune to be captured while trying to cross the Danube in a small boat. This was followed by the good fortune of being exchanged after Austerlitz and promoted to brigade commander. He fought in Prussia and Poland in 1806–07. He was present but not involved at Eylau. His brigade was routed (along with the rest of the division) at Heilsberg during a badly judged charge ordered by Murat. His involvement at Friedland was limited. Watier was next in Spain for four years. Opposed to Wellington, at Fuentes de Onoro in 1811 his horsemen were part of the great cavalry turning movement round Wellington's southern flank that almost secured a French victory. He was promoted général de division in the same year.

Watier was recalled to take command of the 2nd Cuirassier Division for the invasion of Russia. It was a particularly fine formation of over 2,500 men but by the time of Borodino it had lost 50 per cent without being in any major engagement. At that battle his division charged the Great Redoubt, in support of the infantry assault, and were then caught up in a murderous cavalry mêlée behind the redoubt. During the retreat Watier saw what was left of his magnificent division disintegrate. By the time he crossed the Niemen into Poland he commanded less than a squadron – not a single man was mounted. He was in Germany in 1813–14 and present at the taking of Hamburg, remaining there during the subsequent siege until it surrendered in May 1814.

Watier was unemployed after the restoration and had no compunction about rejoining Napoleon in March 1815. He was given the 13th (Cuirassier) Division but it was well under strength at less than 1,400 sabres – due to a scarcity of horses rather than troopers. His division was involved in the pursuit of the Prussians at Ligny and in the massed cavalry assaults on Wellington's line at Waterloo. After four attempts at the impossible his decimated regiments gave up. After the Bourbon's return Watier secured a number of inspectorate posts in the army and gendarmerie. He became a Grand Officer of the Legion of Honour, finally retiring in 1839. He died in Paris seven years later, aged seventy-six.

Delort, Général de Division Baron Jacques Antoine Adrien (1773–1846)

Commanded the 14th (Cuirassier) Division. Delort was another competent cavalry commander whose first allegiance was to the army. He had a good eye for terrain and could pick the moment for a charge with perfect timing. If he had not spent so many years sidelined in Italy and Spain his promotion would surely have been sooner. Initially an infantryman (he enlisted in 1791), he transferred to the cavalry in 1797 after ill health had forced him into temporary retirement. From 1797–1803 he was in Italy, where fine leadership in the field won him promotion to chef d'escadron. It was followed by tedious garrison duties, another promotion and a transfer to the 9th Dragoons as second-in-command. In the Austerlitz campaign he took over the regiment when its commander was killed, and distinguished himself during Murat's great charge at the battle during which Cossacks wounded him twice with lance thrusts.

For the next four years he was in Italy and Spain. It was in Spain that he made his reputation as a resourceful and able tactician. His first opportunity came at a place called Vich in Catalonia. There, in 1810, a superbly timed charge killed or wounded 800 Spaniards and captured another 1000. The following year, in the Army of Aragon, Delort again overwhelmed 700 Spanish cavalrymen but was wounded sufficiently badly to necessitate a period of recuperation in France. He returned in June 1811 and secured a long overdue brigade command. His greatest triumph came in July at Castalla, near Alicante, when, with two infantry battalions and a cavalry squadron (1,200 men), he smashed a Spanish force of 11,000, inflicting losses of over 3000. In April 1813 Delort routed two Spanish infantry regiments and three brigades at Carcagente in June. He was recalled to France at the end of the year and played an important part in Napoleon's last campaign, winning promotion to général de division.

Delort was not recalled to duty after the restoration until Napoleon was actually marching on Paris, when he was then ordered to join Ney in his march south to halt the Emperor. When Ney defected at Auxerre Delort quietly slipped away and did not reappear until the King had fled to Belgium. Napoleon agreed to his taking command of the 14th (Cuirassier) Division. At Ligny his division was not engaged until the evening, when it advanced in support of the Imperial Guard and routed several regiments of Prussian cavalry led by Blücher in person. Blücher was unhorsed but Delort's men failed to notice him and he lived to fight at Waterloo. At that battle Delort's 2nd Brigade and Jacquinot's lancers chased Ponsonby's heavy cavalry back across the valley after they overextended themselves. In the afternoon Ney, misreading some movement in the Allies' line as the start of a withdrawal, ordered Delort to charge. Delort objected. Ney turned to Milhaud and ordered his entire corps forward. It was the start of the destruction of the finest cavalry force in Europe.

Delort had many appointments in the years after Waterloo, until he finally retired in 1841. Five years later he died aged seventy-three.

The Anglo-Allied Commander-in-Chief
FIELD-MARSHAL THE DUKE OF WELLINGTON

APPEARANCE AND HEALTH

Wellington's experience as a general had been gained in India and the Iberian Peninsula, the former prompting Napoleon to give him the derogatory title of the 'Sepoy General'. Wellington had fought some twenty-four battles and sieges prior to Waterloo, perhaps only half the number of his adversary but they had all, bar one (the Siege of Burgos), been victories, the great majority against superior numbers (particularly in India). In 1812 both had faced the ultimate test of generalship – the ability to command in retreat. Wellington had been compelled to pull back from Burgos, only about 120 miles from the French border, all the way to Portugal. He had abandoned Madrid as Napoleon had abandoned Moscow and, although the scale of the suffering and losses were not comparable, Wellington's army was in no fit state to fight in December 1812.

Although only three and a half months older than Napoleon, Wellington undoubtedly looked, and was, by far the fitter of the two in 1815. There was no flabby paunch, no sallow skin, no curtailment of riding and no unintentional dozing off in the middle of the day. Wellington's physical stamina, gained through the long years campaigning in Spain and Portugal, was undiminished. He retained the lean, wiry body of a younger man, brown hair cut short, blue eyes and the unmistakable Roman profile. Although nobody was to hear it that Sunday, he also kept the peculiar laugh that has been likened to a horse with whooping cough, which once

heard was never forgotten. To his officers he was 'the Peer' or 'the Beau', to his soldiers either 'Arty' or 'Nosey'. The Portuguese used to cry 'Douro, Douro' (after his brilliant crossing of the river in 1809) when they saw him, while the Spanish called him the 'Eagle'.

On the night of 15/16 June he had less than three hours sleep and was then in the saddle almost continuously until midnight on the 16th. During that time he had ridden from Brussels to Quatre-Bras, to Frasnes, to Ligny, back to Quatre-Bras and then to Genappe – at least 50 kilometres, possibly 60. That night another three hours sleep was followed by a second day in the saddle, covering over 20 kilometres, and to bed once again at midnight. On 18 June he was up at 3.00 a.m., rode off at 6.00 a.m. and remained mounted for the next sixteen hours. By the end of the battle Wellington had had perhaps nine hours sleep in the previous seventy-two, and had spent at least fifty-five in the saddle. Some of it had been hard, exciting riding, such as his gallop and leap for safety over the crouching bodies and lowered bayonets of the 92nd Highlanders at Quatre-Bras. It was hard on the horse as well as the man.

Wellington rode his favourite eight-year-old chestnut charger Copenhagen. This horse, that had carried him at the battles of Vitoria, the Pyrenees, Toulouse and Quatre-Bras, was to survive Waterloo untouched. He had a reputation as a kicker, and veterans of the Peninsular War who had come too close to his hindquarters before kept a respectable distance. Copenhagen was the foal of the mare ridden by Major-General Thomas Grosvenor at the siege of the city in 1807. Wellington purchased him in Spain from his Adjutant-General, Sir Charles Stewart. Not the fastest horse, not the most comfortable ride, but reliable, steady and with superb stamina. Copenhagen died in 1836, aged twenty-nine, and was buried at Stratfield Saye. Wellington was later to say of him, '… for bottom and endurance I never saw his fellow.' He certainly needed both with the Duke on his back.

Like Napoleon, Wellington was instantly recognizable at Waterloo. Unlike him, however, he did not wear uniform. His dress was drab, in direct contrast to the gold braid and plumes of his jingling cavalcade of accompanying generals and staff. Ironically, its very dullness marked him out for who he was. His black cocked hat with a low crown was similar to Napoleon's, but worn 'fore and aft' rather than square. On it was the black cockade of King George plus three smaller ones in the colours of Spain, Portugal and the Netherlands, indicating the four armies in which he held the rank of field-marshal. At his neck was a white cravat, fastened at the back with a silver buckle. His frock coat was blue like his cloak, which he later claimed to have put on and taken off from anything up to fifty times that day: '… I never get wet if I can help it.' He wore a black sword belt, white buckskin breeches with tasselled top-boots and short spurs. The only other senior personages at Waterloo known to be in civilian clothes were the Duke of Richmond, his son, and General Picton who died with a ball through his top hat.

PLANS AND ORDERS

Wellington's plan for the battle itself was straightforward and is largely apparent from his selection of ground, deployment and events during the battle, rather than from any specific written orders. On the night of 17 June when his second-in-command and cavalry commander, the Earl of Uxbridge, asked what his plan might be, the response was hardly illuminating. 'Well, Bonaparte has not given me any idea of his projects: and as my plans will depend upon his, how can you expect me to tell you what mine are?' Then, patting Uxbridge somewhat patronisingly on the shoulder, he added, 'There is one thing certain Uxbridge, that is, what ever happens, you and I will do our duty.' Years later Uxbridge was to write that the only orders he received from the Duke during the entire campaign were as follows:

• On Uxbridge's arrival in Brussels, 'I place the whole of the Cavalry and Light Artillery of the United Army under your command.'
• A few days later Uxbridge records that Wellington said, "'The Prince of Orange has begged that the Cavalry of HRH's nation should remain under his immediate command. I hope you have no objection to this." I replied, "Not the slightest. I am quite ready to act in any way you please."'
• On 17 June, having decided to withdraw from Quatre-Bras, he ordered Uxbridge, 'to remain in the position of Quatre-Bras as long as I conveniently could, in order to cover the movement of the Army'.
• As the battle started on 18 June the Duke said, 'The Prince of Orange requests that you will take charge of all his Cavalry.'

At Waterloo the Duke gave orders to the infantry or artillery but not to the cavalry. According to Uxbridge, every cavalry movement or charge by an Anglo-Allied formation was made on his orders only. He went so far as to write, 'I felt he [the Duke] had given me *carte blanche*, and I never bothered him with a single question respecting the movements [of cavalry] it might be necessary to make.'

If detailed written orders were lacking, the basic features of Wellington's plan were clear.

• To fight a defensive battle south of the village of Waterloo in the anticipation that Blücher's Prussians, whom he knew had retired on Wavre, would at some stage come in on his left (eastern) flank to assist him.
• In case things went wrong and he was forced to withdraw again, and to guard against a deliberate French turning move via Hal, he positioned 17,000 men in the Hal-Tubize area. In effect, if defeated, he was planning to retire west covering his communications with the coast (and England) at the expense of exposing Brussels.

Tactically:
• To select a suitable defensive position on the Mont St Jean ridge, thus allowing most units to have the advantage of protection from view and fire of a reverse slope.
• If possible, to have a lateral road along or behind the position to allow swift movement of reserves from one part of the front to another.
• To deploy the bulk of his artillery in the front line from the outset, with instructions to destroy attacking infantry or cavalry and not to get involved in counter-bombardment of the enemy's guns.
• To deploy the bulk of his army in the centre and right of the position; he considered this to be his most vulnerable flank (strategically), and the Prussians were expected to arrive on his left.
• To make use of the farms of Hougoumont, La Haie Sainte and Papelotte/La Haie immediately in front of his right, centre and left respectively, as strong points to break up frontal attacks.
• To keep his reserves of infantry and cavalry well back down the reverse slope ready for counterattacks or to plug dangerous gaps.

Wellington planned to fight a typical Peninsular War defensive battle where the enemy could see little of his army, being thus compelled to fire and attack at least partially blind, not knowing for sure what was on the other side of the ridge.

The Selection of the Mont St Jean Position

There is evidence that the selection of the ridge south of Mont St Jean Farm where Wellington gave battle may not, as has almost universally been accepted, have necessarily been the Duke's first choice. According to Lord Fitzroy Somerset, his Military Secretary, writing a year after the battle, it is possible Wellington initially considered what was to become the French ridge (although facing south), with La Belle Alliance as the centre. Fitzroy Somerset stated that at the start of the withdrawal from Quatre-Bras on 17 June Wellington had sent De Lancey ahead with instructions to mark out a defensive position blocking the Charleroi and Nivelles roads south of Waterloo. Seemingly, De Lancey had some discretion. Later that afternoon when the Duke and his staff arrived at La Belle Alliance he halted, thinking this might be the position. Fitzroy Somerset wrote:

> … on arriving near La Belle Alliance he [the Duke] thought it was the position the Qr.M. Genl. would have taken up, being the most commanding ground, but he [De Lancey] had found it too extended to be occupied by our Troops, & so had proceeded further on & marked out a position.

METHOD OF COMMAND

Napoleon was loved, revered, almost worshiped by his soldiers; Wellington was respected by his. His troops had the utmost confidence in his ability as a general. If they saw his familiar profile through the smoke of battle at some crisis point they knew, instinctively, all would be well. But the average company's reaction to seeing him approach was far more likely to be a sergeant's stage whisper of, 'Silence! Stand to your front – here's the Duke', than the waving of shakos or cries of 'Long live the Duke'. He was a disciplinarian, occasionally a stern one, with a somewhat cold, aloof manner, not over-generous with his praise. An example at Waterloo was his omission to mention Colonel Colbourne and the 52nd in his despatch after the battle for the officer's gallantry and skill in repulsing one of the attacking battalions of the Imperial Guard. Whereas Napoleon was inclined to be over-lavish with praise, rewards and honours, Wellington erred towards the other extreme. It is claimed that when, as an old man, Wellington had been asked if there was anything in his life he could have done better, he replied, 'Yes, I should have given more praise'.

There was no doubting his courage or coolness under fire. His calmness, his imperturbability in a crisis, was demonstrated when, in early evening, La Haie Sainte fell. General Ompteda was shot dead near the high road, De Lancey (his quartermaster-general) was mortally wounded by a cannon ball close by, as was one of his most trusted ADCs and personal friends, Sir Alexander Gordon, while to the right both the Prince of Orange and General Alten were down. With his remaining staff clamouring for orders, a poker-faced Duke responded, 'There are no orders, except to stand firm to the last man.'

On the battlefield Wellington rarely, if ever, delegated – and never to the extent Napoleon delegated to Ney or his corps commanders such as Lobau. The strange exception is his complete delegation of control over all the cavalry to Uxbridge. The Duke was seldom static, probably never dismounted, forever dashing about with his staff trailing behind him as he rushed to where he felt his presence was needed. Often he would suddenly wheel round and push back through the jumble of horsemen behind him. He would spend minutes at a time peering through the smoke and confusion with his telescope. At Waterloo, as in many of his previous battles, he paid scant regard to the normal channels of command. We hear virtually nothing at all of II Corps commander Lord Hill, and of the Prince of Orange only when he made a tactical blunder at comparatively low level. Wellington gave his battlefield orders direct, either personally or via a staff officer, to whoever he felt needed them, be they divisional or battalion commanders, or even the soldiers themselves – 'Drive those fellows away', 'There my lads, in with you …', 'You must hold your ground', 'Stand fast!', 'Adam you must dislodge those fellows', 'Go on Colbourne, they won't stand …', 'Now Maitland, now's your time. … Stand up Guards'. This type of 'hands on' leadership is extremely effective when conducted by a general of Wellington's ability and experience. It was made possible by the small size of the battlefield, the fitness and mobility of the commander-in-chief and the fact that he was fighting a defensive battle. Even had he been so inclined, the Emperor could not have led every divisional or corps attack. Even on a cramped battlefield like Waterloo, the attacking general cannot physically dash around encouraging and supervising every assault. Much more than a defender, he is forced to delegate, to use the chain of command.

Not even Wellington could be everywhere. He made frequent use of the forty odd commanders, staff officers and ADCs that crowded round him near the elm tree (by the crossroads in the centre of his position) that became the site of his command post. He scribbled pencil notes on asses' or goats' skin that could be wiped clean and used again. Several are preserved at Apsley House.

Wellington kept tight control. He made quick decisions and he issued orders at every stage of the battle, some examples of which are given below:

• After an early morning reconnaissance of Hougoumont he ordered its reinforcement by the 1/2 Nassau Infantry regiment.
• He gave orders, through the commander of the Royal Horse Artillery (Lieutenant-Colonel Frazer), for Bull's howitzers to fire on the woods south of Hougoumont.
• Instructing the gunners to leave their guns and seek shelter in the infantry squares when the French cavalry reached the ridge.
• Telling Macdonell in Hougoumont to hang on despite the buildings catching fire.
• Reinforcing Hougoumont.
• Bringing in reserves from the rear and extreme right to bolster the centre (for example, the Brunswick battalions and Chassé's 3rd Netherlands Division).
• Personally supervising the repulse of the Imperial Guard attack, and giving orders direct to the brigade commander (Maitland) as to when to fire.
• Ordering the general advance, and the bringing in of the light cavalry from the right flank, to follow up the retreating French.

Wellington seldom gave his subordinates much scope for initiative. He made the decisions, at times even down to battalion level. This was evident at Waterloo. He personally selected the positions of each division, sometimes brigades. A good illustration of how he spelled out the tactical detail of how an operation was to be carried out were his instructions for the withdrawal from Quatre-Bras, written on the battlefield at around 9.00 a.m. on 17 June. These were orders Wellington himself wrote down, with the staff being used as copyists and messengers. An extract reads as follows:

The 6th Division to be collected in columns of battalions, showing their heads only on the heights on the left of the position of Quatre-Bras. The Brunswick Corps to be collected in the wood on the Nivelles road, holding the skirts with their picquets only. The 2nd Division of the troops of the Netherlands to march from their present ground on Waterloo at 10 o'clock. The march to be in columns of half-companies at quarter distance.

Very detailed stuff from a commander-in-chief.

MOVEMENT ON THE BATTLEFIELD

Wellington used the elm tree at the crossroads as the site of his command post, although he was seldom there for long. There is no indication that he or his staff dismounted when near the elm: it was merely a central position from which to watch events while remaining mounted. His corps commanders, foreign representatives, the adjutant-general, quartermaster-general, military secretary, the artillery and engineer commanders, together with over twenty ADCs, made up the great bulk of his tactical headquarters. When the Duke moved they all followed. Distances were short. From the elm to Hougoumont is 1000 metres, from the elm to most parts of the line where the fighting took place is about 750 metres. Wellington and his staff could be at their destinations in ten minutes at most (allowing for battlefield confusion and difficulties and assuming they or their mounts were not hit).

It is impossible to know the precise timings of, or indeed the routes of, Wellington's gallops around the battlefield. It is known that he spent most of his time in the centre and on the right of the position (there is no evidence that he moved east of the Brussels road at all) and that he took shelter in at least two infantry squares during the cavalry charges. An approximation of his known movements on 18 June is given below.

3.00 a.m.	Got up in Waterloo village.
3.15–5.45 a.m.	Wrote letters in house.
6.00 a.m.	Left for battlefield.
7.00–8.30 a.m.	Inspected the line from right (west) to left. This included visiting Hougoumont and ordering its reinforcement.
Around 10.00 a.m.	Second visit to Hougoumont – met Lord Saltoun withdrawing from the Great Orchard.
Noon	On left of centre, pulled back Bijlandt's brigade from exposed position on forward slope.
1.00 p.m.	On right, sent seven companies of Coldstream Guards to reinforce Hougoumont.
1.30 p.m.	To elm and left centre to observe d'Erlon's attack.
mid-afternoon	On right in infantry squares (including Brunswick, but mostly in the combined square of the 2/30 and 2/73) during French cavalry attacks.
6.00 p.m.	In centre around the time La Haie Sainte fell.
8.00 p.m.	On right with Maitland's brigade during Imperial Guard attack.
8.30 p.m.	In centre, ordered general advance.
10.00 p.m.	Met Blücher near La Belle Alliance.

GENERAL HEADQUARTERS AND STAFF

At Waterloo there were some 150 British and KGL officers listed as being part of Wellington's staff. According to the custom of the time these included all general officers down to major-general, commanders of supporting arms, brigade majors and ADCs, in addition to the commander-in-chief's headquarters' staff. The Duke had been highly critical of the competence and lack of experience of many of his staff after he arrived in Belgium. By June, however, this situation had changed (even if Wellington was reluctant to admit it). Of the thirty-three senior staff officers present at Waterloo, thirty-one had experience on the staff in the Peninsular, and of the other two, one had been an ADC for five years.

There was no chief of staff system in the British Army at the time. Staff duties were divided between various departments, with the heads of those departments being comparatively junior officers – compared, for example, to Maréchal Soult and Lieutenant-General Gneisenau both of whom could, and would, have assumed command of their armies on the commander-in-chief being incapacitated at Waterloo. Wellington could not have worked with a chief of staff who was also his second-in-command. The Duke made his own decisions, rarely shared his plans and was seldom influenced by senior staff officers. As the renowned historian Sir Charles Oman aptly put it, 'He [Wellington] did not wish to have a Gneisenau or Moltke at his side: he only wanted zealous and competent chief clerks.' Wellington himself was the *de facto* head of each department.

In Wellington's general headquarters he had the assistance of eight officers (departmental heads) to facilitate the control and administration of his army and the headquarters itself. Most of these department heads had subordinate representatives at corps, division and even brigade level. They were:

• The Adjutant-General (AG) – Major-General Sir Edward Barnes. He was charged with all duties pertaining to unit strengths, parade states, and casualty returns of men and horses. He had overall responsibility for drill, discipline and prisoners (on the latter two he usually worked with the provost-marshal and deputy judge advocate, Lieutenant-Colonel Stephen Goodman). Barnes had a colonel as a deputy (DAG), eleven lieutenant-colonels and majors as assistants (AAGs), and ten captains and lieutenants as deputy assistants (DAAGs). The majority of these officers were attached to corps and divisional headquarters.

• The Quartermaster-General (QMG) – Colonel Sir William Howe De Lancey. Although officially subordinate to the adjutant-general's department, the QMG had far more crucial duties, and the holder of this office was the closest any staff officer came to being a chief of staff. His responsibilities included embarkation, disembarkation, billeting, quartering, route selection for marches, movement, topographical services, reconnaissance and, possibly the most vital of all, the copying and distribution – not the issuing – of orders. At Waterloo De Lancey was officially designated as Deputy QMG but ended up acting as QMG because Major-General Sir George Murray, who Wellington wanted (having filled the post in the Peninsular), had sailed for Canada and could not be recalled in time. De Lancey, who had also been in the Peninsular as DQMG, was initially somewhat disgruntled at this situation, as he was an extremely industrious and competent staff officer. He was killed at Waterloo. His staff, the majority of whom were deployed at subordinate formation headquarters, included seventeen colonels, lieu-

Intelligence Work

The Duke had an extensive network of agents in France, including Paris, and had the inestimable advantage of having the money to pay them. He received almost daily information from his contacts using the express post that operated into Belgium until the French invasion. He also had the services of his former head of intelligence from Spain – Lieutenant-Colonel Colquhoun Grant. When Grant, who had operated behind enemy lines in the Peninsula, was captured (he later escaped) Wellington had said, 'He was worth a brigade to me.' To distinguish him from a less popular John Grant the Spanish guerrillas called him 'Granto el Bueno' – Grant the Good. During the Waterloo campaign Grant was sent, in uniform, to secure information from inside France. There he was able to make effective use of Royalist sympathisers provided by the Comte d'Artois. He returned in time for Waterloo and is listed as an AQMG alongside another Peninsula veteran, Lieutenant-Colonel Sir George Scovell, the code-breaker who was in charge of communications.

tenant-colonels, majors and captains as assistants (AQMGs), and twelve captains and lieutenants as deputy assistants (DAQMGs).

• The Military Secretary (MS) – Lieutenant-Colonel Lord Fitzroy Somerset (who later became Lord Raglan, the ill-fated commander-in-chief in the Crimea). His duties were dealing with all the personal correspondence of the commander-in-chief, reading all incoming reports, keeping the register of incoming and outgoing documents and channelling communications from the non-British formations to the Duke.

• The Commissary-General (CG) – Mr Thomas Dunmore. He was listed as being in Holland and had overall charge of his department in the theatre of operations. The most likely senior commissary officer with the Army was DCG Daniel Ord who, because of the nature of his duties, is unlikely to have been present on the battlefield. The Commissariat was a civilian department representing the Treasury, responsible for providing transport, food, forage and various stores. In conjunction with the Deputy Paymaster-General he acted as the army's banker. Many of his subordinates would have been present on the battlefield. The exact number is not known but the CG's staff in the theatre totalled 126, made up of seven other deputies (DCGs), eighteen assistants (ACGs) and 100 deputy assistants (DACGs), most of whom would have been at corps or divisional headquarters and scattered along the lines of communications.

• The officer commanding the Royal Artillery – Colonel Sir George Adam Wood. Acted as Wellington's artillery adviser and had overall command of all artillery units with the army. Also responsible for the supply of ammunition and arms. At Waterloo Wood was assisted by Lieutenant-Colonel Sir Augustus Frazer who commanded the Royal Horse Artillery units.

• The commanding Royal Engineer – Lieutenant-Colonel Carmichael Smyth. Wellington's adviser on engineering, fortifications, siegecraft, and pontoons. Also the storekeeper for engineering equipment and the pontoon train.

• The Inspector of Hospitals – Sir James Robert Grant. Wellington's former principal medical officer in the Peninsular War, Sir James McGrigor, had been selected for the top post in the military medical hierarchy in London – the new Director-General of the Medical Board. Despite this, he offered to come out to Belgium after his appointment to organize the medical and hospital services. In the event this was not possible. Sir James

Robert Grant (brother of Colonel Colquhoun Grant, Wellington's chief intelligence officer) assumed the duties and may have accompanied the Duke on the battlefield or possibly remained in Brussels. Of the four deputy-inspectors, John Gunning took charge of the field hospital at Mont St Jean farm. Wellington's personal physician was Dr John Hume, who was likely to have accompanied him on the battlefield.

• Headquarters' Commandant – Colonel Sir Colin Campbell. His responsibility was the administration, feeding, security and billeting of the headquarters itself. A frustrating and thankless task.

AIDES-DE-CAMP (ADCS)

These staff officers belonged to a general's 'personal staff'. Their task in war was primarily as messengers for their general. On the battlefield it was one of the most crucial and dangerous jobs in any army. Of the fifty-seven British ADCs at Waterloo, six were killed and twelve wounded. The official allocation of ADCs was – Commander-in-chief four; generals three; lieutenant-generals two; major-generals one. However, at Waterloo several generals had more, plus additional ones that they paid for out of their own pockets (for example Lord Hill had five, four official and one 'extra'). The junior ADCs were often sons of the general, or close relations, or sons of friends or men of importance at home to whom he wished to repay a favour. Their appointment was a personal one, and lasted only as long as the general held command. Captain Lord Arthur Hill, said to be the most overweight young man in the army, was one of three 'extra' ADCs on the Duke's staff. On one occasion near La Haie Sainte when Wellington was exposed to heavy fire, another staff officer commented that Lord Arthur Hill presented an unusually large target, saying of Hill, '[he] remained a little in rear of the Duke, and I suppose just out of the line of fire, otherwise his fat person must have been riddled.'

Senior ADCs at general or corps headquarters were lieutenant-colonels or majors.

BRIGADE MAJORS (BMS)

They were the chief staff officers attached to a brigade headquarters. Their appointment was to the brigade and, unlike ADCs, they remained with the brigade if the commander changed – although they were a part of the general's 'family'. Major Harry Smith of the 95th was the BM of Major-General Lambert's 10th British Brigade at Waterloo. When appointed to a similar position in the Peninsular, Smith recalled asking his commander: 'Have you any orders for the picquets, Sir?' His commander replied, 'Pray, Mr. Smith, are you my brigade-major?' 'I believe so, Sir.' 'Then let me tell you it is your duty to post the picquets and mine to have a damned good dinner for you every day.' There were fifteen British and KGL BMs (including the artillery BM) at Waterloo, of whom five were killed and four (including Smith) were wounded.

WELLINGTON'S GENERAL HEADQUARTERS IN THE FIELD

It is impossible to be precise as to the numbers and names of every officer that formed part of the Duke's tactical headquarters (the group that accompanied him on the battlefield) at Waterloo. However, those listed below either were, or probably were, a part of the cavalcade that attempted to keep up with him as he dashed from one part of the field to another. It includes the corps commanders and some of their staff who undoubtedly rode with, or near, their commander, but does not include all their junior ADCs.

The Duke's Personal Staff

Military Secretary
Lieutenant-Colonel Lord Fitzroy Somerset, 1st Foot Guards, later Commander-in-Chief Crimea

Personal surgeon
Dr. John Hume

Aides-de-Camp
Lieutenant-Colonel J. Fremantle, Coldstream Guards
Lieutenant-Colonel C.F. Canning, 3rd Foot Guards
Lieutenant-Colonel Hon. Sir Alexander Gordon, 3rd Foot Guards
Lieutenant Lord George Lennox, 9th Light Dragoons
The Prince of Nassau-Usingen
Major Hon. Henry Percy, 14th Light Dragoons
Captain Lord Arthur Hill
Lieutenant Lord George Cathcart, 6th Dragoon Guards (killed while GOC 4th Division in Crimea)

CORPS COMMANDERS

Cavalry Corps
Lieutenant-General The Earl of Uxbridge (GOC and 2IC to Wellington)
Major W. Thornhill, 7th Hussars (ADC)
Captain H.B. Seymour, 18th Hussars (ADC)
Captain T. Wildman 7th Hussars (ADC)
Captain J. Fraser, 7th Hussars (ADC)
(Note: Uxbridge and all his ADCs were wounded when he took them with him in the Heavy Cavalry charge)

I Corps
HRH The Prince of Orange (GOC)
Major-General Baron Constant-Rebecque (QMG)
Major-General H.J. van der Wijek (AG)
Lieutenant-Colonel Baron Tripp, 60th Foot (ADC)
Captain Lord John Somerset, brother of Fitzroy Somerset, the Military Secretary (ADC)
Captain Hon. Francis Russell (ADC)

II Corps
Lieutenant-General Lord Hill (GOC)
Lieutenant-Colonel C. Hill, Royal Horse Guards, brother of above (ADC)
Major R. Egerton, 34th Foot (ADC)
Major C.H. Churchill, 1st Foot Guards (ADC)
Captain D. Mackworth, 7th Foot (ADC)
Captain Hon. O. Bridgeman, 1st Foot Guards (ADC)

Commander, Royal Artillery
Colonel Sir George Adam Wood (CRA)
Lieutenant J. Bloomfield (Staff Adjutant)
Lieutenant G. Coles (Staff Adjutant)
Lieutenant-Colonel Sir Augustus Frazer (CRHA)
Lieutenant W. Bell (Staff Adjutant)
Lieutenant-Colonel A. Macdonald (CRHA attached to the cavalry)
Lieutenant-Colonel Sir John May (AAG)
Captain H. Baynes (BM)

Commanding Royal Engineer
Lieutenant-Colonel J. Carmichael Smythe

Adjutant-General's Department
Major-General Sir Edward Barnes (AG)
Major A. Hamilton, 4th West India Regt. (ADC)
Colonel Sir John Elley, Royal Horse Guards (DAG)
Lieutenant-Colonel J. Waters (AAG)

Quartermaster-General's Department
Colonel Sir William Howe De Lancey (DQMG)
Colonel Hon. Alexander Abercromby, 2nd Foot Guards (AQMG)
Colonel F.E. Hervey, 14th Light Dragoons (AQMG)
Lieutenant-Colonel R. Torrens, West India Regt. (AQMG)

Foreign Military Representatives
Field-Marshal Baron de Vincent (Austria)
Lieutenant-General Count Pozzo di Borgo (Russia)
(A Corsican, but one who had a personal hatred of Napoleon)

Lieutenant-General Miguel de Alava (Spain)
Interestingly, de Alava had fought against the British as a naval ADC aboard Admiral Gravina's flagship the *Principe de Asturias* at Trafalgar ten years earlier. In 1808 when Spain rebelled against Napoleonic domination, de Alava became a colonel and served as an ADC to Wellington throughout the Peninsular War. They became close friends and, at the Duke's insistence, he was awarded the Peninsular Gold Cross and Medal with clasps for Badajos, Ciudad Rodrigo, Salamanca, Vitoria and Toulouse.

Major-General Count van Reede (Netherlands)
Major-General Baron von Muffling (Prussia)
Muffling played a key role as Blücher's liaison officer at Wellington's HQ. His equivalent at the Prussian HQ was Lieutenant-Colonel Sir Henry Hardinge.

This gives a total of forty-eight officers and is likely to be a minimum figure, as it excludes some junior ADCs, aides to the foreign representatives and liaison officers. However, at any one time during the battle a number will have been away from the headquarters on various duties, co-ordinating movement, bringing up reserves, deploying artillery or carrying messages. A substantial proportion was wounded. Thus the average size of the staff around Wellington at any given moment was probably around thirty to forty individuals.

Casualties Among British Staff and Generals

Not many senior staff officers or generals survived Waterloo unscathed. Canning and Gordon had been killed, De Lancey mortally wounded while Barnes, and Elley his deputy, were wounded. Among the generals, Picton, Ponsonby, DuPlat, van Merlen and Ompteda were dead, Uxbridge (with all his four ADCs), Cooke, Kempt, Pack, Grant, Dornberg, Adam, Bijlandt, Kielmannsegge and Colin Halkett were wounded. Out of some fifty assistants in the adjutant and quartermaster-generals departments two had been killed and thirteen wounded. Of the sixteen officers commanding cavalry regiments, three were dead and seven injured. Out of twenty-five British battalions commanders, one died and eleven were wounded. As in all battles of that age, rank was no protector of person.

It is not possible to name all the staff at subordinate formation headquarters but the likely appointments are as follows:

Corps HQ	Divisional HQ	Brigade HQ
Commander, 3 or 4 ADCs	Commander, 2 or 3 ADCs	Commander, 1 ADC
1 x AAG	1 x DAAG	1 x BM
2 x DAAG	1 x AQMG	1 x DAQMG
1 x AQMG	1 x DAQMG	1 x DACG
2 x DAQMG	1 x ACG	
1 x DCG		

Anglo-Allied Senior Commanders at Waterloo

Despite his initial derogatory remarks about lack of experience and competence among his senior commanders and staff, by the time the campaign opened Wellington had assembled a group of generals whose experience in many ways matched that of the French. Even the ludicrously young novice commander of Wellington's largest formation, the Prince of Orange, was not new to the noise, confusion and dangers of the battlefield. All but six of the Duke's commanders had served under him in the Peninsular, the six exceptions (Chassé, Collaert, Dornberg, Trip, de Ghigny and Merlen) having fought for the French – Merlen in the Imperial Guard cavalry. The average age of the British major-generals and above was 44.7 (French 43.6), and the average age at death of those surviving the battle was 73.4 (French 72). One lived to be ninety (Kempt) and five others reached their eighties (Byng, Maitland, Halkett, Uxbridge, and Vandeleur). The youngest Anglo-Allied general on the battlefield was the Prince of Orange at twenty-three, but his rank was due entirely to diplomatic niceties (Prince William of Prussia, who commanded the Prussian IV Reserve Cavalry Corps was only eighteen). The next youngest was Adam at thirty-four, with Barnes and Somerset still in their thirties. Picton at fifty-six was the oldest. Short biographical notes follow.

SENIOR STAFF

Barnes, Major-General Sir Edward (1776–1838)

Barnes was the adjutant-general at Waterloo, responsible for personnel, strength and casualty returns, drill, discipline and prisoners of war. A man of bulldog courage, a quick temper and a reputation as a tough disciplinarian. He was not displeased when, at Waterloo, he was referred to as, 'Our fire eating adjutant-general'. He was an infantryman, having served in the 99th Foot (Prince of Wales', Tipperary) and had commanded the 46th Foot (South Devon) in the West Indies. As a lieutenant-colonel he had commanded a brigade at the capture of the French islands of Martinique and Guadeloupe. He served on the staff in Spain and Portugal where he was twice wounded, and led a brigade at the battles of Vitoria, Pyrenees, Nivelle, Nive and Orthez. He led from the front. In July 1813, near the village of Maya in the Pyrenees Barnes put himself at the head of his three battalions and successfully charged six French battalions in what the French commander Général d'Erlon declared to be, 'one of the sharpest affairs ever seen in war'. The following month he did even better at the action at the Pass of Echalar. In dense fog he once more led his brigade unsupported against another of d'Erlon's divisions, with odds of four to one against. Of this attack Wellington was unusually fulsome with his praise: '… in my life I never saw such an attack as was made by General Barnes's brigade upon the enemy above Echalar … it is impossible that I can extol too highly the conduct of General Barnes and these brave troops …'.

Even as adjutant-general Barnes never let slip a chance for action. At a difficult moment at Quatre-Bras, when columns of French infantry were nearing the crossroads, he rode to the front of the 92nd (Gordon Highlanders) and led them in a charge. At Waterloo he rode alongside the Duke where he was one of the numerous staff officers to be wounded.

From 1824–31 Barnes was Governor of Ceylon. By then he must have mellowed somewhat, as he was so popular that his tenure of office was marked by the erection of his statue. For the next two years he was the commander-in-chief in India. Barnes was the army founder of the Army and Navy Club in Piccadilly (the Navy founder being Admiral Bowles). He died in London, aged sixty-two.

De Lancey, Colonel Sir William Howe (1781–1815)

De Lancey was the Deputy Quartermaster-General at Waterloo, and as such was responsible for movement, billeting, reconnaissance, and the copying and distribution of orders. Although only a colonel and DQMG, De Lancey was the nearest any staff officer came to being Wellington's chief of staff. His was the massive task prior to the battle of co-ordinating the movement of the army in accordance with the Duke's instructions. His bride of two months, Lady Magdalene, was with him in Brussels and kept him supplied with strong green tea throughout the night of 15/16 June as he laboriously wrote out all the orders.

De Lancey was a descendant of a Huguenot family that had emigrated to America but had remained loyal during the War of Independence and returned to England afterwards. De Lancey and Wellington had known each other since they were boys. He had been an ADC in India when Colonel Wellesley, as the Duke was then known, commanded the 33rd Foot. He had been on Wellington's staff in the Peninsular as DQMG from 1809–14 with a few periods

The Strongest Man in the British Army

One of the Earl of Uxbridge's ADCs, Captain H.B. Seymour, had the reputation of being the largest and strongest man in the army. He was said to have killed more Frenchmen at Waterloo than any other individual. Allegedly, he was repeatedly insulted in a Paris restaurant a few weeks after the battle by a French officer who did not realize his immense physique. Seymour rose up from his seat, towering like an enormous gorilla over the now seriously alarmed Frenchman, seized his nose with one hand and his lower jaw with the other. With one quick wrench he opened the officer's mouth – and spat down his throat. The humiliated man stumbled away with a broken jaw. Seymour's later military career was limited, and he went on half pay in 1819. Both his father and his son were admirals. Seymour, however, contented himself with becoming the MP for Lisburn.

Death of Colonel De Lancey

Perhaps fate was being kind to Hudson Lowe when Wellington fired him, as his successor, De Lancey, was mortally wounded at Waterloo and died a lingering, painful death. A cannonball grazed him and separated all the ribs on his left side from his backbone – surely a unique injury. He was carried first to Waterloo village and eventually his wife of three months, Magdalene, came to nurse him. Leeches were applied to drain his blood and Magdalene assisted in their application, like the doctors, oblivious of the harm they were doing. Wellington came to see him. The Duke later reminisced, 'Poor fellow! We knew each other ever since we were boys. But I had no time to be sorry. I went on with the army and never saw him again.'

Magdalene watched him die slowly. She later recalled, 'he was restless and uncomfortable; his breathing was like choking, and as I sat gazing at him I could distinctly hear the water rattling in his throat. Soon afterwards a doctor whispered, "He's gone."' Magdalene returned to England delirious with grief but managed to recover sufficiently to remarry within two years, only to die three years later. During that period she wrote a moving account of her experiences, which attracted much complimentary comment from the famous novelist Charles Dickens.

In 1887 her husband, along with fourteen other officers and Sergeant-Major Cotton, were moved from their graves near Waterloo and buried at the new cemetery at Evere. Later the remains of De Lancey, Ensign James Lord Hay and Sergeant-Major Cotton were placed in the vault of the memorial.

---

as acting QMG. Despite many years of copying out letters and orders, the Duke was not always impressed with his ability. In 1813 he wrote to the Military Secretary at the Horse Guards that De Lancey was, '… the idlest fellow I ever met.' General Graham, under whom he served in 1813 and 1814, referred to him as a habitual 'scatterbrain' (although the fact that he kept his job all those years surely means that he must have had his lucid moments).

When Wellington arrived in Brussels in April 1815 to take over command from the Prince of Orange, the QMG was Major-General Sir Hudson Lowe who Wellington regarded as a bumbling incompetent. The Duke wanted Sir George Murray who had been his most competent QMG in the Peninsular – but he had set sail for Canada. A disgruntled De Lancey was persuaded to take the responsibility and do the work without the rank or title. It cost him his life.

He was present at Quatre-Bras. At around 10.00 a.m. on 17 June the Duke sent him back ahead of the army to finalize the selection of a defensive position south of Waterloo village. According to Wellington's Military Secretary (Fitzroy Somerset), he considered the possibility of what was to become the French position, but thought it too extended. At Waterloo he was part of the Duke's entourage as it galloped around the field until, towards the end of the battle, a cannonball passed so close to his chest that it knocked him from his horse and wounded him severely. He was carried from the field in a blanket on the Duke's instructions. He died, tended by his wife, eight days later aged thirty-four. His name is commemorated in Delancey Street, close to Regent's Park in London, and on the island of Guernsey there is a De Lancey Lane, Hill, Park, School and two houses. Even Australia has a De Lancey Street and a Mont De Lancey at Wandin, Victoria.

I CORPS

His Royal Highness The Prince of Orange (1792–1849)

Although only twenty-three at Waterloo, he commanded the largest corps in the Anglo-Allied Army – over 30,000 men made up of two British infantry divisions (1st and 3rd) including Cooke's Guards, two Netherlands infantry divisions (2nd and 3rd), and Collaert's Netherlands Cavalry Division plus fifty-eight guns. It was a most prestigious command given to him for entirely diplomatic reasons. Until Wellington arrived in Brussels in April, the Prince of Orange was the commander-in-chief of all the forces in the Netherlands. It was only after intense pressure and persuasion that his father, the King of the Netherlands, agreed to Wellington taking overall command. Nothing less than I Corps was acceptable by the Prince or his father.

He had been born in The Hague into one of the most distinguished noble houses in Europe. The Princes of Orange had been *stadtholders* (hereditary heads of state) of the Dutch Republic since 1579. The French occupation in 1795 forced the family to flee to England when the young William was only three. Brought up in Yarmouth and Colchester he had a thoroughly English education (later taking his English tutor, Mr Johnson, to the Peninsular War with him). The Prince was commissioned into the Prussian Army at seventeen and two years later made a lieutenant-colonel in the British Army. It was in this rank that he joined Wellington's staff in Portugal in 1811. During this time he was accompanied by the man who had been his military tutor since 1805, and who was to be his QMG at Waterloo, Lieutenant-Colonel Constant-Rebecque. The Prince saw plenty of action during his two years and never lacked courage. The Duke's comment on him was: 'The Prince is a brave young man, but that's all.' In 1813 he was made a major-general in the British Army. Long before Waterloo the Prince had acquired two unflattering nicknames – 'Slender Billy' on account of his long neck, and the 'Young Frog' on account of his high forehead and to distinguish him from his father who was the 'Old Frog.' He was in the forefront of the action at Quatre-Bras and was blamed for giving an order that had two battalions in line instead of square to meet cavalry. The 69th Foot lost a Colour as a result, although the Prince was only partially to blame, as a Major Lindsay of the 69th confused things by giving the wrong word of command for two of the companies.

At Waterloo the Prince was again involved in controversy over an order. When Major-General Alten ordered Colonel Ompteda to counterattack La Haie Sainte with a battalion of the KGL despite the close proximity of French cavalry, he demurred. On hearing this dissension the Prince insisted that Alten's order be obeyed. The command was carried out, but at the cost of Ompteda's life and the destruction of the 5th Line Battalion of the KGL. Not long afterwards the Prince was hit in the shoulder by a musket ball and helped to the rear. The spot where he was wounded is now the site of the Lion Mound. The Prince became King William II of Holland in 1840, dying nine years later, aged fifty-seven.

Constant-Rebecque, Major-General Baron Jean-Victor (1773–1850)

An extremely experienced and competent staff officer who at Waterloo was the Quartermaster-General (Chief of Staff) to the Prince of Orange and to the Netherlands contingents generally.

He was of Swiss origin and had as a young man enlisted for a time in Louis XVI's Swiss Guard. In 1793 he joined the Dutch

Army. When the French overran his country he fled to Britain and in 1805 was selected to become the military tutor of the thirteen-year-old Prince of Orange. In 1811 as a lieutenant-colonel, Constant-Rebecque accompanied the Prince to the Peninsula. Upon the liberation of the Netherlands from the French in 1813 Constant-Rebecque returned home to become chief of staff to the Dutch Army, with the task of creating an efficient force.

On 15 June 1815 it was his quick thinking that led him to disregard Wellington's movement order and ensure the key crossroads at Quatre-Bras were held on 16 June until reinforcements could arrive. During the fighting he rode at the Prince of Orange's side.

At Waterloo he was equally active stemming the flight of Bijlandt's disorganized Belgians and rallying Kruse's Nassauers. He later commented that the endless massed French cavalry attacks during the afternoon, '... rushed like lava between our squares.' Not until the end of the day, as the Anglo-Allied advance was under way, did Constant-Rebecque come near to death when a cannonball carried away his horse's head.

After the war he served in a variety of posts, including his old one of chief of staff to the Netherlands Army. However, he was unable to effect sufficient reform to avoid defeat in the Belgian War of Independence. He was dismissed in 1837 and retired to his estate in Silesia where he died thirteen years later, aged seventy-seven.

Cooke, Major-General George (1768–1837)

Cooke had a small but élite command at Waterloo – the 1st British (Guards) Division. Unlike other formations, it had not been mixed with different units but consisted entirely of Guards battalions which, although strong (1000+ at the start of the campaign), were only four in number. Both brigade commanders were guardsmen, and Cooke had been a guardsman since he was sixteen when, in 1784, he was commissioned into the 1st Foot Guards.

He had fought in Flanders before, in 1794, and in Holland five years later. Promoted major-general in 1811, he spent the next two years in the Cadiz garrison. In 1814 he had commanded one of the attacking columns in the bitter, close quarter, but ultimately unsuccessful, fighting during the assault on Bergen-op-Zoom. At Quatre-Bras his division arrived at around 6.30 p.m. and were thrown in to recapture the Bois de Bossu. His guardsmen pushed through the woods only to be driven back by French lancers after they had exploited too far to the south.

Cooke's two brigades were posted on the right of Wellington's line to the north and north-east of Hougoumont with its orchard and wood, for which the division supplied half the garrison. The men committed to its defence were to be engaged for the entire day in a 'battle within a battle'. Cooke had the misfortune to be severely wounded (losing his right arm) soon after La Haie Sainte fell in the early evening and thus was not in command when his troops played a key role in the final repulse of the Imperial Guard.

Cooke was promoted lieutenant-general in 1821. He died at Harefield, Middlesex in 1837, aged sixty-nine.

Maitland, Major-General Sir Peregrine (1774–1854)

Maitland commanded the 1st British (Guards) Brigade in Cooke's 1st Division. It consisted of two battalions of the 1st Foot Guards: the 2/1 and 3/1. He himself had been commissioned into the 1st Foot Guards as an ensign in 1792 and had remained a guardsman ever since. He fought in Flanders in 1794 and was in action at Lugo and Corunna in 1808–09. He commanded the 1st Guards Brigade at the Battle of the Nivelle in 1813 and the crossing of the Ardour in early 1814. He was promoted major-general the same year.

Maitland's brigade was heavily involved in the fighting for Bois de Bossu at Quatre-Bras and was caught by French lancers in the open ground to the south. In total the brigade lost nearly 500 casualties in this battle. At Waterloo this brigade supplied its light companies for the defence of Hougoumont, with the remainder being deployed in the front line some 400 metres to the north-east of the orchard. The highlight of the battle for this brigade came in the late evening when the Middle Guard launched its 'all or nothing' assault. Maitland's men were in the path of the 3rd Châsseurs of the Guard. As they reached the crest of the ridge, behind which the brigade was lying down, Wellington called out, 'Now Maitland, now's your time!' The brigade stood up, delivered a volley and charged with the bayonet. For their part in repulsing the Middle Guard, the 1st Foot Guards were later renamed the Grenadier Guards, as it was thought (erroneously) that they had defeated the Grenadiers of the Imperial Guard.

Maitland went on to become the commander-in-chief of the Madras Army in 1836 and was in the Cape of Good Hope in 1843. He died eleven years later, aged eighty.

Byng, Major-General Sir John (1772–1860)

Unlike his fellow brigade commander at Waterloo, Byng had not always been a guardsman. He was commissioned into the Duke's former regiment, the 33rd Foot, in 1793. He was one of Lieutenant-Colonel Wellesley's (as Wellington was then known) junior officers in action for the first time at Boxtel in Flanders in 1794. He was wounded in the Irish Rising of 1798. In 1800 Major Byng was serving in America with the 60th Foot (Royal Americans). Four years later he exchanged into the 3rd Guards. By the time he went to the Peninsular in 1811 as a colonel on the staff, he had already been an ADC, an AAG and served on the Copenhagen and Walcheren expeditions.

As a brigade commander he fought at Vitoria, the Pyrenees, the Nivelle (where he was wounded), the Nive, Orthez and Toulouse. The highlight of all this fighting came at St Pierre, on Vieux Mouguerre ridge, in December 1813. He led his brigade in a difficult uphill assault that culminated in Byng personally planting the Colours of the 31st Foot on the heights. For this exploit the Prince Regent was to authorize the augmentation of his family coat of arms with an arm grasping a Colour.

His brigade was fully committed at Quatre-Bras in clearing the Bois de Bossu, where it suffered substantial casualties. At Waterloo much of his command was eventually committed to the defence of Hougoumont, an action that continued throughout the day.

In later years he was to command in Ireland, become an MP for Poole, inherit the title Earl of Stratford and, finally, be promoted field-marshal in 1855. He died five years later, aged eighty-eight – second only to Kempt as the oldest of the Allied Waterloo generals.

Alten, Lieutenant-General Count Charles (1764–1840)

Alten commanded the 3rd British Division at Waterloo that consisted of three brigades, one each of British, KGL and Hanoverian troops. It was a strong formation with over 8000 men. He was the only Hanoverian to command a British division as distinct from a KGL formation. Alten was commissioned into the Hanoverian Foot Guards in 1781. He fought under the Duke of York in the Low Countries in 1793 and 1795, making something of a name for himself as a commander of light troops along the River Lys. After Napoleon's conquest of Hanover he chose to come to England where he obtained a colonel's commission in the KGL, then part of the British service. He saw active service at Hanover in 1805, Copenhagen in 1807, Sweden and the Peninsular, and the Walcheren expedition in 1809, before returning to Spain in 1810 as a major-general.

He gained considerable experience as a brigade and divisional commander in the Peninsula. This included assuming command of the famous Light Division from 'Black Bob' Crauford when he was killed at the Siege of Ciudad Rodrigo in 1812. From then on he saw action in every major battle until the end of the war, including Salamanca, Vitoria, Sorauren, the crossing of the Bidassoa, the Nivelle and the Nive. Wellington was to say of the Light Division under his command that it was, 'the flower of the army, the finest infantry in the world'.

His division was at Quatre-Bras and at Waterloo posted in the centre of Wellington's front line, immediately west of the cross-roads. It was a location that ensured the maximum participation in the battle and fearsome casualties. Alten's men had to stand their ground against artillery, cavalry, infantry and, finally, the Middle Guard. Shortly after the loss of La Haie Sainte at about 6.30 p.m., Alten ordered his KGL brigade commander, Colonel Ompteda, to attack to retake the farm. Ompteda voiced his doubts, as cavalry were close. Unfortunately, this disagreement was heard by the corps commander the Prince of Orange who insisted that Ompteda obey his superior. He did so, but it cost him his life to the French cavalry and the destruction of his 5th Line Battalion, including the loss of its King's Colour.

Alten survived Waterloo unscathed and returned to Hanover to become Minister of War and Foreign Affairs, then inspector-general and, finally, field-marshal in the Hanoverian Army. He died in the Tyrol in 1840, aged seventy-six.

Halkett, Major-General Sir Colin (1774–1856)
Another KGL officer who commanded the 5th British Brigade at Waterloo. Even though it lost heavily at Quatre-Bras it was still a substantial formation, with four (British) battalions totalling around 2,270 all ranks. Although of Scottish descent, Halkett first entered the Dutch Army. He left as a major, and was given authority to raise a battalion of the German Legion for British service. He did so successfully and in 1805 was a lieutenant-colonel commanding the 2nd Light Battalion of the, by then, KGL.

He went to the Peninsular as a colonel commanding a two-battalion brigade of KGL light infantrymen. Halkett was present at most of the hard fought battles, including Albuera, Salamanca, Vitoria and the Pyrenees. He particularly distinguished himself at the start of Wellington's retreat from Burgos in 1812 when, as part of the rearguard, he repulsed a massive French cavalry assault. An eyewitness described his battalions' marksmanship as, 'bringing the enemy down as if they had been partridges'. It was Halkett's brigade that prevented a disaster. He continued to command the KGL light brigade until the end of the war in the Peninsula.

At Quatre-Bras his brigade was badly mauled by cavalry, partly as a result of an unfortunate order from the Prince of Orange. The 69th Foot was caught in line and lost a Colour while the 33rd Foot dashed in disorder into the Bois de Bossu for sanctuary. It was rallied by Halkett personally holding aloft its King's Colour. At Waterloo, as part of Alten's 3rd British Division, his

brigade was under fire near the centre of the line throughout much of the day. His numbers had shrunk so much that when attacked by cavalry the brigade formed only two squares, of two battalions each – the 30/73 and the 33/69. Halkett had four horses shot under him and was wounded twice. There was an awkward incident when his battalions faltered momentarily in the face of the Imperial Guard attack.

In later years Halkett became commander-in-chief of the Bombay Army, Governor of Jersey and then Governor of the Chelsea Hospital. He died aged eighty-two, having lived long enough to see a number of the young officers he knew at Waterloo command large formations in the Crimean War.

Keilmannsegge, Major-General Count (dates not known)
Kielmannsegge commanded the 1st Hanoverian Brigade in Alten's 3rd Division at Waterloo. It was the strongest brigade in the Anglo-Allied Army with five full strength battalions plus two field Jaeger companies. Despite losses at Quatre-Bras, it mustered over 3,300 all ranks. On 16 June the brigade was deployed on the extreme left of Wellington's line to reinforce the 95th Rifles and successfully retook the farm of Piraumont.

At Waterloo the brigade was deployed west of the Charleroi-Brussels road between the 2nd KGL and the 5th British Brigades. From the start Kielmannsegge provided 50 sharpshooters each from the Grubenhagen and Lüneburg Battalions together with 100 men from the 1st Company of the Field Jaeger Corps to help defend Hougoumont Wood. They were posted along the southern edge of the wood south of the Château. During the struggle for La Haie Sainte farm, Kielmannsegge sent his Lüneburg Light Field Battalion to assist the garrison under Major Baring. It was caught en route in the open and scattered by Dubois' cuirassiers. After La Haie Sainte was finally taken, the Allied centre was badly battered by close range cannon fire, a gap opened up and Generals Alten and Halkett were hit, as was Colonel Ompteda, the KGL brigade commander. Kielmannsegge was left to rally the division until he too was wounded.

Collaert, Lieutenant-General Baron J.A. de (1761–1816)
At Waterloo Collaert commanded the Netherlands Cavalry Division. It consisted of one heavy brigade of Dutch and Belgian carabineers under Major-General Trip and two light brigades of Dutch and Belgian hussars and light dragoons under Major-Generals de Ghigny and Merlen, all of whom, like Collaert, had fought for the French for many years. Collaert had been promoted to command a brigade in 1811. His division at Waterloo was deployed well back in reserve behind the centre, on either side of the Brussels road, near Mont St Jean farm. It was a strong division numerically with over 3,600 sabres.

Collaert was very seriously wounded at Waterloo and never really recovered. After months of suffering, he died of his wounds almost exactly a year after the battle on 17 June 1816, aged fifty-five.

Perponcher-Sedlnitzky, Lieutenant-General Baron Henri-Georges (1771–1856)
Born into the minor Dutch nobility Perponcher entered military service while still a teenager, and by 1793 was adjutant to Prince Frederick of the Netherlands. With the French occupation of his country he fled to England with the House of Orange, entering British military service in 1800.

During the Waterloo campaign Perponcher commanded the 2nd Netherlands Infantry Division with over 8,100 men. Its one Belgian and four Dutch battalions formed Major-General van Bijlandt's 1st Brigade, and its five Nassau battalions Major-General Saxe-Weimar's 2nd Brigade. Saxe-Weimar's battalions were particularly strong, averaging well over 800 men each, even after losses at Quatre-Bras.

At the start of the campaign Perponcher concurred with Constant-Rebecque's decision to redirect his division to Quatre-Bras. Saxe-Weimar's brigade initially held the crucial crossroads until reinforced. Perponcher organized the defence of Quatre-Bras and was later complimented by the Duke on his dispositions. The division was involved throughout 16 June, although casualties were comparatively light. At Waterloo his division was divided, with Bijlandt initially deployed in a somewhat exposed position on the forward slope of the ridge just east of the 'Elm Tree' crossroads, and Saxe-Weimar defending Papelotte, La Haie and Frichermont on the eastern flank. Bijlandt's Belgians were shaken by d'Erlon's attack but Saxe-Weimar's Nassauers put up a stout resistance.

After the wars Perponcher was appointed the Dutch ambassador to Prussia, a post he held for twenty-seven years until retiring in 1842. He died in 1856, aged eighty-five.

Chassé, Lieutenant-General Baron David-Hendrik (1765–1849)

A dynamic Dutchman who had spent some five years fighting for the French, rising to the level of brigade commander. His exploits were to earn him the nickname of 'General Bayonet'. He was born of middle class origins and entered the service of the United Provinces as a cadet in 1775. Political indiscretions forced him to flee to France where he became a captain in 1792. Within a year he was a battalion commander in the 30th Demi-Brigade. He transferred back to Dutch service and in 1803 was the colonel of the 2nd Dutch Light Infantry Regiment.

Promoted major-general in 1806, he served briefly in Spain before taking part in Napoleon's Wagram campaign of 1809. The following year he was back in Spain as a brigade commander initially of Dutch troops in the IV Army Corps under Lefèbvre-Desnouëttes. Later he became a French brigade commander in the 2nd Division with d'Erlon as his corps commander. Chassé fought hard in Spain, becoming a highly experienced infantry commander. His brigade was heavily engaged at Durango, Talavera, Vitoria, Maya, Sorauren, during the withdrawal through the Pyrenees, the defence of the river lines of the Nivelle and the Nive, and then at the battles of Orthez and Toulouse. He particularly distinguished himself during the 1814 campaign in France where, for his services in the final battle of Arcis-sur-Aube, he was made a Baron of the Empire. After the Emperor's first abdication Chassé reverted to serving the Kingdom of Holland, and in 1815 was given command of the 3rd Netherlands Infantry Division to lead against his former comrades.

At Waterloo his division had twelve battalions (three Belgian and nine Dutch), six in Colonel Detmer's 1st Brigade and six in Major-General d'Aubreme's 2nd Brigade. Perhaps because Wellington had some misgivings as to the quality of the troops and the loyalty of their general, this division was initially posted well behind the front line, on the extreme western flank near the village of Braine l'Alleud. This was some 2,500 metres from the Duke's elm tree in the centre. The division was not committed to the battle until the end, when the Middle Guard launched its assault. Chassé's division had been moved into reserve behind the right centre and, as the Imperial Guard reached the ridge, he launched Detmer's men in a furious counter-stroke that chased away what was left of the 1/3 and 4th Grenadiers.

From 1819 Chassé was commandant of the fortress at Antwerp, which he defended for two years (1830–32) until forced to surrender to Maréchal Etienne Gérard who had commanded IV Corps at Ligny and Wavre. After retirement he was a member of the Estates-General of the Netherlands. He died aged eighty-four – yet another Waterloo general to become an octogenarian.

Trip, Major-General A.D. (1776–1835)

At Waterloo Trip had command of the heavy cavalry brigade in Collaert's Netherlands Cavalry Division. He had three regiments, the 1st and 3rd Dutch Carabiniers and the 2nd Belgian Carabiniers – in total over 1,200 sabres. Of the three brigade commanders in this division, all of whom had fought for the French, Trip and his men proved the least reliable. Although he performed with some credit in the earlier part of the afternoon, attacking French cavalry that penetrated between the infantry squares, several accounts of his later performance are damning.

During the late afternoon the Earl of Uxbridge placed himself in front of the remnants of the Household Brigade, with Trip's brigade in support, to charge an advancing enemy column supported by cavalry. Somerset's squadrons charged but were driven off by the infantry. As they withdrew, the French cuirassiers advanced and Uxbridge sought to lead Trip's men forward against them. Within a few metres his ADC galloped alongside him to point out that he was alone. Not a man had followed. Uxbridge gave Trip a personal dressing down and tried again but with the same result. The Dutch and Belgian troopers had seen enough, turned about, and rode to the rear in considerable haste and disorder, becoming entangled with two squadrons of the 3rd Hussars of the KGL in the process. However, the veracity of these events is placed in some doubt, as Trip was the only Netherlands cavalry general to be singled out for commendation by Wellington in his despatch.

He died in 1835, aged fifty-nine.

Ghigny, Major-General Baron Charles-Etienne de (1771–1844)

Ghigny commanded the 1st Light Cavalry Brigade in Collaert's Netherlands Cavalry Division. His two regiments combined totalled nearly 1,100 men, with the 4th Dutch Light Dragoons being particularly strong at almost 650 all ranks. The 8th Belgian Hussars mustered less than 450.

He was born in Brussels and first saw active service as a captain in the Belgian Legion fighting under French colours. He went on to amass considerable experience fighting for the French on the Rhine, at Hanover, in Portugal, Spain, Prussia and in Russia. After Napoleon's first abdication Ghigny asked to return home where he was appointed a colonel in the Netherlands Army. In April 1815 he was promoted major-general and later given command of the light cavalry brigade in Wellington's Anglo-Allied force.

His brigade did well in the early afternoon at Waterloo. Having moved forward from reserve near Mont St Jean farm on his own initiative, Ghigny joined with Vandeleur's light cavalry brigade to charge some of Jacquinot's lancers who had just badly mauled the Union Brigade, killing its commander, Major-General

Ponsonby. Ghigny has described this action: 'We caused the whole of the cavalry which was in front of us, composed of lancers [Colonel Bro's 4th Lancers], to retire until it reached the flank of a very numerous battalion [in Durutte's division] formed in square … . As the enemy's fire became very vigorous I ordered the "Retire".' Ghigny then supported Vandeleur in covering the remains of the Union Brigade as it scrambled back to safety. He was also heavily engaged during the afternoon in several counter-attacks against the hordes of French horsemen that penetrated between the Allied infantry squares. The intensity of the combat is illustrated by the fact that his regiments suffered 49 per cent losses, mostly during the vicious mêlées against sabre and lance.

After Waterloo Ghigny spent some time as inspector of cavalry in the army of occupation around Liège. He was promoted lieutenant-general in 1826 and died in 1844, aged seventy-three, and was buried in Brussels.

Merlen, Major-General Baron Jean-Baptiste van (1773–1815)

Merlen commanded the 2nd Netherlands Light Cavalry Brigade at Waterloo, a force of just under 750 sabres. His brigade had two regiments – the 6th Dutch Hussars and the 5th Belgian Light Dragoons.

Merlen's career had, until 1811, been in the Dutch Army where he had risen to the rank of colonel. After Napoleon incorporated Holland into the empire in 1810, Merlen transferred to the 5th squadron of the recently formed Dutch (Red) Lancers of the Guard, officially entitled the 2nd Regiment de Chevau Lanciers de la Garde. The bulk of this regiment had formerly been the Dutch Royal Guards, who kept their predominantly red uniforms, but found themselves with lances and Polish drill sergeants. Merlen fought with them in Russia, where they suffered heavily, and in the struggle for France in 1813–14, rising to general's rank.

After Napoleon's first abdication Merlen returned home and joined the service of the United Netherlands, not realizing that Napoleon would ever return. Nevertheless, when he did so in 1815 Merlen kept his new allegiance and fought his former comrades. Not only did he draw his sword against his old Emperor and his old regiment, but also against his younger brother who was serving in Reille's II Corps. His brigade arrived at Quatre-Bras around 3.00 p.m. and was soon fully committed against Foy's advancing infantry. However, Merlen was caught by the superior numbers of Piré's cavalry and thrown back in some confusion – it was at this time that Wellington was compelled to leap for his life over the crouching 92nd Foot (Highlanders) and take shelter behind their line. The brigade lost 171 men at Quatre-Bras.

At Waterloo the brigade, along with the rest of Collaert's division, was held back in reserve in the fourth line near Mont St Jean farm. It was engaged in the numerous cavalry counterattacks against the French cavalry that swarmed round the infantry squares throughout the afternoon. Merlen was very much the chivalrous officer and gentleman. During one mêlée it was said that he could have captured a French general whom he knew well. Instead he saluted, saying, 'General, this is my side of the battlefield, yours is over there. Take care of yourself; farewell!' Shortly after this Merlen was badly wounded and carried to a shed near Mont St Jean farm where he died two hours later. His last words were that he died at peace, never having harmed anyone. Strange words from a soldier who had seen so many battlefields.

II CORPS

Hill, Lieutenant-General Lord Rowland (1772–1842)

Rowland Hill became one of the very few generals who Wellington trusted with anything like an independent command during the Peninsular War. During the Waterloo campaign he commanded II Corps, the bulk of which was stationed around Hal and Tubize and so took no part in the battle. The only formations of Hill's corps that saw action at Waterloo were the 2nd British Infantry Division and the 4th British Brigade from General Colville's 4th British Division.

Hill was commissioned as an ensign in the 38th Foot (Staffords) in 1790, became a lieutenant in the 53rd Foot (Shropshire) in 1793 and was an ADC to General O'Hara at the defence of Toulon – where a certain French artillery officer named Bonaparte first came to prominence. In 1801 Hill commanded the 90th Foot (Perthshire Volunteers) at the age of twenty-three in Egypt (where he was wounded). He was appointed a brigade commander in the Peninsular in 1808, a divisional commander in 1809 and promoted lieutenant-general in 1812. He took part in most of the major battles in Spain, Portugal and southern France, including Rolica, Corunna, Talavera, Arroyo dos Molinos (Hill's own victory), Merida, Almaraz, Vitoria, the Nivelle, the Nive, Bayonne and Toulouse. His operations were always carried out with care, foresight and consideration for the well being of his troops. He was a kind and charitable man rarely, if ever, known to swear, whom his soldiers affectionately called 'Daddy Hill'. He was created a baron in 1814.

At Waterloo, with his corps split between Hal and in reserve near Mont St Jean, Hill did not have particularly demanding duties or responsibilities. Few accounts of the battle mention him, while one writer has cast doubt (erroneously) on his presence on the field at all. Hill was certainly present throughout the day. When he arrived on the position well before the battle, he was given a rousing welcome from those veterans who remembered him with affection from the old Peninsular days. One recorded:

> On the arrival of General Hill … we all stood up and gave him three hearty cheers, as we had long been under his command in the Peninsula, and loved him dearly on account of his kind and fatherly conduct towards us. When he came among us he spoke in a very kindly manner and enquired concerning our welfare.

The highlight of his day came in the evening when he led Adam's brigade forward against the Imperial Guard, only to have his horse shot and roll over him, giving him severe bruising and slight concussion. Hill had two brothers serving at Waterloo, both officers in the Royal Horse Guards; both were wounded. Lieutenant-Colonel Clement Hill, who was an ADC to his brother, had his leg pinned to his saddle by a sword thrust. Lieutenant-Colonel Sir Robert Hill, who commanded the Royal Horse Guards, was wounded in the arm.

Hill served as second-in-command of the Army of Occupation in France, thereafter retiring to live the life of a country gentleman on his Shropshire estate. When Wellington became Prime Minister in 1828 he accepted the post of Commander-in-Chief of the Army, a position he held for fourteen years. He was made full general in 1825. Within a few months of being made a viscount in 1842 he died at the age of seventy. He was probably the only general to have Wellington's absolute trust. After his death the Duke wrote: 'nothing ever occurred to interrupt for one moment the friendly and intimate relations that subsisted between us'.

Clinton, Lieutenant-General Sir Henry (1771–1829)

The commander of the 2nd British Infantry Division at Waterloo. This division was almost 8000 strong, having British, KGL and Hanoverian brigades.

Clinton's father had commanded the British forces in the American War of Independence. Henry Clinton was commissioned in 1787, served in Holland for the next two years and in 1793 became an ADC to the Duke of York. For the next twelve years his career was far from typical. Promoted lieutenant-colonel in 1795, he was captured by the French and spent two years in captivity (1796–7). In 1799 he served as a liaison officer in Suvorov's Russian Army in Northern Italy. In 1802 Clinton went to India for three years as adjutant-general, then on his return he was once again attached to the Russian Army. Unique among British Waterloo generals he was at the Austro-Russian headquarters at the Battle of Austerlitz in December 1805. Next came a year as the commandant of Syracuse in Sicily. In 1808 he became an MP at the start of a ten-year political career interspersed with periods of military duty in Spain and Portugal.

Clinton was adjutant-general to Sir John Moore during the brief Corunna campaign, and in 1810 was promoted to major-general. The following year, when Wellington was in urgent need of competent general officers, he refused to have Clinton. The British Army historian Fortescue wrote that Clinton, 'for some personal reason, was held to be hopelessly unacceptable to Wellington.' Nevertheless, within a year he was in Spain commanding the 6th Division with some credit at Salamanca, although his frontal assault up the steep slopes of the Greater Arapil cost his division 1,200 men out of 2,800. Twice within the next four months he incurred Wellington's displeasure. On both occasions it involved failure to follow orders. When he marched his column to cross a river at a bridge he had been specifically told not to use, causing a chaotic bottleneck, Wellington was almost speechless with anger. He later commented, 'By God, it was too serious to say anything.' Clinton, however, was a survivor and soldiered on through the remainder of the Peninsular War, receiving promotion to lieutenant-general in 1814, having fought at the Nivelle, the Nive, Orthez and Toulouse.

At Waterloo his division was held in reserve for much of the day behind the right wing, only moving up to the front line mid-afternoon. His 3rd British Brigade under Major-General Adam was to play a prominent part in the repulse of the final Imperial Guard attack.

Clinton died fourteen years after the battle, aged fifty-eight.

Adam, Major-General Frederick (1781–1853)

Adam was only thirty-four at Waterloo and yet commanded the 3rd British Brigade, a strong (almost 3000 men), élite light infantry formation that included the 95th Rifles and the 1/52 under the famous Sir John Colbourne of Peninsula renown. His battalion, with 1,130 all ranks, was the largest in Wellington's army.

Adam's early career, like the Duke's, was an outstanding example of how to work the system of purchase and exchange of commissions to secure rapid promotion. He was commissioned as an ensign into the 26th Foot (Cameronians) by purchase at fourteen. He continued his education and studied at the Military Academy, Woolwich. He became a lieutenant at fifteen and a captain at eighteen in the 27th Foot (Inniskilling), going on active service with them to Holland. This was followed by four months as a company commander in the 9th Foot (East Norfolk) which ended with a swift exchange into the Coldstream Guards. Adam served in Egypt

in 1801, became a major in 1803, and the lieutenant-colonel of the 5th Garrison Battalion the following year. Finally, at the age of twenty-five, he purchased the command of the 21st Foot (Royal North British Fusiliers) in 1805. He had obtained five promotions in six regiments in nine years.

The following year he was appointed the Deputy Adjutant-General in Sicily and was present at the Battle of Maida in 1806. By 1811 he was an ADC to the Prince Regent before being sent to the Peninsula as a brigade commander in the somewhat forgotten east coast theatre of Spain. There he saw action and was wounded twice, on the second occasion his left arm and hand were shattered during his defence of the pass at Ordal in 1813. Adam was promoted major-general the next year.

At Waterloo his brigade, as part of Clinton's division, was kept in reserve behind Wellington's right flank until late mid-afternoon. When called forward it formed in squares on the forward slope east of Hougoumont, where it came under intense artillery fire and was pulled back behind the ridge. Later the brigade played a major role in repulsing the final attack of the Imperial Guard during which Adam was wounded.

In later years Adam became a general and the Governor of the Ionian Islands. He died suddenly of a heart attack at Greenwich railway station in 1853, aged seventy-two.

Picton, Lieutenant-General Sir Thomas (1758–1815)

Wellington once called Picton, the commander of the 5th British Infantry Division at Waterloo, as 'rough, foul-mouthed a devil as ever lived'. He was certainly coarse, moody and impetuous but was also an able commander who had the grudging respect of his troops, if not their love. The Earl of Albemarle described Picton as 'a strong-built man, with a red face, small black eyes, and large nose'. His career was not without its controversies. He was commissioned as an ensign into the 12th Foot (East Suffolk) at thirteen. A captain at twenty, he spent most of the next twelve years on half-pay on his family estate in Pembrokeshire, until in 1794 the urge for action got the better of him and he sailed, on his own initiative, to the West Indies. There he was given a place on the staff of General Abercromby. He took part in the capture of St Lucia and Trinidad in 1796–7, and continued to serve in this unpopular and unhealthy station for over ten years. During this time he secured promotion to brigadier-general and became first military, and then civil, Governor of Trinidad. Then came controversy. Picton was recalled after being accused of condoning the use of torture on a local woman to exact a confession to a crime. Picton returned to England in 1806 to face charges but got off on the technicality that local Spanish law allowed such things.

In 1808 he was a major-general. The following year he took part in the Siege of Flushing and in 1810 was appointed to command the 3rd Division in the Peninsula. At his first inspection he held a court martial for two men of the 88th Foot (Connaught Rangers) for stealing a goat. He stayed to watch their flogging. He then addressed the Regiment in vitriolic terms, reflecting disparagingly on their Irish origin and religion. He told them they would be known in the army as the 'Irish Footpads'. The feud between Picton and the regiment lasted the war. Five years on the 88th refused to subscribe to a presentation plate being given to Picton by the division. A quick-tempered disciplinarian he might be but he never lacked for courage. At Busaco, Fuentes de Onoro and at Badajoz (where he was badly wounded in the storming and consequently invalided home) he led from the front. In 1813 he was knighted and promoted lieutenant-general. At Vitoria he urged his men forward yelling, 'Come on you damned rascals, come on you fighting villains.' His initiative that day undoubtedly contributed to the victory. He took his division through the Pyrenees, into France until the Battle of Toulouse concluded the campaign.

But at fifty-six Picton had had enough of soldiering. He was disgruntled by the fact that, although thanked by the House of Commons seven times for his services, he was not given a peerage. Only with extreme reluctance did he agree to join Wellington to command the 5th British Infantry Division at Waterloo. He had also had a premonition of death – before leaving for Belgium he had lain down in an open grave exclaiming that it was just his size. Before leaving London he made his will. His division lost heavily at Quatre-Bras and he himself had several ribs broken although he concealed the fact. On 18 June he was shot dead through his top hat while leading his men forward to repulse Donzelot's division at about 2.00 p.m. He was one of only two British generals to die at Waterloo, the other being Major-General Ponsonby. Picton had the privilege of three burials – one at Waterloo, then at St George's, London, and finally at St Paul's Cathedral in 1859.

Kempt, Major-General Sir James (1764–1854)

At Waterloo Kempt commanded the 8th British Brigade under his old divisional commander from Peninsula days, Picton. He had almost 2000 men in four battalions – the 1/28 (North Gloucestershire), 1/32 (Cornwall), 1/79 (Cameron Highlanders) and six companies of the 1/95 Rifles.

Kempt had been commissioned at nineteen into the 101st Foot (Duke of York's Irish). By 1794 he was a major, five years later a lieutenant-colonel and ADC to General Abercromby in Holland. He accompanied Abercromby to Egypt in 1800 as his military secretary, being present at the capture of Cairo and Alexandria. He commanded the 81st (2nd Loyal North Lancashire) and fought at the Battle of Maida in 1806. The following year he was QMG to the British forces in North America. In 1809 he was promoted colonel and made an ADC to the King. Kempt was promoted to major-general in 1812 and commanded a brigade in the Peninsula. He was severely wounded at Badajoz but recovered to lead his brigade through until the end of the war. He was in action at Vitoria, the Nivelle, the Nive, Orthez and Toulouse.

Kempt's brigade was fully committed at Quatre-Bras. Lady Butler's famous painting of the battle shows one of his battalions, the 1/28, in square facing French cavalry. At Waterloo his battalions were deployed immediately east of the crossroads in the centre of the line. This was just to the rear (north) of the sandpit that was garrisoned by part of the 1/95 Rifles. Kempt's brigade was actively engaged throughout most of the day, particularly during the repulse of d'Erlon's main assault in the early afternoon. Kempt took over as divisional commander of the 5th Division when Picton was shot.

Kempt had a distinguished career after Waterloo. From 1820–28 he was Governor of Nova Scotia and for the next two years Governor-General of Canada. He became a Privy Councillor, Master-General of the Ordnance, and a full general in 1841. When he died in London, aged almost ninety, he had reached the greatest age of any of his fellow Waterloo generals.

Pack, Major-General Sir Denis (1772–1823)

Pack commanded the 9th British Brigade in Picton's 5th Division at Waterloo. It was a comparatively weak formation with less than 1,700 all ranks in the four battalions, all of which were under 500 strong. The 42nd (Black Watch) had the dubious distinction, with 338 all ranks, of being the weakest battalion in the army. The other battalions were the 3/1 (Royal Scots), the 2/44 (Essex) and the 92nd (Gordon Highlanders).

Their commander was noted as being fidgety, with an irascible temper, although a competent general. Not long after escaping from the Spaniards to Montevideo in South America, a long suffering soldier chalked on a barn door:

> *The devil break the gaoler's back*
> *That set thee loose, sweet Denis Pack.*

He joined the 4th Dragoons as a cornet in 1791 and saw service in Holland and during the expedition to Quiberon Bay in 1795. As a captain he served in the Irish Rebellion. He travelled extensively. In 1805 he took part in the expedition to the Cape of Good Hope; the following year he was in South America where he took part in six actions, was captured, escaped and participated in the landing and subsequent attack on Buenos Aires. In 1808 he was with Wellesley in Portugal and fought at Rolica, Vimiero and Corunna in command of the 71st (Glasgow Highlanders). This was followed in 1809 by action in the Walcheren expedition and the Siege of Flushing. Pack then refused promotion and a command in Canada in order to return to the Peninsula as a lieutenant-colonel commanding a Portuguese brigade. He was present at the Battle of Busaco, the Siege of Ciudad Rodrigo, the Battle at Salamanca, the Siege of Burgos and the Battles at Vitoria, Pyrenees, Nivelle, Nive, Orthez and Toulouse. He was wounded five times during these years and once again at Waterloo.

In June 1815 Pack's brigade suffered heavily at Quatre-Bras, where it was deployed just east of the crossroads. Here it had a severe pounding by gunfire and was subjected to continuous cavalry attacks, one of which briefly penetrated the square of the 42nd. At Waterloo the brigade was posted in the front line some 500 metres east of the 'Elm Tree' crossroads. Here it participated in throwing back d'Erlon's massive infantry assault in the early afternoon. At one stage Pack was obliged to yell at the Gordon Highlanders, 'Ninety-second, you must charge! All the troops in your front have given way!' Charge they did, with a number joining with the Union Brigade cavalry counterattack that smashed the attacking French column.

He later became Lieutenant-Governor of Plymouth before dying in London at the relatively young age of fifty-one.

Lambert, Major-General Sir John (1772–1847)

Lambert commanded the 10th British Brigade at Waterloo, although due to Lieutenant-General Sir Lowry Cole being on his honeymoon Lambert was acting as the 6th British Division commander after his late arrival on the field. This meant that he also commanded Colonel Best's 4th Hanoverian Brigade of four battalions which, until his arrival, had been attached to Picton's 5th Division. Lambert's brigade was an exceptionally strong one, with four battalions. Despite the weakest, the 1/81 (2nd Loyal North Lancashire), being left in Brussels Lambert still had almost 2,300 all ranks with each battalion being well above average strength. His brigade consisted of the 1/4 (King's Own), the 1/27 (Inniskilling), and the strongest, with some 860 all ranks, the 1/40 (Somerset).

Lambert's early career had been with the Foot Guards. He was commissioned ensign in the 1st Foot Guards in 1791 and served in Flanders, being present at the Sieges of Valenciennes and

Dunkirk. Two years later he secured promotion to lieutenant and captain (his next promotion would be to captain and lieutenant-colonel, as this rank structure, peculiar to the Guards, gave its officers seniority over Line lieutenants or captains). In 1794 he was appointed adjutant, served with the Guards during the Irish uprising before getting his company as a captain and lieutenant-colonel in 1801. He took part in the Walcheren expedition, became a colonel in 1810 and a major-general in 1813.

The bulk of Lambert's experience came as a brigade commander in the Peninsular War. His brigade took part in the Battles of the Nivelle, the Nive, Orthez and Toulouse. In January 1815 he had his first brief but bitter experience of high command in America. He was serving under Sir Edward Pakenham during the combined operations off the coast of New Orleans. During the subsequent attack on the city (defended by a rag-bag of American militia, 'irregulars', Indians and with French pirates manning the cannons) Pakenham was shot dead and all other senior generals killed or wounded. Command devolved on Lambert who was forced to accept failure and re-embark the army.

Lambert had only just returned from America in mid-June when he and his brigade were disembarked at Ostend. The brigade marched straight from the ships to Ghent, and thence the 70 kilometres to Waterloo via Brussels (where the 1/81 remained). The brigade had missed Quatre-Bras, only arriving at Mont St Jean around 10.30 a.m. on 18 June. They were placed in reserve near the farm of that name. In the afternoon Lambert was called forward and took up position immediately east of the 'Elm Tree' crossroads. Here they remained until the end of the battle, suffering some 25 per cent casualties, mostly from cannon fire. The 1/27 remained in the same spot the entire time and, literally, died in square (66 per cent became casualties, with sergeants ending up as company commanders).

THE CAVALRY CORPS

Paget, Lieutenant-General Henry William, Earl of Uxbridge (1768–1854)

Paget commanded the Cavalry Corps at Waterloo and would have taken command of the Anglo-Allied Army if the Duke had been a casualty. His corps was large, some 10,000 British and KGL horsemen, divided into two heavy and five light brigades plus the Hanoverian Cumberland Hussars. He also controlled thirty-five guns and a rocket section.

Paget was not of noble birth, being born in London into an unknown and not particularly wealthy family. A year later his father inherited a baronetcy, so his name changed from Henry Bayly to Henry Paget, the son of the new Lord and Lady Paget. When Henry was twelve the family, for unknown reasons, inherited a 100,000 acres of mining land in England and Ireland. Young Henry went to Westminster School and Christchurch College, Oxford. For twenty years (1790–1810) Paget was an MP, first for Carnarvon and then for Milborne Port. In 1793 he started his military career by raising, at his father's expense, the 80th Foot (Staffordshire Volunteers). He fought in Flanders in 1794 and again in 1799, this time as commander of the 7th Light Dragoons. He made his name as a competent cavalry leader in the early part of the Peninsular War while commanding the cavalry of Sir John Moore's army in Portugal and Spain during the Corunna campaign. He won two cavalry actions at Sahagun and Benavente before covering the disastrous retreat to Corunna. The same year he joined the ill-fated Walcheren expedition.

The Earl of Uxbridge's Wound

Most accounts of Waterloo include the statement that Uxbridge had his leg smashed by a cannonball. This is highly unlikely. Firstly, if a cannonball had hit his knee it would have torn the leg from his body; secondly, killed his horse and, finally, the bleeding from such a horrendous wound would have ensured his death from loss of blood before he reached the surgeon. The chances of his being hit a glancing blow, by a bouncing cannonball that had lost much of its velocity is also remote, as the ground was too soft for much bouncing. The probability must surely be that Uxbridge was struck by a shell splinter.

That Paget did not join Wellesley again in the Peninsula was due to his eloping with the general's sister-in-law. Paget deserted his wife, Lady Caroline (known as 'Car') with whom he had eight children, for Lady Charlotte Wellesley (known as 'Char'), the wife of Wellington's brother, Henry. She was to bear him another ten children – Paget's loss of a leg at Waterloo doing little to spoil his performance. The scandal of this affair rocked London society.

When the Earl of Uxbridge, as Paget was then known, arrived to command the cavalry at Waterloo there was some coolness between him and the Duke but no obvious animosity. His command of the cavalry rearguard during the retreat from Quatre-Bras was masterly. As far as Uxbridge was concerned, the highlights of Waterloo were when he launched and led the heavy cavalry (Household and Union Brigades) at d'Erlon's corps, and when he had his right knee smashed by a shell splinter in the closing minutes of the action. He stoically bore the agony of amputation in Waterloo Cottage (now called Château Tremblant) without having to be held down. The leg was buried in the back garden while Uxbridge thereafter gained the nickname 'One-Leg'.

He became the Marquis of Anglesey shortly after Waterloo and in 1828 the Lord Lieutenant of Ireland where he showed himself to be an able administrator, although his obvious favouring of Roman Catholics brought him into conflict with Wellington, who was then Prime Minister. He was made a field-marshal in 1846 and died at the great age of eighty-six some eight years later. His son, Lord George Paget, was second-in-command to the Earl of Cardigan during the famous charge of the Light Brigade in the Crimean War.

Somerset, Major-General Lord Edward (1776–1842)

Somerset was the elder brother of Fitzroy Somerset, the Duke's young military secretary who lost an arm at Waterloo and went on to be the British commander-in-chief in the Crimea. An experienced light cavalryman, he found himself commanding 'heavies' at Waterloo – the 1st British (Household) Cavalry Brigade. It was a weak formation considering it contained four regiments, with only just over 1,300 sabres. The 1st Life Guards had only two squadrons, as did the 2nd Life Guards and the Royal Horse Guards. Only the 1st Dragoon Guards could muster three strong squadrons with over 175 troopers apiece.

This officer, usually known as 'Lord Edward Somerset' had joined the 10th Light Dragoons as a cornet in 1793 and was a captain a year later. He had a brief spell as a major in the 12th Light Dragoons and an even briefer one as an infantryman commanding the 5th Foot (Northumberland Regiment). He served with the cavalry in Flanders in 1799 and throughout the Peninsular War where, for much of the time, he commanded the 4th Light Dragoons.

He made a name for himself at the Battle of Salamanca in 1812 when, at the head of one squadron, he captured five French guns. By the end of the campaign he was commanding a brigade of light cavalry composed of the 7th, 10th and 15th Hussars. He had participated in seven major actions, including Talavera, Salamanca, Vitoria, Orthez and Toulouse.

His regiments played a critical role in delaying the French pursuit through the thunderstorms of the night of 17/18 June, as Wellington's waterlogged infantry marched to the Mont St Jean ridge. At Waterloo his brigade was initially deployed well back in reserve some 250 metres south of Mont St Jean farm and immediately west of the road from Brussels. Somerset's moment of glory came when he charged his brigade into the French cuirassiers protecting the left flank of d'Erlon's massive attack. Somerset survived the battle unscathed, despite his horse being killed by a cannonball, although his brigade did not – they lost some 47 per cent. At the end of the day the Household Brigade had to combine with the Union Brigade to produce a single line of horsemen: the equivalent of one squadron.

Somerset later commanded the British cavalry during the occupation of France and went on to become a full general in 1841. He died the following year, aged sixty-six.

Ponsonby, Major-General Sir William (1772–1815)

Sir William Ponsonby (not to be confused with Lieutenant-Colonel Hon. F.C. Ponsonby who commanded the 12th Light Dragoons) commanded the 2nd British Cavalry Brigade at Waterloo. This was also called the Union Brigade, as it had a regiment each from England, Scotland and Ireland. They were the 1st (Royal) Dragoons, the 2nd Royal North British Dragoons (Scots Greys) and the 6th Inniskilling Dragoons. Although the Union Brigade had only three regiments, they each had three squadrons of about 150 troopers, so it was as strong numerically as the four regiment Household Brigade.

Ponsonby obtained command of the 5th Dragoon Guards in 1803 and then served for three years as a cavalry brigade commander in the Peninsula, being present at Vitoria and the actions through to the end of the campaign. Wellington personally congratulated Ponsonby and his brigade for not joining in the mad scramble for loot after the Battle of Vitoria. His troops had ridden past and ignored a mass of coins scattered beside the Pamplona road. Ponsonby's only concession was to detach a sergeant-major to collect as much as he could for the whole Regiment. He later stumbled in with a sack full of silver, enough for five Spanish dollars each for all 1,300 men. Ponsonby's brigade finished the war with a unique record – no soldier had ever been arraigned before a General Court Martial.

At Waterloo his brigade was posted just south of Mont St Jean Farm, in reserve immediately east of the Brussels road. From there they were launched against the attacking infantry columns of Donzelot and Marcognet. The French disintegrated in chaos with the 105th Ligne losing its Eagle to the combined efforts of Captain Kennedy and Corporal Stiles of the 1st Dragoons. This charge developed into a wild, uncontrolled rush for the French 'Grand Battery'. After several exhilarating minutes sabreing artillerymen, the brigade was struck by the enemy's cavalry counterattack. Jacquinot's lancers inflicted massive damage. Included among the fatalities was Ponsonby. Caught in the soggy ground on a blown and inferior horse he was speared to death with seven lance thrusts. By the end of the day his brigade had lost nearly 50 per cent of its men.

Dornberg, Major-General Sir William (Wilhelm von) (1768–1850)

Dornberg commanded the 3rd British Cavalry Brigade at Waterloo. It was a predominantly German speaking light cavalry formation, with two KGL Regiments and one British totalling 1,400 all ranks. The regiments were the 23rd Light Dragoons, whose commanding officer arrived on the battlefield too late to assume command, and the 1st and 2nd KGL Light Dragoons.

The brigade's commander was German by birth, a competent Hanoverian officer who refused to join the KGL in Britain when Hanover fell to France. Instead, he joined the French service in 1807. By 1809 he had risen to be a royal adjutant and colonel commanding Prince Jérôme's Garde-Jaeger in the Napoleonic State of Westphalia (Napoleon had enthroned his brother Jérôme as king). Dornberg's objective, however, was not to fight for the French but rather to organize a rebellion against them from within the army. The rebellion, when it came in April 1809, was poorly organized and the rebels speedily dispersed (within two days). Dornberg fled to Bohemia disguised as a peasant. He eventually joined the Brunswick Corps and in 1812 was promoted major-general.

During the Waterloo campaign Dornberg's command fulfilled a key function in patrolling the 20 miles of Belgian border south of Mons. Any French advance up the Mauberge–Mons road (Map 5) would clash with his horsemen first. This was the route that Wellington worried about. Dornberg, with his headquarters in Mons, sent a regular stream of reports to Brussels in the days prior to the French advance. However, on 14 June he made an error. A report from an agent, originating from Wellington's spymaster (Colonel Grant) behind enemy lines, indicated clearly that the French were converging on Charleroi and thence, almost inevitably, up the paved road north to Brussels. In passing on the report Dornberg omitted to mention this critical information and the source of the intelligence. This delayed Wellington's decision on where to concentrate his scattered army, thereby giving Napoleon a few more precious hours to thrust north – between his adversaries.

At the start of the battle Dornberg was deployed some 200 metres behind Maitland's Guards, on the right of the Anglo-Allied line. They were engaged during the afternoon in helping to drive off French cavalry that penetrated between the Allied squares, and in the general advance at the end of the battle. Dornberg's casualties amounted to 302, himself being one of them.

He subsequently received promotion to lieutenant-general and for a time served as ambassador at St Petersburg. He died in 1850, aged eighty-two.

Vandeleur, Major-General Sir John (1763–1849)

Vandeleur commanded the 6th British Cavalry Brigade at Waterloo. It consisted of the 11th, 12th and 16th Light Dragoon regiments, each of three squadrons with about 140 all ranks apiece – the 12th and 16th having been under his command in the closing months of the Peninsular War.

Purchase and exchange secured Vandeleur a steady rise in rank from ensign to lieutenant-colonel between 1781 to 1798. In the process he joined four infantry and two cavalry regiments. During those years he served in the West Indies, Flanders and the Cape of Good Hope, finally ending up as a local colonel in command of a cavalry brigade in India in 1802. He did well manoeuvring his horsemen under the swirling red dust clouds of Hindustan as part of Lord Lake's force. In 1803 the Second Maratha War began. While Wellesley was campaigning in the Deccan, Lake was operating in Hindustan. In November of that year Vandeleur at the Battle of Laswari was able to lead his brigade around the Indians' flank before charging in to capture 2000 prisoners.

Made a substantive colonel in 1808 and major-general in 1811, Vandeleur was sent to Spain as an infantry brigade commander in the élite Light Division under Major-General 'Black Bob' Crauford. Crauford was killed at the Siege of Ciudad Rodrigo and Vandeleur was wounded, thus missing the bloodbath at Badajoz. He recovered to fight again at Salamanca and, still in the Light Division, fought at Vitoria and the Nivelle in 1813. In July he was transferred back to the cavalry, assuming command of a light cavalry brigade of two Regiments – the 12th and 16th Light Dragoons. He remained in action until the end of the campaign.

June 1815 saw Vandeleur's brigade screening the Duke's army as it pulled back from Quatre-Bras to the Mont St Jean ridge in the drenching rain of the night of 17th/18th. For most of the battle on the Sunday Vandeleur was posted behind (north of) Papelotte village on the left of Wellington's line. It was something of a backwater for the cavalry until around 2.30 p.m. It was then that the 12th and 16th Light Dragoons, with Vandeleur heading the latter (the 11th remained in reserve), charged into the valley to cover the retreat of the Union Brigade. They clashed with Jacquinot's lancers and both commanding officers were severely wounded, with the 12th sustaining particularly heavy losses. Later in the day as the fighting intensified in the centre and on the right, Vandeleur was positioned behind the right centre, west of the Brussels road. From there he led his brigade forward as part of the general advance in the late evening.

Vandeleur lived to be eighty-seven.

Grant, Major-General Sir Colquhoun (1764–1835)

Commanded the 5th British Cavalry Brigade of over 1,250 all ranks at Waterloo. This light cavalry formation consisted of the 7th and 15th Hussars, plus the 13th Light Dragoons (attached from the 7th Cavalry Brigade) who had replaced the third regiment which was the 2nd Hussars (KGL) who were still patrolling the border. Each regiment had three squadrons.

Grant (not to be confused with his famous namesake, the intelligence officer) could trace his Scottish ancestry back many centuries. He joined the 36th Foot (Herefordshire) as an ensign at the advanced age of twenty-nine, exchanging into the 25th (later the 22nd) Light Dragoons. He served with Wellesley in India, being present at the action at Malavelly and the Siege of Seringapatam in 1799. In 1801 he was a major in the 28th Light Dragoons. The following year he obtained command of the 72nd Foot (Highland) and took them to the Cape of Good Hope where he was wounded in action. A spell as ADC to the Prince Regent was to prove its value in later years. In 1808 he switched back to the cavalry in time to command the 15th Hussars at the Battle of Sahagun and the retreat to Corunna.

He was a huge man, an imposing figure who deserved the nickname, 'the Black Giant'. However, although he did not lack for courage, he was not one of the Duke's favourite generals. At the Battle of Vitoria he commanded a light cavalry brigade which he hurled straight at three French infantry squares supported by cannons. Predictably, the leading squadron of the 18th Light

Dragoons was blown away, forcing Grant to pull back from such foolishness. After the battle his troops were foremost among the looters in the city where fortunes were to be picked up, quite literally, off the ground. Wellington caught the 18th Light Dragoons in the act and was livid, banning all promotions in the regiment. Grant had allowed his brigade to get out of control, and was widely believed to have helped himself generously from the pickings. Whatever the truth, the Duke demanded his recall resulting in Grant being relieved of his command pending a ship to England. However, he never left Spain and, with his powerful friends at the Horse Guards, soon reappeared as a brigade commander for the remainder of the campaign.

At Waterloo Grant's brigade was deployed behind the Foot Guards on the right of the line, with a squadron of the 15th Light Dragoons covering the extreme right flank. His command saw fierce action in the afternoon when, along with other cavalry formations, it was engaged in counterattacking the French cavalry that swarmed around the Allied squares. Grant was wounded himself and had five horses shot under him. His brigade lost 392 men, almost one in three.

Grant was promoted to lieutenant-general in 1830, becoming MP for Queenborough the following year. In 1833 he inherited large estates in Dorset but died two years later, aged seventy-one.

Vivian, Major-General Sir Hussey (1775–1842)

Vivian commanded the 6th British Cavalry Brigade at Waterloo. It was a comparatively strong formation with 1,500 all ranks – the 10th and 18th Hussars each of three squadrons, and the 1st Hussars of the KGL with four. The latter two regiments had been in his brigade at the end of the Peninsular War.

Vivian was an exceptionally well educated officer. He attended Truro Grammar School, Harrow and Oxford, and was a fluent French speaker. He began his military career as an ensign in the 20th Foot (East Devon) aged eighteen, serving in the Flanders campaigns of 1794 and 1799. In 1798 he exchanged into the 7th Light Dragoons as a lieutenant-colonel – it was quite normal for infantry officers to switch to cavalry or vice versa. He commanded the 7th during the retreat to Corunna in 1808–09. He returned to the Peninsula and was present at the crossing of the Nivelle, the Nive, the action at St Pierre, the Battle of Orthez and in the advance on Toulouse where he was wounded and earned a mention in Wellington's despatches. The Duke wrote: 'Colonel Vivian had an opportunity of making a most gallant attack upon a superior body of the enemy's cavalry, which they drove through the village of Croix D'Orade.' Vivian, who was with the 18th Light Dragoons, had been shot in the arm but cantered back to give the order to charge some French cavalry. He raised his sword to signal the advance but the weight of lifting it snapped the bone in his arm and he fell fainting from the saddle. The 18th charged home, however, and were rewarded with a reluctant, 'Well done, the Eighteenth; by God, well done', by the Duke. Wellington had been less pleased with this regiment's excesses after Vitoria.

At Waterloo Vivian was posted on the extreme left flank of the Anglo-Allied line (1,600 metres from the 'Elm Tree'), and patrolled as far east as Smohain village. The brigade had an uneventful day until after the fall of La Haie Sainte when Vivian, on his own initiative, moved behind the centre to help steady what appeared to be a crumbling line. Vivian took part in the general advance at the end of the battle when his regiments were engaged with retreating enemy infantry and cavalry. A squadron of the 10th Hussars had the temerity to charge one of the squares of the Old Guard Grenadiers that was covering the collapse. They were quickly seen off, their commander, Major Howard, being one of the last British officers to die when, having been knocked off his horse in front of the square, a grenadier stepped forward and beat out his brains with repeated blows of his musket butt.

Vivian had a successful and varied career after Waterloo, being MP for Truro in 1820, Inspector-General of Cavalry for five years from 1825, and MP for Windsor the following year. He was promoted lieutenant-general in 1827, became commander-in-chief in Ireland, groom of the bedchamber to King William IV and MP for East Cornwall. The pinnacle of his career was his appointment as the Master-General of the Ordnance and Privy Councillor in 1835. He died seven years later, aged sixty-seven.

The Prussian Commander-in-Chief
FIELD-MARSHAL PRINCE GEBHARD LEBERECHT VON BLÜCHER (1742–1819)

APPEARANCE AND HEALTH

When Blücher fought at Waterloo it was fifty-seven years since he had first put on a uniform, after being commissioned at fifteen into the Swedish service. At seventy-two he was the oldest man on the battlefield. In appearance he looked his age, with weather-beaten, deeply lined face, stained, bushy white moustache and receding hairline, but his appearance belied his toughness, his physical and mental vigour. In 1814 Oxford University conferred on him an honorary doctorate. At the celebratory dinner Blücher remarked, 'Now, if you have made me a doctor, then Gneisenau [his indispensable chief of staff] must be made at least an apothecary.'

In June 1815 Blücher outwardly remained the hard riding, hard drinking, hard swearing hussar he once was. His horse had been killed under him at Ligny two days before, bringing him crashing down under the flying hooves of French cuirassiers. Miraculously, he avoided capture or serious injury. Dazed, shaken and separated from his headquarters but not seriously hurt, he was carried some 10 kilometres to the rear to Gentines. There, a vigorous rubbing down with brandy, coupled with an internal application of champagne, restored his body and mind sufficiently to resume command and make the most important decision of his career – to confirm the march north to Wavre and endeavour to join with Wellington to crush the French.

In strict medical terms 'Papa Blücher', as his soldiers affectionately called him, was far from fit. He was to die within four years of the battle, not of injuries received from the enemy or in falling from his horse, but a combination of advancing age, hard living and a lifelong fondness of the bottle (in particular, gin and rhubarb).

During his long career as a soldier and farmer he had two periods of serious illness. The first, in 1807–08, had been as much mental as physical – at one point he was convinced that he was pregnant with an elephant! The second was after the stress of the 1813–14 campaign in France where he commanded the Prussian forces with commendable tactical talent, and some success, as Napoleon's army was pushed back to Paris. Poor health had then compelled his retirement. Rest revitalized the old soldier, in spirit as well as body. On his recall to duty as commander-in-chief in 1815 his unrelenting hatred of the French, combined with his sense of duty and his aggressive determination, more than compensated for the insidious effects of ageing and alcohol. Blücher the blustering, aggressive commander, combined with Gneisenau, the meticulous, calculating chief of staff, made an effective military marriage.

PLANS AND ORDERS

It had always been the Allies' intention to fight together on the same battlefield. Napoleon's thrust across the Belgian border at the junction of their scattered armies, Blücher's forward concentration and Wellington's less than lightning response, had given the Emperor an opportunity to crush one enemy at Ligny before the other could come to his assistance. For a variety of reasons Napoleon's victory at Ligny was not decisive, the French follow up of Wellington after Quatre-Bras was late, and the follow up of Blücher after Ligny ineffective. Blücher's temporary absence for several hours after his unhorsing at Ligny meant his chief of staff assumed command. Crucially, he decided to withdraw northwards to Wavre and open up alternative communications with Prussia rather than retreat east (see Maps 6 and 7). When Blücher rejoined his headquarters he emphatically endorsed this plan, insisting his army regroup around Wavre with a view to marching to join Wellington. Despite the uncertainty, the defeat and losses at Ligny coming on top of the problems of supply and lines of communication, Blücher stuck with the overall strategic plan – to fight the enemy together.

To do this Blücher needed to issue orders (through Gneisenau) to move his army, or certainly the bulk of it, westwards towards Wellington. Orders were issued for the march as follows (Map 8):

Difficulties within the Prussian Army

It was no mean achievement that Blücher, after a serious setback at Ligny and the loss of another 10,000 deserters immediately afterwards, got his army to join Wellington in time to tip the balance at Waterloo. It was not just the Saxons that were a problem. Even with the improved administration and staff work, serious difficulties included low quality weapons, inexperienced technical personnel (engineers), and many unwilling recruits from the new territories. Following the 1814 peace many Rhineland territories were absorbed by Prussia and were thus required to furnish troops in 1815. This was not popular. The cultured Rhinelanders regarded most Prussians as barbarians. The people of Mainz declared, 'It took only a year of the Prussian regime to make us sorry they [the French] left.' Despite all this, despite the lack of élite units (guards, grenadiers or cuirassiers) the Prussians fought remarkably well at Ligny and Waterloo – much of the credit belonging to the officer corps who proved effective battlefield leaders.

IV Corps (Bülow) – To lead the advance. Task: to attack the French in flank, supposing Wellington was fully committed at Mont St Jean. Depart Dion le Mont at 4.00 a.m. Route: via Wavre then the southern road through Chapelle St Robert, Chapelle St Lambert, Lasne and Bois de Paris. Distance: 16 kilometres.

II Corps (Pirch I) – Task: to attack the French. Route: to follow IV Corps through Wavre and also take the same southern route. Depart location just south of Wavre after the town cleared by IV Corps. Distance: 14.5 kilometres.

I Corps (Ziethen) – Task: to support Wellington's left (eastern) flank and attack the French as the opportunity presented itself. Depart Bierges 2.00 p.m. Route: via the northern road through Rixensart, Grenval, Ohain to arrive in the La Haie area. Distance: 12.8 kilometres.

III Corps (Thielmann) – Task: to follow I Corps with bulk of his force leaving a strong rearguard to watch the French under Grouchy on the Namur road. However, if (as happened) the French pressed their advance, the corps was to defend Wavre, the line of the River Dyle and protect the Army's rear.

These orders did not fully reflect the urgency of the situation while the staff were over optimistic with their time and distance calculations. IV Corps had the furthest to march but was chosen to lead as it had not been engaged at Ligny and was fully up to strength, with over 30,000 men. However, this corps took almost 12 hours to cover the 16 kilometres. Progress of 1.3 kilometres an hour was not unreasonable for so many troops with scores of carts and cannons on a single road that quickly degenerated into a muddy quagmire. Add the fact that the route took them through another corps' bivouac area and through two major bottlenecks (Wavre, where a fire added two hours to the march, and the Lasne defile), they were understandably cautious as they approached the enemy, and the explanation for the snail-like progress becomes clear. In the event, Blücher arrived in time to tip the scales irretrievably against the Emperor – but only just.

METHOD OF COMMAND

The overall effectiveness of the command of the Prussian Army at Waterloo was due to the combination of the battlefield leadership of Blücher coupled with the strategic skill and administrative ability of his chief of staff, Lieutenant-General August von Gneisenau. Blücher possessed, to an astonishing degree, the power of inspiring his troops. He had the will power, the drive, the determination and the sheer guts to carry his army forward despite the setbacks. Blücher did not concern himself with strategic or even tactical planning, but relied on his chief of staff. He himself acknowledged his reliance on Gneisenau:

> Gneisenau, being my chief of staff and very reliable, reports to me on the manoeuvres that are to be executed and the marches that are to be performed. Once convinced that he is right I drive my troops through hell towards the goal and never stop until the object has been achieved – yes, though officers of the old school may sulk and bellyache to the point of mutiny.

Gneisenau took command when Blücher was missing after his fall at Ligny. He made the strategic decision to withdraw north towards Wavre; Blücher later concurred and then rode alongside his soldiers urging them, encouraging them to struggle through the mud and congestion that clogged the route from Wavre to the Waterloo battlefield.

Blücher's answer to virtually any tactical situation was to advance, to attack, and then place himself, like any squadron commander, in front. He was at his best under fire when his quickness of decision and presence of mind more than compensated for his lack of strategic skill. To the delight of his soldiers the leadership of Blücher the field-marshal remained much the same as that of Blücher the squadron commander of fifty years before in Frederick the Great's army. As a captain who knew him well said, 'The general was the same man whom I had known before; rank, fame and years had not affected him in the slightest. He laughed, joked and also swore like any good hussar officer, and for everyone, high or low, general or corporal, he had a coarse joke, an apt jest, but also if he thought necessary, a rebuke.' His soldier's affection was reflected in his nicknames – 'Alte Vorvarts' (Old Forwards) or 'Papa Blücher'.

MOVEMENT TO THE BATTLEFIELD

Bülow's corps started out to join Wellington at 4.00 a.m. on the Sunday with Losthin's 15th Brigade leading, screened by the 2nd Silesian Hussars and accompanied by a 12-pounder battery of guns. At 9.30 a.m. Blücher instructed his ADC to write to Baron Muffling, his liaison officer at the Duke's headquarters.

> … ill as I am [he was still aching from his fall], I will march at the head of my army to attack at once the right wing of the enemy, if Napoleon should attempt anything against the Duke. In case the French do not attack today, I am of the opinion that together we should attack the French Army tomorrow. I desire you to communicate this to the Duke as the result of my rooted conviction.

At around 11.00 a.m. Blücher and his staff set out to join the leading units of Bülow's corps. Within half an hour the increasing roar of the cannonade made it abundantly clear that a battle had been joined in earnest. Along the route to Chapelle St Lambert Blücher was continually halting to urge and encourage his troops, particularly the artillery, as they slipped and struggled, cursed and sweated through the mud. Progress was frustratingly sluggish. Sometime before 1.00 p.m. Blücher caught up with Bülow near Chapelle St Lambert. Here a halt was called to allow Bülow's trailing brigades to catch up. Ahead was the Lasne defile and, quite probably, the enemy. About

Napoleon Spots the Prussians

Most authorities claim that Prussian movement was seen around 1.00 p.m. in the Chapelle St Lambert area some 5 miles north-east of Napoleon's position at Rossomme. In fact the ground is not high enough there to be visible, and the troops spotted were probably those marching near Chapelle St Robert. The Emperor's reaction was swift. The two light cavalry divisions of Domon and Subervie trotted east to reconnoitre. Ahead, with a small escort, went Maréchal de Camp Baron Bernard, one of the Emperor's personal staff officers. He reached the Lasne river and went forward on foot through the woods to observe. He identified Prussian infantry and galloped back to Napoleon. Meanwhile Marbot's 7th Hussars, already deployed in the area, had captured a Prussian hussar. At about 1.15 p.m. he was brought to the Emperor and interrogated, readily admitting that Bülow's corps of 30,000 was on the march. Napoleon immediately despatched Lobau's two infantry divisions to block their approach.

this time the Prussian columns were spotted by Napoleon as they passed Chapelle St Robert. Unbeknown to Blücher, the Emperor sent VI Corps (Lobau) hurrying east to block his march.

At about 2.00 p.m. Blücher, despite the fact that the 14th Brigade was still an hour behind, ordered Bülow to cross the Lasne. His leading units slithered down the defile, across the single bridge, and began to struggle up the steep slopes beyond into the Bois de Paris. Leading the way was a screen of Colonel Schwerin's 6th Hussars. At around 3.30 p.m. the first shots were exchanged on the eastern edge of the wood. Schwerin became probably the first Prussian fatality. By 4.30 p.m. Blücher, watching the massive French cavalry assaults seemingly engulfing Wellington's line from west of the Bois de Paris, courageously insisted that Bülow's attack go in. With his two rear brigades still on the line of march through the wood and the Lasne valley, Bülow sent forward his 15th and 16th Brigades.

GENERAL HEADQUARTERS AND STAFF

The total number of officers at Blücher's headquarters at Waterloo was around fifty, perhaps slightly more, but discounting Lieutenant-Colonel Sir Henry Hardinge, Wellington's liaison officer, whose hand was amputated after being wounded at Ligny. The Prussian General Staff operated under a chief of staff system. In this instance Lieutenant-General von Gneisenau filled the post officially known as Quartermaster-General. He was the second-in-command to Blücher, as well as being responsible for co-ordinating all staff functions. He was also the officer representing the Minister of War with the army, and had jurisdiction (under the commander who took the overall credit or blame for the army's activities) over both operational and administrative matters.

In the field Gneisenau wielded his authority in the name of the commander-in-chief in virtually all military spheres – movement, tactics, deployment, intelligence and logistics (food, clothing, ammunition and accommodation). Blücher made the major decisions after consultation with Gneisenau and others, such as Major-General von Grolmann who headed the staff at the headquarters. Once an important command decision had been made, the staff broke it down into practicalities such as which units were involved, orders of march, routes, timings and resupply. The staff then wrote the orders, distributed them and supervised their implementation. It was, and is, a stressful, twenty-four-hour life that involved considerable use of the pen by senior officers, and of spurs by their juniors.

As with the other two armies, the Prussians had the commanders of the artillery, engineers, medical and provost (military police), together with heads of departments, such as the topographical section, at the Army headquarters.

Blücher's field headquarters at Waterloo

ADCs to Commander-in-Chief
Major Huser
Captain (cavalry) von Jasmund
Captain von Stosch
1st Lieutenant Rothe

Quartermaster-General and Chief of Staff
Lieutenant-General August Graf von Gneisenau

Chief of the General Staff
Major-General von Grolmann

Senior General Staff Officers
Colonel von Pfuel
Colonel von Thile
Lieutenant-Colonel von Witzleben
Captain von Vigny (Engineers)

Assistant General Staff Officers
Major von Bardeleben
Major Knackfuss
Captain Banermeister
Captain Werner
Captain von Oesfeld
2nd Lieutenant von Wussow
2nd Lieutenant O'Etzel
2nd Lieutenant Behrendt
2nd Lieutenant Gerlach

Topographical Service Adjutants
Major von Weyrach
Major von Brunneck
Major Count von Nostitz
Captain Sprenger

Topographical Service Staff
1st Lieutenant Holzwarth
1st Lieutenant Michaelis
Specialist Look

Additional (Volunteer) Staff Officers
Lieutenant-General Count Hochberg
Colonel Prince von Schonburg
Major von Horn
Captain (Cavalry) Count Blücher von Wahlstatt
Captain (Cavalry) Count Holck (Denmark)
Captain Count von Flemming
2nd Lieutenant Zimmer
2nd Lieutenant Nernst
Count Schulenburg-Wolffsburg
Baron Dellmar
Major von Alvensleben
Major von Botticher
Captain Wagner
Captain (Cavalry) Bernard
2nd Lieutenant Meyer
2nd Lieutenant Matton
2nd Lieutenant Muller

Attached Foreign Officers
Major-General van Panhuys (Netherlands)
1st Lieutenant C. Lemmers (Adjutant)
Captain van Delitz

Artillery
General Prince August of Prussia
1st Lieutenant von Rosenberg (Adjutant)

Medical Services
Surgeon-General Voeltzke

Provost
Colonel von Loucey

Prussian Senior Commanders at Waterloo
GENERAL

Discounting Blücher, some thirteen officers of the rank of major-general (the usual rank for a brigade commander) or above reached the battlefield, most of whom might be said to have been actively engaged at Waterloo. Those listed below do not include the two acting cavalry brigade commanders who were killed during the battle (Colonel Schwerin and Lieutenant-Colonel Watzdorf), or those whose units were barely engaged or only in the pursuit (Major-General Brause and Lieutenant-Colonel Sohr). All the officers listed had considerable active service or staff experience. Most had been decorated with Prussia's highest military award, the Pour le Merit, and with the Iron Cross, instituted in 1813. The Prussian system of command within an infantry brigade was to appoint a chief of brigade – a major-general – who commanded the entire formation (infantry, cavalry, artillery and supporting units, as it should be recalled that a Prussian brigade equated to a division in other armies). A full colonel commanded the infantry element within the brigade. An example at Waterloo was the 14th Infantry Brigade, with Major-General von Ryssel the overall commander and Colonel von Funck commanding the infantry battalions. Funck would take over if Ryssel became a casualty.

Gneisenau, Lieutenant-General Count August Graf von
(1760–1831)

Gneisenau was the son of a Saxon artillery lieutenant. He served in the Austrian army and various minor German armies. His early service included a voyage to America to fight for King George III (he arrived too late to see action). He joined the Prussian service as a staff captain in 1786. He was on active service in Poland from 1793–94 and commanded a battalion at Jena in 1806. He made his name for his tenacious defence of Colberg the following year, his exploits being rewarded with Prussia's highest decoration – the Pour le Merit. This incident became famous, to the extent that it inspired Hitler to make a film about it almost 140 years later. Between 1807–13 Gneisenau helped reform and modernize the Prussian Army, which included the establishment of a reorganized general staff corps. For the following two years he was chief of staff to Field-Marshal Blücher in which position he was the sharp strategic brain behind Blücher's aggressive tactics and blustering bravery. It was to be a formidable combination. He was made a count for his services at the Battle of Leipzig in 1813.

The highlights of his Waterloo campaign were, firstly, the decision to march north to Wavre after defeat at Ligny while the fate of Blücher (he had been unhorsed) was unknown, and secondly, the conduct of the relentless Prussian pursuit of the fleeing French after the battle. This he later declared was, 'The most glorious night of my life.'

He later became Governor of Berlin, and in 1831 commanded Prussian forces sent to crush a Polish rebellion. He died of cholera in 1831, aged seventy-one.

IV CORPS

Bülow, General Friedrich Wilhelm Count von Dennewitz
(1755–1816)

Bülow was sixty-years-old at Waterloo (of the generals, only Blücher was older) and, by virtue of his rank as a full general, was senior to all other Prussian corps commanders and the chief of staff. This could have caused problems after Ligny when command devolved onto Gneisenau for several crucial hours when Blücher was missing. However, Bülow's corps had not taken part in Ligny and was still marching to join the army, so arguments over rank could not cloud the critical discussion at the Prussian headquarters on the night of 16/17 June.

Bülow was of distinguished ancestry and good education having studied mathematics, history and geography as a young officer. As a major he turned down the offer of being a tutor to Prince Heinrich (brother of the future King Freidrich Wilhelm III). Unusually for a soldier he was a talented musician. He was also a somewhat short-tempered officer, easily roused to anger even with his superiors. Throughout his career he was noted for directness and being forthright in his dealings with people of all ranks, which sometimes resulted in protracted disputes with very senior officers (including at one stage, Blücher).

He became a cadet at seventeen and a 2nd lieutenant a year later. As a captain he saw continuous action during the years 1793–94, winning the Pour le Merit for leading the storming of a redoubt at the Siege of Mainz. In 1807, as a colonel commanding a fusilier regiment, he was wounded in the arm by a musket ball in action near Waltersdorf. He was promoted major-general in 1808 and served as a brigade commander. During 1813 as a brigade commander with the rank of lieutenant-general, he won an engagement at Zehdenick (awarded the Iron Cross 2nd Class) plus several notable actions at Luckau, Gross-Beeren (Iron Cross 1st Class), and in September of that year defeated Ney at Dennewitz – hence his title of Count von Dennewitz. For his success he was awarded the 'Oak Leaves' to his Pour le Merit. He later fought well against Napoleon at Leipzig and again in 1814 at Laon.

At Waterloo he commanded over 30,000 men in IV Corps. His was the only Prussian corps fully committed to the battle, although his leading units did not debouch from the Bois de Paris until about 4.30 p.m. His battle was the long, hard fought push for Plancenoit. As his formations came up they were flung against the vulnerable French right, initially defended by Lobau. The fighting for Plancenoit was desperate and mostly with the bayonet around the church and in the narrow cobbled streets. Bülow's men first faced Lobau, then the Young Guard and then two battalions of the Old Guard Grenadiers. The struggle for Plancenoit saw the most bitter and protracted fighting of the battle (surpassing Hougoumont and La Haie Sainte in its intensity) with the village changing hands several times.

Bülow died within a year of the victory after an illness of several months. The King ordered every officer in the army to wear a black armband for three days as a mark of respect for his forty-four years of service and especially for his leadership of his corps in the struggle for Plancenoit. A marble statue to his memory was erected in Berlin in 1816.

Hake, Lieutenant-General Albrecht Georg Ernst Karl von
(1768–1835)

Hake commanded the 13th Infantry Brigade at Waterloo. He was reported as an honest, hardworking officer, which perhaps suggests a man being condemned with faint praise. At Waterloo he had been a lieutenant-general for over a year but his command was only a brigade. One wonders what he thought of Pirch I, a mere major-general who had even been promoted to that rank a year after Hake, commanding a corps. Apart from as a very junior officer (lieutenant) when he had won the Pour le Merit in 1792, Hake's career for the next twenty years had been on the general staff. His experience in command of troops on the battlefield had been crammed into one exciting year: 1792. He was present at the actions at Fontoy, Longwy, Pirmasens, the Siege of Mainz and the cannonade of Valmy. The following year he began his staff career as an assistant to a regimental colonel.

As he climbed slowly but steadily up the promotion ladder, Hake served in a wide variety of staff posts. He was a quartermaster, an inspection adjutant on a field-marshal's staff in Berlin, a personal adjutant to Prince Heinrich of Prussia, a member of the staff investigating the conduct of all officers after the crushing defeats of 1806 and a senior official in the Ministry of War. In 1810 he became, as a colonel, head of the engineer corps, with responsibility for the administration of fortresses. By 1812 though, he had become depressed. His tasks were thankless ones, there was plenty of criticism (including some from Gneisenau) and precious little praise. He put in his papers to the King. Within a matter of days he was made a major-general – so he stayed on. The following three years (1813–15) were much better for Hake, even though he was wounded. He was at Leipzig and La Fère Champenoise while his services were again recognized by promotion – to lieutenant-general in May 1814.

At Waterloo Hake's 13th Brigade was third in the order of march of IV Corps from Wavre. As such he did not debouch from the Bois de Paris until after 5.00 p.m. However, there was plenty of fighting left. His was a big brigade (well over 7000 strong) with big battalions. He deployed north of the road to Plancenoit in support of the 15th Infantry Brigade in the advance on the village. His troops were heavily involved in the final attacks just to the north of Plancenoit, mainly against Lobau's corps, that helped, eventually, to secure the village.

In 1819 Hake became Minister of War, a position he kept for fourteen long years. He was promoted full general of infantry in 1825. Ill-health forced his retirement to the softer climate of Italy in 1833. He died near Naples two years later, aged sixty-seven.

Ryssel, Major-General Gustav Xaver Reinhold von (1771–1845)

Ryssel commanded the 14th Infantry Brigade at Waterloo. He was a Saxon by birth and joined the infantry as a ten-year-old cadet in 1781. At nineteen he was commissioned as a 2nd Lieutenant. He saw active service in southern Germany against France in 1796 but did not secure promotion to 1st Lieutenant until he was twenty-seven. He then became a general's adjutant for several years, was wounded in the neck at Jena and was later present at the Siege of Danzig – still a lieutenant in his mid-thirties. However, from 1807 he was noticed. That year he received his captaincy, in 1809 he was a major on the general staff and campaigning in Austria, and the following year he was chief of staff of an infantry division. He had done well. By 1811 he was a lieutenant-colonel and by 1812 a colonel and commander of an infantry regiment.

By this stage of his career he was fighting for the French, as Saxony was then part of Napoleon's empire. In 1812 he led his regiment in the campaign against Russia. His services were rewarded with promotion to major-general in 1813. In the same year he was awarded the Legion of Honour for his actions at the Battle of Bautzen. He was again in action at Gross-Beeren, Dennewitz and Leipzig (all against the Allies, including the Prussians). At this latter battle the Saxon Corps came over to the Allies so Ryssel found himself in the Prussian service – still with the rank of major-general.

Ryssel's brigade was the last infantry formation of IV Corps to reach the Waterloo battlefield. His brigade had been weakened by the detachment of two battalions as part of a covering force south of Wavre. He deployed south of the Plancenoit road, initially in support of the 16th Infantry Brigade. However, he was quickly committed to the evening assaults on the village. His seven battalions were involved in the desperate and bloody struggle against the Young Guard around the church and cemetery. His brigade was later to be thrown out by the two battalions of the Old Guard. His brigade lost almost 1,400 all ranks at Waterloo – almost all in Plancenoit. For his services that day he was awarded the Iron Cross 2nd Class; one wonders if he was wearing his Legion of Honour during the battle.

Ryssel remained in France as part of the Army of Occupation. Five years later he was promoted lieutenant-general. In 1832, suffering ill health, he was promoted general of infantry and pensioned off. He recuperated well in retirement, living on until 1845 when he died aged seventy-four.

Losthin, Major-General Michael Heinrich von (1762–1839)

Losthin was the commander of the 15th Infantry Brigade that was the first Prussian formation to debouch from the Bois de Paris at around 4.30 p.m. At fifty-three he was older than most of his fellow generals. He came from an old Pomeranian family of noble origins and, like so many of his contemporaries, had started his long military career as a cadet while still a young boy (he was eleven). At eighteen he was an officer cadet (*fähnrich*), a year later a 2nd lieutenant. He appears to have had little, if any, regimental soldiering as an officer, going instead into staff appointments while still very junior. He became, as a lieutenant, an 'inspection adjutant' – a junior position on the staff of a general commanding a military district. He was promoted captain in 1789 but continued as an 'inspection adjutant', this time in Warsaw. Nine years later he became a major. The following year he was given command of an infantry battalion. His regimental commander wrote that he had a strong moral character, possessed sound military and mathematical knowledge, could be entrusted with any duty and was a first class staff officer. There was no mention of his command capabilities.

Nevertheless, he must have been above average as in 1801 he was appointed commanding officer of a grenadier battalion. He fought at Jena in 1806 and was awarded the Pour le Merit a year later. By 1813 he was commanding a brigade (the infantry element of it). At Wartenburg he earned himself an Iron Cross 2nd Class and at Leipzig, where he was severely wounded, an Iron Cross 1st Class. A year later after his recovery he was promoted to major-general.

On leaving the Bois de Paris Losthin's nine battalions deployed north of the Plancenoit road and led the push for the village against stiff resistance from Lobau's corps. His brigade was almost continually in action for over four hours. Losses were heavy – some 1,800 (28 per cent).

Waterloo, or Belle Alliance as the Prussian's more accurately called it, marked the end of Losthin's career, although it is not clear why; at fifty-three he was hardly too old to be a general. Within three months he was given the usual end of career package – promotion (to lieutenant-general) and retirement. He died in Silesia in 1839, aged seventy-seven.

Hiller, Colonel Johann Freidrich August Freiherr von (1772–1856)

Hiller had acting command of the 16th Infantry Brigade at Waterloo. He was the son of a Prussian major-general who followed his father into the army – in the circumstances and at that time it is doubtful he could have done anything else even if he had wished to.

He became a boy cadet at twelve (along with his brother who was a year younger) and an officer cadet three years later in 1787. At fifteen he saw action in Holland where he received the first of the four wounds he was to suffer during his career. During the period 1792–95 young Lieutenant Hiller saw considerable action against France. He took part in the cannonade at Valmy, the battle at Kaiserslautern and in at least six minor engagements, in one of which he was wounded for the second time.

After a spell as adjutant to his father he was promoted captain (1802). Two years later he was given a glowing report from his regimental commander. He was complimented on his intelligence, knowledge of languages, mathematics and geometry. His colonel was very pleased with his energy, industry and tactical understanding. He wrote that Captain Hiller, '… deserves to be recommended in every respect.' Despite this fine report in 1804, he was not to make it to major for another seven years. It was a period when Hiller's career stalled. He spent a period in captivity after the fall of Hameln, was placed on half-pay in 1807 and was then appointed as a 'Captain von de Armée', which meant he did not belong to any particular unit. He was given a tedious, backwater administrative job in the town of Pasewalk. In 1810 he was attached to an infantry regiment where he did regimental duties, but remained outside the normal regimental promotion system. He managed to secure a posting as adjutant to a general in 1811 – within three months he was a major.

He was still a staff adjutant when he won the Pour le Merit in action at Eckau in 1812. As a major Hiller did exceptionally well during the two years 1813 to 1814. During this period he reached the rank of colonel, was wounded twice and received the Oak Leaves to his Pour le Merit together with a Russian decoration. He took part in the battles at Gross-Gorschen (wounded), Leipzig, Möckern (seriously wounded), Katzbach and Paris. It was on account of his performance on the battlefield that he was given command, while still a colonel, of the 16th Brigade for the Waterloo campaign.

At Waterloo he deployed from Bois de Paris immediately behind the 15th Brigade. He advanced against Lobau's troops to the south of the Plancenoit road. In the evening Hiller was fully committed to the bitter and protracted struggle for Plancenoit. His men fought hand-to-hand with the Young Guard and then the Old Guard through the streets and around the church. They attacked, were repulsed and attacked again. Their losses exceeded 1,800.

Within three months of Waterloo Hiller was promoted to major-general. The following year he was commander of Stettin on the Baltic coast. A report in 1820, while recognizing his capabilities, considered he had become somewhat conceited. He was promoted to lieutenant-general in 1827 but poor health forced him from active duty three years later. Twenty years afterwards, in his late seventies, the system elevated him again to full general of infantry. He would have been pleased with that. He died in 1856, aged eighty-four.

Sydow, Major-General Hans Joachim Freidrich von (1762–1823)
Sydow commanded the 3rd Cavalry Brigade, the strongest Prussian mounted formation to reach the Waterloo battlefield. He was a cavalry officer who began his service aged thirteen in the Hussar Regiment von Belling in 1775. He fought in the 1793–95 campaign taking part in several minor actions, the Siege of Landau and the Battle of Kaiserslautern. At the latter action he was wounded, his courage being rewarded with the Pour le Merit. For the next ten years he rose steadily on the staff, becoming a major

in 1800. In 1804 Blücher reported that he was an excellent staff officer who, once qualified for command, would go a long way.

He was severely wounded at Jena-Auerstadt but remained with his regiment. In 1809 he was promoted to lieutenant-colonel and assumed command of the Pomeranian Hussar Regiment. However, his Auerstadt wound was giving him problems, sufficient to cause him to quit the service. Nevertheless, in 1813 he felt able to come out of retirement to take command of the Pomeranian National Cavalry Regiment. The next two years saw Colonel Sydow leading his landwehr cavalry units with commendable skill in many of the battles across Germany and France. He was present at Gross-Beeren, Dennewitz, Leipzig, Loan and Paris. For his conduct at the combat near Wittstock he received the Iron Cross 2nd Class, and for his action at the Siege of Zutphen the 1st Class award. He was promoted to major-general three months before Waterloo.

At Waterloo his brigade consisted of five small landwehr cavalry regiments totalling some 1,800 sabres. Apart from the 2nd Neumärk Landwehr Regiment that covered the corps advance from the Bois de Paris, losing some 28 per cent of their strength, his troops saw little serious action. The 2nd Neumärk lost 128 men, the other four regiments only nine between them.

After the campaign he was appointed inspector of landwehr in Köslin. In 1822 he retired from active duty as a lieutenant-general, dying the following year aged sixty-one.

II CORPS

Pirch I, Major-General Georg Dubislaw Ludwig von (1763–1838)

Always referred to as Pirch I to distinguish him from his brother, Major-General Pirch II (who commanded the 2nd Infantry Brigade in I Corps but who did not arrive in time to see any action at Waterloo). He came from a well-established Prussian military family. When only twelve he became a '*gefreiterkaporal*' or 'boy lance-corporal' in the 45th Infantry Regiment of which his father (who later became a general) was the commanding officer. At fourteen he was promoted to cadet with responsibility for carrying the regiment's Colour. The following year he went on active service and in 1782 was made adjutant of his battalion. He spent some nine years as a cadet before, at twenty-three, he was commissioned a 2nd lieutenant. He had undoubted ability as an adjutant since he performed those duties to General von Eckartsberg during the campaign in Holland in 1787 while still a junior officer. He was present at the Siege of Mainz in 1793. Possibly because he had yet to be given the opportunity to prove himself in command of troops in action, it was not until he was thirty-two that he reached the rank of captain. Even then he had yet another spell as adjutant in Silesia.

In 1797 he was promoted major. Then for another nine years he seemingly soldiered on in obscurity. The next significant event in his career was the Battle of Jena in 1806, after which he was a prisoner of the French for two years. Then came promotion to lieutenant-colonel, command (at last) of an infantry unit (2nd West Prussian Infantry Regiment), full colonel in 1812 and the command of a regiment in battle at Gross-Gorschen (Iron Cross 2nd Class, followed by the 1st Class for a series of minor actions), Bautzen, Dresden, Kulm and Leipzig. For his leadership and courage at Liepzig Pirch received the Pour le Merit with Oak Leaves.

He commanded II Corps at Waterloo. It had fought hard at Ligny and suffered accordingly in the defeat and retreat afterwards. Pirch led some 24,000 troops behind Bülow's corps as it slithered through the mud on the tracks from Wavre to the Waterloo battlefield. Starting out at noon Pirch I's leading units did not come into action until nearly 6.00 p.m. By the end of the battle only some 14,500 men from his corps had been engaged.

Within a year of Waterloo Pirch was allowed to retire from active duty on medical grounds (he was almost deaf). He lived quietly in Berlin amongst his family for another twenty-two years before dying peacefully, aged seventy-five. He had outlived his younger brother by fourteen years.

Tippelskirch, Major-General Ernst Ludwig von (1774–1840)

Tippelskirch commanded the 5th Infantry Brigade at Waterloo. He came from an old Prussian family that could trace its origins back to the thirteenth century. He became a cadet in the infantry at eleven and then a *fahnrich* (officer cadet) at twenty. While still in that rank he saw active service in the 1794–95 campaign against France, taking part in the Battle of Kaiserslautern and several minor engagements. As a 2nd lieutenant his skill as a draughtsman/cartographer was utilized drawing plans of the areas around Lingen and Osnabrück when he was detached from his regiment for three years. He was well reported on, although he appears to have suffered from shortsightedness.

In 1804 he joined the general staff as a captain working as an adjutant for General Scharnhorst in Berlin. This was followed by an intense period of active duty as a staff captain and quartermaster-lieutenant. During 1806 and 1807 he fought at the Battles of Jena, Pultusk, Eylau (for which he was awarded the Pour le Merit), Heilsberg and Friedland. In 1807 he was promoted major at the age of thirty-three. There followed administrative duties in Königsberg and as a member of the commission investigating the conduct of officers during the disastrous years of defeat in 1806–07. For four years from 1809 most of his postings were staff appointments, but by 1813 he was promoted to colonel and given command of the infantry element of the Brandenburg Brigade. He led his battalions in the Battles of Gross-Gorschen (Iron Cross 2nd Class), Bautzen, Dresden (Iron Cross 1st Class) and Leipzig. He was promoted major-general only three weeks before Waterloo.

Tippelskirch's brigade had fought long and hard at Ligny. Battalions that had gone into action 800 strong fought at Waterloo with an average strength only just over 500 – four were commanded by captains. The brigade arrived at Waterloo just in time to spearhead the final attack on Plancenoit. They advanced with considerable spirit for the second time in two days into the close quarter, bloody brawl that was (and still is) street fighting. They clashed around the church with the Imperial Guard, eventually forcing them from the village at a cost to themselves of another 350 casualties. Tippelskirch was given the Oak Leaves to his Pour le Merit for his leadership that day.

Despite his achievements at Ligny and Waterloo, Tippelskirch had to wait another ten years before promotion to lieutenant-general. In 1827 he was appointed commander of the Berlin garrison and gendarmerie, a position he kept until his death of an apoplectic stroke in 1840, aged sixty-six. He must have been well respected, as Berliners contributed to a monument over his grave in the garrison cemetery, erected by the gendarmerie.

Krafft, Major-General Karl August Adolf von (1764–1840)

Krafft commanded the 6th Infantry Brigade at Waterloo. He joined the 4th Infantry Regiment as a young cadet of fourteen in 1778. He took his profession very seriously, being well reported on

for his diligent studies. He was employed on staff duties during the campaign in Poland in 1794–95. He then had a five-year stint as an adjutant to the Duke of Brunswick. He was promoted major in 1801. In 1806 he was severely wounded at the Battle of Jena-Auerstadt while commanding a grenadier battalion. It was two years before he was fit enough for further active duty, when he was given command of a fusilier battalion. Promoted lieutenant-colonel in 1810 and colonel two years later, Krafft spent much of this time as commander of the infantry in a Pomeranian Brigade, and in organizing the reserve battalions in Pomerania and Neumärk. He was given command of his own brigade (6th Brigade under Bülow) in early 1813 and promoted major-general six months later.

He was to keep this command for the next two years until after the Waterloo campaign. In 1813–14 he commanded his brigade with skill at several minor engagements, at one of which he earned the Iron Cross 2nd Class. He fought at the Battles of Gross-Beeren, Dennewitz (Iron Cross 1st Class), Leipzig and Laon.

Krafft's brigade was badly mauled in the horrific struggle for the village of Ligny, its strength falling from over 7000 infantry to about 4,200 – a 40 per cent loss. The brigade followed IV Corps from Wavre. After such a battering at Ligny his troops were probably not displeased to arrive on the Waterloo battlefield late (around 7.00 p.m.), too late to become involved in the fight for Plancenoit other than as a reserve for the final (and successful) attack on the village. They suffered negligible losses from artillery fire. His brigade did, however, become more heavily committed to the fighting in France and during the storming of various towns that held out for the Emperor. For his actions during the attack on Namur in October 1815 Krafft received the Pour le Merit. It was in this engagement that Colonel von Bismarck, the uncle of the future German Chancellor, was killed.

Krafft went on to become a lieutenant-general and corps commander. He retired on the grounds of poor health in 1832 with his status and pension enhanced by promotion to general of infantry. He died in Königsberg in 1840, aged seventy-six.

Ziethen, Lieutenant-General Hans Ernst Karl Graf von (1770-1848)

A cavalry officer who, like Pirch I, spent much of his early service up to and including the rank of major, performing the duties of an adjutant. The exception was the two years of 1792–94 when, as a 2nd lieutenant, he saw action as a hussar officer at the storming of Frankfurt, the cannonade at Valmy and the Battle of Kaiserslautern. Ziethen fought well at Jena-Auerstadt in October 1806. Two months later he was made commander of the 4th Hussars. Scharnhorst thought highly of him. Gneisenau, however, disliked him but conceded that he was a competent cavalry commander.

He developed a reputation as an officer not over concerned with personal comforts. He shared the hardships of life on campaign with his men, although he could drive them relentlessly if necessary. Somewhat aloof, with a streak of ruthlessness Ziethen had a good tactical sense and was not frightened of making quick decisions. He distinguished himself during 1813 at the Battles of Gross-Gorschen (Iron Cross 2nd Class), Dresden (Pour le Merit with Oak Leaves) and Leipzig. For gallant service at the engagement at Haynau he received the Iron Cross 1st Class. The following year he fought at Laon.

During the 1815 campaign he commanded I Corps, which was heavily engaged at Ligny, suffering severe losses (6000 plus many deserters during the retreat). Ziethen's task at Waterloo was to march along the northern route from Wavre to the battlefield to link up with Wellington's left flank. He was forced to wait until the other two corps had departed before he could start his march at around 2.00 p.m. Just prior to arriving to join forces with Wellington his corps was diverted south by an ADC with an order from Blücher to go to the assistance of Bülow who was having considerable difficulty in taking and keeping Plancenoit. Muffling, the Prussian liaison officer at Wellington's headquarters, pleaded with him to ignore this new order and keep to the original plan. Ziethen did so – rightly as it turned out. But it was no easy decision to countermand your commander-in-chief's explicit instructions.

By the time his leading units reached the field it was 7.30 p.m. In the confused fighting on Wellington's eastern flank around Papelotte and La Haie farms, Ziethen's men were involved in one or two 'friendly fire' incidents with the Nassauers defending the area. However, it was only his 1st Infantry and 1st Cavalry Brigades that arrived in time to fire shots in anger.

Ziethen was made commander of the Prussian Army of Occupation in France. Later he became Commandant General of Silesia and was promoted field-marshal in 1835. He died in 1848, aged seventy-eight.

Steinmetz, Major-General Karl Freidrich Franziskus von (1768–1837)

Steinmetz commanded the 1st Infantry Brigade at Waterloo. Because his father, a lieutenant-colonel, was killed in action in 1778, all his four sons were automatically accepted as cadets while still boys. Karl Steinmetz entered at thirteen. He became a 2nd lieutenant in a fusilier battalion in 1786. As a young man he was noted for his academic ability and interest in music. For much of the period 1796 to 1803 his talents were employed in drawing maps and plans in the areas of Waldeck and Paderborn. An extract of a report on 1st Lieutenant Steinmetz reads, 'An officer who has been used for several years drawing maps of the country, and with whom we are very content due to his diligence.' Very commendable, but it was not serious soldiering likely to improve his career in those exciting times. Not until he was thirty-seven did he manage to get promoted to captain, and then only in the cadet corps. Another drag on promotion, and something that prevented his entry into the staff corps, was the fact that he was poor. Not only did he not come from a wealthy family, but he had also married young – something that was frowned on by the military establishment and increased his expenses considerably.

In 1806, however, while still a captain he was given acting command of the 2nd Pomeranian Reserve Battalion. This turned out to be the turning point in his otherwise somewhat dull career. Firstly, his battalion was given the duty of guarding the royal family, so his name was registered in high, very high, places. Secondly, in 1807 his unit formed part of the garrison of Colberg and he earned the Pour le Merit for his leadership and skills in the town's defence. Finally, the garrison commander happened to be Gneisenau – destined to become Blücher's chief of staff at Waterloo. His lifelong friendship with Gneisenau dated from this time. Steinmetz's young adjutant during the defence of the town later wrote of his commander's friendliness, kindness, sociable nature and his continuing love of music – he found time to organize concerts during the siege. In 1807 he was promoted major and took command of the Colberg garrison when Gneisenau departed.

As a lieutenant-colonel in 1813–14 he proved his competence in action again and again, fighting with distinction at the Battles of Gross-Gorschen (Iron Cross 2nd Class), Bautzen, Gross-Beeren, Dennewitz, Katzbach, Wartenburg, Leipzig and Möckern (badly wounded). During this period he was promoted to colonel and, only five months later, to major-general.

As with other units (apart from those in IV Corps) Steinmetz's ten battalions had had a rough time at Ligny. His brigade had lost 46 officers and 2,300 men in the meat-grinder fighting through the streets of St Amand. His command had shrunk from over 8000 to less than 5000. At Waterloo his was the leading formation of I Corps that had followed the northern route from Wavre to arrive on Wellington's left flank. He did not arrive until around 7.00 p.m. All his battalions were only 450 or less strong, and only seven reached the battlefield in time to participate in the final moments of the battle. They were engaged in the fighting around Papelotte. For his services at Waterloo and during the French retreat into France Steinmetz received the Iron Cross 1st Class and the Oak Leaves to his Pour le Merit.

Not long after the campaign he developed stomach problems, which led to his early retirement – with the usual sweetener of promotion to lieutenant-general. Despite his sickness he survived for another twenty-one years, dying in Potsdam in 1837 aged sixty-nine.

Treskow II, Major-General Karl Alexander Wilhelm von (1764 – unknown)

Treskow commanded the 1st Cavalry Brigade at Waterloo. He entered the 8th Dragoon Regiment as a youth of fourteen in 1778. Within a year he was on active service in the Bavarian War of Succession. The following year he was an officer cadet. From 1784 until 1807 when he went on half-pay Treskow rose slowly but surely to the rank of major. He was described as 'a good and active officer … with a lot of intelligence, which he has trained with good reading.' He participated in the campaign in Poland in 1795–96 and the Jena-Auerstadt campaign of 1806. There is not much evidence that he shone in any way and, unlike many of his Waterloo contemporaries, he was not awarded any decoration for his service.

He returned to active duty in 1808, becoming commander of the 2nd West Prussian Dragoon Regiment three years later. In 1812 he led his regiment with skill and daring in action at Eckau and Gräfenthal. His conduct earned him the Pour le Merit and promotion to lieutenant-colonel. The following year he was again in action at Luckau (Iron Cross 2nd Class), Gross-Beeren and Dennewitz (Iron Cross 1st Class) and promoted to colonel. Suddenly his career had come to life. In 1814 he got command of a brigade as a colonel and in 1815 of a brigade in I Corps. His promotion to major-general is dated 15 June 1815 – the day the French invaded Belgium. One wonders if he knew of it before Waterloo.

Treskow's horsemen were in action from the outset of the Waterloo campaign, initially screening the Prussian withdrawal from the line of the Sambre and in the fighting around Charleroi. His 2nd Dragoons clashed with the Dragoons of the Imperial Guard near the Bois de Fleurus. At Ligny his brigade was involved in holding off the French in the final stages of the battle. The 2nd Dragoons was one of the regiments led by Blücher in the charge in which he was unhorsed. By the Sunday his command was down to 1,370 – a loss of 32 per cent. At Waterloo his command did not arrive until towards the end of the action. The only regiment to be seriously engaged was the 5th Dragoons, who charged units of Durutte's division as it retreated in the general rout.

The Battlefield

(INCLUDING MEMORIALS)

Yes – Agincourt may be forgot,
And Cressy be an unknown spot,
And Blenheim's name be new:
But still in story and in song,
Shall live the towers of Hougoumont
And the Field of Waterloo.

Sir Walter Scott

General (Maps 8, 9, & 10, pp. 119, 126 & 131)

It may be an exaggeration to say that most of the world has heard of Waterloo – but not too great a one. There are hundreds of Waterloo towns, villages, streets, roads, plus at least one bridge, bay, mountain, a suburb of Sydney and a golf course in the Cayman Islands, strewn indiscriminately around the globe. During the nineteenth century the British scattered the name of the battle that destroyed Napoleon throughout their empire. A Waterloo of some sort exists in such diverse places as Australia, Canada, New Zealand, Trinidad, Suriname, Guyana, Sierra Leone and, more numerously than anywhere else, in the United States of America. The expression, 'to meet one's Waterloo', has gone into the phraseology of the English language as meaning to be finally, and decisively beaten at something, anything. The French have not been happy with this worldwide advertisement of their defeat. In recent times there has been considerable Gallic grumbling by French passengers arriving in London via the 'Eurostar' train through the Channel Tunnel, when they realize their first steps on English soil are at Waterloo Station.

All this, and the battle was not even fought at Waterloo, a village 5 kilometres north of the battlefield. The battle took place in Wallonia, in the French-speaking southern half of Belgium, exactly 20 kilometres south of the capital. This hallowed 15 to 20 square kilometres of farmland is almost exactly bisected, north–south, by the Brussels–Genappe–Charleroi road. It would have been more precise to call it any of the following – the Battle of Plancenoit, La Belle Alliance or Mont St Jean. As battles are traditionally named after the nearest village (or sometimes river) Plancenoit would have been an appropriate name, as prolonged fighting (between French and Prussians) raged back and forth along its cobbled streets and around its church for several hours.

After the battle Wellington rode back to the old coaching inn in Waterloo village that had been his headquarters on the previous night. There he wrote his after-battle despatch to London. As the report originated from Waterloo, the British called the victory the 'Battle of Waterloo'. Neither the French nor the Prussians saw the logic of this, the former preferring Mont St Jean, the latter La Belle Alliance. The Duke's old headquarters now houses the Wellington Museum (see box p. 133).

When the poet Southey was shown round the battlefield he recorded in his notes to *The Poet's Pilgrimage to Waterloo*, 'Our guide [Decoster, see box p. 79] was very much displeased at the name which the battle had obtained in England. "Why call it the Battle of Waterloo?" he said, – "call it Mont St Jean, call it La Belle Alliance, call it Hougoumont, call it La Haye (*sic*) Sainte, call it Papelotte – anything but Waterloo."' He forgot to mention Plancenoit.

The Waterloo Despatch

The victory despatch, penned by the Duke on 19 June in what is now the Wellington Museum in Waterloo, was entrusted to Major the Honourable Henry Percy, 14th Light Dragoons, who was an extra ADC on his personal staff. He tucked the document into a purple velvet handkerchief sachet he had been given at the Duchess of Richmond's ball on 15 June. Percy was also given the Eagles of the 45th and 105th Ligne captured in the battle, to take back to London to lay at the feet of the Prince Regent. Percy was delighted with the honour attached to this assignment and more so as, by tradition, the bearer of the news of victory was always handsomely rewarded financially.

Percy travelled via Ghent to Ostend and thence across the channel and by coach to London, where he arrived at about 10.00 p.m. on 21 June. The despatch was addressed to Earl Bathurst, the Secretary for War. At Number 10 Downing Street Percy was directed to 44 Grosvenor Square (now the Britannia Hotel) where Bathurst was at a dinner party. His coach clattered through the dark streets with the Eagles protruding from the windows on either side. On arrival Percy burst in wearing the same clothes he had worn at the ball six days before and throughout the battle. The news was greeted with wild enthusiasm and Percy dashed off with the Eagles to find the Prince Regent who was at a ball at 16 St James Square. After laying the Eagles at the royal feet, Percy retired exhausted to his father's house at 8 Portman Square.

The Britannia Hotel now has a pleasant bar with a low ceiling, called the 'Waterloo Despatch Bar'. On the wall are two plaques that commemorate Percy's unexpected arrival.

Significance of the battlefield (Map 9, p. 126)

The selection of the battlefield, or at least the general area, was made by Wellington. He had tentatively earmarked the ground south of Waterloo as being highly suitable for a defensive battle on one of his rides over the area in the weeks prior to the opening of hostilities. Whether, when poring over a map in the Duke of Richmond's study in the early hours of 16 June, he drew his thumbnail over the precise position actually taken up two days later, as is contended by some writers, is arguable. He was certainly thinking ahead and indicating the general area in which he would want to hold the French should things go badly at Quatre-Bras.

It is unlikely, however, that the Duke had selected the Mont St Jean ridge as the exact place to fight before the late evening of 17 June. Lieutenant-Colonel Ponsonby, 12th Light Dragoons, declared on numerous occasions after the battle that the Duke had halted several regiments on rising ground just north of Genappe and considered deploying the army there. Sir Hussey Vivian in Siborne's *Waterloo Letters* is quite clear on this point. Ponsonby was stated to have said: 'He [Ponsonby] knew it to be a fact that the Duke had himself halted some Regiments in position on the Brussels side of Genappe, meaning to have halted his Army there, having that town and the small river that runs through it to his front, but that De Lancey, his Quartermaster-General, who had been sent to the rear, came to him and described to him the position at Waterloo [Mont St Jean], and the Duke determined to retire from that on which he was then halted to take up that on which the Battle was fought.'

De Lancey had indeed been sent back from Quatre-Bras on the morning of the 17th to look for a suitable location. De Lancey, who knew the area, had first considered the position later taken up by Napoleon (but facing south), thought it too wide, and moved less than 2 kilometres further north to plan the Anglo-Allied Army's deployment on the low ridge south of Mont St Jean Farm. De Lancey then rode back to Wellington and convinced him to continue back to Mont St Jean.

The position had several cogent strategic, as well as tactical, reasons for selection. First, it directly barred two of the three routes Napoleon might use to march on Brussels. It straddled the two

The Selection of the Mont St Jean Position

There is evidence that the selection of the ridge south of Mont St Jean Farm where Wellington gave battle may not, as has almost universally been accepted, have necessarily been the Duke's first choice. According to Lord Fitzroy Somerset, his Military Secretary, writing a year after the battle, it is possible Wellington initially considered what was to become the French ridge (although facing south), with La Belle Alliance as the centre. Fitzroy Somerset stated that at the start of the withdrawal from Quatre-Bras on 17 June Wellington had sent De Lancey ahead with instructions to mark out a defensive position blocking the Charleroi and Nivelles roads south of Waterloo. Seemingly, De Lancey had some discretion. Later that afternoon when the Duke and his staff arrived at La Belle Alliance he halted, thinking this might be the position. Fitzroy Somerset wrote:

> ... on arriving near La Belle Alliance he [the Duke] thought it was the position the Qr.M. Genl. would have taken up, being the most commanding ground, but he [De Lancey] had found it too extended to be occupied by our Troops, & so had proceeded further on & marked out a position.

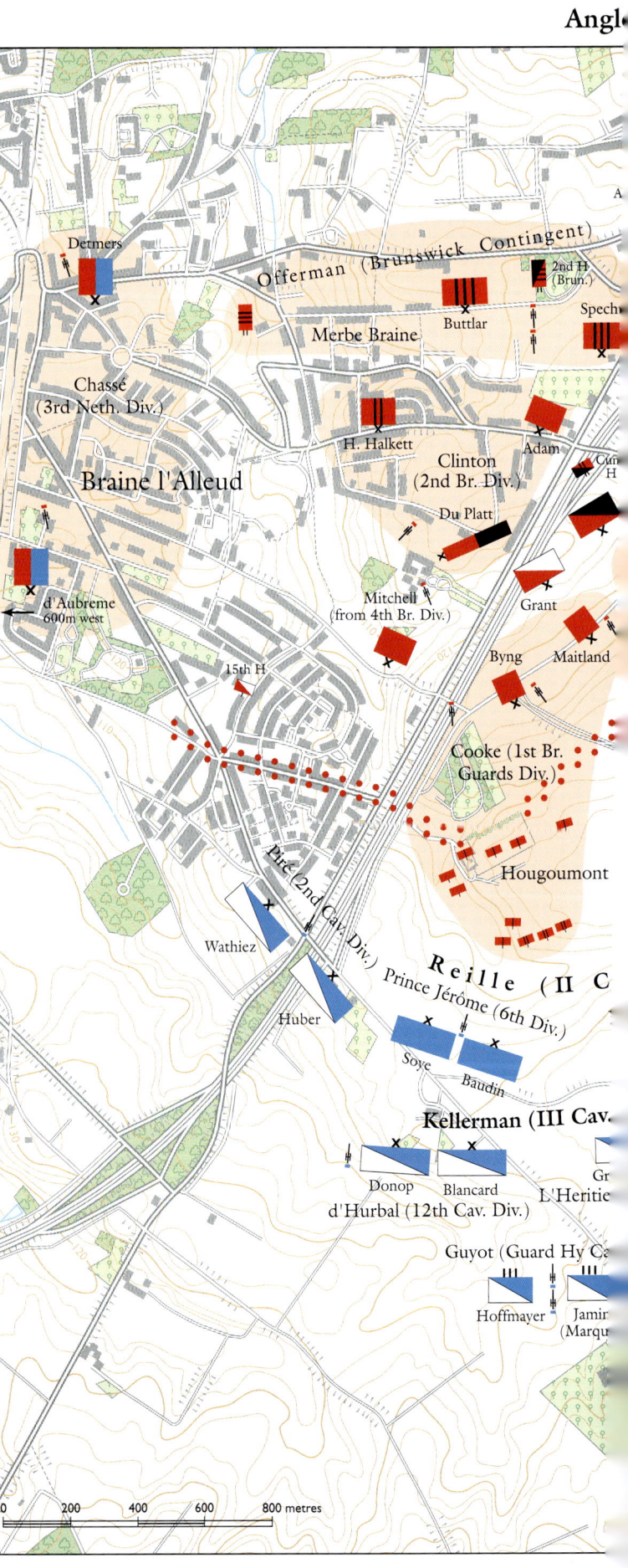

lied and French Deployments at 11.30 a.m.   (shown on modern map)   Map 8

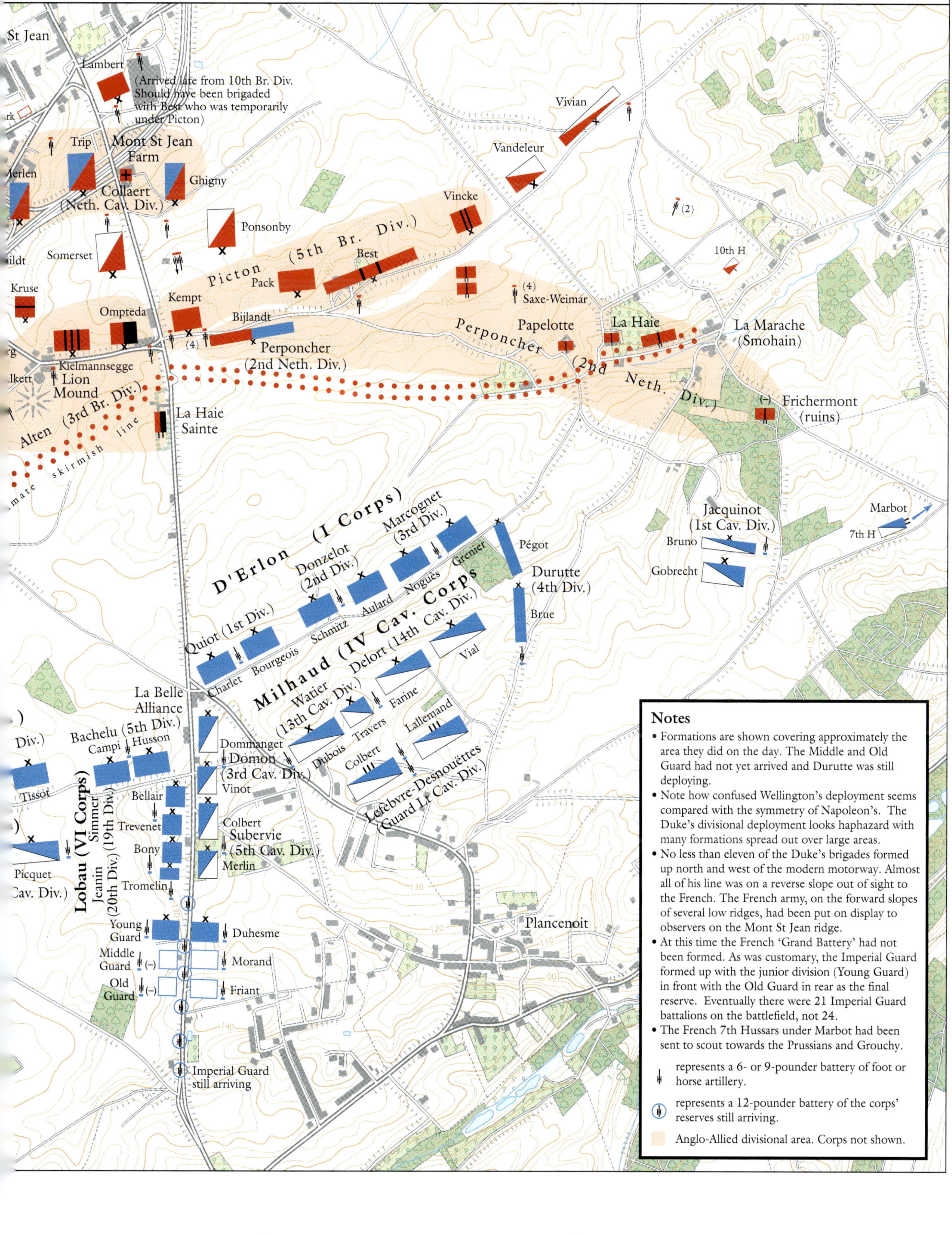

St Jean

Lambert

(Arrived late from 10th Br. Div. Should have been brigaded with Best who was temporarily under Picton)

Trip

Mont St Jean Farm

Merlen

Collaert (Neth. Cav. Div.)

Ghigny

Somerset

Ponsonby

Vincke

Vivian

Vandeleur

(2)

10th H

Kruse

Kempt

Ompteda

Bijlandt

(4)

Pack

Best

Picton   (5th Br. Div.)

Saxe-Weimar

(4)

Perponcher (2nd Neth. Div.)

Perponcher   (2nd Neth. Div.)

Papelotte

La Haie

La Marache (Smohain)

Kielmannsegge

Lion Mound

Alten (3rd Br. Div.)

ultimate skirmish line

La Haie Sainte

Frichermont (ruins)

(-)

D'Erlon   (I Corps)

Quiot (1st Div.)

Donzelot (2nd Div.)

Marcognet (3rd Div.)

Durutte (4th Div.)

Pégot

Brue

Jacquinot (1st Cav. Div.)

Bruno

Gobrecht

Marbot

7th H

Charlet   Bourgeois   Schmitz   Aulard   Noguès   Grenier

Milhaud (IV Cav. Corps)

Watier (13th Cav. Div.)

Delort (14th Cav. Div.)

Vial

La Belle Alliance

Bachelu (5th Div.)

Campi   Husson

Dommanget

Domon (3rd Cav. Div.)

Dubois   Travers   Farine   Lallemand

Colbert

Lefebvre-Desnouëttes (Guard Lt Cav. Div.)

Div.)

Tissot

Lobau (VI Corps)

Simmer (19th Div.)

Jeanin (20th Div.)

Bellair

Trevenet

Bony

Vinot

Colbert

Subervie (5th Cav. Div.)

Merlin

Picquet

Cav. Div.)

Tromelin

Young Guard

Middle Guard   (-)

Old Guard   (-)

Duhesme

Morand

Friant

Imperial Guard still arriving

Plancenoit

Notes

• Formations are shown covering approximately the area they did on the day. The Middle and Old Guard had not yet arrived and Durutte was still deploying.

• Note how confused Wellington's deployment seems compared with the symmetry of Napoleon's. The Duke's divisional deployment looks haphazard with many formations spread out over large areas.

• No less than eleven of the Duke's brigades formed up north and west of the modern motorway. Almost all of his line was on a reverse slope out of sight to the French. The French army, on the forward slopes of several low ridges, had been put on display to observers on the Mont St Jean ridge.

• At this time the French 'Grand Battery' had not been formed. As was customary, the Imperial Guard formed up with the junior division (Young Guard) in front with the Old Guard in rear as the final reserve. Eventually there were 21 Imperial Guard battalions on the battlefield, not 24.

• The French 7th Hussars under Marbot had been sent to scout towards the Prussians and Grouchy.

⊹ represents a 6- or 9-pounder battery of foot or horse artillery.

⊚ represents a 12-pounder battery of the corps' reserves still arriving.

▨ Anglo-Allied divisional area. Corps not shown.

A view of the western half of the battlefield from the summit of Lion Mound

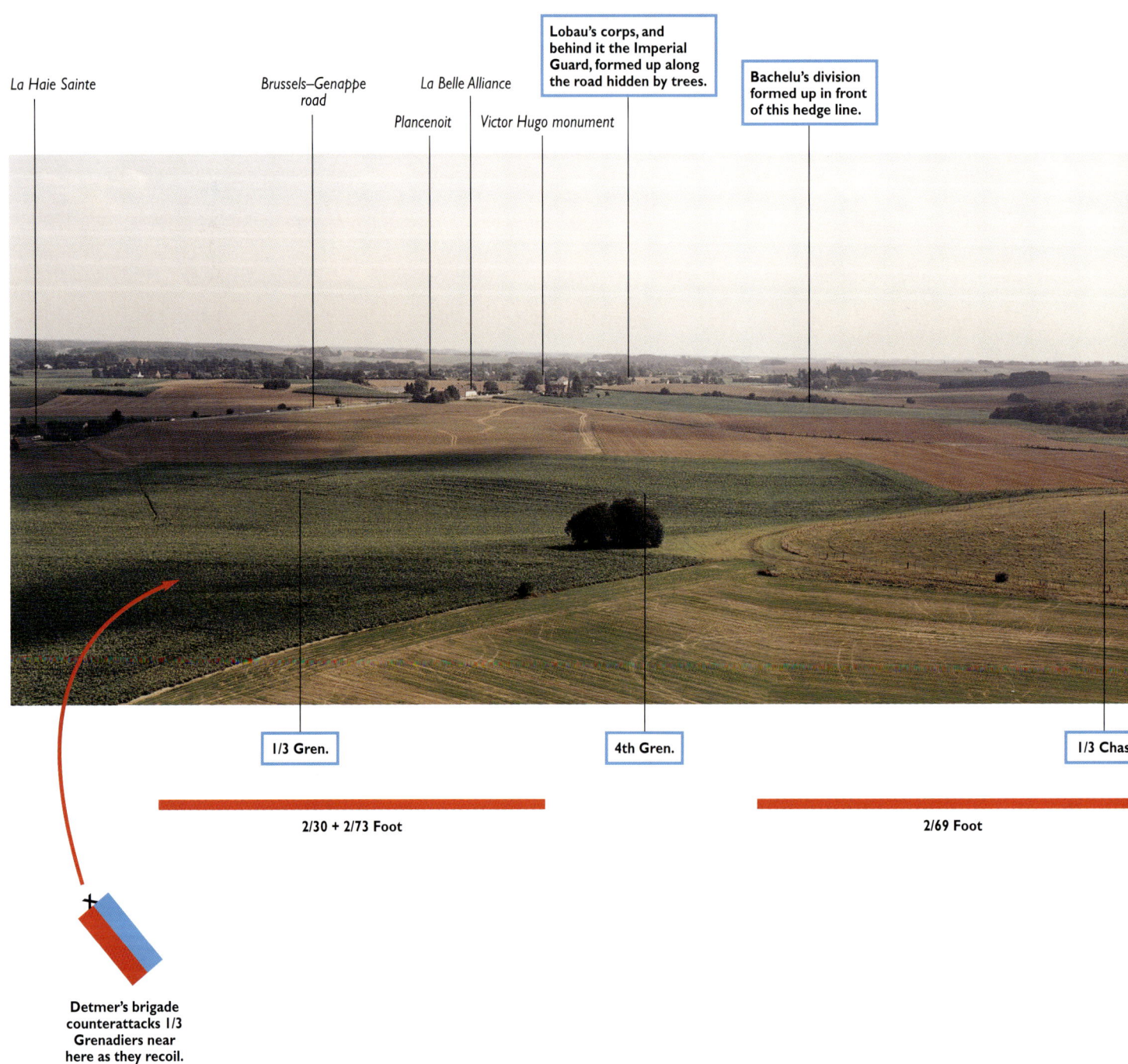

La Haie Sainte

Brussels–Genappe road

La Belle Alliance

Plancenoit

Victor Hugo monument

Lobau's corps, and behind it the Imperial Guard, formed up along the road hidden by trees.

Bachelu's division formed up in front of this hedge line.

1/3 Gren.

4th Gren.

1/3 Chas.

2/30 + 2/73 Foot

2/69 Foot

Detmer's brigade counterattacks 1/3 Grenadiers near here as they recoil.

main roads (one from Genappe and Charleroi, the other from Nivelles) just before they joined at Mont St Jean village. The third possible route from Mons, through Hal, would need a separate force to block it. Secondly, it was the last suitable defensive position south of the Forest of Soignes. This was 8 to 10 kilometres deep, stretching from just south of Brussels to just north of Waterloo village. Although three roads penetrated the forest, and it was not excessively dense, extensive woods prohibited the effective use of cavalry or artillery. Thirdly, Mont St Jean village was only 12 kilometres west of Wavre, where the Prussians were regrouping. Several tracks linked both places, so a halt there facilitated co-operation between, indeed the joining of, Anglo-Allied and Prussian forces.

The tactical attributes of the position are discussed below under **Terrain.**

THE SIZE OF THE BATTLEFIELD (Map 9, p. 126)

The key feature of the Waterloo battlefield was its smallness. The Anglo-Allied and French Armies deployed on an area of undulating agricultural land south of Mont St Jean and north and west of Plancenoit village. It was approximately 5000 metres wide from

The massed French cavalry attacks of the afternoon were confined to the 900 metres between La Haie Sainte and the Hougoumont apple orchard's eastern boundary.

This vegetable field marks the site of the apple orchard that changed hands several times during the day.

'Sunken Way' high water mark of French attacks on Hougoumont.

Kellerman's cuirassiers, and behind them Guyot's heavy Guard cavalry formed up across this forward slope, then devoid of trees.

Foy's division formed up in the rye in front of this hedge line prior to attacking Hougoumont.

Jérôme's division started the battle with an attack on Hougoumont Wood from here.

Piré's lancers guarded the left flank of the French line in this area.

Hougoumont

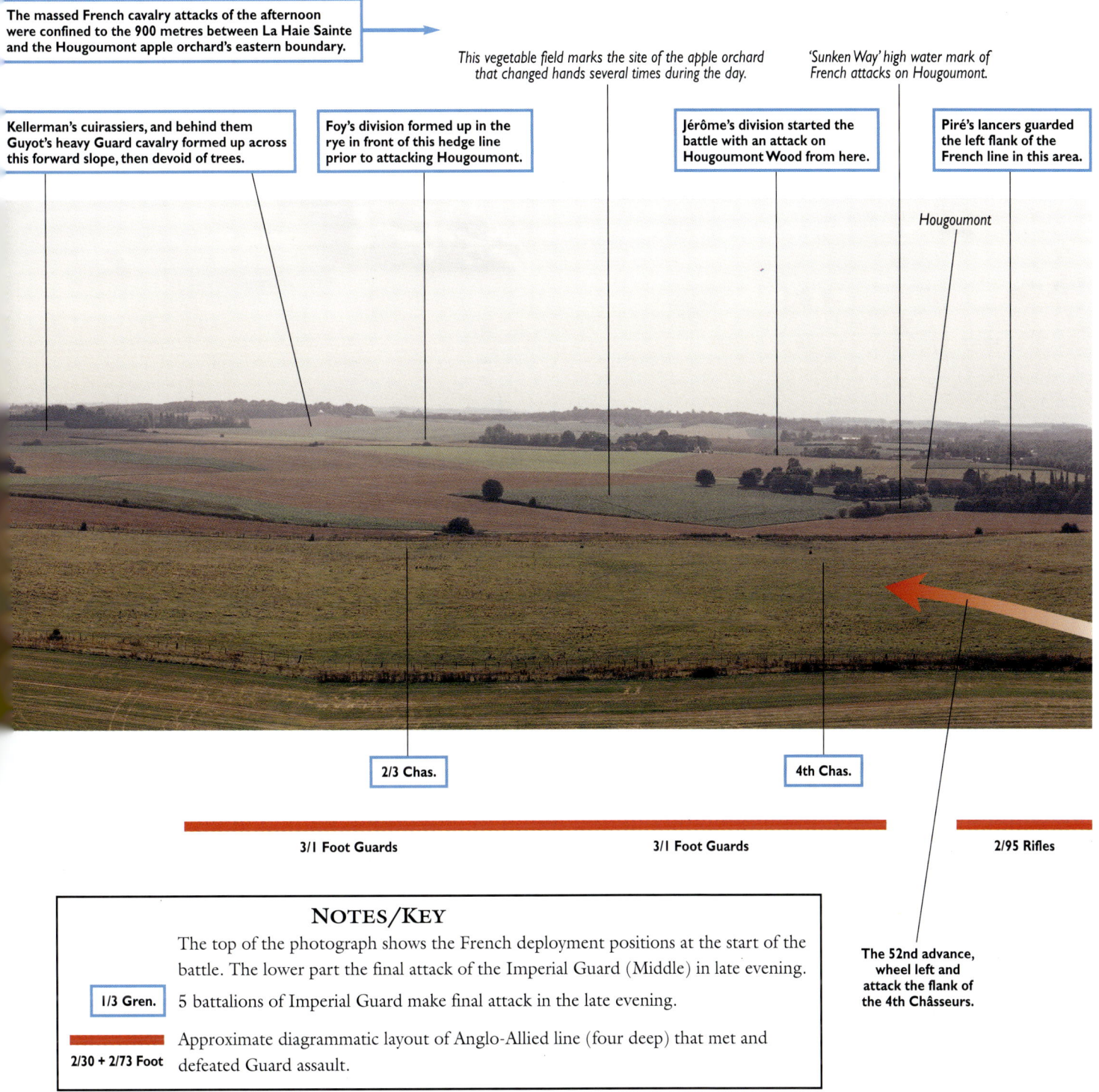

2/3 Chas.

4th Chas.

3/I Foot Guards

3/I Foot Guards

2/95 Rifles

The 52nd advance, wheel left and attack the flank of the 4th Châsseurs.

NOTES/KEY

The top of the photograph shows the French deployment positions at the start of the battle. The lower part the final attack of the Imperial Guard (Middle) in late evening.

| 1/3 Gren. | 5 battalions of Imperial Guard make final attack in the late evening. |

Approximate diagrammatic layout of Anglo-Allied line (four deep) that met and defeated Guard assault.

2/30 + 2/73 Foot

---

just west of Merbe Braine to just east of Frichermont, and 4000 metres deep from Mont St Jean Farm in the north to Rossomme Farm in the south. The actual fighting, however, was confined to a smaller irregular rectangle running for about 3,500 metres east from Hougoumont.

At 11.30 a.m. on that 'Red Sunday' some 150,000 men faced each other across a gap that was never more than 1,200 metres wide and sometimes as little as 300 metres wide. Towards the end of the battle, when all the Prussians that arrived in time were engaged, some 200,000 men, 60,000 horses and 537 guns had

been committed to action inside a combat area measuring approximately 4000 x 4000 metres. Almost 200 years and two world wars later no subsequent battle has managed to cram so many men and animals into so small a space. At the end of the day the dead, the dying and the wounded quite literally carpeted the ground. Men and horses lay in inextricably tangled heaps. In parts of the field it would have been possible to walk across the battlefield from body to body without touching the ground. All this carnage occurred in the space of ten hours (11.30 a.m.–9.30 p.m.). Assuming the total battlefield casualties to be 54,000 (Anglo-Allied 17,000, Prussian

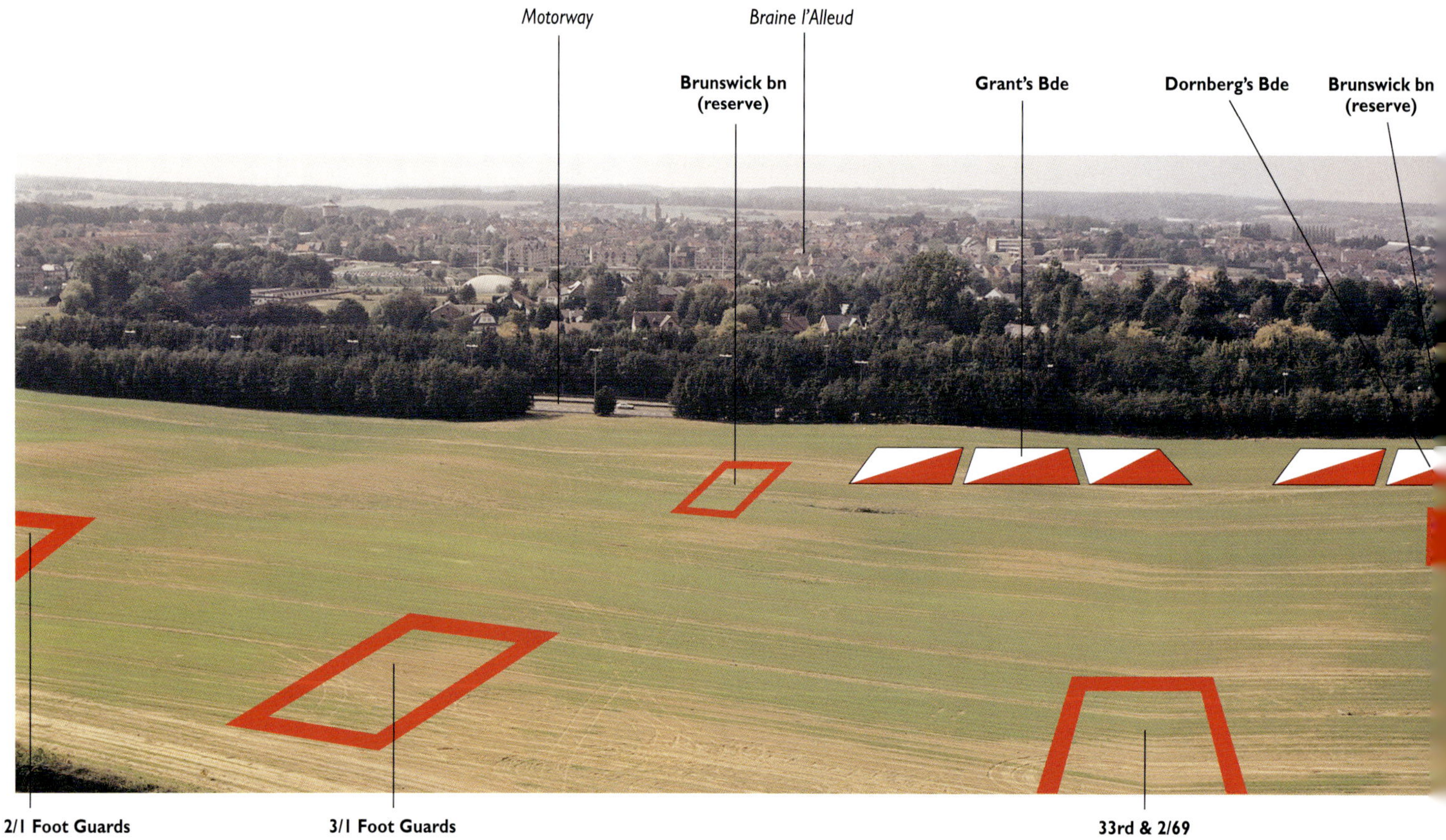

Motorway

Braine l'Alleud

Brunswick bn (reserve)

Grant's Bde

Dornberg's Bde

Brunswick bn (reserve)

2/1 Foot Guards

3/1 Foot Guards

33rd & 2/69

Arenschildt (3rd H KGL)

1/1 Nassau

Merlen's Bde

Bremen & Verden bns.

2/1 Nassau

Joins with image above

Road to Braine l'Alleud

Road to Braine l'Alleud

Hake (Cumberland H)

Brunswick bn
(reserve)

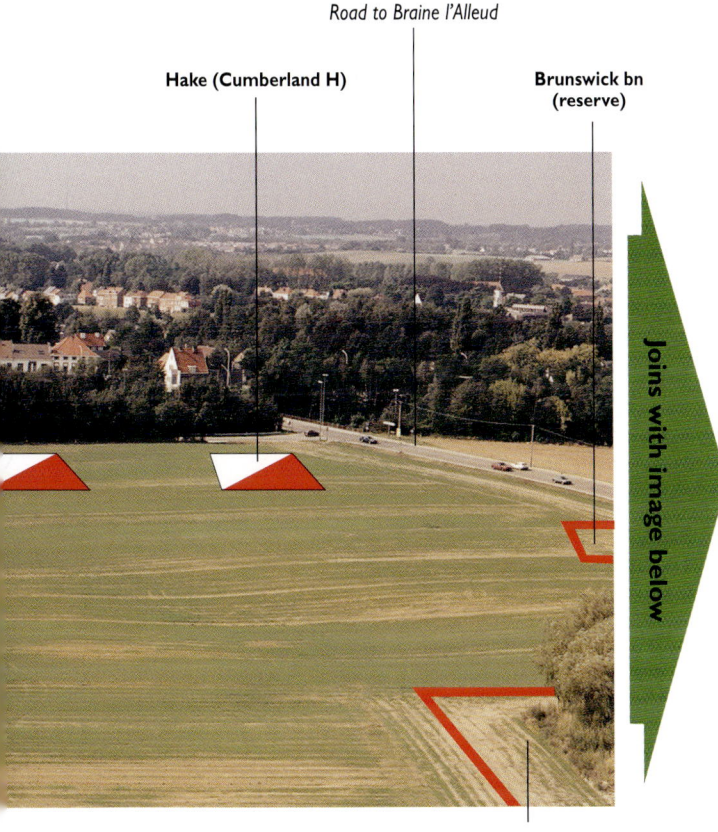

Joins with image below

Panoramic views of reverse slope of Wellington's position showing approximate locations of squares and cavalry reserves at about 4.00 p.m. at the start of the French massed cavalry attacks.

2/30 & 2/73
(Wellington used
this square for
some of the time)

Trip's Dutch/Belgian
Hy Cavalry Bde

3/1 Nassau

York &
Grubenhagen bns

Remnants of
Household &
Union Bdes

5th KGL

8th KGL

1st Lt Bn KGL

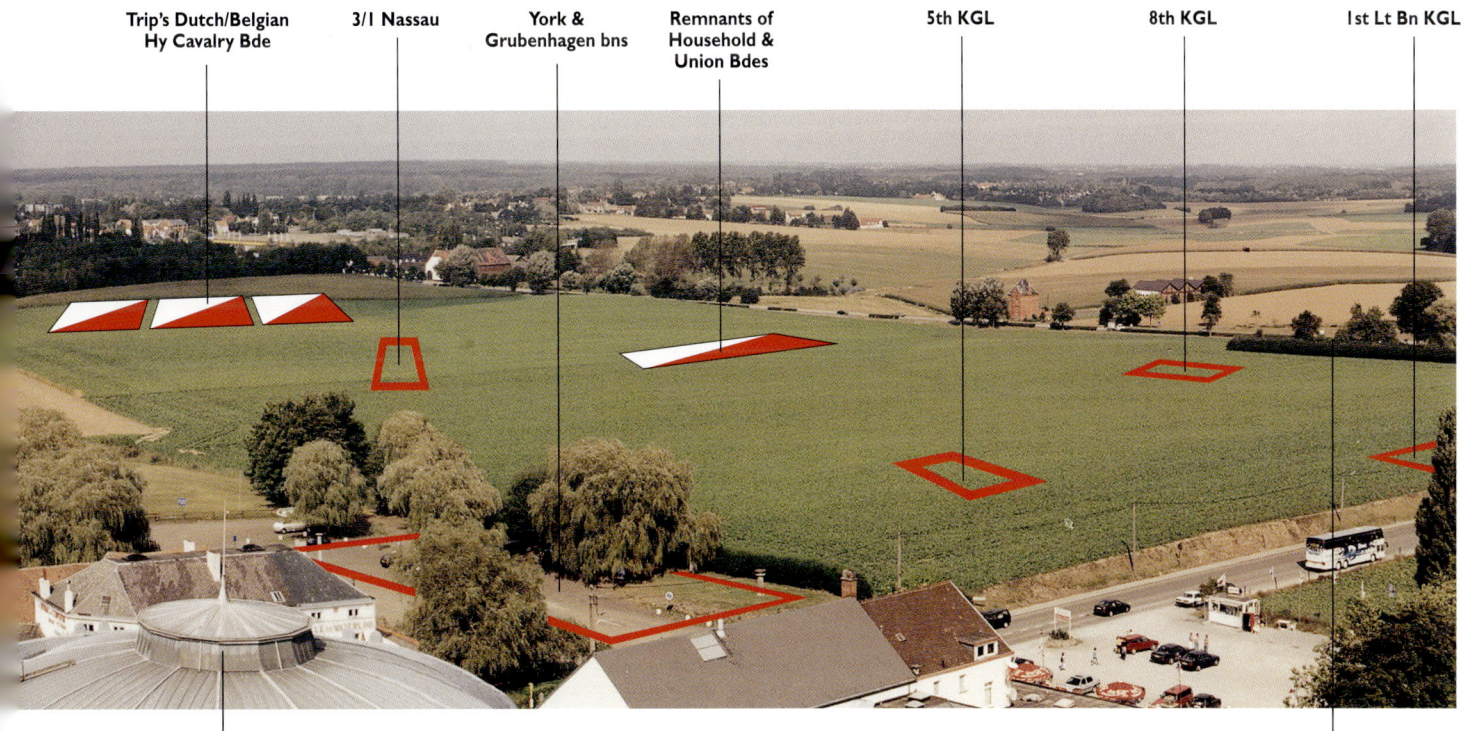

Panorama building

Brussels–Genappe road

A view of the eastern half of the battlefield from the summit of Lion Mound

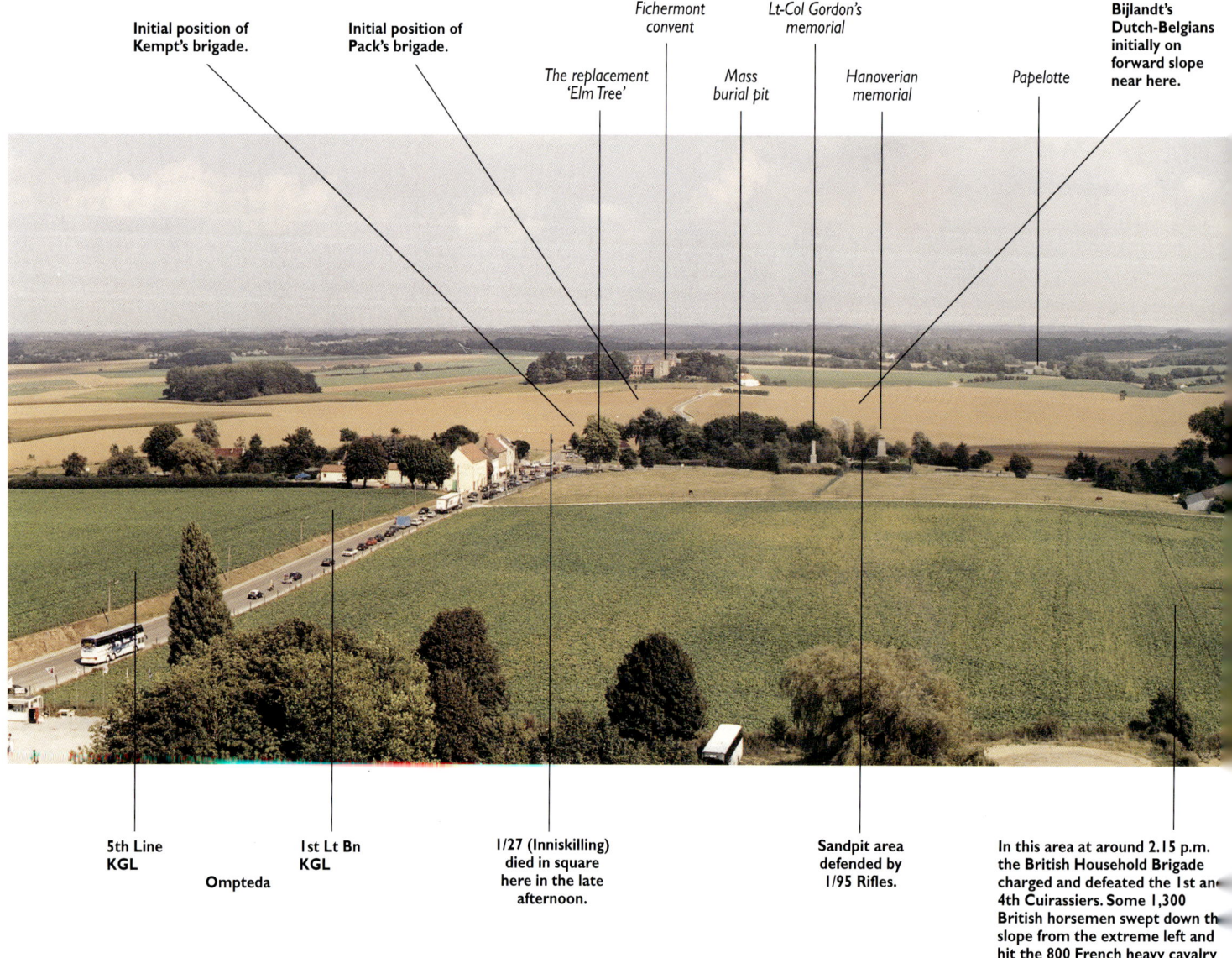

Initial position of Kempt's brigade.

Initial position of Pack's brigade.

Fichermont convent

The replacement 'Elm Tree'

Lt-Col Gordon's memorial

Mass burial pit

Hanoverian memorial

Papelotte

Bijlandt's Dutch-Belgians initially on forward slope near here.

5th Line KGL

Ompteda

1st Lt Bn KGL

1/27 (Inniskilling) died in square here in the late afternoon.

Sandpit area defended by 1/95 Rifles.

In this area at around 2.15 p.m. the British Household Brigade charged and defeated the 1st and 4th Cuirassiers. Some 1,300 British horsemen swept down the slope from the extreme left and hit the 800 French heavy cavalry protecting the left flank of Quiot's attack on La Haie Sainte.

7000, French 30,000, then an average of 5,400 men were hit every hour, 90 every minute, and 1.5 every second of that long summer afternoon and evening.

It is often not appreciated that the battlefield is also one vast, unmarked graveyard. Thousands of dead of all nationalities lie under the surface, some not much deeper than the plough blade's furrow. Several large burial pits were used as mass communal graves for the majority of those killed. One is under the open space in front of the South Gate at Hougoumont, another under the scrub and rubbish that litters the space immediately north of the Hanoverian monument near the old 'Elm Tree' crossroads, and yet another a few metres north, under and around the Belgian monument.

BATTLEFIELD CHANGES

A glance at Maps 8 & 9 (pp. 119 & 126) is enough to show that the battlefield, the area of the actual fighting, has not changed dramatically since 1815. The modern urban sprawl of Braine l'Alleud has been confined to west of the motorway to Brussels that itself marks the eastern edge of the battlefield, as did the old Nivelles road. It is still a farming community. In summer, fields of wheat, rye and corn stand (although not so high) as they did before the battle. The crops are still harvested by farmers from Hougoumont, La Haie Sainte, Papelotte and Plancenoit. The Charleroi road carries heavy traffic now but still follows precisely the same route as when it neatly bisected the combat area. The layout of cross tracks is virtually identical, their surfaces often of the same cobbles, following the same routes and disappearing into the same deep cuttings (particularly south of Papelotte). Plancenoit remains a sleepy, rural village. More houses line the streets and there has been some expansion on the western side, but the old street pattern is easily recognizable on a modern map. The imposing church (reconstructed since the battle), whose spire, peeping above the trees, guided Bülow's Prussians towards their objective, is timeless.

La Haie Sainte defended by 2nd Lt Bn KGL and others.

Durutte's division deployed here.

Marcognet's division deployed here.

Donzelot's division deployed here.

Plancenoit

The French 'Grand Battery' deployed along this ridge.

Main North-South Brussels–Genappe road that bisected both armies.

Note

This photograph shows the French deployment, and some of the Anglo–Allied deployment, on the eastern half of the battlefield at about 1.30pm.

That the field remains easily recognizable today has been due to determined resistance to the demands of various developers and builders over the intervening years. Some encroachment has, however, taken place. Two changes are obvious from the map. The first is the construction of the Lion Mound. This entailed excavating hundreds of tons of soil from near Wellington's crossroads and, with the construction of the Mound, led to the establishment adjacent to it of 'Lion Village', with its tourist facilities. The piling up of so much soil for the Mound has flattened the contours and removed the steep banks from along the roads to the east (except by Lieutenant-Colonel Gordon's monument). The second is that the woods and orchards around Hougoumont have gone, while there are trees to the north of the farm that did not exist in 1815. Some building has also been allowed. There are three modern houses on the western edge of the Brussels–Genappe road, and in 1929 the Fichermont Convent was built 700 metres east of Wellington's 'Elm Tree' crossroads on the old, rough road to Ohain.

The battlefield has come under threat several times in the twentieth century. In March 1914 a Belgian law (the Protection of the Battlefield Law) prohibited demolition or building within an area of 1,347 acres. However, this did not prevent the convent's construction. In 1933 a proposed bill to allow a worker's housing estate was successfully resisted. But the biggest threat was as recent as the 1970s, when it was planned to route the new motorway to Brussels across the field. The counterattack to this outlandish proposal was led by several prominent personalities, including the 8th Duke of Wellington and Field-Marshal Sir Gerald Templar. The motorway now hugs the western edge, running for 2000 metres alongside the old Brussels–Nivelles road.

Despite the changes, today's visitor finds it exceptionally easy to find his way around and identify where and how the battle ebbed and flowed. Ghosts of the soldiers present would be able to pinpoint precisely where they marched, fought, were wounded or died.

Terrain Features of Tactical Importance or Potential   Map 9

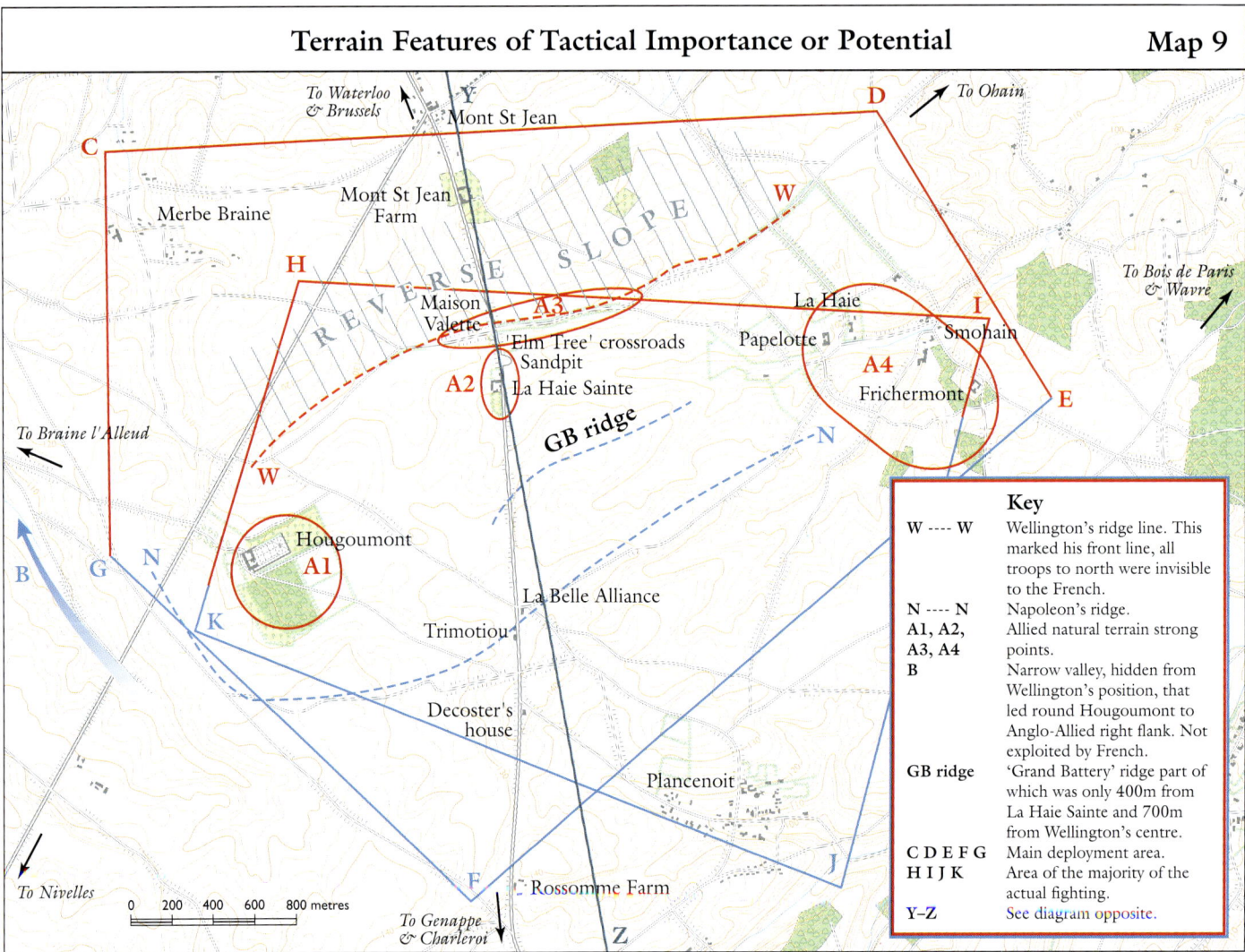

Key

W ---- W	Wellington's ridge line. This marked his front line, all troops to north were invisible to the French.
N ---- N	Napoleon's ridge.
A1, A2, A3, A4	Allied natural terrain strong points.
B	Narrow valley, hidden from Wellington's position, that led round Hougoumont to Anglo-Allied right flank. Not exploited by French.
GB ridge	'Grand Battery' ridge part of which was only 400m from La Haie Sainte and 700m from Wellington's centre.
C D E F G H I J K	Main deployment area. Area of the majority of the actual fighting.
Y–Z	See diagram opposite.

Key Terrain Features (Map 9 above and diagram opposite)

There are eight key terrain features on the battlefield that played, or had the potential to play, important roles in the coming conflict. They were all of significance to both the attacker (Napoleon) and the defender (Wellington). They were as follows:

THE MONT ST JEAN RIDGE

This low ridge, only rising a maximum of 30 metres above the valley floor, ran approximately south-west to north-east some 700 metres south of Mont St Jean Farm. Following its crest was the Braine l'Alleud–Ohain road. It is marked W – W on Map 9 above. This was the Anglo-Allied front line. It stretched for 1,500 metres either side of the paved Brussels–Charleroi road (which cut the position precisely in two). From it those of Wellington's troops on the crest were able to watch the majority of the French army deploying for battle. Until the shooting started, the view across the shallow valley was only partially restricted by undulations, standing crops and some scattered trees. While much of the battlefield was covered in high standing wheat, rye, barley and oats, there were also patches of potatoes, peas, plough, clover – even a low, light green hemp with a pale blue flower. All the ground to the north of this ridge was on a reverse slope and in dead ground to the French. This ridge provided the defending Anglo-Allied Army with protection from view and substantial, although not

complete, protection from artillery fire. When Napoleon gazed through his glass at this ridge he could only see what Wellington wanted him to see – those troops that were on the forward slope or the skyline. The Duke made certain very little was on view.

THE BELLE ALLIANCE RIDGE

This ridge runs from 450 metres south of Papelotte, south-west through La Belle Alliance, curving west and then north-west round Hougoumont before continuing in the direction of Braine l'Alleud. It is marked N – N on Map 9. Along this concave ridge Napoleon deployed his front line. The distance from Wellington's position varied from 350 metres (the Allied troops on the southern edge of the Hougoumont wood) to 1,400 metres. From end to end the French front line stretched for 3,700 metres. La Belle Alliance was only marginally east of centre. The ridge was slightly lower than Wellington's, particularly on the extremities. As the attacker it offered little advantage to the French.

HOUGOUMONT

This walled château/farm with its orchard and wood provided Wellington with a natural strongpoint, an anchor, 400 metres in front of his right flank. Garrisoned, it would compel an attacker to take it before he could threaten the right of the position on the Mont St Jean ridge. If not directly attacked it would channel advancing troops to the east, exposing their flank as they bypassed it moving north.

LA HAIE SAINTE

Another bastion conveniently placed 250 metres in front of Wellington's centre. Coupled with the sandpit 50 metres north and on the other side of the road, it provided the defenders of the ridge with an outpost to disrupt and delay any assault up the main road. The capture of La Haie Sainte was virtually a prerequisite of a successful assault on the centre.

THE 'ELM TREE' CROSSROADS AND THE OHAIN ROAD

This crossroads, in the centre of the Anglo-Allied position, provided an excellent natural defensive position against troops advancing from the south. For about 200 metres the southern and western branches of road were sunk in a steep sided cutting, in places 30 metres below ground level, effectively disrupting the movement of horsemen and guns, and giving useful protection to infantry defenders. The eastern branch, although not a sunken road, had hedges on a low bank running on both sides of the road towards Ohain for some 600 metres, almost to the site of the present Frichermont Convent. Again, this was a barrier to guns and it was a struggle for men or horses to break through. One of Wellington's young ADCs, Lieutenant Cathcart (who was to be killed as a general in the Crimean War), described it thus:

> For about 100 yards, more or less, it was very hollow. At the end going down into the high road [Brussels road] it might have been 10 or even 15 feet deep. I have reason to know it, for there was but one way of going down into it [the Brussels road] from the field at the back of La Haye Sainte, which was very slippery, [and] would admit not more than two horses at a time, and might have been at an angle of 45.

The elm tree that grew in the south-west sector of the cross-roads survived the battle but not the souvenir hunters. A shrewd London businessman bought it for 200 francs. He did a splendid trade in canes, napkin rings and snuffboxes.

THE PAPELOTTE, LA HAIE, SMOHAIN AND FRICHERMONT AREA

This area of sturdily built farms, plus the tiny village of Smohain, provided an extended area of potential strong points in front of Wellington's left flank. Although some distance from the Anglo-Allied ridge (Papelotte 600 metres, Frichermont 1,200 metres) the whole area was typical 'bocage' country – deep sunken lanes, high banks and thick hedges – the sort of terrain that almost 130 years later would cause untold problems to Allied troops in Normandy. These lanes today are virtually unchanged: still deep, dark and gloomy from overhanging foliage. A number would stop a tank, let alone a horseman or cannon. To some English, West Country soldiers they were reminiscent of leafy Devon lanes.

'GRAND BATTERY' (GB) RIDGE

This is a finger of higher ground that points from the Brussels road, halfway between La Belle Alliance and La Haie Sainte, towards Papelotte. From the road it runs north-east for over 1000 metres, gradually dropping into the tangle of lanes around the farm and Smohain. It runs parallel to both the Mont St Jean and La Belle Alliance ridges, and is virtually the same height as the latter. It is 500 metres from the right half of the French front line and 650 metres from thc Anglo-Allied ridge. It is still a bare open ridge, devoid of cover, although on that June Sunday it was covered with

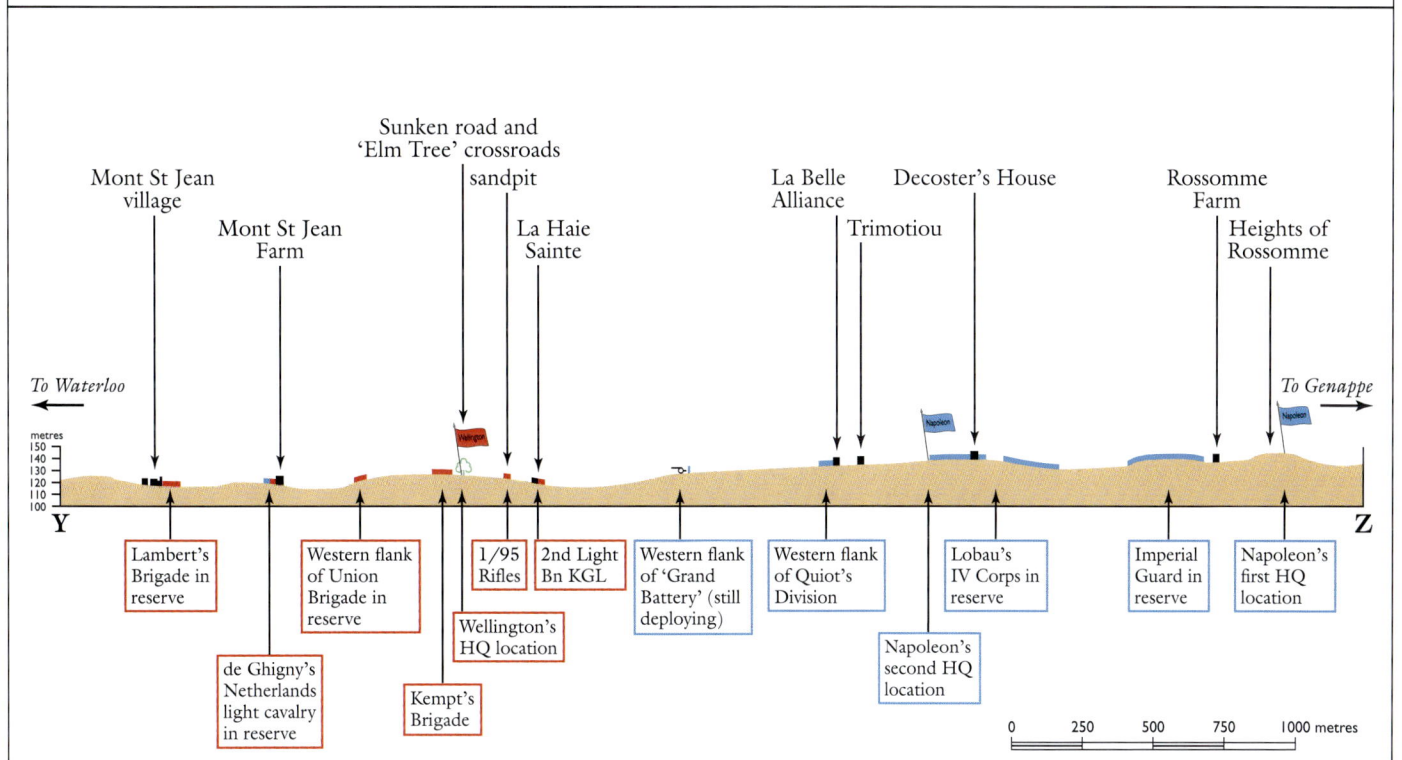

A Cross-section through the Centre of the Battlefield at 12.30 p.m.
(Y–Z on Map 9)

Mont St Jean village

Mont St Jean Farm

Sunken road and 'Elm Tree' crossroads

sandpit

La Haie Sainte

La Belle Alliance

Decoster's House

Trimotiou

Rossomme Farm

Heights of Rossomme

To Waterloo

To Genappe

metres
150
140
130
120
110
100

Y

Z

Lambert's Brigade in reserve

Western flank of Union Brigade in reserve

1/95 Rifles

2nd Light Bn KGL

Western flank of 'Grand Battery' (still deploying)

Western flank of Quiot's Division

Lobau's IV Corps in reserve

Imperial Guard in reserve

Napoleon's first HQ location

de Ghigny's Netherlands light cavalry in reserve

Kempt's Brigade

Wellington's HQ location

Napoleon's second HQ location

0   250   500   750   1000 metres

high, ripening rye. This ridge was to provide Napoleon with an ideal gun platform for his 'Grand Battery'. Forever an artilleryman, the Emperor pushed forward eighty cannons and howitzers to pound Wellington's position from this ridge.

BRAINE L'ALLEUD VALLEY

This narrow valley (marked 'B' on Map 9) leads from behind Napoleon's left, well to the west of Hougoumont and thence to Braine l'Alleud village. It is a valley of great potential. Troops moving along this valley would be unseen from the right half of Wellington's ridge, and unseen from Hougoumont as they marched in the dead ground behind La Belle Alliance ridge. This small valley offered an opportunity, a route to the Emperor to outflank and surprise his adversary. It probably passed unnoticed; it was certainly not used.

Villages

PLANCENOIT (Map 9, p. 126)

(see also Section 9 'Highlights of the Battle')

A small, exclusively farming community located at the head of the Lasne river valley. In 1815 it was the home to some 500 people, virtually all of who decamped with the arrival of the armies. It was the only village on the battlefield and as such became the focal point of all French–Prussian combat. Not a single soldier from Wellington's army set foot in Plancenoit during the battle. Its cobbled streets, walled gardens and solid houses witnessed a monumental struggle for possession during the three hours before darkness and the final French rout. By far the fiercest fighting, with bayonet, sword and clubbed musket, took place around the Roman Catholic Church of Saint Cathérine in the village centre. The church, built on a prominent mound and surrounded by a stone wall, became a strongpoint for both sides. Inside it was crammed with the wounded and dying.

During the late afternoon and throughout the evening the Prussians threw first two brigades, then four and finally five into repeated assaults from the east. In all some 30,000 Prussian infantrymen were eventually committed to what was to prove almost an impossible task, costing them the bulk of their 7000 casualties. Initially the defenders were the five battalions of the 1st Brigade of Simmer's 19th Infantry Division. But as the pressure mounted, Napoleon sent in the Young Guard and Simmer moved to the northern outskirts. The Young Guard had eight battalions under Duhesme. Finally, two battalions of the Old Guard were required to help hold this key village, the loss of which would have meant the surrounding, and probable annihilation, of the French Army. At dusk Imperial Guardsmen still clung to the eastern edge but the village had already changed hands several times.

Plancenoit was not initially garrisoned by the French, although its church (whose clock continued to chime the hours throughout the day) was only 1,200 metres from the Brussels–Charleroi road that exactly bisected Napoleon's army. Frenchmen had sought shelter from the misery of the rain in its houses and barns during the night of 17/18 June. Damp doors and shutters had burned reluctantly as huddled figures sought warmth. But with the dawn the troops were rousted out to trudge, wet and weary, away to their deployment areas. Not until nearly 6.00 p.m. did some of them return to fight among the houses.

Today the village has changed through the increase in population and the building of modern houses, particularly in the west.

These developments have occurred because the village is excluded from the 1914 Protection of the Battlefield Law. Nevertheless, the main street layout remains much as it was at the time, the church still dominating the centre of the village, although the school was not there in 1815 and the modern open square is larger. It is a village full of memories and memorials.

PLANCENOIT MEMORIALS (Map 10, p. 131)

Saint-Cathérine Church

This church is not the identical one that witnessed so much bloodshed on that fateful Sunday, as extensive rebuilding work was undertaken in 1856 that included the reconstruction of the tower and spire. The sketch and photograph below show the differences.

Plancenoit Church in 1815. The spire, jutting above the trees, acted as a guide to the Prussians as they advanced from the east. Some of the most intense fighting of the battle took place around this church.

Saint-Cathérine's Church, Plancenoit today. Notice the rebuilding that has taken place since 1815 and the memorial plaques on either side of the door. Photo: the author

On the wall to the left of the door is a plaque to a twenty-eight-year-old Lieutenant Louis of the Young Guard. It reads:

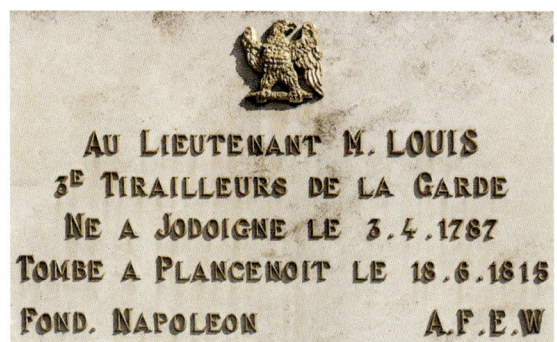

(To Lieutenant M. Louis, 3rd Tirailleurs of the Guard, born at Jodoigne 3.4.1787, fell at Plancenoit 18.6.1815.)

To the right is another to the Young Guard and their commander Général de Division Duhesme who was mortally wounded in the village. It reads:

(In this village of Plancenoit that became famous on 18 June 1815, the Young Guard of the Emperor Napoleon commanded by General Count Duhesme who was mortally wounded.)

Inside the church on the left wall is a white marble plaque dedicated to a young artillery lieutenant from the Old Guard who was killed at the start of the battle. It reads:

A LA MEMOIRE DE
JAQUES CLES ADRE TATTET
LIEUTENANT D'ARTILLERIE DE LA
VIELLE GARDE
MEMBRE DE LA LEGION D'HONNEUR
TUE AU DEBUT DE LA BATAILLE
DU 18 JUIN 1815
A L'AGE DE 22 ANS.

(To the memory of Jaques Cles Adre Tattet, Lieutenant of the Old Guard Artillery, member of the Legion of Honour killed at the start of the battle of 18 June 1815, aged 22 years.)

Also on the wall of the church is a plaque commemorating the efforts of the 1st and 2nd Companies (Batteries) of the 8th Foot Artillery Regiment under Colonel Caron, who were heavily involved from the outset with the defence of Plancenoit. The 1st Company from the 19th Infantry Division (Simmer) was commanded by Capitaine Parisot, who was wounded; the 2nd Company from the 20th Division (Jeanin) by Capitaine Paquet. Both companies had six 6-pounder guns and two 5.5-inch howitzers. It reads:

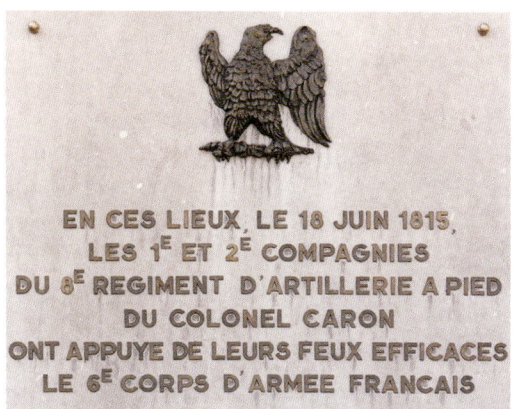

(Near this place on 18 June 1815 the 1st and 2nd Companies of 8th Foot Artillery Regiment under Colonel Caron fought their guns effectively, the French VI Army Corps.)

Prussian Memorial

Close to the triangular road junction on the northern edge of the village, looking back (eastwards towards the Fatherland) down the track from Lasne that Bülow's corps used as their axis of advance, is the Prussian monument. It is a black, Gothic arrowhead surmounted by an Iron Cross (the Prussians instituted the Iron Cross as a decoration for bravery in the field in 1813). It was erected just three years after the battle on a mound once occupied by a French battery. It is the only memorial to the Prussians on the actual battlefield. When French forces marched into Belgium again in 1832 to assist the Belgians in throwing off Dutch rule, they started to destroy this monument but were stopped by their commander, Maréchal Maurice Gérard who had fought under Grouchy during the campaign of 1815. Nevertheless, the monument needed repairs both in 1944 and 1965.

The inscription, written in German, reads:

TO THE DEAD HEROES
THEIR GRATEFUL KING AND COUNTRY
MAY THEY REST IN PEACE
BELLE ALLIANCE 18 JUNE 1815.

Note that the Prussians call it the Battle of Belle Alliance, not Waterloo.

The Young Guard Memorial

This rectangular monument stands on a small island of grass and flowering bushes a few metres south-west of the Prussian monument at the junction of the three roads north of the village. All eight battalions of the Young Guard (tirailleurs and voltigeurs), some 4,750 men, provided the bulk of the defenders of Plancenoit. It commemorates the exceptionally determined resistance of the Young Guard to Bülow's corps in the late afternoon. It reads:

EN CE LIEU
LE 18 JUIN 1815
A 5 HEURES DU SOIR
LA JEUNE GARDE
DE
L'EMPEREUR
OUS LES ORDRES
DU GENERAL COMTE
DUHESME
S'OPPOSA
GLORIEUEMENT
AUX PRUSSIENS
DU
GENERAL BULOW.

(Near this place on 18 June 1815 at 5.00 p.m. the Emperor's Young Guard, under the orders of General Count Duhesme fought gloriously against the Prussians of General Bülow.)

5th Regiment de Ligne

This memorial is located at the cross-roads on the south-east of the village. It commemorates the initial defence of Plancenoit in the area by the two battalions of the 5th Ligne under Colonel Roussille. This Regiment was part of the 19th Division (Simmer) and had fought a delaying action down the Lasne road from the north-east that the Prussians under Bülow had used as their axis of advance. The memorial says: Near this place on 18 June 1815 the 5th Infantry Regiment under Colonel Roussille of Simmer's division, fought heroically against the Prussian corps of General Bülow.

Colonel Roussille

It was one of Roussille's two battalions of the 5th Ligne that had marched to confront Napoleon at the small village of Laffrey, south of Grenoble, over three months earlier. When Napoleon walked forward the troops refused to fire and enthusiastically went over to his cause. The same evening de la Bédoyère's 7th Ligne also defected. Roussille had wanted no part of this defection but was so intensely loyal to his regiment that he begged Napoleon to allow him to keep the command, saying, 'my regiment abandoned me, but I will not abandon it.' He remained the commanding officer and led the regiment against the Prussian advance on Plancenoit. He was killed on the eastern edge of the village. He died, not for the Emperor, not even for France, but for his Regiment.

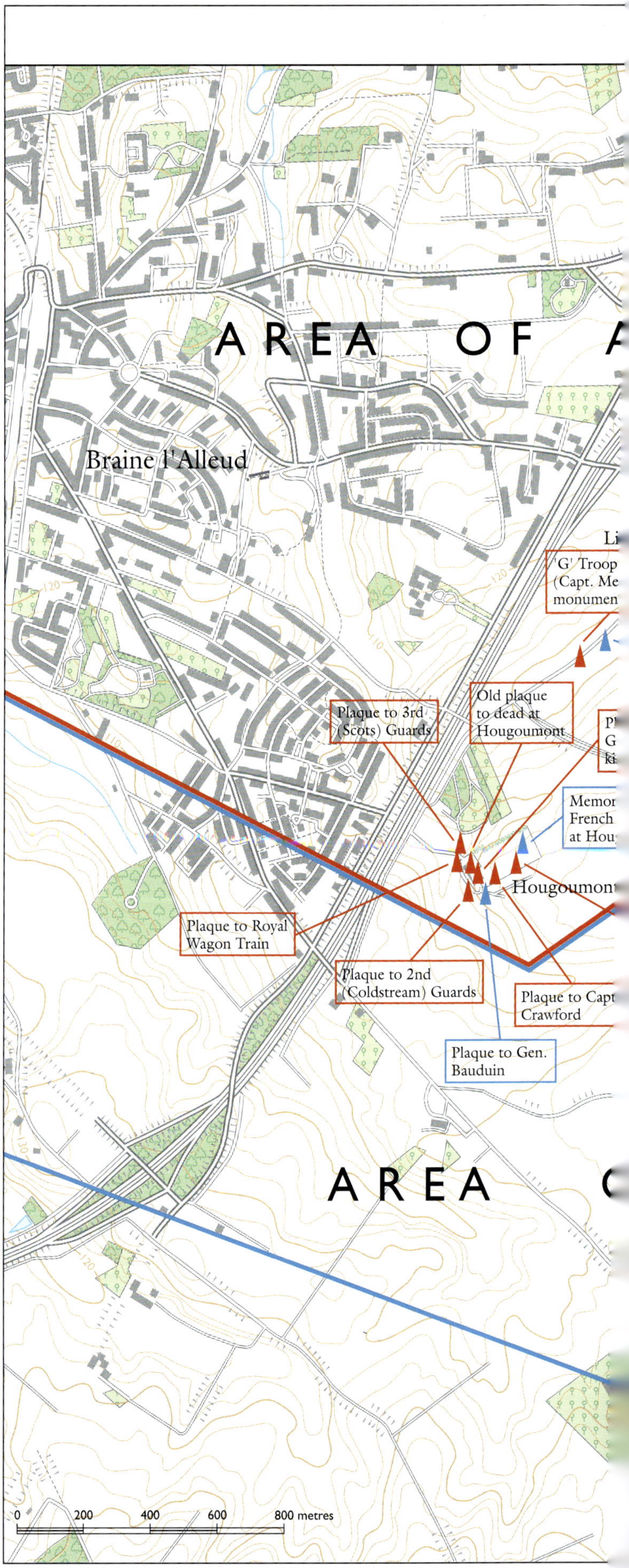

AREA OF A

Braine l'Alleud

Li

'G' Troop
(Capt. Me
monumen

Plaque to 3rd
(Scots) Guards

Old plaque
to dead at
Hougoumont

Pl
G
ki

Memor
French
at Hou

Plaque to Royal
Wagon Train

Hougoumont

Plaque to 2nd
(Coldstream) Guards

Plaque to Capt
Crawford

Plaque to Gen.
Bauduin

AREA

0   200   400   600   800 metres

Battlefield Memorials

Map 10

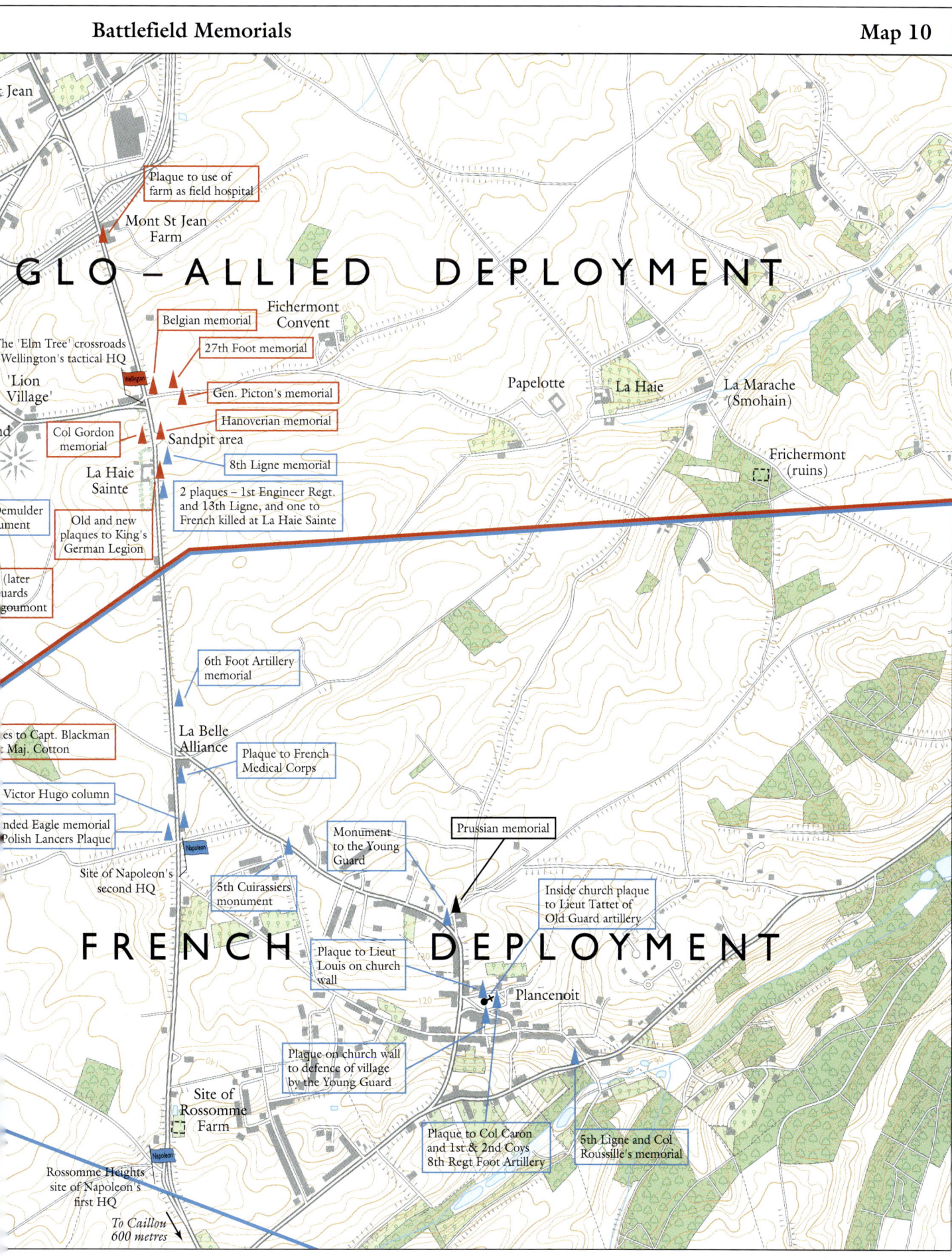

ANGLO – ALLIED DEPLOYMENT

FRENCH DEPLOYMENT

Plaque to use of farm as field hospital

Mont St Jean Farm

The 'Elm Tree' crossroads Wellington's tactical HQ

'Lion Village'

Belgian memorial

27th Foot memorial

Gen. Picton's memorial

Hanoverian memorial

Col Gordon memorial

Sandpit area

8th Ligne memorial

2 plaques – 1st Engineer Regt. and 13th Ligne, and one to French killed at La Haie Sainte

La Haie Sainte

Old and new plaques to King's German Legion

Fichermont Convent

Papelotte

La Haie

La Marache (Smohain)

Frichermont (ruins)

Hemulder ...ment

...(later ...uards ...goumont

6th Foot Artillery memorial

...es to Capt. Blackman ...t Maj. Cotton

La Belle Alliance

Plaque to French Medical Corps

Victor Hugo column

...nded Eagle memorial ...Polish Lancers Plaque

Site of Napoleon's second HQ

5th Cuirassiers monument

Monument to the Young Guard

Prussian memorial

Inside church plaque to Lieut Tattet of Old Guard artillery

Plaque to Lieut Louis on church wall

Plancenoit

Plaque on church wall to defence of village by the Young Guard

Site of Rossomme Farm

Plaque to Col Caron and 1st & 2nd Coys 8th Regt Foot Artillery

5th Ligne and Col Roussille's memorial

Rossomme Heights site of Napoleon's first HQ

To Caillou 600 metres

Braine l'Alleud (Map 10, p. 131)

A village on the north-western edge of the battlefield with a population of some 2,750 people in 1815. It has expanded ten-fold in the intervening 200 years, with many of its inhabitants commuting daily to work in the capital by road and rail. Its houses have encroached in all directions, absorbing the old hamlet of Merbe Braine to the north-east, only being stopped by the autoroute to Brussels (and battlefield protection legislation) that marks the western edge of the battlefield.

Braine l'Alleud marked the extreme right flank of the Anglo-Allied line on the Sunday morning. Wellington posted Lieutenant-General Chassé with the 7000 men of the 3rd Netherlands Division in and around the village. The Duke was uncertain as to the quality of these troops so they were deployed initially in what was likely to be a quiet area. The village saw no fighting; only some forward patrols of Piré's lancers came within striking distance. Towards evening Chassé was brought in to reinforce the centre. The 1st Brigade charged the Middle Guard Grenadiers as they recoiled after their final, desperate assault.

Like Plancenoit, Braine l'Alleud's most famous landmark is its church. The Church of Saint Etienne has a particularly unusual spire atop the tower. It closely resembles the Prussian Army helmet with a spike on top (pickelhaube) that was introduced in the middle of the nineteenth century and worn by German troops as late as World War I. Although at Waterloo the Prussians wore shakos or soft caps, a legend has grown up that Prussian soldiers asked their officers at the start of their march to the battle how they would know if the day was won. The answer was, 'When you see a church tower surmounted by a helmet.' From the road south of La Belle Alliance the Braine l'Alleud church spire (helmet) can be seen.

After the fighting inhabitants of the village came forward to tend the wounded while many cared for convalescents in their homes. The church became a hospital and its role as such is commemorated on a plaque on the exterior wall at the foot of the tower. It reads:

The Church of St Etienne in Braine l'Alleud. Note the spire resembles a late nineteenth-century Prussian helmet.

CETTE EGLISE SERVIT D'HOPITAL AU LENDEMAIN DE LA BATAILLE CHARITABLEMENT LES BRAINOIS VINRENT EN AIDE AUX BLESSES JUIN 1815.

(This church served as a hospital on the day following the battle when the good people of Braine l'Alleud came to tend the wounded, June 1815.) The same words are used inside the church on a bas-relief showing Simon Cyrene helping Jesus carry his cross.

The old Hôtel des Colonnes in Mont St Jean village. Here Victor Hugo stayed in 1861 to explore the battlefield and write the chapter on Waterloo for his famous work Les Misérables. *It was demolished in 1963.*

Merbe Braine (Map 9, p. 126)

A handful of houses and a farm, little more than a hamlet, situated 1,500 metres north of Hougoumont behind Wellington's right flank. It is now a suburb of Braine l'Alleud. On the night of 17/18 June it did no more than provide some shelter and firewood to nearby troops. At the start of the battle Colonel Hew Halkett's four battalions of Hanoverians (part of the 2nd British Infantry Division) were deployed immediately south of this tiny village. In the evening they advanced to the centre to participate in the overthrow of the Middle Guard's attack. The Brunswick Contingent under Colonel Olfermann was also close by at the outset. They later left the vicinity to reinforce the front line in resisting the French cavalry attacks.

Mont St Jean (Map 9, p. 126)

A village, not to be confused with the more famous farm of the same name just 400 metres to the south. It was situated at a critical road junction where the main routes from Nivelles and Genappe (Charleroi) joined before continuing north to Waterloo and Brussels as one highway. The village could have lent its name to the battle, as it was on the Mont St Jean ridge about 1000 metres to the south that Wellington drew up his army and received the French assaults. In 1815 it was a small village of some 300 inhabitants whose homes were grouped around the crossroads. Today it is part of the urban sprawl that continues north to Waterloo, although the key crossroads are still there, if somewhat modernized.

Like the other villages and hamlets nearby, Mont St Jean supplied its share of straw, wood and water to the thousands of troops encamped in the surrounding fields. Late arrivals to the battlefield, such as Major-General Lambert's 10th British Brigade, hurried passed its houses to await events in the fields just south of the village.

Although it was designated by Napoleon as the main objective of Ney's assault, and was within range of his 12-pounder cannons, no Frenchmen (other than prisoners) came near it during the day. Afterwards, its humble homes housed wounded and dying, including Major-General Merlen who, mortally wounded, was carried to a hut in Mont St Jean. In later years Sergeant-Major Edward Cotton, who had fought in the battle as a trooper in the British 7th Hussars, took up residence in the village and became a well-known battlefield guide. He penned most of his book *A Voice from Waterloo* there. A more famous visitor was Victor Hugo who stayed for two months in the Hôtel des Colonnes in the village while exploring the battlefield, preparatory to writing the Waterloo chapter of *Les Misérables.* Despite vehement objections, this old hotel was demolished in 1962. Hugo's bedroom balcony is displayed in the museum at Le Caillou.

Smohain (La Marache) (Map 9, p. 126)

Smohain was, and is, a hamlet rather than a village. It consisted of a handful of houses straddling the head of the brook of the same name, located in the broken ground on the left flank of Wellington's line. Apart from modern houses replacing the old ones, it remains much the same today as in 1815. Its population is still under a hundred but its name has changed to La Marache.

Along with the farms of Papelotte, La Haie and the Château of Frichermont, it was defended during the battle by detachments from Prince Saxe-Weimar's Nassau Brigade. There was continuous probing by French skirmishers from the French 4th Infantry Division (Durutte) throughout the day. In the late afternoon the Prussians joined the action, first from Bülow's corps from the south-east and then, around 7.30 p.m., by Ziethen's advance guard deploying north of the hamlet. They arrived in time to drive off the French shortly before the general rout.

Waterloo (Maps 6 & 7, pp. 32 & 34)

The name first appeared as 'Waterlots' in 1128. It meant 'wet meadows by a stream in a forest'. The hamlet and inns that sprang up at Waterloo were a convenient stopping place for travellers on the road south to Namur and Trier. By the sixteenth century it was a main thoroughfare known as Chemin des Wallons. It was one of the first roads in Belgium to be partly paved. The inhabitants of Waterloo made a living by serving ale, keeping the road in repair, cutting timber in the Forest of Soignes and farming. In 1705 the Duke of Marlborough's army was briefly held in check at Waterloo by a force under Jacques Pastur, a native of the village. On 4 September 1944 the British Guards Armoured Division thundered up the road from the south to liberate it from the Germans.

In 1815 there were around 2000 inhabitants, during World War II about 7000 and today over 28,000. It is now a fully developed, modern town located 15 kilometres south of Brussels and 5 kilometres north of the actual battlefield. Dense housing, shops, supermarkets and streams of roaring traffic link the town to within 500 metres of the battlefield. The village played no part in the battle, no shots were fired in it, or at it, but it gave its name (as far as the British were concerned) to probably the most famous land engagement in history. The battle took the name of the village because the Duke of Wellington used an old inn built in 1705 as his headquarters on the nights before and after the battle. In it he wrote his victory despatch to London and, in a room close by, his ADC and great friend Colonel Gordon died. The inn now houses the Wellington Museum. In the 1950s it almost became a petrol station and there was talk of shipping it stone by stone to America, but in 1958 it was bought by the Belgium State and has been a listed building since 1981.

Opposite the museum are the domed Royal Chapel and adjoining Church of St Joseph. Inside are a host of moving memorials to dozens of the Allied fallen. On the left of the entrance to the church is the following general memorial written on white marble:

IN HONOURED MEMORY OF
ALL BRITISH OFFICERS
NON COMMISSIONED OFFICERS AND SOLDIERS
WHO FELL IN BATTLE
UPON THE 16TH, 17TH AND 18TH OF JUNE 1815
THIS TABLET WAS ERECTED
BY A FEW BROTHERS IN ARMS AND COUNTRYMEN
A.D. MDCCCLVIII.

The Wellington Museum, Waterloo

This museum, housed in Wellington's old headquarters in Waterloo, offers the visitor a host of interesting displays and relics. It is divided into fourteen separate rooms and corridors, each with a specific theme about the battle. They include rooms devoted to the Duke, the room in which Colonel Gordon died, the Netherlands, the Prussians, France, the preservation of the battlefield and 'Waterloo' in the world. Among the relics are the table on which Wellington wrote his despatch, Colonel Gordon's despatch box, Lord Uxbridge's wooden leg, muskets, swords, portraits and a display of maps showing the phases of the battle, together with one highlighting all the places in the world called 'Waterloo'. The garden behind the museum contains several tombstones of British officers and a small tomb that used to contain Uxbridge's amputated leg.

The old inn in Waterloo town, now the Wellington Museum in which the Duke established his HQ on the nights of the 17th and 19th June 1815. Inside are the rooms in which he wrote his victory despatch and where his ADC and great friend Colonel Gordon died.

Farms and other buildings

HOUGOUMONT (Maps 8 and 9, pp. 119 & 126)

(See also Section Nine 'Highlights of the Battle')

In 1815 Hougoumont was a small château and a working farm; today it is just a working farm. Modern Belgian signposts call it 'Goumont', as that is the original name. 'Goumont' is said to originate from the word 'Gomme', meaning resin, which was collected from the stands of pine on the high ground near the château. From this came 'Mont Gomme' – 'Resin Hill'. A château, farm and a 'Bois de Goumont' are depicted on some seventeenth-century maps. The current tenant farmer, Monsieur Roger Temmerman, permits visitors to explore provided they do not enter any buildings or disrupt farming activities.

A realistic impression of what Hougoumont looked like in 1815 is shown in the photograph opposite. It was a compact group of buildings centred around two inner courtyards and containing a small Château (unoccupied and unfurnished at the time of the battle) plus a thriving farm, all enclosed by walls and buildings. A particular joy to the eighty-six-year-old absentee owner (Chevalier de Louville) and the resident farmer (Antoinne Dumonceau) was the elaborate ornamental garden (the present enclosed paddock immediately east of the buildings). This was enclosed by a brick wall on the south and east sides, and to the north by a thick hedge and ditch. Both the farmer and the gardener each had a house inside the compound. The gardener, Guillaume van Cutsem, and his five-year-old daughter were supposedly trapped inside Hougoumont at the start of the battle. Whether he intended to stay to endeavour to

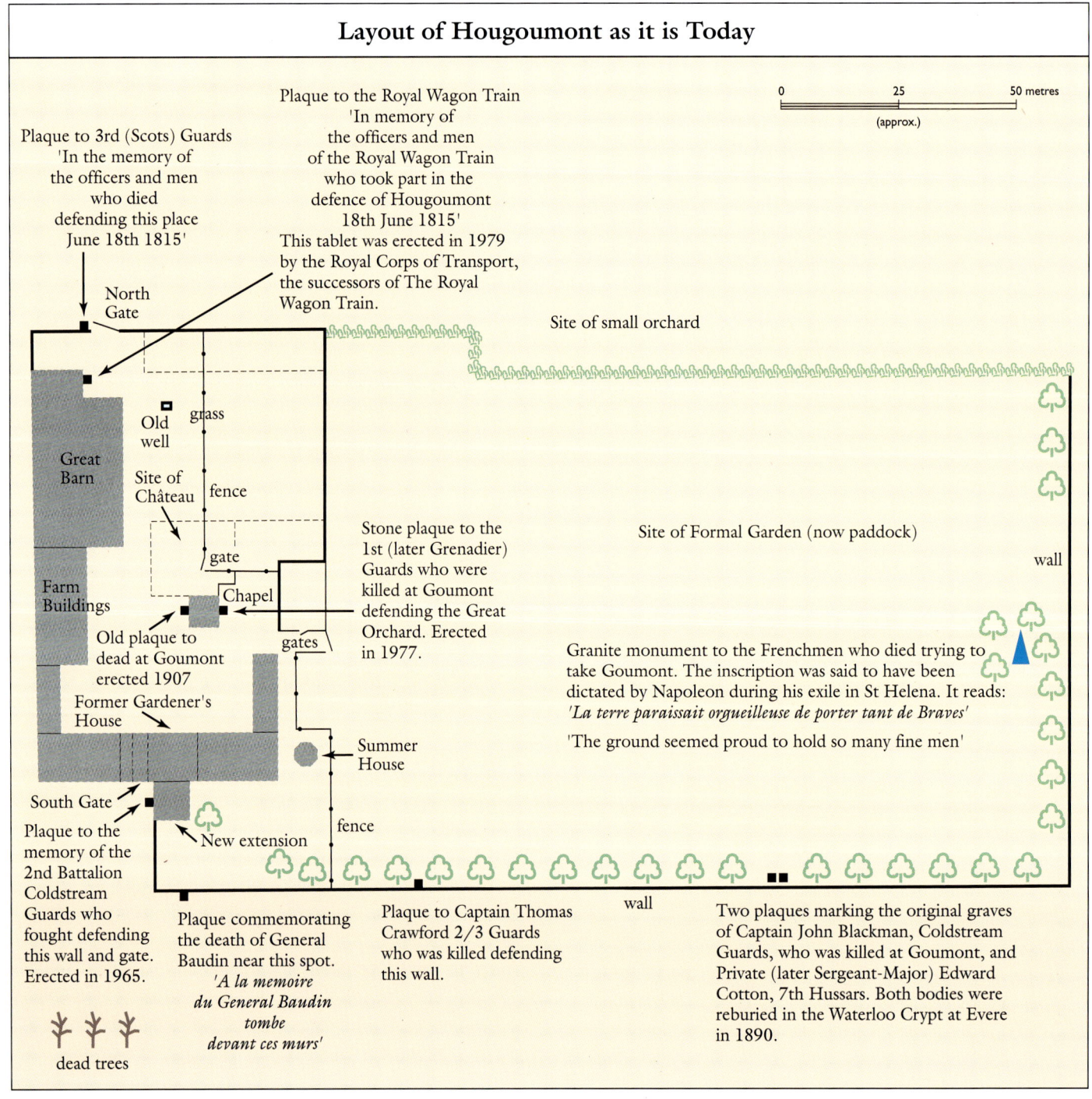

Layout of Hougoumont as it is Today

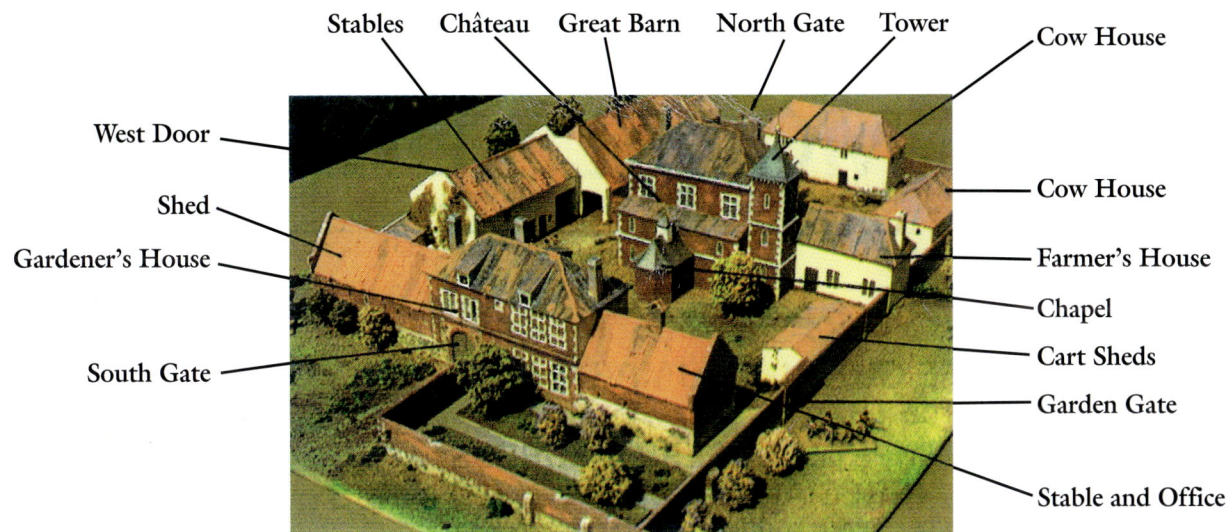

Stables Château Great Barn North Gate Tower Cow House

West Door

Shed

Gardener's House

South Gate

Cow House

Farmer's House

Chapel

Cart Sheds

Garden Gate

Stable and Office

Wargamer's model of Hougoumont in 1815. Although not accurate in every small detail, it gives a good impression of what the château and buildings looked like.

protect his beautiful boxed hedges and colourful flowerbeds, or whether he had mistimed his escape will never be known for certain.

Substantial changes have taken place to Hougoumont in the two centuries since it was fought over so ferociously. The Château, farmer's house and the cow houses adjoining the northern and north-eastern walls have gone – destroyed in the fire that took hold during the battle. The lovely formal gardens are now a grassy paddock and, most obviously of all, the large wood to the south and the extensive apple orchard to the east have disappeared under the plough. Three dead trees 50 metres from the South Gate are all that remain of the once luxuriant wood.

The fight for Hougoumont lasted the entire day. It quickly developed into a battle within a battle. It absorbed assaults by French infantry as a sponge soaks up water. By evening two out of Reille's three divisions had been fully committed at a cost of some 4000 casualties – virtually one in three of those engaged in the six or seven separate attacks. In total about 5,500 men fell dead or wounded within a rectangle 200 x 400 metres. This level of slaughter was only surpassed in Plancenoit. For Wellington, with his Anglo-Allied Army drawn up along the 4,500 metre stretch of the low ridge a few hundred metres to the north, Hougoumont was an ideal advanced post in front of his right flank. By 11.30 a.m. on the Sunday the Duke had garrisoned Hougoumont with some 1,200 Allied troops – a mixture of British guardsmen, Nassauers and Hanoverians tasked with defending the buildings, wood and orchard.

The struggle for Hougoumont is described in Section 9. To walk around the buildings, along the walls or look inside the tiny chapel can, with the aid of the memorials and only a little imagination, be a most rewarding experience.

MEMORIALS (Map 10, p. 131 and diagram opposite)

North Gate

This was the main entrance to the farm during the battle and was approached by a road lined with elms that swept up to the gate somewhat more grandly than it does now. Along this road came reinforcements, galloping ADCs, and the Royal Wagon Train tumbrel with ammunition. To the left of the gate is the start of the famous 'hollow way' that stretches eastwards for over 400 metres and marks the northern boundary of the Hougoumont position. It was the high water mark of the French assaults on the Great Orchard. In 1815 there were two high, wooden gates barring entrance to the Château yard. Like the modern ironwork gates, they opened inwards. To secure them properly required a heavy crossbeam to be placed in iron brackets on either side. It was through this gate that Sous-Lieutenant Legros and a handful of followers made the only (brief) penetration of the compound. At the time of the battle there was a pond to the left of, and close to, the gate. This, coupled with the downpour during the night, had made the low-lying area marshy.

The plaque on the right of the gate commemorates the efforts of the 3rd Foot Guards (later Scots Guards). It reads:

3RD REGIMENT OF FOOT GUARDS
IN MEMORY OF THE OFFICERS AND MEN
OF THE 2ND BATTALION
WHO DIED DEFENDING THIS FARM
JUNE 18TH 1815.

The 'Well of the Dead'

Just inside the North Gate at Hougoumont is the place where Sous-Lieutenant Legros and his gallant comrades who had managed to force their way into the compound before the gates were closed, perished. They died either from the hail of musket shots from the château, or in a series of hand-to-hand fights with sword, bayonet or musket butt. Only a drummer boy was spared – what a story he had to tell in later years as the only Frenchman to have got inside Hougoumont and lived! These dramatic events took place close to the château's well. In 1815 it was an elaborate affair with a tower topped by a dovecote. Today it is merely a hole in the ground. This draw well was made famous by Victor Hugo as the 'Well of the Dead' in his epic *Les Misérables.* He claimed it was stuffed with 300 dead and dying, 'the faint cries of those not yet dead haunting the memory.' However, this was not true. It was carefully excavated in 1985 and not a single human bone was found – just one or two belonging to a horse.

The approach to the North Gate of Hougoumont today. The Great Barn has changed little since 1815. The ground to the left of the gate was boggy and contained a pond. The road leading to the gate was lined with tall elm trees. The path to the right, west of the barn, was the scene of much hand-to-hand fighting and was where Sergeant Fraser, 2/3 Guards, wounded Colonel Cubières.   Photo: the author

Immediately inside this gate, on the wall of the barn on the right, is a plaque commemorating the efforts of a driver from the Royal Wagon Train who managed to bring ammunition to the defenders as they ran low. It reads:

IN MEMORY OF
THE OFFICERS AND MEN
OF THE ROYAL WAGON TRAIN
WHO TOOK PART IN THE
DEFENCE OF HOUGOUMONT
18TH JUNE 1815
THIS TABLET WAS ERECTED IN 1979
BY THE ROYAL CORPS OF TRANSPORT
THE SUCCESSORS OF THE ROYAL WAGON TRAIN

The chapel

Nothing remains of the château but the modern farmer's house (in 1815 the gardener's house); the South Gate and arch are virtually unchanged. Preserved almost precisely as it was, is the tiny chapel that adjoined the château. This is, perhaps, the most poignant place in Hougoumont. Although it survived the fire that destroyed the château, the flames did get inside to reach the large wooden crucifix that then hung above the door. Look inside and you can see that the fire burnt Christ's feet – but nothing more. This was regarded as miraculous and the chapel is a shrine to all those who fought and fell at Hougoumont. Regrettably, at some time the lower right leg of the figure was broken off and stolen.

On the outside western wall is the old original Foot Guards' memorial plaque. It reads:

TO THE MEMORY OF THE BRAVE DEAD
THIS TABLET WAS ERECTED BY HIS
BRITANNIC MAJESTY'S BRIGADE OF
GUARDS, AND BY COMPTE CHARLES VAN BURCH 1907.

On the eastern wall, a more recent plaque reads:

FIRST REGIMENT OF FOOT GUARDS
IN MEMORY OF
THE OFFICERS AND MEN
OF THE LIGHT COMPANIES
OF THE 2ND AND 3RD BATTALIONS
WHO DIED DEFENDING HOUGOUMONT
18TH JUNE 1815
THIS TABLET WAS ERECTED IN 1977
BY THEIR SUCCESSORS OF THE
FIRST OR GRENADIER GUARDS.

Doubtless the chapel is an appropriate place for such a memorial, although it is unlikely that any men of the 1st Guards were actually killed in Hougoumont or the garden (their fight was in the Great Orchard).

The South Gate

The house over the South Gate was the gardener's house in 1815 but it is now a working farmhouse. A small dining extension has been added to the building and juts out onto the eastern side of the gate. On the wall of this extension is a plaque to the Coldstream Guards who defended this gate and the adjoining wall. It reads:

IN MEMORY
OF THE OFFICERS AND MEN OF THE
2ND BATTALION COLDSTREAM GUARDS
WHO, WHILE DEFENDING THIS FARM
SUCCESSFULLY HELD THIS SOUTH GATE
FROM SUCCESSIVE ATTACKS THROUGHOUT
18TH JUNE 1815.

A view of the Chapel, former Gardener's House and the South Gate from the farmyard. Note the draw well at bottom left. In 1815 it was inside a tower topped by a dovecote. Photo: Ken Rowley

The South Gate at Hougoumont. The extension with the memorial to the 2nd Coldstream Guards on the wall was not there in 1815.   *Photo: the author*

A few feet from the corner, where the wall turns east, is another wall-mounted plaque to the French brigade commander of the formation that led the first assault, cleared the woods to the south, and was then stalled in front of the garden wall. Maréchal de Camp Bauduin was shot dead near this spot – he was the first French general to die at Waterloo. The plaque reads:

(To the memory of General Bauduin who fell in front of these walls, 18 June 1815.)

Paddock (formal garden)

The paddock to the east of the buildings was the old formal garden. It contains three memorials. The granite memorial in the clump of trees a few metres from the eastern wall is to the French soldiers killed attacking Hougoumont, although as far as is known none died inside the garden (they never got over the wall). Said to have been dictated by Napoleon in exile on St Helena, it reads:

AUX SOLDATS FRANCAIS
MORTS A HOUGOUMONT
JUIN 1815
LA TERRE PARAISSAIT ORGUEILLEUSE
DE PORTER TANT DE BRAVES.

(To the French soldiers killed at Hougoumont June 1815. The ground seemed proud to hold so many fine men).

Near the centre of the southern wall, a metre or so from its base, are two concrete ground markers. They mark the original graves of Captain John Lucie Blackman, Coldstream Guards, who died defending the wall, and Trooper (later Sergeant-Major) Edward Cotton of the 7th Hussars. Cotton returned twenty years later, married a local woman, and became a well known 'Guide and Describer of the Battle', showing round many officers who had fought there. He wrote a book entitled *A Voice from Waterloo*. When he died in 1849 he was buried beside Blackman. In 1890 the bodies were removed to the Waterloo crypt at Evere, Brussels.

The third memorial inside the paddock is on the south wall about midway between Bauduin's plaque and Blackman's marker. This plaque, partially hidden by trees, is to Captain Thomas Crawford (although he is listed as Crauford in the *Waterloo Roll Call*) of the 2/3 Guards, who was killed in the garden.

LA HAIE SAINTE (Map 10, p. 131 and diagram opposite)

Although the barn was damaged by fire during the battle, and again in 1936, the original walls remained intact and so, today, the buildings round the courtyard are not much changed from 1815. This was, and still is, an important farm. The stone buildings and walls provided the basis of a strong defence and the position of the farm, like Hougoumont, some 250 metres in front of Wellington's line, made it an ideal outpost. Situated thus, in front of the Anglo-Allied centre, meant holding it was critical for the Duke. Equally, without first taking La Haie Sainte every attack on the centre was vulnerable to flanking fire. Some 50 metres north of the farm on the east of the road was another natural defensive position: a sand/gravel pit. Two companies of the 1/95 occupied this position, and their defence of it proved deadly to those troops attempting to break in through the main gate.

The details of the struggle to possess La Haie Sainte are in Section 9. The garrison at the onset of the first attack at around 2.00 p.m. were the six companies of the 2nd Light Battalion of the KGL commanded by Major Baring. They were positioned in the orchard south of the farm, in the compound itself and the kitchen garden to the north. The task of taking it was given to the

A view of the modern La Haie Sainte from the air.

Layout of La Haie Sainte Area Today

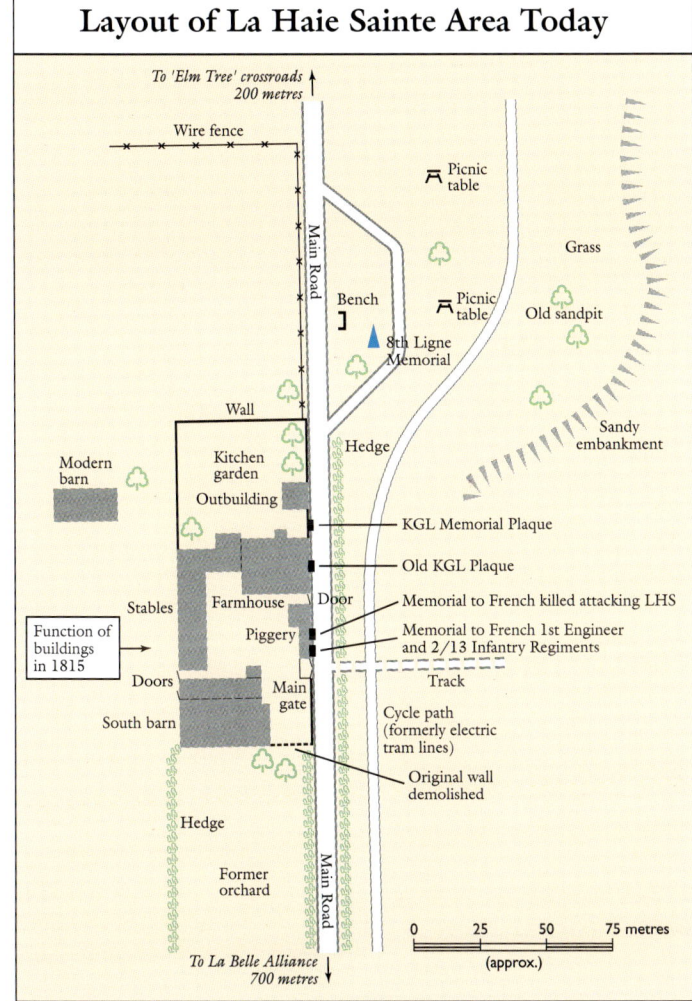

To 'Elm Tree' crossroads 200 metres

Wire fence

Main Road

Picnic table

Grass

Bench

Picnic table

Old sandpit

8th Ligne Memorial

Wall

Sandy embankment

Hedge

Modern barn

Kitchen garden

Outbuilding

KGL Memorial Plaque

Old KGL Plaque

Stables

Farmhouse

Door

Memorial to French killed attacking LHS

Piggery

Memorial to French 1st Engineer and 2/13 Infantry Regiments

Function of buildings in 1815

Doors

Main gate

Track

South barn

Cycle path (formerly electric tram lines)

Original wall demolished

Hedge

Former orchard

Main Road

0   25   50   75 metres

(approx.)

To La Belle Alliance 700 metres

2000 men of Colonel Charlet's 1st Brigade of Quiot's 1st Division. They took the orchard but could get no further. Not until about 6.30 p.m. did the French succeed in taking the farm, mainly due to the defenders running out of ammunition. For Wellington the loss of La Haie Sainte was one of the most critical moments of the battle.

Although it is not normally possible to go inside the compound, visitors can understand the flow of the battle from outside. The French eventually broke in through the stable passage and barn entrance in the west. Shortly afterwards the main gate, underneath the dovecote, was battered down with axes wielded by men of the 1st Engineer Regiment and stormed by the 2/13 Légère from Donzelot's 2nd Division. It is the only place on the battlefield that the French can claim they took by storm, their only entirely successful assault. Both the KGL and the French have plaques on this farm's walls to commemorate a particularly bloody episode in a notoriously bloody battle.

Main gate

It was not until evening that the wooden doors finally gave way under the weight of blows – most of the defenders no longer having ammunition to shoot their assailants. At the cost of many French lives, the farm fell. There are two French memorials on the wall to the right of the main gate commemorating the gallant efforts of those Frenchmen who fought and died at the farm.

A view of La Haie Sainte from the main Brussels–Genappe road. The wall and buildings have changed little over two centuries. The main gate on the left was the one that was finally smashed down as the defenders ran out of ammunition. Note the plaques on the wall, from the left – to the 1st Engineer and 13th Ligne Regiments; to all the French who fell attacking the farm; and the diamond-shaped one to the KGL. Photo: the author

The left hand plaque reads:

LE 18 JUIN 1815
VERS 18H30
LA FERME DE LA HAYE [sic] SAINTE
FUT ENLEVE PAR LE MARÉCHAL NEY
GRAGE AUX ASSAUTS HEROIQUES
DES SAPEURS DU 1ST REGIMENT DU GENIE
DU COLONEL LAMORE
2E COMPANIE DU 2E BATTALION
ET DU 13TH REGIMENT D'INFANTERIE
LÉGÈRE DE LA DIVISION DONZELOT.

(18 June 1815. Towards 6.30 p.m. the farm of La Haie Sainte was captured by Marshal Ney after heroic assaults by engineers of the 2nd Company, 2nd Battalion of 1st Engineer Regiment under Colonel Lamore, and the 2/13 Light Infantry Regiment of Donzelot's division.)

The right hand plaque reads:

A LA MEMORIE
DES COMBATTANTS FRANCAIS
QUI SES SACRIFIERENT HEROIQUEMENT
DEVANT SES MURS DE LA HAIE SAINTE
LE 18 JUIN 1815.

(To the memory of the French soldiers who gave their lives heroically before these walls of La Haie Sainte, 18 June 1815.)

KGL Memorials

Seven years after the battle the defenders of La Haie Sainte, who were only finally driven out when their rifle ammunition was expended, were commemorated by a marble plaque fixed to the wall of the farm house. It was replaced in 1847 by the diamond shaped iron plate that is still there today. It reads:

THE
OFFICERS
OF THE 2ND
LIGHT BATTALION
KING'S GERMAN LEGION
TO THEIR COMRADES-IN-ARMS WHO FELL IN THE DEFENCE OF
THIS FARMHOUSE
ON THE 18 JUNE 1815: MAJOR H. BOSEWIEL
CAPTAIN W. SCHAUMANN
ENSIGN F. VON ROBERTSON
AND 46 NCOS AND RIFLEMEN OF THE 2ND LIGHT BATTALION
RAISED AGAIN BY HIS ROYAL HIGHNESS
CROWN PRINCE GEORGE OF HANOVER ON 18TH JUNE 1847
DEDICATED AT THE SAME TIME
TO THOSE WHO ALSO FELL: CAPTAIN H. VON MARSCHALK
FROM THE 1ST LIGHT BATTALION
CAPTAIN VON WURME
FROM THE 5TH LINE BATTALION
IN RECOGNITION OF THE HANOVERIAN HEROISM THEY SHOWED.

In 1998 another memorial was placed on the kitchen garden wall overlooking the road. This was put up by the town of Bexhill-on-Sea (the home of the KGL during their ten years of service in the British Army) and The Association of Friends of the Waterloo Committee. It reads:

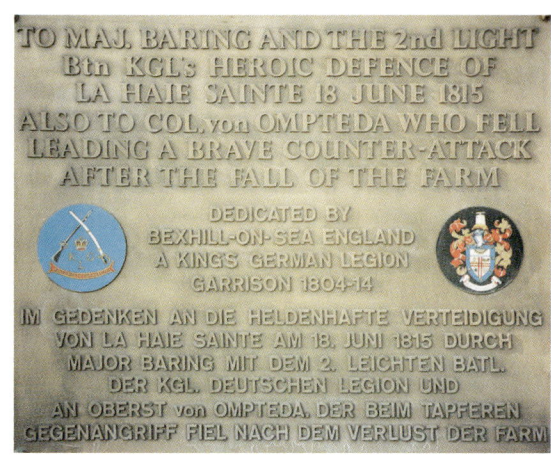

These words are repeated in German underneath.

The 8th Ligne Memorial

The 8th Ligne were part of Durutte's Division, originally posted on the eastern flank in front of Papelotte but pulled to the centre (along with the 29th Ligne) in the evening by Ney to exploit the taking of La Haie Sainte. They clashed with the remnants of Ompteda's Brigade.

Colonel Baron Christian von Ompteda commanded the KGL's 2nd Brigade in the British 3rd Division (Alten). After La Haie Sainte fell Ompteda was ordered to counterattack with the 5th Line Battalion. He demurred, as he had seen French cavalry nearby. The Prince of Orange, who overheard the order, insisted he obey without further argument. Ompteda led the advance and was killed. The battalion was ridden over and chopped up by cuirassiers. Only the battalion's commanding officer, Lieutenant-Colonel Linsingen, and a handful of soldiers survived this debacle unscathed. Ompteda died close to where the French memorial stands. It reads:

EN CE LIEU
LE 18 JUIN 1815
LE 8TH REGIMENT
D'INFANTERIE DE LIGNE
DE LA DIVISION
DURUTTE
ATTAQUA AVEC SUCCES
LA LEGION ALLEMANDE
DU COLONEL
VON OMPTEDA.

(Near this place on 18 June 1815 the 8th Infantry Regiment from Durutte's division successfully attacked the German Legion under Colonel von Ompteda.)

LA BELLE ALLIANCE (Maps 9 & 10, pp. 126 & 131)

The Prussians named the battle after La Belle Alliance. It was a small farm (built in 1770) that doubled as an inn, located almost precisely in the centre of the French front line. Some 1,300 metres north was the 'Elm Tree' crossroads that marked the centre of the Anglo-Allied line. It was not far from this building, built in the angle between the junction of the Brussels–Genappe road and the minor road to Plancenoit, that Blücher and Wellington met after their victory. At one time a marble plaque commemorating this event was fixed to the wall of the house but this is now kept at the Le Caillou Museum. It reads:

BELLE ALLIANCE
RENCONTRE
DES GENERAUX
WELLINGTON ET BLUCHER
LORS
DE LA MEMORABLE
BATAILLE DU XVIII JUIN
M.D CCC XV.

La Belle Alliance as it was shortly after the battle.

(Belle Alliance, the meeting place of Generals Wellington and Blücher after the memorable battle, 18 June 1815.)

Of itself La Belle Alliance had no tactical significance – but it was at the heart of the French position. Napoleon had ridden up to the farm the previous night to watch his enemy bivouac, to count their fires, on the ridge opposite. At 9.00 a.m. he was back making a confirmatory reconnaissance and sending his Imperial Guard's engineer commander, Haxo, to report on any fortifications. Over two hours later it was from near the farm that he reviewed his troops and, from shortly after 2.00 p.m., he watched events unfold from rising ground to the south, close to Decoster's house.

The farm cum inn was owned in 1815 by an inhabitant of Plancenoit called Nicolas Delpierre who sold it the following year to a Scot named Ramsey for 12,500 francs. Its role in the battle was one of makeshift field hospital. Despite its exposed position, scores of French wounded sought shelter inside while medical staff carried out their gruesome business under cannon fire that tore several holes in the roof. A plaque on the outside wall of the small extension commemorates their endeavours. It reads:

A LA MEMOIRE
DU CORPS MEDICAL FRANCAIS
QUI 18 JUIN 1815 ONT DONNE LEUR SOIN LE PLUS DEVOUE.

(To the memory of the French Medical Corps and their care and dedication on 18 June 1815.)

MEMORIALS CLOSE TO LA BELLE ALLIANCE

The Victor Hugo Monument

This is located about 150 metres south of the farm, on the east of the main road. This impressive stone column has been many years in the building, and is still incomplete. The first stone was laid in 1912 and it took until 1956 to reach its present condition, still missing the Gallic cock that was intended to surmount the column. Two world wars and lack of funds are responsible. It is certainly odd that here, at the centre of what was the French position, within a few metres of where Napoleon had his command post, there is no memorial either to him or Ney, but rather to a great French novelist. The chapter on Waterloo in his greatest work, *Les Misérables*, was a masterpiece of writing but contained as much fiction as fact. Not until he was exiled could he bring himself to visit

La Belle Alliance showing the addition of more recent buildings. Note the separate building on the right is an original one.

the battlefield in 1861. Prior to this he had adamantly and frequently refused. He was passionately emotional on the subject: 'It is not only the victory of Europe over France, it is the complete, absolute, shattering, incontestable, final, supreme triumph of mediocrity over genius.' At the base of the column is a large, bronze medallion of Hugo with some lines from his poems.

And this plain, alas! Where one dreams today,
Fled those, before whom the world had fled!

The Wounded Eagle Monument

Located at the crossroads 100 metres south of Victor Hugo's column, on the western side of the main road. This, perhaps the most impressive of the French memorials, depicts a wounded Imperial Eagle with one wing holed by musket balls and canister. In one of its claws is a standard, the other is raised defensively but defiantly towards the enemy. It commemorates the last gallant efforts of the Armée du Nord, but especially the magnificent efforts of the squares of the Old Guard, and the survivors of the

Middle Guard who rallied on them after their repulse in the late evening. These battalions conducted a desperate fighting withdrawal from the valley, past La Belle Alliance and back towards Rossomme. One battalion square, that of the 2/3 Grenadiers was virtually wiped out as it shrank, first to a triangle, and then to a confused, huddled group, before disintegrating. The Wounded Eagle remembers the last agony of the French Army.

The monument is the work of Jean-Leon Gerome, but the location was selected by Comte Albert de Mauroy. He then joined with Gustave Larroumet and the celebrated French historian of the battle, Henri Houssaye, to raise the funds to buy the site. There was criticism at the time that the memorial should be at Ligny, the last French victory rather than Waterloo their last defeat. Houssaye dismissed such opinions with the words, 'We do not want to commemorate the Battle of Waterloo, which was a defeat; we want only to honour the French soldiers who, in this battle of giants, died for their country.' The monument was unveiled 28 June 1904.

The Unveiling of the Wounded Eagle Memorial

The unveiling of this memorial on 28 June 1904 saw a vast crowd of spectators assembled on the battlefield. A fair estimate is 100,000. The Brussels railway station issued 57,000 tickets, and huge numbers flocked in from elsewhere in Belgium and France. Not since the battle had so many people tramped the tracks and fields.

The ceremonies began on a bright summer morning with a Requiem Mass in Plancenoit church to remember the thousands of French soldiers who fell at Waterloo. The Wounded Eagle was to be unveiled mid-afternoon. At 2.00 p.m. the dignitaries and special official guests left Brussels by train for Braine l'Alleud. From there they would continue by the electric tram that ran to the north of the battlefield and thence south, hugging the line of the main road (it is now a cycle path along this stretch) to La Belle Alliance. Here the official party formed up to march the remaining 250 metres to the monument. They included Belgian Gendarmes in full dress blue uniforms with bearskins; a band; the French minister in Brussels, Monsieur Gérard; Lieutenant-General Bruylant, representing the Belgian king; Henri Houssaye, the great French military historian of the battle; and Edouard Detaille, the military artist. Teachers had brought several hundred schoolchildren from the nearby villages, each clutching a small tricolour flag.

The Wounded Eagle memorial to the last agony of the French Army as battalions of the Imperial Guard fought to cover the retreat near La Belle Alliance.   Photo: the author

In the press of people around the monument, draped in the French flag, were many descendants of soldiers who had fought there. Among the most prominent were the grandson of Général de Division Georges Mouton, Comte de Lobau and Baron de

Grandmaison. He bent to place his grandfather's sword at the foot of the monument. Baron Durutte was the grandson of the commander of the 4th Infantry Division in d'Erlon's Corps, whose dreadful wounds to the face had disfigured him for life. Also present were two descendants of the commander of the Young Guard, Duhesme, who died of his wounds received in Plancenoit and who was buried in the churchyard at St Martin at Ways, near Genappe. But most interesting of all was an old woman of 103. Madame Therese Dupuis had been thirteen at the time of the battle and had lived some 15 miles from the field, north-west of Charleroi. She recalled hearing the continuous thunder of the guns, the tramp of men passing her home, of seeing horsemen galloping and doctors tending wounded nearby. The dignitaries rightly made a great fuss of her, although fatigue and emotion overcame her before the end of the speeches and she retired, weeping quietly.

The gendarmes formed a guard around the monument while the band played martial music, the familiar tunes to which the long dead veterans had marched and fought across Europe under the Eagles, and for the last time on that actual spot eighty-nine years before. The artist Detaille made a speech, the tricolour fell to reveal the Wounded Eagle, and Houssaye, with his long black beard, stepped forward to speak. He was fifty-six years old, a veteran himself (he fought in the Franco-Prussian War of 1870–71) and almost overwhelmed with emotion. Forever afterwards Houssaye thought this to be the finest day of his life.

The Polish Lancers' Memorial

This stone memorial has been placed on the ground at the foot of the Wounded Eagle. It commemorates the 1st Squadron, 1st (Polish) Lancer Regiment, under Major Balinski who had commanded them on Elba. At Waterloo these blue-coated lancers fought alongside Colonel Sourd's Red Lancers as part of the Light Cavalry of the Guard. In 1795 Poland had been carved up between Prussia, Russia and Austria, and most Poles saw their best chance of regaining their country by fighting with the French Revolutionary armies. In 1990 their memorial stone was laid; note how the French call the battle 'Mont St Jean'. It reads:

AUX OFFICIERS, SOUS-OFFICIERS
ET SOLDATS
DE L'
ESCADRON POLONAIS
TOMBES A
MONT-SAINT-JEAN
LE 18 JUIN 1815.

(To the officers, NCOs and soldiers of the Polish Squadron who fell at Mont St Jean, 18 June 1815.)

6th Regiment d'Artillerie à Pieds

This French Foot Artillery Regiment, commanded by Colonel Hulot, provided exactly half the cannons and howitzers (forty) of the 'Grand Battery' whose duty it was to soften up Wellington's centre and left prior to, and during, I Corps' (d'Erlon) attack that started around 1.30 p.m. Its contribution to the barrage, that Allied survivors long remembered, came from twenty-four 6-pounders, eight 5.5-inch howitzers provided by the 9th (Capitaine Bourgeois), 10th (Capitaine Cantin), 19th (Capitaine Emon) and the 20th (Capitaine Hamelin) Companies of the Regiment. Additionally, the 11th Company contributed the corps reserve guns under Capitaine Charlet, comprising of six 12-pounders and two 6-inch howitzers. Their efforts are recalled by a memorial stone on the eastern side of the main road to Brussels, about 100 metres north of La Belle Alliance. The inscription reads:

DE LA BELLE ALLIANCE
A PAPELOTTE
LE 18 JUIN 1815
DES UNITES DU 6TH REGIMENT
D'ARTILLERIE A PIED
DU COLONEL HULOT
ONE APPUYE DE LEURS
FEUX EFFICACES
LES ATTAQUES DU
1ST CORPS D'ARMÉE
FRANCAIS.

(From La Belle Alliance to Papelotte on 18 June 1815 the units of Colonel Hulot's 6th Foot Artillery Regiment effectively fired in support of the attacks of the French 1st Army Corps.)

5th Cuirassiers

This regiment was commanded by Colonel Baron Gobert and had slightly over 500 sabres at the start of the battle. It was part of the 14th Cavalry Division under Général de Division Delort, one of the best-equipped and motivated cuirassier formations in the army. Initially in reserve behind the French right Delort was com-

pelled, with considerable reluctance, to join the massed cavalry assaults in mid-afternoon. Lieutenant Demulder of the 5th Cuirassiers has a memorial near the spot where he died on the right of the Anglo-Allied ridge. The Regiment's memorial stone stands on a traffic island, surrounded by a flowerbed of pink roses, halfway down the road from La Belle Alliance to Plancenoit. From their deployment area some 600 metres to the north-east the cuirassiers trotted past this spot at around 3.00 p.m. on their way to join the cavalry attacks on Wellington's infantry squares. The memorial, shown below, reads:

(Near this place on 18 June 1815 the 5th Cuirassiers of Milhaud's cavalry corps left to charge the British infantry squares.)

This memorial, on an 'island' at the road junction leading to Plancenoit, 500 metres SE of La Belle Alliance, supposedly indicates the starting point of the 5th Cuirassiers when they moved off to charge the Anglo–Allied right. In fact the 5th Cuirassiers were some 600 metres to the NE. However, the left flank of the 4th Cuirassiers was only a short distance from here, and most of Milhaud's regiments would have probably filed through the spot en route to their forming up positions for the attack.   Photo: the author

PAPELOTTE (Maps 9 & 10, pp. 126 & 131)

Papelotte was a thriving farm whose buildings were, and still are, grouped around a central yard or compound. During the battle it caught fire and there has been considerable rebuilding since 1815, the most obvious change being the addition of a belvedere (summerhouse built to command a fine view) on top of the main entrance.

It is located at the head of the Smohain brook about 500 metres west of the village of La Marache (Smohain) and 700 metres south of the Ohain–Braine l'Alleud road along which the Duke aligned his front line. The immediate vicinity is a confusing tangle of rough roads

Top left *Papelotte view of the main entrance with belvedere above.*

Above *Sunken lane leading down to La Haie from the Ohain–Braine l'Alleud road. It is typical of the lanes around Papelotte/La Haie and Smohain, and has changed little since 1815. The high hedges and deep cuttings made it impossible country for artillery and cavalry to manoeuvre.*

Left *Papelotte Farm as it is today, showing the outer walls. Photo: the author*

and tracks that run through deep cuttings topped with high hedges. It is infantry country; it is defensive country. These sunken lanes have not changed since the battle and Papelotte remains somewhat isolated and inaccessible. It became (along with La Haie, Smohain and Frichermont) an outpost area in front of Wellington's left wing.

The defence of Papelotte, La Haie, Smohain and Frichermont was the responsibility of Prince Bernard of Saxe-Weimar's 2nd Netherlands Brigade. The six companies of the 3/2 Nassau under Major Hegmann took up positions in and around the farm and its neighbour La Haie. The buildings were occupied and prepared for defence by Captain von Rettburg's Light Company from that battalion. Although French skirmishers from Durutte's Division probed the position for much of the day, it was not until the late afternoon that serious fighting flared around Papelotte. Reinforcements were needed to drive out the attackers. Then, in early evening, one of what the modern media call 'friendly fire' incidents occurred. Prussian troops from 15th Brigade (Bülow's IV Corps) advancing from the south-east mistook von Rettburg's men for Frenchmen as their uniforms were similar, and attacked. A brisk, ten-minute firefight took place with casualties on both sides before the error was discovered.

LA HAIE (Maps 9 & 10, pp. 126 & 131)

Another farm, located about 150 metres east of Papelotte, that played a key role in the defence of Wellington's left flank. Along with Papelotte, Smohain and Frichermont, it formed one of the advanced strongpoints some 700 metres in front of the Duke's line. In 1815, however, it did not lend itself so readily to defence, as it was only one storey high, the walls were of cob (a composition of clay, gravel and straw) that did not stop musket balls, and it had a thatched roof. The whole farm was destroyed by fire in 1910 and was rebuilt of brick with a tiled roof.

A company of the 3/2 Nassau undertook the close protection of the farm. Apart from probing by French skirmishers, it was not until late afternoon that serious pressure was applied in this area.

FRICHERMONT (Maps 9 & 10, pp. 126 & 131)

At the time of the battle Frichermont (modern spelling Fichermont) was a château dating back to the sixteenth century. It was owned by the Duke of Beaulieu. There was a central square tower and at the corners of the walls a smaller round tower. Like Hougoumont it had a formal garden. Around it on three sides were woods, with parkland to the north. Marlborough had used it as his headquarters in 1705. It was destroyed in 1857 and another building constructed on the same spot, which in turn was demolished in 1960 and not replaced. The ruins (some walls and gateposts) are somewhat inaccessible today, being situated among thick woods and overgrown bushes.

The château was much closer to the French right wing and Jacquinot's cavalry (a mere 300 metres away) than the Anglo-Allied left wing that was 1,200 metres to the north-west. It did, however, form the extremity of Saxe-Weimar's position and was occupied by four companies of the 1/28 Orange-Nassau Regiment. Although French cavalry probed the area at around 10.00 a.m., no serious attempt was made by the French to take this position.

MONT ST JEAN FARM (Maps 9 & 10, pp. 126 & 131)

This ancient farm (built in the middle of the twelfth century) is located some 600 metres north of the 'Elm Tree' crossroads and 450 metres south of the village of the same name, on the eastern side of the Brussels–Genappe road. In 1794 the French, under General Lefèbvre-Desnouëttes, fought a sharp engagement at Mont St Jean against an Austrian–Dutch force which they drove back to Brussels.

Here, on 18 June were assembled the senior (staff) surgeons under Dr John Gunning who was a deputy-inspector in the medical service, and the principal medical officer of I Corps at Waterloo. As the main field hospital for the Anglo-Allied Army, during and after the battle it was the scene of indescribable suffering. The inside of the building resembled some hellish abattoir for humans, with amputated limbs thrown in heaps as blood soaked surgeons probed, cut and sawed while their patients (victims), forcibly held down by assistants, shrieked or moaned in torment.

The farm was originally owned by the Knights Templar but had been rebuilt in 1778. Today the main entrance is showing signs of neglect and disrepair. Above the gate there was originally

a square tower. It had been knocked down in 1926 but reconstructed using old stone. Although hit by a number of cannonballs, the farm looked much as it did during the battle until 1992, when an earthquake damaged the tower and it was again demolished. At the time of writing it has not been replaced. The stone plaque on the outside wall to the right of the main gate reads:

IN MEMORY OF
DEPUTY INSPECTOR GUNNING
PRINCIPAL MEDICAL OFFICER OF THE 1ST CORPS
THE SURGEONS AND OTHER MEMBERS
OF THE FIELD HOSPITAL
WHICH WAS ESTABLISHED IN THIS FARM
TO CARE FOR THE WOUNDED OF THE BATTLEFIELD
18TH JUNE 1815
THIS TABLET WAS ERECTED IN 1981
BY THE ROYAL ARMY MEDICAL CORPS.

Rossomme (Maps 9 & 10, pp. 126 & 131)

At the time of the battle Rossomme Farm was situated some 1,500 metres south of La Belle Alliance beside the Brussels–Genappe road, close to where the Rossomme Solarium is now located. It was a farm of about the same size as La Haie Sainte but was burnt down in 1895 and not rebuilt. At the start of the battle the twenty-one battalions of the Imperial Guard were deployed just to the north of the farm on either side of the road. After the battle the farm gave some sort of sanctuary to many French wounded as the routed army streamed past.

Some 250 metres south of where the farm was there is a junction of three roads, where the main road from Brussels swings southeast on its way to Genappe and Charleroi. At this point the road cuts through an east–west ridge called the Heights of Rossomme. On these heights Napoleon established his command post from around

A lithograph of Frichermont as it was in the mid-nineteenth century. The buildings, which were defended by men from the Orange-Nassau Regiment, were never seriously attacked by the French. It was later occupied by Prussians who treated the owner (who remained during the battle) somewhat roughly.   Photo: Hulton Getty

Present day view looking north, from the Heights of Rossomme on the west of the main road where Napoleon had his headquarters until shortly before 2.00 p.m. Note the Lion Mound, the houses in the centre marking the 'Elm Tree' crossroads and, on the right, the Victor Hugo column. The position gives a view of the Anglo-Allied centre but was too far away to control the battle.   Photo: the author

Napoleon on the Heights of Rossomme

Major Lemonnier-Delafosse was an ADC to Général de Division Foy, who later wrote his memoirs. Some time in the early afternoon he was standing at the foot of the Heights of Rossomme, waiting to lead forward some artillery that had yet to arrive. He watched his emperor at work with considerable interest. He wrote:

> Seated on a straw chair, in front of a coarse farm table, he was holding his map open on the table. His famous spyglass in hand was often trained on the various points of the battle. When resting his eye, he used to pick up straws of wheat, which he carried in his mouth as a toothpick. Stationed on his left, Maréchal Soult alone waited for his orders and ten paces to the rear were grouped all his staff on horseback. Sappers of the engineers were opening up ramps around him so that people could reach the Emperor more easily … I left at last, with our artillery and I never saw him again. I have this ever present last memory.

Sketch of Rossomme Farm as it was in 1815.

9.30 a.m. to about 2.00 p.m. It was from here that he set up his table on which his maps were spread, and somebody procured a bale of straw from a barn on which he sat. From this position he sent messages to Grouchy; despatched Colonel Marbot on his reconnaissance; rode forward (and back) to review his troops; gave his final attack orders; ordered the assembly of the Grand Battery; spotted the Prussians on the horizon to the north-east, and sent forward Lobau's corps to counter them. The Emperor set up his headquarters, along with Soult and the entourage of staff officers, on the high ground to the west of the road. The visitor today will find the view from this spot of interest. The trees lining the road are new, so with a telescope the distant heights near Chapelle St Robert, near where the Prussians were first seen at about 1.00 p.m., would have been visible. The view north shows the centre of Wellington's position but not his right or Plancenoit. It was not close enough from which to oversee the battle, so at about 2.00 p.m. Napoleon rode forward.

Le Caillou (Map 10, p. 131)

This farm was located some 3000 metres south of the centre of the battlefield on the eastern side of the Brussels–Genappe road. It was burnt down, along with its adjoining barns, immediately after the battle by vengeful Prussians. A number of French wounded perished in the fires. Two of Napoleon's horses, one being Marengo, were abandoned at the farm. Marengo was sent to England but did not live long – the skeleton can be seen at the National Army Museum in London.

Le Caillou's main interest lies in the fact that it was Napoleon's headquarters on the night of 17/18 June, and that in 1912 the extensively rebuilt and refurbished building was made into a museum. The Emperor had one small room, as the rest of the building was crammed with staff seeking shelter from the driving rain. He slept little. His valet, Marchant, recalled him pacing the room, cutting his finger nails, staring out of the window at the appalling

Napoleon arrives at Le Caillou

The Emperor's second valet de chambre, Louis Saint-Denis, who had joined the Imperial household at eighteen as an under-groom, had accompanied him to Spain, Germany, Russia, Elba, then into Belgium. He had been promoted to 2nd Mameluke (under the famous Raza Roustam) and given the name Ali. He described Napoleon's arrival thus:

The modern day Le Caillou, now a museum containing a number of souvenirs of the Emperor and his army. Photo: the author

It was night, or nearly so, when the Emperor reached the farm of Le Caillou; he set up his headquarters there. As his accommodation was not ready, a bivouac fire was lit near the buildings (which were on the right of the road) and there, lying on a bale of straw, he waited for his room to be made ready to receive him. When he had occupied the small hovel where he had to spend the night, he had his boots pulled off. It was troublesome to pull them off as they had been soaked all day. Then, undressed, he went to bed where he had dinner. He slept little during the night, being disturbed constantly by people coming and going: some came to give him an account of a mission, others to receive orders.

weather and being continually disturbed by the comings and goings of generals and staff. It was here, late at night on the 17th, that orders were issued as to how the army would form up for battle. Here the decision was taken to postpone the attack, the troops were to have their soup and clean weapons – Soult wrote his 5.00 a.m. instructions to that effect. It was here that the Emperor had his 8.00 a.m. breakfast conference with his generals (and was particularly dismissive and scathing of their opinions) on the Sunday morning. When he later rode forward to Rossomme he left behind his treasury wagons, some civil staff and a battalion of the Old Guard (1/1 Châsseurs à Pied) under Major Duuring to guard the area.

Today the museum has several items of interest, including a glass case containing the complete skeleton of a French hussar with a smashed skull and the balls that killed him. In another room is a bronze plaque that names all the important generals and staff who stayed in the farm with the Emperor that night. In the garden east of Le Caillou is an ossuary dedicated in 1912 to house the bones of soldiers discovered on the battlefield. On it is an inscription in Latin that reads:

'FOR THE EMPEROR OFTEN,
FOR THE FATHERLAND ALWAYS'.

In the nearby orchard there is a monument to Major Duuring's battalion. It reads:

THE 1ST BATTALION OF THE 1ST REGIMENT OF
CHÂSSEURS À PIED OF THE IMPERIAL GUARD,
COMMANDED BY MAJOR DUURING, BIVOUACKED IN
THIS PLACE ON THE NIGHT OF 17 TO 18 JUNE. THIS
BATTALION HAD DISTINGUISHED ITSELF AT
MARENGO, ULM, AUSTERLITZ, JENA, FRIEDLAND,
ESSLING, WAGRAM, SMOLENSK, LA MOSKOWA, HANAU
AND MONTMIRAIL.

CHANTELET

Another working farm located 1,100 metres south of Plancenoit at the end of a narrow road that branches east from the main Brussels–Genappe road 250 metres south of Le Caillou. At this farm Maréchal Ney spent the night of 17/18 June. In the late evening, as the French retreat got under way, a detachment of the 1/1 Châsseurs of the Guard from Le Caillou were sent to the farm to check advancing Prussian patrols. There was some skirmishing nearby.

A plaque on the right of the entrance reads:

FERME DU CHANTELET
LE MARÉCHAL NEY
DUC D'ELCHINGEN
PRINCE DE MOSCOWA
LOGEA DANS CETTE FERME
DU 17 AU 18 JUIN 1815.

(Chantelet Farm. Marshal Ney, Duke of Elchingen and Prince of Moscowa stayed at this farm during the night of 17/18 June 1815.)

BUILDINGS

Trimotiou (Map 9, p. 126)

A house, possibly a small farm or farm worker's dwelling located on the western side of the Brussels–Genappe road about 100 metres south of La Belle Alliance. It was one of the four buildings, or small groups of buildings, which bordered this road south of Wellington's line and Rossomme (the others being La Haie Sainte, La Belle Alliance and Decoster's house). It played no part in the battle, but was probably used for shelter and as a source of firewood for the French on the night of the 17th/18th. It also undoubtedly acted as a refuge for the wounded and dying during the battle itself.

DECOSTER'S HOUSE (Map 9, p. 126)

This house was located about 500 metres south of La Belle Alliance, at the junction of the Brussels–Genappe road and a side road leading to Plancenoit. The house itself was of no significance other than it was the home of a Flemish peasant called Decoster. Tradition has it that at about 5.00 a.m. on 18 June French soldiers grabbed the petrified man and forced him to be a guide to Napoleon as to the surrounding terrain. He was mounted, hands tied behind his back, and his horse attached to that of a Châsseur à Cheval from the Emperor's escort. During the battle he was none too happy at the close proximity of a number of cannonballs and instinctively ducked as they passed. On seeing this continuous bobbing up and down the Emperor is alleged to have commented, 'Don't keep bowing like that, this is not the Tuileries!'

In the years immediately following the battle Decoster established himself as a battlefield guide for visitors. As a person who had been in close contact with Napoleon throughout the day and survived unscathed, his fame (and fortune) grew as fresh stories of the battle and the Emperor were concocted and embellished. He is known to have escorted such well-known personalities as the poets Byron, Southey and Sir Walter Scott, the latter being, for a time, completely taken in by his tales. The problem was that a careful investigation of his credentials cast serious doubt as to whether he had actually been a guide at all. A Major Pryce Gordon, who accompanied Sir Walter Scott on his visit, later wrote to the effect that Decoster was a charlatan. When confronted with a blacksmith from La Belle Alliance Decoster was unable to refute that they had been in hiding together some 10 miles away on the day of the battle, and that the large sums he made as a guide enabled him to pay to keep other mouths shut. We will probably never be certain of the real truth.

MAISON VALETTE (Map 9, p. 126)

This small cottage or hut was located on the west of the Brussels–Genappe road about 100 metres north of the 'Elm Tree' crossroads. It was the only building (apart from La Haie Sainte) in the area of this crossroads, and what is now the tourist centre of 'Lion Village'. Near here the 1/95 Rifles bivouacked in the fields on the night before the battle. Their commanding officer, Lieutenant-Colonel Sir Andrew Barnard, made it his headquarters for the night, although not before its thatch had been stripped from the roof. From it were issued the meagre provisions received from Brussels. During the fighting it offered a flimsy shelter to a number of wounded before they were taken back to the field hospital at Mont St Jean Farm. Today the Grill d'Empereur occupies the site.

WATERLOO COTTAGE

A house, now known as Château Tremblant, close to the Wellington Museum in Waterloo. It was here that the Earl of Uxbridge was carried after having his leg smashed by a cannonball at the end of the battle. His leg was amputated, without anaesthetic, and the leg buried in the garden. The story goes that years' later the bones became uncovered when the willow tree planted over them was uprooted in a storm. The 'leg' was then exhibited in a glass case in a small museum. In 1876 General George Paget (Uxbridge's son), who had charged with the Light Brigade at Balaclava, was visiting Waterloo and happened to see his father's leg on display. He was horrified. However, despite diplomatic correspondence at high levels the bones could not be restored to the

family. Instead they were buried in the cemetery at Waterloo in 1880. According to one source the tombstone carried the words:

> *That day when the dead rise again*
> *What a long walk it will be*
> *To go back and join my body*
> *Waiting in England for me.*

Château Tremblant is now in a state of considerable neglect and moves to have it restored have yet to be implemented.

Other Features

THE LION MOUND (Map 10, p. 131)

This famous monument, with its lion as the symbol of both England and Belgium, has dominated the battlefield since its completion in 1826. Its advantages are that if you can climb the 226 steps to the platform around the lion you get a magnificent, panoramic view of the battlefield. Secondly, if as a walker you have problems with orientating yourself or other features, the Lion Mound is invariably there in the distance, marking the right centre of Wellington's line. For those who would have wished the field nearby to retain its original shape, it is a disfigurement, an abomination even.

The monument is dedicated to the Prince of Orange who was wounded near the spot over which it is built, its erection being decided upon by his father, King William I of the United Netherlands, in 1820. It was started in 1823 and completed over two years later. The construction, which was a vast undertaking for the period, involved the movement of well over ten million cubic feet of earth that was taken from between La Haie Sainte farm and the former sunken road that ran east–west from Ohain village, along the front of the Anglo-Allied position. This enormous excavation exercise obliterated the sunken lane that was the predominant tactical feature in the Allied centre, provoking Wellington to exclaim, 'They have ruined my battlefield.' Many of the labourers who toiled ceaselessly for so many months with soil-filled baskets on their backs were, supposedly, *bot'resses liègeoises* – women who normally worked in the Liège coal mines. In total a workforce of 2000, with 600 horses and innumerable carts, was assembled for the task.

The mound is 42.5 metres high with a base circumference of 518 metres. The lion, standing with a paw resting on a globe with its face glaring defiantly at France, was cast in nine separate pieces at the Cockerill works in Liège. It weighs 28 tons and is 4.4 metres

The Lion Mound – as it is today, showing the 226 steps to the top of the mound.

high and 4.6 metres long. It stands on a 4.6-metre high stone pedestal sunk through the height of the mound. Because of lack of roads at the time, the pieces were transported from Liège, first by boat to Dordrecht in Holland, then via the estuary of the Schelde and the Willebroek canal to Brussels harbour. From there they were taken by a wagon drawn by twenty horses to Mont St Jean and each piece inched slowly up the slope for assembly at the summit.

Apart from the Duke, many people at the time and since have condemned its construction. For some it troubled the peace of the dead. The Reverend Falconer visiting in 1825 thought so: '…I picked up a human rib just disturbed from its resting place. I left it where I found it, but the next day in passing over the same ground to go to Namur it was gone; some one … more curious than myself had probably secured it as a relic.' For the French it was a constant reminder of defeat. The pedestal has been painted in the red, white and blue of the French flag, while on another occasion it was decorated with the words, 'Here treason triumphed by chance. Instead of this lion there should be a fox.' During the German occupation in World War II the Luftwaffe installed a radio beacon on the mound.

Today tens of thousands of people of all nationalities and ages clamber to the top every year. The view is well worth the huffing and puffing, although the public telescope is broken.

THE DEMULDER MONUMENT (Map 10, p. 131)

About 250 metres west of the base of the Lion Mound, on the south side of the road to Braine l'Alleud (or Hougoumont) that the Belgians call the Chemin des Vertes Bornes, is a memorial stone to Lieutenant Augustin Demulder. Demulder was an officer in the 5th Cuirassiers and a Belgian who had already been wounded three times (at the Battles of Eylau, Essling and Hanau) during his years in French service. He was thirty years old that Sunday afternoon when he charged the Anglo-Allied squares. He was killed near the memorial, less than 10 kilometres from his birthplace, Nivelles. The stone also commemorates his comrades and marks the high tide for the flood of horsemen that topped the Allied ridge. Each time the cavalry was flung back they left behind heaps of broken bodies, horse and human – in a similar way to seaweed on a beach. The memorial reads:

EN MEMORIE
DU LIEUTENANT
AUGUSTIN DEMULDER
DU 5E CUIRASSIERS
NE A NIVELLES
EN BRABANT EN 1785
CHEVALIER DE LA LEGION D'HONNEUR
BLESSE A EYLAU 1807
A ESSLING 1809
A HANAY 1813
TUE A WATERLOO
ET EN MEMORIE DE
TOUS LES CAVALIERS QUI
CHARGERENT AVEC LUI
LE 18 JUIN 1815
CETTE PIERRE A ETE PLACEE PAR LE
WATERLOO COMMITTEE
EN ASSOCIATION AVEC LA
SOCIETE BELGE D'ETUDES
NAPOLEONIENNES 1986

Captain Mercer's Men get Breakfast

The soldiers of 'G' Troop RHA were among the very few in Wellington's Army to get both a good breakfast and a lavish helping of rum to see them through the day. Mercer had sent an old soldier, a bombardier (corporal), to the rear with wagons to replenish ammunition while it was still dark. He found the road to the rear jammed with wagons of all descriptions, many broken and plundered. Using the initiative and experience that had won him his chevrons, the bombardier loaded up with other things besides ammunition. His find included beef, biscuit, oatmeal and, most welcome of all, casks of rum. His reception back at the Troop was little short of ecstatic. Mercer recorded, 'The rum was divided [between nearly 200 men] on the spot. … The oatmeal was converted speedily into stirabout [porridge], and afforded our people a hearty meal, after which all hands set to work to prepare the beef, make soup, etc.' In a situation familiar to most soldiers, just as the soup was ready the order came to move.

(In memory of Lieutenant Augustus Demulder, 5th Cuirassiers. Born at Nivelles in Brabant in 1785, Chevalier of the Legion of Honour, wounded at Eylau 1807, at Essling 1809, at Hanay 1813, killed at Waterloo. And in memory of all the horsemen who charged with him on 18 June 1815. This stone has been erected by the Waterloo Committee in association with the Belgian Napoleonic Society, 1986.)

MEMORIAL TO 'G' TROOP, ROYAL HORSE ARTILLERY (Map 10, p. 131)

Scarcely 50 metres west of the Demulder monument is another similar stone, marking the last gun position of 'G' Troop RHA. This troop of five 9-pounder guns and one 5.5-inch howitzer was commanded by Captain Alexander Cavalie Mercer who later became a general and who left a fascinating account of his experiences, entitled *Journal of the Waterloo Campaign*. 'G' Troop suffered severely (although not to the extent Mercer described in his Journal), mainly from close range artillery fire after the loss of La Haie Sainte. Mercer recounted a particularly close call when he was talking to (or rather shouting at) Lieutenant Breton who had already had two mounts shot under him (Mercer's had nine wounds). Their horses were standing close to each other, '… his horse stood at right angles to mine, the poor jaded animal dozingly rested his muzzle on my thigh; whilst I, the better to hear amidst the infernal din, leant forward, resting my arm between his ears. In this attitude a cannon ball smashed the horse's head to atoms, and the headless trunk sank to the ground!'

The memorial stone reads:

THIS STONE MARKS THE LAST POSITION
OF G TROOP ROYAL HORSE ARTILLERY
COMMANDED BY CAPTAIN A.C. MERCER
DURING THE BATTLE OF WATERLOO
18 JUNE 1815 FROM HERE THE TROOP
TOOK A CONSPICUOUS PART IN DEFEATING
THE ATTACKS OF THE FRENCH CAVALRY.

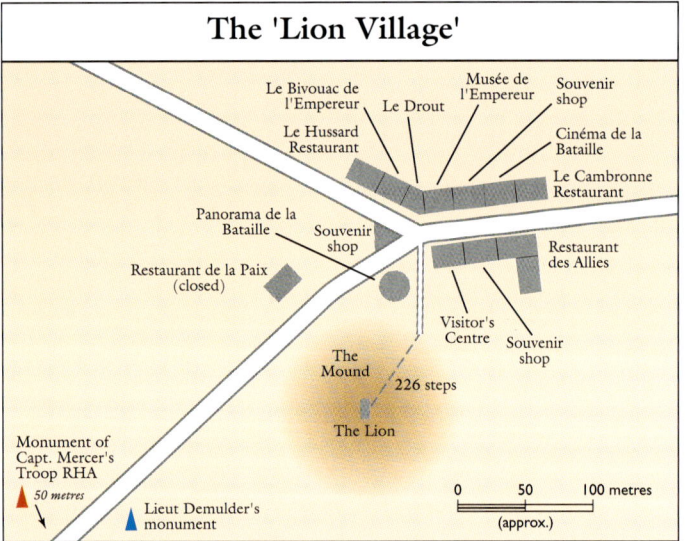

The 'Lion Village'

Le Bivouac de l'Empereur
Le Drout
Musée de l'Empereur
Souvenir shop
Le Hussard Restaurant
Cinéma de la Bataille
Le Cambronne Restaurant
Panorama de la Bataille
Souvenir shop
Restaurant de la Paix (closed)
Restaurant des Allies
Visitor's Centre
Souvenir shop
The Mound
226 steps
The Lion
Monument of Capt. Mercer's Troop RHA
50 metres
Lieut Demulder's monument
0   50   100 metres
(approx.)

'LION VILLAGE' (Map 10, p. 131 and diagram above)

This is the unofficial name given to the buildings to cater for visitors that have sprung up immediately north and east of the Lion Mound. Amongst the inevitable souvenir shops, restaurants, cafés and car parks are the Visitors' Centre and the Panorama. The Visitors' Centre is a good starting place for an overview of the battle. Not only does it have an audio-visual presentation using a 10 square metre model of the battlefield, but also a film of highlights of the battle using re-enactors in appropriate uniforms. There is a well-stocked Waterloo book, card and souvenir shop inside the Centre too.

The Panorama is impressive. Inside the visitor climbs some stairs and finds himself in the midst of the great French cavalry charges. The highlights of the two hours of heroic but fruitless attempts to break the Anglo-Allied infantry squares are realistically painted on a giant panorama 110 metres long and 12 metres high. The building has been there since 1912, the painting being the work of five French artists led by Louis Dumoulin, who developed the inconvenient habit of locking himself in while working.

Opposite the Panorama is a Waxworks Museum containing the life-size impressions of the famous generals who commanded at Waterloo. There is a vignette of Napoleon at breakfast with his generals at Le Caillou at eight o'clock that morning.

THE 'ELM TREE' CROSSROADS (Map 10, p. 131 and diagram right)

This is virtually the exact centre of Wellington's front line. His army stretched away east and west for 1,500 metres on either side of this crossroads. To the north the road ran straight to Brussels via Mont St Jean and Waterloo; to the south was La Belle Alliance and the centre of the French Army. Here Wellington took up his position with his staff when he was not galloping about the field. It is called the 'Elm Tree' crossroads, as in 1815 there was a flourishing, solitary, elm tree in the angle of the southern and western branches of the four roads. It was soon cut down after the battle for saleable souvenirs. Comparatively recently, another tree has been planted – a long overdue replacement.

The nearest the crossroads came to capture was around 6.30 p.m. after the loss of La Haie Sainte. French cannons were hauled into position between the farm and the crossroads and, until the 1/95 Rifles picked off the gunners, did devastating damage to the infantry on the ridge. It was then that the 27th Foot (formed in

square), whose memorial is close to the junction, were cut down in droves by the guns and the hordes of French skirmishers. Near these crossroads, quite early in the battle, General Picton died and, towards the close, Wellington's friend and ADC Lieutenant-Colonel Gordon was mortally wounded near where the Lion Mound now stands but whose memorial is 100 metres south of the crossroads. Under the Belgian memorial just north of the crossroads, and in the scrub and litter filled shallow pit to the south, are two burial pits where countless bodies, Allied and French, were unceremoniously heaped together for mass burial.

In 1815 where these roads crossed was sunk 3 to 4 metres below the surrounding ground. The northern, southern and western branches in particular ran through cuttings for 100 metres or more. All that remains is the steep embankment on either side of the Gordon memorial. Most of the soil from the old cuttings long ago became part of the Lion Mound.

Apart from a cottage called Maison Valette, where the commanding officer of the 1/95 set up his headquarters on the night before the battle, there were no buildings near the crossroads in 1815. The only new construction worthy of note is Le 1815 Hôtel. This is a five-star hotel with superb views over the battlefield from the most expensive bedrooms. The rooms carry appropriate names: Wellington, Picton, Hill, Uxbridge, the Prince of Orange, Napoleon, Ney, Reille, Grouchy, Soult, Lobau, Cambronne, d'Erlon, Blücher, Thielmann and Gneisenau. It even boasts a miniature golf course incorporating models of monuments and farms on the battlefield.

NEARBY MEMORIALS

The Belgian Monument

This impressive monument, a broken pyramid surrounded by a stone wall and approached through an iron gate and up several steps, is located in the angle of the northern and eastern roads. Belgium has always been the country in which armies have clashed throughout history. Therefore, placing the memorial at this crossroads, the centre of Wellington's position at Waterloo, was done deliberately in recognition of Belgium's place in the history of Europe. It was dedicated to the 1,200 or more Belgians who were killed or wounded in the battle in defence of their flag and honour. The inscription reads:

AUX BELGES MORTS LE XVIII JUIN MDCCCXV
EN COMBATTANT POUR LA DEFENSE DU DRAPEAU
ET L'HONNEUR DES ARMES.

(To the Belgians killed on 18 June 1815 in defence of their flag and honour.)

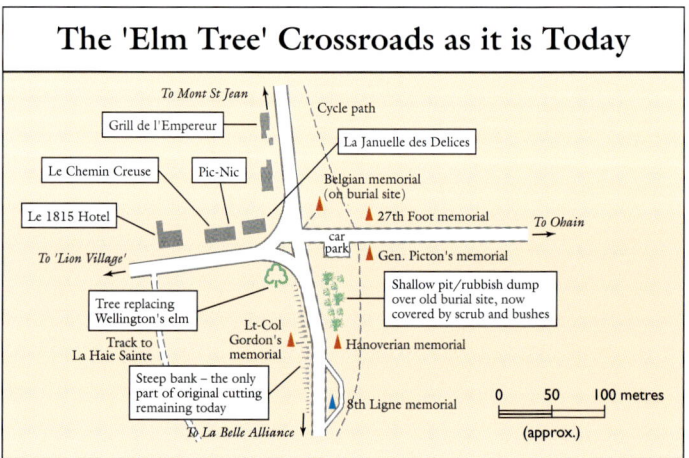

The 'Elm Tree' Crossroads as it is Today

To Mont St Jean
Cycle path
Grill de l'Empereur
La Januelle des Delices
Le Chemin Creuse
Pic-Nic
Belgian memorial (on burial site)
Le 1815 Hotel
27th Foot memorial
To Ohain
car park
Gen. Picton's memorial
To 'Lion Village'
Shallow pit/rubbish dump over old burial site, now covered by scrub and bushes
Tree replacing Wellington's elm
Lt-Col Gordon's memorial
Hanoverian memorial
Track to La Haie Sainte
8th Ligne memorial
0   50   100 metres
Steep bank – the only part of original cutting remaining today
To La Belle Alliance
(approx.)

The Belgian memorial standing at the 'Elm Tree' crossroads on the site of a mass grave of the dead from the battlefield.   Photo: the author

The 27th Regiment of Foot (Inniskilling)

This memorial, some 50 metres east of the Belgian monument, was erected on the 175th anniversary of the battle by the successors of the old 27th Foot, the Royal Irish Rangers. Held in reserve until shortly after 3.00 p.m., this battalion was deployed in square after the loss of La Haie Sainte. This was not because of the threat of cavalry, but because being so close to the crossroads such a formation enabled effective fire to be delivered onto the Brussels road, as well as to the battalion's front. Its densely packed ranks made a target neither French guns nor skirmishers could miss. The battalion, as the memorial confirms, suffered 66 per cent casualties. Of the nineteen officers with the battalion, sixteen were killed or wounded. The 27th was the only Anglo-Allied battalion that went into the action commanded by a captain (John Hare, who had the army rank of major) and came out with sergeants commanding companies. The memorial reads:

IN MEMORY OF THE HEROIC STAND BY
THE 27TH (INNISKILLING) REGIMENT OF
FOOT AT THE BATTLE OF WATERLOO ON
18TH JUNE 1815 WHEN, OF THE 747
OFFICERS AND MEN OF THE REGIMENT
WHO JOINED THE BATTLE 493 WERE KILLED OR
WOUNDED. A NOBLE RECORD OF
STUBBORN ENDURANCE.
OF THEM THE DUKE OF WELLINGTON SAID,
'AH, THEY SAVED THE CENTRE OF MY LINE'
ERECTED BY THEIR SUCCESSORS
THE ROYAL IRISH RANGERS
(27TH INNISKILLINGS, 83RD, 87TH) 18 JUNE 1990.

General Picton's memorial

Lieutenant-General Sir Thomas Picton, commanding the 5th British Division, was shot through the brain near this spot at about 2.00 p.m. He was in the act of urging his troops forward to charge the wavering columns of d'Erlon's infantry. Typically, for Picton was something of a volatile eccentric, he had gone into battle wearing civilian clothes that included a top hat (he was seen wearing a red night-cap at the Battle of Busaco in 1810) and shabby overcoat and carrying an umbrella. Both the top hat and the musket ball that killed him were preserved for posterity. His memorial stone reads:

TO THE GALLANT MEMORY OF
LIEUTENANT-GENERAL SIR THOMAS PICTON
COMMANDER OF THE 5TH DIVISION AND THE LEFT
WING
OF THE ARMY AT THE BATTLE OF WATERLOO
BORN 1758
DIED NEAR THIS SPOT IN THE EARLY AFTERNOON
OF 18TH JUNE 1815 LEADING HIS MEN AGAINST
COUNT DROUET D'ERLON'S ADVANCE.

Lieutenant-Colonel Gordon's memorial

The news of Sir Alexander Gordon's death brought tears to Wellington' eyes since not only were they close friends but he was also one of the Duke's five personal ADCs. Gordon was not killed outright but had his leg smashed by a cannonball while he was near the square of the 2/30 during the attack of the Imperial Guard at the close of the battle. Sergeant-Major Wood of the 30th carried him to what is now the Wellington Museum in Waterloo village, where Dr

Wellington Receives the News of Gordon's Death

When Gordon died in Dr Hume's arms at about 3.30 a.m. on 19 June, the doctor deliberated on whether to wake the Duke. He described what happened:

> I decided to see if he was awake; and going up stairs to his room, I tapped gently on the door, when he told me to come in. He had, as usual, taken off all his clothes, but had not washed himself; and as I entered the room he sat up in his bed, his face covered with the dust and sweat of the previous day, and extended his hand to me, which I took, and held in mine, whilst I told him of Gordon's death, and related such of the casualties as had come to my knowledge. He was much affected. I felt his tears dropping fast upon my hands, and looking towards him, saw them chasing one another in furrows over his dusty cheeks. He brushed them away suddenly with his left hand, and said to me, in a voice tremulous with emotion, 'Well, thank God! I don't know what it is to lose a battle, but certainly nothing can be more painful than to gain one with the loss of so many of one's friends.'

John Hume, Wellington's personal surgeon, amputated his leg at the thigh. It was a hellish operation that Gordon did not survive, although at first he appeared to be recovering, as he spoke briefly to the Duke around 10.00 p.m. and heard the news of the great victory. Some five hours later, however, he died unexpectedly in Hume's arms, probably from shock. Fate had indeed been unkind to Gordon, striking him down in the last moments of the last battle after he had survived for so long at Wellington's side in the Peninsular War.

In 1817 his grieving family erected a memorial half way between the crossroads and La Haie Sainte. It stands at the top of twenty-two steps up from the road (the visitor who climbs them gets a good idea of the depth of the cutting that the road ran through in 1815). At the top is an imposing stone column, the most elaborate British memorial on the battlefield. The inscription, in English and French, is long, effusive and fulsome. It reads:

Epitaphs to Uxbridge's Leg

Several variations of the epitaphs erected to commemorate the burial of the Earl of Uxbridge's leg in the back garden of Waterloo Cottage (Château Tremblant) exist. In ascending order of frivolity, they allegedly read:

> *Here is buried the leg*
> *Of the illustrious and valiant Count Uxbridge,*
> *Lieutenant-General of His Brittannic Majesty,*
> *Commander in Chief of the British, Belgian and Dutch*
> *Cavalry, wounded 18th June*
> *1815, at the memorable battle of Waterloo;*
> *Which by his heroism, contributed towards the*
> *Triumph of the human cause;*
> *Gloriously decided by the brilliant*
> *victory of the said day.*

Next,

> *Here lies the Marquis of Anglesey's leg;*
> *Pray for the rest of his body, I beg.*

And finally,

> *Here lies the Marquis of Anglesey's limb;*
> *The devil will have the remainder of him.*

SACRED TO THE MEMORY OF
LIEUTENANT-COLONEL THE HONOURABLE SIR ALEXANDER GORDON
KNIGHT COMMANDER OF THE MOST HONOURABLE ORDER OF THE BATH . AIDE-DE-CAMP TO FIELD-MARSHAL THE DUKE OF WELLINGTON
AND ALSO BROTHER TO GEORGE EARL OF ABERDEEN
WHO IN THE TWENTY-NINTH YEAR OF HIS AGE
TERMINATED A SHORT BUT GLORIOUS CAREER
ON THE 18TH JUNE 1815
WHILST EXECUTING THE ORDERS OF HIS GREAT COMMANDER
IN THE BATTLE OF WATERLOO
DISTINGUISHED FOR GALLANTRY AND GOOD CONDUCT IN THE FIELD
HE WAS HONOURED WITH REPEATED MARKS OF APPROBATION
BY THE ILLUSTRIOUS HERO
WITH WHOM HE SHARED THE DANGERS OF EVERY BATTLE
IN SPAIN PORTUGAL AND FRANCE
AND RECEIVED THE MOST FLATTERING PROOF OF HIS CONFIDENCE
ON MANY TRYING OCCASIONS
HIS ZEAL AND ACTIVITY IN THE SERVICE OBTAINED THE REWARD OF TEN MEDALS
AND THE HONOURABLE DISTINCTION OF THE ORDER OF THE BATH
HE WAS JUSTLY LAMENTED BY THE DUKE OF WELLINGTON
IN HIS PUBLIC DESPATCH
AS AN OFFICER OF HIGH PROMISE
AND A SERIOUS LOSS FOR THE COUNTRY
NOT LESS WORTHY OF RECORD FOR HIS VIRTUES IN PRIVATE LIFE
HIS INAFFECTED RESPECT FOR RELIGION
HIS HIGH SENSE OF HONOUR
HIS SCRUPULOUS INTEGRITY
AND THE MOST AMIABLE QUALITIES
WHICH SECURED THE ATTACHMENT OF HIS FRIENDS
AND THE LOVE OF HIS OWN FAMILY
IN TESTIMONY OF FEELINGS WHICH NO LANGUAGE CAN EXPRESS
A DISCONSOLATED SISTER AND FIVE SURVIVING BROTHERS
HAVE ERECTED THIS SIMPLE MEMORIAL
TO THE OBJECT OF THEIR TENDEREST AFFECTION
REPAIRED IN 1863 BY HIS BROTHER ADMIRAL THE HONOURABLE J. GORDON
REPAIRED IN 1817 AND 1888 BY HIS GRAND NEPHEW JOHN, 7TH EARL OF ABERDEEN
REPAIRED IN 1857 BY HIS FAMILY.

The abbreviated version on a plaque at the foot of the column reads:

TO THE MEMORY OF THE HON. SIR ALEXANDER GORDON KCB
LT-COL SCOTS GUARDS AND AIDE DE CAMP TO THE DUKE OF WELLINGTON
AFTER SERVING HIS COUNTRY WITH DISTINCTION
HE WAS KILLED AT THE BATTLE OF WATERLOO
18TH JUNE 1815.

Lieutenant-Colonel Gordon's monument. The most elaborate monument to the British, with the most fulsome inscription, on the battlefield. Note the steepness of the cutting through which the 'Elm Tree' crossroads ran in 1815.   Photo: the author

The Hanoverian (KGL) memorial

Opposite the Gordon memorial, on the other side of the road, is an obelisk commemorating the Hanoverians who fell at Waterloo. The State of Hanover was an Imperial dependency during most of the Napoleonic era, and then in 1814 came under the British Crown until the reign of Queen Victoria. Hanoverians were heavily engaged in the counterattacks to take the pressure off the defenders of La Haie Sainte. The memorial was initiated by surviving Hanoverian officers to commemorate their comrades who died in the battle, and was erected in 1818. It was placed on the site of a mass grave said to contain some 4000 bodies of men and horses from both armies.

The inscription reads:

> TO THE MEMORY
> OF THEIR COMPANIONS IN ARMS
> WHO GLORIOUSLY FELL ON THE MEMORABLE
> 18TH JUNE 1815
> THIS MONUMENT
> IS ERECTED BY THE OFFICERS
> OF THE KING'S GERMAN LEGION.

The names of the officers who were killed are listed by battalion on the north and south sides of the monument.

The Bois de Paris (Maps 35 & 36, pp. 384 & 385)

In 1815 this wood was considerably larger than it is today, being some 1,400 metres from north to south and 750 metres from east to west. The wood covered two prominent, steep sided ridges and the intervening valley. It straddled four roads, or rather tracks, that the Prussians marching from Wavre via Lasne used, and the centre of the wood was only 1,500 metres from the French right flank. It had, therefore, considerable tactical importance. The Prussians had enough delays and difficulties reaching the battlefield in time to be of use due to the mud, slippery slopes, defiles, congestion and tangled orders of march, without having to fight for passage of the Bois de Pais as they toiled out of the Lasne defile. Had there been serious opposition in this wood there is little doubt that Waterloo would have been won or lost without their intervention.

The only opposition east of the woods came from Marbot's 7th Hussars, and he skirmished with the Prussian 6th Hussars

The KGL at Bexhill

In 1804 the village of Bexhill on the south coast of England, whose population was not yet 2000, became the adopted home of the exiled Hanoverian troops who formed the KGL. Four battalions of 2,673 men moved into a camp of 25 acres. Initially the local inhabitants regarded the influx of foreign soldiery with some suspicion. However, this did not last long, as the troops were well-behaved, friendly and relationships were boosted by trade. The merchants of Bexhill were among the first to benefit from having so many customers close at hand. The soldiers required food, drink, horses, equipment and boots. Local cobblers soon mastered the art of making the Hessian boot. The village economy boomed. In the ten years that the KGL were based at Bexhill (until they marched away to disband in Osnabrück in 1816) the Parish of St Peter's recorded 108 marriages between local girls and KGL soldiers. A number went with their husbands to Hanover on the legion's disbandment.

The village of Bexhill has now become the town of Bexhill-on-Sea. In 1989 a group of enthusiasts formed the Bexhill Hanoverian Study Group to research the Regiment's stay in the town. There is a small permanent display in the local museum. As recently as 1998 the Group was involved in the unveiling of the commemorative plaque on the wall of La Haie Sainte to the men (many from Bexhill) who fought so long and hard in its defence.

The Hanoverian (KGL) memorial.   Photo: the author

under Colonel Schwerin as they probed west from the Lasne valley. The Prussians had been spotted at about 1.00 p.m. from Napoleon's position and he sent Lobau's cavalry (Domon and Subervie) to confirm the situation and delay the enemy. A short while later Lobau was ordered to take his infantry east. He set out at about 1.30 p.m., the movement masked by the noise and smoke of the 'Grand Battery' firing to support the start of d'Erlon's corps advance. He had something less than 5000 metres to march (mostly on a road) if he was to occupy the Bois de Paris. Allowing for delays, his troops could have covered the distance in less than two hours. Whether or not Lobau was at fault in not pushing on into the wood or whether he had the time is discussed in Section 10 'Myths and Controversies'. As it was, Lobau halted west of the Paris Wood and waited until Bülow's leading units debouched from it at around 4.30 p.m. before engaging the enemy.

Colonel Schwerin's memorial (Map 35, p. 384)

Colonel Count Wilhelm von Schwerin commanded the 1st Prussian Cavalry Brigade, a formation of three regiments, one of whom was not present that afternoon on the eastern edge of the Bois de Paris. Schwerin had put the 6th Hussars in the lead followed by the 1st West Prussian Uhlans. He himself was close behind the leading squadrons. At around 3.30 p.m. the Prussian horsemen, who had already had several running skirmishes with retiring French cavalry (Marbot's 7th Hussars), finally climbed out of the Lasne defile onto

Colonel Count von Schwerin's memorial column. Schwerin was almost certainly the first Prussian killed at Waterloo, or rather on the march to the battlefield. Photo: the author.

the plateau; ahead was the Paris Wood. They immediately came under fire from the trees, having met the advanced squadrons of Lobau's cavalry. The French had brought up a battery of horse artillery, which with its first rounds killed Schwerin as he came forward to assess the situation. He was the first Prussian officer, probably the first Prussian, to be killed at Waterloo.

It is likely that Schwerin was quickly buried, near where he fell. Two years later his family came in search of his remains, which were located with the help of a local woman. They were reburied and the monument erected over them. Schwerin's widow was so grateful for the assistance and kindness of the local people that she gave two church bells to Lasne and 100 Prussian florins a year to the priest to distribute to the poor. These donations continued until her death.

The monument is a 5 metre high stone column, on the base of which is a bronze plaque bearing the words in German:

> WILLIAM, COUNT VON SCHWERIN, KNIGHT AND SUPERIOR OFFICER OF THE KING, FALLEN IN A FOREIGN COUNTRY FOR THE FATHERLAND, DURING THE VICTORY OF 18 JUNE 1815.

THE CONDITION OF THE BATTLEFIELD ON 18 JUNE 1815

Crops

Virtually the entire area was devoted to arable farming, so in June the crops of wheat and rye, although not quite ready for harvest, were ripening and had grown tall. The variety of the these crops grew higher than the modern versions, so much of the battlefield was covered with grain that had grown as high as the withers of the horses: around 1.5 metres or more (although it should be noted that the British 12th Light Dragoons bivouacked in a clover field). After tens of thousands of men and horses along with hundreds of guns had trampled it for several hours, the crops were mostly beaten flat to the 'consistency of an Indian mat', as one officer put it.

At the start, however, these tall crops had a distinct effect on the battle. They restricted visibility. It was easy for an infantryman to stoop or crouch to be invisible, and men who fell wounded were instantly hidden from their comrades as they moved on. Those firing muskets found that their targets, sometimes seen poorly through the heads of waving grain, were smaller and more fleeting. Add to this the dense clouds of smoke, and the range of vision of the average infantry soldier was often measured at a few metres. At Quatre-Bras an officer of the 28th Foot recalled that when his unit was in square a French lancer was sent forward to plant his lance with its pennon in front of the battalion as a marker for his unit to charge on. Early in the day at Waterloo the light company of the 51st Foot was fired on by French skirmishers that had got to within 15 metres of their line under cover of the standing grain. Even towards the close of the battle some crops remained untrampled. Lieutenant Sharpin of Captain Bolton's Brigade (Battery) of guns claims not to have seen the advance of the Imperial Guard until he saw, 'the French bonnets just above the high corn, and within forty or fifty yards of our guns'.

Another inconvenience of these crops was that they, like everything else at the beginning of the battle, were soaking wet. They retained the rainwater so that soldiers pushing through them were immediately drenched again, and powder in the pans of muskets was difficult to keep dry, or even keep in the pan, as the weapon was continually being brushed by thick crops. A musket carefully loaded

The old variety of rye growing on the battlefield in June. Note how high it is and the effect this had on visibility, concealment, and movement in terms of speed and keeping formation.

at the start of an advance was likely to misfire after several hundred metres of struggling through wet wheat. And that advance was certain to have been considerably slower than across open ground, formations being harder to keep, as visibility was restricted, while individual troops found it difficult to maintain dressing or intervals.

Finally, the soaking battlefield, carpeted with high crops, took much longer to dry out – there was also the odd shower in the afternoon as Captain Mercer of the RHA has pointed out in his *Journal*. Whatever sun or breeze there was did not reach the soil. The French hope that a few hours delay would dry the ground was to prove largely wishful thinking.

SODDEN SOLDIERS, SODDEN SOIL

The heavy rain during the twelve hours before the battle ensured that the great majority of men in all armies spent a wet, cold, miserable and sleepless night. The effect of this on delayed deployment by the French is discussed below. Some sought shelter in buildings or barns and many tried to light fires with wet wood, doors ripped from houses, or furniture. The French were particularly prone to this type of looting, and the defenders of La Haie Sainte later that day bemoaned the fact that the barn door had been burnt for warmth a few hours earlier. Most men started the battle wet, exhausted, drained and hungry.

The clay soil held the water, in many low-lying areas dips and hollows contained deep puddles. Everywhere that man or beast went churned up and deepened the mud. Another ingredient that added to the mire were horse droppings – a factor seldom mentioned. Anyone who has mucked out stables in the morning knows what a few horses can produce, multiply this by tens of thousands and you have some inkling of the state of the ground in most bivouac and deployment areas. Not surprisingly, few wanted to lie down during the night, although some cut corn to fashion a sort of mattress. Captain Cotter, a company commander in the 2/69 (South Lincolnshire) preferred, 'standing and walking to and fro during the hours of darkness to lying upon … mud through which we sank more than ankle deep'. Lieutenant Simmons of the 1/95 Rifles, a veteran of the Peninsular War who was to survive being shot through the liver, having two broken ribs and a musket ball in the chest at Waterloo, put the mud to practical use. He 'smeared an old blanket with the clayey mud', put some straw on the ground and pulled the blanket over him.

Apart from making men miserable, the soft, boggy ground had two significant tactical effects on the battle. Firstly, it slowed movement. This was particularly so for horses, guns and wagons. The clay clung to hooves and wheels; they sank in deep and required a conscious effort to pull out. Combined with the thick crops, the slope of the ground and the sunken tracks, there was little galloping at Waterloo. The great French cavalry attacks were mostly launched at a trot, sometimes a walk, on blown horses. It took an hour to drag the Emperor's 'beautiful daughters' (12-pounder cannons) forward and assemble the 'Grand Battery'. Secondly, it took the bounce out of cannonballs. On hard ground roundshot ricochets several times before it loses its lethality. In soft soil the shot usually sinks in and does no damage.

The Sodden Battlefield

Only just before dawn did the downpour ease up. The troops, the ground and the crops were saturated. Tens of thousands of tramping feet, slithering hooves and spinning wheels churned the ground into a sticky, ankle deep quagmire of mud. Those few soldiers lucky enough to have found shelter overnight were soon drenched from pushing through chest-high, waterlogged rye and wheat fields. The sun did not appear, deployment was slow, and the French attack several hours late.

The experience of the British 12th Light Dragoons on the night before the battle was typical of any unit in any army on that battlefield. John Gordon Smith, the regiment's assistant-surgeon recalled, 'We bivouacked in open clover fields, close to … the farm of Mont St Jean. … The adjoining village furnished fuel in abundance. Doors, and window-shutters – furniture of every description – carts, ploughs, harrows, wheel-barrows, clock-cases, casks, tables &c &c, were carried or trundled out to

the bivouac, and being broken up, made powerful fires, in spite of the rain. Chairs were otherwise disposed of. Officers were paying two francs each for them.' Eventually, Smith and his comrades placed bundles of straw on the ground, 'and resolved to establish ourselves for the night under cover of our cloaks; but such was the clayey nature [of the soil] that the rain did not sink in … but rose like a leak in a ship, among the straw, and we were, in consequence, more drenched from below than above.'

The strains of wheat and rye of 200 years ago grew so tall that it sometimes completely concealed infantry or guns. Sergeant Anson of the 42nd Highlanders has described the rye at Quatre-Bras: '… forward we hastened, though we saw no enemy in front. The stalks of rye, like the reeds that grow on the margins of some swamp, opposed our advance; the tops were up to our bonnets, and we strode and groped our way through as fast as we could. By the time we reached a field of clover, we were very much straggled…'.

SMOKE

The muskets and cannons of 1815 produced dense clouds of greyish-white, gunpowder smoke when fired that literally blanketed the battlefield with varying degrees of density. It hung low, needing a stiff breeze to disperse it quickly. Troops were seen fleetingly through gaps in the smoke. Gunners often fired blind into a distant haze. It gave advantage or disadvantage to attacker and defender equally. Men of the 1/4 (King's Own) in square near the 'Elm Tree' crossroads could not see La Haie Sainte when it was lost to the French. Ensign Gronow, who fought as a guardsman with the 3/1 Foot Guards as Sir Thomas Picton did not need him as an ADC, described the inside of that battalion's square as so thick with smoke and the smell of burnt cartridges that he nearly suffocated. At the general advance of Wellington's army at the end of the battle the movement took many units out of a fog in which they had stood for much of the day.

The Battlefield Deployment of the Armies
(Maps 11, 12, 13 & 14, pp. 157, 158, 161 & 162)

GENERAL

In the early morning, sometime between 5.00 a.m. and 6.00 a.m., the scene both on and to the north of the Anglo-Allied ridge has been described thus:

> The light of the sun was obscured by a thick mass of clouds. The woods were dripping wet; the heavy crops made heavier by the moisture; the ground was plashy and yielding, and in the depths of the valleys were wide pools. The air was filled with mist, and as far as the eye could see the whole country was dark silent and dreary. … Soon the men awoke, and the plateau was covered in a moving mass. The soldiers looked cold and blue, dirty and unshaven. … they rose stiff and numbed.

Wellington's Army, with the exception of Lambert's 10th Infantry Brigade that did not arrive at Mont St Jean village until around 11.00 a.m. after a forced march from Ghent, had been in position since the previous night. Minor adjustments were needed, as units had to quit their bivouacs, but there was no major reshuffling required before all formations were able to form up in their battle positions. Virtually all front line units had encamped within a few metres of the ground they would fight on.

The same was not true of the French. At that time virtually the entire army was still short of the battlefield, many units not yet having abandoned their bivouacs. Napoleon wanted an attack at 9.00 a.m. but when he authorized the soldiers to take their soup there seemed little reason to hurry – Wellington would wait, and Grouchy was taking care of the Prussians. Units had scattered, hunting for shelter and firewood during the night. They took time to reassemble. Reille's II Corps had encamped south of Genappe (5 kilometres south of Le Caillou) but had been on the road since daybreak. When Soult's order for the troops to take breakfast and clean muskets was received, a halt was called. Not until 9.00 a.m. did his troops march up past Le Caillou. The son of the farmer there later wrote confirming that at that time troops were still debouching from Genappe. The Imperial Guard did not break camp until 10.00 a.m., while Durutte claimed that he did not bring his division into line on the right of d'Erlon's corps until the opening cannonade was in progress – between about 11.30 a.m. and noon. Few writers (except the poet Sir Walter Scott) have made the point that at 11.00 a.m. the French Army was not yet in line. Napoleon's deliberately ostentatious review of his troops near La Belle Alliance was, in reality, greeting units as they marched up to deploy. Many of Wellington's soldiers have described how they waited and watched as their enemy formed up.

Preparation for battle involved much the same procedure on either side of the valley. Weapons were cleaned and tested, which entailed much firing in the air (particularly noticeable in the Anglo-Allied lines where there was a continuous popping and frequent fusillades of shots), followed by the meticulous, unhurried loading of the first ball to be fired in anger. Ammunition was replenished, horses fed and watered. Those with food available (the minority in both armies) ate it. The French drank their soup.

Soup was not the only liquid drunk before battle. Sixteen-year-old Ensign Keppel in the 3/14 (Buckinghamshire) related how, before attempting to bivouac the previous night, the battalion (of raw young recruits like himself) filed past a large tub full of gin under the watchful eyes of Major Tidy and Quartermaster Ross. Every officer and man got a cupful. Keppel recalled that, 'No fermented liquor that has since passed my lips could vie with that delicious schnapps [gin]. As soon as each man was served the precious contents what remained in the tub were tilted over on the ground.'

With Napoleon's men it was brandy, for those lucky enough to see the supply wagons. It was a tradition in the French Army that brandy be issued before battle. Sometimes the ration was overgenerous. At Genappe the evening before, several French Lancers had been captured after rashly rushing at the British 7th Hussars drawn up blocking the road – they were all found to be drunk.

The French Deployment

A soldier in the Armée du Nord gave a realistic account of the hours before battle:

> About 8 o'clock the wagons arrived with cartridges and hogsheads of brandy; each soldier received a double ration; with a crust of bread we might have done very well, but the bread was not there. You can imagine what sort of humour we were in. This was all we had that day [he seems to have missed out on the soup]. Immediately after the grand movement [deployment] commenced. Regiments joined their brigades, brigades their divisions, and the divisions reformed their corps … our battalion joined Donzelot's division. … Several persons have related that we were jubilant, and were all singing, but it is false. Marching all night without rations, sleeping in the water, forbidden to light a fire, when preparing for showers of grape and canister, all this took away any inclination to sing. We were glad to pull our shoes out of the holes in which they were buried at every step, and, chilled and drenched to our waists by the wet grain, the hardiest and most courageous among us wore a discontented air. It is true that the bands played marches for their regiments, that the trumpets of the cavalry, the drums of the infantry, and the trombones mingled their tones and produced a terrible effect … as for me I never heard anyone sing either at Leipzig or Waterloo.

Anglo-Allied Deployment, Centre and Right, at 11.30 a.m.   Map 11

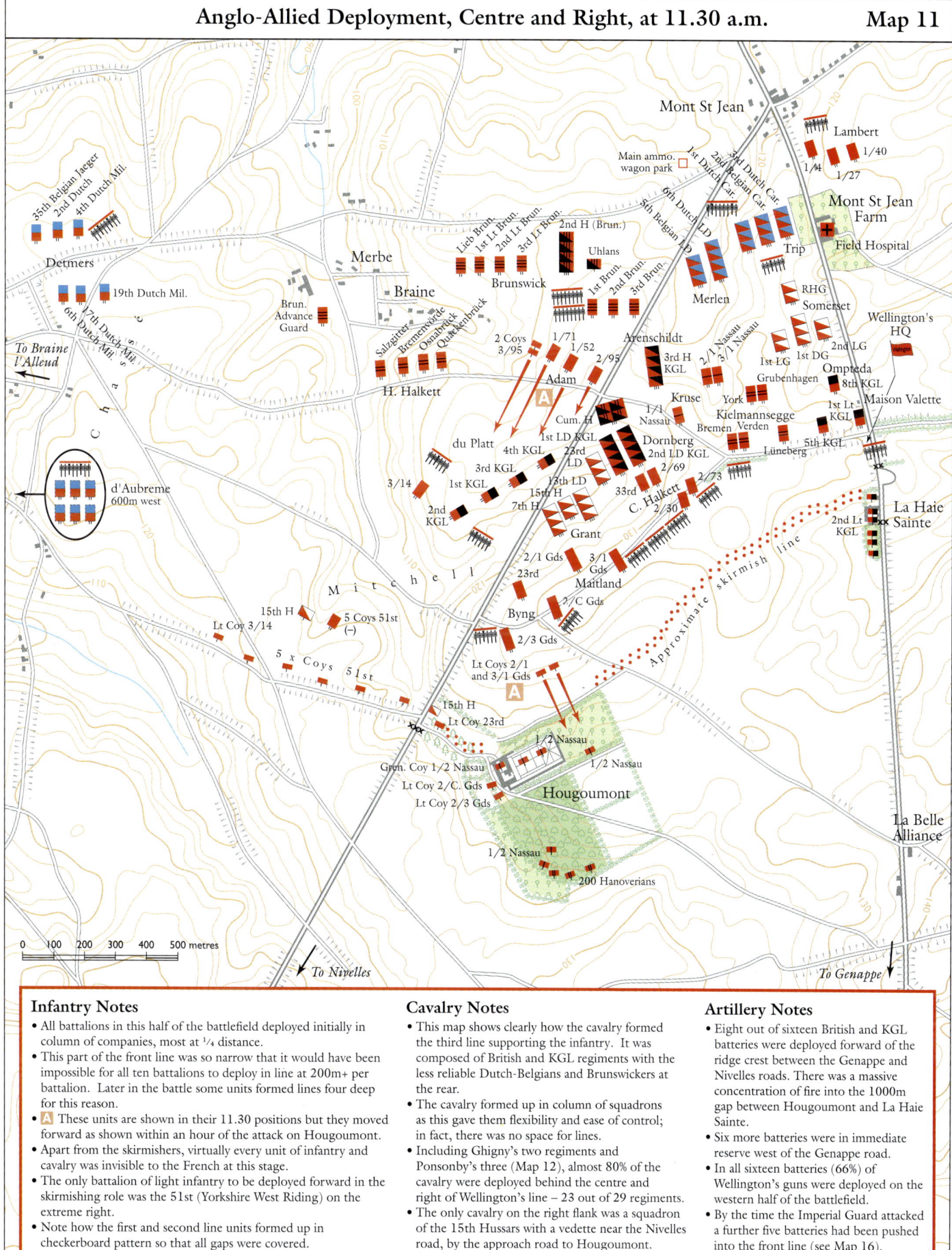

Infantry Notes

- All battalions in this half of the battlefield deployed initially in column of companies, most at ¼ distance.
- This part of the front line was so narrow that it would have been impossible for all ten battalions to deploy in line at 200m+ per battalion. Later in the battle some units formed lines four deep for this reason.
- **A** These units are shown in their 11.30 positions but they moved forward as shown within an hour of the attack on Hougoumont.
- Apart from the skirmishers, virtually every unit of infantry and cavalry was invisible to the French at this stage.
- The only battalion of light infantry to be deployed forward in the skirmishing role was the 51st (Yorkshire West Riding) on the extreme right.
- Note how the first and second line units formed up in checkerboard pattern so that all gaps were covered.

Cavalry Notes

- This map shows clearly how the cavalry formed the third line supporting the infantry. It was composed of British and KGL regiments with the less reliable Dutch-Belgians and Brunswickers at the rear.
- The cavalry formed up in column of squadrons as this gave them flexibility and ease of control; in fact, there was no space for lines.
- Including Ghigny's two regiments and Ponsonby's three (Map 12), almost 80% of the cavalry were deployed behind the centre and right of Wellington's line – 23 out of 29 regiments.
- The only cavalry on the right flank was a squadron of the 15th Hussars with a vedette near the Nivelles road, by the approach road to Hougoumont.

Artillery Notes

- Eight out of sixteen British and KGL batteries were deployed forward of the ridge crest between the Genappe and Nivelles roads. There was a massive concentration of fire into the 1000m gap between Hougoumont and La Haie Sainte.
- Six more batteries were in immediate reserve west of the Genappe road.
- In all sixteen batteries (66%) of Wellington's guns were deployed on the western half of the battlefield.
- By the time the Imperial Guard attacked a further five batteries had been pushed into the front line (see Map 16).

ANGLO-ALLIED DEPLOYMENT (Maps 8, 11 & 12, pp. 119, 157 & 158)

There are several aspects of Wellington's deployment that are worthy of mention, most of which had their origins in the strategic and tactical planning of how the defensive battle would be fought.

• The mixing of national formations and their positioning on the field. Except for the 1st Netherlands Brigade (Bijlandt) the Anglo-Allied front line consisted entirely of British or German troops. In other words, the bulk of his most reliable infantry, under experienced generals, most of whom had fought under Wellington in the Peninsula and were thus fully conversant with his defensive tactics, would take the full force of any frontal assaults. This was pure Peninsula, where Wellington had mixed Portuguese brigades in British divisions and vice versa with remarkable success.

• If the 3rd Netherlands Division (in Braine l'Alleud) is included, the front extended for some 5000 metres from east to west. However, the battle took place on a much narrower frontage of 3000 metres: roughly from Hougoumont to Papelotte/La Haie. The bulk of Wellington's infantry sat astride the Brussels road. In the first two lines within the 3000-metre front were four infantry divisions (1st, 3rd, 5th British, 2nd Netherlands) and the 4th Hanoverian Brigade – in total almost 30,000 men. This gives ten men per metre of frontage – a high density by any reckoning.

• The front line is neatly demarcated by the Hougoumont (Braine l'Alleud) to Ohain road that follows the crest of the ridge

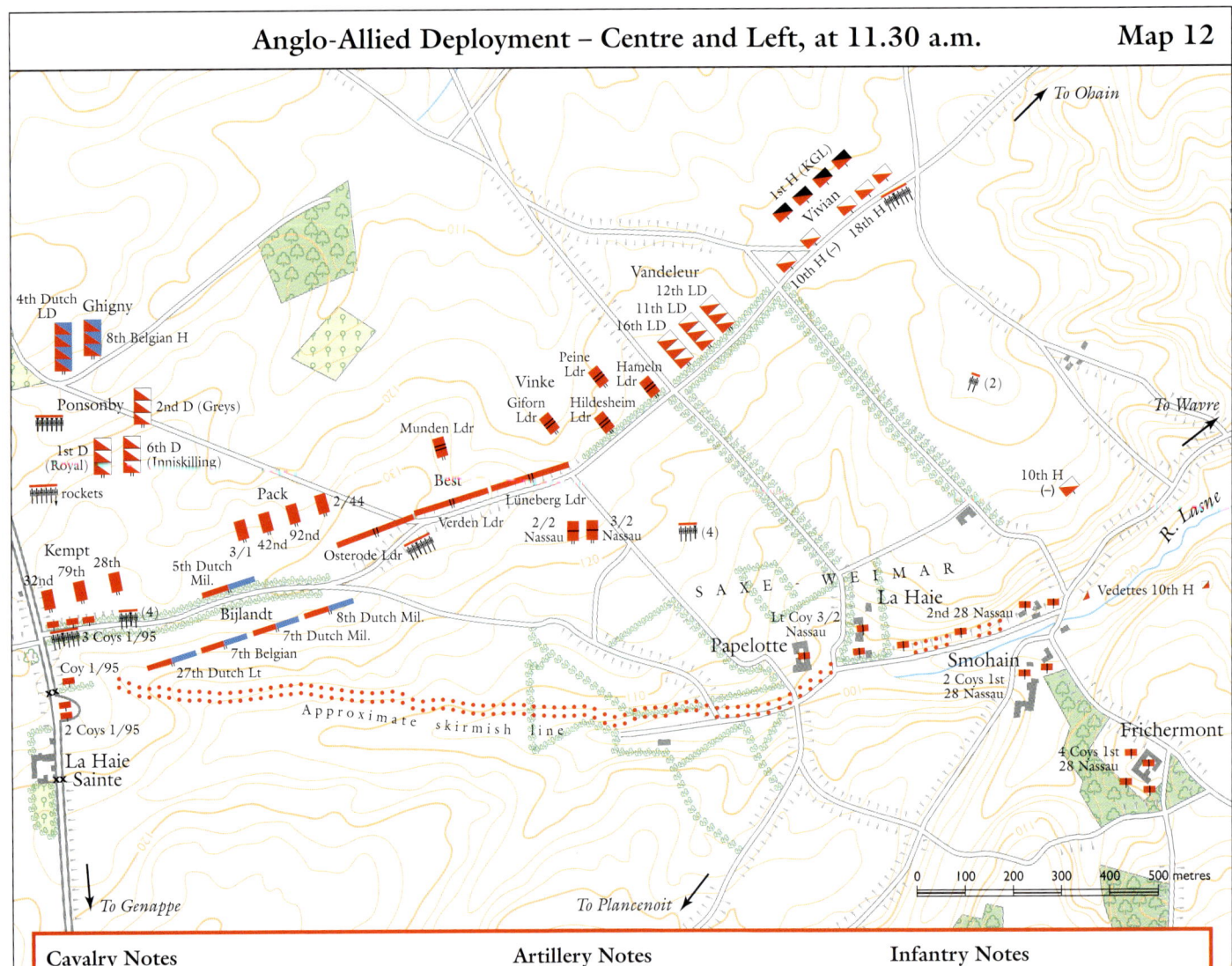

Anglo-Allied Deployment – Centre and Left, at 11.30 a.m.   Map 12

Cavalry Notes

• Vandeleur and Vivian with six regiments (21% of Wellington's cavalry) were the only cavalry to be deployed at the outset in the traditional role of flank protection. With the Prussians expected from this direction Wellington had few concerns about the left.

• The open ground and lack of other troops permitted Vivian to form up with his squadrons in line – his was the only brigade to do so.

• Captain Taylor's squadron of the 10th Hussars was on outpost duty and early in the morning met a Prussian officer with the news that Bülow was marching to the battlefield. He withdrew to the position shown after some of Jacquinot's squadrons probed towards Smohain before the battle started.

Artillery Notes

• Wellington only deployed four batteries in the front line on the eastern half of the battlefield. One other (Gardiner) was on the extreme left and took little part in the battle.

• These four batteries were scattered. The one near the crossroads (Rogers) had restricted fields of fire due to rising ground to its south. Only Whinyate's (rocket) battery was committed from the reserve.

• Despite d'Erlon's unsuitable divisional formation, the weight of gunfire was insufficient to stop them – two of the four attacking divisions reached the ridge, one got north of the Ohain road.

Infantry Notes

• Less than a third (only 25 battalions) of Wellington's infantry were deployed east of the Brussels road.

• Bijlandt's brigade was initially deployed on the forward slope, but either just before or just after the battle started was pulled back behind the hedges along the Ohain road.

• Note that two brigades (Bijlandt and Best) were deployed in line. It is unclear why, as it was not necessary at this stage.

• Note the scattered deployment (over 1,500m) of Saxe-Weimar's Nassau brigade.

A Grenadier Company Commander

At Waterloo the company commander of the Grenadier Company of the 2/73 (Highland) was Captain Alexander Robertson. He was entitled to this prestigious appointment as the senior captain present. He was quite possibly the most senior captain in the Duke's army as he was then, according to Sergeant Morris, sixty years old. Robertson had served with the Fencibles in Ireland and at Copenhagen (1801), Corunna (1809), Walcheren (1809), Barrosa (1811) and had been under fire recently at Quatre-Bras. Despite all this wealth of experience, Morris had a very low opinion of his company commander.

Morris had this to say about his officer's behaviour at Quatre-Bras:

> ... The Colonel ordered two companies out skirmishing; the light company and the company to which I belonged [Grenadier] ... . Our company was unfortunately

commanded by a Captain, sixty years of age; who had been upwards of thirty years in the service ... . He knew nothing of field movements, and when going through the ordinary evolutions of a parade the sergeant was obliged to tell him what to say and do. ... Presently we saw a Regiment of Cuirassiers making towards us, and he was at his wits' end. He became obstinate, too, and would not listen to the suggestions of the sergeants and subalterns, and there is no doubt we should all have been sacrificed, had we not been seen by the Adjutant [Ensign Hay]... .

Robertson was still jittery two days later at Waterloo. Morris again, 'Our poor old captain was horribly frightened, and several times came to me for a drop of something to keep his spirits up. Toward the close of the day he was cut in two by a cannon shot.' A sad end for an officer long past his prime.

---

behind which the great majority of the Anglo-Allied Army formed up. The crucial point being that at 11.30 that morning the French could see one brigade of infantry on the forward slope (Bijlandt), a skirmish line and perhaps a dozen gun batteries – nothing more. While Napoleon knew where his enemy was, some 90 per cent of them were hidden on the reverse slope of the Mont St Jean ridge. Not only were they out of sight but they were also protected from observed artillery fire. With the ridge, the corn and the smoke, any French attack would go in blind.

• Although the 3000 metres of front were strongly held throughout, the bulk of Wellington's force was posted west of the Brussels–Genappe road, a road that bisected both armies with geometrical precision. Always anxious about his right, Wellington had 17,000 men at Hal 12 kilometres to the west, the 7000 men of the 3rd Netherlands Division (Chassé) about 1000 metres west of his right flank in and around Braine l'Alleud and, including Chassé, 47,000 men (64 per cent of his army) behind this right flank. In the event neither the strategic thrust across his lines of communication via Hal, nor the tactical left hook round Hougoumont, materialized. Wellington felt much more secure about his left, which was where the Prussians were and therefore where he anticipated the two armies would eventually join.

• Wellington's deployment of his cavalry was unusual. Conventional military theory (and practice) dictated that cavalry should protect both flanks of an army. At Waterloo seven out of his nine cavalry brigades were deployed behind the centre and right of the position, with none on the west flank. Of these, five (Household, Union and the three Netherlands brigades of Collaert's Division) were massed in two lines directly behind the centre.

• Unlike the French, whose symmetry was almost perfect, the Anglo-Allied deployment looked, indeed was, untidy. The Prince of Orange, commanding I Corps, had units in Hougoumont and

Frichermont, 4000 metres apart round the curve of the position; a cavalry division (Collaert) around Mont St Jean Farm; and an infantry division (Chassé) in Braine l'Alleud. This unlucky young man had troops at every extremity of the position – a situation that rendered effective command highly problematic and was a nightmare for his chief of staff, Constant-Rebecque. In contrast, Lord Hill had only the 2nd British Division (Clinton) and the 4th British Brigade (Mitchell) of his II Corps on the battlefield, the rest being in the Hal-Tublize area. These formations were conveniently concentrated in a small area 600 metres by 600 metres behind the right flank. Some divisions were stretched as well. The 6th Division had its 4th Hanoverian Brigade (Best) in the front line, while the 6th British Brigade (Lambert) that had only just arrived on the battlefield was 1,300 metres to the rear, near Mont St Jean village. Saxe-Weimar's 2nd Netherlands Division was spread out over 2000 metres from Frichermont in the east to Bijlandt's brigade only 400 metres from the 'Elm Tree' crossroads – and he had a battalion detached in Hougoumont. Picton, commanding the 5th British Division, found a brigade (Bijlandt) from another division posted in the middle of his area. In terms of keeping formations together and facilitating command, Wellington's deployment was tangled and confusing.

• The Duke, with the exception of a battery with Vivian on the extreme left flank, stripped his cavalry brigades of their guns and pushed them forward with the rest in front of his infantry. Thirteen batteries (including Gardiner's on the extreme left) were deployed along the front line, just on the forward slope of the ridge so they could see to shoot. Of these, eight were along the front on the west of the Brussels–Genappe road – the right of the position. Forty-eight guns and howitzers posted over 1000 metres of front – almost a smaller version of the French 'Grand Battery'.

• One of the puzzles of Wellington's deployment is whether or not Bijlandt's Netherlands Brigade was the only infantry deliber-

The Quartermaster's Wife

Quartermaster Ross of the 3/14 (Buckinghamshire) had been accompanied by his wife to the battlefield and one can be fairly certain she helped her husband with doling out the gin ration that the battalion received the night before the battle. She was still with the battalion, as Ensign Keppel recounts: 'For some time after the firing began Mrs Ross, our Quartermaster's wife remained with the Regiment. She was no stranger to a battlefield, and had received a severe wound in Whitelock's disastrous retreat from Buenos Ayres (1807) at the time her husband was a sergeant in the 95th. She was at length persuaded to withdraw, and retired to the belfry of Waterloo church.'

ately exposed on the forward slope of the ridge to suffer needless loses from heavy artillery fire. If so, why? This controversy is discussed in detail in Section 10 'Myths and Controversies'.

FRENCH DEPLOYMENT (Maps 8, 13 and 14, pp. 119, 161 & 162)
If Durutte's word is accepted, some French units were still coming up into line after 11.30 that morning. Deployment had been a long and tiring process coming on top of a wretched, sleepless night. Aspects of their deployment of note are:

• On Map 8 the comparison between the muddled, unbalanced looking deployment of the Anglo-Allied army, and the almost perfect balance and geometrical symmetry of the French formations, is instantly apparent. The Brussels–Genappe road split the Armée du Nord exactly in half. Even the Imperial Guard was formed up equally on either side of the road. Give or take a thousand or so, Napoleon had 38,000 men to the east and west of his route to Brussels. His deployment was mostly in full view of Wellington, his staff, some forward infantry, skirmishers and his gunners. The display was deliberate. The Emperor sought to impress, intimidate even, with numbers, with mass. Strains of martial music and cheering could be heard across the 1,300 metres that separated the armies as Napoleon used the prolonged deployment to inspire his own troops and overawe his enemy. Unfortunately for him, only about 15 per cent of the Allies could see what was happening.

• The French deployed in a formation suited to their plan – a solid push up the axis of the Brussels road to take the Mont St Jean crossroads as phase one of a march on the capital. Ney's 'Left Wing' from Quatre-Bras formed the entire front line: an infantry corps 20,000 strong on either side of the road, spread out over 3000 metres in a shallow, concave curve facing north. With some thirteen men to every metre of front the density of French infantry slightly exceeded that of the Anglo-Allied. Light cavalry (châsseurs and lancers) guarded both flanks, heavy cavalry (mostly cuirassiers) were massed behind each leading infantry corps in equal numbers, and in two lines. Behind the centre was the Emperor's first reserve – Lobau's VI Corps with almost 11,000 men. Behind them nearly 20,000 Imperial Guardsmen. A sledgehammer was deployed to shatter the enemy line.

• On Map 8 the deployment shown differs slightly from many previously published maps. Firstly, the two leading frontline infantry corps (Reille and d'Erlon) are formed up just north of, and with their backs to, minor roads. They are often depicted astride or to the south of the roads. This was not the case, as they formed up on the highest ground, or on the forward slope, so that the troops could both see the enemy and be seen by him. Secondly, Jacquinot's cavalry division is usually shown as positioned 300 metres north of where it is shown on Map 8. No self-respecting light cavalry commander would place his horsemen inside a box of deep cuttings, sunken lanes and thick hedges. Some maps show Jacquinot's units charging straight across cuttings and up embankments – a physical impossibility. Certainly, patrols went forward to probe Papelotte or Frichermont, but the bulk of this division formed up well out of the 'bocage' country south and west of those farms. Finally, the Imperial Guard is shown formed up with the Young Guard in front and the Old Guard in the rear. Rarely, if ever, have maps shown the Guard other than with the Old Guard at the front, yet they always had the senior unit at the rear in reserve, or 'left in front' (junior formation leading) as it was called. At Waterloo the Young Guard were sent into Plancenoit,

---

The Imperial Guard Moves into Bivouac

Sergeant Hyppolyte de Mauduit recalled how at around 8.00 p.m. on 17 June the Imperial Guard left the road to the guns and wagons, and moved onto the fields and tracks west of Genappe. It was a night he never forgot:

> The tracks were so deep in mud after the rain that we found it impossible to maintain any sort of order in our columns. In looking for easier paths a large number of men went astray. … During all the marches and counter-marches of that frightful night there was a real helter-skelter. Regiments, battalions, even companies became muddled; and in complete darkness and drenching rain people were hunting vainly for their generals or their officers. … Our greatcoats and trousers were caked with several pounds of mud. A great many of the soldiers had lost their shoes and reached the bivouac barefoot.

A situation any modern soldier would recognize with some sympathy.

Père Lachaise Cemetery – Paris

As First Consul Napoleon gave orders for the Prefect of Paris to buy land outside the city walls for a 'modern and hygienic' cemetery. It was named after King Louis XIV's adviser and confessor, and received its first occupant, a five-year-old girl, in May 1804. It became the most fashionable cemetery in Paris, although today its sprawling memorials and monuments are mostly unattended and crumbling. This 'City of Sepulchres' resembles a huge outdoor museum whose mausoleums and tombs contain scores of famous Frenchmen. Visitors are frequent and, with the aid of a plan purchased at the entrance, it is easy to locate a particular tomb.

A walk along the Chemin Massena reveals the final resting places of numerous Waterloo veterans. Michel Ney is the most illustrious. His tomb is a simple slab with a cross, surrounded on three sides by a wall that bears his effigy. Sometimes fresh flowers are to be found there. The most ostentatious is the 9-metre high statue of Napoleon's divisional commander, Maximilien Foy, who survived the daylong assault on Hougoumont to die of a heart attack at fifty. Nearby sleep Honore Reille and Francois Haxo, the commander of the Imperial Guard Engineers. Other Waterloo veterans include Dominique Larrey, Napoleon's famous surgeon, and Charles de la Bédoyère, the Emperor's ADC who, like Ney, died facing a firing squad. Also buried in this cemetery are François Roguet, Joseph Christiani and François Lallemand of the Imperial Guard, François Kellerman, Marcellin de Marbot who commanded the 7th Hussars that scouted the advancing Prussians, and his brigade commander, Adrien Bruno. Henry Houssaye, the famous French historian of the battle and Victor Hugo's father, General Joseph Hugo, lie among the soldiers who fought there.

French Deployment, Centre and Left, at 11.30 a.m. Map 13

Hougoumont

La Belle Alliance

Piré (2nd Cav. Div.)

6th 1

5th L
Wathiez

1st Ch.à C

6th Ch.à C
Huber

Reille (II Corps)

Bachelu (5th Div.)
Campi
Husson

3/1
2/1
1/1
3/1
2/1

Prince Jérôme
(6th Div.)

Foy (9th Div.)

2/72
1/72
3/3
1/3

3/2
2/2
Soye
1/2
4/2
3/2
2/2
1/2

3/1
1/1
Leg.
Leg.
Leg.
Baudin

3/4
2/4
1/4
2/92
1/92

Leg.
3/100
2/100
1/100
3/93
2/93
1/93

Jamin (Baron)
Tissot

2/61
3/61
1/61

3/108
2/108
1/108

Bellair

2/5
2/11
2/27
2/84
2/5
2/10
2/107

1/5
1/11
3/11
1/27
1/84
1/5
1/10
1/107

Simmer
(19th Div.)

Trevenet

Leg.
Bony
Tromelin

Lobau
(VI Corps)

Jeanin (20th Div.)

Kellerman (W) (III Cav. Corps)

Roussel d'Hurbal (12th Cav. Div.)

3rd Cuir.

1st Car.

L'Heritier (11th Cav. Div.)

8th Cuir.

2nd D

2nd Cuir.
Donop

2nd Car.
Blancard

11th Cuir.
Guiton

7th D
Picquet

Young Guard
Duhesme & Barrois
Guye
2/3T
1/3T
2/1T
1/1T
Chartrand

2/3V
1/3V
2/1V
1/1V

Guyot (Guard Hy Cav. Div.)

Empress's D

Gen. d'Elite

Gren. à C

Hoffmayer

Jamin (Marquis)

Middle Guard
Morand &
Michel

Henrion 4 C
d'Harlet 4 G

2/3C
2/3G
2/2C
1/2C

Mallet
1/3 C
1/3 G
Morvan
2/1 C
1/1 G
Petit

Cambronne

Old Guard
Friant &
Roguet

Pelet
2/2 G
Christiani
2/2 C
1/2 G
1/2 C
1/2 G

Rossomme

Imperial Guard
still arriving

0 100 200 300 400 500 metres

Cavalry Notes

Line cavalry

• Formed up in line on forward slope to give maximum visual effect. Each squadron was in two ranks, each division and brigade in two lines.

• Squadrons had 130–140 men each with a frontage of about 60m. As Napoleon stated Kellerman's corps was spread out between the Genappe and Nivelles roads with the guns on either flank. The total frontage covered was considerable.

• There was a good mixture of cavalry types in the corps – eleven squadrons of cuirassiers, six of carabiners and eight of dragoons.

Imperial Guard

• All squadrons in Guyot's heavy cavalry were up to strength with almost 200 men each. They therefore covered a greater frontage, as shown.

• Unlike line cavalry divisions there was no brigade structure in this division.

• A weak squadron of the Gendarmes d'Elite was attached to this division, although it is uncertain where it formed up.

Infantry Notes

Line Infantry

• Reille's corps covered some 1,500m of front. It was deployed north of the road on the forward slope looking down into the Hougoumont valley. Jerome's division was within 300m of the Hougoumont Wood. Brigades side by side.

• Battalions of II Corps were formed on a two-company frontage in 'columns of attack' with the Voltigeur and Grenadier Companies at the rear. The former to be sent forward as skirmishers just prior to the advance. (See diagram p.194).

• Lobau's VI Corps was closed up very tightly as a reserve formation with battalions in 'column of divisions', a two-company frontage but with the Grenadier Company at the front on the right.

Imperial Guard

• At 11.30 a.m., according to General Petit, the Imperial Guard was still in the process of marching up from the Genappe area. The positions subsequently taken up are shown in outline.

• The 1/1 Châsseurs is not shown on the maps as this battalion was left at Le Caillou to guard the rear headquarters and treasury wagons. As both the 4th Grenadiers and 4th Châsseurs had only one battalion, there was a total of 21 battalions (not 24 as is often stated) on the battlefield.

• While waiting in reserve the battalions formed in column with the four companies one behind the other.

• As always the Guard formed up with junior formations and units at the front. The Grenadiers being at the rear as the last reserve.

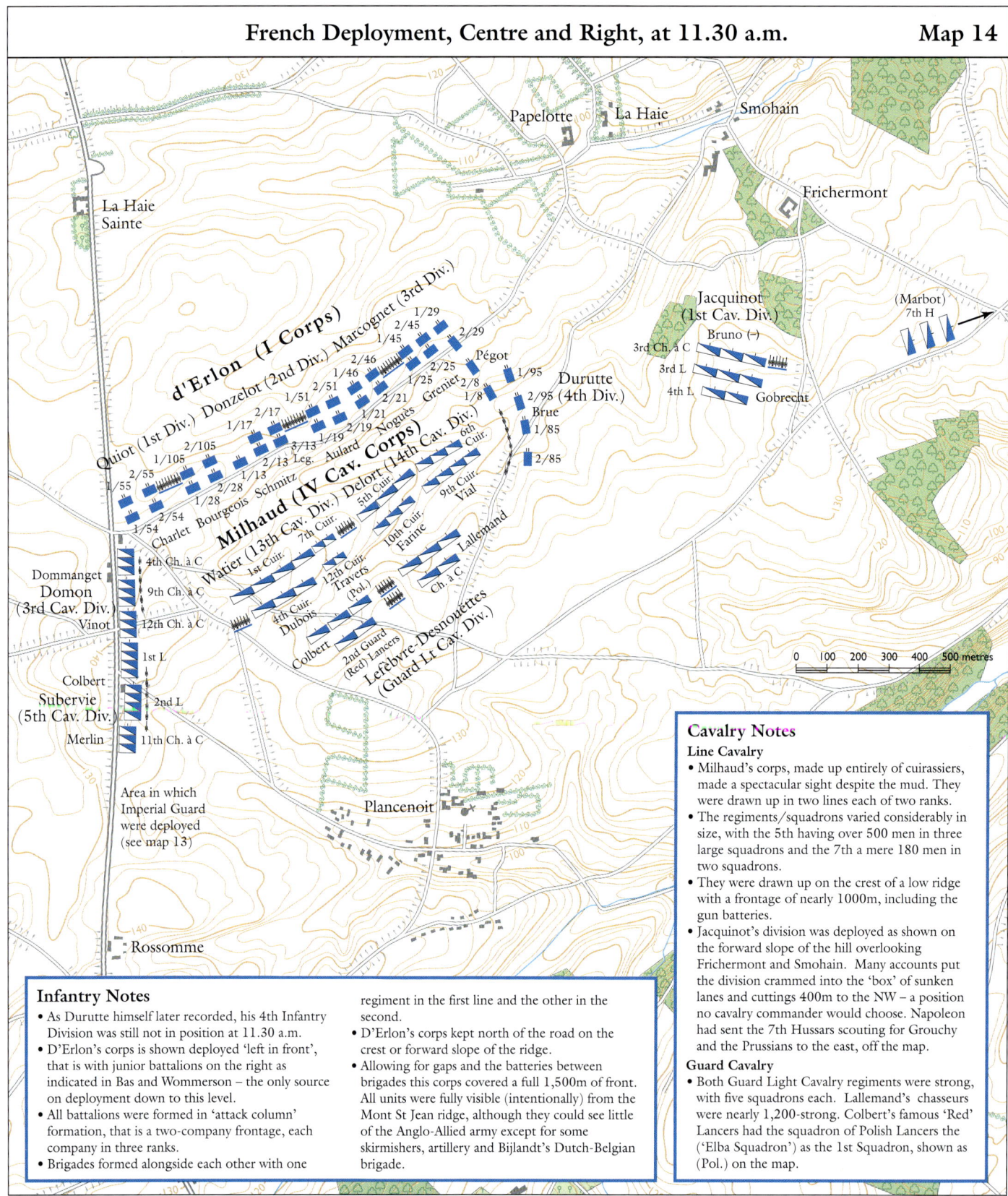

French Deployment, Centre and Right, at 11.30 a.m.   **Map 14**

Cavalry Notes

Line Cavalry
- Milhaud's corps, made up entirely of cuirassiers, made a spectacular sight despite the mud. They were drawn up in two lines each of two ranks.
- The regiments/squadrons varied considerably in size, with the 5th having over 500 men in three large squadrons and the 7th a mere 180 men in two squadrons.
- They were drawn up on the crest of a low ridge with a frontage of nearly 1000m, including the gun batteries.
- Jacquinot's division was deployed as shown on the forward slope of the hill overlooking Frichermont and Smohain. Many accounts put the division crammed into the 'box' of sunken lanes and cuttings 400m to the NW – a position no cavalry commander would choose. Napoleon had sent the 7th Hussars scouting for Grouchy and the Prussians to the east, off the map.

Guard Cavalry
- Both Guard Light Cavalry regiments were strong, with five squadrons each. Lallemand's chasseurs were nearly 1,200-strong. Colbert's famous 'Red' Lancers had the squadron of Polish Lancers the ('Elba Squadron') as the 1st Squadron, shown as (Pol.) on the map.

Infantry Notes
- As Durutte himself later recorded, his 4th Infantry Division was still not in position at 11.30 a.m.
- D'Erlon's corps is shown deployed 'left in front', that is with junior battalions on the right as indicated in Bas and Wommerson – the only source on deployment down to this level.
- All battalions were formed in 'attack column' formation, that is a two-company frontage, each company in three ranks.
- Brigades formed alongside each other with one regiment in the first line and the other in the second.
- D'Erlon's corps kept north of the road on the crest or forward slope of the ridge.
- Allowing for gaps and the batteries between brigades this corps covered a full 1,500m of front. All units were fully visible (intentionally) from the Mont St Jean ridge, although they could see little of the Anglo-Allied army except for some skirmishers, artillery and Bijlandt's Dutch-Belgian brigade.

the remaining Guard units then moved up and the Middle Guard undertook the final assault, while the Old Guard remained in reserve and helped out in Plancenoit. Their tasks all followed logically from their initial formation. Had they been in the reverse order considerable confusion would have resulted when battalions at the rear were required at the front.

- Map 8 shows the deployment at about 11.30 that morning, just moments before the first guns fired at Hougoumont preparatory to Prince Jérôme advancing on the wood (not on the modern map) south of the château and farm. At this time the French artillery batteries were mostly still with their divisions. The process of forming the 'Grand Battery' had not yet started.

SECTION FIVE

The Infantry

But yet, though thick the shafts as snow,
Though charging knights like whirlwinds go,
Though bill-men ply the ghastly blow,
Unbroken was the ring;
The stubborn spearmen still made good
Their dark impenetrable wood,
Each stepping where his comrade stood,
The instant that he fell.
No thought was there of dastard flight;
Linked in the serried phalanx tight,
Groom fought like noble, squire like knight,
As fearlessly and well.

Sir Walter Scott

General

The infantry were by far the most numerous arm and fought the longest and hardest at Waterloo. They therefore suffered the great bulk of the losses (91 per cent of all killed, wounded and missing). In all major battles both before and after Waterloo it has been the same. Only infantry can take or hold ground for any length of time. Without infantry little can be achieved on the ground (a modern example was NATO's failure to prevent ethnic cleansing in Kosovo because governments were too frightened to send in infantry and other ground troops). In general terms the task of the infantry was, and still is, to close with the enemy and destroy him. At Waterloo the Anglo-Allied infantry's primary role was to defend, while that of the French and Prussians was to attack.

The overall structure of the infantry in 1815 was the same whatever the nationality – the foot soldier carried a musket (a few had rifles), bayonet and sometimes a sword. He was grouped into companies, battalions, regiments, brigades and divisions. The drill manuals of each army told the infantryman how to form line, column or square, and how to change from one to the other. The differences were in the detail. The battlefield effectiveness of a battalion of infantry was judged as much on the speed and efficiency with which it could effect formation changes in difficult terrain and under fire, as on its musketry.

Each army had two or three basic types of infantry – guard, line or light. Of the first, Wellington had the 1st British (Guards) Division, Napoleon an entire corps of the Imperial Guard while

Blücher was devoid of such élite troops. Line infantry (French 'Ligne', Hanoverian 'Field', Prussian 'Musketeer') battalions constituted the overwhelming majority of the infantry on the Waterloo battlefield. Most line battalions, except for the Prussians, had one company of troops designated as the 'grenadier' company and another as the 'light' company. Light (French 'Légère', Prussian 'Fusilier') battalions or Rifle (Jaeger) units or companies were primarily for skirmishing or, with the latter, sharp-shooting roles although they could, and did, undertake normal infantry tasks. In practice there was often little difference, particularly within the French Army, between 'line' and 'light' units – they were usually both armed with the musket, had the same organization and could only be distinguished from each other by persons well versed in the details of dress.

By the time the Prussians had all arrived at 7.30 p.m. there were 249 infantry battalions, or their equivalent, committed to the battle. Of these, twenty-six (almost 10 per cent) were élite guard units, of which the French had twenty-two. Forty-one (17 per cent) were light infantry battalions and 182 (73 per cent) line battalions. Only in the Anglo-Allied and Prussian Armies were the infantry also split between regular and reserve (militia or landwehr) battalions. The former had sixty-two regular and twenty-two militia battalions, meaning one in three was a reserve unit. With the Prussians slightly over half were from the reserve – thirty-two out of the sixty-two battalions engaged.

ANGLO-ALLIED INFANTRY

General

Because of misgivings as to the quality of much of his infantry (on which the outcome of any forthcoming battle ultimately depended), the Duke had gone to great lengths to mix the mediocre with the good, and to deploy suspect formations away from likely hot spots (see Map 15, p. 164). Only 30 per cent of his foot soldiers were British and many of these were inexperienced

men not long out of the depots. Even the battalions with Peninsula service had been fleshed out with ex-militiamen to replace droves of discharged, time expired soldiers. Of his 25.5 British battalions formed up that morning, nine had suffered severely at the failed attempt to take Bergen-op-Zoom from the French in March 1814. The 2/44 (Essex) had lost over 200 out of 350 engaged. Of these

Anglo-Allied Infantry Division Deployment 11.30 a.m. 18 June   Map 15

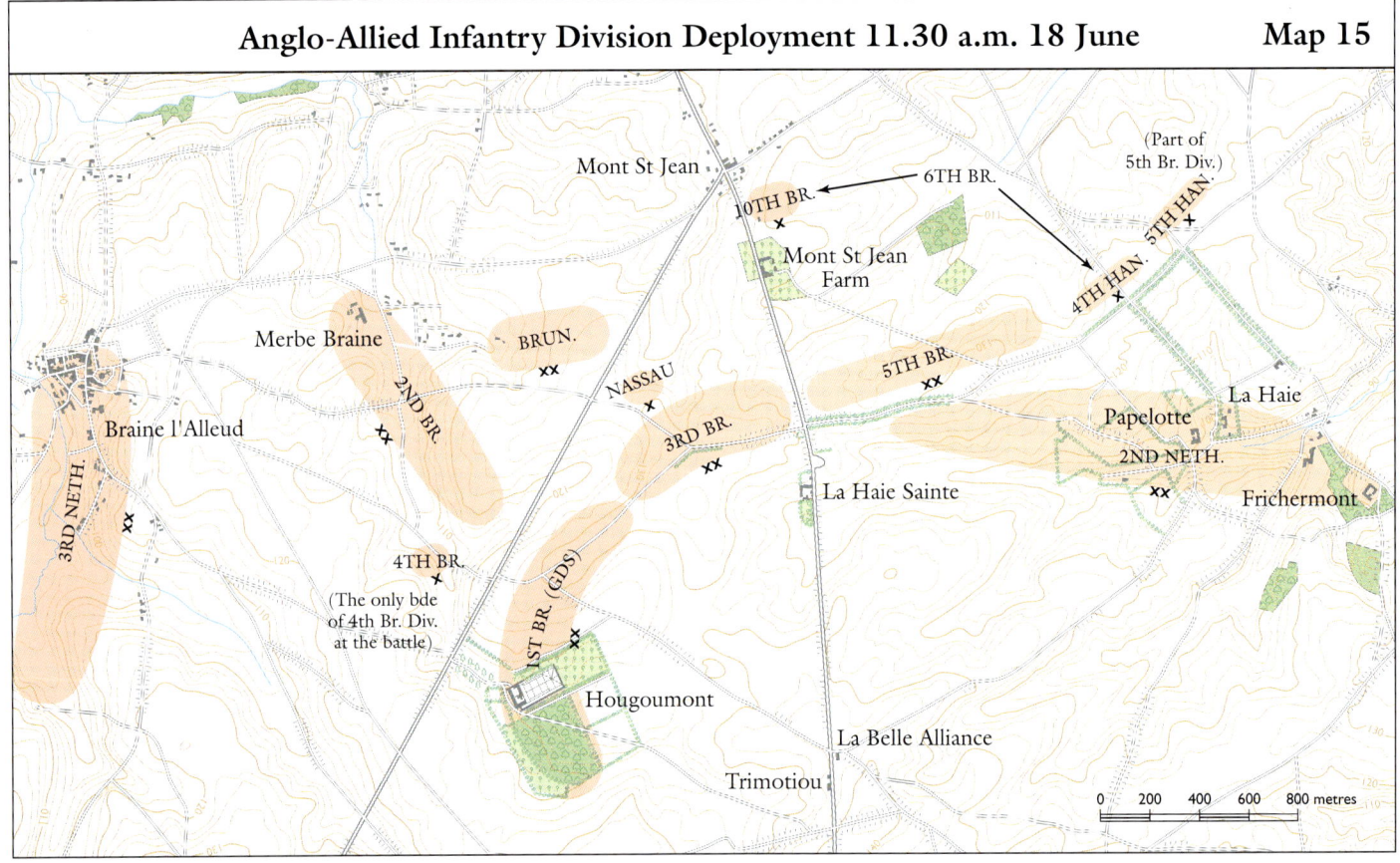

nine, all except one had fought at Quatre-Bras on 16 June, where Picton's 5th Division had lost over 1,500 men – the equivalent of two strong battalions. Here again the 2/44 were mauled, having to fight off cavalry while standing in line back to back, suffering 22 per cent casualties and almost losing a Colour. The 79th (Cameron Highlanders) fared even worse, with losses of 41 per cent at Quatre-Bras, reducing the battalion from over 750 to under 450 at Waterloo. In fact 450 was the average strength of the eight British battalions in the 5th Division, sharply down on the overall battalion average for the army of 640.

The other infantry Wellington had confidence in were the German battalions of the KGL and, to a slightly lesser extent, those from Nassau and Hanover. Interspersed with British units, it was these men that manned the ridgeline south of Mont St Jean. Some 20 per cent of his infantry, however, were in Dutch and Belgian battalions. With the exception of Bijlandt's Brigade (see Section 10 'Myths and Controversies'), which had initially performed with reasonable proficiency at Quatre-Bras, Netherlands infantry formations were placed well out of sight around Braine l'Alleud.

ORGANIZATION

Infantry divisions (Map 8, p. 119)
Wellington had eight infantry divisions plus two semi-independent brigades (the 4th British, from the 4th British Division at Hal, and the Nassau Reserve Contingent). The average divisional combat infantry strength (excluding the semi-independent brigades) was 6,132. The weakest was the 1st (Guards) Division with a mere 3,826 officers and guardsmen. The strongest, over twice the size, was Alten's 3rd British Division with 7,676. The divisions, with their approximate infantry strength (i.e. discounting staff, gunners, and administrative personnel), were:

1st British (Guards) Division – 3,826,
GOC Major-General George Cooke
2nd British Division – 7,550,
GOC Lieutenant-General Sir Henry Clinton
3rd British Division – 7,676,
GOC Lieutenant-General Charles, Count Alten
5th British Division – 6,224,
GOC Lieutenant-General Sir Thomas Picton
6th British Division – 4,958,
Acting GOC Major-General Sir John Lambert
2nd Netherlands Division – 7,143,
GOC Lieutenant-General Baron Perponcher-Sedlnitzky
3rd Netherlands Division – 6,669,
GOC Lieutenant-General Baron David-Hendrik Chassé
The Brunswick Division – 4,953,
Acting GOC Colonel Olfermann

By the end of the day every infantry formation had been engaged, including the 4th British Brigade and the Nassau Reserve Contingent. All available infantrymen had been thrown into the meat-grinder to keep the French from breaking through in the centre. One divisional commander was killed (Picton) and one wounded (Cooke). As far as losses were concerned, the 3rd Division with 3,735 casualties suffered the most. This was due to its position at the very heart of the struggle to the west of the 'Elm Tree' crossroads. There it was embroiled in the protracted defence of La Haie Sainte, took much of the shock of the endless cavalry assaults of the afternoon and, finally, faced part of the Imperial Guard's attack in the evening. The least damaged division at the end of the day was the Brunswick Contingent, which lost only 628 all ranks. Wellington's infantry losses amounted to some 15,426 all ranks, out of a total of about 53,850 (over 28 per cent). By divisions they were:

1st British (Guards)	1,641
2nd British	1,539
3rd British	3,735
5th British	2,943
6th British	1,322
2nd Netherlands	2,098
3rd Netherlands	695
Brunswick Division	628
4th British Brigade and Nassau Reserve	825

Infantry Brigades

Each division was composed of two or three infantry brigades. Wellington commanded nineteen such brigades within the divisional structure, plus two semi-independent brigades – Lieutenant-Colonel Mitchell's 4th British Brigade sent from its parent division at Hal, and Major-General von Kruse's Nassau Reserve Contingent. The twenty-one infantry brigades had an average strength of 2,564. The 4th British Brigade lost the least with 182, the 1st Hanoverian Brigade the most with 1,532.

Battalions

The basic strength of any army was normally calculated by counting the number of infantry battalions in it. The battalion was the primary tactical unit of all infantry formations. Wellington had 84 at Waterloo (4 Guard, 17 Light and 63 Line) with an average strength of 640 all ranks. All battalions were commanded by lieutenant-colonels or majors and were composed of a small headquarters and up to ten companies, usually under a captain, but often with a lieutenant commanding. A British battalion had ten companies, a regular Hanoverian eight, a Netherlands, Nassau or KGL six, and a Hanoverian Militia or Brunswick four. This variation led to considerable differences in the size of companies. A captain in the 1/42 (Royal Highland) that lost nearly 300 men at Quatre-Bras was lucky to command 35 at Waterloo, whereas at the other extreme an officer of the same rank in the Hanoverian

Munden Landwehr Battalion would have about 170. Numbers permitting, companies were usually divided into two sub-divisions, each of two sections. The establishment of the company was normally three or four officers, a similar number of sergeants and corporals, a drummer or bugler and the remainder private soldiers.

All Anglo-Allied battalions, except those from Brunswick or Hanover, had a 'Grenadier' and a 'Light' Company, with the remainder being termed 'Battalion' or 'Centre' Companies. The Grenadier Company was the senior company, supposedly the élite sub-unit with the tallest and strongest soldiers. The company commander was often the senior captain. It formed on the extreme right flank of the battalion line on parade or in battle. It originated in the eighteenth century when the best soldiers were picked to throw grenades – weapons that had long gone out of use by Waterloo. The Light Company always formed on the left, and was the skirmishing company. Composed of the best shots, often smaller, more agile soldiers, it spent much of its time on the battlefield 100–200 metres out in front of the main position opposing enemy skirmishers, or advancing ahead of the battalion. In most line battalions this company was armed like the others with a musket and bayonet – the main exception being the light companies of the KGL line battalions, which had rifles. These light companies and the Grenadier Company did, however, have minor distinguishing features of uniform such as badges, epaulettes or different coloured plumes on their shakos. The remaining companies formed the main line of battle and were numbered from one (on the right) up to eight (as in the case of the British).

WEAPONS

Muskets

A soldier aiming and firing his musket at an enemy over 100 metres away in a battle situation was going to knock him down about once in every thirty shots. If his target was 50–70 metres away then the chances of a hit dramatically increased to one in three. At less than 50 metres, and if firing his shot as part of a volley from his company or battalion, then the results were likely to be devastating. Controlled volleys of musketry fired at close range had great killing power. So also was prolonged, more careful, less flustered firing by

---

Private Clay, 2/3 Guards Bivouacs for the Night 17/18 June

… we marched on until we reached the summit of a hill in a clover field. We halted and there took off our knapsacks. The storm was still continuing with dreadful violence and, thinking that we would be remaining there for the night, we were ordered to pitch our blankets. They had been prepared for such a purpose and had six button holes with loops of small cords … The Company had previously been told off in fours and cast lots to see which two of each four should unpack their knapsacks and pitch their blankets. I was one of the unlucky two and we fixed our muskets perpendicular at each end of the blankets and then slipping the loop of the cord round the muzzle of both muskets … All four of us crept under the cover, taking the remainder of our equipment with us. The storm still continued with equal force and our covering became very quickly soaked …

By this time the shots of the enemy's artillery began to fall among us [from French horse artillery guns that had been

with the advance guard during the pursuit from Quatre-Bras]… our guns … opened up on the enemy. We were immediately called on to assemble, and those whose knapsacks were already packed instantly fell into the ranks and hastened down to a large orchard which belonged to the chateau of Hougoumont. We the wet blanket men were left to strike, pack up and follow them which we found no easy matter. The blankets were exceedingly wet and the buff straps of the knapsacks very slippery and very difficult to pack …

Clay went on to fall up to his neck in a ditch along the sunken lane behind the Great Orchard. How familiar his experiences will sound to the modern infantryman. Two hundred years later nothing much has changed for the foot soldier struggling to keep dry on a filthy night. Just as soon as he had settled down he had to move – an order that always seems to come 'at midnight in the pouring rain', today, just as it did in 1815, and for as far back in history as soldiers care to remember.

Musket Loading Procedure (see diagram opposite)

All the muskets, carbines, rifles and pistols used at Waterloo were muzzle-loading weapons. They fired a spherical lead ball of varying sizes according to the calibre of the piece. The British ball weighed about an ounce and could inflict fearful wounds at close range when the ball flattened slightly on impact, smashing bones, ripping huge holes in muscles, causing massive bleeding and shock.

Cartridges, already made up with powder and ball wrapped in greased paper, were carried in a flapped leather pouch with a slotted wooden interior, each slot containing a cartridge. To load, the soldier held his musket forward horizontally in his left hand (left-handed soldiers had to learn to load, fire and fight right-handed), took a cartridge from his pouch with his right and bit the bullet end off the cartridge, retaining the bullet in his mouth. This was an unpleasant procedure (that forty-odd years later was to trigger the Indian Mutiny) resulting in blackened lips, gritty teeth and the taste of gunpowder and grease. He then pulled back the cock (hammer) one notch to the half-cock position. If the trigger was pulled at this stage nothing would

(supposedly) happen – although the expression 'going off at half-cock' should be remembered. The frizzen was pushed in the direction of the muzzle, opening the priming pan. A small amount of powder was poured from the opened cartridge into the pan, and the frizzen moved into the vertical position, thus sealing the powder. The musket butt was then grounded and the remaining powder poured down the barrel and the ball dropped (or spat) down it. The ramrod was taken from its slots under the barrel, reversed, and with the bulbous end the soldier rammed the empty cartridge paper down the barrel – an awkward manoeuvre with a fixed bayonet. This compacted the wad, ball and powder firmly at the bottom of the barrel; the ramrod was then replaced. The musket was returned to the horizontal, the cock pulled back another notch to 'full-cock', which made the trigger operational. The musket was raised and fired. The cock flew forward, the flint struck the serrated frizzen, the sparks lit the powder in the pan and the flash travelled down the vent and exploded the powder under the ball.

---

numerous skirmishers from about the 75–100 metre range. At Waterloo the leading regiments of d'Erlon's divisions that attacked Picton's battalions attested to the former, and the British 1/27 in particular, to the latter situation. Colonel Hanger writing in 1814 stated: '…[the musket ball] will strike a figure of a man at 80 yards [70 metres] – but a soldier must be very unfortunate indeed who shall be wounded by a common musket at 150 yards [125 metres] provided his antagonist aims at him; and as to firing at a man at 200 … you may as well fire at the moon.' And the colonel was writing about targets on the range, not moving men with the firer partially blinded by smoke and fumbling his drills under the pressure and panic of the battlefield.

At Waterloo, like any Napoleonic battle, seven out of every ten casualties occurred when the opposing sides fought at close range (at under 100 metres) or virtually hand-to-hand. Artillery was the only long-range weapon, and even that was infinitely more lethal at comparatively short ranges. Over 145,000 infantrymen participated in the battle during the nine hours of fighting on that Sunday. All but around 8000 were armed with muskets. Some fired off all their ammunition, some fired hardly at all, but on average it is likely that around twenty-five shots came from each musket. This means, in round figures, some 3.5 million musket shots were fired. Total casualties on the battlefield, especially for the French, are problematic but are unlikely to be much less than 54,000 (see p. 73). Of these losses, around 60 per cent can be assumed caused by cannon fire, carbines, rifles, pistols, swords, lances or bayonets, rather than by musket balls. So, overall, it is estimated that 162 musket shots were needed to inflict an injury.

Flints

All firearms at Waterloo were flintlocks. Without a good flint the musket was as useless as without a cartridge, and could only be used as a club or pike. Consequently, the procurement and care of flints was of vital importance. A high quality flint would continue to produce a good spark for thirty to fifty shots (more than many men would fire in a battle). However, they were easily dropped or lost so each soldier had to carry several spares. During exercises or dry-run drills the French often replaced their flints in the cock with a piece of wood called the *pierre de bois* (wooden stone) in order to save on flints and absorb the shock on the lock mechanism.

The world's best flints came from a tiny village in central France called Meusnes. Prior to the Revolution they had been widely exported. Flint-knapping was a skilled trade and the French artillery kept 168 such tradesmen fully employed.

The muskets of all armies at Waterloo were basically the same – smooth bore, black powder, flintlock weapons with much the same effective range, accuracy and defects. The differences were comparatively insignificant: weight, length of barrel, size of bore. It was only the size of the bore that prevented a Prussian from picking up a French or British musket and using it. His Potsdam musket barrel had a calibre of 19.5mm, the Frenchman's Charleville 17.2mm, while the British Indian Pattern 'Brown Bess' had an 18.7mm calibre. On the other hand a French ball would rattle down the barrel of any musket on the battlefield; the 'windage' might be excessive, but it would fire.

While there was little practical difference in performance on the battlefield, the French musket was technically superior to the 'Brown Bess' as far as maximum range was concerned. This was due to the slightly longer barrel (44.76 inches compared to 42 inches), the lighter ball firing with about the same amount of powder and having less windage. At least one British officer at Waterloo considered the French version of the musket superior to the British. He claimed that, 'their fine, long, light firelocks, with a small bore are more efficient for skirmishing than our abominably clumsy machine …'. He felt the British weapons were, '… of bad quality; soldiers might be seen creeping about to get hold of the firelocks of the killed and wounded, to try if the locks were better than theirs, and dashing the worst to the ground as if in a rage with it.'

There were two indispensable technical skills for infantry to master for success on a Napoleonic battlefield: foot drill and musketry. The former is discussed below, under the heading 'Tactics'. Even effective musketry relied on following set drills, specific actions having to be performed in the correct sequence. The British manual prescribed eleven drill movements to fire a shot. Other things being equal, in a firefight the faster you fired the more likely you were to see off your

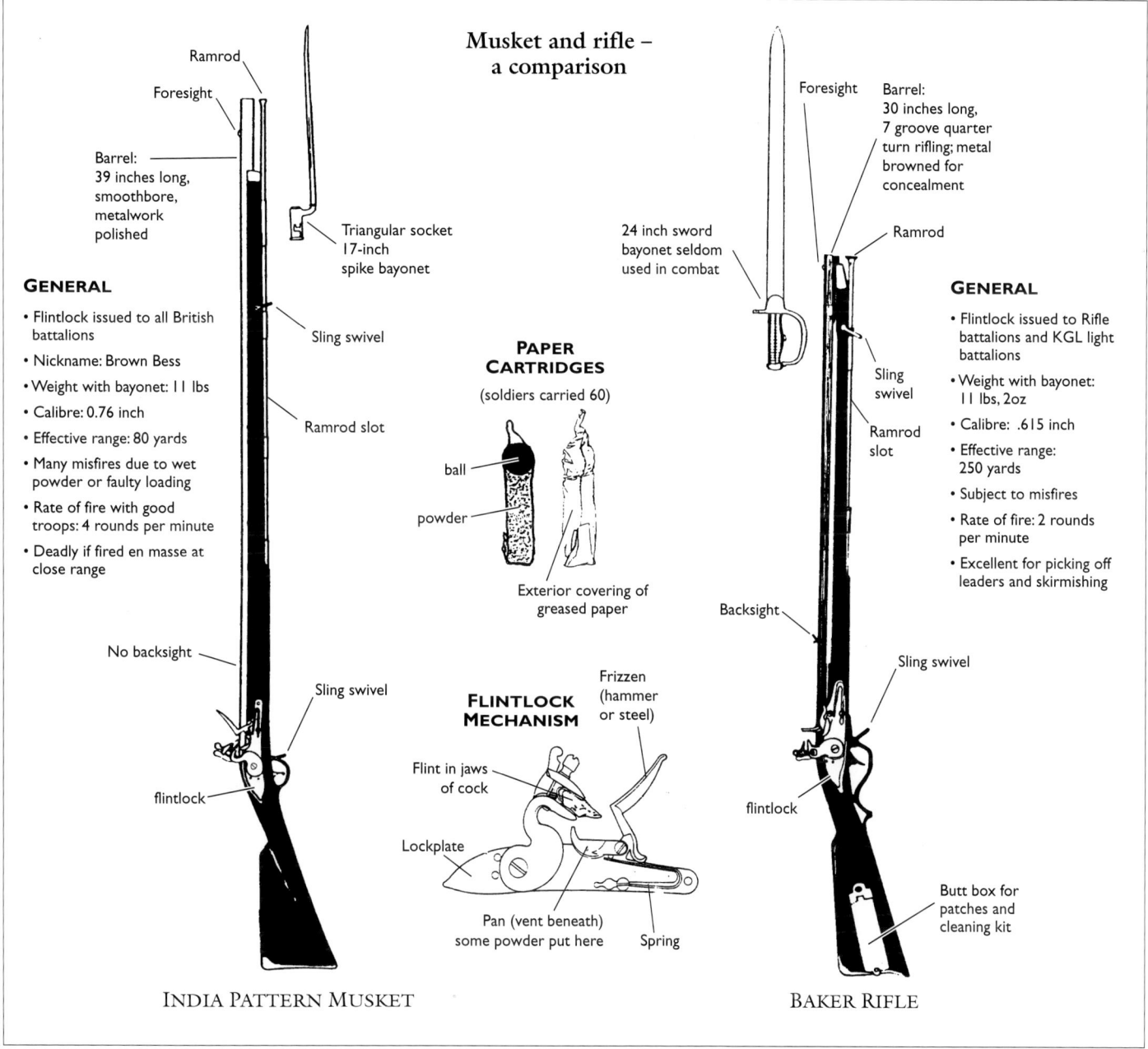

Musket and rifle – a comparison

Ramrod

Foresight

Barrel:
39 inches long,
smoothbore,
metalwork
polished

Triangular socket
17-inch
spike bayonet

GENERAL

- Flintlock issued to all British battalions
- Nickname: Brown Bess
- Weight with bayonet: 11 lbs
- Calibre: 0.76 inch
- Effective range: 80 yards
- Many misfires due to wet powder or faulty loading
- Rate of fire with good troops: 4 rounds per minute
- Deadly if fired en masse at close range

Sling swivel

Ramrod slot

No backsight

Sling swivel

flintlock

INDIA PATTERN MUSKET

PAPER CARTRIDGES

(soldiers carried 60)

ball

powder

Exterior covering of greased paper

FLINTLOCK MECHANISM

Frizzen (hammer or steel)

Flint in jaws of cock

Lockplate

Pan (vent beneath) some powder put here

Spring

Foresight

Barrel:
30 inches long,
7 groove quarter
turn rifling; metal
browned for
concealment

Ramrod

24 inch sword
bayonet seldom
used in combat

Sling swivel

Ramrod slot

GENERAL

- Flintlock issued to Rifle battalions and KGL light battalions
- Weight with bayonet: 11 lbs, 2oz
- Calibre: .615 inch
- Effective range: 250 yards
- Subject to misfires
- Rate of fire: 2 rounds per minute
- Excellent for picking off leaders and skirmishing

Backsight

Sling swivel

flintlock

Butt box for patches and cleaning kit

BAKER RIFLE

---

enemy. Anything less than two or three shots a minute was considered poor. It was possible to speed things up but this involved shortcuts with the drill (such as banging the butt on the ground to get the ball to the bottom of the barrel instead of using the ramrod) but these were risky and usually produced even more inaccurate shooting.

The great majority of British line infantry at Waterloo, and this included the KGL line battalions, were armed with the India Pattern musket whose characteristics are compared with those of the Baker rifle in the diagram above. Nicknamed the 'Brown Bess' this weapon (with minor modifications) had been around for some eighty years. It was named the 'India Pattern' because it was purchased in large quantities from the East India Company at the outbreak of the Napoleonic Wars in an unsuccessful attempt to make up the shortfall in British armouries. It was cheap but sturdy. Improvements were incorporated in a New Land (to distinguish it from the different type used at sea) Pattern musket, but few had been issued before Waterloo. Between 1793 and 1815 it is estimated that about 3 million India Pattern weapons had been produced.

Rifles

Just under 4000 of Wellington's infantry were armed with rifles. The units concerned were:

1/95 Rifles
2/95 Rifles
Two companies 3/95 Rifles
1st Light Battalion KGL
2nd Light Battalion KGL
Three light companies of KGL line battalions
Brunswick Advance Guard Battalion
Two Jaeger companies of Orange-Nassau Regiment
Two Field Jaeger companies of 1st Hanoverian Brigade
One light company Hanoverian Lüneburg battalion
One light company Hanoverian Grubenhagen battalion.

The 95th Rifles and the KGL units were all armed with the Baker rifle, the others with a type of hunting rifle, sometimes a non-standard weapon.

The Baker rifle could deliver both slow, deliberate aimed shots with accuracy up to 200 metres and beyond, or faster musket-type firing using smaller carbine balls. Because the rifle had a grooved (rifled) barrel to twist the ball and give it greater stability, loading was a far slower process than with the musket. The procedure for loading was similar to that of the musket except that instead of using cartridges the rifleman had a powder flask and a pouch of lead balls. Having placed a measured powder charge in the barrel the rifleman took a circular patch of greased cloth from the box in the butt of the rifle, placed it over the muzzle, pressed a ball down into it and drove the ball to the breech with the ramrod. A trained rifleman could expect to fire about half as many shots in a given time as a soldier with a musket. Its inventor, Mr Ezekiel Baker, had added other refinements to facilitate good shooting. These included a shorter barrel that enabled loading in the prone position, a much superior sight, and a scroll type trigger guard giving a better grip for aiming. It proved an excellent weapon for sharpshooters and skirmishers intent on picking off officers or gun crews while out of effective musket range. It was to remain the British Army's rifle for forty years.

At Waterloo, however, the bulk of Wellington's rifle-armed troops were used primarily as line infantry, examples being Major Baring's defence of La Haie Sainte with the 2nd Light Battalion, KGL, and the 1/95 Rifles' defence of the sandpit and sunken road behind. Skirmishing was largely left to the light companies from the line battalions – armed with muskets.

Bayonets

The bayonet was (and still is) largely a psychological rather than a physical weapon. Very rarely did soldiers fence each other with bayonets. Napoleon's Surgeon-General, Larrey, did a study of wounds inflicted in the battles of 1807 and concluded that bayonets inflicted about two per cent of injuries. At Waterloo the incidence of bayonet wounds was probably even less (at two per cent there would have been around 1,100 bayonet casualties), as infantry seldom fought infantry hand to hand. Where fighting was sometimes very close and personal, it was usually the musket that decided the issue, even in Hougoumont, La Haie Sainte and Plancenoit, or during the repulse of the Imperial Guard. For a short while, when ammunition ran out, the defenders of La Haie Sainte did some effective work with the bayonet. Charging infantry or cavalry did not hurl themselves onto a hedge of bayonets. The normal outcome was that one side turned to run after being mauled by cannon and musket fire before the advancing bayonets could draw blood.

At Waterloo the Anglo-Allied infantry had bayonets of between 15–17 inches long with a triangular-sectioned blade attached to a cylindrical socket that fitted the end of the musket barrel. The musket could therefore be fired with the bayonet attached. This was common practice in all armies, perhaps more so with the Prussians who rarely carried their muskets without bayonets being fixed. However, this practice was the not infrequent cause of 'infantryman's hand' – the painful spiking of the right hand during over hasty use of the ramrod.

Rifle-armed troops did not normally carry bayonets. In the British rifle units, such as the 95th, every rifleman had a sword-bayonet (see diagram p. 167) that could literally be used as either, but seldom was.

Swords and sabres

A soldier seen indistinctly advancing on foot through the smoke with drawn sword was invariably an officer – and therefore a worthwhile target. The sword was both a weapon and status symbol. British battalion company officers carried straight bladed swords, light company (and rifle regiment officers) curved bladed, light cavalry type weapons (a sabre rather than a sword). A short-bladed version was also the side arm of all sergeants and bandsmen in a battalion. The number of men killed, or even wounded by an officer wielding a sword was negligible at Waterloo. The adjutant of the 1/95 during the battle, Lieutenant Kincaid, did not think kindly of his sword, describing it as, 'our small regulation half-moon sabre ... better calculated to shave a lady's-maid than a Frenchman's head'. He had drawn his weapon so rarely that at Waterloo it had become rusted into the scabbard.

A few soldiers in the British infantry units and among the German allies also carried swords. This was because the sword was convenient to carry on the belt as a secondary weapon when the soldier had other duties.

Pikes

Except in rifle regiments (where they carried rifles) or in the light companies of battalions (where they had shortened muskets), infantry sergeants were not normally issued with muskets. Instead they carried a 7-foot pike or spontoon with a cross-piece below the point to prevent over penetration. Useful on parade for dressing ranks (the forerunner of the modern sergeant-major's pace stick or sergeant's cane), they required two hands to use and they deprived the battalion of the fire of over thirty muskets. Four spontoon wielding sergeants protected the King's and Regimental Colours carried by two junior ensigns. They were also sometimes known as halberds. The expression 'going to the halberds' meant being flogged, as the unfortunate soldier was tied to a triangle of halberds to receive his punishment. Most sergeants seemed content with this weapon which, like the sword, was something that advertised his rank and status – and was so much easier to clean than a musket. The exception would be the sergeant of the 1/7 (not at Waterloo) who was running with his pike, tripped, caught the point in the ground and fell forward on the butt, which went right through his body.

TACTICS

General

Anglo-Allied infantry tactics at Waterloo were primarily defensive. They were concerned with defending against infantry, cavalry and artillery attacks or any combination of them. The battalion was the tactical unit. It was not until the end of the battle that the great majority of the Duke's infantry was required to advance. For hour after hour throughout the day many units scarcely moved other than to change formation. Battalions came forward from reserve positions but once in the front line on or behind the ridge, or garrisoning Hougoumont or La Haie Sainte, they stayed there. Many soldiers never moved more than 100 metres in any direction, their task always being to hold their ground.

Infantry tactics at Waterloo, and at all other battles before and since, were based on fire and movement. Fire kills; movement gets you into a position from which to deliver the fire. Both these elements required a complete understanding of, and practical competence in, various drills. Given reasonable morale, the soldier that could keep firing two or three shots a minute and change forma-tion quickly within his company, was likely to do well on the bat-tlefield. Most drills were done mechanically, automatically, without thought. Countless hours on the parade ground paid enormous dividends in action. When bodies were being ripped apart, when the confusion, the noise and the fear were unbearable, the fact that a soldier did not fumble his loading or fail to understand a shouted word of command was due, to a great extent, to the repetitive perseverance of his drill sergeant in calmer times. Well drilled and steady was what a general required of his infantry, par-ticularly in defence.

Although the British drill manuals of the day decreed that companies and battalions in line should fight in three ranks, in practice they invariably did so in just two. The KGL, Hanoverian, Belgian, Dutch and Nassau battalions were trained to follow suit, although at Waterloo lines were formed in four ranks on the infre-quent occasions when they were needed because of the limited space available. A two rank line covered considerably more ground than any other formation and enabled every musket to be brought to bear, while neither rank was in danger of suffering casualties from the flustered firing of a third rank.

Other things being equal, the success of tactical (as distinct from individual) musket firing depended on four simple principles, namely:

- Get as many weapons as possible trained on the target.
- Fire in one of several types of controlled volley.
- Not to fire at ranges in excess of 100 metres.
- Reload quickly to get at least one more shot at a closing enemy.

The infantryman in most armies was trained to advance at around 75 paces to the minute in formation. As he neared the enemy he either stopped to exchange fire, retreated, or quickened his pace and came on, trying to reach the opposition with the bayonet. The issue was virtually always decided in the final 100 metres. Provided the attacker did not halt (to fire) in this critical zone, and depending on the ground, the pace and the enthusiasm of the attackers, 100 metres would be covered in around a minute. If the defending infantry (at Waterloo Wellington's) fired first at that range, they would expect to be able to repeat the dose once, hopefully twice, before bayonets were crossed. When d'Erlon's divisions attacked, one volley followed by a counter-charge was often enough to throw them back. In terms of Waterloo, this meant that the French had little to fear from muskets for nine-tenths of their advance. Until the last 100 metres it was mostly artillery that killed.

There were three infantry tactical formations used by all armies at Waterloo: the line, the column and the square. Each had variations and combinations, each could be used by attacker or defender, and different nationalities used slightly different drills to change from one to the other. The tactical skill of the officers lay in anticipating and ordering the right formation for the develop-ing situation. The skill of the NCOs and soldiers lay in the speed and efficiency with which they complied. In simple terms, the line was usually needed to develop maximum firepower (for an attacker or defender); the column was required for moving a unit across the battlefield or when the best formation was still uncer-tain; and the square for defence against cavalry.

In the following paragraphs the 2/30 (Cambridgeshire) bat-talion, nicknamed 'The Three Tens', is used to demonstrate in general terms how any battalion in the Anglo-Allied Army would have formed up in these formations. There were differences in strengths, the number of companies in a battalion and the precise drills used, but the end result was the same – a line, a column, or a square. The 2/30 was a regular battalion that had seen service in the Peninsular War, and had been under fire at Bergen-op-Zoom fifteen months earlier. Because of the unexpectedness of the Waterloo campaign, the urgent need for infantry, and the 1/30 being in India, it was the 2nd battalion that had been fleshed out with new recruits and rushed to Belgium. At Quatre-Bras it had suffered only slightly, losing forty men. It went into action at Waterloo at exactly the average strength (640 all ranks) of Wellington's battalions (although losses and the detachment of its light company later forced it to amalgamate with the 2/73). The 2/30 had its full establishment of officers, although two majors were unusual and most battalions had more than three ensigns.

A battalion in line (Diagram p. 170)

This formation was normally used both to defend a position and in the assault to maximize the number of muskets that could be brought to bear on the enemy. With the 2/30 in two ranks, it meant about 550 muskets deployed (officers, sergeants, drummers and pioneers either could not or did not fire). A number of aspects of this, and indeed any Anglo-Allied battalion drawn up in line, are significant:

- The length of frontage covered – some 210 metres. The Duke would only have required fourteen of his eighty-four battalions to cover the entire 3000 metres of his front with a two-deep line of infantry.
- There was only one pace between the ranks so the line was extremely thin – only some 2 metres deep.
- In an average strength, ten-company battalion, each company was small, with less than sixty muskets. In two ranks, this meant the company frontage was barely 25 metres as each soldier formed up, elbows almost touching, in some 60 centimetres of space. British battalions in particular (as they had a ten company structure) that fell to 400 or less, became barely viable. This happened frequently at Waterloo. The 2/30 had dropped to about 400 by the end of the battle but well before that had been joined with another weak battalion, the 2/73, to form square.
- Three paces behind the second rank was the supernumerary rank, composed entirely of officers and sergeants. Their task was to ensure there was no skulking, holding back or retreating from the ranks in front of them. Another three paces to their rear were the field officers (the lieutenant-colonel and majors) and the adjutant, all mounted, plus the drummers. Behind them, the pioneer section. The Light and Grenadier Company drummers formed behind their own company, but their battalion company comrades were grouped behind Numbers 2 and 7 Companies.
- Company commanders were the only officers in the front line and always stood on the right of their command. In the centre were the King's and Regimental Colours carried by the two junior ensigns and escorted by four sergeants with pikes. The Colour Party divided the battalion into two wings which could, if the situation so demanded, operate as separate tactical entities, usually under the command of a major.
- On the right was the Grenadier Company, on the left the Light Company. Both were supposedly élite sub-units. The Light Company was frequently detached to form a skirmish line some

Typical British Battalion – 2/30 (Cambridgeshire) – Formed in Line

Note on strength
• Diagram shows full strength unit before casualties at Quatre-Bras, sick, etc. had been lost.
• The Battalion lost over 50 at Quatre-Bras, the light company was detached at Waterloo and because it was down to some 450 all ranks it was combined with the 73rd Foot during the battle.

Full parade state
Officers	41
Sergeants	38
Corporals	35
Drummers	14
Soldiers	512
Total	640 all ranks

The above includes non-combatant officers and NCOs plus Maj. Vigoureux and the Light Company who were detached at the start of the battle.

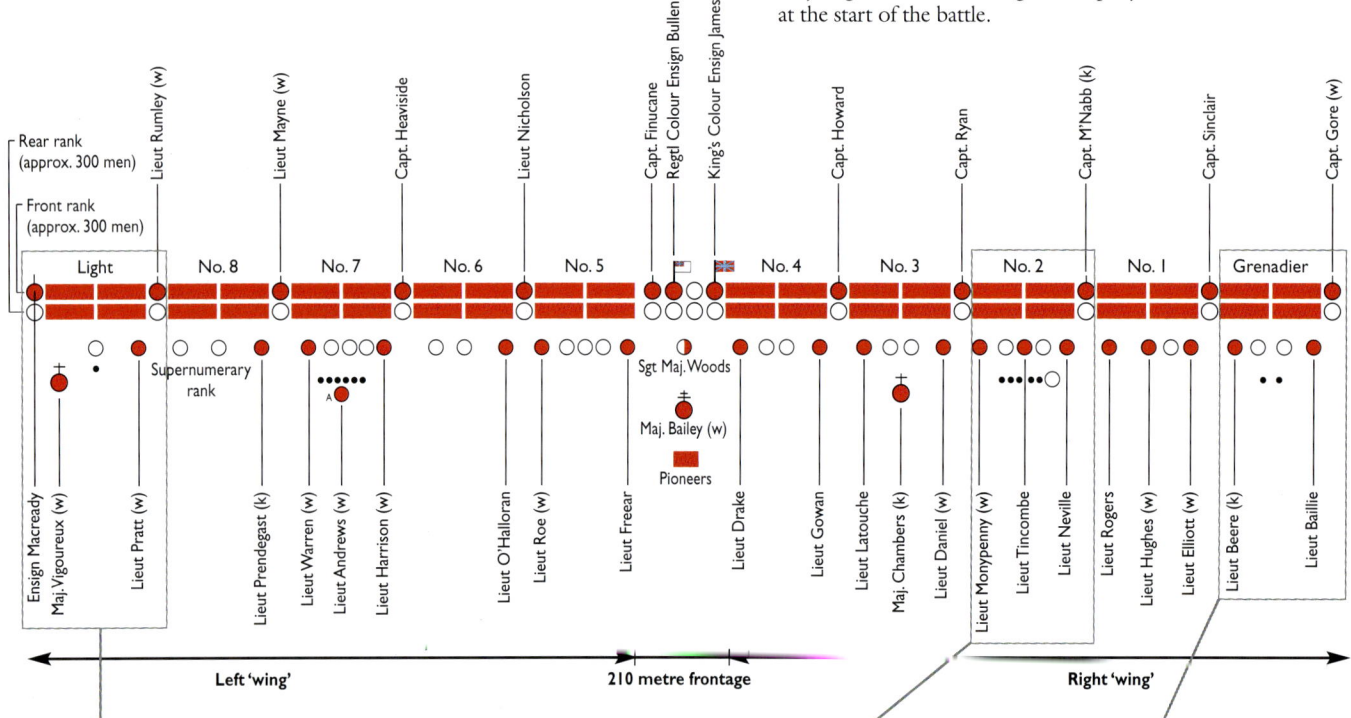

Light Company
• Left of the line, best shots, shorter men trained as skirmishers.
• Armed with muskets, not rifles.
• Fought at Waterloo as part of a skirmishing battalion formed with the light companies of the 33rd, 2/69 and 2/73 commanded by Maj. Vigoureux.

Battalion or Centre Company
• Formed 2 rank line in 2 sub-divisions each of 2 sections
• 4 officers, 3 sergeants, 3 corporals and 52 soldiers
• The Drummer Major (Sgt) and 4 of the drummers are not part of this company
• The company commander always on the right of the front rank
• Company frontage about 20 metres

Grenadier Company
• Elite right flank company with tallest, strongest men
• In 18th century they used to throw grenades
• The 2 drummers belonged to this company
• Two days before at Quatre-Bras this company had lost a popular officer, Lieut Lockwood, who was badly wounded in the head. He later had a silver plate put in his skull with the words 'bomb proof' engraved on it.

Notes
• Typical British 2nd battalion of which there were 8 at Waterloo. Overall strength only marginally above the 630 all ranks average for Wellington's battalions.
• 2/30 was a Peninsular battalion and had fought at Bergen-op-Zoom in March 1814. Suffered slightly at Quatre-Bras (50 casualties).
• 21 Sergeants are shown in the supernumerary rank, although it is possible some would have been on the flanks of companies.
• Maj. Vigoureux is shown with the Light Company, as he took it when detached to form an ad hoc skirmishing battalion with the other light companies in the brigade.

Non-combatant personnel
(On duty at the rear)
🔴 Paymaster Wray
🔴 Quartermaster Williamson
🔴 Surgeon Elkington
🔴 Asst. Surgeon Evans
🔴 Asst. Surgeon Clarke
⚪ Paymaster Sgt Cuthbert
⚪ Quartermaster Sgt Harrison
⚪ Armourer Sgt Artis

Key
🔴 Commanding Officer (M)
🔴 Field Officer (M)
🔴 Company Commander
🔴 A Adjutant (M)
🔴 Subaltern Officer
◐ Sergeant-Major
⚪ Sergeant
• Drummer
(k) Killed at Waterloo
(w) Wounded at Waterloo
(M) Mounted

A British Battalion's Establishment

Virtually no battalions, of any nationality, in the field at Waterloo were identical due to variations in initial strength and wastage through sickness or casualties. Differences were legion. Some battalions had ten companies, others eight, six or four. Some had a band, though most did not. Some had more officers than sergeants, some the other way round; some had two majors, others none, while one, the 1/27 (Inniskilling), was commanded by a captain (with an army rank of major) at the outset and a lieutenant at the end of the day. By then sergeants commanded eight of the remnants of the ten companies. However, at the start of Waterloo a battalion with just under 650 all ranks would be likely to have a battlefield establishment approximately as follows:

Battalion HQ

Combatant officers	Non-combatant officers
1 x Lieutenant-Colonel	1 x Paymaster
1 x Major	1 x Quartermaster
1 x Adjutant (usually a lieutenant)	1 x Surgeon
2 x Ensigns (Colour Party)	1 or 2 Assistant Surgeons

Combatant NCOs	Non-combatant NCOs
1 x Sergeant-Major	1 x Quartermaster-
1 x Drum-Major (Sergeant)	Sergeant
4 x Sergeants (Colour escorts	1 x Armourer Sergeant
detached from companies)	1 x Schoolmaster-Sergeant

Combatant soldiers	Non-combatant soldiers
10 x Bandsmen (possibly)	1 or 2 storemen/assistants
	(possibly)

10 x Companies each with

Combatant officers
1 x Captain
1 x Lieutenant
1 x Ensign

Combatant NCOs	Non-combatant NCOs
1 x Colour Sergeant	Nil
3 x Sergeants	
3 x Corporals	

Combatant soldiers
1 x Drummer
1 x Pioneer
50 x Privates

Such a battalion would have 35 combatant officers, 4 or 5 non-combatant officers, 49 senior NCOs and up to 560 junior NCOs and soldiers. Something over 640 all ranks – slightly above the average for an Anglo-Allied battalion at Waterloo.

200 metres in front of the battalion (see below). At Waterloo the 2/30 sent the Light Company to join with those of the 33rd, 2/69 and 2/73 to form an ad hoc skirmishing battalion under the command of Major Vigoureux (2/30). It was deployed in this role across the front of the brigade.
• A battalion could, and often did, advance in this formation, but it was a slow process and extremely difficult to maintain dressing over broken ground. If caught in line by cavalry, a battalion was certain to be badly cut up, if not destroyed. It had happened to the 2/69 at Quatre-Bras when they lost their King's Colour. At Waterloo the 5th Line Battalion of the KGL suffered the same fate at the hands of French cuirassiers after La Haie Sainte fell.

A battalion in column (Diagrams pp. 172–3)

This formation was primarily used for movement of the battalion across the battlefield, during deployment, or while waiting to move. It was a convenient formation to adopt if it was uncertain what was required of the battalion in the immediate future, as from the column it was comparatively easy and quick to adopt a formation more suitable for firing or fighting – line or square. The great majority of the Anglo-Allied battalions formed in quarter distance columns when they first deployed, and while waiting to see what form the French attack would take. Significant tactical aspects of this formation are:
• It was not normally a fighting formation. If the battalion had to open fire in this formation only the leading company could do so – that is, under sixty muskets. Similarly, for obvious reasons, it was vulnerable to cavalry attack.
• There were several variations of the battalion column. Although it was always formed with a frontage of one company in two ranks (that is 20–25 metres for the average Anglo-Allied unit, except the Hanoverians who used three ranks), the depth of the column depended on the gaps left between the companies in the rear. The right-hand diagram on p. 172 illustrates the four possibilities. With a column at open distance the gaps between the rear rank of the leading company and the rear rank of the next one was the same as the company frontage: say 20 metres. A column at half distance had gaps of 10 metres, at quarter distance 5 metres, and in the close column the troops were virtually treading on each other's heels.
• The area of ground covered by the columns varied considerably with the number of companies in the battalion, the strength of the companies and what type of column it was in. The 2/30, with some 640 all ranks, in open column would occupy a long narrow rectangle of ground with a frontage of about 20 metres and a depth of about 190 metres. However, at quarter distance, which was the formation most commonly adopted among Wellington's battalions on deployment, the frontage would still be 20 metres but the depth less than 50 metres.
• The left-hand diagram on p. 172 shows the 2/30 in its deployment formation at Waterloo. It was formed in a column at quarter distance, ready to move off to the front or to change formation to the front, either into line or square. About two minutes would be needed to complete the change into line, whereas to form square would only take around one minute. Note that Major Bailey has ridden to the front of the column, all company commanders are in front of their companies and Lieutenant Andrews, the adjutant, has ridden to the rear. If not sent out skirmishing, the Light Company would be at the rear with the Grenadiers in the lead.
• The Colours are positioned in the centre of the column, the pioneers out in front to clear away obstacles on the battlefield, and the drummers are paraded in the supernumerary rank behind their own companies.

2/30 in column of companies at quarter distance

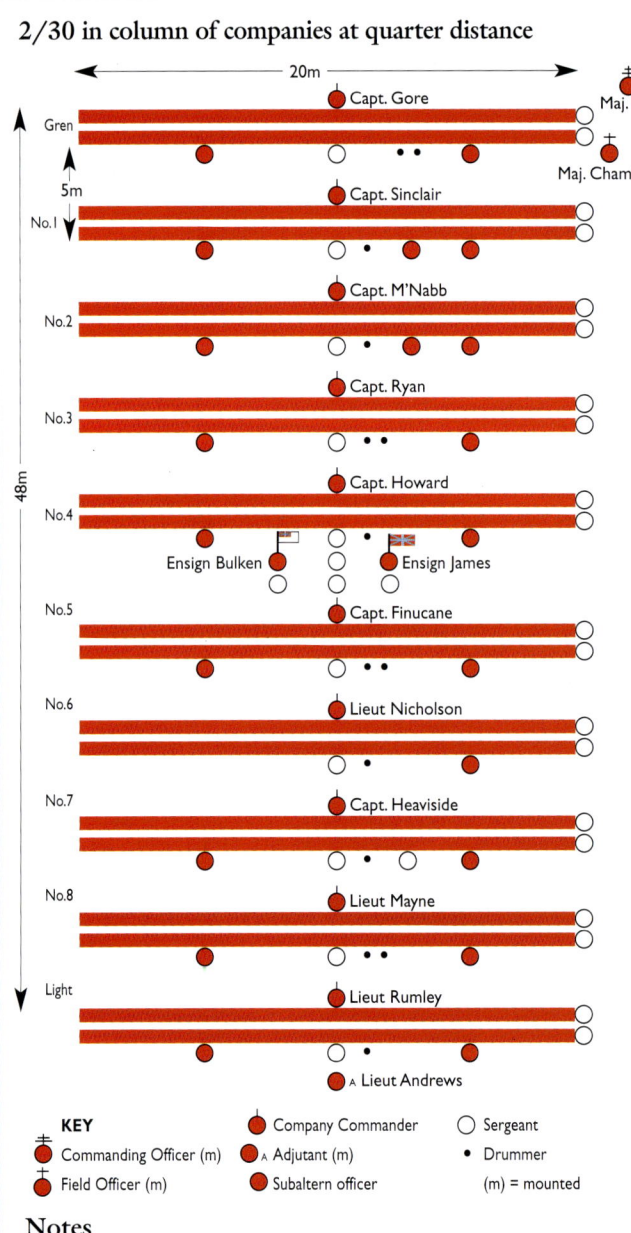

KEY
- ● Commanding Officer (m)
- ● Field Officer (m)
- ● Company Commander
- ● A Adjutant (m)
- ● Subaltern officer
- ○ Sergeant
- • Drummer
- (m) = mounted

Notes
- Some 90% of Anglo-Allied infantry adopted this standard formation on deploying on or behind the ridge. It was a compact, easy to control formation suitable for battlefield movement.
- The battalion could wheel in either direction or move forward (the diagram illustrates the 2/30 ready to advance). It can also quickly change to line or square.
- Note the short frontage and depth.
- From this formation the Light Company with Major Vigoureux went forward to join the skirmishing battalion.
- Battalions with 6 or 4 companies had wider frontage and less depth if of average strength.

Column formations of British (10-company) battalion

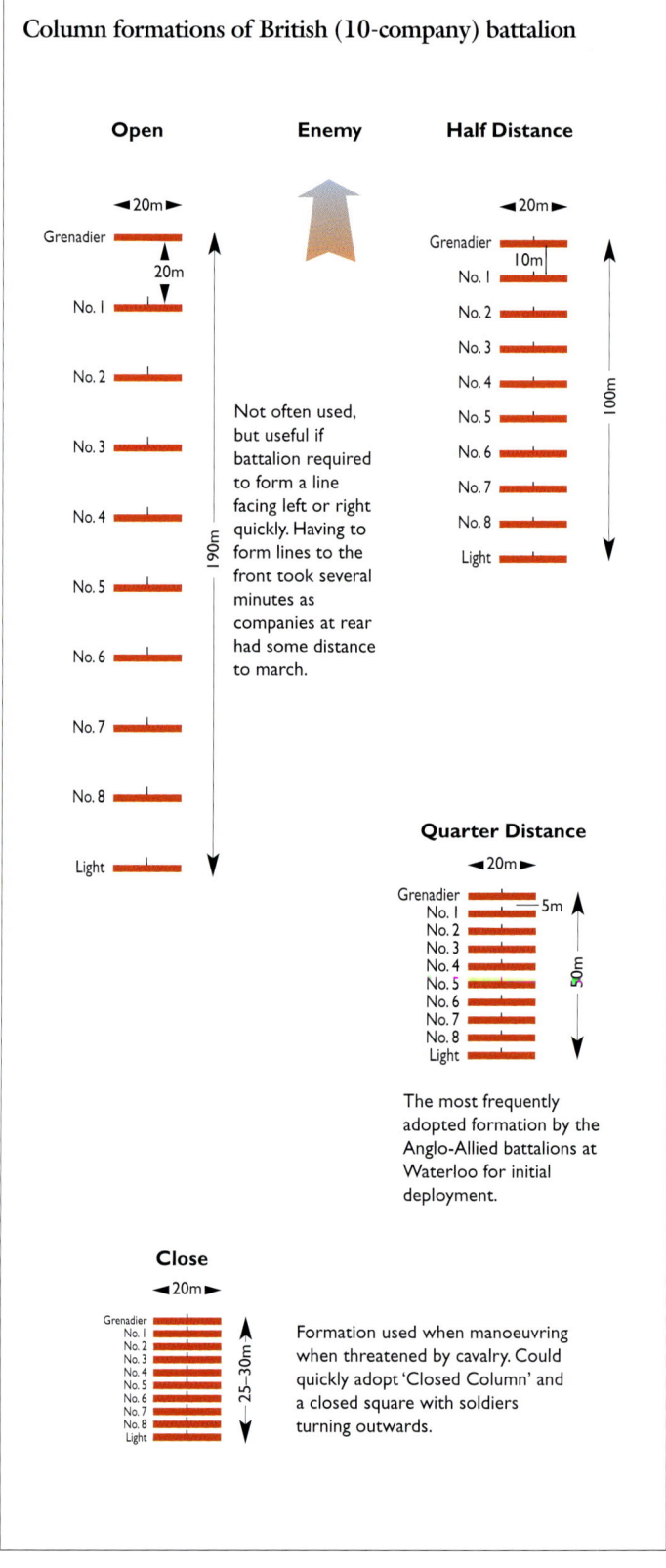

Squares (Diagram opposite)

Wellington's infantry spent a lot of time standing in squares at Waterloo. The price for not being in square when attacked by cavalry was extremely high. Cavalry, particularly heavy cavalry, could smash through a line of infantry, get round its flanks and cut it down from all sides. For this reason skirmishers were never expected to face cavalry. A determined advance by mounted troops would scatter skirmishers with ease, sending them flying for sanctu- ary behind a nearby obstacle or into their own square. If infantry was also caught on the move, and thus unable to fire effectively, the affair could be over in moments rather than minutes. This is precisely what happened to the 5th Line Battalion of the KGL as it was ordered forward in the evening to support La Haie Sainte. Much earlier in the day Donzelot's and Marcognet's divisions had their retreat turned to near rout under the sabres of the British Union Brigade. As well as heavy losses, it cost them each an Eagle.

2/30 forms square from quarter distance column

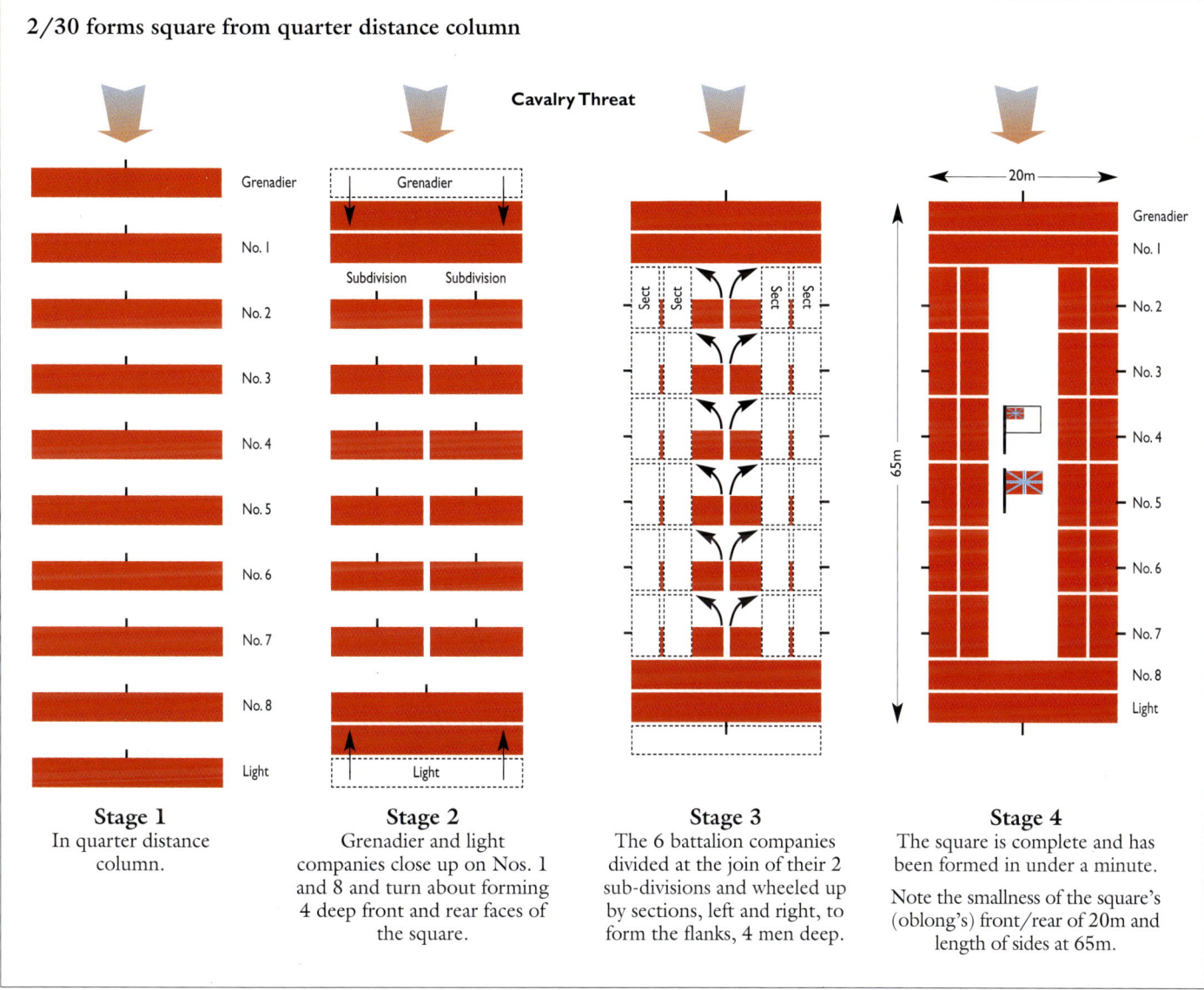

Stage 1
In quarter distance column.

Stage 2
Grenadier and light companies close up on Nos. 1 and 8 and turn about forming 4 deep front and rear faces of the square.

Stage 3
The 6 battalion companies divided at the join of their 2 sub-divisions and wheeled up by sections, left and right, to form the flanks, 4 men deep.

Stage 4
The square is complete and has been formed in under a minute.

Note the smallness of the square's (oblong's) front/rear of 20m and length of sides at 65m.

There were times, however, when it could be decidedly unhealthy to be in square. If the enemy brought up artillery and opened fire (with either canister or ball), the densely packed ranks would be torn apart. Prolonged and heavy skirmisher fire into a target hard to miss could also be unpleasant. The 1/27 (Inniskilling), who did not come forward until the battle was more than half over, died in square from the combined effects of cannon and skirmisher fire. When the remnants moved off at the end of the day their position was unmistakably marked in the mud and crushed corn by their dead – lying in square.

To succeed at Waterloo required considerable tactical skill. The Anglo-Allied brigade and battalion commanders spent much of their time making decisions as to whether to form square, column or, less frequently, line. Because of the massed cavalry assaults by the French, or the threat of them, an irregular chequer-board covered the ground from the centre to the right of Wellington's position for much of the afternoon and early evening.

Depending on the number of companies in a battalion, the square was often, in practice, an oblong. Units of six or ten companies, for example, would form oblongs, battalions with eight or four, squares. The object was to present a hedge of bayonets and muskets, with no gaps or flanks that could be exploited by horsemen. Faced with such a barrier, no horse could be persuaded, no matter how hard its rider dug in his spurs, to force a passage. Battalions that formed line in two ranks formed square in four, as the ranks were doubled up in the process. The outside rank would kneel, those behind stand. The Colours, the colonel, the assistant-surgeon and the drummers would be in the centre of this hollow square (or oblong). It was also the place to which were dragged the dead, the dying and the wounded.

Uniform Distinctions Between Companies in British Battalions

The various companies were normally distinguished in the following ways:

Battalion or centre companies – shoulder straps with worsted tufts; white over red shako plumes; officers wore epaulettes.

Grenadier companies – red 'wings' with white fringes; white shako plumes; officers wore chain or laced 'wings'.

Light companies – 'wings' like the grenadiers; green plumes and shako cords, bugle horn badge.

There were numerous variations on these between regiments.

After heavy losses the 2/30 and 2/73 combine to form column and square.

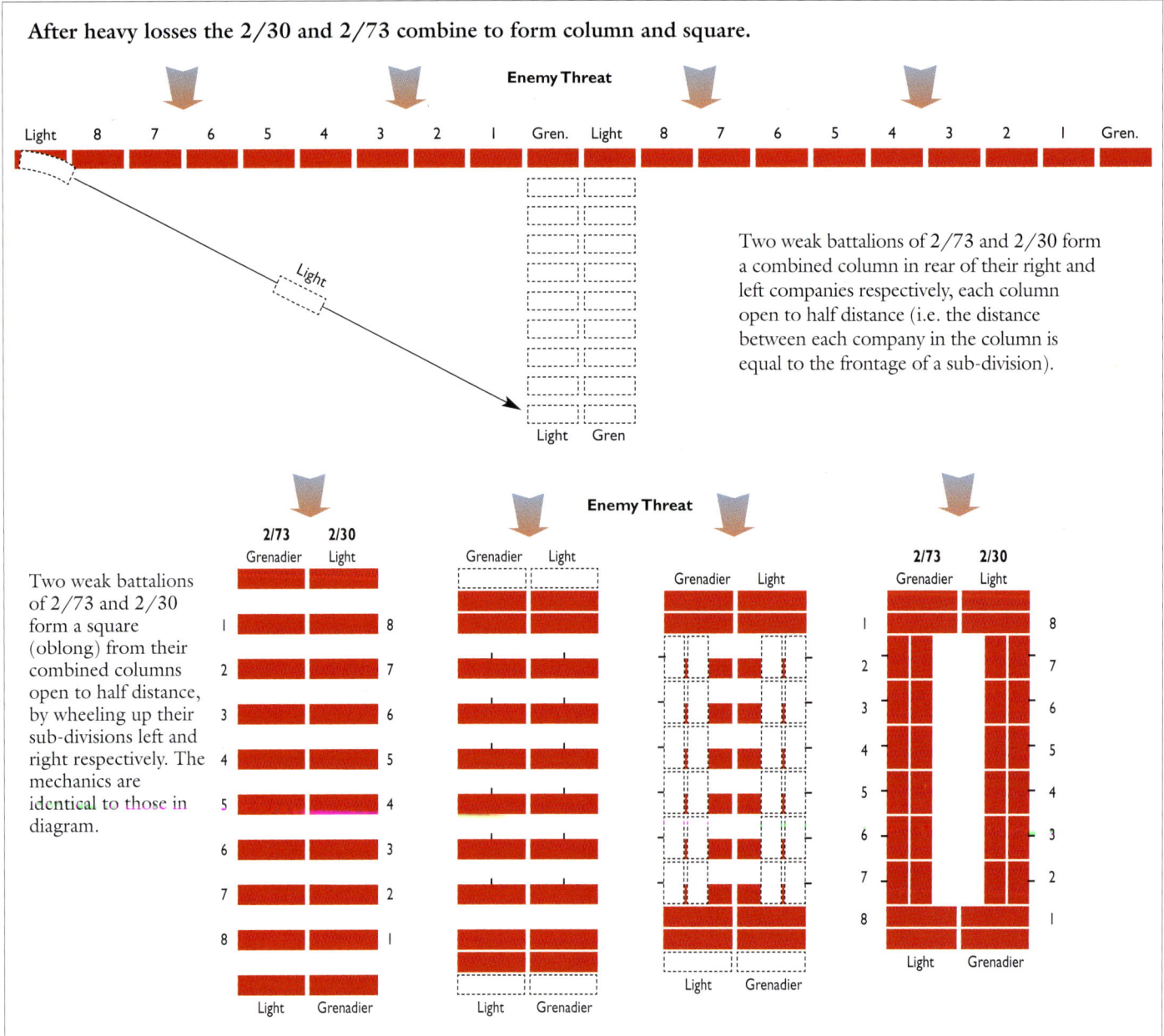

Two weak battalions of 2/73 and 2/30 form a combined column in rear of their right and left companies respectively, each column open to half distance (i.e. the distance between each company in the column is equal to the frontage of a sub-division).

Two weak battalions of 2/73 and 2/30 form a square (oblong) from their combined columns open to half distance, by wheeling up their sub-divisions left and right respectively. The mechanics are identical to those in diagram.

If battalions lost heavily it was feasible, and the drills existed in the manuals, for two units to combine to form one square. Two examples of this at Waterloo were the squares formed by the 2/30 with the 2/73, and the 33rd with the 2/69. The diagrams above illustrate how squares could be formed using the 2/30 and 2/73 as an example.

Skirmishing

This was primarily the task of light infantry, together with the light companies in the line battalions. Such soldiers were better shots, sometimes armed with rifles or slightly improved (shortened) versions of the musket, and received appropriate training to fight under less rigid control than their comrades in the line. Their tactics were fluid and mobile, they took cover behind trees and rocks, and they darted about changing their position. They were trained to fight in pairs well spread out. The skirmisher never fired in volleys; he fired when he could aim properly at a worthwhile target. They were deployed in a loose line in defence, perhaps up to 200 metres in advance of the main position.

Their task when defending was to screen their own main position from attack by enemy units. They did this by peppering away at them as they approached, inflicting casualties, delaying them, confusing them and generally sapping their resolve. If this was done well the chances were that one or two volleys from the main defensive line would repulse the attack. In practice, as at Waterloo, the attacking enemy deployed his own line of advancing skirmishers in front of his main formations, thus the first clash was between skirmish lines. The opportunity to inflict serious damage on the attacking force could therefore be reduced or completely negated.

If the defending skirmishers could not get at the main attacking units, at least they should be able to prevent the enemy skirmishers from approaching their own main position unscathed. A good screen would certainly expect to halt the enemy skirmishers, hopefully drive them back and expose the troops behind. This was the role of the Anglo-Allied skirmish line at Waterloo. If unable to halt the attacking skirmish line, the danger was that it would be able to approach the main position and start inflicting losses and disruption, so that when the main assaulting formation came up it would find its opposition had been softened up. In this situation the problem for a defending battalion was that a thin enemy skirmish line, with individuals firing, dodging and ducking about, did not present a worthwhile target for volley fire. If they fired they would inflict little damage and run the risk of being caught in the middle of loading when the main attack loomed up out of the smoke.

The skirmisher was trained to select his targets. He sought to kill enemy officers (particularly mounted ones) and NCOs. With its leaders down, a unit might hesitate, halt, become demoralized and turn about. Artillery gun crews were also worthwhile victims if any could be found in range. When eventually forced back before a stronger skirmish line, the weight of the main attack or cavalry, the defending skirmishers would retire rapidly to the flanks, back behind their own line or into their own square. He did not always seek safety with his own unit – the nearest one was the best. Skirmishers were very vulnerable to enemy horsemen, especially lancers. A squadron of cavalry could cut up a skirmish line with little loss to itself. If caught in this way the skirmishers were taught to dodge behind obstacles, sham death on the ground or, as a last resort, form a small rallying square (group) with nearby comrades and fight back-to-back.

At Waterloo the Anglo-Allied Army deployed a skirmish line from the outset. It stretched from west of Hougoumont, round the southern edge of Hougoumont wood, across the forward slope of the ridge to La Haie Sainte, and from there due east to south of Papelotte – a twisting route of close to 4000 metres (see Maps 8, 11 and 12). Its average distance from the main position on and behind the ridge was 250 metres. An ad hoc battalion of light companies from the four battalions in Colin Halkett's brigade was formed under the command of Major Vigoureux from the 2/30 (Cambridgeshire). His acting adjutant for the day was one of the 2/30's light company subalterns, Lieutenant John Platt. He left a clear account of his orders, which were:

> To cover and protect our batteries [deployed on, or just over, the crest]. To establish ourselves at all times as much in advance as might be compatible with prudence. To preserve considerable intervals between our extended files for greater security from the fire of the enemy's batteries. To show obstinate resistance against infantry of the same description, but to attempt no formation or offer useless opposition to charges of cavalry, but to retire in time upon the squares in our rear, moving in a direct line without any reference to regiments or nations. When the charge was repulsed to resume our ground.

Wellington's skirmishers were sparsely spread. There were some forty-six battalions in, or just behind, the Duke's front line. Of these, the 1/95 Rifles were employed defending the sandpit, hedge line and ridge in the centre. The four Guards battalions had their light companies defending the buildings, garden and orchard at Hougoumont. The 2nd KGL Light Battalion garrisoned La

A Skirmisher Versus a Lancer

Although generally speaking cavalry, particularly lancers, could destroy a skirmish line with comparative ease, individual infantrymen were taught how to take on a lancer. He had to display considerable coolness and courage but it was nevertheless possible to overcome this much-feared opponent. The foot soldier was taught to continue to face the approaching horseman, remaining still thus providing no clues as to how he was going to react. At the last moment the skirmisher was to spring to his right onto the lancer's left (blind side) and thrust his bayonet into the horse. If attacked by several lancers the soldier was trained to fall down, thrash about for a few moments and feign death. The chances were reasonable that the lancers (or other horsemen) would be distracted by other events, other enemy, and move on.

Haie Sainte, and three Nassau battalions were committed to defending Papelotte, La Haie and Frichermont. This left thirty-seven battalions that might be expected to provide their light companies for the skirmish line. Their combined efforts produced some 3000 men; this included the 600 men of the 51st that was deployed west of Hougoumont – the only battalion of light infantry to be used in its skirmishing role at the outset. This produced about one skirmisher for every 1.3 metres of front to be covered. A very transparent line, although it would be thicker in some places than others, and boosted by the garrisons of the outposts in Hougoumont wood and orchard, La Haie Sainte and the Papelotte and La Haie farms. It did, however, have one considerable tactical advantage – it was deployed down a forward slope with cannons behind it able to fire over the heads of the skirmishers in the shallow valley below. An interesting effect of the high, ripening crops was that skirmishers could not crouch to fire, but could easily conceal themselves to achieve surprise or hide while reloading.

NATIONAL CONTINGENTS

British

General characteristics and organization

The British infantry was organized into Regiments of Foot. By 1815 there were 104, numbered strictly in accordance with seniority – the date of formation. The most senior infantry of the 'line', excluding the Guards, was the 1st of Foot (Royal Scots) whose 3rd Battalion fought at Waterloo in Pack's brigade of Picton's division. It was first raised in 1633 (before the Guards Regiments) and due to its ancient lineage acquired the nickname 'Pontius Pilate's Bodyguard'. The most junior regiment was the 104th (New Brunswick Fencibles) raised in Canada in 1810. Unlike the French or other European armies, a British infantry regiment was not a tactical formation. It was an administrative unit that never took the field. The battalion (normally of ten companies) was the tactical unit. A regiment raised battalions for active duty. Some had only one, others two or three, with the 60th Rifles (not at Waterloo) having seven. In 1815 the British Army had 188 'line' battalions of which just over twenty-five were present on the battlefield.

The fact that some regiments had more than one battalion was originally purely accidental. At the breakdown of the Peace of Amiens in 1803 virtually all regiments had only one. But because such a huge expansion was needed to confront Napoleon, over fifty of those regiments stationed at home were ordered to raise second battalions. Those overseas, far from recruiting grounds, were not so instructed and remained single-battalion regiments (although some did later raise more). As the system developed it became the practice for the 1st Battalion to have the right of preference for active service overseas, with the second battalion remaining at home, its primary function being that of raising drafts to keep its senior partner up to strength. It was unusual for

Conditions of Service

The standard wage for a private was 13 pence a day, or £20 per year. A penny could buy roughly what a pound would buy today but the unfortunate soldier of 1815 actually received less than half his pay in cash. Sixpence a day was stopped for rations and he had additional amounts deducted for barrack damages, loss of kit, contributions to the Chelsea Hospital and other sundries. The Waterloo man was lucky to get his hands on five pence a day or about £7-10-0 a year. He was entitled to a daily issue of a pound of beef and a pound and a half of bread plus, and this was regarded as essential, a pint of wine or a third of a pint of gin or rum.

Year after year of poor food, unhealthy climates and continuous consumption of large quantities of alcohol eventually wore down even the most robust constitutions. The discharge papers of Private Samuel White, who was wounded at Waterloo while serving in the 2/73 (Highland), makes fascinating and not untypical reading:

> Discharged aged about forty-five (he claimed fifty) 14th August 1839, in consequence of being worn out and enfeebled. The Medical Officer's report states: 'His disability is attributable mainly to the climate and partly to tippling. He has been four times in hospital since 1835 with hepatitis, rheumatism, acute contusion and swelled testicles.'
>
> Conduct indifferent. He was tried by a Regimental Court Martial and imprisoned between 19th June and 25th July 1837. Served in the East Indies twenty-one years and two days, and was present at the Battle of Waterloo where he was wounded in the left leg. 5'5½", brown hair, grey eyes, pale complexion. Pension 1s 8d per day.

both battalions to be overseas at the same time, although this happened in the Peninsular War. In the scramble to raise an army in Belgium in 1815 this convention was again ignored. At Waterloo, including the Guards, there were fourteen 1st battalions, eight 2nd and three and a half 3rd – the half battalion being the two companies of the 3/95 Rifles. A regiment was referred to by its number; if it had more than one battalion its number preceded the regimental number – thus the 2/30 was the 2nd Battalion of the 30th (Cambridgeshire) Regiment of Foot.

Regiments (and battalions) were classified as being 'Guards' or 'Line'. Numbered as part of the 'Line' were the light regiments and the highland regiments, both having distinctive dress differences from the bulk of the 'Line', and the former having a specialized battlefield role.

Guards

Four battalions of Foot Guards out of a total of seven fought at Waterloo (for deployment see Map 11). They were the 2/1, 3/1, 2nd (Coldstream) – on maps shortened to 2/C as their motto is 'Second to None', they never acknowledge an abbreviation of 2/2 – and the 2/3 (Scots). Although they were élite units that recruited the biggest and best, and had a deservedly high reputation for drill, discipline and battlefield courage, they never quite attained the status of the French Imperial Guard that became an army within an army. All ranks received higher pay than equivalent ranks in other units. Junior officers were given double ranks to ensure no awkward arguments over seniority with their brother officers in more mundane regiments. Thus a Guard's ensign would be promoted to 'Lieutenant and Captain' and thence to 'Captain and Lieutenant-Colonel' – which explains why accounts of Waterloo have so many lieutenant-colonels dashing around in Hougoumont commanding companies.

The Foot Guards were uniformed like the line infantry but with regimental distinctions. An example of these differences was the arrangement of the strips of lace (gold for sergeants, white for rank and file) across the chest of the scarlet jacket. In the 1st Guards the lace was equally spaced, the 2nd's positioned in pairs, and the 3rd's in groups of three. The present day Guards have followed suit with the grouping of their tunic buttons.

All four battalions had seen service in the Peninsular War but only the 3/1 had been involved in the campaign proper rather than being confined to the environments of Cadiz and the Battle of Barrosa as the other three were. At Waterloo the four light companies, and later the remainder of the 2nd (Coldstream) and 2/3, played a decisive part in the defence of Hougoumont where they were embroiled in intense fighting for much of the day. The 2/1 and 3/1, like the rest of Wellington's right, were in squares resisting cavalry attacks throughout the afternoon. In the evening they played a critical role in defeating the Imperial Guard's final assault. For this the 1st Foot Guards were granted the title 'Grenadier' Guards in the mistaken belief that they had repulsed the French Imperial Guard Grenadiers. They had not; it was the Guard Châsseurs.

These battalions started the campaign with over 1000 men apiece (not unusual for the Guards), but losses at Quatre-Bras meant the average battalion strength at Waterloo was just over 950 all ranks (the average for the army was 640). Losses at Waterloo totalled over 1,600, or some 42 per cent of those engaged. Maitland's brigade of the 1st Foot Guards suffered crippling losses (over 60 per cent), almost double those of Byng's men behind the walls of Hougoumont.

Line

Discounting Guards, Light and Rifle Regiments, sixteen British line battalions fought at Waterloo (for deployment see Maps 11 and 12). They were, in order of seniority:

3/1 (Royal Scots), 1/4 (King's Own), 3/14 (Buckinghamshire), 23rd (Royal Welch Fusiliers), 1/27 (Inniskilling), 28th (North Gloucestershire), 2/30 (Cambridgeshire), 32nd (Cornwall), 33rd (Yorkshire, West Riding – Wellington's old regiment that would be named The Duke of Wellington's Regiment in 1899), 1/40 (Somersetshire), 42nd (Royal Highland), 2/44 (East Essex), 2/69 (South Lincolnshire), 2/73 (Highland), 79th (Cameron Highlanders), and the 92nd (Gordon Highlanders).

In addition, the Guards, the light battalions – with the single exception of the 51st (2nd Yorkshire, West Riding) – all formed and fought as line regiments. These battalions were Wellington's backbone along Mont St Jean ridge. Only six and a half British battalions (from Adam's and Lambert's brigades) were kept in reserve at the start.

All bar three had campaigned in the Peninsular so many still had a proportion of officers, NCOs and soldiers of veteran status.

The British infantryman's personal equipment

Front

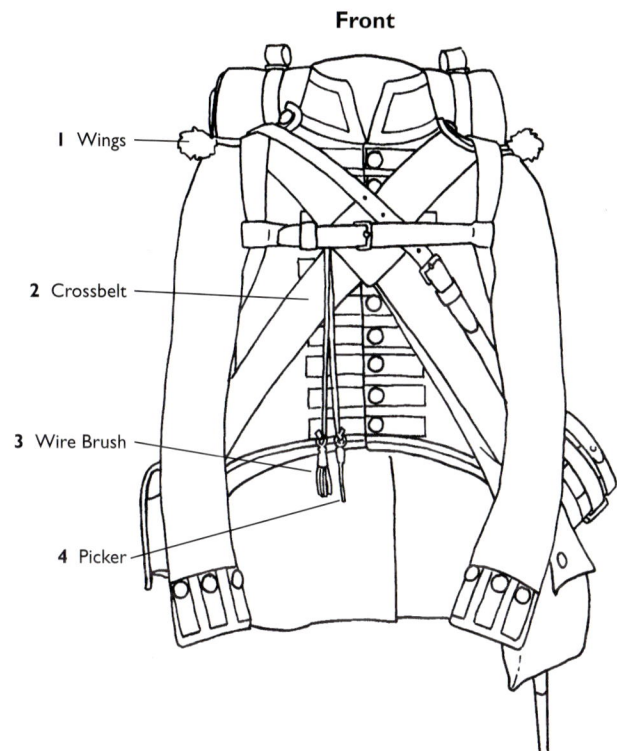

1 Wings
2 Crossbelt
3 Wire Brush
4 Picker

Rear

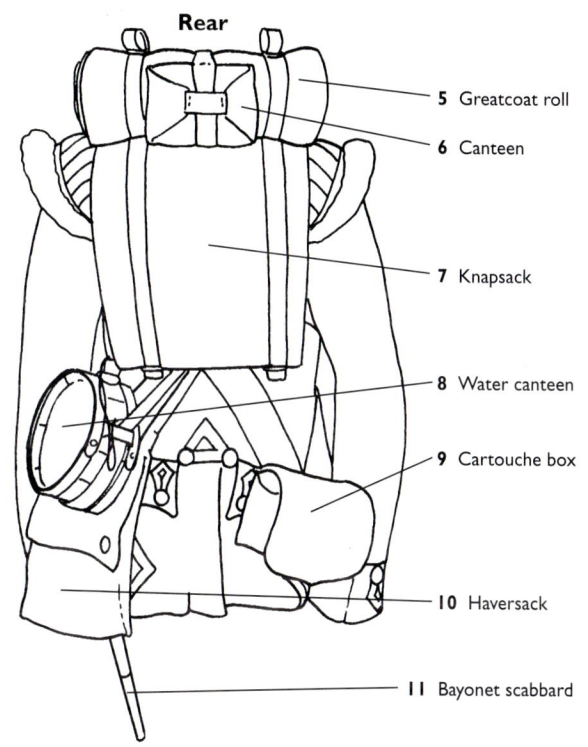

5 Greatcoat roll
6 Canteen
7 Knapsack
8 Water canteen
9 Cartouche box
10 Haversack
11 Bayonet scabbard

Notes

1 The 'wings' on the shoulders indicate a soldier in the Grenadier or Light Company. They were useful in preventing the various shoulder straps from slipping off.

2 The British had two crossbelts, one for the bayonet, the other for the cartouche box, with a belt plate holding them together in the centre. The belts which were white (pipe-clayed), together with the three other straps that went over the chest restricted breathing during a long march or when running.

3 A wire brush was part of the musket cleaning kit and was used for cleaning the priming pan of fouling. Like the picker it was often suspended on a string to avoid loss and facilitate quick use on the battlefield.

4 The picker was a tool for removing the fouling from the touch-hole. Even more than the brush, it was an essential implement to have to hand during prolonged firing.

5 The greatcoat (or blanket) was usually carried as shown on the march. However, the British infantry did not have greatcoats with them at Waterloo as, in accordance with a General Order dated 31 May, they had been packed in bundles of 20 for shipment to Ostend to lighten the soldiers' loads. No doubt the staff had felt they would not be needed in the summer.

6 The canteen was an all-purpose, individual mess tin.

7 The knapsack was black painted canvas stretched over a wooden frame, called the 'Trotter' knapsack after its manufacturer. It was horribly uncomfortable and therefore unpopular. Many soldiers in the Peninsula picked up the softer French cowhide packs and discarded their 'Trotters'. It contained spare shoes, shirts, trousers, stockings, cleaning brushes, pipe-clay and small personal items.

8 The water canteen was wooden, barrel shaped, and an official issue item.

9 The cartouche box was made of leather and contained wood or tin compartments for 60 cartridges. Underneath the flap was a small pocket for spare flints and cleaning tools, although the latter were normally carried on a string (3 and 4 above). To prevent it being obstructed and thus ensure speedy loading, it was the only piece of equipment slung over the left shoulder.

10 The haversack was a simple fabric bag slung over the right shoulder. It was primarily used to carry rations.

11 The bayonet was the only 'blade' type weapon carried by the British infantry soldier, the sword being almost another badge of rank for officers and sergeants in the Colour escort with halberds.

Of the three that had missed the Spanish experience one, the 3/14 (Buckinghamshire), was totally unbloodied, having been formed in 1813 and then having sat in Sicily for a year. No less than fourteen officers and 300 of its rank and file were less than eighteen years of age – mostly lads straight from the plough, a fact that secured them the nickname 'The Peasants'. Only the impassioned pleas of its commanding officer, Major Tidy, had prevented it being left on line of communication duties. The second was, surprisingly, the Duke's former regiment, the 33rd Foot. It had had little excitement since leaving India four years earlier. The third was the 2/69 (South Lincolnshire) who for ten years (1803–13) had been at home, faithfully supplying reinforcements for the 1st Battalion whose soldiers had succumbed at a disturbing rate to the debilitating climate of the West Indies, India and Java.

Both these latter battalions had been severely shaken at Quatre-Bras where the 2/69 lost its King's Colour. They were deployed alongside one another in the second line at Waterloo and, like the 2/30 and 2/73, due to further heavy losses were compelled to combine when forming square.

Many British infantry soldiers had recently campaigned in Spain. A clearer understanding of the maturity and experience of these men is possible if the relevant statistics of a typical unit with recent Peninsula service are examined. The 42nd (Royal Highlanders) had an average age of twenty-seven, ranging from seventeen to forty-four. As might be expected the higher the rank the older the soldier. For drummers it was twenty-three, privates twenty-six, corporals thirty-two and sergeants thirty-six. There were very few men under twenty, even among the drummers. For private

Drummers

Drummers were not necessarily boys. At Waterloo the average age of the drummers in the 2/73 was twenty-three, with the youngest being nineteen and the oldest twenty-seven. They had an average of eight years service each. Often recruited young, they tended to continue their drumming duties well into manhood and were frequently more experienced soldiers than the men they served. There was one drummer on the establishment of every company but a number of battalions had more: the 2/30, for example, had fourteen at Waterloo. Their duties included wielding the lash on soldiers sentenced to be flogged. They were supposed to carry a cat-o'-nine-tails in their pack so that the punishment could be carried out on the march if

necessary. With heavy sentences several drummers would be involved, taking turns to give twenty-five lashes each.

The youngest soldier in the 2/73 at Waterloo was Robert Kyle who, although only seventeen, had already been in the Army for over four years, including two fighting in the Peninsula. After enlistment as a Boy he had done a spell as a Drummer before transferring to Private. He appears to have become one of the Regiment's rogues. When finally discharged in 1838 after twenty-seven years service, he had been imprisoned seven times and had achieved the unusual distinction of being described as of 'bad character' on his discharge papers – a phrase reserved for real villains.

soldiers the average length of service was six years – sufficient to embrace most of the Peninsular War. Many of these men had been with the battalion at five battles in the two years prior to Waterloo (excluding Quatre-Bras). These were the Pyrenees, the Nive, the Nivelle, Orthez and Toulouse. Drummers had served an average of eight years, corporals eleven and sergeants twelve. Their experience was in every way comparable to Napoleon's veterans (except perhaps with those who survived the march to and from Moscow).

Highland Regiments formed part of the line and were distinguished from other battalions by the wearing of a kilt rather than trousers, and a bonnet instead of a shako. The exceptions at Waterloo were the 71st (Highland), which was also a light infantry battalion in Adam's light infantry brigade, and the 2/73 (Highland). Neither regiment wore the kilt or bonnet. A detachment of the 2/73 under Lieutenant Torriano made history at the end of the battle by capturing a French cannon and turning it on the retiring Imperial Guard. It was the last French gun to fire at Waterloo. At the end of the day only five officers out of twenty-seven in the 2/73 were alive and unwounded.

The highlanders in their kilts and bonnets were all in Picton's division to the east of the 'Elm Tree' crossroads. These were the 42nd (Royal Highlanders), the 79th (Cameron Highlanders) and the 92nd (Gordon Highlanders). Although involved with the repulse of d'Erlon's Corps, these battalions did not suffer to the same degree as their comrades west of the crossroads.

Light and Rifle Regiments

The British deployed three battalions designated as light troops at Waterloo. Two of them, the 1/52 (Oxfordshire) and the 71st (Highland), were in Adam's 3rd British ('Light') Brigade. The other, the only one to be used in a light infantry role, was the 51st (2nd

British Infantry as Marines

Several regiments that fought at Waterloo had previous service as marines on board warships. This was not uncommon when there were insufficient Royal Marines for the fleet. The regiments concerned were the 30th, 51st and 69th. The latter had detachments on both the *Agamemnon* and *Captain* when Nelson was commanding. One soldier of the 69th Foot serving on the *Captain* at the Battle of Cape St Vincent led Nelson's boarding party onto the *San Nicolas*. To quote Nelson: 'The soldiers of the 69th regiment, with an alacrity which will ever do them credit, were among the foremost on this service [boarding]. ... A soldier having broken the upper quarter-gallery window, jumped in followed by myself...'. That soldier was Private Matthew Stevens. At Waterloo he was the quartermaster of the 69th. He was also a Scotsman with a sense of humour. When a soldier was struck down at his side by a long shot at the start of the battle he quietly remarked, 'Aweel, it is time for a respectable non-combatant to gang awa!'

Even cavalry were occasionally drafted in to do duty at sea. The 12th Light Dragoons who fought in Vandeleur's brigade had detachments acting, surely with great reluctance, as marines in the Mediterranean in 1795.

Yorkshire, West Riding), part of Mitchell's scattered brigade northwest of Hougoumont (for more precise deployment see Map 11). The 51st saw little action at Waterloo as there was no attempt by Napoleon to turn Wellington's right flank, which is where this battalion spent most of the battle. Only nine soldiers were killed and two officers and twenty men wounded – trifling losses for an infantry battalion at Waterloo. The 1/52 started the battle as the strongest battalion in Wellington's Army, with 1,130 all ranks under the command of Lieutenant-Colonel Sir John Colbourne. Colbourne had commanded a brigade in Portugal, Spain and France, and eventually became Field-Marshal Lord Seaton. One of the most able battalion commanders at Waterloo, he played a vital part in defeating the Imperial Guard in the closing stages of the battle by wheeling his battalion forward and to the left to attack the Châsseurs in flank.

Just under 1,300 officers and men of the 95th Rifles fought at Waterloo, almost 600 became casualties. The 1/95 Rifles had only six companies, totalling barely 400 men. It formed part of Kempt's brigade in Picton's division. The 2/95 also had six companies, but stronger ones, and were in Adam's 'Light' brigade, as were the two companies of the 3/95. Initially this brigade was held 700 metres north of Wellington's right.

The 95th Rifles were only thirteen years old at Waterloo but their reputation for fighting efficiency was a byword throughout the Army. They had won this reputation in the Peninsular War where riflemen had been present at virtually every major battle (they missed Talavera despite marching 65 kilometres in 24 hours) and countless minor engagements. As part of the famous Light Division they had been Wellington's eyes and ears, scouting and screening ahead of every advance and covering every retreat. This role led to their officers drinking an unofficial toast – 'First in the field, and last out of it' – for years afterwards. Their dark green uniforms earned them the nickname 'The Sweeps', their agile skirmishing, 'The Grasshoppers'. Because they usually fought dispersed they carried no Colours, and reacted to whistle blasts or bugle calls rather than the beating of drums. Armed with the Baker rifle, they fought in pairs, loaded crouching behind rocks or trees, could fire from the prone position, and dodged from cover to cover in advance or retirement. Their standard of marksmanship, discipline and unit administration was the envy of the army – not forgetting that riflemen did not have a vast amount of kit that required polishing like other soldiers.

Despite all this, none of the 95th Rifles' units were used in a skirmishing role at Waterloo. They fought as line infantry. Half of the 1/95 defended the sandpit and knoll east of the Brussels road just south of the 'Elm Tree', while the other half lined the hedge bordering the Ohain–Wavre road 150 metres in the rear. The 2/95 and their comrades in the two companies of the 3/95 also fought as conventional infantry, mostly in square repulsing cavalry, until the end when they played an important part in defeating the Imperial Guard.

King's German Legion

By Waterloo the KGL was an integral part of the British Army, having had a depot and base at Bexhill-on-Sea on the Sussex coast since 1804. Lieutenant Lindau, who fought with the 2nd Light Battalion defending La Haie Sainte, later wrote of his happy days at Bexhill, '... the time I spent in England – some eighteen months – was the best part of my life. Never again was I to lead such a carefree and merry life as in the barracks at Bexhill.' The KGL had been founded in 1803 from refugees from the Electorate of Hanover who fled when the French overran their country. As King George III of England was also King of Hanover, it was natural for its émigrés to seek sanctuary in England.

The KGL was built up over several years to an all arms force of some 18,000 men, all volunteers, that by 1815 had fought with distinction at Copenhagen, Flushing, in Pomerania, Sweden, Sicily and, above all, in the Peninsula. Wellington had a high opinion of the KGL, which could be favourably compared with the best British battalions. At Waterloo the KGL fielded eight battalions in two brigades. These were the 1st KGL Brigade under Colonel du Platt consisting of the 1st, 2nd, 3rd and 4th Line Battalions, and Colonel Baron Ompteda's 2nd KGL Brigade with the 1st and 2nd Light and 5th and 8th Line Battalions. They had a combined strength of just under 4,200 all ranks, giving an average battalion strength of 520 – very low considering no KGL infantry had fought at Quatre-Bras. The weakest battalion was Major Baring's 2nd Light, destined to defend La Haie Sainte, with only 403. With the exception of the 8th Line (636), all KGL battalions at Waterloo were weak, being substantially below the army's average of 640. The reason for this was that they had recently been reduced from ten companies to six (four battalion and two flank). The reduction was due to the insistence of the Hanoverian government that KGL troops flesh out their newly raised militia units in early 1815. It meant 91 experienced officers and 104 sergeants were transferred.

The KGL adopted the British battalion organization, uniform (scarlet jackets for line units, dark green for light), drill manual and tactics. They fought in a two rank line, carried two Colours and gave orders in English (except for the Light Battalions). Line battalions were armed with the India Pattern musket, light battalions with the Baker rifle. They did not, however, use flogging as a

punishment. The theoretical war establishment for a KGL company, based on six to a battalion, was:

One captain
Two lieutenants
One ensign
Five or six sergeants
Four corporals
Two or three drummers (buglers in the light infantry)
Ninety-four privates

The above gives a total of 109–111 all ranks per company, or some 660 to a battalion. At Waterloo companies were mostly up to strength with officers and sergeants but well down on soldiers, averaging around eighty-five in each of the six companies.

The 2nd KGL Brigade was the most heavily engaged during the battle. Major Baring's 2nd Light, reinforced by two companies of the 1st Light, the Light Company of the 5th Line and a company of Nassauers, fought almost continuously to defend La Haie Sainte from around 2.00 p.m. until forced to abandon it due to lack of ammunition some four and a half hours later. Shortly after this, Colonel Ompteda was forced to comply with an order to counterattack with infantry in line, despite French cavalry being within striking distance. He himself was killed, while the 5th Line was scattered and cut down by cuirassiers. Earlier in the afternoon the 8th Line had also been caught by the Châsseurs à Cheval of the Imperial Guard and had suffered badly. Ensign von Moreau, carrying the King's Colour, was wounded and so handed it to a sergeant. A French officer then killed the sergeant, taking the Colour into his possession as he did so. Although the French officer was immediately killed, the Colour remained in French hands during the rest of the battle. Some days later it was returned to the battalion by a Hanoverian cavalryman.

The KGL deserved better at Waterloo. They fought long and hard, suffering unnecessary losses due to tactical errors by senior commanders, and were only driven from La Haie Sainte because of a failure of ammunition supply. Casualties amounted to 23 per cent in the 1st Brigade and 30 per cent in the 2nd. The heaviest casualties were in the 2nd Light that lost 50 per cent (202). Surprisingly, according to one parade state, the 5th Line, although scattered with many men initially missing, only lost 162 all ranks, or a comparatively modest 30 per cent.

Hanoverian

By virtue of the fact that King George III of England was also the Elector of Hanover, the state provided a substantial part of the Anglo-Allied infantry at Waterloo – over seventeen battalions, or 21 per cent of the total (excluding the KGL). The Hanoverian line infantry had two different types of battalion, namely 'Field' and 'Landwehr'. The former were composed of volunteers, a proportion of whom had military training and experience; the latter were newly raised militia-type units with soldiers of rudimentary training and no experience. However, these battalions had each received a cadre of veteran officers and senior NCOs from the KGL that went some way towards compensating for the fact that many were reluctant, and mostly youthful and untested, soldiers.

In February 1815 the Hanoverian 'Subsidiary Corps' that was stationed in the Netherlands was restructured. Field and Landwehr battalions were grouped into regiments, each with one Field battalion and three Landwehr. This was the situation on paper, but for Waterloo Wellington separated Field from Landwehr, mixed them up and then grouped them together in different divisions.

Hanoverian drill, tactics and internal organization were similar, but not identical, to the British. They fought in two rank lines, were armed with muskets and bayonets, and carried Colours. There were, however, differences at Waterloo. All Landwehr battalions had only four companies, each of approximately 150 all ranks. Neither regular nor Landwehr battalions had flank (grenadier or light) companies. Instead, in the line battalions, every twelfth man was trained as a skirmisher, while in the light battalions (there were two, the Lüneberg and Grubenhagen Field) all received this training. Additionally, all line battalions had ten sharpshooters (*scharfschutzen*) per company. They formed up on the right of their companies. Orders were given by bugle horn rather than drum. The uniforms were very similar to the KGL, with field battalions wearing red jackets, and the light and jaeger troops green. All officers and sergeants wore yellow sashes round their waists rather than crimson.

The seventeen battalions were grouped into four brigades, each in a different division, as follows:

1st Hanoverian Brigade – Major-General Count Kielmannsegge (took command of the division when Alten was wounded)

> 1st (Duke of York's) Field Battalion
> Grubenhagen Field (Light) Battalion
> Bremen Field Battalion
> Verden Field Battalion
> Lüneberg Field (Light) Battalion
> Two companies of Field Jaeger (sharpshooters)

This brigade contained all five regular field battalions, was the strongest Hanoverian formation with over 3,300 all ranks, and was posted in a key position in Wellington's line (see Map 11). The average battalion strength was 660, making them marginally stronger than the army average. The brigade had three battalions deployed in the front line, just in dead ground below the crest of the ridge, about 350 metres west of the 'Elm Tree'. The other two battalions were in a supporting role in the second line 100 metres to the rear. The fact that the Duke had posted them there (as part of the 3rd British Division under Alten), sandwiched between KGL battalions on their left and British on their right, suggests he had confidence in their steadiness.

This confidence was justified. The brigade fought courageously, taking serious casualties at both Quatre-Bras and Waterloo. The combined losses for both battles were well over 1,500, or 45 per cent of the brigade. The Lüneberg Light was badly cut up by cuirassiers (temporarily losing a Colour) when moving to assist the garrison in La Haie Sainte. Before the start of the battle the brigade had sent fifty men from both the Lüneberg and Grubenhagen Light Battalions, plus the 1st Company of Field Jaegers, to help defend the Hougoumont Wood. All battalions were in square for much of the afternoon, repelling incessant cavalry attacks. They then lost heavily to French guns that had been pushed forward to within 150 metres of their squares after the fall of La Haie Sainte.

3rd Hanoverian Brigade – Colonel H. Halkett

> Bremenvörde Landwehr Battalion
> Osnabrück Landwehr Battalion
> Quackenbrück Landwehr Battalion
> Salzgitter Landwehr Battalion

This all-landwehr brigade was part of the 2nd British Division (Clinton) grouped with a British and a KGL brigade. It was the weakest Hanoverian formation, having only just over 2,500 men, although each battalion averaged a respectable 635 all ranks. Initially, this division was held back in reserve behind Wellington's right with the Hanoverians being at the rear, over 800 metres from the ridge (see Map 11). Later in the afternoon this brigade advanced close to the ridge and had all four battalions in square on the reverse slope north of Hougoumont. The Osnabrück Battalion played a small part in the defeat of the Imperial Guard and later, after he had been captured by Colonel Halkett, took the surrender of Maréchal de Camp Cambronne, the commander of the 1st Châsseurs à Pied of the Imperial Guard. The brigade's losses were comparatively light – 234 all ranks – with the Quackenbrück Landwehr only sustaining fourteen.

4th Hanoverian Brigade – Colonel C. Best

> Verden Landwehr Battalion
> Lüneberg Landwehr Battalion
> Munden Landwehr Battalion
> Osterode Landwehr Battalion

This brigade was another all landwehr formation that was part of the 6th British Division (Lambert at Waterloo), although for much of the battle, it was attached to, and deployed in the area of, the 5th British Divison (Picton) (see Map 12). With almost 2,700 all ranks, its four battalions were well above the average strength, with 675 men apiece. Although it was posted in the front line, it was about 1000 metres east of the 'Elm Tree' on the Anglo-Allied left – a part of the front that did not concern the Duke as much as the centre and right. It was the only formation, apart from Bijlandt's Belgians, whose battalions deployed in line at the outset, rather than column of companies.

Best's brigade saw action at Quatre-Bras from 3.00 p.m. The Verden Landwehr was badly mauled by cavalry at that battle when they were slow to form square. At Waterloo the brigade was not heavily engaged, as even during d'Erlon's corps attack the French brigade that advanced on them (from Durutte's division) failed to get more than his skirmish line into contact before being forced to retire by the retreat of his compatriots on his left. During the short campaign this brigade suffered some 526 casualties, mostly at Quatre-Bras.

5th Hanoverian Brigade – Colonel von Vincke

> Gifhorn Landwehr Battalion
> Hameln Landwehr Battalion
> Hildesheim Landwehr Battalion
> Peine Landwehr Battalion

Another raw landwehr formation of 2,600 men with an average battalion strength of 650 all ranks. Part of the British 5th Division (Picton), it was deployed on the extreme left of the line 1,500 metres east of the central 'Elm Tree' (see Map 12). There were no other infantry units on its left. Wellington had entrusted the defence of 1000 metres of his front line on the left to untried Hanoverian Landwehr units, with no infantry in support behind them – further evidence of the Duke's doubts about his strategic right flank. This brigade saw even less action than Best's. By the battle's end, the only infantry virtually unscathed, because they had not been used, were the two Hanoverian brigades of Best and Vincke, plus the two battalions of Mitchell's brigade, the 3/14 and 51st (Light). Vincke's brigade lost 247 all ranks, with the Hildesheim Battalion only accounting for twenty-four of them.

Brunswickers (Map 11, p. 157)

Hitler's feared SS formations of World War II wore the all black uniform and silver Death's Head skull and crossbones badge of their German forebears in the Duke of Brunswick's 'Black Legion' or 'Black Horde' to give it its more sinister designation. In 1814 the 'Black Duke', as Brunswick was called, disbanded his Legion that had fought for Britain since 1809 and raised a new national army. Units were built up on cadres of veterans from the Peninsular War, where the Brunswick-Oels Regiment had provided semi-independent light infantry companies to most British infantry divisions to beef up their scouting and skirmishing capacity. On Napoleon's return from Elba the Duke offered his 'Brunswick Corps' (still in black uniforms and with line battalions wearing the silver skull on their shakos), to Wellington with himself as commander-in-chief.

There is considerable confusion as to what type of formation the Brunswickers provided. It has been called a 'corps', a 'contingent' and a 'division'. The latter is more accurate. It had a commander-in-chief (the Duke of Brunswick) and a 'brigade' commander (Colonel Olfermann); it had two infantry brigades (sometimes called regiments) plus an independent 'vanguard' battalion, a hussar regiment, a lancer (uhlan) squadron and two batteries of guns. With something in excess of 6,200 men it was too small for a corps but exactly right for a division. Consequently, it is referred to as a division in this book.

In addition to those Brunswickers who had joined the British service as exiles after French dismemberment of their state, some 8000 fought for Napoleon in the Westphalian Army. Many perished in Russia and Spain. It is hardly surprising, therefore, that manpower was short in 1815. The Brunswick Division that marched to Quatre-Bras and Waterloo contained a higher proportion of inexperienced youths than any other formation. The average soldier's age was barely eighteen, while the light battalions had sergeants, sometimes sergeant-majors, of the same age. Even quite senior officers within the battalions were only slightly older. Company commanders of twenty-eight years old and battalion commanders of thirty were commonplace. The Black Duke took a month to march his men to Belgium, arriving under Wellington's command in mid-May.

The Brunswickers fought in a two rank line, every battalion carried a Colour, and each battalion had four companies with a theoretical strength of around 150 rank and file. Except for the Avantgarde Battalion, armed with rifles, all the troops carried muskets and bayonets. The division was organized as follows:

Commander – Colonel Olfermann (initially the 'brigade' commander but took over the division when the Duke of Brunswick was killed at Quatre-Bras).

Avantgarde (Vanguard) Battalion –
Major von Rauschenplat

This rifle-armed battalion of sharpshooters operated independently of the divisional structure and was directly under Colonel Olfermann at Waterloo. It had four companies: two Jaeger companies (mostly veterans from Spain) and two light companies. It was heavily engaged at Quatre-Bras, mostly skirmishing in the Bois de Bossu.

At Waterloo the battalion was initially deployed in reserve immediately west of Merbe Braine village, some 600 metres west of the remainder of the Brunswick Division. Along with the Leib and 1st Light Battalions, it advanced later in the battle to give support to Hougoumont. Its casualties at the end of the day were slight: about sixty.

Light Infantry Brigade – Lieutenant-Colonel von Buttlar

> Leib ('Life' or 'Guard') Battalion
> 1st Light Battalion
> 2nd Light Battalion
> 3rd Light Battalion

With a strength of 2,565 all ranks, at Waterloo battalions had an average of 641 all ranks, down on their establishment mainly on account of losses at Quatre-Bras. The Leib Battalion was broken by artillery fire at Quatre-Bras (although losses of 126 were not excessive), and it was while attempting to rally them that the 'Black Duke' was struck by a musket ball that penetrated his hand, body and liver. He died within minutes, his only words being to his chief of staff, Major von Wachholtz: 'My dear Wachholtz, where is Olfermann?' His loss was deeply felt by the division.

At Waterloo this brigade was held in reserve some 1,500 metres north of Hougoumont before moving forward to support the right wing of Wellington's line. Here they formed squares to repel Ney's cavalry assaults. At times these youngsters appeared shaky, being held together by the efforts of the officers and sergeants pushing, shoving, shouting and thumping them into place. At others they appeared to be holding their own. Ensign Gronow with the 3/1 Guards witnessed a square of Brunswickers deflecting a charge of the French 'Red' Lancers and bringing down an officer's horse that trapped its rider under it. Two Brunswickers darted out to rob the fallen officer before blowing his brains out with his own pistol – a deed that brought forth yells of 'Shame! Shame!' from British troops nearby.

This brigade suffered about 330 casualties, or 13 per cent of its strength.

Line Infantry Brigade – Lieutenant-Colonel von Specht

> 1st Line Battalion
> 2nd line Battalion
> 3rd Line Battalion

This brigade had seen action at Quatre-Bras and, overall, had suffered more severely than the Light Brigade. The 2nd Line Battalion, down to 500 men at Waterloo, having lost 200 on 16 June, was the weakest of all the Brunswick battalions. The brigade started the battle with 1,753 all ranks, with the average battalion being 584. At 11.30

Brunswickers Eat Dogs

In the Peninsular War the Brunswick-Oels troops were sharpshooters wearing green uniforms instead of black. Initially they had excellent German officers with rank and file volunteers, and so established a good reputation for themselves. However, when this source dried up many replacements came from British prisoner-of-war camps. A motley assortment of German, Polish, Danish, Swiss, Dutch and Croatian turncoats was recruited and desertion levels climbed. Sergeant Edward Costello of the 95th Rifles, who had his trigger finger torn off by a musket ball at Quatre-Bras and thus missed Waterloo, has described how relationships plummeted between the 95th and the Brunswickers due to their propensity for eating dogs. He tells how they were, 'gifted with a canine appetite that induced them to kill and eat all the dogs they could get hold of...'. The 95th had a pet dog called 'Rifle' that accompanied them into action and dashed about barking as though it was all a great game. However, he survived the bullets only to be, 'devoured by the insatiable jaws of the Brunswickers'.

A Brunswick Square at Waterloo

Captain Mercer who commanded 'G' Troop of the Royal Horse Artillery has related how during the late afternoon at Waterloo his guns were positioned between two squares of Brunswickers. He described what he saw:

> The Brunswickers were falling fast – the shot every moment making great gaps in their squares, which the officers and sergeants were actively employed in filling up by pushing their men together, and sometimes thumping them ere they could make them move. … Today they fled not bodily, to be sure, but spiritually, for their senses seemed to have left them. There they stood with recovered arms, like so many logs, or rather like the very wooden figures which I had seen them practising at in their cantonments. Every moment I feared they would again throw down their arms and flee: but their officers and sergeants behaved nobly, not only keeping them together, but managing to keep their squares closed in spite of the carnage made amongst them. To have sought refuge amongst men in such a state were madness – the very moment our men ran from their guns I was convinced, would be the signal for their disbanding.

Mercer, like the other battery commanders, had been ordered to run for shelter in the nearest square when the French cavalry came close, and then dash out to man the guns again after the horsemen had been driven off. As we see from the above, Mercer's men stood by their cannons throughout.

a.m. the battalions were formed up in reserve immediately west of the Brussels road, some 1,400 metres north-east of Hougoumont. During the battle they were moved forward to reinforce the right centre and, as the Imperial Guard made its final advance, to support Kruse's Nassauers. There was some hesitancy so Wellington himself rode up to steady them. Their losses at Waterloo just exceeded 500, of which 220 belonged to the 2nd Line Battalion.

Nassauers (Maps 11 & 12, pp. 157 & 158)

The Duchy of Nassau was a German state centred on the city of Wiesbaden, about 200 kilometres south of Hanover on the north bank of the Rhine. After Napoleon occupied the area and formed the Confederation of the Rhine in 1806, some Nassau contingents fought for France in Spain – the Emperor's aptly named 'Spanish Ulcer'. In 1815 the German 28th Orange-Nassau Regiment (two battalions), the 2nd Nassau Regiment (three battalions) and a company of Nassau Jaegers were in the Netherlands as part of the Netherlands Army. They constituted the 2nd Brigade of the 2nd Netherlands Division (Perponcher–Sedlnitzky).

After the peace of 1814 the Congress of Vienna had split up the Napoleonic Duchy into its component states. When the Emperor returned from Elba the Duke of Nassau-Usingen and Nassau-Weilberg sent his 1st Nassau Regiment (three battalions) to join Wellington. It was commanded by Major-General von Kruse. Wellington's intention was to join all his Nassau contingents together into a Nassau Division, but this proved impossible over King William's objections that it would damage the structure and morale of his fledgling Netherlands Army. Kruse therefore retained his command as an independent force of brigade strength in the Duke's reserve.

Apart from the officer corps, which contained a good leavening of experienced men, particularly at the junior level, the Nassauers almost rivalled their fellow Germans, the Brunswickers, for youth and lack of service. Of the 1st Regiment of over 2,800 all ranks, more

than 1000 were recruits with only six weeks in uniform. The Nassauers were the only Anglo-Allied contingent to use regiments as tactical units at Waterloo. The 1st Regiment (of brigade strength) had the somewhat long-winded title of 'The Nassau Reserve Contingent'. The 2nd Regiment with three battalions and the 28th Orange-Nassau Regiment with two, together mustered some 4,500 infantrymen who were grouped as a brigade – by far the largest in the Anglo-Allied Army, even exceeding the British 1st Division in numbers.

Each regiment had an elaborate staff establishment of seventeen officers including, amongst others, three majors, three adjutant-majors, an auditor and seven surgeons, many of whom would be attached to battalions in the field. Among the ninety-four NCOs and soldiers officially on the staff were twenty-two oboists, eighteen sappers, thirty-three Train soldiers and five artisans. Each battalion had six companies – one grenadier, one flanquer (light) and four fusilier. Each battalion carried a Colour. Their uniforms were green (jackets and trousers) with black facings, yellow piping and cross belts. The officers had orange sashes round their waists. Jaegers were armed with rifles, all the rest, including the flanquer companies, had muskets and bayonets. Interestingly, like the French, all NCOs and all grenadier or flanquer company soldiers had swords as well.

At Waterloo troops from Nassau provided over eight very strong battalions, or some 10 per cent of the Duke's infantry. They were deployed at both extremities of the battlefield and in the centre. Nassauers were involved in the defence of Hougoumont, the struggle for the centre (including La Haie Sainte) and the fighting around Papelotte, La Haie and Frichermont.

The Nassau units were organized as follows:

The Nassau Reserve Contingent (Brigade) – Major-General A.H.E. von Kruse

> 1st Nassau Regiment – Colonel E. von Steuben
> 1/1 Nassau
> 2/1 Nassau
> 1st Nassau Landwehr Battalion

This Regiment had only arrived in Brussels eight days before the French crossed the frontier. As an independent formation that had no cavalry or artillery attached, it formed part of Wellington's Reserve Corps, starting the battle with over 2,800 men. Each battalion was bursting with soldiers (mostly recruits) with an average strength of almost 950 – over 300 more than the army average. Six companies of 150 were the norm.

This formation was not involved at Quatre-Bras and consequently went into action at full strength. Wellington posted them in the second line some 200 metres behind the right centre, to the right rear of Kielmannsegge's Hanoverians. It was an important position as there were no infantry behind in support. Until 3.00 p.m. these troops wore white covers over their shakos, which they removed when their commander considered that they provided too easy an aiming mark for French guns. Throughout the afternoon the battalions formed squares to receive a seemingly endless battering from wave after wave of cavalry, interspersed with far more effective cannon and skirmisher fire. For young men with only a few weeks in the army it was an appalling introduction to war. A witness saw a cannonball remove a Nassau officer from his horse so swiftly, so cleanly, that the animal never stirred. On several occasions they were on the point of disintegrating but responded well to the efforts of officers to rally them.

Major-General Constant-Rebecque, chief of staff to the Prince of Orange, later recounted:

> I was often obliged to go to rally the three squares of the Nassau contingent, which were composed of young troops seeing action for the first time, and were often yielding ground. Several times I brought them back at a charge. At one moment, one of these battalions was totally routed by some explosions in the midst of its packed ranks. But by throwing myself in front of them, I succeeded in halting and bringing them back.

In the late afternoon the Flanquer Company of the 2/1 (about 150 men) was rushed to reinforce the over-stretched garrison in La Haie Sainte. Its commander, Captain von Weiterhausen, died on the way. In all some 643 all ranks, of which a high proportion (40 per cent) were killed, became casualties in this regiment.

2nd Netherlands Brigade – Major-General Prince Bernard of Saxe-Weimar

2nd Nassau Regiment – Major F. Sattler *

1/2 Nassau
2/2 Nassau
3/2 Nassau

* The original commander of this regiment was Colonel von Goedecke who was badly injured when kicked by a horse before the campaign got under way. Major Sattler, the commanding officer of 1/2 Nassau, was given the acting appointment and his senior company commander, Captain Büsgen, took over the battalion – and ended up doing a fine job commanding it in Hougoumont.

28th Orange-Nassau Regiment – Colonel, the Duke of Saxe-Weimar

1/28 Orange-Nassau
2/28 Orange-Nassau
One Nassau Volunteer Jaeger Company

It was Saxe-Weimar's battalions that had been south of the vital crossroads at Quatre-Bras late on 15 June when Ney's cavalry advance guard came clattering up the road from Charleroi. It was the Nassauers of his brigade that initially held the French the next day. Had it not been for these battalions Ney would have marched unopposed to Quatre-Bras, thus severing the only direct road link between Wellington and Blücher. For much of the day the Nassauers fought to hold Bois de Bossu on Wellington's right, until eventually they were forced back. In the early evening a Guards' counterattack retook the wood. It was among the trees and undergrowth that the 1/2 Nassau first exchanged shots with Prince Jérôme's infantry. Two days later they would contest another wood south of Hougoumont with exactly the same enemy.

Numerically, Saxe-Weimar commanded the largest brigade in the army at Waterloo, but it was an extraordinarily scattered one that gave him insurmountable control problems. Early on 18 June he was instructed to detach Captain Büsgen with the 1/2 Nassau to help defend the Hougoumont complex of buildings, gardens, woods and orchards. Büsgen joined the Guards' light companies and two companies of Hanoverian sharpshooters. In consultation with the Guards' commanding officer, Captain and Lieutenant-Colonel Mitchell, he deployed his grenadier company in the château buildings, three companies in the garden and two along the southern edge of the wood – one wonders if language was a problem. His brigade commander was nearly 3000 metres away on the other side of the battlefield. Büsgen, who had started the campaign as a company commander, found himself commanding a battalion, cut off

from his own headquarters and endeavouring to co-operate with non-German speaking troops. This battalion acquitted itself well, and remained in and around Hougoumont for the duration of the battle.

On the Anglo-Allied eastern flank the remainder of the 2nd Netherlands Brigade was deployed over a shallow, concave arc that stretched for almost 1000 metres from Papelotte, through La Haie and Smohain village, to the Château of Frichermont. The four companies of the 1/28 Orange-Nassau around Frichermont were far closer to Napoleon's right flank than to Wellington's left. This battalion had its other two companies in Smohain along with troops from their sister battalion, the 2/28 Orange-Nassau, who were strung out westwards from the village to La Haie. The Light Company of the 3/2 Nassau occupied Papelotte. In reserve, 500 metres up the slope to the north-west, were the 2/2 and 3/2 Nassau.

While the action on this flank lacked the ferocity of that on the other side of the battlefield, the Nassauers were continuously engaged with the skirmishers and infantry from the French 4th Division (Durutte). The French got into Smohain and the outbuildings around La Haie and Papelotte from time to time, but reinforcements from the two Nassau battalions in reserve kept them at bay. In the early evening Prussians from Bülow's 15th Brigade pushed up from the south and the Allies finally affected a junction – although not without some mistaken identities and a resultant 'friendly fire' incident.

The total Nassau casualties in the 2nd Netherlands Brigade are estimated at 636 all ranks, or 14 per cent. Interestingly, it was the 1/28 Orange-Nassau defending Frichermont that suffered the least, only losing about sixty men (of whom twenty were missing). The French had never made a serious effort to take it, and the arrival in the vicinity of the Prussians in late afternoon put an end to any slight interest they had in the area.

Netherlands (Maps 8, 11 & 12, pp. 119, 157 & 158)

The Army of the Kingdom of the Netherlands was an uneasy mixture of Dutch, Belgian and Nassau contingents (see above for details of the Nassau units). The mixture was uneasy because the Protestant northerners (Dutch) and the Catholic southerners (Belgians), who mostly spoke French, had only recently been united as a kingdom after some 200 years of separation. It was not a popular marriage. For virtually the entire period of the Revolutionary and Napoleonic Wars both states had been controlled by France. In 1806 the Kingdom of Holland (Northern Netherlands) was created, with Napoleon's brother Louis as monarch until his resignation four years later. Holland was then completely absorbed into France until after Napoleon's defeat at the Battle of Leipzig in 1813. Almost exactly twelve months before Waterloo, the Treaty of London created the new Kingdom of the Netherlands under William VI – he took the title King William I of the Netherlands just three months before the battle.

The Belgians were particularly disgruntled by the new arrangements as they had anticipated independence. Furthermore, many Belgians had been fighting for the French only a year before, making their loyalty to their new army and country somewhat suspect. Two out of the three Netherlands divisional commanders (Chassé and Collaert) plus all three of the cavalry brigade commanders had fought for France. Indeed, even at musket range or through the smoke most Dutch or Belgian units looked confusingly similar to the French, as they all (except the Jaegers in green) wore blue jackets. The Dutch were doubly difficult to recognize as they also had the typically French 'bell-topped' shako; its distinctive silhouette (or lack of it) had been the one sure way of identifying friend from foe at a distance throughout the Peninsular War.

Wellington had a total of seventeen Netherlands battalions at Waterloo (thirteen Dutch and four Belgian), which made up about 15 per cent of his infantry. The men were largely raw recruits with little training and no experience. Many were reluctant soldiers, some (particularly amongst the Belgians) still with pro-French sentiments. They were divided into three Jaeger (one for each brigade at Waterloo), five line and nine militia units (all Dutch). They were theoretically organized into regiments, but in practice they all fielded single battalions. The battalions fought in two rank lines, carried a Colour (although not an individual regimental one) and all types, including the Jaegers, were armed with muskets – another similarity to their enemy. Each battalion had a headquarter staff of fourteen plus six companies: four fusilier, one 'heavy' (grenadier) and one light. With a full establishment each company would have three officers and 126 other ranks. Among the latter were one sergeant-major, four sergeants, one fourrier (clerk/supply NCO), eight corporals, two drummers, one fifer and one sapper. Therefore a battalion at full strength would have some 788 all ranks. As with most other nationalities, no unit mustered a full establishment at Waterloo. Netherlands units were grouped, deployed and used as follows:

2nd Netherlands Infantry Division – Lieutenant-General Baron Perponcher-Sedlnitzky

1st Brigade – Major-General Graf van Bijlandt

> 27th Dutch Jaeger
> 7th Belgian Line
> 5th Dutch Militia
> 7th Dutch Militia
> 8th Dutch Militia

Numerically, with only just over 2,700 infantrymen, this formation was the weakest Netherlands brigade in the Anglo-Allied force after taking serious casualties at Quatre-Bras. The average battalion had around 540 all ranks, the largest being the 7th Belgian Line with 700, the weakest the 5th Dutch Militia with only 220. This militia unit had fought hard at Quatre-Bras, taking Gemioncourt Farm twice, before being driven back after losing over 50 per cent of its numbers. The 27th Jaeger formed a skirmish line along the Gemioncourt Brook while the 5th Militia, supported by the 8th, defended the farm against attacks from Foy, who was unable to take Gemioncourt until reinforced by Jérôme. Although driven back into the Bois de Bossu with heavy losses, these troops generally performed well at Quatre-Bras; the 27th Jaeger lost over 260 – a third of its original strength.

'Friendly fire'

Soldiers have accidentally shot and killed members of their own side since armies first went to war. Only in recent times have incidents received much comment or publicity. When, in the Gulf War for example, casualties inflicted by the enemy were so few, the handful of 'friendly fire' deaths took on a significance they would never have merited otherwise. The modern American military are probably the worst offenders (even discounting the 1000 or so instances of deliberate killing or wounding of their own officers and NCOs in Vietnam, known as 'fragging').

Discounting deliberate 'friendly fire', the problem is basically one of failure to recognize friend from foe. At Waterloo mistakes were made when, in the confusion and drifting smoke, troops suddenly appeared in uniforms of a similar colour or design to those of the enemy. Quick decisions had to be made and when, of necessity, adopting the old adage of 'shoot first and ask questions later', errors occurred. It is a fallacy to think that the Anglo-Allied Army wore red jackets and the French blue. In Wellington's force, for example, British infantry wore red, the artillery dark blue, the light cavalry dark blue, the Nassauers green and the Brunswickers black. The Duke himself said: 'at a distance or in action colours are nothing: the profile and the shape of the man's cap, and his general appearance are what guide us.' The Dutch and Belgian battalions were at the greatest risk of being shot at by their own side, as some were wearing virtually the same uniforms they had used when fighting for the French. Many wore the typical 'bell-topped' shako instead of the straight 'Belgic' ones worn by the rest of the army. The same was true of some of their cavalry regiments, such as the 5th Belgian Light Dragoons whose men wore exactly the same green jackets with yellow facings as the French châsseurs. The overall statistics of uniform colours in Wellington's force are of interest. Approximately 47 per cent wore red jackets, 31 per cent blue, 14 per cent green and 8 per cent black – the majority therefore being in uniforms other than red.

Chassé's two brigades of Netherlands troops were, for a time, mistaken for a French force that had outflanked the Duke's position on the right. Captain Mercer RHA described their sudden appearance:

Suddenly loud and repeated shouts, not English hurrahs, drew our attention. There we saw two dense columns of infantry pushing forward at a quick pace towards us. Crossing the fields, as if they had come from Merke [sic] Braine, everyone pronounced them French, yet still we lingered opening fire on them. Shouting, yelling and singing, on they came right for us, and being now not above 800 or 1,000 yards distant, it seemed a folly allowing them to come nearer unmolested. The commanding officer of the 14th [Major Tidy], to end our doubts, rode forward, and endeavoured to ascertain who they were, but soon returned assuring us they were French. The order was already being given to fire, when luckily Colonel Gould R.A., [sic, Lieutenant-Colonel Gold commanding the divisional artillery] who was standing near me recognised them as Belgians.

The most reliable way of identifying British cavalry at a distance was by looking at the horses' tails. If the tails had been cut short (docked) they were British. The only exceptions were the Life Guards and Royal Horse Guards. Lieutenant-Colonel Sir Henry Hardinge, the British liaison officer at Blücher's headquarters, recognized Wellington and his entourage when the Duke briefly visited the Ligny battlefield by this method. He afterwards told Wellington, 'I saw you, Sir, in the distance as horsemen, and I thought you must be English by the cut tails…'.

At Waterloo there were several instances of 'friendly fire'. One example was when the Prussians started a firefight with the Nassauers near Papelotte. The incident happened as two battalions of the Prussian 18th Regiment from Bülow's IV Corps were moving north to link up with Wellington's left flank. As they approached Papelotte in the close 'bocage' country of sunken lanes and thick hedges they opened fire on Captain von Rettberg's Light Company of the 3/2 Nassau. Rettberg returned fire and counterattacked vigorously before realizing his assailants were Prussians. A number of casualties were inflicted on both sides during this clash that lasted about ten minutes.

There is some controversy over the deployment and conduct of this brigade at Waterloo, which is discussed in detail in Section 10 'Myths and Controversies'. Suffice it to say here that their performance was not as black as has been painted. The brigade was initially deployed in a 450-metre two rank line on the forward slope of the Mont St Jean ridge as a covering force, with its right (western) flank about 200 metres from the elm tree. The seriously weakened 5th Militia was held back in reserve on the ridge. The brigade was later (about noon) withdrawn to line the road and hedge along the crest and was there heavily, if briefly, engaged in a firefight with Donzelot's advancing division. The 7th and 8th Militia retired in some haste and confusion behind the 5th Militia. After reforming (with the help of the Netherlands chief of staff, Constant-Rebecque) they remained in square, out of the action, for the remainder of the day. The 7th Line, however, mostly held its ground and a month later was publicly complimented by the Duke for its conduct that day.

In the course of the fighting at Quatre-Bras this brigade suffered about 890 casualties, many of them missing (possibly prisoners, possibly deserters). It lost over 500 more at Waterloo. In total, during the two battles the brigade lost more than 1,400 all ranks, or 43 per cent of its original strength – sufficient to demoralize many formations. The worst hit was the 5th Dutch Militia who had a particularly bloody initiation to combat, losing 65 per cent of their strength in two days of fighting.

3rd Netherlands Division – Lieutenant-General Baron David-Hendrik Chassé ('General Bayonet')

1st Brigade – Colonel H. Detmers

  35th Belgian Jaeger
  2nd Dutch Line
  4th Dutch Militia
  6th Dutch Militia
  17th Dutch Militia
  19th Dutch Militia

Another strong brigade with over 3000 infantrymen in six battalions, although all six battalions were comparatively weak with an average strength of only 500 all ranks. Two of the battalions, the 2nd Dutch Line and 19th Dutch Militia, could scarcely muster 470 apiece. This brigade was part of the only entirely Dutch-Belgian division in the Anglo-Allied Army. Of its six battalions only the Jaegers were Belgian and four out of the five Dutch battalions were militia units. Wellington had not been permitted to stiffen this division with more experienced troops and, because their reliability was untested (they had not fought at Quatre-Bras), the Duke positioned them well away to the west, virtually off the battlefield around the village of Braine l'Alleud. The 1st Brigade was grouped to the north and north-east of the village.

The brigade had a dull day initially, remaining out of harm's way until around 3.00 p.m. when the whole division was moved through Merbe Braine, out of sight of the French, to approximately the position occupied by Adam's brigade at 11.30 that morning. During this approach to the battlefield they were almost fired on by British units and artillery; their blue uniforms and bell-topped shakos appearing behind the Anglo-Allied line from the extreme right caused considerable, if short-lived, consternation. They remained in their new position for some four hours, often in square as French cavalry passing through the Allied line reached

their vicinity. In the late evening they advanced to play a role in repelling the final attack of the Imperial Guard.

After the loss of La Haie Sainte Wellington reinforced his thinning centre, pushing forward the Brunswickers and bringing Chassé's Netherlands division closer behind the right centre, east of the Nivelles road. As part of the action to defeat the Imperial Guard as it reached the ridge, Detmers' Brigade was launched in column against the 1/3 Grenadiers à Pied. According to an officer in the nearby 2/30 they dashed into the fray cheering, 'Long live the House of Orange! Long live the king!' (the Belgian Jaegers would be unlikely to have joined in). The officer described what he saw: 'a heavy column of Dutch infantry (the first we had seen) passed, drumming and shouting like mad, with their shakos on the top of their bayonets, near enough to our right for us to see and laugh at them.' Funny or not, the charge was a success and the Grenadiers recoiled in disorder (although it has been suggested that the Guard was already on the run). In his dispatch the Duke later wrote that General Vanhope (sic, General Detmers) 'conducted himself much to my satisfaction' – the same phrase he used to describe Major-General Trip's dubious contribution.

The cost of their moment of glory was an overall loss of 400, or 13 per cent of the brigade.

2nd Brigade – Major-General A.K.J.G. d'Aubreme

  36th Belgian Jaeger
  3rd Belgian Line
  12th Dutch Line
  13th Dutch Line
  3rd Dutch Militia
  10th Dutch Militia

This brigade was the strongest of the three Dutch-Belgian brigades at Waterloo, with almost 3,600 infantry. This meant the average strength of the six battalions was a respectable 600, although the 12th Dutch Line with only 430 was hardly viable. It was more of a mixture than the other two brigades, having two Belgian battalions (one of whom was a Jaeger unit), two Dutch line and two militia battalions. The brigade was initially deployed south-west of Braine l'Alleud, well away from the action – although had Napoleon tried to move round Wellington's right flank as he feared he might, this brigade would have borne the brunt of the first clash.

The brigade followed the 1st Brigade when moving across via Merbe Braine during the early afternoon to a position behind the right centre. It was still in this position, formed into three large squares of two battalions each, approximately in rear of Maitland's Guards brigade, when the Imperial Guard launched their assault. They could see nothing of the French but could hear the drumming and yells of 'Vive l'Empereur!' This was enough to unnerve them. There was considerable useless firing off of muskets into the air and, to Vandeleur's cavalry brigade drawn up behind, it seemed they were about to break. Several of Vandeleur's officers rode forward to restore confidence, including the brigade major (Major Childers). Partly through exhortations and threats, partly due to the exertions of their own officers and helped by the Duke himself riding up and saying, 'Tell them the French are retiring', these battalions recovered their composure.

The cost of standing in square for about four hours under intermittent artillery fire was a loss of 284 all ranks, or 8 per cent.

FRENCH INFANTRY

General

'Good infantry is, without doubt, the sinew of an army.' An extract from one of Napoleon's many maxims, and, coming from an artilleryman, an interesting acknowledgement that in the end it is the quality of the foot soldier that usually decides the issue. If, as was the case at Waterloo, the French wanted to seize an objective (the Mont St Jean crossroads), needed to unblock the road to Brussels, it could only be done with infantry attacking, infantry closing with, and destroying the enemy and, finally, infantry occupying ground. Of course, cavalry and guns, particularly the latter, must co-operate and support; but if the Emperor were to march into the Belgian capital it would be his infantry that would get him there.

Captain Jean-Roch Coignet, whom the Emperor had recently appointed as his wagon-master at his headquarters, typified the very best of the French infantry at Waterloo. Coignet was then thirty-eight years old, having served for sixteen continuous years as an infantryman in the Imperial Guard. He joined the army at twenty-three and subsequently fought in every major campaign during Napoleon's reign as First Consul and Emperor: Italy 1800, Austria 1805, Prussia 1806–7, Spain 1808, Austria 1809, Russia 1812, Germany 1813 and France 1814. He fought in thirty-two battles and fourteen other separate actions. He was totally uneducated. As he himself frankly admitted, 'At thirty-three years of age I did not know A from B'. However, he was a holder of the Legion of Honour and had worked his way up through the ranks to corporal, then sergeant, before learning to read and finally being given a battlefield commission as a lieutenant during the Russian campaign. Such was his courage, toughness and experience as an infantryman that his first appointment as an officer on the Emperor's staff was the temporary command of a battalion. Coignet survived Ligny and Waterloo and finished writing his remarkable autobiography at the age of seventy-four in 1850.

Despite the frantic scramble to create a field army in three months, the end product was, overall, a first rate fighting formation. There were weaknesses in the loyalty and competence of the senior officer corps, and march discipline was often poor. The Imperial Guard still creamed off the best but on the battlefield Napoleon had a virtually homogeneous force whose experience of war was unrivalled. It certainly exceeded that of his enemy. Most of the Emperor's soldiers at Waterloo had been serving in the Royalist Army only a few months previously, and before that had spent years under the Imperial Eagles marching and fighting backwards and forwards across Europe. The French Army, like the Anglo-Allied force opposite, may have been wet, dirty, hungry and tired that Sunday morning but many of its soldiers were seasoned campaigners, while most had at least defended France in 1813–14. Virtually all were imbued with considerable faith in, and devotion to, their commander-in-chief. Among the 53,000 infantry assembling for battle were thousands of officers, NCOs and men with similar service to Captain Coignet.

The French infantry were required to attack. They would have to advance under fire, increasing their exposure and vulnerability as they did so, and therefore were likely to suffer more losses than their enemy behind the ridge. The demands on their courage, determination and steadiness would be severely tested. And so it was. Virtually every regiment, every battalion (except Major Duuring's 1/1 Châsseurs à Pied of the Imperial Guard on guard duty at Le Caillou) felt the full weight of enemy musketry and cannon fire at some time during the battle. Of the 103 battalions committed to the action, only the fifteen in Lobau's two divisions had a primarily defensive role – that of halting the approaching Prussians. Even the Young Guard in Plancenoit, and the two battalions of the Old Guard later sent to reinforce them, were sent in initially to attack. Surviving French infantrymen told tales to

---

Napoleon's Wagon-Master at Waterloo

Captain Jean-Roch Coignet is a fascinating example of how a totally uneducated boy who ran away from a brutal home could make good in Napoleon's army. His story is far from unique, as the great majority of French officers, including general officers, had served as soldiers and NCOs, at least in their early careers – the Revolution had seen to that. Marshals Soult and Ney had been both corporals and sergeants (Ney had also been a sergeant-major) before being commissioned.

Coignet's road to success was rough and violent. His family life before he ran away is best described in his own words:

Here is my father's portrait: he was good-natured, sober, and liked nothing so much as shooting, fishing and law-suits; and girls and women of all classes succumbed to his charms. Apart from his three wives [who bore him thirteen children], he was the recognised sire of twenty-eight boys and four girls ... Enough for any man in my opinion. His second wife ... was my mother; the third was our servant. She was eighteen years old and known as The Beauty; consequently she was with child in a fortnight ... As you may suppose this stepmother ruled everything. We poor little orphans were beaten night and day. She choked us to give us a good colour.

Years later, in Russia, his Emperor made him a lieutenant.

On the 13th July he [Napoleon] issued an order for twenty-two non-commissioned officers to be sent to him for promotion to lieutenancy's in the line. We had to be on the square at two o'clock to be presented to the Emperor. ... At two o'clock the Emperor came to review us ... looking every one of these fine looking NCOs all over from head to foot, he said to General Dorsenne, 'These will make fine regimental officers.' When he came to me, he saw that I was the smallest of them all, and the major said to him, 'This is our instructor; he does not wish to go into the line.' – 'What! You do not wish to go into the line?' – 'No Sire; I wish to remain in your Guard.' – 'Very well, I will appoint you to my minor staff.' Then turning to his chief-of-staff, Count Monthion [wounded at Waterloo], he said, 'Take this little "grouser" and let him be attached to the minor general staff.'

The French infantryman's personal equipment

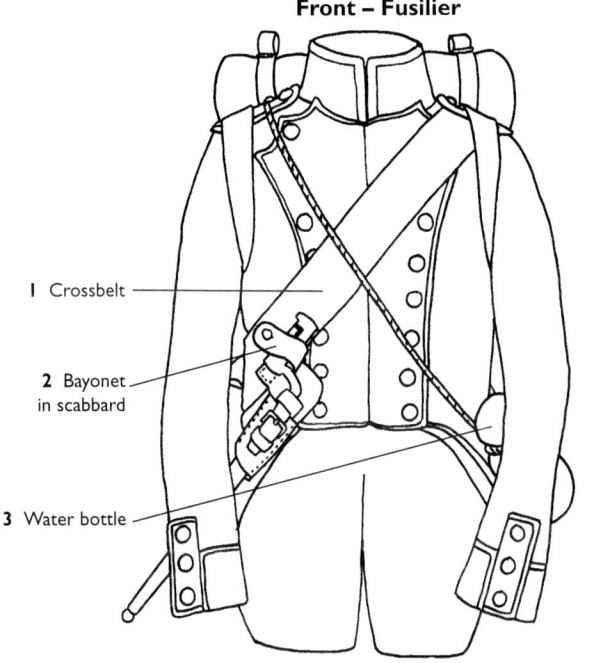

Front – Fusilier

1 Crossbelt

2 Bayonet in scabbard

3 Water bottle

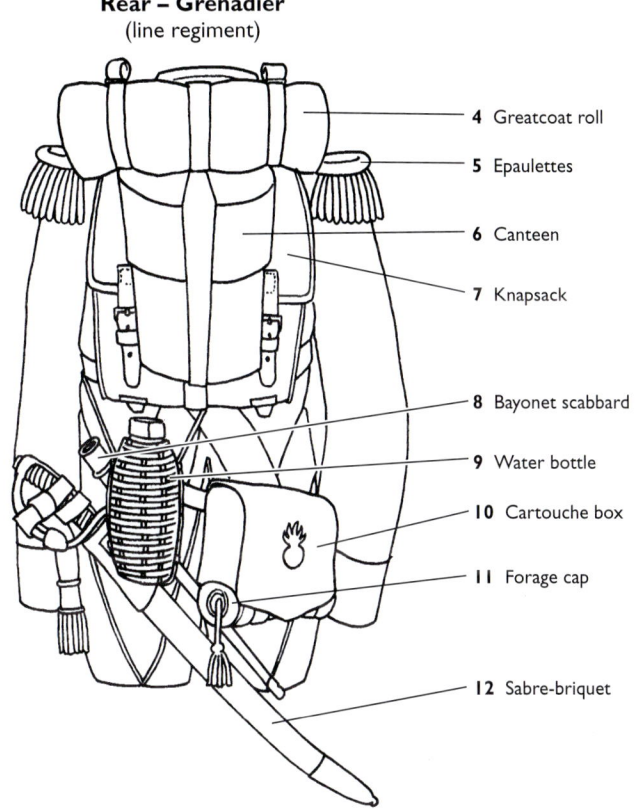

Rear – Grenadier
(line regiment)

4 Greatcoat roll

5 Epaulettes

6 Canteen

7 Knapsack

8 Bayonet scabbard

9 Water bottle

10 Cartouche box

11 Forage cap

12 Sabre-briquet

Notes

1 A single crossbelt slung over the left shoulder to which was attached the bayonet frog at the front. At the rear on the right (not visible in the diagram) was the cartouche box attached to the crossbelt. Note the French fusilier was far less restricted across his chest than his British counterpart.
2 At Waterloo the soldiers in the fusilier companies of the line regiments only had bayonets as side arms – no swords.
3 The French were not issued with water bottles, although they were obviously essential items. Instead the soldier improvised and carried gourds, barrels, metal flasks or glass bottles covered with wickerwork.
4 Almost all paintings of the French infantry attacking at Waterloo show the

soldiers with their knapsacks on but no greatcoat/blanket roll on top. A sodden greatcoat was likely to have been abandoned for weight reasons by troops about to attack but it is uncertain where they were left.
5 The epaulettes signify a soldier in the Grenadier Company.
6 The French canteen or soup plate was larger than the British one and, like the knapsack to which it was strapped, never left the soldier's possession.
7 The cowhide knapsack, with the hair on the outside, was comfortable to wear and even when attacking the troops kept them on. They contained a lot of essential personal items from which the soldier had no desire to be separated. Unless it was properly organized by the staff, to leave knapsacks behind meant certain loss.

8 The bayonet scabbard and sword were both held in the same special frog.
9 The water bottle hung behind the left hip rather than the right to avoid obstructing the opening of the cartouche box.
10 The cartouche box held 35 made-up cartridges, stowed ball-end up, in separate compartments plus a small tin flask of oil. Under the flap was an outside pocket for cleaning kit, spare flints and a piece of greasy cloth. The 'picker' was sometimes kept here or on a light chain from a buttonhole.
11 The French alternative headgear to the shako was a soft, floppy forage cap. This was kept rolled up and strapped underneath the cartouche box.
12 All grenadiers carried the short sabre-briquet (sword) in addition to their musket and bayonet.

their sons and grandsons of struggling forward through wet rye in the teeth of furious fire, trying to get at an enemy they could seldom see, and losing fearfully in the process. Many also recounted the deadly close-quarter, house to house fighting around the church in Plancenoit, the struggle in the apple orchards and at the garden wall at Hougoumont, or capturing the farm of La Haie Sainte.

ORGANIZATION

Infantry Divisions

Napoleon had twelve infantry divisions (the Young, Middle, and Old Guard counting as one each) in the field at Waterloo, com-

pared with the Anglo-Allied equivalent of eight and a half. However, their average strength in combat infantrymen of just under 4,500 was substantially less than the Duke's with over 6000. This is a reminder that overall total numbers of combat infantry available to Napoleon and Wellington on the battlefield were virtually equal – 53,400 to 53,850. Jeanin's 20th Infantry Division with just over 3000 was the weakest. The strongest, with well over double that number, was the 6th Infantry Division under the Emperor's brother, Prince Jérôme, which had almost 7,700 in no less than thirteen battalions. It was the second largest division on the battlefield, but only by a few hundred – the largest being the 3rd British Infantry Division (Alten).

The divisions, discounting attached headquarter staff, gunners and administrative personnel, had approximate strengths as follows:

1st Infantry Division – 3,992,
Acting GOC Maréchal de Camp Quiot du Passage
2nd Infantry Division – 5,077,
GOC Général de Division Baron Donzelot
3rd Infantry Division – 4,002,
GOC Général de Division Baron Marcognet
4th Infantry Division – 3,860,
GOC Général de Division Comte Durutte
5th Infantry Division – 3,986,
GOC Général de Division Baron Bachelu
6th Infantry Division – 7,677,
GOC Général de Division Prince Jérôme Bonaparte
9th Infantry Division – 5,176,
GOC Général de Division Comte Foy
19th Infantry Division – 3,878,
GOC Général de Division Baron Simmer
20th Infantry Division – 3,052,
GOC Général de Division Baron Jeanin
The Young Guard – 4,283,
GOC Général de Division Comte Duhesme
The Middle Guard – 3,587,
GOC Général de Division Comte Morand
The Old Guard – 4,840,
GOC Général de Division Comte Friant

Almost every division was fully engaged at some stage during the battle. All except the Imperial Guard were in action with little respite throughout most of the day. Jérôme and Foy were sucked into the endless attempts to take Hougoumont. Quiot, Donzelot, Marcognet and Durutte, after their initial assault on Wellington's left, were forever trying to renew the attack and take La Haie Sainte, while Simmer and Jeanin spent four or five hours trying to delay the arrival of the Prussians from the east. As was usual with the Imperial Guard reserve, it was committed late in the battle. At Waterloo it was used piecemeal to plug holes, prevent disaster, as a last desperate throw to snatch victory, or to form a rearguard to cover retreat. The Young Guard was sent to retake Plancenoit; then two battalions of the Old Guard were doubled over to help them. Next the Middle Guard attempted to storm the Anglo-Allied centre and right, and finally the remainder of the Old Guard covered the rout.

One French infantry divisional commander was killed, or rather mortally wounded (Duhesme), and six wounded (Durutte, Friant, Foy, Jérôme, Bachelu and Simmer). The difficulties in estimating the French losses at Waterloo have already been discussed. It is impossible to give battlefield losses for each division. All that can be said is that when the divisions mustered for the last time on 26 June they were shadows of their former selves. The average infantry division loss for the period 18–26 June was 62 per cent, with the heaviest losses (72 per cent) being borne by the four divisions of I Corps (d'Erlon) and the least (47 per cent) by the two in VI Corps (Lobau).

Infantry Brigades

The French had two brigades in almost every division, including the Young Guard Division. The exceptions were the Middle and Old Guard Divisions, which cut out the brigade level from the chain of command, each division having four regiments directly under the divisional commander. Discounting these two divisions the average

Breaches of Discipline

The ordinary French soldier who joined the Emperor's cause again in 1815 was usually passionately keen to demonstrate his loyalty, but often used this enthusiasm as an excuse for poor discipline. It was not uncommon for a regiment on parade to demand the dismissal of their colonel, or to publicly complain over the promotion of officers. The 105th Ligne on its march to the frontier demolished a newly built house because it had been decorated with the royalist fleur-de-lis. Its owner had to be jailed to placate the soldiers. Civilians were expected to cheer the Marseillaise and shout *'Vive l'Empereur!'* with enthusiasm. If they did not they were lucky to escape a beating.

But it was in Belgium that looting really got out of hand. On the day before Waterloo the officer responsible for march discipline, Général de Division Radet, wrote angrily to Soult, 'Marauding and pillage are rampant in the Army now, the Guard itself sets the example. Forage magazines have been plundered, horses have been stolen. Plunder has been going on all night in the homes of Belgians who gave us everything willingly and nursed our wounded. The men flatly defy the authority of the gendarmerie. I beg to tender my resignation as Provost-Marshal of the Army.' He nevertheless remained to fight at Waterloo.

strength of a French brigade at Waterloo was 2,270, and was normally commanded by a maréchal de camp. The strongest by far, with numbers exceeding several divisions, was the 1st Brigade of Jérôme's 6th Division under Maréchal de Camp Baudin, with 4,146 all ranks. This brigade opened the battle of Waterloo by spearheading the assault on Hougoumont. The weakest, under Maréchal de Camp Tromelin, was the 2nd Brigade of Jeanin's 20th Division. This formation had a mere 735 all ranks due to the 47th Regiment (half its establishment) being detached in the Vendée. Two brigade commanders were killed (Aulard and Bauduin) and four wounded (Bourgeois, Campi, Guye and Nogues).

Infantry Regiments

As with other nations, the French supposedly numbered their regiments consecutively from the date of formation. The lower the number, the older the regiment and the more senior it was. Nevertheless, in the course of frequent reshuffling, reorganizing and reinforcing constantly necessary as a result of casualties and the changing strategic situation, gaps occurred in the numbering. Some numbers became 'vacant' but were left on the official order of battle – partly to confuse the enemy intelligence as to army strengths.

Excluding the Imperial Guard, the French infantry at Waterloo was divided into regiments d'infanterie de ligne (line infantry) and regiments d'infanterie légère (light infantry). After the First Restoration in 1814 the size of the regular army had been drastically cut back, with the line losing sixty-six regiments and the light being reduced from thirty-seven to fifteen. Both types of regiment were renumbered, the line from one to ninety, the light from one to fifteen. Cutting each regiment to an establishment of only two battalions made further reductions. However, with the return of Napoleon from Elba there was time for a partial revision of the system. Most regiments were rightly proud of their achievements under the Empire; veterans were loyal to their former regiment and its old number under which they had fought for so long. The new royalist numbers meant nothing. Napoleon allowed the regiments to assume their old numbers, and the theoretical establishment was raised to five battalions, the fifth being a depot and training unit.

However, only one Eagle was given to each regiment, to be carried by the 1st Battalion on behalf of the entire regiment.

Although skirmishing tactics had always played a crucial part of French tactics, and this was certainly the case at Waterloo, it was not the sole prerogative of the light infantry regiments. Each line battalion had its voltigeur company but it was not uncommon for the whole battalion to be committed to the skirmish line. In practice it was only minor differences in uniform rather than duties or weapons that differentiated the line regiment from the light regiment. An example at Waterloo was how the great majority of the 1st and 2nd Légère Regiments (with seven battalions) were used in a traditional infantry role in the attack on Hougoumont. Of course, the French light infantryman regarded himself as a superior being to his line comrade but with the things that mattered – weapons, training, morale and leadership – the differences were negligible.

Unlike the British, French infantry regiments were tactical units, normally commanded by a full colonel. The exceptions were the regiments of Grenadiers and Châsseurs of the Old and Middle Guard whose commanding officers were maréchaux de camp (see separate section on the Imperial Guard below). Forty-seven regiments took the field at Waterloo of which twelve were Guard, thirty were Line and five were Light. Their average strength was around 1,150 all ranks, the strongest being the 2nd Légère with 2,294 and the weakest the 85th Ligne with 631. Every regiment had its own headquarters staff that included, among others, an adjutant, quartermaster, surgeon and band. The number of battalions in a regiment varied from two (the great majority) to four (only one). The regiments present at Waterloo (excluding the Imperial Guard) are listed below under their divisions. The first figure in brackets is the approximate all rank strength at the start of the battle, while the second is the number of battalions. This is followed by the name of the commanding officer and, to illustrate its experience of war, a few of the major battles in which it fought prior to 18 June 1815.

LINE REGIMENTS
1st Division
28th (898; 2) Chef de Bataillon Senac – Austerlitz, Eylau, Talavera.
54th (962; 2) Colonel Charlet (acting brigade commander) – Austerlitz, Friedland, Talavera.
55th (1,149; 2) Colonel Morin – Austerlitz, Jena, Eylau, Albuera, Berezina, Dresden, Vitoria.
105th (983; 2) Colonel Gentry (wounded) – Jena, Eylau, Essling, Wagram, Bidassoa. Lost its Eagle at Waterloo.

2nd Division
17th (1,002; 2) Colonel Guerel – Austerlitz, Eylau, Wagram, Moscow, Dresden.
19th (1,032; 2) Colonel Trupel – Danzig, Wagram, Auerstaedt, Eylau, Wagram, Moscow.
51st (1,168; 2) Colonel Baron Rignon (killed) – Austerlitz, Eylau, Friedland, Talavera, Vitoria, Dresden.

3rd Division
21st (1,137; 2) Colonel Baron Carré (wounded) – Auerstaedt, Eylau, Wagram, Moscow, Dresden.
25th (974; 2) Colonel Galté – Austerlitz, Eylau, Wagram, Moscow, Dresden.
45th (1,003; 2) Colonel Chapuset – Austerlitz, Friedland, Talavera, Dresden. Lost its Eagle at Waterloo.

46th (888; 2) Colonel Dupré – Ulm, Austerlitz, Jena, Eylau, Wagram, Moscow, Leipzig, Hanau, La Rothière.

4th Division
8th (983; 2) Colonel Ruelle – Austerlitz, Friedland, Talavera, Vitoria, Wagram.
29th (1,146; 2) Colonel Rousselot – Wagram (where it lost seventy officers and 75 per cent of its men), Danzig.
85th (631; 2, numerically the weakest in the army) Colonel Masson – Auerstaedt, Eylau, Wagram, Moscow, Dresden, Laon.
95th (1,100; 2) Colonel Garnier – Austerlitz, Friedland, Wagram, Medellin (Spain), Ligny.

5th Division
3rd (1,114; 2) Colonel Baron Vautrin (wounded) – Austerlitz, Friedland, Wagram, Quatre-Bras.
61st (830; 2) Colonel Bouge – Austerlitz, Eylau, Wagram, Moscow, Quatre-Bras.
72nd (970; 2) Colonel Thibault (wounded) – Friedland, Wagram, Moscow, Leipzig, Laon, Quatre-Bras.
108th (1,072; 3) Colonel Higonet (wounded) – this regiment was originally raised as the Regiment de l'Isle de France (Mauritius) in 1772. Austerlitz, Eylau, Moscow, Berezina, Ligny.

6th Division
1st (1,766; 3) Colonel Cornebise – Wagram, Salamanca, Dresden, Leipzig, Laon, Paris, Quatre-Bras.
2nd (1,765; 3) Colonel Trippe – Trafalgar (naval duty) it is quite possible this regiment had a few NCOs and men who fought as marines at Trafalgar and soldiers at Waterloo – an experience shared with the 93rd and the 22nd, 34th and 70th Ligne serving with Grouchy. Wagram, Dresden, Leipzig, La Rothière.

9th Division
92nd (1,018; 2) Colonel Tissot (acting brigade commander) – Wagram, Moscow, Quatre-Bras.
93rd (1,461; 3) Chef de Bataillon Massot – another Trafalgar regiment. Wagram, Moscow, Berezina, Dresden, Leipzig.
100th (1,093; 3) Colonel Braun – Ulm, Austerlitz, Jena, Eylau, Friedland, Quatre-Bras.

19th Division
5th (952; 2) Colonel Roussille (killed) – Wagram.
11th (1,176; 3) Colonel Aubrée (mortally wounded) – Ulm, Wagram, Dresden, Leipzig.
27th (821; 2) Colonel Gaudin – Eylau, Friedland, Danzig, Wagram, Arapiles (Salamanca), Dresden.
84th (929; 2) Colonel Chevalier – Ulm, Austerlitz, Wagram, Moscow, Berezina.

20th Division
10th (1,431; 2) Colonel Roussel – Lutzen, Leipzig, Hanau.
107th (735; 2) Colonel Druot (wounded) – Chalon.

LIGHT REGIMENTS
2nd Division
13th (1,875; 3) Colonel Gougeon – Austerlitz, Jena, Eylau, Moscow, Berezina, Dresden.

6th Division
1st (1,852; 3) Colonel Despan-Cubières (wounded) – Lutzen, Leipzig, Paris.
2nd (2,294 – 4, making it the strongest regiment at Waterloo) Colonel Maigros (wounded) – Austerlitz, Friedland, Corunna, Arapiles (Salamanca), Vitoria, Paris.

9th Division
4th (1,604; 3) Chef de Bataillon Damamm (wounded) – Ulm, Friedland, Corunna, Arapiles (Salamanca) Vitoria, Dresden, Leipzig.

20th Division
5th (886; 2) Colonel Curnier – Wagram, Nivelle, Dresden, Leipzig.

Battalions
On paper it appears Napoleon had 104 battalions available at Waterloo: twenty-three Imperial Guard, fifteen Light and sixty-six Line. However, the actual number available on the battlefield was two less than this. Due to losses at Ligny the 1st and 2nd Battalions of the 4th Châsseurs à Pied of the Guard combined at Waterloo and fought as one. In addition, the Emperor left the 1st Battalion of the 1st Châsseurs à Pied to guard his rear headquarters, baggage and treasury chest at Le Caillou. Some sources claim that there were twenty-four battalions in the Guard. This is not correct, as the 4th Grenadiers à Pied only managed to raise one battalion for the campaign. The average strength of a French battalion at Waterloo was 520. The strongest with 841 was the combination of the 1/4 and 2/4 Châsseurs à Pied, the weakest with a mere 246 was the 3/100 Ligne, closely followed by the 3/108 Ligne with 251. Interestingly, nine battalions had less than 400 all ranks but only two Imperial Guard battalions slipped below 500.

A battalion was normally commanded by a chef de bataillon. The line and light battalions had six companies and the Imperial Guard four. In the regiments of the line one company was composed of voltigeurs (skirmishers), one of grenadiers and four of fusiliers. In the light infantry one company consisted of voltigeurs, one of carabineers (equivalent to grenadiers) and four of châsseurs. In line regiments the fusilier (i.e. 'battalion'/'centre') companies were distinguished by dark blue shoulder straps piped red, the grenadiers by red epaulettes and the voltigeurs by epaulettes of various combinations of green and yellow. Light infantry generally wore all blue uniforms with white metal buttons (the line had brass), green epaulettes for châsseur companies, red for carabineers and yellow for voltigeurs. Officers had silver lace to distinguish them from the line regiments with gold. Regiments had their own minor differences and combinations. With the exception of the Grenadiers and Châsseurs of the Imperial Guard, the headdress of the French infantry was the conveniently recognizable bell-topped shako. However, due to uniform shortages many battalions had varying numbers of soldiers in a motley assortment of uniforms at Waterloo, some with civilian clothes under their jackets, different coloured trousers and a wide range of military headgear.

The strength of companies varied considerably. The captain commanding could have anything from over a hundred men down to forty, with the average being eighty-five. Senior ranks within the company were one captain, one lieutenant, one sous-lieutenant, one sergeant-major and three sergeants. The company was split into two sections and, when in line on parade or in action, formed up in three ranks – making the frontage of a French unit somewhat shorter than an Anglo-Allied one of similar numbers.

In summary the main differences between the Emperor's and the Duke's battalions were that the former were more numerous, had a far higher percentage of veterans in them, but were smaller and fought in three ranks when in line or square.

French and British Infantry Ranks – A Comparison

FRENCH	BRITISH
Maréchal	**General**
Général de Division	**Lieutenant-General** or **Major-General**
Maréchal de Camp	**Brigadier** (modern) – British brigades were commanded by major-generals
Colonel – usually commanded a regiment	**Colonel** – usually on staff
Major – Guard COs or staff officers	**Lieutenant-Colonel** – usually commanded a battalion
Chef de Bataillon – commanded a battalion	**Major** – second in command of a battalion
Capitaine – company commander	**Captain** – company commander
Lieutenant – company officer	**Lieutenant** – company officer
Sous-Lieutenant – company officer	**Ensign** – company officer
Premiere Porte-Aigle – Eagle bearer, usually a lieutenant who had been promoted from NCO rank for bravery	**Ensign** carrying the Colour
Adjutant-sous-officier	**Battalion sergeant-major** – modern Regimental Sergeant Major (RSM)
Sergent-Major	**Colour-Sergeant**
Sergent	**Sergeant**
Fourrier – an administrative NCO	**Sergeant**
Caporal	**Corporal**

WEAPONS

Muskets

Virtually the entire French infantry corps carried the musket as their primary arm. Napoleon himself had ordered the recall of experimental issue rifles in 1807 as he regarded them as expensive and too slow to load. As was noted in Section 1 'The Campaign', there had been serious setbacks in the rush to supply the number of muskets required. However, at Waterloo the great majority had a version of the Year IX that had gradually replaced the original 1777 model. It was often called the 'Charleville' (not Charleroi as is sometimes suggested), which was one of the places where it was manufactured. Like every other musket on the field it was a flintlock weapon and of a similar weight, effective range, and suffered from the same loading, firing and handling problems. It had a slightly smaller calibre, which ensured it could not be used by either Wellington's or Blücher's soldiers.

The first shot fired with a musket in battle was likely to be the most accurate. This was because the barrel would be clean, the flint new and the loading drill precisely and carefully completed without undue haste. Once that shot had gone difficulties accumulated with consequent loss of effectiveness and, finally, the inability to fire at all until remedial action could be taken. The list of problems is impressive, and gives a clear insight into some of the stresses afflicting the infantryman at Waterloo – several of them more worrisome for Frenchmen in a three rank line than his enemy in two, or for skirmishers firing individually. The problems were:

• Having fired the first shot the soldier must stop to reload, or continue with an empty musket – either of which might be unhealthy.

• After the first shot loading was likely to be rushed. The stresses and fearful events of the battlefield, along with the confusion and noise induced errors. The better drilled the soldier, the less likely he was to make mistakes. Nevertheless, there can have been few infantrymen at Waterloo that did not make, or see made, one or more of the following human errors:

 ＊ Forgetting to remove the ramrod from the barrel before firing. The ramrod became as lethal as any ball but subsequent loading was problematic.
 ＊ Putting the paper cartridge down the barrel ball first. This meant the musket could not be fired as the powder was on top of the ball. The remedy was to fix what the French called a tire-ball (corkscrew) on the end of the ramrod and worry the cartridge back out – a lengthy, frustrating and unnerving experience under fire.
 ＊ Spiking your right hand (there was no such thing as a left-handed musket so everyone fired from the right shoulder) on the bayonet due to over hasty use of the ramrod.
 ＊ Forgetting the musket was already loaded and ramming a second cartridge down the barrel. The subsequent firing would inevitably be more injurious to the firer than the enemy.
 ＊ Forgetting to close the pan after pouring a small amount of powder into it prior to ramming the cartridge down the barrel. The powder in the pan would fall out or be blown out by wind and the musket would not fire.
 ＊ Forgetting to hold the butt tightly into the shoulder before firing – in which case the mule-like kick would probably knock the firer back into the rank behind.

• As firing continued so the chances of some technical problem occurring increased. The more one fired the greater the odds that something would go wrong with the next shot. Possibilities included:

 ＊ Flintlock weapons 'missed fire' on average once every nine or ten shots. Either the flint failed to spark or the priming merely 'flashed in the pan' without setting off the powder in the bottom of the barrel. Either way, no shot could be fired and the flint had to be adjusted or replaced or the musket reprimed.
 ＊ About once in every twenty shots there was a good chance of a 'hang fire'. This was caused by the powder in the barrel burning slowly and taking several seconds to explode. The danger was that it would do so just as the firer relaxed and brought the weapon down to check the cause of the failure to fire.
 ＊ After continuous firing for some time the musket barrel became extremely hot – too hot to touch – making the pouring of gunpowder down it a hazardous undertaking.
 ＊ With every shot some fouling was left in the barrel. This steadily accumulated, eventually making it impossible to ram a ball down until the barrel had been cleaned.

• Quite apart from what the enemy was doing, being involved in a firefight was a brutal and bruising experience. The noise was deafening, the smoke blinded you, every time you fired the butt slammed hard into your shoulder and particles of half-burnt powder stung your face. Biting the cartridge dried the mouth, leaving you with gritty teeth and tongue and a bitter taste. If a soldier survived a long firefight he would still be suffering from a badly bruised shoulder, partial deafness, burnt cheeks, stinging eyes, a headache and a raging thirst.

• In the worst circumstances a firer stood a chance of being accidentally shot by his comrades, particularly by those in the third rank of a line. With all the jostling and movement of reloading and firing it did not take much of a mistake by a rear rank soldier to bring down his friend in front – a 'hang fire' was especially hazardous. The situation was such that a man could literally 'get away with murder'. Possibly a few did. However, since long before Waterloo the French had realized the dangers of third rank men firing muskets. Their 1791 Regulations specified that third rank soldiers load muskets for those in front. Even this was found impractical, as no soldier likes to part with his weapon in action,

Barrels Too Hot to Handle

Continuous firing of a musket over a period of five to ten minutes rendered the barrel too hot to touch. There was then a real danger of prematurely exploding cartridges with the consequent disabling of the firer. However, waiting for the barrel to cool in the midst of battle was not without its problems, so most soldiers resorted to holding the musket by the sling for reloading and chancing a cartridge 'cooking off'. According to Captain Coignet (Napoleon's wagon-master at Waterloo) the French had more unconventional solutions. When this happened at the Battle of Marengo Coignet recorded: 'Our muskets were so hot it became impossible to load for fear of igniting the cartridges. There was nothing for it but to piss into the barrels to cool them, and then to dry them by pouring loose powder and setting it alight unrammed.' Modern soldiers have been known to adopt the first part of this technique.

Various weapons used at Waterloo

1 British pattern 1796 heavy cavalry sword
2 British India pattern musket – shortened barrel and long bayonet
3 Prussian model 1809 musket
4 French heavy cavalry sword
5 British light dragoon pistol
6 French cavalry pistol
7 British 1796 light cavalry officer's sword
8 British Baker rifle
9 French infantry musket 1777 with later modifications
10 French light cavalry sword

while the men in the front two ranks lacked confidence in muskets they had not loaded themselves. All this was largely academic at Waterloo, as the occasions during the battle when the French had to fire in line were extremely limited.

It is not often appreciated how dangerous it was for a third rank to be firing. The French Maréchal Saint-Cyr attributed no less than 25 per cent of infantry casualties to this cause. In Napoleon's later campaigns when large numbers of recruits were in the firing line the problem became acute. So many of these injuries occurred at the Battle of Bautzen and Lutzen that at first the Emperor thought the recruits were inflicting these wounds on themselves to escape further service.

Mousquetons

This weapon had a shorter barrel than the musket and consequently a shorter range. It was lighter, easier to handle and was the equivalent of the Anglo-Allied carbine. The French issued it initially to light cavalry (hussars and châsseurs à cheval) plus gendarmes, artillery and supply train soldiers. Later musicians and pioneers (sapeurs) in the infantry also received it, as did heavy cavalry.

Bayonets

All French infantry carried a triangular sectioned bayonet about 40 centimetres long. The occasions on which they used it at Waterloo were few, being largely confined to the close fighting in Plancenoit village by the Young Guard and two battalions of the Old Guard.

Pistols

Flintlock pistols were not an infantryman's weapon, although some officers used the short-barrelled gendarmerie pistol as a side arm of personal choice in addition to their sword. It could be carried in a holster or pocket and the bore was slightly smaller so the ball had a tight fit; this was necessary as the weapon was always carried with the muzzle pointing downwards. The porte-aigle (Eagle-bearer) was also often armed with a brace of pistols, as was the sapeur sergeant. They were point-blank weapons, although it was not recommended to stick it into an opponent's body and then pull the trigger due to the possibility of it exploding.

Swords

Officers of fusilier companies carried straight bladed swords (epées) while those in the light infantry or from grenadier or voltigeur companies had ones with curved blades. The French infantryman's sword was the sabre-briquet. It had a blade about 65 centimetres long with a single branch brass guard, and was carried in a black scabbard. It was an additional weapon to his musket and bayonet. With variations it was carried by all senior NCOs and soldiers except those of the fusilier companies of line regiments. The sapeur's briquet had a saw-edged back to the blade. It was exceptional for infantry of any nationality at Waterloo to fight with a sword.

Halberds

It is uncertain whether the French at Waterloo carried these weapons. Each of the second and third porte-aigles (the two sergeants tasked with protecting the Eagle-bearer) were supposed to carry halberds with long streamers attached to frighten horses. British witnesses who participated in the fighting to capture the Eagles of the 45th and 105th Regiments make no mention of halberds being used.

TACTICS

General

As has been stressed above, the French infantry tactics at Waterloo were all, or almost all until the end, about attacking. A successful infantry attack usually involves some or all of certain basic elements:

- Concentration of a superior force against the objective.
- Achieving some form of surprise.
- Movement to the objective.
- Maximum covering fire, support and co-operation from other units and arms.
- Fighting to take the objective.

Details of the French tactics are covered in Section 9 'Highlights of the Battle', where the major assaults are examined. Here it is sufficient to say that in general terms the French only partially secured superiority of numbers, never achieved surprise, had movement problems, sometimes lacked sufficient support from other arms and arrived at the objective too weakened to take it.

French infantry commanders were faced with three main tactical decisions during the movement phase of their assault. Firstly, what formation to adopt for the approach to the objective? Secondly, whether to press on in that formation onto the enemy position or change it just prior to contact (if they did make a change, when precisely to do so)? Thirdly, should they halt when in range and get involved in a stand-up firefight or rush in immediately with the bayonet?

The French manuals advocated that a battalion should change formation into line as they neared the enemy and thus be able to develop its full weight of fire. The problem for the commander was that this took several minutes and involved centre companies halting. The decision as to the exact moment to give the order to change was usually fraught with problems. Given too soon and the advance was slowed needlessly while the battalion, now spread over 150 metres, became unwieldy, far more prone to disruption by natural obstacles and the pace dropped as officers and NCOs struggled to maintain the dressing. Given too late (i.e. when within 100 metres of the enemy) and the situation became even worse, as the battalion was likely to be caught in a hail of fire as it struggled to change formation – invariably a recipe for disaster. With these difficulties in mind it was helpful for the commander to be able to see the enemy. At Waterloo (and in many previous Peninsula battles) this was seldom possible as, in addition to the dense smoke, Wellington's battalions were usually disconcertingly invisible in dead ground during the attackers' approach.

At Waterloo the French infantry used one of three formations for the approach to their objective, normally preceded by a cloud of skirmishers up to 100–150 metres in advance of the main body. The three formations adopted were:

- The battalion column of attack (Diagram p. 194) – companies in three rank lines on a two company frontage. This formation was used for the advance by Reille's II Corps on Hougoumont, and d'Erlon's I Corps attacks subsequent to his initial assault on Wellington's centre and left.
- Divisions in column of battalions (Diagram p. 195) – all battalions in a division in three rank lines one behind the other, almost treading on each other's heels with only about 5 metres between battalions. This was used by the great majority of the thirty-three battalions of d'Erlon's corps in its initial attack on the Anglo-Allied centre and left. It was a spur of the moment, unfamiliar formation, not in the French drill or tactics regulations.
- Battalion squares. These were used by the Imperial Guard battalions that made the final attack on Wellington's position.

1st Battalion 92nd Ligne formed in column of attack at half distance

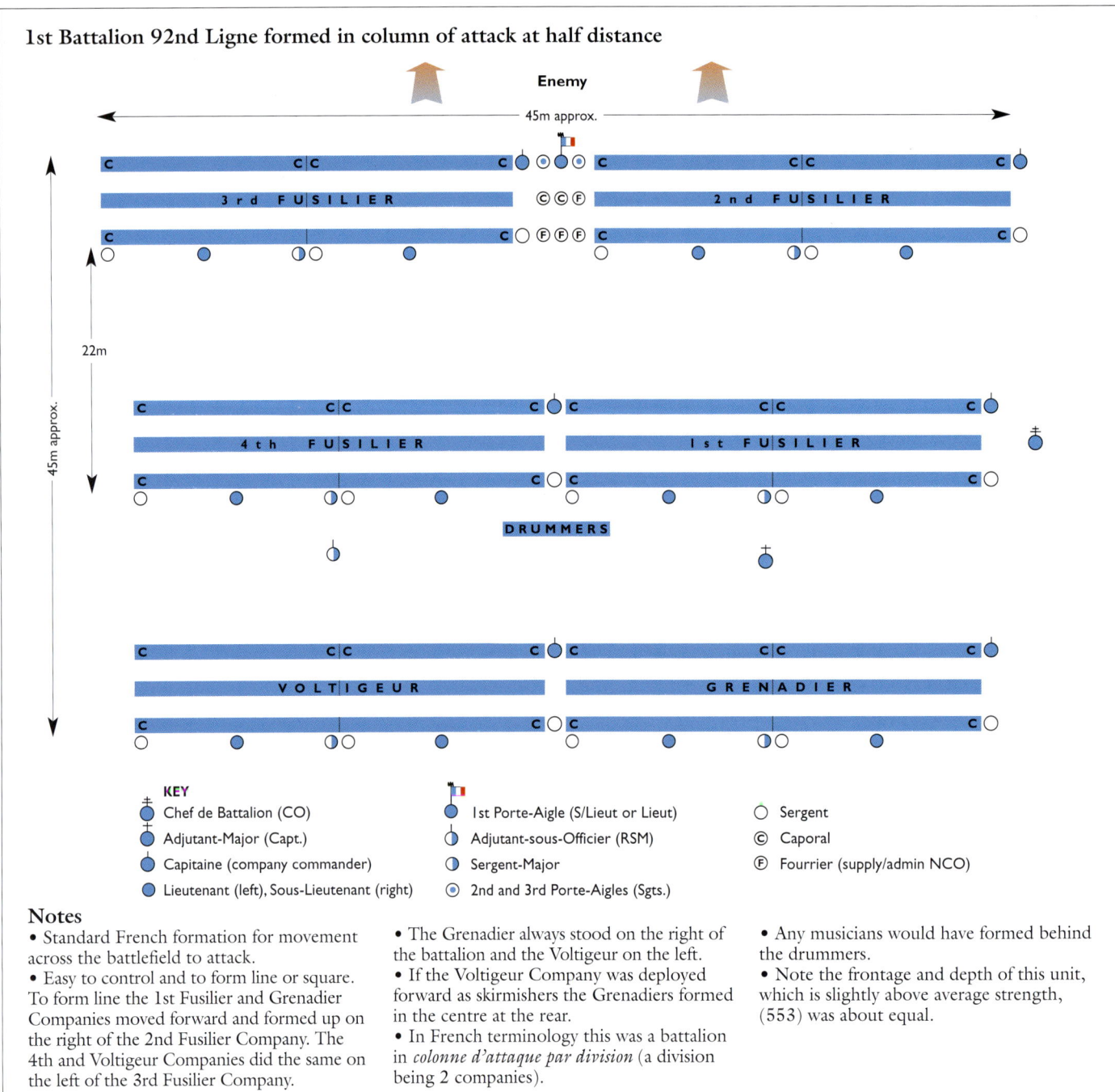

KEY

‡ Chef de Battalion (CO)	1st Porte-Aigle (S/Lieut or Lieut)	○ Sergent
† Adjutant-Major (Capt.)	Adjutant-sous-Officier (RSM)	© Caporal
Capitaine (company commander)	Sergent-Major	Ⓕ Fourrier (supply/admin NCO)
Lieutenant (left), Sous-Lieutenant (right)	◉ 2nd and 3rd Porte-Aigles (Sgts.)	

Notes

- Standard French formation for movement across the battlefield to attack.
- Easy to control and to form line or square. To form line the 1st Fusilier and Grenadier Companies moved forward and formed up on the right of the 2nd Fusilier Company. The 4th and Voltigeur Companies did the same on the left of the 3rd Fusilier Company.

- The Grenadier always stood on the right of the battalion and the Voltigeur on the left.
- If the Voltigeur Company was deployed forward as skirmishers the Grenadiers formed in the centre at the rear.
- In French terminology this was a battalion in *colonne d'attaque par division* (a division being 2 companies).

- Any musicians would have formed behind the drummers.
- Note the frontage and depth of this unit, which is slightly above average strength, (553) was about equal.

Attackers had to maintain their formation on the move despite the difficulties of the terrain and regardless of taking casualties. Considerable reliance was placed on the troops morale, forceful leadership by officers and NCOs, combined with an instinctive knowledge of the drills by all ranks. Each formation used by the French at Waterloo is discussed below.

A battalion in column of attack (Diagram above)

This was the most commonly used French formation for advancing to the attack. Its French title was battalion in '*colonne d'attaque par division*', a division (in this case) being two companies. It was easy to control, giving the commander the option of speedily forming line to open fire or assault, of forming square if threatened by cavalry or, if the enemy seemed to be wavering as they got close, just to keep going and charge forward with the bayonet.

Its disadvantage was that it could not develop much fire to the front. It was intended as a movement only formation. The example used in the diagram is the 1st Battalion 92nd Ligne that had 553 all ranks and was on the right of Foy's divisional line for his attack on Hougoumont. Points to note are:

- The narrow frontage for two companies of around 45 metres that facilitated control but only allowed some 120 muskets out of over 500 to be brought to bear to the front.
- The battalion is at half distance, which means the gap between companies (i.e. from rear rank of the 2nd Fusilier Company to the rear rank of the 1st Fusilier Company) is equal to half their frontage, or about 20 metres. With companies at this distance apart it was easy to form line or square quickly.
- In this formation the rear companies were always the grenadiers and voltigeurs, which allowed them to come up on the right and

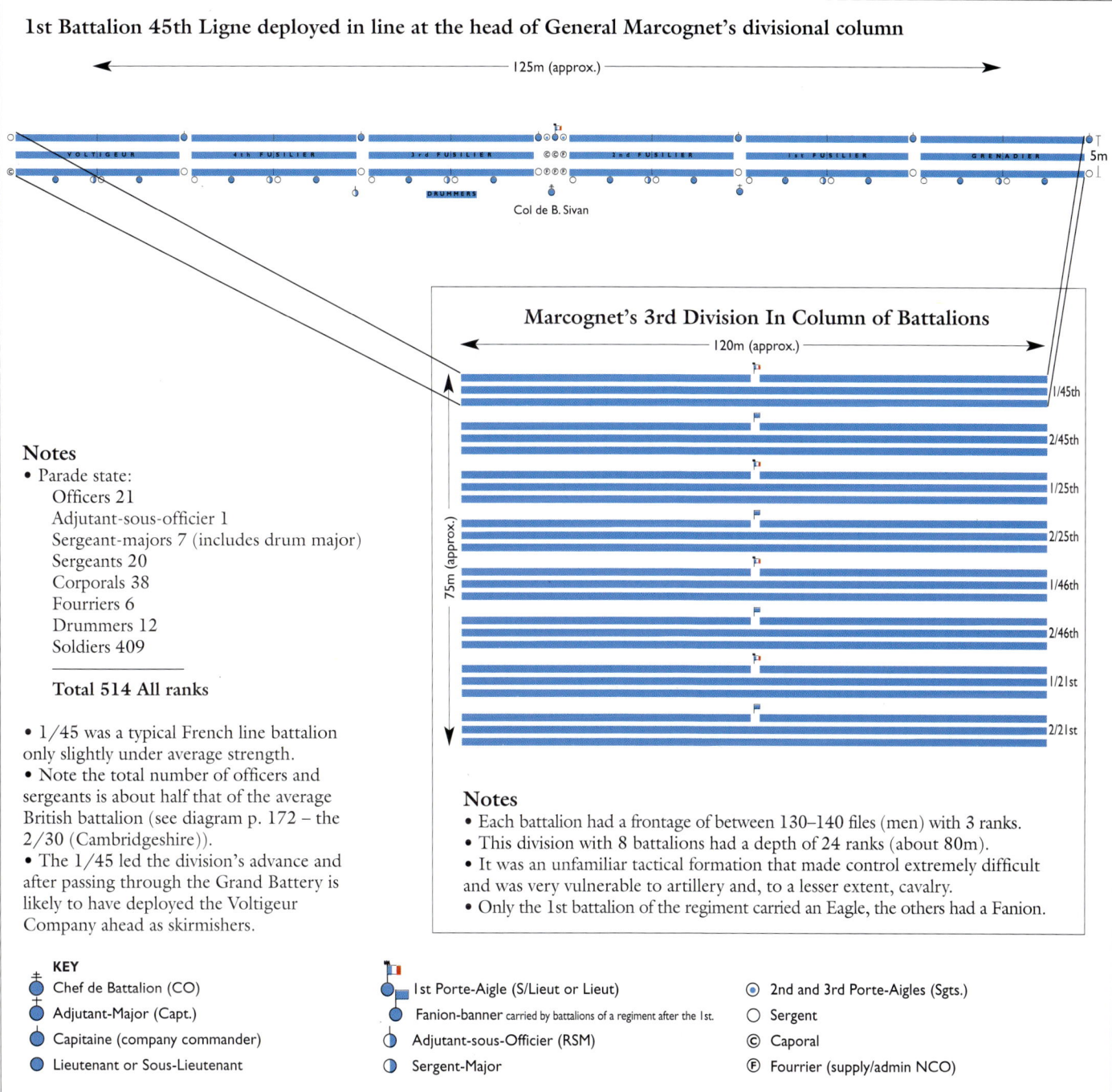

1st Battalion 45th Ligne deployed in line at the head of General Marcognet's divisional column

125m (approx.)

VOLTIGEUR   4th FUSILIER   3rd FUSILIER   2nd FUSILIER   1st FUSILIER   GRENADIER

5m

DRUMMERS

Col de B. Sivan

Marcognet's 3rd Division In Column of Battalions

120m (approx.)

75m (approx.)

1/45th
2/45th
1/25th
2/25th
1/46th
2/46th
1/21st
2/21st

Notes
• Parade state:
  Officers 21
  Adjutant-sous-officier 1
  Sergeant-majors 7 (includes drum major)
  Sergeants 20
  Corporals 38
  Fourriers 6
  Drummers 12
  Soldiers 409

Total 514 All ranks

• 1/45 was a typical French line battalion only slightly under average strength.
• Note the total number of officers and sergeants is about half that of the average British battalion (see diagram p. 172 – the 2/30 (Cambridgeshire)).
• The 1/45 led the division's advance and after passing through the Grand Battery is likely to have deployed the Voltigeur Company ahead as skirmishers.

Notes
• Each battalion had a frontage of between 130–140 files (men) with 3 ranks.
• This division with 8 battalions had a depth of 24 ranks (about 80m).
• It was an unfamiliar tactical formation that made control extremely difficult and was very vulnerable to artillery and, to a lesser extent, cavalry.
• Only the 1st battalion of the regiment carried an Eagle, the others had a Fanion.

KEY
- Chef de Battalion (CO)
- Adjutant-Major (Capt.)
- Capitaine (company commander)
- Lieutenant or Sous-Lieutenant
- 1st Porte-Aigle (S/Lieut or Lieut)
- Fanion-banner carried by battalions of a regiment after the 1st.
- Adjutant-sous-Officier (RSM)
- Sergent-Major
- 2nd and 3rd Porte-Aigles (Sgts.)
- Sergent
- Caporal
- Fourrier (supply/admin NCO)

left of the line respectively if required. Similarly, the 1st and 4th Fusilier Companies could quickly come up to the right and left of the centre companies. The resultant line would be numbered from right to left with the senior (grenadier) on the right flank.
• At Waterloo the voltigeur company was invariably sent forward at the outset of an advance to provide a skirmish line. The voltigeurs of the 1/92 Ligne performed this role, and when it did so the Grenadiers remained centrally at the rear as a reserve during the advance.
• While there are some minor differences in the positioning of individuals, French officers and NCOs took up similar locations to their counterparts in Anglo-Allied battalions. Company commanders were always in front, on the right, of their command while the other company officers and most sergeants formed a fourth supernumerary 'rank'.

A battalion in line (Diagram above)
There were very few instances at Waterloo when a French battalion deployed in line. The exception was when, at about 1.30 p.m., d'Erlon's corps of four divisions, thirty-three battalions, almost 20,000 infantrymen, formed up to advance across 600 metres (from the 'Grand Battery') of high-standing crops to assault the centre and left of Wellington's line. Entire divisions of eight or nine battalions, each deployed in lines of three ranks, moved off with the battalions closed up one behind the other. Details of this attack, together with the tactical consequences of this formation, are discussed in Section 9 'Highlights'. The diagram depicts the leading battalion of Marcognet's 3rd Infantry Division, 1st Battalion 45th Ligne (who lost their regiment's Eagle in the attack) in detail. Significant aspects of the French battalion in line are:

• The length of frontage was only about 125 metres. This was substantially less than an average Anglo-Allied unit; the 2/30 in line at full strength covered 210 metres of ground. The reasons for this are that French battalions were on average much smaller (520 all ranks compared with 640) and formed line in three ranks, not two.

• In terms of firepower available to the front, the 1/45 had around 450 muskets in total whereas the 2/30 had a hundred more. If the French had deployed in line, a third of these muskets might not have been able to fire. As far as Waterloo is concerned this disadvantage was not as serious as it might have been, as instances of French battalions in line having a musketry duel with an Anglo-Allied or Prussian battalion also in line, are hard to find. Even the protracted firefight after the loss to the French of La Haie Sainte between the attackers and the defending battalions of Lambert's and Kempt's brigades was not between opposing lines of formed battalions. Rather, it was between less tightly formed men who crouched behind a hedge (British) or behind a knoll (French), many firing from the kneeling position – in effect a much reinforced skirmish line.

• Because the French battalion had only six companies, each was slightly stronger than British battalions with ten: over eighty men compared with around sixty. These six companies were each divided into two sections. Two companies together were called a 'division'. A battalion column 'par division' meant a battalion column on a two-company frontage (as in Diagram p. 194).

• The fact that most French battalions had only about half the number of officers and sergeants compared to a British battalion is partially explained by the smaller number of companies, plus the fact that it was not uncommon for British companies to have four officers. The British also had two junior officers carrying the Colours, whereas there was only one porte-aigle (an officer) carrying an Eagle in each French regiment.

• There were a number of obvious similarities between French battalions in line and those of their enemies. Netherlands, Nassau and KGL all had six companies, company commanders all stood in the front rank on the right, there was a supernumerary rank of officers and sergeants at the rear of companies, and the commanding officer, drummers and Eagle/Colours were all positioned in the same place.

Squares

The formation of hollow squares by the French was almost entirely confined to Imperial Guard battalions in the late evening. Napoleon commanded an attacking army, and squares were defensive formations. Unusually, the square was adopted as a movement formation by the Guard units when they advanced on Wellington's right. This was almost certainly for fear of being caught by cavalry on the move – as they had seen happen earlier when the British Household and Union Brigades had carved up d'Erlon's infantry. However, there was an alternative: a column of companies, well closed up. For the Imperial Guard battalions this would have meant the four companies in line, in three ranks, one behind the other with minimal distance between the companies. From this formation a 'closed' square could quickly be formed. The leading company would halt. Those behind would close right up, and the fourth company (at the rear) would turn about while the three files on both flanks turned outwards. This would produce a tightly packed oblong well able to see off horsemen; the time taken was less than half a minute.

Some sources suggest the Guard did attack in column of companies, citing the supposed awkwardness of moving in squares, plus the fact that most Anglo-Allied witnesses described their attackers as coming through the smoke in columns. This controversy is examined in depth in Section 10 'Myths and Controversies'. In practice, squares were not particularly difficult formations to use for movement. The front and rear companies merely marched in line – in the case of the Imperial Guard, with a frontage of about forty to forty-five men (30–35 metres). The companies forming the flanks had it even easier, as they marched forward in 'column of threes'. Inside was the commanding officer, supernumerary officers and NCOs, the Eagle or Fanion (flag) party and the drummers. Like the column of companies, it was vulnerable to cannon fire or prolonged musketry, and it was not suitable as an assault formation. The commanders of the five assaulting squares would have the usual decision to make as they approached the enemy: when do I change formation? Do I halt and open fire? Or do I push on?

Apart from these attacking hollow squares, the reserve battalions of the Old Guard that did not participate in the final attack formed squares for the more usual defensive purposes. Several became rocks amidst a sea of fleeing soldiery as defeat overwhelmed the French at 9.00 p.m. For a time the Emperor himself sought sanctuary in such a square.

Methods of Delivering Musket Fire

An infantry battalion in line had a number of options as to how to open fire. That chosen depended on the tactical situation, the proximity of the enemy, whether they were infantry or cavalry and the training of the unit. Several permutations were possible, but the three basic methods were:

• battalion fire
• company/platoon fire
• file fire

Battalion fire involved the whole line (each rank) blasting off one devastating, simultaneous volley, probably followed immediately by a bayonet charge if the enemy were close. Alternatively, volleys could be given by ranks thus preserving some reserve while reloading took place.

Company or platoon fire meant that companies fired volleys in succession – from the right or left along the line, or from both flanks inwards. This meant that the battalion could produce fire from some part of the line almost continuously. It was common practice with British and Prussian battalions. Again, it was feasible to combine company fire with firing by ranks. To maintain this type of firing required a high level of training.

File fire was, in effect, 'fire at will'. A file (of two or three men depending on the number of ranks) fired and reloaded as quickly as possible and continued firing. In a three rank line either the front rank knelt or (with the French) the third rank reloaded muskets and passed them forward. Although a battalion was able to keep up continuous firing, it varied in volume, was patchy and difficult to control – especially stop. Most protracted firefights sooner or later devolved into both sides firing 'at will'.

Skirmishing

Skirmishing was the primary duty of the voltigeur companies in the line or light battalions, although with the latter all companies were theoretically skirmishing troops. In practice, and certainly at Waterloo, the light battalions often fought as ordinary infantry. For example, of the fifteen light infantry battalions there is little evidence to suggest that any one complete unit was used to provide skirmishers for a brigade attack. They, along with the line battalions, used their voltigeur companies for this duty. There had been no attempt to divide the light infantry evenly among the formations. There was no particular reason why II Corps (Reille) should have ten light battalions and I Corps (d'Erlon) only three. If light infantry were expected to provide the skirmishing force for the line infantry then I Corps' main attack would have merited a different distribution of these 'specialist' battalions.

Generally the French skirmisher screen was stronger than the British. This was because with a six-company battalion the French deployed one sixth as skirmishers whereas the British used only a tenth. Thus a French battalion of 520 would produce about 80 skirmishers, while the British with 640 would provide only 60. In a clash between skirmish lines in front of the main position, other things being equal, the Anglo-Allied force would be pushed back. This is precisely what happened when d'Erlon deployed his skirmishers to clear the way for his thirty-three battalions. If all contributed their voltigeur company, then up to 2,600 men would have spread out in the rye fields once they had passed through the 'Grand Battery'. There would have been around 1.7 French skirmishers for every metre of front. Opposing them would have been a far thinner line of around 1,100 or 0.75 men per metre.

Not all these men would be spread out across the front. The French tactics were to keep back up to a third in a group under the company commander as a reserve. These men would be used to reinforce the line ahead, as messengers with orders or, if attacked suddenly by cavalry, as the nucleus of a rallying square. As the skirmish line approached the main position, and the enemy skirmishers retired, there was the problem of these men masking the fire or progress of the main force coming up behind. Whistle blasts would signal the withdrawal, which was done by running back through the gaps in the advancing battalions. If this was impossible, the voltigeurs were trained to lie flat and let the troops pass over them.

THE IMPERIAL GUARD INFANTRY

'There is no temple without a God, no throne without a Guard'

General

The Imperial Guard was formed in 1804 from the old Consular Guard. It was the Emperor's personal creation. He vetted all recruitment, all promotions, all privileges, every detail of their duties and their uniform. It grew to become an army within an army. It had infantry (foot grenadiers and châsseurs), heavy cavalry (horse grenadiers and dragoons), light cavalry (horse châsseurs and lancers), foot artillery, horse artillery, gendarmerie, marines, engineers, plus artillery and equipment trains. Its expansion was remarkable. From 12,000 in 1805 to 56,000 in 1812, it then, despite staggering losses in Russia, expanded again to 102,000 by 1814 – although not without considerable dilution of entry standards for the junior regiments. These regiments became known as the Middle Guard and Young Guard to distinguish them from the original Old Guard. They included Dutch, Polish,

Italian and, most exotic of all, Mameluke units. Four ultra loyal and experienced 'Colonels-General' had charge of the major components of the Guard – the Foot Grenadiers, the Foot Châsseurs, the Cavalry and the Artillery and Marines – but the soldiers remained the Emperor's men.

Over ten years of continuous campaigning Napoleon had deliberately and skilfully cultivated a close personal bond between himself and his Guard. This was particularly so with the Old Guard regiments (1st and 2nd Grenadiers and 1st and 2nd Châsseurs). These men had mounted guard at the Emperor's palace, been on duty at state banquets and guarded his headquarters in the field. The Emperor knew hundreds of them by name, remembered their faces, stopped to speak to them on sentry duty, praised, admonished, promoted and rewarded them. In return he secured their devotion. They were his children, to whom he listened as if he was the captain commanding their company.

A Guard corporal steps in front of the Emperor at a review. When he speaks to request leave, and an advance of 300 francs, to visit his sick mother he does not say, 'Your Majesty' or 'Sire' but '*Mon Empereur*', which, to the corporal, is just another military rank. Napoleon grants him leave and directs his staff that he be given a draft on the treasury for 1000 francs. The corporal, however, knowing it could take months for the bureaucracy to produce the money, respectfully asks for a smaller amount from unit funds. His Emperor produces a handful of gold coins and tells him to 'Push off!' The corporal would speak of that incident, that kindness, for the rest of his life.

The Guard had indeed thrived on its privileges. Pay was more than double that in the line regiments. A grenadier in the Guard received 80 centimes a day, his counterpart in the line 30; a corporal 2 francs 22 centimes, which was not that much lower than a Line sous-lieutenant with 2 francs 77 centimes. Each rank in the Guard was equivalent of one higher rank in the Line. Thus a Guard corporal equated to a sergeant, a sergeant to a sergeant-major and a captain to a chef de bataillon. Being the equal of a Line sous-lieutenant, the Guard sergeant-major could swagger around town wearing an officer's sword, silk stockings and carrying a cane. The Guard had the best barracks, better food, civilian cooks in camp, and their own special supply train in the field. Each guardsman had his own soup bowl instead of having to share a communal cooking pot with others. The Guard had its own hospital at Gros-Caillou near Paris, where the menu included white bread, chicken, fish and baked potatoes. All hospital staff were carefully selected and under the direction of the Chief Surgeon of the Imperial Guard (and later of the Grande Armée), Baron Larrey.

A Line regiment had to give way to a Guard regiment on the line of march. Regulations required it to halt, present arms and sound a salute that the Guard merely acknowledged as it tramped passed. These perks and privileges aroused resentment. A standing joke in the army, that carries with it a hint of the animosity that existed between the 'haves' and the 'have nots', was that in the Guard, 'asses have the rank of mules'. The Old Guard in particular was fiercely proud of their distinctions that set them apart from lesser men. Their curling moustaches, that Napoleon forbade them to wax, their larger packs, better quality uniforms, towering, dark brown bearskins, brass fittings on their muskets, their tattooed hands and their huge gold earrings announced to all that they were the élite of the élite. However, not everyone was favourably impressed by their appearance. The British artist

Imperial Guard – Items of Headdress, Arms and Equipment

Three Views of the Grenadiers' bearskin

Red copper, metal front plate with Imperial Eagle and Crown above its head. A flaming grenade in each lower corner.

Cloth cockade tricolour (blue, red, white) behind which was attached a tall red plume for reviews.

Red cloth patch with white cotton grenade in centre.

This bearskin has been stripped of its plume and the white woollen cord that was looped diagonally across the front and rear. That illustrated is as worn at Waterloo by the 1st, 2nd and some of the 3rd Grenadiers. The Châsseurs did not have the metal plate at the front or the red patch on the crown. It was said that the plate caused premature baldness among many guardsmen – it had to be a tight fit as there was no chinstrap.

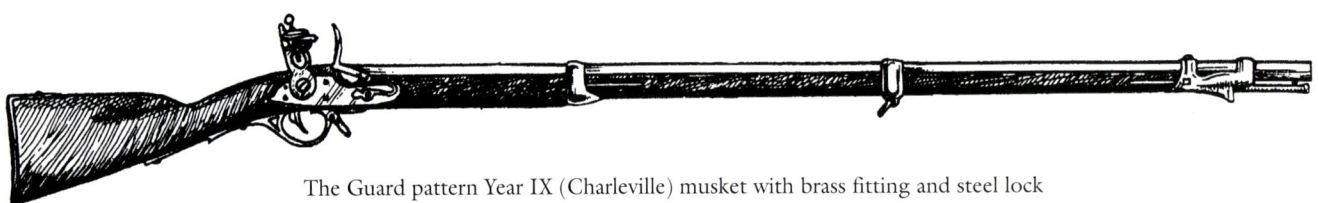

The Guard pattern Year IX (Charleville) musket with brass fitting and steel lock

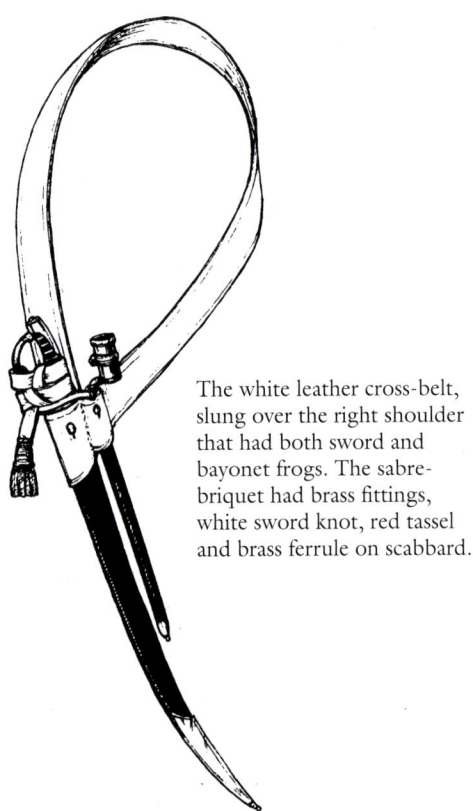

The white leather cross-belt, slung over the right shoulder that had both sword and bayonet frogs. The sabre-briquet had brass fittings, white sword knot, red tassel and brass ferrule on scabbard.

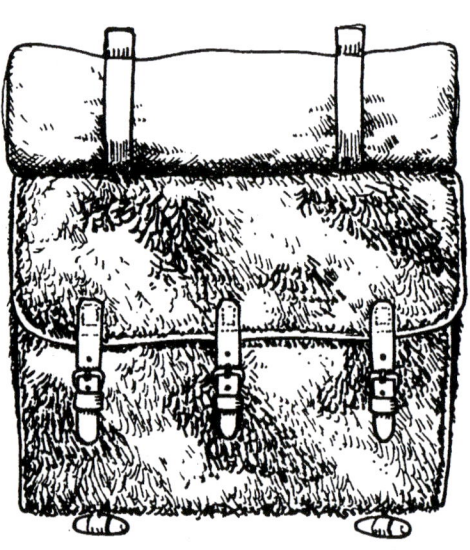

The calfskin knapsack was larger than the normal infantry issue and had three (instead of two) white closing straps and buckles. It was a comfortable and popular pack, much sought after by the British and others.

Benjamin Haydon saw them on duty at Fontainebleau in 1814. He wrote:

> More dreadful looking fellows than Napoleon's Guard I have never seen. They had the look of thoroughbred, veteran, disciplined banditti. Depravity, recklessness, and bloodthirstiness were burned into their faces ... Black mustachios, gigantic bearskins, and a ferocious expression were their characteristics.

Whenever the Emperor went to war the Guard was present. As at Waterloo it was both his strategic campaign, and his battlefield tactical, reserve. It became the practice not to commit the Old Guard except as the ultimate last resort. At Borodino, when the battle and campaign hung in the balance, Napoleon refused to use his Guard, remarking, 'And if there should be another battle tomorrow where is my army?' The 'Young Guard', however, was raised to fight. It always led in the approach to battle, and was the first of the Guard formations into action, while the Old Guard invariably waited and watched. Russia apart, where exhaustion, starvation and the cold killed infinitely more than the enemy, the Guard suffered fewer losses in battle than other formations. The Gendarmerie d'Elite, the Guard's military police, saw so little action and suffered so few battle casualties that they were given the nickname 'The Immortals'.

Even at Waterloo Napoleon hesitated to commit Old Guard battalions. It was the Young Guard that was sent to Plancenoit, the Middle Guard that mounted the final attack while, with the exception of two battalions that retook Plancenoit, the Old Guard was held back. It guarded the treasure chest and rear headquarters at Le Caillou; it covered the rout. The square of the oldest of the Old, the 1st Battalion of the 1st Regiment of Grenadiers gave sanctuary to their Emperor as it fought its way through the chaos from La Belle Alliance towards Le Caillou. Its commander, Major Loubers, had always been a grenadier. He had been a captain in the Elba Guard, had marched with Napoleon to Paris, and at Waterloo held the most prestigious command for an officer of his rank in the army. In 1840, in his old uniform of the Elba Guard, Loubers was among those marching for the last time behind the hearse of his Emperor as his body, brought back from St Helena, was taken to its final resting place at Les Invalides.

The Guard restored – March 1815

With the first abdication the Bourbons abolished the Guard. Napoleon was permitted to take a token military force to Elba. He took some 600 men, selected from a host of volunteers. They came from Foot Grenadiers, Foot Châsseurs, Horse Châsseurs, lancers, artillery, engineers and marines. Most marched the 1000-kilometre route via Lyons, the Mont-Cenis pass into Italy and thence to Savona to embark on British boats for Elba. They formed the Napoleon Battalion, drilling and parading under the white banner with the red diagonal and golden bees. The monotony did not last. Within nine months of landing on Elba on 26 May 1814, they were starting out on another long march back to Paris. Around this tiny nucleus Napoleon resurrected his Guard.

As early as 13 March, before he had reached Paris, Napoleon reconstituted the Guard. By 28 March he had recalled most of the old half-pay soldiers of the Guard and put in motion the creation of additional regiments of the Young Guard. Napoleon wanted 35,000 men – a target he was unable to meet. Not all discharged veterans returned. A levy of two officers and twenty men from

each line regiment proved insufficient for the Old Guard. The 1st Regiments (of Grenadiers and Châsseurs) were filled up with twelve-year men from the 2nd Regiments. These in turn recruited eight-year veterans from the Line, while former Young Guardsmen and those with four years service went to the 3rd Regiments. The Young Guard was recruited with difficulty from retired men, volunteers and Corsican flankers.

At 11.00 a.m. on 1 June the Guard artillery at the Tuileries commenced firing a 101-gun salute as the Emperor, in 'fancy dress' (his Emperor's ceremonial robes included a violet cloak and plumed hat), left the palace for a special ceremony on the Champs de Mars. He was to present new Eagles and flags to his army. The procession was long and impressive. Headed by Red Lancers and Châsseurs à Cheval, there were nineteen coaches, the Emperor's drawn by eight horses and surrounded by four mounted marshals (Soult, Ney, Jourdan and the recently appointed Grouchy). Jingling and clattering behind were personal staff, Gendarmes d'Elite, horse grenadiers and dragoons. At the Ecole Militaire 200 Eagles and 87 flags of the National Guard were massed in front of an altar. Of the Eagles, only two were destined for the Guard – the Grenadier and Châsseur regiments would get one each to be carried by the 1st Battalions. Mass was celebrated, cannons crashed, a loyal address was read out, and the 'Te Deum' sung. Then the Eagle-bearers came forward. The Emperor addressed them: 'I entrust these Eagles with the national colours to you. Will you swear to die in their defence? And you, soldiers of the Imperial Guard, do you swear to surpass yourselves in the coming campaign, and die to a man rather than permit foreigners to dictate to the Fatherland?' Predictably, the response was, 'We swear! *Vive l'Empereur*!'

Napoleon had mustered over 13,500 Guard infantry for his Armée du Nord. Some 12,700 fought for him at Waterloo.

Organization (see Structural Organization diagram page 54)

The organization of the Guard infantry at Waterloo can seem confusing. This arises from the fact that the senior half of the Grenadier Division (the four Grenadier Regiments) and the senior half of the Châsseur Division (the four Châsseur Regiments), constituted the Old Guard while the junior halves made up the Middle Guard. Although organized for administrative purposes into divisions of grenadiers and châsseurs, at Waterloo the Guard fought in division sized formations grouped as 'Old', 'Middle' and 'Young' Guards. The Old Guard comprised the 1st and 2nd Regiments of Grenadiers and Châsseurs, the Middle Guard the 3rd and 4th Regiments of Grenadiers and Châsseurs, and the Young Guard the 1st and 3rd Regiments of Tirailleurs and Voltigeurs. As was customary, the Guard marched to battle and formed up in reserve, with the junior formation (the Young Guard) in front, then the Middle Guard, and finally the Old Guard at the rear as the last reserve. With the exception of two Old Guard battalions, this is the order in which they were sent into action as the battle developed at Waterloo.

In June 1815 the Guard infantry was top-heavy with generals. There were fifteen generals of the rank of maréchal de camp (general of brigade) or higher for 12,700 guardsmen – one general for every 847 lower ranks. Generals commanded seven regiments, of which two had only one battalion.

There were twenty-one battalions of Guard infantry on the battlefield at Waterloo – eight Young Guard, six Middle Guard and seven Old Guard. All were organized into four companies of 130–150 all ranks. In May the Emperor had authorized the officer

The French Eagle, National Colour (Standard) and Fanions (flags)

A month after being proclaimed Emperor in May 1804, Napoleon decided on the emblem of Empire. He considered the cock and the lion but rejected both in favour of an eagle with wings spread. It became the design of the Great Seal of State and the emblem of the army and navy. In the army the Eagle would be carried on top of a pole with a standard underneath. The Eagle was of supreme importance. When writing on the subject to Maréchal Berthier he stressed that it was the priceless symbol of France and the Empire, while the standard below it was of lesser importance and could be replaced if necessary.

During the Empire two models were produced, in 1804 and 1815, although in the latter case it was a copy of the former but less finely moulded in the rush before the campaign started. The Eagle had both wings spread and the head turned to its left. In its claws it grasped a thunderbolt and in this respect it mirrored the Eagle of the Romans at the height of their empire; Napoleon had great admiration for the Roman Army and it is highly likely that this is why he chose the eagle. The Eagle was cast in bronze and then gilded with ormolu (a gold coloured alloy). It was 8 inches high and fastened to a plinth 2 inches deep. The plinth had the metal numerals indicating the number of the regiment attached at the front and rear. Guard Eagles had a badge indicating the arm, for example a grenade for grenadier regiments, instead of a number. It weighed just over 4 pounds. At Waterloo the infantry carried thirty-seven Eagles into battle (two Imperial Guard, thirty-five line regiments) and lost two. Because the Consular Guard, and then the Imperial Grenadier and Châsseur Guard regiments, were normally in barracks in Paris or on palace duties, their Eagles were kept in a room next to the throne room in the Tuileries. They were only taken out for state occasions, reviews or when going on campaign.

Initially, every infantry battalion (and cavalry squadron) received an Eagle and its accompanying standard. In 1804 this meant that 909 were presented. Every unit had to send its commanding officer with four officers, ten NCOs and soldiers to the presentation on 5 December. Despite the cost involved and the expansion of the army, it was not for another seven years that this lavish scale of issue was cut back. By the end of 1811 Napoleon decreed that only the 1st battalion (and 1st squadron) of each regiment would have an Eagle. These units would carry it on behalf of the entire regiment.

The other battalions or squadrons carried a fanion (flag) of distinguishing colours – 2nd battalion white, 3rd red, 4th blue, 5th green, 6th yellow, 7th violet and 8th sky blue. They were one metre square, plain, like a coloured tablecloth, carried by a sergeant and intended to be merely guides or markers to assist with drill movements. Inevitably, this situation did not last as commanding officers defied regulations to introduce more ornate designs and decorations, including battalion identification. Not only did the fanion then become something more deserving of the position of honour at the head of the column, but it also became worth capturing.

Over the years regiments gained an increasing number of battle honours but it was impossible to display them on the 1804 type of standard (drapeau). This difficulty was not overcome until an official of the War Ministry's Bureau of Inspection pointed to the simple tricolour flag that flew over the Tuileries when the Emperor was in residence. An enthusiastic Emperor accepted the idea immediately and the first orders for manufacture were signed the next day. The first new Colours, with battle honours embroidered on them, were despatched to line regiments in April 1812 – in time to be carried into Russia. The Guard, however, kept its 1804 pattern standards until the following year.

The pre-1815 Colour of the 1st Grenadiers is in the French Army Museum in Paris. On its face are the words:

and NCO establishment for the Guard to be increased because he wanted 200 guardsmen in a company. Thus a company (in addition to the captain and lieutenant) would have two sous-lieutenants instead of one, six sergeants instead of four, twelve corporals instead of eight and four drummers (often corporals) instead of two. In practice, this proved too optimistic for the Waterloo campaign, and Guard battalions fought with an average of sixteen officers.

Diagram p. 202 shows how the Guard formed up on either side of the Brussels–Genappe road. It also indicates, in outline, how each battalion was eventually used in the battle. It was not until after midday that every unit was in this position. Despite their late arrival they were in for a long wait (until around 6.00 p.m.) to get into the action.

The Young Guard

This division mustered nearly 4,300 infantrymen under the overall command of Général de Division Comte Duhesme. His second-in-command was Général de Division Comte Barrois. It was organized into two brigades, each having two regiments – one of tirailleurs and one of voltigeurs. Each regiment had two battalions. The eight battalions had an average strength of 535 all ranks, with the strongest being the 1/1 Voltigeurs with 615 and the weakest 1/3 Voltigeurs with 480. The division stood, or rather sat on their packs, listening to the roar of battle on either side of the Brussels road for over six hours before being rushed into Plancenoit village to halt the advancing Prussians.

The Middle Guard

This division moved into position with just under 3,600 under the command of Général de Division Comte Morand, with Général de Division Comte Michel as his second-in-command. The Middle Guard was the weakest (by about 700) of the three Guard formations. It was not organized into brigades but operated by regiments. There were only six battalions in this formation as the 4th Grenadiers had not managed to raise a second battalion before hostilities started, while the 4th Châsseurs had lost heavily at Ligny so its two battalions joined to form one strong unit at Waterloo. The average battalion strength was almost 600 – high because there were only six battalions. Five of them took part in the final assault on Wellington's line.

The Old Guard

With over 4,800 infantrymen this was the strongest Guard formation at Waterloo. Like the Middle Guard, its tactical formation was the regiment rather than the brigade. The commander was Général de Division Comte Friant with Général de Division Comte Roguet as his second-in-command. The eight battalions had an average strength of slightly over 600, the strongest being the 2/1 Châsseurs with 654 all ranks and the weakest the two battalions of 2nd Grenadiers with about 545 apiece. Only seven of these battalions actually deployed and fought on the battle-

GARDE
IMPERIALE
L'EMPEREUR
NAPOLEON
AU 1er REGIMENT
DES GRENADIERS
A PIED
On the reverse are the following names:
MARINGO, ULM
AUSTERLITZ, JENA
EYLAU, FRIEDLAND
ECKMUHL, ESSLING
WAGRAM, SMOLENSK
MOSCOWA,
VIENNE, BERLIN,
MADRID, MOSCOU

After Waterloo all the standards issued to the Imperial Guard, except one, were destroyed. The exception belonged to the Guard Horse Artillery. Strangely, it has battle honours on the face and city names on the reverse – no salutation or regimental title.

Until 1808 the duty of carrying the Eagle in battle went to the senior sergeant-major – today's regimental sergeant-major in the British Army. Close protection was provided by the fourriers (administrative/clerical NCOs). These duties were especially dangerous as the Eagle attracted fire and invited attack. As Colonel Elting so aptly puts it in *Swords Around a Throne,* '…heavy casualties among the colour guard played havoc with the battalion's paperwork.' In that year the Emperor decided to create the new post of porte-aigle (eagle-bearer) in every regiment. It was to be filled by a lieutenant promoted for his courage and strength, having ten years service, or the campaigns of Ulm, Austerlitz, Jena and Friedland to his credit. He was

armed with a sword and two pistols. On either side on parade or in battle were the 2nd and 3rd porte-aigles. These were veterans, big men renowned for their strength and bravery but probably too illiterate or dull for promotion. They ranked as sergeants but drew a sergeant-major's pay and were armed with halberds.

The bravery, devotion and ingenuity shown in the protection of the Eagles was exceptional. The commanding officer of the 125th Ligne, Chef de Bataillon Tremanger, was captured in Russia in 1812 but somehow managed to keep and conceal the Eagle and standard for two years and bring them back to France. A cavalry regiment lost its Eagle at the Battle of Borodino. Before the retreat began, officers from the regiment returned for a final search for it on the cold, deserted battlefield. The Eagle was miraculously discovered inside the skeleton of a long dead horse. The dying porte-aigle had stuffed it up the anus of the dead animal.

At Waterloo the 84th Ligne, under Colonel Chevalier in the 19th Infantry Division, had a particular honour. Its Eagle had a silver plaque attached to its staff with the inscription '*Un Contra Dix*' ('One Against Ten'). This distinction had been given to the regiment for defeating 10,000 Austrians in 1809. The 105th Ligne, which was to lose its Eagle at Waterloo, had once saved the Eagle of the 14th Ligne. This had happened at Eylau when the Eagle had been sent spinning into the snow when hit by a cannonball. It was spotted by a grenadier of the 105th who darted forward to recover it from under the hooves and bayonets of the attacking Russians.

After Waterloo the Bourbons did their best to see that all Eagles and standards were destroyed. Most units did it themselves. In some regiments the officers burned the standards before mixing the ashes with wine and drinking them down. Those in the Swiss 2nd Foreign Regiment tore the standard into strips with each officer keeping a piece. The colonel then tossed the Eagle into the dark waters of the Garonne River.

field, as Napoleon left the 1/1 Châsseurs at Le Caillou. Apart from the two battalions (1/2 Grenadiers and 1/2 Châsseurs) sent to retake Plancenoit at about 7.15 p.m., the Old Guard did not come in to action until the French retreat was under way; their squares then took on the impossible task of covering the flight of the army.

IMPERIAL GUARD REGIMENTS

The overall commander of the entire Imperial Guard corps at Waterloo was the Emperor himself. He made all the tactical decisions regarding its movement and tasks. His permission was needed before a single battalion was committed. The nominal acting commander and chief of staff to the Guard, the man who saw to it that the Emperor's instructions were carried out and supervised the general administration of the corps, was Général de Division Comte Drouot. A first rate artillery general and administrator, he was described by Marshal Macdonald as, 'the most upright, honest man I have ever known, well educated, brave, devout and simple in his manner'. Had Waterloo gone the other way Drouot would assuredly have received his baton. The tactical organization of the Guard infantry at Waterloo was based on the three divisions of Young, Middle and Old Guards. Notes on the regiments in each, in order of seniority, are given below:

The Old Guard Division (Général de Division Friant with Général de Division Roguet as second-in-command)

1st Regiment of Foot Grenadiers (Grenadiers à Pied)

Under the command of Maréchal de Camp Baron Petit, this was the most senior regiment of the Guard – the original 'Grumblers', as veterans were called. Petit had the duty at Waterloo of commanding the last reserve of the Guard during the rout of the army. Thirty-five years later he was still alive and Honorary President of the Imperial Guard Association. The strict entry standards had been maintained (although with difficulty). These soldiers had an average age of thirty-five and were over 1.65 metres tall. All had twelve years' service, four out of five had the Legion of Honour and a third had fought in over twenty campaigns.

This regiment had a new Eagle, carried by the 1st Battalion on behalf of all grenadiers in all four regiments. It also had managed to raise a full band of twenty-four musicians led by a musician playing (shaking) a *chapeau chinois* (the English called it a 'Jingling Johnny' – an elaborate pole with a hat like top with bells attached), and bass and snare drums. It was this regiment that formed two battalion squares near La Belle Alliance as the Middle Guard attack was repulsed. Drummers and musicians continuously played the grenadier's regimental march, 'La Grenadiere', to try to rally their retreating comrades. The regiment went to war in

The Imperial Guard infantry and artillery form up in reserve north of Rossomme between 11.00 a.m. and noon

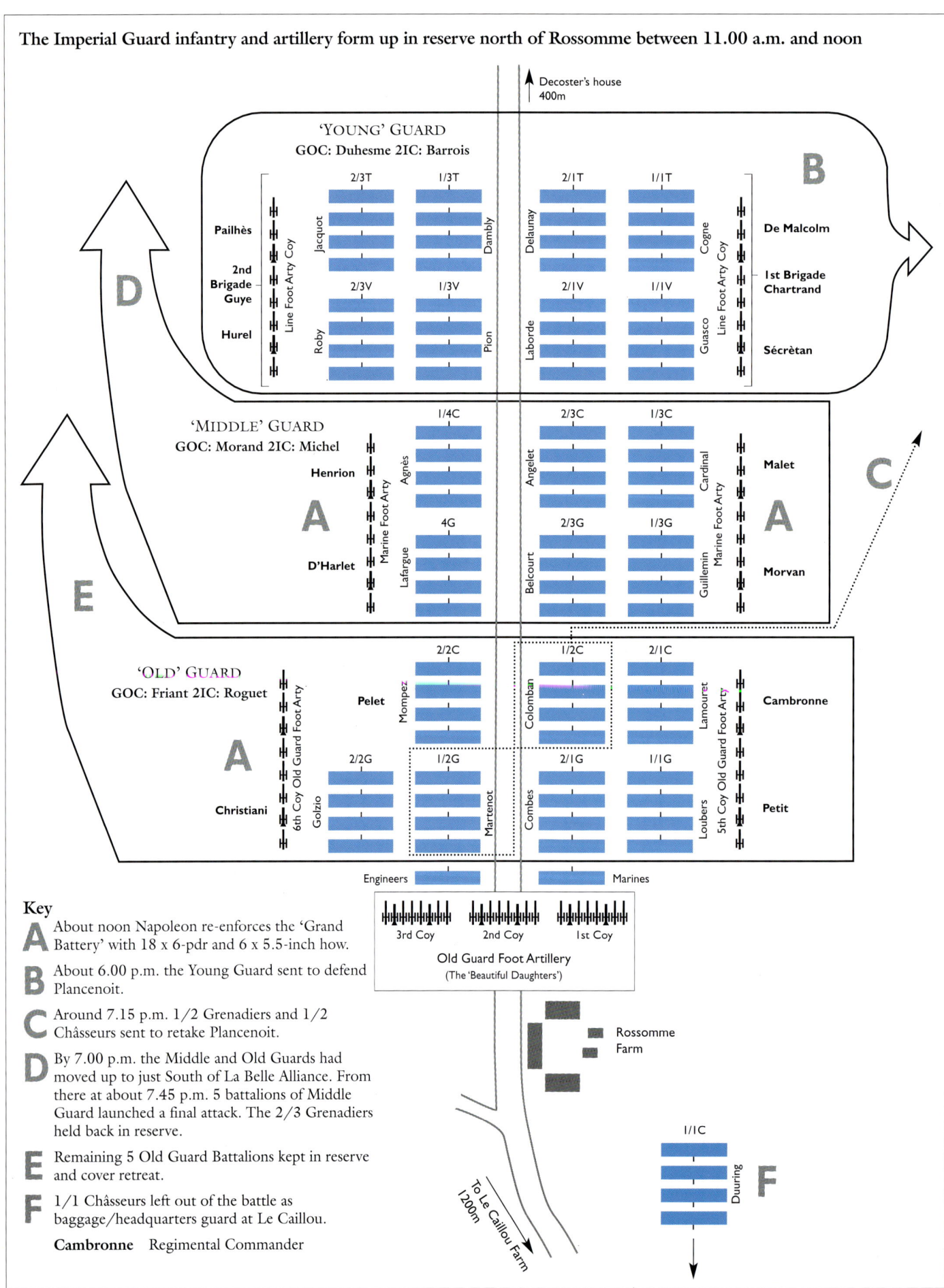

↑ Decoster's house
400m

'YOUNG' GUARD
GOC: Duhesme 2IC: Barrois

B

2/3T 1/3T 2/1T 1/1T

Pailhès

2nd Brigade Guye

Hurel

Jacquot   Dambly   Delaunay   Cogne

2/3V 1/3V 2/1V 1/1V

Roby   Pion   Laborde   Guasco

Line Foot Arty Coy

De Malcolm

1st Brigade Chartrand

Sécrètan

Line Foot Arty Coy

D

'MIDDLE' GUARD
GOC: Morand 2IC: Michel

A

1/4C 2/3C 1/3C

Henrion

D'Harlet

Agnès   Angelet   Cardinal

4G   2/3G   1/3G

Lafargue   Belcourt   Guillemin

Marine Foot Arty

Malet

Morvan

Marine Foot Arty

A

C

E

'OLD' GUARD
GOC: Friant 2IC: Roguet

A

2/2C   1/2C   2/1C

Pelet

Christiani

Mompez   Colomban   Lamouret

2/2G   1/2G   2/1G   1/1G

Golzio   Martenot   Combes   Loubers

6th Coy Old Guard Foot Arty

5th Coy Old Guard Foot Arty

Cambronne

Petit

Engineers   Marines

Old Guard Foot Artillery
3rd Coy   2nd Coy   1st Coy
(The 'Beautiful Daughters')

Rossomme Farm

To Le Caillou Farm
1200m

1/1C

Duuring

F

Key

A About noon Napoleon re-enforces the 'Grand Battery' with 18 x 6-pdr and 6 x 5.5-inch how.

B About 6.00 p.m. the Young Guard sent to defend Plancenoit.

C Around 7.15 p.m. 1/2 Grenadiers and 1/2 Châsseurs sent to retake Plancenoit.

D By 7.00 p.m. the Middle and Old Guards had moved up to just South of La Belle Alliance. From there at about 7.45 p.m. 5 battalions of Middle Guard launched a final attack. The 2/3 Grenadiers held back in reserve.

E Remaining 5 Old Guard Battalions kept in reserve and cover retreat.

F 1/1 Châsseurs left out of the battle as baggage/headquarters guard at Le Caillou.

Cambronne   Regimental Commander

Cantinières

As with the British Army, the French allowed a certain number of wives to accompany each battalion. Their numbers varied, as did their reputation and virtues. Like their counterparts behind the ridge of Mont St Jean, their purpose was to wash, mend, cook, fetch firewood and water and, in battle, help the surgeons. Colonel John Elting in his book *Swords Around the Throne* provides a splendid pen-picture of them:

> A rough, tough, sunburned lot with saw-edged voices and vocabularies that made grenadier topkicks wince, they were quick foragers and skilful improvisers of meals and shelters, a sisterhood of long, hard roadways and the rain. In desperate fights they risked death running into the ranks with drink for soldiers half choked from biting cartridges, and with aprons full of ammunition when their men's pouches were emptying.

One is known to have become a duchess. She married a Sergeant Lefèbvre, little thinking he would one day be a marshal and Duke of Danzig. She was fond of scandalizing society ladies by describing how she used to do the soldiers' washing.

Many cantinières were present at Waterloo, probably the most famous being Marie Tête-de-Bois (wooden head) who was a cantinière with the 1st Grenadiers à Pied of the Imperial Guard. She had reputedly served in seventeen campaigns. Her first husband, a drummer, had died sixteen months earlier when Napoleon defeated Blücher at the Battle of Montmirail. A little over a month later she lost her son at the fall of Paris. By June 1815 she had recovered sufficiently to marry another grenadier called Chactas. As the Imperial Guard moved up from near Rossomme in the early afternoon, a cannon ball cut her in two, spattering her new husband with blood. The regiment scratched a shallow grave for her in the roadside ditch. A corporal erected a rough wooden cross with the epitaph: 'Here lies Maria, Cantinière of the 1st Grenadiers of the Old Imperial Guard, dead on the field of honour 18 June 1815. Passerby, whoever you may be, salute Maria.' Within a few hours a Prussian shell struck down Grenadier Chactas and, within a few days, his wife's grave had been demolished.

---

the correct uniforms: half-belted 'Imperial blue' greatcoats, blue trousers, dark brown bearskin bonnets and large Guard knapsacks. They carried muskets with brass fittings and their sabre-briquets were of regimental pattern. Mustachioed, wearing their hair in queues and gleaming gold earrings, their sleeves covered in long-service stripes they looked, despite the rain and mud, exactly what they were – picked men, the Emperor's best.

This regiment had led the right-hand column that smashed its way through Ligny village at the end of that battle two days earlier. Before the assault went in, General Roguet shouted, 'Warn the Grenadiers that the first man who brings me a prisoner will be shot!' He did not have to carry out his threat. Later, in the failing light, with dead or dying all round, with the Prussians in flight the 1st Grenadiers' band struck up a tune that had been played countless times across the continent over the previous fifteen years: '*La Victoire est a nous*'. It was the last time it was ever heard on a battlefield.

The Regiment consisted of two strong battalions:

1/1 Grenadiers. Commanded by Major Loubers, it was the senior infantry battalion in the army and had some 640 all ranks. Among the officers was a Captain Deleuze who had made his entire career in the Grenadiers. At forty-four Deleuze was the oldest captain in the corps, the holder of the Legion of Honour and a pension worth 1,800 francs – which he lived to collect. This battalion was entrusted with the Grenadiers' Eagle, although it was destined to remain in reserve throughout the battle. By evening it had formed square with the 2/1 on either side of Decoster's house, where it provided sanctuary to the Emperor, General Friant and several staff officers during the rout of the army. As it slowly withdrew to Le Caillou it opened fire several times on Frenchmen to keep from being overwhelmed.

2/1 Grenadiers. Commanded by Major Combes (an Elba officer) it was of a similar strength to the 1/1 Grenadiers (640). It had fought at Ligny but was, like its sister battalion, kept in reserve at Waterloo until called upon to form part of the rearguard.

2nd Regiment of Foot Grenadiers (Grenadiers à Pied)

This regiment was commanded by its Colonel-Commandant, Maréchal de Camp Baron Christiani – a long serving grenadier officer who, as a colonel in 1811, had been commandant of the Old Guard NCO school at Fontainebleau. He had done well as the commander of the 2nd Old Guard Division in the battles for France the previous year. Entry requirements were the same as for the 1st Regiment. Uniforms, equipment and weapons were more or less standard Guard pattern. With 34 officers and about 1,060 soldiers, it was not as strong as the 1st Regiment by some 200 men.

It had fought hard at Ligny as the leading regiment in the attack on the village late in the evening. At Waterloo the regiment was divided, with one battalion being sent to help retake Plancenoit shortly before 7.00 p.m. and the other, with Christiani at its head, going forward as a support battalion for the Middle Guard's final assault on Wellington's line. Its two battalions were:

1/2 Grenadiers. Commanded by Major Martenot it had some 545 all ranks. With the 1/1 Châsseurs it was destined to carry out a spectacular counterattack that cleared the village of Plancenoit of all Prussians just as they seemed certain to burst through Napoleon's right flank and cut the Brussels–Genappe road.

2/2 Grenadiers. Under Major Golzio, it was of approximately the same size as the 1st Battalion (545). Held in reserve until the evening it was moved forward in square behind, and in support of, the Middle Guard's assault. It then suffered severely in trying to withdraw in the face of Wellington's general advance.

1st Regiment of Foot Châsseurs (Châsseurs à Pied)

This regiment was commanded by Maréchal de Camp Vicomte Cambronne; he was the man who had led the Elba battalion on its trek through France and Italy to join Napoleon on his tiny island. As he stepped ashore Napoleon greeted him with outstretched hand and the words, 'Cambronne, I have had some bad moments waiting for you, but now that we are together again all is forgotten.' Cambronne was commandant of the Guard on Elba before leading them on the long march back to Paris in March 1815. He refused divisional command at Waterloo in order to remain with his beloved châsseurs, although he did accept the appointment of Grand Officer of the Legion of Honour. He was wounded and captured at the end of the battle in circumstances described in Section 10 'Myths and Controversies'.

The 1,300 all ranks of the 1st Châsseurs included men from the King's Royal Corps of Châsseurs, light infantrymen from the line, and veterans of the Russian campaign (although most were soldiers who had joined in 1813). The regiment had its Eagle, drummers and a band of twenty-four musicians. The regimental march, 'La Carabiniere' was heard through the storm of battle at Ligny and Waterloo. The soldiers wore, for the most part, their correct, regulation châsseur uniform, which closely resembled that of the grenadiers. The easiest way of telling them from their grenadier comrades was to look at the tall bearskin caps – if they had a copper metal plate with an eagle in front, or a red cloth patch behind, they were grenadiers; if not, they were châsseurs. Their equipment and muskets were Guard pattern.

This senior regiment of châsseurs, part of the Old Guard and entitled to the nickname 'Grumblers', was never fully committed to the fight at Waterloo. As the 1/1 Châsseurs (that normally was entrusted with the Eagle) remained at Le Caillou, it is likely that it was carried on the field by the 2nd Battalion. This battalion went forward to support the Middle Guards' final attack but did not participate in the actual assault. Nevertheless, its square was badly shot up during the retreat from the field. Its two battalions were:

1/1 Châsseurs. With 650 all ranks it was almost the strongest Guard battalion in the corps (second only to the amalgamated battalion of the 1/4 and 2/4 Châsseurs). The 1/1 was commanded by Major Duuring, one of the most loyal officers in the corps. He was a Dutchman, formerly the commander of the 3rd (Dutch) Grenadiers (in 1811 part of the Imperial Guard). His loyalty to his regiment, to his Guard and to his Emperor far outweighed any qualms he may have had in fighting his own countrymen. As the senior battalion, the 1/1 was normally entrusted with the Eagle of the Châsseurs. However, there is strong evidence that as this unit was being left out of battle, charged with the security of Le Caillou and the treasury wagons, that the Eagle (carried by a Lieutenant Martin) was under the protection of the 2/1 Châsseurs at Waterloo. During the night it was Duuring's hard task to fight off the pursuing Prussians, stem the flood of fugitives and to escort, along with other Guard remnants, Napoleon (and the Eagle of the Grenadiers that had become isolated in the confusion) back to Fleurus.

2/1 Châsseurs. Another big battalion of around 650 all ranks. Its commander, Major Lamouret, a former Napoleon Battalion company commander, had been the first man ashore from Elba on 1 March. Captain Lamouret's opponent then had been a customs' official. A few hours later he broke his leg escaping from captivity. By June he had recovered and was assigned the position of battalion commander. At Waterloo he took over escort duties for the Eagle of the Châsseurs as the 1st Battalion was not present on the battlefield. Late in the evening he marched his battalion, in square, up the slope towards Wellington's line in support of the Middle Guard's final assault. Thereafter the battalion was caught up in the costly chaos of retreat. During this time his battalion lost cohesion and became scattered to the extent that Lieutenant Martin, the Eagle-bearer, took refuge in the square of the 2/2 Châsseurs. Martin guarded the Eagle well, although he was unable to rejoin the remnants of his unit until he reached Laon.

2nd Regiment of Foot Châsseurs (Châsseurs à Pied)

The commander was Maréchal de Camp Baron Pelet who had been a key aide to Marshal Ney with the rearguard during the retreat from Moscow. He served with the Old Guard through the bitter battles to defend France in 1813–14. Pelet was the officer who, from the hundreds of clamouring volunteers, selected those guardsmen who would accompany Napoleon to Elba. At Waterloo he became involved in the bloody brawl for the streets of Plancenoit, personally stopping some of his enraged soldiers from slitting the throats of Prussian prisoners, although he was unable to save them all.

Most of the soldiers' uniforms, equipment and arms were recognizable as Guards' pattern, and, with nearly 1,200 all ranks, both battalions were comfortably above the army average in strength. At Ligny the regiment had been sent with the Young Guard to support Vandamme's corps in its struggle for the villages of St Amand and Le Hameau. At Waterloo, after waiting for over six hours sitting, smoking and dozing on the damp ground in reserve, the regiment was split. At around 7.00 p.m. the 1st Battalion, along with the 1/2 Grenadiers, was rushed to sort out the crisis developing in Plancenoit – a task they achieved with stunning success against heavy odds. The 2nd Battalion was later moved up in square to support the Middle Guards' final attempt to break the Anglo-Allied line. It did not participate.

Interestingly, it was a châsseur from the 2nd Regiment who became the oldest Imperial Guard infantry survivor of the battle. This was a soldier called Vivien who died at Lyons in 1892, aged 106.

1/2 Châsseurs. With 581 all ranks this battalion was of above average strength. It was under the command of Major Colomban who, as a sergeant, had been commissioned into the châsseurs thirteen years earlier. After the desperate close quarter combat of St Amand and Le Hameau two days before, this battalion again did much of its fighting through the cobbled streets of Plancenoit with clubbed muskets and the bayonet. The involvement of some of its men in the massacre of prisoners until stopped by their regimental commander illustrates the vicious brutality of the fighting in the village, much of it around the church.

2/2 Châsseurs. Another reasonably strong unit with around 580 all ranks. It was under the command of Major Mompez. The battalion remained uncommitted throughout the day until late evening. It was then moved up in square to the foot of the slope south-west of La Haie Sainte as part of the second line supporting the Middle Guard's final assault. It did not join the assault but was caught up in the confusion of the withdrawal. It was supported for a time by cavalry, and fell back in good order to La Belle Alliance. Here it gave shelter to Lieutenant Martin, the Eagle bearer of the Châsseurs.

Marines of the Guard (Marins de la Garde)

Although not part of the Old Guard, they were nevertheless formed as early as 1803 and deployed immediately in rear of the Old Guard at Waterloo. *Marins de la Garde* means 'sailors' of the Guard and, although operating at Waterloo as soldiers, they retained their naval ranks. Thus Captain Preaux who commanded the equipage (company) of 107 marines was more accurately a *lieutenant de vaisseau* (ship), his sergeant-major a *maitre* (mate) and his sergeants *contre-maitres*.

They had an illustrious history. Originally raised as a five-company battalion, they served as a unit or in detachments throughout 1805–07. In 1808 they were almost destroyed at the Battle of Baylen in Spain. Despite this, a company marched into Russia and served during the defence of France in 1813–14. They were 'jacks of all trades' and were used to man boats, build bridges, and took on engineering tasks, as well as fighting as infantry. They wore blue jackets and trousers with black leather cross-belts and a bell-topped shako covered in a black waterproof cloth. Officers wore bicorn hats, single-breasted blue coats with gold lace. The marines were armed with dragoon muskets, bayonets and their own design of sabre. They had a fanion but not an Eagle at Waterloo.

At Ligny, with the Engineers of the Guard, they formed a small assault column that stormed the eastern part of the village. At Waterloo the company formed up behind the 1st Grenadiers and remained in reserve until the very end of the battle when they fought as infantry helping to cover the retreat.

The Middle Guard Division (Général de Division Comte Morand with Général de Division Comte Michel as second in command)

The 3rd Regiment of Foot Grenadiers (Grenadiers à Pied)

This regiment was almost 1,200 strong and was under the command of Maréchal de Camp Baron Poret de Morvan. Morvan was a veteran of Italy and Santo Domingo; he had fought with the Young Guard Division at Craonne and had been badly wounded at Laon – he was hit again at Waterloo. With Ney and Friant he walked ahead of the 1/3 Grenadiers in the last desperate attempt of the Middle Guard to break Wellington's line.

This was a new regiment raised as recently as 8 April. There had been insufficient time and funds to ensure all these grenadiers were correctly dressed in the full Guard uniform. This was particularly noticeable with the headdress. Some had bearskins, but many marched with an odd assortment of shakos, bicorn hats or forage caps (*bonnet de police*). Some used cord instead of musket slings, while many muskets were line issue (lacked the brass fittings).

At Ligny this regiment had formed part of the left-hand column that attacked the village towards the end of the battle. At Waterloo it remained in reserve until the evening before moving forward to take part in the final assault. It formed two battalion squares but only the 1/3 actually advanced on the Anglo-Allied position, the 2nd Battalion being held back and positioned by the Emperor in reserve between La Haie Sainte and Hougoumont.

1/3 Grenadiers. A strong battalion with about 580 all ranks under the command of a former Young Guard commander who had fought well at Leipzig, Major Guillemin. This battalion was the right flank battalion of the Middle Guard's assault on Wellington's line. It was pushed back by the charge of Detmers' Dutch-Belgian brigade just as it reached the ridge – although some evidence suggests that the Dutch-Belgians were merely chasing an already defeated battalion rather than breaking it themselves.

2/3 Grenadiers. Of the same strength as the 1st Battalion, it had as its commander Major Belcourt, an officer well known to the Emperor as he had commanded the grenadier battalion charged with his personal protection for a period during the defence of France the previous year. At Waterloo Napoleon posted this unit in square on a slight rise in the ground between La Haie Sainte and Hougoumont, where it had great difficulties in holding off the Anglo-Allied general advance after the Middle Guard's repulse. It was badly shot up, losing over 200 men. The square was reduced to a tattered triangle when they were attacked by British cavalry, infantry from Hougoumont, and surrounded and shelled with grapeshot.

The 4th Regiment of Foot Grenadiers (Grenadiers à Pied)

This was the most recent grenadier regiment, being barely six weeks old at Waterloo. As such it had problems, not only with getting the correct uniforms but also in recruiting sufficient manpower. By the time the regiment left Paris for the war it had only raised one battalion. In many cases the uniforms resembled those worn by the provincial National Guard, with greatcoats of a variety of shades of blue, grey, and even beige. Many soldiers had been transferred from the Young Guard and so had their uniform, with shakos, line muskets and knapsacks.

The regimental commander was Maréchal de Camp Baron d'Harlet, another long serving Guards' officer who had fought at Eylau, in Russia, Spain and France.

This regiment was in the heavy fighting for the village of Ligny, while at Waterloo its single battalion took part in the Middle Guard's attack at the close of the battle. Led by the wounded d'Harlet, it reached the ridge where, for a few brief moments, it seemed as if it might push aside the British 2/30 and 2/73 battalions. It was not to be, and the battalion tumbled back down the slope from about where the Lion Mound now stands.

1/4 Grenadiers. This single battalion had about 520 all ranks and was commanded by Major Lafargue. While participating in the final assault, as it breasted the Mont St Jean ridge, Lafargue fell mortally wounded. Within moments a possible breakthrough had been turned into defeat.

The 3rd Regiment of Foot Châsseurs (Châsseurs à Pied)

Another recently raised regiment (8 April) that had made up the numbers by transfers from the Young Guard. Like its sister regiment in the grenadiers, it marched to battle in a motley collection of uniforms and headgear.

Its commander, Colonel Malet, had been a drum-major before commissioning in 1802, when the old Consular Guard was transformed into the Imperial Guard. He had been soldiering in various regiments since 1795, including the Foot Guides of Italy as well as the Consular Guard. He was the holder of the Legion of Honour, had been wounded three times (at Lodi, Acre and Essling), and had followed his Emperor from Italy to Egypt, Marengo, Vienna, Madrid, Moscow, Dresden, Paris and Elba. On Elba Malet had been the deputy commander of the Napoleon Battalion under Cambronne. He was mortally wounded at Waterloo, falling at the head of his regiment as it reached the Anglo-Allied position – he would probably have considered it a fitting end to twenty years of fighting for his Emperor.

The 3rd Châsseurs had fought at Ligny assisting Vandamme's corps, and the Young Guard in the struggle for St Amand.

1/3 Châsseurs. An average strength battalion commanded by a veteran officer who had, like the overwhelming majority of French officers, served in the ranks. Major Cardinal was killed at the same time as his colonel was shot as they breasted the ridge near the foot of the Lion Mound.

2/3 Châsseurs. It had a strength of 530 all ranks and was commanded by Major Angelet. If any Frenchman had a charmed life it was Angelet. When he fell wounded during Blücher's defeat at the Battle of Craonne in 1814, it was for the eleventh time – he came through Ligny unscathed, but was hit yet again at Waterloo. He led from the front, outside his battalion square, up the slope to the enemy line in the closing minutes of the battle. The 2/3 was forced back by the sudden sweep of fire from Maitland's Guards who rose from the mud and matted rye in which they had been lying a mere 30 metres away; they had given the indestructible Angelet his twelfth wound.

The 4th Regiment of Foot Châsseurs (Châsseurs à Pied)

Like their comrades in the 4th Grenadiers, this regiment had only one battalion at Waterloo, although for a different reason. A second battalion had been raised for the campaign but both units had suffered heavy losses at Ligny in the fighting for the villages of St Amand and Le Hameau. Because of this they amalgamated to make one large battalion of over 800 all ranks at Waterloo.

The regimental commander was Maréchal de Camp Baron Henrion. He had been promoted general on the same day as van Merlen (now commanding the 2nd Netherlands Light Cavalry Brigade on the other side of the hill), just prior to the invasion of France in 1813. At the Battle of Montmirail Henrion had handled the 2nd Châsseurs with consummate skill, forming them into squares as if on a parade ground, in time to beat off sustained cavalry charges.

Like the 3rd Châsseurs, there were not twenty men in a company that were dressed the same, and all carried the cheaper Charleville musket with its iron fittings.

They had fought at the end of the day at Ligny supporting Vandamme's corps. Again at Waterloo it was in the closing stages that they advanced in square, the left flank battalion of the five Middle Guard units that Napoleon ordered forward as his last gamble. Shot at in front and hit in flank by the British 52nd Foot, their assault collapsed, Henrion falling wounded.

1/4 and 2/4 Châsseurs. This battalion, 'big' because of the amalgamation, had over 800 all ranks. It was commanded by Major Agnès and had as its surgeon the famous Maugras, ex-Polish Lancers, who was himself wounded tending casualties at Austerlitz and had been Surgeon-Major of the Guard at Jena in 1806. The regiment's adjutant-major (captain staff officer) had been a soldier in the Swiss Guard twenty-eight years before, later becoming a corporal in the Consular Guard. Agnès was killed at Waterloo leading his men forward to the final assault.

The Young Guard Division (Général de Division Comte Duhesme with Général de Division Comte Barrois as second in command)

Napoleon reconstituted the Young Guard in early April 1815 by reforming the former tirailleur and voltigeur regiments originally created during the period 1809–13. The Young Guard received the same pay as the Line infantry but had the various Guard insignia, drum beats and were exempt from the more mundane fatigues.

Regiments left on campaign wearing blue-grey greatcoats with red epaulettes for the tirailleurs and green for the voltigeurs. They wore the bell-topped shakos, some covered with a waterproof oilskin cloth. As only officers and NCOs carried a sword or sabre-briquet, the guardsmen had only the one cross-belt to which the bayonet scabbard was attached. Their muskets were the usual Line issue. Neither the tirailleur nor voltigeur regiments had Eagles at Waterloo, but they did have drummers and fifers. Both brigades had some musicians equipped with instruments 'found' in the châsseurs' magazine, but not a full band.

The entire division was committed to the fight at Ligny where they were needed on the French left to support Vandamme's corps in its struggle for the villages of St Amand and Le Hameau. At Waterloo the whole division was again the first Guard formation into action when, at around 6.00 p.m., it was sent to hold Plancenoit. It spent the remainder of the battle fighting for this village.

The division was divided into two brigades; the 1st Brigade under Maréchal de Camp Chartrand, who survived the battle only to be shot for treason later, consisted of two regiments:

1st Tirailleurs

Slightly over 1,100 strong, this regiment was under the command of Colonel Trappier de Malcolm who later became a general under Louis-Philippe.

1/1 Tirailleurs. About 560 strong under Major Cogne.

2/1 Tirailleurs. 550 strong under Major Delaunay.

1st Voltigeurs

A large regiment of over 1,200 all ranks under the command of Colonel Sécrètan who had been wounded as a captain at the Battle of Essling in 1809 when the Young Guard had lost 25 per cent of its strength. He had fought in Spain as a battalion commander and took over a brigade in the defence of Paris in 1814.

1/1 Voltigeurs. Over 600 strong commanded by Major Guasco, an officer who had been with Napoleon on Elba and marched to Paris with him.

2/1 Voltigeurs. Slightly over 600 strong, this battalion was under Major Laborde who had been the adjutant-major on Elba and, like Guasco, had accompanied the Emperor all the way to Fontainebleau.

The 2nd Brigade was a weaker formation, having over 400 men less than the 1st Brigade. It was commanded by Maréchal de Camp Baron Guye who had been wounded at Craonne but recovered in time to take part in the defence of Paris. It was composed of two regiments:

3rd Tirailleurs

Under 1000 strong commanded by Colonel Pailhès. He had fought at Austerlitz, served as an ADC in Spain and commanded the 4th Tirailleurs during the retreat from Moscow. In later years he was promoted general by Louis-Philippe.

1/3 Tirailleurs. 500 all ranks commanded by Major Dambly.

2/3 Tirailleurs. 488 all ranks commanded by Major Jacquot.

3rd Voltigeurs

Also under 1000 strong commanded by Colonel Hurel.

1/3 Voltigeurs. 480 all ranks commanded by Major Pion.

2/3 Voltigeurs. 487 all ranks under Major Roby.

Imperial Guard Infantry – The Reckoning

Although none of the Guard was sent into action until about 6.00 p.m., over six hours after the battle had started, every battalion was required to fight, and fight hard. Each division was committed to meet a crisis and, because of this, found itself involved in the most intense and desperate clashes at Waterloo.

The Young Guard fought the longest (for nearly three hours) in Plancenoit. Theirs was a particularly protracted and bitter struggle, much of it at close quarters. The severity of fighting is reflected in the table opposite which gives the numbers of those who attended the final musters between the 23–26 June – only 14 per cent of the Young Guard infantry paraded. The Middle Guard was used to try to snatch a last minute victory by advancing slowly up an open slope, in squares, into withering blasts of cannonball and canister fire. With the exception of the two battalions sucked into Plancenoit and the one left at Le Caillou, the Old Guard battalions were shredded in their heroic attempts to stop the Anglo-Allied general advance. Several of these battalions lost half of their strength in half an hour. Major Belcourt, commanding the only Middle Guard battalion (2/3 Grenadiers) not involved in the final assault, saw his command cut from about 580 to 200 in this period.

The table below shows the estimated all rank strengths of the Guard infantry at the start of the battle, the strength at the final muster a week later and the percentage of those then present.

	strength on 18 June	strength on 26 June	% present
1st Grenadiers	1,280	644	50
2nd Grenadiers	1,090	374	34
1st Châsseurs	1,307	588	45
2nd Châsseurs	1,163	375	32
Total Old Guard	**4,840**	**1,981**	**41**
3rd Grenadiers	1,164	201	16
4th Grenadiers	520	100	17
3rd Châsseurs	1,062	165	15
4th Châsseurs	841	244	29
Total Middle Guard	**3,587**	**710**	**20**
1st Voltigeurs	1,219	196	16
3rd Voltigeurs	967	146	13
1st Tirailleurs	1,109	83	8
3rd Tirailleurs	988	164	16
Total Young Guard	**4,283**	**589**	**14**
Total of all Guard infantry	**12,710**	**3,280**	**26**

Barely a quarter of the Imperial Guard infantry were available for duty a week after Waterloo. Of the twelve regiments, seven had shrunk to less than 20 per cent of their former strength; the 1st Tirailleurs with 8 per cent could only muster a weak company. The Young Guard had been hit hardest (a reflection on the length of time they fought in Plancenoit), with the Old Guard (still in reserve at the end and therefore in action for the shortest time) being the least severely mauled. Of the regimental commanders and above, three were killed (Duhesme, Michel and Malet) and six wounded (Friant, Morvan, Cambronne, Guye, Henrion and d'Harlet). All officers in the 3rd and 4th Châsseurs and 4th Grenadiers were either killed or wounded.

With the restoration of the King the remnants of the Guard were broken up, scattered throughout France, across Europe, into Turkey and America. Some were fleeing the 'white terror' (the Bourbons ruthless revenge on the more ardent Bonapartists) that had Chartrand shot, others merely seeking anonymity and obscurity. To earn a living some men served the King. Louis-Philippe later recalled Guard veterans still fit enough to serve, so men such as Roguet, Petit, Morvan, Barrois, Guye, Henrion and d'Harlet donned a uniform again. Pailhès and Trappier, survivors of the carnage in Plancenoit, both became generals.

Like all old soldiers, the Guard did not forget their days of glory. Old uniforms were kept in cupboards, medals polished and hung over mantlepieces and stories of battles grew in the telling. Above all 'He' was remembered. Similarly, Napoleon, exiled to St Helena, remembered his beloved Guard. In his will he left 200,000 francs to be divided among the amputees of Ligny and Waterloo, with double to the Guard and quadruple to former members of the Napoleon Battalion. Another 300,000 was to be distributed specifically to the officers and men of the Guard who served on Elba, or their widows and children – the shares of amputees and severely wounded to be double.

An Imperial Guard officers' association was set up and regular reunions held. At a dinner in 1845 General Schramm, their president, eulogized their commander at Waterloo, Drouot, who had died the previous year. In 1850 General Petit was made president of the association and, with ranks thinning rapidly, proposed that former senior NCOs of the Guard, who at the time had ranked as officers in the Line, be eligible to join. Ten years later survivors received the St Helena Medal from Napoleon's nephew, then the Emperor. A handful of men hung on into their dotage. Vivien, a soldier who had fought so desperately in Plancenoit with the 2nd Châsseurs, died in 1892 at Lyons aged 106. And a Lieutenant Markiewicz of the Polish Lancers lived in three centuries. He was born in Cracow in 1794, fought in Russia, charged at Waterloo and was still alive in 1902. Despite their losses in the last battle, the Imperial Guard took a long time to fade away.

PRUSSIAN INFANTRY

General

The overall performance of the Prussian infantry at Waterloo was far higher than might have been expected from a force with over 50 per cent of its battalions landwehr (militia/reserve) units. Despite this, each had a fair proportion of veterans who had seen service during the prolonged fighting of 1813–14 that ended with the final advance on Paris. That it did so well was even more remarkable, as the Prussian infantry (like the French) was required to attack – often more demanding of morale and courage for any troops than defending. Bülow's IV Corps was the first to reach the eastern extremity of the battlefield at around 4.30 p.m., and it was his command that did most of the serious fighting in the push towards, and repeated attacks on, Plancenoit over the next four hours. Out of his force of thirty-four battalions, two-thirds (twenty-three) were landwehr units whose opponents for the final two hours were the Imperial Guard.

An impartial observer who understood the problems faced by the Prussian Army during its formation and over the last few weeks in the field could be forgiven for having doubts as to its likely performance in the coming clash. As he watched Bülow's worn out, mud-caked infantry hauling themselves metre by metre out of the Lasne defile at little over a kilometre an hour, he could have been looking at an army in retreat. But for the determination, loyalty to the allied cause and strategic clear sightedness of the Prussian high command, they might well have been straggling east away from the war, rather than west towards it. Two days before they had been defeated at Ligny with the loss of nearly 19,000 men; the previous day nearly another 10,000 disaffected Rhinelanders had disappeared towards Liège. In two days the army had shrunk by 29,000, or 22 per cent. Before that, in early May, prior to a shot being fired, their Saxon contingent of 14,000 had been dismissed in disgrace following a mutiny. It had been a bleak start for the Prussians.

Many of the difficulties stemmed from the fact that following the 1814 armistice most Rhineland territories had been absorbed by Prussia after a long period of French occupation. And Rhinelanders

The Prussian infantryman's personal equipment (line regiment musketeer)

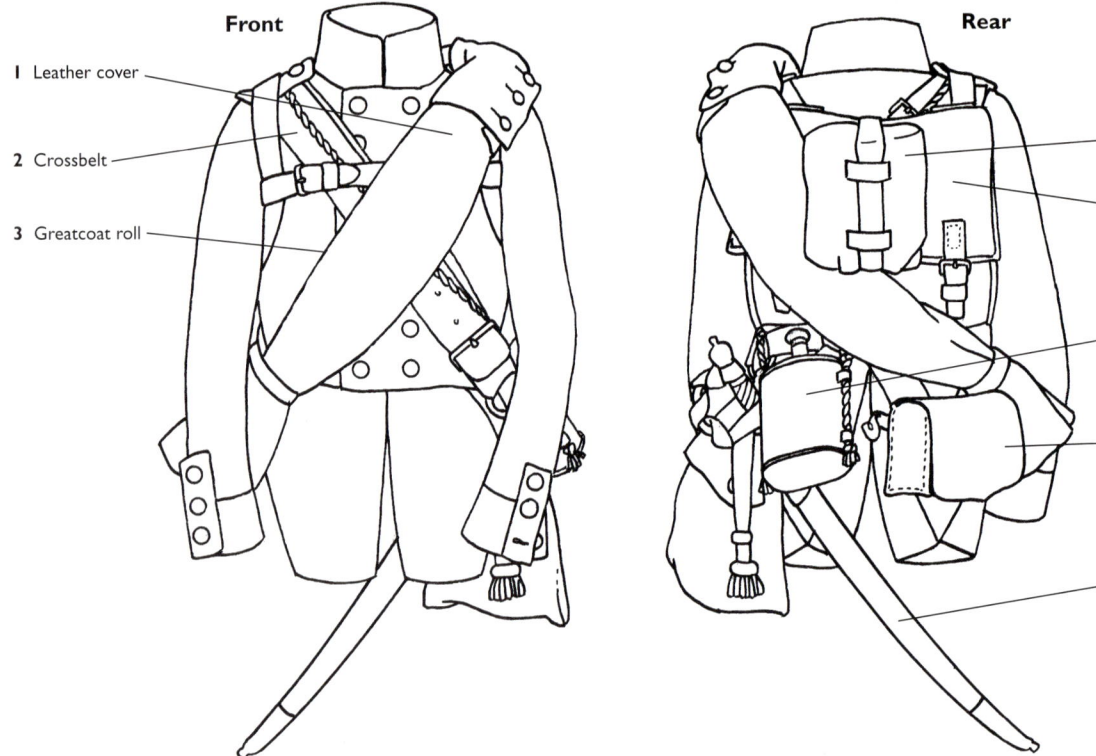

Front

1 Leather cover
2 Crossbelt
3 Greatcoat roll

Rear

4 Canteen
5 Knapsack
6 Water bottle
7 Cartouche box
8 Sword

Notes

1 This piece of leather cloth was wrapped around the greatcoat roll to help keep it from working loose and slipping off the shoulder.

2 A single crossbelt slung over the right shoulder to which was attached the sword frog.

3 The greatcoat/blanket roll was often carried over the left shoulder rather than on top of the knapsack. This method was popular with the Prussians, and items of clothing or other small personal belongings inside acted as quite effective protection from sword cuts.

4 The canteen, like the French, was strapped to the outside of the knapsack.

5 The Prussian knapsack was sometimes made of goat or calfskin like the French and had the usual fastenings of buckle straps like a satchel.

6 Again, like the French, the Prussian soldier had to pick up the best he could by way of a water bottle.

7 The cartouche box was leather and like those of other nationalities contained cartridges and cleaning tools.

8 All line regiments' infantrymen carried a sword. Interestingly, they did not have bayonet scabbards as it was the practice to always have bayonets fixed.

---

had never liked Prussians. The people of Mainz claimed, 'It took a year of the Prussian regime to make us sorry they [the French] had left.' They objected to being required to fight for arrogant Prussians. The Silesians drafted into landwehr regiments soon acquired the highest desertion rate in the army – but, perversely, they fought with remarkable tenacity and courage at Waterloo. There had been a massive rationalization of the army, with old regiments disappearing, unfamiliar new names and numbers handed out, the recall of disgruntled soldiers only recently discharged, and the drafting of reluctant recruits to fill landwehr battalions. Many came from territories that had been part of the French Empire for two decades – some soldiers probably spoke French better than German. Compounding all this were the empty coffers of the Prussian treasury. Equipment, uniforms, food and fodder cost money but the quartermasters in the field could only offer dubious paper receipts.

That the morale of the majority of the Prussian Army withstood the rigours of the field and the shock of Ligny was due to the high quality of leadership at all levels. The officer corps, many themselves inexperienced, coped remarkably well with the problems of campaigning and battle. At the top the combination of 'Papa' Blücher's 'hands-on' leadership, courage, and implacable hatred of the French, with the strategic and administrative talents of his chief of staff, Gneisenau, ensured the army did not break despite the series of setbacks.

ORGANIZATION

Infantry Brigades (Maps 35, 36, 37 & 38, pp. 384, 385, 387 & 392) As stated previously, the Prussian brigade was the equivalent of a French or Anglo-Allied division. Its commander was usually a major-general, but could be a lieutenant-general (13th Brigade) or a colonel (14th and 16th Brigades). All, except for the 1st Brigade, had one or two squadrons of cavalry under command for scouting; most had some jaeger detachments or rifle troops, and each had a battery of artillery in direct support.

The Prussian brigades that, in whole or in part, fought at Waterloo are listed below with the number of infantry (38,000) that were actually engaged (or came under fire):

I Corps – Lieutenant-General Count Hans von Ziethen
1st Infantry Brigade – 2,920, Major-General Karl von Steinmetz
II Corps – Major-General von Pirch I
5th Infantry Brigade – 4,840, Major-General Count von Tippelskirch
6th Infantry Brigade – 4,188, Major-General von Krafft
7th Infantry Brigade – 1,650, Major-General von Brause
IV Corps – Major-General Count Bülow von Dennewitz
13th Brigade – 6,833, Major-General von Hake
14th Brigade – 5,493, Major-General von Ryssel
15th Brigade – 6,105, Major-General von Losthin
16th Brigade – 5,955, Colonel Hiller von Gartringen (acting)

Private, 2nd (Coldstream) Foot Guards

Private, 92nd (Gordon) Highlanders

Rifleman, 95th Rifles

PLATE 1 – *Anglo-Allied Infantry*

Private, 52nd
(Oxfordshire)
Light Infantry

Ensign, 27th (Inniskilling) Regiment

Private, 28th (North Gloucestershire) Regiment

PLATE 2 – *Anglo-Allied Infantry*

Private, 2nd Light Battalion, King's German Legion

Private, 4th (Dutch)
National Militia

Officer, 1st Battalion,
2nd Nassau

Grenadier Corporal,
7th (Belgian) Infantry

PLATE 3 – *Anglo-Allied Infantry*

Private, Hanoverian
Osnabrück Landwehr

Private, Hanoverian
Feld-Battalion Verden

Officer, Hanoverian Lüneburg Light Battalion

PLATE 4 – *Anglo-Allied Infantry*

Private, Prussian
1st Silesian Landwehr

Private, Prussian 2nd Battalion 18th Regiment

Sergeant, Brunswick
1st Line Battalion

PLATE 5 – *Prussian Infantry*

Officer, Châsseurs à Pied,
Imperial Guard

Private, 1st Grenadiers à Pied, Imperial Guard

Officer, 3rd Voltigeurs,
Imperial Guard

Private, 1st Tirailleurs, Imperial Guard

PLATE 6 – *French Infantry*

Voltigeur, 1st
Light Infantry

Eagle-Bearer,
45th Regiment

Grenadier Sergeant,
72nd Regiment

PLATE 7 – *French Infantry*

Trooper,
7th (Queen's Own) Hussars

Officer,
11th Light Dragoons

Bugler/Trumpeter,
1st Life Guards

PLATE 8 – *Anglo-Allied Cavalry*

Sergeant, 6th (Inniskilling) Dragoons

Trooper, 1st Light Dragoons,
King's German Legion

Trooper, Hanoverian
Duke of Cumberland's Hussars

Trooper, 3rd Hussars,
King's German Legion

PLATE 9 – *Anglo-Allied Cavalry*

Trooper, 8th (Belgian) Hussars

Trooper,
4th (Dutch)
Light Dragoons

Trooper,
2nd (Belgian)
Carabiniers

Trooper, 1st (Dutch) Carabiniers

PLATE 10 – *Anglo-Allied Cavalry*

Trooper,
Châsseurs à Cheval, Imperial Guard

Trooper,
Empress's Dragoons, Imperial Guard

Trooper,
2nd (Red) Lancers, Imperial Guard

PLATE 11 – *French Cavalry*

Trooper,
7th Dragoons

Trooper, Grenadiers à Cheval, Imperial Guard

Trooper, 8th Cuirassiers

PLATE 12 – *French Cavalry*

Maréchal de Logis, 1st Châsseurs à Cheval

Trooper, 4th Lancers

Trooper, 7th Hussars

PLATE 13 – *French Cavalry*

Trooper,
6th (2nd Silesian) Hussars

Officer,
1st West Prussian Uhlans

Trooper,
1st Pomeranian Landwehr

PLATE 14 – *Prussian Cavalry*

Driver,
Royal Wagon Train

Sergeant-Major,
Royal Foot Artillery

Gunner, Royal Horse Artillery

PLATE 15 – *Anglo-Allied Artillery/Others*

Driver,
Artillery Train

Gunner,
Foot Artillery

Gunner,
Horse Artillery

PLATE 16 – *French Artillery/Others*

These eight brigades fought at Waterloo, although only half – the four in IV Corps (Bülow) – were heavily engaged. All arrived piecemeal, being committed to the action the moment they reached the battlefield. The first to appear from the Bois de Paris were Losthin's 15th and Hiller's 16th Brigades. Like everyone else, they had endured a wet and miserable night, been paraded before 4.00 a.m., and arrived at the eastern extremity of the battlefield after over twelve hours on the move. These troops had marched 17 kilometres (from Dion le Mont, south-east of Wavre) averaging just under 1.5 kilometres to the hour (not quite one mile per hour). These brigades had done nothing but march since the campaign started three days before. From their cantonments around Liège many had covered over 70 kilometres towards Ligny, only to be diverted towards Wavre as most of the army streamed north after its defeat.

At 4.30 that afternoon they began the 2000-metre fighting advance towards Plancenoit. An hour later the 13th Brigade (Hake) cleared the Bois de Paris and came forward to reinforce the leading formations (15th and 16th Brigades). It was followed by the 14th Brigade (Ryssel), which had left two battalions on detachment south of Wavre. The 13th was quickly drawn into the fight against Lobau's troops, helping to push them slowly back across the open ground north-east of Plancenoit. The 14th was destined to become embroiled with Hiller's 16th Brigade in a close combat battle with the Young Guard for, perhaps appropriately, the graveyard around the church in Plancenoit. It was later thrown out of the village by two battalions of the Old Guard.

Behind Bülow's IV Corps came the three brigades of Pirch I's II Corps, the 5th, 6th and 7th, that would eventually reach the battlefield. The seven brigades of these two corps had been moving along a single road. An endless snake of soldiers, guns and wagons occupied every one of the 12,000 metres back to Bierges. There were all the frustrations of a long march, continual stopping, starting and concertinaing – the 'hurry up and wait' phenomena so familiar to infantrymen down the ages. The leading formation of II Corps, Tippelskirch's 5th Brigade, debouched from the Bois de Paris shortly after 6.30, just as Bülow's troops were regrouping after being ejected from Plancenoit by the Old Guard. The brigade was immediately ordered to spearhead another assault on the village. The prospect of more ferocious street fighting cannot have been good news to battalions down to 500 strong, some commanded by captains, as a result of the recent struggle for Ligny.

As the 7th Brigade (the third in the corps order of march) under Major-General Brause had straggled passed the tiny roadside chapel at St Lambert, a staff officer from Blücher diverted it south. It was to be a flank guard that would advance on the village of Maransart along the south bank of the Lasne. It turned out to be an easy mission. Only the leading battalion (2nd Elbe Landwehr) could claim to have been under fire at Waterloo. The 8th Brigade (Bose) never made it in time to see any action.

Arriving even later, by the more northerly route that led to Wellington's left (eastern) flank, were the advance elements of Ziethen's I Corps. At around 7.00 p.m. the 1st Brigade under Major-General Steinmetz appeared on the road from Ohain. This brigade had suffered harshly in the days before Waterloo and had shrunk from almost 8000 men to fewer than 5000 – it had lost 46 officers and 2,300 men amongst the houses and along the narrow, cobbled streets of St Amand (near Ligny). Within half an hour of arriving, its two leading regiments (12th and 24th Infantry) were committed to the fighting around Papelotte and La Haie. The third regiment (1st Westphalian Landwehr)

probably considered itself fortunate to arrive too late to see action. The regiments that saw action at Waterloo, together with their strengths and commanding officers, are given below. Noticeably, those that fought at Ligny are well under 2000 strong.

1st Brigade
12th Infantry – 1,460, Lieutenant-Colonel von Othegraven
24th Infantry – 1,460, Major von Laurens

5th Brigade
2nd Infantry – 1,630, Major von Cardell
25th Infantry – 1,580, Major von Helmenstreit
5th Westphalian Landwehr – 1,630, Major von Roebel

6th Brigade
9th Infantry – 1,650, Major von Schmidt
26th Infantry – 1,008, Colonel von Reuss
1st Elbe Landwehr – 1,530, Colonel von Bismarck

7th Brigade
2nd Elbe Landwehr – 1,650, Major von Reckow

13th Brigade
10th Infantry – 2,393, Colonel von Lettow
2nd Neumärk Landwehr – 2,074, Major von Braunschweig
3rd Neumärk Landwehr – 2,366, Major von Schmalensee

14th Brigade
11th Infantry – 1,438, (one battalion detached) Major Count von Reichenbach
1st Pomeranian Landwehr – 1,640, (one battalion detached) Lieutenant-Colonel von Brandenstein
2nd Pomeranian Landwehr – 2,415, Major von Pewels

15th Brigade
18th Infantry – 2,400, Colonel von Loebell
3rd Silesian Landwehr – 1,930, Major von Thile
4th Silesian Landwehr – 1,775, Lieutenant-Colonel von Massow

16th Brigade
15th Infantry – 2,445, Colonel von Creilsheim
1st Silesian Landwehr – 1,800, Major von Fischer
2nd Silesian Landwehr – 1,710, Lieutenant-Colonel von Blandowski

The Prussians lost some 7000 all ranks at Waterloo, of which just over 6,600 (94 per cent) were infantrymen. Of these, over 6000 (90 per cent) were in the brigades of IV Corps, where one man in four was destined to be killed, wounded or go missing. In summary, the approximate infantry casualties are given below:

Brigade	Strength on arrival	Losses (approximate)	Percentage
1st	2,920	300	10
5th	4,840	300	6
6th	4,188	35	1
7th	1,650	5	-
13th	6,833	970	14
14th	5,493	1,395	25
15th	6,105	1,795	29
16th	5,955	1,825	31
Totals	**37,984**	**6,625**	**17**

Regiments

Like those of the French, the Prussian regiments were tactical units. There were twenty-one at Waterloo, divided between the regular line regiments (ten) and landwehr militia (eleven). The Prussians did not have guard or grenadier units. Each regular regiment had two musketeer (line) battalions and one fusilier (light) battalion – many also had small, company sized detachments of jaeger troops as sharpshooters. The landwehr had three musketeer battalions. A regiment was supposedly a colonel's command, but heavy losses at Ligny meant that at Waterloo only five had colonels, four had lieutenant-colonels and twelve had majors as commanding officers.

The strongest was the 15th Infantry with some 2,445 all ranks. The weakest, due to losses at Ligny, was the 26th Infantry Regiment with only 1,008. The regiments that led the advance to Plancenoit, and were involved in the subsequent two to three hour fight for the village, suffered the most. The 18th Infantry Regiment (15th Brigade) had the highest losses: over 800, or 33 per cent. The 15th Infantry Regiment with 660, or 27 per cent, suffered the next biggest loss.

Battalions

A total of sixty-one Prussian battalions, plus another battalion's worth of jaeger and Silesian sharpshooters, reached the battlefield of Waterloo in time to claim genuine participation in Napoleon's ultimate defeat. They were divided into nine Fusilier (light), twenty Musketeer (line) and thirty-two Landwehr (militia) battalions. They had an average strength of 615. There were eleven battalions with 800 or more all ranks (full war establishment). The intensity of the fighting at Ligny was clear from the fact that every battalion at that battle went into action at Waterloo with a strength of 550 or less. Colonel von Reuss's three battalions had under 350 apiece – only 44 per cent of their proper war establishment.

The battalions, all of which had the same basic internal organization, were normally under the command of a major, but at Waterloo in a number of battalions that had fought at Ligny the senior officer was a captain. Each had a small headquarters staff, part of which was the Colour party. Officially, every battalion was supposed to carry two Colours but this did not happen at Waterloo. The Colour was carried by a junior officer, normally a 2nd lieutenant called a *fahnentrager*, escorted by two corporals (*unteroffizier*). Every battalion had four companies, each of which was divided into two platoons, or zuge, (singular zug), which were numbered consecutively through the three battalions in a regiment – that is one to twenty-four. Within a Prussian battalion of 800 all ranks every company would have around 200 made up of a captain, a 1st lieutenant, three 2nd lieutenants, a sergeant-major (*feldwebel*), three sergeants (*sergeanten*), eleven corporals (*unteroffiziere*), twenty lance-corporals (*gefreite*), two drummers/horn players and 157 soldiers. At Waterloo many of the battalions in Bülow's IV Corps had companies of almost this number, although those companies in a battalion of average strength (615) had only 150 all ranks. At the other extreme those in the battalions of the 26th Infantry Regiment had shrunk to around seventy-five. The reason for this was that although the peacetime establishment of a Prussian battalion was about 630 (which allowed about 150 men per company), on mobilization the establishment was automatically increased by the addition of fifty soldiers per company. Casualties at Ligny meant that the infantry elements of I and II Corps that fought at Waterloo did so at their peacetime strength.

A musketeer battalion was a line battalion while a fusilier battalion was, although armed with the same musket, a light unit trained to function as such. In theory, battalions in the landwehr regiments were also categorized in the same manner. As late as 8 June 1815 Blücher issued an instruction to all brigade commanders that landwehr regiments that had not yet done so were to designate one battalion as the light battalion. This unit, as well as third ranks, was to be well trained in skirmishing and individual combat. He had left it a little late. Nevertheless, the Prussians had moved a long way towards having all-purpose infantry. Blücher also stipulated that nine battalion brigades would, as a rule, deploy for a set piece attack (such as on Plancenoit) – although tactical circumstances, strengths and casualties could mean modifications.

Most Prussians had blue uniforms. Even the landwehr, once the most wretchedly clothed and equipped militia in Europe, wore reasonable uniforms at Waterloo, with the distinctive white 'Landwehr Cross' on the front of their black cloth cap (*schirmutze*). What usually distinguished the Prussian infantryman, seen fleetingly through the smoke, was his blanket/greatcoat roll tied over his left shoulder. It was also possible to tell a musketeer from a fusilier by his equipment. The former had white leather equipment and his cartridge pouch was worn on the hip; his fusilier comrade had black equipment while his cartridge pouch was attached to the front of his waist belt.

WEAPONS

At least 95 per cent of Prussian infantry carried the musket, there being no difference between that carried by the musketeer or the fusilier. It was the Potsdam version first manufactured in 1782. It had a slightly larger calibre and weight than both the French and British muskets but its rate of fire and range were virtually the same. Unlike other armies, the Prussian infantryman had no bayonet scabbard and so kept his bayonet on the end of his musket for most of the time. It would be interesting to know how many accidents this caused, particularly when using a ramrod.

Swords were carried by all officers, sergeants, corporals, drummers, musicians and line regular fusiliers.

TACTICS

General

Like the French, the Prussian tactics at Waterloo were offensive. They were attacking and, initially, when they emerged from the Bois de Paris, advancing to contact the enemy and screened by cavalry. The leading formations of Bülow's corps were required to advance, to push back Lobau's troops and threaten Napoleon's right flank and rear. Later they, and those that followed, were involved in the most dreaded type of infantry combat – street fighting and house clearance. 'Fighting in built up areas' (FIBUA), as it is called in modern military terminology, was what taking Plancenoit involved. Street fighting soaks up soldiers as a sponge does water, and by late evening even the small village of Plancenoit had thousands of troops from both sides crammed into its narrow streets, engaged in a struggle for every house, alley, garden and the churchyard. There was no possibility of keeping formations; battalions and companies mixed and mingled in a confusing press of bodies, noise and smoke. Gone were the lines and columns of open ground (although they have to be depicted this way on the maps), in their place small groups and individuals fired at each other at ranges of 5 metres or less, then wielded butt and bayonet as they contested every house, every room. It was the tactics of a massive ale-house brawl where the sergeant and the corporal were of more use than the officer. Unlike their comrades in the other corps that had fought at Ligny, Bülow's troops had not tasted this sort of combat before.

Attack Formations – General

By 1815, although the Prussian infantry was divided into musketeer and fusilier battalions, they had virtually become all-purpose infantry. This meant that all, including landwehr units, were expected to fight in line or to provide skirmish troops according to the circumstances. While the fusiliers were the first choice of a brigade commander who needed skirmishers, his musketeer units could, and frequently did, provide their own. They did it by deploying their third rank soldiers as skirmishers. The key features of this system in use at Waterloo were:

• All Prussian infantry formed in close order did so in three ranks, but the third rank did not fire. It was used to reinforce the other two, extend the line if necessary and provide skirmishers. The Infantry Regulations of 1812 makes it clear that the second rank took a pace to the right so that it could fire through the gaps in the first rank while the third took a pace back and stood fast. The biggest and strongest formed the first rank and 'the most nimble and best shots are selected for the third'.
• All infantry was supposed to be able to operate in open or broken country against dispersed or close order troops. Every unit (battalion) or sub-unit (company) had to be capable of providing skirmishers (from their third rank) or of fighting in close order.
• If a fusilier battalion was available it was likely the whole unit would be used forward in the skirmishing role. If this was insufficient then a musketeer battalion could also be used.
• The actual skirmish line would be two-deep, with about half the unit kept 100 paces behind as supports or reserve in a close order, two rank line. At Waterloo a fusilier or musketeer battalion of 800 men in the skirmishing role would deploy one zug (platoon) from each company (almost 400 men) forward to provide the actual skirmishers, with the other four zuge 100 paces behind as supports. This formation would cover some 200 metres of front.

The attack column (angriffskolonne)

When Prussian infantry marched onto the battlefield it normally did so in the zug column. To advance to the attack a battalion would adopt the double zug attack column. Points to note are:

• The soldiers in the zuge were in three ranks, and they were generally formed closed up with the rear rank of the leading zuge only about two feet in front of the first rank of the zug behind. In this formation a full strength zug of nearly 100 would cover a frontage of about 22 metres, so the double zug column's frontage would be around 45 metres and slightly under 20 metres deep. This formation was very vulnerable to artillery fire but could produce a line extremely quickly (see diagram p. 212).

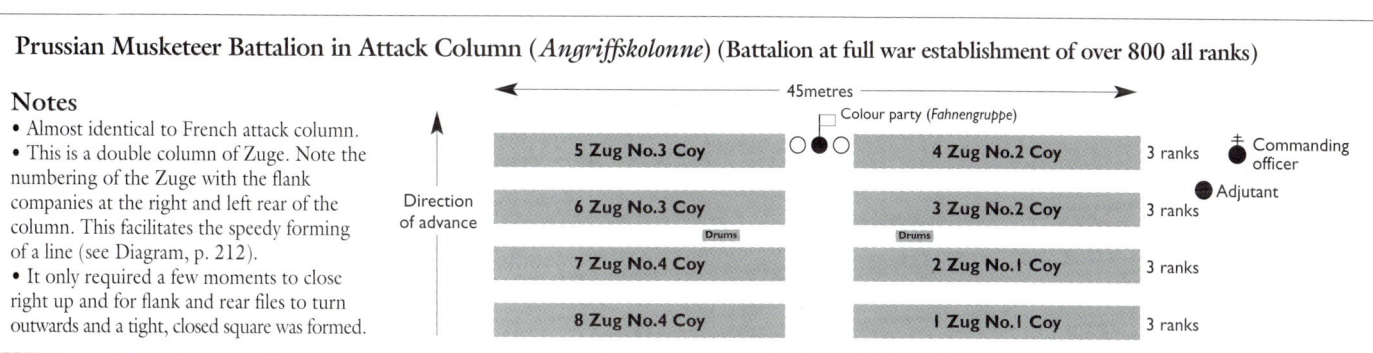

Prussian Musketeer Battalion in Attack Column (*Angriffskolonne*) (Battalion at full war establishment of over 800 all ranks)

Notes
• Almost identical to French attack column.
• This is a double column of Zuge. Note the numbering of the Zuge with the flank companies at the right and left rear of the column. This facilitates the speedy forming of a line (see Diagram, p. 212).
• It only required a few moments to close right up and for flank and rear files to turn outwards and a tight, closed square was formed.

45 metres

Colour party (*Fahnengruppe*)

Direction of advance

5 Zug No.3 Coy	4 Zug No.2 Coy	3 ranks
6 Zug No.3 Coy	3 Zug No.2 Coy	3 ranks
7 Zug No.4 Coy	2 Zug No.1 Coy	3 ranks
8 Zug No.4 Coy	1 Zug No.1 Coy	3 ranks

Drums

Commanding officer
Adjutant

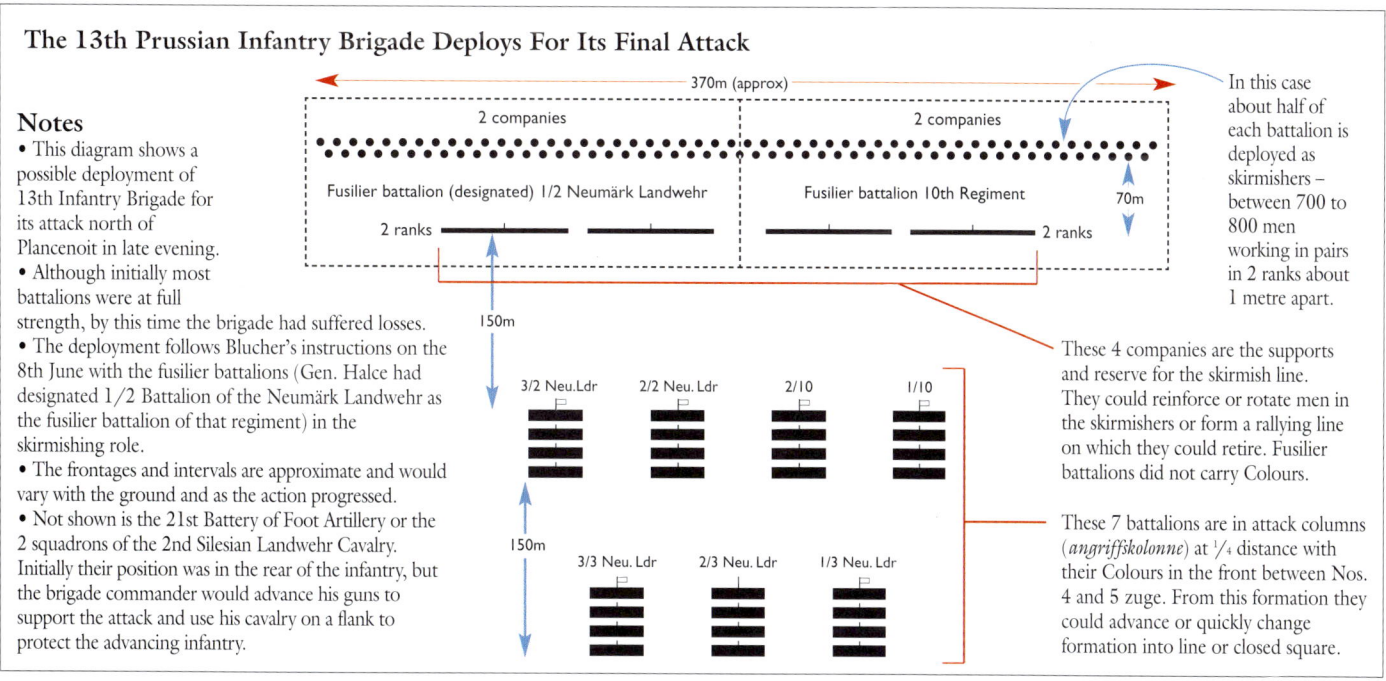

The 13th Prussian Infantry Brigade Deploys For Its Final Attack

Notes
• This diagram shows a possible deployment of 13th Infantry Brigade for its attack north of Plancenoit in late evening.
• Although initially most battalions were at full strength, by this time the brigade had suffered losses.
• The deployment follows Blucher's instructions on the 8th June with the fusilier battalions (Gen. Halce had designated 1/2 Battalion of the Neumärk Landwehr as the fusilier battalion of that regiment) in the skirmishing role.
• The frontages and intervals are approximate and would vary with the ground and as the action progressed.
• Not shown is the 21st Battery of Foot Artillery or the 2 squadrons of the 2nd Silesian Landwehr Cavalry. Initially their position was in the rear of the infantry, but the brigade commander would advance his guns to support the attack and use his cavalry on a flank to protect the advancing infantry.

370m (approx)

2 companies   2 companies

Fusilier battalion (designated) 1/2 Neumärk Landwehr   Fusilier battalion 10th Regiment

2 ranks   2 ranks

70m

150m

3/2 Neu.Ldr   2/2 Neu.Ldr   2/10   1/10

150m

3/3 Neu.Ldr   2/3 Neu.Ldr   1/3 Neu.Ldr

In this case about half of each battalion is deployed as skirmishers – between 700 to 800 men working in pairs in 2 ranks about 1 metre apart.

These 4 companies are the supports and reserve for the skirmish line. They could reinforce or rotate men in the skirmishers or form a rallying line on which they could retire. Fusilier battalions did not carry Colours.

These 7 battalions are in attack columns (*angriffskolonne*) at 1/4 distance with their Colours in the front between Nos. 4 and 5 zuge. From this formation they could advance or quickly change formation into line or closed square.

Prussian Battalion Forming Line From Attack Column

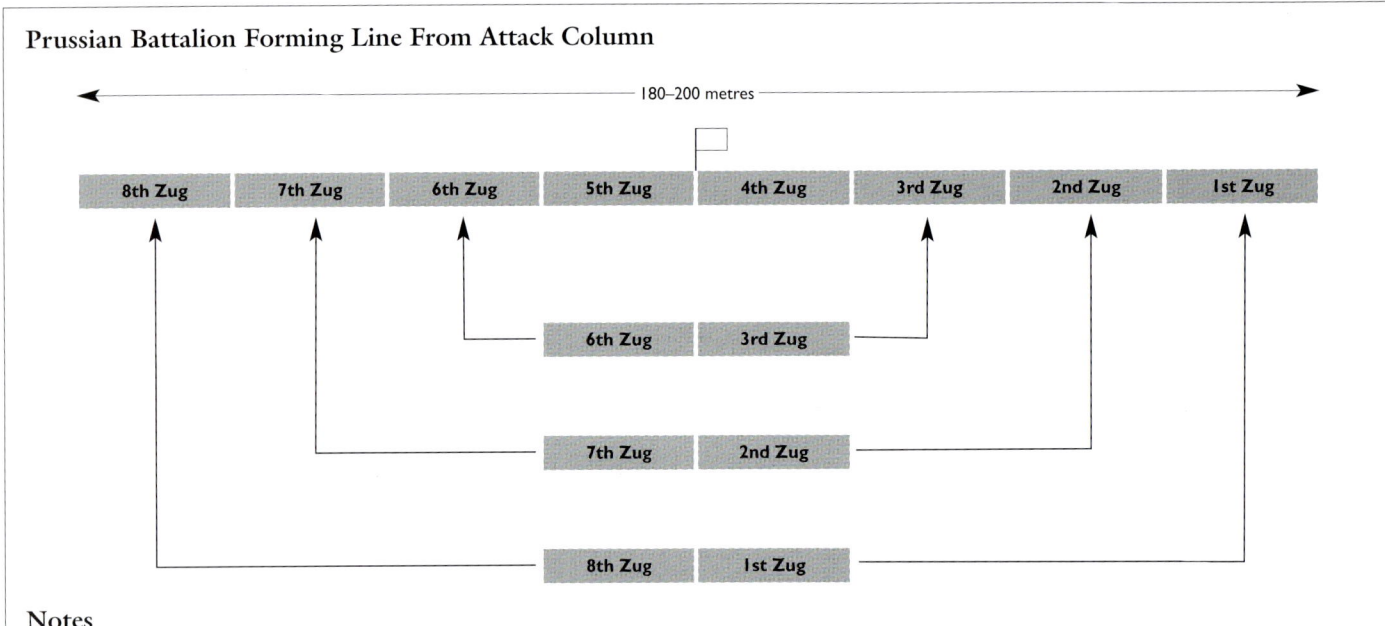

Notes

• The battalion used the attack column to advance across the battlefield. On nearing the enemy it would endeavour to deploy into line for the fire fight or the assault. This formation change took about 1.5 minutes to complete in reasonable conditions.

• The drums/horns formed behind the Colours and the CO and Adjutant took position behind the 4th Zug.

Prussian Company in three Ranks (part of a battalion in close order line)

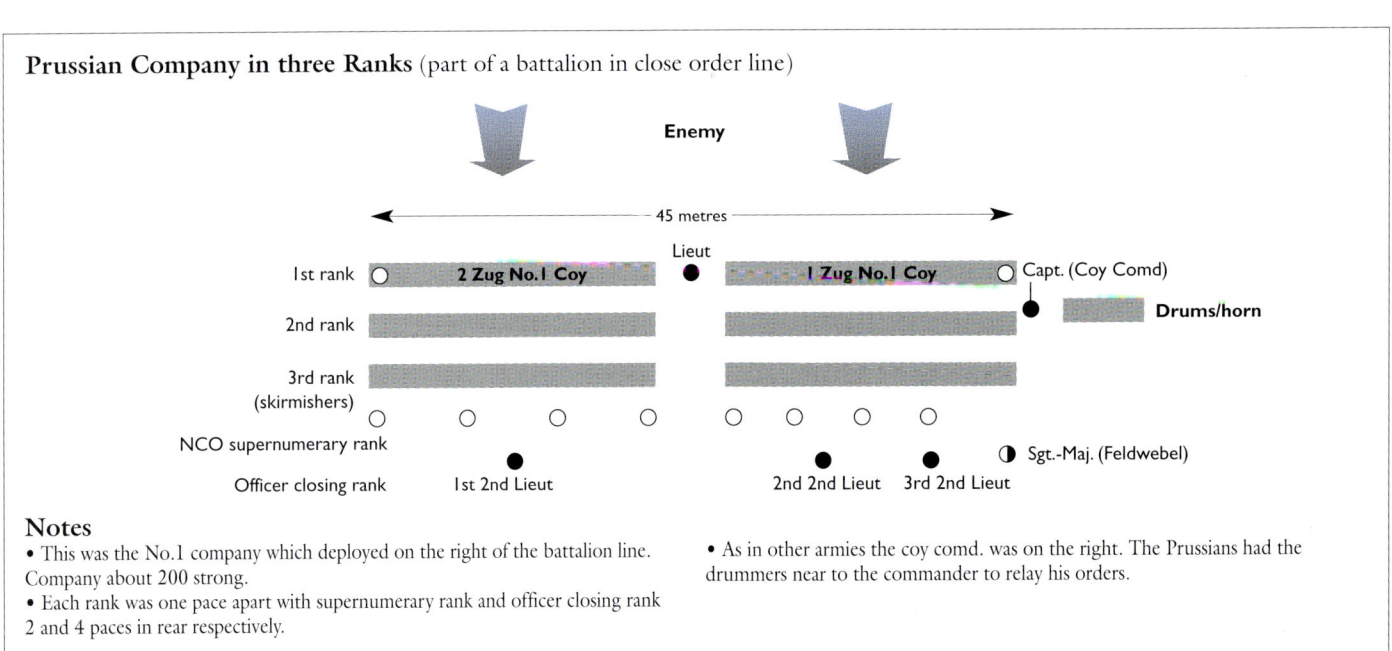

Notes

• This was the No.1 company which deployed on the right of the battalion line. Company about 200 strong.
• Each rank was one pace apart with supernumerary rank and officer closing rank 2 and 4 paces in rear respectively.

• As in other armies the coy comd. was on the right. The Prussians had the drummers near to the commander to relay his orders.

• This formation was virtually identical to the French column of attack and was primarily intended for movement across the battlefield prior to forming a three rank line for a firefight or an assault. Battalions attacking Plancenoit soon lost all resemblance to any particular formation as they reached the village.

The line (Diagram above)

As with the line in other armies, it was intended for use in a firefight or assault (bayonet charge). The third rank did not fire but could be used to reinforce the first two. At Waterloo a Prussian battalion of average strength (615) would extend over some 150 metres.

Squares

The Prussians did not use the hollow square when attacked by cavalry. Their 1812 regulations abolished it in favour of a dense column formed by the zuge in the attack column closing right up and the flanking files turning outwards. This had the advantage of being easy to form in a matter of seconds, although its vulnerability to any type of fire was frighteningly high. Another issue was that there was no room in the centre for casualties to be treated, and control of such a densely packed body was extremely difficult.

The Cavalry

Beneath their fire, in full career,
Rush'd on the ponderous cuirassier,
The lancer couch'd his ruthless spear,
And hurrying as to havoc near,
The cohort's eagles flew.
In one dark torrent, broad and strong
The advancing onset roll'd along,
Forth harbinger'd by fierce acclaim
That, from the shroud of smoke and flame,
Peal'd wildly the imperial name!

Sir Walter Scott

General (Maps 8, 11, 12, 13 & 14, pp. 119, 157, 158, 161 & 162)

Waterloo is often thought of as an infantry battle in which dense formations of French foot soldiers marched repeatedly across the valley that separated the armies only to be blown away by Allied musketry. Infantry hugely outnumbered other arms and certainly suffered the most. Artillery probably inflicted the most casualties (see Section 7 'The Artillery') but it was the cavalry that provided the really dramatic highlights of the battle. It is impossible to know for sure how many cavalry attacks or counterattacks were made during the nine-hour struggle, but the number certainly exceeds thirty. They have been deliberately called 'attacks' rather than 'charges', as the number of occasions when cavalry units got their horses to a gallop, even a canter, were rare to the point of being almost non-existent.

From around 1.30 p.m. when d'Erlon's corps began its long walk through the wheat fields until the French rout streamed past La Belle Alliance, cavalry regiments were in action somewhere on the battlefield. For nearly two hours during the afternoon French cavalry totally dominated events. In that time over 8000 horsemen were funnelled through the 900 metre Hougoumont–La Haie Sainte gap to try again and again to break Anglo-Allied infantry squares. Some 3000 Allied horsemen were eventually drawn into this contest. It was magnificent, it was courageous, it was high

drama – but it failed. Never again were so many cavalry deployed to fight so desperately in so confined a space. Neither the American Civil War nor the Franco-Prussian War would match it.

In the morning Napoleon's superiority in cavalry was significant but not seriously so – some 2,250, with the Emperor fielding, in round figures, 15,600 horsemen, the Duke 13,350. But by the time the Prussians brought their 7000 onto the field, the French mounted arm had been broken as a fighting force. By evening, after the last Prussians had arrived, 36,000 cavalrymen divided into 267 squadrons in 73 regiments had been committed to the battle.

At 11.30 that morning all the Anglo-Allied regiments were invisible to their enemy. However, the French cavalry were, for the most part, formed up on the forward slopes of low ridges. Despite the filthy, mud-spattered uniforms, they had presented an impressive spectacle when they paraded en masse, almost knee to knee, squadron after squadron, regiment after regiment, in a huge arc from south-west of Hougoumont to the fringes of the Frichermont estate.

Virtually every type of cavalry fought at Waterloo. The roll-call of the French horsemen was perhaps the most diverse. On the flanks stood châsseurs à cheval, lancers and hussars. Grouped behind the centre and flanks were Imperial Guard grenadiers à cheval, dragoons, more châsseurs, red lancers, gendarmes d'élite – even a handful of

---

Cavalry Horses

The command, control and administration of a cavalry regiment were more complex and demanding than that of an infantry battalion. Without fit horses, a mounted unit verged on worthless. There is considerable military wisdom in the saying that, 'horses have no patriotism: soldiers fight without bread, but horses insist on oats'. Most troopers had to be closely supervised to ensure sufficient care was given to their animals. In barracks it was easy for officers and NCOs to insist on 'horses first, men second' when it came to feeding, watering, grooming, checking shoes and avoiding saddle sores. Not everything could be left to the veterinarian and the farriers who, in a cavalry unit, were as important as the surgeon and his assistants.

On campaign, even a short one like Waterloo, insistence on 'horses first' could soon start to slip. Few soldiers could maintain the standard set by Private Melet of the Empress's Dragoons of the Imperial Guard who rode his beloved 'Cadet' at Waterloo. They had been inseparable for nine years. Cadet had carried him through twelve major battles and countless lesser engagements. They had ridden together across Prussia, Poland, Spain, Austria, Spain again, Russia, Saxony and France. During the retreat from Moscow Melet would ride into Russian lines at night to steal forage for Cadet, and invariably brought back a prisoner as well. Sadly, they were finally separated at Waterloo when Melet was wounded and Cadet killed.

mamelukes. Finally there was the flash of armour from twelve regiments of cuirassiers and two of carabineers. The Anglo-Allied Army mustered heavy guard cavalry – Life Guards, Horse Guards and Dragoon Guards, heavy dragoons, light dragoons, hussars and some Dutch and Belgian carabineers. The Prussians added more hussars, dragoons, lancers (uhlans) and landwehr cavalry. Unfortunately, the mud and the clouds dulled the colours, destroying much of the glitter.

This bewildering array of titles is confusing. Cavalry was supposedly divided into two types – heavy and light – according to their primary wartime role. Inevitably, this was too simple; so there was a third category, the so called 'medium' cavalry that came somewhere between the two, but was expected to do the job of either depending on the circumstances. These were the dragoons (originally mounted infantry). At Waterloo the cavalry, categorized by type, was as follows, with dragoons and landwehr units partially under the heading that indicates their role in the battle:

	Heavy	Medium	Light
Allied	Life Guards		Light Dragoons
	Horse Guards		Hussars
	Dragoon Guards		
		Dragoons	
French	Grenadiers à Cheval		Châsseurs à Cheval
	Empress's Dragoons		Lancers
	Cuirassiers		Hussars
	Carabineers		
		Gendarmes d'Elite	
		Dragoons	
Prussian			
		Dragoons	Lancers (Uhlans)
			Hussars
			Landwehr

Heavy cavalry regiments tried to enlist large men and put them on large horses; some wore cuirasses but all had imposing helmets or bearskin caps. Their role on the battlefield was shock action: the charge. They were not normally required to do the more mundane, off the battlefield tasks of their medium or light comrades. They considered themselves a superior body, often kept in reserve for the right moment to be launched in a decisive charge. However, this restricted role sometimes led to a less than rigorous training schedule resulting in unfit, overweight horses and riders. The light cavalry were usually leaner and fitter. As their name implies, they were smaller men on smaller horses due to their primary tasks requiring mobility and endurance.

These light horsemen provided the eyes and ears of the army. They were the cavalry's 'jack of all trades'. They reconnoitred, patrolled, screened, skirmished, provided outposts, escorted, foraged and pursued. On the battlefield they were often found on the flanks – Vandeleur's and Vivian's light dragoons and hussars on the Anglo-Allied left; Piré's châsseurs and lancers on the French left and Jacquinot's châsseurs, lancers and hussars on the right. Nevertheless, light cavalry were expected, if the opportunity arose, to attack both infantry and heavier horsemen – as happened at Waterloo. Medium cavalry were neither heavy nor light in the conventional sense, but were expected to perform the tasks of both. Dragoons were medium cavalry. Because they were less expensive to mount, maintain and pay, in many ways they tended to be the 'poor man's' heavy cavalry. As shown in the table on the left, all three armies used their dragoons at Waterloo in the heavy role. Britain called most of their light cavalry regiments 'light dragoons'.

Cavalry were grouped into formations with the same titles as infantry, although the numbers in cavalry formations (as distinct from units) were always far lower than their infantry equivalents. Again, like infantry formations, most divisions had artillery attached and under command on campaign. Although cavalry corps had divisions and brigades within them, their battlefield strength was often assessed by counting the number of units (regiments) or even sub-units (squadrons) present.

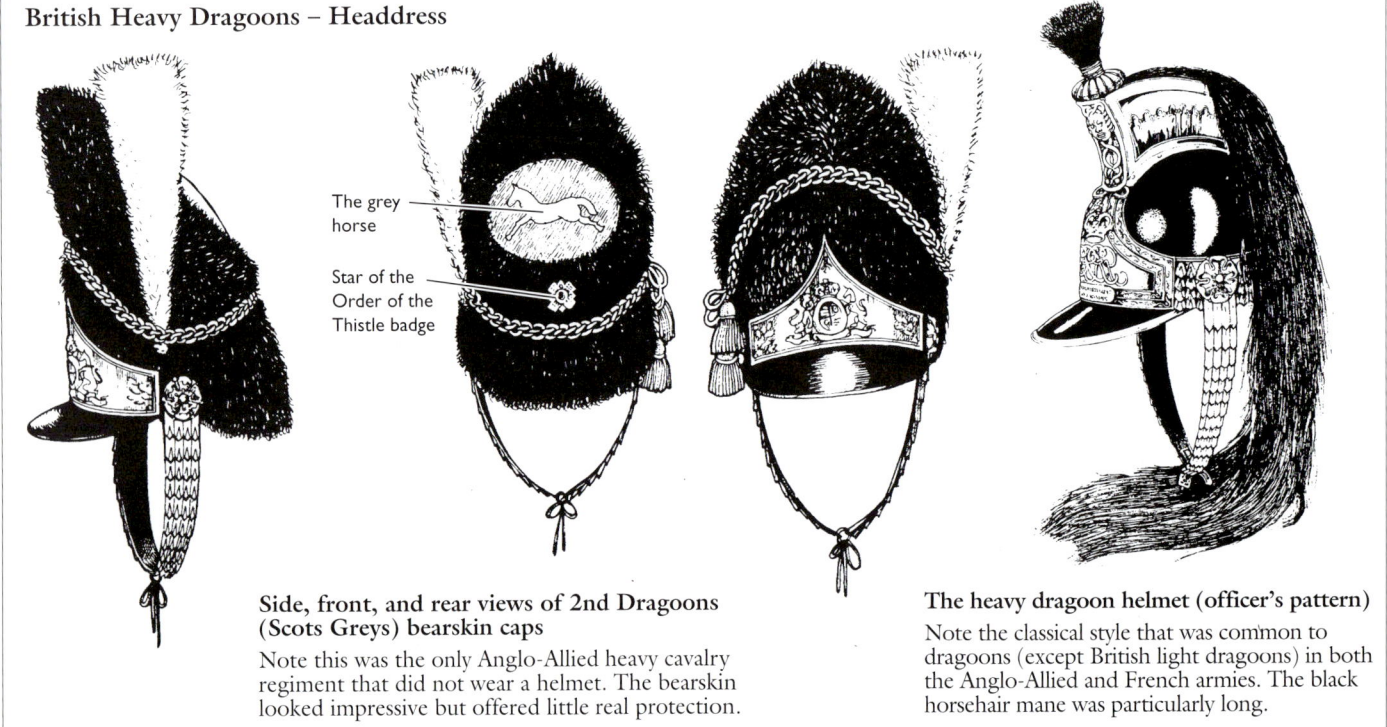

British Heavy Dragoons – Headdress

The grey horse

Star of the Order of the Thistle badge

Side, front, and rear views of 2nd Dragoons (Scots Greys) bearskin caps
Note this was the only Anglo-Allied heavy cavalry regiment that did not wear a helmet. The bearskin looked impressive but offered little real protection.

The heavy dragoon helmet (officer's pattern)
Note the classical style that was common to dragoons (except British light dragoons) in both the Anglo-Allied and French armies. The black horsehair mane was particularly long.

ANGLO-ALLIED CAVALRY

General

It has been said that Wellington was essentially an infantry general. His victories in India (with the exception of Assaye) had been infantry victories, as had those in Portugal and Spain. Initially in the Peninsula he had been starved of horsemen by a parsimonious home government, while most of Portugal and much of Spain were unsuitable for large scale mounted operations. Even on the central plateau, which was certainly cavalry country, it was only at Salamanca that one of the Duke's heavy cavalry brigades charged decisively.

The Duke had a generally low opinion of the battlefield tactical ability of his cavalry officers. Once a regiment was launched into action it tended to get out of control, was reluctant to rally and, after a small success, preferred to dash wildly off in pursuit – only to be badly cut up by a more judiciously controlled enemy reserve. Wellington had not forgotten the 20th Light Dragoons after Vimeiro, the 23rd Light Dragoons at Talavera, the 13th Light Dragoons at Campo Mayor or General Slade's cavalry brigade at Maguilla. After the latter fiasco Wellington wrote, 'I have never been more annoyed than by Slade's affair. Our officers of cavalry have acquired a trick of galloping at everything. They never consider the situation, never think of manoeuvring before an enemy, and never keep back or provide for a reserve…'. At Waterloo Wellington's Household Brigade was to suffer severely and the Union Brigade was almost destroyed after making precisely the same error.

With nearly 13,400 men, over 18 per cent, about one man in five of Wellington's army at Waterloo was a cavalryman – a higher proportion than he was accustomed to commanding. Unlike the French there was, with one exception, no cavalry divisional structure in the Anglo-Allied cavalry. The Earl of Uxbridge, in addition to being the Duke's second-in-command, commanded a cavalry corps of two heavy and five light brigades – well over 9000 horsemen. Until after the first shots were fired when the Prince of Orange added it to Uxbridge's command, the exception was Lieutenant-General Collaert's Netherlands Cavalry Division of three brigades (one heavy, two light), with over 3000 horsemen. In addition, the Brunswick contingent fielded nearly 1000 men in a hussar regiment and uhlan squadron.

Of the twenty-nine regiments present, sixteen were British and four were KGL units. Of these only three – 1st (King's) Dragoon Guards, 2nd Royal North British Dragoons (Scots Greys) and 6th Dragoons – had not seen service in the Peninsula. The only regiments to see action at Quatre-Bras were Merlen's 6th Dutch Hussars and the 5th Belgian Light Dragoons (both losing quite heavily), plus the 2nd Brunswick Hussars with their accompanying squadron of lancers (uhlans). The next day, however, one KGL and nine British regiments were involved in the skilful delaying action to cover the army as it pulled back to Mont St Jean. Into the night of 17 June, in drenching rain and sometimes violent thunderstorms, numerous successful regimental and squadron actions were fought alongside horse artillery batteries to keep the French at bay. Casualties were negligible (about 115 all ranks, of which 46 belonged to the 7th Hussars), so almost all regiments took the field at Waterloo without previous loss.

The cavalry of the British Army during the Napoleonic Wars was divided into two components. First, the Household Regiments: heavy men on heavy horses, whose primary functions were to protect the sovereign and perform ceremonial duties for the Royal Household or state occasions. These regiments seldom served overseas. Second, comprising the great majority, were the dragoon regiments of various types. The KGL, which formed a part of the British Army, had only dragoons. No cavalry wore armour, no cavalry carried lances and, until 1806–7, no hussars existed. The dragoons were categorized as dragoon guards, heavy dragoons and light dragoons. Even the 7th, 10th, 15th and 18th Hussars were still entitled 'light dragoons' on official documents, with the word 'hussars' in parenthesis afterwards. Their conversion had only meant a change in uniform style, their training and utilization remaining the same. In this book, however, they are referred to as 'hussars'.

Casualties among the Anglo-Allied cavalry totalled over 3,850, or 29 per cent of those deployed on the battlefield.

Wellington's Cavalry during the Withdrawal to Mont St Jean

The skilful tactics of Wellington's cavalry and horse artillery ensured that the Duke was able to make a clean break from Napoleon during the afternoon and night of 17 June after the battle at Quatre-Bras had ended in stalemate. A number of spirited actions took place at Genappe and elsewhere, several in drenching rain amid the flash of lightning and crash of thunder mixing with those of the guns. The ten regiments that played a part in this withdrawal were:
1st Life Guards, Royal Horse Guards (Blues),
1st (Royal) Dragoons, 2nd Dragoons (KGL),
11th Light Dragoons, 13th Light Dragoons,
23rd Light Dragoons, 1st Hussars (KGL),
7th Hussars and the 18th Hussars.

ORGANIZATION

Cavalry Divisions (Maps 8, 11 & 12, pp. 119, 157 & 158)
The only formation grouped as a cavalry division was the Netherlands Cavalry Division under Lieutenant-General Baron J.A. de Collaert. It was a numerically strong formation with 3,305 all ranks that included one heavy (Trip) and two light brigades (Ghigny and Merlen), plus half a battery (three guns and one howitzer) of horse artillery. All three brigade commanders, together with the divisional commander, had previously fought for the French. Merlen's 2nd Light Brigade had been pushed around by French chasseurs at Quatre-Bras, taking substantial losses. At Waterloo the division was initially deployed well back in reserve behind the centre, on either side of the Brussels road near Mont St Jean Farm. This formation was heavily engaged during the afternoon in counterattacking against the French cavalry as they swept around and behind the infantry squares. Despite its losses two days earlier, despite its commanders and many of the soldiers having fought for the French, this division performed far better than Wellington had perhaps anticipated. At 33 per cent overall

divisional casualties were high and included the death of Merlen and the severe wounding of Collaert (who died of his wound a year later). The brigades in this division were:

• **Netherlands Heavy Cavalry Brigade** (1,237) – Major-General Trip
1st Dutch Carabineers (446 in three squadrons) – Lieutenant-Colonel Coenegracht
2nd Belgian Carabineers (399 in three squadrons) – Colonel Bruijn
3rd Dutch Carabineers (392 in three squadrons) – Lieutenant-Colonel Lechleitner

This brigade fought well in supporting the infantry squares during the afternoon and made several successful attacks on French cuirassiers, led by Trip in person. They were the 7th and 12th Cuirassiers of the French 2nd Brigade commanded by a Belgian officer, Travers de Jevers. Some sources suggest that later, when ordered to charge again by Uxbridge's ADC, Trip refused and his brigade turned about. This alleged cowardly behaviour is hard to substantiate and difficult to reconcile with the fact that Trip was the only Netherlands' cavalry commander to receive a commendation in Wellington's despatch. The words used were that Trip,

'... conducted himself much to my satisfaction.' Coming from the Duke this was praise indeed. The formation lost 221 all ranks (18 per cent) – a comparatively low figure by Waterloo standards.

• **1st Netherlands Light Cavalry Brigade** (1,086) – Major-General Ghigny
4th Dutch Light Dragoons (647 in four squadrons) – Lieutenant-Colonel Renno
8th Belgian Hussars (439 in three squadrons) – Lieutenant-Colonel Davivier

This brigade was relatively small due to having only two regiments, one of which was under strength at the outset. On the initiative of the brigade commander it went forward to help cover the retreat of the two British heavy brigades when they were chased away from the French 'Grand Battery'. The brigade was later moved across to the west of the Brussels–Genappe road. From there it became embroiled in the cavalry actions of the afternoon as the Anglo-Allied cavalry counterattacked the French horsemen when they penetrated between and behind the infantry squares. The brigade suffered severely, losing 533 all ranks, which at 49 per cent was the highest proportional loss of any of the Duke's cavalry formations.

Cavalry March Rates

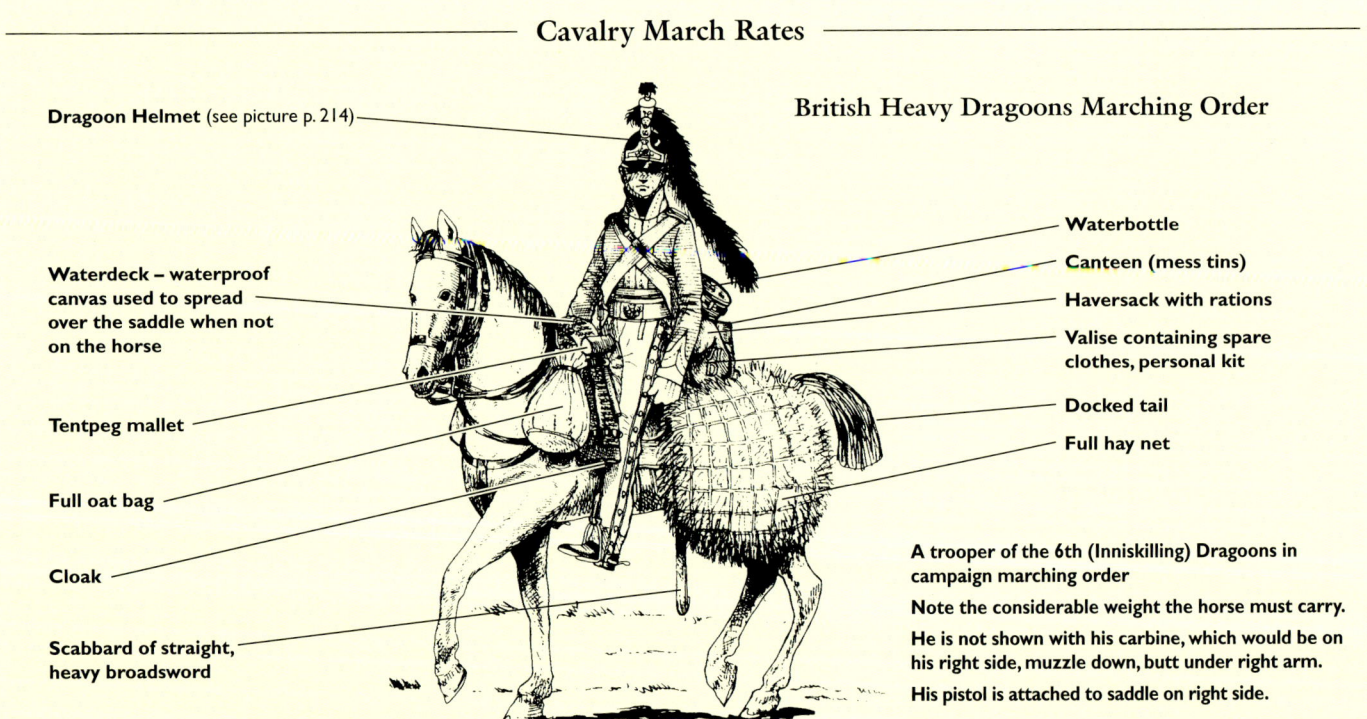

British Heavy Dragoons Marching Order

Dragoon Helmet (see picture p.214)

Waterbottle

Canteen (mess tins)

Haversack with rations

Valise containing spare clothes, personal kit

Waterdeck – waterproof canvas used to spread over the saddle when not on the horse

Docked tail

Full hay net

Tentpeg mallet

Full oat bag

Cloak

Scabbard of straight, heavy broadsword

A trooper of the 6th (Inniskilling) Dragoons in campaign marching order

Note the considerable weight the horse must carry.

He is not shown with his carbine, which would be on his right side, muzzle down, butt under right arm.

His pistol is attached to saddle on right side.

At a normal walk horsemen did not move at a much greater pace than infantrymen. A person can comfortably lead a walking horse on foot without either getting fatigued. In military terms this meant that along a reasonable road or track a cavalry unit moving at the walk would expect to cover 4 kilometres in the hour – an infantry battalion only slightly less. Only when the horses were made to step out, into a brisk walk, was the distance covered noticeably different – about 6 kilometres to the infantry's 4. At a forced march pace the cavalry would expect to do 10 kilometres an hour to the infantry's 5–6. In columns of fours along a road, 1000 horsemen would cover about 750 metres of road space. Rough guides such as this were helpful for

cavalry patrols in estimating numbers of troops seen on the march in the distance.

A cavalryman seated on his horse occupied a metre of frontage. This meant that a three-squadron regiment of about 450 men, such as the 6th (Inniskilling) Dragoons, formed up in column of squadrons (each squadron having two ranks) would occupy between 65–75 metres of front. The same regiment, with all squadrons in line, would need at least 200 metres with the men knee to knee and no gaps between squadrons. With this in mind it is easy to understand how little room there was for deployment by Wellington's regiments with seventeen cavalry regiments packed into the Brussels–Nivelles, Brussels–Genappe and Ohain road triangle.

• **2nd Netherlands Light Cavalry Brigade** (741) – Major-General Merlen
6th Dutch Hussars (470 in four squadrons) – Lieutenant-Colonel Bereel
5th Belgian Light Dragoons (271 in three squadrons) – Lieutenant-Colonel de Merex

Another small brigade – due to losing over 300 at Quatre-Bras. Like Ghigny's brigade, it performed very creditably at Waterloo. In the early afternoon the brigade advanced to help throw back d'Erlon's infantry, and supported the 12th Light Dragoons against Jaquinot's lancers. Later it was involved with other formations in checking the French cavalry that had penetrated behind the infantry squares. Its casualties were exceptionally severe for a cavalry unit, amounting to 371 (34 per cent), including the brigade commander who was mortally wounded by a cannon ball. After he fell the remnants of the brigade were divided, the 5th Belgian Light Dragoons being attached to Ghigny's brigade and the 6th Dutch Hussars to Trip's.

Cavalry brigades not under divisional command
(Maps 8, 11 & 12, pp. 119, 157 & 158)
There were only nine properly constituted cavalry brigades in Wellington's army as the two-regiment 7th British Brigade had attached the 15th Light Dragoons to the 5th Brigade, and the Hanoverian Brigade had only one regiment present. They had an average strength of 1,282. The strongest was Vivian's 6th British Cavalry Brigade (1,504), the weakest, having lost 320 men at Quatre-Bras, was the Netherlands 2nd Light Cavalry Brigade (741). Add in the Brunswick Hussars and uhlan squadron and the army had the equivalent of ten brigades. Brigades consisted of two, three or four regiments and were categorized as heavy or light formations.

Directly under the Earl of Uxbridge were two heavy and five light brigades with the support of thirty-five guns and howitzers plus a rocket troop. They were as follows:

Heavy Brigades
• **1st British (Household) Cavalry Brigade** (1,319) – Major-General Somerset
1st Life Guards (255 in two squadrons) – Lieutenant-Colonel Ferrior
2nd Life Guards (235 in two squadrons) – Lieutenant-Colonel Lygon
Royal Horse Guards (Blues) (246 in two squadrons) – Lieutenant-Colonel Hill
1st (King's) Dragoon Guards (583 in three squadrons) – Lieutenant-Colonel Fuller

This brigade of guard cavalry was seriously under strength at the start of the battle. Its Waterloo highlight was the destruction of Delort's cuirassiers protecting the left flank of d'Erlon's corps attack. It lost almost half its men (632) and horses.

• **2nd British (Union) Cavalry Brigade** (1,332) – Major-General Ponsonby
1st (Royal) Dragoons (435 in three squadrons) – Lieutenant-Colonel Clifton
2nd Royal North British Dragoons (Scots Greys) (444 in three squadrons) – Lieutenant-Colonel Hamilton
6th (Inniskilling) Dragoons (543 in three squadrons) – Lieutenant-Colonel Muter

The brigade was called the 'Union' Brigade as it consisted of regiments representing England, Scotland and Ireland. All were dragoon regiments, designated as 'heavies'. Although each regiment had three squadrons, it was still well below the war establishment. Its Waterloo highlight was the scattering of Donzelot's and Marcognet's divisions as they attacked the Anglo-Allied ridge, and the subsequent uncontrolled dash to the French 'Grand Battery' – for which they paid a high price. Like the Household Brigade, they lost dramatically – 616, or 46 per cent, including the brigade commander.

Light Brigades
• **3rd British Cavalry Brigade** (1,401) – Major-General Dornberg
23rd Light Dragoons (341 in three squadrons) – Major Cutliffe
1st Light Dragoons (KGL) (540 in four squadrons) – Lieutenant-Colonel Bülow
2nd Light Dragoons (KGL) (520 in four squadrons) – Lieutenant-Colonel Jonquieres

This was a predominantly German brigade with the KGL regiments almost up to strength. It was not involved at Quatre-Bras but took part in covering Wellington's withdrawal to Mont St Jean on 17 June. The 23rd fought without their usual commanding officer who arrived back from Brussels too late to resume command. No particular highlight during the battle. Although Dornberg was among the wounded, the brigade's casualties were comparatively light – 310 (22 per cent).

• **4th British Cavalry Brigade** (1,315) – Major-General Vandeleur
11th Light Dragoons (442 in three squadrons) – Lieutenant-Colonel Sleigh
12th Light Dragoons (433 in three squadrons) – Lieutenant-Colonel Ponsonby
16th Light Dragoons (440 in three squadrons) – Lieutenant-Colonel Hay

A typical all British brigade that had seen some action during the withdrawal to the Mont St Jean position the previous day. Positioned on the left of the line 600 metres north of Papelotte. Its tasks in the battle were not of great significance. It helped cover the retreat of the Union Brigade, supported the centre in the latter part of the afternoon and finally became involved in a series of actions against the retreating French rearguards. Losses amounted to 319 (23 per cent).

• **5th British Cavalry Brigade** (1,267) – Major-General Grant
7th Hussars (362 in three squadrons) – Lieutenant-Colonel Kerrison
15th Hussars (450 in three squadrons) – Lieutenant-Colonel Dalrymple
13th Light Dragoons (455 in three squadrons) – Major Boyse

This brigade had a regiment, the 2nd Hussars KGL, still away watching the frontier. The 13th Light Dragoons from the 7th British Cavalry Brigade replaced it for Waterloo. All these regiments had considerable experience in Spain. The 7th Hussars had several clashes with the French during the withdrawal from Quatre-Bras, losing around forty-six men in the process. It deployed a squadron of the 15th Hussars to help watch the right flank from just west of Hougoumont. The Brigade's main action during the battle was a series of attacks on French cavalry in support of Wellington's infantry squares. Artillery fire and these clashes were costly, the brigade suffering 392 casualties (31 per cent).

• **6th British Cavalry Brigade** (1,504) – Major-General Vivian
10th Hussars (452 in three squadrons) – Lieutenant-Colonel Quentin
18th Hussars (447 in three squadrons) – Lieutenant-Colonel Murray
1st Hussars KGL (605 in four squadrons) – Lieutenant-Colonel Wissell

This brigade was posted initially on the extreme eastern flank, 1,800 metres from the 'Elm Tree' crossroads. Because of its comparative isolation it was the only cavalry brigade that kept its horse artillery battery under command for the battle. It was also the only formation that consisted entirely of hussars. All regiments had served in the Peninsula. It was not heavily engaged at Waterloo, only being brought into the centre towards the end of action. However, it did execute several cavalry charges against rearguard infantry units during the French rout. Its losses were the lightest of any cavalry brigade – 208 (14 per cent). The 1st Hussars KGL probably had the least casualties of any Allied unit of comparable size at Waterloo – ten, of which only one was killed.

• **7th British Cavalry Brigade** (712) – Colonel Arenschildt
3rd Hussars KGL (712 in four squadrons) – Lieutenant-Colonel Meyer

This originally two-regiment brigade had to detach the 13th Light Dragoons to bring the 5th Brigade up to full strength. The 3rd Hussars KGL was the strongest cavalry regiment in the army and was led into action against cuirassiers by the brigade commander personally during the afternoon. Its losses amounted to 136 (19 per cent).

• **Hanoverian Cavalry Brigade** (516) – Colonel Estorff (not present at Waterloo)
Duke of Cumberland's Hussars (516 in four squadrons) – Lieutenant-Colonel Hake

The other two regiments – the Prince Regent's Hussars and the Bremen and Verden Hussars – were both at Hal. The Cumberland Hussars sat on their horses (most reserve cavalry units dismounted) in reserve behind Dornberg's brigade for much of the afternoon. During this time they suffered about sixty casualties, almost entirely from artillery fire coming over the crest of the ridge 400 metres to their front. These losses proved too much for them and they disgraced themselves by refusing to advance at a crucial moment in the early evening. They then fled to Brussels, spreading the news that the French were on their heels and causing temporary consternation in the capital.

Cavalry Regiments

The cavalry regiment was the tactical unit of the mounted arm for all three armies engaged at Waterloo. Wellington had twenty-nine of them divided into ninety-three squadrons. The average strength of an Anglo-Allied cavalry regiment was 460 all ranks, and of squadrons 143. The largest was the 3rd Hussars KGL with 712, while the smallest was the 2nd Life Guards whose two squadrons mustered a mere 235. The basic statistics, by cavalry type, are shown in the following table:

Type	Regiments	Squadrons	Numbers	% (of all cavalry)
Guards	4	9	1,319	10
Heavy dragoons	3	9	1,332	10
Light dragoons	9	30	4,089	31
Hussars	10	35	5,137	38
Carabineers	3	9	1,237	9
Uhlans (lancers)	-	1	235	2
Totals	**29**	**93**	**13,349**	**100**

The Duke, therefore, had ten heavy cavalry regiments, or just over a third of his mounted troops. The remaining nineteen regiments were 'lights'. However, these figures on their own do not reflect the true proportions. No less than three heavy regiments had only two squadrons, so in terms of actual numbers of troopers (3,888 heavy and 9,461 light) the actual proportions were 29 per cent heavy and 71 per cent light. Only six light regiments were deployed in their traditional role as flank protection, with twenty-three heavy and light being massed behind the centre and right of the position in direct support of the infantry along the ridge. While in reserve the cavalry, with the exception of the Cumberland Hussars, dismounted to lessen the likelihood of casualties from 'overs' (shells), and to rest the horses.

In terms of the national mounted contributions to the Anglo-Allied force, the details of regiments are provided in the table below:

Nationality	Regiments	Squadrons	Numbers	% (of all cavalry)
British	16	45	6,473	48
KGL	4	16	2,377	18
Brunswick	1	5	919	7
Hanoverian	1	4	516	4
Dutch	4	14	1,955	15
Belgian	3	9	1,109	8
Totals	**29**	**93**	**13,349**	**100**

Nassau did not provide any cavalry.

Cavalry regiments were invariably commanded by lieutenant-colonels, with a slightly larger headquarters than an infantry battalion (incorporating a veterinary surgeon and saddler sergeant) to reflect it having as many horses to administer to as men. At Waterloo each regiment had between two and four squadrons, varying in strength from 112–180. All the six German speaking regiments plus the two Dutch light dragoon regiments had four squadrons. Each squadron was further divided into two troops and four half-troops. Within the British Army, including the KGL, the official establishment for a cavalry regiment was ten troops (five squadrons). Each troop was supposedly composed of one captain, one or two lieutenants, one cornet (cavalry ensign or 2nd lieutenant), one troop sergeant-major, one farrier, four sergeants, four corporals, one trumpeter and eighty-five troopers – a total of 100 all ranks. The senior captain, who in the British service also commanded his troop, commanded a squadron. The theory was that a regiment went to war with three, preferably four squadrons, leaving one depot or reinforcement squadron at home. At Waterloo, as noted above, only the KGL regiments fielded four squadrons, while the 1st and 2nd Life Guards and the Royal Horse Guards could only raise two each. The theoretical squadron strength of some 200 all ranks was never achieved. The average during the battle was 145, with the 2nd Life Guards going into action with around 112 per squadron.

Household and Dragoon Guard regiments carried square standards on parade instead of Colours, with other regiments having swallow-tailed guidons. However, they were not taken on campaign and consequently were not carried at Waterloo.

Household and Guard Regiments

All three Household Cavalry Regiments were present at Waterloo. They were called 'Household' regiments as they were raised to protect the sovereign. Over the years this meant they were confined to duties in London and state ceremonial. Because of this they missed out on much overseas active service, only travelling abroad when the sovereign did so. However, they were highly prestigious regiments and extremely costly to maintain with an officer corps virtually entirely from the more wealthy nobility. All regiments were heavy cavalry.

• The Life Guards

They were the most senior regiment in the Army, although not the oldest, being formed as 'Horse Guards' by the future King Charles II while in exile in 1659. In 1674, following a threat on his life, Charles gave the special task of protecting himself and his queen to the Life Guards (hence the new title). A decree enjoined them to, 'attend the King's person on foot wheresoever he walk, from his rising to his going to bed, and this to be performed by one of the three captains ...'. Unlike the modern Life Guards who wear gleaming cuirasses on ceremonial occasions, they were not worn at Waterloo. When they subsequently adopted body armour they were nicknamed the 'Tins'. In 1815 they wore scarlet jackets, grey trousers with a red stripe, a magnificent 'Roman' style helmet with black wool crest and a tall, white over red plume (farrier's plumes were black). Troopers were armed with the 1796 pattern, straight sabre, carbine, bayonet and pistols in holsters in front of the saddle. The regiment was mounted on large, black horses with manes brushed to the left to distinguish them from the 'Blues' who brushed them to the right. Overall casualties were severe, totalling 244 out of 490 all ranks engaged. Of these, the 2nd Life Guards suffered the most with 158 – reflecting their getting caught up in the mad dash to the 'Grand Battery' and subsequently being hit by counterattacking cuirassiers and lancers. During this action two officers were captured (Captain Irby and Lieutenant Waymouth) – it was an extremely rare occurrence for an Allied soldier, let alone an officer, to be taken prisoner at Waterloo.

• The Royal Horse Guards (The Blues)

This regiment had its origins in Cromwell's New Model Army. Formed in 1650 it fought against the king in 1651, although with the restoration it became part of the Household troops with the title Royal Horse Guards. Unlike all other British Guard regiments whose uniforms were scarlet, the Royal Horse Guards wore blue – hence

Life Guard Incidents

• The commanding officer of the 1st Life Guards, Lieutenant-Colonel Ferrior, supposedly led eleven charges (attacks) during the battle before falling seriously wounded.
• Captain Kelly of the 2nd Life Guards killed an officer of the French 1st Cuirassiers. He dismounted in the heat of the action and cut off his victim's epaulettes as a souvenir.
• Corporal Shaw of the 2nd Life Guards was a huge man and a well-known prize-fighter. Before the battle he was seen guzzling gin, which had the effect of enraging him to the extent that he cut down at least ten opponents until his sword broke. He hurled the hilt at his enemy before snatching off his helmet to use as a club. He was cut down and then shot, crawling away to bleed to death on a dunghill during the night.
• Cornet Story of the 1st Life Guards had an extraordinary encounter during the first charge. Years previously he had been captured by the French and kept as a prisoner at Verdun for seven years. During the charge at Waterloo he was about to strike down a French infantryman when the soldier threw down his musket shouting, '*Monsieur, ne me tuez pas; je vous connais à Verdun; sauvez-moi la vie en grace!*' Story recognized the man, spared him and his comrade (also from Verdun) and sent them to the rear as prisoners.

their nickname, 'The Blues'. Apart from this obvious difference the uniforms, arms and type and colour of horses ridden were much the same as the Life Guards. The regiment lost a total of ninety-nine all ranks (46 per cent) at Waterloo, but only one officer was killed (Major Packe), seven wounded and one captured (Lieutenant Tathwell).

• 1st (King's) Dragoon Guards

Of seven Dragoon Guard regiments this was the only one at Waterloo. With 583 all ranks it was the strongest British cavalry regiment at the battle. All the dragoon guard regiments had originally been raised as 'Horse' and thus were considered to have 'Household' status. However, between 1746 and 1788 they were converted to regular heavy dragoons but were allowed to retain 'guards' in their title. Unlike the Life Guards and Royal Horse Guards, this regiment had seen no active service in the Peninsula, having been kept at home since 1803. It had a tough fight ahead of it on 18 June, but the inexperience of its officers and men was not evident in their performance (except when they got carried away by initial success and were caught up in the gallop to the French guns, thus becoming vulnerable to the subsequent counterattack).

Their uniform was a scarlet jacket, dragoon helmet and blue facings. They were armed with the straight, heavy sword, carbine and pistols. They suffered the highest losses of any Anglo-Allied cavalry regiment at Waterloo (with the exception of the 8th Belgian Hussars), probably because there were more of them and they were heavily engaged. Some 279 all ranks were listed as casualties (48 per cent). They included seven officers killed, one of whom was the commanding officer, Lieutenant-Colonel Fuller, and 124 missing – mostly men who 'disappeared' trying to get back from the 'Grand Battery'.

Heavy Dragoon Regiments

The 1st (Royal) Dragoons, 2nd Dragoons (Scots Greys) and the 6th (Inniskilling) Dragoons were the three regiments of heavy dragoons that formed the Union Brigade. Originally, like all dragoon regiments, they were intended for use as mounted infantry – which supposedly entailed most movement on horseback and most fighting on foot. Long before Waterloo, however, dragoons had ceased, except on rare occasions, to fight as infantrymen and were invariably employed on all cavalry duties. Dragoons became thought of as 'medium' cavalry. At Waterloo the regiments in the Union Brigade were classified and armed as 'heavies' for use as shock troops. Heavy dragoon weapons were the weighty, straight cavalry swords, carbines, bayonets and pistols.

• 1st (Royal) Dragoons

Another very senior regiment raised in 1661 by the Earl of Peterborough. It had five years' Peninsula experience but was somewhat under strength with three squadrons of about 140 all ranks in each. The highlight of the battle for this regiment, as for the others in the brigade, was the charge that broke up Donzelot's division and resulted in the capture by Captain Kennedy Clark and Corporal Stiles of the Eagle of the French 105th Regiment (see Section 10 'Myths and Controversies'). The 'Royals', as they were usually known, lost most of their men during the disorganized withdrawal from the 'Grand Battery'. Losses are recorded as 198, or 45 per cent.

• 2nd (Royal North British) Dragoons (Scots Greys)

This regiment traced its origins back to 1678 and gained considerable distinction during Marlborough's victories at Blenheim, Ramillies, Oudenarde and Malplaquet. It had not, however, seen service in the Peninsula. The regiment was easily distinguished from the other red-jacketed heavy cavalry by its grey horses and the bearskin caps it wore instead of helmets. Originally the caps were cloth, mitre-shaped grenadier caps, but towards the end of the seventeenth century bearskin was substituted for cloth, though the traditional shape was retained. This regiment was badly cut up during the retreat from the 'Grand Battery'. The dying commanding officer, Lieutenant-Colonel Hamilton, was reported to have held his reins in his teeth after having both arms lopped off shortly before being shot through the heart. Hamilton's place was taken by Major Clarke, followed by Major Hankin after Clarke was hit and, finally, for the last three hours, by the senior captain, Edward Cheney, who had five horses shot from under him in twenty minutes. The regiment's real claim to fame, however, was the capture of the Eagle of the French 45th Line (Marcognet's division) by the 1.9-metre giant, Sergeant Ewart.

Total losses amounted to 201 all ranks (45 per cent), including one commanding officer dead and two wounded – the fourth, unlike his horses, coming through unscathed.

• 6th (Inniskilling) Dragoons

This regiment got its name after being raised in 1689 for the defence of the town of Enniskillen in Ireland. Later, when mounted on black horses in Scotland, they were nicknamed 'The Black Dragoons'.

Although it had fought well at Dettingen and Fontenoy in the middle of the previous century, it had no recent Peninsula experience. When Major-General Ponsonby was killed near the 'Grand Battery' Lieutenant-Colonel Muter of the 6th Dragoons became acting commander of the brigade. Major Miller took over the regiment but was later severely wounded so, by the end of the day, Captain Madox was acting commanding officer. The only serving Italian officer in the Duke's army rode with this regiment. He was a junior lieutenant called Paul Ruffo who was wounded and listed as missing. Years later Ruffo became Prince Castelcicala, Neapolitan Minister to England. At the last Waterloo banquet in London in 1852 the Prince sat at Wellington's right at the top table.

The 6th Dragoons lost 217 all ranks at Waterloo (48 per cent of the regiment), reflecting the intensity of the brigade's action during the early afternoon and the effectiveness of a well-timed enemy counterattack.

Light Dragoon Regiments

There were nine light dragoon regiments at Waterloo, including two KGL, one Dutch and one Belgian, with a total strength of almost 4,100 sabres. The strongest was the 4th Dutch Light Dragoons with 647 all ranks, the strongest British (excluding KGL regiments) the 13th Light Dragoons with 455. The weakest was the 5th Belgian Light Dragoons with 271. During the battle all regiments were used in the shock role: counterattacking enemy cavalry or, to a lesser extent, infantry.

With the single exception of the 5th Belgian Light Dragoons who wore green, the uniform jackets of these cavalrymen were blue. All British regiments had adopted the bell-topped shako. Uniform differences were in the detail – the cuffs, the collars and the braid. Brief notes on each regiment are given below:

• 11th Light Dragoons

Not heavily engaged. It was kept in reserve when the rest of Vandeleur's brigade went forward to attack Durutte's division and

---

Union Brigade Incidents

• Private Smithies rode in Major Dorville's squadron of the 1st (Royal) Dragoons. He afterwards penned a fascinating account of what it was like to fight hand-to-hand with cuirassiers:

> The cuirassiers, you will recollect, had coats of steel, whilst we had no such protection; and then again their swords were much longer ... On we rushed at each other, and when we met the shock was terrific. We wedged ourselves between them as much as possible, to prevent them from cutting, and the noise of the horses, the clashing of swords against their steel armour, can be imagined only by those who have heard it. There were some riders who had caught hold of each other's bodies – wrestling fashion – and fighting for life, but the superior physical strength of our regiment soon showed itself ... It was desperate work indeed, cutting through their steel armour...

• Many Union Brigade officers realized the dangers of the wild, uncontrolled charge to the 'Grand Battery'. As one of them stated:

> Our men were out of hand. Every officer within hearing exerted themselves to the utmost to reform the men; but the helplessness of the enemy offered too great a

temptation to the Dragoons, and our efforts were abortive. It was evident that reserves of Cavalry would soon take advantage of our disorder ... if we could have formed a hundred men we could have made a respectable retreat, and saved many; but we could effect no formation, and were as helpless against their attack as their Infantry had been against ours. ... Those whose horses were best, or least blown, got away. ... It was in this part of the transaction that almost the whole of the loss of the Brigade took place.

• One the many minor miracles of Waterloo was the survival of Troop Sergeant-Major Marshall of the 6th Dragoons during the charge to the 'Grand Battery'. While cutting at a cuirassier on his right, his bridle arm was broken by a sword cut on his left. More enemy moved in, unhorsing him with a lance thrust through his side. He lost consciousness for a while then, as he dragged himself towards a riderless horse, another trooper cut him several times with his sword. To add insult to injury a French artilleryman rested his foot on Marshall's body as he rammed his gun. For two days and three nights he lay on the field with nineteen lance and sabre wounds. He survived to spend seven years on a pension of two shillings a day in Belfast.

cover the retreat of the Union Brigade after their attack on the 'Grand Battery'. Took part in the general advance at the end of the day. Losses 76 (17 per cent).

• 12th Light Dragoons

As part of Vandeleur's brigade this regiment advanced to attack Durutte's division in flank and then assisted in covering the retreat of the Union Brigade after their reckless charge to the 'Grand Battery'. In the process the regiment became engaged with French lancers. The commanding officer, Lieutenant-Colonel Ponsonby, was seriously wounded and left for dead. Losses 111 (26 per cent).

• 13th Light Dragoons

Formed part of Grant's brigade and was involved with a number of counterattacks on French cavalry that had penetrated between the infantry squares. Commanded by Major Boyse because Lieutenant-Colonel Doherty was ill in Brussels with what was described as 'West Indies' fever. Losses 111 (24 per cent).

• 16th Light Dragoons

Like the 12th, they took part in the attack on Durutte's division and the covering of the withdrawal of the scattered Union Brigade. Lieutenant-Colonel Hay, who had been wounded at Salamanca and received the Gold Medal for the Peninsula, was so badly injured at Waterloo that he could not be moved for eight days. Young Cornet Beckwith was to make his name, not at Waterloo, but at Bristol sixteen years later. As a major he acquired a reputation for ruthlessness in the crushing of the Bristol riots while leading dragoons in their policing role. The 'riots were not suppressed until many of the ringleaders and their followers had perished, some by being cut down by the cavalry when charging through the streets'. Losses 32 (7 per cent).

• 23rd Light Dragoons

This was the smallest British light dragoon regiment, with only 341 all ranks present. It formed part of Dornberg's brigade and was involved in supporting the infantry squares, particularly that of the 33rd Foot, during the massive French cavalry assaults of the late afternoon. This regiment was commanded by Major Cutcliffe, as Lieutenant-Colonel the Earl of Portarlington was absent, arriving late and consequently fighting as a trooper with the 18th Hussars. Losses 80 (23 per cent).

• 1st Light Dragoons KGL

As part of Dornberg's brigade it was primarily engaged in supporting the infantry squares by counterattacking the French cavalry. Losses 153 (28 per cent).

• 2nd Light Dragoons KGL

The third regiment in Dornberg's brigade. In action supporting infantry squares against cavalry. Losses 86 (16 per cent).

• 4th Dutch Light Dragoons

With 647 all ranks it was the largest light dragoon regiment in the Anglo-Allied army. As part of Ghigny's brigade it crossed to the east of the Brussels road and advanced against French lancers to help in covering the hasty retreat of the Union Brigade. It was then heavily involved during the afternoon with counterattacking French cavalry that had penetrated between the infantry squares. Losses were high – 249 (38 per cent).

• 5th Belgian Light Dragoons

As part of Merlen's brigade it had been heavily engaged at Quatre-Bras and lost about 171 men. This meant it was the weakest cavalry regiment in the Duke's army with a mere 271. It was used in the main for supporting the infantry squares by engaging French cavalry. After Merlen was killed the regiment was attached to Ghigny's brigade. Losses 157 (36 per cent).

Hussar Regiments

Hussars considered themselves an élite branch of the light cavalry arm, claiming to epitomize the cavalry spirit: gallant, daring and reckless to the point of stupidity. The renowned French light cavalryman General Antoine Lasalle declared, 'A Hussar who isn't dead at thirty is a blackguard'. He himself often charged waving his long pipe rather than his sabre, but was uselessly killed at the end of the Battle of Wagram, aged thirty-four.

Wellington had ten hussar regiments, including two KGL, one Dutch, one Belgian, one Brunswick and one Hanoverian unit. The strongest was the 3rd Hussars KGL with 712 all ranks. The strongest British regiment was the 10th Hussars with 452. The 7th Hussars with only 362 at the start of the battle was the weakest. Throughout Europe hussars wore very similar uniforms, characterized by the dolman, a short tail-less jacket decorated with braid, and the fur-trimmed pelisse hanging from the shoulder (or worn as a jacket). With the sole exception of the Brunswick Hussars in black, the Anglo-Allied hussars had blue jackets, all liberally covered in gold or silver braid under the mud. Most wore bell-topped shakos. All were armed with a slightly curved, light cavalry sabre, carbine and pistols.

• 7th Hussars

Wellington's cavalry commander, the Earl of Uxbridge, was the Colonel of the 7th Hussars (his old regiment) and wore their uniform at Waterloo. Private Edward Cotton rode with the 7th that day, rose to be a sergeant-major and, twenty years later, married a local Belgian woman and became a battlefield guide. He wrote a fascinating little book called *A Voice from Waterloo*. He was eventually buried in the garden at Hougoumont but his body was later moved, along with others, to the vault in the cemetery at Evere near Brussels.

Like most regiments, the soldiers were often unrecognizable due to the filthy condition of their uniforms. Captain Verner of the 7th wrote that the men were, 'so covered in mud that it was

The Belgian 5th Light Dragoons

At Quatre-Bras this regiment suffered heavy losses (170) in its first fight with its former allies, the French. Its brigade commander, Merlen, had fought against Wellington in Spain, but he led it into action with considerable élan on 16 June. At Quatre-Bras the regiment attacked (in support of its brother regiment) against the 6th Châsseurs of Piré's division. The French recognized the uniforms of their old comrades (which were remarkably similar to their own) and advanced with sabres pointing down – a sign that they would not attack – and called on the Belgians to ride through their ranks and rejoin their old colours. Merlen would have none of it and ordered a charge but, although repulsed, there were no defections. Regrettably, as the regiment pulled back it was mistaken for the French and subjected to considerable 'friendly fire' that knocked over another forty men.

utterly impossible to distinguish a feature in their faces or the colour of the lace of their dress…'.

The 7th Hussars had fought hard while covering the withdrawal of the centre column from Quatre-Bras. They had charged French lancers at Genappe, but they lost more men than any other cavalry regiment on 17 June and started Waterloo as the weakest hussar regiment with a mere 362 all ranks. During the battle the regiment was involved in helping to repel the French cavalry assaults that lapped around the infantry squares during most of the afternoon, and in the general advance at the end of the day. Losses were high, 198 (55 per cent), second only to the 8th Belgian Hussars in terms of percentage.

- **10th Hussars**

These light cavalrymen were easily recognizable by their large, bell-topped scarlet shakos. The regiment was part of Vivian's brigade on the extreme left flank. Captain Taylor's squadron was posted on outpost duty in and beyond the village of Smohain where he intercepted the Prussian officer bringing the news of the march of Bülow's corps to the battlefield. Riding with them was an interesting character called Lieutenant William Hamilton. Not long after the battle he left the Army to become a priest and a teacher, spending many years at Elizabeth College in Guernsey. He was a great favourite with the boys on account of his genial personality and fund of Waterloo tales. Every year on 18 June the Reverend Hamilton came into school wearing his Waterloo Medal on his clerical coat. The boys, 'used to drag him into the playground, and cheer him till we made him cry and we were hoarse.'

The 10th only came into action at the end of the day but fought well in the final advance against the French cavalry and infantry rearguards. It was then that their only officer to be killed was lost: Major Howard. Losses 94 (21 per cent), of which one officer was killed and two wounded.

- **15th Hussars**

The second hussar regiment wearing red bell-topped shakos instead of the usual black. Although their losses were not excessive at Waterloo, this regiment had no less than four commanding officers during the course of the day. Lieutenant-Colonel Dalrymple was wounded; Major Griffith was killed; Captain Thackwell wounded and yet another officer, Captain Hancox, took over. Captain Thackwell had joined as a cornet in 1800 and was to serve in the same regiment for thirty-two consecutive years, the last twelve as the commanding officer. However, he was fortunate to survive his Waterloo wounds. After taking command he was hit on the left forearm so was forced to hold the reins in his right

hand, with his sword hanging by the sword knot. Another shot smashed into his right arm so forcing him to take the bridle in his teeth. He was soon compelled to hand command to Captain Hancox. Thackwell, who lived through the amputation of his left arm at the shoulder, soldiered on to become Inspector-General of Cavalry in 1854.

Before the start of the battle the regiment detached a squadron on outpost duty west of Hougoumont, so for most of the day it fought as a two-squadron unit. It was involved in supporting the infantry squares during the afternoon. Losses were 83 (18 per cent), almost all from the two squadrons on the main position.

Death of Major Howard 10th Hussars

It is likely that Major Howard was the last Anglo-Allied officer to be killed at Waterloo. His death occurred in the last few minutes of the action during the British cavalry attack on the French rearguards as the bulk of the army fled the field. Howard commanded a squadron of the 10th Hussars and was ordered by Vivian to attack a square of the Old Guard in conjunction with a Hanoverian battalion that was advancing nearby. The infantry for some reason did not participate; but Howard led his men forward, accompanied by Vivian, in a hopeless attempt to break a square of veteran infantry. The hussars charged up to the bayonets, muskets were fired, pistols banged and horses shied away from impact with the steel points. Howard was shot through the mouth, falling from his horse a few feet from the square, probably unconscious. A French guardsman immediately darted out from the square and pounded Howard's head with the butt of his musket.

The following morning a Sergeant Plowman with a burial party from the regiment recognized Howard and immediately buried him in a field of clover. He later had to identify the spot when it was requested that Howard's body be removed to England for burial at Streatham about six weeks after the battle. In 1879 his remains were moved again and interred in the family mausoleum at Castle Howard in Yorkshire.

- **18th Hussars**

This regiment was deployed on the eastern extremity of the Anglo-Allied line, over 2000 metres from the 'Elm Tree' crossroads and 900 metres north of La Haie farm, with vedettes (small mounted patrols) even further east towards Ohain. It was the only cavalry regiment that formed up with its squadrons in line as opposed to column due to the availability of unlimited space. Its isolation saved lives. The French guns had other targets so, like the rest of Vivian's brigade, the men sat on the wet ground unable to see what was happening under the dense clouds of smoke to the south-west.

It was not until the evening that the brigade moved behind the centre and the 18th Hussars became involved in the attacks on the retiring enemy. Despite this, the regiment still suffered 104 casualties (23 per cent) but only two officers were wounded.

- **1st Hussars KGL**

Lieutenant-Colonel Wissell's 600 German hussars were another regiment in Vivian's brigade that suffered little at Waterloo, spending most of the day sitting listening to the roar of battle over 2000 metres away and unable to play any part. Even at the end when the brigade was engaged with the French cavalry and infantry rearguards, the regiment was in support rather than in the forefront of the attacks. The result was that the 1st Hussars KGL had the lowest casualties of any regiment or battalion in either Wellington's or Napoleon's armies at Waterloo: ten – one officer wounded, one soldier killed, five soldiers wounded and three missing. These amounted to 1.5 per cent of the regiment.

- **3rd Hussars KGL**

This regiment formed part of the 7th British Cavalry Brigade under Colonel Arenschildt. When the 13th Light Dragoons were detached to reinforce the 5th British Cavalry Brigade this formation became a brigade in name only. That it was on its own was to some extent compensated for by being the strongest cavalry regiment in Wellington's force, with 712 all ranks. Posted behind the right centre it suffered from artillery fire and was employed, under the personal leadership of the brigade commander, in attacks on French cuirassiers during the afternoon. It acquitted itself well in the confusion of charge and counter-charge that surged around the infantry squares. Losses 136 (19 per cent).

• 2nd Brunswick Hussars and Uhlan Squadron

This regiment and the lancer squadron (under Major Pott) were part of the Brunswick Contingent, and as such had fought at Quatre-Bras two days earlier. It was there that the Duke of Brunswick had been shot dead at the head of his troops. The same fate met Major Cramm, the commander of the Brunswick Hussars, although their overall losses at Quatre-Bras were only 46.

At Waterloo both the black uniformed regiment and the squadron were initially kept well back in reserve behind the right centre, some 800 metres from the Mont St Jean ridge. They saw some action later in the day during the French massed cavalry attacks, but were never fully committed. Losses were 78 (11 per cent) for the Hussars and 13 for the Uhlans, none of whom were killed.

• Cumberland Hussars

This regiment was composed of young Hanoverian gentlemen of considerable social standing and wealth but little military experience. They all furnished their own horses and equipment. They were positioned behind the right centre in reserve. While waiting and watching the battle develop, they took some casualties from artillery fire that they found disconcerting. During the crisis when La Haie Sainte fell they began to falter and, although repeatedly ordered forward by Uxbridge's ADC, Captain Seymour of the 18th Hussars, they refused to move and shortly afterwards fled the field. They cleared a passage back to Brussels with their swords, where they caused alarm by claiming the French were just behind them. A number of individuals, however, remained on the field to fight with other units. Lieutenant-Colonel Hake was dismissed the service. Losses 61 (12 per cent).

• 6th Dutch Hussars

This regiment was part of Merlen's Netherlands Cavalry Brigade that had been engaged at Quatre-Bras where they took heavy casualties, reducing their strength to 470. Initially held in reserve behind the centre, west of Mont St Jean Farm, it was committed to heavy fighting in support of the infantry squares during the late afternoon. After the death of their brigade commander, Merlen, they were attached to Trip's heavy cavalry brigade. They proved a steady regiment that fought well, remaining in action despite sustaining a high level of casualties. Losses 214 (45 per cent).

• 8th Belgian Hussars

This regiment was easily distinguishable by its pale blue uniform and silver braid. It formed part of Ghigny's brigade that, considering its possibly suspect commitment to the cause, fought with considerable distinction throughout the afternoon. Despite staggering losses of 285 (65 per cent) – the highest percentage casualty rate for any unit in the Duke's army – it continued to do its duty to the end.

Carabineers

The 1st and 3rd Dutch and 2nd Belgian Carabineers formed the Netherlands Heavy Cavalry Brigade under Trip. All three wore blue jackets with different facings and the high crested 'Roman' style helmet with wool crest and plume. They were kept in reserve immediately west of Mont St Jean Farm. They initially fought well when committed to the action against French cavalry during the afternoon, but some accounts say they later left the field. If this is so, it is difficult to understand why Wellington commended Trip in his despatch (see box p. 117). Losses were:
1st Dutch Carabineers 102 (23 per cent)
3rd Dutch Carabineers 63 (16 per cent)
2nd Belgian Carabineers 156 (39 per cent)

The Flight of the Cumberland Hussars

It was Captain Seymour, an ADC to the Earl of Uxbridge and reputedly the strongest man in the British Army, that brought the order to Lieutenant-Colonel Hake that his regiment, which was then retiring without orders, was to return and advance. Hake protested that his men were all volunteers, owned their own horses and that he had little confidence in them. He made no attempt to stop the rearward movement. Seymour then appealed to the second-in-command to turn the men about – again without result. In desperation the huge captain grabbed the colonel's bridle and spoke forcefully and bluntly, trying to shame Hake into obeying. It was a useless task, so Seymour reported back to Uxbridge. The general sent his ADC back to order the Hussars to at least reform out of fire across the highroad. Instead of halting, the regiment dug in its spurs and headed for Brussels. To be fair, it was said that a number of officers and soldiers were ashamed of this behaviour and left the ranks to join other units for the remainder of the day. The bulk of the regiment reached Brussels and cantered through the Place Royale causing some panic with their shouts that the French were on their heels. Hake was later court-martialled and dismissed from the service.

WEAPONS

Swords and Sabres (Diagram p. 224) All the Anglo-Allied cavalry, except for one squadron of Uhlans with lances, carried swords/sabres as their primary weapon. There were variations in their length of blade, degree of curvature, weight and balance, style of hilt and the amount of protection it gave the hand. As with the cavalry who wielded them, sabres were broadly divided into heavy or light weapons. In the Duke's force his heavy cavalry (Household, Union and Netherlands Heavy Brigades) carried heavy swords while the remainder (light dragoons and hussars) had lighter sabres. In general terms (there were exceptions) the heavy weapons were intended primarily for thrusting, the light for cutting. The cavalrymen certainly could, and did, do both with either type, and many sabres were designed for both purposes. Part of the problem was that there was a considerable difference of opinion as to whether the thrust or the cut was the most effective way of incapacitating an enemy.

Wellington's British heavy cavalry carried the 1796 pattern heavy broadsword in a metal scabbard (Diagram p. 224), much like the Netherlands' Carabineers. They were made in Birmingham, with the scabbard stamped, 'Warranted Never to Fail' – an inaccurate guarantee. It was an exact copy of a 1775 Austrian sword, with a 35-inch, massive straight blade and a hatchet point (only one side of the blade being curved at the tip). This made penetration unnecessarily difficult. Before Waterloo the heavy cavalry were ordered to, 'grind the backs of their swords' to make the tip into the more effective spear point.

To Cut or Thrust?

The debate on this issue was never satisfactorily resolved. Proponents of the thrust could point to the fact that a stab wound penetrates deeply, pierces vital organs, causes internal bleeding and invariably cripples, if not kills, an opponent with one wound. One stab in the body was frequently mortal, whereas a man with several cuts might fight on – even one with twenty could survive. The epitome of the daring light cavalry officer was Colonel Antoine de Brack, nicknamed 'Mademoiselle' on account of his good looks and elegance. Writing after the Napoleonic Wars he advised cavalrymen,

> It is the point alone that kills; the others serve only to wound. Thrust! Thrust! As often as you can: you will overthrow all whom you touch, and demoralize those who escape your attack, and you will add to those advantages that of always being able to parry and never [be] uncovered.

Use of the point was usually advantageous in a charge where the sword was supposed to be held extended with a straight arm. With a compact formation, riding knee to knee, the thrust was really the only practical offensive movement. However, once contact was made, once the line 'threaded' with the enemy, once individuals fought their independent duels then, instinctively, slashing tended to take over. Most thrusts were made at the opponent's body. If aimed at the chest the sword was supposed to be held so that the blade was parallel to the ground. This allowed it to slide between the ribs without getting stuck in the bones. If a sword could not be withdrawn the victorious trooper could find himself with serious problems.

A grim example of these difficulties was experienced by Captain Morris of the 17th Lancers who rode in the charge of the Light Brigade almost forty years after Waterloo. Until that moment Morris had been an ardent supporter of the thrust. He had galloped at his enemy with sword-arm outstretched, dipped the point under the Russian's defence and, within a split second, the blade had penetrated the man's body. The momentum slammed the hilt home against his chest. The sword was sticking out of the Russian's back and jammed tight in bone and muscle; in falling the body almost jerked Morris from his saddle. He was effectively tied to the corpse, anchored to the spot and bent double trying to withdraw the blade. He was reluctant to let go of the hilt and disentangle his sword knot, so for some moments he continued his tussle with the dead body. Seeing his predicament more enemy closed in. A piece of bone was sliced from his scalp, he fell from his horse, was cut again and stabbed by a lance – he then surrendered, and survived. He later remarked, 'I don't know how I came to use the point of my sword, but it's the last time I ever do.'

British Swords used at Waterloo

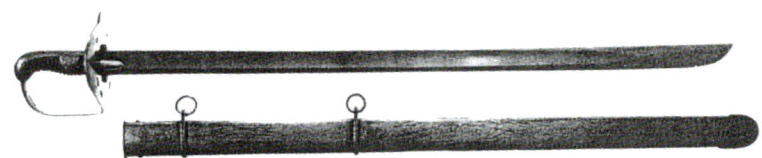

British 1796 pattern Heavy Cavalry sword

According to British training manuals this was primarily a cutting weapon.

The hatchet point makes thrusting unnecessarily difficult.

A heavy weapon with the point of balance towards the hilt to make it easier to wield.

Not popular – more a bludgeon than a blade.

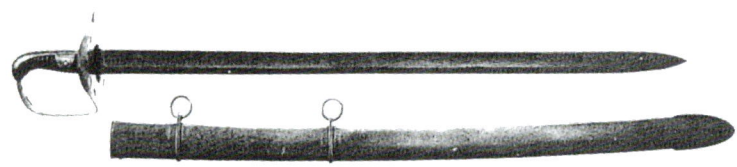

British 1796 Heavy Cavalry sword with spear-point

Although expected to cut rather than thrust, British cavalry were supposed to go in with the point, arm extended, when charging.

Before Waterloo regiments had their armourers grind the backs of the blades to make a spear-point to facilitate the thrust.

The drawback of the metal scabbard was it tended to rust easily, the sword rattled in it, the blade was blunted by too frequent drawing and it tended to bend out of shape (like the one illustrated).

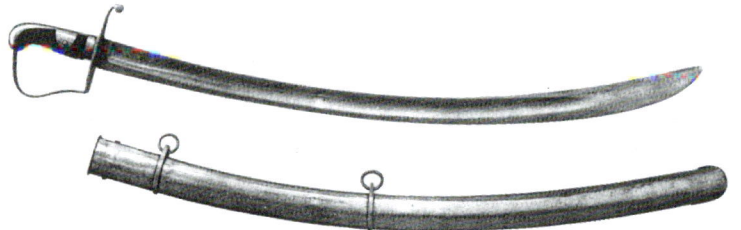

British 1796 Light Cavalry sabre

Specifically designed for slashing, with the weight towards the point.

The combination of the balance, broadness and pronounced curve of the blade towards the point made this a particularly lethal cutting weapon.

It was much feared by the French in the Peninsular – a well executed blow could take off an arm with ease.

An officer described it as a, 'lumbering, clumsy, ill-contrived machine. It is too heavy, too short [and] too broad ...'. If it had a keen edge and was wielded by a powerful arm, a blow from this weapon was extremely damaging, with bones likely to be broken in the arms or shoulders and helmets crushed.

The British cavalry manual – the *Rules and Regulations for the Sword Exercise of Cavalry* issued in 1796 – was in principle in favour of the cut over the thrust as it considered the latter too easy to parry. It conceded, however, that the thrust was a good way to dispatch a fleeing enemy, as he was virtually helpless, in no way able to see, let alone parry, what was coming. Moreover, the thrust was sometimes useful against infantry who were disadvantaged by their lower level. However, if the cut was officially the best way for cavalry to kill the French, the authorities had not given the heavy cavalry the best weapon with which to do it. It was too weighty for any prolonged 'cut and thrust' mêlée; the point of balance was towards the hilt to ease the strain on the wrist, rather than towards the tip to give weight to a cut. In addition it was straight (always best for thrusting), did not have a spear-point (unless ground down) and tended to lose its edge with frequent drawing from or replacing in the steel scabbard. The final drawback was the inner edge of the large disc hilt that chafed the hand when carried. This led to many swords having this part removed.

Captain Bragge of the 3rd Dragoons writing of the cavalry combat at Bienvenida in the Peninsula stated, 'It is worthy of remark that scarcely one Frenchman died of his wounds though dreadfully chopped, whereas twelve English Dragoons were killed on the spot and others dangerously wounded by thrusts.' In summary, it was too much the blunt bludgeon, too little the flashing blade.

With the 1796 pattern, light cavalry sabre Wellington's light dragoons and hussars were far better armed for slashing. The weight was towards the point, the blade was 33 inches long (measured in a straight line from hilt to point), broader towards the point, with a pronounced upwards sweep reminiscent of the Indian tulwar; all are features facilitating the cut. This sabre had done excellent service in the Peninsula, where the French dreaded it for the fearsome wounds it inflicted. A well-honed blade deftly wielded by a strong arm could sever a limb with a single blow. A French general had even protested that it should be banned after witnessing the damage it could do.

Lances – see under French cavalry weapons p. 246

Carbines (Diagram below)

The carbine was a short-barrelled, cavalry firearm carried by all mounted troops (corporals and privates), both heavy and light, in Wellington's army. The only exceptions were the best shots in the 10th Hussars who were issued with the Baker rifle carbine, which they used to good effect on at least one occasion during the retreat from Quatre-Bras. Carbines had a belt fitting that allowed the weapon to be hung on a spring-clip from a shoulder belt. They were short-range weapons designed to give horsemen the ability to skirmish on foot as well as mounted. Although it was possible for a regiment to fire volleys of carbine fire, it was a method seldom used. Firing the weapon from the saddle was, for obvious reasons, wildly inaccurate, and reloading on the move a lengthy, frustrating and almost impossible exercise. Carbines were designed to take bayonets, although the Duke's heavy cavalry were ordered to leave theirs at home, while the light dragoons and hussars did not normally carry them. Virtually all cavalrymen went through years of campaigning without ever having the need to fix bayonets to fight – they were an oft discarded encumbrance, handy around the campfire, but worthless on the battlefield. Even with the carbines themselves the times when they could be usefully fired at Waterloo were rare. In the Peninsular War the British cavalry general, Stapleton Cotton, ordered the Household Cavalry not to carry carbines, 'as these troops can never be called upon to skirmish, and the horses have already a sufficient load to carry.'

British Carbines

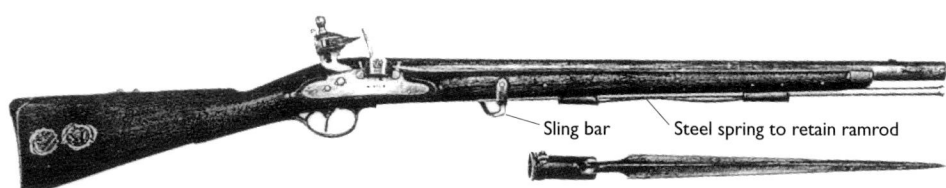

Sling bar   Steel spring to retain ramrod

The Nock pattern Heavy Cavalry carbine

Carried by the household and union brigades at Waterloo, hung from the sling bar and placed in a holster in front of the saddle on the right side.

Cumbersome, impossible to fire accurately while mounted and were, at one stage, discarded by the heavy cavalry in the Peninsular War.

A bayonet was issued but not carried at Waterloo.

Ramrod retained by engaging with underside of fore-end cap

The Eliott Light Cavalry carbine

Although dating from 1773 some light cavalry still carried it at Waterloo.

The ammunition was not compatible with the musket and it was too long and heavy to handle properly when mounted.

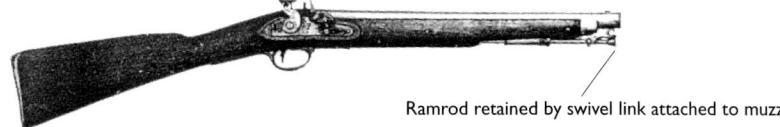

Ramrod retained by swivel link attached to muzzle

The Paget Light Cavalry carbine

Issued in late 1812 this weapon was a considerable improvement on the Eliott carbine as it was lighter, shorter, and more handy for a mounted man.

The swivel link permanently attaching the ramrod below the muzzle was another useful feature.

British Pistols

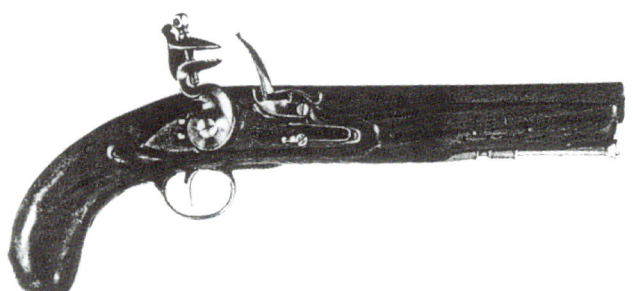

The 1796 pattern Heavy Cavalry pistol

The majority of cavalrymen did not see much merit in having two firearms, and would probably have abandoned the pistol given the option.

This type had the same bore as muskets.

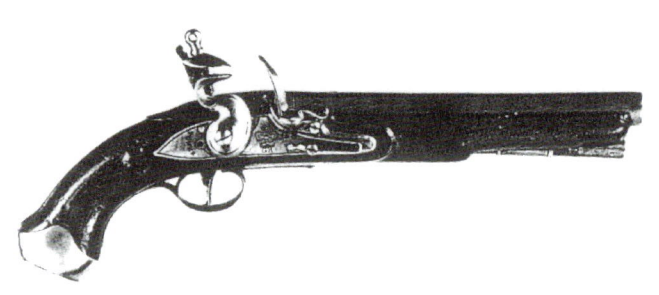

The Light Cavalry pistol

This had the same bore as the carbine.

At Waterloo the Household troops and the heavy dragoons of the Union Brigade were armed with the 1796 Nock heavy carbine. It weighed 8 pounds, had a barrel length of 28 inches and a bore of 0.76 as part of an attempt to standardize ammunition size throughout the army. The overall length of the weapon was 3 feet 5½ inches. It was carried muzzle down, suspended from the pouch bandolier by a sling bar and placed in a small bucket attached to the front of the saddle on the right side. Early versions were fitted with the highly effective, but expensive, screwless lock. The problem of the ramrod working loose from the pipes, thus being dropped and lost, was overcome by riveting a strip of steel spring between the two pipes, the inward curve of which held the ramrod firmly in place.

The light cavalry at Waterloo were mostly armed with the Paget carbine, although some are likely to have still had the older Eliott pattern that had been the standard issue in the British service since approval in 1773. The Eliott flintlock carbine had a 28-inch barrel with a bore of 0.66 inches, which meant its ammunition was not compatible with the musket – a considerable inconvenience. When the ramrod was pushed home it was prevented from falling out by a device that engaged in the lip on the underside of the brass fore-end cap.

The more common, lighter pattern weapon issued to the light cavalry was the Paget carbine that was accepted in 1808 but did not go into production until four years later – hence not all British light cavalry had it at Waterloo. It was much shorter and handier than the Nock carbine, with a 16-inch barrel (although this reduced its range and made it resemble an elongated pistol). The ramrod was permanently mounted on a swivelling link beneath the muzzle to prevent it from being dropped while reloading. The 16th Light Dragoons had a folding butt version that they may have carried at Waterloo.

Pistols (Diagram above)

Pistols were issued to all cavalry present at Waterloo. Most had one (a few had two) carried in holsters in front of the saddle. They were used in action even less than the carbines, the main constraints being the extremely limited range, plus the fact that the firer used only one hand and was riding a moving horse. Unless the pistol was point-blank or within inches of an enemy's body, a miss was a virtual certainty. It was less risky to use a sword. Giving the cavalryman

two firearms, each of which required different cartridges, was not a practical or popular decision; the cavalry had pleaded in vain with the authorities to abandon them. An attempt made to use the carbine cartridge by shaking half the powder out for use in the pistol was seldom a good solution. Done in haste this often resulted in too little or too much powder – in the latter case the explosion blew the weapon out of the firer's hand. The firing of pistols (and carbines) at Waterloo was rare; most was done by the French cavalry that attacked the Anglo-Allied squares in the afternoon. Individuals, unable to get their mounts to face the hedge of bayonets, banged off a few futile shots from a few metres away. Captain Mercer RHA described how individual cuirassiers would ride up to his guns, fire their pistol (or carbine) at his gunners, then ride away to reload.

Henry Nock, the prolific English gun-maker of the times, produced the British heavy dragoon pistol with a 9-inch barrel but with the same bore as the musket – the Household Cavalry got a refined version. The light dragoons were given a pistol of the same length with a carbine bore, but there were a bewildering variety of the weapons available, large numbers of which were privately purchased by officers.

TACTICS
General

Although Wellington fought a defensive battle at Waterloo, his cavalry attacked. With the sole exception of the Cumberland Hussars, all of his twenty-nine regiments were called upon to take the offensive during the long afternoon and summer evening. It bears repeating that cavalry cannot effectively defend other than by attacking. For cavalry to stand to receive an attack was tantamount to accepting defeat. On a battlefield the horseman relied on weight and momentum, so to remain stationary was to surrender these assets before sabres were crossed. Although the Anglo-Allied Army was on both the strategic and tactical defensive at Waterloo, its cavalry attacked or, more accurately, counterattacked. They never stood to receive the French assaults.

The Duke's horsemen were required to undertake virtually every type of action that could be asked of cavalry. They attacked infantry in column, infantry in square and they pursued fleeing infantrymen and cavalrymen. They fought against armoured cuirassiers and against lancers. They also charged French guns.

From shortly before 2.00 p.m. until nearly 9.00 p.m. the only time Wellington's cavalry were not required somewhere was after the loss of La Haie Sainte until the repulse of the Middle Guard – a period of about two hours.

There were two unusual features of cavalry action at Waterloo. The first was that lack of space and the density of the troops on the ground made it difficult for cavalry regiments to deploy into a line, and almost, but not quite, impossible for a brigade to do so. This was particularly true in the triangle formed by the Brussels–Genappe, Brussels–Nivelles and the Ohain roads. Over 25,000 men and twelve gun batteries were packed into this area of less than half a square kilometre before a shot was fired. During the afternoon Wellington rushed reinforcements into this triangle from both east and west as the French poured thousands more cavalry into the cauldron of confusion that this area had become. It was there that many of the Anglo-Allied cavalry counterattacks took place. But they were small affairs, with local commanders being able to deploy a regiment but more often two or sometimes even single squadrons.

The second unusual feature was that, contrary to popular belief and artists' brushes, full-bloodied Allied cavalry charges at the gallop occurred only in pursuit or at the end of the battle in following up a retreating enemy. A combination of the closeness of the enemy, the obstacles in the way (troops, guns, ammunition caissons, sunken roads and hedges), the slope of the ground, the soggy soil (especially the ploughed patches) and the wet crops reduced most attacks to a trot.

A final point of general interest was that, like the infantry, cavalry normally achieved their best results in combination with guns, which is why all Anglo-Allied mounted formations had a Royal Horse Artillery (RHA) battery or equivalent attached. However, at Waterloo the Duke removed all except one of these batteries (from Vivian's brigade) and subsequently placed them in a static role with the foot artillery along the ridge (see Section 10 'Myths and Controversies').

Discounting skirmishing, which was not normally a battlefield task of cavalry, the mounted arm used only two basic formations: the column and the line. Each had its variations and limitations, each was used at Waterloo and, as with the infantry, the skill of the commander was to choose the right one and give the right order for change at the right moment. These formations are discussed below using the British 12th Light Dragoons to demonstrate how Wellington's cavalry regiments, with minor differences, manoeuvred during the battle.

The 12th Light Dragoons was a regiment that had seen continuous service in the Peninsula from July 1811 through to the end of the war. For the final two years in Spain they had been brigaded with the 16th Light Dragoons under Major-General Vandeleur – who was delighted to have them back for Waterloo. The veterans among the 12th were even more delighted that Lieutenant-Colonel the Honourable Frederick C. Ponsonby, their commander in Spain, was once more sitting on his horse in front of them. He was one of the most experienced regimental cavalry commanders in the army,

---

Lieutenant-Colonel Frederick Ponsonby's Unique Experience

As commanding officer of the 12th Light Dragoons, Ponsonby led them in a charge onto the flank of part of Durutte's division as it attacked the Mont St Jean ridge at about 2.00 p.m. French lancers attacked his unit and Ponsonby was fortunate to survive his wounds. He later described his experience:

In the mêlée I was disabled instantly in both arms … I was carried on by my horse, till, receiving a blow on my head from a sabre, I was thrown senseless on my face to the ground. Recovering, I raised myself a little to look round, when a lancer passing by exclaimed, 'Tu n'est pas mort, coquin,'['You're not dead, you rascal'] and stuck his lance through my back. My head dropped, the blood gushed into my mouth, a difficulty of breathing came on, and I thought all was over. Not long afterwards a tirailleur came up to plunder me, threatening to take my life. I told him that he might search me … he found three dollars … [he] was no sooner gone than another came for the same purpose; but assuring him that I had been plundered already, he left me … [shortly afterwards] an officer … stooped down … saying he feared I was badly wounded … I expressed a wish to be removed to the rear. He said it was against the order to remove even their own men … I complained of thirst, and he held his brandy bottle to my lips, directing one of his men to lay me straight on my side, and place a knapsack under my head. He passed on into the action, and I shall never know to whose generosity I was indebted, as I conceive, for my life. … another tirailleur came and knelt and fired over me, loading and firing many times, and conversing with great gaiety all the while; at last he ran off saying, 'Vous serez

bien aise d'entendre que nous allons nous retirer; bon jour, mon ami.'['You will be pleased to hear we are going to retire; good day, my friend.'] … It was dusk when two squadrons of Prussian cavalry … passed over me in full trot, lifting me from the ground and tumbling me about cruelly. … had a gun come that way it would have done for me. … I thought the night would never end. Much about this time I found a soldier of the Royals [1st Dragoons] lying across my legs, who had probably crawled thither in his agony; his weight, convulsive motions, noises and the air issuing through a wound in his side, distressed me greatly … it was not a dark night, and the Prussians were wandering about to plunder … several of them came and looked at me. About an hour before midnight I saw a soldier in an English uniform coming towards me … He said he belonged to the 40th Regiment [Lambert's brigade], but had missed it. He released me from the dying man. Being unarmed he took up a sword from the ground, and stood over me … At 8 o'clock in the morning some English were seen … a cart came for me. I was placed in it and carried to a farm-house … and laid in a bed from which poor Gordon [Lieutenant-Colonel Sir Alexander Gordon, the Duke's ADC and personal friend] had just been carried out [dead]. … I had received seven wounds … I was saved by continual bleedings, one hundred and twenty ounces in two days, besides the great loss of blood on the field.

It was a second miracle that he survived the loss of blood while in the surgeon's care. Ponsonby became a major-general and lived for another twenty-two years.

Typical British Light Cavalry Regiment – 12th Light Dragoons

Formed in close column of squadrons (troop frontage) at outset of battle with 'left in front' (No.3 squadron leading)

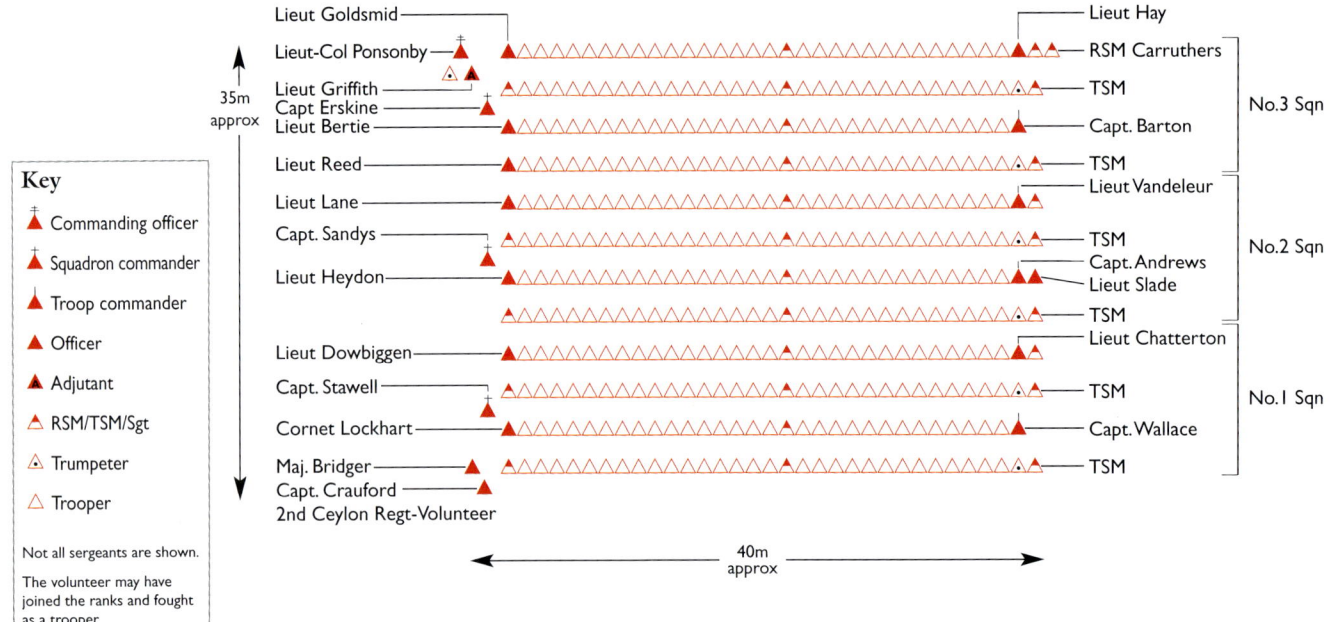

Key

▲ Commanding officer
▲ Squadron commander
▲ Troop commander
▲ Officer
▲ Adjutant
△ RSM/TSM/Sgt
△ Trumpeter
△ Trooper

Not all sergeants are shown.

The volunteer may have joined the ranks and fought as a trooper.

General Notes

• Typical British light cavalry regiment of which there were 9 plus 4 KGL. With a strength of about 433 the 12th LD were somewhat under the average strength (460) of an Anglo-Allied cavalry regiment.
• The 12th LD had fought in the Peninsular. It took part in the attack on Durutte's division and in covering the withdrawal of the Union Brigade. Ponsonby was badly wounded and had a miraculous escape (p. 227).
• Losses amounted to 111 (26 %). Only 2 officers were killed – Lieut Bertie and Cornet Lockhart, but Capt. Sandys later died of his wounds.

Formation Notes

• Close column of squadrons was the formation adopted by virtually all cavalry prior to the battle. It was usually on a half-squadron (troop) frontage.
• Riders were in loose files – i.e. about 6" between boots. Ranks were half a horse's length apart (just over a metre).
• The 3 senior captains were 'squadron officers' i.e. squadron commanders. They also retained command of their troops, which were known by the commander's name i.e. 'Capt. Sandys' Troop' or 'Capt. Barton's Troop'.
• Maj. Bridger took command of the regiment when Ponsonby was badly wounded.

Non-combatant personnel

Paymaster Otway
Quartermaster Sidley
Surgeon Robinson
Asst. Surgeon Smith
Veterinary Surgeon Castley
Paymaster Sergeant Isaac
Armourer Sergeant Goulding
Saddler Sergeant McIntosh
On duty at rear

Parade State

Officers	26
Sgt-Majs/Sgts	34
Corporals	24
Trumpeters	7
Farriers	6
Soldiers	336
Total	**433**

Includes non-combatant personnel

---

having fought throughout the Peninsular War. Wellington did not generally have much time for cavalry officers or cavalry regiments, but Ponsonby and the 12th were among the very few exceptions. He is reputed to have remarked that, 'In Spain the Germans [meaning the KGL], the 14th Light Dragoons [not at Waterloo] and perhaps the 12th under Fred Ponsonby, were the only regiments that knew their duty and did not get into scrapes of every description.'

The regiment had embarked at Ramsgate and landed at Ostend on 3 April. They marched inland and were billeted among the villages around Renaix on 8 April to await events. They were not engaged at Quatre-Bras. Although part of the rearguard screening the army's withdrawal on 17 June, they again avoided serious contact and suffered no losses. At Waterloo they started the day with 433 all ranks (somewhat under the average strength of 460). The twenty-six officers included the non-combatants. Like all other British light cavalry regiments, they mustered three squadrons – one squadron short of a proper war establishment.

A regiment in closed column (Diagram above)

Like virtually every other cavalry regiment, Ponsonby formed the 12th in a close column after moving into position on the reverse slope of the ridge north of Papelotte. The squadrons were closed right up on a half squadron, or troop, frontage, which meant some thirty troopers sitting side by side in each rank (two ranks per troop). With about 6 inches between riders they were in 'loose' files – as distinct from knee to knee. On each flank there was an officer 'covered' by a sergeant (or corporal) in the second rank. The ranks were only half a horse's length apart, with the gap between squadrons barely noticeable at one horse's length. It was, therefore, a densely packed formation with no room for a super-numerary (third) rank as with a line. The squadron officers (squadron commanders, Captains Stawell, Sandys and Erskine), who nominally remained troop commanders as well, formed on the left flank of their squadrons. Ponsonby, his adjutant (the recently commissioned Griffith) and his trumpeter stood to the left of the leading troop. The actual frontage depended on the number of men in a troop. The 12th covered some 35–40 metres with a depth of slightly less. Once formed up, the regiment dismounted (and sat or lay down) to rest the horses. They could see nothing of the enemy and little of their own army due to their position in dead ground – although undoubtedly Ponsonby and other officers walked up to the ridge crest to peer through the hedge that bordered the Ohain road.

This formation was primarily for movement and deployment. It was easy to control, not so vulnerable to being broken up by obstacles, made it difficult for enemy at a distance to estimate the strength of the unit (due to its narrow frontage). It also facilitated a speedy deployment into the primary fighting formation – the line. It was common practice, as at Waterloo, for cavalry to adopt this formation in their assembly areas while awaiting developments. Some units may have changed formation to stand in a column with a full squadron frontage after the battle got underway – provided there was the space to do so. In this diagram the 12th Light Dragoons is shown formed with what was known as the 'left in front', that is with Captain Stawell's No.1 Squadron at the rear of the column. The manuals decreed that the senior squadron must be on the right of any line formed, so the drills for changing into line from column varied depending on which squadron was in the lead. According to the regulations, movements in the presence of the enemy were carried out at a trot or gallop (in most circumstances 'gallop' here meant 'canter', a word never seen in the cavalry manuals).

The closed column was avoided when attacking as the density and depth of the formation ensured that a single well-placed cannonball would knock down dozens of men and horses. Also, if sabres were crossed then only the leading ranks could join the mêlée, while the long flanks invited a counter-charge. Nevertheless, like all rules this one was made to be broken. In an emergency situation, where a unit had been surprised or there was no time to form line or the ground prevented it, then an attack in column was sometimes unavoidable.

A cavalry regiment in line (Diagram below)
Squadrons, regiments, even brigades of cavalry sought to fight in lines. Invariably, in all armies a line was two ranks of horsemen frequently riding knee to knee with the heads of the horses in the second rank only a metre from the hindquarters of the first. Looked at from the front such a line, even advancing at a trot, presented a military spectacle that had few equals. The line ensured the greatest number of sabres or lances were brought to bear on the enemy and the wide frontage helped in outflanking the enemy (or avoiding being outflanked). There were, however, two serious drawbacks.
• The longer the line the more difficult it was to control. Before a line advanced the commanding officer designated the 'squadron of direction' – usually the centre squadron if three were in line. The squadron commander had to keep precisely behind and a horse's length away from his colonel. The other squadron commanders had to keep in line with the officer commanding the 'squadron of direction'. The half-squadron officers (troop officers) riding on the

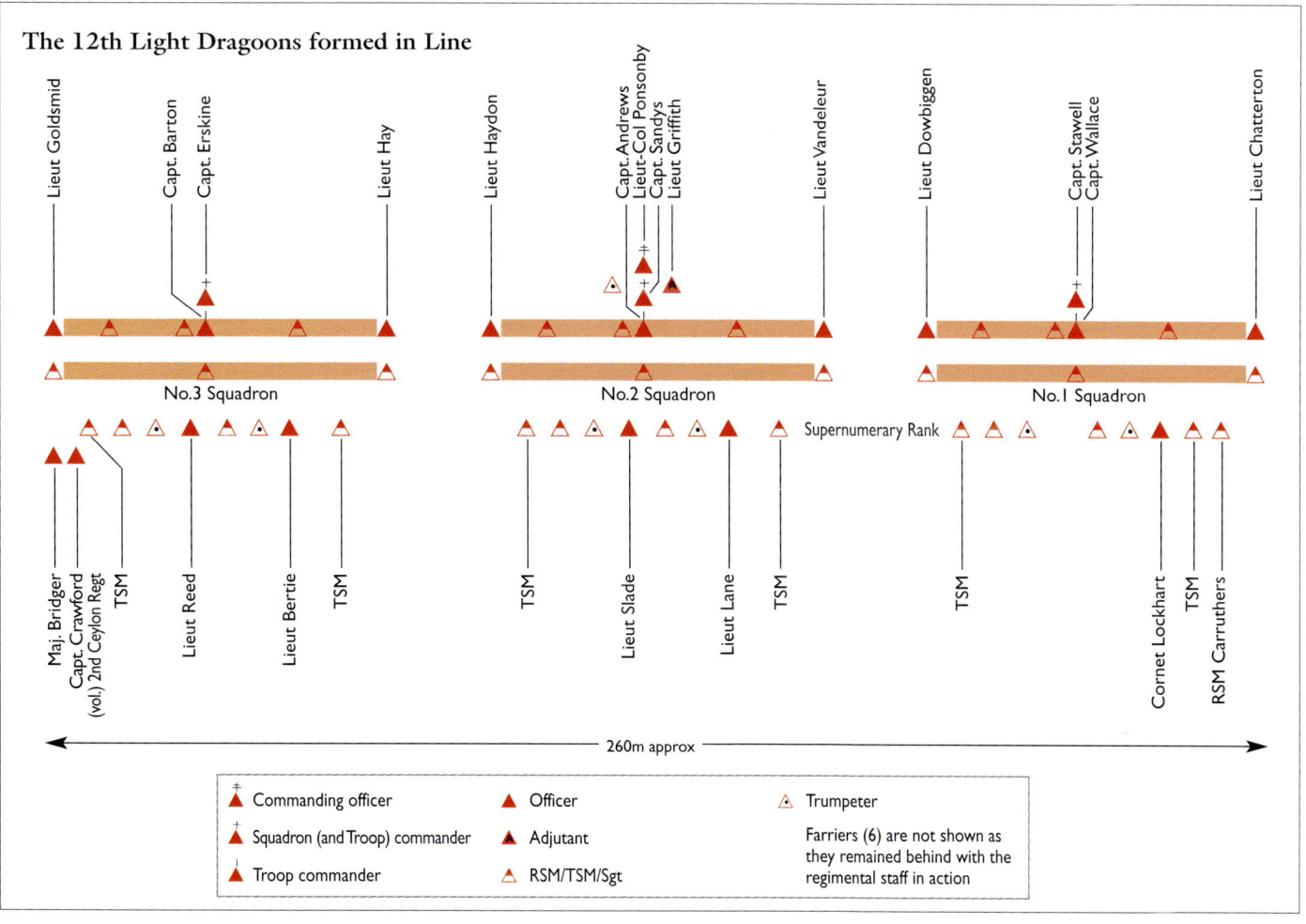

The 12th Light Dragoons formed in Line

A Regiment forms line from close column (1)
(The regiment forms on the head of the column)

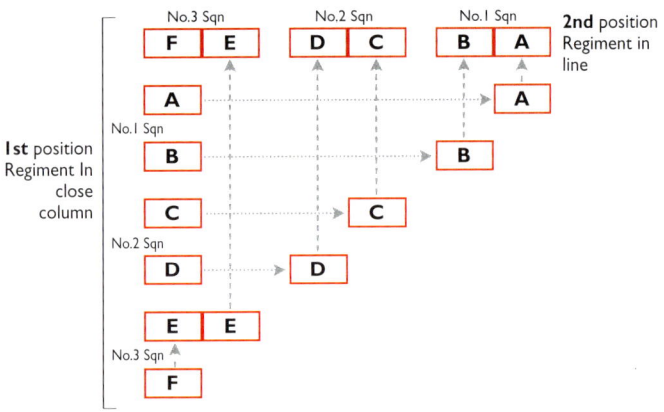

Notes
• The distances between troops in close column have been exaggerated for clarity.
• The regiment in line (in 2 ranks) would have covered a frontage of about 260m, including the gaps between squadron.
• The time required to complete this manoeuvre was something under 3 minutes.

A Regiment forms line from close column (2)
(The regiment forms on the centre squadron)

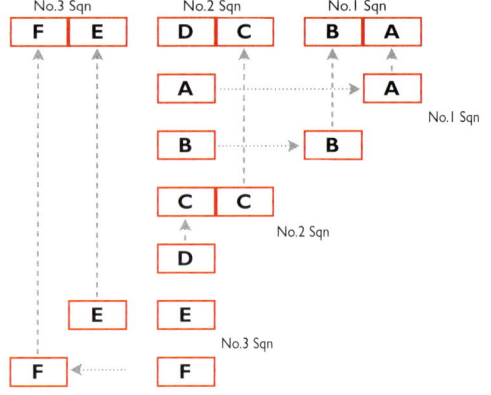

Notes
• With this method the regiment forms on the centre squadron (No.2 Sqn.) but No.1 Sqn. is always on the right in the line.
• The length (frontage) of the line is the same and was the formation used preparatory to advancing to charge.
• The time required to make the change was about 2–5 minutes.

flanks and in the centre of the front rank had to keep the line dressed (straight). All this was not too difficult over a short distance – in Hyde Park or at a trot if the unit had been extensively drilled in peacetime. At Waterloo, as with any battlefield, lines soon became ragged and formations disordered. In practice, the British system of having only one officer in front of the squadron was not conducive to forward control of the front rank. This was one reason why British cavalry tended to race away, as there were insufficient officers out in front to keeping the leading rank in check.

• The second problem was invariably the ground. The 12th Dragoons' three squadrons in an unbroken line with no gaps between squadrons occupied some 200 metres of frontage. If such a line advanced more than 100 metres at Waterloo it would encounter obstacles – slopes, dips, roads, hedges, embankments, cuttings, trees, orchards or buildings. Add to these other friendly units of infantry, artillery or cavalry, and the sheer impossibility of maintaining a long line over any distance becomes obvious.

In combination these problems ensured that lines of advancing Anglo-Allied cavalry composed of more than two squadrons were a rarity; both the Household and Union Brigade's advances were short, and quickly broken up by a sunken road, hedges and the La Haie Sainte enclosure.

As the diagram opposite shows, there were actually four types of line that cavalry commanders might adopt. They were:

The single line (Diagram A opposite)
Either all squadrons (or regiments, but this never happened at Waterloo) were packed together so that a continuous 'curtain' of horsemen was formed, or the squadrons had gaps of about a third of their frontage between them. It was the latter that was the usual practice in 1815. The Diagram on p. 229 shows the 12th Light Dragoons drawn up in this formation. The gaps between squadrons are 25 metres with the total frontage being 260 metres – a long line. The commanding officer (Ponsonby) rode in front of the centre squadron with his adjutant and trumpeter. One horse's

length behind him was the squadron commander (Captain Sandys) of the 'directing squadron' (No. 2 Squadron). Troop officers were positioned in the centre and on the flanks of the front ranks of squadrons, covered by sergeants or corporals. No standards were carried at Waterloo. A third, or supernumerary (sometimes called a serrefile), rank formed two horse's lengths behind the second rank. It was composed of officers, troop sergeant-majors, sergeants and trumpeters. On the extreme right was the regimental sergeant-major. The six farriers were usually at the rear with non-combatant regimental staff, left out of action. It is uncertain where Major Bridger and Captain Crauford (of the 2nd Ceylon Regiment) rode, but it is likely that they were behind the left flank as shown.

Examples of this formation being used (with all three squadrons in line), at least at the outset, include the advance of the 1st Dragoon Guards (Household Brigade) against the French cuirassiers west of La Haie Sainte, and the 12th Light Dragoons attack on the flank of Durutte's division.

The double line (Diagram B opposite)
This was used when a squadron or regiment was deliberately held back to create a second line to support the first. Within a three-squadron regiment one would form the second line; if the regiment had four squadrons then they would often be divided equally between the two lines. In most circumstances this was a better tactical formation than the single line since it provided a specifically designated reserve or support. If attacking infantry, this second line would be about 200 metres behind the first. If cavalry were being charged, the supports would be double that distance to the rear. The second line (also in two ranks) could either directly reinforce/support the first, manoeuvre to a flank, divide into two halves (troops) and operate on both flanks, or cover the withdrawal of the leading squadrons. It was a flexible system that many British units in the Peninsula had neglected to their cost, incurring the Duke's anger. After Waterloo Wellington personally wrote out detailed instructions on how the cavalry must deploy, not just two lines, but three in any attack.

Somerset's Household Brigade was initially formed up with one regiment (Royal Horse Guards, the Blues) in support behind the other three – the only other formation to do so was Vivian's hussar brigade on the extreme left. Nevertheless, once the order of advance was given the Blues were not held back but quickly merged into the front line in their fight with Dubois' cuirassiers. Lieutenant-Colonel Robert Hill, commanding the Blues, was later emphatic, perhaps suspiciously so, that his regiment was in the front line, saying that he recalled the commanding officer of the 1st Life Guards (Major Ferrior) killed on his right as they advanced to the charge. In fact there would not physically have been room for the Blues to be with the other three regiments in the first line at the start – the combined nine squadrons would have needed over 800 metres of frontage. The regiment did not, however, hold back to properly fulfil the role of supports but piled straight into the mêlée as soon as it could.

The echeloned line (Diagram C below)

It was an attack formation much favoured by many cavalrymen as offering several advantages over the straight line and being particularly suited to attacking infantry. Its merits were:

• It enabled the cavalry to deliver an attack in two directions: straight ahead or diagonally to one side. By wheeling the squadrons a quarter left or right a new line of attack was possible.

• The enemy was hit by a series of successive shocks as the squadrons (or regiments) hit home at intervals.

• The echelons behind could wait for the leading squadron to draw the first enemy volley and then charge home before reloading was complete.

• The rear echelons could be held back until the result of the first echelon's assault was clear. This could facilitate exploiting a weakness, attacking an exposed flank as the enemy moved forward to envelop the first echelon, or to cover a withdrawal.

• It was far easier to manoeuvre formations in echelon, squadrons could quickly form line or column, the direction of an advance could be swiftly altered, and the formation could pass through friendly units without becoming entangled or disorganized.

The only possible example of this formation being adopted at the outset was within the Union Brigade. The 2nd Dragoons (Scots Greys) were echeloned back to the left of the 6th Dragoons (Inniskilling) and 1st (Royal) Dragoons. However, there is good reason to suppose that the Scots Greys were intended to form a second line of supports, rather than being deliberately echeloned back – otherwise all three regiments would have been in echelon. More importantly, Captain Phipps of the 1st Dragoons later stated that he overheard Uxbridge telling the brigade commander as they came forward into line that, 'The Royals and Inniskillings will charge, the Greys support.' Whatever the truth of the matter, like the Blues in the Household Brigade, the Greys quickly moved into the first line and became embroiled in the attack on d'Erlon's divisions as they reached the ridge and in the subsequent dash to the 'Grand Battery'.

The checkered line (Diagram D below)

There is no evidence that this formation was used by any cavalry formation during the battle. It was a variation on the echeloned line to be used by cavalry units covering a withdrawal by the lines successively retiring through the gaps in the line behind. British cavalry during the withdrawal of the army used it on 17 June.

Various Cavalry Attack Formations   (The diagram shows either a 3 regiment brigade or 3 squadron regiment)

A **Single Line**	B **Double Line**	C **Echeloned Line**	D **Checkered Line**
Enemy	Enemy	Enemy	Enemy

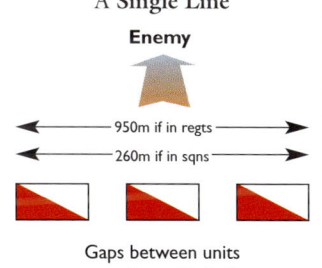

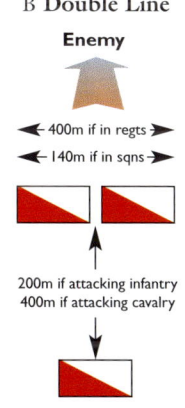

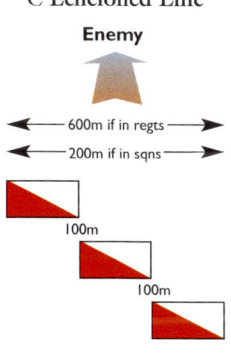

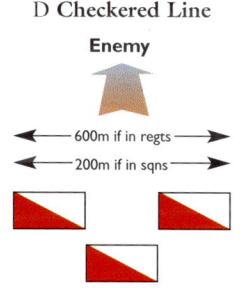

• This 2 rank line was seldom possible at brigade level due to ground restrictions.
• A formation favoured by British cavalry commanders for a full-blooded charge at the enemy.
• Difficult to use at Waterloo due to the confined space, particularly for a 4 sqn regiment.
• Used initially by Union Brigade Regiments when attacking Donzelot's and Marcognet's divisions.
• Wellington disapproved of its use without supports/reserves.

• A better formation as there is a distinct second line in support.
• The second line could be used to support the first, exploit and take advantage, manoeuvre to a flank, divide into troops and protect both flanks.
• After Waterloo Wellington went one further and insisted that cavalry attacks be undertaken by 3 lines.
• Used by Household Brigade (with the Blues in 2nd line) in their attack on Dubois' cuirassiers.

• The objective was to submit the enemy to a series of successive shocks as the regiments/squadrons hit home at intervals.
• Partially used at the start of the Union Brigade's attack on d'Erlon's columns as they crested the ridge.
• The Greys started their advance echeloned to the left rear of the 6th Dragoons but quickly came into line.

• A variation of the line formation with similar objectives as the echelon formation.
• It is doubtful if it was used at Waterloo.

TYPES OF ANGLO-ALLIED CAVALRY ACTION AT WATERLOO

Cavalry versus Infantry

When Wellington's horsemen attacked French infantry they were invariably doing so against units that were not prepared to receive a mounted assault. In other words, they had been caught in column, on the move, disorganized by cannon and musket fire, or had started to withdraw. Not surprisingly, all these attacks were successful. Each involved scores of individual combats in which the mounted man on his horse wielding a sabre had a decided moral and physical advantage over the frightened foot soldier with his musket (probably unloaded) and bayonet. On the only occasion when Anglo-Allied cavalry tried to break up infantry ready to receive them in square they failed. This did not occur until the end of the day when reserve battalions of the Old Guard covered the rout of the French Army. It was the French cavalry that spent the afternoon trying to break into infantry squares. Their attempts and the tactics involved are discussed below.

The Union Brigade's attack on the infantry columns of Quiot, Donzelot and Marcognet as they reached and came over the ridge in the early afternoon, is the best example of the Duke's cavalry catching infantry unprepared and tumbling them to ruin as a result. The timing of the attack was exactly right. The French had just completed a long advance under heavy artillery fire in vulnerable formations against an enemy they could not see, suffering severe losses and becoming disorganized. Then, at the moment when the attackers thought they had breached the line, they were hit by 1,300 heavy horsemen. In the resulting debacle and flight two French Eagles were lost and 2000 prisoners taken. On a smaller scale similar events took place when Vandeleur's light cavalry charged into the flank of part of Durutte's division a little further to the east. These attacks proved nothing new, merely underlining the centuries old truth that cavalry that catches unprepared infantry will invariably destroy them.

Cavalry versus Cavalry

As already emphasized, cavalry attacked by cavalry must themselves attack if they are not to surrender the moral and physical advantage to the enemy. In every instance of Anglo-Allied cavalry clashing with the French it was the consequence of a French attack and an Allied response. However, although there were numerous such engagements, large and small, mostly around and behind the Anglo-Allied infantry squares during the afternoon, none of them produced the popular impression of a cavalry clash: two solid lines smashing into each other at the charge. Not only did it not happen at Waterloo, but it is also difficult to find any historical example. If two walls of horsemen approached each other at speed they did not collide head on. The instinct of the horses to swerve or pull up was always stronger than the pain of the spur or the pull on the bit. Often one side would lose its nerve and turn about before the horses balked at self-destruction. Almost inevitably one side would have greater determination, greater morale or greater numbers than the other. The weaker-willed formation would often become disordered and break off the charge. The French tactical analyst of the mid-nineteenth century, Colonel Ardent du Picq, considered that, 'three quarters of the time this will happen at a distance, before they can see each other's eyes'. Another outcome that occurred more often if the riders were in a loose formation with some room between horses was that the lines rode through each other, or 'threaded'.

Throughout the Napoleonic Wars it was far more common for two opposing bodies of cavalry to meet at a trot or even a fast walk, rather than at a charge or a gallop. In these circumstances there was more likelihood of an actual mêlée. Both sides met in a hand-to-hand fight with the combatants seeking out individual opponents. This was the common scenario at Waterloo.

The primary example of two bodies of advancing heavy cavalry meeting head on during the battle was when the Household Brigade took on the flank guard of d'Erlon's attack (Baron

---

The Charge

As has already been mentioned in the main text, the instances of Anglo-Allied cavalry delivering a full-blooded charge at the gallop at Waterloo are hard to find above squadron level. The sequence of the work up to the charge was straightforward and set out in the manuals. First the walk, then the trot, gallop and finally the charge itself sounded on a trumpet. The British (and the French) did not specify the distances to be covered at the walk or trot, merely stating that the gallop should commence 250 yards from the enemy and the charge from 80. The cramped conditions of the Waterloo battlefield and the numerous obstacles made a long advance infeasible and a gallop of 250 yards a virtual impossibility.

• The British 1812 Regulations make a number of interesting points on the ideal charge – many of which were not followed at Waterloo. The salient ones were:

• On the charge being sounded the gallop was increased so long as the unit did not become disordered: the fastest horses were supposed to be held in check for the slowest so that all the line arrived together.

• At the instant of shock (there seldom, if ever, was a direct collision of bodies or horses) the trooper's body should be sitting well back, his horse not restrained by the bit but spurred forward

and given his head. With regard to the attitude of the trooper the manual has this to say, 'rising in the stirrups, and pointing the sword, will always occasion a shake in the squadron; it will naturally be done when necessary.'

• The importance of the uniform velocity of the unit was stressed along with the need to carefully follow the commander and maintain dressing. 'The spur as much as the sword tends to overset an opposite enemy; when one has nearly accomplished this end, the other may complete it.' This was the theory – the practice was never so neat and exact. Care had to be taken to ensure horses were not blown when they reached the enemy.

• Although a part of the unit might have been sent to pursue a broken foe, the bulk must immediately rally and collect itself for further orders – something the British cavalry seldom remembered.

• If a charge failed then the remnants must retire to make way for the supports, moving to the rear to rally under the protection of others.

• The regulations emphasized that even if the distance separating the squadron from the enemy was short, it should never receive an attack standing stationary. Some forward movement was vital prior to contact – 'otherwise its defeat is inevitable'.

Dubois' 1st and 4th Cuirassiers), west of La Haie Sainte. According to Captain Kelly of the 1st Life Guards (who killed an officer of the 1st Cuirassiers and then dismounted to cut off his epaulettes) the two lines, 'came together like two walls, in the most perfect lines he ever saw'. Whatever Kelly may have seen, it was not two bodies moving at great speed. The French were coming up the slope having ridden through high standing crops, or boggy ground for much of their 1,400 metre advance, consequently their line was ragged and their horses moving at a fast walk at best. The British Household Brigade was even more disorganized. They had to pass in rapid succession through or around several Hanoverian and KGL battalions, cross a road, 'too wide to leap, and the banks too deep to be easily passed', move through or around the British guns of Ross's battery, before finally confronting the French. At this moment the squadrons needed to briefly collect themselves before trotting down the slope into the leading cuirassiers that were less than 100 metres away. Lieutenant Waymouth of the 2nd Life Guards (who was wounded, and became one of the very few officers captured by the French at Waterloo), later wrote that, 'a short struggle enabled us to break through them, notwithstanding the great disadvantage arising from our swords, which were a full six inches shorter than those of the cuirassiers.'

Cavalry versus Artillery

A detailed discussion of the use of artillery at Waterloo is contained in Section 7, these paragraphs being confined to Anglo-Allied cavalry attacking French guns. This occurred only once during the battle when the disorganized, somewhat depleted Union Brigade swept on to the 'Grand Battery' after routing d'Erlon's divisions.

Of all troops probably the most vulnerable to cavalry at close quarters were the artillery. Once mounted men got in amongst the gunners they caused mayhem. The cavalry dreaded the terrible toll cannons could take of them as they approached. Once among the gun crews, however, they showed no mercy, flailing away at virtually defenceless men. This is what happened when the British heavy cavalry had a few brief minutes among the advanced French gun line only 600 metres south of the Mont St Jean ridge. Corporal John Dickson of the Scots Greys recalled what happened with considerable feeling:

> Then we got among the guns, and we had our revenge. Such slaughtering! We sabred the gunners, lamed the horses, and cut their traces and harness. I can hear the Frenchmen yet crying 'Diable!' when I struck at them, and the long-drawn hiss through their teeth as my sword went home. Fifteen of their guns could not be fired again that day. The artillery drivers sat on their horses weeping aloud as we went among them; they were mere boys, we thought.

Typically, the Union Brigade had done precisely what Wellington was so critical of the British cavalry for doing – ruining a successful action (completing the rout of d'Erlon's corps) by careering off in pursuit and then getting badly cut up by the inevitable counter-stroke. This came in the form of nearly 900 cuirassiers under Baron Farine, 700 lancers under Baron Gobrecht plus the 365 men of Colonel Woestine's regiment of châsseurs à cheval. The Union Brigade was almost destroyed as an effective force.

Even the cavalry's brief victory spree among the guns had no lasting effect. The 'Grand Battery' was not put out of action, nobody on the Allied ridge noticed any lasting reduction of fire, and French artillery continued to be the biggest killer of Wellington's troops. All this was due to the failure of the Union Brigade to spike the guns (drive a metal spike into the vent of the cannons), probably (like the French) because they did not carry any. Corporal Dickson thought fifteen guns were permanently put out of action, others have suggested forty (half the total strength of the battery). In fact, depleted gun crews were replaced by other troops, mostly infantry, and horses were not crucial for the operation of guns firing from a fixed position – manpower replaced horsepower, and the undamaged cannons were quickly in action again.

The cavalry in pursuit

Anglo-Allied cavalry units were involved in pursuit twice on the battlefield of Waterloo. The first occasion was the Union Brigade's chase after the routing divisions of d'Erlon's corps, which continued up to the gunline of the 'Grand Battery'. The second was late evening when the light cavalry of Vivian's brigade, supported by those of Vandeleur, followed up and pursued the retreating elements of the French Army as it struggled to leave the battlefield, only covered by a few stubborn squares of the Old Guard.

Cavalrymen enjoyed a pursuit, particularly if the fugitives were infantry. The elation of the chase, the adrenalin pumping, the feeling of invincibility, the comparative ease of the killing; all these factors combined to make a pursuing horseman a frighteningly powerful figure. Well-mounted enemy cavalry could often get away but an infantryman's back was a temptingly easy target for sword or lance. A close pursuit of a fleeing enemy always produced lop-sided casualty statistics – 20:1 in favour of the pursuer was not exceptional. There was nothing the fleeing soldiers could do unless they could break away and gain an opportunity to rally. To fight back meant the soldier stopping, turning and facing the unknown menace behind, probably on his own. Few dared to take this risk. The infantryman's best recourse was to fall down and sham death. The speeding horse behind would instinctively try to avoid trampling him, its rider would have difficulty reaching him with his sabre, while even a lancer might be distracted by an easier target.

The Union Brigade's pursuit of d'Erlon's infantry was short, but not sweet. Nor was it intended. The brigade commander's extra ADC, Major Evans of the 5th West India Regiment (who later became General Sir De Lacey Evans and a divisional commander in the Crimean War), later wrote:

> … Sir William Ponsonby did his best to prevent the further advance up the opposite ridge and towards the left of the French cannon, and so did all the officers of any discretion about him; but finding that we were not successful in stopping the troops, we were forced to continue on with them in order to continue our exclamations to halt, as we all, except I suppose the Cornets, saw what would happen.

Ponsonby was one of the many who paid with their lives for the failure to rally the foolishness of the wild, undisciplined pursuit to the French guns. Scattered and isolated they were hit by a French counter-stroke of cuirassiers, châsseurs and lancers – the pursuers became the pursued.

At the end of the day the light cavalry pursuit fared considerably better than that of their heavy comrades. It was a controlled affair, with Vivian's hussars leading the cavalry advance of the victorious Anglo-Allied Army against a fleeing enemy who presented only a few pockets of serious resistance. It was a short, tactical pursuit confined to the battlefield. The strategic pursuit south was handed to the much fresher Prussian cavalry.

The cavalry as skirmishers

In general terms cavalry might expect to skirmish prior to the start of a battle, and infantry during the course of it. The cavalry's mobility made them, especially the light cavalry, the army's screen, its scouts and a major provider of information. This work often required them to skirmish (fight) for information or to prevent the enemy obtaining it. The light cavalry (with horse artillery) provided an army's advanced guard and rearguard. On 17 June and well into the night, through violent thunderstorms and drenching rain, British light cavalry and horse artillery skirmished with the advancing French from Quatre-Bras, through Genappe and northwards towards La Belle Alliance. They were not, however, employed as skirmishers during the battle – this duty was handed to the infantry.

On the Duke's extreme left the 10th Hussars pushed a piquet south through Smohain which maintained vedettes further out. The 1st Hussars KGL had posted similar patrols to the east and along the Ohain road. At the western end of the line east of Hougoumont a squadron of the 15th Hussars did similar duty alongside some light infantry from the 51st Foot. This cavalry was not required to skirmish on the battlefield.

The Duke's directions on cavalry tactics

The performance of the heavy cavalry at Waterloo confirmed Wellington's frustrations. Within the Union Brigade in particular the officers had failed to organize the attack with a reserve and supports held well back, lost control, and had been unable to rally their troops. The result was that the brigade had fallen for the oldest trick in the book – it had been caught disorganized on winded horses by a well-timed counterattack. The result was that the two brigades between them barely made a respectable sized regiment. After the battle the Duke issued a directive entitled 'Instructions to Officers commanding Brigades of Cavalry in the Army of Occupation'. The essential elements were:

• There must always be a reserve to exploit success or cover a withdrawal. This reserve to be not less than half the force available. At Waterloo there had been no reserve.

• A cavalry force attacking should do so in three lines with the first and second deployed, the reserve kept in column. At Waterloo there were two lines that quickly merged into one.

• Against cavalry there should be 400–500 yards between the lines and the reserve. When charging infantry the gaps should be reduced to 200 yards. At Waterloo the gap between the two lines was barely 100 metres against both cavalry (Dubois' cuirassiers) and infantry (d'Erlon's divisions).

• When the leading line charged, the supporting (second) line should follow at a walk to avoid being involved in the initial mêlée – 'order in the supports must be rigidly kept – they are useless if they have got into confusion…'. At Waterloo all surged forward at best speed and the second line rushed immediately into the hand to hand fight.

THE FRENCH CAVALRY

General

Archduke Charles of Austria was a man with considerable experience of fighting Napoleon's cavalry. He once explained the reason for their success on so many battlefields (despite an overall decline in quality of men and horses during the three years prior to Waterloo) as being due to their élan, their ability to charge no matter what the circumstances. He claimed, 'The French cavalry was, on the whole, poorly mounted and poorly equipped; its men were awkward horsemen. Yet it outclassed its opponents simply because, when the order rang out and trumpets clarioned "Charge!" it put in its spurs and charged all out, charged home!' They certainly tried to live up to this reputation at Waterloo. For almost two hours throughout the late afternoon some 8000 horsemen were committed to charge, charge, and charge again at the Anglo-Allied infantry squares and gun batteries. Today's visitors to the Panorama in 'Lion Village' can gaze in astonishment and admiration at a circular mural 110 metres long by 12 metres high depicting the action at the height of these charges. However, despite the Archduke, despite the artist's brilliant brushwork, for reasons discussed below (pp. 249–51) they did not actually charge home. Regiments and squadrons did not come on at a gallop, but at a trot or brisk walk.

The heyday of Napoleonic cavalry was the period from 1805–7. Those were the years of the campaigns on the Danube, into Prussia and across Poland: the days of the Emperor's dazzling victories on the Ulm, at Austerlitz, at Jena-Auerstadt, at Eylau and at Friedland. It was a period before the cavalry was diluted by having to recruit thousands of foreigners and raise foreign regiments. The Guard cavalry was comparatively small but élite, horses and remounts were plentiful, every corps had its light cavalry division, while the massive cavalry reserve of the Grande Armée exceeded 10 per cent of the total. The years that followed those times saw a dramatic decline in standards and numbers.

It started with the 'Spanish ulcer'. Napoleon's dragoons and light cavalry were needed in their thousands in the seemingly everlasting (six years), costly side-show (for the Emperor) of the Peninsular War. Next came Russia. The cavalry never recovered from the loss of horses. Nine out of ten cavalrymen who survived walked much of the way home; most of those who rode did so on tiny, but tough, Russian ponies, their boots scuffing the ground. Cavalry units without horses formed up to fight as infantry with carbines, cuirassiers picked up lances to use as pikes, châsseurs harnessed surviving horses to sleighs and formed 'wagon laagers' at night. Some

500 officers who still had horses were formed into what became called the 'Sacred Squadron', with generals commanding troops.

The following year (1813) the French cavalry lacked trained horses and trained riders. Weapons, helmets and equipment were in short supply. The army's operations were badly handicapped by the dearth of competent light cavalry for scouting, screening and foraging. In 1814 the situation worsened. Colonel Elting in *Swords Around a Throne* quotes General Pajol's description of his cavalry at one engagement: '... many men and horses had not been with the army for more than fifteen days. Not only were the riders incapable of handling their horses and weapons properly, but even of holding the reins in one hand and their sabre in the other; some even needed both hands to turn their horses right or left.' Nevertheless, on this occasion they did what Archduke Charles so admired and dug in their spurs – thereby gaining a small but stunning victory.

The climax to the cavalry's misfortunes (as with the rest of the army) was the inevitable cut back – the premature peace dividend – during Napoleon's short sojourn on Elba. Line cavalry regiments were reduced from 110 to 56. Although the two regiments of carabineers survived, the dragoons lost nine (from twenty-four to fifteen), the châsseurs sixteen, and the cuirassiers two. Six hussars regiments were retained, as were all six of the lancers. That

Napoleon and his staff were able to field so formidable an array of 15,600 horsemen that performed so creditably at Waterloo speaks volumes for his, and their, energy, zeal and organizing ability. Because the number of differing types of French horsemen at Waterloo can confuse the unfamiliar reader, they will be clarified in detail before describing the battlefield organization and tactics employed – a slightly different format from that used with the Anglo-Allied cavalry.

TYPES OF FRENCH CAVALRY (INCLUDING WEAPONS)
General

The French fielded seven different types of cavalry on the battlefield, eight if you count the Gendarmes d'Elite half squadron. They were divided almost equally between heavy and light horsemen – at Waterloo all French dragoons were used in the heavy role. Purely by accident, the 15,580 horsemen were almost exactly evenly divided between 'heavies' (7,798) and 'lights' (7,782). The most numerous type in terms of regiments was the cuirassiers with twelve, but they had virtually the same overall strength as the châsseurs à cheval with only eight regiments – just over 4,100 each. Of Napoleon's horsemen almost one in five was a lancer while, apart from one Uhlan squadron, Wellington had none. In contrast

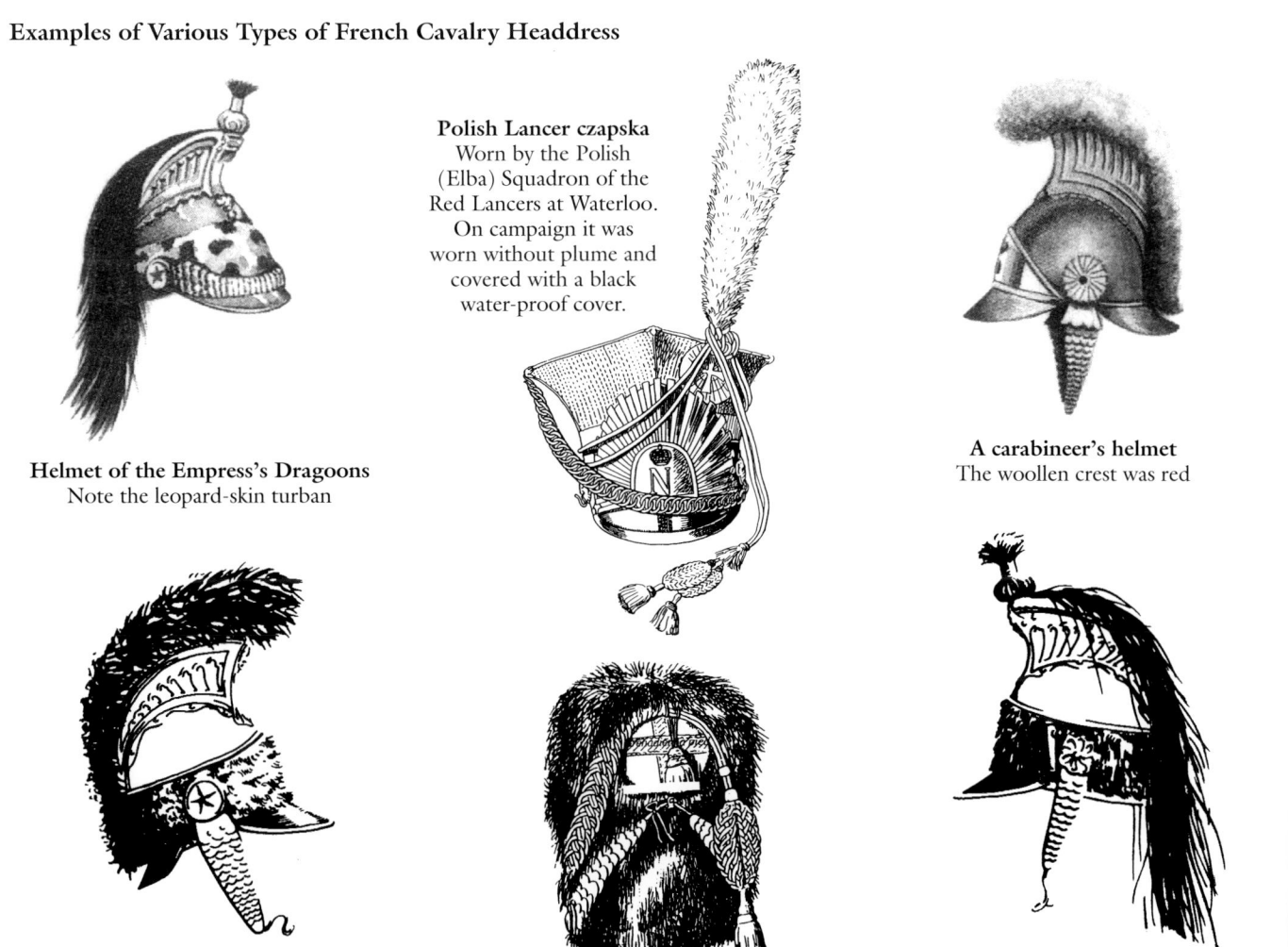

Examples of Various Types of French Cavalry Headdress

Helmet of the Empress's Dragoons
Note the leopard-skin turban

Polish Lancer czapska
Worn by the Polish (Elba) Squadron of the Red Lancers at Waterloo. On campaign it was worn without plume and covered with a black water-proof cover.

A carabineer's helmet
The woollen crest was red

A lancer's helmet
In reality a dragoon's helmet with a neck peak and black crest

Bearskin of Grenadiers à Cheval of the Imperial Guard

A dragoon helmet
The turban was brown fur, the horsehair mane was black

the Emperor had but one regiment of hussars (the 7th) to the Duke's ten. The table below gives an overall breakdown of types:

Type	Regiments	Squadrons	Numbers	% (of all cavalry)
Heavy cavalry				
Cuirassiers	12	35	4,123	26
Carabineers	2	6	847	6
Dragoons	3	12	1,926	12
Grenadiers à Cheval	1	4	796	5
Gendarmes d'Elite		0.5	106	1
Total heavy	**18**	**57.5**	**7,798**	**50**
Light cavalry				
Châsseurs à Cheval	8	28	4,109	26
Lancers	7	25	3,234	21
Hussars	1	3	439	3
Total light	**16**	**56**	**7,782**	**50**
Grand total	**34**	**113.5**	**15,580**	**100**

As with the other armies, the French cavalry's tactical unit on the battlefield was the regiment, divided into two, three, four or five (normally a depot squadron) squadrons. The campaign establishment was four squadrons, so those with two were dangerously weak. At Waterloo five regiments had just two squadrons; fifteen had three; twelve had four and two had five (Guard Châsseurs and Lancers). Each regiment had its own headquarters staff under the colonel. According to circumstances this staff consisted of some or all of the following – two chefs d'escadron (majors), one adjutant-major (captain), one paymaster/quartermaster, one surgeon-major, one adjutant, one brigadier-trompette (corporal trumpeter), one veterinary surgeon and six maitres (cobblers, tailors, armourers and saddlers).

Squadrons in all regiments were divided into two companies, each under a captain – the senior commanded the squadron. The companies were further divided into two troops and four divisions. When moving along a road a squadron would usually be in column of fours. Within each regiment the 1st Company of the 1st Squadron was the Elite Company, with the necessary embellishments to its dress to distinguish its members from the rest. This company had the honour of carrying the Eagle. The cavalry did not have the system of porte-aigles like the infantry so the Eagle was carried by a highly decorated, veteran maréchal de logis (sergeant).

With one or two exceptions French heavy cavalry wore blue jackets and their light comrades green. There were fourteen regiments with blue as the predominant colour, seventeen with green.

The odd ones out were the carabineers in white, a dreadfully impractical colour – which showed every tiny mark but more importantly for the wearer's morale, magnified even a small amount of blood loss to frightening proportions. Then there were the 2nd Light Horse Lancers of the Guard in their bright red jackets, although the Polish squadron was in blue.

Heavy Cavalry
Cuirassiers (Maps 13 & 14, pp. 161 & 162)
General
'The cuirassiers are of greater value than any other type of cavalry.' So said Napoleon to Maréchal Bessières in 1808. Cuirassiers were an élite. Big men, originally at least 1.8 metres tall, they had to have served in three campaigns and have twelve years service before they could be accepted. For officers it was a prestigious arm of the service, second only to the Imperial Guard (strangely, Napoleon never had cuirassiers in his Guard). Selection procedures were rigorous, sometimes intriguing. Regiments of cuirassiers, often augmented by carabineers, provided the Emperor with one of his most formidable battlefield weapons. They were classified as élite troops entitled to red epaulettes and plumes, plus a flaming grenade insignia on their saddlecloths and coat-tails together with an extra five centimes pay a day (called the 'sou of the grenade').

A fully armed and equipped cuirassier wearing body armour weighed around 309 pounds. He needed to be mounted on an exceptionally powerful horse (only obtainable in Normandy). The purpose of cuirassier formations was to smash through a weakened line, exploit a breakthrough or destroy a wavering army. For this reason they were normally held in reserve, or at least in the second line – as at Waterloo. They were nicknamed Napoleon's 'Gros Freres', his 'Big Brothers'. Such troops were best used en masse. To facilitate this regiments were invariably grouped together in brigades, divisions and even corps. At Waterloo Milhaud's 4th Reserve Cavalry Corps had eight regiments in four brigades in two divisions – almost 2,800 glittering horsemen. The other four regiments formed two brigades in Kellerman's 3rd Reserve Cavalry Corps. They were the Napoleonic equivalent of a modern tank division, with an identical role.

Armour
The cuirassier's helmet was a steel cap surrounded by a turban of black fur, with a copper crest surmounted by a black horsehair mane. Helmets differed in points of detail between regiments – some had plumes of various colours on the left side but these were only worn by officers at Waterloo.

A Cuirassier in Close Combat

In individual combat the cuirassier (or carabineer) did not necessarily have the advantage over other types of horsemen. His chest and back were fairly immune from cuts or thrusts, but the weight was tiresome and the armour restricted his arm movements. A fight against a more agile light cavalryman did not always go the cuirassier's way. An effective method of securing a decisive advantage over such a heavyweight was to kill or maim his horse. Once thrown in the mud it was a slow struggle to get up. Even on his feet the big boots and heavy armour rendered him an easy victim. Private Cotton (later sergeant-major and battlefield guide) of the British 7th Hussars witnessed a fight between a cuirassier and a hussar. He described what happened: 'A hussar and a cuirassier had got entangled in the mêlée, and met in the plain in full view of our line; the hussar was without cap and bleeding from a wound in the head, but that did not hinder him from attacking his steel-clad adversary. He soon proved that the strength of cavalry consists in good swordsmanship … and not in being clad in defensive armour … after a few wheels a tremendous fencer made the Frenchman reel in the saddle … a second blow stretched him on the ground, amidst the cheers of the light horseman's comrades [the 3rd Hussars KGL], who were ardent spectators of the combat.'

The Cuirass – a Help or a Hindrance?

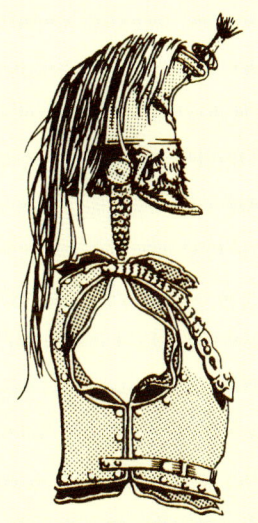

Cuirass and helmet side view

Antoine Faveau of the Cuirassiers had the misfortune to be struck by a cannonball at Waterloo

Cuirass and helmet front view

Most major European armies had followed the French and formed cuirassier regiments by 1815. They seemed the ultimate shock weapon. Britain, however, was the exception and had no cuirassiers at Waterloo but quickly issued them to the Household Cavalry after the battle – they still wear the cuirass today on ceremonial duties in London. The arguments for and against centred around the following:

For

• The physical protection the armour gave saved lives and thus reduced casualties.

• The morale boost it gave the wearer, who felt more secure and thus able to face more dangerous situations with confidence.

• The adverse morale effect it had on the enemy to see solid lines of these huge, glittering men on equally huge horses approaching – they looked invincible.

• They were essential to counter the enemy's cuirassiers as no other horsemen could be counted to stand against them in close combat.

Against

• They were expensive troops to equip and maintain.

• The problems of finding sufficient strong horses and men, particularly towards the end of a long campaign. For many recruits a cuirass was a burdensome encumbrance, and it took considerable experience to feel reasonably comfortable in it. In 1809 even some officers were caught discarding cuirasses – they were forced to wear the trooper's version and pay for the cost of new ones.

• The excessive weight of armour and equipment rendered the soldier slow moving, less agile and very vulnerable if he lost his horse or was even slightly wounded.

• They were seldom able to charge at more than a trot due to the state of the ground or when faced with an incline – Waterloo was a prime example – which tended to negate the weight and force of their attacks.

As with the cut versus thrust argument, both sides had convinced advocates. Despite the cuirassiers' courageous but largely unsuccessful performance at Waterloo, together with Wellington's scathing comments on unhorsed cuirassiers looking like so many turtles on their backs, the British Army adopted them.

The cuirasses (back and breastplates) were made of steel with gilded copper rivets around the edges, weighing about ten pounds. They were designed to stop or deflect penetration by pistol balls, sword, lance or bayonet, and in this they enjoyed some success. They took the wearer some time to get used to and tended to restrict arm movement but gave him a comfortable feeling of security. Against a musket shot this was almost always misplaced. Despite its pigeon breasted shape, a cuirass offered little protection at under 100 metres. Originally each breastplate was subjected to a severe test by the military before acceptance from the manufacturers. It had to be 'proved' by resisting three musket shots at 30 paces. Perhaps not surprisingly few passed this stringent trial. After some wrangling, economics triumphed and cuirasses had only to deflect one shot at longer range. When the cuirassiers repeatedly charged the Anglo-Allied infantry squares at Waterloo, several soldiers commented on the noise of balls hitting (and often penetrating) the breastplates as being like hail stones striking a glass pane. A cannon ball went through a cuirass as a thrown stone through a sheet of paper (see Antoine Faveau's cuirass above). The 11th Cuirassiers went into battle at Waterloo without cuirasses because they could not be procured in time.

Uniforms

It was difficult to distinguish between cuirassier regiments unless one was either close enough to see the buttons, which were flat, white metal and bore the regimental number, or knew the colour code of the facings (lapels, collars and cuffs). This was due to all regiments wearing dark blue tunics, linen or hide overalls of a grey/brown colour and high black boots. The facing colours were in groups of three. The senior regiment of each group wore the facing colour on both collar and cuffs, the second senior on cuffs only and the third on collar only. The colours of the regiments at Waterloo were:

1st, 2nd and 3rd	scarlet
4th, 5th and 6th	aurore (pale gold tinged with pink)
7th, 8th and 9th	primrose
10th, 11th and 12th	pink

Various French Cavalry Weapons

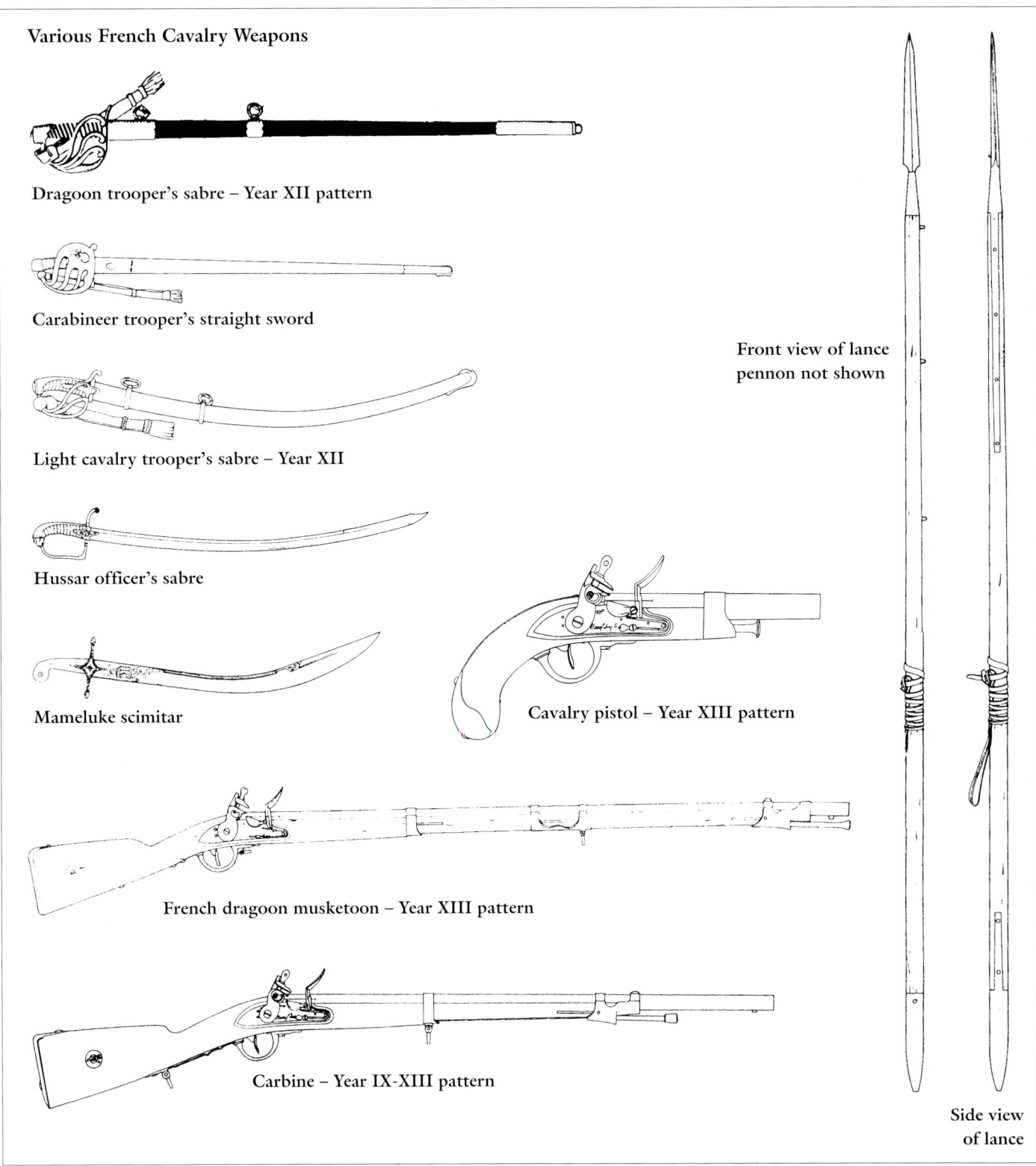

Dragoon trooper's sabre – Year XII pattern

Carabineer trooper's straight sword

Light cavalry trooper's sabre – Year XII

Hussar officer's sabre

Mameluke scimitar

Cavalry pistol – Year XIII pattern

Front view of lance
pennon not shown

French dragoon musketoon – Year XIII pattern

Carbine – Year IX-XIII pattern

Side view
of lance

Their trumpeters had no armour and a white flowing tail to their helmets. They had jackets of imperial livery decorated with lace and red epaulettes. This was a style Napoleon had made standard throughout the infantry and cavalry.

Weapons (Diagram above)

By 1815 the cuirassier's main armament was the XIII pattern, heavy, 97-centimetre twin-guttered blade carried in an iron scabbard. Although sharp bladed it was intended mainly as a thrusting weapon. The cuirassier was trained to concentrate on the parry and thrust and, when charging, to do so with the sword-arm extended (no bent elbows), leaning forward over his horse's neck. Until 1812 the only firearms carried by cuirassiers were two pistols, but in that year they were issued with a cavalry musketoon complete with cross-belt and bayonet. These were of considerable value during the march to and from Moscow. At Borodino 6000 horses were killed and within five days of the retreat some 30,000 more had died. Thereafter most cuirassiers marched, fought and died on foot.

Historical background

All cuirassier regiments at Waterloo could trace their origins back to the fifteenth century, the most senior (the 1st) being formed in 1645, the most junior (the 12th) in 1688. Since Austerlitz they had fought with distinction across Europe. All twelve had ridden into Russia. During the brief restoration in 1814 they had been absorbed into the King's army with appropriate royalist titles – for example, the 1st were called the Cuirassiers du Roi, the 2nd the Cuirassiers de la Reine. With Napoleon's return from Elba they switched sides again.

Mobilization problems centred around procuring enough strong horses. By Waterloo the 2nd, 7th, 11th and 12th could still only mount two squadrons apiece. During the previous three days all regiments had seen action either at Fleurus, Ligny or Quatre-Bras. At the latter Kellerman had led a charge of the 8th and 11th in which his horse had been killed and he had only regained French lines by being half-carried, half-dragged back, clinging to the stirrups of two troopers. In a subsequent, more successful attack, they had dispersed the British 69th Foot, taking its one remaining Colour. Shortly afterwards this trophy was presented to Ney by an immensely proud trooper of the 8th Cuirassiers named Lami. At Ligny the 9th had twice ridden over the unhorsed Prussian commander-in-chief, Blücher, without realizing it.

Organization at Waterloo

Despite the mud-caked boots, filthy overalls and tarnished breastplates, the corps of cuirassiers was the Emperor's showpiece for the battle. They were split between two corps as shown here:

3rd Reserve Cavalry Corps – GOC Général de Division Comte Kellerman
11th Cavalry Division – GOC Général de Division Baron L'Heritier
2nd Brigade – GOC Maréchal de Camp Baron Guiton
8th Cuirassiers (300 in three squadrons) – Colonel Garavaque

11th Cuirassiers (241 in two squadrons without cuirasses) – Colonel Courtier
12th Cavalry Division – GOC Général de Division Baron d'Hurbal
2nd Brigade – GOC Maréchal de Camp Donop
2nd Cuirassiers (311 in two squadrons) – Colonel Grandjean
3rd Cuirassiers (480 in four squadrons) – Colonel Lacroix

4th Reserve Cavalry Corps – GOC Général de Division Comte Milhaud
13th Cavalry Division – GOC Général de Division Comte Watier
1st Brigade – GOC Maréchal de Camp Baron Dubois
1st Cuirassiers (465 in four squadrons) – Colonel Comte Ordener
4th Cuirassiers (314 in three squadrons) – Colonel Habert
2nd Brigade – GOC Maréchal de Camp Baron Travers de Jevers
7th Cuirassiers (180 in two squadrons) – Colonel Richardot (the smallest regiment in the army)
12th Cuirassiers (258 in two squadrons) – Colonel Thurot
14th Cavalry Division – GOC Général de Division Baron Delort
1st Brigade – GOC Maréchal de Camp Farine du Creux
5th Cuirassiers (518 in three squadrons) – Colonel Gobert (the largest cuirassier regiment)
10th Cuirassiers (359 in three squadrons) – Colonel Lahuberdiere
2nd Brigade – GOC Maréchal de Camp Baron Vial
6th Cuirassiers (285 in three squadrons) – Colonel Martin
9th Cuirassiers (412 in four squadrons) – Colonel Bigarne

Battlefield highlights

• At around 2.00 p.m. Dubois' brigade (1st and 4th Cuirassiers) was tasked with advancing to protect the western flank of d'Erlon's massive corps attack on the Anglo-Allied centre and left. On the French left the fighting swirled around La Haie Sainte. Immediately west of this farm the cuirassiers attacked and destroyed the Lüneberg Light Battalion that was rushing to assist La Haie Sainte,

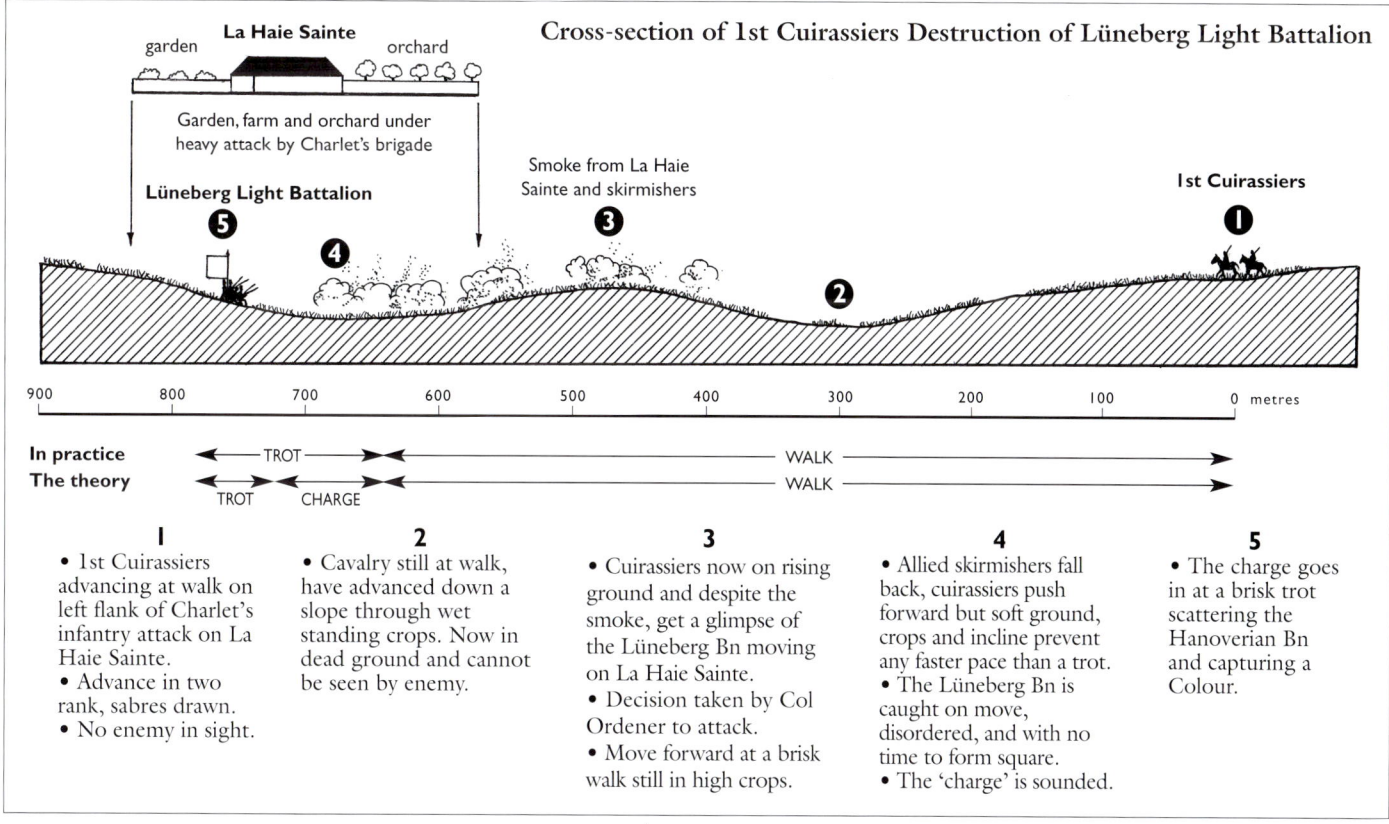

Cross-section of 1st Cuirassiers Destruction of Lüneberg Light Battalion

La Haie Sainte
garden   orchard

Garden, farm and orchard under heavy attack by Charlet's brigade

Lüneberg Light Battalion

Smoke from La Haie Sainte and skirmishers

1st Cuirassiers

❺ ❹ ❸ ❷ ❶

900   800   700   600   500   400   300   200   100   0 metres

In practice — TROT — WALK —
The theory — TROT — CHARGE — WALK —

1	2	3	4	5
• 1st Cuirassiers advancing at walk on left flank of Charlet's infantry attack on La Haie Sainte. • Advance in two rank, sabres drawn. • No enemy in sight.	• Cavalry still at walk, have advanced down a slope through wet standing crops. Now in dead ground and cannot be seen by enemy.	• Cuirassiers now on rising ground and despite the smoke, get a glimpse of the Lüneberg Bn moving on La Haie Sainte. • Decision taken by Col Ordener to attack. • Move forward at a brisk walk still in high crops.	• Allied skirmishers fall back, cuirassiers push forward but soft ground, crops and incline prevent any faster pace than a trot. • The Lüneberg Bn is caught on move, disordered, and with no time to form square. • The 'charge' is sounded.	• The charge goes in at a brisk trot scattering the Hanoverian Bn and capturing a Colour.

capturing their Colour and killing Colonel Klenke, their commander. Some cuirassiers reached the Ohain road on the crest of the ridge to the west of the 'Elm Tree' crossroads, but got into difficulties by the unexpected appearance of the steep cutting through which the road ran. A counterattack by the Household Brigade drove Dubois' men back with substantial loss.

• By about 2.30 p.m. d'Erlon's corps was retiring in confusion, harried by the Union Brigade and some of the Household Brigade. The British squadrons galloped up to and through the French 'Grand Battery', cutting down numerous gunners and drivers. They had however, overreached themselves and Travers' Brigade (7th and 12th Cuirassiers) counterattacked south of La Haie Sainte. At the same time Farine's Brigade (5th and 10th Cuirassiers), along with lancers from Jacquinot's division, charged from the south and south-east. Wellington's Union Brigade was almost destroyed as an effective force.

• The climax of the battle for all cuirassier regiments was the series of cavalry assaults on the Duke's right, which took place between about 4.00 p.m. to nearly 6.00 p.m. Milhaud's regiments led the attack but were soon followed by Kellerman's. These attacks eventually sucked in around 8000 horsemen and as such constituted what was probably the largest assault by cavalry in so confined a space during the entire Napoleonic Wars.

Carabineers

General

These two regiments, although not armoured until 1809–10, had always been classified as heavy cavalry. Despite often being within the same division as cuirassiers, they had a prickly pride in their assumed superiority over all other cavalry except the Guard. This attitude had become a carabineer characteristic, ingrained during a hundred or more years of close association with the French monarchy – they both survived the first restoration in 1814, largely due to their royalist background. They had been pampered, being granted many royal perks and privileges such as never being given corporal punishment, never having to do guard duty and always parading on the right of the line or the head of the column. Traditionally, carabineers had always ridden black horses. Despite the remount problems, they remained 'black horse' regiments at Waterloo.

As their name implies, their origins were linked to their use of the carbine. In 1679 all cavalry regiments were required to select

two men in each company to be armed with rifled carbines and train as snipers. In 1690 they were grouped together into one company in each regiment as specialists in dismounted action, skirmishing and outpost duties. Three years later King Louis XIV took the next step and grouped the companies into the Royal Regiment of Carabineers. In 1778, almost a hundred years later, the second regiment was formed.

Armour

The carabineers' helmet was of yellow copper, with iron chinstrap scales and a headband with the letter 'N' in front. The crest had a scarlet comb instead of the cuirassiers black plume. The officers' version was more elaborate and was made from red copper and silver.

Like the helmet, their cuirasses were virtually identical in design to those worn by the far more numerous cuirassiers. The differences were in the detail. Those of the troopers were covered with a sheet of brass, the officers' red copper. The effect was quite startling. When well burnished and catching the sun they could easily be mistaken for gold.

Uniforms

Early in the Revolution the carabineers had been compelled to change their title and their uniform in an attempt to disassociate them from their monarchist past. They briefly became 'Grenadiers à Cheval' and lost their cocked hats, which were replaced by grenadier's bearskins. The new title did not last, but the bearskins remained for nearly seventeen years. This was despite the incompetence (or parsimony) of the military bureaucracy in failing to provide the bearskins with chinstraps. It was not until Napoleon noticed how many suffered head wounds (at Aspen-Essling and Wagram) due to both the poor protection they offered and how easily they fell off that, in 1809, he ordered them first to be given chinstraps and, shortly afterwards, helmets and cuirasses. While welcoming the loss of the bearskins, being forced to wear a cuirass was felt by many to be an insult to their courage.

Shortly afterwards, their uniform was changed (not without further grousing and grumbling) from blue and red to white – a particularly impractical colour for the field and consequently in a dreadful state on the morning of 18 June. Dark grey overalls replaced breeches on campaign. Like cuirassiers they wore long black riding boots.

Cuirassier Officer's Selection Test

One French cuirassier regiment had in its heyday instituted a particularly demanding test for would-be officers. Candidates were given three horses, three bottles of champagne and three willing wenches. They were then given three hours to drink the champagne, bed the ladies and ride a rough 20-mile course. The order in which these were accomplished was immaterial.

Kindly Carabineers

French soldiers were normally master scavengers, ruthless looters with years of experience in living off the countryside. This was the way they secured the bulk of their food and fodder: by requisition, threat or outright theft. It was often the only way to survive, as the French military supply system varied from rudimentary and inadequate to non-existent. To have a French unit billeted on a village was often to condemn the inhabitants to ruin. History, however, records a unique exception.

In 1800 the 1st Carabineers were billeted on the poor German town of Eichstedt. The citizens had just been ordered to produce a massive 'contribution' to the military coffers so the

arrival of a cavalry regiment was greeted with utter dismay. The town's authorities proposed to sell their church's sacred vessels to raise funds. The carabineer commander, whose name unfortunately is not known, unsuccessfully appealed to his superiors to have the 'contribution' cut. Failing in that, he and his officers raised a substantial sum by digging into their own pockets to meet most of the levy. This was an unprecedented act of generosity. The people of Eichstedt were so amazed and delighted that for many years afterwards, as the wars flowed back and forth across Europe, they celebrated an annual mass for the 1st Regiment of Carabineers.

One Advantage of Long Swords

The French cavalry swords and sabres were often slightly longer than the British counterparts. The extra reach this gave made it easier for them to strike or stab any person lying on the ground. Not only wounded troops lay on the battlefield but others who shammed death in order to escape from the swords or lances of their enemy. Modern writers have frequently claimed that only lancers had a realistic chance of striking a prone man. This was not so. The cavalry sabre was about the same length as a polo stick with which riders have no difficulty hitting a small ball. Several witnesses at Waterloo are quite clear on this issue.

• Lieutenant Kincaid, the adjutant of the 95th Rifles, stated: 'The French eventually broke and fled, pausing only to stab wounded allied troops as they rode over them. It made me mad to see the cuirassiers in their retreat, stooping and stabbing at our wounded men.'

• Captain Wallace of the 1st (King's) Dragoon Guards tells us: 'When charging at Waterloo, a French trumpeter was passed lying on the ground. Few of the regiment [1st Dragoons] forbore to have a slash at their fallen enemy as they galloped past.

I did not slash at him but the trumpeter slashed at me!'

• When fighting on foot against Kellerman's cuirassiers at Quatre-Bras Major Menzies of the 42nd Foot fell to the ground wounded. As he made to get up a cuirassier officer rode up and attempted to despatch him with his sword. As he stooped from his saddle, the major seized his leg and managed to pull him off his horse on top of him. A lancer rode up and tried to rescue his officer but only succeeded in spearing the Frenchman instead of Major Menzies, who continued to lie there for about ten minutes. When he was eventually carried off he was found to have sixteen wounds from both sword and lance blows – most received while on the ground.

• For a really accomplished horseman like Captain Llewellyn of the 28th Foot hitting a man on the ground with a sword posed few problems. Once in the Peninsula while galloping after some retreating French he spotted an open portmanteau full of silver cutlery lying open on the ground. As he thundered past he bent low from the saddle and scooped up a handful of antique silver.

Weapons

Early in the Revolution both regiments had handed over their carbines to some unarmed infantry and continued to do duty with sword and pistol until re-arming themselves with musketoons from a captured Austrian arsenal. At Waterloo carabineers carried long sabres with a slightly curved blade in black leather scabbards, the Year IX model cavalry musketoon, bayonet, crossbelt, cartridge-pouch and a pistol. Like the cuirassiers' straight sword, the length of the carabineer's weapon enabled him to stab or slash a fallen or prone man by bending low over his horse's neck.

Historical background

Despite their reputation for disdainful arrogance, these two regiments had fought with distinction in all the major campaigns and battles of the previous ten years. Their prettiness on parade was more than matched by their horsemanship and bravery on the battlefield. They fought at Austerlitz, Friedland, Essling and Wagram. They went into action at Borodino in 1812, and at Dresden, Leipzig and Hanau the following year. Finally, they defended France at Montmirail, Craonne, Laon and Reims. It was an impressive record, but no more so than many regiments present that Sunday morning in Belgium. However, the small size of the corps at Waterloo (under 850 men) meant that only a handful of veterans could claim to have ridden with it throughout those years. They arrived too late to be engaged at Quatre-Bras on 16 June.

Organization at Waterloo

There had never been more than two carabineer regiments in the French Army. They were both present at Waterloo in d'Hurbal's 12th Cavalry Division, part of Kellerman's 3rd Cavalry Corps fighting, as usual, alongside cuirassiers. The 1st Brigade, under Maréchal de Camp Blancard, was composed of:
1st Carabineers (434 in three squadrons) – Colonel Rogé
2nd Carabineers (413 in three squadrons) – Colonel Beugnat

Battlefield highlights

The carabineers might well have missed the carnage that resulted from the endless series of cavalry attacks that swept around Wellington's infantry during the late afternoon had it not been for the direct order and personal intervention of Ney. Kellerman's recent experience at Quatre-Bras had confirmed his misgivings as to the wisdom of using cavalry on their own to attack infantry in square. When reluctantly forced to be a party to reinforcing the failure on Mont St Jean ridge, he had specifically ordered the carabineers to remain in a hollow near Hougoumont and not advance further without his authority. Sometime later Ney spotted this brigade and rode over, yelling angrily at the brigade commander, Blancard, to attack at once. The marshal shouted down his protests, pulled rank, thus forcing the carabineers into the maelstrom on the ridge.

The Dragoons (Map 13, p. 161)
General

Like their counterparts in other armies, the French dragoons were originally mounted infantry using their small horses as a means of transport to the battlefield, then dismounting to fight on foot. By 1800, however, dragoons were decidedly cavalry – a medium cavalry expected to undertake any mounted mission. At Waterloo all three regiments present were classified as heavy cavalry whose primary role was shock action and thus were no more required to dismount to fight than any other cavalry unit.

Uniforms

The tunics, or 'habits' as the French called them, were all of a similar 'middle' green colour, with the Imperial Guard Dragoons (the Empress's Dragoons) having a somewhat darker shade. The different regiments could only be distinguished by persons knowledgeable in the minutiae of dress, in particular the combinations of green, red, carmine, rose, white and yellow used for the facings – these included lapels (turnbacks), collars, cuffs and cuff flaps. The 2nd Dragoons had red and green, the 7th all carmine, the Guard green, red and white.

The distinctive headgear of the dragoons was their brass, neo-Grecian style, helmet with its black horsehair (white for trumpeters) plume. Troopers had a brown fur turban around it, officers and all Guard dragoons an imitation leopard skin one. Grey linen breeches were worn on campaign with high black boots complete with blackened iron spurs.

Weapons

The 2nd and 7th had the Year XII pattern straight, heavy sword in a black leather scabbard, those of the Guard being slightly curved. All had two pistols, the Year IX musketoon and bayonet.

Historical background

During the period 1800–06 Napoleon was not able to mount all his dragoons. Two divisions of dismounted dragoons were formed for the planned French invasion of England. Although dressed and equipped as infantry, with drums as well as trumpets, these troopers were expected to carry their riding boots, bridles and saddles across the Channel so they could mount captured horses. When the idea of invasion was abandoned the Grand Armée turned east, with the foot dragoons being given the task of protecting the baggage train and artillery park. This dismounted division was derided as the 'wooden swords' or 'walkers'.

From 1808 onwards the Emperor poured twenty-four out of thirty dragoon regiments into Spain. In that unforgiving war, where the guerrilla's sudden ambush, the pistol shot in the dark, the partisan's knife and sickness cost the French armies up to 500 men a week, the dragoons learned their trade.

The 2nd Dragoons had spent five years in Portugal and Spain from 1808–13, engaged at Medellin, Talavera and Vitoria before, to their infinite relief, they were ordered home – to fight in the defence of France in the following year. In the brief Waterloo campaign the regiment had come up too late to join the corps commander (Kellerman) in his charge at the head of Guiton's cuirassiers at Quatre-Bras. Their sister regiment, the 7th Dragoons, missed Spain, fighting instead in Italy, at Wagram, Borodino, Dresden and La Fère-Champenoise. For the same reason as the 2nd they saw no action at Quatre-Bras.

The Empress's Dragoons were formed as part of the Imperial Guard cavalry in 1806 from mounted regiments of the line, with officers culled from the Grenadiers and Châsseurs à Cheval of the Guard. The Emperor 'presented' them to his wife with the name Regiment de Dragons de l'Emperatrice. From 1807 wherever the fighting was most critical, this regiment was involved, even sending two squadrons to Spain in 1808 and again two years later. They were in action at Essling, at Wagram, in Russia, at Bautzen, Leipzig and Hanau. At Hanau a Captain Sachon (who commanded a squadron at Waterloo) led a hundred dragoons in a wild charge that upset three infantry squares, thus winning his major's epaulettes. A year later, again with only a squadron, Sachon forced the surrender of 500 Russians near Montmirail, in France.

The Empress's Dragoons had started the Waterloo campaign commanded by Général de Division Baron Letort, who was standing in for Général de Division Ornano (wounded in a recent duel). Unnecessarily, but typically, Letort put himself at the head of two duty squadrons of dragoons ordered into action by the Emperor at Fleurus on 15 June and got himself severely wounded – he died in agony on 17 June, his family becoming a beneficiary in Napoleon's will. For the remainder of the campaign Colonel Hoffmayer com-manded the Empress's Dragoons. He was an officer lucky enough to survive an ambush by 4000 Cossacks outside Moscow three years earlier. He led them gallantly forward at Ligny and Waterloo.

Organization at Waterloo

Over 1,900 dragoons fought for the Emperor at Waterloo. The two line regiments formed a brigade in L'Héritier's 11th Cavalry Division in Kellerman's corps. The Empress's Dragoons had as comrades the Grenadiers à Cheval in Guyot's Guard Heavy Cavalry Division. The regiments were:

1st Brigade – GOC Maréchal de Camp Baron Picquet
2nd Dragoons (593 in four squadrons) – Colonel Planzeau
7th Dragoons (517 in four squadrons) – Colonel Léopold
Imperial Guard
Empress's Dragoons (816 in four strong squadrons) – Colonel Hoffmayer

Battlefield highlights

An exhausting and costly afternoon attempting to break into Anglo-Allied squares on Mont St Jean ridge.

Grenadiers à Cheval (Map 13, p. 161)
General

These were typical heavy horsemen on big, black horses with all the swagger and authority that went with belonging to the senior Guard cavalry regiment. Originally the minimum height for entry was 1.68 metres (above average for the time). Put such men on a high horse, and give him a towering bearskin to wear, and you have an imposing, if not threatening, figure. Like their infantry counterparts, these mounted grenadiers were far better paid, far more privileged and far more pampered than any line soldier. Their haughtiness and superior attitude towards 'lesser' military beings secured them the nickname of 'The Gods'. They were also sometimes known as 'Big Heels' or 'Giants'.

Uniforms

On 18 June 1815 these once magnificent horsemen had, like much of the army, lost their shine. There was a shabbiness, a lack of uniformity in the long lines of wet and dirty horsemen that stood in their squadrons in reserve behind Kellerman's corps. Most wore blue, single-breasted undress coats; some had their grubby, off-white cloaks on, some had them rolled across their shoulder, others on the front of the saddle. While most had their bearskins, few were ornamented. The remainder wore an assortment of hats or forage caps. All, however, still boasted the two insignia of a Grenadier of the Imperial Guard: the hair tied tightly in a queue and the glint of gold in their ears. Only the trumpeters stood out as reminders of more generous times in their sky-blue uniforms, white bearskins and grey horses.

Weapons

These consisted of the heavy, curved cavalry sabre with a grenade incorporated in the hilt, a brace of pistols plus a dragoon musket and bayonet.

Historical background

The regiment was first raised as a light horse unit in 1799, but by 1804 they had been named the Grenadiers à Cheval de la Garde Imperiale. Their original strength was 1,018 organized in four squadrons each of two companies. Thereafter they rode across Europe and into Russia, being present at all major engagements with their Emperor. They fought to defend France in 1814. As General Jamin's 'Giants' they charged at Ligny. They did the same at Waterloo, along with the rest of the cavalry. Captain Mercer RHA remembered them. He had just brought his troop of guns into position on the ridge during the French cavalry attacks. Some Horse Grenadiers led the first assault on his guns. 'These grenadiers à cheval were very fine troops, clothed in blue uniforms without facings, cuffs or collars. Broad, very broad buff belts, and huge muff caps [bearskins] made them appear gigantic fellows.'

Organization at Waterloo

Grouped with the Empress's Dragoons to form the Guard Heavy Cavalry Division under Guyot.
Grenadiers à Cheval (796 in four squadrons) – Général de Division Jamin, Marquis de Bermuy

Highlights at Waterloo

They were not required until late afternoon when they, along with the rest of the Guard cavalry, were dragged into the mounted onslaught against the Anglo-Allied ridge.

Gendarmes d'Elite (Map 13, p. 161)

These were the military police of the Imperial Guard, originally formed as an élite squadron of gendarmerie for duty in Paris and largely composed of former army NCOs. In 1802 the squadron was incorporated into the Imperial Guard due to repeated attempts to assassinate Napoleon. It was usual to reinforce the squadron with 'auxiliaries' from the National Gendarmerie for a particular campaign. Their primary duty was the close protection of the Emperor, his baggage and his residence, and as such they did not often come under fire in a major battle. With so few casualties over the years they became known as the 'Immortals'. They did, however, become frequently involved in small-scale skirmishes with bandits, marauders or against enemy partisans on the lines of communication. They were highly disciplined, dedicated, ruthless – men to be feared by draft-dodgers or villains skulking anywhere near the Emperor or his property.

They formed a small part of the Guard heavy cavalry, were mounted on black horses, wore blue tunics with scarlet facings, grey breeches, black riding boots and a bearskin headdress devoid of decorations. Hurriedly regrouped for Waterloo they wore 'the most uniform dress possible'. They were armed with a slightly curved, heavy cavalry sabre, pistols and a musketoon. There was only a half-squadron of 106 all ranks present at Waterloo, commanded by a Captain Dyonnet. They formed up on the right of the Grenadiers à Cheval as a tiny part of Guyot's Guard Heavy Cavalry Division. With the Grenadiers they trotted up the slope into the chaos around the enemy's infantry squares – they were to prove that they were, after all, mortal.

Light Cavalry

Chasseurs à Cheval (Maps 13 & 14, pp. 161 & 162)
General

Châsseurs à Cheval provided the bulk of Napoleon's light cavalry. They were a relatively new branch of the cavalry, having only come into existence in 1779.

There were twenty-nine regular regiments eventually, with eight (including the Guard) present at Waterloo. Their tasks were those common to all light cavalry – scouting, screening, foraging, escorting, raiding, pursuit and, when necessary, charging knee to knee. They were a vital part of Napoleon's information seeking intelligence apparatus. Châsseurs provided much of an army's strategic and tactical protection: the patrols and picquets that prevented enemy reconnaissance. The Emperor had very firm views on how they (and hussars) should conduct themselves. When writing to Maréchal Berthier in 1812 he stated: 'A colonel of châsseurs or hussars who goes to sleep, instead of spending the night in bivouac and remaining in constant communication with his picquets, deserves to be shot.'

Uniforms

It was supposedly cheaper to uniform and equip châsseurs than other types of cavalry, which may be part of the reason for their popularity with the authorities when it came to expansion. Nevertheless, during the twenty-five years prior to Waterloo there were at least eighteen different styles of châsseur headdress – mostly a confusing mixture of caps, shakos and bearskin colpacks (hussar style caps). The bewildering variety of plumes and pompoms that went with them makes trying to differentiate between the regiments an unrewarding exercise. At Waterloo it is even likely that the 1st Châsseurs were still wearing the dragoon-type helmets that the Bourbons had insisted they wear after the first restoration the previous year.

If their headdress was variegated and complex, their uniform was simple and easily recognizable – both the tunic and overalls were dark green. The facings of regiments differed, élite companies had red epaulettes and officers silver, but a French cavalryman in dark green (and wearing a shako) at Waterloo was a châsseur. A splash of red in the ranks indicated a trumpeter, except those in the 12th who wore light blue.

Interestingly, the uniform of a colonel of the Châsseurs à Cheval of the Imperial Guard was Napoleon's favourite form of dress; he wore it at Waterloo under his grey overcoat, and numerous paintings show him in it. Six years later he was buried in it.

Weapons

Their primary weapon was the decidedly curved cavalry sabre. This was supplemented by the carbine, bayonet and pistol. Châsseurs were often required to use their carbines, both mounted and on foot, as skirmishers. Their most extraordinary dismounted action occurred in 1796 on the River Po. A body of châsseurs commandeered some skiffs and rowed out to successfully board six river boats carrying over 500 Austrian infantry.

Historical background

Châsseurs were involved in every major campaign in Europe of the Napoleonic Wars. As the eyes and ears of the army, they had to be. They were present at virtually all the decisive battles. At least one, often several, of the Waterloo regiments were in action on the Ulm, at Austerlitz, Essling, Jena, Eylau, Friedland, Wagram, Borodino (all eight regiments), Dresden, Leipzig and the prolonged defence of France in 1813–14. The 11th had a brief sojourn in the Iberian Peninsula, fighting at Fuentes d'Onoro before being recalled to ride into Russia. The huge distances involved in the march on Moscow ensured every available light cavalryman was pressed into service.

For the invasion of Belgium in 1815 the 1st, 3rd, 6th and Guard Châsseurs were all in Ney's left wing of the army. Piré with the 1st and 6th (and his lancers) charged Wellington's position at

Cavalry Use of Carbines and Pistols

Some of the French cavalry at Waterloo did try to make use of their carbines (or musketoons) and pistols when their horses baulked at the bayonets. It was a wasted effort. Carbines might be useful when stationary, dismounted or on patrol or picquet duty, but firing from the saddle (unless the muzzle was almost touching the target) was inevitably a futile exercise. The reasons are worth highlighting.

• Carbines and pistols, particularly the latter, were extremely inaccurate weapons. If the firer was mounted, aiming became more difficult; if he was moving as well it was impossible, with the barrel being jerked around and the trooper having no control over where his shot went.

• In order to partially overcome this problem of aiming, the cavalryman had to approach very close to his enemy before firing – with the obvious attendant risks this entailed. Having got close to the opposition he then had to let go of his sabre to handle his carbine. With the enemy so close this could be foolish if he was suddenly required to defend himself hand-to-hand in a mêlée.

• In close proximity to the enemy on a battlefield the carbine was usually a fire and forget weapon. The trooper fired one shot and then forgot about it as there was seldom the opportunity to reload – an impossible task if jigging around in the saddle and trying to control a horse with the enemy nearby.

the crossroads where his regiments for a time caused havoc, cutting up an unformed Hanoverian battalion. The 3rd, with Jacquinot as part of d'Erlon's corps, spent 16 June wandering between the battlefields of Quatre-Bras and Ligny. In the evening, although poised on the Prussian's right flank, they were restricted by Durutte's caution (his division did not march back to Quatre-Bras with the rest of d'Erlon's corps) from playing a part in the closing moments of the battle. The Guard Châsseurs were held in reserve all day at Quatre-Bras and were not committed to support either Piré or Kellerman when they made their desperate, and almost successful, charges.

With the Emperor at Ligny were the 4th, 9th and 12th in Domon's division and the 11th with Subervie. All three of Domon's regiments were committed at the end of the day and routed two Prussian cavalry brigades as they fell back from St Amand village. They were at the forefront of Napoleon's pursuit of Wellington on 17 June and the first troops to arrive in front of Mont St Jean ridge – prompting the Duke's artillery to open fire, thus unmasking and confirming his position. The 11th saw no serious action until Waterloo.

Organization at Waterloo

There were just over 4,100 chasseurs on the battlefield, in eight regiments. The strongest was the Guard Châsseurs (nicknamed 'Invincibles' or 'Cherished Children') with 1,197, the smallest the 12th with 318. They were grouped as follows:
Guard Light Cavalry Division – GOC Général de Division Comte Lefèbvre-Desnouëttes
Guard Châsseurs à Cheval (1,197 in four squadrons) – Général de Division Baron Lallemand (his brother Henri took command of the Guard artillery on the death of Deveaux de Saint Maurice).
1st Cavalry Division – GOC Général de Division Jacquinot
1st Brigade – GOC Maréchal de Camp Baron Bruno
3rd Châsseurs (365 in three squadrons) – Colonel Marquis de la Woestine
2nd Cavalry Division – GOC Général de Division Comte Piré
1st Brigade – GOC Maréchal de Camp Baron Huber
1st Châsseurs (485 in four squadrons) – Colonel Simoneau
6th Châsseurs (560 in four squadrons) – Colonel Fandouas
3rd Cavalry Division – GOC Général de Division Baron Domon
1st Brigade – GOC Maréchal de Camp Baron Dommanget
4th Châsseurs (337 in three squadrons) – Colonel Baron Desmichels
9th Châsseurs (362 in three squadrons) – Colonel Baron du Kermont
2nd Brigade – GOC Maréchal de Camp Baron Vinot
12th Châsseurs (318 in three squadrons) – Colonel de Grouchy

5th Cavalry Division – GOC Général de Division Baron Subervie
2nd Brigade – GOC Maréchal de Camp Merlin
11th Châsseurs (485 in three squadrons) – Colonel Baron Nicolas

Battlefield highlights

The Guard Châsseurs, led by Lefèbvre-Desnouëttes, spearheaded the second wave of cavalry attacks against the Duke's position between La Haie Sainte and Hougoumont. When the battle started to go against the French Lefèbvre-Desnouëttes, whose fanaticism for the Emperor made surviving defeat intolerable, tried to get himself killed but only succeeded in being wounded.

The 3rd Châsseurs were involved, as part of Jacquinot's division, with supporting Durutte's infantry on the eastern flank, and in the fighting withdrawal in the face of the Prussian advance during the late afternoon. The 1st and 6th, somewhat battered after Quatre-Bras, were with Piré on the opposite flank under orders to support the attack on Hougoumont and guard the army's left flank.

As part of Lobau's VI Corps, the 4th, 9th, 11th and 12th Châsseurs were initially in reserve behind the centre. With the approach of the Prussians they were switched at about 1.15 p.m. to the eastern flank as part of the force sent to block them. Together they participated in a series of effective delaying actions, at one stage scattering Crown Prince William's uhlans and hussars in a decisive charge. They were ultimately pushed back to the north of Plancenoit.

Hussars (Map 14, p. 162)
General

As with châsseurs, Napoleon expected his hussars, like all soldiers, to be able to turn their hand to any duty. As he once told his chief of staff (Berthier), '[General Sebastiani] must remind his hussars that a French soldier must be a cavalryman, infantryman and artilleryman; that he is required to lend his hand to everything and anything.'

Uniforms

The hussar's love of his uniform, his delight in the detail of dress and the bewildering diversity of costume, colour, lace, braid and headdress that every regiment took so much pride in, made them excessively expensive troops. Despite the insatiable demand for light cavalry as the French armies swept back and forth across Europe and into Russia, the number of hussar regiments raised was only fourteen. For twenty years from 1794 not a single new hussar regiment was created, while two (11th and 12th Hussars) had been converted to dragoons. The reason was cost. It was far cheaper to dress and equip châsseurs, dragoons, even lancers, all of whom were quite capable of doing what hussars did and just as effectively. In other words, they were a luxury. Only the 7th fought at Waterloo.

The basic hussar uniform was fundamentally different, more elaborate than that worn by other types of cavalry. It consisted of a short, heavily braided shell-jacket (called a dolman), tight Hungarian riding breeches, calf-length Hungarian boots, and a second, fur-trimmed jacket slung on the left shoulder – the pelisse. The pelisse was, like the dolman, well endowed with gold or silver braid and bright buttons. It was worn in cold weather as a short overcoat, although it was not uncommon for it to be left in the depot or baggage wagons on campaign. Headgear consisted of shakos with complex permutations of shape, size and colour, or bearskin colpacks for the élite companies. At Waterloo the 7th Hussars had dark blue dolmans and overalls with a broad red stripe down the leg, shakos of the same colour with the élite company still wearing the colpack.

By tradition the French hussars were almost as concerned with their hair as with their uniforms. Magnificent, luxuriously long and curling moustaches were the hallmark of a veteran hussar; boyish recruits (including the young Marbot) had them painted on with blacking. Queues were worn, as were braided love-locks called *cadenettes* worn dangling in front of each ear, kept straight by lumps of lead (or a gold coin) tied in the ends. If necessary, horsehair *cadenettes* were fixed to the soldiers' own hair. Probably by Waterloo the 7th had abandoned the queues and *cadenettes* – but not the moustaches.

Weapons

The 7th Hussars had the curved, light cavalry sabres together with pistols, musketoons and bayonets – although, as with most cavalry, there is considerable doubt as to whether they bothered to take bayonets on campaign. As with other cavalry officers, NCOs and trumpeters did not carry the musketoon.

Historical background

The hussars originated from the Hungarian light horsemen, the 1st Hussars being formed as far back as 1720 with the 2nd, 3rd, 4th and 5th raised before the Revolution. The 6th–13th were all formed in the three years 1792–95. Of these, the 11th and 12th were quickly converted to dragoons and the 13th only lasted a year. It was reformed in 1813 along with the creation of the 14th. Those regiments that served throughout the Empire saw plenty of action. There were hussars in every theatre of war, they were represented at virtually all major battles across Europe and into Russia.

The 7th Hussars were at Austerlitz, Eylau, Jena-Auerstadt, Wagram, Borodino, Lutzen, Bautzen, Leipzig, Hanau and the defence of France in 1813–14. Perhaps there were a few veterans at Waterloo that remembered the days in 1806 during the Jena-Auerstadt campaign when they were under General Lasalle in the 'Infernal' Brigade. That was when they marched around 800 kilometres in twenty-four days, took part in scores of engagements and captured Stettin (prompting Napoleon to remark, 'If your light horsemen can capture fortified places in this way, I shall have to disband my engineers, and melt down my siege guns').

As they formed part of Jacquinot's division at Waterloo, the 7th did not see action at either Ligny or Quatre-Bras but was involved in closely pressing Wellington's rearguards as he pulled back to Mont St Jean on 17 June.

Organization at Waterloo

The 1st, 4th, 5th, 6th and 7th Hussars took part in the Waterloo campaign but only the 7th fought at the battle, the remainder being with Marshal Grouchy. The 7th was brigaded with the 3rd Châsseurs à Cheval under Maréchal de Camp Baron Bruno in Jacquinot's 1st Cavalry Division.

7th Hussars (439 in three squadrons) – Colonel Baron Marbot

Battlefield highlights

By mid-morning Napoleon had sent the 7th Hussars to probe well to the east of the French position in the direction of Grouchy and the Prussians. Marbot captured a Prussian hussar, who was taken to the Emperor at around 1.15 p.m. and confirmed that the troops just seen near Chapelle St Robert were indeed Prussians (Bülow's corps) advancing on the French right and rear. Marbot's men had been the first French troops to make contact with the Prussians in the Lasne valley. He recalled one of those encounters:

> The head of the Prussian column approached, though very slowly. Two times I threw back into the valley the hussars and lancers that preceded it. I strove to win time by holding the enemy at bay as much as possible. The enemy could only debouch with great difficulty from the muddy, sunken tracks in which he was engaged.

Later Marbot pulled back to join Domon and Subervie's cavalry west of the Bois de Paris. He then became involved in the fighting withdrawal back towards Plancenoit.

Lancers (Maps 13 and 14, pp. 161 & 162)
General

Lancers were light cavalry as their French title '*chevau-legers lanciers*' makes clear. As such their duties were the same as any other light cavalry, the difference being in their being armed with a lance (in addition to other cavalry weapons). This changed their fighting characteristics, discussed below under 'Weapons'.

Napoleon's lancers at Waterloo were divided into two types according to their original nationality. First, the French lancers, or line regiments, that had been converted from dragoon regiments during 1811–12. Second, the foreign lancers, Dutch and Polish, that had been incorporated into the Imperial Guard.

Uniforms

All the six line regiments of lancers at Waterloo wore green jackets and overalls with brass helmets, fur turbans (imitation panther-skin for officers) topped with black wool crests. The only sure way of telling a lancer from a dragoon regiment was to see if lances were carried (at least by the front rank). This difficulty is not surprising as all these six regiments were originally dragoons. Although differences developed in colours of turnbacks and facings, the conversion had been cheap and easy – issue lances and give extra training. The 2nd Guard (Red) Lancers had their magnificent scarlet tunics (trumpeters white) and Polish style, square-topped, scarlet *czapskas*, although at Waterloo these exotic and costly headdresses almost certainly had protective covering. The single squadron of Polish Lancers had dark blue tunics with crimson facings and crimson *czapskas*. All Guard lancers wore an ankle length boot, described as a Mameluke boot, instead of the normal high, black riding boots.

Weapons

Originally these regiments were to be armed only with lances, sabres and two pistols. Sergeants and ten men in each company were to have carbines instead of lances and corporals were to carry a hatchet instead of a pistol in their right holster – officers never carried lances. These arrangements reflected the old Polish system of arming the front ranks with lances, the second with carbines. However, the Emperor intervened. All lancers were to retain musketoons and bayonets. The extra weight of the weapons and ammunition overloaded the horses. Major de Brack (nicknamed 'Mademoiselle' on account of his good looks, who formed part of Napoleon's close escort after the battle with twenty-five Red Lancers) had personal experience of the effect of this edict. He wrote how his lancers, 'weary of marching almost all the time on foot to spare their horses, gave in all the more readily to their good sense … and got rid of half the load. The officers closed their eyes, endeavouring to keep as many lances as possible.' In 1813 the lance was supposedly issued to the front rank only in line with the old Polish custom. During the rush to recruit and equip in the weeks prior to the invasion two years later, Colbert, commanding the Guard Lancers, complained that musketoons, lances and 300 pistols were lacking for his regiment alone. The balance of evidence suggests that the lance was only issued to the front ranks of each company at Waterloo, although no mention of this is made in most accounts of the battle – the official 1813 distribution of weapons to lancers is given in the box below.

The lance itself was about 2.7 metres long and weighed 7 pounds. It had a steel point, a blackened wood staff, leather wrist-strap and steel ferrule. The pennon, attached below the point, was swallow-tailed and coloured red over white. In action some commanding officers had it tied to the staff and covered as they felt that fluttering on the end it made it easier for an opponent to follow and thus parry the point. Similarly, at a distance they considered that it easily identified the unit, particularly for enemy gunners. Nevertheless, other officers thought that the lowered lance with pennant flapping frightened enemy horses as lancers closed in. It was, like the thrust or cut controversy, another argument of detail about which light cavalrymen could not always agree.

France was the country that reintroduced the lance to Western Europe, having experienced its effectiveness in the hands of the Cossacks and Poles. In 1809 Napoleon ordered that the Polish Light Horse, raised two years earlier, would be armed with the lance. Within three years he had three regiments of Guard lancers and nine

of Line lancers. Other countries followed – but not Britain until after Waterloo. At Waterloo 21 per cent of Napoleon's cavalry were lancers. With the Prussians nearly 5000 more were deployed on the battlefield. They were pitted against infantry and against sword armed cavalry, experiencing both success and failure. The merits and problems of using this weapon are listed below – it was yet another weapon that had both its ardent advocates and detractors.

Advantages

• The adverse morale effect it had on the enemy. It was a sobering sight, particularly for an infantryman or gunner, to be on the receiving end of a squadron of charging lancers. To hear the thunder of the hooves, to feel the ground vibrate and to see the long line of lances suddenly sweep down with levelled points and still remain steady was sometimes too much for ill-trained troops. It was the thought of the impact, the knowledge of the extended reach of the weapon, and the fear of the dreadful wounds it could inflict.
• The lance projected a metre beyond the horse's head. This meant it outreached the bayonets of enemy infantry. If for some reason the foot soldier in square could not fire his musket (it was unloaded or in heavy rain), the lancer could stand off and thrust his weapon with impunity – although not with much force.
• It was a killer. Although some soldiers survived as many as seventeen or eighteen lance wounds at Waterloo, the momentum of the horse meant that to be skewered in the body by a lance was invariably fatal. It was the moving horse that gave real power to the thrust.
• It was the ideal weapon for pursuit or for use against a prone man. Fleeing infantry were exceptionally easy victims. The backs of fleeing cavalry were equally tempting targets but they had to be caught and then, due to the approximately equal speed of the horses, a thrust lacked the same force as that delivered to a running man.

Disadvantages

• It was not thought to be so effective against cavalry, especially if there was a mêlée involving individual combat, when the horsemen were more or less stationary. In these circumstances the sabre was a handier weapon, so lancers were also given sabres for this reason – although it was uncommon for a lancer to abandon his lance (it was considered an unworthy act). A stationary lancer had serious problems with his cumbersome 2.7 metre pole. If his clumsy poke were to be parried (not difficult, as it was easy to see coming) the

---

Official Weapon Distribution for French Lancers in 1813

Because only the first rank of lancers would normally have the chance to use the lance effectively (a fact that had been borne out by experience in Russia), weapons were redistributed in April 1813. They were issued as follows to a company of 125 men:

1st rank
Two sergeants each with a sabre and two pistols
Four corporals each with a sabre, a musketoon, a bayonet, a pistol and a lance
Forty-four troopers each with a sabre, a pistol and a lance

2nd rank
Four corporals and forty-four troopers each with a sabre, a musketoon, a bayonet, and a pistol

3rd or supernumerary rank
One sergeant-major, two sergeants, one farrier each with a sabre and two pistols
Three trumpeters each with a sabre and a pistol
Two farriers each with a sabre and a pistol
Nine troopers each with a sabre and a carbine
Nine troopers each with a sabre and a lance

This distribution meant the numbers of weapons carried was – 125 sabres, 109 pistols, 52 musketoons, 52 bayonets, 9 carbines and 57 lances. Altogether a highly complex, confusing and probably unworkable arrangement. However, it is very probable that at Waterloo only about half the men in French lancer regiments carried a lance.

Colonel Baron Jean Baptiste Sourd

He commanded the 2nd Chevau-Legers Lanciers at Waterloo. A truly amazing officer who had fought in Russia, in the battles in France and around Paris in 1813–14. He was present at Quatre-Bras, but it was on 17 June that he demonstrated his iron willpower, his almost superhuman ability to bear pain.

He became embroiled in the mêlée in the crowded main street of Genappe when the tightly packed lancers were at a disadvantage against the sword swinging British cavalry. His right arm was slashed no less than six times. Napoleon's Guard surgeon, Larrey, saw him with his smashed arm hanging uselessly. He had lost a lot of blood. Larrey amputated immediately. Sourd was given a slug of brandy and a musket ball to bite on while the surgeon cut off his arm by the roadside. The bloody stump was bandaged and Sourd prepared to rejoin his unit. At this stage Ney arrived to tell Sourd that he was recommending to the Emperor that he be promoted to replace General Colbert who had been wounded at Quatre-Bras (in the event Colbert continued in command). Still in agonizing pain Sourd dictated a note to his Emperor. According to the French historian Houssaye, it read: 'The greatest favour you could grant me is to allow me to remain colonel of my regiment of lancers, which I hope to lead again to victory. I refuse the rank of general. May the great Napoleon forgive me! The rank of colonel is everything to me.' He led his lancers at Waterloo throughout the next day and took part in the massive cavalry attacks during the afternoon.

Sourd lived to be a general under Louis Philippe and died in 1849, aged seventy.

lancer would be exceptionally lucky to avoid the slashing sabre. Furthermore, parrying a sharp sabre with a wooden pole could not be done too often without it being weakened, if not broken.

• The lance was not best suited for sentry duty or scouting; the pennons gave away your position and the pole was continually snagging when moving through trees or scrub. It was well-nigh impossible to fire a carbine and hold a lance, which meant that either the mounted lancer never used his carbine or that skirmishing had to be left to those who had firearms but no lances – an annoying complication.

• The thrust could sometimes be too effective. It was not uncommon for a lancer to impale an opponent. It was then almost impossible to withdraw the lance. The likelihood was that the falling body would drag the lancer down, or at least bring him to a halt, with a tightly twisted wrist-strap and embedded lance anchoring him to a corpse.

• It took a lot of extra training to produce a competent lancer. A British training manual produced some years after Waterloo stated that he had to master fifty-five different exercises with his lance – twenty-two against cavalry, eighteen against infantry, with fifteen general ones thrown in for good measure.

Historical background

The Emperor made the decision that his armies needed more lancers in 1811. As he had thirty regiments of dragoons, the easiest, quickest, and above all cheapest way to have an instant force of lancers was to give the weapon to some dragoon regiments and change their titles. This he did in 1811. Six dragoon regiments became Chevau-Legers Lanciers numbered 1–6. The following converted:

1st Dragoons – 1st Lancers
3rd Dragoons – 2nd Lancers
8th Dragoons – 3rd Lancers
9th Dragoons – 4th Lancers
10th Dragoons – 5th Lancers
29th Dragoons – 6th Lancers

Two years prior to this mass conversion Napoleon had created the first lancer regiment in the Imperial Guard after the Battle of Wagram by converting (giving lances to) his Polish Guard light cavalry regiment. From 1811 it was officially known as the 1st Regiment de Chevau-Legers Lanciers de la Garde. In 1812 Napoleon also converted the Dutch Hussars of the Guard to lancers. They became the 2nd Regiment de Chevau-Legers Lanciers de la Garde but were better known as the Red Lancers on account of their dazzling uniforms.

All these regiments (except the 2nd in Spain) fought in Russia, at Dresden, Leipzig, Hanau and in the defence of France in 1813–14. In the three days prior to Waterloo the 1st, 2nd, 3rd and 4th were on the periphery of the Ligny battlefield where they saw little serious action. The Red Lancers with the 5th and 6th were at Quatre-Bras. The latter two regiments greatly distinguished themselves under Piré in fierce fighting around the crossroads – their numbers were consequently thinned before Waterloo.

Organization at Waterloo

Napoleon had seven lancer regiments at Waterloo, in twenty-five squadrons (including the Elba Squadron), giving a total of about 3,234 all ranks. They were grouped as below:

Guard Light Cavalry Division – GOC Général de Division Comte Lefèbvre-Desnoüettes
2nd Guard Light Cavalry Lancer Regiment (880 in five squadrons, of which the 1st was the Elba Squadron of Polish Lancers under Major Balinski) – Lieutenant-Colonel Baron Jerzmanowski
1st Cavalry Division – GOC Général de Division Baron Jacquinot
2nd Brigade – GOC Maréchal de Camp Gobrecht
3rd Lancers (406 in three squadrons) – Colonel Martigue
4th Lancers (296 in two squadrons) – Colonel Bro
2nd Cavalry Division – GOC Général de Division Comte Piré
2nd Brigade – GOC Maréchal de Camp Baron Wathiez
5th Lancers (412 in three squadrons) – Colonel Jacqueminot
5th Cavalry Division – GOC Général de Division Baron Subervie
1st Brigade – GOC Maréchal de Camp Count Colbert
1st Lancers (415 in four squadrons) – Colonel Jacquinot (brother of the GOC 1st Cavalry Division)
2nd Lancers (420 in four squadrons) – Colonel Sourd (despite having his right arm amputated on 17 June [see box above])

Battlefield highlights

Because of their deployment on the flanks of the army, the only lancers to get swept into the great cavalry versus infantry fight for the Anglo-Allied centre-right were the 2nd Lancers of the Guard – the former Dutch Red Lancers. During the course of an attack on a square of Brunswickers an officer fell trapped under his wounded horse, he himself being unhurt. Two Brunswick soldiers darted forward to rob him of his valuables before putting one of his own pistols to the head of the struggling man and blowing out his brains. This cowardly killing was greeted by shouts of 'Shame! Shame!' from nearby British infantry.

On the French right flank the 3rd and 4th Lancers took part in the counterattack against the Union Brigade when it over-reached itself in charging out of control into the 'Grand Battery'. The lance was used with great effect against this scattered and disordered brigade. Among its victims was the British brigade commander Major-General Ponsonby, who was finished off by a lancer from the 4th called Urban. Urban dismounted to take Ponsonby's sword; many years later the sword was returned to Ponsonby's descendants.

Also moved to the extreme right were the 1st and 2nd Lancers who, as part of Subervie's division, fought the Prussians as they emerged from the Bois de Paris. From around 4.30 p.m. to late evening they participated in the skilful delaying tactics, trying to keep Bülow's corps at bay while their Emperor strove for a decision elsewhere. At the head of the 2nd, in terrible pain, rode the one-armed and unarmed Colonel Sourd.

Some 3000 metres away, to the west of Hougoumont, the 5th and 6th Lancers under Piré had a quieter, relatively less exciting battle.

The Mamelukes

A squadron of Mamelukes was added to the Imperial Guard in 1801. It was a polyglot mixture of Muslims of various races and colours, all uniformed in an exotic oriental dress with a turban. Their recruitment was widespread and included Georgia, Circassia, the Crimea, Arabia, Syria, Egypt, Abyssinia, Darfur, Albania, Turkey, Hungary, Malta, Tunisia and Algeria. Two of their officers were from Bethlehem. Only their fourriers (clerical/administrative NCOs) were French and did not wear the same uniform.

Their primary weapon was the Turkish scimitar (sabre) with a very pronounced curve, carried in a leather scabbard. Tucked in their waist sash was a brace of pistols and a long dagger. Initially these troops had been issued with blunderbusses but they were eventually replaced with the standard cavalry musketoon. Mamelukes fought magnificently at Austerlitz and were rewarded with their own Eagle. They served in Poland, Spain (twice), at Wagram and in Russia. They were exceptionally skilful riders, able to do virtually anything with their horses. As swordsmen they put the fear of Allah into their opponents with their reputation of being able to decapitate a man with a single blow from their razor-sharp scimitars. They also sharpened their stirrup irons, the more effectively to kick any unsuspecting infantryman or horse that pressed too close.

In April 1815 Napoleon issued an Imperial Decree stating that the Châsseurs à Cheval of the Guard would be augmented by a Mameluke squadron of two companies. The special uniforms were ordered and according to the quartermaster's registers many of them were issued. Nevertheless, although a number joined prior to Waterloo they appear to have been taken onto the rolls of the Guard Châsseurs or Lancers in an indiscriminate way rather than as a separate squadron. No contemporary witnesses mention a Mameluke squadron at the battle, so it is most likely that they fought as individuals in the ranks of the Guard Châsseurs à Cheval, like Major Renno and Captain Abdallah (both Mameluke veterans), or in the Red Lancers.

TACTICS
General

With the possible exception of Piré's division on the French left, every cavalry regiment was called upon to carry out several attacks during the course of the battle. The great majority of these occurred during the afternoon when the entire uncommitted heavy cavalry reserve (III and IV Cavalry Corps) plus all the Guard Cavalry were hurled piecemeal, in a series of wave attacks against Wellington's infantry squares. Their task was to smash a hole in the Anglo-Allied right. When these assaults were at their height three light cavalry divisions (1st, 3rd and 5th) began their long battle to help hold the Prussians at bay on the French right.

Several factors are worthy of note, namely:

• The Emperor's cavalry, like the Duke's, fought every permutation of mounted action likely to be seen on a battlefield (except pursuit). At various stages regiments were called upon to charge cavalry, to charge infantry in square and infantry in line, to counterattack against cavalry, to attack guns, to fight delaying actions and sometimes to skirmish.

• The French cavalry divisions, unlike the Anglo-Allied mounted formations, kept their horse artillery batteries under command and thus had them available to support their operations (see Section 7 'Artillery'). A possible exception at Waterloo was the two horse batteries with Kellerman's corps. There is evidence to suggest that Napoleon personally ordered them forward into a static role to support Reille's attacks on Hougoumont.

• Like all other units, mounted or otherwise, they found the battlefield frustratingly confined, full of obstacles, inclines and boggy ground. Only rarely was there space to deploy a brigade, more often regiments attacked with only two squadrons in line, sometimes only one. Seldom could a squadron attack at more than a trot or brisk walk. With certain rare exceptions most attempts to gallop were done by generals, staff officers and ADCs.

A squadron of the 1st Cuirassiers, typical of the heavy squadrons that fought against Wellington's cavalry and infantry, is examined below to illustrate how most French cavalry were organized and commanded.

A French cuirassier squadron in battle order (line)
(Diagram opposite)

The diagram represents No.2 Squadron of the 1st Cuirassier Regiment under Colonel Ordener drawn up in a two rank line, the horsemen with knees almost touching. This regiment was, with a strength of 465 all ranks, of about average size for French cavalry regiments generally, with a war establishment of four squadrons, each of about 113 all ranks. This regiment had suffered little thus far in the campaign, so the squadron shown has its full complement of eight officers. However, it had a tough time at Waterloo. It clashed, with squadrons in the formation shown, with the Household Brigade west of La Haie Sainte while doing duty as flank guard to d'Erlon's massive attack. It also led the way at the start of the afternoon's cavalry assaults.

Points of note are:

• The high proportion (1:13) of officers and their position in a squadron about to attack the enemy. Five officers are out in front of the squadron. In addition to the squadron commander there is an

No. 2 Squadron 1st Cuirassiers Deployed in Line

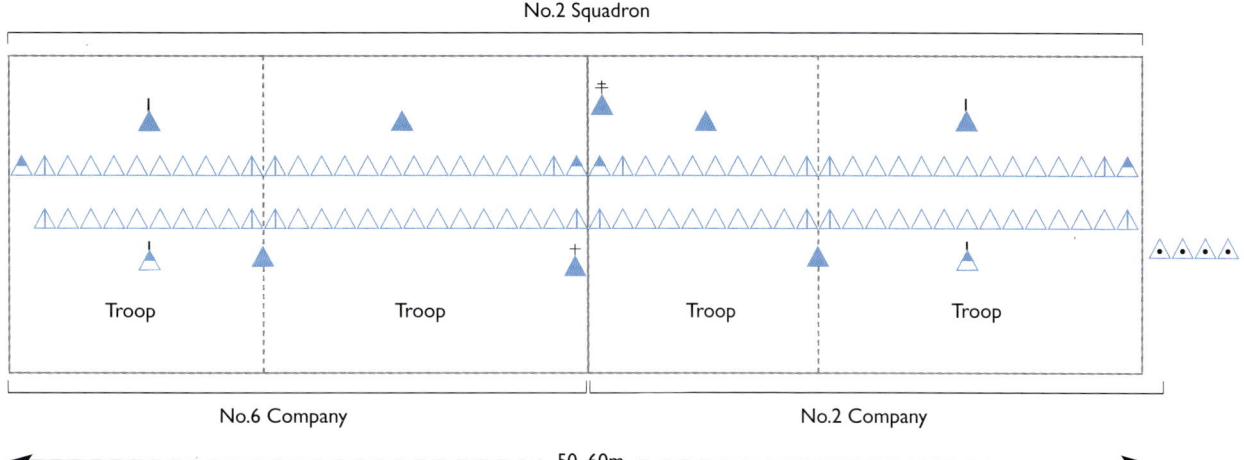

No.2 Squadron

Troop   Troop   Troop   Troop

No.6 Company   No.2 Company

50–60m

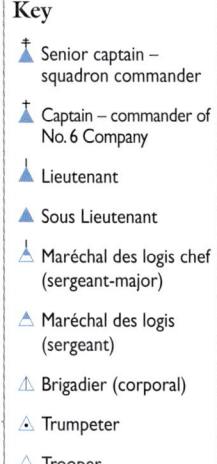

Key

‡ Senior captain – squadron commander

† Captain – commander of No. 6 Company

Lieutenant

Sous Lieutenant

Maréchal des logis chef (sergeant-major)

Maréchal des logis (sergeant)

Brigadier (corporal)

Trumpeter

Trooper

Notes

• This squadron of cuirassiers is drawn up in battle order in a two rank line, riders virtually knee to knee. Note the numbering of the two companies, each of which was split into two troops.

• In the example shown, the squadron is depicted with a full complement of eight officers at the start of the battle.

• An important feature is high proportion of officers out in front. This was normal for French cavalry who put the emphasis on forward control – the officers in front could keep the pace down, hold back the front rank, and thus more easily prevent surging forward and loss of control. Note the contrast with the British who only had one officer in front.

• The senior of the two captains commanded the squadron. The establishment of a company

was 1 captain, 1 lieutenant, 2 sous lieutenants, 1 maréchal des logis chef, 2 maréchal des logis, 8 brigadiers, 2 trumpeters, and in the example given, 79 troopers.

• Not shown are the 2 fourriers and 2 farriers that would usually have been kept in the rear.

• As with all cavalry, the squadron would carry out normal movement in different types of column. They were:

1 The *colonne serre* – squadrons in two rank line one behind the other

2 The squadrons with a company frontage

3 The squadrons with a troop frontage

4 The squadrons with a half troop (division) frontage

5 The squadrons in column of fours – the formation used when moving off the battlefield on roads

Parade State

Officers	8
M de L C	2
M de L	4
Brigadiers	16
Trumpeters	4
Troopers	79
Total	**113**

Excludes fourriers and farriers

---

officer in front of each of the four possible manoeuvre elements (troops). Here the French are putting the emphasis on forward control. These officers could ensure that their sub-units went in the desired direction at the desired speed. This greatly assisted alignment. It made it more difficult for the first rank to surge forward. The troopers (and the horses) had a leader in front who set the pace, making it easy to follow. This is in direct contrast to the British (see Diagram p. 229) whose cavalry squadrons had but one solitary officer in front. This was one of the reasons that British cavalry so often got out of control (as at Waterloo) and dashed ahead too soon.

• There are no officers in the leading (or second) rank. The business of controlling lateral movement is given to the NCOs. The squadron, the companies and the troops each have an NCO on both flanks. Their task was to keep alignment (dressing), act as guides when wheeling and to prevent any lateral 'loosening' of the files as they advanced. Again, quite different from the British who put about 60 per cent of their officers in the front rank.

• Discounting the trumpeters, there is not much of a supernumerary rank – just three officers and two maréchal des logis chef (sergeant-majors). The French did not give much importance to

these 'file-closers' whose task it was to chivvy men forward, prevent backsliding or outright desertion in the face of the enemy. The contrast with the British, and particularly with the Prussians (Diagram p. 256) is marked.

• A squadron of this strength, with about fifty men in each rank, would cover a frontage of up to 60 metres depending on whether there were a few inches between the knees or not. Stronger squadrons, like those in the Imperial Guard, would cover a greater distance. The depth remained constant at about 5-6 metres.

The cavalry charge

Like the manuals of all European armies, those of the French advocated that a cavalry unit advancing to the attack should start out slowly at the walk, but build up to an all out gallop (the charge) in the last 80 or so paces – this was the procedure developed by Frederick the Great. The French regulations envisaged the following sequence of events:

• The cavalry, possibly in a stationary position, receives the order to attack. Sabres are drawn and the unit moves forward at the walk in a two rank line.

When to Draw Sabres?

Regulations stipulated that sabres be drawn at the very start of an attack. In practice this procedure was usually followed, although there was a body of opinion that felt strongly that this was a mistake as it threw away a moral advantage. They argued that the best time for sabres to be drawn was just a few moments before contact. The reasoning was persuasive:

• Drawing the sabres early indicated to an observant enemy that the unit was about to attack. This prevented surprise and gave the enemy the maximum time to prepare – change formation, begin a counter-charge or move away.

• Conversely, if the sabres remained in their scabbards, the opposition could not be certain as to the significance of any movements at the start of an advance.

• If sabres were drawn in unison in the last moments of the charge it had an intimidating effect on those at the receiving end. The sudden flash of blades in the air followed by the levelling of points within seconds of impact was a frightening sight.

• For the riders drawing their weapon at the moment they drove home their spurs with the enemy only a few seconds away added a brief but vital boost to the adrenaline rush, thereby giving the attacker extra strength and élan at the crucial moment.

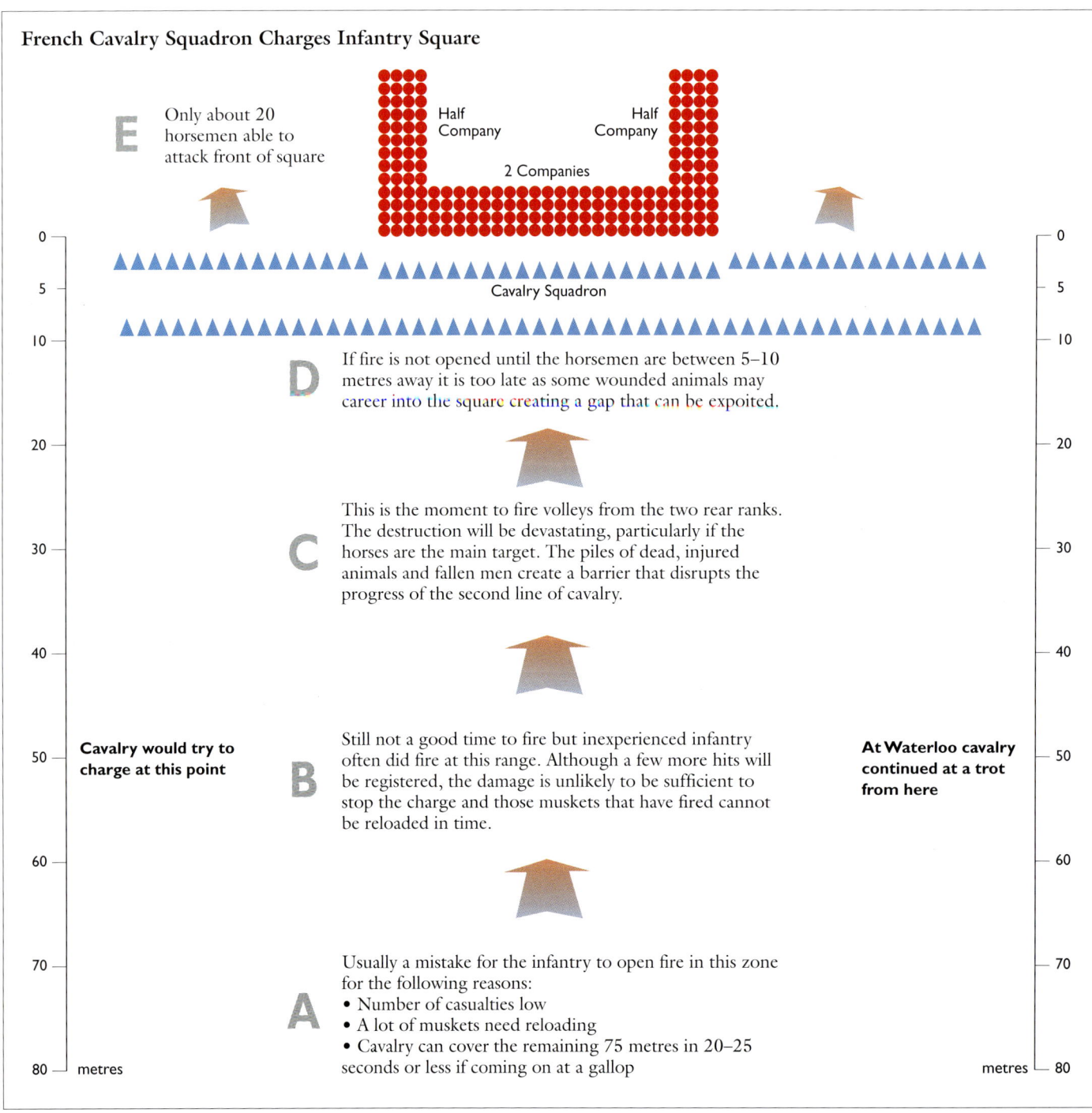

French Cavalry Squadron Charges Infantry Square

E — Only about 20 horsemen able to attack front of square

Half Company   Half Company

2 Companies

Cavalry Squadron

D — If fire is not opened until the horsemen are between 5–10 metres away it is too late as some wounded animals may career into the square creating a gap that can be expoited.

C — This is the moment to fire volleys from the two rear ranks. The destruction will be devastating, particularly if the horses are the main target. The piles of dead, injured animals and fallen men create a barrier that disrupts the progress of the second line of cavalry.

Cavalry would try to charge at this point

B — Still not a good time to fire but inexperienced infantry often did fire at this range. Although a few more hits will be registered, the damage is unlikely to be sufficient to stop the charge and those muskets that have fired cannot be reloaded in time.

At Waterloo cavalry continued at a trot from here

A — Usually a mistake for the infantry to open fire in this zone for the following reasons:
• Number of casualties low
• A lot of muskets need reloading
• Cavalry can cover the remaining 75 metres in 20–25 seconds or less if coming on at a gallop

metres

The Cavalryman Confronts the Infantry Square

The 3rd and 4th ranks are the main firing ranks. The most effective method was for one rank to fire when the approaching cavalry reached 40m and the other 30m.

The first two ranks are from the Grenadier Coy, the rear two from No.1 Coy (see Diagram p. 173).

The cavalryman is unable to reach the infantry with his sabre. A lancer could stab the front rank man and possibly the second.

The horseman is outnumbered here 4:1, but in reality it was usually nearer 8:1.

The second rank soldier would be primarily a bayonet man reserving his fire.

The kneeling man in the front rank would not normally fire except in a dire emergency.

Note the horse is rearing up slightly – it is refusing to go into the bayonet hedge.

That the cavalryman has got this close to the square indicates the infantry opened fire too soon.

• After about 40 paces (25 metres) the line would get the order to trot. The troopers were to advance in silence so best to hear words of command above the noise of battle. Officers would pass on the orders and the leading rank would take their direction and pace from the officers out in front.

• The trot would continue until the line was within 100 metres of the enemy. At this point the commander would increase the pace to a controlled gallop and the line, with the riders still knee to knee, would surge forward while still maintaining dressing.

• When within 50 metres of the enemy the commander would order the trumpeters to sound the charge and the unit would dig in its spurs and gallop flat out for their opponents – the '*charge a la sauvage*', the 'wild charge'. The troopers were to stand up in their stirrups and give the horse a loose rein, while the men in the front rank were to hold their sabres pointed ahead in outstretched arms, those in the rear holding theirs above their heads. At this point the cavalrymen were supposed to yell '*Avancez!*' (forward).

• In those last 50 metres the officers out in front were to hold back slightly to let the leading rank catch them up. This was to avoid being an isolated, obvious target at close range. The supernumerary rank officers or NCOs at the rear, who until that moment had been concentrating on preventing any falling back, spurred forward to catch up the second rank and join the mêlée.

In practice, the French cavalry were renowned for conducting their charges (attacks) at the trot or even the walk. This was particularly true of the heavy cavalry, although all would endeavour to raise a gallop if the enemy turned their backs in flight. There was a considerable body of French opinion that rated the charge at the trot the superior method.

Attacking infantry in square

For two hours during the late afternoon at Waterloo some 8000 French horsemen in twenty regiments were given the task of smashing a hole through the Anglo-Allied centre-right. The attacks were repeated over and over again as fresh regiments were thrown in when those that had gone before were repulsed or retired. Not a single square was penetrated. Wellington's infantry stood their ground. During those two hours the number of casualties caused by sabre, lance or even carbine or pistol shot was negligible. The infantry came to dread the intervals between the

Lancers Attack an Infantry Square

Colonel Marbot of the 7th Hussars had witnessed a strange and frustrating stand-off between his 23rd Châsseurs and Prussian infantry in square two years previously at the battle of Katzbach. As at Waterloo, it had been very wet and the ground was too soft for the cavalry to work up much speed. Marbot described the scene:

Our situation and that of the enemy infantry before us was truly ridiculous, for we were eyeball to eyeball without being able to do each other the least harm, our sabres being too short to reach the Prussians whose muskets would not go off [due to being wet].

At this point Colonel Perquit arrived with his 6th Lancers.

… whose long weapons, outreaching the enemy's bayonets, at once killed many Prussians. During that terrible combat you could hear the ringing voice of the brave Colonel Perquit, crying with a strong Alsatian accent; 'Thrust, lancers. Thrust.'

attacks rather than the attacks themselves, as they were then exposed to demoralizingly effective artillery fire. Once they realized they could see off the cavalry with comparative ease, the infantrymen welcomed the respite they offered from the guns. Ensign Macready in the 30th Foot recalled his men muttering, 'Here come those damned fools again', as they prepared to receive yet another assault.

The French cavalry officers attacking a square had to break in somehow – by luck, good judgement or a combination of both. There had to be a breach in the hedge of bristling bayonets and, if there was gap, it had to be exploited instantly. Once horsemen got inside a square it was all over for the infantry. However, the problems for the cavalry to overcome could seem insurmountable:

• Firstly, simple mathematics was against the cavalry when they attacked a square. An average strength battalion with 640 men formed a rectangle four ranks deep. This meant that on the short (one company wide) side there were some 120 soldiers, all of whom could fire, all of whom contributed bayonets to the hedge. They covered a frontage of about 20 metres. The most horsemen that the French could bring to face them were perhaps forty in two ranks. As only one rank could attack at a time, some six bayonets confronted a single sabre or lance – discouraging odds.

• Neither horses nor humans, especially the former, could be persuaded to throw themselves onto bayonets. No matter how determined the rider, how fast the approach or how sharp the spurs, the horses either swerved away or pulled up before contact.

• Even if a sabre armed cavalryman could close right up to the face of the square he could not strike the men behind the bayonets – he did not have the reach. Either he or his mount was far more likely to be spiked than he was to inflict any damage. A lancer had a better chance, although he was still outnumbered by at least four or five to one. One of De Brack's 'Red' Lancers at Waterloo found the situation so frustrating that he 'stood up in his stirrups and hurled his lance like a dart; it passed through an infantry soldier, whose death would have opened a passage for us, if the gap had not been quickly closed'.

• Once the first attacks failed then subsequent efforts became less and less likely to succeed, as not only did the infantry's morale improve with success but the piles of dead and dying animals and men formed a barrier over which it was difficult to pass.

Unless the cavalry could bring up guns (something the infantry dreaded) to blast holes in the squares, they had to rely on their enemy making a mistake, luck, or officers able to exploit the fleeting chance when it came. Any combination of the following could provide the opportunity:

• The square was composed of inexperienced troops (or more importantly inexperienced officers) whose morale had been shaken by previous losses. They were unsteady troops, some of whom might turn to seek shelter inside the square, thus creating confusion and the sought after gap in the hedge.

• The infantry fired too soon, that is at about 100 metres. The result would be few casualties and a lot of empty muskets, particularly if the side of a square had fired a volley (this was unlikely with competent officers). The cavalry could cover the intervening ground in 20–30 seconds.

• The infantry fired too late – at less than 10 metres. In these circumstances there was a chance that a wounded or dying horse whose momentum carried it forward would be oblivious of the bayonets and collapse into the square. Some second rank troopers could exploit the resultant gap.

Unfortunately for the French, Wellington's infantry did not make these errors, or if they did they could not be turned to good account. Waterloo was the final example, hammered home on scores of battlefields over the past two decades that, other things being equal, a cavalry charge against infantry in square would be thrown back 99 times out of 100. To keep repeating the process merely multiplied the horsemen's casualties. Some quotes from Waterloo veterans make relevant reading.

• Captain William Eeles of the 3/95 Rifles (whose brother was killed while acting as brigade major to Major-General Kempt):

A British Square under Cavalry Attack

Ensign Rees Gronow's 1st Battalion, 1st Foot Guards was not present at the battle. Gronow had joined Picton's headquarters as an extra ADC but as he was really surplus to the general's needs he was sent to join the 3rd Battalion at Waterloo. He fought as a soldier without any officer responsibilities. He has left a vivid description of what it was like inside an infantry square during the long afternoon of cavalry attacks and persistent artillery fire:

During the battle our squares presented a shocking sight. Inside we were nearly suffocated by the smoke and smell from burnt cartridges. It was impossible to move a yard without treading upon a wounded comrade, or upon the bodies of the dead; and the loud groans of the wounded and dying were most appalling.

At four o'clock our square was a perfect hospital, being full of dead, dying and mutilated soldiers. The charges of the cavalry were in appearance very formidable, but in reality a great relief, as the artillery could no longer fire on us; the very earth shook under the enormous mass of men and horses, I shall never forget the strange noise our bullets

made against the breast-plates of Kellerman's and Milhaud's cuirassiers, six or seven thousand in number [an exaggeration], who attacked us with great fury. I can only compare it, with a somewhat homely simile, to the noise of a violent hailstorm beating against panes of glass.

The artillery did great execution; but our musketry did not at first seem to kill many men, though it brought down a large number of horses, and created indescribable confusion. The horses of the first rank of cuirassiers, in spite of all the efforts of their riders, came to a standstill, shaking and covered with foam, at about twenty yards' distance from our squares, and generally resisted all attempts to force them to charge the line of serried steel. On one occasion two gallant French officers forced their way into a gap momentarily created by the discharge of artillery; one was killed by Stables the other by Adair …

In the midst of our terrible fire, their officers were seen as if on parade, keeping order in their ranks, and encouraging them. Unable to renew the charge, but unwilling to retreat, they brandished their swords with loud cries of 'Vive l'Empereur!'

Training the Horses

Getting a horse to do something it does not want to do is difficult; getting it to do something that frightens it is almost an impossibility. All nations endeavoured to train their cavalry horses to charge up to and into steady infantry. Field days were held in which the cavalry were made to charge a line or square of friendly troops. Naturally, before impact on the line either the horses were pulled up or allowed to swerve round the flanks. Sometimes they were allowed to pass through gaps in the line. On the battlefield it was found that this type of training merely reinforced the animals' instinct of self-preservation. The horses had been trained to stop or swerve to avoid contact. Many officers felt this was the preferred option for most of the riders as well. It is impossible to know how many horses were made to fall on the infantry bayonets at Waterloo – one suspects few, if any. Sergeant-Major Cotton of the 7th Hussars was of the same opinion, and was later to write:

> Not a single individual set an example of soldier-like devotedness by rushing upon the bristling bayonets … Of the fifteen thousand [it was 8000] French horsemen, it is

doubtful whether any perished on a British bayonet, or that any of our infantry in square fell by the French cavalry's sabres.

After Waterloo Maréchal Marmont came up with an improved system of training the horses. The friendly infantry were more spread out than on the battlefield so as to permit the horsemen passing between individual files. The cavalry then 'charged' at a walk and went through the ranks. This was repeated again and again. The pace was increased to a trot, canter and finally a gallop. The amount of musket fire (without ball) was similarly gradually increased in volume. In this way it was hoped the horses would be well accustomed to the noise and smoke, and would expect to be ridden up to and through the infantry. This training technique came too late for Waterloo. The next full-blooded cavalry charge was undertaken thirty-nine years later when the British Light Brigade charged some 2000 metres against a Russian artillery battery at Balaclava in the Crimea. They overran the guns.

… kept every man from firing until the Cuirassiers approached within thirty or forty yards [precisely the best moment to fire] of the square, when I fired a volley from my company which had the effect, added to the fire of the 71st, of bringing so many horses [particularly with cuirassiers soldiers were ordered to fire at the horses] to the ground, that it became quite impossible for the enemy to continue their charge.

- Wellington, speaking of the squares, remarked that they, 'would not throw away their fire till the Cuirassiers charged, and they would not charge until we had thrown away our fire.' A stalemate situation with all the advantages to the infantry.
- Lieutenant-Colonel Reynell, commanding the 71st Foot referred to the cavalry charges as, 'repeated *visits* from [the] Cuirassiers. I do

not say *attacks*, because these Cavalry Columns on no occasion attempted to penetrate our Square, limiting their approach to within ten or fifteen yards of the front face, when they would wheel about, receiving such fire as we could bring to bear…'.
- An engineer officer sheltering inside the square of the 79th Foot:

> No actual dash was made upon us. Now and then an individual more daring than the rest would ride up to the bayonets, wave his sword about and bully; but the mass held aloof, pulling up within five or six yards, as if, though afraid to go on, they were ashamed to retire. Our men … when they heard the sound of cavalry approaching, appeared to consider the circumstance a pleasant change (from being cannonaded!)

PRUSSIAN CAVALRY

General

Like the rest of the Prussian Army, the cavalry had been beset with mobilization difficulties. Manpower shortages were acute, but the scarcity of horses was worse. Remount depots had been emptied due to the enormous demands of the campaigns in 1813–14. There were problems with the Poles who were either reluctant to sell their animals to Prussians, or put the price up to extortionate levels. The King threatened to requisition the horses if they were not sold for a fair price. Despite squeezing horses from every available source, a number of regiments did not start the campaign with the 450 animals the establishment required.

There were three administrative categories of Prussian cavalry. The first were the thirty-six regular line regiments that formed the backbone of the cavalry element of the army. These included four guard, four cuirassier, eight dragoon, twelve hussar and eight uhlan (lancer) regiments. Of these, ten were present at Waterloo but there were no guard or cuirassiers among them – the Prussians had no heavy cavalry at all at Waterloo. The second were the thirty-three landwehr (militia) regiments. These were all light cav-

alry units, some of whom were armed with the lance. Eight landwehr regiments fought at Waterloo. The third category consisted of the ersatz regiments that formed the cavalry's depot and training units but did not take the field.

Blücher brought a total of 7000 horsemen onto the battlefield, representing 14 per cent of his force at Waterloo – one soldier in seven was a cavalryman. This compared with Wellington's 18 per cent and Napoleon's 21 per cent. Each army corps had a cavalry commander with responsibility for the cavalry brigades (like the infantry there were no divisions) in the corps. In addition to the cavalry brigades it was the usual practice for each infantry brigade to have one or two squadrons of cavalry attached and under command for scouting and screening duties. This system meant that Blücher had no central cavalry reserve under his direct command like Napoleon, or indeed Wellington.

Of the eight infantry brigades at Waterloo all had two squadrons with the exception of the 1st Brigade which had none and the 6th that had one. The 11th Hussars, the Elbe Landwehr

Cavalry and the 2nd and 3rd Silesian Landwehr were broken up for these duties.

As was to be expected it was the cavalry with Bülow's IV Corps that bore the brunt of the cavalry action during the battle. The two brigades with I and II Corps did not arrive until later and thus several units did not participate until the pursuit during the night.

ORGANIZATION

Cavalry brigades

I Corps

1st Cavalry Brigade (1,180) – GOC Major-General von Treskow II
2nd Dragoons (290 in three squadrons) – Lieutenant-Colonel von Woiski
5th Dragoons (340 in four squadrons) – Major von Osten
4th Hussars (270 in three squadrons) – Major von Englehardt
3rd Uhlans (280 in three squadrons) – Lieutenant-Colonel von Stutterheim

This brigade had fought in the delaying action along the line of the Sambre and around Charleroi on 15 June. The 2nd Dragoons had a brush with the Empress's Dragoons of the Imperial Guard near the Fleurus Wood. At Ligny the brigade suffered from artillery fire in an exposed position. The 2nd Dragoons was one of the regiments led by Blücher in a charge in which he was unhorsed during an attempt to rally his forces. It did not arrive at Waterloo until around 7.30 p.m., having lost 32 per cent of its strength in three days. It was therefore weak numerically, with three of its four regiments being well under 300 strong. They were perhaps fortunate that only the 5th Dragoons saw action in the final minutes at Waterloo.

II Corps

2nd Cavalry Brigade (1,060) – acting GOC Lieutenant-Colonel von Sohr
3rd Hussars (537 in four squadrons) – Major von Klinkowstroem
5th Hussars (523 in four squadrons) – Major von Arnim
11th Hussars (300 in three squadrons) – Major von Romberg *
Elbe Landwehr (300 in two squadrons) – Lieutenant-Colonel von Reibnitz*

* These regiments had their squadrons on detached duties with the 5th, 6th and 7th Infantry Brigades. This meant the brigade had only two regiments under direct command at Waterloo. Although present on the battlefield from around 6.30 p.m., the brigade was not committed until the pursuit phase.

IV Corps

1st Cavalry Brigade (1,215) – acting GOC Colonel Count von Schwerin
6th Hussars (575 in four squadrons) – Colonel von Eicke
1st West Prussian Uhlans (640 in four squadrons) – Lieutenant-Colonel Beier

This brigade had one regiment (10th Hussars) detached with two infantry regiments and two guns under Colonel Ledebur, south of Wavre. Like the rest of the corps, this brigade had not seen any action so far during the campaign. The 6th Hussars led the corps advance from the Lasne valley. Colonel Schwerin was probably the first Prussian (certainly officer) to be killed in the first clash with the French near the Bois de Paris. The brigade supported the 15th Infantry Brigade in the advance on Plancenoit.

2nd Cavalry Brigade (450) – acting GOC Lieutenant-Colonel von Watzdorff
8th Hussars (450 in three squadrons) – Major von Colomb

In effect this was not a brigade but a single regiment, as the 8th Dragoons did not join the army until late June. Despite this the regiment was heavily engaged in the advance on Plancenoit.

3rd Cavalry Brigade (1,836) – GOC Major-General von Sydow
1st Neumärk Landwehr (364 in three squadrons) – Major von Sydow (brother to the GOC)
2nd Neumärk Landwehr (426 in three squadrons) – Major Count von Haslingen
1st Pomeranian Landwehr (304 in three squadrons) – Major von Blankenburg
2nd Pomeranian Landwehr (316 in three squadrons) – Major von Kameke
1st Silesian Landwehr (426 in three squadrons) – Major von Schill
2nd Silesian Landwehr (330 in four squadrons)* – Major von Schallern
3rd Silesian Landwehr (315 in four squadrons)* – Major von Falckenhausen

* Neither of these regiments are counted in the brigade total as they were split up among the infantry brigades.

This was the strongest Prussian cavalry brigade at Waterloo and an all landwehr formation. The 2nd Neumärk covered the deployment of the 16th Infantry Brigade west of the Bois de Paris, and the 1st Pomeranian supported the 15th Infantry Brigade on its advance towards Plancenoit. Apart from this the brigade saw little fighting at Waterloo.

Regiments

General

The Prussians deployed eighteen cavalry regiments with sixty squadrons onto the battlefield before the French turned in rout at about 8.30 p.m. The last to arrive were the four in Major-General Treskow's brigade. As they had taken a bruising from guns and heavy cavalry at Ligny, it is unlikely that they were disappointed in missing the highlights. Nevertheless, the 5th Dragoons (the strongest regiment in the brigade with 340) made a spirited attack on Durutte's demoralized battalions as they joined the rest of the army in retreat. Of these regiments ten were regular and eight landwehr. The strongest was the 1st West Prussian Uhlans with 640 all ranks, the smallest the 4th Hussars with 270. The average size of a regiment was 388 – substantially below the French or Anglo-Allied cavalry regiments. Squadrons averaged 116 all ranks. No cavalry regiment at Waterloo carried a Standard.

Details of the regiments are set out in the table below:

Type	Regiments	Squadrons	Numbers	% (of all cavalry)
Hussars	6	21	2,655	38
Dragoons	2	7	630	9
Uhlans	2	7	920	13
Neumärk Landwehr	2	6	790	11
Pomeranian Landwehr	2	6	620	9
Silesian Landwehr	3	11	1,071	16
Elbe Landwehr	1	2	300	4
Totals	**18**	**60**	**6,986**	**100**

It is problematic trying to calculate accurately the losses in killed, wounded, and missing of each cavalry regiment at Waterloo. However, in general terms they were extremely light and in total were between 320–350, some 4.5–5 per cent. The highest losses were suffered by the 2nd Neumärk Landwehr with around 122, followed by the 8th Hussars with 66. The 1st Neumärk Landwehr had only one man killed. Some regiments almost certainly had no casualties at all.

Uniforms and Weapons

The hastily raised new cavalry units were a hotchpotch of former regiments, often formed by taking squadrons from several different old regiments. This, not surprisingly, led to an odd mixture of uniforms as many of these units went to war in 1815 wearing their old ones. There was little uniformity: as many as six different uniforms and styles could be seen in the same regiment. This being so, the details below are only a guide as to what the majority in the various categories were wearing. There was also some confusion over weapons. An example, an extreme one perhaps, being the 8th Uhlans which was a lancer unit but fought at Ligny and Wavre in their old hussar uniforms and without lances. There was also a problem with their pistols. The regiment was issued cartridges that did not fit the pistols, necessitating a hasty scramble to remake them to the right size.

A statistic not often appreciated was that over half (53 per cent) of the Prussian cavalry on the battlefield were lance armed (as all landwehr cavalry regiments carried the lance). They had more lancers at Waterloo than the French. If the fact that all troopers in the Prussian regiments carried lances is taken into account, whereas in the French only the front ranks did so, it is likely that up to 1,500 more Prussians actually carried a lance than Frenchmen.

Dragoons

They wore a standard pattern shako usually covered on campaign with a black waterproof cover. Their jacket was normally the light blue, thigh length *litewka* with the distinctive regimental facing colours. Grey overalls were worn by all ranks. Although seldom depicted with them in contemporary drawings, the Prussian dragoons were armed with a carbine and pistols, as well as their slightly curved sabre in a metal scabbard.

Hussars

Their uniforms were typical of hussars in any army: they had the heavily braided dolman and pelisse. Of the regiments at Waterloo the 3rd, 5th, and 8th Hussars wore a dark blue dolman and pelisse, the 4th brown, and the 6th and 7th green. Their headdress was the shako with the ubiquitous black cloth cover and grey overalls. Weapons were a heavy curved sabre in a metal scabbard and pistols.

Uhlans

The 1st and 3rd Uhlans present at Waterloo were original Uhlan regiments and so their uniforms were similar, having dark blue coats, black shakos and grey overalls. As was noted above, the Uhlan regiments formed later were not uniformly dressed, or even armed in at least one case. The lance, with swallow-tailed pennon (black over white), was their primary weapon. They also carried the curved cavalry sabre and pistols – but not carbines.

The Prussian Iron Cross Award

The highest Prussian award was the order Pour le Merite that had been instituted by Frederick the Great; but in March 1813 a second level of gallantry award was created – the Iron Cross (1st and 2nd Class). It was to remain a highly prestigious German order until the end of World War II, by which time Hitler had instituted several higher grades.

One of the earliest winners was an artillery veteran who saved the life of both the King of Prussia and the Tsar of Russia. A French shell had landed close to these two commanders-in-chief as they were conversing during the Battle of Bautzen in May 1813. Seeing the shell still sparking on the ground this gunner hurled himself on it and extinguished the fuse with his hands. The King called out to him to ask his name, saying, 'You shall be rewarded my brave fellow. Here on the spot I promote you to be an officer.' The artilleryman was humble in his thanks but protested he could not be an officer as he was illiterate or otherwise he would by now have been a corporal. However, he shrewdly seized the once in a lifetime opportunity to add, 'Your Majesty, however, will not, I hope be displeased, if I mention that the pay of an officer would make my family and myself happy for life.' The King not only authorized the request but gave an Iron Cross as well. The Tsar, who also owed him his life, bestowed on him the coveted Order of St George.

Landwehr

Again, there was some variety of dress within regiments. Although uniforms were generally dark blue, some troopers were in the long coats (*kollet*) others had the shorter *litewka*. The shako was the most common headdress, although the Neumärk regiments had the 'English' stovepipe variety instead of the usual bell-shape. All had a white cross (the landwehr insignia) on their caps. The 3rd Silesian had the Polish style *czapska* headdress. Although not always made clear by writers on the Prussian Army, the landwehr cavalry were lance armed, as were the attached volunteer Jaegers. In addition they had a curved sabre and pistols.

TACTICS

Command and control

The Prussians had worked hard for a number of years on improving and developing their staff and command and control systems. The cavalry system in use at Waterloo illustrates the improvements. Within each army corps there was a cavalry reserve force, usually two or three cavalry brigades. These were quite separate from the squadrons attached to and under command of the infantry brigades. The cavalry brigades had their overall commander (with his own staff) at corps headquarters. Thus the corps commander had only to give his orders concerning cavalry to the one man instead of to each brigade commander. The reserve cavalry commanders at Waterloo (all were eventually present on the battlefield) were:

I Corps – Lieutenant-General von Roeder
II Corps – Major-General von Wahlen-Jurgass
IV Corps – General Prince William of Prussia

Tactics

The Prussians paid particular attention to the combined arms battle, the details of which were set out in a manual (called the *1812 Reglement*). Blücher had issued a detailed reminder of how he expected brigades to operate tactically ten days prior to the battle. Cavalry were to precede the vanguard on the line of march (the 6th Hussars performed this function ahead of IV Corps' march from the Lasne valley). They would deploy behind the infantry on the battlefield but were ready to operate on either or both flanks

No.1 Squadron 6th Prussian Hussars Deployed in Line

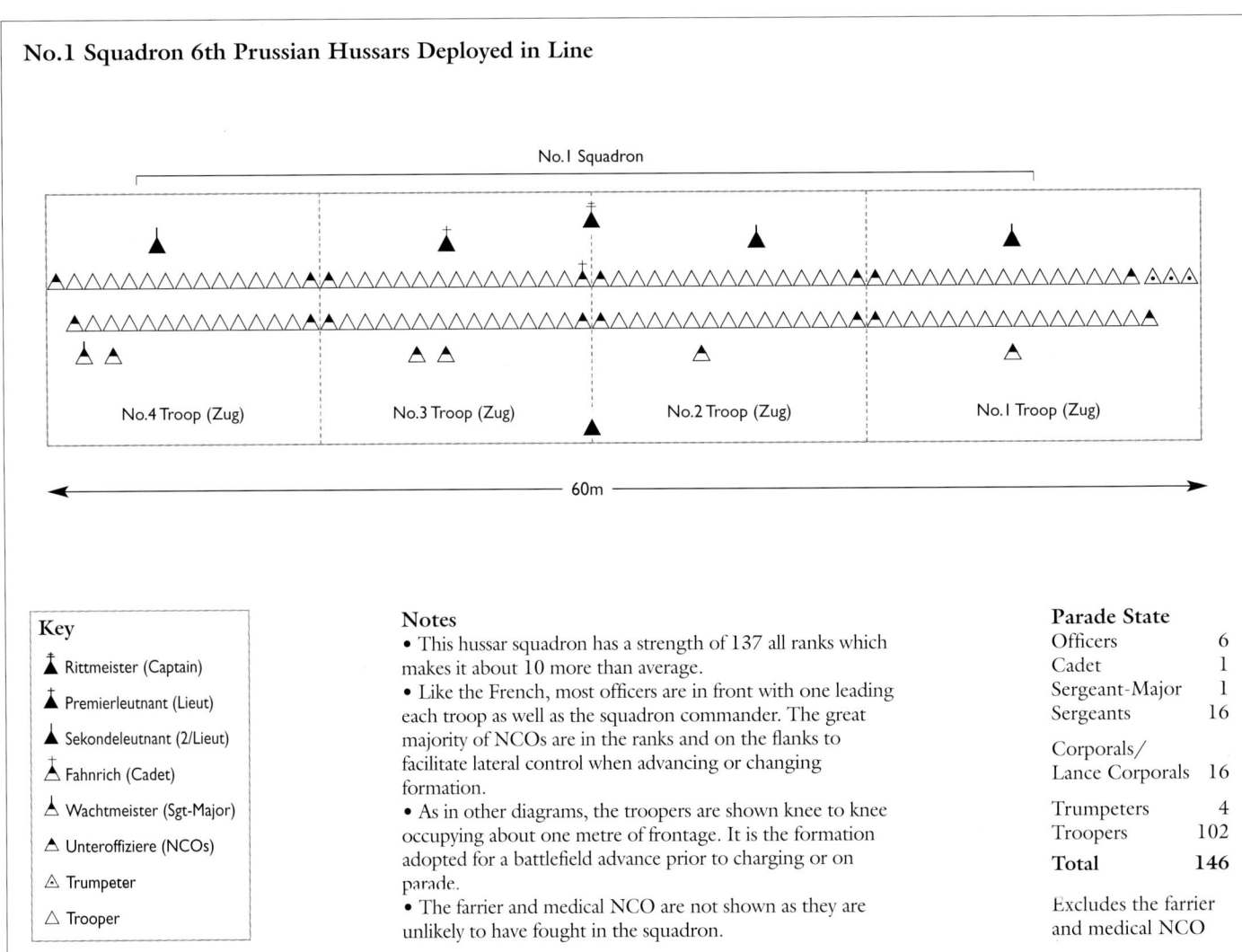

Key

- 🔱 Rittmeister (Captain)
- ♠ Premierleutnant (Lieut)
- ▲ Sekondeleutnant (2/Lieut)
- ♰ Fahnrich (Cadet)
- ↟ Wachtmeister (Sgt-Major)
- △ Unteroffiziere (NCOs)
- △ Trumpeter
- △ Trooper

Notes

- This hussar squadron has a strength of 137 all ranks which makes it about 10 more than average.
- Like the French, most officers are in front with one leading each troop as well as the squadron commander. The great majority of NCOs are in the ranks and on the flanks to facilitate lateral control when advancing or changing formation.
- As in other diagrams, the troopers are shown knee to knee occupying about one metre of frontage. It is the formation adopted for a battlefield advance prior to charging or on parade.
- The farrier and medical NCO are not shown as they are unlikely to have fought in the squadron.

Parade State

Officers	6
Cadet	1
Sergeant-Major	1
Sergeants	16
Corporals/ Lance Corporals	16
Trumpeters	4
Troopers	102
Total	**146**

Excludes the farrier and medical NCO

in support of the infantry as required by the circumstances. Each cavalry brigade had its own horse artillery battery. The system was flexible. It worked well during the advance across the open undulating countryside between the Bois de Paris and Plancenoit.

Organization

As with other armies, the Prussian cavalry regiment had its own small staff at headquarters. In theory the regimental commander was a full colonel, but at Waterloo this was the exception rather than the rule. In fact only the 6th Hussars had a colonel (Eike), four had lieutenant-colonels (1st West Prussian Uhlans, 3rd Uhlans, 2nd Dragoons and the 2nd Elbe Landwehr Cavalry) and the remaining thirteen had majors. According to the official establishment the headquarters would have a major, adjutant, regimental quartermaster and a medical officer. NCOs included a saddle maker and two armourers.

Each regiment supposedly had four squadrons divided into four troops (zuge). Of the eighteen regiments that arrived on the battlefield seven had four squadrons, ten (including all except one of the landwehr units) had three and one, the Elbe Landwehr, had only two. The 3rd, 4th, 5th and 6th Hussars plus the 5th Dragoons had detachments of around thirty mounted Jaegers attached specifically to undertake dismounted skirmish or outpost duties.

The 1808 squadron establishment is given below while how they formed up in line is depicted in the diagram above, which was laid down in the *1812 Reglement Preussische Kavallerie*.

One Rittmeister (captain)
One Premierleutnant (lieutenant)
Four Sekondeleutnant (2nd lieutenant)
One Wachtmeister (sergeant-major)
One Portepee-fahnrich (cadet or senior NCO standard-bearer, although no standards were carried at Waterloo)
One Sergeante (sergeant)
Nine Unteroffiziere (corporals)
Twelve Gefreite (lance-corporals)
Ninety-eight Troopers
Three Trumpeters
One Medical NCO
One Farrier

This gives a total of six officers and 127 other ranks. The Prussian squadrons at Waterloo had an average strength of 116 all ranks, so most were not seriously deficient at the start of the battle (Waterloo was the first time IV Corps had seen action). When the squadron deployed in line the position of the officers and NCOs was markedly similar to those taken up in French squadrons. Unlike the British, emphasis was placed on forward control by having five out of six officers out in front of the leading rank. There is an NCO on the flanks of each rank of the squadron, and the troops with all junior NCOs in the ranks. Again, like the French, less emphasis is given to having strong supernumerary rank.

SECTION SEVEN

The Artillery

Three hundred cannon-mouths roar'd loud;
And from their throats with flash and cloud
Their showers of iron threw.

Sir Walter Scott

General (Maps 16, 17, 18 & 19, pp. 274, 275, 294 & 295)

There were certainly plenty of guns and howitzers at Waterloo. By the time the Prussians brought their 134 pieces onto the battlefield the total was 537 (Wellington 157, Napoleon 246). Of these, comparatively few were actually destroyed (incapable of firing given a detachment and ammunition). Overall there was about one artillery piece for every 372 soldiers present. The French had the highest ratio with 1:315, the Anglo-Allied Army 1:466 and the Prussians 1:366. In simple terms there were three categories of artillery that travelled with an army on campaign – foot, horse (collectively called 'field' artillery) or siege. Only the first two were present at Waterloo.

With foot artillery, as the name implies, the guns were intended to accompany and support the army from semi-static positions on the battlefield. Although the guns, howitzers, and necessary wagons were horse drawn, the gunners marched on foot. They were intended to support an infantry formation. Horse, or 'flying' artillery, was first adopted by the Russians, who succeeded in using it to spring several unpleasant surprises on Frederick the Great. Frederick quickly copied the idea but, despite elaborate secrecy, was unable to maintain a European monopoly for long. Horse artillery was mobile artillery with all guns, vehicles, gunners and drivers mounted. Their role was to keep up with the cavalry, to be able to give them support from a flank, to move rapidly from one position to another, and to be able to get out of action quickly.

Although artillery was grouped in regiments for administrative purposes, both foot and horse fought in units of six or eight pieces (a piece being a gun or howitzer). Confusingly, most nationalities at Waterloo gave these groupings different names. They were 'batteries' to the Prussians, KGL, Brunswickers, Hanoverians, Dutch and Belgians, but 'brigades' to the British foot artillery, 'troops' to the British horse artillery and 'companies' to the French. In this book, unless discussing a specific unit, artillery are referred to as operating in batteries. Wellington deployed twenty-four batteries plus two guns, Napoleon thirty-four and Blücher seventeen.

Types of ordnance (pieces) at Waterloo

All armies used the following types of artillery:

GUNS (CANNONS)

Smooth bore, muzzle-loading guns of brass or iron differentiated by the weight of the projectile they fired. For example, a 6-pounder fired a six-pound ball (round shot). The Anglo-Allied Army fielded 6- and 9-pounders, the French 6- and 12-pounders (the largest field artillery piece in use) and the Prussians 6- and 12-pounders. Guns, indeed all artillery, were mounted on a wooden framework bound with iron that was supported by two large wheels, known as the 'carriage'. At the rear of the carriage, to stabilize the gun and to allow it to be attached to the two-wheel limber, was the 'trail'. The trail in use by all guns at Waterloo, except those of the British, was the double trail constructed with two separate, parallel pieces of timber. British guns had adopted the 'block' trail – a single baulk of timber, which lightened the carriage thus facilitating moving or re-aiming the gun.

All guns were direct, line of sight weapons, which meant the gunners had to see the target to ensure effective fire. The longer the barrel, the greater the accuracy at longer ranges; the bigger the charge, the bigger the bang and the greater the velocity. The trick was to manufacture field guns that balanced these considerations with overall weight and therefore tactical mobility. The gun was primarily used to smash its target by the weight and velocity of the projectile on impact. Using round shot, it could be used against 'soft' targets (humans or horses) or 'hard' ones (guns, buildings, bridges, fieldworks, wagons or thin walls). At Waterloo there were few worthwhile hard targets for the gunners on either side.

The range varied with the size of the gun, thus the heavier the piece the longer the effective range due to the increased muzzle velocity. All guns could fire at greater ranges, and occasionally did so, but these maximums were not effective battlefield ranges, and no self-respecting artillery officer would waste ammunition by opening fire at targets much in excess of 900–1000 metres. The maximum and effective ranges of the guns in use at Waterloo

British 6-pounder gun and 5.5-inch Howitzer

6-pounder gun   5.5-inch Howitzer

firing round shot, shell or canister (see ammunition types below) were, in metres:

Gun	Max. effective range	Most effective range	Canister (up to)
British 6-pdr	1000–1,300	600–700	350–400
French 6-pdr	1,300	700	400–450
Prussian 6-pdr	1,500	600–700	400
British 9-pdr	1,700	800–900	450
Prussian 12-pdr	2000	900	550
French 12-pdr	1,800	900	600

At Waterloo none of the 12-pounder guns got within canister range of the enemy. The 6-pounders could be expected to open fire at a worthwhile target (one they could actually see) at around 600–700 metres with shot or shell, and at 400 with canister. The British 9-pounder could add 200 metres to the former and 50 to the latter. The 12-pounders could reach out to 900 metres and still expect to hit the target. These most effective range zones for visible targets are marked on Maps 16 & 17, pp. 274 & 275. It should be emphasized that artillery fire killed at much greater ranges than these.

Cannonballs could ricochet and shells were lobbed over ridges, as at Waterloo, well above the normal effective ranges.

As with musketry the rate of fire was crucial, depending on the training, amount of recoil and physical fitness of the gunners. Anything less than two shots a minute was considered poor for the lighter guns; three shots was good, more than that was exceptional. Serving the guns was exhausting work due to the need to haul the gun back into position after every shot. On firing, the gun leapt back several feet and, with soft ground (as at Waterloo), quickly dug itself into a bed of mud. Dragging over a ton (with 12-pounders, two tons) of timber and metal back into position for realignment every thirty seconds during firing soon sorted the men from the boys. With prolonged firing, the rate invariably fell no matter how well trained the artillerymen. Waterloo was a protracted and intense struggle, with many of the French and Anglo-Allied gunners getting only brief respites from the need to keep firing. It is a fairly safe assumption that the overall average rate of artillery fire, in all three armies, was about two shots a minute with the 6- and 9-pounders. The heavy 12-pounders needed more muscle power but even with larger detachments, the rate of fire was usually less than for the lighter pieces.

A Firing Accident in 1811

As a unique illustration of how interdependent the duties of spongeman and ventsman were, none can better that told in the book *The Life of Alexander Alexander*, published in 1830:

> One occurrence I witnessed was almost incredible: a Portuguese governor arrived at Colombo, early in the year 1811; on the firing of the salute, Gunner Richard Clark was blown from the mouth of his gun right into the air, and alighted upon a rock at a considerable distance in the harbour, yet escaped without a bone being broken, almost unhurt. It was the most miraculous escape I ever witnessed; he was but an awkward soldier at the best; the gun of which he was No.1 [at that time No.1 was the spongeman] went off by accident. The gun was just loaded when she went off, through the negligence of Clark in not sponging properly. He was not at his proper distance, like the other man [loader], nor yet near enough to receive the whole flash. To the astonishment of everyone, he was seen
>
> in the air, the sponge-staff grasped in his right hand, the hammerhead downwards, which first struck the rock as he alighted on his breech. The rock was thickly covered with seaweed. A party was sent down to bring up the body, as all concluded him killed on the spot; he was brought up only stunned and slightly singed, and was at his duty again in a few days; while No.5 [at that time the ventsman] who served the vent, had his thumb, with which the motion-hole [vent] is stopped during loading, so severely burned, it was feared he must have lost it, and it was only saved by the skill of the surgeon. … If the gun goes off in loading, the thumb is witness whether he [the ventsman] did his duty or not, if it is burned he receives praise, if it is not he is punished. The thumb is sometimes so severely injured that amputation is necessary.

By Waterloo ventsmen's thumbs were protected by leather thumb-stalls.

Spiking Guns

There was only one gun of any army known to be spiked at Waterloo, and that was done deliberately by the British sergeant in charge of one of Major Rogers' 9-pounders (at about the time General Picton was shot) when he thought his gun was about to be overrun. It was later taken to the rear to have the spike drilled out. Although it rarely happened, the sergeant's action was in accordance with his training – that it was imperative to prevent a gun falling into enemy hands. Not only defending troops might have to spike their own guns, but attackers that overran artillery positions and captured ordnance were supposed to spike them if they could not be pulled away. This did not happen at Waterloo. Neither the British Union Brigade nor any of the French cavalry made any attempt to spike guns when they overran enemy batteries during the battle. Wellington, in giving orders for gun detachments to run for cover inside nearby squares thus abandoning their cannon, was taking a serious risk of having his guns disabled – he got away with it, as the French cavalry either had no spikes or were too busy to dismount and use them. Interestingly, the French could have used the British spikes, two of which were kept in the left axle box of every gun or howitzer. Had any Frenchman known this and had made the effort he had only to lift the lid – there was even a hammer and mallet in the limber boxes if nothing else was to hand!

There were several different ways to disable a gun – some took much longer and had more lasting effect than others. Methods used included:

• Spiking – the quickest way, for use in battle where time and opportunity were fleeting. It entailed driving a tapered steel spike down the vent at the rear of the barrel. The French spikes were six-sided, with each splay having upward pointing teeth or barbs.

A spike could be drilled out, but this was not a task that could be carried out quickly in action. Another method was to ram a mixture of ordinary gunpowder and fuse powder, of about a third of the weight of the ball used, down the barrel. Next, two balls or a cylinder of wood were rammed hard down and the whole lit from the muzzle end. The resultant explosion often forced the spike from the vent – much as a champagne cork pops from a well-shaken bottle.

• An alternative, which took slightly longer, was to drive a cylinder of hard wood down the barrel followed by a round shot wrapped in felt. This package was extremely hard to remove, the most usual method being to push burning charcoal down the raised barrel to burn away the felt. It could be a long and frustrating process, as the felt was not readily combustible and there was little oxygen at the bottom of the barrel to feed the flames.

• More rough and ready measures involved sawing off the trunnions, firing another cannonball at the barrel, or smashing a wheel, although with the latter it could often be speedily replaced with a spare.

• If the barrel was made of brass, as most were, and there was plenty of time, the barrel was taken off its carriage and supported at each end while a large fire was lit under the centre. As the heat intensified, so the copper in the metal began to melt, with the barrel eventually sagging in the middle.

All that was ever done at Waterloo to take out captured artillery was to disable the gunners, the horses and cut the traces of the teams. These proved ineffective as infantrymen could replace gunners if necessary, while horses were only required if the guns were to be moved a substantial distance.

HOWITZERS

These pieces that had replaced the old mortars on the battlefield relied on high angle fire at the longer ranges and canister if the enemy closed in. Howitzers had short, stubby barrels and so did not fire round shot. There were four types of howitzer deployed at Waterloo: the 5.5-inch (British and French), the 6-inch (French), the 7-pounder (Prussian) and the 10-pounder (Prussian). With the exception of the 7-pounders and 10-pounders, these measurements reflected the diameter of the bore. All such ordnance had the double trail carriage.

Their primary role was to lob shells at the enemy, their secondary one being to help out with canister in emergencies. Howitzers were of little use against hard targets that required a massive impact to destroy them, but the exploding shell they fired could be deadly against troops in the open or, more importantly, against enemy hidden by low hills or undulating ground. Because of this facility, the howitzer detachment did not necessarily need to see the target to open fire effectively. The well-known British inclination to conceal themselves behind ridges gave added significance to the howitzer for their enemies – as was the case for the French at Waterloo.

The effective battlefield ranges were marginally greater than those of the gun. Those of the 5.5-inch, 6- and 7-pounder were around 800 metres with shell and 450 with canister, the 10-pounder reaching out to 900 and 500 respectively. Similarly, and for the same reasons, the howitzer detachments that kept up a rate of fire of two shots a minute over a period of time were doing well.

There were 134 howitzers deployed at Waterloo by the time the battle ended – 25 per cent of all the artillery on the field. The French, Prussian, Dutch and Belgian gun batteries all had two howitzers each; the British, KGL and Hanoverian had one; a single British battery (Major Bull's) was a specialist howitzer unit of six pieces, and the Brunswick artillery had none. The distribution of howitzers at Waterloo is shown in the table below:

Howitzer	Anglo-Allied	French	Prussian
5.5-inch	30	58	–
6-inch	–	12	–
7-pounder	–	–	28
10-pounder	–	–	6
Totals	**30**	**70**	**34**

Even with Bull's Troop, only 19 per cent of Wellington's artillery were howitzers, whereas the French had 28 per cent and the Prussians 25 per cent. At Waterloo this was no disadvantage to the Duke, as the French presented direct, line of sight targets throughout the battle. Conversely, the Emperor would be grateful for the high proportion of howitzers that could reach the reverse slope of Mont St Jean ridge.

ROCKETS

The British deployed one rocket troop (see pp. 265–7).

Firing Drills (Diagrams opposite and p. 262)

A competent artillery detachment could bring their piece into a firing position, unlimber, drive off the limber team and unload the trail chest of ammunition in about a minute. The gun or howitzer could come into action immediately on the command to load, continue firing until told to stop, and then be limbered up again ready to move in about two or three minutes if necessary. The procedures, the actions of every individual in the detachment, were reduced to drills. Every drill had been repeated a thousand times in training. Every movement had to be done in precisely the right order, every action had to be exact. Short cuts cost lives – one tiny spark could lead to fatalities. This was why all implements used by the gunners were made of wood or copper.

In the British artillery there were five men directly involved with loading and firing. With the French the number varied depending on the calibre of the ordnance, while the gunners were often assisted by infantrymen drafted in from the nearest unit to help manhandle the piece or hump ammunition – for example, a 12-pounder would have eight gunners and, if lucky, seven infantrymen. What follows, however, was the British system.

The NCO (either a sergeant or corporal) was the detachment commander, known as No.1. No.2 was the sponge-man, No.3 the loader, No.4 the ventsman and No.5 the firer. Four other members of the detachment were responsible for keeping the loader supplied with the right type of ammunition. After a shot had been fired the piece jumped back anything up to six feet. The whole detachment (including the men carrying ammunition) were needed to haul it back into position using drag ropes hooked onto the carriage and wheel hubs – this was the really exhausting business.

The duties and drills for firing were as follows:
• **No.1** – His responsibilities were command and supervision of the detachment plus laying (aiming). He had to align the piece, traverse it, raise or lower the barrel with the elevating screw, and make final adjustments. Good laying and judging range came from experience. It had to be done while squinting along the top of the barrel in between traversing (moving the trail) with a handspike (lever) – a task that needed two men before lighter trails were introduced. To do all this he needed to see the target. At Waterloo this was the reason why the Anglo-Allied artillery in the front line were, unlike the infantry, mostly positioned on the forward slope of the ridge – they needed to see what was happening. Even so, their targets were either obscured or fleeting for much of the time due to undulations in the ground, the tall crops and, above all, the dense clouds of smoke. Detachment commanders had difficult jobs.
• **No.2** – The spongeman stood in front and to the right of the muzzle. His equipment was a wooden bucket of water and a sponge-rammer. The latter was a long wooden staff with a cylinder wrapped in sheepskin at one end, and a similar cylinder of bare wood at the other that was dished to fit the projectile. Smart spongemen marked the staff so they knew when a round was in the bore – this helped to prevent double loading by mistake in the excitement of action. Once a shot had been fired and the gun dragged back from its recoil, the No.2 dipped his sponge in the bucket and thrust it down the barrel, the object being to extinguish any burning fragments before another charge was loaded. After the No.3 had put the next round (cartridge and projectile) in the barrel the No.2 reversed his staff and rammed both down the bore. These were not the most popular of duties.

British RHA 9-Pounder with Team Limbered Up Ready to Move

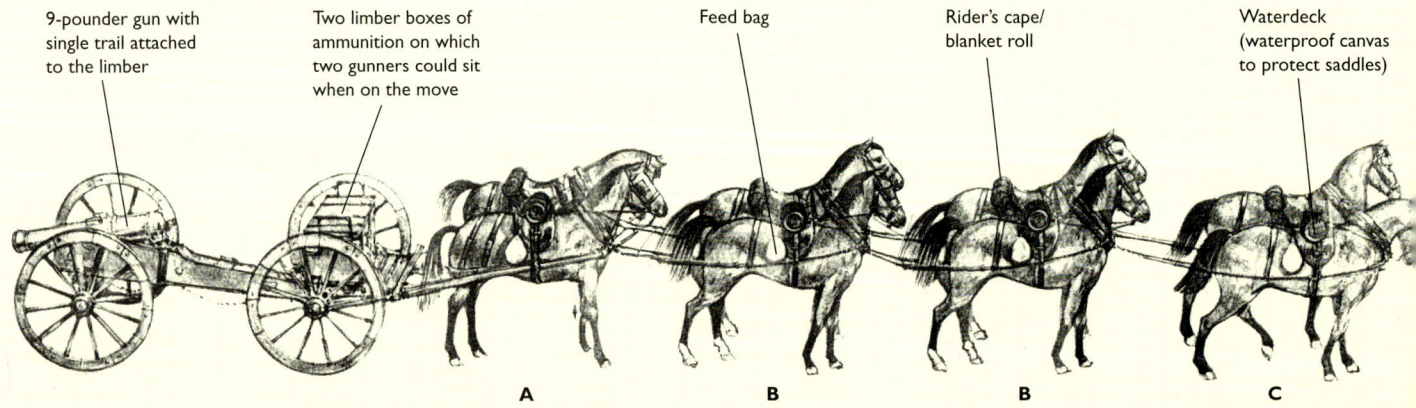

9-pounder gun with single trail attached to the limber

Two limber boxes of ammunition on which two gunners could sit when on the move

Feed bag

Rider's cape/ blanket roll

Waterdeck (waterproof canvas to protect saddles)

A   B   B   C

Notes
• Mercer's 9-pounders had eight horses pulling each gun at Waterloo, although they could be drawn by six.
• The nearside (left) horses were ridden by soldiers of the Corps of Artillery Drivers.
• All the horses shown are what are known as 'ride and drive' horses in the modern RHA. This distinguishes them from officers' 'chargers' that never have to pull guns. For many generations now RHA horses have come from the Irish Republic, although this was not necessarily the case at Waterloo.

A – The two 'wheeler' horses in the shafts of the limber – double shafts were unique to the British.
B – The 'centre' horses.
C – The 'leader' pair, often the largest horses.

British RHA 9-Pounder Gun Detachment Ready to Serve the Gun

No.2. – Spongeman.
He sponged out the barrel after every shot after dipping his sponge in the water. After No.3 had put the projectile in the muzzle he pushed it down the barrel with the rammer.

No.4 – Ventsman.
A key member of the detachment. He was equipped with a thumb stall, pricker and firing tubes. It was vital he put his thumb over the vent before the No.2 rammed the projectile. He also pricked the cartridge through the vent and then inserted the firing tube.

No.3 – Loader.
After the barrel had been sponged he placed the cartridge, followed by the projectile in the barrel to be rammed home by No.2.

No.5 – Firer.
He had the least onerous duties. He was equipped with a portfire. Depending on his orders he would apply his portfire to the firing tube in the vent, thus firing the gun.

No.1 – Detachment commander (a sgt).
Aligns gun, makes adjustments with elevating screw. Needed to see the target before firing.

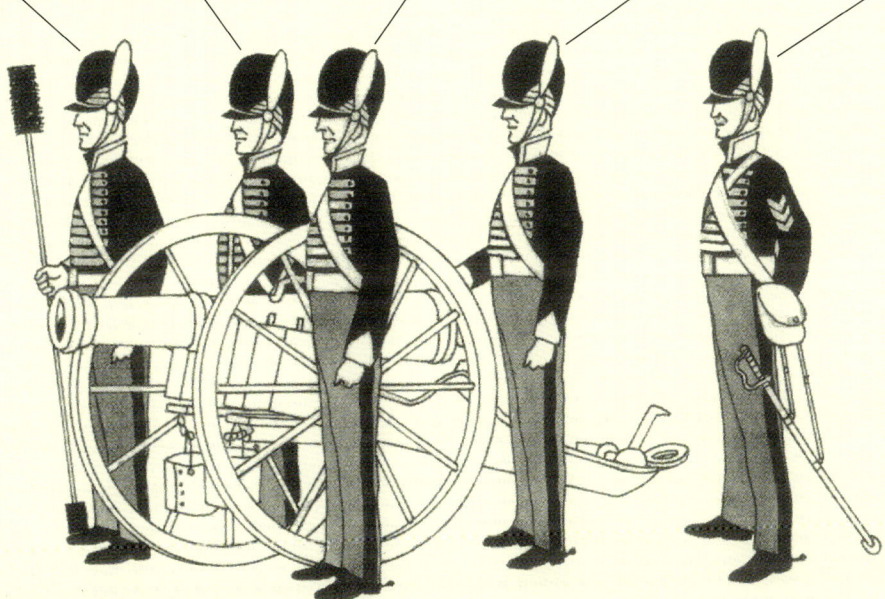

• **No.3** – The loader's position was at the front to the left of the muzzle. After the barrel had been sponged the No.3 placed the cartridge followed by the projectile in the barrel to be rammed home by the No.2. At the same time the No.4 placed his thumb over the vent. The passage of the cartridge, round and rammer down the bore created an air current out of the vent if it was not blocked. This could ignite any small hot embers left after the swabbing – with nasty consequences for the spongeman in particular.

• **No.4** – The ventsman stood behind the wheel of the carriage on the right of the trail (his French counterpart on the left). His equipment consisted of a leather thumb stall, a pricker (sharp rod) and firing tubes. These tubes were made of quill or stiff paper and filled with mealed powder moistened with spirits of wine. They came in different lengths with the bottom end cut slantwise to assist in piercing the cartridge. The top end was capped with flannel steeped in saltpetre and spirits of wine so that the cap did not have to be removed before firing.

   No.4 had to have his wits about him and watch what was going on intently. As soon as the loader lifted the projectile to the muzzle he had to place his thumb over the vent for the reasons explained above. With the clamour of battle going on all round it was easy to forget, or not do it at precisely the right moment. The penalty, if things went badly wrong and there was a premature explosion, was not that the barrel burst killing the detachment, but that the spongeman lost his hands. In the British service tradition had it that the spongeman was entitled to hit the ventsman over the head with his staff if he failed to 'serve his vent'.

   Next, after the round and cartridge had been rammed down together, the No.4 pushed his pricker through the vent, thus

piercing the cartridge at the bottom of the barrel. This action was immediately followed by his inserting a firing tube in the vent, which was angled at 101 degrees, allowing the tube to be blown clear on firing. With prolonged firing, as at Waterloo, there was the possibility of the vent becoming so hot that it was impossible to insert the firing tube without it exploding prematurely. The solution was to use a bucket of water to cool it down, but there was seldom any to spare. The only alternative was to stop firing temporarily – which was one of the reasons why guns were not deployed individually.

• **No.5** – The firer stood behind the wheel to the left of the trail (French firer on the right) and had perhaps the easiest, or the least strenuous, of duties in the detachment. His equipment was a portfire: a stiff paper tube 16.5 inches long filled with a composition that burned at the rate of one inch a minute. Spares were carried inside the lid of the limber boxes. It was lit from the linstock, a forked stick holding a length of even slower burning match alight at both ends; one was stuck in the ground between and behind every two pieces (a division). Depending on his orders, the No.5 would apply his portfire to the firing tube as soon as the ventsman had inserted a firing tube in the vent, or await an order from the No.1 who in turn might be awaiting the order from the officer in command of his division (pair of guns). Unless the firing was continuous (as it was for much of the time at Waterloo) the firer would then cut the burning end off his portfire with the portfire-cutter attached to the trail – this avoided unnecessary sparks flying around the gun position and lengthened the life of this piece of equipment.

Various Gunners' Tools and Accessories

French 12-pounder sponge and rammer

All nationalities used the double-ended rammer. The sponge was often sheep's wool, the rammer of wood.

French powder scoop and 'worm' or wad hook

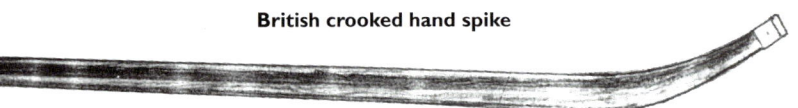

The powder scoop for loose gunpowder measuring was virtually obsolete by Waterloo.
The 'wormer' was used by the rammer to extract wads of unburnt cartridge, or faulty charges.

British crooked hand spike

Used by the No.1 (NCO) to lever the trail round to aim the piece.
A task requiring two men until lighter trails were introduced. Some hand spikes were straight.

French forked and straight linstocks

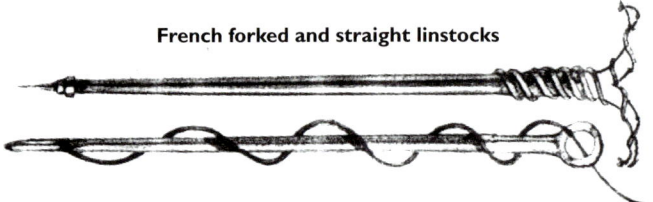

Used for holding the slow match, which was lit and linstock thrust into
the ground close to the guns. The portfire was lit from it during action.

Shot gauges

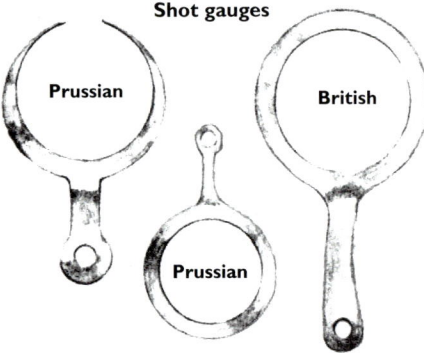

Prussian

British

Prussian

Used to check the size of shot if uncertain if it
would fit in a barrel. Enemy shot could be fired
back so sometimes checking was necessary.

British portfire cutter

This was used to trim off
the burning end of the slow
match during any lull in the
firing to reduce the risk of
accidental explosions. This
large example was attached
to the right side of the trail
behind the barrel.

Water bucket

One or two buckets were hung from
the axle-tree in front of the gun. The
sponge was soaked in water before
use. Buckets were wooden or leather.

Thumb stall

A key piece of equipment for the
ventsman to protect his thumb which
he was continually required to place
over the red-hot vent.

Vent prickers or priming wires

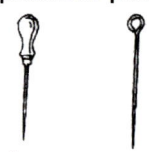

Used by the ventsman to push down the
vent to puncture the charge (cartridge)
bag thus making ignition more certain.

Portfire cutter

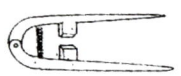

Small spring-loaded cutters.

Artillery Ammunition (Diagram p. 265)

GENERAL

By 1815 only canister ammunition was 'fixed' or 'ready' ammunition, i.e. the projectile and propellant were joined in one. Other types were fired with the cartridge still separated from the projectile. Gone were the days of scooping up loose powder with a ladle – this had been abandoned except for adjusting the range of mortars that were on a fixed elevation of 45 degrees. The correct weight of powder (normally about a third of the weight of the projectile) was placed in a serge or flannel bag that had been stiffened and the weave sealed by boiling in glue. The mouth of the bag was tied with string. The projectile (round shot or shell) was secured by two tinned iron straps to a circular 'dished' piece of wood, of the same diameter as the bore, called a 'sabot'. The British secured the straps to the wooden sabot with copper tacks. With canister the sabot was inserted into the mouth of the powder bag and tied up with the string. Additional string was used around the top and middle to ensure it kept its shape and could be rammed down the barrel without difficulty. With other ammunition the cartridge was placed in the barrel first, followed by the projectile, and both rammed down together.

ROUND SHOT

About 70–80 per cent of all projectiles carried by the three armies at Waterloo were round shot. This was because it was multi-purpose ammunition, equally effective at smashing all likely battlefield targets. This solid iron ball was a fearsome killer of men and horses. Sixteen-year-old Ensign Keppel of the raw and inexperienced 3/14 Foot, whose ancestors had fought under Marlborough at Blenheim and the Duke of Cumberland at Fontenoy and Culloden, came under cannon fire for the first time during the afternoon. He witnessed a bugler of the 51st Foot being hit:

> … a round shot took off his head and spattered the whole battalion with his brains [it was in square], the colours and the ensigns in charge of them coming in for an extra share. One of them, Charles Fraser, a fine gentleman in speech and manner, raised a laugh by drawling out, 'How extremely disgusting!' A second shot carried off six of the men's bayonets, a third broke the breastbone of a Lance-Sergeant [Robinson], whose piteous cries were anything but encouraging to his youthful comrades.

Keppel lived to see the Crimean War, the Indian Mutiny, the American Civil War, the Franco-Prussian War, the Zulu War, the First Boer War and General Gordon's death in Khartoum before, a general himself by this time, he died in 1891 aged ninety-two, one of a tiny handful of Waterloo veterans.

Artillery officers liked firing round shot into columns of troops, or infantry in square, where one cannon ball at the right angle could plough through twenty ranks with ease, bowling men over like so many helpless skittles. Ricocheting round shot was deadly on hard flat ground as it kept low and did not lose its lethality until after at least the third bounce. Even a ball that had ricocheted several times and was trundling over the ground like a cricket ball would break a leg or ankle. Unfortunately for the gunners at Waterloo, the ground was too soft for more than an occasional ricochet at best.

COMMON SHELL

This was a hollow iron sphere containing gunpowder ignited by a fuse that was lit by the flash of the propellant charge. The shell was an anti-personnel (or anti-horse) projectile, as the fragments of iron flung out from an exploding shell did no real harm to hard targets. The ideal target was a body of troops in the open, the best bursting point overhead and slightly in advance of the target (see Diagram p. 269). The knack was in the selection and cutting of the fuse to get the right burning time for the range. This was a frequent cause of error, with the shell bursting too soon or too late, or landing on the ground still spluttering. Not that any of these things necessarily rendered the shell ineffective, but the lethality was thereby often reduced – it was not unknown for a brave and quick-witted soldier to extinguish the fuse of an unexploded shell that landed nearby.

At Waterloo, as throughout the Napoleonic Wars, shells were fired by howitzers, not guns. The howitzer's high angle firing enabled them to seek out troops that were concealed from the gunners by ridges or woods. A further advantage was that the shells could be fired over the heads of advancing friendly troops. French shells sought out targets in the Hougoumont wood and orchard, on the reverse slope of Mont St Jean ridge, and supported d'Erlon's divisions with overhead fire as they advanced through the corn to assault Wellington's centre and left. Shells could also be fired to ricochet, causing consternation as they bounced around near the enemy fizzing and spitting. Shell bursts among cavalry were especially effective, as not only did the flying metal cause casualties, but also the noise of the explosions terrified the horses.

CANISTER OR CASE SHOT

This ammunition was appropriately named, as it was a canister filled with balls for use against close range targets. It was the universal projectile of last resort, designed to destroy an enemy as he closed in on the defenders. It was fired by either guns or howitzers and was, in effect, a giant shotgun cartridge. There were two types: 'heavy' and 'light'. The first contained fewer and heavier balls than the second and was effectively able to reach out to about 600 metres. The light canister was invariably fired at ranges under 400 metres, preferably in the last 150 and in conjunction with sustained musket fire.

Canister consisted of a thin tin cylinder slightly smaller in diameter than the bore of the piece that would fire it. The cylinder would be packed with balls and sawdust – the British light canister for a 6-pounder contained eighty-five 1.5-ounce balls, the heavy variety forty-one 3.5-ounce balls, with the French varying between 2 and 4 ounces. At the bottom was a wooden sabot to which the cartridge was attached. The cylinder was topped with an iron lid and wire-loop carrying handle. As the projectile left the barrel, the pressure of the charge and the relaxation of the confining pressure of the barrel caused the canister to disintegrate, allowing the balls to be hurled forward in an ever-expanding cone. The diameter of the cone was about 32 feet at 100 metres, 64 feet at 200 metres and 96 feet at 300 metres. In other words, it was difficult to miss at close range. Often, as at Waterloo, the last two or three rounds fired would be double-shotted – where the piece was loaded either with a round shot and then a canister on top of it, or two canister rounds. This technique caused carnage among the French cavalry attacking the Anglo-Allied right during the late afternoon, heaping up a tangle of horses in front of the infantry squares. On hard ground ricochet firing could also produce dramatic results.

Some writers confuse canister with grapeshot, a type of projectile not used at Waterloo. Grapeshot was a number of iron balls packed round an iron column attached to a circular sabot and covered with canvas bound with string. It was only used by naval forces or siege train artillery during the Napoleonic Wars.

'CARCASS' PROJECTILES

This was an incendiary projectile common to most armies of the period, fired from howitzers. It was used by the French, on the personal instructions of the Emperor, to set fire to the buildings and barns at Hougoumont. It was oblong-shaped and made from canvas reinforced with iron hoops and bound with cord. It contained a mixture of turpentine, resin, tallow, sulphur, saltpetre and antimony, which was poured into the shell and allowed to harden. The fuse, containing gunpowder, was ignited by the propellant charge. The shell could burn for up to twelve minutes, depending on the calibre, and was virtually impossible to extinguish. Because the likelihood of needing it on the battlefield was small, only a very few were carried in the ammunition wagons.

SPHERICAL CASE OR SHRAPNEL

This type of artillery ammunition was unique to Britain. Henry Shrapnel invented it in 1784 – the shell eventually bearing his name, as it still does today. It consisted of a hollow iron sphere filled with musket balls and gunpowder ignited by a fuse. The number of musket balls varied considerably – 27–85 for the 6-pounder, 41–127 for the 9-pounder and 153 for the 5.5-inch howitzer.

It was primarily an airburst weapon, the object being to shower the enemy with musket balls at a far greater range than muskets could ever reach. If the burning time of the fuse was accurately calculated, it was a potent addition to the British armoury, proving to be very much a British 'secret weapon' – one that the French would have used to good effect on Wellington's stationary units behind the ridge had they possessed it.

Experiments established that some musket balls travelled up to 350 metres from the point of burst.

'AMMUNITION WITHOUT ORDNANCE' OR ROCKETS
(Diagram p. 266)

Rockets were another British 'secret weapon' that was used at Waterloo. They were first brought into service by Colonel William Congreve, an officer in the Hanoverian service with the patronage of the Prince of Wales. Wellington, however, was entirely sceptical of their value. The incendiary, heavy naval version was first used in earnest at Boulogne in 1806. The British burnt down the port, although they had been aiming at the ships in the harbour, thus revealing their major shortcoming: a lack of accuracy. A year later a rain of 40,000 rockets reduced much of Copenhagen to ashes. Afterwards the Duke was to comment when asked if he would deploy them, 'I do not wish to set fire to any town, and I do not know of any other use for rockets.' It was against his better judgement that one section was deployed at Waterloo – even then the so-called 'Rocket Troop' still had five 6-pounder guns instead of the usual six.

The lighter, battlefield version (6- and 9-pounders used at Waterloo) had a number of advantages over conventional artillery. It did not require the 'inconvenience' of a gun to fire, hence 'ammunition without ordnance'. There were also a remarkable variety of rockets available, including shells, solid shot, canister, incendiary, signal rockets and even illuminating parachute flares. They could fire over 3000 metres, were cheap to make, could be fired faster than any gun, could go where any infantryman could go and made a fearful noise in flight. Nevertheless, these impressive assets were often negated by their infuriating tendency to have a mind of their own when airborne. Especially disconcerting was an occasional inclination to boomerang. Despite this, they could produce spectacular results against raw troops, horses or as a total surprise at short range.

Wellington's Dislike of Rockets

Captain Mercer, who commanded 'G' Troop RHA during the battle, described an incident in his *Journal of the Waterloo Campaign* that perfectly illustrates the Duke's dislike of rockets:

> Captain Whinyates having joined the army with the rocket troop, the Duke, who looked upon rockets as nonsense, ordered that they should be put into the store, and the troops supplied with guns instead. Colonel Sir G. Wood [the Duke's artillery commander at Waterloo], instigated by Whinyates, called on the Duke to ask permission to leave him his rockets as well as guns. A refusal. Sir George, however, seeing the Duke was in a particularly good humour, ventured to say, 'It will break poor Whinyates heart to lose his rockets.' 'Damn his heart, sir! Let my orders be obeyed.' was the answer thundered in his ear...

Later he must have relented, as Whinyates certainly had his rockets and five 6-pounder guns at Waterloo.

The best description of rockets being used that illustrates the reasons for the Duke's scepticism of their value, is when Captain Mercer RHA watched them come into action on the road north of Genappe during the retreat on 17 June:

Meanwhile the rocketeers had placed a little iron triangle in the road with a rocket lying on it. The order to fire is given – port-fire applied – the fidgety missile begins to sputter out sparks and wriggle its tail for a second or two, and then darts forth straight up the chausée. A gun stands right in its way, between the wheels of which the shell in the head of the rocket bursts, the gunners fall right and left and, those of the other guns taking to their heels, the battery is deserted in an instant. Strange; but so it was. I saw them run, and for a few minutes afterwards I saw the guns standing mute and unmanned, whilst our rocketeers kept shooting off rockets, none of which ever followed the course of the first. Most of them, on arriving about the middle of the ascent, took a vertical direction, whilst some actually turned back upon ourselves – and one of these followed me like a squib until its shell exploded, actually put me in more danger than all the fire of the enemy throughout the day. Meanwhile the French artillerymen, seeing how the land lay, returned to their guns and opened a fire of case shot on us...

British 9-Pounder Gun and 5.5-inch Howitzer and Ammunition

British 5.5-inch Howitzer

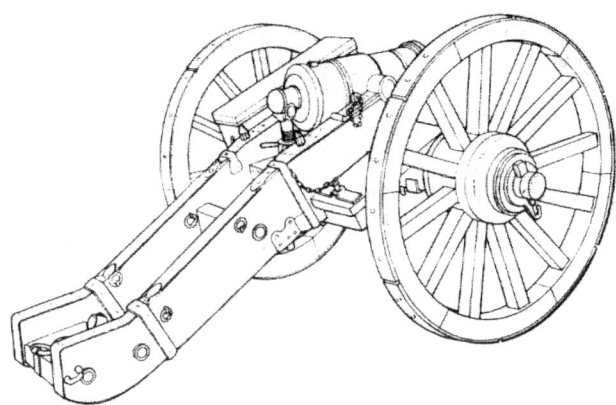

British 9-pounder gun

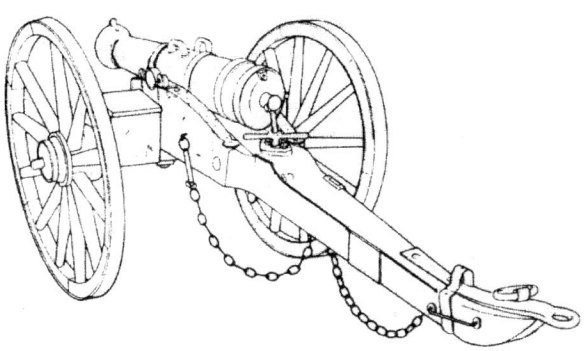

- Normally each battery (horse and foot) had one howitzer. The British RHA had one battery of 6 howitzers.
- They were particularly effective in firing the new spherical case (shrapnel) which neither the French nor Prussians possessed.
- Note the 'stubby' barrel for high-angle fire and the heavier double trail. Wellington deployed 30 howitzers at Waterloo – only the Brunswick artillery did not have any.

- The heaviest field artillery gun deployed by Wellington at Waterloo. Originally introduced to counter the French 8-pounder (not used at Waterloo).
- The Anglo-Allied army had 60 of these guns in the field out of 157 artillery pieces.
- Substantially heavier than the 6-pounder, these guns were drawn by 8 horses at Waterloo, although 6 could be used.
- Note the gun has a single trail, which reduced the overall weight and facilitated realigning/traversing after each shot.

Common shell

 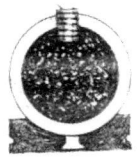

- Only fired by howitzers at Waterloo.
- Cut-away drawing shows gunpowder only (compare with spherical case) the effectiveness depending on shards of the casing hitting the target.
- Often exploded on the ground. The soft soil at Waterloo frequently nullified most of its effects as it buried itself before exploding.

Round shot

- Fired by all guns but not the howitzer.
- This ball has been fixed to the wooden sabot (shoe) by tin straps, which fall away after firing.
- The great majority of shots fired by artillery at Waterloo were round shot.

Canister

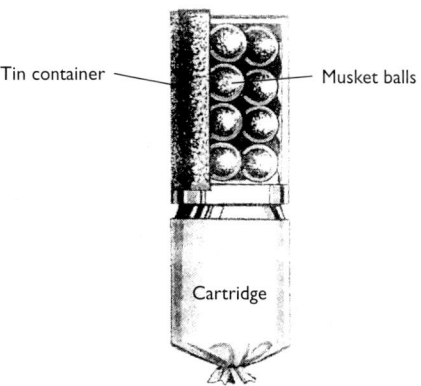

Tin container — Musket balls

Cartridge

- Fired by all ordnance at close range targets.
- This large 'shotgun' ammunition was lethal against dense formations and was sometimes loaded with a round shot for even more devastating results.
- It was the only artillery ammunition that usually came 'fixed' – that is with the cartridge attached to the projectile.

Spherical case
(shrapnel)

 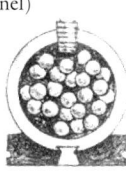

- Neither the French nor Prussians had this shell which was intended to burst in the air showering balls on the troops below.
- It proved effective at Waterloo and was used by all British ordnance.
- The knack was to time the fuse accurately so that the burst occurred at the right moment.
- Fired by both guns and howitzers.

The British RHA Rocket Section at Waterloo

This drawing shows the Rocket Section of Captain Whinyates' RHA Troop on the line of march. The standard limber was used with 4 horses drawing it and the rocket 'car'. Two gunners rode in the car which carried 60 rounds of 12-pdr rockets with the sticks, in half lengths in boxes along each side of the car.

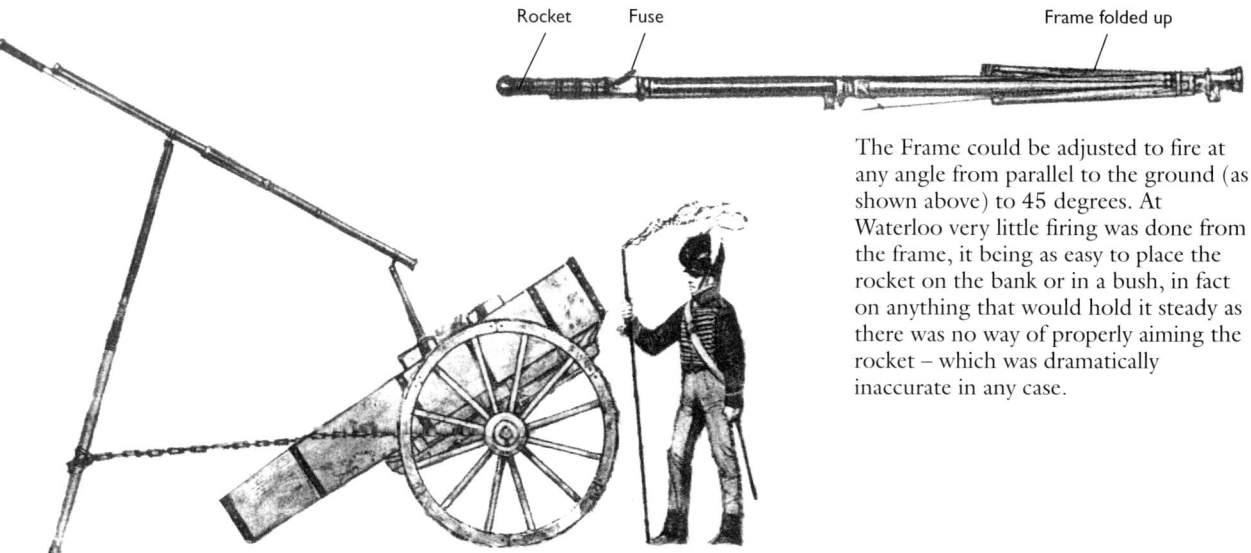

Rocket   Fuse   Frame folded up

The Frame could be adjusted to fire at any angle from parallel to the ground (as shown above) to 45 degrees. At Waterloo very little firing was done from the frame, it being as easy to place the rocket on the bank or in a bush, in fact on anything that would hold it steady as there was no way of properly aiming the rocket – which was dramatically inaccurate in any case.

This illustration shows a 12-pdr rocket ready on its frame for a high angle shot. Captain Dansey, the 2nd Captain of this Troop at Waterloo, later wrote: 'We had with the Troop a great awkward lumbering carriage with an apparatus called a Bombarding Frame for heavy rockets … I recollect seeing it with its great long frame cocked up in the air, at an angle of about 45 degrees, firing away… I am sure the NCO in charge of it did bring the carriage into action quite of his own accord…'.

There were a great variety of projectiles that could be propelled by a rocket. The light rockets (6, 9, 12 and 18lbs) came in 3 sections – charge, projectile and stabilizing stick. All exploding rockets (they could fire round shot) had external paper fuses, which were ignited by the propellant flash, the fuse being cut to the correct length before loading. This fuse was also connected to the bursting charge by a quick match held in a tube fixed to the outside of the rocket.

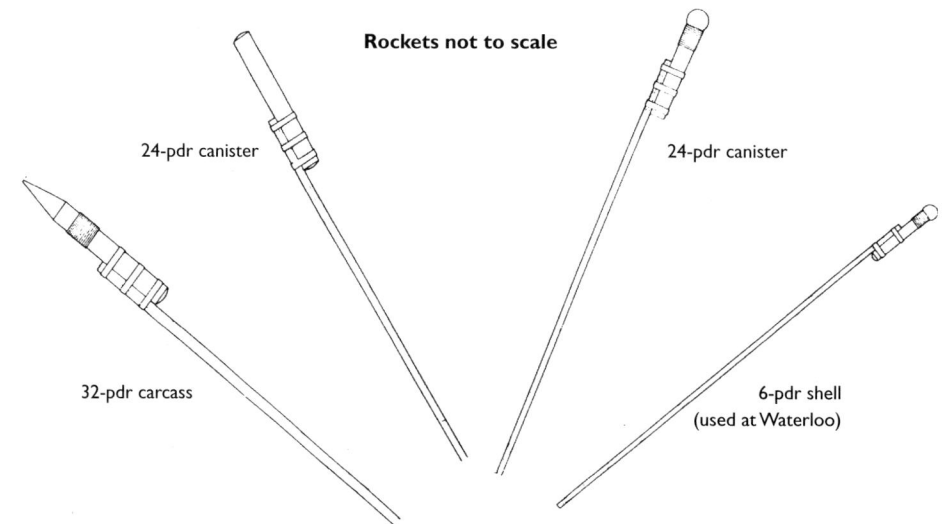

Rockets not to scale

24-pdr canister

24-pdr canister

32-pdr carcass

6-pdr shell
(used at Waterloo)

The 2nd Rocket Troop

This troop, as was customary at the time in the RHA, was called 'Captain Whinyates' Troop'. At Waterloo it fired many more projectiles from its guns than it launched rockets. The figures are – round shot 309, spherical case 236, canister 15, but only 52 rockets. This makes an average of 112 rounds from each of the 6-pounders that made up the bulk of the troop. One big advantage with rockets was that they did not need teams of horses to pull them around, limbers were unnecessary, wagons were virtually superfluous, except for heavy rockets for bombarding towns or fortifications from long range. One man could fire off light rockets on the battlefield far more quickly than five gunners could fire a 6-pounder. He only had to lean the stick on a slope, place it on the ground or push it in a bush or hedge, light the fuse and stand clear. Although these rocket heads were heavier and the sticks longer, it posed no more problems than launching a modern rocket on bonfire night.

The troop consisted of five 6-pounders, the whole divided into thirteen sections, each carrying eight 6-pound rockets. Captain Dansey RHA, the second captain, later recalled that with the troop there was also a:

> … great awkward lumbering carriage, with an apparatus called a Bombarding Frame for heavy rockets; my impression is that at the time of our advance with the Guns, this carriage did not go to the front with us, but I recollect our seeing it, with its great long frame cocked up in the air, at an angle of about 45 degs., firing away.

Dansey goes on to say that the NCO in charge was firing on his own initiative and that Whinyates ordered him to stop. As Whinyates himself makes no mention of this spectacular event (nor does any one else), there must be some doubt as to the reliability of Dansey's memory after nearly thirty years. Whinyates has described how the personnel of the troop carried the rockets:

> Each mounted man carries a fasces [bundle] of three or four rocket sticks in a bucket in a similar manner to the mode lances and Dragoon carbines are carried. These sticks were carried on the right side of the horse. Besides these the centre of the Threes carried a small trough on his saddlebag, in which the rocket was laid when fired, and every man in the Rocket Sections carried rockets in his holsters.

The rockets looked like and worked on much the same principle as modern firework rockets. As with shells, it was the burning time of the fuse that dictated the range. They could be fired at an angle from a tripod, along a bank or stuck in a hedge for longer range, or along the ground against closer targets. Captain Whinyates, commanding the Rocket Troop at Waterloo, gives an interesting, if brief account of when they fired along the ground:

> When halted and brought into action, they dismounted from their horse to fire ground rockets, that is rockets not laid at angles of elevation, but rockets that ricocheted along the ground. There were crops of high standing grain in front of the Rocket Sections when the men dismounted, which screened all objects in front, and the rockets were fired through them in the direction of the Enemy's troops…

This is one of the few references as to what was a common problem, particularly in the earlier stages of the battle – how the tall crops hindered vision for the man on his feet.

AMMUNITION SUPPLY AND EXPENDITURE

All three armies at Waterloo had similar systems of carrying and replenishing ammunition on the battlefield. It was based on a proportion of projectiles being with the gun at all times, carried either in a box on the piece (called the axle box or trail chest) or in boxes on the limber, or both. When the gun came into action these boxes were kept beside the piece while the gun teams (horses) with the limbers were taken about 30 metres to the rear, preferably under cover. About 50 metres behind the gun teams and limbers would be the first line of ammunition wagons (caissons) with their teams, at least one for each gun. Another 50 metres further back might be a second line of ammunition wagons; a hundred metres back again the administrative wagons for the battery such as those carrying spare wheels, a forge, spare carriage, tools or infantry ammunition. There were variations with different nationalities (the French had more caissons for howitzers

as they had two per battery and, as with most things, the Imperial Guard had more wagons per gun than the line artillery).

Each had a system designed to bring the ammunition forward to those who needed it. Re-supply was from the rear (2nd line cchclon) to the front – if a detachment had to go looking for ammunition something had gone wrong. It was usual practice for just one wagon to go forward to replenish the battery at a time as this lessened the risk of wagons being damaged or horses killed. An empty wagon would be replaced from the second line and would go to the main park at the rear to stock up again. There does not appear to be any evidence to suggest that many artillery batteries in any army at Waterloo actually ran out of ammunition. However, Major Lloyd of the British Foot Artillery and Captain Mercer of the British RHA were getting anxious at one stage, and the British batteries that had been in the front line all day may have been perilously close. At the start of the battle it is safe to say that most guns or howitzers had around 130–150 projectiles of various types at the battery position or close behind in the wagons. Many had much more than this, particularly the Imperial Guard. As most artillery were guns, more stocks of round shot (about 70–80 per cent) than of other projectiles were held. However, the loads were carefully calculated so that shell, canister and, for the British, spherical case were sufficient even for such an intense battle as Waterloo, where artillery was constantly in action throughout the engagement. Shortages were most likely to occur due to the destruction of wagons, the killing of horses or detachments. Captain Duncan in his *History of the Royal Artillery 1872* states that a number of guns stopped firing, not from lack of ammunition, but 'from incessant firing' – the problem of overheating.

Few attempts have been made to calculate ammunition expenditure during the battle, one of the exceptions provided by Duncan, who states that the British artillery expended 10,400 rounds. There were seventy-seven British pieces at Waterloo, so the average expenditure was 135 per gun or howitzer – comfortably within the amount normally available in the field. Firing at a

--- **The Corps of Royal Artillery Drivers** ---

Until 1793 guns and wagon teams for the movement of artillery were in the hands of hired civilians. This was a wretched arrangement that frequently saw drivers abandoning their animals as soon as they heard the first bang on the battlefield. In that year the Corps of Royal Artillery Drivers was formed. This new organization came under the Master General of Ordnance. It was a military organization under its own officers and was, supposedly, a disciplined body. However, it quickly developed a reputation as 'a nest of infamy', as one officer described it in the Peninsula. There was a lot of drunkenness, absence and outrage, which the Corps' junior officers, who were often commissioned without purchase from artillery NCOs, frequently failed to curb.

The Corps was organized into troops (eleven in 1810, but only four in June 1815), each under a captain commissary. Each troop was split into five sections under lieutenants' commissary and consisted of ninety drivers supported by a number of craftsmen such as smiths, farriers, cartwrights, wheel makers and harness makers. Since the number of drivers was well in excess of the number required by a battery, the drivers were always split up, seldom serving under their own officers who remained responsible for their welfare and administration. Discipline and morale suffered.

At Waterloo about half of the 5,300 artillerymen in Wellington's army were drivers belonging to this Corps or to similar national organizations within the different contingents. There were ten Corps officers present at the battle, none of whom were killed or injured – one captain-commissary (William Humphreys), eight first lieutenant-commissaries, one of whom was the Corps adjutant (Jordan) and one second lieutenant-commissary. At Waterloo they served well, with their teams and wagons very much under fire, despite the reverse slope of the Duke's position. Their casualties were about equal to those of the gunners.

---

rate of about two shots a minute means that the average British battery was actually in action firing for only sixty-seven minutes (possibly less) during a battle lasting eight hours. As with most battles, short periods of extremely intense activity were interspersed with much longer periods when the artillery were not engaged or firing was sporadic. Batteries that were in the front at the outset fired far longer than those initially in reserve or on the flanks.

Using the above figures as a guide for the rest of Wellington's artillery, together with Napoleon's and Blücher's, a rough approximation of the total ammunition expenditure would be as shown below:

• Wellington – The seventy-seven British pieces were, with the exception of Gardiner's Troop, heavily engaged and averaged 135 rounds – total 10,400. Some of the remaining eighty weapons, such as those of the KGL, were fully committed in the front line, others were not. A reasonable average for them would be eighty rounds per piece – total 6,400.
• Napoleon – Like the Duke, a mixture of at least eighty guns and howitzers (in the 'Grand Battery') that were heavily engaged over a prolonged period, others perhaps less so or for shorter periods. Assuming these eighty weapons fired the same average number of shots as the British front line artillery, this would total 10,800. The remaining 166 pieces might have averaged sixty rounds (there is little hard evidence that the Guard's 12-pounders fired at all) – total 9,960.
• Blücher – His 134 pieces did not start arriving until late afternoon, some did not appear until the action was almost at an end. A generous estimate of the average Prussian gun's ammunition consumption might be thirty-five rounds – total 4,700.

The above gives an overall total of over 42,000 (42,260) artillery rounds of all types (excluding rockets) fired at Waterloo – an average of seventy-eight rounds per gun/howitzer, or the equivalent of about 40–45 minutes continuous action by all pieces. This seems a reasonable estimate considering there were long periods when a proportion of the guns did not, or could not, fire. For the Anglo-Allied artillery, examples of this were the reserve batteries until committed; after d'Erlon's attack there was little in the way of targets for the guns east of the Brussels–Genappe road to fire at as Wellington had forbidden counter-battery fire; and while the enemy cavalry swarmed round the infantry squares. For the French, the reserve batteries of the Guard; VI Corps guns had little to do until the Prussians arrived; during the massed cavalry attacks.

CASUALTIES CAUSED BY ARTILLERY

Although it is impossible to know for certain, it seems likely that, overall, artillery fire was the single most effective means (certainly for the French) of inflicting casualties at Waterloo. The relevant factors are:

• The Anglo-Allied Army lost approximately 17,000 during the battle, or 23 per cent of the troops engaged. The eighty guns and howitzers of the 'Grand Battery' were in action for much of the battle – they only temporarily ceased firing after the Union Brigade charge, and were subjected to negligible counter-battery fire. There were many veterans who testified that it was the French guns they feared most of all. The massed French cavalry attacks were regarded by some as a welcome relief from the gunfire. During these assaults the horsemen never broke into any square, were rarely able to cross sword or lance with bayonet, and themselves inflicted negligible casualties with pistol or carbine. Wellington's cavalry was almost never exposed to musket fire until the last few minutes of the battle. His infantry was only subjected to intense or prolonged musket fire (and then only a small proportion of it) during the fighting at Hougoumont, La Haie Sainte and from the French skirmishers generally. If these factors are accepted, then it is reasonable to assume that up to two-thirds of the Duke's losses may have been from artillery fire, totalling around 11,000 casualties.
• The French casualties are particularly difficult to estimate as no records of actual battlefield losses were (not surprisingly) ever kept. However, the approximate figure of 30,000 (excluding prisoners) was suggested above (see box p. 73) which represents almost 40 per cent of those engaged. D'Erlon's corps attack suffered mainly from the Allies' guns on the ridge as his divisions approached. The Anglo-Allied infantry could not be seen and only fired as the French came over the crest. A high proportion

(possibly half) of the French cavalry losses during the afternoon were from artillery fire, a lot of it canister at close range. At the end the Imperial Guard's assault was staggered by gunfire before being finished off with musket ball and bayonet. On the other hand, a high proportion of Reille's losses, sustained in his endless efforts to take Hougoumont, would have been from musket fire, as would also be the case during the struggle to capture La Haie Sainte. Again, the bitter infantry fighting in the streets of Plancenoit resulted in losses from bullet and bayonet rather than shot or shell. On balance, the probability is that the French casualties from gunfire were proportionately less than the Anglo-Allied. A figure of about 45 per cent – 14,000 losses – seems a fair estimate.

• The Prussians lost 7000 men, a total of 14 per cent of the troops actually engaged. In view of the intensity of the infantry fighting at close quarters in Plancenoit that absorbed most of IV Corps in the evening, it is likely that artillery fire inflicted a lower percentage of casualties than was the case with the French. Probably not more than a third of the Prussians fell to gunfire – around 2,300.

Some interesting statistics emerge from the above tentative analysis. The Anglo-Allied and Prussian artillery together fired some 21,500 rounds and inflicted approximately 14,000 casualties – one casualty for every one-and-a-half rounds fired. The French fired almost the same number (20,760) and caused losses of around 13,300 – also one-and-a-half shots for each casualty. Overall, at Waterloo each gun or howitzer fired an average of seventy-eight shots. At one-and-a-half rounds for every hit, this would mean artillery inflicted just under 28,000 casualties – which coincides with the calculations above. Contemporary and modern analysis has concluded that for every one-and-a-half artillery rounds fired on Napoleonic battlefields, about one casualty would result. Waterloo would seem to bear this out.

Factors Affecting Artillery Usage and Effectiveness

Artillery batteries were probably the most effective units used at Waterloo in terms of casualties inflicted. An average battery with about 175–200 men fired some 470–625 projectiles (depending on whether it had six or eight pieces) and, at the rate of one and a half shots for one hit, could claim to have killed or wounded between 300–400 of the enemy. The large number of pieces deployed (537), together with the huge number of potential targets (almost 200,000 men) crammed onto a small battlefield, made it easier for a shot or shell to find its target. However, it is important to make the point that for the first three or four hours French artillery fire in particular was negated by the fact that their enemy was behind a crest line. Additionally, the soggy ground had yet to dry sufficiently to allow cannonballs to bounce, or prevent some shells from burying themselves. The more important factors affecting artillery fire at Waterloo are discussed below.

TYPES OF FIRE (Diagram below)
Direct fire
With direct fire the gunner had to see what he was firing at. The shot went 'directly' from the gun in a straight line to the target. All guns (as distinct from howitzers) were basically flat trajectory weapons and therefore relied on direct fire. Direct fire ammunition was the round shot – the most commonly used round on the battlefield at that time. Although a gun's barrel could be elevated (by using the elevating screw), doing so by more than three or four degrees negated the dismembering effect of a flat trajectory round shot where the solid iron ball skimmed the ground at less than a man's height and faster than the speed of sound.

Ricochet fire
This was a type of direct fire used mostly by guns firing round shot or canister. Howitzers could also use it with shells, but at close range canister was the more deadly. The gunner aimed to hit the ground just in

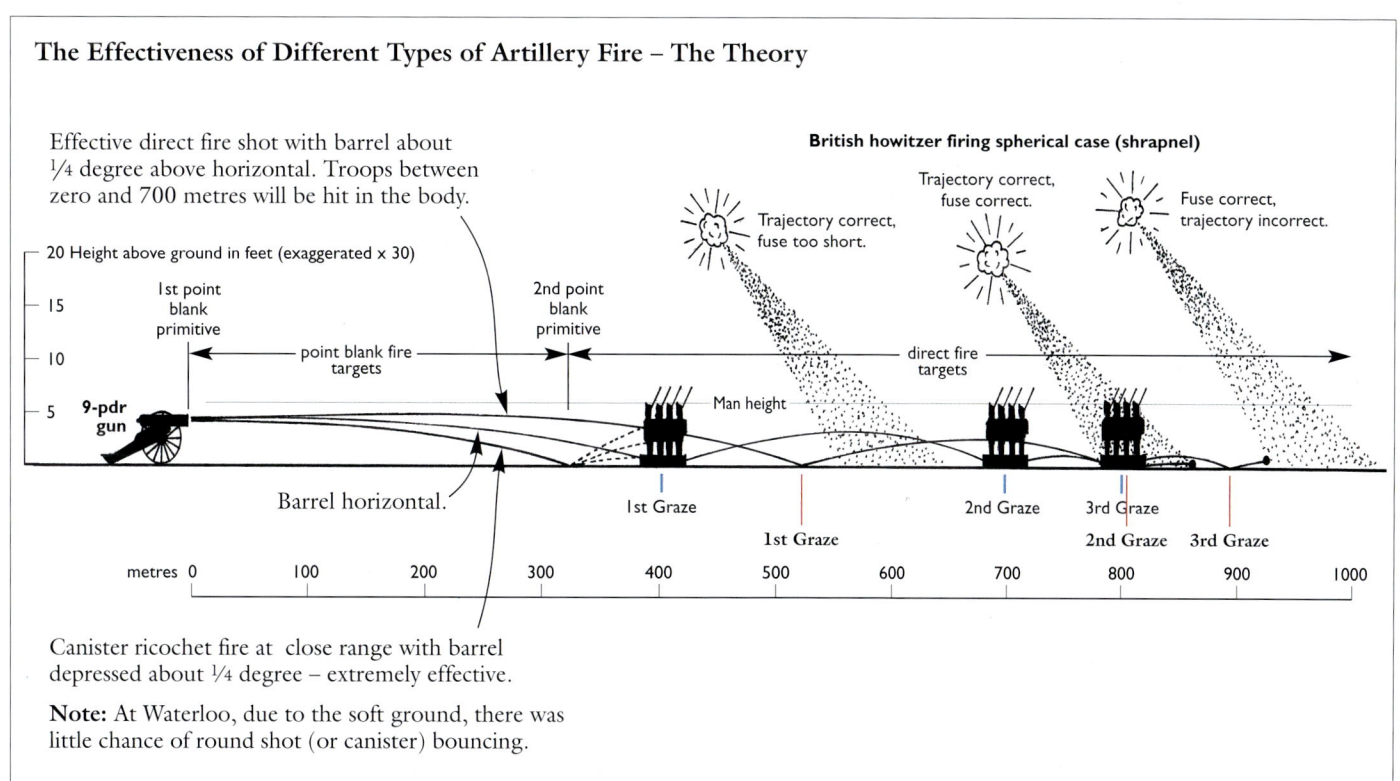

The Effectiveness of Different Types of Artillery Fire – The Theory

Effective direct fire shot with barrel about ¼ degree above horizontal. Troops between zero and 700 metres will be hit in the body.

British howitzer firing spherical case (shrapnel)

Trajectory correct, fuse too short.
Trajectory correct, fuse correct.
Fuse correct, trajectory incorrect.

20 Height above ground in feet (exaggerated x 30)

1st point blank primitive

2nd point blank primitive

point blank fire targets

direct fire targets

Man height

9-pdr gun

Barrel horizontal.

1st Graze

1st Graze

2nd Graze   3rd Graze

2nd Graze   3rd Graze

metres   0   100   200   300   400   500   600   700   800   900   1000

Canister ricochet fire at close range with barrel depressed about ¼ degree – extremely effective.

Note: At Waterloo, due to the soft ground, there was little chance of round shot (or canister) bouncing.

front of the target so that the ball (or balls) bounced, hitting the enemy at about chest height and continued bouncing another two or three times before rolling to rest. It was designed to maximize the bowling alley effect. It was best used on dry, level ground – the gunner hoping for several bounces, as with a flat stone skimmed across the surface of a pond. These conditions did not exist at Waterloo.

If a 9-pounder gun fired with the barrel horizontal, the ball would strike the ground (the technical term was 'first graze') at just under 400 metres. The next bounce would be at around 700 metres, with the third another 100 metres further on – thereafter it was probably rolling, but still capable of injuring anybody who got in its way. Out to the second bounce the ball would be slightly less than 5 feet from the ground. After that it was knees and feet that were most vulnerable. A fractional elevation of the barrel by a quarter of a degree was enough to extend the distance of the 'first graze' by up to 150 metres. Further elevation and the shot would be travelling above a man's height, which therefore negated much of the lethality of the shot. When ricochet firing was used it was more effective if the barrel was depressed slightly, the gun aimed in front of the target so that all 'grazes' occurred within 600–700 metres.

Point blank fire

The expression to fire at 'point blank' range is well known and in common use today. Its modern usage means to shoot at extremely close range, from only a few feet (or even inches) from the target – a miss being impossible. There was a lot of point blank fire at Waterloo, but in 1815 it was a technical term used by the artillery. Although the British and French had slightly different ways of calculating it, the principles were the same.

If a gun was fired with the barrel horizontal to the ground, the trajectory of the round shot was a parabola. When the ball left the barrel it was forced very slightly above the line of sight (this being a straight line from the muzzle to the target). It occurred just as the round shot left the barrel and was called the 'first point blank primitive'. The 'second point blank primitive' was the point at which gravity pushed the ball below the line of sight. For a 6-pounder this

would happen at about 350 metres. For artillerymen, point blank fire meant shooting at any target between the first and second 'point blank primitives' – not quite so close as its modern meaning. With targets beyond this distance it was necessary to increase the elevation of the barrel to obtain the range for a direct hit. This was the gunner's technical differentiation between 'point blank' and 'direct' fire. With the former the barrel was simply horizontal, with the latter calculations were needed to get the right range. For much of the time at Waterloo the Anglo-Allied guns were firing point blank or with barrels slightly depressed, whereas those in the French 'Grand Battery' were using direct or indirect fire.

Indirect fire

This was artillery fire at targets out of sight of the gunners. Modern artillery fire is almost entirely indirect, with the target often several kilometres away over the horizon. At Waterloo it was in its infancy and only effectively employed by howitzers firing shells (or with the British spherical case). The high angle fire of the howitzers enabled the 'Grand Battery' to lob shells over the crest of the Mont St Jean ridge to hit the troops sheltering on the reverse slope, or to hurl incendiary shells into Hougoumont. Wellington made good use of Major Bull's Troop of six howitzers to drive back French infantry assaults by raining shells and shrapnel onto Hougoumont Wood.

Guns could theoretically use indirect fire with barrels at high elevation and firing shells, but it was not recommended. If round shot was fired at a high angle, it was a waste of ammunition as either the ball plunged straight into soft ground so that unless a man was standing on that spot it did no damage, or, if the ground was hard, it bounced high over the enemy's heads.

Counter battery fire

As its name implies this type of fire entailed using artillery to fire at, and hopefully destroy or at least neutralize, the enemy's artillery. The general consensus of the time (with a few exceptions) was that artillery was best employed on the battlefield against infantry or cavalry. Only if the opposing guns were exposed and there were no

---

The Effects of the French Artillery Bombardment

Ensign Leeke of the 1/52 Foot, who carried one of the Colours at Waterloo, stated that Peninsula veterans had never experienced such a battering by artillery as they faced that day. The worst was when they formed square on the forward slope north-east of Hougoumont to receive the French cavalry attacks – which came as a welcome relief from the gunfire. It was a large battalion and formed two squares, initially almost concealed in the tall rye that had yet to be trampled down. The French guns were about 700–800 metres to the south of the squares. The British batteries were behind the squares and firing over them – at one stage faulty fusing of shrapnel shells caused some to burst over the 52nd which inflicted casualties – it was stopped when an officer dashed back to the guns to inform them what was happening. This is what young Leeke had to say:

> The standing to be cannonaded, and having nothing else to do, is about the most unpleasant thing that can happen to soldiers in an engagement. I frequently tried to follow with my eye, the course of the balls from our own guns, which were firing over us. It is much more easy to see a round shot passing away from you over your head, than to catch sight of one coming through the air towards you, though this also occurs

occasionally … I distinctly saw the French artilleryman go through the whole process of sponging out one of his guns and reloading it; I could see that it was pointed at our square, and when it was discharged I caught sight of the ball, which appeared to be in a direct line for me. I thought, Shall I move? No! I gathered myself up, and stood firm with the Colour in my right hand [he commented that both Regimental Colours had been shot up badly during the Peninsular War, and at Waterloo were 'little more than bare poles']. I do not know exactly the rapidity with which cannon balls fly, but I think that two seconds elapsed from the time I saw this shot leave the gun until it struck the front face of the square. It did not strike the four men in rear of whom I was standing, but the poor fellows on their right. It was fired at some elevation, and struck the front man about the knees, and coming to the ground under the feet of the rear man of the four, whom it most severely wounded, it rose and, passing within an inch or two of the colour pole, went over the rear face of the square without doing further injury. The two men in the first and second rank fell out outward, I fear they did not survive long; the two others fell within the square.

Captain Mercer Defies the Duke's Order Forbidding Counter-battery Fire

While waiting in reserve on a ridge behind Wellington's right flank (Map 16), Mercer was foolishly tempted into firing at Piré's horse battery, thus flouting the Duke's specific orders. He opened up at a target some 700 metres away. Later, he described what happened:

> About this time [probably between 2.00 p.m. and 3.00 p.m.], being impatient of standing idle, and annoyed by the batteries on the Nivelles road [west of Hougoumont], I ventured to commit a folly, for which I should have paid dearly had our Duke chanced to be in our part of the field. I ventured to disobey orders, and open a slow deliberate fire at the battery, thinking with my 9-pounders soon to silence his 4-pounders [they were 6-pounders]. My astonishment was great, however, when our very first gun was responded to by at least half-a-dozen gentlemen of very superior calibre whose presence I had not even suspected, and whose superiority we immediately recognised by their rushing noise and long reach, for they flew far beyond us. I instantly saw my folly, and ceased firing, and

> they did the same – the 4-pounders [6-pounders] alone continuing the cannonade ... The first man of my troop touched was by one of these confounded long shot [Gunner Hunt]. I shall never forget the scream the poor fellow gave when it struck. It was one of the last they fired, and shattered his left arm to pieces as he stood between the waggons. That scream went to my very soul, for I accused myself of having caused his misfortune.

It is puzzling to know which these heavy French guns could have been. Piré, on the extreme French left, deployed his own 6-pounders across the Nivelles road and advanced them after the start of the battle. It was fire from them that initially annoyed Mercer. According to him, his firing prompted a response from much heavier guns firing round shot. The only heavier pieces were the 12-pounders that were Reille's Corps reserve – but at that time they were over 2000 metres to the east forming part of the 'Grand Battery'. Perhaps Mercer was mistaken as to their calibre – we shall never know.

other available targets would it be deemed worthwhile to indulge in counter-battery fire. Part of the problem was that it required pinpoint accuracy, which was only possible if the range was known precisely; otherwise a lot of ammunition was going to be wasted and would not be available for more pressing, vulnerable, softer targets. Artillery officers were trained to calculate the range by watching for the muzzle flash and counting the number of seconds between it and the sound of the firing. This was then multiplied by 369 yards (340 metres) to give the range. If counter-battery fire was sanctioned, it was usually more effective if all the guns in the firing battery concentrated on one enemy piece at a time, destroying it and moving on to the next.

Wellington expressly forbade counter-battery fire at Waterloo. Captain Mercer disobeyed these instructions briefly when he was goaded by gunfire from a French horse artillery battery west of Hougoumont. There were other examples later in the battle when some French guns came close to the Allies' position. Because of this order, the French 'Grand Battery' got off lightly on their ridge only 600 metres from the Duke's line west of the Brussels–Genappe road. It was used by these French guns against the Anglo-Allied artillery on the forward slope of the ridge, particularly at the outset, as few other worthwhile targets were visible.

TERRAIN

• All the gun batteries had to be out in the open in order to fire. With direct fire weapons this was inevitable. Wellington had to position his artillery on the forward slope of the ridge, whereas he could attempt to shelter his infantry and cavalry on the reverse slope – at least until the attackers were close. Similarly, the French 'Grand Battery' was totally exposed along a low ridge that ran for over 1000 metres within 600 metres of the eastern half of the Anglo-Allied position.

• The Duke's use of a reverse slope position for virtually his entire army (except his guns) from the outset undoubtedly saved many lives. Most of the Anglo-Allied artillery teams, limbers and ammunition wagons were in dead ground to the French gunners so they could only see the actual guns for much of the battle. This factor reduced the effectiveness of the 'Grand Battery's' fire, as a

high proportion of round shot buried itself in the forward slope or flew over the heads of the troops behind the ridge. It was fortunate for the French that they had two howitzers to a battery rather than one, otherwise the effectiveness of their preparatory bombardment would have been even less lethal than it was.

• The softness of the soil at Waterloo after the heavy rain cut the effectiveness of round shot in particular. Had the ground been hard and dry, ricochet shots would have been possible and far more deadly. As it was, the waterlogged ground made them something of a rarity. Coupled with the slopes and undulations, which necessitated the French firing upwards and the Allies downwards, many round shot caused no casualties, merely ploughing into the ground without grazing. The only victims would be soldiers unlucky enough to be standing in the ball's path before it hit the ground.

• The tall standing crops, although they did not cover the entire field, restricted the vision of many gunners, especially the French. This factor was more serious at the outset of the battle before large areas had been flattened, which would have been the case by around 4.30 p.m. after the French cavalry attacks got underway. With thick wheat or rye standing over 5 feet in height, double the height of the present-day varieties, no crouching gunner could aim his piece as the stalks were higher than the barrel of the gun.

VISIBILITY

Restrictions on visibility produced by the undulations of the ground and crops have already been touched on under the heading of 'Terrain', but the greatest obscurity was caused by smoke. This was always a feature of battlefields before the introduction of smokeless powder, and affected not just gunners but every man on the field. A vast amount of smoke was created at Waterloo, as the firing of all weapons was intense, continuous and confined to a small area. If the infantry, who rarely opened fire above 100 metres, could not see much of their target, they had only to level their muskets into the smoke and some of their balls would find their mark. This was not the case with artillery. Firing at much longer ranges required the NCO who aimed the piece to see the target if ammunition was not to be wasted, or if friendly troops

The Effectiveness of French Artillery Fire

If anyone doubts the lethality or horror that French gunfire invoked then they should read the accounts of the men who saw it, heard it, felt it and feared it. Lieutenant Hugh Wray of the 1/40 Foot, a battalion that did not come forward to the front (near the 'Elm Tree' crossroads) until mid-afternoon states:

> We had three companies almost shot to pieces, one shot killed and wounded twenty-five of the 4th Company, another of the same kind killed poor Fisher, my captain and eighteen of our company … another took the 8th [Company] and killed or wounded twenty-three … At the same time poor Fisher was hit I was speaking to him and I got all his brains [over me as] his head was blown to atoms.

> Captain Fisher's decapitation brought forth at least one piece of battlefield humour from a soldier who had obviously been no stranger to his company commander's anger in the past. He exclaimed, 'There goes my best friend!' Wray heard this and, not knowing the sarcasm behind the comment, stepped forward

to take the captain's place saying, 'I will be as good a friend to you.' This produced a few grim smiles from those nearby.

The British battalion that suffered the most at Waterloo, primarily from artillery fire, was the 1/27 Foot (Inniskilling). As part of Lambert's Brigade, this battalion, like the 40th Foot, did not reach the front until about 3.30 p.m. and so had missed half the battle. It more than made up for this in the next four hours. Some 700 all ranks marched up to take position in the north-east angle of the crossroads. From this position they never moved other than to change from column to square and back again countless times. There they received the most vicious pounding from French guns (not to mention musketry fire from skirmishers) of any unit in the army. The results were appalling. Of the nineteen officers present two were killed and fourteen wounded – one (Lieutenant George Macdonald) who survived three wounds was still doddering around as an ancient general in 1871. Soldier casualties amounted to 463. Of these, 103 were killed and 360 wounded. In total this battalion suffered 479 casualties, or 68 per cent of its strength.

were in front. After every shot the gun had to be hauled forward again and realigned with dense clouds of smoke drifting over the position. Waiting for the smoke to thin was one of the constraints on maintaining a reasonable rate of fire.

No accounts of Waterloo give an indication of the strength or direction of the wind that day. There must have been some breeze as the rain clouds and thunderstorms moved away. In June the prevailing wind is from the west. It is reasonably likely, therefore, that the smoke at Waterloo was blown from west to east. If this were the case, visibility would be generally better in the western half of the battlefield. East of the Brussels–Genappe road one would expect the 'Grand Battery' gunners, especially those on the right of the line, to be cursing the smoke with justifiable vehemence.

THE EFFECTIVENESS OF DIFFERING CALIBRE/TYPE OF ARTILLERY PIECE

It is often assumed that the bigger the gun the better, that in a battle if one side had more 12-pounders or 9-pounders than the other, then those guns are going to give that force the edge as far as artillery was concerned. In other words, a detachment firing a 6-pounder, other things being equal, is going to do less damage to the enemy than one firing a large piece. This assumption is only true if two other factors apply. Firstly, if range is a major consideration, since the larger guns fired further with greater accuracy. Secondly, if the guns were firing at 'hard' targets that demanded the maximum 'smashing' effect. Neither of these factors were much in evidence at Waterloo.

Waterloo was a small battlefield. Over 80 per cent of artillery firing was conducted at ranges of 700 metres or less – in many cases much less. The French 'Grand Battery' was only 600–800 metres from much of Wellington's line. The Duke's guns east of the Brussels–Genappe road could not fire effectively at d'Erlon's divisions until they came into view after passing through the 'Grand Battery'. It was a similar story west of the road, where much of the artillery fire against the massed French cavalry assaults was at point blank range with canister as well as round shot. Within those ranges all guns and howitzers were equally effective against soft targets. A 6-pounder cannon ball ripping

through an infantry or cavalry unit is not going to kill or maim less than a ball with a one-inch greater diameter coming from a 12-pounder. With canister there were more balls in each 12-pounder shot than in that of a 6-pounder. However, this was balanced by the fact that the smaller gun could fire three times while its heavier cousin struggled to manage two.

All guns were equally accurate out to 700 metres. At Waterloo only the French, more especially at the beginning, directed some of their fire against artillery (they could not see many alternatives). Also, surprisingly little effort was made by the French, apart from setting some buildings at Hougoumont on fire with howitzers, to smash gates or walls with gunfire either there, or at La Haie Sainte. These were the only 'hard' targets readily available.

Because of the nature of the battle, the French use of heavier 12-pounders did not give them an edge in terms of effectiveness against the targets engaged. This point is seldom made. In a comparatively close range battle like Waterloo, where virtually all targets are made of flesh and blood, it is not the weight of shot that makes a difference but the number of pieces firing, the rate of fire and the skill of the gunners.

THE EFFECTIVENESS OF THE ROUNDS AT THE TARGET

Despite the problems of visibility, despite the use of reverse slopes, despite the mounting casualties of men and horses, despite the increasing exhaustion of the gunners, artillery was still the most effective killer at Waterloo. How was it able to inflict approximately one and a half casualties for every shot fired? The probable answer lies in a combination of factors.

• The large number of guns deployed (537, or one gun to every 370 men). The considerable number of rounds fired – about 42,000 – meant that throughout the eight hours of fighting some eighty-eight guns fired every minute or, put another way, a shot was landing somewhere every one and a half seconds – and killing or injuring one and a half men!

• Many of the targets, particularly in the Anglo-Allied and French armies, were vulnerable to artillery fire because they formed in close formations. The French attacked over long distances, usually in dense columns or even squares (the Imperial Guard's final assault). For two hours in the afternoon 8000 horsemen ebbed and flowed into the 1000-metre funnel between Hougoumont and La Haie Sainte, providing Wellington's gunners with a target they could not miss. The Duke's orders ensured that artillery ammunition was reserved for soft infantry or cavalry targets. The majority of Wellington's troops were stationary for most of the time, repeatedly changing from battalion or regimental column to square and back again, on much the same patch of ground.

• The French made use of their additional howitzers to lob shells onto the reverse slope of Mont St Jean ridge. The ranges at which artillery was used were relatively short, so all guns could be put to good use. There was considerable use made of canister – an excel-lent killer – at close ranges, particularly against the French attacks. The use of spherical case (shrapnel) by a large proportion of Wellington's gunners proved its worth.

• When an artillery round, be it round shot or shell, hit a soft tar-get, it made a bloody mess. One musket ball fired at a 100-metre range or less, and hitting its target, might knock over one man or one horse. One round shot might bowl over three, four, ten, or sometimes many more, decapitating, tearing off limbs or even cut-ting a man in two. A bursting shell or spherical case would shower iron shards and balls at troops nearby, again with a good chance of a number striking home. As with musket shots, many artillery rounds missed, but those that hit, or narrowly missed, wreaked a fearful toll.

ANGLO-ALLIED ARTILLERY (Maps 16 & 17, pp. 274 & 275)

General – Composition and Deployment

Wellington's artillery played, like the rest of the army, a largely defensive role at Waterloo. It did, however, make a major contri-bution to the eventual outcome. There were a total of 157 pieces available to the Duke (another twenty-two were at Hal), divided into twenty-four batteries (plus two guns from a Belgian battery that had lost heavily at Quatre-Bras). Wellington made several cru-cial decisions (two of which were controversial) regarding the overall deployment and use of his artillery. These were:

• The great majority of horse artillery batteries were taken from their normal cavalry formations and, during the battle, put in the front line in a static role ('batteries of position') alongside foot artillery batteries. Initially, six horse batteries were in the front line along with six foot batteries (see Section 10 'Myths and Controversies').

• There was to be no counter-battery fire by Anglo-Allied artillery. Wellington wanted to conserve ammunition to defeat infantry and cavalry attacks. Destroying enemy guns took a long time and required a lot of accurate firing – and even if successful it was not necessarily a battle winning tactic.

• To concentrate his guns and howitzers on his right, that is on and behind the 1,500 metres of ridgeline between the Brussels–Genappe and Brussels–Nivelles roads. Originally, sixteen batteries were posi-tioned either just forward of this part of the ridge or held in reserve behind or to the right flank. By 4.30 p.m. three more (Bull, Rogers and Sinclair) had been moved from the east to the west of the Brussels–Genappe road that split his position in half. This left only thirty-three guns and howitzers (out of the 157) east of the road to cover 2000 metres of front.

• The detachments of batteries facing close attack were to aban-don their pieces and seek shelter in infantry squares rather than remain with, or attempt to withdraw, their guns. This was contrary to all current artillery teaching and tactics (see Section 10 'Myths and Controversies'). Not all batteries or individuals complied, some remaining to man their guns or take refuge under them.

In terms of manpower serving his artillery, including drivers, Wellington had, in round numbers, slightly over 5000 men. As with other armies, his artillery was divided into horse and foot. His horse artillery numbered about 2,750 all ranks, the foot 2,450. In terms of ordnance, this was divided into thirteen batteries of horse gunners with eighty-three pieces, and just over eleven foot batteries with seventy-four guns and howitzers. The British Royal Horse Artillery batteries kept their guns in action with an average of 171 men each (the lowest of all nationalities), whereas the overall aver-age strength of an Anglo-Allied battery, including gunners, drivers and those fetching and carrying ammunition, was almost 220. Looked at another way, an average of thirty-three men were avail-able at the start of the battle to keep every gun or howitzer firing.

The Duke deployed 127 guns (sixty-seven 6-pounders and sixty 9-pounders) together with thirty 5.5-inch howitzers – slightly over five guns to every howitzer. By the time the French massed cavalry attacks got underway he had positioned at least seventy-two guns and howitzers along his front line between the two Brussels roads. This meant one piece for every 21 metres of that part of the line.

Neither the Dutch, Belgian or Brunswick artillery had 9-pounders, while only three of the eight RHA batteries had received the 9-pounder in time for Waterloo.

A general comparison of the Anglo-Allied artillery by nation-alities is given in the table below.

Nationality	Batteries	Men	6-pounder	9-pounder	5.5" how.	Total (pieces)
British						
RHA	8	1,368	20	15	12	47
Foot	5	1,095	–	25	5	30
KGL						
Horse	2	450	–	10	2	12
Foot	1	215	–	5	1	6
Dutch						
Horse	2	460	12	–	4	16
Belgian						
Foot	2 (+2)	735	14	–	4	18
Hanoverian						
Foot	2	475	5	5	2	12
Brunswick						
Horse	1	167	8	–	–	8
Foot	1	205	8	–	–	8
Totals	24 +2 guns	5,170	67	60	30	157

Points to note are:

• The British provided the great bulk of the horse gunners – ten batteries, including two KGL batteries, that were part of the British

Wellington's Artillery, Initial Deployment and Subsequent Moves (West)   Map 16

Battery	9-pdr	6-pdr	5.5" how.	Total guns
British				
Royal Horse Artillery (RHA)				
Lt-Col Ross 'A' Troop	5		1	6
Maj. Beane 'D' Troop		5	1	6
Lt-Col Webber-Smith 'F' Troop		5	1	6
Capt. Mercer 'G' Troop	5		1	6
Maj. Ramsey 'H' Troop	5		1	6
Maj. Bull 'I' Troop			6	6
Capt. Whinyates 2nd Rocket Troop		5	Rocket section	5
Totals RHA	15	15	11	41
Royal Foot Artillery (RFA)				
Maj. Lloyd	5		1	6
Maj. Rogers	5		1	6
Capt. Sandham	5		1	6
Capt. Bolton	5		1	6
Capt. Sinclair	5		1	6
Totals RFA	25		5	30
KGL (Horse & Foot)				
Maj. Kuhlmann (Horse)	5		1	6
Maj. Sympher (Horse)	5		1	6
Capt. Cleeves 1st Foot Bty	5		1	6
Totals KGL	15		3	18
Brunswick (Horse & Foot)				
Maj. Moll (Horse)		8		8
Capt. Heinemann (Foot)		8		8
Totals Brunswick		16		16
Dutch/Belgian (Horse)				
Capt. Petter (½ bty)		3	1	4
Capt. Gey van Pittius (½ bty)		3	1	4
Totals Dutch/Belgian		6	2	8
Grand Totals	55	37	21	113

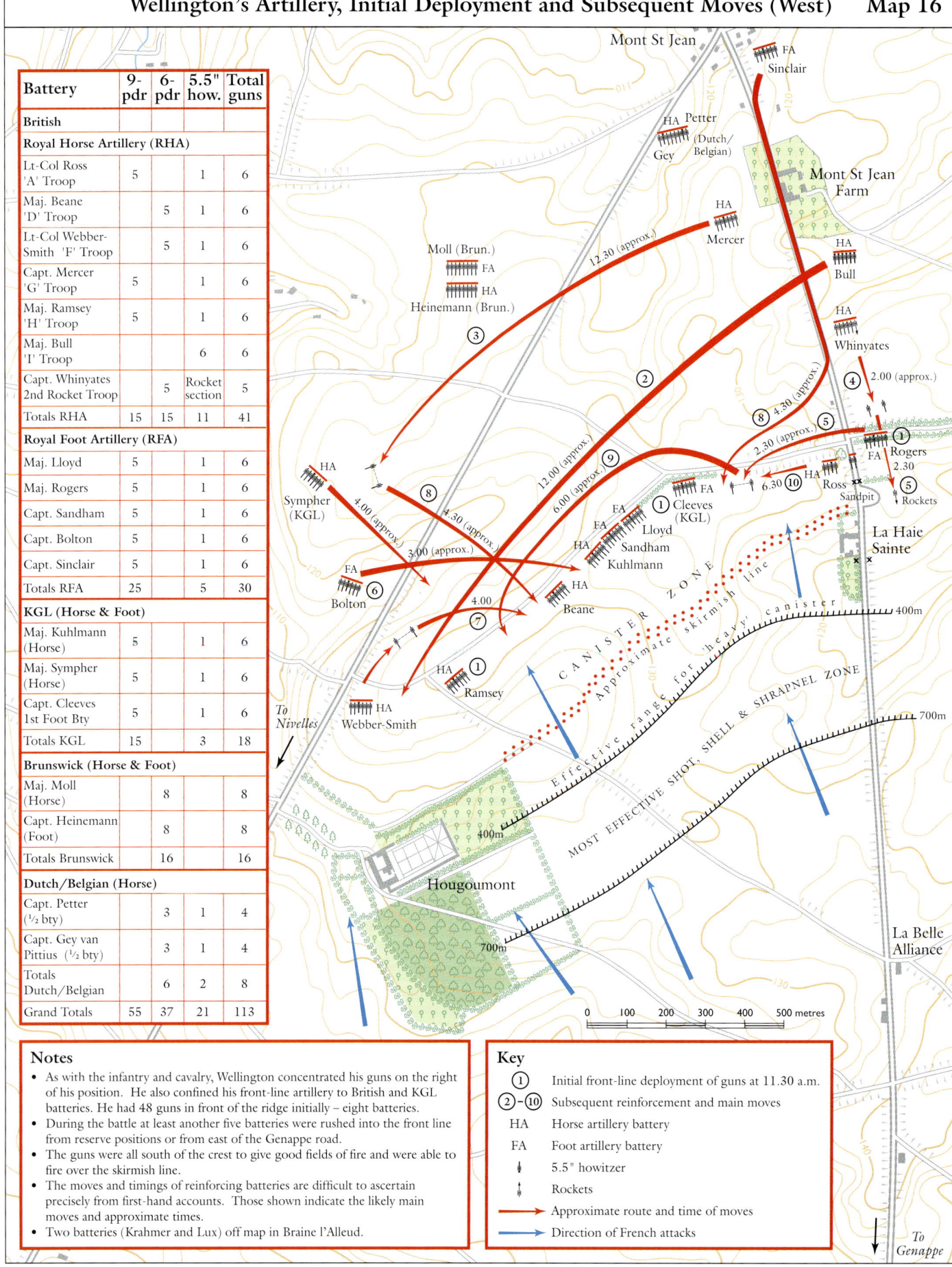

Notes
- As with the infantry and cavalry, Wellington concentrated his guns on the right of his position. He also confined his front-line artillery to British and KGL batteries. He had 48 guns in front of the ridge initially – eight batteries.
- During the battle at least another five batteries were rushed into the front line from reserve positions or from east of the Genappe road.
- The guns were all south of the crest to give good fields of fire and were able to fire over the skirmish line.
- The moves and timings of reinforcing batteries are difficult to ascertain precisely from first-hand accounts. Those shown indicate the likely main moves and approximate times.
- Two batteries (Krahmer and Lux) off map in Braine l'Alleud.

Key
- (1) Initial front-line deployment of guns at 11.30 a.m.
- (2)–(10) Subsequent reinforcement and main moves
- HA Horse artillery battery
- FA Foot artillery battery
- 5.5" howitzer
- Rockets
- Approximate route and time of moves
- Direction of French attacks

Wellington's Artillery, Initial Deployment and Subsequent Moves (East)   Map 17

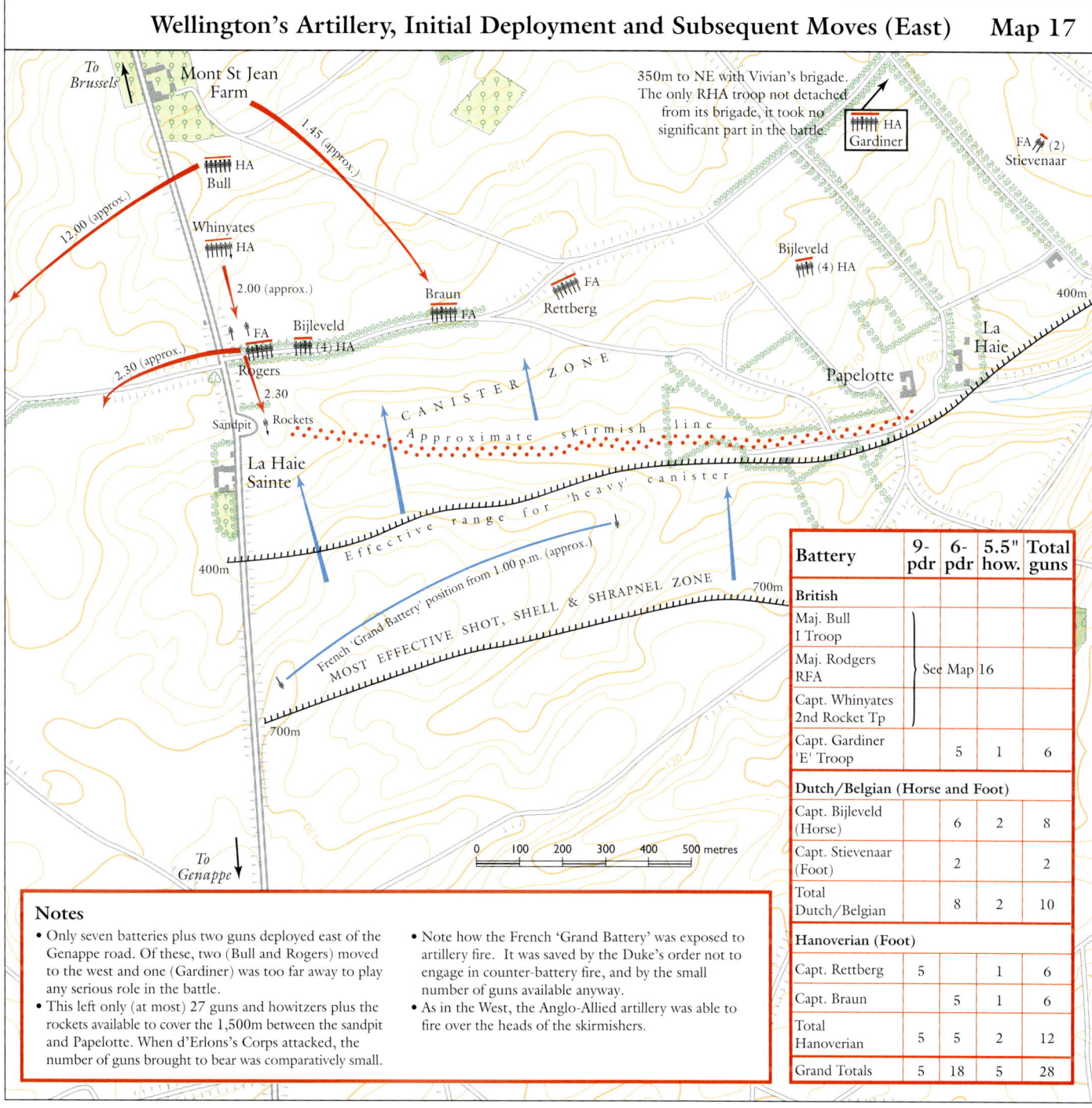

Battery	9-pdr	6-pdr	5.5" how.	Total guns
British				
Maj. Bull I Troop				
Maj. Rodgers RFA	See Map 16			
Capt. Whinyates 2nd Rocket Tp				
Capt. Gardiner 'E' Troop		5	1	6
Dutch/Belgian (Horse and Foot)				
Capt. Bijleveld (Horse)		6	2	8
Capt. Stievenaar (Foot)		2		2
Total Dutch/Belgian		8	2	10
Hanoverian (Foot)				
Capt. Rettberg	5		1	6
Capt. Braun		5	1	6
Total Hanoverian	5	5	2	12
Grand Totals	5	18	5	28

Notes

- Only seven batteries plus two guns deployed east of the Genappe road. Of these, two (Bull and Rogers) moved to the west and one (Gardiner) was too far away to play any serious role in the battle.
- This left only (at most) 27 guns and howitzers plus the rockets available to cover the 1,500m between the sandpit and Papelotte. When d'Erlons's Corps attacked, the number of guns brought to bear was comparatively small.
- Note how the French 'Grand Battery' was exposed to artillery fire. It was saved by the Duke's order not to engage in counter-battery fire, and by the small number of guns available anyway.
- As in the West, the Anglo-Allied artillery was able to fire over the heads of the skirmishers.

Army. Wellington relied on his British and KGL artillery just as he did with his British and German infantry and cavalry. All except for two batteries (Gardiner on the extreme left and Whinyates with his rockets) were used on the right of the line, west of the Brussels–Genappe road.

- The Belgian and Hanoverian only had foot artillery, and the Dutch only horse artillery.
- Stievenart's Belgian battery had lost four guns at Quatre-Bras, so it is uncertain how many men he had with the remaining two at Waterloo.
- The Dutch, Belgian and Brunswick batteries (six) all had eight pieces per battery, unlike all the others with six. The Dutch and Belgian units followed their old French system and had two howitzers per battery.

COMMAND AND CONTROL (Diagram p. 276)

Wellington had wanted to have Lieutenant-Colonels Frazer and Dickson, his two old artillery commanders from the Peninsula, with him at Waterloo. However, although Frazer was available, Dickson, the nominal commander of 'G' Troop RHA, still with the regimental rank of captain, was not. He did join later, but by then the only appointment available was as commander of the Battering Train. Instead, Wellington got Colonel Sir George Wood, an officer he did not know well, as his overall artillery commander.

The Duke had very decided views on how the artillery was to fight the battle. He would often overrule his senior gunner officers. An example of this was his refusing to countenance Lieutenant-Colonel Frazer's plan to group all the 'heavy drags' (as the RHA's

British Artillery Officers – An Exclusive Group

The artillery is the oldest arm in the British Army, dating back to the sixteenth century. The Royal Regiment of Artillery was established in 1716. It was independent of the rest of the army in that it was the responsibility of the Board of Ordnance, under the Master General of Ordnance, rather than the army commander-in-chief. This greatly annoyed Wellington.

Artillery officers were very much educated professionals. Like engineers, they did not, could not, buy their commissions or promotion. To obtain a commission in the Royal Artillery (or Royal Engineers) a young man first had to attend the Royal Military Academy at Woolwich and pass competitive examinations. The subjects taught included mathematics, fortification, gunnery, drawing, mapping, chemistry, musketry and fencing. However, the effects of all this excellent education was often negated by the small size of the corps and the fact that promotion, all promotion, was by seniority rather than merit.

Gunner officers tended to be old for their rank. It took them about three times as long to reach major than infantry or cavalry

officers – even during wartime. Many became frustrated after a fruitless wait for dead men's shoes, retiring still junior officers after years of service. In 'G' Troop RHA at Waterloo its commander, Mercer, was the only one of the five officers to obtain promotion above captain. The problem was acknowledged by the authorities, and a partial remedy – brevet rank – instituted for senior captains for particularly meritorious service. Brevet rank was an army rank, which, although it carried extra pay, was not a regimental rank. This was the reason so many British battery commanders at Waterloo held ranks one or two higher than captain – the established rank for the job. Eight out of the thirteen battery commanders with a regimental rank of captain had brevet ranks in 1815. Bull, Ramsay, Beane, Lloyd and Rogers were majors, while Webber-Smith, Ross and Gardiner were lieutenant-colonels. Five of the ten survivors eventually made it to general or higher (Webber-Smith, Gardiner, Whinyates and Mercer became generals, while Ross became the first Royal Artillery officer to reach the rank of field-marshal).

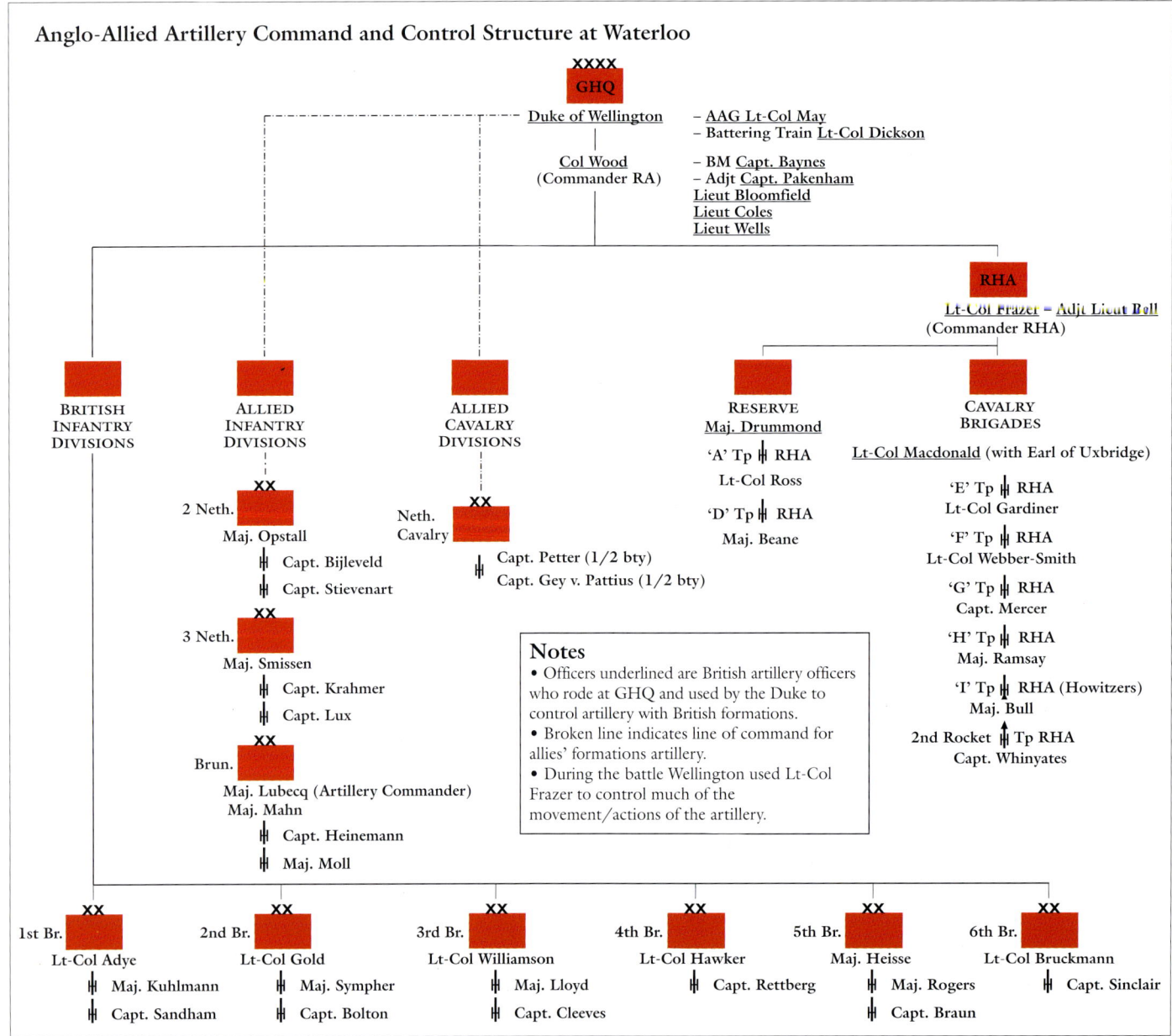

Anglo-Allied Artillery Command and Control Structure at Waterloo

GHQ (XXXX)

Duke of Wellington
- AAG Lt-Col May
- Battering Train Lt-Col Dickson

Col Wood (Commander RA)
- BM Capt. Baynes
- Adjt Capt. Pakenham
Lieut Bloomfield
Lieut Coles
Lieut Wells

RHA
Lt-Col Frazer – Adjt Lieut Bell (Commander RHA)

BRITISH INFANTRY DIVISIONS

ALLIED INFANTRY DIVISIONS
- 2 Neth. — Maj. Opstall
  - Capt. Bijleveld
  - Capt. Stievenart
- 3 Neth. — Maj. Smissen
  - Capt. Krahmer
  - Capt. Lux
- Brun. — Maj. Lubecq (Artillery Commander) / Maj. Mahn
  - Capt. Heinemann
  - Maj. Moll

ALLIED CAVALRY DIVISIONS
- Neth. Cavalry
  - Capt. Petter (1/2 bty)
  - Capt. Gey v. Pattius (1/2 bty)

RESERVE Maj. Drummond
- 'A' Tp RHA — Lt-Col Ross
- 'D' Tp RHA — Maj. Beane

CAVALRY BRIGADES
Lt-Col Macdonald (with Earl of Uxbridge)
- 'E' Tp RHA — Lt-Col Gardiner
- 'F' Tp RHA — Lt-Col Webber-Smith
- 'G' Tp RHA — Capt. Mercer
- 'H' Tp RHA — Maj. Ramsay
- 'I' Tp RHA (Howitzers) — Maj. Bull
- 2nd Rocket Tp RHA — Capt. Whinyates

Notes
- Officers underlined are British artillery officers who rode at GHQ and used by the Duke to control artillery with British formations.
- Broken line indicates line of command for allies' formations artillery.
- During the battle Wellington used Lt-Col Frazer to control much of the movement/actions of the artillery.

- 1st Br. — Lt-Col Adye
  - Maj. Kuhlmann
  - Capt. Sandham
- 2nd Br. — Lt-Col Gold
  - Maj. Sympher
  - Capt. Bolton
- 3rd Br. — Lt-Col Williamson
  - Maj. Lloyd
  - Capt. Cleeves
- 4th Br. — Lt-Col Hawker
  - Capt. Rettberg
- 5th Br. — Maj. Heisse
  - Maj. Rogers
  - Capt. Braun
- 6th Br. — Lt-Col Bruckmann
  - Capt. Sinclair

9-pounder guns were called), plus Bull's six howitzers into a central artillery reserve at the start of the campaign. This would have been the British equivalent of the French 'Grand Battery', consisting of fifteen 9-pounders and nine howitzers. Instead he insisted on their being divided up among the cavalry brigades like the 6-pounders. At Waterloo, however, he reversed his own decision and centralized the RHA batteries.

The decision to strip the British cavalry brigades of their horse artillery and deploy them as batteries of position was made sometime late on 17 June or early on 18 June. Without these seven batteries (discounting Gardiner) he did not have sufficient reliable artillery to cripple the massive attacks he rightly anticipated would be thrown at him. Whether he positioned the batteries personally or left it to Lieutenant-Colonel Frazer is uncertain, but the latter is quite likely as Frazer was, for a gunner, comparatively well trusted by the Duke. Frazer was certainly very involved with directing the comings and goings of the guns during the battle, and he appears to have played a more prominent role in this than the British artillery commander Colonel Wood. For example, it was Frazer who, early in the battle, anticipated the need for howitzers with which to hit the French in Hougoumont Wood. He sent orders to bring them forward and then reported their arrival to the Duke. The Duke's decision not to engage in counter-battery fire paid dividends, although there were occasions when it was ignored not only by Mercer, but by some batteries desperate to reduce the French gunfire in the intervals between the cavalry attacks.

The artillery staff system appears cumbersome in that the overall British artillery commander was Colonel Wood who had Lieutenant-Colonel Frazer under him commanding the RHA, which was divided into the batteries with the cavalry and the reserve. The Netherlands and Brunswick divisions had their own artillery commanders and staff within their headquarters.

ORGANIZATION

As with the cavalry and infantry, Wellington's artillery units had the same basic organization regardless of their nationality: they operated as batteries of six to eight guns, the great majority including one or two howitzers. Each army at Waterloo had its foot and horse batteries, the latter being fully mobile with all personnel either mounted or able to ride (precariously and uncomfortably) on the limbers or wagons. The men of each battery (both horse and foot) were divided approximately equally between the gunners (detachments) who fired the piece and the drivers, who were responsible for the horses (teams) that pulled them and the caissons/wagons. Overall, the average strength of an Anglo-Allied battery was over 200 all ranks – gunners plus drivers. British gunners were armed with musket and bayonet but did not carry a sword in the field. All drivers carried a light cavalry sabre (but at one time they had been unarmed).

All batteries consisted of the guns and howitzers, the limbers (small wheeled platforms pulled by the team and attached to the trail of the gun for movement), the ammunition wagons (the French called them caissons) and a number of administrative wagons (forge, spare wheels, baggage, forage and stores). There were usually about six artillery officers to a battery, plus a surgeon, with the other ranks being split between gunners, drivers and a much smaller number of specialists (farriers, smiths, wheelwrights and collar makers).

A typical Anglo-Allied horse artillery battery that had its fair share of the action at Waterloo was 'G' Troop RHA commanded by Captain Mercer. Its organization is discussed below. The numbers of personnel, horses, wagons, ammunition stocks, expenditure and casualties follow, as far as possible, those given by Captain Mercer in his *Journal of the Waterloo Campaign*.

'G' Troop Royal Horse Artillery (Diagram p. 278)
General

'G' Troop was one of twelve such RHA troops (batteries). As these gunners were mounted and normally fought alongside cavalry, they took the term 'troop' from the cavalry. Eight took part in the Battle of Waterloo. The RHA was itself a part of the far larger Royal Regiment of Artillery, which included all the foot or 'marching' units, as their pedestrian comrades were called. Mercer's troop was one of only three that had managed to exchange their old 6-pounders for five 9-pounders after arrival in Belgium; it retained

---

Wellington's Hostility towards the Artillery

With the exception of two or three artillery officers who had served him well in the Peninsula, such as Frazer and Dickson, the Duke was particularly cool towards gunner officers. In fact the corps as a whole found it unusually hard to win praise, or even recognition, no matter how much it contributed to victory. His attitude had hardened during his time in Portugal and Spain where he had run through five artillery commanders before he had Dickson transferred from Portuguese service in 1813. After five years Wellington at last had a gunner of his choosing. Dickson went on to win approval by commanding the artillery to the Duke's satisfaction (no mean achievement) at Vitoria, San Sebastian, the passage of the Bidassoa, Nivelle, Nive and Toulouse. Wellington was annoyed at having to accept Colonel Wood instead of Dickson for the Waterloo campaign – although he did have the grace to mention him in his Waterloo despatch.

The other source of annoyance was from some artillery officers' habit of communicating direct to the Master General of the Ordnance in England on matters that Wellington considered his concern as commander-in-chief in the field. For almost 200 years the RHA have never really forgiven Wellington for his previous harsh treatment of Captain Ramsay, a particularly courageous and well-liked officer who was killed at Waterloo. On one occasion in Spain in June 1813 Wellington had ordered Ramsay to place his guns in 'a position of readiness', emphasizing that he was not to move from it unless ordered by Wellington himself. Ramsay remained immobile for twelve hours before a staff officer finally arrived to order him into action to meet a developing crisis in the battle. Unfortunately, on his way the Duke spotted him and flew into a rage, relieving him of his command and placing him under arrest on the spot. It was Frazer who, a few days later, caught Wellington in a good mood and persuaded him to reinstate Ramsay. The Duke almost certainly realized he had been unjust, as he approved Ramsay's brevet rank of major a few months later.

Despite this, at Waterloo the incident still rankled in Ramsay's mind. Before the battle started, Wellington rode past 'H' Troop and, quite out of character, called out, 'Hulloa Ramsay'. Ramsay did not reply. His acknowledgement was to bow down in an exaggerated manner until his nose touched the mane of his horse. A few hours later he was dead.

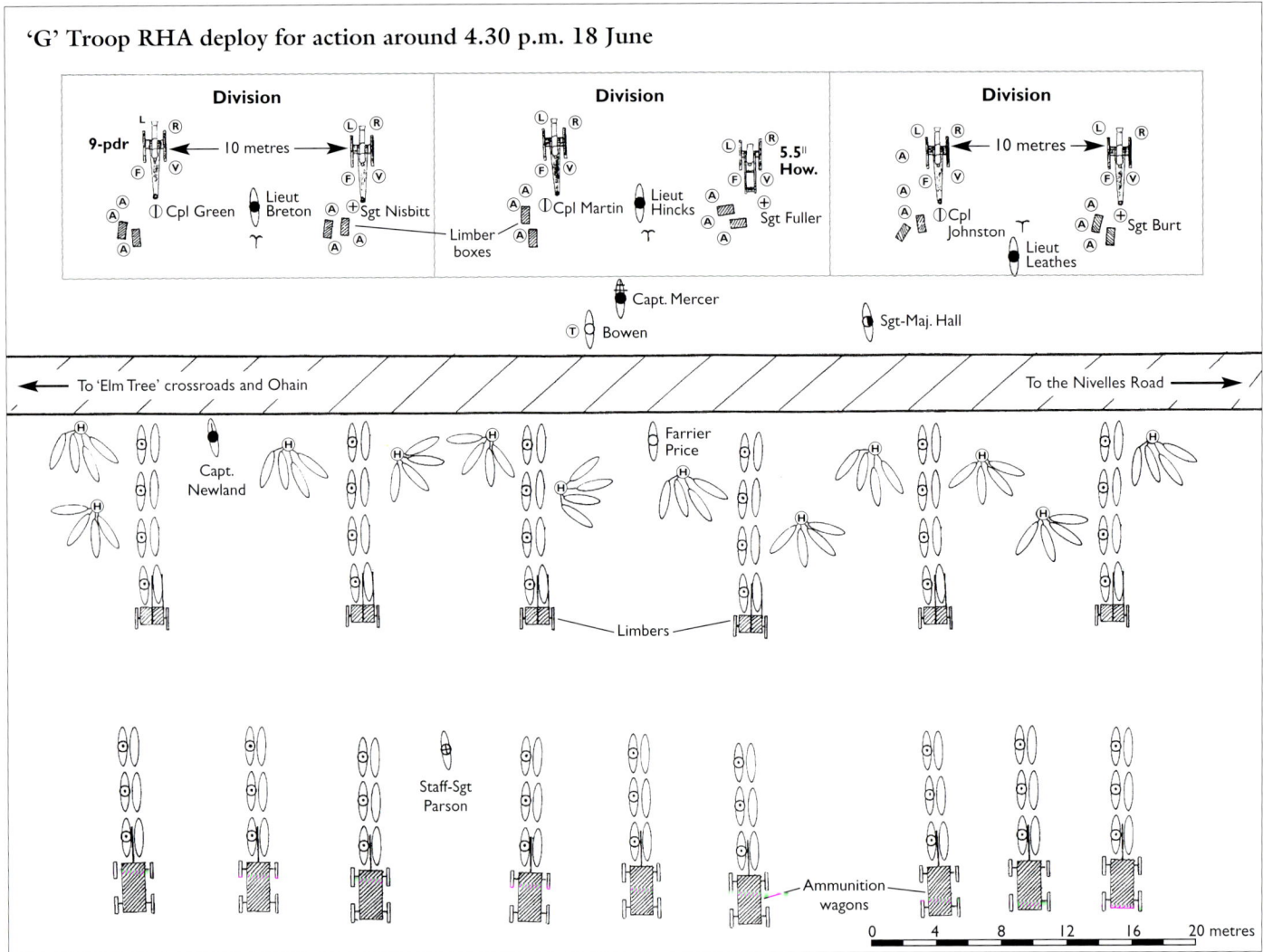

'G' Troop RHA deploy for action around 4.30 p.m. 18 June

Notes

• This diagram shows the likely layout of 'G' Troop RHA under Captain Mercer when they were brought forward to the front line after the start of the massed French cavalry attacks (see Map 16). The Troop was deployed a few metres forward, south of the ridge road to Ohain. It was critical to be on the forward slope in order to see the enemy. The gun position occupied about 60-65 metres, with some 10 metres between each piece. The two ammunition boxes carried on the limbers have been dumped beside the guns before the teams withdrew with the limbers.

• The Troop was divided into three divisions and six sub-divisions of one piece each. Each division was under the command of a subaltern officer.

• There were ten gunners (including either a sergeant or corporal) in each detachment. The NCO and four gunners fired the gun, three gunners humped ammunition from the limber boxes to the loader (all eight would be involved in hauling the piece back into the firing position after each recoil). Two gunners (possibly those riding on the limber boxes) were detailed off as horseholders to take the detachment's horses a short distance to the rear just north of the road.

• The teams and limbers were withdrawn from the gun position north of the road but, as was the drill with the RHA, did not pull back an

appreciable distance. Normally, horse artillery would not expect to be firing from one position for long and so their limbers were kept close for a quick move out of action. Teams of eight horses drew all 9-pounder guns and limbers, the near side (left) horse being ridden by a driver.

• Behind the limbers was a line of nine ammunition wagons. They are shown close behind the limbers but may have been another 20 metres further back. Each wagon had a team of six horses, again the near side ones ridden by drivers. It was the task of the second captain, assisted by the sergeant-major and staff-sergeant, to ensure a controlled flow of ammunition to the guns. There was a staggered system of supplying the guns so that not all wagons were emptied at the same time. Once two or three were empty they had to make the 1,800m round trip to the army's main field park 400m south-west of Mont St Jean village. An officer or senior NCO may have accompanied them.

• The specialist wagons are not shown as they were further to the rear.

• Not all the personnel or horses are shown in the diagram (there were some with the specialist wagons) but sufficient to demonstrate how crowded (perhaps 150 men and 150 horses) the troop was into a space about 60 metres by 50 metres – presenting a target not easy to miss.

Key

‡ **Troop Commander**
● **Second Captain**
● **Subaltern Officer**
◑ **Troop Sergeant-Major**
⊕ **Sergeant (No.1 on gun)**
◐ **Corporal (No.1 on gun)**
Ⓣ **Trumpeter**
Ⓥ **Ventsman**
Ⓛ **Loader**
Ⓡ **Rammer**
Ⓕ **Firer**
Ⓗ **Horse holder**
Ⓐ **Ammunition carrier**
⊙ **Driver**
Υ **Forked Linstock**

the single 5.5-inch howitzer. Three of the other troops still had 6-pounders and a howitzer, one had 6-pounders and a rocket section, the other six howitzers. The troop could, if the tactical circumstances warranted it, be divided into half-troops, each under a captain. When operating as a troop it was split into three 'divisions' of two pieces each, which in turn were divided into six 'sub-divisions' – individual pieces with their ammunition wagons. The organization and deployment during the battle is best described under sev-

eral headings, namely – officers, soldiers, horses, ammunition, deployment, battle highlights and casualties.

Officers

The troop had its correct establishment of officers – two captains and three lieutenants. They were:

1 Captain Alexander Cavalie Mercer. He was the thirty-one-year-old son of an engineer general who had been stuck as a captain since 1806. He counted himself lucky to have command of a troop at Waterloo, as he was officially only the 'second captain' of 'G' Troop. The substantive commander, Captain Dickson, with the army brevet rank of lieutenant-colonel, was commanding the Battering Train while the acting commander, yet another brevet lieutenant-colonel, Macdonald, had been taken by Frazer as his deputy. In addition, of all the RHA troop commanders, Mercer was the only one not to have seen Peninsula service. The last time he had seen action was seven years earlier at the debacle at Buenos Aires. However, he was to perform admirably on 18 June, survive unscathed, attain general's rank and live to be eighty-five – long enough to see the conclusion of the American Civil War.

2 Captain Robert Newland. He was acting as second captain in the troop. This meant he was second-in-command, commanded a half-troop of three pieces if necessary and had responsibility for ammunition re-supply in action. He had been a captain for less than a year. Although he too survived the battle, he was still a captain sixteen years later when, disillusioned, he retired by selling his commission.

3 Lieutenant Henry Leathes. The son of an army officer. As the senior lieutenant he commanded the right hand division of two 9-pounders. Another officer perhaps beginning to feel disgruntled with the sluggish promotion in the artillery, as he had already been a lieutenant for nine years, many of them in the Peninsula. He resigned four years after the battle.

4 Lieutenant John Hincks. Another army officer's son. He commanded the centre division of the troop: the 5.5-inch howitzer and a 9-pounder. Unscathed at Waterloo, Hincks, with seven years seniority in his rank, managed to secure promotion to captain by 1826 when he retired on half pay.

5 Lieutenant John Breton. Commanded the left division of two 9-pounders during the battle. He had three horses shot under him but was himself untouched. He retired, still a lieutenant, in 1820.

Two other specialist officers were attached to the troop. The first was Assistant-Surgeon Richard Hichens whose military career was to be a relatively brief one (five years), going on to half pay nine months after Waterloo, but living until 1866. The second was Assistant-Commissary Coates. This officer had experience in the Peninsula and was attached to the troop after arrival in Belgium with responsibilities for procuring food and fodder. Whether he was present at the battle is uncertain, but it is likely he was, although, as with other officers of his Department, it would not have entitled him to the Waterloo Medal or the prestigious 'W' before his name in the Army List. There is some doubt as to whether Mercer actually received a Waterloo Medal, although his entitlement is absolutely clear.

Soldiers

'G' Troop's strength of five officers (it had lost the sixth, Lieutenant Bell, who was acting as adjutant to Lieutenant-Colonel Frazer) and 187 other ranks at Waterloo meant that it was well up to establishment. It does not, however, appear to have been allocated the extra eight gunners to which it was entitled when it exchanged its 6-pounders for 9-pounders – the additional drivers were forthcoming. The personnel were divided approximately equally between the Royal Horse Artillery NCOs and soldiers who manned the guns (not all of whom rode horses), and the men attached from the Corps of Royal Artillery Drivers who rode the horses pulling the guns, limbers and wagons. Not until 1822 did drivers become an integral part of every troop. Mercer has listed precisely the men he

commanded at the start of the campaign. The troop was in action during the retreat on 17 June but suffered no losses. While one or two men may have been away sick, the likelihood is that the numbers were much as Mercer stated in his *Journal*. They were:

NCOs
Two Staff-Sergeants
Three Sergeants
Three Corporals
Six Bombardiers

Of the two staff-sergeants, one was acting as the troop sergeant-major. The sergeants each had charge and were the No.1 of a piece of ordnance. In action a sergeant commanded, from the right, the first, third (usually the howitzer) and fifth pieces. The three corporals had the same responsibilities with the remaining three guns. The bombardiers were the equivalent of the modern lance-corporal with, in this case, two in each detachment. All these men were mounted.

Gunners and drivers. 'G' Troop had eighty gunners. Of these, sixty were actual gun detachments, each of the eight gunners riding their own horses plus two seated on the limber. In action, of the ten NCOs and men in the detachment, two were detailed as horse holders (usually those on the limber boxes), each taking four animals to the rear of the position. The remaining gunners were available as replacements; some would have ridden spare horses, others riding the horses drawing the specialist wagons. There were eighty-four drivers attached to the troop. Of these, twenty-four rode the near side (left-hand) of the four pairs of horses pulling the guns (and limbers), and another twenty-seven rode the near side horses of the ammunition wagons.

Specialist personnel. Of these Mercer had the following:
One Farrier
Three Shoeing Smiths
Two Collar-Makers
One Wheel-Wright
One Trumpeter (and one supernumerary)

Their tasks are self-explanatory. The establishment allowed for only two shoe-smiths and one carriage-smith. Mercer apparently had three of the former but none of the latter – possibly a lapse of memory, as carriage-smiths were important individuals. These soldiers travelled with the wagons, although the farrier (Mercer says two, although he only had one) and one collar-maker were mounted as they needed to be more mobile.

Horses

There were some 220 horses and six mules (for the officer's baggage) with 'G' Troop at the start of the battle. They were either riding horses carrying men, or draught horses pulling the guns and wagons, or spare animals which were probably a mixture of both. They were as follows:

• Riding horses. These totalled seventy – the officers had seventeen (every officer had three, except the surgeon who had two); one each for the two staff-sergeants; 48 for the gun detachments (these included twelve NCOs), and three for specialist personnel.
• Draught horses. Some 120 in total – forty-eight pulling the six limbers (and guns); fifty-four hauling the nine ammunition wagons, and eighteen pulling the remaining wagons (four horses each, except the carriage wagon that required six).
• Spare horses numbered thirty according to Mercer.

Normally, when a battery was in action the team of horses drawing the limber was taken some 30 metres to the rear after dumping the two limber boxes of ammunition with the gun. This was standard procedure for guns of position (foot artillery). With horse gunners, certainly with the British RHA, this was not always the case. The RHA were trained to have their limbers, with the teams hooked in, standing close behind the guns. They were then instantly ready to move. On the single order 'Mount!' the gun would be away and out of action in a matter of moments. Mercer (and probably other RHA troops) modified this drill at Waterloo. The officers remained mounted (Lieutenant Breton had three horses shot under him) while with the guns. The limber teams, however, were taken back just behind the crest of the ridge, a few metres to the rear – although they were still exposed at least for some of the time, as one of Mercer's leading drivers, Miller, was shot by a cavalryman with a carbine. Even this did not save many of the horses in 'G' Troop. Crippling damage was done when a French battery got within 400 metres to fire shot after shot into the teams:

> The rapidity and precision of this fire was quite appalling. Every shot almost took effect, and I certainly expected we should all be annihilated. Our horses and limbers, being a little retired down the slope, had hitherto been somewhat under cover from the direct fire in front; but this plunged right amongst them, knocking them down by pairs, and creating horrible confusion. The drivers could hardly extricate themselves from one dead horse ere another fell, or perhaps themselves. The saddle-bags, in many instances were torn from the horses' backs, and their contents scattered over the field. One shell I saw explode under the two finest wheel-horses in the troop – down they dropped.

At the end of the day Mercer had lost sixty-nine horses (32 per cent) plus an unknown number of wounded. When Wellington gave the general advance in the late evening Mercer did not have enough horses to move.

Ammunition

Like most other Anglo-Allied artillery batteries, 'G' Troop carried its immediate ammunition requirements in two separate locations (unlike the 6-pounder, no ammunition was carried in an axle box). These were in two limber boxes carried on the limber (in more modern parlance 'F' echelon ammunition), and in the ammunition wagons ('A' echelon). In the wagons the ammunition was stored in two limber boxes and a larger amount in the body of the wagon. With the British artillery at Waterloo there were nine ammunition wagons for a six gun battery – one for each piece and one extra for each 'division'. The normal practice was for the limber boxes (from the limber) to be left with the gun and the limbers withdrawn a short distance to the rear, hopefully under cover. The ammunition wagons would be 50 metres or so further back in rear of the limbers. Further back still, perhaps another 50–100 metres, would be the wagons with the forge, baggage, spare carriages or wheels wagons ('B' echelon). However, it all depended on the tactical situation, the ground and the location of neighbouring units. The overriding consideration for Mercer and his fellow battery commanders was to ensure a speedy replenishment of the guns and, at the same time, try to shield his men, horses and ammunition from enemy fire. At Waterloo most of the front line batteries had their guns on the forward slope (so they could see to shoot), with the limbers, wagons and horses a short distance back on the reverse slope. The best description of the 'system' during the battle is that written by Major Rudyard who, at Waterloo, was the second captain (responsible for ammunition supply) of Major Lloyd's Brigade (battery) of foot artillery:

> My horses, ammunition wagons, were in the rear of our Guns under cover of a little hollow [limbers and wagons were seemingly together] between us and our squares of infantry. The forge cart, artificer's stores, and such like were in the rear all out of fire. When ammunition was to be replenished [wagons were empty], a Subaltern conducted such wagons as could be spared. They were supplied from the depot in the wood, and returned without delay. The ground we occupied was much furrowed up by the recoil of our Guns and the grazing of the shot, and many holes from the bursting of shells buried in the ground. As horses were killed or rendered unserviceable, the harness was removed and placed on the wagons, or elsewhere. Our men's knapsacks were neatly packed on the front and rear of our limbers and wagons, that they might do their work more easily.

It is difficult to be exact with the amount of ammunition carried at the start of the battle. Mercer thought fifty rounds were carried in the two limber boxes of each gun but this is hard to verify and he does not specify the type. The number given in Straith's *Treatise on Fortifications and Artillery* and in Captain Griffith's *Artillerist's Manual* (4th Edition, published 1847) is thirty-two in the two boxes on the limber. The table below gives the likely typical loads for a 9-pounder in an RHA Troop at Waterloo.

	Ball	Shell	Canister	Spherical Case	Total (per gun/ wagon)
Axle box (each)	*Ammunition was not carried in the single axle box*				
Limber boxes (2)	18	–	8	6	32
Limber boxes (2 carried on wagon)	18	–	8	6	32
Ammunition wagon	56	–	–	8	64
Totals for a 9-pounder	92	–	16	20	128
Totals for troop* (9-pounders)	608	–	96	128	832
5.5" Howitzer	–	48	16	60	124 (+2 carcass)
Grand total for troop	608	48	112	188	956

* Calculated on the basis of seven wagons for 9-pounders, two for howitzers.

Ammunition expenditure was extremely heavy for those guns in the front line such as Mercer's. Wagons were sent back to the wagon/ammunition park some 300 metres south-west of Mont St Jean village (Map 16) during the action as soon as they became empty. It was a round trip of over 3,200 metres (two miles) for batteries deployed on the extremities of Wellington's line. Even with an officer or senior NCO chivvying them along, it would not have taken much under an hour. 'G' Troop fired a total of 700 rounds, mostly during a period of intense fighting (4.30 p.m.–8.30 p.m.), averaging 117 per piece. Although this was just within the likely ammunition holding of the troop, undamaged wagons would have been sent to the rear to replenish. It was slightly under the estimated average for the whole army, but then Mercer did not come into action in the front line until well after 4.00 p.m. Also the severe losses among his horses, the exhaustion of his detachments and overheated cannons would slow the rate of fire as the battle progressed.

Side elevation of British 9-pounder gun and limber

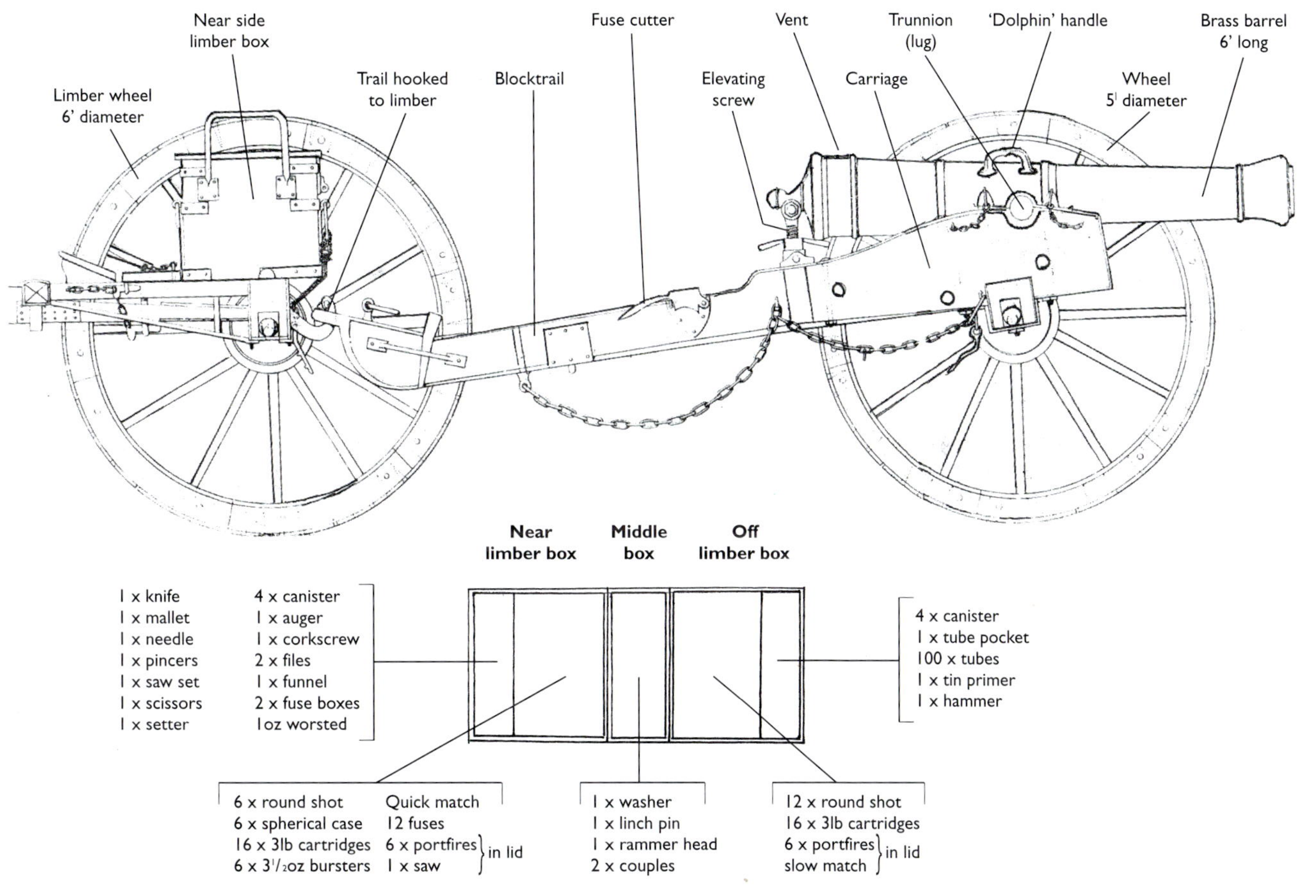

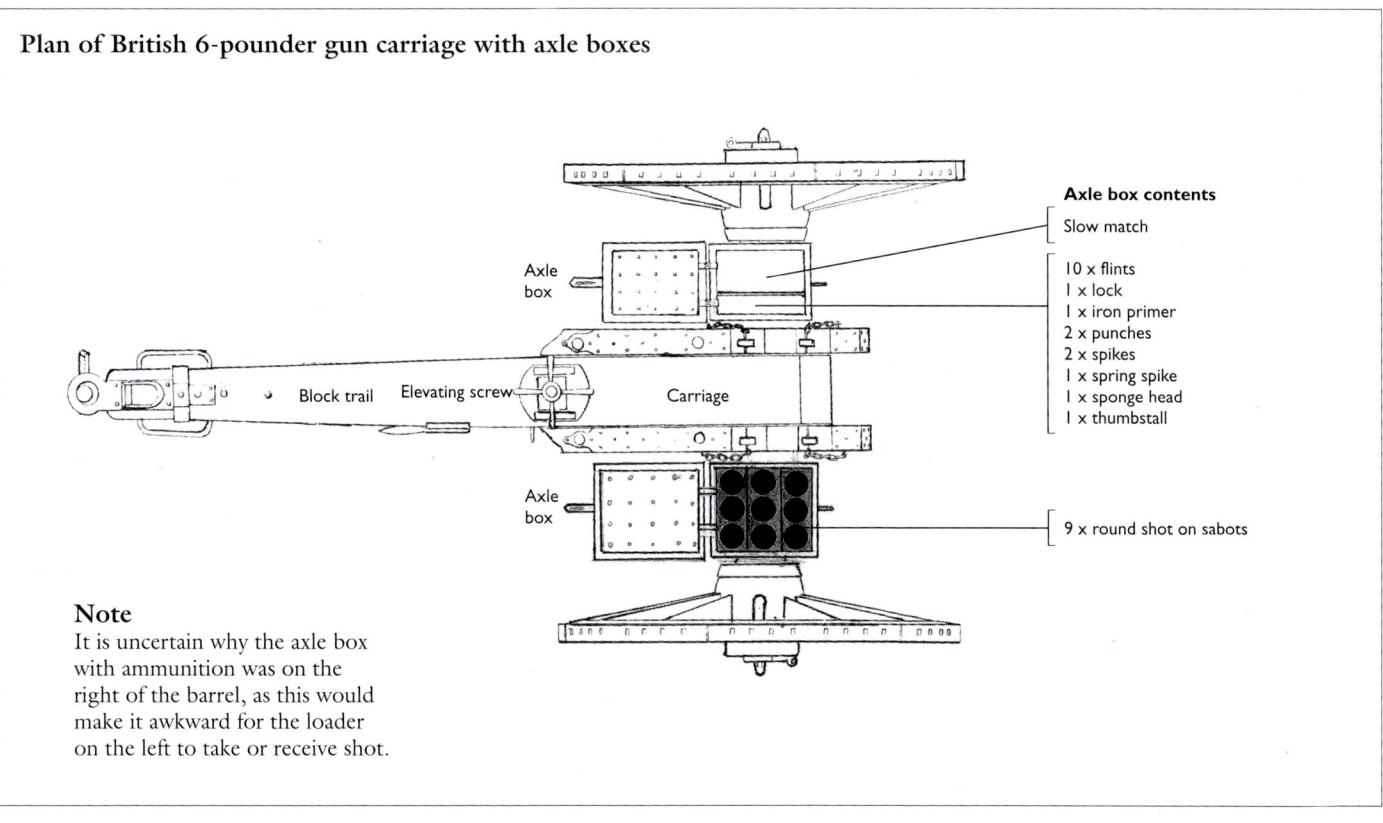

Near side limber box · Fuse cutter · Vent · Trunnion (lug) · 'Dolphin' handle · Brass barrel 6' long · Limber wheel 6' diameter · Trail hooked to limber · Blocktrail · Elevating screw · Carriage · Wheel 5' diameter

Near limber box · Middle box · Off limber box

1 x knife · 4 x canister
1 x mallet · 1 x auger
1 x needle · 1 x corkscrew
1 x pincers · 2 x files
1 x saw set · 1 x funnel
1 x scissors · 2 x fuse boxes
1 x setter · 1oz worsted

4 x canister
1 x tube pocket
100 x tubes
1 x tin primer
1 x hammer

6 x round shot · Quick match
6 x spherical case · 12 fuses
16 x 3lb cartridges · 6 x portfires } in lid
6 x 3½oz bursters · 1 x saw

1 x washer
1 x linch pin
1 x rammer head
2 x couples

12 x round shot
16 x 3lb cartridges
6 x portfires } in lid
slow match

Plan of British 6-pounder gun carriage with axle boxes

Axle box contents
Slow match
10 x flints
1 x lock
1 x iron primer
2 x punches
2 x spikes
1 x spring spike
1 x sponge head
1 x thumbstall

9 x round shot on sabots

Axle box · Block trail · Elevating screw · Carriage · Axle box

Note
It is uncertain why the axle box with ammunition was on the right of the barrel, as this would make it awkward for the loader on the left to take or receive shot.

Deployment and highlights

Mercer's troop had been left in reserve west of Mont St Jean Farm until after 12.30 p.m. – he thought he had been forgotten. Eventually Lieutenant Bell (one of his subalterns acting as adjutant to Lieutenant-Colonel Frazer) arrived and brought the troop forward to a position on the right, behind the second line (Map 16). It was from this location that he briefly disobeyed Wellington's orders and indulged in some counter-battery fire against Piré's guns. It was here also that Gunner Hunt became his first casualty.

'G' Troop remained in this position for over two hours, witnessing the start of the French cavalry attacks and temporarily mistaking the approach of Chassé's Netherlands Division for French. His troop was well closed up to the extent that he was able to watch one of his wagons being struck by a cannon ball. Then, probably between 4.30 p.m. and 5.00 p.m., Frazer rode up yelling, 'Left limber up, and as fast as you can'. The troop was desperately needed to fill a gap in the frontline among the infantry squares. As they rode forward Frazer briefed Mercer on the Duke's order that if hard pressed by cavalry they should abandon their guns to seek refuge in the nearest square. Frazer positioned the guns between two squares of Brunswickers. The teams, limbers and wagons that were a few metres down the reverse slope of the ridge came under heavy artillery fire from a battery that had been pushed forward to within about 350 metres of Mercer's position. During this period his unwounded gunners became so exhausted that they lacked the strength to run the guns up to re-aim after each shot. This meant they gradually recoiled backwards:

> They [the guns] had retreated nearer to the limbers; and as we had pointed our two left guns towards the people [the gun battery] who were annoying us so terribly, they soon came together in a confused heap, the trails crossing each other, and the whole dangerously near the limbers and ammunition wagons, some of which were totally unhorsed, and others in sad confusion from the loss of their drivers and horses, many of them lying dead in their harness attached to their carriages.

Of particular interest with this account is the evidence it provides for the closeness of the teams, limbers and ammunition wagons to the guns – for most of the time the drivers and horses were as exposed as the gunners.

Casualties

In terms of actual losses to the troop the final tally was nowhere near as horrendous as Mercer's account suggests. In fact, the fatalities among the men were miraculously light. According to official returns only five were killed, four of them being drivers. Other casualties are, however, listed variously as 'sick absent' or 'sick'. Some, perhaps most of these, were wounded. For 'G' Troop they totalled eighteen other ranks (gunners and drivers). The total casualties for the troop were 23 out of 192 all ranks committed to the battle, or 12 per cent – hardly crippling losses considering the intensity of the fighting around Mercer's gun position and the weight of fire supposedly falling on it. Perhaps the most amazing fact was that the only gunner killed in 'G' Troop at Waterloo appeared to be the unfortunate Gunner Butterworth who lost both arms (and subsequently bled to death) through an accident. Out of over 200 horses Mercer claimed to have 140 animals 'dead, dying or severely wounded'. The official muster, however, shows only sixty-nine killed, which is about three times more than

the other RHA troops. One must suppose Mercer was inclined to exaggerate and elaborate in his later writings, perhaps partly due to his feeling hard done by, as he received no recognition or decoration for his actions during the battle. It was a grievance he carried with him into old age.

ORDER OF BATTLE AND ACTION SUMMARY BY NATIONALITIES (Maps 16 & 17, pp. 274 & 275)

British

Royal Horse Artillery

• 'A' Troop – Lieutenant-Colonel Sir Hew Ross with five 9-pounders, one 5.5-inch howitzer, 180 all ranks. Deployed in the front line in the centre of Wellington's line from the outset. In action on and just west of the 'Elm Tree' crossroads. After the loss of La Haie Sainte the troop moved 150 metres further west and was engaged in the repulse of the Imperial Guard; by this stage only three guns could be moved.

• 'D' Troop – Major Beane with five 6-pounders, one 5.5-inch howitzer, 180 all ranks. Posted in the front line, in the centre-right of the position, throughout the action. Heavily involved with the repulse of the French cavalry and Imperial Guard attacks. Beane was killed and Lieutenant Cromie died two days later while undergoing the amputation of his legs that had been smashed by a cannon ball.

• 'E' Troop – Lieutenant-Colonel Sir Robert Gardiner with five 6-pounders, one 5.5-inch howitzer, 180 all ranks. Posted on the extreme left of the Anglo-Allied line with Vivian's light cavalry brigade. More spectators than participants until the end of the battle when they opened fire on French fugitives. They also briefly suffered from 'friendly' Prussian artillery fire in the general confusion at the end.

• 'F' Troop – Lieutenant-Colonel Webber-Smith with five 6-pounders, one 5.5-inch howitzer, 107 all ranks. Initially deployed on the extreme right (west) of the line, close to the Nivelles road, in support of the Hougoumont garrison where it was on the receiving end of effective French guns until their infantry secured the wood. Later moved east some 500 metres into the centre of the front line east of the crossroads. Heavily engaged against cavalry and later Imperial Guard attacks.

• 'G' Troop – Captain Mercer with five 9-pounders, one 5.5-inch howitzer, 192 all ranks. For deployment and highlights see above.

• 'H' Troop – Major Ramsay with five 9-pounders, one 5.5-inch howitzer, 180 all ranks. Posted on the right of the front line north of Hougoumont orchard. It was in action in this position throughout the day, losing Major Ramsay (the darling of the RHA) to a musket ball early on. Frazer buried him on the field during a lull in the action, but three weeks later his body was removed to Scotland for reburial by a distraught father who lost three sons in eight months. The troop maintained its position, playing a critical role in resisting the cavalry and Guard assaults. With two officers killed and two wounded out of five, it suffered the highest officer casualties of any Anglo-Allied battery.

• 'I' Troop – Major Bull with six 5.5-inch howitzers, 180 all ranks. Initially this specialist troop was in reserve but was soon called forward to bombard the French, attacking through Hougoumont Wood, with spherical case, Bull attesting to the effectiveness of this ammunition. Later moved slightly to the rear and east, taking up a position on the right of Ramsay's troop for the remainder of the action. Had a number of howitzers that had to cease firing due to overheating.

• 2nd Rocket Troop – Captain Whinyates with five 6-pounders, one rocket section, 181 all ranks. Initially in reserve north-east of the crossroads but sent forward when Ponsonby's heavy cavalry attacked. The gunners were ordered south of the Ohain road to fire rockets along the ground from close to the sandpit. The troop's guns were also heavily engaged throughout the day. Lieutenant Strangways was badly wounded but survived to become a brigadier in the Crimean War where he was killed by a shell at the Battle of Inkerman.

Royal Artillery (Foot)

These batteries (called brigades) took the name of their commander at the time.

• Captain Sandham's Brigade – with five 9-pounders, one 5.5-inch howitzer, 215 all ranks. Attached to the 1st British Infantry (Guards) Division. Despite being in the same position in the front line all day, all five officers with this troop remained unscathed. This troop claims to have fired the first Anglo-Allied cannon shot of the battle – a claim disputed by other units, including Captain Cleeves's battery of the KGL.

• Captain Bolton's Brigade – with five 9-pounders, one 5.5-inch howitzer, 217 all ranks. Attached to the 2nd British Infantry Division, which was not engaged at Quatre-Bras. At the outset of Waterloo this brigade was in the second line west of the Nivelles road on the extreme right of the main position. Later moved into the front line to the left of Beane's troop and was engaged in the repulse of the Imperial Guard. At this time Bolton was killed by a cannon ball. Minutes later Captain Napier received eight wounds from a bursting shell.

• Major Lloyd's Brigade – attached to the 3rd British Infantry Division with five 9-pounders, one 5.5-inch howitzer, 200 all ranks. Saw action at Quatre-Bras. At Waterloo it remained in the same position in the centre of the front line, west of the Genappe road, throughout the battle. Lloyd died a lingering and painful death from his wounds six weeks after the action.

• Captain Sinclair's Brigade – attached to the 6th British Infantry Division with five 9-pounders, one 5.5-inch howitzer, 200 all ranks. Not involved at Quatre-Bras. At Waterloo remained in reserve near Mont St Jean until about 4.30 p.m. when it was sent to the front line 350 metres west of the Genappe road. From there it was engaged against the French cavalry and Imperial Guard.

• Major Rogers' Brigade – attached to the 5th British Infantry Division with five 9-pounders, one 5.5-inch howitzer, 263 all ranks. In action at Quatre-Bras. At Waterloo formed just east of the 'Elm Tree' crossroads. From this position the brigade fired on Quiot's attacking column, although the rising ground to their immediate front restricted their field of fire. Around the same time that General Picton was killed and the position seemed about to be overrun, the NCO in charge of one gun had it spiked (the only known incident of this happening at Waterloo). It was taken to the rear to have the spike drilled out but never returned. The brigade was moved to the west of the road but could, in the later stages of the action, only move three guns due to the loss of so many horses. 2nd Lieutenant Wilson, who was standing close to Picton when he was shot dead, ultimately became the last survivor of Rogers' brigade, dying as a major-general in 1876.

King's German Legion

At Waterloo the KGL artillery was part of the British Army, and as such the internal establishment of personnel, guns, howitzers and ammunition wagons was almost identical to those of the Royal Artillery or RHA. All three batteries had 9-pounders. It is not possible to know the precise casualties for each battery but overall losses amounted to eighty-one all ranks (and fifty-one horses) or twenty-seven casualties per battery. These are very light losses considering the intensity of the action. The only officer killed was Lieutenant Manners of the RA who was attached to Captain Cleeves's battery from Major Rogers' battery.

Horse Artillery

• 1st Horse Artillery Battery – Major Kuhlmann with five 9-pounders, one 5.5-inch howitzer, 225 all ranks. Attached to the 1st British (Guards) Division, this battery had seen action at Quatre-Bras on 16 June where it had engaged Kellerman's cuirassiers, as it was to do again at Waterloo. It was deployed in the centre of the front line, west of the Genappe road, where it remained throughout the day, taking part in the repulse of the French cavalry and Imperial Guard.

• 2nd Horse Artillery Battery – Major Sympher with five 9-pounders, one 5.5-inch howitzer, 225 all ranks. Attached to the 2nd British Infantry Division, which was not involved at Quatre-Bras. At Waterloo it was held back in the second line, behind the right of Wellington's position. With the approach of Chassé's division to replace it, the 2nd division was moved up to reinforce the front line. Sympher's battery advanced with it to engage French cuirassiers who charged home forcing the gunners to take shelter among Du Platt's infantry or under the gun carriages. It then came into action again at or near the front line, but its exact position relative to the other batteries is impossible to determine.

Foot Artillery

• 1st Foot Battery – Captain Cleeves with five 9-pounders, one 5.5-inch howitzer, 215 all ranks. Attached to the 3rd British Division, which saw action at Quatre-Bras. At Waterloo it was deployed in the front line some 400 metres west of the Genappe road, with Major Lloyd's guns on its right. This battery had been in action at Quatre-Bras. It later was one of the batteries that claimed to have fired the first Anglo-Allied artillery round of the battle when it fired three rounds per gun at French infantry (possibly from Foy's or even Bachelu's divisions) moving diagonally across Wellington's front towards Hougoumont. It was subsequently embroiled in the fighting against the enemy cavalry and Imperial Guard assaults.

Dutch/Belgian

Like their cavalry and infantry compatriots, the Netherlands artillery was dressed, equipped and organized on almost identical lines to the French, for whom many of them had fought until recently. Their batteries were composed of six guns and two howitzers, and the personnel split between the gunners and those of the Artillery Train responsible for moving the guns and wagons. By an unfortunate coincidence the two batteries most heavily engaged at Quatre-Bras (one had lost six of its eight guns) were those posted in the front line from the outset at Waterloo – although both were east of the Genappe road, the relatively quieter half of the battlefield after 3.00 p.m. It is not possible to separate the losses sustained at Quatre-Bras from those at Waterloo or those suffered by individual batteries. However, the Dutch/Belgian artillery as a whole lost 166 all ranks, giving an average per battery of about forty. All Stievenart's were lost at Quatre-Bras.

Horse artillery

• Belgian Horse Battery – Captain Krahmer de Bichen with six 6-pounders, two 5.5-inch howitzers, 210 all ranks, including the train personnel. Attached to the 3rd Netherlands Infantry Division. This battery had not been engaged at Quatre-Bras and did not come into action at Waterloo until the end of the day. As the Imperial Guard attack neared the crest of the ridge, Krahmer's battery was ordered forward by General Chassé. It came into action in support of the square of the 30th and 73rd Foot that appeared on the verge of recoiling. Ensign Macready inside the square was convinced it was the coming into action of this battery at very close range that saved the situation in that part of the line.

• Dutch Horse Battery – Captain Bijleveld with six 6-pounders, two 5.5-inch howitzers, 219 all ranks, including the train personnel. Attached to the 2nd Netherlands Division, this battery was deployed in half-batteries of three guns and one howitzer each. One half-battery was posted on the forward slope of the front line less than 200 metres east of the 'Elm Tree' crossroads. It was part of Major-General Bijlandt's brigade deployed initially in line in an exposed position despite this formation, including the gunners, having had a battering at Quatre-Bras. The second half-battery was with Saxe-Weimar's brigade, posted on the forward slope some 300 metres north-west of Papelotte – a location that turned out to be something of a backwater. The first four guns were, however, engaged against d'Erlon's attack during the early afternoon.

• Dutch Horse Battery – Captains Petter and Gey van Pittius. This battery operated in two half-batteries, each with three 6-pounders and one 5.5-inch howitzer, with a combined strength of 241 all ranks, including artillery train personnel. They were part of the Netherlands Cavalry Division under Lieutenant-General Collaert. These half batteries were not involved at Quatre-Bras. At Waterloo they were initially kept in reserve with their division a few hundred metres south-east of Mont St Jean village, close to the wagon/ammunition park. They supported their division when it was heavily engaged against the French cavalry that penetrated between the squares during the afternoon.

Foot artillery

• Belgian Foot Battery – Captain Stievenart, originally six 6-pounders and two 5.5-inch howitzers and 258 all ranks, including train personnel but, due to losses at Quatre-Bras (the battery was overrun), only two guns were available at Waterloo. They were part of Saxe-Weimar's brigade and were deployed, well out of harm's way, on the extreme left flank, 500 metres north-east of La Haie. There they saw no action and suffered no further losses.

• Belgian Foot Battery – Captain Lux, six 6-pounders, two 5.5-inch howitzers, 267 all ranks, including train personnel. Although part of Chassé's division, this battery was attached to Major-General d'Aubreme's brigade and was, although present, not seriously engaged at Waterloo.

Brunswick

The two batteries with the Brunswick Contingent (Division) were armed with 6-pounders and both had been present at Quatre-Bras where the Duke of Brunswick had been killed. They are recorded as having suffered twenty-seven casualties at Waterloo. Major Mahn commanded the divisional artillery.

Horse artillery

• Brunswick Horse Battery – Captain von Heinemann with eight 6-pounders, 167 all ranks. Initially deployed in reserve behind Wellington's right. They were engaged later in the day supporting the Brunswick infantry squares when they formed to receive cavalry.

Foot artillery

• Brunswick Foot Battery – Major Moll with eight 6-pounders, 205 all ranks. At the outset they formed up with the Brunswick Contingent in reserve behind the Duke's right and, like the horse battery, were only in action briefly supporting their infantry in the late afternoon.

Hanoverian

There were only two foot artillery batteries at Waterloo, both attached to Hanoverian infantry brigades within British divisions. One battery (Braun's) saw action at Quatre-Bras. Total losses for Waterloo were thirty-five all ranks.

Foot artillery

• Foot battery – Captain Braun with five 6-pounders, one 5.5-inch howitzer, 237 all ranks. Attached to the 5th Hanoverian Infantry Brigade, which formed part of the 5th British Infantry Division. The battery saw action at Quatre-Bras. At Waterloo it was deployed on the forward slope of the ridge 700 metres east of the 'Elm Tree' crossroads, near the angle formed by the junction of the Ohain and Papelotte roads. From here it was in action against Marcognet's and Durutte's columns when they attacked early in the afternoon.

• Foot Battery – Captain von Rettberg with five 9-pounders, one 5.5-inch howitzer, 238 all ranks. This battery was isolated from its parent formation, the 6th Hanoverian Brigade in the 4th British Infantry Division, as it had remained in the Hal area. At Waterloo it formed up on the left of Braun's battery and, like it, was engaged mainly during the early afternoon against the right of d'Erlon's corps attack.

Casualties

As with most estimates of losses at Waterloo, it is impossible to claim precise accuracy, as the sources are meagre and often unreliable. Nevertheless, from the evidence available it appears that, despite the ferocity of the fighting and the exposed position of many of the Anglo-Allied gun positions, artillery casualties were remarkably light. The best estimate of total losses is 414 made up as below.

British	105
KGL	81
Dutch/Belgian	166
Brunswick	27
Hanoverian	35

This is a mere 8 per cent of the 5,300 artillerymen (gunners and drivers) in Wellington's army at the beginning of the day. A possible explanation may lie in the well-documented fact that counter-battery fire was not always effective in that it took a long period of accurate (pinpoint) shooting to cripple a well-sited battery.

FRENCH ARTILLERY (Maps 18 & 19, pp. 294 & 295)

General

At Waterloo Napoleon, the soldier who by training and instinct was a gunner, found himself up against an infantryman (Wellington) and a cavalryman (Blücher). The Emperor had a prodigious memory for all things connected with artillery, being able to recall, at the height of his power certainly, the exact calibre and location of innumerable batteries scattered across his empire (another more recent dictator, Hitler, had a similarly amazing memory for technical trivia). Napoleon was a great advocate of using guns en masse. Their fire was to be concentrated. His own maxim made this point:

> In a battle like a siege, skill consists in converging a mass of fire on a single point: once combat is opened, the commander who is adroit will suddenly and unexpectedly open fire with a surprising mass of artillery on one of these points, and is sure to seize it.

When compared with some of his earlier battles the number of French guns and howitzers at Waterloo (246) was verging on inadequate by Napoleon's standards. Six years earlier, to support his assault across the Danube, he amassed 550 pieces of ordnance (including some siege guns) on the island of Lobau and its neighbouring islets. The Imperial Guard battery alone counted 102 guns. The 'Grand Battery' at Waterloo (see p. 296) was, by comparison, a mediocre effort.

The comparison is not entirely fair. In 1815 the raising of a formidable artillery arm was beset by the same frustrating difficulties as those confronting the infantry and cavalry. There was so little time. There was also a depressing dearth of trained men, guns, ammunition, equipment, materials and, above all, horses – although the Old Guard gunners, always fussy and pernickety about tradition, somehow managed to acquire black horses to pull their cannons. The Young and Middle Guards had to make do with five Auxiliary Foot Artillery companies attached from the line and manned by men from the 1st Battalion of the 1st Regiment of La Corps des Canonniers de la Marine (one was a horse battery that was attached to VI Corps for the campaign). On those critical days in June they were not found wanting. The Emperor had intended that all horse artillery batteries have eight pieces, but lack of horses forced him to accept six. It was normal French practice for every infantry division to have one foot and one horse battery attached; for Waterloo they had to make do with a single foot battery. The usual infantry corps reserve with two or more 12-pounder batteries was similarly cut to one. Inevitably, the Imperial Guard was not required to make such sacrifices in terms of numbers, and thus retained two batteries for each division, including the cavalry.

ORGANIZATION (Diagram p. 286)

Despite the efforts of several English language writers to convince us otherwise, the French artillery at Waterloo was not equipped or organized on the old Gribeauval system of 1776. This had seen a major rationalization of the then chaotic artillery arm, with the field artillery being equipped with 4-, 8- or 12-pounder cannon. However, there was not a single 4- or 8-pounder on the field at Waterloo. The artillery was equipped in accordance with the Year XI (1803) System. The French guns at the battle were exclusively 6- or 12-pounders. Out of 178 guns (as distinct from howitzers) 142 were light 6-pounders. In total Napoleon brought 246 pieces of ordnance to the battlefield divided into thirty-four batteries. The foot batteries (twenty-two) consisted of six guns and two howitzers, the horse of four guns and two howitzers. A 6-pounder battery would have had two 5.5-inch howitzers, a 12-pounder two 6-inch howitzers. The French with 28 per cent, therefore, had a higher proportion of howitzers than the Anglo-Allied Army. Of the balance, 58 per cent were 6-pounders and 14 per cent the heavy 12-pounders. The detailed distribution is shown in the table below:

Formation	Batteries	6-pdrs	5.5" how.	12-pdrs	6" how.	Totals
Imperial Guard (Drouot)	13	52	20	18	6	96
I Corps (d'Erlon)	6	28	10	6	2	46
II Corps (Reille)	5	22	8	6	2	38
VI Corps (Lobau)	6	24	10	6	2	42
III Reserve Cavalry Corps (Kellerman)	2	8	4	–	–	12
IV Reserve Cavalry Corps (Milhaud)	2	8	4	–	–	12
Totals	34	142	56	36	12	246

Points of interest are:
- With about 6,500 artillerymen (gunners and train personnel) one of the Emperor's batteries had an average strength of 191 all ranks compared with the Duke's 220.
- The French fielded one gun or howitzer for every 315 men, the Anglo-Allied force one for every 466. As usual the Guard had more artillery than other formations, 1:208, with VI Corps, which was only 50 per cent of the strength of the other corps, having 1:250. The weakest in terms of artillery support was II Corps, which could only muster one gun for every 531 men – about one per battalion.
- Napoleon employed about twenty-six men to keep one piece in action. Wellington required thirty-three.

The French artillery structure of 1815 closely followed that of pre-Restoration days. Like the rest of the army, every branch of the artillery listed below was duplicated within the Imperial Guard. Acute shortages, however, meant that in the desperate scramble to mobilize for the campaign in Belgium, Desvaux de Saint Maurice (overall commander of the Guard Artillery) was compelled to transfer in whole units from the Line Artillery while marines manned four foot batteries and one horse battery (detached to VI Corps) within the Guard. The main components of the artillery arm were:
- Artillerie à cheval – Horse artillery
- Artillerie à pied – Foot artillery
- Pontonniers – pontoon bridging troops
- Ouvriers and armuriers – artificers and armourers
- The Train d'artillerie – the artillery drivers who owned and rode the horses that pulled every gun, caisson and wagon.

French Artillery Organization and Allocation for Waterloo

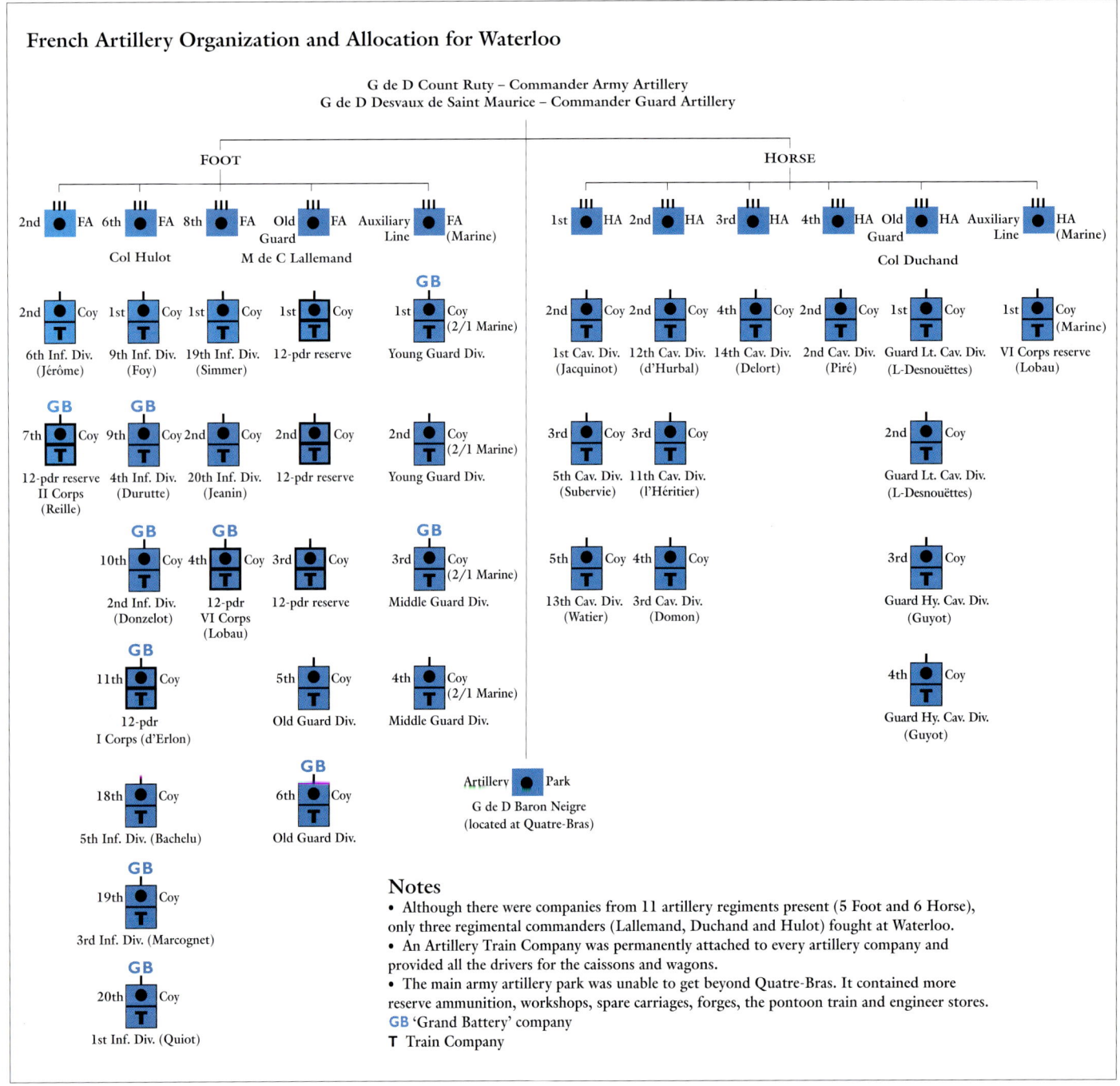

G de D Count Ruty – Commander Army Artillery
G de D Desvaux de Saint Maurice – Commander Guard Artillery

FOOT

2nd FA   6th FA   8th FA   Old Guard FA   Auxiliary Line FA (Marine)

Col Hulot   M de C Lallemand

2nd Coy — 6th Inf. Div. (Jérôme)
1st Coy — 9th Inf. Div. (Foy)
1st Coy — 19th Inf. Div. (Simmer)
1st Coy — 12-pdr reserve
GB 1st Coy (2/1 Marine) — Young Guard Div.

GB 7th Coy — 12-pdr reserve II Corps (Reille)
GB 9th Coy — 4th Inf. Div. (Durutte)
2nd Coy — 20th Inf. Div. (Jeanin)
2nd Coy — 12-pdr reserve
2nd Coy (2/1 Marine) — Young Guard Div.

GB 10th Coy — 2nd Inf. Div. (Donzelot)
GB 4th Coy — 12-pdr VI Corps (Lobau)
3rd Coy — 12-pdr reserve
GB 3rd Coy — Middle Guard Div.

GB 11th Coy — 12-pdr I Corps (d'Erlon)
5th Coy — Old Guard Div.
4th Coy (2/1 Marine) — Middle Guard Div.

18th Coy — 5th Inf. Div. (Bachelu)
GB 6th Coy — Old Guard Div.

GB 19th Coy — 3rd Inf. Div. (Marcognet)

GB 20th Coy — 1st Inf. Div. (Quiot)

HORSE

1st HA   2nd HA   3rd HA   4th HA   Old Guard HA   Auxiliary Line HA (Marine)

Col Duchand

2nd Coy — 1st Cav. Div. (Jacquinot)
2nd Coy — 12th Cav. Div. (d'Hurbal)
4th Coy — 14th Cav. Div. (Delort)
2nd Coy — 2nd Cav. Div. (Piré)
1st Coy — Guard Lt. Cav. Div. (L-Desnouëttes)
1st Coy (Marine) — VI Corps reserve (Lobau)

3rd Coy — 5th Cav. Div. (Subervie)
3rd Coy — 11th Cav. Div. (l'Héritier)
2nd Coy — Guard Lt. Cav. Div. (L-Desnouëttes)

5th Coy — 13th Cav. Div. (Watier)
4th Coy — 3rd Cav. Div. (Domon)
3rd Coy — Guard Hy. Cav. Div. (Guyot)

4th Coy — Guard Hy. Cav. Div. (Guyot)

Artillery Park
G de D Baron Neigre
(located at Quatre-Bras)

Notes
- Although there were companies from 11 artillery regiments present (5 Foot and 6 Horse), only three regimental commanders (Lallemand, Duchand and Hulot) fought at Waterloo.
- An Artillery Train Company was permanently attached to every artillery company and provided all the drivers for the caissons and wagons.
- The main army artillery park was unable to get beyond Quatre-Bras. It contained more reserve ammunition, workshops, spare carriages, forges, the pontoon train and engineer stores.

GB 'Grand Battery' company
T Train Company

The division of all field artillery into foot and horse followed the same principle as other armies. With the foot artillery all personnel were supposed to walk, including the company officers. However, rank had its privileges, so it was rare to see a company commander unmounted. Also, for those for whom promotion had proved elusive, a regulation allowed lieutenants over fifty years old to have horses. There were twenty-two foot batteries (the French called them companies) at Waterloo with 174 pieces. The remainder (twelve) were horse artillery batteries with seventy-two pieces whose gunners and train personnel rode. The foot gunners carried musket, bayonet and briquet, the horse gunners sabre and carbine, and the train personnel carbine, pistol and briquet.

Foot and horse artillery were organized into regiments, each with a commander and staff. There were companies from eleven different artillery regiments at Waterloo but only three regimental commanders. Lallemand commanded the Old Guard Foot Artillery Regiment and Duchand the Horse. The single line artillery commander was Colonel Hulot, a man of immense experience and courage whose regiment and name feature on the memorial beside the Brussels–Genappe road 200 metres north of La Belle Alliance. His 6th Foot Artillery Regiment provided companies for six infantry divisions and the 12-pounders of I Corps reserve. Artillery regiments, however, were entirely administrative units composed of anything up to twenty-eight companies (batteries) of gunners. These companies were attached (with a train company), in a seemingly haphazard manner, to infantry or cavalry formations. Those with heavier guns (12-pounders) were invariably kept as the corps or army (a Guard privilege) reserve.

The pontonniers originated in 1792 from a motley collection of ill-disciplined Rhine River boatmen. Although the task of assembling pontoon boats for bridge building was an engineer's task, as French engineers repeatedly reminded their Emperor, Napoleon kept them as a branch of the artillery because of its greater resources, better workshops, more horses and skilled workmen. Three battalions had been formed with from six to fourteen companies apiece. Their greatest claim to glory was at the crossing of the Beresina River during the retreat from Moscow. Scores froze to death toiling waist deep in icy water to build the bridge that saved the Grande Armée. Among those who succumbed to the cold was their commander, the son of a sergeant and a soldier since he was nine, General Jean Eble. Pontonniers, with their plodding wagons piled with flat-bottomed boats, beams, timber planking, ropes and anchors, marched into Belgium, but with so many intact bridges over the Sambre they were largely redundant. At Waterloo they remained in the main artillery park near Quatre-Bras.

Artificers and armourers were the specialist workmen. Their skills were endlessly in demand. The ouvriers were responsible for constructing and repairing artillery vehicles. As such, most were at the park at Quatre-Bras.

Artillery train personnel were of roughly equal strength as the gunners (about ninety all ranks after allowing for some losses at Ligny and Quatre-Bras) in every battery in the field. They were easily distinguishable from their blue uniformed artillery comrades by their iron-grey jackets. These men rode the horses that hauled the guns and caissons into action. They faced exactly the same dangers on the battlefield as the gun detachments they served. The artillery train was renowned for its efficiency. As with other armies, the French had relied on civilians until 1800. This had proved at best unreliable, at worst disastrous in action. The successful formation of the train saved, so Napoleon claimed, Fr.2 million a year. It was organized in battalions, with companies allocated to artillery companies on a semi-permanent basis. In the past there had been Dutch train units, even Prussian ones, serving the Emperor. Without them a battery could not fire, it could not move. Severe losses in 1813 caused infantry and cavalry soldiers invalided out with hand wounds to be drafted into the train – although how they managed to handle a stiff harness or a frightened horse with disabled and frozen fingers is unclear. In addition to serving alongside the guns, train personnel were to be found driving the assortment of wagons that made up the artillery parks.

Caissons

With the introduction of the Year XI System to improve and rationalize the previous Gribeauval System, the old 12-pounder caisson was adapted to carry ammunition for all types of ordnance. It was a long (4-metre), narrow-bodied wagon, painted olive green, with a sloping top that was hinged to open. The interior was divided into watertight compartments (containers) designed to hold ammunition, supposedly without deteriorating, for prolonged periods. The compartments' configuration could be adjusted to accommodate the type, or types, of projectiles being carried. The rear pair of wheels were larger than the pair at the front and there was a spare (usually of the larger variety) carried at the rear. Shovels and a pick were attached to the sides with a detachable toolbox carried at the front. It was common practice, if numbers permitted, to assign an artificer to each caisson. Four horses, the two near side ones being ridden by train soldiers, drew a caisson.

Despite modifications, these vehicles were far from satisfactory. Complaints included the lack of any springs (suspension) that caused continuous jolting and jarring of the ammunition, resulting in its deterioration. There was insufficient protection against humidity, but perhaps the most important drawback of all was that it could be a struggle for four horses to pull it – particularly off good roads or up steep inclines. If one or two animals were injured or killed and replacements were not immediately available, the caisson was immobile. Interestingly, six horses, which allowed for losses, drew the British wagons. This would have been impossible for the French at Waterloo due to the scarcity of horses and the demands of the cavalry and guns. These caissons could hold about 100 projectiles for the guns or seventy-five for the howitzers.

Ammunition caisson

Spare wheel

Tool box

Notes
• These were long (4-metre) narrow wagons with hinged tops.
• Usually pulled by 4 horses, it contained between 100–110 projectiles, a spare wheel (large) at the back and had shovels and a pick fastened on the side.

• Both the horses and large wheels could be used to replace losses or damage on the guns.
• Over 200 of these caissons took up a lot of space in rear of the 'Grand Battery'.

COMMAND AND CONTROL

Napoleon was his own master gunner – his artillery commander at Waterloo was virtually ignored. There was little he did not know about the tactical or technical details of artillery, the latter including the manufacture of both cannons and ammunition. It was Napoleon who in 1803 appointed a special committee to recommend changes to the Gribeauval system. Its great contribution to French gunnery had been the introduction of the elevating screw, which enabled the range to be altered by turning the screw to raise or lower the breach. However, as an artillery lieutenant the young Bonaparte had been exposed daily to the system's deficiencies. Among them were the need for wheels of twenty-five differing sizes, a different size of caisson for every calibre of gun, heavy and unwieldy limbers, neither of which had seats for the gunners and consequently made for an uncomfortably dangerous ride for those brave enough to cling on. Long before Waterloo the Emperor had simplified and dramatically improved the system.

Before and during the action it was the Emperor that oversaw the positioning of the guns. It was his decision to concentrate a massed battery to prepare the way for his first main assault, to smash a hole in the enemy line as he had done on so many of his battlefields. He decided its composition and location. He gave it its target and task. It was Napoleon that ordered up howitzers to set fire to the buildings in Hougoumont. But it was also Napoleon who clung to his 'beautiful daughters' (the Guard 12-pounders) until the end of the battle, reluctant to commit them even when the Middle Guard climbed the Mont St Jean ridge in the late evening. It was the Emperor who failed (except on the eastern flank where he had difficulty seeing what was happening) to ensure that sufficient guns always supported, co-operated with, advanced with and fought with the infantry and the cavalry. The all arms battle was as much a key to success in 1815 as it is today. At Waterloo it was patchy.

His subordinate artillery commanders were equal in courage, if not always in competence. Those of rank or particular significance during the action were:

Général de Division Baron Charles Ruty
Army artillery commander

Général de Division Comte Jean Desvaux de Saint Maurice
Guard artillery commander

Général de Division Baron Gabriel Neigre
Artillery Park commander

Général de Division Baron Henri-Marie Noury
VI Corps artillery commander

Maréchal de Camp Baron Henri Lallemand
Deputy Guard artillery commander

Baron Ruty

Forty-one years old at Waterloo, his face disfigured by a musket ball that had smashed his jaw almost twenty years earlier, Ruty had been a professional gunner since leaving the Artillery School at Châlons in 1792. He was then commissioned into the 2nd Foot Artillery Regiment (there were two batteries of his old regiment present on the morning of 18 June with II Corps) at the start of a long and active career. He served for three years in Egypt, fighting at the Battles of the Pyramids, Mount Tabor and Aboukir. His appointments during those momentous years of Empire building

French Artillery Company (Battery) and Train Organization

As much of the French artillery had been in action at Ligny or Quatre-Bras, there would have been some losses in most companies and amongst train personnel. Therefore few units would have been exactly the strength given here, which is the full establishment.

6-Pounder Horse Artillery Company (four guns and two howitzers)

One Captain – company commander
One Captain – second captain
Two Lieutenants
One Master Sergeant (equivalent to the British sergeant-major)
Four Sergeants
One Fourrier (administrative/clerical NCO)
Four Corporals
Four Metal workers
Four Ouvriers (artificers)
Twenty-four Cannoniers 1st Class
Thirty-five Cannoniers 2nd Class
Two Trumpeters
One Shoeing Smith

Total four officers and eighty other ranks.

In action a gun detachment usually consisted of an NCO as No.1 with six gunners. The additional men, sometimes drafted in from nearby infantry units, were 'helpers' to hump ammunition and add muscle to the drag ropes when moving the gun short distances or after recoil. There was no real difference in the firing drills or duties of the detachment members from that of a British RHA troop (or artillery of any nation). What slight variations existed were confined to the French ventsman and firer being on opposite sides of the gun to their British counterparts. A *coffret* (trail box) of six to eight rounds was placed on the ground to the left of the trail. This was the only ammunition not carried in the caissons. The limber consisted of a light A-frame on wheels, which did not carry either ammunition or gunners. It was normally kept within 20–30 metres behind the gun line, drawn by a team of six horses driven by train personnel. With the horse artillery these drivers often remained mounted and held the horses of the gunners. Each 6-pounder gun was supported by two caissons (ammunition wagons), each howitzer or 12-pounder by three. As usual, the Guard got more than line units. They were supposed to have three caissons for 6-pounders, and five for howitzers and 12-pounders. Four horses pulled caissons with drivers from the attached train.

Foot Artillery Company (six guns and two howitzers)

The main difference in establishment from the horse company were the additional four 1st Class and thirteen 2nd Class cannoniers. Instead of two trumpeters there were two drummers but no shoeing smith. The total establishment was four officers and eighty-eight other ranks.

Train Company

One company was attached to and came under the command of an artillery company. For this reason it did not have any officers at this level, each train company having a master-sergeant (sergeant-major) in charge. Its responsibility was to move the guns, caissons and wagons. A company consisted of about 100 personnel made up of:

One Master Sergeant	Sixty Soldiers 2nd Class
Four Sergeants	Two Shoeing Smiths
One Fourrier	Two Harness Makers
Four Corporals	Two Trumpeters
Twenty-four Soldiers 1st Class	

Plan View of French 12-Pounder and Detachment

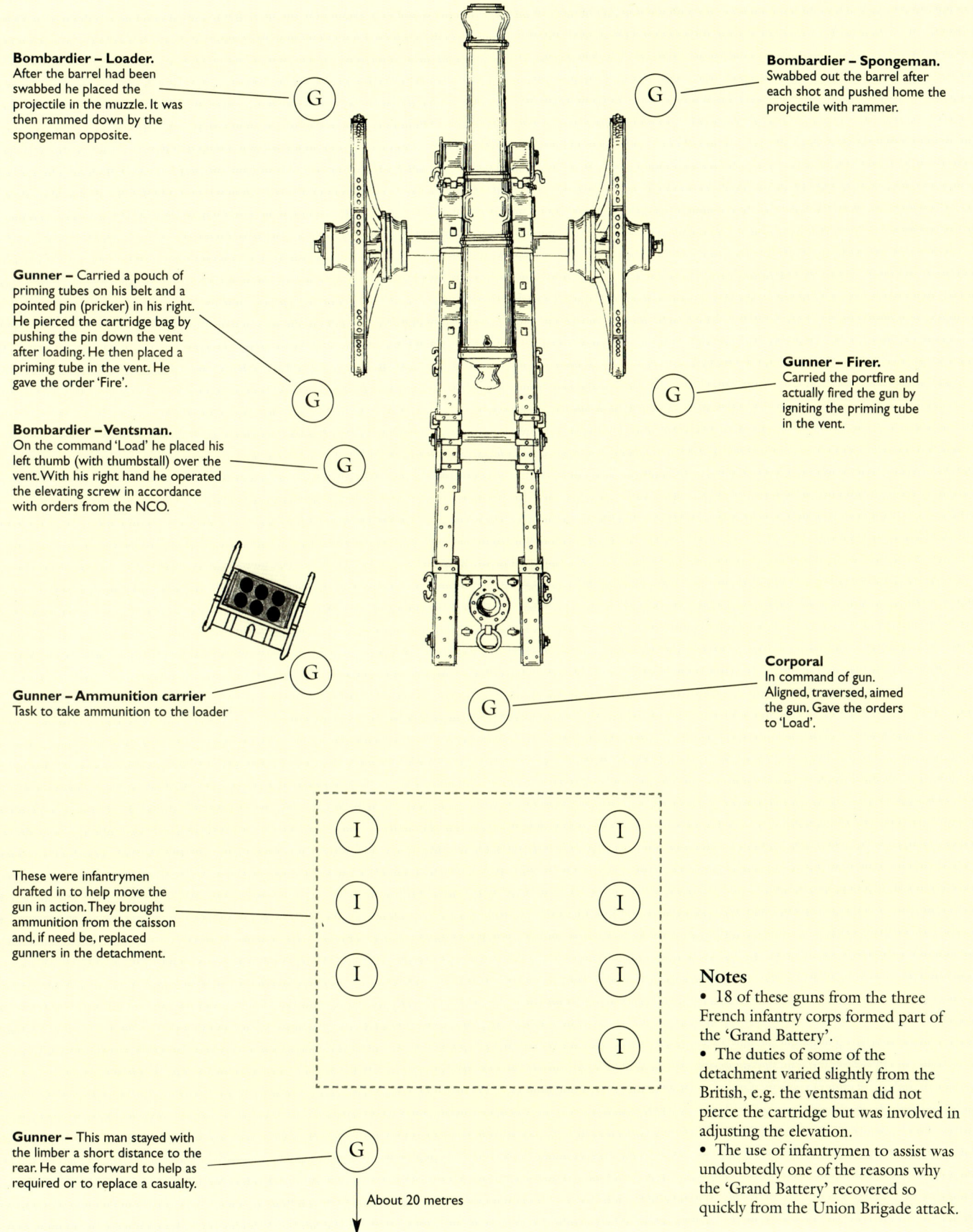

Bombardier – Loader.
After the barrel had been swabbed he placed the projectile in the muzzle. It was then rammed down by the spongeman opposite.

Gunner – Carried a pouch of priming tubes on his belt and a pointed pin (pricker) in his right. He pierced the cartridge bag by pushing the pin down the vent after loading. He then placed a priming tube in the vent. He gave the order 'Fire'.

Bombardier – Ventsman.
On the command 'Load' he placed his left thumb (with thumbstall) over the vent. With his right hand he operated the elevating screw in accordance with orders from the NCO.

Gunner – Ammunition carrier
Task to take ammunition to the loader

Bombardier – Spongeman.
Swabbed out the barrel after each shot and pushed home the projectile with rammer.

Gunner – Firer.
Carried the portfire and actually fired the gun by igniting the priming tube in the vent.

Corporal
In command of gun. Aligned, traversed, aimed the gun. Gave the orders to 'Load'.

These were infantrymen drafted in to help move the gun in action. They brought ammunition from the caisson and, if need be, replaced gunners in the detachment.

Gunner – This man stayed with the limber a short distance to the rear. He came forward to help as required or to replace a casualty.

About 20 metres

Notes
• 18 of these guns from the three French infantry corps formed part of the 'Grand Battery'.
• The duties of some of the detachment varied slightly from the British, e.g. the ventsman did not pierce the cartridge but was involved in adjusting the elevation.
• The use of infantrymen to assist was undoubtedly one of the reasons why the 'Grand Battery' recovered so quickly from the Union Brigade attack.

General Charles de Gaulle's Comments on the Decline of French Artillery

In his book *France and her Army* the late General de Gaulle made some interesting comments on French Napoleonic artillery, ammunition expenditure and the general deterioration in that arm as the long wars took their toll on quality as well as quantity. By way of comparison, at Waterloo French guns fired an estimated 21,000 projectiles. De Gaulle wrote:

> Napoleon endeavoured to compensate for the progressive deterioration in the quality of his troops by increasing their armaments. Thus in 1806 he estimated that he needed 3,000 serviceable cannon; in 1809 he wanted double that number. Every campaign saw an increase in the general artillery reserve. At Austerlitz the French fired 50,000 rounds; at Wagram they fired 96,000; at Moscowa, over 100,000; at Dresden the artillery of the Guard alone hurled 48,000 projectiles. The great artillery men of the Empire, Senarmont, Lariboisiere, Drouot [acting commander of the Guard at Waterloo] excelled in these mass actions and were able, at first, to make up for lack of skilled troops by superior fire-power. But material wore out and replacements became progressively poorer in quality. The armaments industry suffered from lack of men who, in any case, were badly paid. Botched work became more and more frequent. Twelve hundred cannon had been left behind in Russia and almost as many at Kulm, on the Katzbach and at Leipzig, without counting those that were abandoned by the roadside in Germany, Spain and Italy, and even France. For the wood of which the gun-carriages and wheels were made, instead of being seasoned, as formerly, for ten, twenty or thirty years, now came from newly cut timber; as a result it warped, split and bent.

Realizing this debilitating state of affairs, it is only more remarkable what Napoleon, his generals and staff were able to achieve in the few short weeks available in 1815.

included regimental, corps and army artillery commander, commandant of an artillery school and director of artillery parks. He campaigned in Austria, Prussia, Poland, Spain, Germany and France. He fought at Friedland, Albuera, at the sieges of Ciudad Rodrigo, Almeida and Cadiz (where he invented a new siege mortar that later bore his name). He was the Grande Armée's artillery chief of staff in 1813, and fought at Leipzig, remaining loyally at Napoleon's side until the first abdication in 1814.

Despite this, he quickly changed his colours under the Bourbons and secured an appointment to the 'Committee for War'. Ruty stayed loyal to the King until the very last moment after Napoleon's escape from Elba. At one point he was quite prepared to turn his guns on Napoleon's troops, but was thwarted by the gunners' refusal to co-operate. Napoleon preferred to remember his long years of service to the Empire, and appointed him artillery commander of the Armée du Nord – much to the disgust of many who suspected the ease with which he swapped sides.

It proved a poor appointment. Ruty seemed out of his depth and largely ignored by his Emperor and the generals that had his ear such as Drouot and Desvaux of the Guard. At Waterloo he did nothing of significance; he was a lightweight, seemingly cold-shouldered or bypassed. Napoleon was said to treat him as a clerk. Few, if any, of the hundreds of accounts of the battle that have been written mention Ruty – other than to acknowledge he was there. All this probably stemmed from a lack of trust in his loyalty. After Waterloo, like so many other generals, he quickly went back to the Bourbons. He served several years in the Artillery Inspectorate. He became a Peer of France and a commander of the Order of Saint Louis before dying in 1828 at the comparatively young age of fifty-four.

Comte Desvaux de Saint Maurice

The young Desvaux learned the rudiments of his profession at the same time and place as Ruty – the Châlons Artillery School. Thereafter their paths did not cross until June 1815. In the early days of the Revolution Desvaux fought in the Army of Italy; he crossed the Alps and saw action at Marengo; switched from foot to horse artillery and rose to colonel and the command of the 6th Horse Artillery Regiment. He was in Austria with Marshal Marmont, wounded during the Ulm campaign in 1805, a prisoner of war briefly in 1806 and back in Italy in 1809. He took part in the Austrian campaign of 1809. It was his guns that supported Macdonald's assault at Wagram, which won for him the plum appointment of forming and commanding four companies of Imperial Guard Horse Artillery. He led them into Russia in 1812 – although he brought very few back out again. In 1813 he commanded the eighty-piece battery at Lutzen that supported the Young Guard attack that broke the Allies' line – something he would try to repeat at Waterloo. He fought his guns with skill and success at Leipzig and Hanau.

Although he accepted service under the king, as a former Guard officer his loyalty was suspect. Within two months he was sidelined on half pay. He rallied to Napoleon with enthusiasm. His reward was the task of reconstructing and commanding the Guard Artillery. During the campaign in Belgium his batteries were divided up among the various Guard formations, only leaving him with personal control over the Emperor's 'beautiful daughters'. At Ligny his massed guns were in action all day against the Prussian positions centred on the village of Ligny itself. At Waterloo he was given overall command of the 'Grand Battery'. He directed their fire at Wellington's centre but, due to his target being largely invisible on the reverse slope, they did not inflict the damage necessary to ensure an opening for the infantry. Shortly after the British Union Brigade had been seen off, as he was reorganizing the battery and drafting in infantry to replace fallen gunners, he was cut in half by a cannonball. It was a grim ending for a soldier who had barely been scratched in twenty-three years of war. His remains were lost in the confusion of defeat and were presumed buried in one of the unmarked mass graves on the battlefield.

Baron Neigre

Neigre's father had been a sergeant in the Metz Artillery Regiment. As a boy he knew no life except that of barracks and the crack of cannons, so it was unremarkable that he followed his father into the regiment as a gunner in 1790, aged sixteen. It was a good time to be a gunner. Neigre was a sergeant himself within two years and, two years after that, a captain of one of the innumerable independent artillery companies that flooded the armies of the early Revolutionary Wars. By 1797 his career had taken a slight change of direction when Captain Neigre took charge of a bridging train of pontonniers. His most outstanding success in the field came in the December of 1800 when he was tasked with building a bridge across the freezing water of the 200-metre wide Inn River in Germany. The unknown captain launched his boats and built his bridge, thus allowing the infantry to storm over within just two hours – a time deemed impossible. From then on his new posts and promotion came largely within the complex system of artillery administration, trains and parks. He became an expert in the less than glorious but critical fields of artillery supply, maintenance and logistics. His fine reputation was such that he was head of the Artillery Park for the invasion of Russia. Keeping 1,200 guns moving and supplied over such distances against 'General Winter' as well as the Russians was an undertaking of daunting magnitude. The retreat saw him promoted to general of brigade and a year later to general of division.

He was the obvious choice as commander of the Artillery Park for the Armée du Nord. When Napoleon fought at Ligny and Quatre-Bras Neigre was at Charleroi, supervising the forward movement of the hundreds of wagons that made up the park.

During the final clash at Waterloo he was doing much the same near Quatre-Bras. As the flood of fugitives arrived that night, Neigre desperately sought to rally enough men to organize a defence of the crossroads. Wagons were used to construct a barricade. He awaited in vain for the arrival of Girard's division from Fleurus. With only a handful of assorted soldiers Neigre was overwhelmed, knocked to the ground and trampled underfoot.

Afterwards he was appointed to the Bourbon's Central Committee of the Artillery. But he had no stomach for persecuting his former comrades. As head of the Council of War set up to try Drouet d'Erlon *in absentia* for treason, he quickly dismissed the case for lack of evidence. In 1832 he supervised the bombardment of Antwerp, an event that saw the firing (with surprisingly little effect) of a 1000-pound mortar shell. He remained in the army until his death in 1847, aged seventy-three, by which time he had been given the somewhat less demanding duties of Director of Powders and Saltpetres.

Baron Noury

Noury was another senior officer who began his military career as a cadet, this time at the Douai Artillery School. The ten years from his commissioning until 1801 were unspectacular but earned him

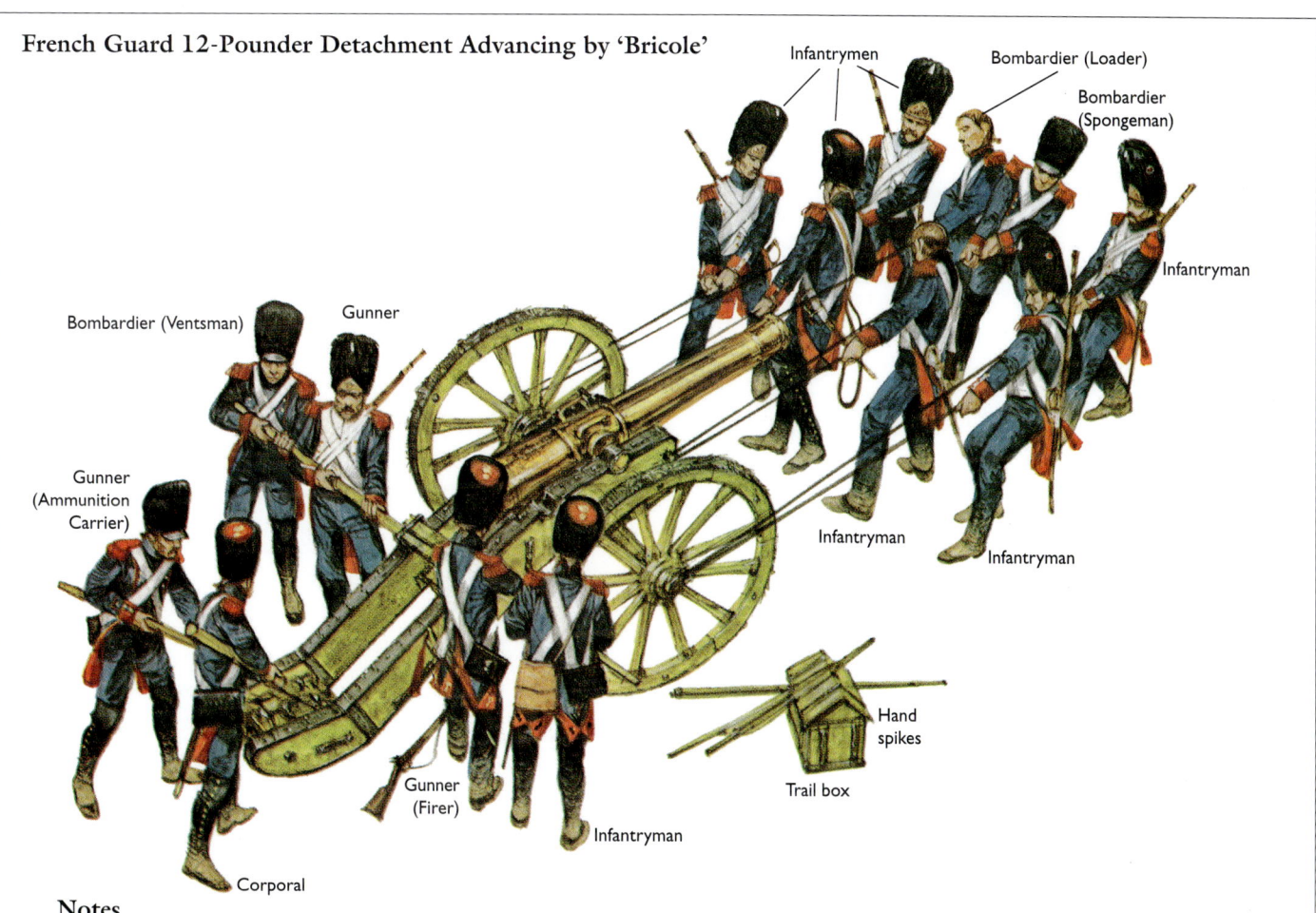

French Guard 12-Pounder Detachment Advancing by 'Bricole'

Infantrymen

Bombardier (Loader)

Bombardier (Spongeman)

Infantryman

Bombardier (Ventsman)

Gunner

Gunner (Ammunition Carrier)

Infantryman

Infantryman

Gunner (Firer)

Hand spikes

Trail box

Infantryman

Corporal

Notes

• This method of moving the gun by hand (by 'bricole') required all the detachment using drag ropes and hand spikes. It was often necessary after firing to re-position the gun before the next shot, and goes a long way towards explaining why the 12-pounder could not normally fire at a much better rate than one shot a minute.

• This sketch shows an Imperial Guard Foot Artillery detachment with some infantry (Grenadiers) manhandling the gun. Note the corporal has another gunner to assist in adjusting the alignment of the heavy trail.

• Although these 'Beautiful Daughters' were present at Waterloo, it is uncertain when or if they came into action.

steady promotion to the rank of chef de bataillon (major). In 1802 he spent a year as director of artillery on the island of Elba. Service with the Grande Armée between 1805–8 saw Noury prove himself a capable staff officer, gain promotion to colonel and command of the 2nd Foot Artillery. He took part in the Prussian and Polish campaigns, fought at Jena, and in 1807 became colonel of the 2nd Horse Artillery (both his former regiments had companies at Waterloo). For the next four years Noury served first in Spain at the Siege of Saragossa, then on the Danube fighting at Aspern-Essling and Wagram, then back to Spain. Next, a year at the Rennes Artillery School as commandant before yet another posting to Spain where his talent was needed to secure the fall of Figueras. His sound reputation as a gunner secured him a transfer to the prestigious Imperial Guard Artillery for the march on Moscow. He fought at Borodino, and was one of the last to leave Moscow at the start of the infamous retreat. Before doing so he blew up a large part of the Kremlin. In 1813 his positioning of the guns was instrumental in the successful repulse of the enemy at Dresden. Eventually he had an appointment on the artillery staff at Leipzig.

The Bourbons soon put him on half pay due to the general reduction in the army, so he welcomed Napoleon's return and the command of VI Corps artillery for the battles in Belgium. His guns did not play a part at Ligny as Lobau was late in arriving. At Waterloo he handled his batteries with considerable skill and effectiveness against the Prussians. He lost his 12-pounders to the 'Grand Battery' but retained control over two foot and three horse artillery batteries (thirty-four guns and howitzers). He deployed them west of the Bois de Paris where they were in action for the best part of four hours, during which time they were gradually forced back to Plancenoit. The criticism often levelled at the French high command that they failed to co-ordinate the actions of the guns with that of the other arms did not apply on the eastern flank under Lobau and Noury. Between them they conducted a fine fighting withdrawal, with the artillery playing its full part. Noury lost all his remaining guns after the general collapse of the French in the late evening.

Within a year of the peace Noury was appointed to the new Artillery Inspectorate. There he served for over twenty years. Two years after going on half pay in 1837 he died, aged sixty-eight.

Baron Henri Lallemand

Henri was the younger brother of François Lallemand who commanded the Châsseurs à Cheval of the Imperial Guard at Waterloo. His career got off to a slow start and was much in the shadow of his elder brother's more exciting exploits. After being commissioned into the 1st Foot Artillery Regiment he served in Egypt and was present at the battle of Aboukir and the siege of Alexandria. However, he remained a sous-lieutenant for five years, only gaining promotion in 1802. He then built a reputation as a sound organizer and trainer while posted to his regiment's depot at Metz. Although he missed Austerlitz, he succeeded in getting a transfer to the Guard Foot Artillery as a company commander in 1806. He served in Spain, then Germany, where he gained another promotion. It was at Wagram that he finally made his name on the battlefield. His battery was part of a massed battery that traded shots for hours with the Austrian guns opposite. Lallemand's leadership was of a high order and his gunners kept firing despite mounting losses. He was later rewarded by being made a Baron of the Empire. As a major in Russia he again showed inspiring leadership at Smolensk and Borodino, but most notable were his efforts to keep his guns moving during the retreat. He became chief of staff of the Guard Artillery, and fought at Lutzen, Bautzen and Leipzig. Largely due to his personal efforts, 166 guns were brought back across the Rhine. During the defence of France in 1814 he played crucial roles at Brienne, Montmirail and Laon.

Although he served the Bourbons briefly, it was without spirit or enthusiasm as he stalled with the disbandment of his beloved Guard artillery. In March 1815 he joined a plot with his brother, d'Erlon and Lefèbvre-Desnouëttes to raise the garrisons of northern France against the King the moment they heard of Napoleon's landing from Elba. He acted prematurely and unsuccessfully, being quickly arrested, along with his brother, and jailed. Luckily for him Napoleon's return was a triumph. He spent the next few months frantically re-establishing, recruiting and equipping the Guard Artillery for the campaign in Belgium. His reward was his appointment as second-in-command of the Guard Artillery and direct command over their foot batteries.

During the battle he was initially involved in co-ordinating the fire on Hougoumont. On Desvaux's death he assumed command of

---

The Fate of Baron François Lallemand (Brother of Henri)

François Lallemand commanded the Châsseurs à Cheval of the Imperial Guard. His exploits in the years following the battle make interesting reading and are not untypical of the later lives of a number of the Emperor's more ardent followers. Tony Linck in his book *Napoleon's Generals – The Waterloo Campaign* has described him:

> An inspirational and brave leader, respected by all who served under him, Lallemand also became one of those tragic punch drunk Bonapartists who in later life took loyalty to a ridiculous extreme.

After Waterloo Lallemand remained with Napoleon on board the Royal Navy ship *Bellerophon* in Torbay harbour while the former Emperor's fate was debated. When it was decided Napoleon would be sent into exile on St Helena, Lallemand's offer to accompany him was declined. He tried to escape from England but was arrested in Plymouth and shipped to Malta where he was imprisoned in Fort Manuel. Meanwhile, he was tried *in absentia*

and condemned to death in Paris for treason. The British released him and he spent some months in Turkey and Egypt before arriving in America. There he founded a Bonapartist colony in Texas for fugitives from the 'White Terror'. He was joined by his brother, Henri. When driven from Texas by the ravages of yellow fever he settled for a time in Louisiana.

In 1823 he returned to Europe to offer his support to the Junta in Cadiz that had risen against the Bourbons. The rebellion quickly collapsed at the first whiff of French musket smoke. Lallemand moved to Brussels where he soon ran out of money and friends. He returned to the United States, becoming a French teacher in New York. To his great delight the Bourbons were overthrown and he was able to return to France in 1830. Within a few months his rank and privileges were restored and he joined the Army General Staff. He served in the Cavalry Inspectorate, was commander of the 17th Military Division in Corsica and the 10th at Toulouse. By the time he died of a heart attack in Paris in March 1839, aged sixty-four, he had been made a Grand Officer of the Legion of Honour.

French 6-inch Howitzer

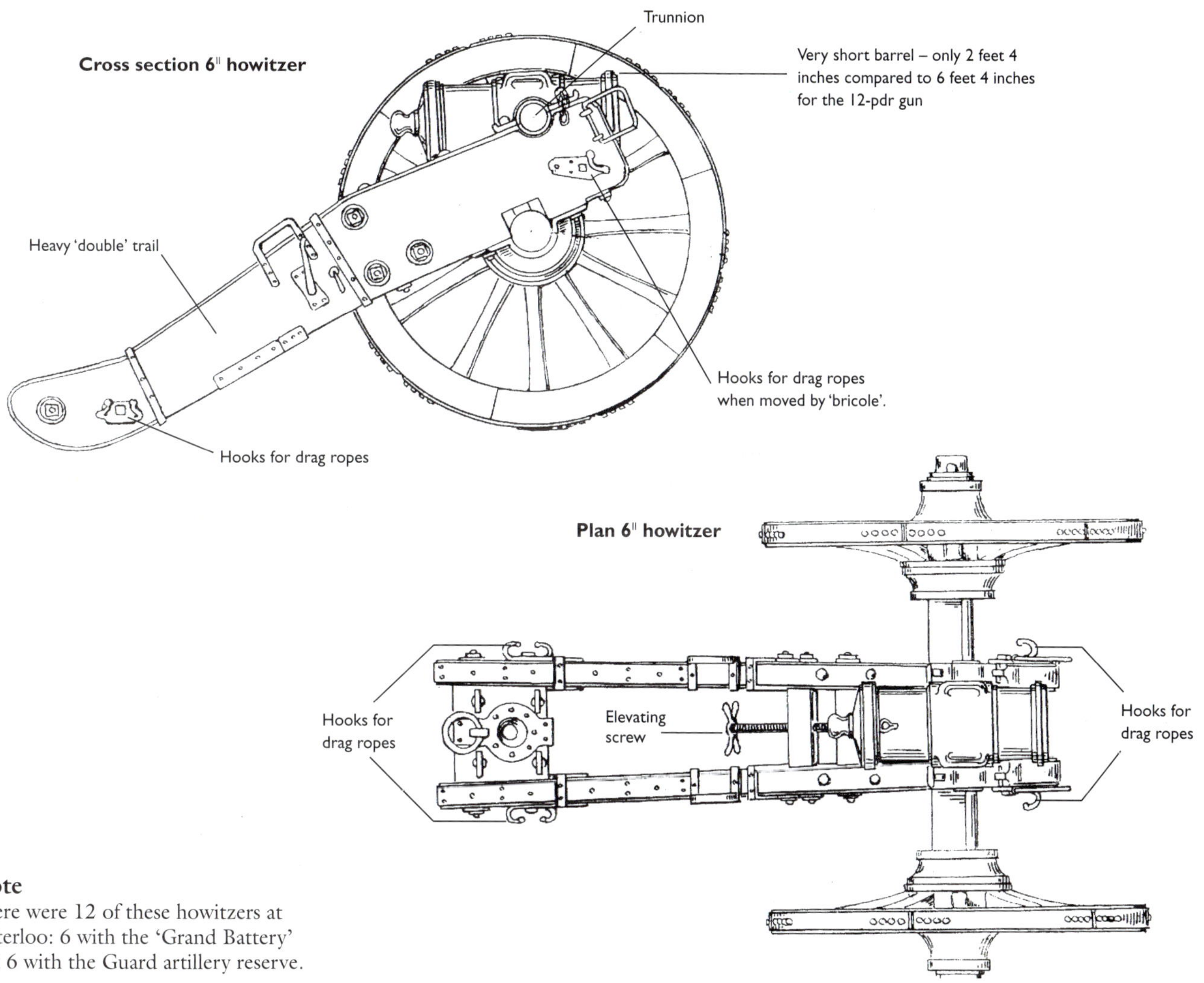

Cross section 6" howitzer

Trunnion

Very short barrel – only 2 feet 4 inches compared to 6 feet 4 inches for the 12-pdr gun

Heavy 'double' trail

Hooks for drag ropes when moved by 'bricole'.

Hooks for drag ropes

Plan 6" howitzer

Hooks for drag ropes

Elevating screw

Hooks for drag ropes

Note
There were 12 of these howitzers at Waterloo: 6 with the 'Grand Battery' and 6 with the Guard artillery reserve.

the Guard Artillery and spent much time directing the fire of the 'Grand Battery' during the latter part of the afternoon. Some sources say he refused a request to allow two Guard Horse Artillery batteries to support the cavalry charges. Be that as it may, some Guard guns did advance with the Middle Guard in its final desperate attempt to break the Anglo-Allied line. In the final stages Lallemand was wounded.

He was later arrested but escaped to America where, in Texas, he founded a colony of French fugitives who dreamed and planned of freeing their old Emperor from St Helena. Their colony was run on strict military lines. They slept in their cloaks, woke to the sound of drums beating reveille and called all the roads in the camp after famous French victories. It all came to naught – yellow fever was a much more deadly enemy than their opponents on any battlefield had been. Lallemand and his brother moved close to Philadelphia where they joined more exiles, including Joseph Bonaparte, Vandamme and Grouchy. There he married, settled down, caught dysentery and died at the age of forty-six in 1823.

One of Napoleon's 'Beautiful Daughters' (12-Pounder Gun)

French Artillery Deployment West of the Genappe Road, Initial Positions and Subsequent Moves   Map 18

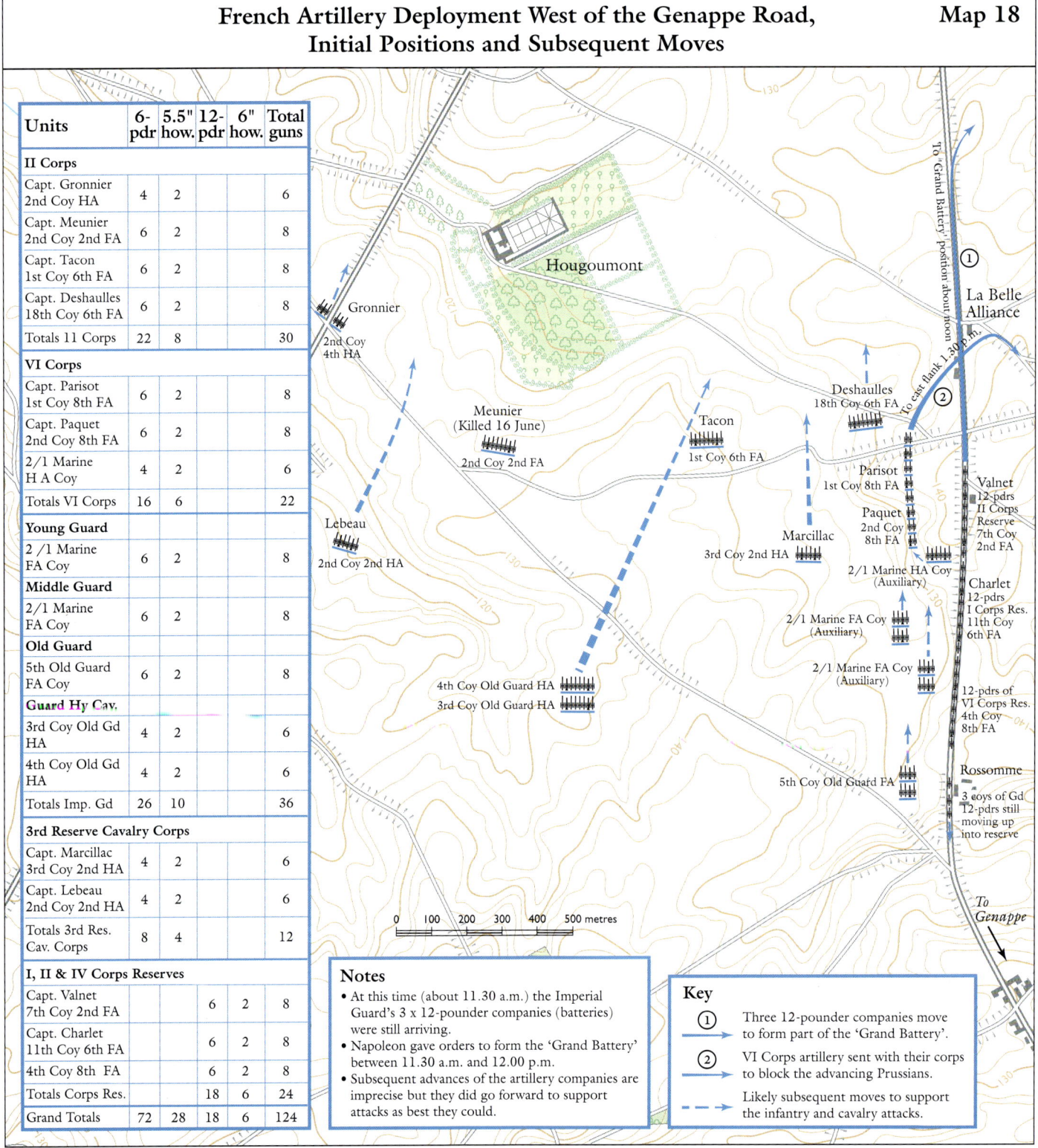

Units	6-pdr	5.5" how.	12-pdr	6" how.	Total guns
II Corps					
Capt. Gronnier 2nd Coy HA	4	2			6
Capt. Meunier 2nd Coy 2nd FA	6	2			8
Capt. Tacon 1st Coy 6th FA	6	2			8
Capt. Deshaulles 18th Coy 6th FA	6	2			8
Totals 11 Corps	22	8			30
VI Corps					
Capt. Parisot 1st Coy 8th FA	6	2			8
Capt. Paquet 2nd Coy 8th FA	6	2			8
2/1 Marine H A Coy	4	2			6
Totals VI Corps	16	6			22
Young Guard					
2 /1 Marine FA Coy	6	2			8
Middle Guard					
2/1 Marine FA Coy	6	2			8
Old Guard					
5th Old Guard FA Coy	6	2			8
Guard Hy Cav.					
3rd Coy Old Gd HA	4	2			6
4th Coy Old Gd HA	4	2			6
Totals Imp. Gd	26	10			36
3rd Reserve Cavalry Corps					
Capt. Marcillac 3rd Coy 2nd HA	4	2			6
Capt. Lebeau 2nd Coy 2nd HA	4	2			6
Totals 3rd Res. Cav. Corps	8	4			12
I, II & IV Corps Reserves					
Capt. Valnet 7th Coy 2nd FA			6	2	8
Capt. Charlet 11th Coy 6th FA			6	2	8
4th Coy 8th FA			6	2	8
Totals Corps Res.			18	6	24
Grand Totals	72	28	18	6	124

Notes
- At this time (about 11.30 a.m.) the Imperial Guard's 3 x 12-pounder companies (batteries) were still arriving.
- Napoleon gave orders to form the 'Grand Battery' between 11.30 a.m. and 12.00 p.m.
- Subsequent advances of the artillery companies are imprecise but they did go forward to support attacks as best they could.

Key
- ① Three 12-pounder companies move to form part of the 'Grand Battery'.
- ② VI Corps artillery sent with their corps to block the advancing Prussians.
- Likely subsequent moves to support the infantry and cavalry attacks.

DEPLOYMENT (Maps 18 & 19, above and opposite)
By the time the first French guns opened fire on Hougoumont and the ridge behind at around 11.30 a.m. the army artillery deployment was still incomplete. The deep mud was one of the reasons why the battle opened some two-and-a-half hours late. Napoleon's senior artillery officers had all advised delay. The ground was seriously hampering the movement of guns. The long columns of cannons, caissons and wagons were confined to the roads, indeed, they had absolute priority on the roads, particularly

the one from Genappe to Brussels. While the Emperor and his generals conferred over breakfast at Le Caillou, substantial elements of his artillery were still struggling slowly forward south of Genappe. Several hours would be needed for the guns to get up and the ground to become less boggy.

The six batteries of 12-pounders and 6-inch howitzers had the greatest problems due to weight, especially if they were forced to leave the road. Just one battery with its associated caissons and wagons would, in single file, take up at least 120 metres of road. So

French Artillery Deployment East of the Genappe Road, Initial Positions and Subsequent Moves

Map 19

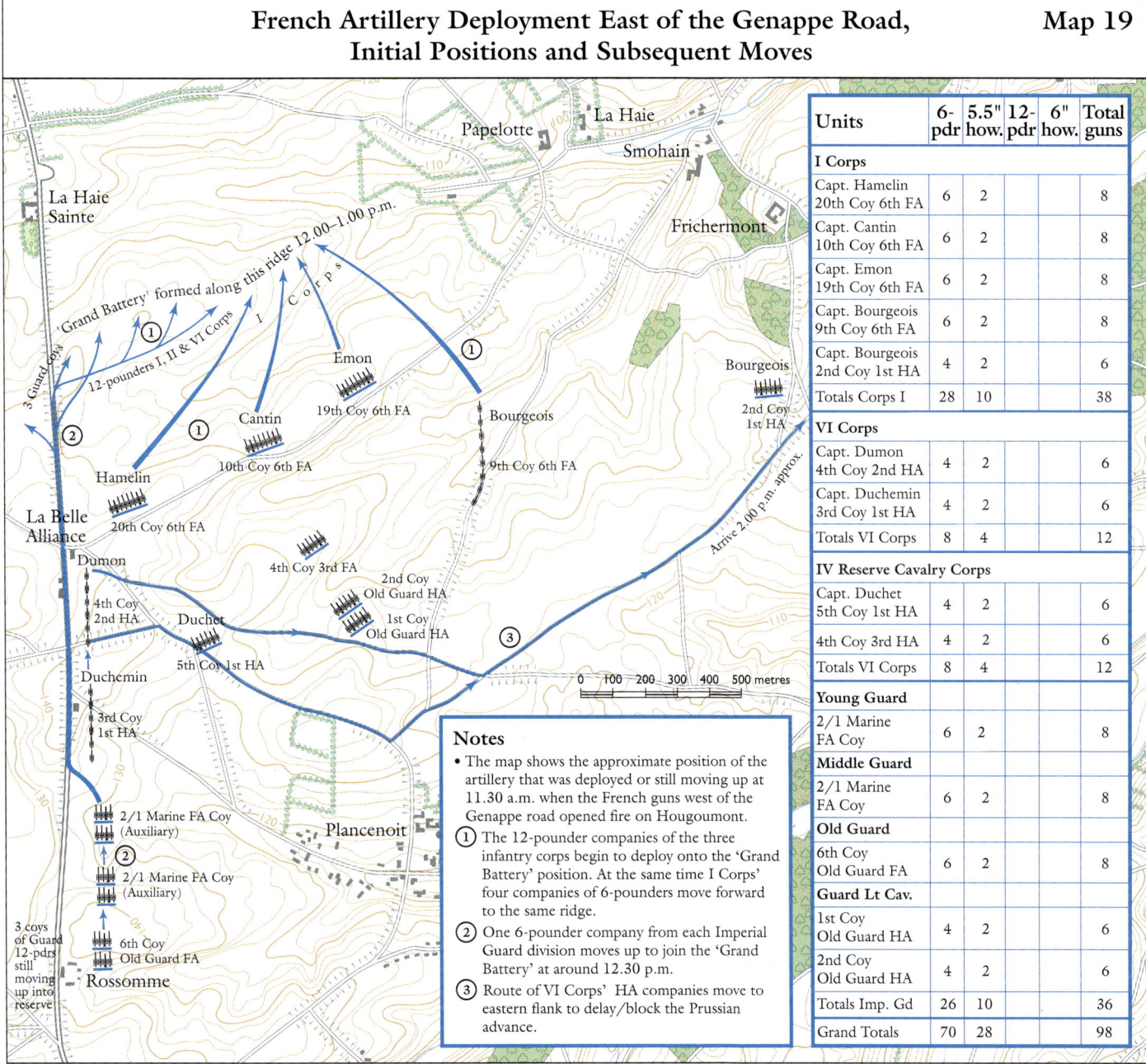

Units	6-pdr	5.5" how.	12-pdr	6" how.	Total guns
I Corps					
Capt. Hamelin 20th Coy 6th FA	6	2			8
Capt. Cantin 10th Coy 6th FA	6	2			8
Capt. Emon 19th Coy 6th FA	6	2			8
Capt. Bourgeois 9th Coy 6th FA	6	2			8
Capt. Bourgeois 2nd Coy 1st HA	4	2			6
Totals Corps I	28	10			38
VI Corps					
Capt. Dumon 4th Coy 2nd HA	4	2			6
Capt. Duchemin 3rd Coy 1st HA	4	2			6
Totals VI Corps	8	4			12
IV Reserve Cavalry Corps					
Capt. Duchet 5th Coy 1st HA	4	2			6
4th Coy 3rd HA	4	2			6
Totals VI Corps	8	4			12
Young Guard					
2/1 Marine FA Coy	6	2			8
Middle Guard					
2/1 Marine FA Coy	6	2			8
Old Guard					
6th Coy Old Guard FA	6	2			8
Guard Lt Cav.					
1st Coy Old Guard HA	4	2			6
2nd Coy Old Guard HA	4	2			6
Totals Imp. Gd	26	10			36
Grand Totals	70	28			98

Notes

- The map shows the approximate position of the artillery that was deployed or still moving up at 11.30 a.m. when the French guns west of the Genappe road opened fire on Hougoumont.
- ① The 12-pounder companies of the three infantry corps begin to deploy onto the 'Grand Battery' position. At the same time I Corps' four companies of 6-pounders move forward to the same ridge.
- ② One 6-pounder company from each Imperial Guard division moves up to join the 'Grand Battery' at around 12.30 p.m.
- ③ Route of VI Corps' HA companies move to eastern flank to delay/block the Prussian advance.

Napoleon's 'beautiful daughters' together with the 12-pounders of the three corps would occupy over 700 metres of road space. The entire French artillery (guns, teams, caissons and wagons) would, if all on a single road, produce a monumental snake at least 4 kilometres long. It was a lengthy process involving much shouting and swearing, stopping and starting, considerable sweating and a fair amount of skill by staff, commanders and soldiers to keep even short columns moving and then get them off the road into their deployment areas. Little wonder Waterloo did not start on time.

In fact, during the approach march artillery batteries moved with the divisions to which they were attached rather than in one enormous column of guns and wagons. As far as was possible, commanders and staff tried to ensure that their guns were on roads or tracks while their cavalry and infantry moved either across country or marched parallel to the road. It was vital, for obvious reasons, to at least have the lighter guns forward with their parent formation. The corps' reserves of artillery, in this case the 12-pounders, could move at the rear of the corps or the army in some circumstances. As shown on Map 18, all the 12-pounders were still on the road (the Guard's guns were well south of Rossomme) and had not yet deployed to their corps areas at 11.30 a.m. when the first shots were fired. Had the 12-pounders of the three infantry corps not been diverted to the intended position of the 'Grand Battery' at about this time, it is quite likely that these heavier guns would have remained halted on the main road for some hours, at least until the battle developed and suitable tasks presented themselves.

Staff officers were despatched at about 11.30 a.m. to the commanders of the artillery units that Napoleon had decided would make up the 'Grand Battery'. In many cases they met them on the move and had merely to indicate their new destination. Deployment of the French artillery cannot be said to have been complete until the 'Grand Battery' had taken up its position. Details of its composition, deployment, tasks and effectiveness are among the aspects of this battery described in the following paragraphs.

THE FRENCH 'GRAND BATTERY' (Map 20, p. 298)

General

As in so many of the Emperor's battles, the massing of artillery was intended to play a central part in the French plan to smash a hole in the enemy's centre. Through this hole infantry (d'Erlon's I Corps), and supporting cavalry, could attack with every chance of success. This tactic had been proved a battle winner across Europe. At Waterloo the number of guns was small in comparison with Wagram or Borodino, for example, but the principle of concentrating fire was the same. However, the 'Grand Battery' at Waterloo failed to achieve its initial aim. Its preliminary bombardment was ineffective, it inflicted few losses, it did not shake the enemy's morale – with the result that a four division infantry assault was seen off with comparative ease in little over thirty minutes. The reasons are explained below.

Composition

The precise units that formed the 'Grand Battery' were decided by Napoleon. In effect, he reinforced I Corps' foot artillery, including its reserve of 12-pounders, with some of the other corps' 12-pounders (from II and IV Corps) plus three batteries of Guard foot artillery. It was composed of:

Ordnance

Forty-two 6-pounders (eighteen from the Guard)
Eighteen 12-pounders (none from the Guard)
Six 6-inch howitzers (with the 12-pounder batteries)
Fourteen 5.5-inch howitzers

This gives a total of eighty pieces (sixty guns and twenty howitzers). One howitzer for every three guns was a high proportion.

Ammunition stocks

The French did not possess spherical case (shrapnel) so the stock of ammunition readily available to this Battery was divided approximately in to 69 per cent round shot, 18 per cent shell and 13 per cent canister. As the range and suitability of the target precluded its effective use, little if any canister was fired by this Battery. The amount of ammunition available at the guns (in the trail boxes) and in the caissons immediately to the rear is estimated, based on the average holdings of I and II Corps (whose stocks are known). Each trail box held about ten round shot, and each caisson between 100–110 projectiles. The approximate stock available to the 'Grand Battery' at the start of the battle was:

Round shot 15,300
Shell 4000
Canister 3000

The total number of projectiles available was about 22,300. If all these guns and howitzers each fired 150 shots during the battle (fifteen above the Anglo-Allied average), the total ammunition expenditure would have been approximately 12,000 rounds of shot and shell – comfortably within the initial holding of 19,300. Therefore, it is highly unlikely that any gun ran out of ammunition.

Limbers, caissons, wagons and horses

By the time the 'Grand Battery' opened fire, or within a short time thereafter, the gentle, 400 metre wide valley between the guns and d'Erlon's divisions formed up in rear was covered with some 350 limbers, caissons and wagons drawn by nearly 1,500 horses. In addition to the limber for each gun or howitzer, there were two caissons of ammunition for every line 6-pounder, three caissons for every line howitzer and 12-pounder, with the Guard batteries having three for their guns and five for their howitzers. Map 20 shows most of these deployed in three lines in the dead ground behind the Battery. Because of the difficulties of scale, the horses have not been shown and the caissons appear slightly closer together than they would have been on the ground. Nevertheless, with the addition of over 700 train personnel, together with the fourth line of specialist wagons (carrying spare wheels, carriages, mobile forges, artificers and tools, plus some infantry ammunition), there was a considerable body of vehicles, horses and soldiers keeping the guns in action. This body, and the gun line, presented a considerable obstacle to the advance of the infantry in the rear.

Personnel

In total, based on the all rank establishment of a foot battery, allowing for some losses at Ligny and Quatre-Bras and assuming that some infantry were drafted in to help manhandle the guns, the number of personnel serving the 'Grand Battery' was probably between 1,800–2000. This figure includes:

• 20 senior officers and their staff. These included Général de Division Desvaux de Saint Maurice who supervised and controlled the deployment and firing until killed; Maréchal de Camp Henri Lallemand (he took over on Desvaux's death), and Colonel Hulot whose regiment provided five of the ten batteries.
• 30–35 company officers with the guns.
• 70–80 NCOs (sergeants and corporals)
• 600 gunners in the detachments.
• 400 infantrymen drafted in to hump ammunition and help drag the guns.
• 700–750 train personnel riding/driving the horses, caissons and wagons.

Deployment (Map 20, p. 298)

Orders were issued for the assembly of the 'Grand Battery' at around 11.30 a.m. while a number of batteries, including the 12-pounders, most of the Guard's guns and Durutte's, were still on the move. It was also the time that Prince Jérôme's division from II Corps began its attack on Hougoumont Wood. From this time until the Battery opened fire at around 1.00 p.m. the eighty pieces and all their associated ammunition caissons were assembling along the ridge on which the gunline was to be established. It took time for the guns and their vehicles to move into their deployment area off the road, across the soft, muddy ground and through the high-standing wet crops.

The open ridge selected for the Battery's deployment made an ideal gun platform. It stretched for 1,200 metres from just east of the Brussels–Genappe road (and 400 metres north of La Belle Alliance) before it finally dipped down into the narrow valley leading to Papelotte. It ran in a roughly south-west to north-east direction, paralleling both the French and Anglo-Allied main positions. Although it was slightly lower than the Anglo-Allied ridge, it was about the same height as the French army's position 400 metres to its south. Between the Battery and the French line was a shallow valley that provided concealment and protection for most of the vulnerable supporting ammunition caissons, wagons

——— Anglo-Allied Units in the Target Area During its Preliminary Bombardment (Map 20, p. 298) ———

Target area A

One company 1/95 Rifles
Captain Cleeves's Battery KGL Foot Artillery
Lieutenant-Colonel Ross's 'A' Troop RHA
Major Rogers' Brigade Foot Artillery
Captain Bijleveld's Battery of Dutch-Belgian Foot Artillery (half battery only)
Captain Braun's Battery Hanoverian Foot Artillery
Captain Rettberg's Battery Hanoverian Foot Artillery
In addition there would have been some skirmishers, although it is likely they were mostly too far down the forward slope to have been hit by this artillery fire and skirmishers were seldom a worthwhile target for guns.

Target Area B

32nd Foot
79th Foot
28th Foot
Three companies 1/95 Rifles
27th Dutch Light Infantry

7th Belgian Line Infantry
5th Dutch Militia
7th Dutch Militia
8th Dutch Militia
3/1 Foot
42nd Foot
92nd Foot
2/44 Foot
Osterode Landwehr Battalion (Hanoverian)
Verden Line Battalion (Hanoverian)
Lüneberg Line Battalion (Hanoverian)
Bremen Line Battalion (Hanoverian)
Grubenhagen Line Battalion (Hanoverian)
York Line Battalion (Hanoverian)
1st KGL Light Battalion
5th KGL Line Battalion
8th KGL Line Battalion

This gives a total of twenty-two battalions, of which only eight were British. The majority of troops under this preliminary bombardment were German.

---

and the hundreds of horses. By pushing the guns 400 metres forward in front of the main position, the range to their target (the Mont St Jean ridge line) was reduced to between 600–800 metres. This put much of the enemy's front line comfortably within effective range of all the ordnance in the Battery. In front of the gunline the ground fell away into another valley before climbing a little more steeply to the Mont St Jean ridge. There would therefore be a time, as the advancing French infantry crossed this valley, when the Battery could provide some overhead supporting fire.

This ridge (hereafter referred to as 'Battery Ridge') had one potential problem from the French viewpoint – the guns along it seemed very exposed, isolated almost, so far in front of the army. The risk, however, was not as great as might be supposed, as the French were going to attack and they could assume with a fair degree of certainty that their enemy would remain on the defensive. The plan was for the French infantry to move ahead of the Battery in the opening moves of the battle. Napoleon obviously did not envisage these guns being attacked. He was proved wrong when the British heavy cavalry galloped up to the Battery and started slashing at the gunners and drivers, but this was a disorganized and unplanned attack that was soon driven off. The other minor difficulty on this ridge was that many of the guns could not be properly aimed due to the tall rye and wheat that stood higher than the guns' muzzles. The movement of horses and men subsequently flattened most of it but initially it is likely that company officers had to organize some trampling down in front of a number of guns.

The deployment of the batteries along the ridge in terms of where in the line specific batteries were placed is tentative. The positions shown on the map are likely possibilities but no source gives details of how the mixture of units was deployed. The four foot batteries of I Corps are on the right in the same order as their parent infantry divisions behind them. Next is d'Erlon's 12-pounder reserve battery, which is likely to have been the next to

arrive on the ridge. Then come the two other 12-pounder batteries, with VI Corps' on the right as it was probably the closest of the two when the order came to form the Battery. This puts all the 12-pounders in the centre of the Battery. On the left are the Guard's three batteries, which must surely have been the last to arrive from the rear. The extreme left-hand battery is that of the Old Guard, as it was the last formation to march up after the action started at Hougoumont. It is likely that this battery did not complete its deployment until nearly 1.00 p.m.

So as not to present too inviting a target, battery commanders would deploy their guns with about 10 metres between them. They could be pushed closer, but there is no reason to suppose they were along 'Battery Ridge'. A deployed eight-gun battery would therefore have had a frontage of about 80 metres and with a similar 10-metre gap between batteries. The 'Grand Battery' covered slightly more than 1000 metres of ridgeline. Before smoke spoiled the view it must have made a splendid sight.

The target

On Map 20, p. 298 the target area of the 'Grand Battery' has been drawn as a rectangle some 1,200 metres wide and 375 metres deep. This is the area in which the great majority of the round shot and shells probably fell. The range to the target area varied, it being shorter in the east than in the west. Thus the 9th Company of the 6th Foot Artillery on the right was only 450 metres from the forward edge of the area and 700 metres from its rear. On the other end of the line the Old Guard Foot Artillery Company was 700 metres from the forward edge and 1000 metres from the rear.

The area on the map has been divided into two. The first, Area A, shows that part of the target area falling on the forward slope of Mont St Jean ridge. This area received the bulk of the hits but contained the least enemy. Area B is over twice the size of Area A. It is on the reverse slope and as such was hidden from the French gunners' view. It received considerably fewer direct hits than Area A.

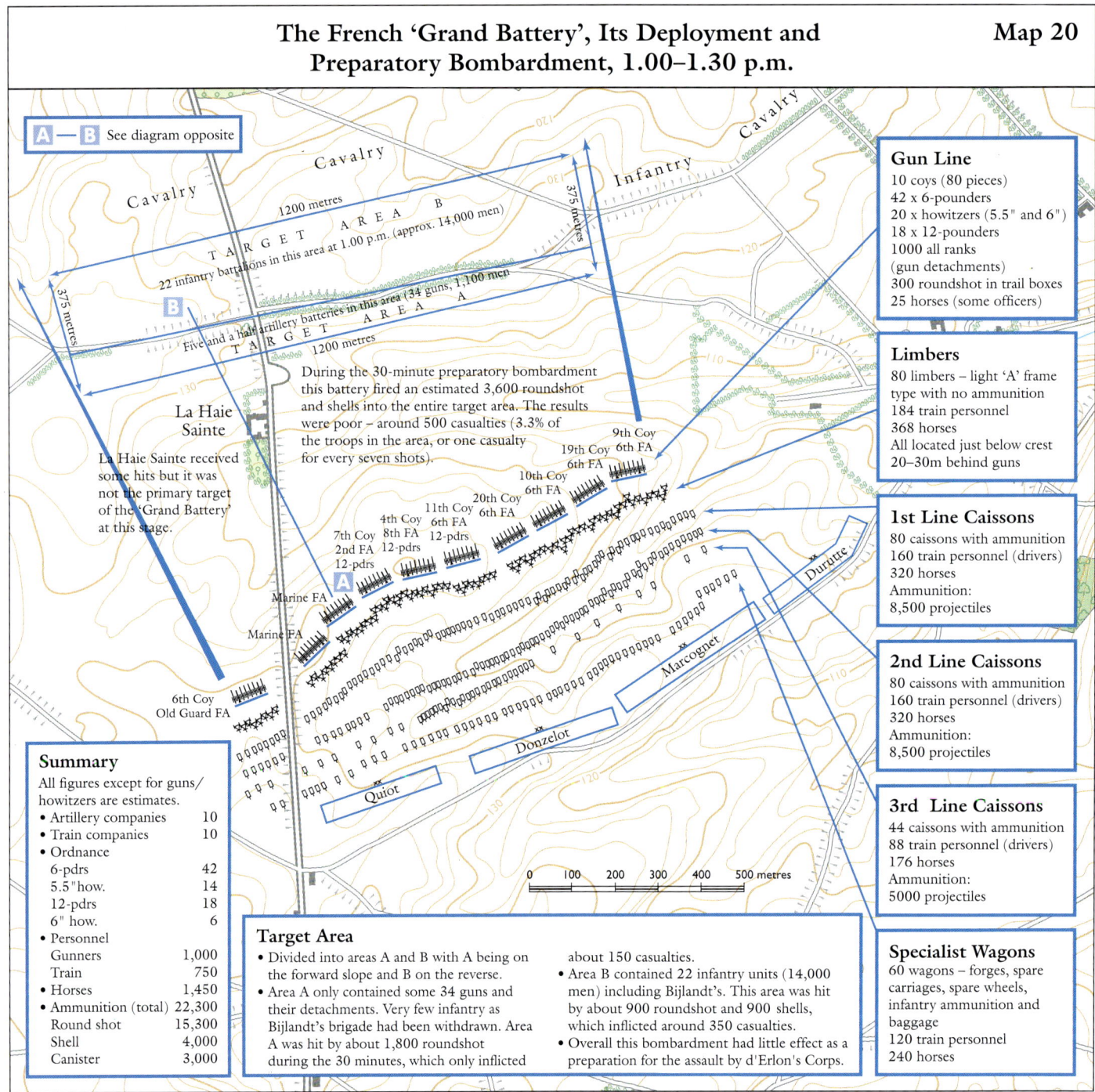

The French 'Grand Battery', Its Deployment and Preparatory Bombardment, 1.00–1.30 p.m.

Map 20

A — B See diagram opposite

Cavalry

Cavalry

Cavalry

Infantry

1200 metres

TARGET AREA B

22 infantry battalions in this area at 1.00 p.m. (approx. 14,000 men)

375 metres

375 metres

Five and a half artillery batteries in this area (34 guns, 1,100 men)

TARGET AREA A

1200 metres

La Haie Sainte

La Haie Sainte received some hits but it was not the primary target of the 'Grand Battery' at this stage.

During the 30-minute preparatory bombardment this battery fired an estimated 3,600 roundshot and shells into the entire target area. The results were poor – around 500 casualties (3.3% of the troops in the area, or one casualty for every seven shots).

9th Coy
19th Coy 6th FA
6th FA
10th Coy
6th FA
20th Coy
6th FA
11th Coy
4th Coy 6th FA
7th Coy 8th FA 12-pdrs
2nd FA 12-pdrs
12-pdrs

Marine FA

Marine FA

6th Coy
Old Guard FA

Durutte

Marcognet

Donzelot

Quiot

0 100 200 300 400 500 metres

Gun Line
10 coys (80 pieces)
42 x 6-pounders
20 x howitzers (5.5" and 6")
18 x 12-pounders
1000 all ranks
(gun detachments)
300 roundshot in trail boxes
25 horses (some officers)

Limbers
80 limbers – light 'A' frame type with no ammunition
184 train personnel
368 horses
All located just below crest
20–30m behind guns

1st Line Caissons
80 caissons with ammunition
160 train personnel (drivers)
320 horses
Ammunition:
8,500 projectiles

2nd Line Caissons
80 caissons with ammunition
160 train personnel (drivers)
320 horses
Ammunition:
8,500 projectiles

3rd Line Caissons
44 caissons with ammunition
88 train personnel (drivers)
176 horses
Ammunition:
5000 projectiles

Specialist Wagons
60 wagons – forges, spare carriages, spare wheels, infantry ammunition and baggage
120 train personnel
240 horses

Summary
All figures except for guns/howitzers are estimates.

• Artillery companies	10
• Train companies	10
• Ordnance	
6-pdrs	42
5.5"how.	14
12-pdrs	18
6" how.	6
• Personnel	
Gunners	1,000
Train	750
• Horses	1,450
• Ammunition (total)	22,300
Round shot	15,300
Shell	4,000
Canister	3,000

Target Area
• Divided into areas A and B with A being on the forward slope and B on the reverse.
• Area A only contained some 34 guns and their detachments. Very few infantry as Bijlandt's brigade had been withdrawn. Area A was hit by about 1,800 roundshot during the 30 minutes, which only inflicted about 150 casualties.
• Area B contained 22 infantry units (14,000 men) including Bijlandt's. This area was hit by about 900 roundshot and 900 shells, which inflicted around 350 casualties.
• Overall this bombardment had little effect as a preparation for the assault by d'Erlon's Corps.

The effectiveness of the 'Grand Battery's' preliminary bombardment

As a massed battery firing to soften up the enemy preparatory to an infantry attack that was to smash the Anglo-Allied centre, pave the way for the seizing of the Mont St Jean crossroads and the march on Brussels, it was a singular failure. Why did the thirty minutes uninterrupted bombardment by eighty guns and howitzers only inflict around 500 (3.3 per cent) casualties among the 15,000 or more men at the receiving end? The explanation lies in a combination of factors discussed below.

Ammunition expenditure

Accounts that actually discuss the matter put the length of time of the initial bombardment at about thirty minutes, probably from 1.00–1.30 p.m. Assuming that the twenty-four 12-pounders and 6-inch howitzers fired one shot a minute, in thirty minutes some 720 projectiles were fired. The fifty-six 6-pounders would have fired at about twice that rate, which is some 3,360 rounds. This gives a bombardment of 4,080 round shot and shell, or an average of fifty-one firings per piece. However, this does not take account of the effect of smoke slowing the re-aiming process after each shot, or the increasing fatigue of the gun detachments as they sought to sustain a continuous rate of fire. These factors would reduce the overall rate. The average number of shots per piece over the period was probably nearer to forty-five than fifty-one. As no canister was fired, the bombardment would have probably consisted of about 2,700 round shot and 900 shells.

Target Area A (Map 20 opposite and Diagram below)
This comparatively narrow strip was all on the forward slope so the troops and guns in it were visible to the French gunners (smoke permitting). It was this area that the gunners were actually aiming at with direct fire. It is reasonable to assume that virtually all the shots striking this area were round shot fired from the guns (as distinct from the howitzers). It is also likely that about two-thirds of these balls struck the forward slope while the balance grazed or flew over the ridge. As noted above, some 2,700 round shot were fired in total, meaning that about 1,800 hit the forward slope.

The length of the target area was 1,200 metres, so over the thirty minutes there were only 1.5 hits per metre of front – a very thin spread in terms of quantity and time. As the ground was soggy, cannonballs rarely ricocheted but buried themselves in the earth if they did not hit an object or person. In addition to these factors, this target area had few troops in it. The only infantry formation initially deployed on the forward slope had been the Dutch-Belgian brigade under Bijlandt, but this was withdrawn to the crest or just behind it before, or at the start of, the bombardment (see Section 10 'Myths and Controversies'). All that remained in direct line of fire, the only targets visible to the French gunners peering along the barrels, were six batteries of artillery (thirty-four pieces) along with their detachments and drivers – about 1,100 men (Anglo-Allied skirmishers are excluded as they were never a worthwhile artillery target). During the entire battle, casualty returns for these batteries indicate they suffered some 300 casualties. As the intense fighting had switched to the western half of the battlefield by 3.00 p.m., it is reasonable to assume that 150 of these losses may have occurred during the 'Grand Battery's' initial bombardment. In this area, therefore, it is likely that the 'Grand Battery' only inflicted about one casualty for every twelve shots hitting Area A.

Interestingly, the tactical importance of La Haie Sainte as an outpost protecting Wellington's centre, and which was to prove such a difficult nut to crack, went virtually unnoticed by the French gunnery officers. Although it was hit, it did not, at this stage, receive the pounding it deserved – a pounding that might have rendered it untenable.

Target Area B (Map 20 opposite and Diagram below)
Over twice the size of Area A, Target Area B was invisible to the French gunners. It was entirely in dead ground on the reverse slope of the Mont St Jean ridge. This was why Wellington selected it. It was ideally suited to give some protection to his troops from artillery fire. Of equal importance was the issue that Napoleon and his generals had no idea of what was on the other side of the ridge, where troops were concentrated or any movements carried out. As far as his gunners in the 'Grand Battery' were concerned, they were firing blind into this target area, hoping that their shots would do enough damage. They were using indirect fire without the modern technology to make it accurate.

Two types of shot fell into this area. Firstly, the 'overs' of round shot that had just cleared, grazed or bounced (the state of the ground precluded many of these) over the crest. About a third (900) of the cannon balls fired might be expected to have done this. Secondly, virtually all the high angle shells fired from the howitzers landed in, or burst over this part of the target area. The estimated figure for shells fired is 900. Taking account of the area of Target Area B and the number of shots of all types hitting it (1,800), there was an overall hit rate of one for every 169 square metres – an area measuring about 13 metres by 13 metres. Again, a thin scattering rather than a deluge.

Standing, sitting or lying in this area at about 1.00 p.m. were twenty-two infantry battalions (about 14,000 men). Mostly they were in column of companies at quarter distance – fairly well

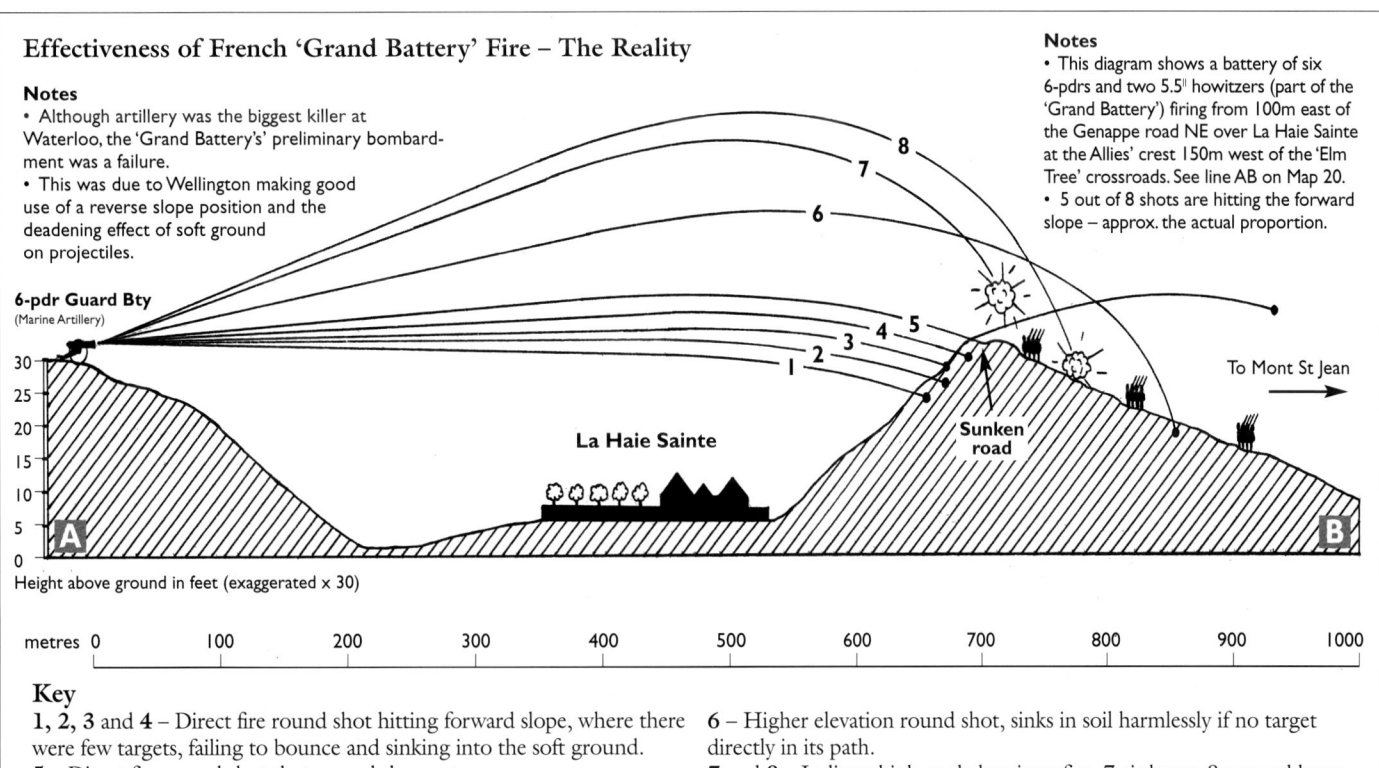

Effectiveness of French 'Grand Battery' Fire – The Reality

Notes
• Although artillery was the biggest killer at Waterloo, the 'Grand Battery's' preliminary bombardment was a failure.
• This was due to Wellington making good use of a reverse slope position and the deadening effect of soft ground on projectiles.

Notes
• This diagram shows a battery of six 6-pdrs and two 5.5" howitzers (part of the 'Grand Battery') firing from 100m east of the Genappe road NE over La Haie Sainte at the Allies' crest 150m west of the 'Elm Tree' crossroads. See line AB on Map 20.
• 5 out of 8 shots are hitting the forward slope – approx. the actual proportion.

6-pdr Guard Bty
(Marine Artillery)

La Haie Sainte

Sunken road

To Mont St Jean

Height above ground in feet (exaggerated x 30)

metres 0   100   200   300   400   500   600   700   800   900   1000

Key
1, 2, 3 and **4** – Direct fire round shot hitting forward slope, where there were few targets, failing to bounce and sinking into the soft ground.
5 – Direct fire round shot that grazed the crest.

6 – Higher elevation round shot, sinks in soil harmlessly if no target directly in its path.
7 and **8** – Indirect high angle howitzer fire. 7 air burst, 8 ground burst.

A view of the centre/left of Wellington's position from the 'Grand Battery's' ridge

La Haie
Sainte

Hanoverian
memorial

Sandpit
area

Out of sight on reverse slope
Kempt's Brigade.

**Bijlandt's Dutch/Belgians initially formed
here, but were withdrawn behind ridge
into gap between Kempt and Pack
before main French bombardment.**

Out of sight on reverse slope
Pack's Brigade.

Fichermont
convent

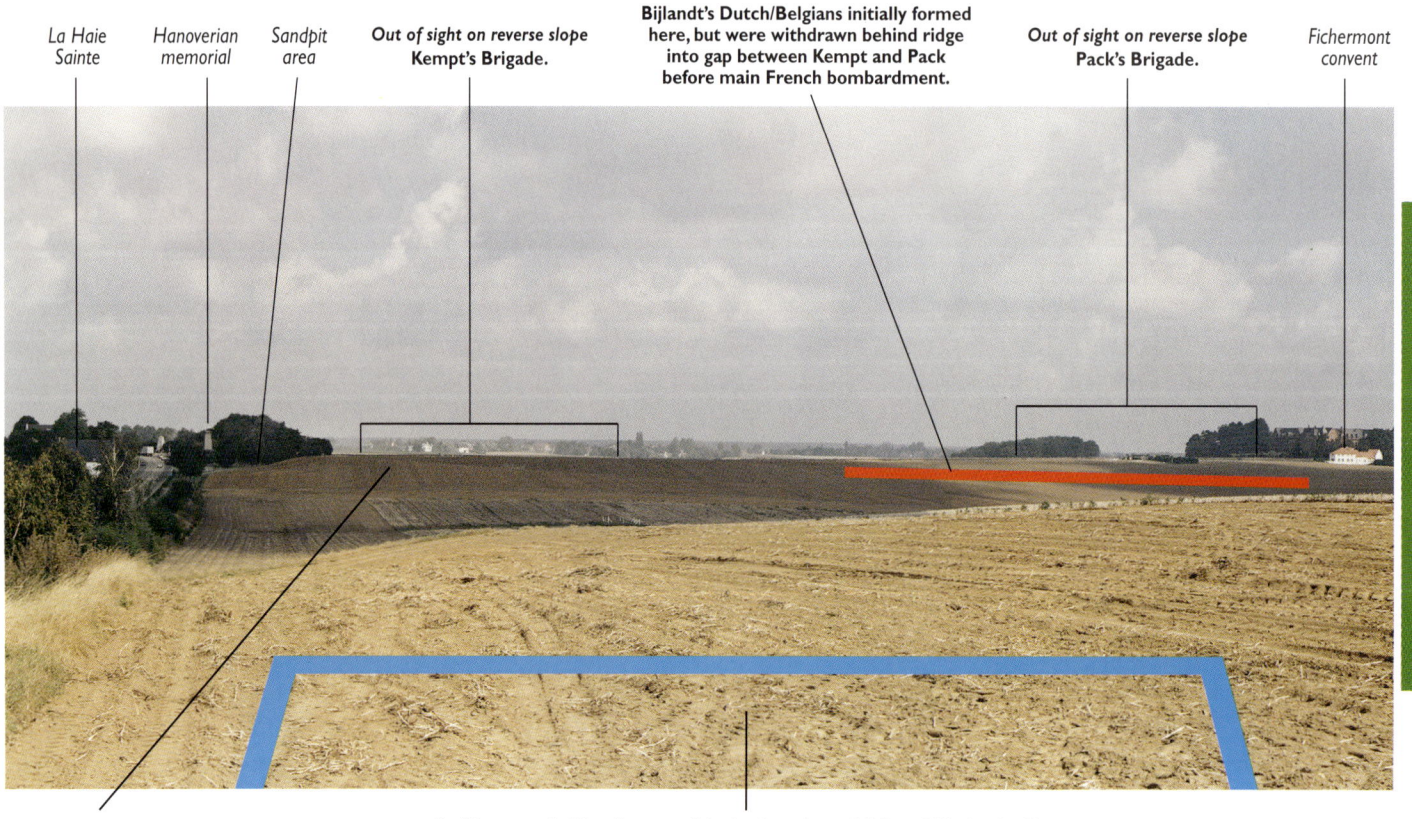

Joins here with image below

**This small 'sandpit' ridge shielded the
main ridge from fire and view for over
200m east of the 'Elm Tree' crossroads.
On it was a company of the 1/95 Rifles.**

Position occupied by a battery of 6-pdrs from Imperial Guard Marine Artillery.

Note how difficult it is to see anything of the target.

A view of the 'Grand Battery's' position – looking east

**At the extreme eastern end of the position
was No. 9 Coy of Col Hulot's 6th Regt FA.**

*Papelotte
La Haie
Smohain*

Joins here with image above

**In this area were
the limbers,
caissons and
wagons.**

**In the foreground were the 6-pdrs
from the Guard's Marine Artillery.**

**In the centre of the position
were the 12-pdr batteries.**

closed up. The losses suffered by all these units during the battle amounted to 3,350. During that thirty-minute bombardment, with some balls flying over their heads and some shells burying themselves in the mud before exploding, it is most unlikely that more than a tenth of these casualties were a result of the 'Grand Battery's' preliminary bombardment. This would indicate perhaps 350 killed or wounded – one shot in five being effective.

Conclusions

These may be summarized as:

• Some 3,600 shots were fired into the area during the thirty-minute bombardment.
• Of these, about half hit the forward slope, the other 1,800 falling on the reverse slope part of the target area.
• There were over 15,000 troops in the target area, of which an estimated 500 (3.3 per cent) were hit during the bombardment

i.e. one shot in seven was effective.
• This low level of losses was due to:
– Most troops being hidden from the gunners by ground and smoke.
– The ridge protected the great bulk of the troops from at least 50 per cent of the shots fired.
– The soft ground tended to absorb both round shot and shells that landed (there was little rolling or ricocheting).
– The relatively small number of shots fired into a large area.

Let an officer of Picton's division who stood under the bombardment have the final say:

> A furious fire of artillery from the whole line opposite to Picton's burst upon us. The greater part, fortunately, went over our heads, carrying one off here and there. This fire was much too high; the old hands said it was meant to intimidate, as usual.

PRUSSIAN ARTILLERY (Maps 37 & 38, pp. 387 & 392)

General

The problem facing the Prussian General Staff in March and April 1815 was not so much procuring the ordnance for the forthcoming campaign, but in finding trained men to use them and horses to pull them. The war cabinet had decreed that the army required seventy-six batteries, twenty more than had been available the previous year. So despite the dramatic decline in manpower following the armistice of 1814, more men were needed for more guns than before. Eventually, Blücher's Army of the Lower Rhine took the field with thirty-eight out of the forty-eight batteries that this army was supposed to have. The Prussian Commander-in-Chief of Artillery, Prince August of Prussia, even wanted to go as far as drafting in semi-invalids to make up numbers. The King overruled him, although a number of the least infirm were allowed to join the Laboratory Columns tasked with the manufacture of ammunition. Artillery recruitment was, however, opened up to volunteers from the infantry or cavalry, which provided uniformed manpower but not trained gunners.

Finding trained personnel for many of the new 12-pounder batteries proved impossible. Nine of them were forced to accept infantry reservists, train personnel and men from East Prussian infantry depot battalions. None of these fought at Waterloo, but three were in action at Ligny where their performance was, not surprisingly, unimpressive.

Blücher's forces had four army corps, each of which had an artillery commander who assigned the batteries to the infantry and cavalry brigades (divisions) as required for the campaign or operation. He would keep a number of batteries in reserve – always the 12-pounders, sometimes 6-pounders as well.

Exactly thirty-eight Prussian batteries marched into Belgium – 304 pieces of ordnance (forty-eight 12-pounder guns, sixteen 10-pounder howitzers, one hundred and seventy-four 6-pounder guns and sixty-six 7-pounder howitzers). They were approximately equally divided among the four army corps. Three of these corps

received a severe battering at Ligny. After a seesaw struggle for several small villages, they were eventually driven off the field by inferior numbers of superior troops. Their artillery, in action throughout the battle, had suffered appreciable losses (twenty-one guns); one battery in II Corps (Captain Bully's) lost all its guns and howitzers. This was why IV Corps, which had yet to see a shot fired in anger, was put in the lead for the march to join Wellington at Waterloo. Despite the Lasne defile, the bottleneck at the bridge, the steep hills, the rutted tracks and deep mud en route, all the batteries of IV Corps reached the battlefield in time to participate. Of the seventeen batteries that reached the field, eleven were with IV Corps. Of the other six, two arrived so late it is doubtful if they fired a shot. The estimated numbers and general location of the Prussian ordnance at around 8.30 p.m. on 18 June was as follows:

On the Waterloo battlefield – 134 pieces
En route to the Waterloo battlefield – 106 pieces
On the Wavre battlefield – 41 pieces
On detached duty – 2 pieces

The twenty-one missing pieces had been lost at Ligny or in the scramble to get away afterwards.

COMPOSITION

As with other armies, the Prussians had foot and horse artillery. Like the French, they were equipped with light 6-pounders and the heavier 12-pounders, but the howitzers in the light batteries were 7-pounders, while those with the heavy batteries were 10-pounders. There were six horse batteries (all 6-pounders) and eleven foot batteries (including three 12-pounders) present at Waterloo. The distribution is shown in the table below of the ordnance that reached the battlefield before the French fled.

each battery but with no allowance made for reserves. Calculations assume all ordnance was pulled by six horses except 12-pounders, which had eight, while all caissons needed four.

6-pounder foot battery – 72
6-pounder horse battery – 200, of which just under half would be
    draft animals
12-pounder foot battery – 112

Ammunition

Artillery ammunition was available to the guns from four sources at Waterloo.

The first was that carried in the trail chest on the gun or howitzer itself. This allowed it to come into action the moment it was in position; a few round shot and two or three canister could be grabbed straight from the box. The second was from the limber. The Prussian limber was larger than the French and carried ammunition in boxes. This was the 1st line reserve, which was readily available to the battery. In action the limbers and teams were kept close behind the guns. These boxes could be off-loaded and carried to the guns within a matter of seconds. The third reserve supply, or 2nd line, was held in the caissons. These wagons held a substantial number of rounds (see below) and were the principal ammunition source for the guns in battle. They were deployed in one or two lines perhaps 30–40 metres behind the limbers – it depended on the ground or if they could find some cover. The final supply was held with the munitions (park) column of the brigade. These twenty or more wagons were grouped together to the rear of the brigade. It was from this source that empty caissons came to replenish their supplies. The approximate holdings were:

Foot 6-pounder gun
Trail chest – 9 round shot, 3 canister
Limber – 45 round shot, 25 canister
Caisson – 143 round shot, 45 canister
Total per battery – 610 round shot, 258 canister

Foot 7-pounder howitzer
Trail chest – 6 shell, 4 canister
Limber – 14 shell, 6 canister
Caisson – 60 shell, 20 canister, 3 incendiary shell, 2 illuminating
Total per battery – 160 shell, 60 canister, 6 incendiary,
    4 illuminating

Horse 6-pounder gun
Trail chest – 9 round shot, 3 canister
Limber – 45 round shot, 15 canister
Caisson – 90 round shot, 25 canister
Total per battery – 664 round shot, 208 canister

Horse 7-pounder howitzer – as for foot 7-pounder howitzer

Foot 12-pounder gun
No trail chest
Limber – 12 round shot, 9 canister
Caisson – 70 round shot, 25 canister
Total per battery – 492 round shot, 118 canister

Foot 10-pounder howitzer
No trail chest
Limber – 4 shell, 1 canister
Caisson – 36 shell, 8 canister, 2 incendiary, 2 illuminating
Total per battery – 152 shell, 34 canister, 8 incendiary,
    8 illuminating

Points of interest:
• About 54 per cent of Prussian artillery ammunition was round shot, 29 per cent canister and 17 per cent shell.
• The Prussians brought about 15,750 projectiles (round shot, canister and shells) onto the Waterloo battlefield that were readily available to the 134 pieces. This excludes the stocks held with the munitions' columns, which would have more than doubled this figure. However, the amount available within the immediate battery area appears quite light (averaging less than 120 per piece) compared with the French 'Grand Battery' with over 270 per piece.
• The Prussians had far fewer (but larger) ammunition caissons moving with the battery than either the French or Anglo-Allied artillery. The comparison with the French is startling. One of Napoleon's line foot 6-pounder batteries of eight pieces had eighteen caissons following it and forming up behind it in action. A similar Prussian battery had four plus two rack wagons, although they carried more.
• Artillery ammunition expenditure was discussed above on p. 268. Overall, the Prussians fired about 4,700 projectiles – thirty-five rounds per gun or howitzer (many fired much more, a number may not have fired at all). So despite the seemingly low immediate stocks, they easily met their requirements at Waterloo.

Deployment

It took a long time for all the batteries (seventeen) to deploy onto the Waterloo battlefield. The first to come into action was almost certainly Captain von Zincken's 6-pounder horse artillery battery with the 1st Cavalry Brigade of IV Corps. This formation under Count Schwerin clashed with French cavalry on the eastern edge of the Bois de Paris at around 3.30 p.m. Thereafter the Prussian guns arrived piecemeal with their parent formations from 4.30 p.m. until around 8.00 p.m. or even later. Apart from the late arrivals the batteries were fed into the fight (mainly for Plancenoit) as and when they appeared off the line of march. No attempt was made to group the batteries, as the Prussians were fighting an offensive, and therefore mobile, battle. Batteries moved and fired in support of the infantry and cavalry during the long and bitter struggle, first to reach Plancenoit, and then to take it. If it was uncertain on which flank to deploy the guns at the start of an advance or attack, then it was usual to split the battery in two with half on either flank.

Casualties

Losses among the Prussian artillery at Waterloo were negligible. A total of 102 all ranks were killed or wounded, or 4 per cent of those present. No officers died and only two were wounded. The three 12-pounder batteries of IV Corps artillery reserve incurred the highest number of losses (thirty-six). This tiny proportion of casualties reflects not that most batteries were not fully committed, but rather that the French gunfire was concentrated on the attacking infantry units.

Other Arms and Services

Engineers and Pioneers

GENERAL

There were very few engineers or pioneers at Waterloo. The combined total for all three armies barely exceeded 2000. They were specialist troops who earned their extra pay attacking fortified places, constructing permanent works, tunnelling, mining, building bridges or field defences and road repair, rather than firing muskets on a battlefield. All engineer officers received technical training at appropriate military schools. They played a particularly crucial role in the supervision of siege operations. With the exception of the French, all the armies that met at Waterloo had marched into Belgium with an inadequate establishment of technical troops. Napoleon mustered some twelve companies totalling over 1000 men, Wellington slightly over 800, and Blücher under 400.

These special troops went by a variety of names, most of which give a reasonable clue as to their duties. There were engineers (always officers), pioneers, sappers, miners, pontooneers (somewhat perversely often classified as artillery troops), artisans and staff corps personnel. During the three days prior to the battle it was the French who had the most need for engineers or pioneers from the outset; they were advancing, they needed to cross rivers, they needed to know the state of the roads – they needed the mobility that these specialist troops were trained and equipped to help provide. For this reason Napoleon pushed his engineer companies and pontooneers up with his advance guard units, on the heels of his light cavalry, when he crossed the Belgian border.

The few Prussian pioneers were totally inadequate for route repair at the Lasne defile or along the muddy tracks leading from Wavre through the Bois de Paris to the battlefield. The Prussian ability to keep moving on that endless march depended on the sheer determination of the infantry and artillery to keep going.

ANGLO-ALLIED ENGINEERS

General

The role of Anglo-Allied engineers at Waterloo could only have been one of supervising the constructing of field fortifications, barricades or strengthening buildings, as Wellington intended to fight a defensive battle. There is little evidence to suggest that they did any of these things, or even that most of the men who would normally be expected to do this work were actually on the battlefield – no Sappers and Miners are listed on the Waterloo Medal Roll, for example. Attempts to prepare the buildings at Hougoumont, La Haie Sainte or Papelotte were left to the infantry garrisons. It was a similar story with the hasty barricades of branches and bushes thrown across the Genappe and Nivelles roads.

Wellington's engineer troops were a somewhat fragmented organization at Waterloo, consisting of:

Royal Engineer staff
Royal Sappers and Miners
Staff Corps personnel
Dutch-Belgian engineer detachment.

Royal Engineers

The Corps of Royal Engineers was composed exclusively of officers. In 1813 there were only 262 in the entire army. Those with Wellington at Waterloo formed an engineer staff, or pool of officers, at headquarters under Lieutenant-Colonel Carmichael Smyth, who later became Governor of British Guiana. During the Peninsular War with its innumerable sieges, bridge building and route reconnaissance requirements, engineer officers were in constant demand. During siege operations their duties often required them to be at the forefront of the assault – Lieutenant John Sperling, who was the adjutant of the Corps at Waterloo, had led the 'Forlorn Hope' (the leading troops in the attack on a breach in a fortress) the previous year at the storming of Bergen-op-Zoom. A total of 102 served in the Peninsula, of whom twenty-four were killed in action and one died of exhaustion – a higher percentage than for the infantry.

The Master-General of Ordnance controlled the Corps, not the commander-in-chief at Horse Guards – an arrangement that was of considerable satisfaction to the former and frustration for the latter. The officers, all trained at Woolwich, belonged to a tiny but exclusive family, whose members were better paid than infantry officers of equivalent rank. They wore long-tailed red jackets with 'Garter blue' facings of velvet, bicorne hats, carried straight swords and a telescope – a piece of equipment (and status symbol) as important to them as any naval officer. Because there were so few of them, promotion vacancies were distressingly scarce, so they waited for dead men's boots with considerable impatience, although the Peninsular War had helped. This lack of scope for promotion was reflected in their rank structure. An officer might expect to rise from 2nd lieutenant to lieutenant, second captain, captain, major (but only brevet rank), lieutenant-colonel and colonel. Exceptionally, one or two made general, but many more became grey-haired captains on half pay.

There were sixty-one engineer officers posted to the Netherlands in 1815 but only eleven were actually present at Waterloo. In practice the Royal Engineers played an insignificant

Wellington's Waterloo Map

This map, which eventually ended up in the Royal Engineers' Museum at Chatham, was allegedly the one used by the Duke to mark the Mont St Jean position. It is a large map, measuring some 4 feet by 3 feet that shows the country around Waterloo. It was hastily put together in Brussels, from original sketches made in the field by Royal Engineer officers, by Captain Oldfield RE, the engineer brigade major. He gave it to Lieutenant Waters to take to Wellington at Quatre-Bras on 16 June. Waters almost did not make it. With the map stuffed in his sabretache he set off. En route he was chased and almost ridden down by French cavalry. In the course of an exciting gallop Waters managed to extricate himself but lost his horse (and the map). However, the luck of this very worried young officer held and the horse was found quietly grazing nearby. Waters eventually reached the Duke's headquarters at Quatre-Bras.

When the Duke asked for the map Waters duly handed it over and watched as Wellington made some pencil marks near La Haie Sainte (that are still visible) indicating a likely defensive position for the army. The Duke then handed the map to his Quartermaster-General, Sir William De Lancey, with instructions to check the location and get the army into a suitable position. As we know, De Lancey considered the La Belle Alliance ridge (facing south) a possibility before deciding the Duke's suggestion was better. De Lancey was mortally wounded at Waterloo and the map, soaked in his blood, was removed from his pocket and given to Lieutenant-Colonel Carmichael Smyth during the subsequent advance on Paris. It remained among his family papers until 1914 when it found its way to the Royal Engineers' Museum.

role at the battle due to the lack of any requirement for, or time to construct, field fortifications. Only Lieutenant-Colonel Carmichael Smyth is recorded as making a contribution to the victory. Acting on the Duke's instructions, he had made a detailed survey of the Mont St Jean position the previous year, which facilitated a speedy deployment on the night of 17/18 June. Only Lieutenant Pringle, a Peninsula veteran, was wounded at Waterloo.

Royal Sappers and Miners

This formation was originally called the Royal Military Artificers and Labourers but dropped the 'and Labourers' in 1798 before becoming the Royal Sappers and Miners in 1813. They provided the tradesmen (carpenters, bricklayers, miners, smiths and masons, etc.) for the wide variety of work that the engineer officers directed and supervised. Any large-scale digging, dragging and lifting was done by civil labour or, inevitably, the infantry. As their title implies, their speciality was siegecraft – constructing saps, burrowing under walls, setting off mines or fighting claustrophobia and enemy miners in dark tunnels. They had done particularly well in the Peninsula at

San Sebastian in 1813, with the companies operating under engineer officers. As noted above, Lieutenant Sperling led the storming party, many of whom were Sappers and Miners, into the assault at Bergen-op-Zoom. In this case it involved, not attacking a breach in a wall, but cutting down palisades, crossing ditches, planting ladders against the wall and mounting the ramparts.

By 1815 they had become an infinitely more effective body than their disreputable forebears in the Royal Military Artificers. Ten companies were located in the Low Countries in the spring of that year, two (after the battle, five) of which were part of the pontoon train. The pontoon train personnel included a number of Flemish seamen who supposedly had local knowledge of the inland waterways, rivers and coastal navigation. The approximate establishment of a company of Sappers and Miners was one sub-lieutenant, four sergeants, three corporals, four second corporals (later lance-corporals), two drummers and sixty-four privates. The ten companies in the Netherlands amounted to ten officers and 772 other ranks.

From 20 June Lieutenant-Colonel Carmichael Smyth issued orders that each British infantry division would have a brigade (com-

Royal Engineer Officers at Waterloo

The following officers were present at the battle:
Lieutenant-Colonel Carmichael Smyth – Commander, Royal Engineers. Just prior to the commencement of the action he had occasion to put the officer in command of the Sappers and Miners company from Hal under arrest for failing to construct field works near Braine l'Alleud. He ended his career as Governor of British Guiana.
Captain Sir George Hoste
Captain John Oldfield – The engineer brigade major at Waterloo. He put together the map of the Waterloo area used by Wellington to mark on the Mont St Jean position. Oldfield subsequently rose to the rank of general.
2nd Captain Frank Stanway – As a lieutenant at the siege of Badajos three years before, this officer had led a party at night to blow a breach in the San Roque dam. He placed the explosives, lit the fuse and retired to await results. Nothing happened. It was the moment any officer in charge of a demolition dreads. Have I miscalculated? Do I wait a little longer? Do I go back and check; if I do will it explode as I get close? Stanway went back. Falling

water had dampened the slow match. Stanway relit it and was soon rewarded by a monumental crash – but no wall of water. The earth bank at the foot of the dam had protected it from the full force of the blast.
2nd Captain Alexander Thomson
Lieutenant William Pringle – The only engineer known to have been wounded at Waterloo.
Lieutenant Marcus Waters – The officer who took Captain Oldfield's map to the Duke at Quatre-Bras.
Lieutenant Francis Head – He rose to be Lieutenant-Governor of Upper Canada and was to survive Waterloo for sixty years.
Lieutenant Francis Gilbert
Lieutenant John Sperling – The corps adjutant at Waterloo. He had led the 'Forlorn Hope' with great gallantry at the storming of Bergen-op-Zoom in 1814. On 17 June he took the message to the Sappers and Miners at Hal ordering them to work on field fortifications at Braine l'Alleud – a task they failed to carry out (see box opposite).
Lieutenant Douglas White

pany) of about eighty all ranks attached to it, with their own drivers, tools, engineer stores and wagons, some of which carried sufficient spades, picks and axes to keep an infantry battalion busy. In April, May and June, however, circumstances had dictated that the companies were located where there was urgent work to be done. Under the overall direction of Lieutenant-Colonel Carmichael Smyth, they were tasked with improving the fixed defences along the French–Belgian border, the line of the River Scheldt, and to prepare inundations (flooding) west of that river. They were widely scattered, with junior NCOs or even privates supervising the work of large gangs of unenthusiastic civilian labourers; some 20,000 were employed. Hal was the depot from which these companies were equipped. In the weeks prior to the battle they made a significant contribution to the defences of Wellington's right flank from Ostend to Mons – an area of great sensitivity for the Duke.

Although the Sappers and Miners now wore scarlet jackets with dark blue facings (changed in 1813 from blue jackets, as the sappers were forever being mistaken for Frenchmen), the soldiers did not receive their muskets until shortly before the battle. Corporals carried swords, while sergeants bore halberds as well. In total, Wellington's army had almost 800 Sappers and Miners, 550 drivers from the artillery and hired Belgian civilians (the weak link in the system, described as 'ignorant of their duty and many of them of bad characters'). Over 1000 horses pulled their 160 engineer wagons, including the pontoons.

At Waterloo the sappers and miners were not engaged. Some should have been at work the night before at Braine l'Alleud (see box below), others could have usefully helped prepare Hougoumont and La Haie Sainte for defence. Of the three companies known to have been ordered to Mont St Jean, two arrived too late for the battle. One, under Sub-Lieutenant Johnston, was later to receive high praise for the efforts it made to reach the battlefield. At 2.00 a.m. on 18 June when Johnston started out, he was some

---

Wellington's Pontoon Train

Although it was not present at the battle, the composition of the Anglo-Allied Pontoon Train makes interesting reading. It was massive. To make a bridge over a river of under 100 metres wide required:

80 pontoons	348 Flemish drivers
8 engineer officers	105 seamen
4 sub-lieutenants commanding	861 horses – enough to mount two cavalry regiments
197 sappers	
5 field trains	4 wheel carriages
32 civil artificers	4 boats
2 lieutenants commanding	16 Flanders wagons
167 Royal Artillery drivers	4 forge carts

---

50 kilometres from Waterloo. He marched his men at a killing pace to arrive at the village, despite the congestion on the road from Brussels, fourteen hours later at about 4.00 p.m. – an achievement any infantry unit would have been proud of. The company remained at Waterloo village until the evening when it withdrew slightly along the Brussels road. Despite Carmichael Smyth's commendations and persistent applications by the troops, neither Johnston nor his men were awarded the Waterloo Medal. A company of soldiers had sat in the village after which the battle was named for over half the action but were not entitled to the medal.

The company that failed to carry out the digging of field works at Braine l'Alleud did, however, arrive at the village in time for battle. However, due to the fact that they did not arrive in time to carry out their orders, none of the company were recommended for the Waterloo Medal. These two incidents explain why no names of soldiers of this corps feature on the medal roll. The other companies were still employed in the rear and to the west on the lines of communication. A substantial number were with the siege train.

Siege train personnel were divided between I and II Corps, the Reserve Corps and the Pontoon Train – the latter under the command of Major Tylden RE at Malines, 20 kilometres north of Brussels. Each had engineer officers, about 150 sappers, several artificers, around thirty-five Flemish civilian drivers, fifteen wagons and a forge. The Pontoon Train had considerably more (see box above). None of these units appeared on the battlefield. However, a number from this corps were to meet Napoleon in very different circumstances a few months later, when a half company of Sappers and Miners was stationed on St Helena as part of the garrison-cum-jailers.

Royal Staff Corps

This small corps was formed in order to give the Horse Guards direct control over an engineer service. It was entirely designed to circum-

---

The Hal Sappers and Miners Company Fails to Construct Field Works

Regrettably, the only task known to have been given to engineer or pioneer troops at Waterloo, the Sappers and Miners company posted at Hal, was not carried out. Because of this failure the company commander, Lieutenant Faris, was put under open arrest, his men were not recommended for the Waterloo Medal and, according to Captain Oldfield RE, no sappers were available to put La Haie Sainte into a state of defence.

Early on 17 June Wellington had ordered Lieutenant-Colonel Carmichael Smyth to strengthen the position in front of Braine l'Alleud on the extreme western flank with earthworks. Carmichael Smyth sent his adjutant, Lieutenant Sperling, to Hal with instructions for the Sappers and Miners based there to carry out the task. Sperling arrived at Hal at 5.00 p.m. and passed the order to the lieutenant in command. The company commander, Lieutenant Faris, was told to move off within an hour and construct the necessary field works. It was 15 or 16 kilometres by road,

depending on the route taken – perhaps a four-hour march, five at the most. The lieutenant and his men arrived at Braine l'Alleud some fourteen hours later having, according to Faris, got lost in the Forest of Soignes during the night and then sheltering from the rain in Waterloo village until morning. The first person the unfortunate lieutenant met in Waterloo village the next day as he was starting out for Braine l'Alleud was Carmichael Smyth. There was an ugly scene, which ended in Carmichael Smyth putting Faris under open arrest. By the time the company arrived where it was supposed to be it was too late to do anything worthwhile. There is little doubt that Faris had been late leaving, as if he had started at six there would still have been another two-and-a-half hours of daylight, making it difficult for him to miss his way. During darkness, in dense woods in the pouring rain, missing a vital turning was not difficult. When the drenched troops reached Waterloo village the temptation to seek shelter proved too much.

vent the frustrations of having the Master-General of Ordnance run the army's engineers as a personal fiefdom. By 1809 it was a battalion-sized organization of ten companies that could be deployed around the world as circumstances required. The men were trained, equipped, dressed and armed as infantry but had a primary responsibility for field defences or fortifications. The soldiers' duties overlapped with those of the Royal Staff Corps, and those of their officers with the Royal Engineers.

With only ten companies scattered in widely separated locations, there was insufficient manpower in the Staff Corps to undertake major works unassisted. In fact, all personnel in the corps were classified as 'supervisors'. Muscle power was supposed to be provided by civilians or the infantry. The rank structure and pay was designed to reflect the supervisory nature of their duties. Each company had a sergeant-major, quarter-master sergeant and the rank of sergeant-overseer. There were no junior NCOs, but a 1st class private acted as a sergeant in charge of unskilled workers (civil or military), a 2nd class equated to a corporal and a 3rd class to a lance-corporal – he got more pay than an infantry private.

They had proved useful in Spain. It was a Staff Corps officer, Lieutenant-Colonel Henry Sturgeon, who had masterminded the construction of the famous bridge of boats near the mouth of the Adour in 1813. In March the following year, however, Sturgeon is said to have got himself deliberately shot at the outposts after incurring the Duke's displeasure.

In April 1815 four companies were sent to Belgium (another arrived in late July). Their usefulness at Waterloo is not apparent. As with Sappers and Miners, there is little evidence to suggest Staff Corps personnel were present at the battle – again no mention in the medals rolls or casualty returns, and no work assigned to them. Intriguingly, however, the Corps was awarded the battle honour 'Waterloo'. One source states that the Corps was attached to the Quartermaster-General's department and had, '18 officers and 256 other ranks present and under arms'. If correct, this would account for the battle honour. Yet *The Waterloo Roll Call* lists only nine officers as being actually present at the battle, the senior being Lieutenant-Colonel William Nicolay who eventually became a major-general and Governor of Mauritius in 1832. In addition there were three captains, three lieutenants and two ensigns. Four of these held deputy-assistant quartermaster-general posts on the headquarters' staff. This was a junior staff appointment, and the officers concerned (two captains and two lieutenants) were attached to various divisional headquarters. Several were used as military police directing the flow of units through the various bottlenecks on the route back from Quatre-Bras on 17 June. Captain Thomas Wright and Lieutenant George Hall were wounded. One of the others, twenty-year old Lieutenant Basil Jackson, had the distinction of living to be one of the oldest Waterloo survivors. He rose to the rank of colonel, wrote *The Military Life of the Duke of Wellington*, and died in 1889 at the age of ninety-four. Longevity was a family trait as his father, also Basil Jackson, was a fifty-eight year old captain in the Royal Wagon Train at Waterloo, dying at the age of ninety-two.

Dutch-Belgian Engineer Detachment

Although the Dutch-Belgians fielded a battalion of five companies, two of which were sappers, two miners and one pontooneers, the detachment at the battle was far smaller. I Corps engineers were provided with a weak company of sixty-eight all ranks under Captain Esau. There is no record of their task or performance during the battle.

FRENCH ENGINEERS
General

France's engineer service had been stronger, better equipped and organized than those of her enemies for many years, although at the height of the Empire there were never more than 10,000 engineer troops under arms, including an Engineer Train. They were organized into sapper battalions of up to 1,800 men and smaller, independent miner companies. They were all well trained under professionally qualified officers. Like their counterparts in other countries, their responsibilities were both destructive and constructive. The former involved siege-work, demolitions and mining, the latter building and maintenance of fortifications, bridges and roads. From 1809 every French army corps had one battalion of sappers and one company of miners under command. This establishment included 35 wagons carrying 1,700 pick-axes, 170 miners' picks, 1,700 spades, 680 axes and various hand tools and demolition equipment. For most construction projects the engineers supervised the work of labour battalions or civilians.

The main branches of what were regarded as the 'engineer' troops of the Empire were:

The Corps Imperial du Genie
- Headquarter and engineer officer corps
- Sapeurs (sappers)
- Mineurs (miners)
- Train du Genie (engineer train)
- Sapeurs-Ouvriers (engineer-artificers)
- Pionnier (labour) units
- Sapeurs-pompiers (firemen)

Headquarter and engineer staff officer corps

Engineer officers were supposedly graduates (although up to a third of captains in the sapeur and miner units were not) of engineering schools. This body of officers was 384 strong in 1803. It included three generals of division and six of brigade. The best remembered was General Maximilien Caffarelli, nicknamed 'Jambe de Bois' on account of his wooden leg. These officers had a wide range of duties. They were mostly scattered across Europe and in outposts of the Empire overseeing the maintenance, improvement and expansion of a vast network of fortresses. It was a monumental task with no ending, far beyond the capacity of the engineer troops available. Other officers were administering the engineering works (on bridges and roads, for example) within a '*direction*' (district) or '*sous-direction*' (sub-district) into which France and her colonies were divided. Still others undertook topographical reconnaissance along France's frontiers.

At Waterloo the twenty-two senior engineer commanders and staff were posted at army and corps headquarters as follows:

Army Headquarters
Général de Division Baron Joseph Rogniat – Commander-in-Chief of army engineers.
Colonel Baudrand – Engineer Chief of Staff
Colonel Bonne – Director Topographical Service
Captain Coffinal – Assistant
Captain Bellonnet – Assistant
Captain Robert Saint-Vincent – Assistant

Imperial Guard
Général de Division Baron Francois Nicolas Haxo – Commander, Imperial Guard Engineers. Haxo merits some additional comment.

General of Brigade (Maréchal de Camp) Louis Marie Joseph Maximilien Caffarelli du Falga

Louis Caffarelli was probably the most well-known and well-remembered (he was mortally wounded at the Siege of Acre in 1799) of Napoleon's engineer officers. He was first commissioned in 1775 aged nineteen, but enjoyed mixed fortunes under the Revolution, being cashiered several times and imprisoned once. Nevertheless, he was a thoroughly competent officer, becoming a companion of the young Bonaparte who always called him 'Max'. His left leg was removed by a cannon ball on the Rhine front. It was quickly replaced by a wooden one and Caffarelli was promoted general of brigade. Always a popular figure with his men he was thereafter referred to as 'General Jambe de Bois'.

A strong bond of friendship developed between Caffarelli and Napoleon in Egypt. They visited the ancient sites together.

On one occasion while exploring the ancient canal between the Mediterranean and the Red Sea their guides got lost and both were nearly drowned. Caffarelli had difficulty swimming and lost his wooden leg – although a spare was available back at his headquarters. At the Siege of Acre in 1799 homesick soldiers would exclaim, 'Caffarelli's alright – he's still got one foot in France!' Always in the siege lines supervising operations, Caffarelli was frequently exposed to enemy fire. Perhaps inevitably, a Turkish musket ball smashed his arm. The amputation was messy and agonizing. Napoleon visited his friend almost hourly, but infection set in and Caffarelli died of blood poisoning and shock. Napoleon wept. He was of the opinion that, 'France has lost one of her best citizens and science one of her most devoted servants'. Later he took Caffarelli's heart back to Paris.

A great man at a siege (particularly in Spain), his bravery under fire was never in doubt; he led his Engineers and Marines of the Guard in the taking of the main bridge at Charleroi on 15 June. His loyalty to the Emperor was, however, questionable. A chest wound, capture and nine months in a German jail, from which he was not released until June 1814, made him particularly servile and anxious to ingratiate himself with the Bourbons. Within three weeks of his return to Paris he was made a Chevalier de Saint Louis. March 1815 saw him commanding the engineers in Ney's force that was sent to block Napoleon. When Ney defected to his old Emperor, Haxo returned to the King, opting to go into exile with him. However, at the Belgian border his enthusiasm waned and he slipped away, and, with amazing gall, offered his services to Napoleon. Due to the urgent need for experienced senior engineer officers Napoleon accepted his offer.

His appointment, however, as commander of the engineers of II Corps, which was normally a general of brigade's post, must have been a deep disappointment. He must have been puzzled but delighted when, exactly a week before Waterloo, he got his old job back with the Imperial Guard. He was present at Ligny. At Waterloo his main task was to carry out a morning reconnaissance of Wellington's line to locate any field fortifications. His ride revealed the barricade across the Brussels road near La Haie Sainte. He reported to the Emperor, quite rightly, that there were no field works protecting the position. He neglected to emphasize that Wellington's army was, for the most part, entirely hidden on the reverse slope of the ridge – but then the Emperor was quite capable of seeing that for himself. One modern writer has criticized Haxo for not pointing out the 'weakness' of the Duke's left (eastern) flank. This is unfair, as Haxo, like everybody else, could not see what was on the other side of the hill on the left, centre or right of the enemy position. He also probably realized, as would anyone who walks the ground today, that the Anglo-Allied left was well protected by outposts at Papelotte, La Haie and Smohain, not to mention the tangle of hedgerows and sunken lanes all round – altogether something of an attackers' nightmare.

Haxo, true to form, was one of the first to suggest capitulation after the Allies arrived on the outskirts of Paris. He was itching to try his fortunes again with the Bourbons. They took him back. As a member of a court martial, he condemned to death a former Guard general. He became Inspector-General of Fortresses for the Northern Frontiers and, under Louis Philippe, fought again in Belgium in 1831 and in Holland the following year where he oversaw the successful siege of Antwerp. He died in Paris in June 1838, aged sixty-four.

I Corps

Maréchal de Camp Baron Garbe, Commander, Corps Engineers
Colonel Baraillon, Corps Engineer Chief of Staff
Chef de Bataillon Morlaincourt, Commander 2nd Battalion, 1st Engineer Regiment
Chef de Bataillon Quellard, Second-in-Command 2nd Battalion, 1st Engineer Regiment
Lieutenant Grimouville, regimental staff
Lieutenant Vieux, regimental staff

II Corps

Maréchal de Camp Baron de Richemont, Commander, Corps Engineers
Colonel Daulle, Corps Engineer Chief of Staff
Chef de Bataillon Repecaud, Commander 1st Battalion, 1st Engineer Regiment
Captain Sticker, regimental staff
Captain Levavasseur, regimental staff
Captain Noizet, regimental staff
Lieutenant Ythier, regimental staff

VI Corps

Maréchal de Camp Sabatier, Commander, Corps Engineers
Colonel Constantin, Corps Engineer Chief of Staff

Sapeurs

The bulk of the French engineer corps was sapeurs. Originating from 1793, sapeurs were formed into battalions of eight companies, each company having four officers and, by 1806, about 150 other ranks. Like other members of the engineer corps, sapeurs wore blue foot artillery uniforms and shakos with black velvet facings, scarlet piping and yellow buttons. They were armed with musket, bayonet and briquet (short sword). In the field it was normal for a sapeur battalion to be allocated to an army corps, with some of the companies attached to the divisions. Each company had its caisson carrying tools and equipment for building trestle bridges. Because their tasks during an advance involved bridging, route clearance and repair, they normally marched (often with pontooneers) immediately behind the advance guard. In retreat they were to be found with the rearguard demolishing bridges, laying mines or constructing obstacles.

After the restoration of the monarchy in 1814 the Bourbons restructured and reduced the sapeurs to three regiments of two battalions. Each battalion had five companies of sapeurs and one of miners. Napoleon accepted this organization on his return to Paris in March 1815. During the planning for the campaign the Emperor had been meticulous in his study of the river systems in the Netherlands. He was determined that his advance would not be slowed by lack of bridging equipment or pontoons. He crossed the Belgian frontier with over 1000 sapeurs from the 1st and 3rd Engineer Regiments plus a small contingent of Guard Sapeurs. This force was organized as follows:

Imperial Guard

One company of Sapeurs du Genie de la Garde under Major Bergeres – 112 all ranks.

One company of Marines of the Guard under Captain Preaux – 107 all ranks.

The Guard engineers were only five years old at Waterloo, having been formed in 1810 as firemen for the Imperial palaces. Firefighting was also their main duty on campaign, when six horse-drawn pumps accompanied them in the field with Imperial headquarters. The intervening years prior to Waterloo saw their expansion to battalion size and the undertaking of more 'engineering' tasks, but with only the 1st Company retaining Old Guard status. They are usually remembered by their elaborate 'firemen's' helmet. Made of iron, with a brass comb, chinscales, eagle plate, black horsehair crest and red plume, these men cut an impressive figure; however, only a handful, if any, wore them at Waterloo. The official establishment for a company was three officers, four sergeants, one fourrier, eight corporals, eight artisans, thirty-six sapeurs 1st class, eighty-eight sapeurs 2nd class and two drummers. Major Bergeres' company could only muster 75 per cent of its full establishment.

Although not sapeurs, the marines were grouped with them to form a small battalion for the 1815 campaign. This unit was well up behind the French cavalry when they were stalled by the Prussian defenders of the main bridge over the Sambre at Charleroi on 15 June. Vandamme's infantry should have been available to uncork the bottle but due to poor staff work they had been late starting. Napoleon himself arrived at the bridge and grabbed the only available foot soldiers – the Guard Engineers and Marines. Under the directions of Haxo they quickly cleared the bridge, allowing the cavalry screen to clatter across and the advance to continue.

At Ligny the Guard Sapeurs, still combined with the Marines of the Guard, formed a small assault column as part of the Guard's attack on Ligny. They captured part of the eastern section of the village. Likewise at Waterloo this unit had no engineering tasks and was used as extra infantry, kept in reserve with the Old Guard Grenadiers. They saw action covering the retreat of the army.

I Corps

2nd Battalion 1st Engineer Regiment under Maréchal de Camp Morlaincourt was a weak unit with only 351 all ranks and an average company strength of seventy. This battalion had attached Companies 1–4 to the infantry divisions. The 5th Company remained as corps reserve. The companies were deployed as follows:

No.1 Company under Captain Emon 1st Division (Quiot)

No.2 Company under Captain Chiappe 2nd Division (Donzelot)

No.3 Company under Captain Daigremont 3rd Division (Marcognet)

No.4 Company under Captain Parentin 4th Division (Durutte)

II Corps

1st Battalion 1st Engineer Regiment under Chef de Bataillon Repecaud had strength of 431 with companies averaging eighty-six all ranks. Companies 1–4 were attached to divisions as shown below, with No.5 Company held in reserve.

No.1 Company under Captain Lenoire 5th Division (Bachelu)

No.2 Company under Captain Cossiere 6th Division (Prince Jérôme)

No.3 Company under Captain Le Pecheur de Branville 7th Division (Girard – this division was with Grouchy)

No.4 Company under Captain Leroux-Douville (he was wounded, and the only engineer officer casualty at Waterloo) 9th Division (Foy)

VI Corps

1st Battalion 3rd Engineer Regiment. This was a small regiment of only three companies, two of which were not at Waterloo.

No.1 Company under Captain Toliot 19th Division (Simner) – ninety-five all ranks

No.2 Company under Captain Euzenate had been left at Laon awaiting further orders

No.3 Company under Captain Ferrey was attached to the 21st Division (Teste) serving with Grouchy

There is no real evidence to suggest that any of the French engineers had a particular battlefield role at Waterloo. They were present with their divisions and, if employed at all, it was likely they used their muskets rather than their spades.

Miners

As with miners in other nation's armies, these troops were usually highly trained specialists. They were mainly recruited from civilian miners already well versed in the techniques and hazards of working underground. Not only did they face the enemy in countermining operations, but the equally dangerous threats of flooding, cave-ins and asphyxiation. They were rewarded by Napoleon for these additional risks by being deemed the élite of all French engineer troops. They paraded on the right of the line – the position of honour; they were better paid and, because their duty was particularly unhealthy, there were limits set on the time they could spend on active duty in the field. When not on campaign, miners were usually given the task of demolishing obsolete or captured fortifications.

By 1813 there were two miner battalions each of six companies, although these were administrative units as the companies were invariably deployed independently. During the drastic Bourbon reductions to the army in 1814 the miners did not escape. Each of the six battalions of sapeurs was to have a sixth company of miners. However, sieges were never going to be an immediate priority for Napoleon in Belgium, so miner companies did not appear in the Armée du Nord's order of battle.

Train du Genie

Napoleon was to find that reliance on hired civilians and requisitioned wagons was not an effective way of moving large amounts of equipment on campaign for either the artillery or engineers. In 1806 he formed a small military Engineer Train. By 1811 it had six field companies plus a depot. Like all train troops, they wore iron-grey uniforms. Engineer train troops had black facings to distinguish them from the artillery train's dark blue and the supply

Pionniers Noirs

These men were Haitian blacks, many shipped to France as prisoners of war after General Leclerc had easily overrun the island in 1802 – although yellow fever later made him pay a crippling price. Having been assembled in France, they were taken in batches to Italy to be organized into two battalions of pioneers. At the Siege of Gaeta in 1806 they were offered a few sous for every unexploded enemy shell they could procure. An observer wrote:

> These negroes would follow through the air with greedy looks the enemy's bombshells for which they were paid; reaching them as they fell, they would dash upon them and pull out the burning fuse unless its premature explosion happened to kill them during this dangerous and not too lucrative sport.

Napoleon appointed a mulatto of great strength and bravery as their commander. His real name was Joseph Damingue but his size ensured him the nickname 'Hercule'. Hercule had made an impression as a junior officer in Italy but he was illiterate and Napoleon's elevation of him to colonel to command the Pionniers Noirs was a perfect example of a man being promoted above his ceiling. Hercule demanded, and got, an Eagle for his unit – much to the annoyance of the Miners who were not allowed one. However, his regime was slack and his men became surly and indifferent to their duties. Hercule was pushed, not altogether unwillingly, into early retirement in 1805; Napoleon allowed him to go on full pay. The unit was 'given' to the Kingdom of Naples as the 7th Line Regiment with the somewhat ridiculous alternative title of 'Royal Africa'. Nevertheless, a stricter commanding officer was able to make it into a reasonably competent unit. It saw service in Germany in late 1813. A Sergeant Burgogne commented on how strange it was to see so many black men, the sapeurs in white bearskins, standing shivering on parade in the snow.

train's brown. Although the train advanced into Belgium for repair and potential bridging duties, it was not on the battlefield at Waterloo.

The Imperial Guard also maintained its own Equipment Train, which in 1815 consisted of five companies with an established strength of two officers and eighty-three other ranks. Whether or not the train reached the battlefield is doubtful, it being more likely that it was halted in the vicinity of the Artillery Park at Quatre-Bras.

Sapeurs-Ouvriers

The original company of these specialist tradesmen was raised in 1811 to staff the new engineer arsenal at the Fortress of Metz. Its task was the manufacture and repair of engineer equipment. In 1815 the Guard had its own small section of twenty ouvriers under a captain. It may have been present at the battle, but if so, its role was of no significance.

Pionnier (labour) units

These units were employed on pick and shovel work behind the lines. They were not normally used in a combat zone and none were present in Belgium in 1815. A strange assortment of pionnier battalions was raised from punishment units, soldiers condemned to hard labour, foreigners, blacks from Haiti and, most commonly, prisoners of war. No less than thirty-eight prisoner of war battalions (mostly Spanish) were available in early 1811. Fifteen were working on fortifications, fifteen on roads and bridges, and eight at naval bases. Even then Napoleon demanded more, fifteen more, for work on the Channel coast. As well as the pionniers noir (see box above) there were pionnier blancs recruited from Austrian prisoners who did not wish to return home.

Sapeurs-pompiers (firemen)

They have been described as the 'engineer's poor city cousins'. They originated from the old Paris civilian fire service. By 1814 they had been militarized and expanded to a battalion of 600 men, including a band and drummers – wearing an iron and brass helmet instead of a shako. They paraded on the left of the line and marched at the rear of the column. They fought well during the defence of Paris in 1814, but were not involved in the campaign in Belgium the following year.

PRUSSIAN ENGINEERS
General

The Prussian engineer units were usually termed 'pioneers' and consisted of field companies of about 100 all ranks with two-thirds sappers and one-third pontooneers. In April 1815 General Rauch, the Chief of Engineers for the Army, stipulated that every army corps would take the field with two pioneer companies. With all the conflicting demands of reorganizing and recruiting for the army as a whole, this was an unrealistic target. When Blücher marched into Belgium each of his corps had one pioneer company. At Waterloo there was a maximum of 366 pioneers present, with the probability that only those with IV Corps (170) reached the battlefield in time to see any action.

Deployment

Engineer staff was deployed at army and corps headquarters as follows:

Army HQ

There were no senior engineer or pioneer officers at army headquarters, only one engineer, Captain Vigny, serving as a staff officer plus a small topographical section with 1st Lieutenant Holzwarth, 2nd Lieutenant Michaelis and Specialist Look.

I Corps HQ

Staff – 1st Lieutenants Beyer and Wittich
Topographical section – 2nd Lieutenant Krauser, Specialist Preuschen

II Corps HQ

Staff – Colonel Aster (corps chief of staff and commandant of the pioneers)
2nd Lieutenants Schubert and Polack
Topographical section – 2nd Lieutenants Elsner, Kuhne, Obuch and Geissler

IV Corps

Staff – 1st Lieutenant Buschbeck, 2nd Lieutenant Becherer

Topographical section – 2nd Lieutenants Binder and
   Schonermarck

Specialists Schelle and Fischer

The table opposite shows the Prussian pioneer unit deployment for the Waterloo campaign. Each unit includes a small detachment (column) of artisans.

Formation	Unit	Commander	Officers	ORs	Total
I Corps	1st Fd Pioneer Coy	1st Lieut Giese	2	103	105
II Corps	3rd Artisans Co.	1st Lieut Bunkowski	1	16	17
	7th Fd Pioneer Coy	1st Lieut von Uthmann	2	72	74
IV Corps	6th Artisan Co.	Sgt-Maj. Kruger	–	19	19
4th Coy	Mansfeld Pioneers	Capt. Nauck	4	147	151
Totals			9	357	366

The artisan column attached to I Corps was at Maestricht.

THE WOUNDED AND MEDICAL SERVICES

General

The scale of the task confronting all medical services initially swamped them. By the end of that 'bloody' Sunday between 35,000–40,000 men of all nationalities were lying wounded in the trampled crops, in ditches, in makeshift field hospitals or en route to Brussels and elsewhere. Thousands lay moaning piteously where they fell; thousands more were stumbling along, clutching desperately at their wounds as their life oozed from their bodies. Hundreds crawled or dragged themselves to the roadsides. All were in constant terror of the looter's knife. Some had the benefit of comrades, carts or even wheelbarrows to carry them. This crippled mass of humanity demanded urgent medical aid. There was not one barn, stable, farm, church, courtyard or house within a mile radius of the battlefield that did not have men bleeding and dying on its floors. Assistant-Surgeon William Gibney of the 15th Hussars later described the situation as, 'hideous, each house was packed to overflowing, every room was full … and little relief was given, often none … [no one had expected] so prolonged and bloody a battle.' Wellington wrote in his dispatch to London, '… such an action could not be gained without a great loss; and I am sorry to say ours has been immense…'. It was to be his last and bloodiest battle.

This insoluble battlefield problem of scale was made infinitely more difficult as the burden of tending and treating the overwhelming majority of all Waterloo wounded fell on the British and Belgians. Wellington's army occupied the battlefield, too exhausted and mauled to move; Napoleon's army fled; and Blücher's largely disappeared into the night in pursuit. Understandably, perhaps, the fleeing and pursuing troops took most of their medical staff but left behind their wounded. Then on the following afternoon the Anglo-Allied Army began its march on Paris, taking with it most of the 200 or so regimental surgeons and their assistants that accompanied their units – they were likely to be needed for further fighting. They left behind a depleted and exhausted medical staff. A number of French medical officers, including the chief surgeon of the Imperial Guard, Baron Larrey, were captured and gave valuable assistance over the coming weeks. But the problems remained daunting.

That so many survived their wounds and the agonizing, shocking trauma of amputation without anaesthetic was certainly in part due to the services of the Belgian (and to a lesser extent Dutch) civilian medical services and the ad hoc, spontaneous response of the Belgian rural population near the battlefield. They formed a rudimentary service of medical orderlies, nurses and general assistants. Undoubtedly some were battlefield scavengers, some were more inclined to help Frenchmen, and many resented being drafted in to

---

Survival Rate of the Waterloo Wounded

A reasonable estimate of this statistic is possible, as certain approximate figures are known. The likely overall number of casualties (dead and wounded) on the battlefield was around 54,000, perhaps slightly more (Wellington 17,000, Napoleon 30,000 and Blücher 7000). Some of those initially badly wounded would have died later during the day, before they could be moved or received any treatment. Based on other actions, it is a fair assumption that some two-thirds of total casualties were wounded who survived the battle. This gives a total figure of 36,400 men requiring medical treatment (Wellington 10,200, Napoleon 22,000 and Blücher 4,200). An overall estimate of 36,000 is probably not far out.

Lieutenant-General Sir Neil Cantlie published a book entitled *History of the Army Department* in 1973, in which he gives an assessment of the British wounded that received hospital attention in Belgium after the battle. Based on official contemporary reports he stated that 856 patients out of 9,528 died from their wounds. This is a surprisingly small death rate of nine per cent. It speaks well of the hospital care and treatment given, drastic though it invariably was, but above all of the inordinate toughness, will-power and sheer guts of so many of the injured.

Of course many died before reaching hospital because of the seriousness of their wounds, slowness of evacuation and poor hygiene, but in general terms the survival rate of those who reached a hospital was good.

A 9 per cent death rate of wounded men reaching hospital can be compared favourably with more modern wars. With American casualties reaching hospital, the death rates in twentieth-century conflicts were:

World War I – 8 per cent
World War II – 4 per cent
Korean War – 3 per cent
Vietnam – 1.5 per cent
Falklands (British wounded) – nil

The extremely low percentage in Vietnam and nil in the Falklands reflects the huge advances in surgical techniques – use of antibiotics, blood transfusions, nursing care and helicopter evacuation. Even so, the medical staff in the hospitals of Belgium in the weeks following Waterloo did remarkably well, judged not only by the standards of the time but also from those pertaining a hundred or more years later.

A Wounded Man Often a Loss Multiplier

Even today with swift casualty evacuation, often by helicopter, a wounded soldier causes greater loss to his unit than his comrade who has been shot dead. Many armies teach that, if possible, it is better to wound an enemy than kill him outright. This is because:

• A wounded soldier in great pain and groaning or screaming is bad for the morale of his close comrades. They do not like what they see and it can generate considerable fear – a highly contagious emotion.
• Soldiers near the wounded man may either stop advancing, or expose themselves in trying to pull him to safety. In the first case several men are out of the attack instead of just one; in the latter, several more targets are presented to the enemy.
• Several men will be needed to carry the injured soldier to the rear or to medical aid. The temptation is for his immediate comrades to do this, some because he is their friend, some perhaps as a good excuse to leave the battle. Either way, the unit has lost the use of three or four men instead of just one.

At Waterloo all troops were instructed (as they are today) not to help their comrades to the rear. Many soldiers in Wellington's army chose to disregard these orders. Streams of walking wounded made their way to the rear, the more serious ones helped by their comrades (according to the Reverend Gleig 'more numerous than the wounded'). There was no organized system of casualty evacuation and helping the wounded was a good excuse for some to leave the battle. Certainly, it was commonplace to see wounded officers with 'attendants' carrying or supporting them as they left the field. Assistant-Surgeon Gibney of the 15th Hussars personally organized the evacuation of his badly wounded commanding officer, Lieutenant-Colonel Dalrymple, from the field hospital at Mont St Jean to Waterloo. Gibney accompanied him to the rear. He later wrote that he was pleased to leave a 'room that was more than dreadful … [it being] crowded to excess with wounded officers…'. Seemingly, in many cases, the privileges of rank were extended to priority medical treatment – at least on or near the battlefield. Moffat, the assistant-surgeon of the British 7th Hussars, noted that his regimental surgeon (David Irwin) was summoned from the field hospital at Mont St Jean to attend to his Regimental Colonel (the Earl of Uxbridge, Wellington's cavalry commander). Irwin was not seen again for several days as he accompanied Uxbridge to Brussels, thus depriving the regiment of their surgeon. The majority of the men moving north along the road to Brussels during the action were unwounded. When Wellington wrote his despatch after the battle a footnote was added giving the number of troops missing as 1,875 – mostly men who had gone to the rear with wounded comrades and had been dilatory about returning.

---

dig (sometimes at bayonet point) and fill mass graves. Nevertheless, the majority of those inhabitants who lived nearby provided what help they could. They guided the wounded to shelter, they opened up their barns, often their houses, and priests gave over their churches as temporary field hospitals (the church in Braine l'Alleud has a plaque on the wall to commemorate this). Nuns became nurses while ordinary peasants gave their blankets, their sheets, their food and their water. It was an extraordinary display of generosity.

Brussels became the centre for the collection of wounded of all nationalities during June and July. The mayor of the city instructed all inhabitants to provide clothing and blankets on pain of having sick billeted on them if they did not respond. But they did respond – magnificently. The ladies of the city hugely impressed Sergeant Costello of the 95th, who came to Brussels on 20 June looking for treatment for his shot-away trigger finger:

… thousands of wounded French, Belgians, Prussians and English arrived; carts, wagons, and every other obtainable vehicle were continually arriving heaped with sufferers. The wounded were laid, friend and foes indiscriminately, on straw, with avenues between them, in every part of the city, and nearly destitute of surgical attendance. The humane and indefatigable exertions of the fair ladies of Brussels, however, greatly made up for this deficiency; numbers were busily employed – some strapping and bandaging wounds, others serving out tea, coffee, soups, and other soothing nourishments; while many occupied themselves stripping sufferers of their gory and saturated garments, and dressing them in clean shirts and other habiliments; … many of the fairest and wealthiest of the ladies of that city now ventured to assert their pre-eminence on the occasion.

Brussels provided five hospitals for Anglo-Allied patients and others for French. The overflow went by river barge to Antwerp where Deputy Inspector Summers Higgins was the senior medical officer. There they were allocated to both hospitals and hotels.

Dozens of Belgian civilian surgeons offered their services, as did some Dutch. The head of the medical services of the Dutch-Belgian Army, J. Fr. Kluyskens and his staff made a major contribution. Captured French surgeons, including 'the great Larrey', worked in hospitals accommodating their own countrymen. A number of eminent surgeons arrived from England, notably Charles Bell (both an anatomist and artist), George James Guthrie ('the English Larrey') and John Thomson, the Professor of Military Surgery at Edinburgh University. All available medical personnel co-operated, totally disregarding the nationality of their fellow surgeons or the patients under their care. A London barrister in the city remarked, 'Something, if possible, beyond the average care for the sick and hurt, appeared to me to animate all the medical men for the care of wounded of Waterloo; their zeal made no distinction on whether their countrymen or the enemy.'

As the experience of being wounded was pretty much identical no matter what army the soldier was in, as were the problems of evacuation, treatment and the suffering endured, the medical aspects of Waterloo discussed below apply to all casualties even though examples are of one nationality.

THE WOUNDED

During the Battle

Discounting for a moment the awful pain of a wound, discounting the shock and fear of death, there were a number of other factors present on the Waterloo battlefield (and other battlefields) that added considerably to the trauma of being injured. They were:

• If unable to walk, the soldier faced the prospect of remaining for hours before he could be taken to the rear. His comrades were not normally allowed to leave the line or square to assist him. He had to rely on the bandsmen detailed as stretcher-bearers or the

A Surgeon Speaks

Many French wounded lay for days on the field before being taken to hospital in Brussels. The veteran Peninsula surgeon of the 30th Foot (Cambridgeshire), J.G. Elkington (twice a prisoner of the French and present at Talavera, Fuentes d'Onor, Ciudad Rodrigo, Badajoz, Salamanca, Burgos and Quatre-Bras), rode out onto the battlefield to search for French wounded on 21 June. He found plenty – but also missed some. Incredibly, according to *Wellington's Surgeon-General* by R.L. Blanco, 'there were wounded survivors discovered who had lain on the ground exposed to the elements for nearly two weeks after Waterloo'. The British surgeon Charles Bell tried to save them and later wrote of his experiences amputating on French casualties:

> I found that the best cases, that is, the most horrid wounds left totally without assistance, were found in the hospital of the French wounded. This hospital was only forming; they were even then bringing these poor creatures in from the woods. It is impossible to convey to you the picture of human misery continually before my eyes … At six o'clock [in the morning] I took the knife in my hand, and continued incessantly at work until seven in the evening; and so the next day, and again on the third.
>
> And all the decencies of performing surgical operations were soon neglected; while I amputated one man's thigh, there lay at one time thirteen, all beseeching to be taken next; one full of entreaty, one calling upon me to remember my promise to take him, another execrating. It was a strange thing to feel my clothes stiff with blood, and my arms powerless with the exertion of using the knife…

regimental surgeon being near, and not too busy to give him (very basic) attention. The Netherlands brigade defending the Papelotte area drafted in engineer troops to locate and carry wounded to the surgeons, as they had nothing else to do. For anything other than rudimentary attention, casualties had to get back to Mont St Jean Farm where the majority of urgent surgery could be carried out.

• The man lying wounded on the ground risked being hit again. Many soldiers at Waterloo were wounded several times, often fatally. Some of this re-wounding (or killing) was deliberate. After the French finally captured La Haie Sainte all the wounded lying helpless in the buildings were brutally bayoneted. Prior to this, French lancers had ridden around spearing the bodies of Union Brigade men who had been unhorsed in their charge on the 'Grand Battery'. One soldier survived eighteen such wounds, while a number were eventually brought in with ten or more. Lieutenant-Colonel Ponsonby, commanding the British 12th Light Dragoons, survived to recount his experience. He was lying injured near the French lines when a lancer riding past noticed him move. '*Tu n'est pas mort, coquin!*' (You're are not dead, rascal!) he exclaimed, at the same time jabbing his lance into Ponsonby's back. Another notorious example was the bayoneting of French wounded by the Prussians near Rossomme during the French flight after the battle. In fact, any wounded Frenchman was extremely lucky to live if a Prussian discovered him in the chaotic aftermath of Waterloo.

• There was also a good chance at Waterloo that a wounded man unable to walk or crawl could be hidden from view, and therefore assistance. This was particularly true in those areas of the battlefield where the high standing crops had not been well flattened. Wounded skirmishers were especially vulnerable, as were attackers whose assault had been beaten back, leaving them isolated in a dip or hollow between the armies. They were still finding wounded on the Waterloo battlefield four days after the battle.

• For obvious reasons, to be left lying badly injured for hours, even days, hugely increased the likelihood of death through loss of blood and shock. It also exposed the unfortunate soldier to the battlefield scavengers, both civil and military, that picked over the bodies. The dead were easily robbed, so a wounded man was a nuisance to many of these murderous villains – a quick slash with a knife or thrust with a bayonet was all that was needed. This was assuredly the fate of men from all sides who lay out during the night of 18/19 June.

Transportation

An isolated, wounded man might sit up, shout, moan or crawl to a road or towards his comrades to attract attention, but having been found there was always the problem of transport. It was supposedly the bandsmen's (not the drummers') duty to bring in the wounded during a battle. They provided an entirely inadequate body of stretcher-bearers – their numbers were derisory, they had no stretchers and they had no training. They half-lifted, half-dragged the injured to the nearest surgeon, who could be only a few metres away in the centre of a square, or 1000 metres' distance in a field hospital. Those that could not stand were carried on makeshift stretchers made from pieces of wood, a blanket or a door ripped from its hinges; some, the fortunate few, got a ride on a horse, a spare caisson, cart or wagon.

After the battle an assistant surgeon of the 7th Hussars, James Moffat, collected together as many of his regiment's wounded as he could find. He then gathered a party of soldiers to round up, at gunpoint, Belgian peasants who were busying themselves pillaging the dead. With this disgruntled workforce Moffat had his wounded carried to Mont St Jean field hospital. However, it was but the first stage of the 17-kilometre journey back to Brussels. Every wounded man that made it to Brussels did so on his feet, on a horse or some sort of vehicle. The forty-eight British spring wagons (ambulances) did not arrive at Mont St Jean until the morning of 19 June. This was due to their having been employed taking the Quatre-Bras wounded to Brussels. When they attempted to come south again their passage was blocked by the tangle of vehicles, lightly wounded, and panicky skulkers that flowed from the battlefield to the city throughout the 18th. At Mont St Jean village the officer in charge of these wagons, whose orders were to follow the army, was about to take the Nivelles fork when the Principal Medical Officer on the spot (John Gunning) insisted he head straight for the battlefield. For four days they were occupied bringing British and KGL wounded to the hospitals in Brussels.

There is little doubt that as far as treatment on, or transportation from, the battlefield was concerned, wounded Frenchmen were very much at the back of the queue. Some kept themselves alive by eating the flesh of the dead horses. As one British staff officer wrote many years later:

I remember to have seen in some published accounts, that the wounded of our allies and of the French were brought in indiscriminately with our own. ... But I fear we cannot lay claim to so much merit. ... the wounded of the British and King's German Legion troops were first attended to, then those of the Hanoverians. The Brunswickers, Dutch and Belgians had their several ambulances, or hospital wagons, by which their own wounded were provided for; but those of the French were left for the wagons of the peasantry to pick up... . I have reason to believe that it was not until the fourth day after the battle that the last French were taken up ... Neither does it appear that any food was regularly supplied to them; but several peasant women were seen wandering about laden with pitchers of water and bread... .

Certainly the overwhelming majority of the wounded that filled the churches and houses in Plancenoit and Braine l'Alleud were French. However, those several thousand wounded Frenchmen that finally arrived in Brussels were given equal attention (often by French surgeons).

Amputations

One of the most memorable things about the Waterloo wounded of all sides is the incredible fortitude of so many soldiers in unimaginable agony. Probably most screamed and twisted desperately against the hands that held them to the table, but a significant proportion did not. Surgeons had no anaesthetic available other than perhaps some mixture of opium tincture, laudanum and alcohol. At Waterloo even the supplies of the latter were gulped down in a matter of minutes. The surgeons were forced to rely on the sheer willpower of the patient, reinforced by the strong arms of the assistants to hold him still. An assistant-surgeon of the 1st Life Guards later wrote:

Our work behind the lines was grim in the extreme, and continued far into the night. ... the silent horror of the greater part of the sufferers was a thing I shall not forget. When one considers the hasty surgery performed on such an occasion, the awful sight the men are witness to, knowing that their turn on that blood-soaked operating table is next, seeing the agony of the amputation ... then one realises what our soldiers are made of.

Another outstanding example of this sort of courage was related by Sergeant Costello of the 95th who watched a surgeon at work while awaiting his turn in a Brussels hospital. A Frenchman was making a dreadful noise as a surgeon probed his shoulder to find a musket ball. Nearby, a Royal Dragoon was actually holding his own arm as the surgeon cut if off, all the while calmly spitting tobacco juice onto the floor. The Frenchman's yells annoyed the dragoon. As the arm came away he lifted it up and, 'Struck the Frenchman a smart blow across the breast with the severed limb, holding it at the wrist. "Here take that, and stuff it down your throat and stop your damned bellowing".'

As one hospital assistant, Isaac James, said at the end of three days and nights work after the battle, 'We had lots of arms and legs to chop off'. A recent work entitled *Medic: Evolution du Service de Sante Militaire* edited by R. Reynaert (1997) contains a chapter called 'Waterloo 1815 – Traumatology of the Wounded', written by E. Evrard. This is based on a paper written by the head surgeon of the Dutch-Belgian Army, J. Fr. Kluyskens, concerning operations conducted by himself or under his direction. According to this document, the British carried out some 500 amputations during and immediately after the battle in the field hospital at Mont St Jean and in the one established in Waterloo village. The British surgeon Charles Bell, who came to Brussels after the battle, personally amputated, or supervised the amputation of, 380 limbs in hospital, while Kluyskens himself claims 300. These are staggering statistics. Evrard considers the total amputations for June and July exceeded 2000. If one includes operations conducted elsewhere (by the French during the battle for example), then 3000 may be nearer the mark.

The above figures relate to the number of men who lost limbs to the surgeon's saw and knife, not to the number who lived to tell about it. Sir Neil Cantlie in his modern study of the records considered that some 12 per cent of limb injuries led to amputation – a lower figure than we might expect. For primary amputations (operations carried out quickly without any serious attempt to save the limb) the mortality rate was about 30 per cent. With secondary ones (those done later once gangrene or other complications had set in) the death rate was 45 per cent. Some 27 per cent of Charles Bell's primary amputation patients died, as did 47 per cent of his secondary ones. Overall, about a third of soldiers whose limbs were amputated as a result of Waterloo wounds died on the table or before leaving hospital – perhaps 1000 men.

The speed of execution of an amputation depended on the skill of the surgeon and the sharpness of his instruments. Understandably some were better than others. For the man on the table it often meant the difference between seemingly endless agony or death

Surgical Instruments

The catalogue of instruments of the medical profession in the age of amputation without anaesthetic makes frightening reading. They included amputating saw, knife, metacarpal saw (a small saw for tackling small bones such as those of the fingers or toes), scalpel, screw tourniquet, curved needles, a tenaculum for lifting arteries or veins, catheters (flexible or rigid silver tubes), circular saw (trephine) for removing part of the bone from the skull, and instruments for draining fluid.

Charles Bell, who operated on so many wounded after Waterloo, was a man skilled in the use of his instruments and immune to the hellish sights and sounds around him. A soldier in Spain has described how the surgeons worked during and after a battle:

They [the surgeons] were stripped to their shirts and bloody ... a number of doors, placed on barrels, served as temporary tables, and on these lay the different subjects upon whom the surgeons were operating. To the right and left were arms and legs, flung here and there without distinction, and the ground was dyed with blood. Doctor Bell was going to take off the thigh of a soldier of the 50th, and he requested I would hold down the man for him. He was the best-hearted man I ever met ... and with much composure was eating almonds out of his waist-coat pocket, which he offered to share with me ... The operation ... was the most shocking sight I ever witnessed; it lasted nearly half an hour, but his life was saved.

from shock, and recovery. For a straightforward operation one minute for an arm, two for a leg was considered good – ten minutes for either was not. The man under an inexperienced surgeon's knife could only pray he fainted. All medical men agreed that multiple fractures of the femur (thighbone) represented the most serious difficulties. Two-thirds of such cases were expected to die. Larrey watched the eminent British surgeon George Guthrie operate on a Frenchman whose right thigh had been totally smashed by a cannon ball. It was a horrendous undertaking for both the surgeon and the soldier as it involved disarticulating the remains of the femur at the hip joint. In an amazing combination of skill and an iron will the man recovered. Some years later the old veteran was to meet Larrey again at the Hotel des Invalides in Paris.

Medical officers considered that early amputation (primary amputation) was the only chance of survival for a man with a smashed limb. Such wounds, with splintered bones, torn tissue and with pieces of uniform embedded in them, were highly vulnerable to sepsis. A quick amputation above the injury would usually avoid these complications, leaving the soldier with a relatively simple wound. Unfortunately, the surgeons' enthusiasm for amputation cost many men limbs they might otherwise have kept. Lieutenant-Colonel Hamilton commanding the 2/30 had a narrow escape after being badly wounded at Quatre-Bras. Three times the surgeon tightened the tourniquet round his leg, three times he was called away to more desperate cases. It was then decided not to chop and Hamilton lived to walk again.

Gangrene, or more accurately hospital gangrene (known at the time as 'hospital rot'), took its toll in the hospital wards after Waterloo. Anaerobic germs transmitted by surgeons and other staff moving from patient to patient caused it. Once a soldier was infected in the overcrowded conditions, with no attempt at isolation, epidemics were inevitable.

Bleeding a patient, even one that had lost considerable quantities of blood from his wound, was commonplace. It was an accepted treatment for all manner of ailments – amputees being no exception. Of course, this practice often hastened the end of a dying man or killed one that would otherwise have lived. Even non-medical personnel had confidence in it. Lieutenant-Colonel Ponsonby of the 12th Lancers suffered seven wounds but considered he was saved by copious bloodletting (120 ounces in the two days following the battle). He later remarked, 'I had received several wounds; a surgeon slept in my room and I was saved by excessive bleeding.' Ponsonby survived his wounds despite the bleeding; Colonel De Lancey, the Duke's Quartermaster-General, did not. Struck a glancing blow by a cannon ball that smashed his side, separating his ribs from his backbone, De Lancey at first showed signs of recovering. His wife, who drove out from Brussels to be at his side, nursed him. However, ten days after the battle he died. His wife later wrote that the surgeons bled him constantly, 'wishing also thereby to make the recovery more complete'.

ANGLO-ALLIED MEDICAL SERVICES
Organization

While it is true that the organization for the evacuation and treatment of Wellington's wounded was initially overwhelmed by the magnitude of the task on the battlefield, once casualties reached a base hospital their chances of surviving rose dramatically. Although the number of wounded was huge, the number who eventually survived once admitted to a hospital was remarkably high. Sir Neil

Cantlie quotes figures produced in April 1816 showing that there were almost 7000 British casualties requiring hospital treatment after Waterloo. Of these, just over 5000 (74 per cent) rejoined their units. The figures make for surprising reading.

Total cases	6,831
Rejoined	5,068
Discharged from the army	506
Posted to veteran battalions	167 (not fit for active duty)
Amputations	236 (survived amputations on the date in question)
Remaining in hospital	854

The British Army's medical service, at least in the top echelons, was a civilian organization. At its head was the Medical Board, composed of the Director-General, the Physician-General, the Surgeon-General and the Inspector-General of Hospitals. At the time of Waterloo the man who had just taken up the comparatively new appointment of Director-General of the Medical Board (comparable to a modern 'chief executive') was Sir James McGrigor, Wellington's former Inspector-General of Hospitals in the Peninsula. There he had proved himself a dedicated and able medical administrator. It was McGrigor who set up prefabricated, portable hospitals to move behind the army as it advanced, thus reducing the distance wounded must travel in unsprung carts on rutted roads. The Medical Board had responsibility for examining and appointing military physicians and surgeons, administering all general and field hospitals and auditing the provision of medicines and hospital supplies.

There were two other gentlemen, not members of the Medical Board, who played a key role (for good or ill) in the system. The Apothecary-General was a hereditary post with responsibility for furnishing medicines and drugs. The Purveyor-General supplied the hospitals with all their other equipment and needs. It was a system pregnant with the potential for conflict, confusion, inter-departmental rivalry and jealousies.

Hospitals had their own staff of surgeons, assistant-surgeons, apothecaries and purveyors but there was no nursing service as such, reliance being placed on regimental soldiers attached from their units. By 1815 the transportation needs of the wounded had been partially met by the introduction of spring wagons that could take up to eight lying casualties. Forty-eight were available in Belgium. With a total maximum lift of under 400 casualties this was woefully inadequate for anything other than a minor engagement. They were normally allocated to divisions.

There was a body of medical staff officers that included inspectors, deputy inspectors, apothecaries and purveyors. They were military personnel, found at the various headquarters down to divisional level, responsible for organizing the medical facilities within the formation to which they were attached. During a battle some would open up and supervise the running of field hospitals, a good example being Deputy-Inspector John Gunning, the principal medical officer at I Corps headquarters. He was in charge of the field hospital at Mont St Jean farm – his name appearing on the commemorative plaque on the wall today.

Each infantry battalion, cavalry regiment or artillery battery had its own medical officer and assistants. The artillery surgeons belonged to the Ordnance Medical Department. All horse units (including foot artillery) had veterinary surgeons. This was the system in use throughout the Duke's army at Waterloo, and not just with British units. The full medical establishment for a British battalion was one surgeon (ranking as captain) and two assistant-surgeons (ranking as lieutenants). Not all infantry units at Waterloo had their full complement, but many did. For example, the 2/30 (Cambridgeshire) had the veteran from Spain, Surgeon John Elkington, plus Assistant-Surgeons John Evans and Patrick Clarke. The 23rd Foot (Royal Welch Fusiliers) had a particularly strong medical team with Surgeon John Dunn, who had held the rank for twelve years, having three assistant-surgeons under him. On the day they only had eighty-three wounded to worry about. Compare this with the vastly overstretched two assistant-surgeons with the 1/27 (Inniskilling) who had to try to cope with 373 wounded in the space of four hours during the afternoon. The battalion was shredded in square, mostly by artillery fire, and the centre was covered by dead, dying and wounded. Never before or afterwards did the two young medical officers, Gerald Fitzgerald and Thomas Mostyn, have to experience such horrors. Mostyn had begun his medical career as a hospital assistant five years earlier and was still serving forty years later at the time of the Crimean War. He had eight clasps to his Peninsula medal, had fought at Plattsburg in America (in 1814), Quatre-Bras and Waterloo – an old soldier indeed.

The 28th Foot, destined to suffer 138 wounded, had to get by with one assistant-surgeon, Patrick Lavens. Lavens was not destined for a meteoric rise in the medical profession; he remained an assistant-surgeon for another thirteen years before finally quitting as surgeon of the 14th Light Dragoons in 1843, after thirty-two years as a unit medical officer. Units with horses had a veterinary surgeon instead of one assistant-surgeon. An interesting example was the veterinary surgeon of the Royal Horse Guards, John Siddall. He joined the regiment at seventeen, became the veterinary officer eight years later and continued to serve in the same regiment for fifty-two years – surely a record. He died in 1856, aged sixty-nine, the last surviving Waterloo officer of the Royal Horse Guards.

Unit medical officers were military men, with the British wearing a combination of regimental and medical style uniforms. Their single-breasted red jackets had embroidered loops across the chest but the facings were usually of regimental colour or pattern. Medical staff wore bicorne hats, regimental surgeons usually the headdress of their unit, both with black plumes. All medical officers carried a sword as a status symbol rather than as a weapon. The regimental surgeons were entitled to a mule or packhorse to carry their instruments, plus a cart for bedding and medical supplies. Each assistant had a small medical satchel (an 1815 first-aid kit) containing a few instruments, bandages and a tourniquet but no amputating knives.

Deployment

The competence and humanity of the medical officers varied considerably. In the scramble to prepare for the final campaign against Napoleon the Medical Board had great difficulty providing sufficient surgeons for the line. Many veteran surgeons from the Peninsular War were on half pay, had entered civilian practice or could not be located in time. Nevertheless, on the day, most units fought at Waterloo with sufficient surgeons in terms of numbers, although their quality was sometimes questionable. The Board was compelled to recruit civilians who had never seen action and were totally unprepared for the horrifically mutilated bodies they would be expected to deal with during the battle. Even medical students were put into uniform and sent to war. A sergeant of the 94th Foot in the Peninsula was of the opinion that many 'were thrust into the army as a huge dissecting room, where they might mangle with

impunity, until they were drilled into an ordinary knowledge of their business'. A handful of the young assistant-surgeons with line units at Waterloo may well have fitted Donaldson's description. The Board tried, with a measure of success, to ensure that line units had at least one experienced medical officer. Those of no experience of battle, such as the young Denis Murray whose appointment as an assistant-surgeon with the 16th Light Dragoons was not confirmed until four days after the battle, were sent to units with accomplished surgeons over them. At Waterloo Murray was working under a veteran (Isaac Robinson) who had been an army surgeon since 1804. Despite this considered deployment, there were undoubtedly men whose bodies were cut and probed by novices – the ultimate on-the-job training. Nevertheless, as noted above, once a soldier was admitted to a hospital in Brussels or elsewhere, his chances of living through his ordeal were good.

Medical resources for the Anglo-Allied Army in the Netherlands in June 1815 were deployed at follows:
• Base or line of communication military hospitals. These were established at Antwerp, which was destined to take much of the overflow from Brussels after Waterloo. Then Ostend, the Duke's port of disembarkation at the start of his main line of communication east and south-east. Next, 45 kilometres east, was Bruges, then Ghent and finally Brussels. There was also a hospital set up at Louvain, 30 kilometres north of Wavre, which was destined to handle mainly Prussian casualties. Wellington's headquarters was initially in Brussels, and hospitals in this city were intended to care for the bulk of the seriously sick or wounded during the planned advance into France. Overall responsibility for medical arrangements rested with the Duke's principal medical officer Sir James Robert Grant MD, who ranked as an inspector of hospitals. He was the brother of Lieutenant-Colonel Colquhoun Grant, Wellington's masterful and adventurous intelligence officer. Sir James was highly qualified, with a vast experience of military medicine in the field. He was one of the very few officers to serve continuously from the start of the Revolutionary Wars against France in 1793. At Waterloo he rode with the Duke's headquarters as the overall medical commander. He was accompanied by Wellington's personal friend and physician, Deputy-Inspector John Hume.
• Medical staff. All nations in the Duke's army supplied medical officers to the various national corps, contingents or divisional headquarters. They were senior medical officers (at corps level in the British service deputy-inspectors of hospitals) responsible for all medical arrangements within the formation to which they were attached. When a battle was fought it was these officers who would be expected to establish field hospitals in the rear of the fighting. The primary example at Waterloo was that at Mont St Jean under the control of Deputy-Inspector John Gunning. Some forty-six senior medical staff left England for duty with Wellington's army in Belgium during the campaign. Of these, twenty-two are known to have been present at the battle and subsequently received the Waterloo Medal. They were:

One Inspector (Grant)
Four Deputy-Inspectors (John Gunning, William Taylor, Stephen Woolriche, and John Hume)
One physician (George Denecke MD who was the senior medical officer with the British 3rd Division and had been slightly wounded at Quatre-Bras)
Eleven surgeons (mostly deployed at divisional headquarters)
Four assistant-surgeons

One apothecary (William Lyons, the only British apothecary to receive the Waterloo Medal. He probably rode with the general headquarters or assisted at Mont St Jean Farm)

Once the battle developed, most of the above medical officers staffed the Mont St Jean field hospital or the one set up at Waterloo village.

• The Ordnance Medical Department. These medical officers were attached to the various British foot and horse artillery batteries (brigades and troops). Each gunner unit in Anglo-Allied Army had one surgeon or assistant-surgeon plus a veterinary surgeon. In the British artillery there were four surgeons, three assistant-surgeons and ten second assistant-surgeons present with their batteries at Waterloo. The senior surgeon was Edward Simpson who had precisely two years' experience. He went on to become a senior surgeon before retirement in 1844. No less than eleven of his medical colleagues never received any further promotion, most being retired on half pay within a year or two of the battle. These included Captain Mercer's medical officer, Assistant-Surgeon Richard Hichins, who was on half pay within ten months of the battle. Interestingly, it was the most junior, Second Assistant-Surgeon Stewart Chisholm, who was to have the longest and most successful career in army medicine. He rose to be Staff Surgeon 1st Class in 1855 and died in 1862.

• Unit medical officers. Assuming that every infantry and cavalry unit had an average of two medical officers, there were about 200 surgeons and assistant-surgeons deployed with Wellington's army at Waterloo. With those attached to the artillery batteries plus the medical staff officers, there were just over 300 medical officers present at the battle. This represents one for every 243 men or one surgeon for every 34 of the approximately 10,200 wounded. There were also about thirty-five veterinary surgeons with the army. British infantry and cavalry units were accompanied by thirty-eight surgeons and sixty-eight assistant-surgeons.

• At Waterloo it was common practice for at least one assistant-surgeon to remain in action with his unit with the task of administering immediate first aid, applying dressings and tourniquets to control haemorrhage. The surgeon would establish a small regimental aid post some short distance in rear of the line utilizing any nearby barn or building if possible. Notable exceptions to this usual practice were the medical officers with the 1/95. Lieutenant Kincaid, the adjutant, described their aid post thus:

When we first took possession of the knoll [east of the sandpit], before the battle began, there was almost a hedge of bushes and underwood, with a tall tree in the centre, lining the abrupt face of it on our side. We cut down most of the bushes to form an abatis across the road, and our two Medical Officers [there were three with the battalion] took post behind the tree as the most secure place for their operations. The tree was a naked one with a bushy top. One of the first of the enemy's round shot struck it about two-thirds up, bringing the whole bushy part down on their devoted heads and nearly smothering them among the branches.

During the battle regimental surgeons usually joined with others from their brigade to form a joint aid post. Examples of these regimental/brigade aid posts or dressing stations are the buildings at La Haie Sainte, the chapel at Hougoumont, the roadside hut immediately north of the 'Elm Tree' crossroads and outbuildings or houses in Mont St Jean and Merbe Braine villages. The field hospital in Mont St Jean farm was set up and run by medical staff officers with assistance from some regimental surgeons from nearby units. Another ad hoc field hospital was established in Waterloo when the village was flooded by the overflow from Mont St Jean and those struggling to make it back to Brussels direct from the battlefield.

• Ambulance wagons. There were some forty-eight of these available to the British formations, driven by soldiers of the Royal Wagon Train, plus additional ones with their Allies. They were late arriving at Quatre-Bras and were all committed to evacuating casualties to Brussels throughout 17 June. On 18 June they could make no headway against the flood of men and wagons streaming north, so they could not be used at Waterloo until the following day, when the magnitude of the task engulfed them.

Battlefield reality

The medical organization was first put to the test at Quatre-Bras – where it was quickly found wanting. It was not just a case of too many wounded and too few medical men, although this was exposed as the critical weakness. The desperate rush to deploy the army, the forced marching and the piecemeal arrival of formations and units on the battlefield meant that most medical supplies, and the ambulance wagons, were still far to the rear when Ney attacked

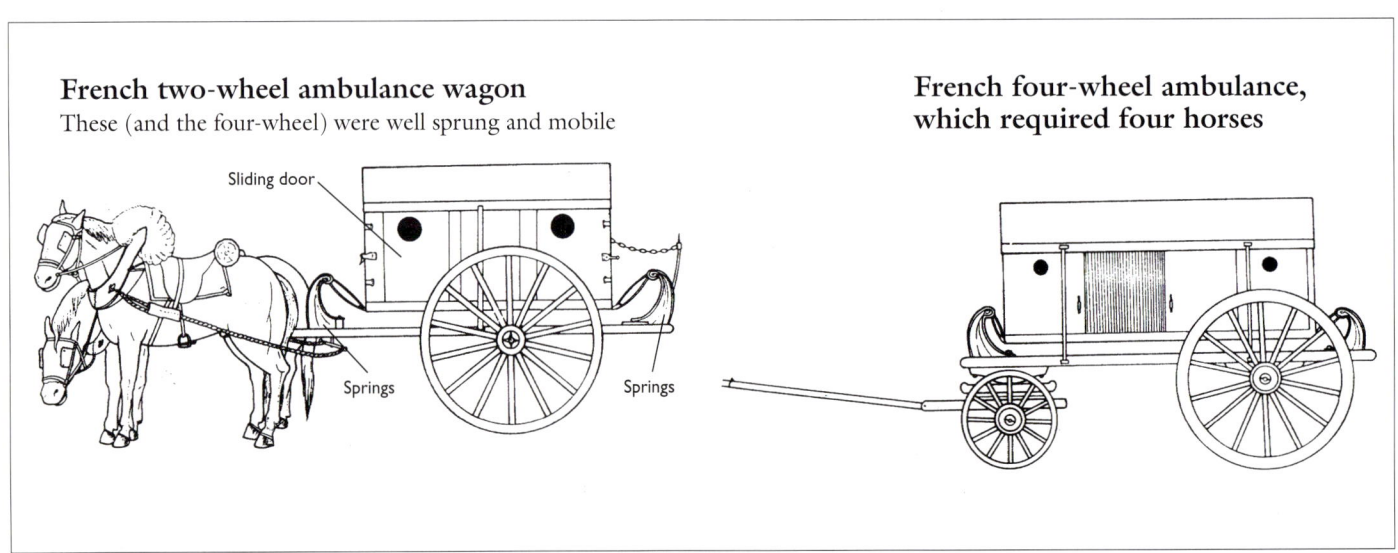

French two-wheel ambulance wagon
These (and the four-wheel) were well sprung and mobile

Sliding door

Springs   Springs

French four-wheel ambulance, which required four horses

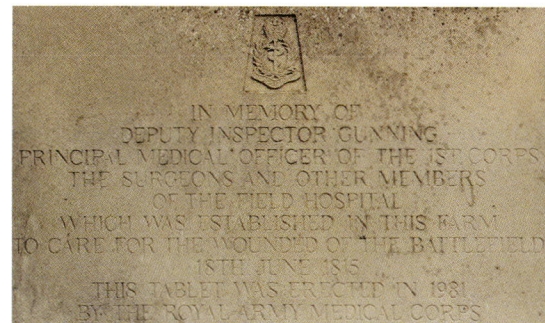

The plaque on the wall of Mont St Jean farm commemorating its use as a field hospital under Deputy-Inspector John Gunning. Photo: the author

The western side of Mont St Jean farm – Wellington's main field hospital during the battle. This picture shows the farm more or less as it was in 1815 with the tower over the central entrance.

the crossroads. Most casualties pleaded in vain for attention. Even walking wounded found it verging on the impossible to get to a surgeon. Sergeant Costello, minus his trigger-finger, had no hope of even a rough dressing at a barn crammed with injured all clamouring for help. Sergeant Morris of the 2/73 doubted if a surgeon would get to see a man who had both arms torn off before he bled to death. Assistant-Surgeon John Haddy James with the 1st Life Guards was appalled by his own helplessness, the total inadequacy of the contents of his medical bag. He watched in horror as dozens of wounded crawled from the battlefield. 'I was unable to do anything for these wounds as I had no sort of medical supply with me, and could only watch their painful progress with useless pity.' It was the same at Waterloo but on a much grander scale.

Despite many of the regimental surgeons being under fire throughout the battle, only one British medical officer is known to have been wounded at Waterloo. This was Assistant-Surgeon John Stewart serving with the 92nd Foot (Gordon Highlanders). Surgeons Whymper and Good both survived nine hours in Hougoumont without a scratch.

FRENCH MEDICAL SERVICES

Organization

Napoleon used the temporary pause in hostilities brought about by the Peace of Amiens in 1802 to try to bring some order and efficiency to his military medical services. He was partially successful. A French soldier who was sick or wounded expected to be treated by one or both of two associated organizations. They were the Service de Sante and the Administration des Hopiteaux Militaires.

Service de Sante

This was a uniformed military organization divided into three main departments: medecins (physicians), chirugiens (surgeons) and pharmaciens (pharmacists). All wore a blue uniform, with physicians having black velvet facings, surgeons crimson, and pharmacists green. Surgeons, as might be expected, took care of wounds and obvious injuries, but they also had responsibility for treating 'external diseases'. Pharmacists prescribed, prepared and actually administered medicines. The ranks or grades within the service depended on training, skill and seniority. In the first grade were the

Gunner Butterworth's Cruel Death

Gunner Butterworth was the rammer on one of Captain Mercer's 9-pounders. He was possibly the first casualty of the troop at Waterloo. His injuries were horrific and accidental. Mercer described what happened: 'He had just finished ramming down the shot, and was stepping back outside the wheel, when his foot stuck in the miry soil, pulling him forward the moment the gun was fired. As a man naturally does when falling, he threw out both his arms before him, and they were blown off at the elbows. He raised himself a little on his two stumps, and looked up most piteously in my face. To assist him was impossible – the safety of all, everything, depended upon not slackening our fire, and I was obliged to turn from him. … I afterwards learned that he had succeeded in rising and was gone to the rear; but on inquiring for him next day some of my people who had been sent to Waterloo told me that they saw his body by the roadside near the farm of Mount St Jean – bled to death!'

Had tourniquets been applied immediately he might have made it to the field hospital and quite possibly survived.

Sergeant-Major Marshall 6th Dragoons (Inniskilling)

Marshall was a troop sergeant-major in the 6th Dragoons who charged with the Union Brigade, smashed through Donzelot's division and careered on up to the French 'Grand Battery'. During the counterattack by Farine's cuirassiers a sword blow broke Marshall's left arm. As he rode on, a lance thrust pierced his side and he felt two more blows, one of which shattered his right thigh. He fell from his horse and briefly lost consciousness. When he came round horses were galloping wildly around and over him. He lay hugging his wounds and feigning death for several minutes until he spotted a riderless horse nearby. He dragged himself towards it. As he caught hold of a stirrup to pull himself up he was cut down from behind with a final swipe from a sword. From then on he lay still, actually in among the French artillery position. Marshall, losing blood, in great pain drifted in and out of consciousness while the French guns fired over him. He was so close to the artillery that at one time a gunner rested his foot on Marshall while he reloaded. He was to survive his nineteen wounds and three nights on the battlefield, living for another ten years.

The French Cure Crush Injuries, Blindness and Tetanus

In 1808 Maréchal Lannes was badly crushed when his horse fell on him on an icy mountain road. He had difficulty breathing, his stomach was swollen and giving great pain, there was extensive bruising over his body and he was unable to move. A medical officer supervised the following unique experience for the marshal. A huge sheep was stunned and skinned alive; Lannes was stripped and smeared with a lotion of camphorated camomile oil then sewn inside the hot, bloody skin. His arms and legs, which were outside the skin, had steaming flannels applied to them while he drank weak lemon tea with plenty of sugar. Lannes then actually went to sleep for two hours wrapped in this revolting blanket. When he woke the skin was removed and the marshal submitted to being rubbed down with a mixture of camphorated brandy and milk of almonds, given regular massage and frequent hot baths. In five days he was back in the saddle – although whether because or in spite of his treatment must remain uncertain.

The French surgeon Larrey examined a thirteen-year-old English drummer boy who had been captured during the British retreat to Corunna in 1808. He was found to be blind. Larrey prescribed warm baths, massages with camphorated wine and the burning of small pieces of moxa (downy plant material from wormwood) on his temples. After the seventh treatment he recovered his sight.

Sometimes an effective treatment for tetanus (lockjaw) was to knock out one or two front teeth and feed the patient through a straw. Alternatively, in severe cases, cauterizing the wound with white-hot irons often did the trick – the jaws relaxed and the wound healed.

medecins/chirugiens/pharmaciens-major; in the second were the aides-major. These grades were not equated to an army rank although the holders had the courtesy status of officers – so they wore a sword, but no epaulettes.

The third class was the sous-aides-major that were originally young, conscripted medical students or qualified NCOs. In the Grande Armée they had been given carbines and quickly earned the nickname '*carabines rouges*'. As the Empire's armies expanded, and as campaigns like that in Russia took their toll, replacing medical officers became acutely difficult. Part of the solution was to bring in more of these youngsters. A substantial number volunteered to avoid conscription into more dangerous arms. After three months basic training they were let loose on the soldiery. An exasperated Emperor was to declare in 1812 that his useless surgeons did more damage than the Russian artillery. Despite this damning comment, some learned fast, attended medical schools and secured competency and promotion.

Finally, there were the élève-chirugiens and élève-pharmaciens – students who had the necessary qualifications but needed on the job training

Administration des Hopiteaux Militaires

This organization supervised and ran the extensive network of permanent military hospitals that had been set up in France and elsewhere during the Empire. In 1814 there were eleven large and seventeen smaller permanent military hospitals. At the height of the Empire there had been many more. In 1806–7, for example, six such hospitals plus a convalescent depot were established around Warsaw. Their quality varied, depending on the zeal of the commissaires de guerre who were in charge. Some were splendid, others let twelve men die in succession on the same bed, or the staff consumed the wine and half the meat intended for the patients. For a while, in Madrid, the hospital had 3000 beds on four floors but no latrines for any of them. For the sick or wounded it was just one more chance they must take in the lottery of whether they survived or not.

Some civilian hospitals were given extra funds provided they made beds available for a specified number of soldiers.

As with other armies, the French had had great difficulty in setting up anything like an efficient body of medical orderlies. Initially they had been civilians provided by a contractor. They were worse than useless, robbed their patients, accepted no authority and spent their time avoiding danger or their duties. In 1809 Napoleon put them into uniform (brown with red facings), organized as ten companies of d'infirmiers d'hopiteaux. Armed and equipped as infantry, they were expected to collect wounded after a battle and help in the hospitals. There was little improvement. In late 1813 the Emperor ordered another shake up. A hospital battalion, modelled on that of the Imperial Guard, was to be set up. It consisted of ten companies of infirmiers officered by surgeons, with 160 caissons for medical supplies and 480 two-wheel ambulances. Such an organization was to support forty field hospitals. Theoretically this battalion could provide second line medical treatment and casualty evacuation for forty divisions as it was these personnel and vehicles that formed the divisions d'ambulance, one of which was usually attached to each division in the field.

Army, corps and divisional headquarters each had Service de Sante medical officers on their staff. Every corps had attached to it sufficient medical officers, infirmiers, wagons, ambulance vehicles and supplies to form a division d'ambulance. At full strength such an 'ambulance' had one physician, five surgeons, two pharmacists, twenty or more infirmiers and up to ten ambulance wagons. Their job was to establish a field hospital not far to the rear of the fighting line in any convenient building. It was here that the first battlefield surgery was to be carried out. Further forward, the treatment of wounded was in the hands of the regimental medical staff. They would set up a small regimental aid post perhaps less than 100 metres from the fighting in a sheltered dip or behind a bank. Here the intention was to give urgent first aid. French medical officers were often under heavy fire and occasionally got involved in the fighting. A Surgeon-Major Pons of the 14th Ligne was well remembered as having twice rallied walking wounded and led them in a successful counterattack. Many had the Legion of Honour. A regimental aid post with a surgeon-major, three aides-major, four sous-aides-major and one medical caisson would be up to establishment – and a rarity.

Deployment

Like all other branches of the Armée du Nord, the medical service was well under strength at Waterloo. Therefore, it is unlikely that the number of regimental medical officers with infantry and cavalry units much exceeded 150, including the Imperial Guard. To these must be added perhaps fifty with the artillery. At divisional level working at the hurriedly improvised field hospitals would possibly be another seventy-five, giving an estimated total of between 275–300.

At Napoleon's headquarters overall charge of the medical services had fallen to the widely known and admired Baron Larrey, as the substantive director, Baron Pierre François Percy, had suffered a severe attack of angina at Ligny (he survived another ten years). Larrey must have been pleased, as it had been a disappointment not to get the post at the start. He retained his duties as head of the Imperial Guard medical services. Also riding with the Emperor's entourage was his personal surgeon, Baron Yvan. Although names are available, details of the officers and men at corps or divisional level have proved impossible to verify. However, it can be assumed that as far as was possible with the limited numbers, skeleton divisions d'ambulance were deployed with the divisions as they crossed the Belgian frontier on 15 June and that they remained with them during the following days. Certainly, wounded flooded into La Belle Alliance, Decoster's house, Plancenoit church and the houses in that village. These were the probable sites of the field hospitals, as were Rossomme and Le Caillou farms. Regimental aid posts were undoubtedly established, as it was a standard procedure, but their locations can only be guesswork. The ground just south of the roads running east and west from La Belle Alliance marking the French front line is likely to have been used by some. Undoubtedly, houses in Plancenoit were taken over for this purpose.

There is real evidence to suggest that the French ambulance system failed at Waterloo. A young staff officer attached to Prince Jérôme's headquarters was shocked as he watched the wounded steaming back from Hougoumont Wood:

Soon … we saw the men who had carried their wounded comrades to the ambulances return with downcast faces saying, 'It is dreadful, we have no more ambulances. Only the carriages remain, without teams of horses.' This is what

had happened. The Emperor, pressed to organise transport at the moment of opening the campaign, had issued a decree that a postillon and horses from each relay post were to be put at the disposal of the War Administration to provide the teams and drivers of ambulance carriages. These makeshift drivers, most of whom had never heard gunfire, became nervous under the fire of the English batteries, unharnessed their horses or cut the traces and galloped off … This heartbreaking sight had a dismal effect on the troops.

Battlefield reality

Although it is impossible to be precise with the numbers of French wounded at Waterloo, it is reasonable to assume that about two-thirds of total casualties (30,000, excluding prisoners) would have been wounded. On this basis some 20,000 Frenchmen were injured during the battle.

It is also likely that a seriously wounded Frenchman, particularly if he was unable to walk, was more likely to die of his wounds through delayed evacuation or lack of attention than casualties of other nationalities. The reasons for this were:

• The French attacked. With the possible exception of the fighting in Plancenoit both infantry and cavalry units advanced up to, and occasionally beyond, the Anglo-Allied front line – and then were driven back. Their wounded were strewn over the ground over which they advanced and then retired. Most got left behind. A large number of walking wounded undoubtedly struggled back, but those that could not move or were only able to crawl were often doomed to lie unattended for hours, if not days.

• When the French finally fled from the battlefield they took most of their medical staff with them and left most of their wounded behind. They were abandoned to the mercies of the looters and the victors.

Baron Jean Dominique Larrey

By 1815 Larrey was forty-nine years old and the Chief Surgeon of the Imperial Guard. His name was a by-word among all nations as one of the outstanding surgeons of his day and a man of great humanity. Initially he had entered the navy, but at twenty-one became an auxiliary surgeon with the marines. In 1792 he completed his medical training and joined the Army of the Rhine. While in the field he invented 'flying ambulances' – two or four wheel carriages with springs capable of carrying two or four stretcher cases each. They substantially reduced jolting and jarring and became the envy of other armies. His career took him all over Europe and into Russia. He was decorated by Napoleon for stamping out a typhus epidemic in Italy but was wounded at the Siege of Acre. At Alexandria he had all his horses killed to ensure his sick and wounded never went short of food. Eventually he was promoted Chief Surgeon of the Imperial Guard and awarded the Legion of Honour.

He was in charge of all the hospitals at Austerlitz, Eylau (where he operated for hours on end in the freezing cold), Essling, Wagram, on the Berezina and at Bautzen. At Wagram his popularity with the troops, but not their commanders, received another boost when he again killed horses for food, and heated soup in cuirasses before supervising the removal of 10,000 wounded to Vienna. The Emperor made him a baron. He also served in Spain where he endeared himself to a thirteen-year-old British drummer boy who went blind after capture. Larrey's medicines and care seemingly restored the

lad's sight. In 1812 he was promoted to Chief Surgeon of the Grande Armée.

At Waterloo he was back in his old post as Chief Surgeon of the Imperial Guard. At the end of the battle he had the misfortune to be wounded with two sabre cuts and then stabbed by a Uhlan's lance. He was captured, stripped of his valuables, hands bound behind his back before being taken to General Bülow. His captors were adamant they had caught Napoleon! As Larrey himself later explained, 'My build, a grey coat I was wearing, gave me a certain resemblance to the Emperor…'. He was to be led away for execution when a Prussian surgeon recognized him. Still doubtful, Bülow sent Larrey to Blücher who recognized him instantly and, immensely grateful for having once saved his own son's life, treated him with great respect. When he had recovered he was first sent to Louvain where he worked on French casualties before being moved to Brussels for similar duties.

Napoleon always referred to him as, 'My virtuous Larrey' or 'the soldier's friend'. He left Larrey a sizeable sum in his will. After the war Larrey devoted much of his time to writing on surgery and the treatment of wounds. Eventually the Bourbons restored his pension and appointed him Chief Surgeon of the Royal Guard. The Emperor's final words on him as he lay on his sick bed on St Helena were, 'An honest man withal – in fact the greatest man I have ever known.' Larrey himself died, aged seventy-six, at Lyon. A statue of him stands in front of the church of Val-de-Grace in Paris.

French casualty evacuation system – theory and practice at Waterloo

IN THEORY

An infantry division of 4 regiments in the line.

A soldier is hit. He either walks to the RAP or is carried by men from the regiment so detailed.

The Regimental Aid Post. Set up in a sheltered place close behind the regiment. Function – immediate first aid, bandaging, apply tourniquet. In 4 battalion regiment. Composed of 1 x surgeon–major, 3 x aides major, 4 x sous-aides-major, 1 x medical caisson.

Walking wounded continue back to Divisional Field Hospital. Others carried in 2-wheeled wagons, driven by 'infirmiers' sent forward from Div. Fd Hosp.

Established further back but still on the battlefield. Here the first surgery (amputations) would be carried out. Use made of nearby buildings for shelter. Staffed by a 'Division d'Ambulance' – 1 x physician, 5 x surgeons, 2 x pharmacists, 20+ 'infirmiers', up to 10 ambulance wagons.

A civil contractor had responsibility for collecting the wounded and moving them from hospital to hospital as directed by medical officers.

A permanent military hospital run by the 'Administration des Hopiteaux Militaires' on the lines of communications.

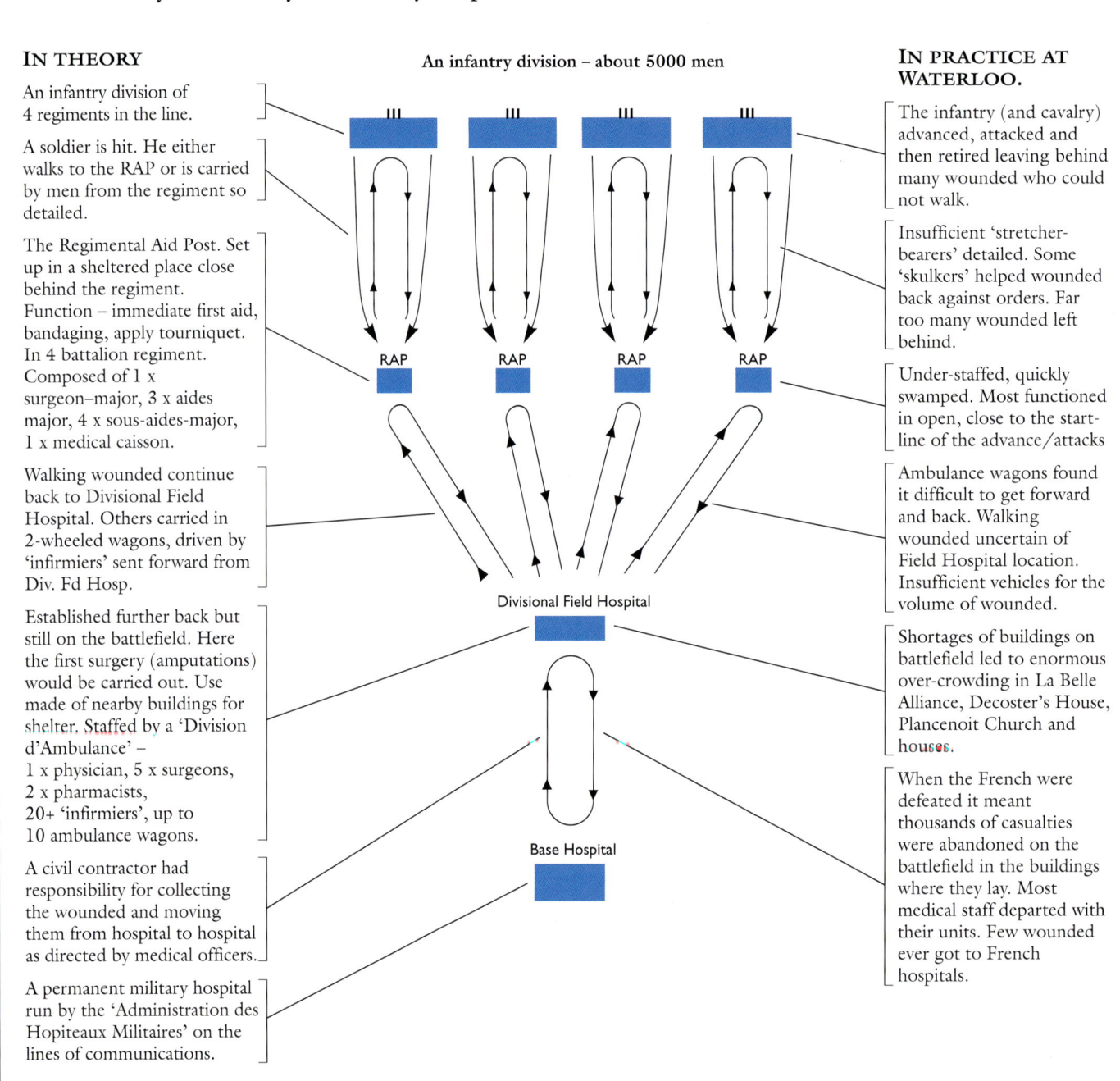

An infantry division – about 5000 men

RAP   RAP   RAP   RAP

Divisional Field Hospital

Base Hospital

IN PRACTICE AT WATERLOO.

The infantry (and cavalry) advanced, attacked and then retired leaving behind many wounded who could not walk.

Insufficient 'stretcher-bearers' detailed. Some 'skulkers' helped wounded back against orders. Far too many wounded left behind.

Under-staffed, quickly swamped. Most functioned in open, close to the start-line of the advance/attacks

Ambulance wagons found it difficult to get forward and back. Walking wounded uncertain of Field Hospital location. Insufficient vehicles for the volume of wounded.

Shortages of buildings on battlefield led to enormous over-crowding in La Belle Alliance, Decoster's House, Plancenoit Church and houses.

When the French were defeated it meant thousands of casualties were abandoned on the battlefield in the buildings where they lay. Most medical staff departed with their units. Few wounded ever got to French hospitals.

The Battlefield on 19 June

Major Harry Smith of the 95th Rifles, who was the brigade major to Major-General Lambert's brigade at Waterloo, rode over the field the next day. He later wrote:

I had been over many a field of battle, but with the exception of one spot at New Orleans and the breach at Badajos, I had never seen anything to be compared with what I saw. At Waterloo the whole field from right to left was a mass of dead bodies. In one spot, to the right of La Haye Sainte, the French cuirassiers were literally piled on each other; many soldiers not wounded lying under their horses; others fearfully wounded, occasionally with their horses struggling upon their wounded bodies. The sight was sickening, and I had no means or power to assist them. Imperative duty compelled me to the field of my comrades, where I had plenty to do to assist many who had been out all night; some had been believed to be dead, but the spark of life had returned.

This is an interesting example of the French wounded being, understandably, at the bottom of the pile for evacuation the next morning.

Intendant-General Baron Antoine Noel Bruno Daru

Daru was a soldier turned statesman of considerable intelligence, diplomatic skill and administrative ability, which he combined with a lifelong love of literature and poetry. Born in 1767, he entered the artillery when he was only sixteen years old, but early in the Revolution Daru switched to commissary duties. After a brief spell as commissary to the troops defending the Brittany coast against English raids he was thrown into prison as a suspected royalist. Released after the fall of Robespierre, he gained quick (almost meteoric) promotion. By 1799 he was the chief commissary to Massena's army in Switzerland.

In 1805 Daru became the Commissary of the Grande Armée that marched into Central Europe. After Austerlitz he assisted in the drawing up of the Peace of Schonbrunn and secured the position Intendant-General. After Friedland he drafted the Treaty of Tilsit and became the de facto Governor of Prussia. When criticized for being so outspokenly against Napoleon marrying Marie Louise of Austria instead of a French woman, the Emperor responded, 'No matter, I want an enlightened and vigilant administrator and Daru is precisely

that. He has judgement, intellect, the power to be decisive and a body and mind of iron.'

He was appointed Secretary of State in 1811 and marched on Moscow the following year, in charge of the hugely complex administrative juggernaut that was supposed to keep the Grand Armée supplied. He worked miracles with what was available and suffered the atrocious hardships of the retreat. He was particularly scathing of Maréchal Murat (also the King of Naples) when he abandoned his command in the snow to head home for the Italian sunshine.

As Minister of War in 1813, it was largely due to his tireless efforts that the Emperor was able to raise new armies. He was Intendant-General once again for the Waterloo campaign, riding in Napoleon's headquarters – although in this case he might have been better able to use his talents at Charleroi uncorking the supply bottleneck. After the second restoration the Bourbons soon forgave his past loyalties and he was made a peer. However, he spent the final years of his life writing a seven-volume history of Venice, a history of Brittany, and translating and composing poems. He died in 1829, aged sixty-two.

French Wounded

Ensign Charles Mudie of the 3/1 Foot (Royal Scots) kept a diary of his experiences at Waterloo. In it he described the desperate situation of many of the French wounded after the battle.

> Our Brigade [Pack's] was close to the farm of Belle Alliance – the ground all round was covered with their killed and wounded, which latter implored us to bring them water, but we had it not to ourselves. I went to the Farm in search of wood and water. It was literally crammed with wounded French whose misery it was awful to see; many crawling from the field to get into the barn dragging a shattered limb behind them. … This spot happened also to abound in French cuirasses. They proved extremely serviceable, the men using them for frying pans. At 5 in the morning we

walked over the field and back to our old position, the numbers of killed and wounded exceeded belief, particularly near the road where the dead and dying were promiscuously heaped…

The next day Mudie walked down the Genappe road for about a mile south of La Belle Alliance:

> We walked about a mile on the road the French had retreated by. Several cottages on the road were crammed with their wounded and dying whom it was almost impossible to come near, their wounds already emitting an unwholesome smell. … Fatigue parties were ordered to carry off the wounded … and place them under the cover of some old sheds. Three or four hours made very little difference in the appearance of the field.

• The advancing Prussians were in a vengeful mood and much more likely to bayonet an injured Frenchman than bandage his wounds.

• Even when Wellington's army scoured the battlefield for casualties, priority for evacuation and treatment at an aid post or field hospital was, first their own officers, then their men and last, if he was lucky, a Frenchman. Not until he was back in a base hospital in Brussels was his treatment on a par with that given to the Allies' wounded.

These hazards facing the French wounded at Waterloo were, for some, lessened by the generous treatment offered to them by the local Belgian population, particularly in Braine l'Alleud. A high proportion of these people resented the merger of their country with the Dutch and went out of their way to help fallen Frenchmen.

PRUSSIAN MEDICAL SERVICES

Organization

For the Waterloo campaign the Prussian medical services adopted a similar system to the French in that each regiment had medical officers sufficient for at least one surgeon or assistant to be attached to all units. They were assisted by orderlies or stretcher-bearers (krankentrager) in grey uniforms with blue facings, black gaiters and armed with swords. The officers wore infantry-style uniforms with dark blue facings piped red, and shakos. The second echelon of medical support were the mobile field hospitals, of which there were sufficient staff and vehicles for one to be attached to each brigade (division). At corps level II and IV Corps had resources for setting up a main field hospital. As with all the armies at the battle, medical personnel, supplies and transport were totally inadequate for the tasks that confronted them.

Burial of the Dead (1)

An estimated total of 54,000 men were either killed or wounded at Waterloo. Of these, approximately a third were killed outright or died on the field before they could be removed. Added to the heaps of human remains were the bodies of thousands of horses. To bury around 18,000 bodies and countless dead animals was a monumental task requiring a large labour force. It was not a popular duty. Most of the corpses had been stripped of valuables and uniforms. A staff officer later wrote:

> … many in the course of a few days became horrible objects; such as lay exposed to the sun turning nearly black, as well as being much swollen, while those lying about Hougoumont, in the shade of its trees, retained their natural whiteness.

> The scene was altogether too nauseating for a party of English ladies and gentlemen who arrived to see the sights – 'they flew away like so many scared doves'.

Large groups of local peasants were compelled to form the burial parties. An eyewitness reported:

> Entirely to clear the ground of dead men and horses occupied a period of ten or twelve days, and this disgusting duty was performed entirely by the peasantry. The human bodies were for the most part thrown into large holes, fifteen or twenty feet square; while those of the animals were generally honoured with a funeral pile and burned. To drag the large carcasses, some of which were inflated to an enormous bulk, was a work of great labour.

Many bodies were thrown into the nearest ditch or cutting and covered over to no great depth. Massed graves are thought to exist a few metres south of the south gate at Hougoumont; near the Belgian memorial immediately north of the 'Elm Tree' crossroads; just a few metres north of the Hanoverian memorial; and under what was formerly the sandpit. These were areas near which corpses lay particularly thickly along the high water mark of the French attacks.

Burial of the Dead (2)

An eyewitness of the dreadful scenes on the battlefield on 19 June recorded what he saw and had his writings published in *The Mirror of Literature, Amusement and Instruction* in January 1829. An extract is worthy of repeating:

> This general burying was truly horrible – large square holes were dug about six feet deep, and thirty or forty young fellows stripped to their skins were thrown into each, pell mell, and then covered over in so slovenly a manner that sometimes a hand or foot peeped through the earth. One of these holes was preparing as I passed, and the followers of the army were stripping the bodies before throwing them in, whilst some Russian Jews were assisting in the spoliation of the dead, by chiselling out their teeth, an operation they performed with the most brutal indifference. The clinking hammers of these wretches mingled with the occasional report of pistols from different corners of the field – I was informed that the Belgians were killing wounded horses. Hundreds of these fine creatures were galloping over the plain, kicking and plunging, apparently mad with pain, whilst the poor wounded wretches who could not get out of their way tried to escape from them but in vain.

Deployment

Prussian medical resources were allocated as follows:

Army Headquarters

Chief Medical Officer – Surgeon-General Voeltzke
Blücher's personal medical officer – Surgeon-Major Bieske
Medical staff officer – Regimental Surgeon Stein

I Corps

Principal Medical Officer – Surgeon-Major Weber
No.1 Mobile Field Hospital – Surgeon-Major Dr Schulz
No.2 Mobile Field Hospital – not known
No.5 Mobile Field Hospital – Surgeon-Major Hagen
No.12 Mobile Field Hospital – Surgeon-Major Dr Bischoff

II Corps

No.1 Field Hospital – Surgeon-Major Dr Fricke
No.4 Mobile Field Hospital – Surgeon-Major Dr Beggerow
No.8 Mobile Field Hospital – Surgeon-Major Dr Starcke

IV Corps

No.4 Main Field Hospital – Divisional-Surgeon Dr Peterson
No.9 Mobile Field Hospital – Surgeon-Major Flist
No.10 Mobile Field Hospital – Surgeon-Major Ritter
No.11 Mobile Field Hospital – Surgeon-Major Below

It is impossible to be certain how many medical personnel or mobile hospitals actually reached the battlefield before the French retreat. All that can be said is that none of the mobile field hospitals attached to I Corps arrived before the end of the fighting, as the leading units did not appear until about 7.30 p.m. It is possible that Nos.4 and 8 were deployed by II Corps and almost certain that Nos.9, 10 and 11 with IV Corps were receiving casualties during the battle. All the regimental and battalion medical officers of the units that reached the battlefield were undoubtedly present. In terms of numbers, the total of Prussian medical officers at Waterloo is estimated to be around 175. They had to cope with about 5,250 casualties (wounded), a substantial number of whom were left behind when the Prussians became responsible for the pursuit of the French.

SUPPLY SERVICES

General

With all armies supply units are usually rear echelon troops not normally involved in fighting. They are basically responsible for the provision and transportation of food, fodder, drink (wine or spirits) and ammunition. They operate along an army's lines of communication moving supplies up to the troops in the field. Some units are involved with delivery of supplies onto a battlefield, particularly ammunition, but most work behind the lines securing provisions or moving them from depot to depot. These were their roles at Waterloo. Although some supply troops were present on the battlefield on 18 June it is impossible to say with certainty how many, as it was never accurately recorded.

In general terms it is true to say that the great majority of soldiers of all the armies involved went into action on empty stomachs. They had been marching and fighting for two or three days, with food wagons relegated to the rear of the order of march. They had not caught up by the morning of 18 June. Most men had long since eaten the rations they had carried on their person. With ammunition it was a different matter. Here, with one or two minor exceptions, we can be fairly certain that shortages of musket or artillery ammunition did not seriously affect units at Waterloo. The infantryman carried sufficient in his pouches to see him through the day, and if he did run short there were plenty of dead or wounded comrades with some left, and the ammunition wagons were not far in the rear.

A point to be remembered when considering ammunition expenditure is that the defender invariably used more musket rounds than the attacker. In the context of Waterloo Wellington's infantry fired off more shots per man overall than the French. This is because they were defending and for much of the afternoon firing at cavalry who could not respond in kind. A French infantryman in the front rank of Donzelot's division was required to advance and attack over 1000 metres behind a screen of skirmishers before he had a chance of one shot at a worthwhile target. His comrades behind in the rear ranks of the column would not have fired at all before the enemy line was reached. The defenders behind the crest, in line, would have got off at least one shot, possibly two.

The only two occasions when ammunition supply became a critical factor in the outcome of an action was for the defenders of Hougoumont and La Haie Sainte. In the former case replenishment arrived and the post was held, in the latter it did not and the post was lost.

BRITISH SUPPLY SERVICES

General

There were two organizations responsible for supplies of food, fodder and ammunition reaching the majority of Wellington's men at Waterloo – the Commissariat and the Royal Wagon Train. The former was responsible for the provision of the supplies, which included the employing of contractors and the hiring of wagons as required. The latter's task was to transport them, assisted by the vehicles of the contractors.

The Commissariat

The buying, storing, forwarding and issuing of supplies were thankless tasks. Commissaries, as the officers of this organization were called, were civilians ultimately answerable to the Treasury. They were a much maligned body. Despite seldom coming under fire, commissaries led an extremely stressful and frustrating life. Both senior and regimental army officers often gave them a hard time for failing to achieve the impossible. An assistant-commissary attached to a division was expected to make daily provision for approximately 10,500 pounds of bread (or 7000 pounds of biscuits), 7000 pounds of meat and 7000 pints of wine or spirits. In the Peninsula Picton had his commissary officer report personally at 3.00 a.m. every morning. These red-jacketed young men were sometimes lads of only sixteen years of age. Prior to 1810 young men of no administrative skill, business knowledge or mathematical ability could join the Commissariat with officer status. After that date new entrants were obliged to successfully complete at least a year as a commissary clerk before promotion. Assistant-Commissary-General Tupper Carey, who was in charge of supplying the 2nd British Division at Waterloo at twenty, had already earned seven clasps to his Peninsular Medal (these medals were not actually awarded until 1848); he later rose to be a commissary-general.

Not all commissaries were as competent as young Carey. They dispersed large sums, usually in the form of receipts, for every purchase of goods or services and had to keep meticulous accounts of public money. Auditors would probe and question for years after transactions had been completed. Even death was no escape from debts, as they were passed down to dependants! Perhaps, not surprisingly, many commissariat officers were not over-scrupulous and did not come from the best elements of the commercial world. As one remarked, 'Gentlemen, if a commissary is expected to starve in the midst of all his stores, then the devil take the whole business.' The number of commissaries dismissed for irregularities during the Peninsular War was high. In 1810 two of its most senior officers were doing time in Newgate prison (Commissary-Generals Alexander Davidson and Valentine Jones). It was almost expected of a commissary to defraud the public.

By 1815 commissariat grades had been equated with military ranks. The senior commissariat officer with Wellington in Belgium was Commissary-General Thomas Dunmore who equated with a brigadier-general. At corps headquarters there would be a deputy-commissary-general (lieutenant-colonel or major), at division an assistant-commissary-general (captain), and with a brigade a deputy-assistant-commissary-general (lieutenant). Commissary clerks were considered the equivalent of a sergeant-major. During the Waterloo campaign junior commissary officers were attached to Royal Horse Artillery troops – 'G' Troop's was Deputy-Assistant-Commissary-General William Coates. However, he is not listed among the six commissaries present during the battle. With infantry battalions or cavalry regiments, Coates' job was undertaken by the quartermaster.

In June 1815 there were 105 British commissary officers deployed in the Netherlands – one commissary-general, eight deputy-commissaries-general, eighteen assistant-commissaries-general and seventy-eight deputy-assistant-commissaries-general. Of these, we can only be certain that six were present on the battlefield at Waterloo. The overwhelming majority was to the rear, struggling to bring order to the chaos behind the lines and force a passage for their supplies (particularly rations). Some were at Hal while others, of more senior rank, were dispersed back along the lines of commu-

British Commissaries at the Battle not Granted the Waterloo Medal

Only six commissary officers are known for certain to have been at the battle, although it is likely there were others. None of them were granted the Waterloo Medal, and none allowed the prestigious 'W' before their name in the Army List, although in later years those who had served in the Peninsula had the 'P' before their names. Those Peninsula officers who lived until 1848 were granted the Military General Service Medal 1793–1814 when it was issued so long after the events it commemorated.

Assistant-Commissary Carey was particularly incensed by the unfairness of this decision, which he blamed directly on the Duke. According to Carey, Wellington refused to allow the commissary officers the Waterloo Medal because ration supplies did not get through on 17 or 18 June. Carey maintains that supplies were available but the civilian drivers panicked and abandoned their wagons – something for which he maintained commissary officers were not responsible. It was a sensitive issue on which Carey, and presumably others, felt strongly. He wrote:

> … but it is not the case, as was asserted, that they were without it [food] on the 18th. The Duke, nevertheless, got angry without reason, and in consequence we were deprived of the Medal, though it was given to a division of the army at Halle [Hal] in observation, which never heard the cannonade of the action [true, this was an extraordinary decision which caused much ill feeling], as well as to many officers and men who were not actually in the field but only on the effective returns of their corps. Had he made the least inquiry he would have found that there was a vast quantity of supplies in wagons near

Waterloo equal to several day's consumption for the whole army, which, as I have described, became useless owing to the panic occasioned by the followers of the army, and for which the Commissariat were in no way responsible…

A thoroughly aggrieved Carey cannot resist a final crack at an undoubtedly disagreeable side of the Duke's character:

> In the Duke's character there is a defect, which at times showed much inconsistency in taking prejudices against individuals [Captains Ramsey and Mercer of the RHA spring to mind], which, when once established, could never be removed by any explanation, and by which several deserving officers, and I may include my own department, suffered most unjustly.

The Commissariat officers at Waterloo, four of whom reached the rank of commissary-general, were:

Deputy-Commissary-General
Gregory Haines – became commissary-general and had eight clasps to his Military General Service Medal.
Randal Routh – later knighted and became commissary-general.

Assistant-Commissary-General
Tupper Carey – also became commissary-general with seven clasps to his Military General Service Medal.
Alexander Dallas – another Peninsula veteran who became a distinguished clergyman in Ireland
C. Purcell

Deputy-Assistant-Commissary-General
Gilbert Dinwiddie – he also eventually became commissary-general

nication or in Brussels. Somewhat unjustly, those commissariat officers who were present at the battle were not granted the Waterloo Medal, presumably because they were technically civilians. It must have caused considerable anger but was never reversed, even in 1848 when, like army veterans, former Commissariat officers were granted the Military General Service Medal with Peninsula clasps.

Some officers of the Field Train Department of the Ordnance assisted the Commissariat with the stocking and forwarding of ammunition. Only three officers of this organization are known to have been present at the battle and who received the Waterloo Medal. They were Assistant-Commissaries Samuel Tibbs, Edward Sparkes and Richard Bant. The former had served throughout the Peninsular War and eventually received fourteen clasps to his Military General Service Medal. This was almost a record, but not quite. Two men are known by name (James Talbot of the 45th Foot and Daniel Loochstadt of the KGL and 60th Rifles) to have received fifteen, although there were a number that equalled this amazing achievement.

The Royal Wagon Train
The Royal Wagon Train had responsibility for the transport of all supplies of food, fodder, ammunition and the operation of a rudimentary ambulance service utilizing 'spring wagons'. It had been formed in 1799 for service in Holland from men drafted in from the cavalry, with senior artillery NCOs being commissioned as subalterns. Later expansion brought the number of troops to fourteen, with almost 2000 all ranks. It was sent to Spain but proved totally inadequate to make much impression on the staggering transportation problems of that war. Their reputation was not good. A commissariat officer wrote of their commander in the Peninsula, Major-General Digby Hamilton: 'Fat General Hamilton of the wagon train has also turned

up here with his useless wagon corps…'. Their uniform was initially blue, and this, combined with their dubious reputation, quickly gave rise to their acquiring the nickname 'Newgate Blues' after the infamous prison of that name. In 1811 they were issued with red jackets with blue facings. All soldiers were armed with carbines and bayonets, while the officers carried the light cavalry sabre.

For the Waterloo campaign eight British troops, supported by another four Hanoverian troops, were deployed in the theatre of operations and attached to the Quartermaster-General's Department. The British troops were composed of over 1000 all ranks, 1,440 horses, 100 spring wagons, five stores, five mobile forges and twenty-seven forage wagons. Even this substantial train could not cope with the huge demand for transport, so large numbers of local wagons with civilian drivers had to be hired by the Commissariat.

It is impossible to be sure how many Royal Wagon Train personnel were present at the battle, as many wagons were unable to get through to Mont St Jean until 19 June. Nevertheless, the *Waterloo Medal Roll* lists nine officers and 265 other ranks receiving the medal. This would indicate that perhaps three of the eight troops were involved in the action. However, the *Waterloo Roll Call* lists twelve Royal Wagon Train officers at the battle, the senior being Lieutenant-Colonel Thomas Aird. The remainder comprised of two captains, seven lieutenants and two cornets. In addition, the Waterloo contingent had a surgeon and veterinary surgeon attached.

The only incident of importance involving Royal Wagon Train personnel that was recorded, was the resupplying of the Hougoumont garrison with ammunition by a solitary driver and wagon. The driver, Private Joseph Brewer, unhesitatingly made the dash for the north gate of the château under a hail of fire. He survived to tell the tale and was later allowed to transfer to the 3rd

Foot Guards in recognition of his gallant act. This incident seemingly occurred late in the afternoon, by which time the garrison was dangerously low on ammunition, having been firing for over four hours. Brewer's timely arrival, which quite possibly saved the situation, is commemorated by a plaque erected in 1979 by the Royal Corps of Transport, the then successors of the Royal Wagon Train.

The officer responsible for sending Brewer on his way was Captain Horace Seymour of the 18th Hussars and ADC to the cavalry commander, the Earl of Uxbridge. This is the same Seymour who was reputedly the strongest man in the British Army and had the confrontation with Colonel Hake and the Cumberland Hussars. Seymour was later to write:

> Late in the day of the 18th, I was called by some officers of the 3rd Guards defending Hougoumont [Ensign Barclay Drummond, their acting adjutant, who later became a general and Groom-in-Waiting to the Queen], to use my best endeavours to send them musket ammunition. Soon afterwards I fell in with a private of the Wagon Train in charge of a tumbril on the crest of the position. I merely pointed out to him where he was wanted, when he gallantly started his horses, and drove straight down the hill to the Farm, to the gate of which I saw him arrive. He must have lost his horses, as there was a severe fire kept on him. I feel convinced to that man's service the Guards owe their ammunition.

There are not many references to ammunition supply in Wellington's army at Waterloo. A rare exception is an officer in Picton's 5th British Division who mentions in an article that the battalions had all but run out of ammunition by late afternoon. He describes the replenishment:

> About this time our ball cartridge was all expended, and no supply being at hand the skirmishers were called in, seeing which, those of the enemy came on in the most daring manner step by step. The ammunition cart was brought as quickly as possible to the height [ridge], and the horses being withdrawn, it was left there for us. Every man sent for a cask as a supply was either killed or wounded. ... Sergeant Connor, of the Royals, who at last whipped out a cask, shouldered it, and came running towards us with it, when down he tumbled with a bad wound in the heel; he however managed to throw the barrel so as to make it roll down the slope towards our post, on which we immediately resumed the offensive...

THE FRENCH SUPPLY SERVICES

The Intendance Service

The Intendance was the logistics corps of the French Army. It was Napoleon's equivalent of Wellington's commissariat and was responsible for the same tasks – that of procuring the wherewithal for the army to eat, drink and fight. It was a semi-military organization, sometimes referred to as the 'Administration'. Its officers wore blue jackets, with different coloured facings depending on which branch of the organization they belonged to, red waistcoats, breeches, bicorne hats and carried an epée type sword. Intendance other rank personnel were termed ouvriers d'administration. They were dressed in blue or iron-grey coats, waistcoats and breeches, and were armed like the infantry, including a sabre.

There were five main branches or departments with differing procurement and supply responsibilities. The *vivres-pain* supplied bread, dried vegetables, salt, wine and brandy. The *vivres-viande* provided the meat ration through local purchase, requisitioning or from beef cattle on the hoof following the army. The *fourrages* were responsible for fodder (hay, straw or grain). This was bulky and heavy so provision was often contracted out – an extremely unreliable expedient. The *chauffage* supplied fuel and candles for barracks, permanent camps or fortresses. This branch was not involved in field operations. The fifth department was the *habillement* charged with providing uniforms and items of equipment.

As might be expected, the combat troops looked on Intendance personnel as thieves and cowards, which in most cases they were. Almost without exception, these officials were racketeers of some sort. Many were fat men in comfortable billets, far more concerned with getting rich than meeting their supply obligations. De Brack, a cavalry officer, wrote: 'I made eight campaigns in the time of the Empire, and always with the outposts; I did not see during all that time one single commissaire de guerres [a senior Intendance officer]; I did not receive a single ration from the army's depots.' A common *vivres-viande* scam was to requisition (seize) a poor peasant's cow but, for a suitable remuneration, leave the rich farmer's alone. Then, out of greed and idleness, allow the requisitioned animals to die from lack of feed or water. In 1809 twelve Intendance employees were shot for selling the soldiers' wine ration.

Just occasionally there were exceptions. Maréchal Davout once approved the recommendation for one of his commissaires des guerres for the Legion of Honour for his care of the wounded. In Russia, at the crossing of the Beresina Commissaire des Guerres, Antoine Delahaye had his horse shot under him and his leg broken while repeatedly forcing his way across blocked bridges to save the wounded.

The gross inefficiencies of the supply system were one of the main reasons why the French armies of the period foraged for their needs. This meant living off the surrounding countryside, scrounging, stealing and generally devouring everything edible for miles around like a huge swarm of locusts. This gave Napoleon's armies a far greater strategic mobility in Europe than their enemies who relied primarily on endless, plodding and vulnerable supply columns. The problem with too much reliance on what the countryside could provide was that an army had to keep on the move; if it concentrated in one area for more than a week or so it was quickly stripped of produce and the soldiers began to get hungry. An army also had to concentrate to fight, so no large force could go entirely without some supply trains for long. In inhospitable countries like Russia or Spain they were indispensable. Spain, for example, has been described with great accuracy as a country where large armies starved and small ones got beaten.

The Train des Equipages

This was the French equivalent of the Royal Wagon Train. Its task was to transport supplies. After the campaign in Russia in 1812 the Train was reorganized into twelve four-company battalions, each battalion with 140 wagons. Captains commanded battalions, sous-lieutenants companies. Each company has seven NCOs, four craftsmen, eighty drivers, thirty-six wagons and 161 horses. Uniforms were iron grey and all ranks (including officers) were armed with carbines and sabres (briquets). In addition, officers and NCOs were supposed to carry a brace of pistols. The Imperial Guard had its own Train des Equipages – five companies strong for the Waterloo campaign.

The French Wine/Brandy Ration and British Gin

Within the French Army wine, usually vin rouge, had a number of uses other than the obvious one. It was used to flavour the soldiers' soup, soften his rock-hard biscuits, as a restorative, as an antiseptic and to deaden pain. Spanish wine, which was virtually the only type the French could not stomach, was recommended as good for cleaning muddy boots. Wine that was issued via the Intendance rarely arrived in its original state. It had invariably been diluted with water, the trick being to disguise this fact by adding the right amount of pure alcohol or salt to bring out the flavour. It was even known for watery wine to be given a kick by adding sulphuric acid or arsenic!

Brandy was more popular. Called 'eau de vie', the daily ration was what kept the veterans going through a protracted campaign. As with wine, it could be 'doctored'. Sometimes substitutes, such as a mixture of alcohol and water enlivened with pepper or ginger and given something of the right colour with tea or caramel, were swallowed without too much fuss. Some barrels were broken open before Waterloo and a proportion of Frenchmen went into action suitably fortified. The French assumed the British did the same. Afterwards Assistant-Commissary Carey had difficulty convincing a French commissary officer that the British custom was to consume their alcohol (if available) after, rather than before, an action.

Carey had got it wrong as far as Waterloo and the 3/14 Foot were concerned. Ensign Hon. George Keppel described what happened with his battalion:

> Prior to taking up our position for the night [17 June] the regiment filed past a tubful of gin. Every officer and man was, in turn, presented with a little tin pot full. No fermented liquor has since passed my lips could vie with that delicious schnapps. As soon as each man was served the precious contents that remained in the tub were tilted over on to the ground.

At Waterloo

Apart from a few battalion or regimental supply wagons (barrels of brandy having priority) that may have miraculously kept up with the marching troops, there is little evidence of Intendance or Train des Equipages personnel being present at the battle. The only certain exception was the officer in overall charge of administration and supply: Intendant-General Baron Antoine Daru, who rode with Napoleon's Imperial staff. Daru was a man of outstanding integrity and ability in a branch of the service where these attributes were seldom seen. He had started his career as a teenage cadet and by 1813 had risen to Minister of War (see box p. 323).

On the morning of Sunday 18 June the great bulk of Daru's hundreds of supply wagons were still stuck at the Charleroi bottleneck. This was due to several factors, mostly outside his control. Firstly, the train had been kept at the rear of the advancing army for sound reasons of mobility. Supply wagons blocked roads, and the need for speed and surprise was paramount, with priority on these routes going to guns and their ammunition wagons. Secondly, the state of the roads was poor due to the torrential rain on the night of 17 June, which had converted them into mud slides. Thirdly, the congestion on the main route forward was appalling. And finally, the drivers were generally disinclined to expose themselves to the dangers of shot and shell.

As has been described above, the Armée du Nord spent much of the night before the battle in undisciplined and unsuccessful foraging for food, wood and warmth. The situation was so bad that the commander of the Gendarmerie, Baron Radet, resigned his position (although he remained with the army). Like their opponents, most French soldiers fought at Waterloo with empty bellies. Even when Napoleon gave orders that the troops were to halt on the line of march for their breakfast soup, not many had anything worth eating left in their pouches.

After the French defeat the wagons were still at Charleroi. Napoleon sent orders for them to turn round and withdraw. The messenger found the garrison commander drunk and insensible. Movement of any sort was delayed and confused with the result that the train was overtaken by the retreating army and many vehicles were lost.

THE PRUSSIAN SUPPLY SERVICES

The defeat at Ligny and the hasty retreat north to Wavre had thrown the Prussian supply services, with the exception of those with IV Corps that had not been engaged, into turmoil. However, the need to put IV Corps, which was the furthest from Mont St Jean, in the lead for the march to join Wellington played havoc with its supply columns as well. Supply columns were, quite rightly, kept well to the rear of the various army corps. The difficulties of the terrain, mud and the Wavre and Lasne bottlenecks made progress of the marching columns, particularly the guns, frustratingly slow. In the event the Prussian units that reached the battlefield had left their supply columns, with the exception of ammunition wagons, far behind.

As with the other arms and services, supply staff (commissariat) and supply columns were attached to each corps. They were:

- A supply and bakery unit
- A horse supply depot
- Three or four supply columns

For the Waterloo campaign the Prussian supply was organized as follows:

Army headquarters

Head of Commissariat – Major-General van Panhuys
Adjutant – 1st Lieutenant Lemmers

I Corps
Senior Commissary – name not known
No.3 Supply and Bakery Unit – Captain von Stromberg
No.13 Supply Column – Captain von Moerner
No.15 Supply Column – Captain von Zagorsky
No.17 Supply Column – Captain von Massow

II Corps
Senior Commissary – Prescher
No.2 Supply and Bakery Unit – 2nd Lieutenant von Machui
Horse Supply Depot – Captain von Karwinski
No.4 Supply Column – 1st Lieutenant Josl
No.5 Supply Column – Captain von Brandt
No.6 Supply Column – 1st Lieutenant von Sanitz

IV Corps
Senior Commissary – de Rege
No.4 Supply and Bakery Unit – commander not known
Horse Supply Depot – 1st Lieutenant von Lewetzow
No.8 Supply Column – Captain Baron von Stillfried
No.21 Supply Column – 1st Lieutenant Petzold
No.31 Supply Column – commander not known
No.32 Supply Column – commander not known

The Highlights

Sound, sound the clarion, fill the fife!
To all the sensual world proclaim,
One crowed hour of glorious life
Is worth an age without a name.

Sir Walter Scott

General

It is not intended to describe the battle blow by blow. Rather the six main highlights will be examined:

- The struggle for Hougoumont
- The French I Corps' (d'Erlon) attack, including the subsequent Anglo-Allied and French cavalry counterattacks
- The massed French cavalry attacks
- The struggle for La Haie Sainte
- The struggle for Plancenoit
- The Imperial Guard's final assault

The views, feelings, experiences and actions of some of the participants will feature in the 'boxes' that accompany each section. The highlights themselves will be broken down into:

- Outline of events
- The tactical significance of the action
- The forces engaged
- Plans, intentions and orders
- Special features
- Other headings relevant to a particular highlight

The Struggle for Hougoumont (Maps 21–25, pp. 337-341)

The trumpets sound, the banners fly,
The glittering spears are ranked ready,
The shouts of war are heard afar,
The battle closes thick and bloody.

Robert Burns

Outline of events

The buildings, garden, orchard and wood of Hougoumont were defended by British Guards, Nassauers and a few Hanoverians from the first cannon shot at about 11.30 a.m. until the Imperial Guard recoiled almost nine hours later. Throughout that time Reille's corps mounted a series of attacks in a vain effort to capture this strongpoint. The first two assaults were the most determined and came closest to success. By shortly after midday the wood to the south of the buildings was taken and not fully recovered until the closing stages of the battle. At around 1.00 p.m. the French made their only penetration of the defences at the North Gate – one officer (Sous-Lieutenant Legros) with about thirty men smashed their way in, only to be shot down after the gates were closed behind them.

For the remainder of the day the substantially reinforced French launched a succession of attacks with perceptively diminishing enthusiasm. They took and then lost the Great Orchard. By mid-afternoon they had set fire to the château, farmer's house and most sheds and barns, but still the only Frenchmen inside the garden or the buildings were corpses – except for a drummer boy who was spared after getting inside the northern farmyard with Legros' party. Evening saw Wellington's general advance sweep back into the wood. Hougoumont's defenders were, by then, hugely outnumbered by the dead, dying and wounded from both sides. This epic struggle has been aptly described as a 'battle within a battle'.

Looking out through the North Gate. Sous-Lieutenant Legros and about thirty Frenchmen forced their way through this gate. Photo: the author

Closing the North Gate

This gate had been deliberately left open to allow free and speedy access for friendly troops. By 12.30 p.m. Macdonell had been pushed back along the west side of the buildings, so his companies used the North Gate through which to withdraw, under pressure, into the northern courtyard of the château. Dashwood's 2/3 Guards were the last inside and only just closed the double gates before the French arrived.

There was no time to secure the gates properly. Shots were fired through the woodwork, shattering the arm of Lieutenant and Captain Evelyn. Within moments heavy axe blows combined with the pressure of a dozen bodies forced them open. The axe was wielded by Sous-Lieutenant Legros of the 1st Company, 2nd Battalion, 1st Légère Regiment. A powerful man known as L'enfonceur, formerly an engineer who had risen through the ranks, Legros burst into the compound at the head of his men. There was some desperate hand-to-hand fighting. A number of defenders fled into buildings, barns and even some low pigsties, before turning to shoot from windows or doors into the mêlée. Lieutenant Diederich von Wilder (a Nassau officer in the Grenadier Company) was chased as far as the farmer's house. There he had the traumatic experience of having his hand chopped off at the wrist by a Frenchman with an axe – whether it was Legros is not known.

Wellington was within a whisker of losing Hougoumont. Macdonell, near the gate leading to the garden, instantly realized that the gates must be closed at any cost to stop more Frenchmen pouring in. Yelling at three nearby officers (Captain and Lieutenant-Colonel Wyndham, Ensigns Hervy and Gooch,

The North Gate as it appeared when photographed in 1850. Drawing by John Mollo.

all Coldstreamers) to join him, he dashed towards the gate. Near the well another six soldiers (Sergeants Fraser, McGregor and Aston plus Private Lester, all 2/3 Guards, together with two more Coldstreamers, the Irish brothers Corporals James and Joseph Graham), joined him. While some heaved on the gates, others fought with bayonets or swords to beat back more of the enemy as they arrived. Slowly, the gates were pushed together, barricaded and the crossbar dropped into position. Frustrated by the closure, at least one Frenchman clambered onto the shoulders of a comrade and, leaning over the wall, took aim at Captain and Lieutenant-Colonel Wyndham. Wyndham, who was holding Corporal James Graham's musket, calmly handed it back to Graham who took a quick shot at the Frenchman. Both fired simultaneously, but it was the Frenchman who dropped out of sight with a ball through his brain.

With no reinforcements arriving the thirty or so Frenchmen in the yard were doomed. Within five minutes Legros and his comrades lay dead. The only one allowed to live was the young drummer boy – who had somehow lost his drum.

Hours later at the end of the day as the French fled the field, Wyndham is said to have spotted Prince Jérôme in his carriage trying to escape. He allegedly leaped through one door as the Emperor's brother jumped from the other, thereby narrowly missing capturing him. The other interesting anecdote is that after the closing of the gate incident, for the rest of his life Wyndham could never bear to shut a door. As a result he would often sit in a howling draught for hours on end – a habit that did not appear to undermine his health since he lived to be seventy.

The Tactical Significance (Diagram p. 332)

Wellington's ridge south of Mont St Jean was endowed with three natural outposts or strongpoints, of which Hougoumont was the largest – the others being La Haie Sainte and the Papelotte/La Haie/Smohain area. They acted as three breakwaters jutting out from the flanks and centre of his main position. Occupied, they would divide, channel and weaken the force of frontal attacks, just as breakwaters do with an advancing tide. Occupied by the enemy, they would seriously threaten the main position, providing ideal bases from which to launch strong assaults from not much above musket range.

Hougoumont required little work to make it a formidable place to assault; the large wood to the south screened most of the buildings from the French view. It also provided good cover for infantry who could move around quite freely since there was no undergrowth. Most importantly, the wood (and to a lesser extent the Great Orchard) prevented the French from firing round shot or canister at the buildings or garden walls in preparation for an attack, except from the west. The thick, high hedges were a boon to the defenders and a curse to the attackers. They were just as effective a barrier as a man-made barricade. The significance to

both sides of the hedge along the southern edge of the Great Orchard is demonstrated by Private Clay, who later described how he had to cut loopholes in it.

The walls and buildings only required strong arms and pick-axes to provide loopholes – a number were knocked in the garden walls, but there would have been more had there been sufficient tools. Poking holes with bayonets in a brick wall is a frustratingly slow business, although Lieutenant Graeme, serving with the 2nd Light Battalion of the KGL in La Haie Sainte, stated emphatically that they sent their pioneers across to Hougoumont on the evening of 17 June to help prepare defences.

In order to bring sufficient muskets to bear on the wood (which if lost would provide a covered approach to within 20 metres of the wall), platforms had to be constructed on the inside to allow soldiers to fire over the top. This was a much more stressful undertaking than pushing a muzzle through a hole in the wall. These preparations were extended along the eastern wall facing the Great Orchard. The height of the wall, nearly 2 metres, was of considerable significance to the attackers, as there was no means of climbing over other than being pushed up by, or clambering on the backs of, one's comrades. Many gallant Frenchmen tried. The few that succeeded

Hougoumont – Château and Buildings June 1815

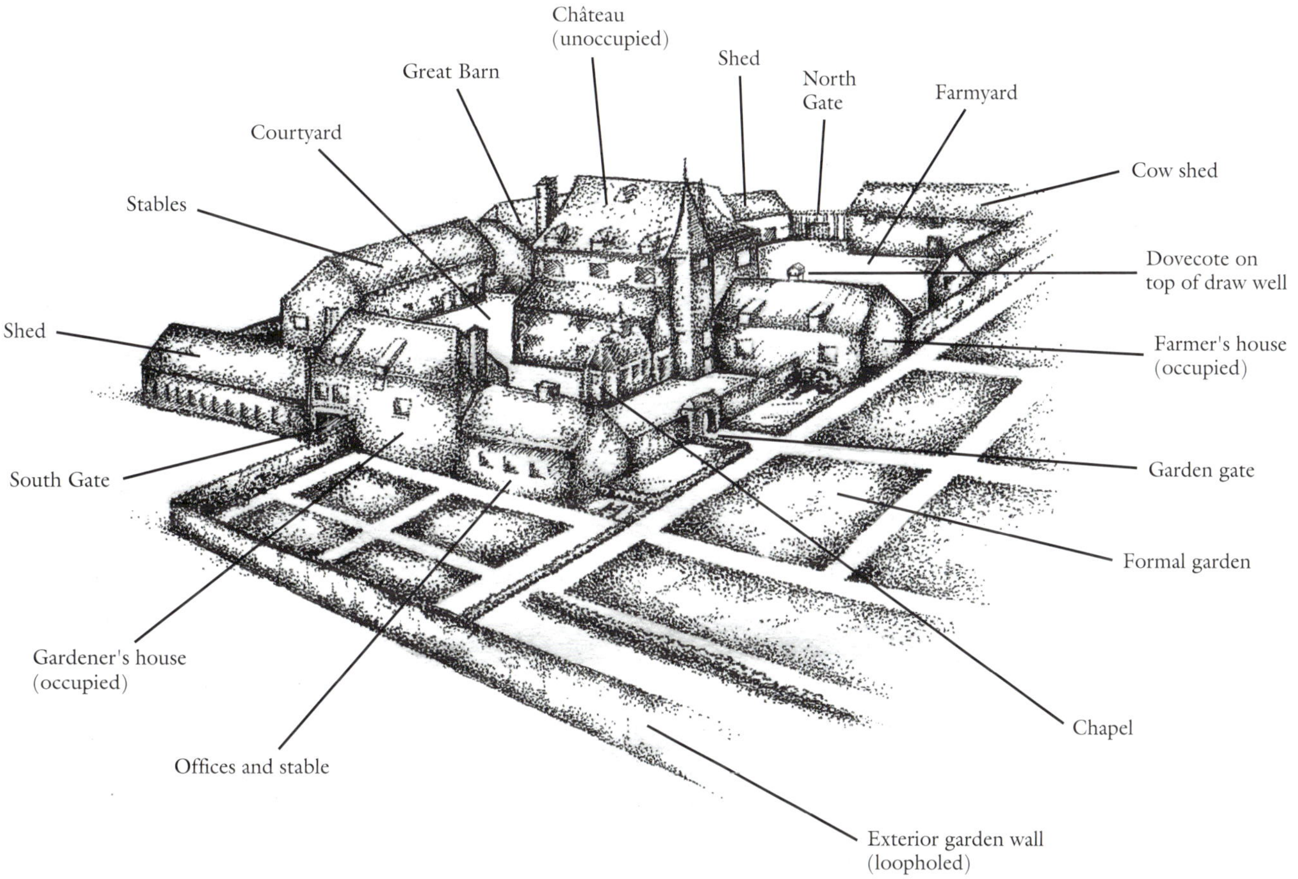

Château
(unoccupied)

Great Barn

Shed

North
Gate

Farmyard

Courtyard

Cow shed

Stables

Dovecote on
top of draw well

Shed

Farmer's house
(occupied)

South Gate

Garden gate

Gardener's house
(occupied)

Formal garden

Offices and stable

Chapel

Exterior garden wall
(loopholed)

Note: Virtually the only buildings to survive the fire were the chapel
and the buildings separated from the rest of the complex along
the southern side – shed, gardener's house, offices and stable.
Wounded were scattered throughout the buildings – a number
perished in the flames.

*Looking east along
what was the Sunken
Way, to the right was
the Small Orchard, to
the left the rising
ground up to the main
Allied position on the
ridge. It was the
rallying point for
Saltoun's companies,
the high water mark for
the French assaults and
the forming up place
for counterattacks.*

Photo: the author

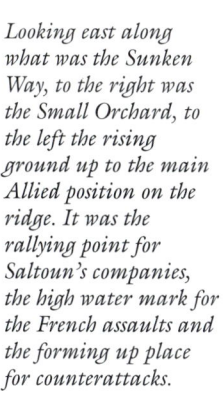

Terrain Features of Tactical Importance or Potential – Hougoumont in 1815

The Buildings

1. North gate initially left open, site of only French penetration of the compound.
2. Stabling and cow sheds.
3. Well, with dovecote over the top.
4. Great Barn. Burnt down between about 3.00–4.00 p.m.
5. Archway with door linking the northern and southern courtyards.
6. The Château, it was unoccupied and unfurnished. Burnt down.
7. Chapel. Miraculously escaped the fire, the flames only charring the wooden statue of Christ on the cross inside the wooden door.
8. Farmer's House. Occupied and in use. Burnt down.
9. Store sheds. 9A small west door.
10. Garden Gate. Used by defenders to move men between the buildings and formal garden.
11. Gardeners House and offices. In use prior to the battle. With the chapel the only building to escape the fire.
12. The South Gate. An arched passageway with doors at both ends.
13. Store shed.

Kitchen Garden

This narrow strip of land enclosed by hedge is clearly described by Private Clay as a kitchen garden. In it the Light Companies of the 2/C and 2/3 Guards were deployed to meet the first French attack. The second main attack drove them inside the farm.

The Haystack

Behind this haystack Private Clay (2/3 Guards) sought shelter while he fired at the enemy in the wood. He was so engrossed he failed to notice his comrades had withdrawn inside the farm via the north gate.

It caught fire quite easily in the battle. Nearby a mass grave was dug the next day for hundreds of corpses in the area.

The Wood

The wood was some 300 metres long (north-south) and 250 metres wide, defended by about 470 green uniformed Hanoverians and Nassauers.

It was soon captured by the French and remained in their hands for most of the day.

It screened the buildings from view and artillery fire from the south, but was no obstruction for infantry. Lieut and Capt. Ellison later wrote 'It had no underwood [undergrowth] and was easily traversed in all parts by Light Infantry'.

The château/farm garrison

The initial garrison inside the building was the Grenadier Coy of 1/2 Nassau.

With the second main French attack the Light Companies of the 2/C and 2/3 withdrew inside the buildings.

Subsequently another 7 companies of the 2/C reinforced the defenders of the building and formal gardens.

The North Gate

Through this gate came reinforcements, ADCs and the ammunition tumbril. Some walking wounded also left by this gate.

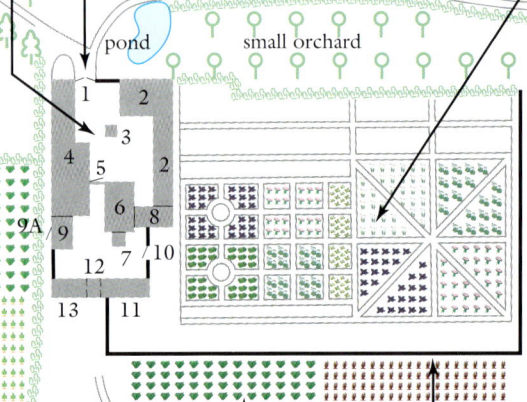

'The killing ground'

This 30-metre wide, 200-metre long strip of ground was where most Frenchmen died. Every attempt to cross it and scale the wall opposite failed. By the end of the battle it was almost impossible to walk along the northern edge of the wood without stepping on a body.

This strip of land is shown on Craan's map as a vegetable garden.

The Garden walls

A 7-ft high brick wall enclosed the southern and eastern sides of the formal garden. Vulnerable to artillery fire it was impervious to musket balls. It was these walls that enabled the defenders to repulse six times their number.

Many loopholes had been knocked through both walls and platforms constructed to allow soldiers to fire over the top. A handful of Frenchmen fell dead into the garden.

Sunken Way

This track with a thickset hedge on the south side, formed a convenient rallying point for Allied troops when driven from the Great Orchard.

The ground was low-lying and very marshy.

The track formed the high water mark of French attacks in this area.

Formal Garden

An elaborately laid out ornamental garden with shrubs, flowers and many small paths.

Defended initially by one company of 1/2 Nassau. Subsequently reinforced by several companies of the Coldstream Guards.

Gate

Intended to give access between wood, fields and orchard, this gate had been blocked by defenders.

Nevertheless, it was a focal point for movement, between wood and orchard.

Ensign Standard stated, 'the ditch at the corner of the wood (by gate) was full of dead bodies'.

Great Orchard

An apple orchard about 200 metres square. Defended initially by about 250 men from the 1/2 Nassau Regiment, but for most of the battle by the Light Companies of the 2/1 and 3/1 Guards under Lord Saltoun. He was eventually relieved by most of the 2/3 Guards under Hepburn.

This orchard changed hands several times during the day. The high water mark of the French attacks was the northern hedge that borders the 'sunken way'.

The defenders on the eastern hedge were able to fire into the flanks of the French cavalry as they made their massed assaults in the late afternoon.

After the battle all the apple trees had been shot to pieces and the orchard generously covered with red, green and blue uniformed bodies.

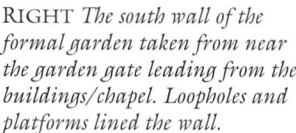

ABOVE *The SE corner of the garden wall. The trees on the skyline mark the Allied right wing. In this area were the initial positions of the 2/C and the 2/3 Guards battalions with Bull's howitzer battery firing into the woods behind the camera. The light green trees in the middle distance mark the Sunken Way while the vegetable field was part of the apple orchard.*

Photo: the author

RIGHT *The south wall of the formal garden taken from near the garden gate leading from the buildings/chapel. Loopholes and platforms lined the wall.*

Photo: the author

merely fell dead inside rather than outside the garden. The only alternative for the French infantryman was to bang away at the tiny loopholes or the heads of the defenders that kept bobbing up over the wall like so many snap targets on a modern firing range. The gap between the wall and the wood was a true killing zone. The northern boundary of the garden was not, as many maps indicate, a wall but a hedge. On this occasion it was of no tactical importance as the French never (except for a fleeting appearance at the North Gate) got round to the rear of Hougoumont.

Hougoumont presented the Duke with other advantages. Firstly, because it conferred so many advantages on those who occupied it, Hougoumont could be defended by comparatively few men (see p. 336). Secondly, unless captured, it would funnel any major attack on his right into the 950-metre gap between the east-

ern hedge of the orchard and La Haie Sainte. To avoid effective enfilade musket fire from these strongpoints, the gap would be squeezed to around 650 metres. Thirdly, substantial supporting artillery fire could be brought down on attacking columns. Even those in the wood did not escape, as within the hour of the first shot, Bull's troop of six howitzers was raining shrapnel through the trees with demoralizing effect. Bachelu's 5th Division never reached Hougoumont because their advance was driven back by the weight of artillery fire from the combined batteries on the ridge west of the 'Elm Tree' crossroads.

All the tactical advantages that Hougoumont gave to its defenders were denied to its attackers. To the French they became deadly disadvantages. Napoleon never intended its capture (see p. 336) although such a success would have secured the left flank

A view of 'the killing ground' looking east from near the South Gate. The large tree and fence on the right marked the hedge line and edge of the wood. Scores of men fell all along this narrow strip of grass. Photo: the author

of any subsequent assaults on the Duke's centre-right. To attack Hougoumont was an infantryman's job. The wood, the Great Orchard and the buildings all required close quarter bullet and bayonet fighting to clear. Such combat is extremely costly, particularly without the support of guns.

The French efforts to give direct support by artillery to their infantry were so small as to be almost non-existent. A single howitzer was pushed forward, probably from the 3rd Company 2nd Horse Artillery, to a position near the gate between the wood and the Great Orchard (Map 24, p. 340). Lord Saltoun tried to capture it, but although it undoubtedly fired some canister, it seems to have had little effect. The only artillery success, instigated by the Emperor in person, was when carcasses fired from howitzers set fire to most of the buildings. None of the gates, walls or buildings would have withstood cannon fire. With a modicum of determination, a battery could have been pushed forward on the west or even the east of Hougoumont. Comparatively few shots would have been sufficient to punch large holes in any of the defences that were proof against musket balls. One wonders why it never happened.

For Napoleon, it was far from essential to secure Hougoumont. It could, with difficulty, be ignored; it could be outflanked in the west; or subjected to a feint attack in the hope of drawing off some of Wellington's reserves. It was the latter role that Napoleon assigned to it – without much success.

Wellington's Artillery Fire

Not all of the Duke's artillery firing in support of Hougoumont fired into the wood like the howitzers. Many cannons refrained from doing so. Some, however, could not resist the tempting but long range (1,500 metres) and high angle shoot at the infantry in the open waiting to advance – Foy's and Bachelu's divisions. Bachelu's chief of staff, Colonel Toussaint-Jean Trefcon, expressed surprise that his troops were hit even though they were, 'unengaged and quite a respectable cannon-shot away'. Foy's ADC, Major Lemonnier-Delafosse, not only recalled his division coming under fire, but also Kellerman's cavalry formed up behind him. The cannon balls had little velocity left but were a nuisance:

Behind us in reserve was the brigade of carabiniers on which the cannon-balls which passed over us went to fall. To get out of their range, this brigade moved to their left [further behind Hougoumont wood], which provoked General Foy to laugh, 'Ha! Ha! The big boots don't like the rough stuff.' We received the cannon-balls standing firm. They covered us with mud and the soaked ground, by conserving the marks of their paths, looked like a field ploughed by the wheels of carts. This was lucky for our line, for many of the projectiles buried or muffled themselves while rolling along this muddy soil.

The Forces Engaged

There is considerable uncertainty as to the precise numbers of troops committed to attacking and defending Hougoumont during the course of the battle. The figures at the start (11.30 a.m.) are reasonably clear for both sides, as are the reinforcements sent in during the next three hours or so. What happened after that until the end of the battle is far less certain. The uncertainties are twofold:

• Many sources claim that by the end of the day the entire French II Corps had been sucked into the struggle for Hougoumont – some 18,000 infantrymen. This is difficult to justify. The figure hinges on whether Bachelu's division was drawn in. It is clear that at least his leading brigade attempted to advance on Hougoumont from the south-east around mid-afternoon. To reach the wood or Great Orchard these battalions had to advance 1000 metres diagonally across the Anglo-Allied front. As they neared their objective they came under sustained and accurate artillery fire (round shot and shrapnel) from Wellington's batteries along the ridge. The attack broke up without reaching Hougoumont. At the end of the day Bachelu's division became involved in other operations against Wellington's centre. For these reasons this division has not

hope of drawing off some of Wellington's reserves. It was the latter role that Napoleon assigned to it – without much success.

been included in the number of French troops that actually assaulted Hougoumont.

• The second difficulty involves the number of troops Wellington sent to assist the garrison. During the afternoon there is no doubt that as the whole of Byng's 2nd Brigade got drawn forward into Hougoumont, the Duke moved up reserves from the rear to strengthen and support his front line. Several sources indicate that Brunswick, Hanoverian and Nassau units moved in the direction of Hougoumont. This is correct but there is no evidence that any of these troops were actually engaged defending the place. Being musket-armed soldiers, they needed to come down the forward slope into the compound, orchard or wood to be of any use – they did not do so until the battle was virtually over. Possibly between 7.00–7.30 p.m. or later the 2nd KGL, Colin Halkett's Hanoverians, the

French Fail to Use their Guns Effectively

Writing in 1836 in the *United Service Journal* under the name 'W', a British officer who fought at Hougoumont emphasized how fortunate the defenders were that the French failed to use their guns against the western flank of the château and farm, which was unprotected by the wood. It is probable that this error cost them success at Hougoumont. 'W' wrote:

On the French side of the house and garden, coming down close to both, was an open but thickly planted wood of about five acres. Upon this wood did the successful issue of the defence and real strength of the post entirely depend; for the house and garden, although proof against musketry, could not have stood for ten minutes against the fire of a few pieces of field-artillery, but, ill-built, must have tumbled down and buried its defenders in the ruins. Neither could the orchard

have been kept for one moment after the fall and occupation of the house and garden … But the wood entirely screened the house, garden and offices from the sight and operation of the enemy's artillery: rendering mud-cemented [incorrect] walls – through which their shots would have passed like brown paper – thus equal for the purposes of the defence, to the strongest fortification. Owing to the existence of this wood, the troops occupying the house and garden enjoyed a complete exemption from the storm of shot and shells which fell with such fury on the other parts of the [main] position. Except an ill-directed shell, which occasionally passed over, and now and then a discharge of grape [canister], which was lost among the branches of the trees, the attack and defence consisted entirely of musketry.

Colonel Cubières Meets Sergeant Fraser

Maréchal de Camp Bauduin commanded the 1st Brigade of Jérôme's division and had the dubious honour of leading the first attack on Hougoumont Wood. Like the other French senior officers, he led the way into the wood conspicuously mounted on a horse. One of the Jaegers or Hanoverian sharpshooters easily picked him out. Within minutes he had been shot dead. Command of the brigade devolved onto the commanding officer of the 1st Légère, Colonel Cubières.

After about an hour the 1st Brigade cleared the wood and Great Orchard but was held up by the walls around Hougoumont. Jérôme sent in his 2nd Brigade under Soye. His arrival allowed Cubières to lead the fight against Macdonell to the west of the buildings. The weight of numbers slowly drove the Guards back, out of the kitchen garden and along the path outside the west wall towards the North Gate. It was on this path that Cubières came up against thirty-three-year-old Sergeant Ralph Fraser of the 2/3 Guards. Fraser was very much the tough, old sweat veteran NCO who had served and fought in Egypt, Hanover, Copenhagen and the Peninsular War. He had twice been seriously wounded. The colonel took a swing at the sergeant with his sword, which Fraser avoided and lunged upwards with his halberd (as light company

Looking along the western side of the 'Great Barn'. The dead trees are all that is left of the wood to the south of the buildings. The open ground was the kitchen garden area in which the light companies of the 2nd (Coldstream) Guards and the 2/3 Guards were initially deployed. Colonel Cubières was unhorsed and wounded by Sergeant Fraser on the path running along the wall of the barn. Photo: the author

sergeants did not normally carry halberds there is some doubt as to what weapon he used). Cubières was wounded and knocked, or pulled, from his horse. Instead of killing him Fraser leapt on the colonel's horse and rode back to the North Gate through which most of his comrades were withdrawing.

The wounded Cubières survived and later became a general, a baron and Governor of Ancona in Italy. He forever remained grateful to Fraser and the other Guards who spared him. By a strange turn of fate Colonel Woodford, who later became a field-marshal, met Cubières in 1832. Inevitably talk turned to Waterloo. Woodford later wrote, 'He says we forbore to fire upon him, and he owes us much for many good years since. I have some recollection of the circumstance, of which he always makes a great deal.'

Fraser, who minutes later helped to close the North Gate, received a special medal for his gallantry but, surprisingly, was discharged three years later 'in consequence of long service and being worn out'. He was only thirty-eight. The medical authorities had made a very poor diagnosis – Fraser was good for another forty-seven years. He became a Bedesman at Westminster Abbey, dying at the outbreak of the American Civil War in 1862, aged eighty-five.

Brunswick Advance Guard, and the Leib and 1st Light battalions advanced into and drove the French out of the orchard and most of the wood. Because this happened so late in the battle and none of these units were involved in the actual defence of the position, they have not been included in the defenders' strength.

In light of the above, the comparison of relative strengths, reinforcements and very approximate timings are given below (no attempt has been made to include casualties):

Estimated time	French	Anglo-Allied
11.30 a.m.–12.30 p.m.	4,000 (7 bns)	1,200 (equivalent to 2 bns)
12.30–1.30 p.m.	3,500 (6 bns)	9 companies (equivalent to 1 bn)
	2,500 (5 bns)	–
1.30–2.30 p.m.	2,700 (6 bns)	6 companies (but 2 withdrawn)
Totals	12,700 (24 bns)	2,600 + (equivalent to 4.5 bns)

In terms of infantrymen actually fighting for possession of Hougoumont, by early afternoon the French outnumbered the Anglo-Allied force 5:1. Put another way, Reille had committed over 23 per cent of his Emperor's infantry in comparison to Wellington's 5 per cent. With artillery it is impossible to be certain as to the number of guns or batteries actually supporting the defence of, or attacks on, Hougoumont. The French probably employed five batteries (thirty-four pieces), initially. However, once their infantry took the wood, the great majority of firing in support of II Corps took the form of counter-battery fire. The Duke brought up to eight or nine batteries (including Bull's six howitzers) into action within the first hour. There is no doubt that others joined in later when they did not have more pressing targets to engage (and ammunition stocks allowed), or that it was artillery fire that inflicted at least as many losses as musket balls on the attackers. The combination of howitzers and spherical case (shrapnel) proved ideal against an enemy concealed from view in the wood. And it was gunfire that prevented Bachelu's division from effectively joining the struggle.

Plans, Intentions and Orders

Wellington's plan was to hold Hougoumont. When he visited the château for the second time that morning, his orders to Captain and Lieutenant-Colonel Macdonell were equally simple: 'defend the post to the last extremity'. The French intentions with regard to Hougoumont were much less clear.

Napoleon's attack order, timed at 11.00 a.m., makes his original intentions for the army quite plain. It is straightforward, short and with the overall objective clearly set out. This order was dictated by the Emperor, written by Soult and addressed to all corps commanders. To understand the French activities at Hougoumont it needs to be stated in full:

> Directly the army has formed up, and soon after 1 p.m., the Emperor will give the order to Marshal Ney and the attack will be delivered on Mt. S. Jean village in order to seize the cross-roads at that place. To this end the 12-pdr. Batteries

of II and VI Corps will mass with that of the I Corps. These 24 guns will bombard the troops holding Mont S. Jean, and Count d'Erlon will commence the attack by first launching the left division [Quiot], and, when necessary, supporting it with other divisions of I Corps. The II Corps [Reille] will also advance keeping abreast of the I Corps. The company of the Engineers belonging to I Corps will hold themselves in readiness to barricade and fortify Mt. S. Jean directly it is taken.

Added in pencil to a copy of the order, in Ney's handwriting, was the note: 'Count D'Erlon will note that the attack will be delivered first by the left instead of commencing from the right. Inform General Reille of this change.' This order and Ney's addition have considerable bearing on the French actions at Hougoumont:

• Napoleon's orders for the army's attack at 1.00 p.m. make no mention of Hougoumont. Both leading corps (under Ney) were to make frontal advances, keeping abreast of each other, after a preliminary artillery bombardment. The objective was Mont St Jean village. D'Erlon was to start the attack with his left division. If this order had been followed, Hougoumont would have come under attack after 1.00 p.m. as part of the general advance of the two leading corps. As we know, this is not what happened.

• As Ney wrote in his hurried note, there was a change to the original order shortly after it was issued. Almost certainly it was related to Hougoumont. In the Emperor's first order Reille would have read that the attack would begin with the right-hand corps (d'Erlon), leading with his left division. This had been altered to the battle starting with the left corps (Reille).

• There is no surviving written record of these changed orders, which were possibly verbal. Without new orders there is no way that Reille would have dared to open the battle instead of d'Erlon, and do so one-and-a-half hours early.

• Soon after issuing his original order, Napoleon changed his mind. The overall objective remained the same but the method of achieving it was altered. Firstly, he increased the weight of the preparatory bombardment by adding three batteries of Guard Artillery to the 'Grand Battery'. Secondly, he decided to launch a preliminary, limited attack on Hougoumont to hopefully draw in some of Wellington's reserves before d'Erlon made the main assault.

Napoleon never intended to get bogged down in Hougoumont. He had no wish to see 23 per cent of his infantry dragged into a costly struggle for an objective that was almost irrelevant to the overall plan. There was no need to capture Hougoumont, and Napoleon's second orders reflected that. Reille in passing on his orders to Prince Jérôme merely told him, 'to occupy the low ground south of the wood, maintaining in front a strong line of skirmishers'. That twenty-four battalions ultimately became embroiled was partially the fault of Jérôme in committing his entire division in desperate attempts to take the château and garden when this was not in his orders. More at fault, however, was his corps commander for not stopping him, and then making

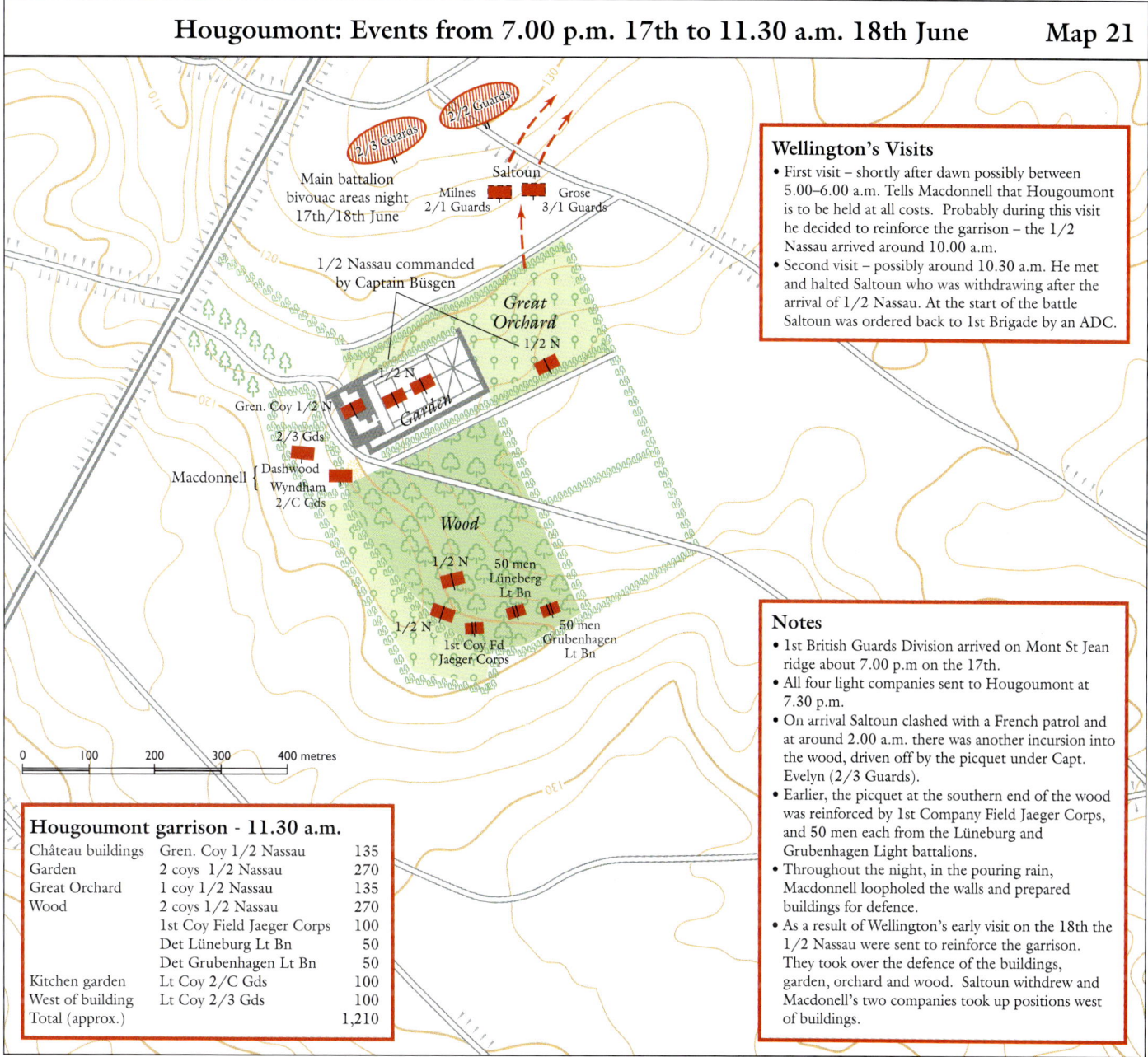

Hougoumont: Events from 7.00 p.m. 17th to 11.30 a.m. 18th June   Map 21

Main battalion bivouac areas night 17th/18th June

Milnes 2/1 Guards   Saltoun   Grose 3/1 Guards

1/2 Nassau commanded by Captain Büsgen

Great Orchard

1/2 N

Gren. Coy 1/2 N

Garden

1/2 N

2/3 Gds

Macdonnell { Dashwood Wyndham 2/C Gds

Wood

1/2 N   50 men Lüneberg Lt Bn

1/2 N   50 men Grubenhagen Lt Bn

1st Coy Fd Jaeger Corps

0	100 200 300	400 metres

Wellington's Visits
- First visit – shortly after dawn possibly between 5.00–6.00 a.m. Tells Macdonnell that Hougoumont is to be held at all costs. Probably during this visit he decided to reinforce the garrison – the 1/2 Nassau arrived around 10.00 a.m.
- Second visit – possibly around 10.30 a.m. He met and halted Saltoun who was withdrawing after the arrival of 1/2 Nassau. At the start of the battle Saltoun was ordered back to 1st Brigade by an ADC.

Notes
- 1st British Guards Division arrived on Mont St Jean ridge about 7.00 p.m on the 17th.
- All four light companies sent to Hougoumont at 7.30 p.m.
- On arrival Saltoun clashed with a French patrol and at around 2.00 a.m. there was another incursion into the wood, driven off by the picquet under Capt. Evelyn (2/3 Guards).
- Earlier, the picquet at the southern end of the wood was reinforced by 1st Company Field Jaeger Corps, and 50 men each from the Lüneburg and Grubenhagen Light battalions.
- Throughout the night, in the pouring rain, Macdonnell loopholed the walls and prepared buildings for defence.
- As a result of Wellington's early visit on the 18th the 1/2 Nassau were sent to reinforce the garrison. They took over the defence of the buildings, garden, orchard and wood. Saltoun withdrew and Macdonell's two companies took up positions west of buildings.

Hougoumont garrison - 11.30 a.m.
Château buildings	Gren. Coy 1/2 Nassau	135
Garden	2 coys 1/2 Nassau	270
Great Orchard	1 coy 1/2 Nassau	135
Wood	2 coys 1/2 Nassau	270
	1st Coy Field Jaeger Corps	100
	Det Lüneburg Lt Bn	50
	Det Grubenhagen Lt Bn	50
Kitchen garden	Lt Coy 2/C Gds	100
West of building	Lt Coy 2/3 Gds	100
Total (approx.)		1,210

the situation worse by sending in Foy's division. He even tried to reinforce failure by ordering Bachelu forward – it was, perhaps, ironic that Anglo-Allied gunfire prevented this folly.

Special Features

Command and control

Wellington took considerable interest in what happened at Hougoumont. He visited the place twice before the battle, he probably selected the commander (Macdonell), he decided on the garrison being reinforced by the 1/2 Nassau, he issued the orders for its defence personally to Macdonell, and he watched events closely for the first hour and a half from the ridge behind the château. It is likely that he gave the instructions to Byng regarding the reinforcement of the garrison during that time. When Bull arrived with his howitzers Wellington briefed him as to the delicate indirect fire task he wanted carried out. He later sent Major Hamilton (ADC to the Adjutant-General) to the château with orders to, 'hold the position to the very last, and on no account to

give it up or abandon it'. During the afternoon, when his attentions were elsewhere, he still found time to send explicit written instructions on what to do about the burning buildings – instructions that would have seemed more appropriate coming from a sergeant rather than the commander-in-chief (see box p. 94).

At Hougoumont the command set-up was confusing. This was due to several factors. The first was that reinforcements came piecemeal, with senior officers arriving without the knowledge of the whereabouts of those already there, or whether their seniority placed them in command. Because of the extraordinary double rank system in the Guards, at about 2.30 p.m. there were two colonels (Woodford and Hepburn whose seniority was exactly the same to the day) and nine, possibly ten lieutenant-colonels, all inside the buildings and garden. When Woodford arrived he declined to assume command from Macdonell. But Macdonell could not physically command what was happening in the Great Orchard, so the fighting in that area was led by Lord Saltoun until he withdrew on the arrival of Colonel Hepburn and the final reinforcements from the 2/3 Guards.

Hougoumont: Events from 11.20 a.m.–12.30 p.m.   Map 22

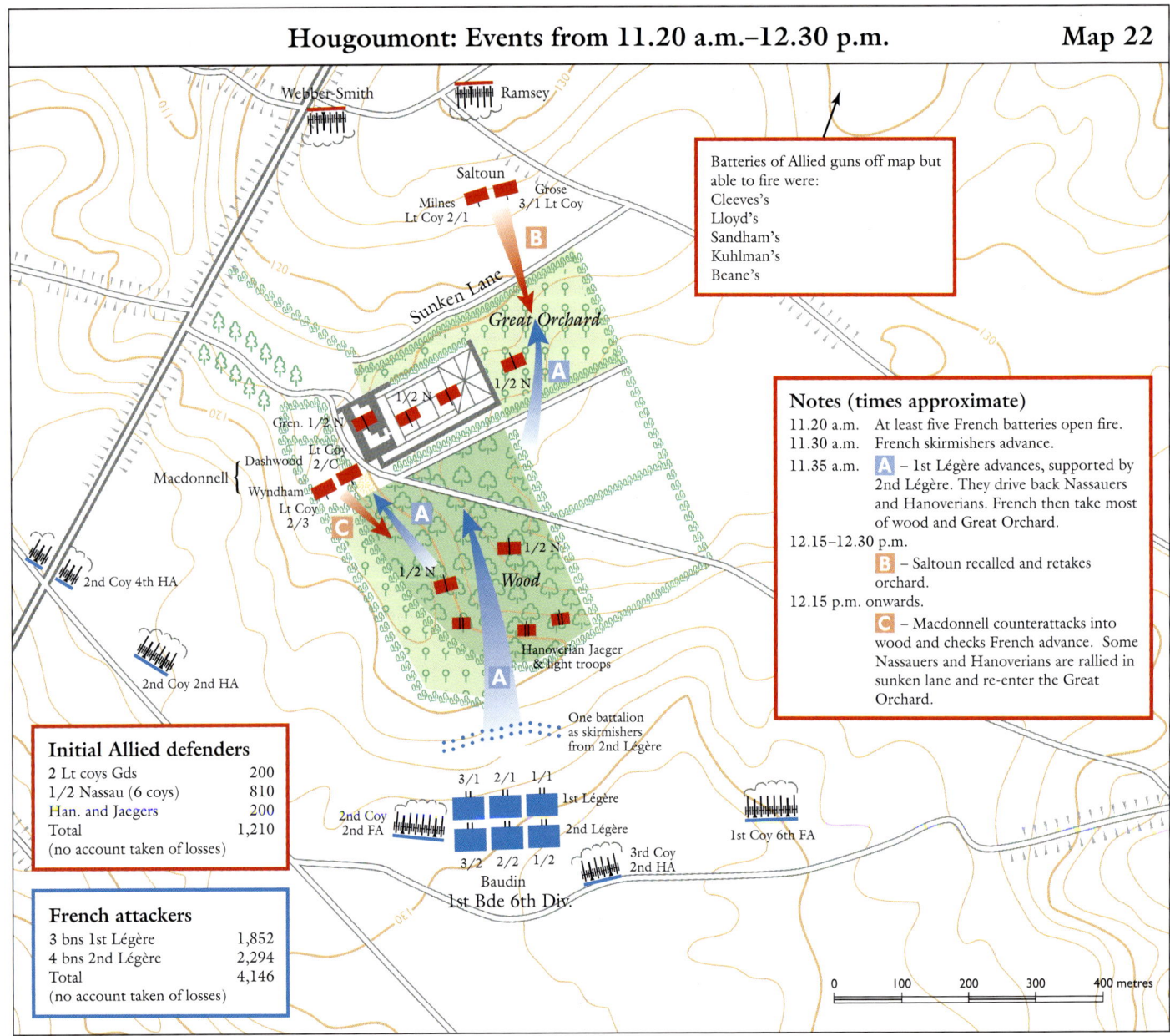

Webber-Smith

Ramsey

Saltoun

Milnes
Lt Coy 2/1

Grose
3/1 Lt Coy

B

Batteries of Allied guns off map but
able to fire were:
Cleeves's
Lloyd's
Sandham's
Kuhlman's
Beane's

Sunken Lane

Great Orchard

1/2 N

A

1/2 N

Gren. 1/2 N

Lt Coy
2/C

Dashwood

Macdonnell {

Wyndham
Lt Coy
2/3

C

A

1/2 N

1/2 N

Wood

2nd Coy 4th HA

1/2 N

2nd Coy 2nd HA

Hanoverian Jaeger
& light troops

One battalion
as skirmishers
from 2nd Légère

Notes (times approximate)

11.20 a.m.   At least five French batteries open fire.
11.30 a.m.   French skirmishers advance.
11.35 a.m.   **A** – 1st Légère advances, supported by
2nd Légère. They drive back Nassauers
and Hanoverians. French then take most
of wood and Great Orchard.
12.15–12.30 p.m.
B – Saltoun recalled and retakes
orchard.
12.15 p.m. onwards.
C – Macdonnell counterattacks into
wood and checks French advance. Some
Nassauers and Hanoverians are rallied in
sunken lane and re-enter the Great
Orchard.

Initial Allied defenders

2 Lt coys Gds	200
1/2 Nassau (6 coys)	810
Han. and Jaegers	200
Total	1,210
(no account taken of losses)	

French attackers

3 bns 1st Légère	1,852
4 bns 2nd Légère	2,294
Total	4,146
(no account taken of losses)	

3/1   2/1   1/1

1st Légère

2nd Coy
2nd FA

2nd Légère

3/2   2/2   1/2

3rd Coy
2nd HA

1st Coy 6th FA

Baudin
1st Bde 6th Div.

0   100   200   300   400 metres

The British Guards Companies Defending Hougoumont

By mid-afternoon eighteen companies of Guards had been committed to the fight for Hougoumont. They included sixteen from the 2nd British (Guards) Brigade (Byng) but only two from Maitland's 1st British (Guards) Brigade. However, on the arrival of the final reinforcements from the 2/3 Guards the light companies of the 2/1 and 3/1 were withdrawn. At no time were there more than about 2,200 guardsmen of all ranks defending Hougoumont. The companies present in or around Hougoumont for at least some of the time were:

2nd Battalion, 1st Foot Guards
Light Company Captain and Lieutenant-Colonel W.H. Milnes

3rd Battalion, 1st Foot Guards
Light Company Captain and Lieutenant-Colonel Lord Alexander Saltoun (In practice Saltoun commanded both light companies of the 1st Foot Guards, with Lieutenant and Captain E. Grose leading the 3rd Battalion company)

2nd Battalion (Coldstream) Guards – Colonel A. Woodford
Grenadier Company Captain and Lieutenant-Colonel D. Mackinnon
No.1 Company Captain and Lieutenant-Colonel J. Macdonell (Macdonell, despite being junior to Woodford and Mackinnon, had command of the defence of the buildings and garden for much of the battle. Lieutenant and Captain T. Sowerby then commanded his company)
No.2 Company Ensign The Hon. J. Forbes (Forbes was the senior ensign in the battalion and the only officer in the company, the usual company commander and the other subaltern being on the staff)
No.3 Company Ensign H. Vane (Responsibility was thrust unexpectedly on this young man – who had only been commissioned for fifteen months – when his company commander, Lieutenant and Captain T.S. Cowell, reported sick on 17 June and was sent to Brussels. Vane was, however, assisted by Ensign The Hon. W. Forbes, the younger brother of No.2 Company commander)
No.4 Company Captain and Lieutenant-Colonel The Hon. E. Acheson.

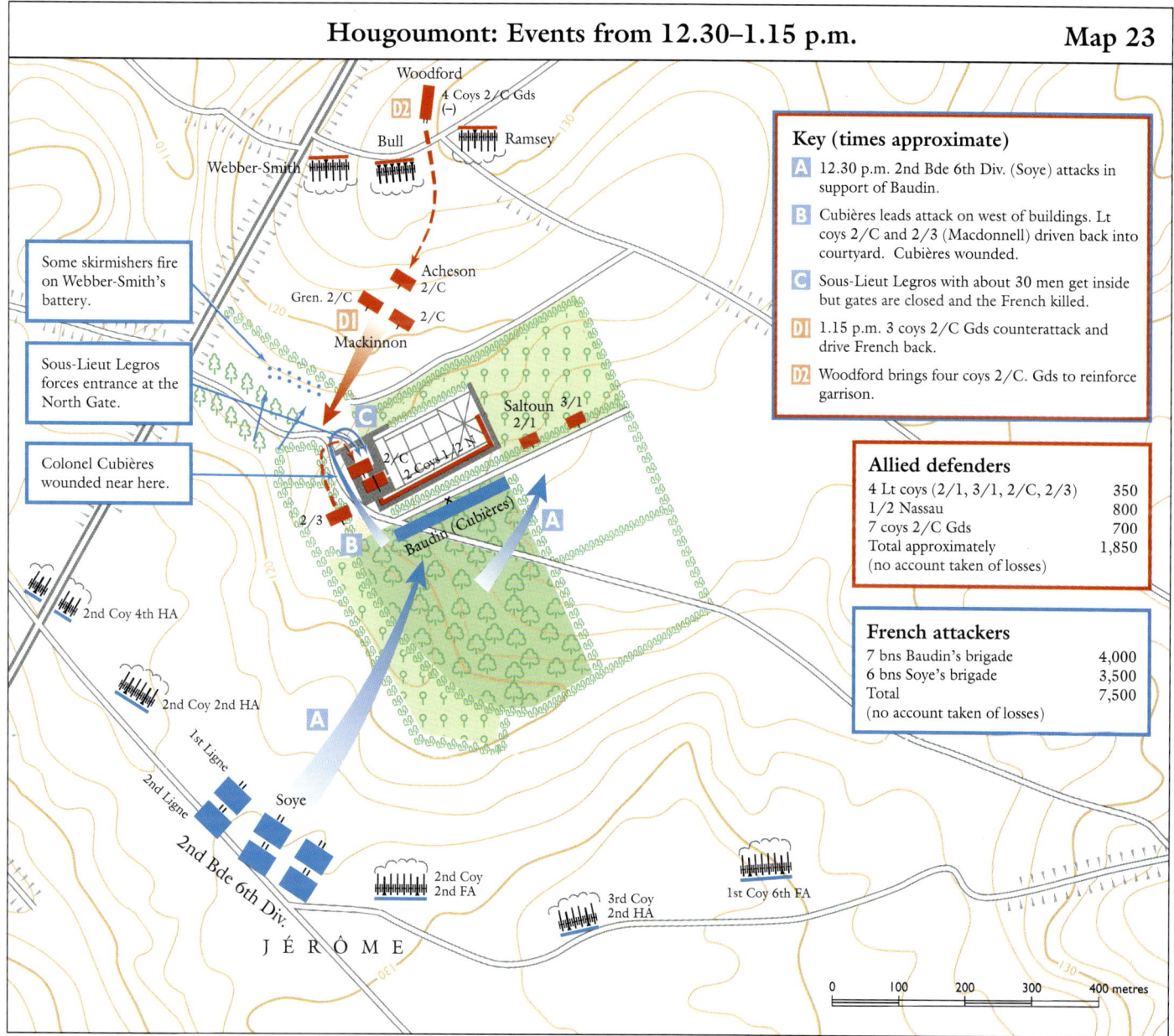

Hougoumont: Events from 12.30–1.15 p.m. — Map 23

Woodford
4 Coys 2/C Gds (–)
D2
Bull
Webber-Smith
Ramsey

Some skirmishers fire on Webber-Smith's battery.

Acheson 2/C
Gren. 2/C
2/C
D1
Mackinnon

Sous-Lieut Legros forces entrance at the North Gate.

Colonel Cubières wounded near here.

Saltoun 3/1
C
2/1
2/C 2 Coy 1/2 N
B
2/3
Baudin (Cubières)
A

2nd Coy 4th HA
2nd Coy 2nd HA
A
1st Ligne
2nd Ligne
Soye
2nd Bde 6th Div.
J É R Ô M E
2nd Coy 2nd FA
3rd Coy 2nd HA
1st Coy 6th FA

Key (times approximate)

A 12.30 p.m. 2nd Bde 6th Div. (Soye) attacks in support of Baudin.

B Cubières leads attack on west of buildings. Lt coys 2/C and 2/3 (Macdonnell) driven back into courtyard. Cubières wounded.

C Sous-Lieut Legros with about 30 men get inside but gates are closed and the French killed.

D1 1.15 p.m. 3 coys 2/C Gds counterattack and drive French back.

D2 Woodford brings four coys 2/C. Gds to reinforce garrison.

Allied defenders

4 Lt coys (2/1, 3/1, 2/C, 2/3)	350
1/2 Nassau	800
7 coys 2/C Gds	700
Total approximately	1,850
(no account taken of losses)	

French attackers

7 bns Baudin's brigade	4,000
6 bns Soye's brigade	3,500
Total	7,500
(no account taken of losses)	

0   100   200   300   400 metres

(Lieutenant and Captain K.L. Blackman, whose initial gravesite inside the garden wall is still marked with a plaque, was in this company)

No.5 Company Ensign R. Bowen

No.6 Company Captain and Lieutenant-Colonel H. Wyndham

No.7 Company Remained on ridge as Colour guard, Lieutenant and Captain G. Bowles

No.8 Company As above, Captain and Lieutenant-Colonel H. Dawkins

Light Company Lieutenant and Captain R. Moore

Note: Surgeon W. Whymper is known to have been in Hougoumont, and it is likely that Assistant-Surgeons G. Smith and W. Hunter were with him

2nd Battalion, 3rd Foot Guards (later Scots Guards) – Colonel F. Hepburn

Grenadier Company Captain and Lieutenant-Colonel F. Home

No.1 Company Captain and Lieutenant-Colonel E. Bowater

No.2 Company Lieutenant and Captain H. Hawkins (Fifteen years later this young officer, who had commanded a company at Waterloo, and had already been in the rank four years, was still a

lieutenant and captain – richer officers having purchased over him)

No.3 Company Captain and Lieutenant-Colonel D. Mercer

(At around 2.00 p.m. Mercer commanded Nos.3 and 4 Companies when they were sent down from the ridge to reinforce Saltoun in the Great Orchard. During this time he handed over his company to Lieutenant and Captain C.J. Barnett.

No.4 Company Lieutenant and Captain W. Drummond

No.5 Company Lieutenant and Captain E.B. Fairfield

No.6 Company Lieutenant and Captain W. Moorhouse

(Moorhouse was the only officer in this company during the battle, as Ensign The Hon. E. Stopford was an ADC to the brigade commander and Ensign The Hon. G. Anson had the misfortune to be posted with the baggage guard at Waterloo village)

No.7 Company Thought to be with the Colours on the ridge, Lieutenant and Captain Hon. H. Forbes

No.8 Company As above, Captain and Lieutenant-Colonel C. West

Light Company Captain and Lieutenant-Colonel C. Dashwood

Note: Surgeon S. Good was in Hougoumont, as most probably were Assistant-Surgeons J.R. Warde and F.G. Hanrott

Hougoumont: Events from 1.45–2.45 p.m.   Map 24

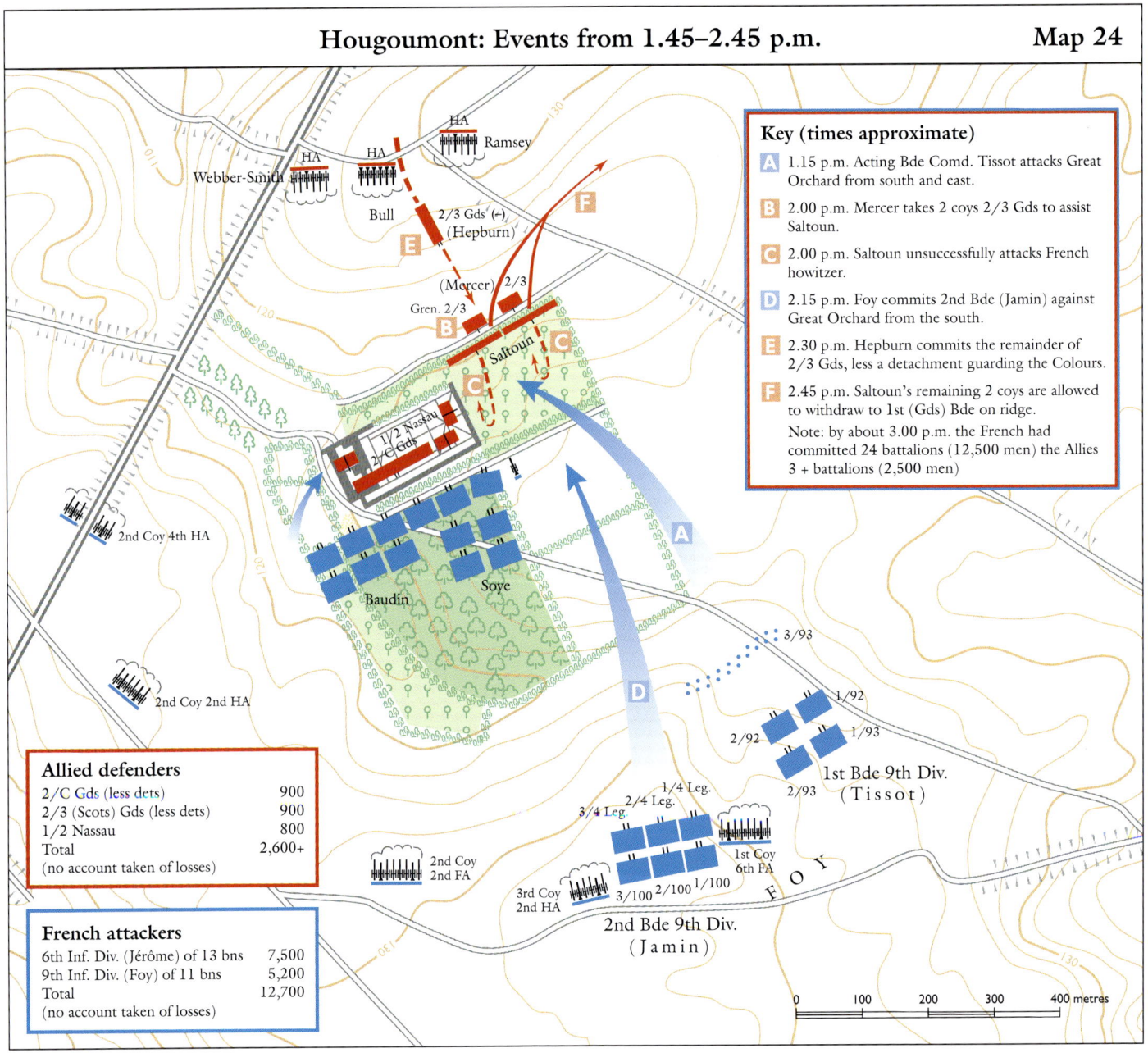

Key (times approximate)

A 1.15 p.m. Acting Bde Comd. Tissot attacks Great Orchard from south and east.

B 2.00 p.m. Mercer takes 2 coys 2/3 Gds to assist Saltoun.

C 2.00 p.m. Saltoun unsuccessfully attacks French howitzer.

D 2.15 p.m. Foy commits 2nd Bde (Jamin) against Great Orchard from the south.

E 2.30 p.m. Hepburn commits the remainder of 2/3 Gds, less a detachment guarding the Colours.

F 2.45 p.m. Saltoun's remaining 2 coys are allowed to withdraw to 1st (Gds) Bde on ridge.

Note: by about 3.00 p.m. the French had committed 24 battalions (12,500 men) the Allies 3 + battalions (2,500 men)

Allied defenders

2/C Gds (less dets)	900
2/3 (Scots) Gds (less dets)	900
1/2 Nassau	800
Total	2,600+
(no account taken of losses)	

French attackers

6th Inf. Div. (Jérôme) of 13 bns	7,500
9th Inf. Div. (Foy) of 11 bns	5,200
Total	12,700
(no account taken of losses)	

Lord Saltoun (1785–1853)

Alexander George Fraser was the sixteenth Baron Saltoun who won undying fame at the age of thirty commanding the two light companies of the 1st Foot Guards in the Great Orchard at Hougoumont. He was originally commissioned into the 42nd Foot but purchased a 1st Foot Guards vacancy at enormous cost to his father in 1804 when he was nineteen. In 1815 he was a Captain and Lieutenant-Colonel but only ninth in seniority among those of his rank in the regiment. He was actually the company commander of the Light Company of the 3/1 Foot Guards and saw action with it again during the repulse of the Imperial Guard in the late evening. He had four horses shot under him during the day but remained unscathed. His leadership during the battle became something of a legend. Wellington was supposed to have described him as, 'a pattern to the army both as a man and soldier'. He survived Waterloo untouched but several days later when involved in the attack on Peronne la Purcelle a musket ball struck him on his breeches' pocket. Fortunately the force of the blow was taken by

some five-franc coins. Saltoun was badly bruised. He went on to command a brigade in the First Opium War against China in 1842 before eventually rising to lieutenant-general and colonel-in-chief of the Coldstream Guards. Archibald Forbes, a war correspondent who died in 1900, told of a visit he made as a boy with his father to a house in Scotland at the mouth of Glen Rothes. While waiting outside the house he was greeted by:

A very queer-looking old person, short of figure, round as a ball, his head shrunk between very high and rounded shoulders and with short stumpy legs. He was curiously attired in a whole-coloured suit of gray; droll-shaped jacket the great collar of which reached far up the back of his head, surmounted by a pair of voluminous breeches which suddenly tightened at the knee.

The young Forbes mistook him for the butler. He was of course *the* Lord Saltoun of Waterloo fame, looking somewhat decrepit for a man in his early sixties. He died in 1853 aged sixty-eight.

Hougoumont: Events from 2.45–7.30 p.m.   Map 25

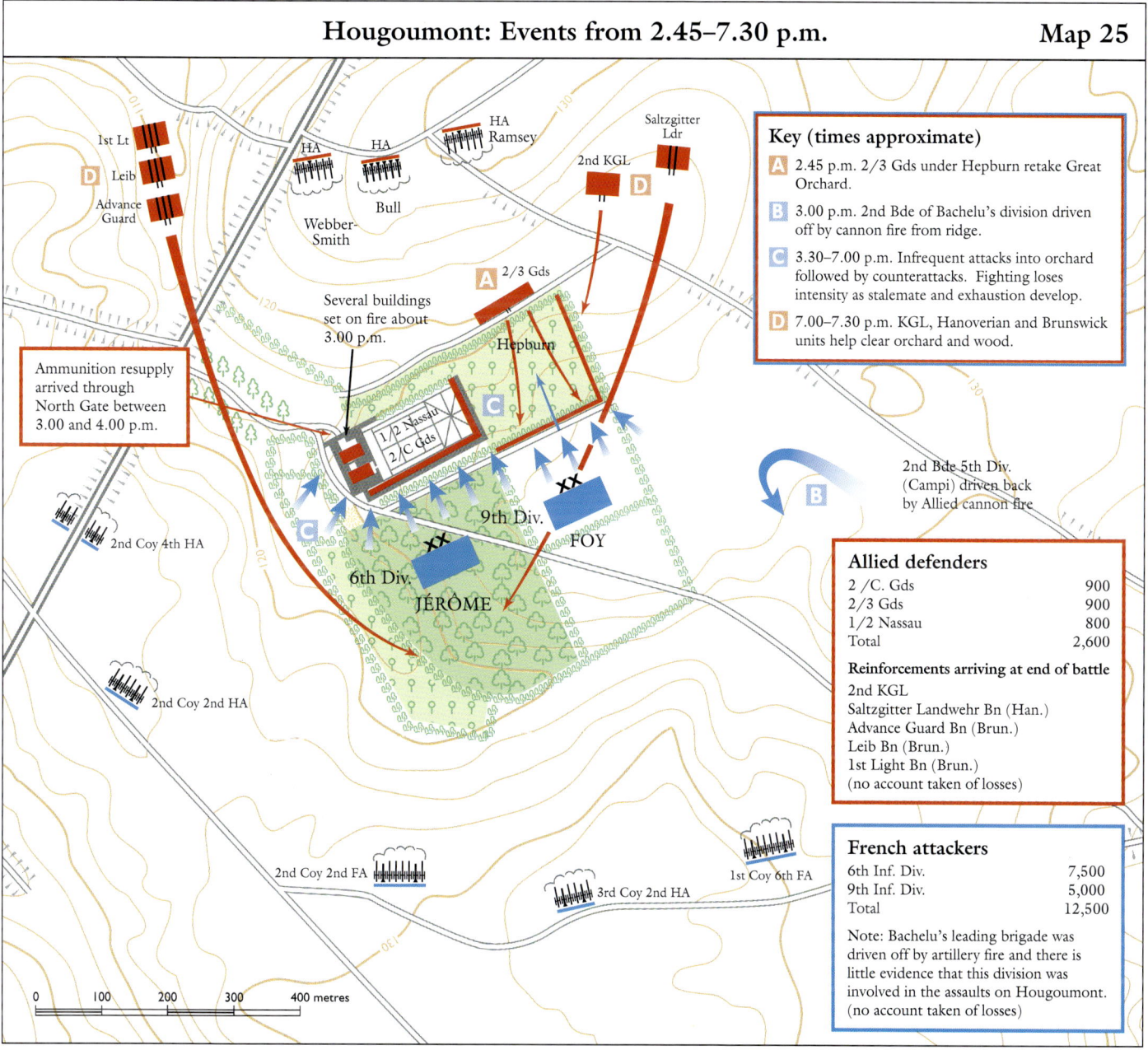

Key (times approximate)

A 2.45 p.m. 2/3 Gds under Hepburn retake Great Orchard.

B 3.00 p.m. 2nd Bde of Bachelu's division driven off by cannon fire from ridge.

C 3.30–7.00 p.m. Infrequent attacks into orchard followed by counterattacks. Fighting loses intensity as stalemate and exhaustion develop.

D 7.00–7.30 p.m. KGL, Hanoverian and Brunswick units help clear orchard and wood.

Several buildings set on fire about 3.00 p.m.

Ammunition resupply arrived through North Gate between 3.00 and 4.00 p.m.

2nd Bde 5th Div. (Campi) driven back by Allied cannon fire

Allied defenders

2 /C. Gds	900
2/3 Gds	900
1/2 Nassau	800
Total	2,600

Reinforcements arriving at end of battle
2nd KGL
Saltzgitter Landwehr Bn (Han.)
Advance Guard Bn (Brun.)
Leib Bn (Brun.)
1st Light Bn (Brun.)
(no account taken of losses)

French attackers

6th Inf. Div.	7,500
9th Inf. Div.	5,000
Total	12,500

Note: Bachelu's leading brigade was driven off by artillery fire and there is little evidence that this division was involved in the assaults on Hougoumont. (no account taken of losses)

At that stage things became even more muddled. Because Byng had assumed command of the division when Sir George Cooke was severely wounded, Hepburn (in Hougoumont) was now the acting brigade commander. Despite this, he did not take overall command at Hougoumont. Indeed, Wellington gave much of the credit for the remaining hours of the defence of the position in his despatch to Captain and Lieutenant-Colonel Home of the 2/3 Guards. He was even junior to Macdonell. This bewildering situation partly arose when Major Hamilton arrived with orders for Macdonell to find only Home in the courtyard. Hamilton understandably asked, 'Do you command here?', to which Home responded, 'I believe so. I have seen no officer superior to myself. It has been reported to me that Colonels Macdonell and Woodford are not to be found [they were in the garden].' Fortunately this bizarre state of affairs did not affect the conduct of the defence.

Throughout the battle Captain Büsgen, the acting commander of the 1/2 Nassau whose troops made up a sizeable propor-tion of the garrison, was unaware of who his commander was. In his written account he stated:

> Neither when I was [first] detached, nor during this period [of the attacks on Hougoumont] was any commander under whose orders I was placed, named to me. … I saw no other troops [other than the Coldstream Guards] sent to support the battalion under my command. I do not know if and what other troops were later sent to support this position. Due to the continuous fighting and the view restricted by trees, hedges and walls, I could not observe what was happening at a distance.

The French did not have quite the same sort of difficulties. Reille, as corps commander, failed to ensure the Emperor's younger brother carried out his orders – perhaps because he was such a close relative. Prince Jérôme, despite his relationship to Napoleon, was only the commander of a division, albeit the largest one in the army. He allowed his eagerness for glory to cancel out any modicum of tactical ability he may have possessed – despite

The Arrival of the 1/2 Nassau

Seldom, if ever, does an account of the struggle for Hougoumont mention the fact that for almost an hour, during the first and most powerful French attack that resulted in the loss of the wood and part of the Great Orchard, there was almost certainly not a single British Guardsman in the buildings, formal garden, Great Orchard or wood. All these locations were defended by the 1/2 Nassau under Captain Büsgen, assisted by some 200 Hanoverians. The only British Guardsmen present were the Light Companies of the 2nd (Coldstream) Guards and 2/3 Guards under Macdonell, both deployed west of the château in the kitchen garden area – only 160–170 men, as both battalions had suffered losses at Quatre-Bras. The Light Companies of the 2/1 and 3/1 Guards under Lord Saltoun had been withdrawn after the arrival of the 1/2 Nassau. In other words, as the Nassauers moved into Hougoumont the Guards pulled out, half to rejoin their battalions on the ridge (Saltoun) and half to a position west of the buildings (Macdonell). Having toiled all night in the rain preparing the place for defence and then being ordered to hand it over to the Nassauers must have provoked more than a few unprintable comments from the guardsmen.

Captain and Lieutenant-Colonel Daniel Mackinnon, who led the Grenadier Company of the 2nd (Coldstream) Guards at Hougoumont and later wrote their official history, has made this little known event abundantly clear:

> At ten o'clock the light companies of the Guards [i.e. all four companies] were relieved by a battalion of 800 Nassau light troops: part of this corps was stationed in the lofts, buildings, yards and out-offices; the remainder, with the Hanoverian Yagers [who had arrived the previous night], were distributed in the orchard and wood. Lord Saltoun then joined the second brigade on the [main] position.

Lieutenant-Colonel Macdonell with his companies moved to the right [west] of the chateau.

A staff officer had guided the 1/2 Nassau to Hougoumont at around 10.00 a.m. on 18 June. He gave the order to Lord Saltoun to hand over his responsibilities for the defence of the Great Orchard and rejoin his battalion. Saltoun conducted Captain Büsgen around the orchard area before marching back up the ridge. On his way he met the Duke riding down for his second look at Hougoumont. Wellington halted the two companies. On being told where they were going he seemed not to have authorized their withdrawal. He instructed Saltoun to remain where he was until further orders. Shortly after the battle started an ADC rode up and told Saltoun to continue back to his brigade. Almost the moment he arrived he was hurriedly sent back, as the Nassauers were losing the Great Orchard.

Captain Büsgen, who was commanding the battalion as Major Sattler had taken over command of the regiment, had this to say of the situation on his arrival:

> … the farm and the garden were unoccupied. A company of Brunswick Jaeger stood at the furthest edge of the wood. … I immediately undertook the necessary deployment for the defence. I had the Grenadier Company occupy the buildings, and sent two companies to the vegetable garden [formal garden] next to them. I placed one company behind the hedge of the orchard, moved the voltigeurs into line with the Brunswick Jaeger [southern edge of wood] and placed one company in reserve a little to the rear [of the Jaegers].

Büsgen goes on to add that after the first French attack had been thrown back the Jaeger company 'rejoined its Corps in the main position'.

the pleas of his chief of staff, Guilleminot. Reille did nothing to stop Jérôme and himself abandoned the lessons of his considerable experience, ignored his orders and flung in Foy's division.

Napoleon's attention was soon distracted by far more crucial events to the east, but he did insist on pushing forward the two horse artillery batteries belonging to Kellerman in order to bolster the opening bombardment of Hougoumont. Later he found time to order howitzers to fire incendiary carcasses into the château complex – with good effect. Had he been able to devote more time to his left, no doubt the artilleryman in him would have ensured that guns were brought to bear on the buildings. This was the other major failing of the French command at Hougoumont.

Ammunition and Casualties

There was a lot of ammunition expended at Hougoumont. Not surprisingly, the troops in the buildings and garden ran short during the afternoon and it was only the timely arrival of the gallant Private Brewer of The Royal Wagon Train with his cart that prevented a critical situation becoming a disastrous one. The maximum number of soldiers defending the buildings, garden and Great Orchard at any one time was around 2,600. Each man would have started out with some fifty balls on his person. Because of the intensity of the fighting, the need for virtually every man to be in the firing line coupled with the length of time the action continued (with varying intensity up to nine hours), there is little

doubt that the average soldier had to replenish his ammunition during the afternoon. From this it is not too fanciful to assume the average musket-armed guardsman or rifle-armed jaeger fired at least fifty times during 'the battle within a battle' (some will have fired many more, others less). That represents 130,000 shots.

How much damage did those musket balls do? Again we come up against the difficulty in assessing French casualties. Most sources state as a bald fact that 5000 Frenchmen fell dead or wounded at Hougoumont but without justifying this number. This figure is a sixth of the entire army's losses (30,000) or 39 per cent of those actually attacking Hougoumont. Probably a quarter were hit by artillery fire, with the rest (3,750 plus) the victims of musketry – thirty to thirty-five shots to secure a hit.

Assuming that some 12,700 Frenchmen from Jérôme's and Foy's divisions were fully engaged for some of the time at Hougoumont and that they each carried about thirty-five rounds, it is safe to say that there was no need for many of these men to start scrabbling around for extra ammunition. There would have been between 400,000–450,000 rounds with the attacking troops. The deployed skirmishers would have kept up a steady fire over prolonged periods, but of those twenty-four battalions committed not more than five or six would have been actually firing at any one time – there was just not enough room. Not all battalions were involved from the beginning; there were lulls and, even when attacking the buildings or garden, firing by individuals would be slow. Furthermore, as happens in all battles, a proportion of soldiers would hardly have fired at all. This was due to the crush, confusion, smoke and lack of worthwhile targets (most of the enemy being behind a wall or in a building) and the inevitable hanging back by some. On average, a French soldier attacking Hougoumont would have been doing well to fire more than fifteen times. This gives an ammunition expenditure of over 190,000 shots. Put another way, on average, about 350 French muskets were firing every minute throughout the nine hours. How effective was it?

The quick answer is – not very. This answer is easier to give than that concerning the defenders' musketry. Apart from a tiny handful, musket balls caused almost every casualty inflicted on the defenders. In one important way the troops in Hougoumont had it easier than the rest of the Duke's army on the ridge – they were subjected to very little effective artillery fire. Also, the casualty returns for the Guards at Waterloo are known. The figures below indicate the estimated casualties inflicted while the units were at Hougoumont:

2nd (Coldstream) Guards	308	(29 per cent)
2/3 Guards	239	(23 per cent)
Light Company 2/1 Guards	30	This company was withdrawn to the ridge before 3.00 p.m. (23 per cent)
Light Company 3/1 Guards	30	Withdrawn as above (25 per cent)
1/2 Nassau	200	Estimate based on 25 per cent casualties. (Total casualties for the three battalions of the 2nd Nassau Regiment were 472)
Hanoverians and Jaegers	40	Estimate based on 25 per cent casualties
Total	847	(almost 33 per cent of the troops engaged)

These figures suggest that it took 224 French musket shots to secure a hit. This is not such a poor performance as it seems. Most defenders were behind cover of some sort for much of the time, if only a hedge or a tree. The majority were behind brick walls. When a Frenchman fired at a defender he was either trying to hit the head and shoulders of a man who kept bobbing up from behind a wall, or he was shooting at a tiny loophole only a few inches across. Add to this the fear, the noise, the confusion, the smoke, the inaccuracy of his weapon and the firer's need to be quick (he was far more vulnerable than his target 30 metres away), it is little wonder his shots invariably missed.

D'Erlon's Corps Attack (Maps 26, 27 & 28, pp. 344, 348 & 353)

And louder still, and still more loud,
From underneath that rolling cloud,
Is heard the trumpet's war-note proud,
The trampling and the hum.
And plainly, and more plainly,
Now through the gloom appears,
Far to the left and far to the right,
In broken gleams of dark-blue light,
The long array of helmets bright,
The long array of spears.

Lord Thomas Macaulay

The advance

At about 1.00 p.m. the roar of eighty cannons was carried by the westerly wind to Wavre 15 kilometres away. Marshal Grouchy noticed the perceptible increase in tempo 20 kilometres to the east. He dismissed urgings to march to the sound. However, due to the wind direction nothing was heard at Hal to the west. It was the softening up bombardment preparatory to what was intended as the Emperor's masterstroke of the day. Some thirty minutes later four infantry divisions stepped out into the soggy crops to walk the 1,100 or so metres to Wellington's line east of the Genappe road – their first objective. For the first 500 metres each of the thirty-three battalions marched in file, twisting, turning, threading their way through the dense jumble of hundreds of artillery horse teams, caissons, limbers and wagons that fed the 'Grand Battery'. They were executing what tacticians call a 'passage of lines'. Ahead, the guns continued to fire as fast as the detachments could reload. The infantry, approaching from behind, were deafened by the thunderous roar, blinded as to what lay ahead by the dense banks of smoke that drifted slowly from left to right. Shouted orders were impossible, every man followed those in front. Riding at the head of each battalion was its commanding officer.

As the leading battalion of each division reached the gunline, firing ceased. Each division had to clear the guns and form up in their assault formation (see below). It took time – perhaps as much as ten to fifteen minutes. Every battalion ordered forward their voltigeur company to form a dense skirmish line of more than 3000 men – almost three men per metre of front. Now the advance proper began. On the left was Quiot's 1st Division, then,

---

Hougoumont After the Battle

A visitor on the day after the battle described the Great Orchard thus:

I came first upon the orchard, and there discovered heaps of dead men, in various uniforms; those of the Guards in their usual red jackets, the German Legion [the 2nd KGL had attacked through there in the evening], and the French dressed in blue mingled together. The dead and the wounded positively covered the whole area of the orchard; not less than two thousand men had fallen there. The apple-trees presented a singular appearance; shattered branches were seen hanging about their mother-trunks in such profusion that one might suppose the stiff-growing and stunted tree had been converted into a willow. Every tree was riddled and smashed…

In the wood the scene was similar:

Every tree in the wood is pierced with balls; in one alone I counted the holes where upwards of thirty had lodged … huge piles of human ashes, dreadfully offensive in smell, are now all that remains of the heroes … The poor countryman who, with his wife and family, occupied the gardener's house still inhabit a miserable shed among the deserted ruins. The buildings of Hougoumont were infinitely more shattered [burnt] than those of La Haie Sainte …. In one spot fifty dead bodies lay close together … Near this was a black scorched place where 600 human corpses found in the grounds were collected and burned … [this mass burial pit was near where the haystack used to be near the South Gate].

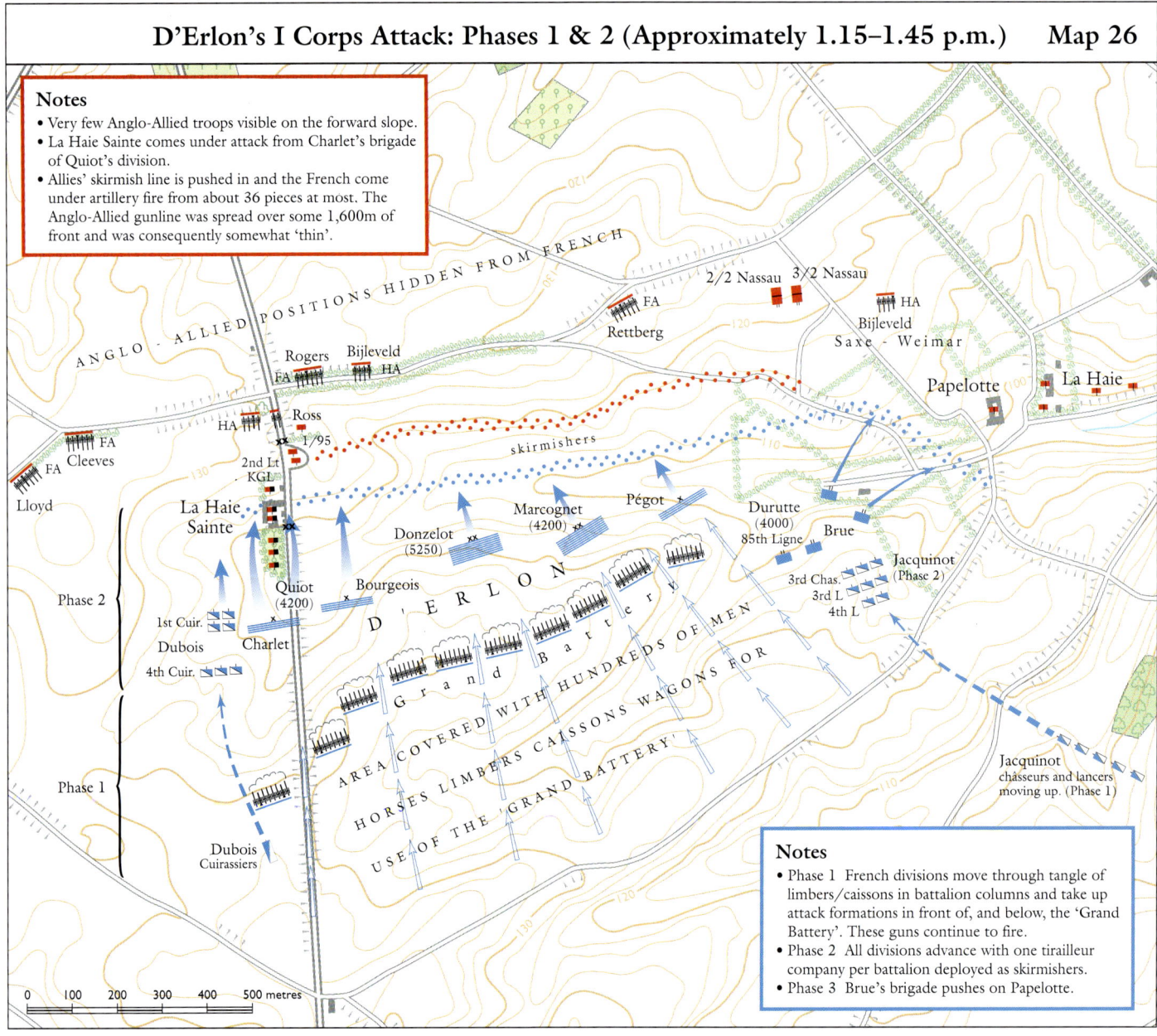

D'Erlon's I Corps Attack: Phases 1 & 2 (Approximately 1.15–1.45 p.m.)   Map 26

Notes
- Very few Anglo-Allied troops visible on the forward slope.
- La Haie Sainte comes under attack from Charlet's brigade of Quiot's division.
- Allies' skirmish line is pushed in and the French come under artillery fire from about 36 pieces at most. The Anglo-Allied gunline was spread over some 1,600m of front and was consequently somewhat 'thin'.

Notes
- Phase 1 French divisions move through tangle of limbers/caissons in battalion columns and take up attack formations in front of, and below, the 'Grand Battery'. These guns continue to fire.
- Phase 2 All divisions advance with one tirailleur company per battalion deployed as skirmishers.
- Phase 3 Brue's brigade pushes on Papelotte.

moving off at short intervals, Donzelot (2nd Division), Marcognet (3rd Division) and finally, Durutte (4th Division). The corps was echeloned back from the left and spread over 1000 metres of open, undulating farmland. There was wild cheering, sixteen Eagles were lifted high, young boys thrashed their drum skins, and the men marched in dense divisional columns, slowly and steadily with shouldered arms. Gaps between formations were seldom greater than 150 metres. Riding at the front was Marshal Ney and the corps commander, d'Erlon, with their staff. As soon as the columns descended into the shallow valley in front of the Anglo-Allied line, the 'Grand Battery' guns opened up again. It was fire and movement on a grand scale – very comforting for the infantryman who was not to know it was doing so little damage at the receiving end (see pp. 298–301).

The invisible ceiling of cannon balls and shells could continue for perhaps another 250 metres of the advance. Long before this, however, the deadly effect of the enemy's guns was felt. Cannon balls and canister tore through the tightly packed ranks, sweeping away whole files of a dozen or more men at a time. The only order

heard, screamed by officer or NCO alike, was 'Close up! Close up!' There was little to see through the swirling smoke ahead for the survivors in the leading ranks of the two centre divisions as they climbed the final slope. There was no line of infantry, no guns, only a thin line of red-jacketed skirmishers banging away and falling back. Behind them a hedge could be glimpsed.

Not long after 2.00 p.m. most of I Corps were within a few metres of the crest. For the last 100 metres they had been hit by heavy musket as well as cannon fire. More men collapsed, there was hesitation, and the Eagles faltered. But officers yelled, waved their swords and the advance staggered forward again. The leading battalions of Bourgeois' brigade on the left crossed the hedge and the road behind. Donzelot's division could almost touch the hedge, while Marcognet was within 50 metres of the crest. On the extreme left Charlet's brigade of Quiot's division had surrounded La Haie Sainte and taken the orchard and kitchen garden. Beyond that, west of the Genappe road, Dubois' cuirassiers had smashed a battalion of Hanoverians sent to assist the defenders of La Haie Sainte. On the eastern extremity one brigade of Durutte's division

The farm, much as soldiers in Bourgeois' brigade would have seen it over standing crops if they looked left as they approached the ridge during d'Erlon's first attack.

was climbing the slope while the other pushed towards Papelotte. As the French breasted the rise, four battalions of Netherlands infantry fell back in disorder (the fifth remained steady). Weakened at Quatre-Bras and demoralized by almost an hour of artillery fire, most of Bijlandt's men could not stand to face the French only 30 metres away. Their retreat opened up a 250-metre gap along the crest.

To the watchers back on the main French position the battle appeared won. The skyline and forward slope of the ridge were dark with d'Erlon's infantry. The leading Prussians were still well over two hours away. For the remainder of the day it is arguable that Napoleon never came closer to winning Waterloo.

The significance and statistics of d'Erlon's attack

This corps attack was intended to win the battle for the French. Subsequent efforts were mostly piecemeal, disjointed or badly co-ordinated. Even when La Haie Sainte finally fell after 6.00 p.m., the fleeting opportunity it offered was lost as the Emperor clung to his only reserve, the remaining battalions of his Guard, refusing to commit them. After d'Erlon fell back at about 2.15 p.m. Napoleon became more and more concerned for his right rear as the Prussian build up and pressure on Plancenoit increased.

Napoleon and Ney have frequently been criticized for failing to ensure all arms co-operation in their attacks at Waterloo. With d'Erlon's advance, however, there was no lack of co-ordination

A view of Wellington's centre/left from Donzelot's divisional start line

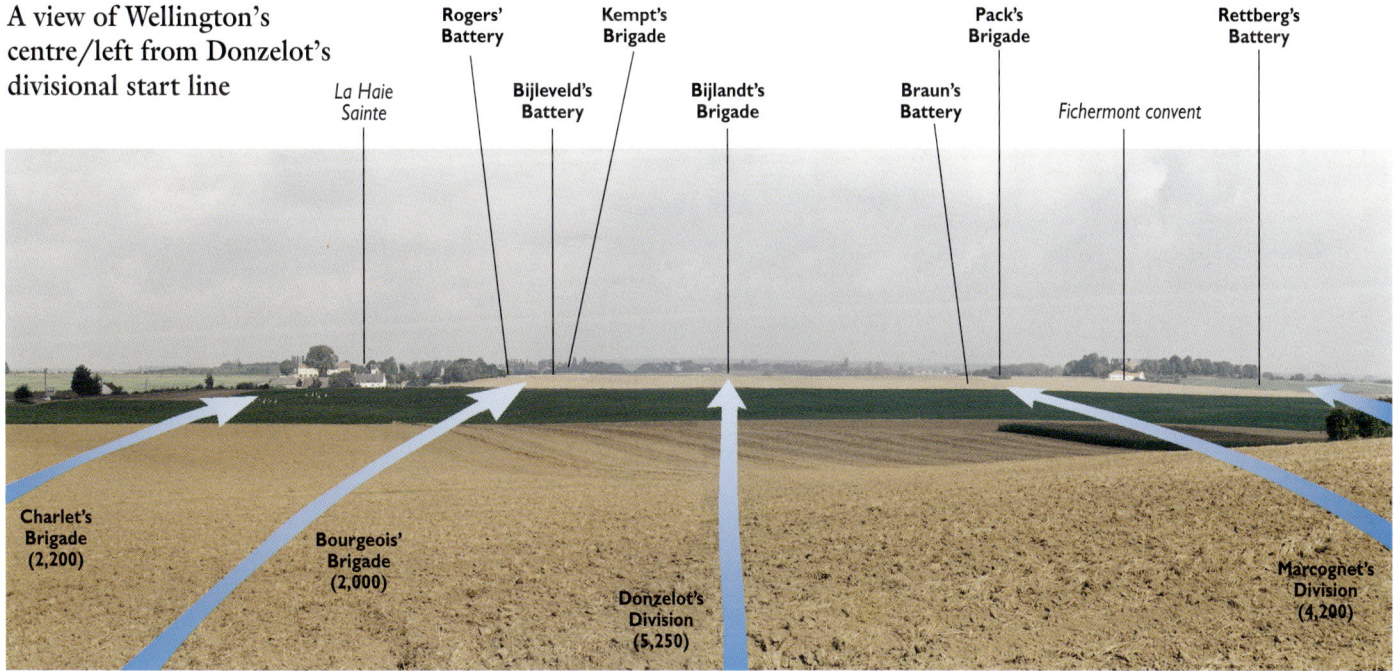

La Haie Sainte · Rogers' Battery · Bijleveld's Battery · Kempt's Brigade · Bijlandt's Brigade · Pack's Brigade · Braun's Battery · Fichermont convent · Rettberg's Battery

Charlet's Brigade (2,200) · Bourgeois' Brigade (2,000) · Donzelot's Division (5,250) · Marcognet's Division (4,200) · Pégot's Brigade of Durutte's Division (2,100)

Notes

• D'Erlon's Corps of four divisions advanced in echelon from the left, starting with Charlet's attack on La Haie Sainte.
• The ploughed field in the foreground was covered in gun limbers, horse teams, caissons and wagons, through which the divisions had to pass before taking up their assault formations.
• The 'Grand Battery' was deployed all along the dark green cabbage field.

Inside d'Erlon's Columns

A conscript in the 25th or 45th Ligne in Marcognet's column, who described his approach to the hedge as slow due to the softness of the ground, went on to say:

> As we mounted on the other side [of the valley] we were met by a hail of balls [initially canister] from above the road at the left. If we had not been so crowded together, this terrible volley would have checked us. ... Two batteries [Braun and Rettberg] now swept our ranks, and the shot from the hedges a hundred feet distant pierced us through and through. A cry of horror burst forth, and we rushed on the batteries ... thousands [an exaggeration] of Englishmen rose up from the barley, and fired their muskets almost touching our men, which caused a terrible slaughter ... we

should have been dispersed over the hillside like a swarm of ants if we had not heard the shout 'Attention, the cavalry!' Almost at the same instant a crowd of red dragoons on grey horses swept down on us ... those that had straggled were cut to pieces without mercy. ... They came down between the divisions, slashing right and left with their sabres, and spurring their horses into the flanks of the columns in order to break them, they were too deep and massive for that [but] they killed great numbers and threw us into confusion. ... The worst was that at that moment their foot soldiers rallied and recommenced their fire, and they were even so bold as to attack us with the bayonet [probably referring to the 92nd Foot]. Only the first two ranks made a stand. It was shameful to form our men in that manner.

between the infantry, artillery and, to a lesser extent, the cavalry. A massive gun battery, including twenty-four 12-pounders, was assembled to prepare the way with a prolonged bombardment. The guns continued to fire over the heads of the advancing troops for as long as possible. Cavalry protected the flanks. In the east Jacquinot's light horsemen moved forward to watch that flank, while in the west Dubois' brigade of cuirassiers advanced alongside the infantry. The French had also achieved concentration. No less than 17,000 infantry, supported by eighty guns and flanked by 800 heavy cavalry west of the Genappe road were directly involved in this attack. This represented a third of the Emperor's artillery and infantry on the field.

As Napoleon could not see what was on the other side of the hill, it was more by luck than judgement that he was hitting the weakest part of the Duke's line. For every infantryman, every cav-

alryman and every gun Wellington had deployed east of the Genappe road, two were to the west of it. His concern was always his right, and yet the main French stroke would come on his centre-left. Discounting the four battalions drawn off on each flank (at La Haie Sainte and Papelotte), twenty-five French battalions of so far unbloodied but enthusiastic soldiers were converging on a part of the Anglo-Allied front, some 800 metres in length, and manned by thirteen battalions and three and a half artillery batteries. When Bourgeois' leading soldiers crashed through the hedges bordering the Wavre (Smohain) road, they could not know that they would be the only French infantrymen (except prisoners) to glimpse what was on the other side of the ridge.

When the corps first deployed along the north side of the La Belle Alliance–Papelotte track, it did so with brigades side by side in their four divisions. The regiments formed up with their two

Durutte's skirmishers view of Papelotte as they advanced at the start of d'Erlon's attack. Photo: the author

battalions in column of attack (Diagram p. 194), again side by side. The corps stretched for some 1,600 metres (almost exactly a mile) north-east from La Belle Alliance. The only source that gives a clue to as to what order the battalions formed up is De Bas and de Wommersom's *La Campagne de 1815* (Brussels, 1908–9). In it, a diagram shows Quiot's division deployed with the 1st Brigade (Charlet) on the left and the 2nd (Bourgeois) on the right. In other words, the senior brigade is on the left, which is not the conventional way formations deployed, as the position of honour was on the right. Within brigades the junior regiment is in front, the senior in the second line (Map 14, p. 162). *The Waterloo Companion* has accepted this arrangement and extrapolated it to the other divisions. Consequently, this deployment puts the 45th and 105th Ligne at the head of their columns, which seems appropriate as both lost their Eagles.

When the advance began regiments and battalions filed forward, picking their way through the clutter of caissons and wagons and then the gunline itself. The 'Grand Battery' stopped firing while the divisions sorted themselves out into their assault formation, and voltigeur companies (approximately eighty to ninety men each) deployed forward to form a skirmish line. These formations were unusual (they are discussed in detail in Section 10 'Myths and Controversies'). They were solid blocks of men, each battalion deployed in a three-rank line closed up one behind the other (Marcognet's division is depicted in the Diagram on p. 195). With battalions averaging around 535 all ranks (460 without the voltigeur company), each would cover a front of about 120 metres with a depth of 5 metres. An eight-battalion division like Marcognet's would have a frontage of 120 metres and a depth of twenty-four ranks, or about 75 metres – a solid looking, unwieldy rectangle called a 'column'. Donzelot, with nine battalions, would have a depth of twenty-seven ranks. The frontage of the corps contracted to about 1,200 metres by the time it got beyond the guns and was ready to move off in its assault formation. The gaps between divisions were initially about 250 metres.

The corps did not advance in line together. In accordance with Napoleon's order the attack began on the left. Within 100 metres Charlet's brigade of Quiot's division separated from Bourgeois' brigade (it was probably formed up as a separate column). It crossed the Genappe road on its left and became embroiled in the struggle for La Haie Sainte that was to continue with varying degrees of intensity for the next four hours. Bourgeois continued northwards, came under heavy rifle fire from the 95th Rifles in the sandpit and knoll to its east causing it to slow, veer slightly right, outflanking the 95th and compelling their withdrawal, before reaching the crest. At the head of the column was the 105th Ligne. Catching up slightly to the right rear was the largest column of all: Donzelot, led by the 17th Ligne. To its right rear again, perhaps five minutes behind, was Marcognet with the Eagle of the 45th Ligne still in the centre of the leading regiment. On the extreme right Durutte had only sent his 1st Brigade (Pégot) at the main enemy position. Keeping the 85th Ligne in reserve, he pushed skirmishers and the 95th Ligne forward towards Papelotte – which he succeeded in taking, albeit briefly.

As these divisions advanced in echelon, so they converged, with the lateral gaps between them shrinking considerably. When they hit the Anglo-Allied ridge they did so over a distance of under 800 metres. Gaps between columns varied from less than 100 metres to not more than 200 metres.

That this attack failed was due to the combination of four factors. They were:
• The generally ineffective French artillery fire due to the Anglo-Allied units being behind the ridge, with infantry lying down and cavalry dismounted.
• The considerable damage inflicted by even the few guns on the dense, tight formations in which the French advanced.
• The steadiness and fire discipline of the six or seven battalions of British infantry that checked the advance just behind the crest.
• The perfect timing of the cavalry counterattack by the Union Brigade, which caught the French totally by surprise as they staggered around in the smoke and confusion, uncertain what to do or where to go.

Timings
The timing of this attack and its ultimate repulse is significant in relation to understanding how the battle progressed. An approximation is given below:
• The 'Grand Battery's' preparatory bombardment – about thirty minutes from 1.00 p.m.
• The divisions move forward 500 metres through the gunline – fifteen minutes from 1.30 p.m.
• The divisions form up into assault formation – five to ten minutes from 1.45 p.m.
• The divisions advance at five-minute intervals from 1.55 p.m.
• Time taken to cover the 600 metres to the crest under heavy fire, moving uphill through patches of thick, wet standing crops and trying to keep formation, from fifteen to twenty minutes. This means that Bourgeois and Donzelot might be expected to hit the hedge on the ridge from between 2.15 p.m. to 2.20 p.m. Marcognet might have been five minutes behind but Pégot's brigade never reached the ridge before the others were thrown back.
• Time spent on the crest before being driven back – five minutes at most, from 2.20 p.m.
• The Union Brigade charge down the forward slope, the dispersal and rout of the attackers and the British cavalry's dash to the 'Grand Battery' – ten minutes from 2.25 p.m.
• The French cavalry counterattacks which cut up and drive back the scattered Union Brigade – ten minutes from 2.35 p.m.

If these estimates are not too far out, d'Erlon's attack (excluding the bombardment), repulse, and the Union Brigade's defeat took about an hour-and-a-quarter from start to finish – from 1.30 p.m. to 2.45 p.m.

THE ANGLO-ALLIED RESPONSE (Maps 27 & 28, pp. 348 & 353)
West of the Brussels–Genappe road
Infantry
To the west of this road, directly opposing Charlet's 2000 infantrymen and Dubois' 780 cuirassiers, were Ompteda's KGL brigade of 2,150, Kielmannsegge's Hanoverian brigade with 3,300 bayonets and Major Baring's 400 KGL light troops in La Haie Sainte. Behind, in reserve, were Somerset's 1,300 heavy horsemen of the Household Brigade. All these troops, except for skirmishers, were out of sight, even to Dubois' cuirassiers. Within a few hundred metres Charlet's four battalions became sucked into a struggle for La Haie Sainte, initially with some success among the apple trees in the orchard. Outnumbering the defenders by over three to one, they quickly swarmed round the farm on four sides. Wellington, on seeing the

D'Erlon's I Corps Attack:
Phase 3, the Crisis of the Entire Battle (1.45–2.15 p.m.)

Map 27

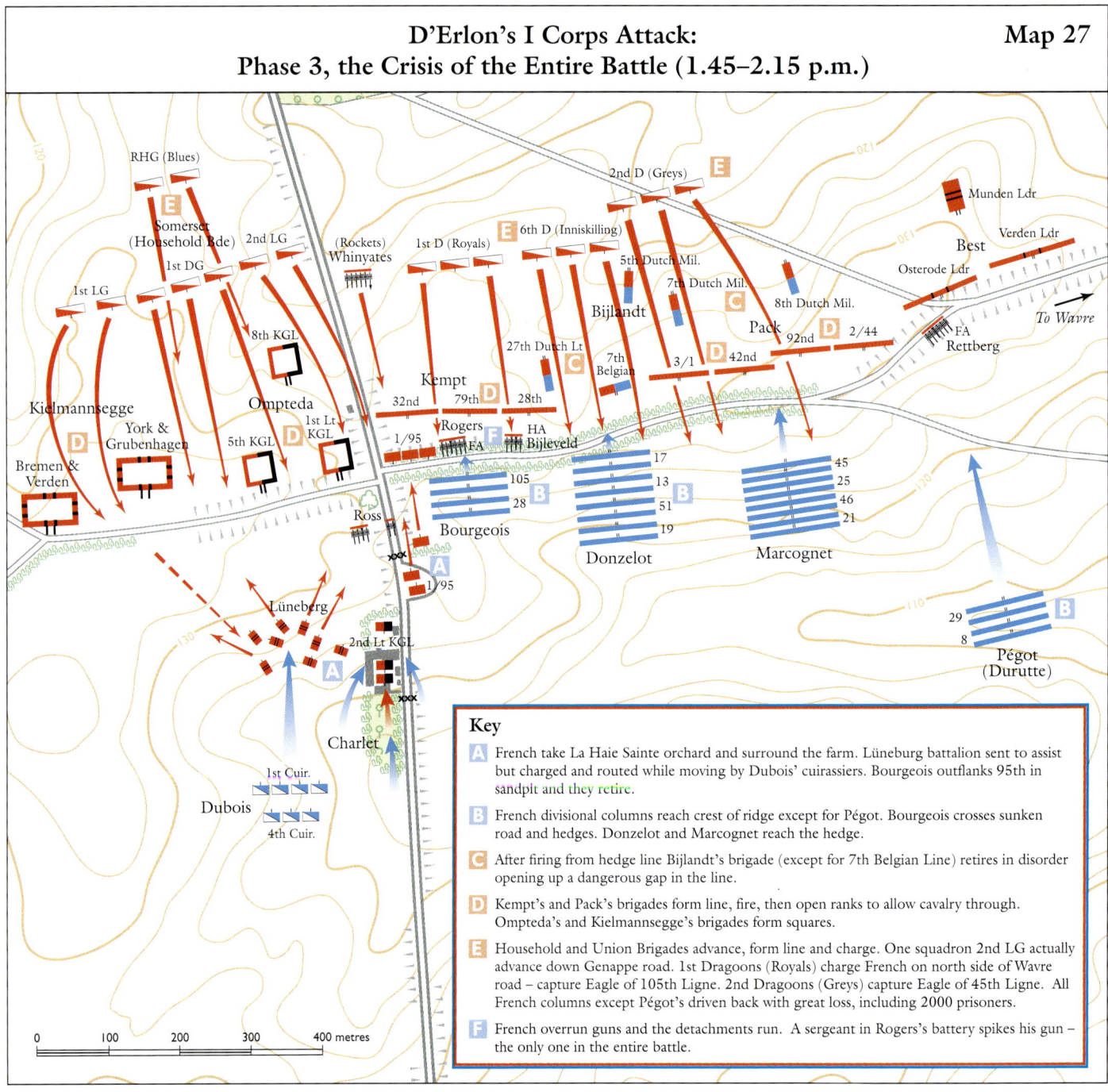

Key

A French take La Haie Sainte orchard and surround the farm. Lüneburg battalion sent to assist but charged and routed while moving by Dubois' cuirassiers. Bourgeois outflanks 95th in sandpit and they retire.

B French divisional columns reach crest of ridge except for Pégot. Bourgeois crosses sunken road and hedges. Donzelot and Marcognet reach the hedge.

C After firing from hedge line Bijlandt's brigade (except for 7th Belgian Line) retires in disorder opening up a dangerous gap in the line.

D Kempt's and Pack's brigades form line, fire, then open ranks to allow cavalry through. Ompteda's and Kielmannsegge's brigades form squares.

E Household and Union Brigades advance, form line and charge. One squadron 2nd LG actually advance down Genappe road. 1st Dragoons (Royals) charge French on north side of Wavre road – capture Eagle of 105th Ligne. 2nd Dragoons (Greys) capture Eagle of 45th Ligne. All French columns except Pégot's driven back with great loss, including 2000 prisoners.

F French overrun guns and the detachments run. A sergeant in Rogers's battery spikes his gun – the only one in the entire battle.

strength of the attack on La Haie Sainte, ordered its reinforcement by the Lüneburg Field (Light) Battalion from Kielmannsegge's Hanoverian brigade. Deploying into line, Lieutenant-Colonel von Klencke mounted and led his men across the 200 metres that separated them from the farm around which there was considerable confusion and smoke. Ahead, Klencke could see a shaky skirmish line falling back in haste, some men running for shelter in the farm and numerous French infantrymen on their heels. What the unfortunate colonel could not see until too late was the flash of light on scores of breastplates – Dubois' approaching cuirassier squadrons (Diagram p. 239).

Dubois' advance had been partially hidden by several undulations of ground south-west of La Haie Sainte's orchard. He led two regiments (1st and 4th Cuirassiers), seven squadrons, 780 heavy élite cavalrymen. He tried to move forward at a trot but they had come a long way and the ground was uphill, soft and muddy under the wet crops,

so that even a trot was difficult at times. As he crested the slight rise west of the farm Dubois saw the answer to any cavalryman's prayer – infantry soldiers in the wrong formation, getting entangled in the confusion around the farm, seemingly unaware of his presence and less than 200 metres away. He did not have to think. Trumpets shrilled, spurs sank in and the brigade, with the four squadrons of the 1st Cuirassiers in the leading line, plunged forward at their best pace. A few moments of hacking and slashing, and the Lüneburg battalion was shattered with Klencke among the wounded. Dubois' men pushed on up the slope, cutting down the laggards and the wounded. Within a few minutes they were within 50 metres of the crest, trying to regain some sort of formation on blown horses.

Beyond the crest three battalions of Germans (Ompteda's KGL brigade) and three of Hanoverians (Kielmannsegge's brigade) had formed square.

The cavalry

Lord Somerset, commanding the Household Brigade, liked to know what the enemy was doing so earlier that morning sent a subaltern from each of his four regiments to the crest of the ridge 300 metres to his front. They were to report events. Meanwhile, his men dismounted in column of squadrons. On the left near the Genappe road were the two squadrons of the 2nd Life Guards, mustering a mere 235 all ranks. In the centre were the three squadrons of the 1st Dragoon Guards with 580 sabres. On their right were two more squadrons of the senior regiment, the 1st Life Guards, with 255 men. Behind, in the second line were the two squadrons of the Royal Horse Guards (The Blues), 246 strong. Somerset had slightly over 1,300 heavy cavalrymen – substantially more than Dubois – but in worryingly weak regiments.

Almost certainly it was Uxbridge who gave the order for the two heavy cavalry brigades to charge at about 2.20 p.m. It is strange that the Duke, who thought nothing of giving instructions direct to battalion or even battery commanders, should have nothing to do with this critical decision, but there is no evidence to suggest he did; he had specifically delegated command of the cavalry to Uxbridge prior to the battle. Credit for what was a perfectly timed counterstroke seemingly belongs solely to Uxbridge. He saw the French advance while he had been away on the right checking on other cavalry formations, galloped back and told Somerset to form line and be ready to charge cuirassiers, then still out of sight. He then dashed across the Genappe road to tell Ponsonby with the Union Brigade the same thing. Somerset's subalterns had already alerted him to events over the crest so he had already anticipated the order. His men were mounted: seven squadrons in the first line, two in the second. A few minutes later Uxbridge returned and placed himself in front of the left-hand squadron of the 2nd Life Guards. He gave the order. Somerset's trumpeter, sixteen-year-old John Edwards, sounded 'walk march'.

The Household Brigade was able to advance up the reverse slope of the ridge without too much hindrance from infantry units blocking its way, as they had all formed squares. Nevertheless, there was no question of them charging just yet. Firstly, they still could not see whom they were attacking as there was no enemy in view. Secondly, 'the first obstacle they encountered was the road which runs along the top of the ridge, that was too wide to leap, and the banks too deep to be easily passed'. Thus Major Naylor, who commanded the centre squadron of the 1st (King's) Dragoon Guards, later described it to Lieutenant Waymouth, 2nd Life Guards. As the brigade neared the top, the right half of the first line got ahead of the 2nd Life Guards on the left. These two squadrons were squeezed towards the jumble of obstacles around the crossroads. They were slowed and fell behind the remainder of the front line.

As the 1st Life Guards and 1st (King's) Dragoon Guards reached the crest, they saw their enemy for the first time, less than 100 metres down the slope. Unfortunately, they could not charge until they had negotiated the sunken road and scrambled up the far bank. By the time these five squadrons had done so and young Trumpeter Edwards had sounded the charge, the distance between the opposing lines was very short indeed – but the British had the impetus of the slope. According to Captain Kelly of the 1st Life Guards, 'the Brigade, and the Cuirassiers too, came to the shock like two walls … A short struggle enabled us to break through them, notwithstanding the great disadvantage arising from our swords, which were full six inches shorter than those of the cuirassiers…'.

This cavalry combat was the only one of its kind at Waterloo. Heavy cavalry charging heavy cavalry, five British squadrons with about 840 sabres (the 2nd Life Guards and Royal Horse Guards were not in the initial clash) attacking seven squadrons of cuirassiers with around 780 sabres. The French advantages – longer swords, and cuirasses; the British – an element of surprise and a short downhill rush. The short, sharp mêlée that ensued was a swirling mass of individual fights, horseman against horseman. The noise of sword on sword, and sword on helmet or cuirass was described later by Somerset as resembling 'so many tinkers at work'. Private Hodgson of the Life Guards took part in this whirlpool of thrusting and cutting just west of La Haie Sainte. The first enemy he encountered was an Irishman in French service. Hodgson described his opponent closing on him, yelling, 'Damn you, I'll stop your crowing'. He felt frightened, as he had never fought anybody with swords. The first cut he gave was on the cuirass, which Hodgson thought was silver lace, the shock nearly breaking his arm. Watching the cuirassier he found he could move his own horse quicker so he dropped the reins and guided his own mount with his knees, waiting for the renegade Irishman to make a point (thrust). When he did so Hodgson turned his horse, swung his sword and neatly chopped off his opponent's sword hand. He then thrust his point into the man's throat and 'turned it round and round'.

Within two or three minutes Dubois' men had had enough. They turned to flee, pursued by the wildly excited British horsemen who had now been joined by their second line: the two squadrons of the Royal Horse Guards. A number of cuirassiers on the French right turned east and, in a frantic effort to get away, scrambled down into the sunken road near the sandpit. They careered down it in a confused, tightly packed mass towards La Belle Alliance, only to become entangled with some of their retreating infantry comrades.

On the left of the Household brigade line were the two squadrons of the 2nd Life Guards. On the extreme left was Lieutenant Waymouth commanding the left half squadron. In this position he found that he had to force his horse down the embankment onto the Brussels-Genappe road north of the 'Elm Tree' crossroads. As he later wrote:

> … my recollection is distinct that I crossed the road in rear and to the left of La Haie Sainte. … in crossing the road I had to get my horse down a bank of perhaps some three feet or so, and then to go along the road some yards before I could find a place to mount the opposite bank…

Most of the 2nd Life Guards crossed to the east of the Genappe road, north of La Haie Sainte, and immediately became embroiled with the cuirassiers who had fled down the road.

La Haie Sainte split the Household Brigade. The 2nd Life Guards advanced and attacked (they could not charge in the restricted space around the sandpit, farm, barricade and in the sunken road). Cornet Marten of the 2nd Life Guards recalled becoming mixed up in amongst French infantry, stating, 'I am equally confident that all this took place with us on the left of the Genappe road, from our having to jump over trees on that road, which I afterwards learned had been placed there by the 95th Rifles [as a barricade]'. At least one squadron, possibly two, of the 1st Dragoon Guards ended up east of the road after pursuing fleeing cuirassiers round the farm and orchard of La Haie Sainte. Many officers and men from both regiments became caught up in the mad dash with the Union Brigade to the 'Grand Battery'.

Looking towards La Belle Alliance from the Allied ridge where the Household Brigade counterattacked Dubois' cuirassiers. The hollow in the middle distance to the right of the bushes was the scene of this fierce cavalry clash. Photo: the author

East of the Brussels–Genappe road
The infantry

Unknown to d'Erlon, his attack was aimed primarily at the 5th British Infantry Division under the eccentric (he wore a top hat at Waterloo), short-tempered firebrand Lieutenant-General Sir Thomas Picton. As the French infantry approached the hedge along the ridge, Picton had but a few minutes before his premonition of death would be fulfilled – he was shot through the head, dying as he toppled from his horse. The 5th British Division was large – some 9,500 all ranks if Best's 4th Hanoverian Brigade that was attached pending the arrival of the 6th British Division is included. To these formations must be added the 2,900 infantrymen of Bijlandt's Netherlands Brigade.

However, this large division had to cover some 1,400 metres of ridgeline. As the French advance progressed it moved in to the left, so that by the time Bourgeois' brigade hit the hedge, the actual objective (frontage) of the corps had shrunk to 800 metres. This western stretch was defended from the right by Kempt's brigade (28th, 32nd, 79th and 95th Foot), Bijlandt's brigade (27th Dutch Jaeger, 5th, 7th, 8th Dutch Militia and the 7th Belgian Line) and Pack's brigade (1st, 42nd, 44th and 92nd Foot). As the skirmishers fell back, the batteries of Rogers, Bijleveld and Braun continued to fire over their heads for a long as possible. The Netherlanders in the centre were lining the hedge. As they opened up with their muskets, the two British brigades on either side and 50 metres to the rear of them began to change from battalion column of companies to line. As yet, apart from the 95th deployed forward on the right, all Kempt's or Pack's men could see ahead was swirling smoke. Occasionally perhaps through the crash of cannons and banging of muskets one could hear the

continuous rattle of side drums and faint cries of, '*En avant! En avant! Vive l'Empereur!*'

As Donzelot's division came up to the hedge in the centre of Picton's position, a Lieutenant Scheltens in the 7th Belgian Line described two incidents of the close quarter fighting that stuck in his memory throughout his life:

> Our battalion opened fire as soon as our skirmishers had come in. The French column was unwise enough to halt and begin to deploy [the battalions were already deployed]. We were so close that Captain Henry l'Olivier, commanding our grenadier company, was struck on the arm by a ball, of which the wad, or cartridge paper, remained smoking in the cloth of his tunic. ... One French battalion commander had received a sabre cut on his nose, which was hanging down over his mouth. 'Look,' he said to me, 'how they do for us!' The good fellow might have fared much worse.

But Bijlandt's brigade could not hold. Watching from behind the left flank of the Netherlanders was Lieutenant Hope of the 92nd Foot. He described what he saw:

> … the Belgians, assailed with terrible fury, returned the fire of the enemy for some time with great spirit … then partially retired from the hedge. At the entreaty of their officers, the greater part of them returned to their posts, but it was merely to satisfy their curiosity, for they almost immediately retired again without firing a shot. The officers exerted themselves to the utmost to keep the men at their duty, but their efforts were fruitless.

The Netherlands brigade, apart from one battalion (the 7th Belgian Line which mostly held its ground and was congratulated publicly by the Duke a month after the battle), poured back leaving a dangerous gap along the ridge. They were eventually rallied by the chief of staff to the Prince of Orange, Major-General Constant-Rebecque. Some were used to escort prisoners to Brussels, many disappeared, but none returned to the action that day.

According to Lieutenant Shelton of the 28th Foot, Kempt's brigade (in line) was rushed forward to the hedge, fired a volley into it, scrambled through and charged forward into Bourgeois' column. At about the same time the 1st Dragoons came up from behind, negotiated a difficult passage through the infantry and the hedge, and swept forward to crash into the French infantry. Further east Pack's brigade did not attack the French until they had crossed over the road and hedge along the crest line. Initially the French threw the highlanders of the 42nd into some confusion. Major de Lacy Evans, ADC to the Union brigade commander (Ponsonby) and who would himself command a division in the Crimean War nearly forty years later, was emphatic afterwards that Donzelot's column crossed the road and hedge before being hit by the British cavalry counterattack. Lieutenant Winchester of the 92nd Foot later wrote:

> ... Sir Denis Pack calling out at the same time, '92nd everything has given way on your right and left and you must charge this column', upon which he ordered four deep [line] to be formed and closed in to the centre. The Regiment, which was then within about twenty yards of the column, fired a volley into them. The enemy on reaching the hedge at the side of the road had ordered arms, and were in the act of shouldering them when they received the volley from the 92nd. The Scots Greys came up at this moment, and doubling round our flanks and through our centre where openings were made for them, both Regiments charged together...

In summary, Bourgeois' brigade had reached the hedge, Donzelot's division had just crossed the hedge, Marcognet's division was almost at the hedge and Pégot's brigade (of Durutte's division) was still perhaps 100–200 metres from it when the infantry of Bijlandt's brigade abandoned the ridge. Within a few moments Kempt's and Pack's brigades in the second line were heavily engaged and advancing when most battalions had to get out of the way as best they could as the Union Brigade surged up the slope and through them.

The cavalry

The maps that accompany many accounts of the Union Brigade's charge, and indeed some famous paintings, give the impression that these regiments conducted a mad gallop down the forward slope of the ridge, smashed into the approaching French columns, scattering them before sweeping on up to the 'Grand Battery'. Such maps and pictures do not reflect the fact that the majority of d'Erlon's infantry had reached the crest before being hit by Ponsonby's squadrons. In other words, most of the Union Brigade's charging was done uphill, on the reverse slope and after negotiating routes through or round the British infantry battalions. The horsemen then had to cross the hedges and road that lined the ridge. Consequently, very few cavalrymen could raise a gallop before engaging the enemy. Several participants have made this point clear. Major de Lacy Evans had this to say:

As the enemy advanced up to the crest of the position on their side, the Heavy [Union] Brigade was also moved up on ours. Our Brigade came up to one hundred yards in rear of the little sunken road and hedge. I communicated the order for this movement myself. We waited there for a few minutes till the head of the Enemy's Column [Donzelot] had just crossed the sunken road – as I understood – to allow our Infantry to pass round the flanks of Squadrons, and also that the Enemy should be a little deranged in passing the road, instead of our being so, had we charged across the road.

Captain Kennedy Clark, who commanded the centre squadron of the 1st (Royal) Dragoons, confirms the situation:

> At this moment many of the Artillery (I believe all) were ordered to leave, or did leave their Guns, which were stationed behind the hedges, and they passed through the intervals of our Squadrons. The Infantry that, I presume had previously lined the hedges were wheeled by Sections to their left [to get them out of the way] ... the French column [Bourgeois], the head of which had at this time passed both hedges unchecked ... . From the nature of the ground we did not see each other until we were very close, perhaps eighty or ninety yards. The head of the column appeared to be seized with a panic, gave us a fire which brought down about twenty men, went instantly about and endeavoured to regain the opposite side of the hedges...

Kennedy Clark is absolutely emphatic on this crucial point:

> ...they [the enemy] had forced their way through our line – the heads of the Columns were on the Brussels side of the double hedge... . In fact the crest of the height had been gained, and the charge of the Cavalry at the critical moment recovered it. ... The charge [of the Union Brigade] took place on the crest, not on the slope of the ridge, though it was followed up to the hollow ground between the two positions.

A point of particular interest that occurred as the French reached the ridge was that as the gun detachments ran for cover, one gun in Rogers' battery was spiked by its sergeant. It was the only known incident of its kind at Waterloo. Kennedy Clark makes it clear that the artillery west of the Brussels–Genappe road initially took up firing positions behind the hedge.

On the left flank of the brigade the Scots Greys had a similar experience. Lieutenant Wyndham's description of the situation indicates that Marcognet's column had virtually reached the crest before it was hit by the Greys: 'We afterwards wheeled into line and went, in not the most regular order, over and through the hedge ... encountering at the same [time] the French fellows who had formed themselves at the hedge...'.

The impact of nine squadrons of heavy cavalry (over 1,300 sabres) striking the three French columns as they reached the ridge was decisive. The blow was not, however, delivered at a gallop by many. Major de Lacy Evans described approaching the enemy 'at a moderate pace'. Major Miller of the 6th (Inniskilling) Dragoons comments: '... so over the hedge I went, and waited a moment or two for the men to collect, and then we were into the Column in a second.' There was obviously no time to work up anything more than a trot. Miller continues, 'From our scattered state getting over the hedges I do not conceive we should have made any impression on our opposing columns had they not been inclined to retire...'. Lieutenant Winchester of the 92nd Foot stated that the 'Scots Greys actually walked over this Column...'. The French regiments had been severely mauled by cannon on their approach march, they had been checked by some short range musket volleys and were disorganized and confused when the cavalry struck. This counterattack may have been scattered and disrupted by obstacles but it was straight out of the tactical manuals with regard to timing. In this respect it could not have been bettered. At the moment of triumph, with the ridgeline east of the Genappe road almost in French hands, the Union Brigade swept some 11,000 infantrymen back the way they had come. Big men on big horses, supported initially by some infantry (the 92nd Foot in particular) chased d'Erlon's divisions up to the 'Grand Battery' 600 metres south of the ridge. In the process the Union Brigade took some 2000 prisoners and captured the Eagles of the 45th and 105th Ligne.

The following morning a British staff officer walking down the forward slope over which d'Erlon had advanced noted that, 'their track up the slope and near the crest of it was marked distinctly by their packs and accoutrements, which still lay on the ground as thrown off, in a long line or chain, and I counted about forty brass drums, mostly all of which were on the reverse flank of the column...'. What is never mentioned in accounts of these heavy cavalry charges is that a number of British cavalrymen were taken prisoner by the French. The precise number is not known but is unlikely to have been more than a handful. In the 2nd Life Guards Captain the Honourable Henry Irby and Lieutenant Samuel Waymouth were both taken prisoner. Irby managed to escape from a cellar in which a number of prisoners were confined in the general confusion of the French defeat. Unfortunately, Waymouth was badly wounded prior to capture in the fight with Dubois' cuirassiers, so it was some days before he was released.

THE FRENCH CAVALRY COUNTERATTACK

By the time the Union Brigade had passed the southern end of the La Haie Sainte orchard it had been joined by the 2nd Life Guards and many from the 1st (King's) Dragoon Guards from the Household Brigade. Allowing for losses, and some commanders being able to rally at least part of their regiments, perhaps 1,500 inextricably mixed horsemen careered south. They had 'lost all regularity in the eagerness of the pursuit.' Major de Lacey Evans described what happened with honest clarity:

> In fact, our men were out of hand. The General of Brigade, his Staff, and every officer within hearing, exerted themselves to the utmost to reform the men; but the helplessness of the Enemy offered no greater temptation to the Dragoons, and our efforts were abortive.

There was nothing more exhilarating, nothing gave a cavalryman a greater adrenaline rush than to see the back of a fleeing enemy. The red-jacketed British heavy cavalry surged through the

---

The Rocket Troop in Action

Lieutenant Warde was an officer serving with Major Ross's Troop of the RHA at Waterloo. From his position close to the Genappe road to the north of the sandpit Warde was in a good position to observe the Rocket Troop come into action after the repulse of d'Erlon's attack. He wrote:

> The Rocket Troop was composed of five light six-pounders, and the Troop told off into thirteen Sections, each Section carrying eight six-pound rockets. Soon after coming into position, Major Whinyates received orders to advance with the thirteen Sections, with a view of checking the advance of a Brigade of the Enemy's Cavalry. Major Whinyates moved a trot within range of three hundred yards, and fired volleys of rockets, and in ten minutes the French Brigade were in total disorder and dispersed...

The Capture of the Eagle of the 45th Ligne

Sergeant Charles Ewart of the 2nd Dragoons (The Greys) took this Eagle when his regiment charged Marcognet's division. About a month after the battle Ewart himself described what happened in a letter:

> It was in the first charge I took the Eagle from the enemy; he and I had a hard contest for it; he thrust for my groin – I parried it off, and I cut him through the head; after which I was attacked by one of their Lancers, who threw his lance at me, but missed the mark by my throwing it off with my sword by my right side; then I cut him from the chin upwards, which went through his teeth.

Next I was attacked by a foot soldier who, after firing at me, charged me with his bayonet; but he very soon lost the

combat, for I parried it and cut him down through the head; so that finished the contest for the Eagle.

Ewart was ordered to take his trophy to Brussels so had no further involvement in the battle. He was rewarded with an ensign's commission in the 5th Royal Veteran Battalion – NCOs granted battlefield commissions for gallantry were never allowed to become officers in their own regiment. Ewart retired on a pension of five shillings and ten pence a day in 1821 when his battalion was disbanded. He died in 1846.

The Eagle and Standard of the French 45th Ligne, captured by Sergeant Charles Ewart of the Greys. They are now held in the United Services Museum in Edinburgh Castle. Photo: Philip Haythornthwaite's collection

D'Erlon's I Corps Attack: Phases 4 & 5 (2.15–2.30 p.m.)   Map 28

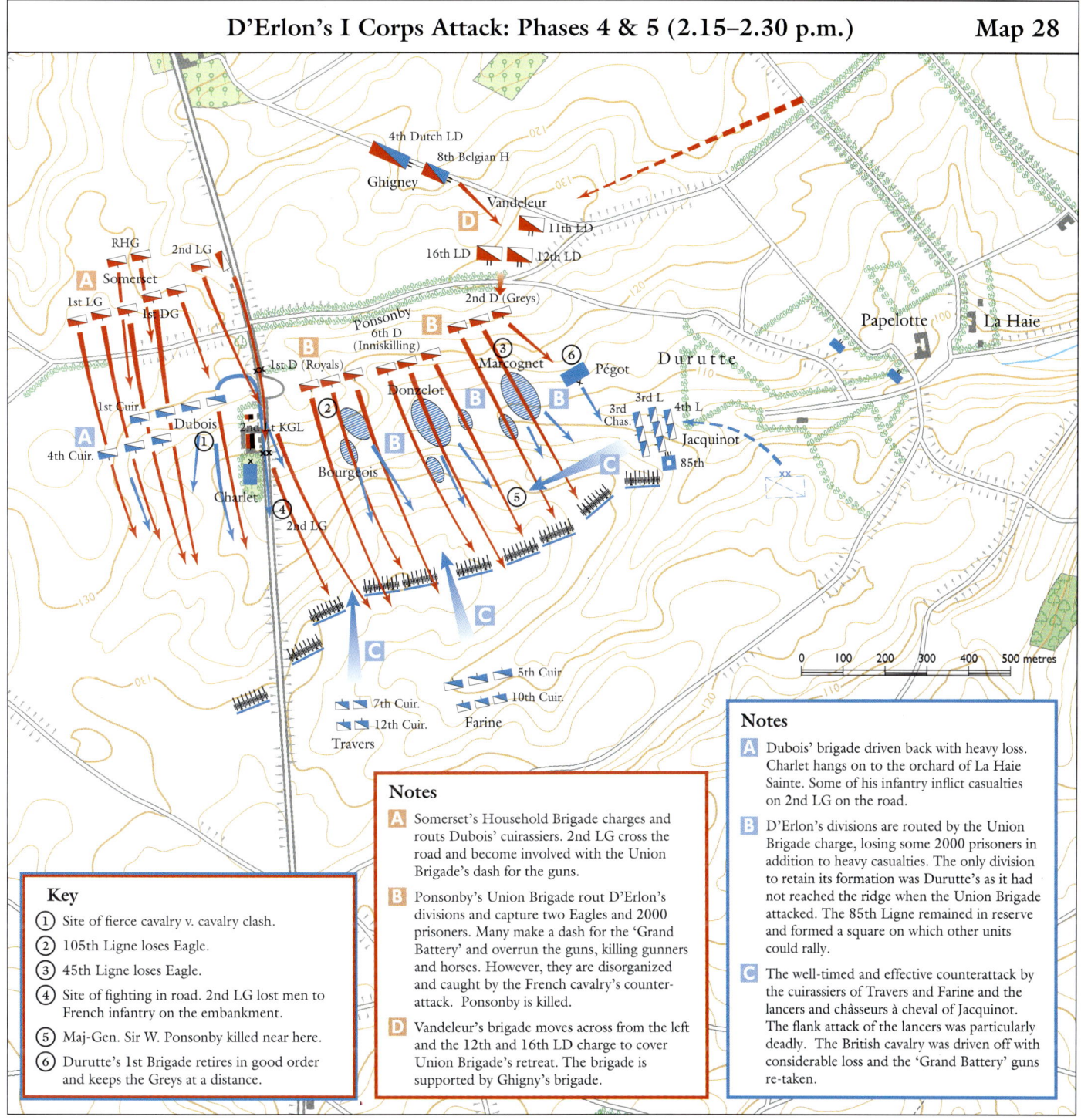

Key

1. Site of fierce cavalry v. cavalry clash.
2. 105th Ligne loses Eagle.
3. 45th Ligne loses Eagle.
4. Site of fighting in road. 2nd LG lost men to French infantry on the embankment.
5. Maj-Gen. Sir W. Ponsonby killed near here.
6. Durutte's 1st Brigade retires in good order and keeps the Greys at a distance.

Notes

A. Somerset's Household Brigade charges and routs Dubois' cuirassiers. 2nd LG cross the road and become involved with the Union Brigade's dash for the guns.

B. Ponsonby's Union Brigade rout D'Erlon's divisions and capture two Eagles and 2000 prisoners. Many make a dash for the 'Grand Battery' and overrun the guns, killing gunners and horses. However, they are disorganized and caught by the French cavalry's counterattack. Ponsonby is killed.

D. Vandeleur's brigade moves across from the left and the 12th and 16th LD charge to cover Union Brigade's retreat. The brigade is supported by Ghigny's brigade.

Notes

A. Dubois' brigade driven back with heavy loss. Charlet hangs on to the orchard of La Haie Sainte. Some of his infantry inflict casualties on 2nd LG on the road.

B. D'Erlon's divisions are routed by the Union Brigade charge, losing some 2000 prisoners in addition to heavy casualties. The only division to retain its formation was Durutte's as it had not reached the ridge when the Union Brigade attacked. The 85th Ligne remained in reserve and formed a square on which other units could rally.

C. The well-timed and effective counterattack by the cuirassiers of Travers and Farine and the lancers and châsseurs à cheval of Jacquinot. The flank attack of the lancers was particularly deadly. The British cavalry was driven off with considerable loss and the 'Grand Battery' guns re-taken.

---

shallow valley, hacking and slashing at anything in reach, until most of them rode up to the long line of guns that was the 'Grand Battery'.

With winded horses that were out of control, groups of riders, even individuals, plunged in amongst the cannons and beyond. Corporal Dickson of the Greys never forgot the next few minutes. 'Then we got among the gunners, and we had our revenge. Such slaughtering! We sabred the gunners, lamed the horses, and cut the traces and harness. I can hear the Frenchmen crying, "Diable!" when I struck at them, and the long drawn out hiss through their teeth as my sword went home.' Much of the 'Grand Battery' was out of action – at least temporarily. Many gunners

were cut down, perhaps several hundred horses maimed, but to the guns themselves nothing could be done; not one horseman had the means or inclination to spike a single gun. Infantrymen could replace injured gunners, and horses were not needed to keep firing from a static position.

The price of being the only Anglo-Allied troops to actually reach the French position throughout the battle was prohibitive. The Union Brigade and half the Household Brigade were about to be hit by three counter-strokes every bit as perfectly timed as theirs had been fifteen minutes earlier. Almost 2,400 heavy and light cavalry were thrown at them from the front and their left (eastern) flank.

The Capture of the Eagle of the 105th Ligne

Captain Kennedy Clark of the 1st (Royal) Dragoons, with the assistance of Corporal Stiles of the same regiment, captured the Eagle of the 105th Ligne in Bourgeois' brigade. There was to be considerable acrimonious argument as to which of these two individuals actually secured the Eagle (discussed in Section 10 'Myths and Controversies'), but Kennedy Clark's account is as follows:

> When I first saw it [the Eagle] it was perhaps about forty yards to my left and a little in my front. I gave the order to my Squadron, 'Right shoulders forward, attack the Colour,' leading direct on the point myself. On reaching it I ran my sword into the Officer's right side, a little above the hip joint. He was a little to my left side, and he fell to that side with the Eagle across my horse's head. I tried to catch it with my left hand, but could only touch the fringe of the flag, and it is probable that it would have fallen to the ground, had it not been prevented by the neck of Corporal Stiles' horse … . Corporal Stiles was Standard Coverer; his post was immediately behind me, and his duty to follow wherever I led. … on running the Officer through the body I called out twice together, 'Secure the Colour, secure the Colour, it belongs to me.' This order was addressed to some men close to me, of whom Corporal Stiles was one. On taking up the Eagle, I endeavoured to break the Eagle off from the pole with the intention of putting it into the breast of my coat; but I could not break it. Corporal Stiles said, 'Pray, sir, do not break it,' on which I replied, 'Very well, carry it to the rear as fast as you can, it belongs to me.'

The woefully under-strength 2nd Cuirassier Brigade from Watier's 13th Cavalry Division under Maréchal de Camp Travers was first. The 7th and 12th Cuirassiers could barely muster four squadrons of about 440 men between them. Travers led them forward to the east of the Genappe road. They immediately engaged a mixture of mostly British Life Guards and some Dragoon Guards. The second counterattack was launched about 300 metres to the east of Travers. It consisted of the much stronger (about 875 all ranks) six squadrons of Maréchal de Camp Farine du Creux's 1st Cuirassier Brigade of Delort's 14th Cavalry Division. Colonel Gobert's 5th Cuirassiers, with 165 men in each of his three squadrons, were a particularly powerful force. They heavily outnumbered their comrades in the 10th Cuirassiers who rode forward with them. The third, and by the majority of accounts the most deadly counter-stroke, came in from the eastern flank.

During d'Erlon's advance and subsequent retreat Jacquinot had quietly moved his light cavalry division forward so as to protect the otherwise dangerously exposed right flank of I Corps. When the French infantry began their retreat his division was probably on the spur overlooking Papelotte, as shown on Map 26. From there it was not much over 300 metres to be in an ideal position from which to charge the British cavalry in their flank. This is precisely what he did. At the risk of belabouring the point, it is worth stressing what Jacquinot did not do. Almost without

A sunken lane south of Papelotte. Modern battle maps often show Jacquinot's cavalry charging straight across this lane when they counterattacked the Union Brigade – an impossibility. Photo: the author

A view of Jacquinot's counter-stroke against the Union Brigade

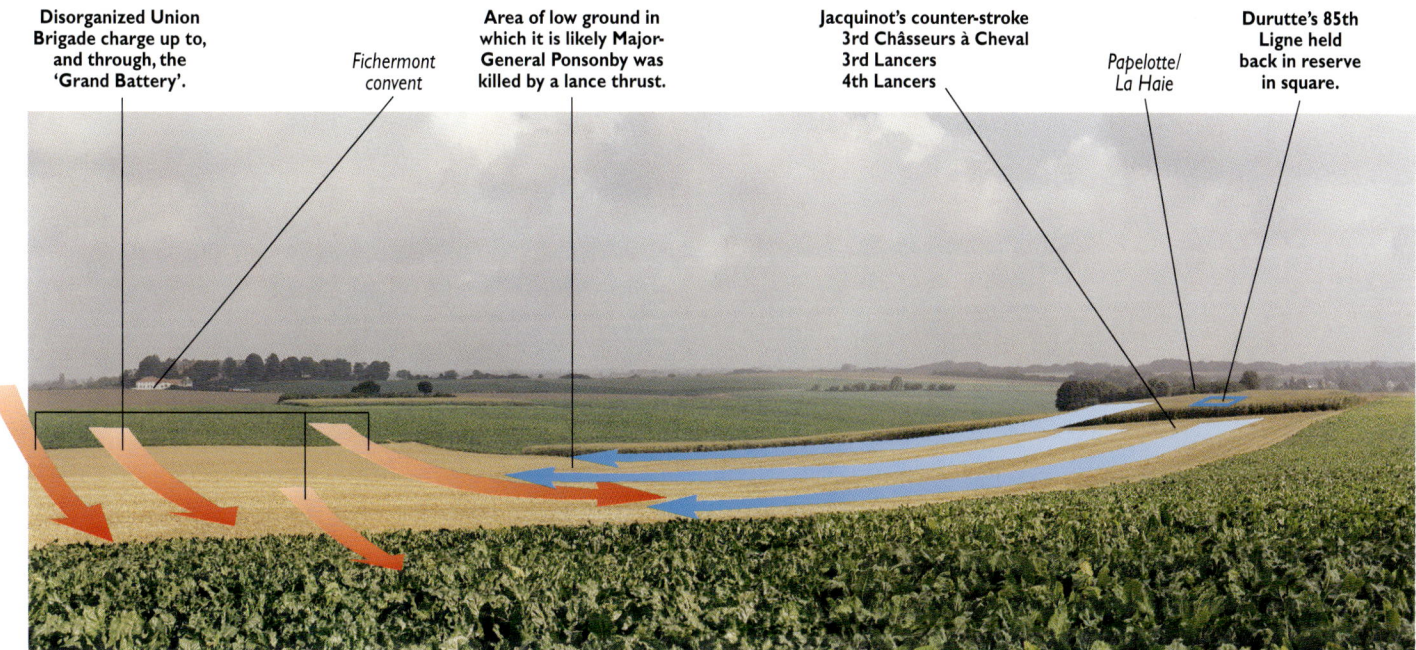

Disorganized Union Brigade charge up to, and through, the 'Grand Battery'.

Fichermont convent

Area of low ground in which it is likely Major-General Ponsonby was killed by a lance thrust.

Jacquinot's counter-stroke 3rd Châsseurs à Cheval 3rd Lancers 4th Lancers

Papelotte/ La Haie

Durutte's 85th Ligne held back in reserve in square.

Note: The 'Grand Battery' was deployed approximately along the line of the cabbage field.

exception, accounts of his attack that are illustrated with maps show his regiments charging full tilt for 800 metres across the tangle of sunken roads, tracks and thick hedges south of Papelotte. It was, and still is, bocage country. These obstacles would stop a modern tank let alone a horseman. Jacquinot was far too experienced a cavalry commander to let his squadrons become enmeshed in such difficulties.

The French counter-stroke was perfectly timed. Ten squadrons of cuirassiers, three of châsseurs à cheval and five of lancers, in all nearly 2,400 horsemen, rode into the disorganized and exhausted British cavalry. It was no real contest. Most accounts of this part of the action highlight the ruthlessness of the 700 men of the 3rd and 4th Lancers. Colonel Bro de Commeres, who commanded the latter regiment, was wounded in the mêlée. In his memoirs he has left a somewhat colourful account of those few minutes that saw the death of Major-General Ponsonby, the Union Brigade commander, and the destruction of much of what was left of his brigade:

> I found myself lost for a moment in the powder smoke. When I came out of it, I noticed some English officers surrounding Second-Lieutenant Verrand, eagle-bearer. Rallying some horsemen, I rushed to help him. Sergeant Urban killed General Ponsonby with a lance thrust. My sabre cut down three of his captains. Two others were able to flee.
>
> I returned to the front to save my adjutant-major. I had emptied my second pistol when suddenly I felt my right arm paralyzed. ... A dizzy spell compelled me to seize the mane of my horse. I was strong enough to say to Major Perrot 'Take command of the regiment!' General [Charles] Jacquinot came up and, seeing the blood flooding my clothes, supported me and said 'Withdraw!' ... Having to leave my squadrons made me weep with anger.

The remnants of the British heavy cavalry that could do so scrambled to get back out of the valley. Some succeeded but many were less fortunate. On blown horses, whose hooves sank a foot deep in the mud, those that raised a trot were doing exceptionally well. The British evacuation of the valley was covered by the forward deployment of Vandeleur's Light Cavalry Brigade that had moved in from the left flank. The 12th and 16th Light Dragoons advanced to attack the French lancers. The 11th Light Dragoons remained on the ridge in support. Although not fully committed to the action, de Ghigny's brigade of Netherlands light cavalry was also brought forward from near Mont St Jean Farm. The withdrawal saw the forward deployment of Captain Whinyates' rocket troop followed by a spectacular display of fireworks. According to Maréchal Ney's ADC, Colonel Heymes, the troop 'fired more than 300 rockets at us [an exaggeration], which first astonished and then amused us without doing us the least harm'. Ensign Mountsteven, serving in the 28th Foot, claimed, 'the first rocket which I saw thrown, made a slight mistake, and came nearly into the centre of our ranks instead of those of the enemy'.

Although Wellington's British heavy cavalry had suffered unnecessarily in their wild rush for the French guns, the casualty figures do not support quite so depressing a picture as most accounts portray. Overall, by the end of the battle the Household Brigade had lost a total of 589 all ranks (45 per cent), and the Union Brigade virtually the same with 612 all ranks (46 per cent). In reality, when the survivors reorganized in the rear of the centre there were probably fewer men present than the following morning when casualty lists were compiled and numerous 'stragglers' had had time to trickle in. Although Wellington may have lost the effective use of two brigades of heavy cavalry, he had thrown back Napoleon's main set-piece attack that had been intended to win the battle for France.

The French Massed Cavalry Attacks on the Anglo-Allied Squares

> One charge to another succeeds,
> Like waves that a hurricane bears;
> All day do our galloping steeds
> Dash fierce on the enemy squares.
> At noon we began the fell onset;
> We charged up the Englishman's hill,
> And madly we charged it at sunset –
> His banners were floating still.
>
> William Makepeace Thackeray

Wellington was once asked what was the bravest action he had ever witnessed in battle. His response was, 'The repeated charges of the French cavalry at Waterloo'.

General

This phase of the battle lasted almost two hours – from about 4.00 p.m. to nearly 6.00 p.m.. At the start of this phase Napoleon still had, if his formations were handled well, a reasonable chance of winning the battle; at the end of it Prussian pressure on Plancenoit was draining away his last reserves (the Imperial Guard infantry) and threatening the very existence of his army. These attacks were to be the most spectacular highlight of the day. Nobody who saw them disputed that. As old men, Wellington's infantry survivors took the sight of 8,500 horsemen, mostly in gleaming cuirasses and burnished helmets, with them to their graves. One such man, Ensign Rees Gronow, who lived for fifty years after the battle, was in the square of the 3rd Battalion of the 1st Foot Guards. He later wrote:

> Not a man present who survived could have forgotten in after life the awful grandeur of that charge. You perceived at a distance what appeared to be an overwhelming, long moving line, which, ever advancing, glittered like a stormy wave of the sea when it catches the sunlight. On came the mounted host until they got near enough, whilst the very earth seemed to vibrate beneath their thundering tramp. One might suppose that nothing could have resisted the shock of this terrible moving mass. They were the famous cuirassiers, almost all old soldiers, who had distinguished themselves on most of the battlefields of Europe...

But they failed to break a single square.

Maréchal Ney ordered them, Maréchal Ney led them (losing three horses in the process), but he did so as a result of an error of judgement. At about 3.30 p.m. he had instituted another assault on La Haie Sainte by infantry which failed (see pp. 368–70), and he rode forward to peer through the swirling smoke at the centre of the enemy position. What he saw, fleetingly and indistinctly, was Wellington pulling several units back into more protected reverse slope locations, wounded and wagons going to the rear, plus numbers of prisoners being escorted away from the line. Ney could not know why these troops were going back, he only saw what seemed substantial numbers of men leaving the ridge. He misinterpreted this rearward movement as the line beginning to crack. An ADC was sent galloping away for heavy cavalry – cuirassiers. This order was to be put in motion the largest and most prolonged series of cavalry attacks in so confined a space of the Napoleonic Wars.

THE FRENCH ASSAULTS (Maps 29 & 30, pp. 357–8)

Statistics

In total, by some time after 5.00 p.m. the French had committed nearly 9000 horsemen (no attempt has been made to assess casualties) to attacking through the 950-metre wide gap between Hougoumont and La Haie Sainte (both of which were under attacks of varying intensity throughout the cavalry onslaughts). These figures meant that only a small proportion of cavalry could form the front or leading wave of any massed advance. A single horseman requires a minimum of about a metre of space. The mathematics of the situation dictated that the great majority of the attackers would be in successive, follow-up waves. This was what happened since available space dictated formations. Regiments advanced in squadron columns with frontages varying according to the strength of the squadrons (formed in two ranks). The largest squadrons, occupying over 100 metres, were in Napoleon's favourite regiment, the Châsseurs à Cheval of the Guard – which with almost 1,200 sabres was larger than most cavalry brigades. The smallest were in the much-depleted 7th Cuirassiers, whose two squadrons only required some 30 metres of frontage.

In all twenty regiments, sixty-seven squadrons participated. This represents 62 per cent of the French cavalry on the battlefield. Of these, twelve regiments were cuirassiers. If one adds the carabiniers, who also wore the cuirass, then over 60 per cent (some 6000) of the attacking horsemen were armoured. Only 9 per cent were lancers, although the strikingly colourful uniform of Lieutenant-Colonel Jerzmanowski's Red Lancers has perhaps attracted more attention from writers and artists than their numbers (880) justify. Among them was the élite 1st Squadron made up of Poles (wearing blue) from the Elba Squadron under Major Balinski. Baron Lallemand commanded the largest regiment, the Châsseurs à Cheval of the Imperial Guard, almost 1,200 strong. The smallest independent sub-unit to charge was under a grey-haired ex-ranker: a former infantryman turned gunner turned policeman-cum-cavalryman, Captain Dyonnet. He led the small squadron of about 100 men of the Gendarmes d'Elite.

At least twelve artillery batteries, probably seventy-six guns and howitzers, supported the attacks. It is impossible to be certain exactly which batteries these were but the possibilities include:
• The two batteries on the western end of the 'Grand Battery', at least one of which was west of the Genappe road
• The three divisional foot batteries of Reille's II Corps
• Two horse batteries sent forward earlier from Kellerman's Corps by Napoleon
• The two horse batteries of Milhaud's IV Reserve Cavalry Corps, which almost certainly accompanied their divisions when they moved across from the east of the Genappe road
• The two Guard horse batteries that would have accompanied Lefèbvre-Desnouëttes' Guard light cavalry in their move

It is possible to discern two main phases to these assaults. Phase 1 (Map 29) was the first advance and attack by Milhaud's entirely cuirassier corps together with Lefèbvre-Desnouëttes' Guard Light Cavalry Division. This took place at around 4.00 p.m. and comprised over 4,800 horsemen in ten regiments, thirty-four squadrons. It had the support of a fierce preliminary bombardment. Phase 2 (Map 30) saw the introduction of Kellerman's III Reserve Cavalry Corps and Guyot's Guard Heavy Cavalry Division. These came into action shortly before 5.00 p.m. and comprised another ten regiments (two were initially held back in reserve), thirty-three squadrons

Ney's First Massed Cavalry Attack, around 4.00 p.m.   Map 29

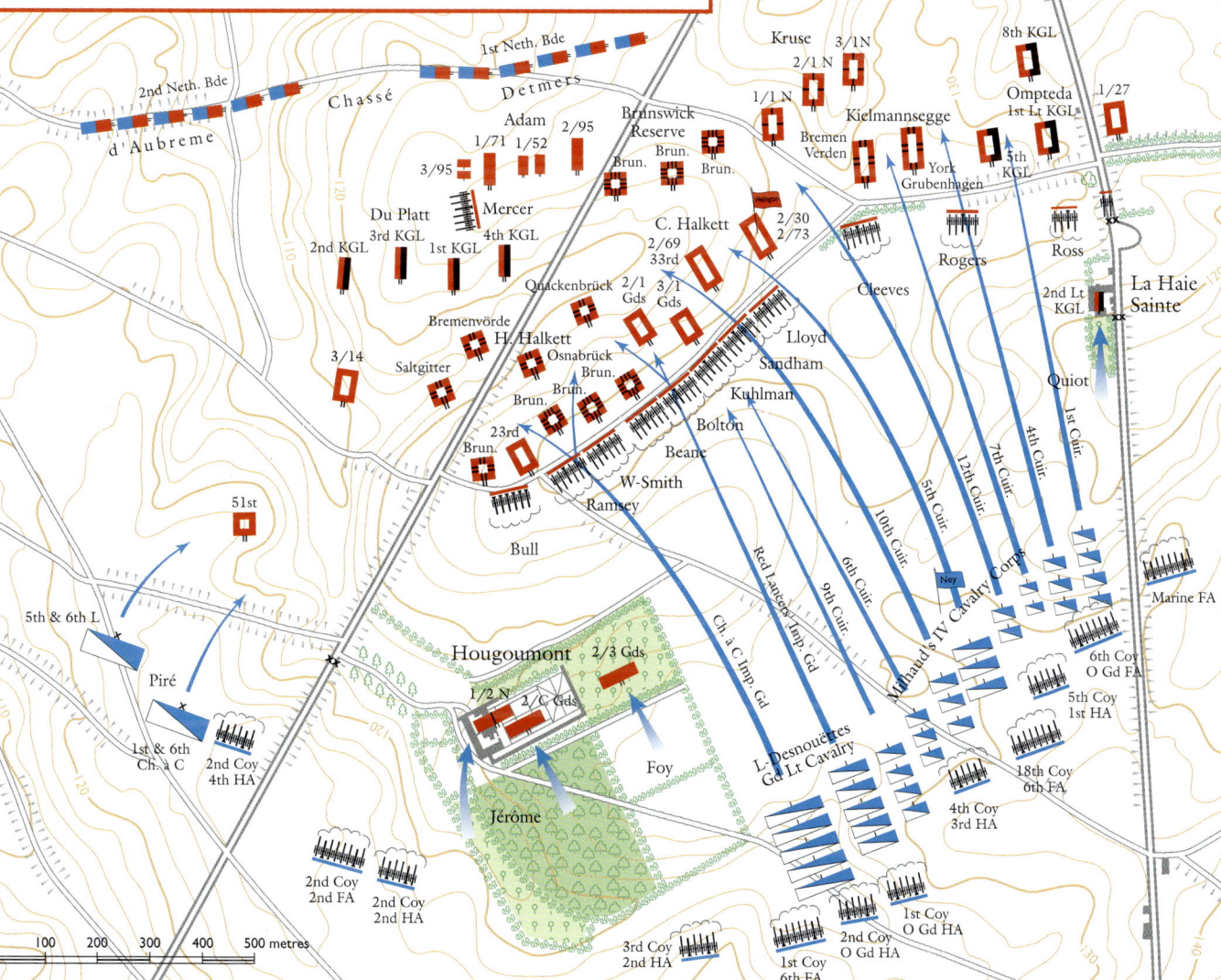

Notes

- The map shows the probable location of Anglo-Allied infantry units at the time of the first French cavalry attack. Depending on the strength of each battalion, the number of companies, and whether it combined with another unit, the battalions formed squares or rectangles.
- Formations changed frequently from column to square and back again according to the tactical situation. Adam's and Du Platt's brigades probably remained in column during the first attack.
- Initially, within the main road triangle some 22 squares (13,000–14,000 infantry men) faced the first attack. They were backed up by eighteen cavalry regiments of greatly varying size and quality (8000 sabres). These have not been shown to avoid confusion and overcrowding the map.
- Some eleven batteries (65 guns/howitzers) were able to bring fire to bear on the advancing mass of horsemen.
- The Netherlands Divisions under Chassé was in the process of arriving from Braine L'Alleud at about this time or slightly earlier.

Notes

Statistics

- 10 regiments (8 cuirassiers), 34 squadrons, about 4,400 of all ranks. Total frontage about 800m.
- Frontage of squadrons (in two ranks) varied according to strength from about 30m to over 100m (Ch. à C of Imp. Gd)
- Artillery in support was at least eleven batteries – probably about 76 guns and howitzers. Batteries probably included:
  - 2 at western end of 'Grand Battery'
  - 3 divisional foot batteries of Reille's corps
  - 2 horse batteries previously sent forward from Kellerman
  - 2 horse batteries brought up with Milhaud's cavalry corps
  - 2 Guard horse batteries with Lefèbvre-Desnouëttes.

- Map shows all regiments advancing in echelons of squadron columns with the cuirassiers on the right, the light cavalry of the Guard on left, as described by Houssaye.
- Both Hougoumont and La Haie Sainte were still under attack.
- The attack was preceded by a heavy artillery bombardment that continued over the cavalry's heads as they moved into the valley ahead.
- Piré made threatening moves on the left but did not charge.
- The advance proceeded at a trot, often a walk, over boggy ground and through standing crops – it was led by Ney.
- The 1st, 4th 7th and 12th Cuirassiers had already been in action shortly beforehand with the 1st and 4th attacking again over the same ground.

The Height of the French Cavalry Attacks, around 5.00 p.m.   Map 30

Notes

- The map shows the approximate positions of Anglo-Allied squares around 5.00 p.m. – the height of the French cavalry assaults.

A - A After the earlier attacks Wellington pushed forward Adam's brigade in front of the Brunswick squares.

B - B These indicate the numerous counterattacks by Anglo-Allied cavalry against the French horsemen as they penetrated between and behind the front-line squares. Not all were successful. Trip's Dutch/Belgian heavy cavalry failed at least once and the Cumberland Hussars fled to Brussels.

C Du Platt's KGL were also brought forward to the area behind Hougoumont.

- The Anglo-Allied artillery did most of the damage to the French. By this time they had been reinforced by Mercer and Sinclair.

Notes

- It is impossible to portray on a map the complexity and confusion of these massed cavalry attacks, albeit all carried out at a trot or walk. No squares were broken and virtually the only casualties inflicted on the squares were by artillery fire. Certainly the French horse batteries were advanced and fired when the horsemen fell back to regroup.

A The second major assault by an additional 8 regiments, 27 squadrons, 4000 men. Of these, over half were in big regiments of dragoons and grenadiers à cheval.

B Milhaud's and Lefèbvre-Desnouëttes' horsemen rally before rejoining the fray. These attacks became a series of disjointed regimental and squadron affairs.

C Kellerman ordered Blancards' carabiniers to remain in reserve near Hougoumont. Later a furious and frustrated Ney forced them into the action. At that stage 20 regiments, 67 squadrons, over 10,000 horsemen had been committed.

D At about 5.30 p.m. Bachelu's division and a brigade from Foy were sent forward. It was too late to achieve anything on the main Allied positions. If these 6,500 men had been used earlier their chances would have been far better.

- It was the French horse batteries that did the damage to the Anglo-Allied infantry. Several were pushed well forward and fired effectively while the cavalry regrouped in the valley east of Hougoumont.

Map labels: Mont St Jean Farm, 2nd Dutch 35th Belgian, 4th Dutch Mil., 6th Dutch Mil., 17th Dutch Mil., 19th Dutch Mil., Chassé, Trip, Merlen, Remnants of Household & Union Brigades, Ghigny, 8th KGL, Kruse, 2/1 N, 3/1 N, 1/1 N, Kielmannsegge, Grubenhagen, York, Ompteda, 5th KGL, 1st Lt KGL, 1/27, Bremen Verden, BRUNSWICK RESERVE, Brun., Arenschildt, Dornberg, Cleeves, Sinclair, Rogers, Ross, 12th Dutch, 13th Dutch, 3rd Belgian, 36th Belgian, C. Halkett, Ney, 3rd Dutch Mil., 10th Dutch Mil., Brun., Quackenbrück, 2/69, 33rd, 2/30, 2/73, 11th Cuir., 8th Cuir., 7th D, 2nd D, La Haie Sainte, 3rd KGL, 2nd KGL, 4th KGL, Du Platt, 1st KGL (Grant), 2/1 Gds, 1 Gds, Lloyd, 2nd Cuir., 2nd Lt KGL, Bremenvörde, H. Halkett (Grant), Kuhlman, Bolton, Sandham, 2/95, Kellerman, 3/14, Osnabrück Brun., Brun., Beane, 3rd Cuir., 13th LD & 15th H, Saltgitter, 23rd Brun., W-Mercer, 1/52, Adam, 1/52, 9th Cuir., 12th Cuir., 7th Cuir., 1st Cuir., Mitchel, W-Smith, Ramsey, Bull, Gren à C, Guyot, Emp. D, 'Red Lancers', 4th Cuir., 51st, 3/95, 1/71, 5th Cuir., 6th Cuir., 10th Cuir., Quiot, Piré, Hougoumont, 2/3 Gds, 1/2 N, 2/C Gds, Foy, Chas. à C Imp. Gd, Jérôme, 2nd Car., 1st Car., Blancard, Tissot (Foy), Bachelu

0 100 200 300 400 500 metres

around 4,500 all ranks. Between and after these main assaults there were numerous other, less sustained attacks as formations and regiments rallied and returned to the fray, but these relied more on the initiative and determination of individual brigade and regimental commanders than on the higher command.

Command and control

There is some disagreement over whether or not Napoleon authorized these massive attacks or whether the responsibility was Ney's. There is no doubt that Ney insisted on the first assault, but did the Emperor order the huge reinforcement by Kellerman and Guyot? Ney undoubtedly thought he saw an opportunity, decided that to exploit it he needed heavy cavalry and sent the necessary order by ADC to Milhaud's Corps. The ADC went straight to a brigade commander, Farine, instead of Milhaud (the corps commander) or Farine's divisional commander, Delort. The 5th and 10th Cuirassiers moved forward. They did not get far. Delort halted them. He later explained what happened:

> I halted Brigadier-General Farine's brigade, which was heading for the great plateau on the direct order of Marshal Ney and without my involvement. I enjoined Farine not to leave the division and pointed out to him that I only received orders from the general who commanded the corps to which my division belonged. During this dispute [with the ADC], which suspended the movement of the brigade, Marshal Ney came in person, bubbling over with impatience. Not only did he insist on the execution of his first order but he demanded the two divisions [Delort's and Watier's] in the name of the Emperor. Still I hesitated … I pointed out that heavy cavalry should not attack infantry which was posted on heights, had not been shaken and was well placed to defend itself. The marshal shouted 'Forwards, the salvation of France is at stake!' I obeyed reluctantly.

Typically impatient of delay or queries to his orders, Ney galloped frantically about the battlefield, using his rank to countermand divisional and corps commanders' orders, desperately trying to galvanize, rally and lead by example. It was Ney who later countermanded Kellerman's orders to his brigade commander, Blancard, to keep his carabiniers in reserve. Accompanied by his loyal ADC, Colonel Heymes, Ney placed himself at the forefront of the attacks. Miraculously, despite reaching the Anglo-Allied line himself, he remained unscathed. His horses were less fortunate. Of the five mounts killed under him at Waterloo, three died during these cavalry assaults. The British Foot Guards officer, Major Horace Churchill who was ADC to Lord Hill, wrote nine days after the battle:

> Marshal Ney was with his cavalry and I was within 20 paces of him. I could not get 6 of our cavalry to follow me or we must have taken him. He was alone with about 6 orderlies. I hollered out to our rascals, but nothing could get them to face him…

Churchill did not have a high opinion of the performance of many of Wellington's cavalry regiments at Waterloo.

An impressive number of French generals led their troops forward. The tally is nineteen, including one marshal, seven généraux de division and eleven maréchaux de camp. Ney was uninjured, but four divisional commanders were wounded; of the brigade commanders one was killed (Jamin, who fell dead over a British gun) and nine wounded. Only Vial among the brigade commanders was untouched. Some 74 per cent of the French generals who rode ahead of their men in these cavalry charges became casualties – a creditable reflection on their courage and belief in leading from the front.

Lieutenant O'Grady of the British 7th Hussars commented on how quickly the French lost proper control and how units became mixed and muddled: 'The French cavalry were in the first instance Cuirassiers and in Squadron but they soon became mixed with Cavalry of all arms and returned in masses of more or less size [than a squadron].'

Some tactical aspects of the attacks

As Sergeant-Major Cotton, a Waterloo veteran who fought with the British 7th Hussars as a private, was to say, 'Of the fifteen thousand [it was about 9000] French horsemen, it is doubtful whether any perished on a British bayonet, or that any of our infantry in square fell by the French cavalry's sabres'. Cotton was right. No Anglo-Allied squares were broken. Most suffered heavy losses not from swords or lances but from cannon fire. The cavalry attacks that lasted for nearly two hours failed. Some of the reasons for this are discussed below.

• Numbers were against the French. Although 9000 horsemen seems a lot, they were pitted against at least twenty-five infantry squares of up to 14,000 men who were ready to receive them. The French deployed over seventy guns to support their cavalry but Wellington had at least sixty-five opposing them. Then, to clinch a numerical superiority, the Duke had almost 8000 horsemen immediately available to counterattack – some of these regiments proved ineffective. Overall, discounting the artillery whose numbers on either side were about equal, the French attacked some 22,000 men with 9000. It has always been a rule of the military thumb that an attacker needs superiority of 3:1 to give a reasonable chance of success. These odds can be reduced, if not reversed, if the attacker achieves surprise – but this did not happen at Waterloo. At

---

Duty with the Colours Sometimes Unpopular

Although it was the duty of subaltern officers (usually the two most junior ensigns) to carry a regiment's Colours in action (and indeed on parade in peacetime), two or three sergeants could expect to be detailed as the Colour escort. This was to protect both the Colours and the officers bearing it – who were obvious targets in a mêlée and had of necessity to fight one-handed while clinging to the Colour with the other. The casualty rate among these young officers and sergeants was high so, although the duty was honourable, it was not necessarily popular, particularly with senior NCOs. Eventually, the British infantry instituted the rank of 'Colour-Sergeant', ranking above a sergeant but below a sergeant-major. Sergeant William Lawrence of the 40th Foot (in square east of the Genappe road) was none too keen on receiving this duty:

> About four o'clock I was ordered to the Colours. This, although I was used to warfare as much as any, it was a job I did not at all like; but still I went as boldly to work as I could. There had been before me that day fourteen sergeants already killed and wounded while in charge of these Colours, with officers in proportion, and the staff and Colours were almost cut to pieces.

squadron level the numerical situation facing the French horseman when he confronted the infantry in square is shown diagrammatically on p. 250. He was invariably outnumbered by at least 4:1, often more.

• All the attacks lacked pace; there was no momentum. To break into an infantry square requires a gap, even a small one, to be created in a side by gunfire or by a horse being forced into the infantrymen and then collapsing on them. To create or exploit a gap requires the riders to dig in their spurs, gain some impetus and force a reluctant animal to rush upon bristling bayonets or exploding muskets. It cannot be achieved at a walk, or even a trot, and not without plenty of foolhardy determination on the part of the riders.

The French cavalry almost certainly never got above a trot; they never actually closed with a square mostly preferring to swerve round the sides or halt, mill around, wave their sabres and fire off the occasional carbine shot. As Ensign Gronow, who was inside the 3/1 Foot Guards square, said:

> When they got within ten or fifteen yards they discharged their carbines, to the cry of 'Vive l'Empereur!' but their fire produced little effect... . The result was that when the cavalry had discharged their carbines, and were still far off, we occasionally stood face to face, looking at each other inactively, not knowing what the next move might be.

A British staff officer is equally emphatic about the French failure to attempt to charge home:

> ... I doubt whether any attack amounting to actual collision took place during any of the so-called charges of cavalry. For my own part, I many times saw masses of horse advance to within thirty or forty yards of the squares, when, seeing the determined firmness of the latter, they invariably edged away and withdrew.

Several factors ensured the attackers never raised even a canter, let alone a gallop. Firstly, they were moving uphill for at least 300–400 metres as they approached the crest of the ridge. Secondly, the ground was soft and soggy, mostly covered with wet corn and the horses and riders were heavy. Thirdly, Wellington's artillery knocked over scores of horses as they advanced, thus creating confusion, piles of bodies, riderless animals careering about and wounded men struggling to get to the rear – a situation guaranteed to further delay those still unscathed. And fourthly, as they reached the crest many had to force their way through a virtual barricade of guns that had been temporarily abandoned by their detachments.

• After the initial massed advance it became increasingly difficult for the French officers to exercise control, to co-ordinate attacks or recognize and concentrate on possible weak spots. Added to the chaos, the casualties, the noise and the smoke was the fact that regiments quickly became split up as a squadron swung left round a square while those that followed might have halted or gone right. The checkerboard layout of many of the squares enabled fire to be brought to bear at close range and from two directions at once. Some horsemen rode between and around the squares, others sought to retire, some halted facing the infantry while more squadrons came up over the ridge behind and became entangled with those in front. Squadron officers moved to the front with great gallantry, urging their men to attack; but their efforts were confined to the handful of individuals nearby, and even with these, their shouts went largely unheeded. Again, the British staff officer comments:

> Sometimes they would halt and gaze at the formidable triple row of bayonets, when two or three individuals might be seen to leave their places in the ranks [these were mostly officers], striving by voice and gesture to urge them forward; placing their helmets on their swords, they waved them aloft, a bootless display of gallantry; for the fine fellows they addressed remained immoveable...

There must always be some doubt whether, throughout this period, a French sword ever actually crossed with an Anglo-Allied bayonet.

• Partly because the great majority of the attacking horsemen wore cuirasses, a number of infantry squares had orders to fire low, at the horses. The horses were larger and softer targets. To knock one over was as effective in stopping an attack as hitting the rider. A dying animal crashed down bringing the cuirassier with it. The cavalryman, winded, bruised, perhaps trapped under his mount, struggled to get up in his huge boots and weighed down by his armour. He had ceased to be a useful soldier. His ambition was to retire rapidly, something he found both dangerous and difficult. A British sergeant who had ordered his men to fire at the horses described the result as, '... a most laughable sight to see these guards [they were not Guards] in their chimney armour – trying to run away, being able to make little progress and many of them being taken prisoner by those of our light companies who were out skirmishing'.

The cavalryman's dead horse meanwhile had added to the obstacles confronting his following comrades. During the afternoon scores of dead and dying animals littered the slope, in places piled sufficiently high to act as barriers. A badly wounded horse would often remove its rider from the action just as effectively as a dead one. They might rear up, stumble, career off in any direction, become unmanageable and disrupt the squadron formation. Not infrequently their pain-induced antics would throw the rider. Shooting at horses was rewarding. The animals' instinct of self-preservation also caused difficulties. As young Gronow explained:

> ... our musketry did not at first seem to kill many men; though it brought down a large number of horses, and created indescribable confusion. The horses of the first rank of cuirassiers, in spite all of the efforts of their riders, came to a stand-still, shaking and covered with foam, at about twenty yards' distance, and generally resisted all attempts to force them to charge the line of serried steel.

• The French use of artillery during, or rather before and in between, these mounted assaults was extremely effective and was feared by those at the receiving end far more than any number of horsemen waving swords. A Royal Engineer, sheltering in an infantry square, made this point clearly:

> No actual dash was made upon us ... the mass held aloof, pulling up within five or six yards, as if, though afraid to go on, they were ashamed to retire. Our men soon discovered they had the best of it, and afterwards, when they heard the sound of cavalry approaching, appeared to consider the circumstance a pleasant change (from being cannonaded)!

One of the commonest reasons why the French failed at Waterloo is given as their neglect of combined arms attacks, their inability to ensure tactical co-operation between infantry, cavalry and artillery. There are several instances at Waterloo where this criticism is unjustified. With these cavalry assaults they made extremely successful efforts to ensure the horsemen were supported by a large number of guns and howitzers. Some twelve batteries (seventy-six guns and howitzers) were used in a ferocious preliminary bombardment as the cavalry regiments formed up. While the horsemen descended into the valley and moved up the lower slopes of the ridge, the artillery opened up again. A number of horse batteries were pushed forward to closer ranges after the initial assault and canister was used. When the cavalry came back into the valley to rally and reorganize, the periods between attacks were utilized by the French gunners to inflict heavy losses on the enemy squares. As noted above, it was guns not sabres that killed or wounded Wellington's infantry during those two hours. The French artillerymen were unable to fire from a flank, they were unable to get their guns up the crest due to the horrendous congestion and confusion. There was literally no room for them on the slope. Nevertheless, they softened up the target at the start, fired overhead in support and hammered away at the ridge whenever they saw a chance through the smoke.

Reasons for failure

Despite all the valid reasons given above for the French cavalry's lack of success, there remains a distinct possibility that Ney could have triumphed on the ridge that afternoon. Two serious omissions prevented it. They were:

• The French failure to spike the Anglo-Allied cannons. This basic error had enormously damaging consequences, not just for the cavalry attacks but probably for the outcome of the entire battle. The French horsemen overran sixty-five or more cannons, not once but several times. By shortly after 4.00 p.m. Wellington had lost all his artillery that was deployed against these massed attacks, almost half his guns. He had lost his most effective killer of the enemy at the very moment that they had gained his position. Without them he must fight one-handed. The Duke himself had insisted his gunners abandon their pieces if in danger of being overrun. He took the calculated risk that the French would not have either the means or the will to disable his guns. He was right. Not a single gun was touched, not a single cuirassier, lancer, dragoon or châsseur had a spike, a nail or a mallet. Not a single officer or NCO thought to use pistol ramrods instead of spikes, get the cannons overturned or rolled or dragged down the slope, or even break rammers. Some rammers were left in the rush for safety as evidenced by Major Lloyd's use of one when he returned to his guns on his own after a charge had been repulsed. Instead the guns remained perfectly ser-

viceable and were used time after time as successive attacks were beaten back and came on again to face the same weight of fire that had decimated them a few minutes earlier. It was a major blunder, the significance of which is seldom understood or mentioned.
• The French failure to support their horsemen with infantry. Ney initially led nearly 5000 cavalry up onto the Mont St Jean ridge. He had taken Wellington's artillery, he had forced his infantry into squares – vulnerable to cannon and musket fire – but his guns could not get close enough, and instead of an infantry division coming up the slope behind, there were countless more cavalry. The attacks developed into the repeated reinforcement of failure by more of the same: cavalry. There was at least one infantry division (Bachelu) plus one of Foy's brigades (Tissot), some 6,500 infantry, that had not been sucked into the Hougoumont meat-grinder operation, which, with a little tactical forethought, could have been sent trudging up the slope on the hooves of the horsemen. With anything like decent timing they would not even have been subjected to much artillery fire during their approach up the exposed forward slope. The use of these troops did eventually occur to Ney and they were ordered forward, but not until late afternoon when the cavalry attacks had almost exhausted themselves and all regiments were crippled. Adam's brigade blew this infantry attack away with little difficulty. Another of those countless battlefield might-have-beens of Waterloo.

The Effectiveness of the French Guns

Ensign Macready, who ended the battle commanding the light company of the 30th Foot, has given a graphic account of how French guns were so much more effective than any other arm.

After this [the French cavalry attacks] had lasted some time, some French artillery trotted up our hill [portion of the ridge], which I knew by the caps to belong to the Imperial Guard; and I had scarcely mentioned this to a brother officer, when two guns unlimbering at a cruelly short distance, down went the portfires and slap came their grape [canister] into the square. They immediately reloaded, and kept up a most destructive fire. It was noble to see our fellows fill up the gaps after each discharge. I had ordered up three of my lights bobs [infantrymen], and they had hardly taken their places when two falling sadly wounded, one of them (named Anderson) looked up in my face, uttering a sort of reproachful groan, when I involuntarily said, 'By God! I couldn't help it.'

A friend of his, Lieutenant Rogers, who later emigrated to Canada and drowned while fishing in the Detroit River, recalled these two guns well. 'Never shall I forget those two guns. Every discharge made a regular gap in the square. It surprised me with what coolness our men and the 73rd closed them up.'

THE ANGLO-ALLIED DEFENCE (Maps 29 & 30, pp. 357–8)
General

The Duke conducted a highly successful defence of his centre and right against massive and sustained cavalry attacks during the late afternoon. They were all delivered frontally against the strongest part of his line. He was able to combine the operations of his three arms perfectly, with his guns taking a demoralizing toll as the horsemen approached, his infantry fully prepared to receive cavalry in two lines of squares, all backed up by numerous cavalry poised to counterattack at the crucial moment. His infantry suffered severely from cannon and howitzer fire but not at all from swords or lances. Due to a skilful combination of defensive tactics and some major failings on the part of the French leadership, the outcome was never really in doubt. The flower of the French mounted arm did not recover from their two-hour mauling on the ridge.

Statistics

The massed French cavalry advance took place up the slope of the ridge between Hougoumont and La Haie Sainte – a distance of almost 1000 metres. As the attackers breasted the ridge they passed through a long line of guns and then, immediately, crossed the Ohain road that formed the southern side of the triangle formed

View of French cavalry attacks seen from Adam's brigade position at around 5.15 p.m.

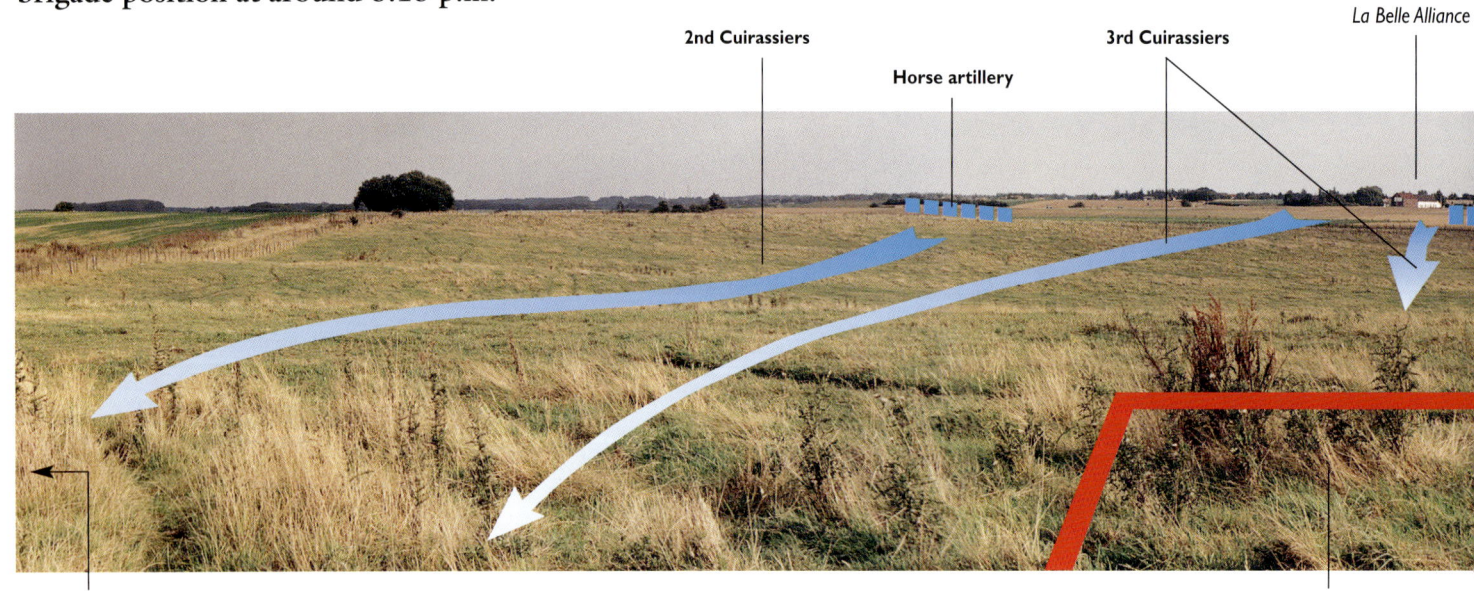

2nd Cuirassiers

Horse artillery

3rd Cuirassiers

La Belle Alliance

2/95 Square

Left wing 1/52 Foot

View of western part of ridge showing approximate positions at first French cavalry attack

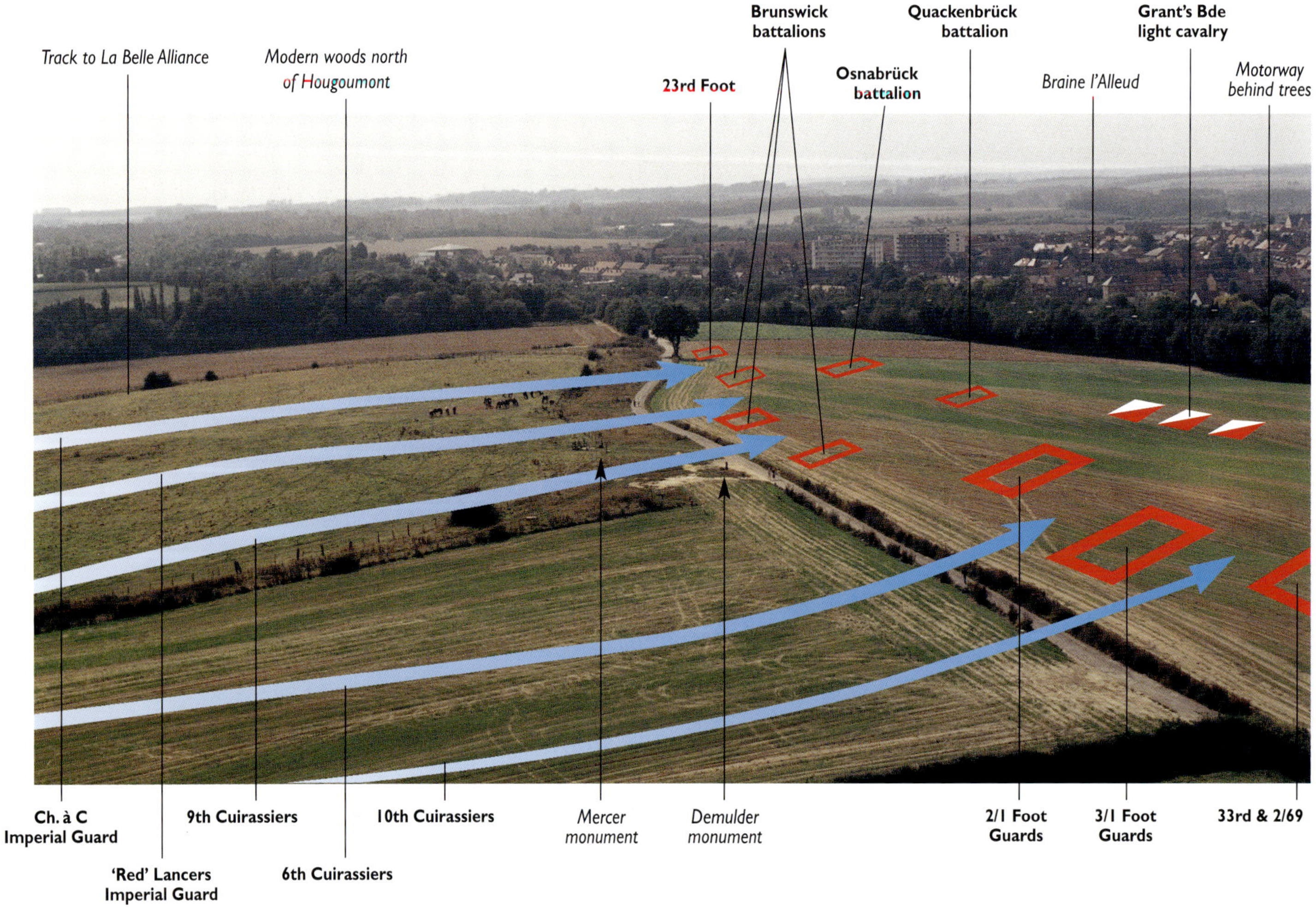

Track to La Belle Alliance

Modern woods north of Hougoumont

Brunswick battalions

Quackenbrück battalion

Grant's Bde light cavalry

23rd Foot

Osnabrück battalion

Braine l'Alleud

Motorway behind trees

Ch. à C Imperial Guard

9th Cuirassiers

10th Cuirassiers

Mercer monument

Demulder monument

2/1 Foot Guards

3/1 Foot Guards

33rd & 2/69

'Red' Lancers Imperial Guard

6th Cuirassiers

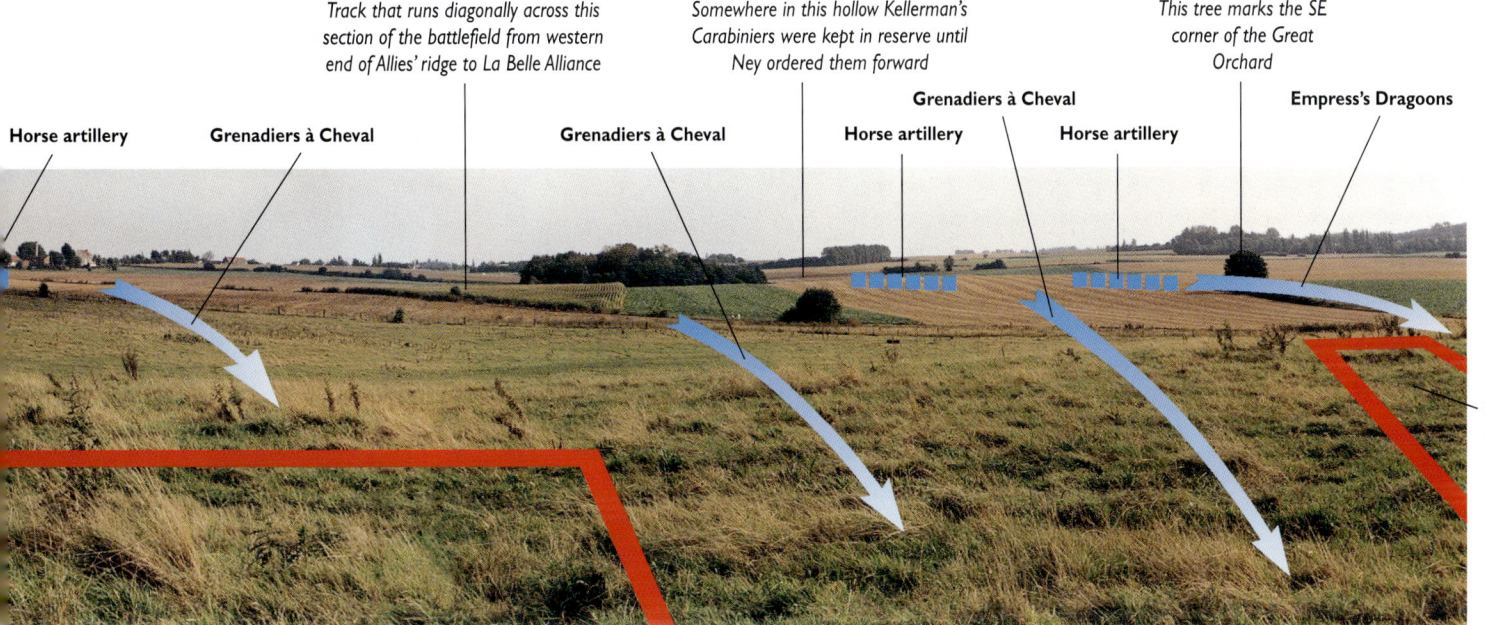

Track that runs diagonally across this section of the battlefield from western end of Allies' ridge to La Belle Alliance

Somewhere in this hollow Kellerman's Carabiniers were kept in reserve until Ney ordered them forward

This tree marks the SE corner of the Great Orchard

Grenadiers à Cheval

Empress's Dragoons

Horse artillery

Grenadiers à Cheval

Grenadiers à Cheval

Horse artillery

Horse artillery

Right wing 1/52 Foot

with the Nivelles and Genappe roads that joined at Mont St Jean village. The actual fighting during this phase of the battle took place virtually entirely inside this triangle, 90 per cent of it in the southern half. Inside Wellington had initially deployed some twenty-six infantry battalions in twenty-two squares, the equivalent of fifteen cavalry regiments plus another three (that were used) just outside the triangle in the north. In terms of men these represented 13,000–14,000 foot soldiers supported by around 7000 horsemen. Along the southern face, just south of the Ohain road, were some sixty-five guns and howitzers strung out in eleven batteries (Rogers' battery only had five, as the sixth had been spiked by its own sergeant earlier). They were to be reinforced by at least two more batteries during the afternoon. After the action had been under way for some time the Duke brought up Du Platt's KGL Brigade and Adam's Brigade from outside the triangle.

It was the front line of squares formed in a rough checker-board pattern on the reverse slope of the ridge that took the brunt of the assaults. At 4.00 p.m. seventeen battalions had formed into thirteen squares along this line. Colin Halkett's four battalions, being low on numbers, had paired off to form two large squares (rectangles), the 2/30 with the 2/73 and the 33rd with the 2/69 (who had lost a Colour at Quatre-Bras). Similarly, in Kielmannsegge's Hanoverian Brigade the Bremen had combined with the Verden, and the York with the Grubenhagen. The squares were spread over almost 1,400 metres of front, from north of Hougoumont to the 'Elm Tree' crossroads; the attackers could spread out slightly after passing through the Hougoumont–La Haie Sainte funnel. This meant that there was approximately one infantry square in every 100 metres of front.

Wellington's front line of squares was mixed in terms of nationalities. There were two squares of British Foot Guards, three of British line regiments, four (probably) Brunswick, two Hanoverian and two KGL. Wellington was relying on British and German troops to take the first shock, although there was perhaps something of a question mark over the reliability of the Brunswickers and Hanoverians. His second line of infantry was initially composed of nine squares, all German speakers, two Hanoverian, three Brunswick, three Nassau and one KGL. West of the road triangle there were the equivalent of another eleven-and-a-half battalions, of which those in Du Platt's and Adam's brigades remained in close column of companies rather than squares, until they moved to the front later in the action.

The cavalry, instantly available should the enemy penetrate too far behind the squares, consisted of the following:

Grant's brigade – 7th Hussars, 15th Hussars, 13th Light Dragoons
Dornberg's brigade – 23rd Light Dragoons, 1st and 2nd Light Dragoons, KGL
Hake's Cumberland Hussars
Arenschildt's 3rd Hussars, KGL
Merlen's brigade – 5th Belgian Light Dragoons, 6th Dutch Hussars
Trip's brigade – 1st and 3rd Dutch Carabiniers, 2nd Belgian Carabiniers
British Household and Union Brigades – equivalent to one or two regiments

The above were quickly reinforced by Ghigny's brigade (from east of the Genappe road) of the 4th Dutch Light Dragoons and 8th Belgian Hussars. Also available were the 2nd Brunswick Hussars deployed north-west of the triangle. Of all these, thirteen regiments were light cavalry, only five heavy. If the Duke's cavalry were to be required to cross swords with French horsemen, mostly light cavalry would be pitted against their predominantly armoured enemy.

The initial eleven batteries of artillery that took such a fearful toll of the French as they climbed the slope were composed of six horse artillery and five foot artillery units. These deployed thirty-nine 6-pounders, ten 9-pounders and sixteen 5.5-inch howitzers. One horse battery (Mercer) and one foot battery (Sinclair) later reinforced the front line, bringing the totals to thirty-nine 6-pounders, twenty 9-pounders and eighteen 5.5-inch howitzers – an overall total of seventy-seven pieces of ordnance. They were spread over the 1,400 metres of ridge, averaging around one piece for every eighteen metres, although in the western half of the line they were packed closer than that. It is noteworthy that of the thirteen batteries known to have come into action on the crest, eleven were British and the other two KGL.

Sergeant Tom Morris Recalls

Sergeant Morris of the 1/73 later wrote some fascinating recollections of his service in the Peninsular and at Waterloo, including some anecdotes of his time in the two-battalion square in which he served. The man kneeling next to him in the front rank had a speech defect so that each time the French cavalry approached he would yell, 'Tom, Tom; here comes the *calvary*!' Another soldier had been wounded in the head and the flow of blood over his face blinded him. Morris watched as this man leaped up and dashed away, thinking to find the field hospital at the rear. However, as he could not see he ran forward:

> ... he was actually rushing into the thickest of the battle, calling out loudly and most piteously for

relief. He met the cuirassiers who were again advancing, and the foremost of them cutting the poor fellow down with the sword, the rest of them rode over him.

Morris also witnessed a fallen cuirassier trying to kill himself. Whether this act was to bring relief from the unbearable agony of a wound or the shame of failure will never be known, but he struggled for some moments to commit suicide with his sword. The length of the weapon and his prone position rendered his efforts futile. He turned instead to a nearby bayonet, placed it under his stomach and rolled on it – an unpleasant way to go.

Command and control

During this phase of the battle Wellington still retained his tight control. Although he and his staff, indeed all senior officers, were compelled to seek shelter inside squares when the cavalry approached the ridge (the Duke spent some time in the square of the 2/30 and 2/73), this did not prevent decisions being taken and orders given. An example of this is the bringing forward of Du Platt's brigade to a position of support north of Hougoumont, and Adam's brigade through the Brunswick squares to form a new front line north-east of the Great Orchard. Wellington, however, did not order the cavalry counterattacks. Uxbridge initiated these. Divisional and brigade generals sought sanctuary in the most convenient square, as did staff, engineer, Royal Wagon Train, commissariat or any other individual, senior or otherwise, whose duty found him near the front at that time.

Inside a square, command was exercised from the centre where the commanding officer sat on his horse and the two young officers with the Colours stood. Decisions on the type of musket fire to be delivered (by ranks, by files, whole volleys from a side of the square) were mostly made by the company commanders with their companies. The crucial question of when to fire was usually the square commander's decision, at least for the first time. Captain William Eeles, with a company of the 3/95 Rifles with the square of the 1/71 during the latter part of the afternoon, has described how he as a company commander exercised fire control:

> I ... kept every man from firing until the Cuirassiers approached within thirty or forty yards of the Square, when I fired a volley from my Company which had the effect, added to the fire of the 71st, of bringing down so many horses and men ... that it became impossible for the Enemy to continue their charge.

He then goes on to make the point, repeated and reiterated countless times during and about the Napoleonic Wars: 'I mention this merely to prove how perfectly impossible it is for Cavalry to arrive in sufficient force against Infantry, so as to be at all dangerous, if the Infantry will only be steady, and give their fire all at once.' He might have added 'at close range'.

Some tactical aspects of the defence

During the initial attacks, probably for at least forty-five minutes, the front line infantry squares were all on the reverse slope. This allowed Wellington's artillery an uninterrupted shoot as the cavalry approached, concealed the Anglo-Allied units from view until the

horsemen breasted the ridge and gave some protection, although not as much as is sometimes supposed, from the French artillery fire. As the cavalry came over the crest they were immediately within effective musket range of at least one square. The checkerboard formation of some of the squares made it impossible for the enemy to avoid coming under fire from both front and flank as they penetrated between the squares. The battalions were able to give each other what modern military manuals consider a key principle of defence: mutual support.

• It should not be assumed that all the infantry battalions stood continuously in square for the two hours of these attacks. The British were particularly good at drill on the battlefield and quite capable of speedily forming line from square and vice versa. A number of battalions took the opportunity of doing so, almost impudently, if the situation warranted it. Sergeant-Major Cotton (then a private in the 7th Hussars), who was sitting on his horse only a short distance behind the front line, later made this point:

> ... our squares often wheeled up into line, four deep, [as they were in a square] to make their fire more destructive on the French cavalry when retiring: on this the Cuirassiers would suddenly wheel round to charge; but our infantry were instantly [a slight exaggeration] in square, and literally indulged in laughter at the disappointment and discomfiture of their gallant opponents.

• Despite the fact that the Brunswick Contingent had suffered quite severe losses, including their commander, at Quatre-Bras, and their morale was somewhat suspect as a result, Wellington brought them forward from the reserve. About four battalions (it is uncertain which ones) were deployed just below the ridge on the right of the front line. They replaced the two Foot Guards' battalions (2nd Coldstream and 2/3 Guards) that had by this time been fully (less Colour protection companies) committed to Hougoumont. The Duke was taking a calculated risk, but he supported them on either side with British battalions (23rd Foot, 2/1 Foot Guards). In the event, the Brunswick squares appeared very shaky to Captain Mercer later in the afternoon, but they had at least stood their ground during the first attacks – prior to Adam's brigade advancing to positions in front of them.

• Provided an infantry battalion remained in square, it was virtually safe from cavalry. However, when infantry co-operated with the cavalry it became a difficult matter of judgement for the defending commanders to know when to change formation. If they got it wrong they could see their battalion destroyed within minutes. This is what happened to the 5th KGL during the massed French cavalry attacks. The 3rd British Division commander, Lieutenant-General Alten, saw some of the French infantry attacking La Haie Sainte during a slight lull in the cavalry onslaught as a threat to the line. He ordered Colonel Ompteda to deploy the 5th KGL, who were in square, and attack the infantry. Ompteda demurred. The French cavalry may not have been visible but he knew they were only a short distance away down the forward slope. At this moment the Prince of Orange rode up and insisted Ompteda obey the order, despite the colonel repeating his reservations. The 5th KGL deployed and advanced with Ompteda at their head. They were ridden over by cuirassiers. A desperate struggle ensued for possession of the battalion's King's Colour. The officer carrying it was killed and the sergeant who grabbed it from him was wounded.

Although no square was actually broken during these attacks, one or two came close. Major-General Constant-Rebecque, the chief of staff to the Prince of Orange, had personally to rally the three squares of the 1st Nassau Regiment. As they formed part of his own national Netherlands contingent, his critical comments are likely to be accurate. However, it was artillery fire not cavalry that caused the problem. Constant-Rebecque wrote:

I was often obliged to go to rally the three squares of the Nassau contingent (Kruse's brigade), which were composed of young troops seeing action for the first time, and were often yielding ground. Several times I brought them back at a charge. At one moment one of these battalions was totally routed by some explosions in the midst of its packed ranks. But by throwing myself in front of them, I succeeded in halting and bringing them back.

The Square of the 5th KGL

In his *History of the King's German Legion* Beamish quotes an interesting incident during the cavalry attacks on the square of the 5th KGL formed about 200 metres west of the 'Elm Tree' crossroads.

A body of cuirassiers made repeated attacks on the square formed by the fifth line battalion of the legion; after each unsuccessful charge, they retired into a hollow where they were protected from the fire of the square, while the commanding officer, with great coolness remained in observation on a little rising ground, moving his horse about *en vedette*, and watching for a favourable opportunity to renew the attack. Colonel Ompteda, who was in the square, called upon several of the men to rid him of the Frenchman's observation, but all the shots failed, and for the fifth time, the charge was repeated. At length a rifleman of the first light battalion, named John Milius, who had been severely wounded and brought into the square, hearing what was required, begged that he might be carried to the front. Here the devoted soldier, although with a broken leg and faint from the loss of blood – levelling his trusty rifle, brought the officer lifeless from his horse with the first shot.

• Sometime around 5.00 p.m. the Duke ordered Du Platt's KGL brigade forward through the front line, close enough to the north of Hougoumont to be able to support the garrison as required. More significantly, he also brought up Adam's brigade through the Brunswick squares. The brigade was required to deal with French infantry advancing east of Hougoumont (Foy and Bachelu's divisions), and then to remain in squares (four, as the large 1/52 of over 1,100 strong split into two wings) on the forward slope of the ridge to face the continued cavalry assaults. Wellington was probably keen to screen the Brunswick squares who were looking increasingly jittery (Map 30, p. 358). These squares were well spread out over almost 500 metres, somewhat isolated and worryingly vulnerable to the French guns. They were echeloned back from the right (1/71) near the Great Orchard to the 2/95 Rifles on the left with the two 1/52 squares in the centre. The Anglo-Allied batteries behind them along the western part of the ridge had to fire over their heads – the firing of shrapnel being particularly problematic. Ensign William Leeke, the most junior subaltern in the 1/52 who was to survive Waterloo for another sixty-four years, had this to say of the situation:

The old officers, who had served during the whole of the Peninsula war, stated they had never been exposed to such a cannonade as that which the 52nd squares had to undergo on this occasion… . Our own artillery [probably Bolton, Beane, Mercer and Webber-Smith], on, or just under the crest of our position, were also firing over our heads the whole time… . Some shrapnel shells burst short, and wounded some of the 52nd men; but the firing of these shells was discontinued, on our sending notice of what they were doing to the artillery above us.

The Belated French Infantry Attack

Ney left employing infantry in support of his cavalry until too late, until the horsemen were exhausted and, in many regiments, a broken force. When Bachelu's division and Foy's brigade (commanded by Tissot) moved off they did so with little or no cavalry support and straight into heavy cannon and then musket fire – it became something of a turkey shoot. It was a doomed attempt that should have been made over an hour earlier. General Foy recalled what happened:

I kept my left flank at the hedge [the eastern boundary of Hougoumont]. In front of me I had a battalion deployed as skirmishers. When we were about to meet the English, we received a very lively fire of canister and musketry. It was a hail of death. The enemy squares [including Adam's

brigade] had the front rank kneeling and presenting a hedge of bayonets. The columns of Bachelu's division fled first and their flight precipitated the flight of my columns. At this moment I was wounded. A ball passed through the top of my right arm; the bone was not touched. After being hit I thought that I had only a contusion and stayed on the battlefield. Everyone was fleeing. I rallied the debris of my division [brigade] in the valley adjacent to the wood of Hougoumont. We were not followed.

In this abortive attack Général de Division Bachelu was wounded by a shell splinter in the head and his horse was killed. The same shell also injured one of his brigade commanders, Maréchal de Camp Campi.

• Uxbridge had his problems with some of the cavalry when he wanted to launch them in counterattacks. Early on he had been concerned with the threatening moves on the right flank by Piré's lancers and horse artillery battery. He ordered Grant over to the far right to manoeuvre to counter them. Grant sent the 13th Light Dragoons and 15th Hussars. This reaction was enough to halt Piré. While they were away Uxbridge brought up Trip's three carabinier regiments – the 1st and 3rd Dutch and 2nd Belgian Carabiniers. Uxbridge later described what happened:

> Seeing a Corps [of cavalry] formed for attack and advancing, I brought forward a Brigade of Dutch Heavy Cavalry, and they promised to follow me. I led them beyond the ridge of the hill, a little to the left of Hougoumont. There they halted, and finding the impossibility of making them charge, I left them and retired.

His ADC, Captain Seymour, had this to say of the same incident:

> … as to the conduct of the Dutch Brigade of Heavy Cavalry, the impression still on my mind [twenty-seven years later] is that they did show a lamentable want of spirit, and that Lord Anglesey [Uxbridge] tried all in his power to lead them on, and while he was advancing, I believe I called his attention to the fact of his not being followed.

Apart from this incident and the disappearance of the Cumberland Hussars, Uxbridge's cavalry did their duty admirably.
• The Duke's orders to his gunners to abandon their pieces if closely pressed and seek shelter in the nearest square were, with one certain exception, obeyed. The exception was Mercer. According to him, to run for shelter in the two nearby jittery Brunswick squares would have invited disaster: 'To have sought refuge amongst men in such a state were madness – the very moment our men ran from their guns I was convinced, would be the signal for their disbanding.'

As the French neglected to spike or otherwise incapacitate any

of the abandoned guns the detachments were able to return and open fire again as the horsemen retired to regroup. One of the battery commanders who sought safety in the square of the 3/1 Foot Guards was Major Lloyd. With him was a Staff Corps officer, similarly sheltering, who witnessed a very gallant act by the major. When the enemy withdrew, Lloyd saw his guns standing untouched and rode back to them alone. The Staff Corps officer quickly joined him. Lloyd seized a rammer and tried one of the pieces, which to his surprise was loaded. He fired the gun with some effect at the enemy who were only 150 metres away. He fired a second gun. Still none of his detachment had returned. Lloyd could not find another charge to reload and, as he was bemoaning the fact, the Staff Corps officer's horse was hit. The animal became uncontrollable and bolted to the rear carrying its rider with it. Lloyd was later killed.

The Struggle for La Haie Sainte (Maps 31, 32, 33 & 34, pp. 369, 370, 374 & 378)

> When thou hast reach'd La Haye, survey it well:
> Here was the heat and centre of the strife;
> This point must Britain hold whate'er befell,
> And here both armies were profuse of life:
> Once it was lost, – and then a stander-by
> Belike had trembled for the victory.
>
> Southey

Outline of events
'La Haie Sainte' has the intriguing literal English translation of 'The Sacred Hedge'. It has nothing to do with the large numbers of corpses littered round the farm after the conflict, or the role played by the hedges in its defence, as it carried this name before the battle. It is a strange name for a farm and its origin remains a mystery – at least to the present writer.

The Unsteadiness of Some Brunswick and Other Squares

Captain Mercer's troop of 9-pounders was posted slightly in front of and between two squares of Brunswick infantry during the latter half of the French cavalry attacks. To him they appeared near to dissolving in panic. He was convinced that to abandon his guns and seek shelter in their ranks would precipitate a rush to the rear. It was no surprise when Wellington pushed up Adam's brigade through these squares onto the forward slope. Mercer's description of what he saw pulls no punches:

> The Brunswickers were falling fast – the shot every moment making great gaps in their squares, which the officers and sergeants were actively employed in filling up by pushing their men together, and sometimes thumping them ere they could make them move. … There they stood, with recovered arms, like so many logs, or rather like the very wooden figures which I had seen them practising at in their cantonments. Every moment I feared they would again throw down their arms and flee; but their officers and sergeants behaved nobly, not only keeping them together, but managing to keep their squares closed in spite of the carnage made amongst them. To have sought refuge amongst men in such a state were

madness – the very moment our men ran from their guns I was convinced, would be the signal for their disbanding.

A Waterloo staff officer writing his recollections of the battle many years later in the *United Services Journal* supports Mercer in his concerns as to the reliability of some squares, although he merely refers to them as 'foreigners', which is unhelpful. He was, however, referring to squares in the second line, so they could have included Nassauers (Major-General Constant-Rebecque had problems with them), Hanoverians or more Brunswickers. He wrote:

> Had they [the French cavalry] thought it worthwhile to fall resolutely on a few of the squares in the second line, doubtless some of them would have been broken; for I repeatedly noticed unsteadiness amongst them, and men running from them to the rear. It was amusing to see at times several starting from an angle of a square, and immediately one or two Staff Officers would gallop off to intercept them in their flight, who always succeeded in driving them back to their colours. I assisted in this duty more than once, and was surprised at the readiness with which the foreigners returned as soon as we got in their rear.

Sketch of La Haie Sainte in 1815

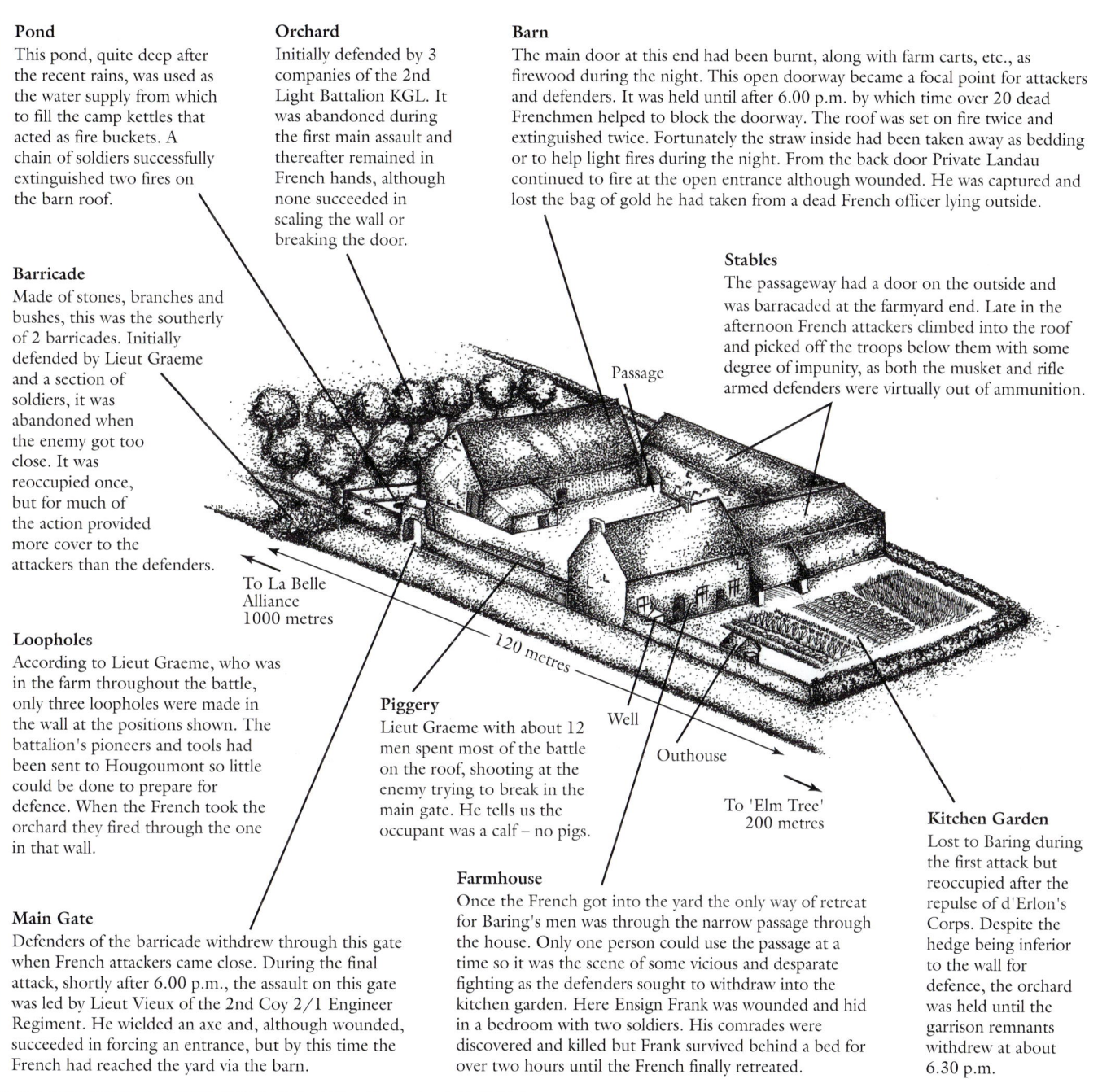

Pond

This pond, quite deep after the recent rains, was used as the water supply from which to fill the camp kettles that acted as fire buckets. A chain of soldiers successfully extinguished two fires on the barn roof.

Orchard

Initially defended by 3 companies of the 2nd Light Battalion KGL. It was abandoned during the first main assault and thereafter remained in French hands, although none succeeded in scaling the wall or breaking the door.

Barn

The main door at this end had been burnt, along with farm carts, etc., as firewood during the night. This open doorway became a focal point for attackers and defenders. It was held until after 6.00 p.m. by which time over 20 dead Frenchmen helped to block the doorway. The roof was set on fire twice and extinguished twice. Fortunately the straw inside had been taken away as bedding or to help light fires during the night. From the back door Private Landau continued to fire at the open entrance although wounded. He was captured and lost the bag of gold he had taken from a dead French officer lying outside.

Stables

The passageway had a door on the outside and was barracaded at the farmyard end. Late in the afternoon French attackers climbed into the roof and picked off the troops below them with some degree of impunity, as both the musket and rifle armed defenders were virtually out of ammunition.

Barricade

Made of stones, branches and bushes, this was the southerly of 2 barricades. Initially defended by Lieut Graeme and a section of soldiers, it was abandoned when the enemy got too close. It was reoccupied once, but for much of the action provided more cover to the attackers than the defenders.

Passage

To La Belle Alliance 1000 metres

120 metres

Loopholes

According to Lieut Graeme, who was in the farm throughout the battle, only three loopholes were made in the wall at the positions shown. The battalion's pioneers and tools had been sent to Hougoumont so little could be done to prepare for defence. When the French took the orchard they fired through the one in that wall.

Piggery

Lieut Graeme with about 12 men spent most of the battle on the roof, shooting at the enemy trying to break in the main gate. He tells us the occupant was a calf – no pigs.

Well

Outhouse

To 'Elm Tree' 200 metres

Kitchen Garden

Lost to Baring during the first attack but reoccupied after the repulse of d'Erlon's Corps. Despite the hedge being inferior to the wall for defence, the orchard was held until the garrison remnants withdrew at about 6.30 p.m.

Main Gate

Defenders of the barricade withdrew through this gate when French attackers came close. During the final attack, shortly after 6.00 p.m., the assault on this gate was led by Lieut Vieux of the 2nd Coy 2/1 Engineer Regiment. He wielded an axe and, although wounded, succeeded in forcing an entrance, but by this time the French had reached the yard via the barn.

Farmhouse

Once the French got into the yard the only way of retreat for Baring's men was through the narrow passage through the house. Only one person could use the passage at a time so it was the scene of some vicious and desparate fighting as the defenders sought to withdraw into the kitchen garden. Here Ensign Frank was wounded and hid in a bedroom with two soldiers. His comrades were discovered and killed but Frank survived behind a bed for over two hours until the French finally retreated.

This farm was successfully defended by the green-jacketed, rifle-armed 2nd Light Battalion, KGL under Major George Baring from the start of d'Erlon's attack at around 1.30 p.m. until forced to abandon the post some five hours later. The battalion formed part of Colonel Ompteda's 2nd KGL Brigade in Lieutenant-General Alten's 3rd Division. Baring was an experienced officer with at least ten years active duty. He had served on the expedition to Hanover (1805), the Baltic (1807 and 1808), the Scheldt (1809) and had completed two three-year stretches in the Peninsula (where he was wounded at the bloodbath of a battle at Albuera in 1811). He had command at Waterloo because the lieutenant-colonel, David Martin, although in Belgium was, for some reason, not present. Baring survived Waterloo unscathed

(although his horses did not), eventually becoming a major-general in the Hanoverian service and Commandant at Hanover.

He was reinforced during the afternoon by the equivalent of four companies from the 1st Light Battalion, KGL, the 5th Line Battalion, KGL, and troops from the 1/2 Nassau Regiment, the latter all the way from Hougoumont. Throughout their five hours at La Haie Sainte the garrison was, like Hougoumont, subjected to a series of heavy assaults in which the attackers hugely outnumbered the defenders. Throughout this time the farm was under continuous fire, at the very least from skirmishers. There were slight lulls when the prolonged main attacks were pushed back, and communication with the main line, some 200 metres to the rear, was possible during these periods. The main assaults with their approximate timings are given overleaf:

Looking across the farmyard from the main gates towards the farmhouse and stables. The right-hand farmhouse door was the start of the passage through to the kitchen garden.

Ground Plan of La Haie Sainte in 1815

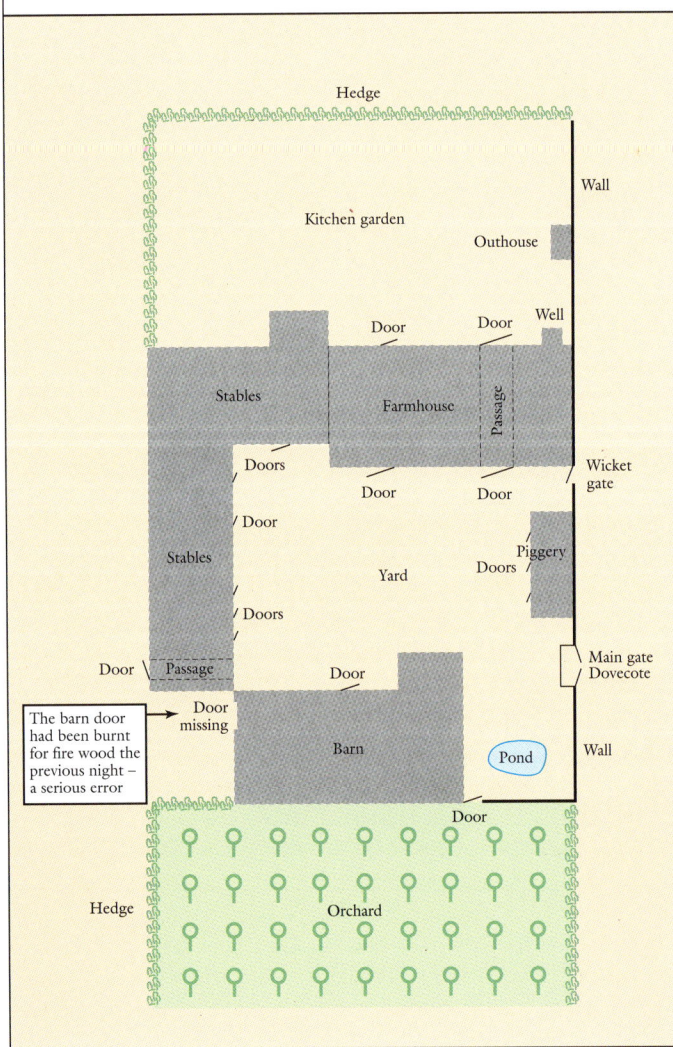

Hedge

Wall

Kitchen garden

Outhouse

Well

Door   Door

Stables   Farmhouse   Passage

Doors   Wicket gate

Door   Door

Door

Stables   Piggery
                Doors

Yard

Doors   Main gate
                Dovecote

Door   Passage   Door

The barn door had been burnt for fire wood the previous night – a serious error

Door
Door missing

Barn   Pond   Wall

Door

Hedge   Orchard

• 1.30 p.m.–2.30 p.m. The farm came under direct attack by Colonel Charlet's brigade of Quiot's 1st Infantry Division. Both the orchard and kitchen garden were lost but the defenders retired into the farm buildings and were able to beat off further attacks. The first shot of this assault broke the bridle of Baring's horse, the second killed his second-in-command, Major Bosewiel. Losses during this first hour were high and included three officers killed and six wounded. The divisional commander, seeing the farm surrounded by smoke and blue-coated infantry, ordered up the Lüneberg (light) Battalion under Lieutenant-Colonel von Klencke to counterattack so that they might relieve the pressure on the defenders. Baring, with some of his troops, was outside the buildings and they merged with the Lünebergers at the moment they were struck by Dubois' exultant cuirassiers. Von Klencke was killed, his men (with some of Baring's) fled back towards the main position, while others scrambled back into the farm. It was a disaster for the Lüneberg battalion, which ceased to exist as a fighting unit.

• 3.00 p.m.–5.00 p.m. The renewed attacks began after about thirty minutes, during which the defenders were shelled and subjected to skirmisher fire. They used this relative pause to reorganize defences and absorb reinforcements sent at Baring's request. Two rifle-armed companies of the 1st Light Battalion, KGL arrived under Captains von Gilsa and Marschalck. They were detailed to hold the garden while the bulk of the much reduced 2nd Battalion remained in the buildings. No attempt was made to reoccupy the orchard. Two companies of the 1/95 Rifles provided some extra support on the eastern side by the reoccupation of the sandpit. The fresh attacks were sustained, courageous and prolonged. Baring described it thus:

> … this [assault] followed in the same force as before;
> namely, from two sides by two close columns, which, with
> the greatest rapidity, nearly surrounded us, and, despising
> danger, fought with a degree of courage which I had never
> before witnessed in Frenchmen. … [They threw] themselves

The Struggle for La Haie Sainte: Phase 1, 1.30–2.30 p.m.   Map 31

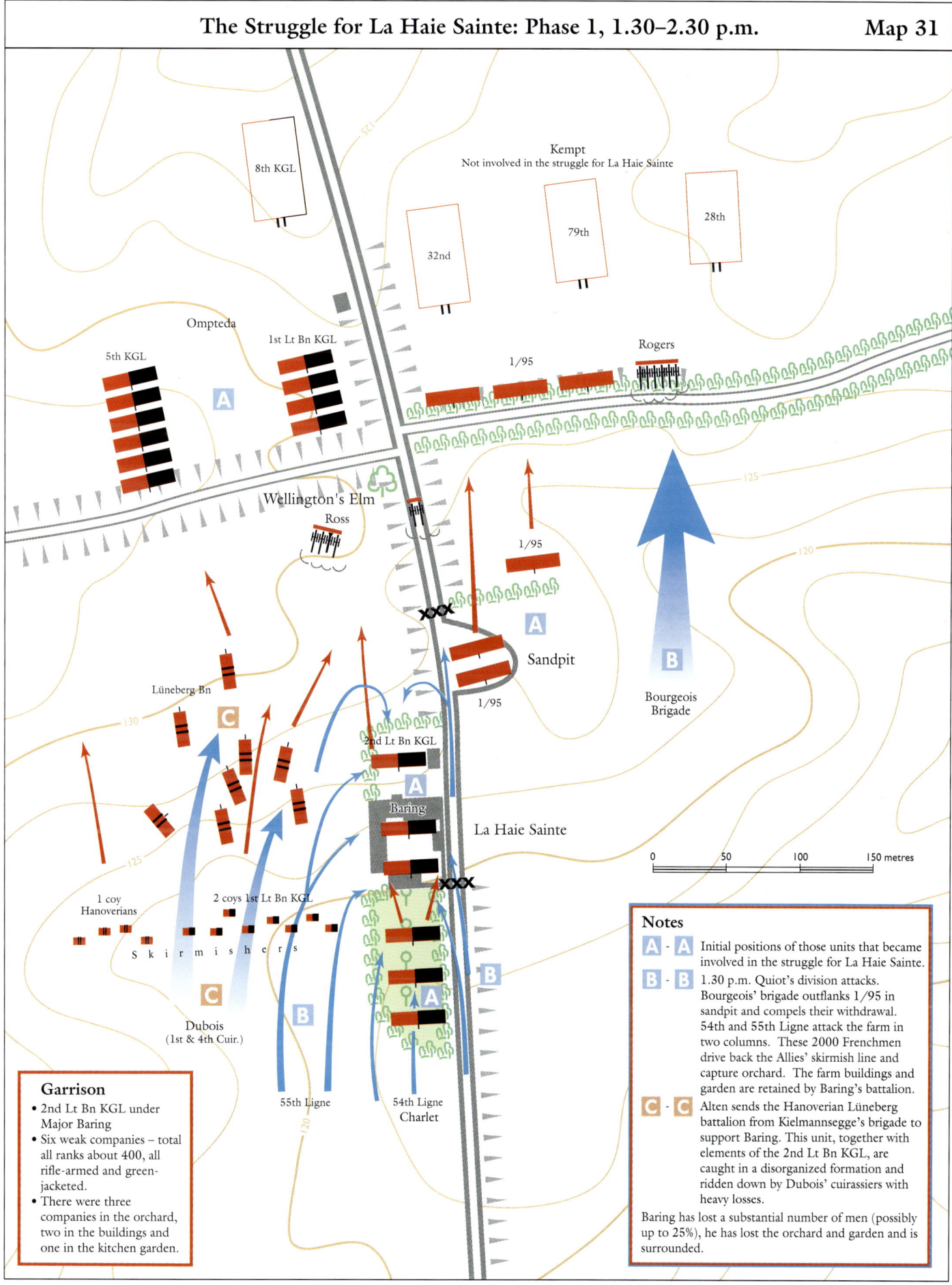

8th KGL

Kempt
Not involved in the struggle for La Haie Sainte

32nd

79th

28th

Ompteda

5th KGL

1st Lt Bn KGL

Rogers

1/95

A

Wellington's Elm
Ross

1/95

A

Sandpit

B

1/95

Bourgeois
Brigade

Lüneberg Bn

C

2nd Lt Bn KGL

Baring

A

La Haie Sainte

1 coy
Hanoverians

2 coys 1st Lt Bn KGL

S k i r m i s h e r s

C

A

B

Dubois
(1st & 4th Cuir.)

55th Ligne

54th Ligne
Charlet

B

0   50   100   150 metres

Notes

A - A Initial positions of those units that became involved in the struggle for La Haie Sainte.

B - B 1.30 p.m. Quiot's division attacks. Bourgeois' brigade outflanks 1/95 in sandpit and compels their withdrawal. 54th and 55th Ligne attack the farm in two columns. These 2000 Frenchmen drive back the Allies' skirmish line and capture orchard. The farm buildings and garden are retained by Baring's battalion.

C - C Alten sends the Hanoverian Lüneberg battalion from Kielmannsegge's brigade to support Baring. This unit, together with elements of the 2nd Lt Bn KGL, are caught in a disorganized formation and ridden down by Dubois' cuirassiers with heavy losses.

Baring has lost a substantial number of men (possibly up to 25%), he has lost the orchard and garden and is surrounded.

Garrison

• 2nd Lt Bn KGL under Major Baring

• Six weak companies – total all ranks about 400, all rifle-armed and green-jacketed.

• There were three companies in the orchard, two in the buildings and one in the kitchen garden.

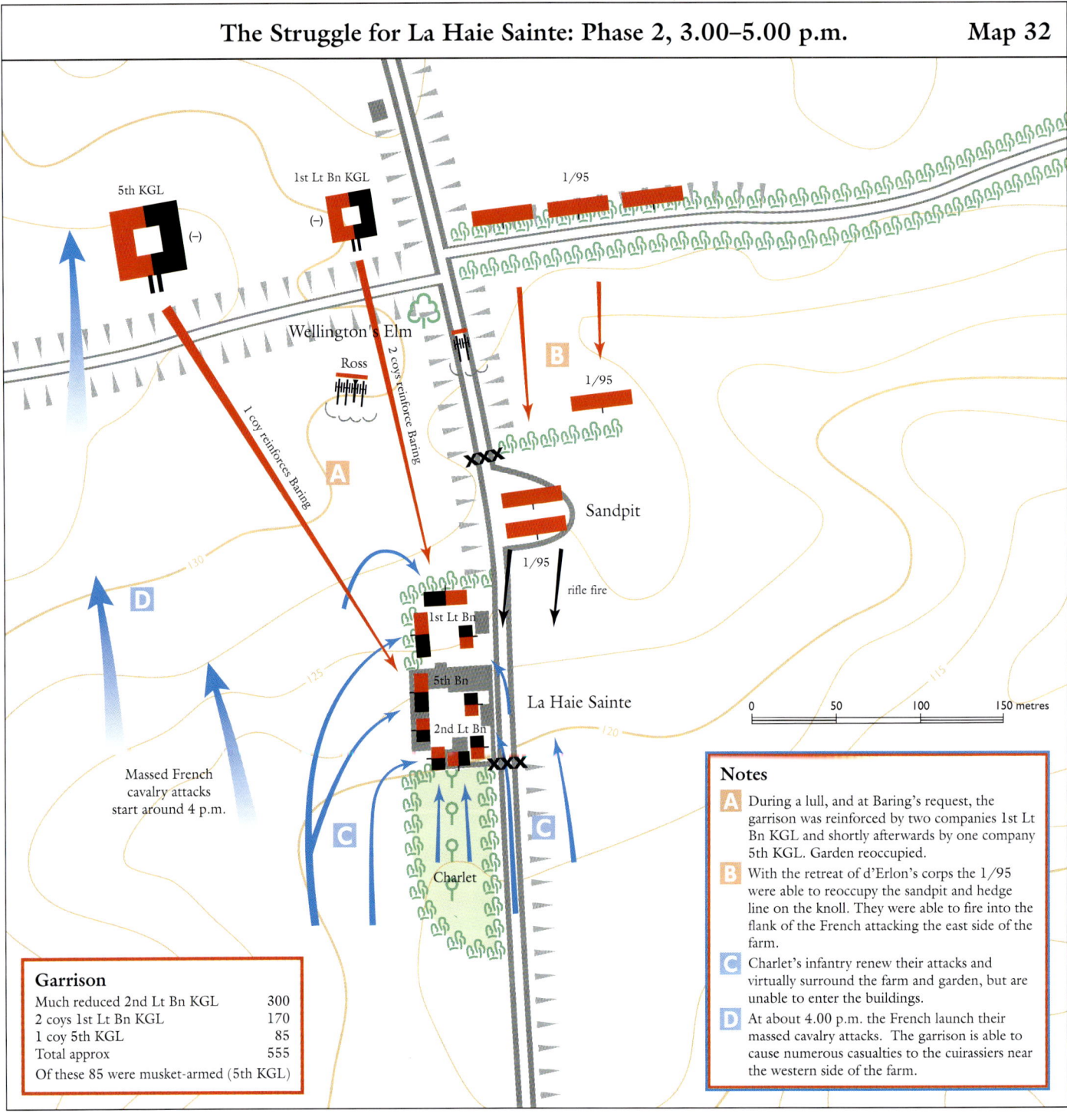

The Struggle for La Haie Sainte: Phase 2, 3.00–5.00 p.m.   Map 32

5th KGL

1st Lt Bn KGL

1/95

Wellington's Elm

Ross

1 coy reinforces Baring

2 coys reinforce Baring

A

B

1/95

Sandpit

1/95

rifle fire

D

1st Lt Bn

5th Bn

La Haie Sainte

2nd Lt Bn

Massed French
cavalry attacks
start around 4 p.m.

C

C

Charlet

0   50   100   150 metres

Notes

A During a lull, and at Baring's request, the garrison was reinforced by two companies 1st Lt Bn KGL and shortly afterwards by one company 5th KGL. Garden reoccupied.

B With the retreat of d'Erlon's corps the 1/95 were able to reoccupy the sandpit and hedge line on the knoll. They were able to fire into the flank of the French attacking the east side of the farm.

C Charlet's infantry renew their attacks and virtually surround the farm and garden, but are unable to enter the buildings.

D At about 4.00 p.m. the French launch their massed cavalry attacks. The garrison is able to cause numerous casualties to the cuirassiers near the western side of the farm.

Garrison

Much reduced 2nd Lt Bn KGL	300
2 coys 1st Lt Bn KGL	170
1 coy 5th KGL	85
Total approx	555
Of these 85 were musket-armed (5th KGL)	

against the walls, and endeavouring to wrest the arms from the hands of my men through the loopholes; many lives were sacrificed to the defence of the doors and gates; the most obstinate contest was carried on where the gate was wanting [the barn] … . On this spot seventeen Frenchmen already lay dead, and their bodies served as a protection to those who pressed after them…

Shortly after the arrival of the 1st Light Battalion companies the Light Company of the 5th Line Battalion, KGL was also hurried down to bolster the garrison. The company commander, Captain von Wurmb, never made it; he was killed by cannon fire en route. Interestingly, these were the first red-coated, musket-armed

troops to arrive. Prior to this, La Haie Sainte, the sandpit and knoll immediately on its east were exclusively defended by *les coquins verts* (the rascals in green) with rifles.

At around 4.00 p.m., while the attacks on the farm continued, Baring and his men saw the huge masses of French cavalry start their advance on Wellington's right and centre. Dubois' cuirassiers again rode past the western side of the farm, suffering severely as they did so from well-aimed fire from the defenders of the buildings and garden. By 5.00 p.m. the infantry assaults were at last slackening, then, as the cavalry finally accepted they could not break the infantry squares and stopped attacking, there was a brief respite for Baring and his much depleted garrison.

Looking south from the main Allies' position held by the 1/95 Rifles in the centre, on the horizon is the Victor Hugo Monument (column). The buildings immediately in front are La Belle Alliance. Note the knoll in the foreground, which was held by a company of the 1/95 behind a hedge. The sandpit was among the trees on the right, with La Haie Sainte just beyond.

Photo: the author

Looking back from the knoll to the main position (marked by the hedge), which was lined by three companies of the 1/95. Bourgeois' brigade and Donzelot's divisions suffered severely over this last 150 metres before they reached the ridge.

Photo: the author

Looking at La Haie Sainte from the knoll/sandpit area held by the 1/95 Rifles. It clearly shows how effective their flanking fire into the French attackers must have been.

Photo: the author

• 5.00 p.m.–6.00 p.m. This was the final phase of the defence. Baring was acutely short of rifle ammunition (see below and Section 10 'Myths and Controversies'). He was to receive no replenishment throughout the struggle, despite five separate and increasingly desperate appeals. Although ammunition was not forthcoming, more men were. About 150 men from the Light Company of the 1/2 Nassau Regiment arrived. They were green-jacketed but carried muskets, which meant that by this time Baring had only about half his force rifle-armed. Of almost equal value as the muskets were the Nassauers' large camp kettles. Shortly after their arrival the French succeeded in setting fire to the barn roof, but there was no means of carrying water from the pond to the blaze. Baring found the solution: 'I tore a kettle from the back of one of the men; several officers followed my example, and filling them with water, they carried them facing almost certain death, to the fire. The men did the same … and the fire was thus luckily extinguished.' The process had to be repeated later to put out a second fire.

The greatest pressure continued to be on the defenders of the open entrance to the barn. It was partially blocked with farm equipment and the bodies of the dead but, with ammunition dwindling, Baring was worried the unequal struggle to cross the threshold could not continue. Baring singled out one soldier fighting in the barn for special mention – a skirmisher named Frederick Lindau. Lindau had been in the barn virtually all afternoon. Earlier on he had the gall to rifle the pockets of a French officer killed at the entrance, his daring being rewarded with a bag of gold coins. He was wounded in the head twice but continued to fight, despite blood pouring down his face through a loose bandage. He stood well back from the open doorway, towards the rear of the barn, and calmly pumped shot

after shot through the doorway into the mob outside. Baring personally told him to withdraw to have his wounds better dressed but Lindau refused with the words, 'He would be a scoundrel that deserted you, so long as his head is on his shoulders'. Lindau was later unable to retire from the farm and was captured. He lived to tell his story but lost his gold.

• 6.00 p.m.–6.30 p.m. There was a final lull in the attacks before the shortage of ammunition, heavy casualties, utter exhaustion and renewed attacks by fresh troops combined to give the farm to the French. Baring sent off his fourth request for ammunition, having calculated that his men were down to three or four cartridges each. As his men attempted to block up holes in the walls made by artillery fire, Baring realized the next attack was likely to be the last as far as his defence was concerned: 'I was not capable of sustaining another attack in the present condition. All was in vain! [his last request for ammunition was unheeded] With what uneasiness did I now see two enemy columns again in march against us!'

The French had brought across Pégot's comparatively fresh brigade from Durutte's 4th Infantry Division on the eastern flank to support Ney's final assault on La Haie Sainte. It was spearheaded, however, by the three battalions of the famous 13th Légère under Colonel Gougeon from Donzelot's 2nd Infantry Division. The attackers succeeded in breaking down the outer door of the passage through the stables, but some wild fighting with butt and bayonet in the narrow confines pushed them back for a time. Yet another request for ammunition was sent off (the fifth). Frenchmen had climbed up onto the roof of the stables to calmly fire down into the yard at soldiers, for the most part, unable to reply. At last, after some five hours of failure, the

KGL Officers in La Haie Sainte

2nd Light Battalion
Majors – George Baring, A. Bosewiel
Captains – E. Holtzermann, W. Schaumann
Lieutenants – F. Kessler, C. Meyer, O. Lindam, B. Riefkugel, A. Tobin, T. Carey, E. Biedermann, G. Graeme, S. Earl, W. Timmann (Adjutant)
Ensigns – F. von Robertson, G. Frank, W. Smith, L. Baring
Surgeon – G. Heise
There were eighteen combatant officers with this 400 strong battalion giving an average of 2.5 officers per company. The company commanders were the two captains and the first four named (senior) lieutenants.

1st Light Battalion
Captains – von Gilsa, von Marschalck
Lieutenants – Kuntze
Ensign – Baumgarten
There were two officers with each company sent to the farm.

5th Line Battalion
Captains – von Wurmb
Lieutenants – Witte, Schlager
Ensigns – Walther
All four officers were with the one company, although Wurmb was killed before he reached the farm.

Lieutenant Graeme's Experiences

Graeme was an officer in the Hanoverian service and was serving with the 2nd Light Battalion, KGL at Waterloo. He was in La Haie Sainte throughout the struggle. At the start of the first French attack Graeme was posted at the barricade across the road by the orchard wall from which he was soon compelled to retire into the farm. After the first assault had been driven back he wrote:

A party of our men sallied out and pursued the crowd [of retreating French infantry] a considerable way up towards La Belle Alliance. None [of the French] passed through our abatis, as we afterwards returned, and I placed my men behind it as before.

The ground was literally covered with French killed and wounded … . The French wounded were calling out

'Vive l'Empereur!' and I saw a poor fellow lying with both his legs shattered, trying to destroy himself with his own sword, which I ordered my servant to take from him.

At this moment a curious circumstance occurred. … We perceived a single French Cuirassier riding down the *chausee* towards us. As he approached he waved with his sword, so that I said he must be a deserter, and would not allow my men to fire. He rode close up to the abatis, and raising himself in his stirrups as looking to see what was behind it, then wheeled round his horse and galloped back to the French position, and in the hurry I believe the gallant fellow luckily escaped our shots which were sent after him.

The rear view of La Haie Sainte as seen by countless French infantrymen. The small door on the right did not exist in 1815. The large black door into the barn was the one burnt the previous night. This entrance was open throughout the action and the scene of much vicious hand-to-hand fighting. At least 20 bodies partially blocked the entrance and approaches. The left door led into a passageway through the stables. As in the barn, there was much bayonet fighting in the passage once the door was beaten down around 6.00 p.m. Many Frenchmen climbed onto the stables' roof and fired down into the yard.

Photo: the author

La Haie Sainte is among the trees in the centre right (grey roof). The wire fence marks the boundary of the Orchard. Dubois' cuirassiers, the Household Brigade, Colonel Charlet's brigade and the 13th Légère all knew the shallow valley ahead. All this area was thick with the bodies of men and horses after the battle.

Photo: the author

The main gate and farmhouse from the Genappe road. This was the approach of the French engineers under Lieut Vieux who eventually broke down the gate with an axe.

Photo: the author

enemy charged through the open entrance into the barn. At about the same time the main gate fronting the Genappe road was smashed down by French engineers led by a Lieutenant Vieux wielding an axe – how similar to Legros' assault on the Hougoumont gate. Vieux died as a colonel in 1836 at the Siege of Constantine in Algeria.

Baring could delay the order he had dreaded all afternoon no longer: 'Inexpressibly painful as the decision was to me of giving up the place … I gave the order to retire through the house into the garden'.

As in the stables, the passageway through the house was the scene of some vicious fighting due to its narrowness restricting access to single file. The pursuing French were disinclined to be merciful. Baring states, 'The passage through the house being very narrow, many of the men were overtaken by the enemy, who vented their fury upon them in the lowest abuse, and the most brutal treatment.' Ensign Franks, probably the last officer to retire through the farmhouse, was lucky to survive (see box p. 378). The defenders spent only a few minutes in the garden before Baring realized that with the buildings in enemy hands it was untenable. He immediately authorized the remnants of his command to make their way back to the main position singly or in small groups. The French did little to hinder their escape, so the survivors of this gallant and memorable defence returned to their parent units.

Aspects of tactical significance

The factors that influenced the struggle for La Haie Sainte that gave it its importance or dictated the tactics are summarized below:

• Its location in front of the centre of Wellington's line gave the farm huge tactical importance to both attackers and defenders. For the French to gain possession meant they had secured a springboard from which to launch a final attack on the Duke's centre – their first battlefield objective. Their aim was to break through in the centre as the quickest route to the Mont St Jean crossroads and an open road to Brussels. If the French did not occupy La Haie Sainte, Wellington's centre was almost certainly safe. Unlike Hougoumont, whose possession was not critical to either side, La Haie Sainte was

vital to both. However, in Anglo-Allied hands it acted as a breakwater to every French advance splitting it, delaying it and damaging it with flanking fire. It was an outpost that could, and did, disrupt any attack on the Duke's centre. A garrison of 400 indicates that it is likely Wellington underestimated its importance, at least initially. And whoever ordered Baring's pioneers and tools to Hougoumont on the night of 17/18 June had not got his tactical thinking straight. Not until late in the afternoon was the relative tactical importance of these two obvious to all, evidenced by the switching of 150–200 men (2/1 Nassauers) from Hougoumont to La Haie Sainte. The bungled ammunition supply (discussed in Section 10) was another indication that the Anglo-Allied high command only belatedly appreciated the significance of this outpost.

• Tactically, the value of the farm was enhanced by the close proximity of the sandpit and knoll on its north-east flank. Three companies of the 1/95 Rifles manned these positions. At the start of the action troops in the sandpit were concealed from the approaching French columns by the high-standing crops. When the battle got underway the 95th had an excellent shot from the rising ground and knoll down the eastern side of the farm. With the longer range and better accuracy of the rifles they could inflict losses on enemy as far away as the road alongside the orchard. Similarly, Baring's men could fire on troops advancing on the sandpit or knoll. The positions mutually supported each other. The fact that the troops in all these positions were rifle-armed, at least at the outset, considerably increased their tactical effectiveness.

• Even with three companies (under 200 men of Baring's battalion) it quickly proved impossible to hold the orchard. The swarms of French skirmishers backed up by 2000 soldiers of the 54th and 55th Ligne surrounded not only the orchard but the entire farm. The perimeter of the orchard, discounting the side along the buildings, was some 300 metres long – too much to expect 200 men to defend against such superior numbers with only a hedge as a barrier. The kitchen garden was regained and held throughout the action after the first French assault had been repulsed. That it was not taken again was due to several factors. Firstly, it had more

Captain Whinyates' Rockets in Action

In a vain attempt to save La Haie Sainte Lieutenant Dansey, RHA of Whinyates' Troop advanced with two guns and some rockets directly towards the farm. Leaving the guns to the rear, Dansey proceeded along the Genappe road with the rockets. He later recounted what happened:

When I was detached from the Troop, I had two guns as well as rockets, and I went to the front along the high road to look for a place, or rather to form an opinion as to where it would be best to come into action, and I went near the abatis [northern one], and the fire of musketry was very hot, and I resolved

not to attempt to bring the Guns up. I went back and ordered the men to get their rockets and follow me on foot with them. Lieutenant Wright took a rocket under his arm, and we all went to the front to the abatis and stuck the rockets among the bushes of it. The moment we began firing I was wounded by a musket ball, and Lieutenant Wright had some buttons knocked off his jacket…

Looking south towards La Belle Alliance from approximately the position of the northernmost barricade across the road. Here Lieut Dansey's gunners stuck their rockets in the branches before firing. They had a good shoot.

Photo: the author

The Struggle for La Haie Sainte: The Farm is Taken by the French   Map 33

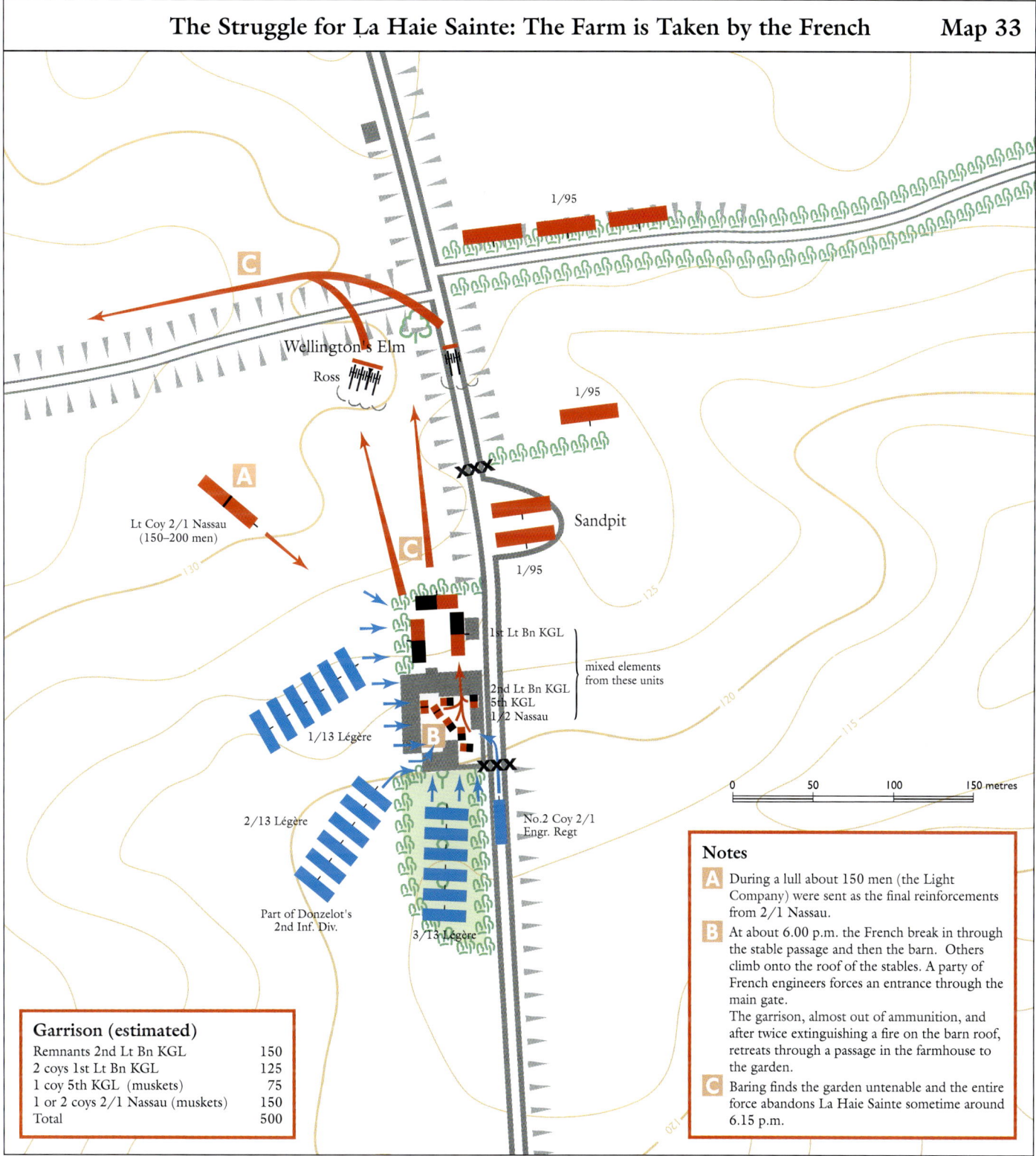

Wellington's Elm

Ross

1/95

1/95

C

A

Lt Coy 2/1 Nassau
(150–200 men)

C

Sandpit

1/95

1st Lt Bn KGL

mixed elements
from these units

2nd Lt Bn KGL
5th KGL
1/2 Nassau

1/13 Légère

B

2/13 Légère

No.2 Coy 2/1
Engr. Regt

Part of Donzelot's
2nd Inf. Div.

3/13 Légère

| 0 | 50 | 100 | 150 metres |

Notes

A During a lull about 150 men (the Light Company) were sent as the final reinforcements from 2/1 Nassau.

B At about 6.00 p.m. the French break in through the stable passage and then the barn. Others climb onto the roof of the stables. A party of French engineers forces an entrance through the main gate.
The garrison, almost out of ammunition, and after twice extinguishing a fire on the barn roof, retreats through a passage in the farmhouse to the garden.

C Baring finds the garden untenable and the entire force abandons La Haie Sainte sometime around 6.15 p.m.

Garrison (estimated)

Remnants 2nd Lt Bn KGL	150
2 coys 1st Lt Bn KGL	125
1 coy 5th KGL (muskets)	75
1 or 2 coys 2/1 Nassau (muskets)	150
Total	500

defenders than the orchard: initially there were well over 200, mostly from the 1st Light Battalion KGL that was substantially stronger than the 2nd. Secondly, they were defending a much smaller perimeter: only 100 metres of thick hedge and 40 metres of wall. Thirdly, these troops could count on fire support from the main position less than 200 metres away, and from the 1/95 Rifles in the sandpit. Finally, by the time the later French attacks had reached the garden their numbers and enthusiasm had been reduced and they were literally exposed to fire from all directions.

• Preparations for the defence of the buildings were dangerously hampered by two important factors, each equally serious. The burning of the barn door was an example of negligence or lack of supervision by officers or NCOs that is hard to understand, no matter how wet and miserable the soldiers. One wonders why the barn door and not the others? Farm carts that could have been used as barricades were also destroyed in the futile, but understandable, desire to keep warm and dry. The other error was the sending of the pioneers with their tools to Hougoumont. Some senior officer had neglected to tell

Baring he was to be responsible for defending the farm until the morning of 18 June, although with a little thought it must have seemed a highly likely task. Whoever made the decision to remove the pioneers from La Haie Sainte was deciding that the defence of Hougoumont had priority – a strange decision considering the farms' respective locations. Because Baring lacked both tools and timber, the loopholes were few and there were no platforms built behind the walls. Lieutenant Graeme makes the point:

> We had no loopholes excepting three great apertures, which we made with difficulty when we were told in the morning that we were to defend the farm. ... Later in the day the Enemy got possession of the one near the pond, and fired in upon us.

This meant that shooting over the walls was often not possible, and seriously restricted through them. Graeme and his men had to lie or kneel on the roof of the piggery in order to fire at enemy on the road or attacking the main gate.

• For the attacking French the problems were almost identical to those at Hougoumont, although on a smaller scale. There were the same walls and hedges to be climbed or broken through, the same wooden doors to be smashed open (interestingly in both cases this was achieved by an officer wielding an axe), and the same exposure to fire from soldiers behind cover who made difficult targets to hit.

Forces engaged

As at Hougoumont, the struggle for La Haie Sainte was an extremely one-sided affair, numerically speaking. Discounting casualties, at no time during the five hours of fighting did the garrison reach more than 800 all ranks. The actual fighting strength was always much less due to casualties and this situation is shown in the table below (p. 377). With the French, each assault numbered at least 2000, often more. They had the option, which they took up, of continuously reinforcing, replacing and relaunching their attacks with little or no diminution of numbers. An estimate of the forces engaged is given below.

Anglo-Allied

The initial garrison consisted of the 2nd Light Battalion, KGL a weak unit with barely 400 all ranks present. There were six rifle-armed companies, each about sixty-five strong. The defence of the orchard was given to three companies of just under 200 men. The buildings had two companies totalling 130 men, and the kitchen garden one company of about sixty-five.

This garrison was responsible for defending a total perimeter of almost 700 metres – about one man for every 1.75 metres. When the orchard was abandoned the perimeter was cut by half. Reinforcements were sent as the action progressed. They consisted of:
• Two companies of the 1st Light Battalion, KGL, each about eighty-five strong. They were rifle-armed and posted in the garden along with some men (probably a weak company) from Baring's battalion. At this stage the garden would have had around 220 defenders.

• The light company of the 5th Line Battalion, KGL, approximately another eighty-five all ranks. These soldiers wore red jackets and carried muskets.
• The Light Company 1/2 Nassau Regiment from Hougoumont – about 150 all ranks, again red-jacketed and musket-armed.

All the soldiers defending La Haie Sainte were Germans and all were light infantrymen (although not all wore green or used rifles). Of the 800 all ranks that fought there, 570 (71 per cent) were rifle-armed, and 230 (29 per cent) had red jackets and muskets. However, these statistics do not take account of casualties. It was not until after 5.00 p.m. that the 150 Nassauers arrived, by which time the number of active defenders had shrunk considerably. At this stage, as the ammunition shortage became acute, the number of rifle- and musket-armed troops must have been about equal.

Corporal Henry Muller, 1st Light Battalion, KGL

Muller was in one of the light companies that were sent to reinforce the garrison in La Haie Sainte. His company was posted in the kitchen garden. During one of the French advances Muller, who was one of the best shots in the battalion, sought permission to go to the end of the garden to pick off the French officers leading the attacking columns. Permission was given so he took two comrades (Sasse and Schlermann) along to keep him supplied with loaded rifles. His first shot brought a senior officer tumbling from his horse and his subsequent ones did further damage. Later another assault came in led by an officer on foot. Muller bowled him over and the advance petered out.

The French

It is impossible to be as precise with the number of attackers as with the defenders, since sources are not always clear as to which formations or units participated in each main assault. Regiments and battalions were regrouped, reinforced and replaced to keep up the pressure. We can be fairly certain, however, that the following formations and units participated:
• Colonel Charlet's 1st Brigade of Quiot's 1st Infantry Division. This formation, (of four battalions) of 2000 all ranks launched the first attack on the farm as part of d'Erlon's advance.
• Maréchal de Camp Baron Schmitz's 1st Brigade of Donzelot's 2nd Infantry Division. This was a powerful five-battalion formation of nearly 3000 all ranks, although by the time it became involved at La Haie Sainte it had suffered substantial losses. It was the three battalions of the 13th Légère that finally broke into the farm buildings shortly after 6.00 p.m.
• Maréchal de Camp Pégot's 1st Brigade of Durutte's 4th Infantry Division. Despite the pressure from the Prussians, this formation was brought across from the French right in the early evening to support the attacks on Wellington's centre. Pégot had about 2000 men in four battalions and it is possible he supported the final assault on La Haie Sainte.
• Other French units may have been involved. Certainly the 2nd Company, 2/1 Engineer Regiment smashed in the main gate.

It is not unreasonable to suggest that over the course of the five hour fight Ney committed up to 7000 men in some thirteen battalions, although it was not physically possible for more than four battalions (2000 men) to attack the buildings and garden at one time.

The table below gives an approximate comparison of the strength of the defenders and attackers of the farm over the period from the first attack to its fall. The numbers endeavour to take account of losses, which were heavy, particularly during the first assault. It will be seen that at no time did Baring have more than the equivalent of one battalion available and that he was always outnumbered by at least 4:1.

Approximate time	Anglo-Allied		French	
	Battalions	Men	Battalions	Men
1.30 p.m.–2.30 p.m.	1 (weak)	400	4	2000
3.00 p.m.–5.00 p.m.	1	500	4	2000
5.00 p.m.–6.00 p.m.	1	550	4	2000
6.00 p.m.	1 (weak)	450	4	2000

Special features

Command and control

Baring remained in command at the farm throughout. His immediate superior was his brigade commander, Colonel Ompteda, until he was killed. His divisional commander was Lieutenant-General Alten, who was wounded shortly after the farm fell. Similarly, his corps commander, the Prince of Orange was hit about the same time. It is not possible to know for certain who was giving the orders that effected the garrison. It is likely that Ompteda ordered forward the reinforcement companies from the battalions in his brigade, but he would not have had the authority to send the Nassau light company from Hougoumont. Nor would Alten. It was probably either the Prince of Orange or Wellington. The divisional commander intervened in support of La Haie Sainte twice, both times with unfortunate consequences. He sent forward the Lüneberg battalion, then, with the support of the Prince of Orange, the 5th Line battalion, KGL. Both counterattacks were chopped up by French cuirassiers. Baring made the decision to finally abandon the farm.

On the French side Ney had overall, on the spot, control of all the attacks on the Anglo-Allied centre, including La Haie Sainte. It was he that kept pushing d'Erlon's divisional commanders to renew the attacks. The only possible exception is the final assault that took the farm. There is some evidence to suggest that Napoleon insisted it must be taken at any cost. If so, it is probable that he authorized Ney's switching of Pégot's brigade from the right flank. Attacks were led by brigade, regiment and battalion commanders from the front. Ney himself was much in evidence urging on the troops or yelling at their commanders.

Death of Colonel Ompteda

The Prince of Orange had insisted that Ompteda obey his divisional commander (Alten) and send the 5th Line Battalion to counterattack in an effort to retake the farm. The battalion, with the colonel at its head, was ridden down by cuirassiers, much as the Lüneberg Battalion had a few hours earlier. Ompteda appears to have got well ahead of the battalion as he approached the enemy. Captain Berger of the 5th Line described what happened:

> I saw that the French had their muskets pointed at the colonel, but did not fire. The officers struck the men's barrels up with their swords. They seemed astonished at the extraordinary calm approach of the solitary horseman, whose white plume showed him to be an officer of high rank. He soon reached the enemy's line of infantry before the garden hedge. He jumped in [to the garden], and I clearly saw how his sword strokes smote the shakos off. The nearest French officer looked on in admiration without attempting to check the attack. When I looked round for my company I found I was alone. Turning my eyes again to the enemy, I saw Colonel Ompteda, in the midmost throng of the enemy infantry and cavalry, sink from his horse and vanish.

> The powder marks on his collar indicated that he had been shot through the neck at very close range. His ADC, Lieutenant von Brandis, recovered his body the next day. As for the 5th Line Battalion, KGL, Lieutenant Kincaid, the adjutant of the 1/95 Rifles, described their demise briefly but accurately, '… the cuirassiers broke in among them, and so complete was the surprise that they were annihilated almost without firing a shot'.

Ammunition resupply

The failure of ammunition supply was what forced Baring to abandon the farm. He requested it five times without success. As this is a controversial issue that merits detailed study, it is dealt with in Section 10 'Myths and Controversies'.

Casualties

A maximum of 800 men was sent to La Haie Sainte; between 400–450 came out at the final withdrawal. Baring states that when he assembled the remnants of his own battalion at the end of the battle he had forty-two effectives. However, the actual casualties of the 2nd Light battalion, KGL are recorded as 202 all ranks (Siborne). The difference is probably accounted for by the fact that his men withdrew from the farm singly or in small groups, becoming scattered on the main position and going in search of ammunition. When all those 'missing' or lightly wounded had reported, some the following day, there were considerably more than forty-two present. Nevertheless, 50 per cent casualties in a small battalion was crippling. Of the reinforcements that went in (400), between 200 and 250 came out unscathed. It is therefore estimated that the casualties suffered by the garrison during the defence of the farm were between 350–400 (probably nearer 400) or 43–50 per cent.

It is not possible to even guess at the French losses at La Haie Sainte, although they are likely to have been at least double that of Baring's.

Overall situation after La Haie Sainte was taken by the French

At 6.30 p.m. a second window of opportunity had opened up for the French, the first being when two divisions of d'Erlon's corps had reached the ridge east of the Genappe road over four hours earlier. Now Ney needed more infantry for a final push. He brought forward a horse battery to a position close to La Haie Sainte, from which it blasted the ridge with canister until sharpshooters in the 1/95 Rifles picked off the gunners. Although Pégot's brigade and other units attacked, they failed to break through. Ney sent his ADC, Colonel Heymes, to the Emperor for more troops. An exasperated Napoleon snapped, 'Troops! Where does he expect me to get them? Does he expect me to make them?' He was exaggerating somewhat, as at this time only the Young Guard had been committed to Plancenoit. Nevertheless, the struggle for that village was at its height; if he lost the village he lost the battle, so to give Ney his only reserve was a gamble Napoleon refused to take.

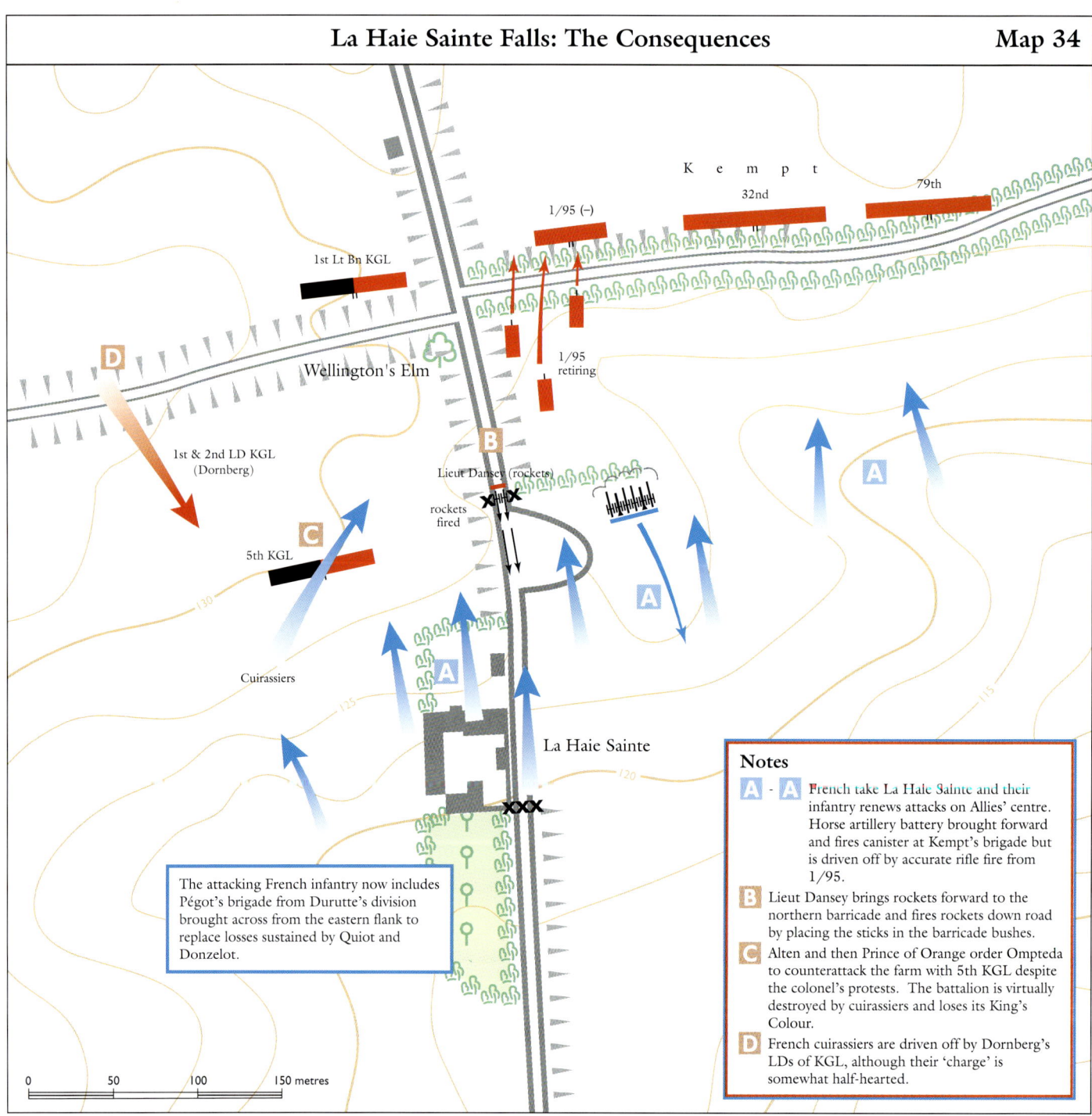

La Haie Sainte Falls: The Consequences   Map 34

K e m p t

79th

32nd

1/95 (-)

1st Lt Bn KGL

1/95
retiring

D

Wellington's Elm

1st & 2nd LD KGL
(Dornberg)

B

Lieut Dansey (rockets)

A

rockets
fired

C

5th KGL

A

Cuirassiers

A

La Haie Sainte

Notes

A - A French take La Haie Sainte and their
infantry renews attacks on Allies' centre.
Horse artillery battery brought forward
and fires canister at Kempt's brigade but
is driven off by accurate rifle fire from
1/95.

B Lieut Dansey brings rockets forward to the
northern barricade and fires rockets down road
by placing the sticks in the barricade bushes.

C Alten and then Prince of Orange order Ompteda
to counterattack the farm with 5th KGL despite
the colonel's protests. The battalion is virtually
destroyed by cuirassiers and loses its King's
Colour.

D French cuirassiers are driven off by Dornberg's
LDs of KGL, although their 'charge' is
somewhat half-hearted.

The attacking French infantry now includes
Pégot's brigade from Durutte's division
brought across from the eastern flank to
replace losses sustained by Quiot and
Donzelot.

0   50   100   150 metres

The Fighting in the Farmhouse

A few days after the battle Lieutenant Graeme wrote, left-handed
as he had been hit in the right arm, to his mother recounting the
last few desperate minutes of the scramble to get through the
house into the back garden.

We all had to pass through a narrow passage. We wanted to
halt the men and make one more charge [before
withdrawing], but it was impossible; the fellows were firing
down the passage. An Officer of our Company [Ensign
Franks] called to me 'Take care' … He [the Frenchman] was
about five yards off, and levelling his piece just at me, when
this Officer stabbed him in the mouth and out through his
neck; he fell immediately.

But now they flocked in … An Officer and four soldiers came in
first; the Officer got me by the collar, and said to his men, 'C'est ce
coquin.' Immediately the fellows had their bayonets down, and
made a dead stick [thrust] at me, which I parried off with my sword,
the Officer always running about and then coming to me again and
shaking my collar [probably wanting to take him prisoner], but they
all looked so frightened and pale as ashes, I thought, 'You shan't
keep me' and I bolted off through the lobby; they fired two shots
after me, and cried out 'Coquin', but did not follow me.

Franks, who had undoubtedly saved Graeme's life, hid upstairs
behind a bed. Although two wounded soldiers in the same room
were bayoneted, Franks remained undiscovered.

The struggle for Plancenoit (Maps 35, 36 & 37, below and pp. 384 & 385)

The tide has turned: the roar is dying fast.
Each lessening wave breaks shorter than the last;
And France, the life blood ebbing from her veins,
Feebly, yet furious still, for victory strains.

G.E. Scott

THE APPROACH TO PLANCENOIT

When the leading Prussian battalion of Colonel von Loebell's 18th Regiment cleared the western edge of the Bois de Paris it could be said to have arrived, at last, on the battlefield of Waterloo (called Belle Alliance in Prussian history books). It was about 4.30 p.m. The soldiers had been on the move for over twelve hours, covering the 20 kilometres from their sodden, miserable overnight halt south-east of Wavre at slightly over 1.5 kilometres an hour. They were men who had been marching for the best part of three days from their cantonments around Liège. These troops were part of General Count Bülow von Dennewitz's IV Corps which was spearheading the Prussian drive to link up with Wellington and roll up the French right wing by cutting off their escape. As it turned out, linking up with Wellington was easy, attacking Napoleon's flank was not – because it involved taking the village of Plancenoit.

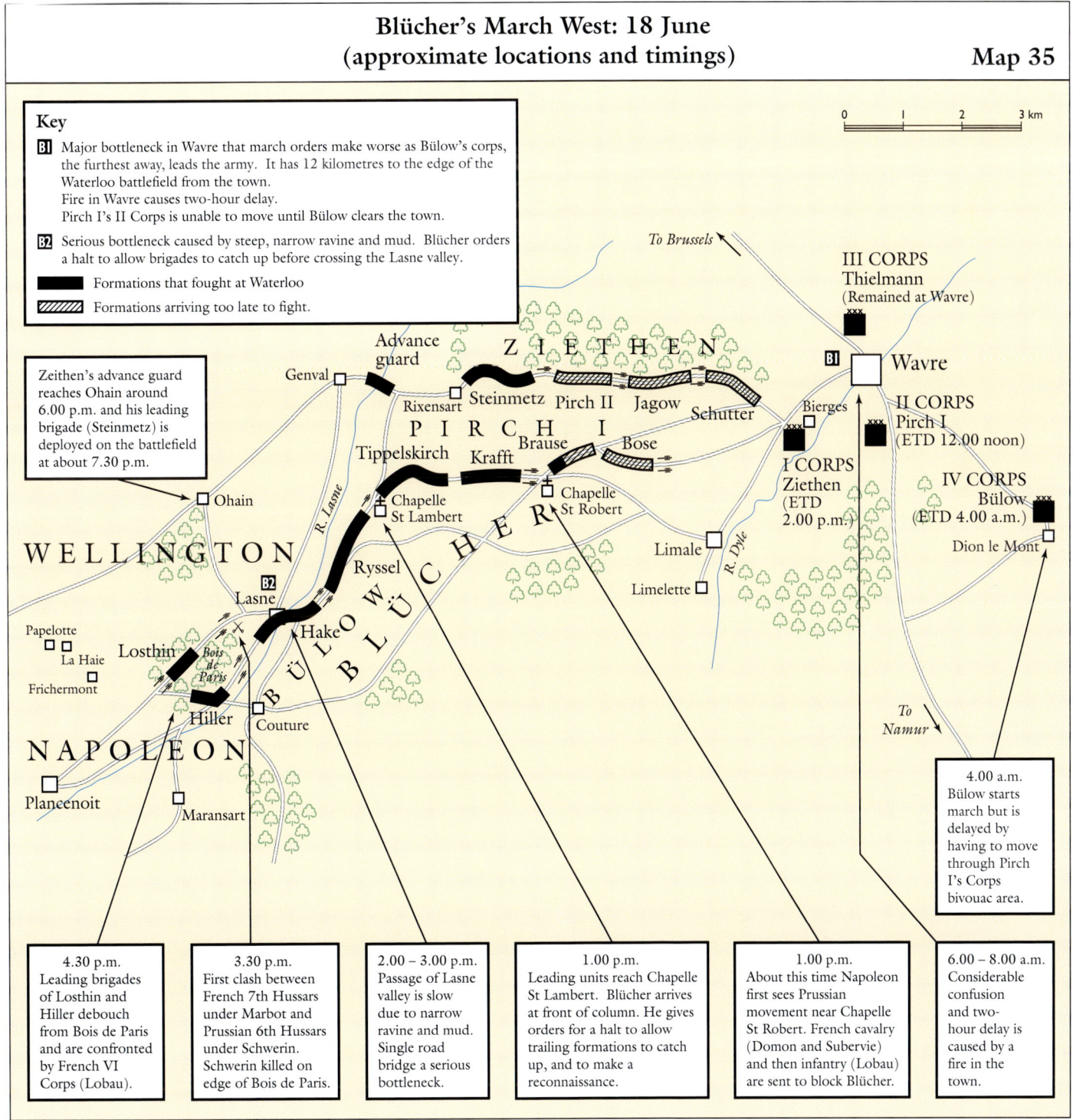

Blücher's March West: 18 June (approximate locations and timings)

Map 35

Key

B1 Major bottleneck in Wavre that march orders make worse as Bülow's corps, the furthest away, leads the army. It has 12 kilometres to the edge of the Waterloo battlefield from the town.
Fire in Wavre causes two-hour delay.
Pirch I's II Corps is unable to move until Bülow clears the town.

B2 Serious bottleneck caused by steep, narrow ravine and mud. Blücher orders a halt to allow brigades to catch up before crossing the Lasne valley.

▬ Formations that fought at Waterloo

▨ Formations arriving too late to fight.

Zeithen's advance guard reaches Ohain around 6.00 p.m. and his leading brigade (Steinmetz) is deployed on the battlefield at about 7.30 p.m.

4.00 a.m. Bülow starts march but is delayed by having to move through Pirch I's Corps bivouac area.

4.30 p.m. Leading brigades of Losthin and Hiller debouch from Bois de Paris and are confronted by French VI Corps (Lobau).

3.30 p.m. First clash between French 7th Hussars under Marbot and Prussian 6th Hussars under Schwerin. Schwerin killed on edge of Bois de Paris.

2.00 – 3.00 p.m. Passage of Lasne valley is slow due to narrow ravine and mud. Single road bridge a serious bottleneck.

1.00 p.m. Leading units reach Chapelle St Lambert. Blücher arrives at front of column. He gives orders for a halt to allow trailing formations to catch up, and to make a reconnaissance.

1.00 p.m. About this time Napoleon first sees Prussian movement near Chapelle St Robert. French cavalry (Domon and Subervie) and then infantry (Lobau) are sent to block Blücher.

6.00 – 8.00 a.m. Considerable confusion and two-hour delay is caused by a fire in the town.

A Prussian 12-pounder Battery's March to Waterloo

Captain von Reuter commanded the No.6 Battery of 12-pounders, part of I Corps' (Ziethen) artillery reserve. He had had a tough time at Ligny and lost a gun. His guns were again in action with the rearguard during the retreat to Wavre on 17 June. His battery followed the northern route to Waterloo via Ohain but he did not arrive until late when the French were in retreat. He also did not open fire. In his account he recalled the terrible state of the road, the urgency, the desperate efforts needed to keep moving. Although a foot battery, at the start he had his men mounted on the gun carriages. At best he was able to trot; more often he moved at a walk. As they slowly overtook infantry units on the road these troops made way for him. Reuter comments that the infantry seemed in good spirits with bands playing. They greeted his guns with cheers and shouts of 'Hurrah! Here come our gallant 12-pounders!'

Reuter remembered that he timed his arrival on the edge of the battlefield on a soft summer evening, saying that, 'at this moment the moon rose.' It was evident that a great victory had been won, but any sense of triumph was spoiled for Reuter by the plight of the wounded:

> The wounded, as we came rushing on, set up a dreadful crying, and holding up their hands entreated us, some in French and some in English, not to crush their already mangled bodies beneath our wheels. It was a terrible sight to see those faces with the mark of death upon them, rising from the ground and the arms outstretched towards us. Reluctant though I was, I felt compelled to halt, and then enjoined my men to advance with great care and circumspection. And soon I saw that I could in any case have no share in the glory of the day, for the enemy had begun to break and fly on all sides.

Reuter and his surgeon were to spend the night tending the wounded near where they halted – his compassion was the exception rather than the rule.

It was IV Corps that had been chosen for these key roles as it had missed the mauling at Ligny. Since early morning the 30,000 troops and eighty-six guns under their sixty-year-old general, who had been made Count of Dennewitz after defeating Ney at the place of that name two years previously, had been toiling along, or at the side of, a single track, often knee deep in mud. Blücher himself had been riding up front, cajoling and encouraging as the men heaved at the cannon wheels, leaned forward into the slopes or slithered in the mud. When Loebell's troops at the head of the infantry column had reached Chapelle St Lambert at around 1.00 p.m. the tail had not long left Wavre. At this stage the worst part of the march was still to come. The final 5 kilometres involved the plunge down into the narrow Lasne valley defile and a gruelling climb out before pushing on through the Bois de Paris. Luckily, neither the Lasne valley nor the Bois de Paris contained Frenchmen. This information had been passed to Bülow some two hours earlier by Prussian cavalry patrols, one of which had actually spoken to Captain Taylor of the British 10th Hussars who was on picquet duty on Wellington's eastern flank. From then on the Duke was aware that IV Corps was on its way – this was before a single musket had been fired in anger at Mont St Jean.

It was at St Lambert that Blücher had ordered a halt. Although confident that the French were not on the other side of the Lasne river, or even in the Bois de Paris, the back end of Bülow's corps had to be given a chance to catch up. The 18th Regiment sank gratefully to the ground. Even the hugely increased tempo of gunfire coming from the battlefield ahead that marked the start of the bombardment by the 'Grand Battery' did not force an immediate resumption of the march. During the next hour several important events took place, which had profound effects on the course of the battle of Waterloo:
• On the battlefield Napoleon's main assault by d'Erlon's corps, which was to seize the Mont St Jean crossroads and unblock the road to Brussels, failed. Had it succeeded, as it nearly did, the Prussians would have arrived too late to affect the issue.
• At about 1.00 p.m. Napoleon, scanning the hills to the east through his telescope, spotted movement. A score of staff officers swung their glasses to the spot. Most accounts claim he had seen the Prussians at Chapelle St Lambert, but from where he was on the hill by Rossomme this is unlikely. What the Emperor had seen was probably part of IV Corps crossing an open patch of ground at Chapelle St Robert. There was little speculation as to its identity, as it was impossible for it to be Grouchy. Napoleon gave orders for the 3rd and 5th Cavalry Divisions under Domon and Subervie respectively, both from Lobau's VI Corps, to move east to investigate.

Within fifteen minutes eight squadrons of lancers and twelve of châsseurs were trotting along the track that led east, then north-east, from La Belle Alliance. At almost the same time a patrol from Colonel Marbot's 7th Hussars brought in a captured Prussian hussar. He quickly confirmed the bad news – a Prussian corps was approaching. It was a serious threat that Napoleon could not ignore. A considerable force of infantry and guns was needed immediately on the extreme eastern flank. An ADC spurred up the road towards La Belle Alliance to set the whole of VI Corps on the move. Lobau began his march around 1.30 p.m. He followed his cavalry just as d'Erlon's divisions began their attack. The absence of this corps deprived Napoleon of all his infantry reserves (apart from the Imperial Guard) at the outset of the battle. It was, almost certainly, the most crucial single factor that prevented the French from snatching a victory at Waterloo.
• A conference was held at Chapelle St Lambert between Major-General von Muffling (Blücher's representative at Wellington's headquarters) who had ridden over from Mont St Jean with several staff officers, and Bülow and Prince Wilhelm (commander of the Cavalry Reserve). At this moment they were unsure of how Napoleon would attack, so a plan was devised for three possibilities. If the French attacked the Duke's right, the Prussians would march to join him via Ohain. If they attacked his centre and left, the Prussians would advance on the southern track (that ended in Plancenoit) to hit the enemy's right. If the French themselves turned east towards Chapelle St Lambert and the Prussians, then Wellington would advance to strike them in their exposed left flank. Muffling rode back to Wellington, and Bülow informed Blücher of the agreed options.

From 2.00 p.m., for an hour, Losthin's brigade struggled through the Lasne defile. Up ahead was Colonel Count von Schwerin's 1st Cavalry Brigade, minus Lieutenant-Colonel von Ledebur's 10th

Hussars who were on detached duties south of Wavre. Schwerin himself was close behind the leading squadrons of the 6th Hussars under Colonel von Eike. At around 3.30 p.m the first serious skirmish between the Prussians and the French occurred on the eastern fringes of the Bois de Paris. Marbot's 7th Hussars, probably reinforced by cavalry from Domon or Subervie, together with a battery of horse artillery, opened up on the Prussian horsemen. The unfortunate Schwerin probably became the first Prussian killed at Waterloo. He was hurriedly buried in a shallow grave. Two years later his remains were reburied beneath the monument that marks the spot today. The inscription, in German, reads: 'William, Count von Schwerin, knight and superior officer of the King, fallen in a foreign country for the Fatherland, during the victory of 18 June 1815'.

The French cavalry pulled back, abandoning the Bois de Paris to the Prussians. It was approaching 4.30 p.m. From the western edge of the wood it was possible to see in the distance, beyond the intervening French, that Wellington's line was seemingly being overwhelmed by masses of horsemen. The decision was taken to press on. There was no time to wait for the two rear brigades (the 13th and 14th) who were still negotiating the Lasne valley to catch up.

Some 1,200 metres to the south-west of the wood Lobau's VI Corps sat astride the road to Plancenoit. The infantry and guns had been waiting for nearly two hours (whether or not this was wasted time and Lobau would have been better to advance further east into the Bois de Paris or Lasne valley is discussed in Section 10 'Myths and Controversies'). It was a good defensive position. Protected by woods on either flank, the infantry divisions were deployed around a triangle of tracks, the northern arm of which led to Frichermont and Smohain. In the south was Simmer's 19th Infantry Division, to the north Jeanin's somewhat weaker 20th.

Cuttings on either side of the tracks provided excellent cover for men with muskets. Lobau had chosen the highest point on the road to Plancenoit. In front of the position the ground sloped down gently to where the Prussians would debouch from the Bois de Paris. It was open country with some standing crops. At the time it was occupied by the six regiments of cavalry from Domon's 3rd and Subervie's 5th Cavalry Divisions. Some twenty-eight artillery pieces had been brought forward. If any of the French infantry turned round they would see, poking up through the trees, just over a mile away, the spire of Plancenoit church. It was to become a marker for the Prussian advance and the scene of probably the bitterest fighting of the entire battle.

By around 4.30 p.m. Bülow's 15th Brigade (Losthin) had deployed north of the Plancenoit road. It was soon followed by the 16th Brigade (Hiller) to the south. Losthin sent two battalions towards Frichermont to protect the right flank of the advance and to link up with Wellington's left. Hiller did the same in the south, his two battalions heading down into the Lasne valley aiming to follow it through Virère Wood to the south of Plancenoit. For the next hour and a half the Prussians pushed resolutely south-east, with the French fighting hard not to give ground. Lobau could expect no help and, as his Emperor was fond of saying, 'God is on the side of the big battalions'. Bülow, however, was able to feed in more and more troops as they came up from the rear. By 5.30 p.m. his entire corps had cleared the Bois de Paris – 30,000 men – along with the Cavalry Reserve. By about 5.00 p.m. he had taken the high ground and the triangle of tracks on its summit. Now, for the first time, most of the Waterloo battlefield was visible and, of particular importance, the Prussians could see their main objective. In another hour they were in position to launch their first attack on the village.

The Bois de Paris. It was along this track that Bülow's IV Corps advanced to the eastern edge of the battlefield. Photo: the author

The approach to Plancenoit – from the Prussian viewpoint

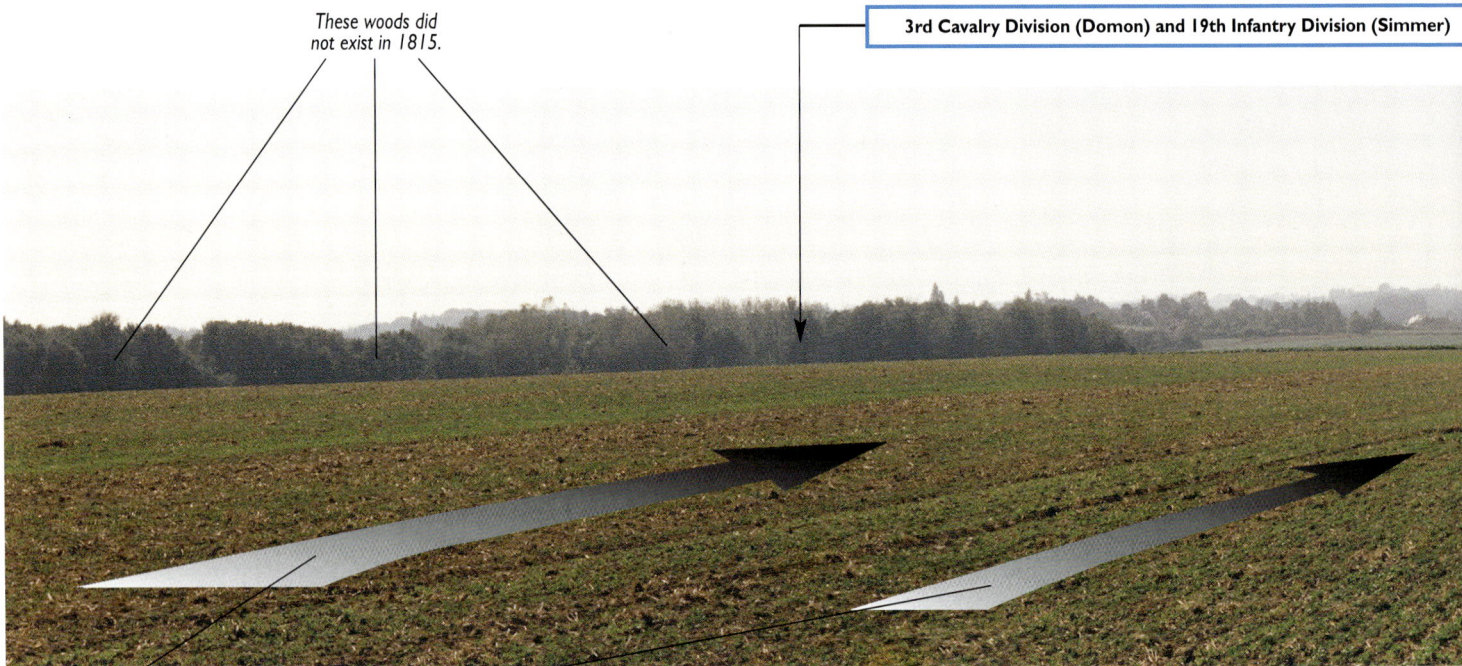

These woods did not exist in 1815.

3rd Cavalry Division (Domon) and 19th Infantry Division (Simmer)

16th Brigade (Hiller) advanced on the left of the road.

Brutality Inflicted on the Wounded of Both Sides

The fighting in Plancenoit was of a particularly merciless nature. The hatred between French and Prussian was intense. To be captured by either side, even if wounded, often meant an unpleasant death. Some French guardsmen had captured some Prussians from the 15th Regiment and Silesian Landwehr and had slit the throats of several when General Pelet arrived and furiously put a stop to it. The surviving prisoners were placed under the protection of bearded chậsseur sappers.

The British staff officer, Lieutenant Jackson, described the unfortunate fate of Frenchmen who fell into Prussian hands during the rout:

After passing La Belle Alliance some of our people became mingled with the Prussians, and the latter were firing in a very disorderly manner; I was also amongst them, and really thought myself in considerable danger of being shot. As to the unhappy Frenchmen who lay about wounded, they met with no mercy. I got clear of the Prussians as soon as I could, and was glad to find myself with a whole skin among the 52nd, which was one of the most forward regiments.

5th Cavalry Division (Subervie) and 20th Infantry Division (Jeanin)

This wood did not exist in 1815.

Joins here with image above

15th Brigade (Losthin) advanced on right of the ro

Plancenoit church spire

5th Cavalry Division (Subervie) and 20th Infantry Division (Jeanin)

Joins here with image below

Road from Lasne and the Bois de Paris – Prussian axis of advance.

15th Brigade (Losthin)

• Note the very open nature of the ground, suitable for infantry, cavalry and guns.

• The Prussians reached this area by about 5.00 p.m. with the church spire in Plancenoit clearly visible at a distance of about 1,400 metres. An hour later they launched their first attack on the village.

1st Cavalry Division (Jacquinot) in this area.

Lion Mound

La Haie Sainte

'Elm Tree' crossroads

THE FIGHT FOR THE VILLAGE

Shortly before 6.00 p.m. the first all-out assault on Plancenoit began. It was preceded by a heavy concentration of artillery fire by five or six batteries. The village itself was attacked by five battalions of Hiller's 16th Brigade while Losthin's 15th advanced to the north. Ten battalions, around 6,500 men, surged forward. Defending the houses, gardens and churchyard were nine weak battalions (under 4000) of Simmer's 19th Infantry Division. The six battalions of Jeanin's 20th Infantry Division lined the road running north from the village. It was much weaker than the 19th, with barely 3000 all ranks. Over half its strength was in the 10th Ligne, the largest regiment in the French Army. Among the regiment's 1,400 men were veterans who had, within the last two years, fought in Spain, Italy and with the Grande Armée at Lutzen, Bautzen, Leipzig and Hanau.

The attackers were resisted in every house, in every street, from behind every wall, and with particular determination by the defenders of the cemetery wall round the church. It turned into a strongpoint whose retention or capture became the focus of much of the fighting for the next two hours. Today it is the centre of an open square, but in 1815 it was not as large and a number of the houses were closer, so some attackers could get within a few metres of the cemetery walls under cover of buildings. The French had brought cannons and howitzers into the streets where close range blasts of canister would blow away opposition as a gale does autumn leaves. Despite this, in their first attack the Prussians succeeded in taking the church and much of the village. Weight of numbers slowly pushed the French back. Colonel Roussille, commanding the 5th Ligne (it was a battalion of his regiment that had first confronted, and then gone over to, Napoleon in the south of Grenoble three months earlier), was killed in the south of the village.

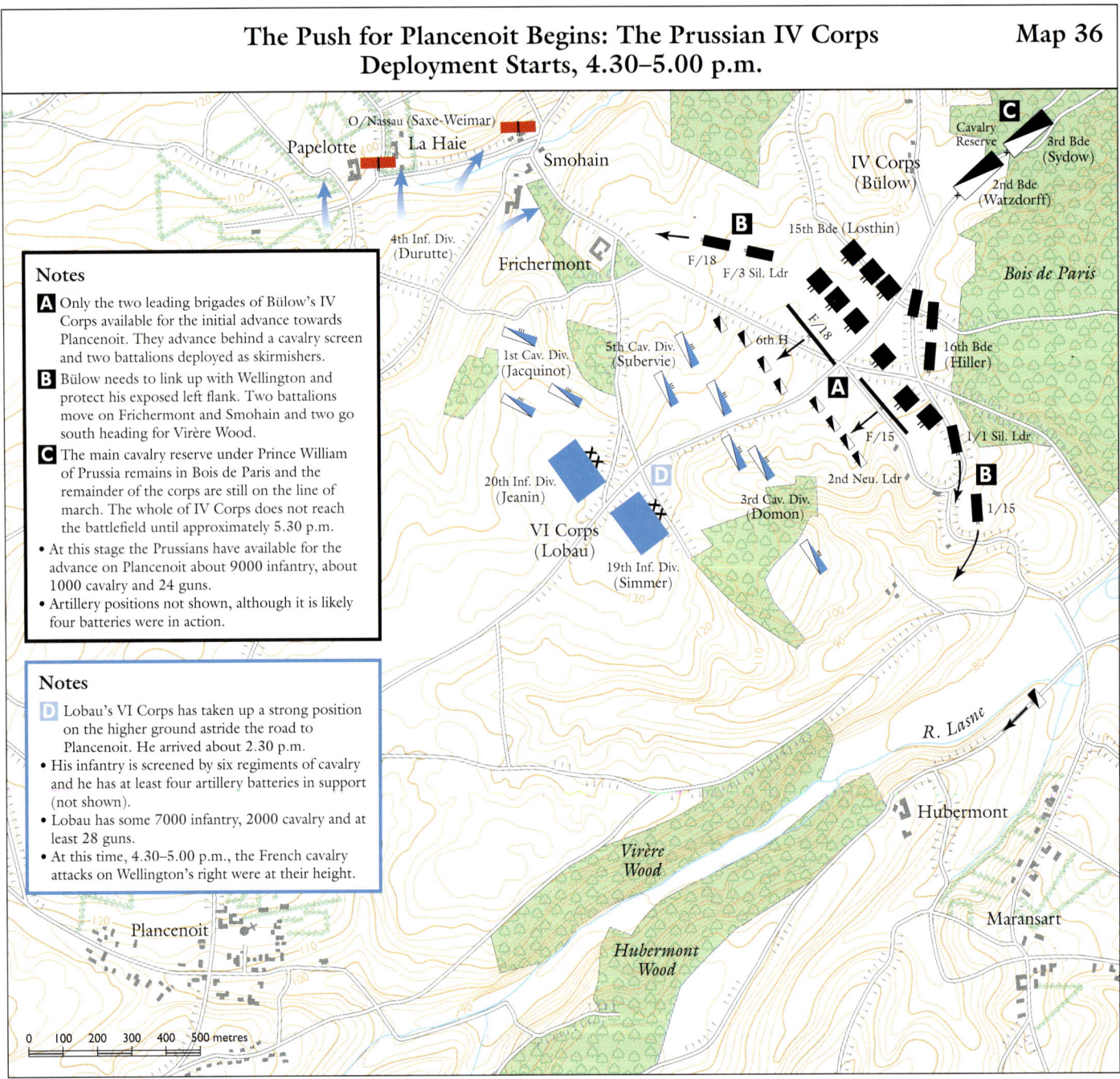

The Push for Plancenoit Begins: The Prussian IV Corps Deployment Starts, 4.30–5.00 p.m.   Map 36

Notes

A Only the two leading brigades of Bülow's IV Corps available for the initial advance towards Plancenoit. They advance behind a cavalry screen and two battalions deployed as skirmishers.

B Bülow needs to link up with Wellington and protect his exposed left flank. Two battalions move on Frichermont and Smohain and two go south heading for Virère Wood.

C The main cavalry reserve under Prince William of Prussia remains in Bois de Paris and the remainder of the corps are still on the line of march. The whole of IV Corps does not reach the battlefield until approximately 5.30 p.m.

• At this stage the Prussians have available for the advance on Plancenoit about 9000 infantry, about 1000 cavalry and 24 guns.

• Artillery positions not shown, although it is likely four batteries were in action.

Notes

D Lobau's VI Corps has taken up a strong position on the higher ground astride the road to Plancenoit. He arrived about 2.30 p.m.

• His infantry is screened by six regiments of cavalry and he has at least four artillery batteries in support (not shown).

• Lobau has some 7000 infantry, 2000 cavalry and at least 28 guns.

• At this time, 4.30–5.00 p.m., the French cavalry attacks on Wellington's right were at their height.

For nearly five hours the Imperial Guard infantry reserve had sat in the mud and crops on either side of the Genappe road. But by 6.00 p.m., with Prussian infantry in the streets of Plancenoit and their cannon shots striking the main road, Napoleon's rear had become frighteningly vulnerable. The Prussians had to be pushed back and the Imperial Guard were the only troops to do it. For the Emperor there would be no half measures. He ordered Duhesme, the incorrigible looter, the crude, brutal general who had been dismissed from his post in Spain for involvement in torture, to take the Young Guard into Plancenoit. He led eight battalions, some 4,750 men, mostly volunteers from Paris and Lyons. Within half an hour these young voltigeurs and tirailleurs had cleared the village. A plaque beside the main entrance to the church commemorates their courage against the odds.

Hiller regrouped and came on again, this time with the close support of the 1/11 and 1/1 Pomeranian Landwehr from Ryssel's

14th Brigade. He later had this to say of the attempt to retake the village:

Overcoming all difficulties and with heavy losses from canister and musketry, the troops of the 15th Infantry and 1st Silesian Landwehr penetrated to the high wall around the churchyard held by the French Young Guard. These two columns succeeded in capturing a howitzer, two cannon, several ammunition wagons and two staff officers along with several hundred men. The open square around the churchyard was surrounded by houses, from which the enemy could not be dislodged in spite of our brave attempt. A firefight continued at fifteen to thirty paces which ultimately decimated the Prussian battalions. Had I, at this moment, the support of only one fresh battalion at hand, this attack would indeed have been successful.

It was not until the 14th Brigade took over the assault just before 7.00 p.m. that the Prussians were able to wrest most of the village, including the churchyard, from the Young Guard. Ryssel had a strong brigade of seven battalions, five of which were 800 strong. These 5,500 men were comparatively fresh, well supported by Hiller's battalions and eager for the fight. They were enough to secure all but a few houses of Plancenoit by 7.15 p.m. Once again Napoleon was within a whisker of being surrounded, his line of retreat severed. Once again his only answer was the Imperial Guard.

But this time there were only two battalions of the Old Guard that could be spared. They were dispatched to retrieve a desperate situation piecemeal, with perhaps a ten or fifteen minute interval between battalions. With the Emperor's authority Général de Division Charles Morand, the commander of the Chasseurs à Pied of the Imperial Guard, sent the following order to Maréchal de Camp Jean Pelet:

Take your first battalion to Plancenoit where the Young Guard is being beaten. Support it and hold the position … Keep your troops together and well in hand. If you attack the enemy employ a single division [two platoons] with bayonets.

Pelet led the 1/2 Chasseurs of the Guard, under their commanding officer Major Coloban, down the approach road to the western edge of the village. They had over 800 metres to traverse; the situation was critical so it is tempting to assume most of it was done at the double.

As he neared the village a series of incidents brought home to Pelet the seriousness of the situation. First he rode past the wounded commander of the French in Plancenoit: Duhesme. He had been hit on the head by a musket ball and could only remain in the saddle by being held there by guardsmen in rotation. Duhesme was to die of his wound two days later in Genappe. Next he met Maréchal de Camp Chartrand, commander of the

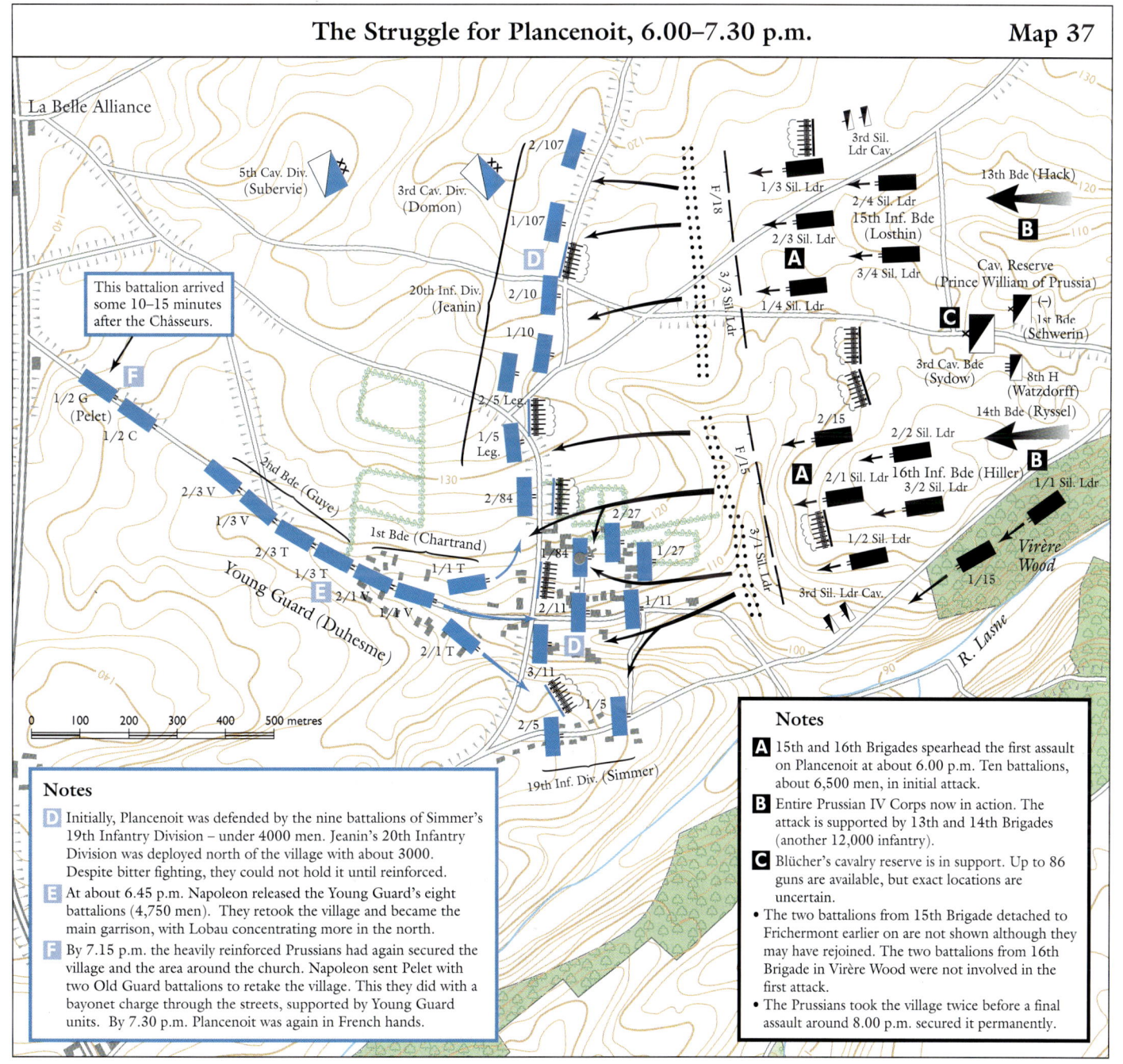

The Struggle for Plancenoit, 6.00–7.30 p.m.   **Map 37**

This battalion arrived some 10–15 minutes after the Chasseurs.

Notes

D Initially, Plancenoit was defended by the nine battalions of Simmer's 19th Infantry Division – under 4000 men. Jeanin's 20th Infantry Division was deployed north of the village with about 3000. Despite bitter fighting, they could not hold it until reinforced.

E At about 6.45 p.m. Napoleon released the Young Guard's eight battalions (4,750 men). They retook the village and became the main garrison, with Lobau concentrating more in the north.

F By 7.15 p.m. the heavily reinforced Prussians had again secured the village and the area around the church. Napoleon sent Pelet with two Old Guard battalions to retake the village. This they did with a bayonet charge through the streets, supported by Young Guard units. By 7.30 p.m. Plancenoit was again in French hands.

Notes

A 15th and 16th Brigades spearhead the first assault on Plancenoit at about 6.00 p.m. Ten battalions, about 6,500 men, in initial attack.

B Entire Prussian IV Corps now in action. The attack is supported by 13th and 14th Brigades (another 12,000 infantry).

C Blücher's cavalry reserve is in support. Up to 86 guns are available, but exact locations are uncertain.

• The two battalions from 15th Brigade detached to Frichermont earlier on are not shown although they may have rejoined. The two battalions from 16th Brigade in Virère Wood were not involved in the first attack.

• The Prussians took the village twice before a final assault around 8.00 p.m. secured it permanently.

The leading battalions of the 16th Brigade (Hiller) attacked up this slope at 6.00 p.m. The church remained their marker, their objective and for many their grave. Photo: the author

The road from Lasne and the Bois de Paris finally reaches the northern outskirts of Plancenoit. The Prussian memorial is in the centre of the trees where the road disappears. Photo: the author

The Prussian's Final Assault on Plancenoit, 8.00–8.30 p.m.   Map 38

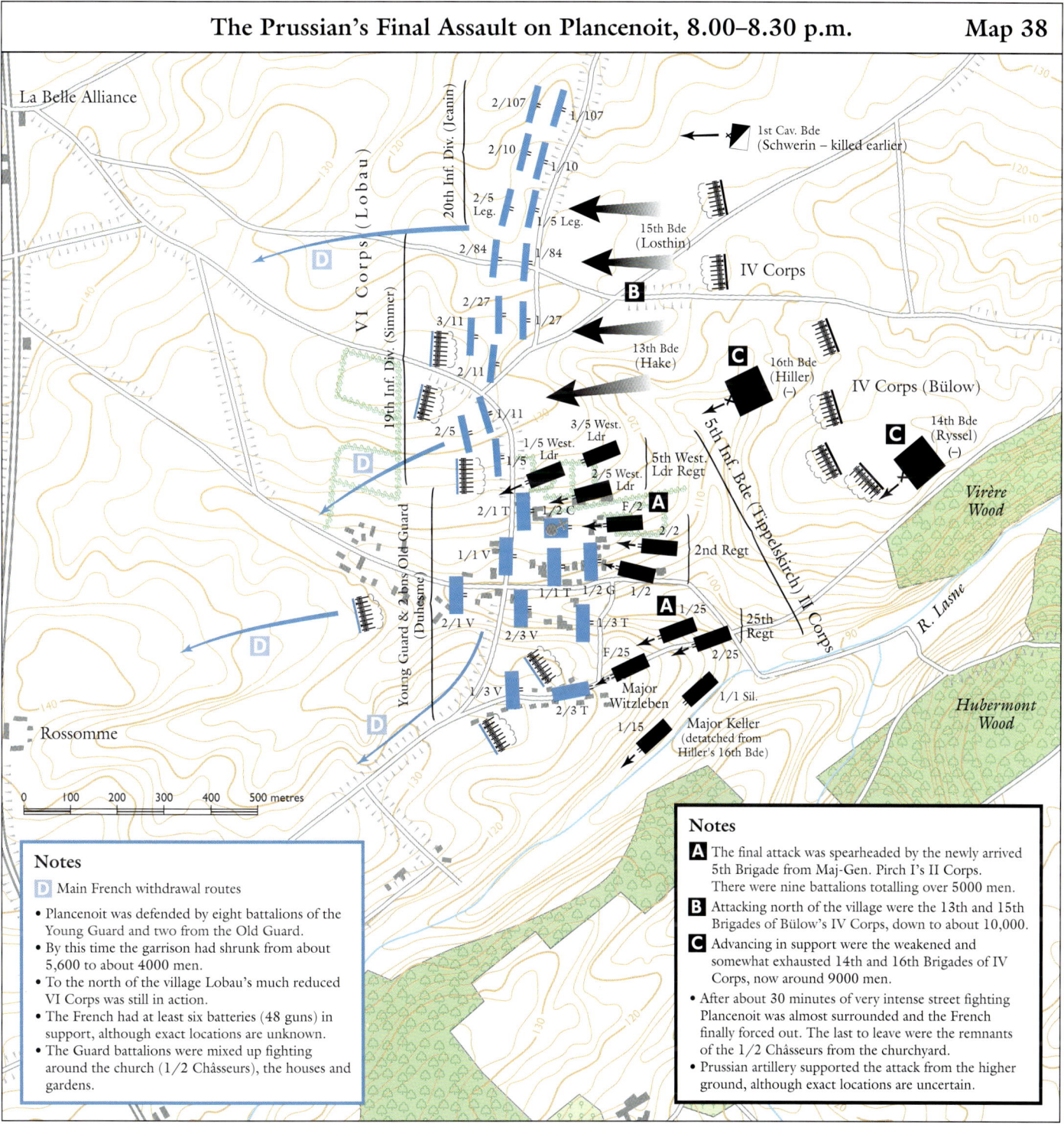

Notes

D Main French withdrawal routes

- Plancenoit was defended by eight battalions of the Young Guard and two from the Old Guard.
- By this time the garrison had shrunk from about 5,600 to about 4000 men.
- To the north of the village Lobau's much reduced VI Corps was still in action.
- The French had at least six batteries (48 guns) in support, although exact locations are unknown.
- The Guard battalions were mixed up fighting around the church (1/2 Châsseurs), the houses and gardens.

Notes

A The final attack was spearheaded by the newly arrived 5th Brigade from Maj-Gen. Pirch I's II Corps. There were nine battalions totalling over 5000 men.

B Attacking north of the village were the 13th and 15th Brigades of Bülow's IV Corps, down to about 10,000.

C Advancing in support were the weakened and somewhat exhausted 14th and 16th Brigades of IV Corps, now around 9000 men.

- After about 30 minutes of very intense street fighting Plancenoit was almost surrounded and the French finally forced out. The last to leave were the remnants of the 1/2 Châsseurs from the churchyard.
- Prussian artillery supported the attack from the higher ground, although exact locations are uncertain.

Young Guard's 1st Brigade. An agitated and breathless Chartrand claimed the situation virtually out of control, with the Prussians now in possession of the village. As if to verify this, a large mob of voltigeurs came running up the road in full flight. Behind them, fuming at his inability to stop their onslaught, was the commander of the 3rd Voltigeurs, Colonel Hurel. The arrival of the châsseurs was, however, enough to stop the rot. The leading company of the 1/2 Châsseurs under Captain Peschot sent forward a platoon to charge the Prussians advancing down the street. The second platoon supported them. As the momentum of the attack faltered, fresh companies were brought forward and the châsseurs succeeded in reaching the churchyard. The fighting was ferocious, at close range, with bayonet, butt and boot taking over from musket ball, as many soldiers had no time to reload after firing. Pelet, stripped to his shirt, was a prominent target on his mare Isabelle and could never understand how he remained untouched: 'I saw muskets aiming at me forty paces away. I can not imagine how they did not shoot me twenty times.'

Just as Pelet was starting to despair of being able to maintain his position and rally the voltigeurs and tirailleurs, the 1/2 Grenadiers à Pied arrived. Their rush forward with the bayonet (and Drum-Major Stubert clubbing his opponents with his mace) tipped the scales in favour of the French. Plancenoit once again belonged to Napoleon's army. They held it for nearly an hour. This was long enough for their

IV Corps' March to Waterloo

Hilaire Belloc, writing some seventy years ago in his immensely readable book *Six British Battles*, was a great admirer of Bülow's achievement in the first three days of the campaign. What he wrote is worth repeating.

Bülow, it must be remembered, commanded no less than 32,000 men. The fatigues and difficulties attendant upon the progress of such a body, most of it tied to one road, will easily be appreciated. …

The greater part of the Fourth Corps had spent the first night in the open; all of it had spent the second night on the drenched ground. Upon the third day, the Sunday of Waterloo, this force, though it lies furthest from the field of Waterloo of all the Prussian forces, is picked out to march first to the aid of Wellington, because it had had no fighting and is supposed to be 'fresh'. … It does not get through Wavre until something like eight o'clock, and the abominable conditions of the march may be guessed at from the fact that its centre [actually its head] did not reach St Lambert until one o'clock, nor did the last brigade pass through that spot until three o'clock [it was later]. Down the steep ravine of the Lasne and up on the westward side of it was so hard a business that … the brigades did not begin to debouch from the woods at the summit until after four o'clock. …

In about forty-eight hours, therefore, this magnificent piece of work had been accomplished. It was a total movement of over fifty miles for the average of the corps – certainly more than sixty for those who had marched furthest – broken only by two short nights, and those nights spent in the open, one under drenching rain. The whole thing was accomplished without appreciable loss of men, guns or baggage, and at the end of it these men put up a fight that was the chief factor in deciding Waterloo.

The Lasne defile, with the village church in the centre. The Prussians descended this slope, crossed the river (hidden by trees) at the bridge and continued to advance uphill into the wooded slope on the horizon on the left. Photo: the author

A view of Plancenoit from where the Imperial Guard rested in reserve alongside the Genappe road. The church spire is visible on the horizon on the right. Photo: the author

Emperor to make his final throw with what was left of his Guard. Only when this last desperate assault on Wellington's line recoiled in ruins did the resistance in Plancenoit crumble irretrievably.

By then the Prussians had launched the 5th Brigade of Pirch I's II Corps into the struggle. These additional nine battalions (5000 infantrymen) had began to arrive on the battlefield around 6.30 p.m. and had moved up to support Bülow. At shortly before 8.00 p.m. they led the attack that would take the shattered and burning village for the last time. It was a three-pronged assault. To the north of the church were the 5th Westphalian Landwehr under Major von Roebel; in the centre, striking for the church itself, was the 2nd Regiment under Major von Cardell; to the south, advancing along the road that topped the ridge overlooking the Lasne river, was Major von Helmenstreit's 25th Regiment. Gradually, reluctantly, the Imperial Guard gave way. Casualties had been horrendous. When the 1st Tirailleurs paraded again a week after Waterloo only 92 out of 1,100 were present, the majority having fallen at Plancenoit in and around the churchyard. North of the village Lobau's men began to join the rush to the rear, Prussians poured in from every direction, they all but cut off the village in the south, Wellington ordered a general advance. Nevertheless, Pelet and his châsseurs maintained discipline and fell back under heavy fire. He later wrote:

> … outside the village I found myself in a terrible confusion of men who ran for their lives while shouting, 'Stop! Stop! Halt! Halt!' Those who shouted most loudly ran the fastest. These noises were accompanied by cannon shots and musketry, which gave legs to the laziest.

As the victorious Prussians marched from the village towards La Belle Alliance, a band struck up Luther's famous hymn 'Now thank we all our God'.

The forces engaged

Except at the outset when the Prussians first cleared the Bois de Paris and deployed to begin their advance, when the numbers were almost equal, the French were always outnumbered by at best 2:1 and at worst 4:1. By the end of the day Bülow's entire corps of over 30,000 men and eighty-six guns plus Pirch I's leading brigade of another 5000 were available to take or surround Plancenoit. During the struggle for the village the Prussian infantry available (and it was entirely an infantry task to take it) rose from around 9000 to 31,000. During the same period from 4.30 p.m. to 8.00 p.m. the French could only reinforce their defenders from 7000 to 13,000. In terms of battalions, the Prussians made use of some forty-three, the French twenty-five, although theirs were invariably weaker units. As it was a close quarter fight in a built up area (the only one on the battlefield), the struggle absorbed troops as a sponge soaks up water. Being in such a confined area the Prussians could only use a comparatively small proportion of their units in the assault at any one time. This favoured the defenders, as did the ability to fire from behind walls or from inside houses. It was the Prussian ability to sustain the struggle with massive injections of manpower, to keep renewing the attacks with fresh units that proved irresistible – even for the Imperial Guard.

Casualties

Only infantry losses are considered in these comments. As with all casualties, particularly the French, it is only possible to make informed estimates. In total the advance to, and struggle for, Plancenoit probably cost around 11,000 casualties (killed and wounded). Of these, some 6,350 were Prussian and 4,500 French. With this type of fighting the defenders would not be

---

Order – Counter-order – Disorder: The Arrival of I Corps on the Battlefield

Due to confusion and some heated arguments between staff officers, the leading brigade of I Corps (Steinmetz) almost missed the end of the battle. As the advanced guard of the corps reached Ohain at around 6.00 p.m. the chief of staff, Lieutenant-Colonel von Reiche, rode forward to prepare the way for the corps to join the battle. He spoke to Muffling, Wellington's Prussian liaison officer who had been sent to the left flank to co-ordinate the arrival of the Prussians. Muffling briefed Reiche that his corps was urgently needed on the eastern flank, as the Anglo-Allied Army was struggling to hold on. Reiche undertook to speed up the arrival of the Prussians. He rode back and gave the necessary instructions to the advance guard. He then rode back to the battlefield where he repeatedly told Saxe-Weimar's hard-pressed Nassauers to hang on since reinforcements were about to arrive.

On returning to the advance guard to hurry them along he found that a Captain von Scharnhorst from Blücher's staff had arrived with orders for I Corps to turn south and reinforce IV Corps who were having problems regaining Plancenoit from the Young Guard. A heated exchange ensued between Reiche and Scharnhorst. Reiche later wrote:

> I pointed out to him that everything had been arranged with Muffling, that Wellington counted on our intervention close to him but von Scharnhorst did not want to listen to anything. He declared that such were Blücher's orders and that if I did not obey, I would be held responsible [as indeed he would]. Never had I found myself in a similar predicament in any

moment in my career. On one hand, our troops were in peril in the direction of Plancenoit; on the other, Wellington counted on our help. I was in despair at this dilemma. General Ziethen was nowhere to be found. Moreover, this was the moment at which the head of the column of I Corps had to know what it should do. It had even passed the point where it ought to turn off towards Blücher, when General Steinmetz, who commanded the advance guard of I Corps, seeing me conferring with the head of the column, charged at me, shouted at me, as was his custom, and without wanting to hear my explanation, ordered his advance guard to retrace their steps to the fork and to head towards Plancenoit. Fortunately, at that very moment General Ziethen appeared and after having listened to me, he corrected the march of his troops towards Wellington's left flank.

At the crucial moment of decision a desperately worried Muffling galloped up, having seen the Prussian troops turn away. His urging undoubtedly helped Ziethen make up his mind. It was the correct decision in the circumstances.

Steinmetz's leading units came into action sometime after 7.30 p.m. They advanced on Smohain and attacked southwards. Their arrival coincided with the Middle Guard's advance on Wellington's right centre. The French, who had been deliberately given the false news that it was Grouchy who had arrived, were quickly disillusioned. Their morale cracked, the Guard recoiled and the rout began.

expected to lose as much as the attackers. These estimates are based on the following:

Prussian

According to casualty returns, their losses at Waterloo were about 7000. Almost all of these (91 per cent) occurred in the advance to, and struggle for, Plancenoit. Of the infantry formations involved in these operations, the casualties were, in round figures:

5th Brigade (Tippelskirch)	350	(only involved in the last attack)
13th Brigade (Hack)	1,000	(14 per cent)
14th Brigade (Ryssel)	1,400	(24 per cent)
15th Brigade (Losthin)	1,800	(28 per cent)
16th Brigade (Hiller)	1,800	(29 per cent)
Total	6,350	

French

As with all French casualties, the only figures available are the strengths of the formations at the start of the battle and those for the musters held 23–26 June. The fight for Plancenoit involved Lobau's VI Corps, the Young Guard and two battalions of the Old Guard. The great majority of the battlefield losses of these formations occurred during the struggle for the village (or the withdrawal to it). About 4000 of Lobau's men mustered on 26 June, so his campaign losses amount to about 3000, or 43 per cent. Of these, it seems reasonable to assume some 2000 occurred around Plancenoit and its approaches.

The Young Guard was destroyed in Plancenoit. Their eight battalions went in at around 6.00 p.m., having been in reserve all day,

almost 4,300 strong. Only a tiny fraction, 598 (14 per cent), paraded on 26 June. The actual figures given for those attending their last muster were:

1st Voltigeurs: 196; 3rd Voltigeurs: 146; 1st Tirailleurs: 92; 3rd Tirailleurs: 164; **Total**: 598

Allowing for losses and 'desertions' during the week following the battle, a figure of 2,500 may be a little on the low side for Plancenoit casualties.

Based on these estimates the defence of Plancenoit cost the French about 4,500 killed and wounded. Add to these a proportion of the Prussian casualties, and the ruins of the village that evening must have resembled a giant slaughterhouse with perhaps 5000–6000 bodies of dead and dying lying in its streets, gardens, houses and, above all, in the churchyard and church itself.

The tactical significance of Plancenoit

The threat to and struggle for this village had a most profound effect on Napoleon's conduct and the eventual outcome of the battle. The Prussian advance/assault on this village was the single biggest factor that cost the French a victory at Waterloo. Of particular significance were:

• The absolute necessity for the Emperor to commit all of VI Corps, which was his first reserve, to the extreme eastern flank at the outset of the battle. His force available for attacking his main enemy was instantly reduced by over 10,000 men. This meant that for the main battle, which had yet to begin in earnest, Napoleon had less men than Wellington – and an attacker should outnumber a defender by 2:1, if not 3:1 to have a reasonable chance of success. The need to

A view from behind the churchyard wall in Plancenoit. This was the scene of the most bloody conflict. The wall is the original one behind which so many Frenchmen and Prussians sheltered, fought over and died alongside. Photo: the author

use so many troops in this way came as a total surprise and because it was unexpected it must have made for a worrying start to the battle.

• The position of Plancenoit behind Napoleon's right centre and less than 1000 metres from his main line of communication (the Genappe–Brussels road) made its possession of supreme importance to the French. If Plancenoit was lost, the battle was lost; if the battle was lost, so was the campaign and with it the Emperor's throne. Tactically the village was in a valley and overlooked by higher ground from all directions. This put the Prussians at a slight advantage that was increased by the fact that their axis of advance along the road from Lasne led straight to their objective. Once they pushed Lobau off his initial position on the high ground with the triangle of tracks, it was downhill all the way to Plancenoit.

• When the French finally took La Haie Sainte sometime between 6.15 p.m. and 6.30 p.m. it opened up a small window of opportunity on the Mont St Jean ridge. Ney saw it and demanded infantry to exploit it. They were not forthcoming, primarily because of the situation in Plancenoit. At this time the Prussians' first attack on the village was going in. Not only that, but Lobau's troops were getting the worst of it. Napoleon could not ignore what the loss of Plancenoit would mean, he could not delay, he was compelled to deal with this threat before anything else. It is clear that he realized the gravity of the situation since he sent not a regiment, not a brigade, but all eight battalions of the Young Guard to secure the village.

• Plancenoit changed hands twice before finally being lost by the French. Each time Napoleon only regained it by using up his last reserve – the Imperial Guard. He had started the day with an infantry reserve of thirty-six infantry battalions on the battlefield (Imperial Guard twenty-one, Lobau fifteen). Keeping Plancenoit cost him twenty-five of them. By the time he launched his last attack his reserves had been drained away by this thorn in his side. In the event only eight battalions of fresh troops were committed to the last attack on Wellington's ridge, of these only five were in the front line.

The Imperial Guard's final attack (Maps 39, 40, 41, 42 & 43, pp. 392, 396, 397 & 400)

> On came the whirlwind – like the last,
> But fiercest sweep of tempest blast –
> On came the whirlwind – steel-gleams broke
> Like lightening through the rolling smoke;
> The war was waked anew.

> Sir Walter Scott

Outline of events

For over six hours Napoleon had tried in vain to smash a hole in Wellington's centre. Twice he had come within a whisker of success: through d'Erlon's attack and the capture of La Haie Sainte. Now, with dusk and the Prussians closing in, one final throw of the dice remained – the Imperial Guard infantry, or rather what was left of it. The Emperor himself led them to the start line 500 metres south of La Haie Sainte and west of the Genappe road. The Guards' band marched up the road playing the same tunes that had signalled their presence on more than fifty battlefields across Europe and beyond. They had never known defeat. When they moved off Napoleon rode up the road as far as the orchard south of La Haie Sainte. There he handed over to Ney.

Eight battalions (the leading five from the Middle Guard, the other three from the Old Guard) were committed to the attack, five

in the first line and three in the second. A horse artillery battery under the personal control of the Old Guard Artillery commander, Lieutenant-Colonel Duchand, advanced with the first line. Duchand had divided his guns into four sections positioned between the squares. A Marshal of the Empire led the advance and there was an Imperial Guard's general for every battalion. The Emperor insisted a ninth battalion (the 2/3 Grenadiers under Major Belcourt) be posted as a reserve on rising ground about midway between Hougoumont and La Haie Sainte. Maréchal de Camp Petit, who had kissed his Emperor an emotional goodbye in the courtyard at Fontainebleau less than a year before, remained in command of the 'oldest of the old': the 1st and 2nd Battalions of Grenadiers. The former carried the Regiment's Eagle. They were posted, in square, on either side of the Genappe road south of La Belle Alliance, not far from Decoster's house. There an artillery battery together with the Guard Engineers and Marines joined them. By tradition these battalions were never committed except in the direst circumstances. Within an hour they were required. The 1/1 Châsseurs under Major Duuring were left out of battle entirely. Back at Le Caillou it was his duty to guard the Emperor's baggage and treasury. Two battalions of the Old Guard and all eight of the Young Guard were in Plancenoit.

All the battalions formed up in squares, advanced in squares and attacked in squares, as they had no wish to be caught on the move by cavalry. Whether or not they were open or closed squares is uncertain. The argument as to whether the Guard advanced in columns rather than squares and then attempted to deploy into line on the ridge is discussed in Section 10 'Myths and Controversies'. There were no skirmishers deployed from these battalions. Senior officers rode or walked ahead. Each battalion's drummers were in the centre. The painting of the 2/3 Châsseurs by Jean Auge as they begin their long haul up the slope to the crest, behind which Maitland's Guards are lying down, is an excellent example of an open square. Each battalion averaged 600 men, so each side would contain around 150 in three ranks. The frontage would have been about 35 metres with an open square. They moved off in echelon from the right, the 1/3 and 4th Grenadiers leading with Ney, Friant and several ADCs riding in front. The Guard marched with shouldered muskets, bayonets fixed, officers with drawn swords and drummers beating the *pas de charge*.

The advance began at around 7.30 p.m. Within twenty minutes it was all over. It was not, however, purely an Imperial Guard effort as is the impression given by some writers. ADCs had been sent galloping to d'Erlon and Reille. Their divisions were to cooperate and march back again over the familiar valley to their front. Donzelot's men would advance on the immediate right of the Guard, west of the Genappe road. Général de Division Dejean and Maréchal de Camp de la Bédoyère, who had brought over the 7th Ligne to Napoleon at Grenoble, were sent down the divisions to tell them that the renewed heavy firing on the eastern flank signalled the arrival of Grouchy. The Emperor knew full well it did no such thing; it was done to boost morale at a critical moment. It had the desired results – temporarily. In effect this attack was as near a general advance, spearheaded by the Guard, that the French achieved at Waterloo. Some cuirassiers and a hotchpotch of Guard cavalry moved forward in support, but the main supporting arm was the artillery. It is uncertain precisely which batteries advanced, but the Guard Horse Artillery was among them. As always in this battle, it was the guns that did the most damage. Again and again

Napoleon's Final Fling: The Imperial Guard Advances, around 7.30 p.m.   Map 39

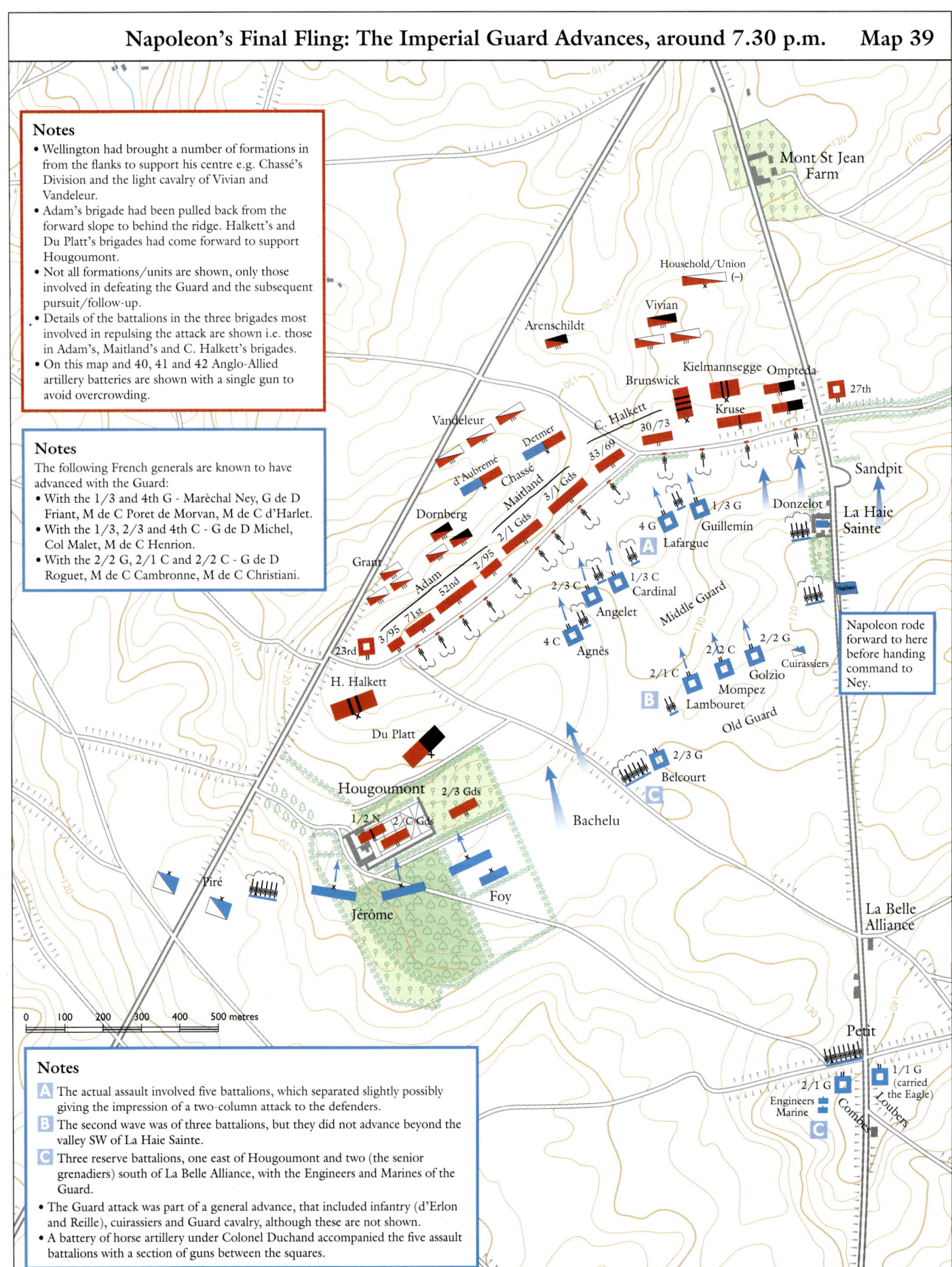

Notes

- Wellington had brought a number of formations in from the flanks to support his centre e.g. Chassé's Division and the light cavalry of Vivian and Vandeleur.
- Adam's brigade had been pulled back from the forward slope to behind the ridge. Halkett's and Du Platt's brigades had come forward to support Hougoumont.
- Not all formations/units are shown, only those involved in defeating the Guard and the subsequent pursuit/follow-up.
- Details of the battalions in the three brigades most involved in repulsing the attack are shown i.e. those in Adam's, Maitland's and C. Halkett's brigades.
- On this map and 40, 41 and 42 Anglo-Allied artillery batteries are shown with a single gun to avoid overcrowding.

Notes

The following French generals are known to have advanced with the Guard:
- With the 1/3 and 4th G - Marèchal Ney, G de D Friant, M de C Poret de Morvan, M de C d'Harlet.
- With the 1/3, 2/3 and 4th C - G de D Michel, Col Malet, M de C Henrion.
- With the 2/2 G, 2/1 C and 2/2 C - G de D Roguet, M de C Cambronne, M de C Christiani.

Napoleon rode forward to here before handing command to Ney.

Notes

A The actual assault involved five battalions, which separated slightly possibly giving the impression of a two-column attack to the defenders.

B The second wave was of three battalions, but they did not advance beyond the valley SW of La Haie Sainte.

C Three reserve battalions, one east of Hougoumont and two (the senior grenadiers) south of La Belle Alliance, with the Engineers and Marines of the Guard.

- The Guard attack was part of a general advance, that included infantry (d'Erlon and Reille), cuirassiers and Guard cavalry, although these are not shown.
- A battery of horse artillery under Colonel Duchand accompanied the five assault battalions with a section of guns between the squares.

one reads of Anglo-Allied units suffering acutely from round shot, shells and canister. The Imperial Guard was nobly supported by its gunners. In particular, the battery under Duchand was handled with superb courage and audacity, coming into action within less than 100 metres of the ridge and causing great execution among Colin Halkett's brigade.

Along the ridge Wellington was moving his reserves, bringing formations in from the flanks, although whether this was directly due to the arrival of a defector to Adam's brigade is uncertain. Less than half an hour before the Imperial Guard advanced, a colonel of cuirassiers, who had already twice charged the Anglo-Allied line, trotted up the slope towards Colbourne's 52nd Foot yelling '*Vive le Roi! Vive le Roi!*' He rode up to Colbourne saying words to the effect, 'That scoundrel Napoleon is with his Guard over there. He will be upon you shortly.' Many years later this officer, an ardent royalist, visited the battlefield and told the then ex-Sergeant-Major Cotton, who was a battlefield guide, that he delayed desertion as he had wanted to bring over some of his men. Wellington rode down the line, the centre and right of which had been strengthened by the arrival of Vivian's and Vandeleur's brigades of light cavalry plus Chassé's Netherlands Division of twelve battalions – 7000 men, of whom over half were militia. Wellington was pulling in formations that had so far been sheltered from the action. Chassé ('General Bayonet') was dependable but his men were young and untested, with the loyalty of the Belgian battalions particularly suspect. Until mid-afternoon they had been posted at Braine l'Alleud, well out of danger.

By this time the Duke's batteries along this sector of the ridge had suffered severely. They had lost men and horses while numerous guns were disabled. The surviving detachments verged on collapse from exhaustion. Many had been firing and loading, humping and heaving with little respite for at least six hours. After the loss of La Haie Sainte Captain Mercer described what happened when a French battery unlimbered on higher ground only 400 metres from his left flank:

> The rapidity and precision of this fire were quite appalling. Every shot almost took effect and I certainly expected we should all be annihilated. Our horses and limbers, being a little retired down the [reverse] slope, had hitherto been somewhat under cover from the direct fire in front; but this plunged right amongst them, knocking them down by pairs, and creating horrible confusion. … The whole livelong day had cost us nothing like this. Our gunners too … were so exhausted that they were unable to run the guns up after firing … they [the guns] soon came together in a confused heap, the trails crossing each other … I sighed for my poor troop – it was already but a wreck.

Both Kuhlmann and Cleeves's batteries, in the centre of the position, were short of ammunition and were in the process of replenishing as the Guard came forward. This partly explains Ensign Macready's (30th Foot) bitter comment: 'To my thinking, no body of the French army could have passed over our front so little molested as the Imperial Guard. When they passed where were the well-served batteries that had thundered on … The soldiers of Lloyd, Cleeves … In both cases all silent.' Although the gunfire brought to bear on the Guard was less intense than earlier, Macready exaggerated somewhat. He seems unaware of the excellent shooting of Krahmer's Belgian battery that had been rushed

forward by Chassé to take position on the right of Lloyd. Despite Macready's complaints, despite their losses and fatigue, it was cannon fire that caused the squares advancing on Maitland's part of the line to, 'bend under the stroke like corn smitten by the wind'.

Ten minutes steady marching brought the two Grenadier battalions to within easy musket range of Colin Halkett's brigade that had just changed formation from square into a four deep line. On their right Donzelot's leading units began to push up the slope against the visibly shaky Brunswickers and, to the Brunswickers' left, Kruse's Nassauers. Wellington personally steadied the Brunswickers and Kruse was able to halt, indeed drive back, the attacking French. The 1st and 2nd Battalions advanced in column to follow up but, as Kruse's own account states, '… perhaps because the Crown Prince was wounded [this would not have been known to the majority of the men] a wave of panic hit the young soldiers and at the moment of their greatest victory, the battalion [2nd] fell into confusion and retreated.' It was rallied back behind the ridge.

As the 1/3 and 4th Grenadiers came up the final few metres of the slope they were confronted by the seriously depleted battalions of the 30th, 73rd, 33rd and 69th Foot. They had lost men at Quatre-Bras and had combined to make two squares to face the previous cavalry assaults. The Grenadiers' approach impressed young Ensign Macready in the light company of the 30th:

> Our Colours were ordered to the rear [the 69th had lost one at Quatre Bras and the 33rd nearly so] … Our square was ordered to open out from its rear face, and wheel up right and left into line four deep … when a column [square] of the Imperial Guard … came over our ridge in splendid order. As they rose step by step before us, with their red epaulettes and cross belts put on over their blue greatcoats, and topped by their high, hairy caps, and keeping time, and their officers looking to their alignment … I certainly thought we were in for very slashing work.

Lieutenant Rogers of the same regiment remembered how, 'The square now formed a line four deep – almost at the same moment we saw the hairy caps over the rise of ground. It was a column of the Imperial Guard'.

Before the Grenadiers reached the ridge Maréchal Ney had been forced to walk when his fifth horse collapsed beneath him, while Général de Division Friant was hit and forced to leave the field – convinced the Guard were about to secure a resounding victory. A mixture of men from Yorkshire, Lincolnshire, Cambridgeshire and the Scottish Highlands faced French Grenadiers of the Guard at 40 metres. According to Macready, the brigade commander (Colin Halkett) shouted for silence and instructed one volley on the order, followed by port arms. He later wrote:

> They [the Guard] halted and fired – I think badly. We returned the volley – ported – and, giving a hurrah! came to the charge. Our surprise was inexpressible when through the clearing smoke we saw the backs of the Imperials flying in a mass. We stared at each other as if mistrusting our eyesight. Some guns from the rear of our right [Krahmer] poured in grape [canister] among them, and the slaughter was dreadful. Nowhere did I see carcasses so heaped upon each other. I never could account for their flight…

Modern view of the Anglo-Allied ridge from the perspective of the Imperial Guard's advance

2/1 Guards

3/1 Guards

Joins here with image below

2/3 Châsseurs

2/95 Rifles

Flank attack by 52nd Foot

4th Châsseurs

Notes

- From this viewpoint the steepness of the slope becomes very apparent. It was sufficient to slow both infantrymen, horsemen and guns, particularly when the ground was covered in wet wheat.
- The crest was lined by the Allies' gun batteries, all of which had a good shot. However, most, if not all, Wellington's infantry were invisible to the French and vice versa.

Ensign William Leeke Awaits the Guard's Advance

Leeke was the most junior officer of his battalion at Waterloo and as such had the duty of carrying the Regimental Colour. He left the army in 1824, went to Cambridge and was ordained as a priest. He survived the battle by sixty-four years.

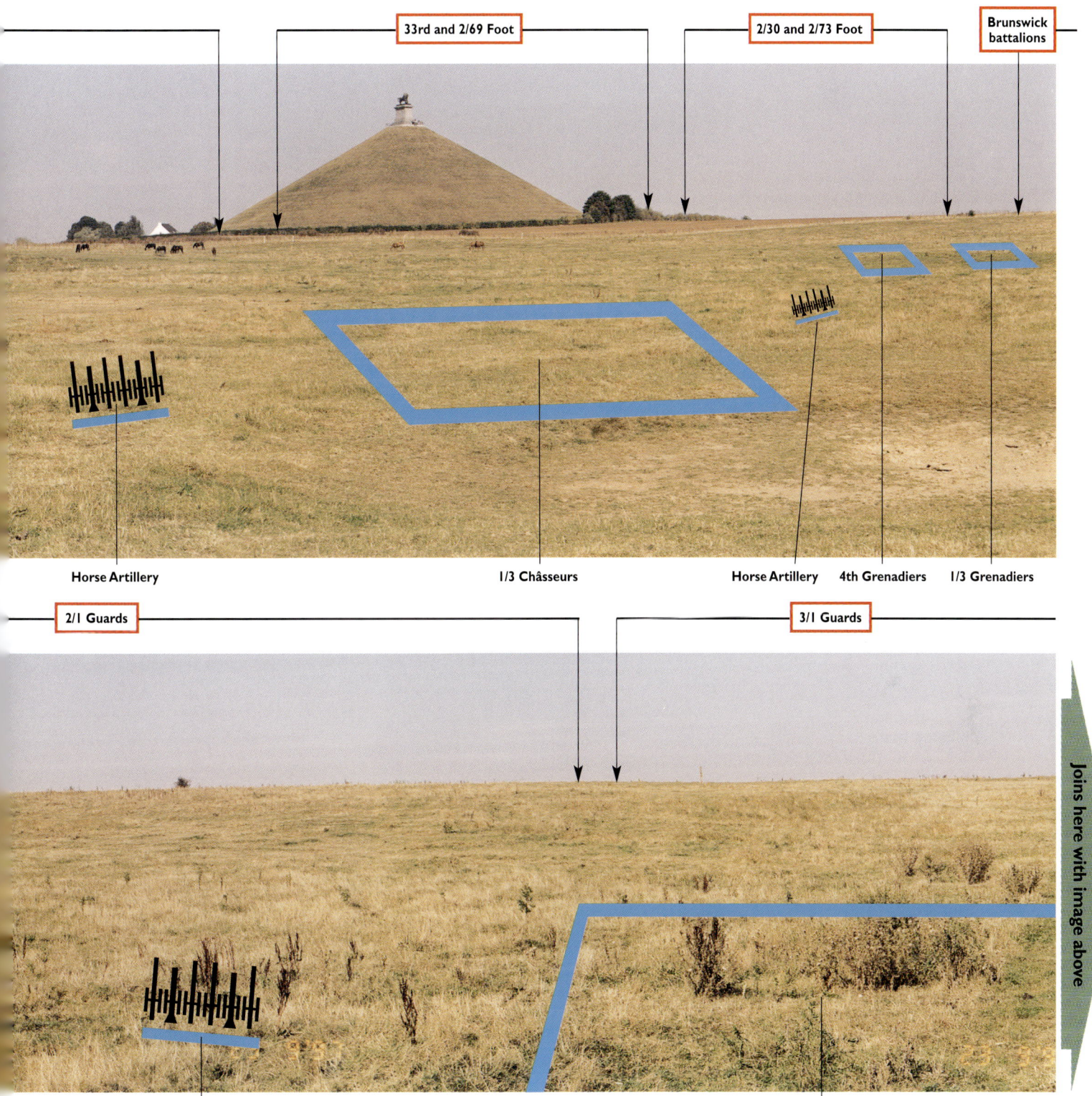

33rd and 2/69 Foot

2/30 and 2/73 Foot

Brunswick battalions

Horse Artillery

1/3 Châsseurs

Horse Artillery

4th Grenadiers

1/3 Grenadiers

2/1 Guards

3/1 Guards

Joins here with image above

Horse Artillery

2/3 Châsseurs

It was now getting on for seven o'clock. The 52nd formed line four deep … The regiment stood about forty paces below the crest of the position. … The roar of round-shot still continued … One of these … came rolling down gently towards us like a cricket ball, so slowly that I was putting out my foot to stop it, when my colour-sergeant quickly begged me not to do so, and told me it might have seriously injured my foot [as indeed it would]. Exactly in front of me lay, at a distance of two yards a dead tortoise-shell kitten. It had probably been frightened out of Hougoumont, which was the nearest house to us … The circumstance led me to think of my friends at home. …

In front of our left company were several killed and wounded horses; some of the latter were lying, some standing, but some of both were eating the trodden down wheat or rye, notwithstanding that their legs were shot off, or that they were otherwise badly wounded. … There was a peculiar smell at this time, arising from a mingling of the smell of the wheat trodden flat down with the smell of gunpowder. … a French cuirassier officer came galloping up the slope and down the bank in our front, near to Sir John Colborne, crying 'Vive le Roi!'

'La Garde Recule': Phase 1, Approximately 7.30 p.m. — Map 40

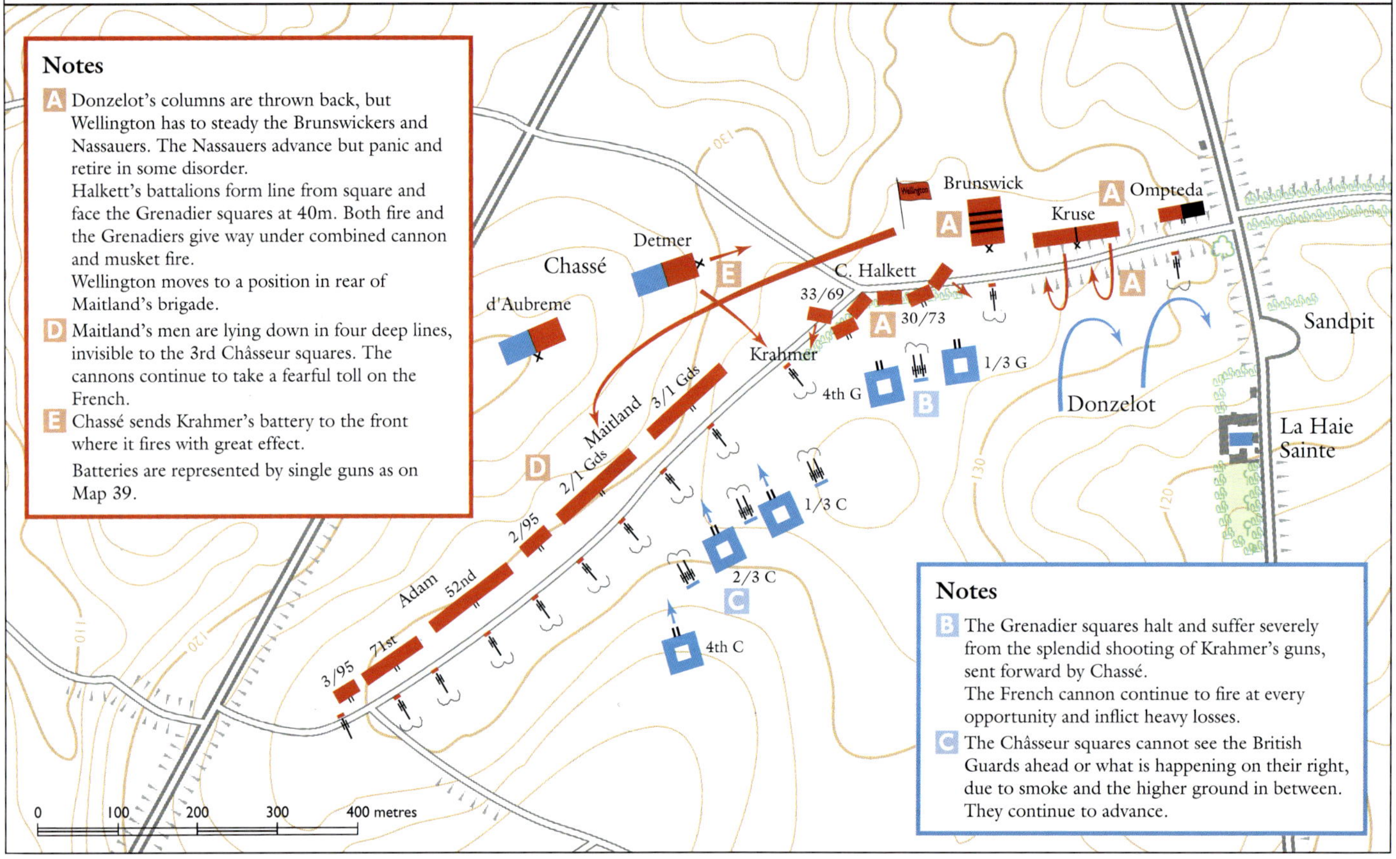
Notes
A Donzelot's columns are thrown back, but Wellington has to steady the Brunswickers and Nassauers. The Nassauers advance but panic and retire in some disorder.
Halkett's battalions form line from square and face the Grenadier squares at 40m. Both fire and the Grenadiers give way under combined cannon and musket fire.
Wellington moves to a position in rear of Maitland's brigade.
D Maitland's men are lying down in four deep lines, invisible to the 3rd Châsseur squares. The cannons continue to take a fearful toll on the French.
E Chassé sends Krahmer's battery to the front where it fires with great effect.
Batteries are represented by single guns as on Map 39.
Notes
B The Grenadier squares halt and suffer severely from the splendid shooting of Krahmer's guns, sent forward by Chassé.
The French cannon continue to fire at every opportunity and inflict heavy losses.
C The Châsseur squares cannot see the British Guards ahead or what is happening on their right, due to smoke and the higher ground in between. They continue to advance.
Brunswick
Ompteda
Kruse
Detmer
Chassé
C. Halkett
33/69
30/73
d'Aubreme
Krahmer
1/3 G
4th G
Sandpit
Donzelot
La Haie Sainte
Maitland
3/1 Gds
2/1 Gds
2/95
1/3 C
2/3 C
4th C
Adam
52nd
71st
3/95
0
100
200
300
400 metres

'La Garde Recule': Phase 2, Approximately 7.45 p.m. — Map 41

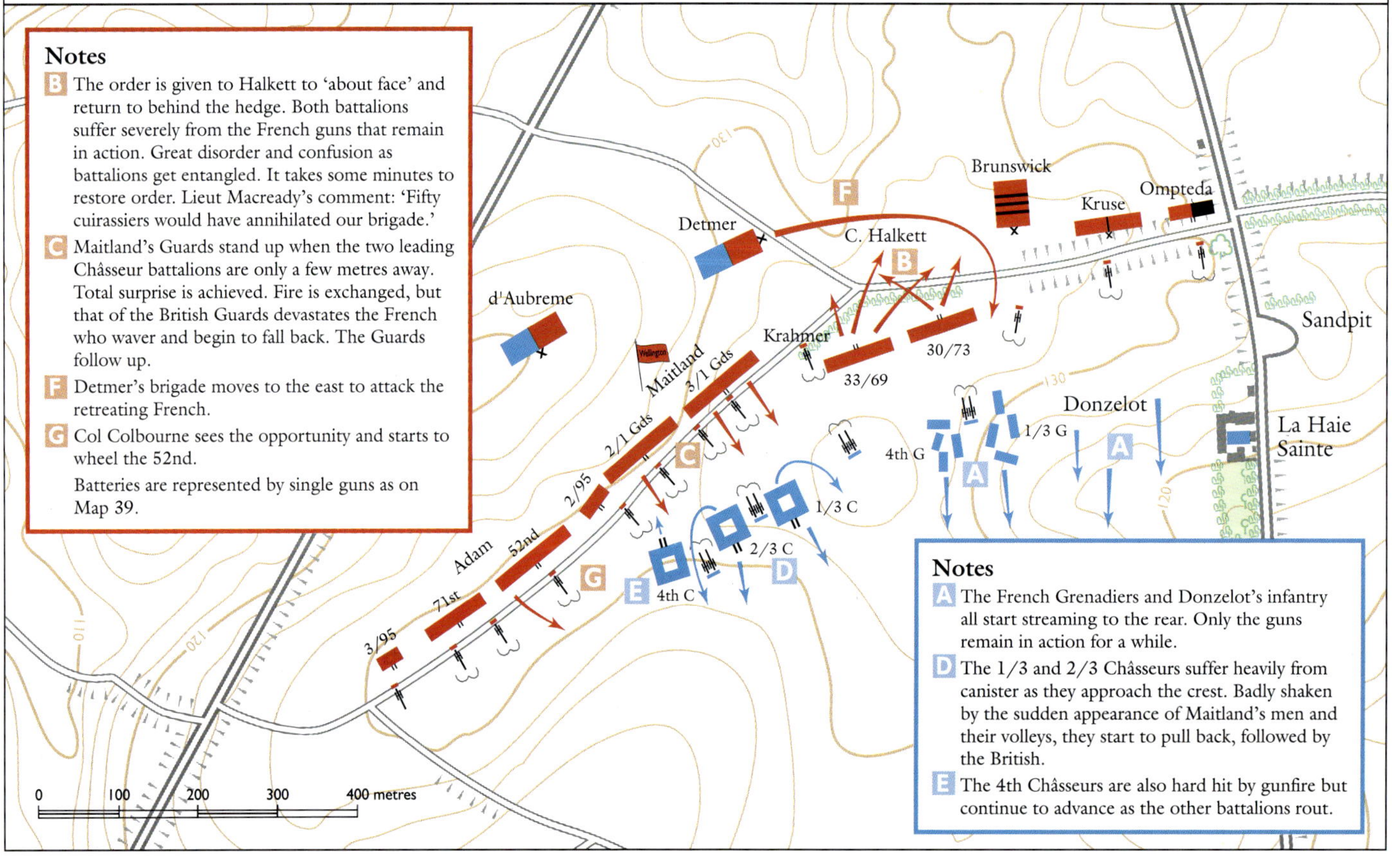
Notes
B The order is given to Halkett to 'about face' and return to behind the hedge. Both battalions suffer severely from the French guns that remain in action. Great disorder and confusion as battalions get entangled. It takes some minutes to restore order. Lieut Macready's comment: 'Fifty cuirassiers would have annihilated our brigade.'
C Maitland's Guards stand up when the two leading Châsseur battalions are only a few metres away. Total surprise is achieved. Fire is exchanged, but that of the British Guards devastates the French who waver and begin to fall back. The Guards follow up.
F Detmer's brigade moves to the east to attack the retreating French.
G Col Colbourne sees the opportunity and starts to wheel the 52nd.
Batteries are represented by single guns as on Map 39.
Notes
A The French Grenadiers and Donzelot's infantry all start streaming to the rear. Only the guns remain in action for a while.
D The 1/3 and 2/3 Châsseurs suffer heavily from canister as they approach the crest. Badly shaken by the sudden appearance of Maitland's men and their volleys, they start to pull back, followed by the British.
E The 4th Châsseurs are also hard hit by gunfire but continue to advance as the other battalions rout.
Brunswick
Kruse
Ompteda
Detmer
C. Halkett
d'Aubreme
Krahmer
30/73
33/69
Sandpit
Donzelot
1/3 G
4th G
La Haie Sainte
Maitland
3/1 Gds
2/1 Gds
2/95
1/3 C
2/3 C
4th C
Adam
52nd
71st
3/95
0
100
200
300
400 metres

'La Garde Recule': Phase 3, Approximately 7.50 p.m. Map 42

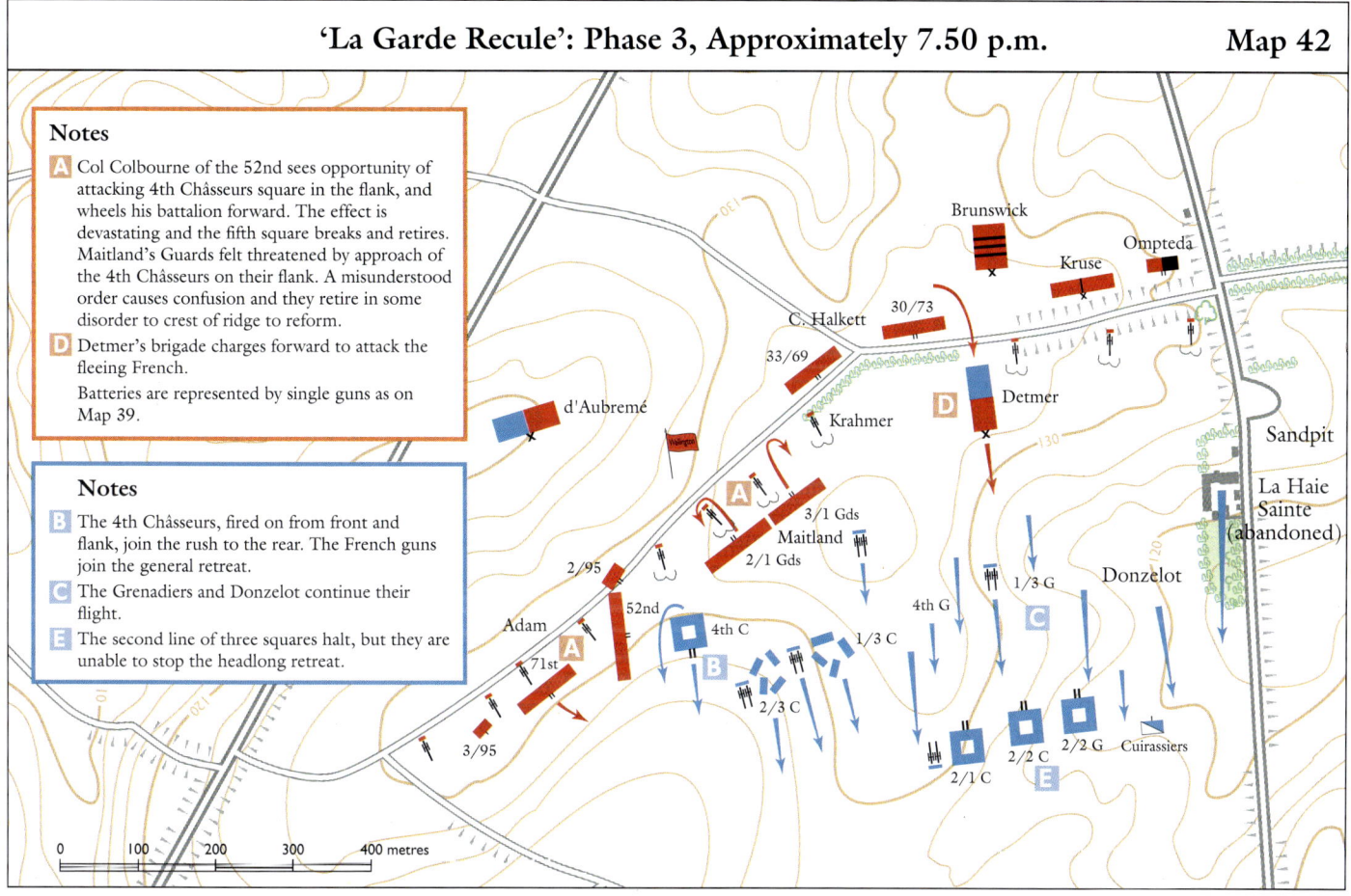

Notes

[A] Col Colbourne of the 52nd sees opportunity of attacking 4th Châsseurs square in the flank, and wheels his battalion forward. The effect is devastating and the fifth square breaks and retires. Maitland's Guards felt threatened by approach of the 4th Châsseurs on their flank. A misunderstood order causes confusion and they retire in some disorder to crest of ridge to reform.

[D] Detmer's brigade charges forward to attack the fleeing French.

Batteries are represented by single guns as on Map 39.

Notes

[B] The 4th Châsseurs, fired on from front and flank, join the rush to the rear. The French guns join the general retreat.

[C] The Grenadiers and Donzelot continue their flight.

[E] The second line of three squares halt, but they are unable to stop the headlong retreat.

Now the second incident of panic occurred among the victors (the first being Kruse's Nassauers confused rush back to the ridge). The order was given to Halkett's men to about face, probably to get back behind the hedge and crest, which was obeyed. However, Duchand's gunners had not fled and continued to fire shot after shot into the retiring British. Heavy casualties and chaos ensued. The 30th and 73rd became entangled with the 33rd and 69th and the whole becoming 'a mere mob' as they stampeded for shelter. As Macready so aptly put it, 'Fifty cuirassier would have annihilated our brigade…'. There were perhaps five minutes before order was restored when a final small window of opportunity opened. Fortunately for the Duke there were no troops to take it.

A few minutes later, again according to the informative Macready who was just a lad of seventeen at the time, Detmers' brigade from Chassé's division came up and charged down the slope. From the way Macready describes their appearance it would seem they made their attack on an already fleeing enemy rather than into a formed square, which most accounts maintain. Macready's version makes it clear that by the time Detmers charged, serious opposition had gone and the 30th were about to pile arms for a well-earned rest. He wrote:

> A heavy column of Dutch infantry (the first we had seen) passed, drumming and shouting like mad, with their shakos on the top of their bayonets, near enough to our right for us to see and laugh at them, and after this the noise went rapidly away from us. Soon after we piled arms, chatted, and lay down to rest.

One suspects the laughter was occasioned by the enthusiasm of the charge when the enemy had largely disappeared in flight, or perhaps the less than serious way the Dutch went to war with their shakos on the ends of their muskets.

The next Guard units to hit the ridge were the 1/3 and 2/3 Châsseurs à Pied. Both had shrunk substantially as a result of the sustained, if less intense, cannon fire over their 750-metre approach. Nevertheless, they remained steady, still in square, drums still beating and officers shouting encouragement. The more thoughtful among them might have wondered why there were no infantry ahead. With shouldered arms they came on up to the crest, puzzled perhaps, certainly apprehensive. The reason for the seeming lack of opposition was that Wellington had ordered Maitland's Guards' brigade to lie down. When the French were a mere 25 metres away the Duke shouted, 'Now Maitland! Now's your time!' Over 1,400 infantrymen in a four deep line stood up, virtually shoulder to shoulder, spread over about 250 metres. They delivered a shattering volley. Down went the regimental colonel, Michel; down went battalion commanders Cardinal and Angelet together with some twenty officers and 200 guardsmen. Artillery fire had cost them dearly. The first musket volley knocked over 20 per cent of those still standing. It was too much, even for these veterans; the square staggered and began to disintegrate. The British Guards moved forward with the bayonet to confirm the rout.

Yet again a triumphal bayonet charge ended in confusion and a hurried retirement. This time it was the arrival of the last Imperial Guard's square, the 4th Châsseurs, looming up through the smoke on Maitland's right flank that gave cause for concern. Maitland gave the order to halt and reform which, seemingly, was understood by the 2/1 Guards on the right but misunderstood by

Panic in Colin Halkett's brigade

Unlike many, Macready, who had been an ensign in the 30th Foot at Waterloo, was quite prepared to admit that there was confusion and panic in British battalions during the battle. In his *Journal* he described what happened after the Middle Guard Grenadiers had been driven back, the battalion had advanced to follow up, but the French guns continued to take their toll:

> There was a hedge in our rear, to which it was deemed expedient to move us, I suppose, for shelter from the guns. We faced about by word of command, and stepped off in perfect order. As we descended the declivity the fire thickened tremendously, and the cries from the men struck down, as well as from the numerous wounded on all sides of us who thought themselves abandoned, was terrible. … Prendergast [Lieutenant] of ours was shattered to pieces by a shell; McNab [Captain] killed by grape-shot [he was an extra ADC to General Picton but after Picton was killed returned to his battalion], and James [Ensign] and Bullen

> [Ensign] lost all their legs by round-shot during this retreat. … As I recovered my feet from a tumble, a friend knocked up against me, seized me by the stock [stiff leather collar], and almost choked me, screaming, (half-maddened by his five wounds and the sad scene going on), 'Is it deep, Mac, is it deep?' At this instant we found ourselves commingled with the 33rd and 69th regiments; all order was lost, and the column (now a mere mob) passed the hedge at an accelerated pace. The exertions of the officers, added to the glorious struggling of lots of the men to halt and face about, were rendered to no avail by the irresistible pressure … they [the officers] were themselves jammed up against them and hurried on with the current, literally for many yards not touching the ground. … I cannot conceive what the enemy were about during our confusion. Fifty cuirassiers would have annihilated our brigade…

Once back behind the hedge and crest the brigade sorted itself out.

the 3/1 on the left as an order to form square. This was understandable considering the distance involved from one end of the line to the other, the noise, smoke and confusion of even a short bayonet charge. As the battalions were now somewhat isolated out in front of the ridge they were highly vulnerable to a cavalry attack, so officers might well have been expecting a 'form square' order. However, the result was a typical example of the old army adage 'order – counter-order – disorder'. It ended in the brigade retreating in confusion to their original position where they quickly sorted themselves out. Nevertheless, another little window had opened, only to be slammed shut before any advantage could be taken of it. The French lacked the cavalry and the will to do so.

Despite the debacle in the squares to its front and right, the 4th Châsseurs continued forward. Maréchal de Camp Henrion and the battalion commander Agnès must have been encouraged by the obvious confusion among the British Guards. If so, it was short-lived. They were suddenly called upon to face the strongest battalion in Wellington's army (over 1000 bayonets) formed in line on their left flank. Its volley brought the 4th Châsseurs to a staggering halt. Agnès was shot dead about this time. The Anglo-Allied counter-stroke was launched on the initiative of the battalion commander of the 52nd Foot, Colonel Colbourne, an officer of considerable talent who had commanded a brigade in the Peninsula and was destined to become Lord Seaton and a field-marshal forty-five years later.

Along with the rest of Adam's brigade, the 52nd had been withdrawn back to the ridge after the French cavalry attacks had finally petered out. Wellington considered these battalions too exposed. As the Imperial Guard squares approached, Colbourne spotted the vulnerability of the western formation. He briefly discussed his intention with his second-in-command, Major Rowan (later to be knighted and appointed Chief Commissioner of the Metropolitan Police). Colbourne took the following action:

> I ordered our left hand Company to wheel to the left, and formed the remaining Companies on that Company. … This movement placed us nearly parallel with the moving Columns of the French Imperial Guards. I ordered a strong Company to extend in our front [as skirmishers], and at this

moment Sir F. Adam rode up, and asked me what I was going to do. I think I said, 'to make that Column feel our fire.' Sir F. Adam then ordered me to move on, and that the 71st should follow, and rode away towards the 71st.

The 4th Châsseurs did not join the general retreat immediately: for a minute or two they exchanged fire with the 52nd. It was effective fire. As Colbourne admitted:

> The 52nd suffered severely from the fire of the Enemy; the loss of skirmishers was severe, and the two Officers of the Company were wounded. The right wing of the 52nd lost nearly one hundred and fifty men during the advance [follow up of the Imperial Guards retreat]; the Officer carrying the Regimental Colour was killed.

It was Adam's brigade, with the 52nd in the van, which spearheaded the infantry follow up of the retreating Imperial Guard. When there was some hesitation due to the battalion mistaking the 23rd Light Dragoons (Dornberg's brigade) for French (and firing on them) Wellington, who had ridden up behind Colbourne and witnessed the incident, shouted, 'Never mind! Go on! Go on!' The Duke had also ordered up Hew Halkett's Hanoverian Brigade. Halkett personally led forward the 600 strong Osnabrück Landwehr Battalion under Major Munster, while his other three battalions became involved in retaking the Hougoumont orchard and wood. Leading the cavalry advance were Vivian's three regiments of light cavalry, followed by that of Vandeleur. Vivian's men in particular made several spirited charges and had something of a field day among the fleeing Frenchmen. All along the line, on both sides of the Genappe road the French were in retreat. Within a few minutes it became a *sauve qui peut* flight. However, six battalions of the Imperial Guard were not initially swamped in the rush to the rear.

At this stage a junior officer of the 52nd recalled being sent ahead of the battalion with a section of about twenty-five men to chase away some French guns. Within a few moments, as he cleared the swirling smoke, he faced the three unbroken squares of the second line that had halted south-west of La Haie Sainte and, unbeknown to him were probably still under the direct command of the Emperor. He described what he saw:

... I was clear of the Imperial Guards smoke, and saw three squares of the Old Guard within four hundred yards farther on. They were standing in a line of contiguous squares with very short intervals, a small body of cuirassiers on their right, while the guns took post on their left. ... They were standing in perfect order and steadiness ... The section advanced to within 200 metres of the squares and halted until joined by the main body of the 52nd.

The officer continued:

Up to this moment neither the guns, the squares of the Imperial Guard, nor the 52nd had fired a shot. I then saw one or two guns slewed round to the direction of my company and fired, but their grape [canister] went over our heads. We opened our fire and advanced; the squares replied to it, and then steadily faced about, retired. ... the cuirassiers declined the contest and turned. The French proper right square brought up its right shoulders [inclined to the left] and crossed the chausee [Genappe road], and we crossed it after them.

It was during this controlled retreat by the 2/1 Châsseurs, 2/2 Châsseurs and 2/2 Grenadiers that Maréchal de Camp Cambronne, the commandant of the Châsseurs, who had refused promotion before Waterloo in order to remain with his regiment, supposedly made his famous response to shouts for the square of the 2/1 Châsseurs to surrender. This issue is discussed in Section 10 'Myths and Controversies'. What is reasonably certain is that during this time, before the squares crossed the Genappe road, Cambronne was both wounded and captured. The capture was effected by no lesser person that Colonel Hew Halkett, the Hanoverian brigade commander, who was at that time with the Osnabrück Battalion alongside the 52nd, treading on the heels of the French. He has described how it happened:

During our advance we were in constant contact with the French Guards, and I often called to them to surrender. For some time I had my eye upon, as I supposed, the General Officer in command of the Guards (being in full uniform) trying to animate his men to stand.

After having received our fire with much effect, the Column left their General with two Officers behind, when I ordered the sharpshooters to dash on, and I made a gallop for the General. When about cutting him down he called out he would surrender, upon which he preceded me [to the rear], but I had not gone many paces when my horse got a shot through his body and fell to the ground. In a few seconds I got him on his legs again, and found my friend, Cambronne, had taken French leave in the direction from where he came. I instantly overtook him, laid

hold of him by the aiguillette [shoulder cords], and brought him in safety and gave him in charge to a sergeant of the Osnabruckers to deliver to the Duke...

Halkett makes no mention of Cambronne being wounded. Nevertheless, most sources claim he was hit in the face by a musket ball. If this was the case, it must have been a spent ball as he was agile enough when attempting to escape capture.

By this time Wellington had ordered a general advance. The flood of French fugitives followed by the flood of victorious Allies failed to swamp all the squares of the Imperial Guard. Belcourt's 2/3 Grenadiers were soon isolated, surrounded by their enemy. Attacked by infantry, cavalry and smashed at close range by canister shells, this battalion of 580 all ranks was never completely broken. With men dropping at every step, by the time it had reached La Belle Alliance the square of three deep had shrunk to a tiny triangle with ranks of two deep. Almost miraculously Belcourt remained untouched. At this stage the order was given to fire a final volley and to break up into groups to make their way to the rear. Most of the survivors reached Rossomme where they heard the drummers of the 1st Grenadiers rallying stragglers to the Eagle by continuously beating 'La Grenadiere'.

A square that had disintegrated by the time the remnants reached La Belle Alliance was Cambronne's 2/1 Châsseurs. Near there Eagle-Bearer Martin (the 1st Châsseurs Eagle was carried at Waterloo by the 2/1 Battalion, as the 1/1 was left out of the battle at Le Caillou) took refuge in the square of the 2/2 Châsseurs under Mompez. The single battalion of the 4th Grenadiers, its commander mortally wounded, disappeared almost entirely. Harlet, himself injured, had seen all his captains and lieutenants fall dead or wounded. A group of his soldiers hustled their general into Belcourt's square for temporary shelter.

The two rocks upon which the chaos, confusion, panic and tide of fugitives could make no impression were the squares of the 1/1 and 2/1 Grenadiers. Posted on either side of the Genappe road south of La Belle Alliance, they never moved, even firing on Frenchmen who tried to force their way in for sanctuary. Under their commandant, Maréchal de Camp Petit, they numbered thirty-two officers and nearly 1,200 Grenadiers. These 'old mustaches' averaged thirty-five years of age, a third had fought in twenty to twenty-five campaigns, and four out of five wore the coveted Legion of Honour. Almost unique among the Imperial Guard infantry at Waterloo, all their uniforms were regulation pattern, half-belted overcoats, blue trousers, high bearskin bonnets and Old Guard pattern packs. They carried brass-mounted muskets and sabres. Their twenty-four musicians were led by a 'Jingling Johnny'

The 1st Regiment of Grenadiers of the Imperial Guard Quits the Battlefield

Maréchal de Camp Petit, who commanded the 1st Grenadiers, wrote a detailed account of the Guard's attack and retreat. In it he has described how these two battalions abandoned the battlefield:

The Emperor galloped back and placed himself inside the square of the 1st Battalion of the 1st Regiment of Grenadiers. The whole army was in the most appalling disorder. Infantry, cavalry, artillery – everybody was fleeing in all directions. Soon no unit retained any order except the two squares formed by this regiment's two battalions posted to right and left of the main road. On orders from the Emperor, their commander, General Petit [he wrote in the third person] had the 'Grenadiere' sounded to rally those guardsmen who had been caught up in the torrent of fugitives. The enemy was close at our heels, and, fearing that he might penetrate the squares, we were obliged to fire at the men who were being pursued and who threw themselves wildly at the squares. This was one evil we had to incur in order to avoid a greater one.

It was now almost dark. The Emperor himself gave the order for us to leave our positions, which were no longer tenable.... The two squares withdrew in good order, the 1st Battalion across country, the second along the road.

The French Retreat Begins: Main Events and Incidents · Map 43

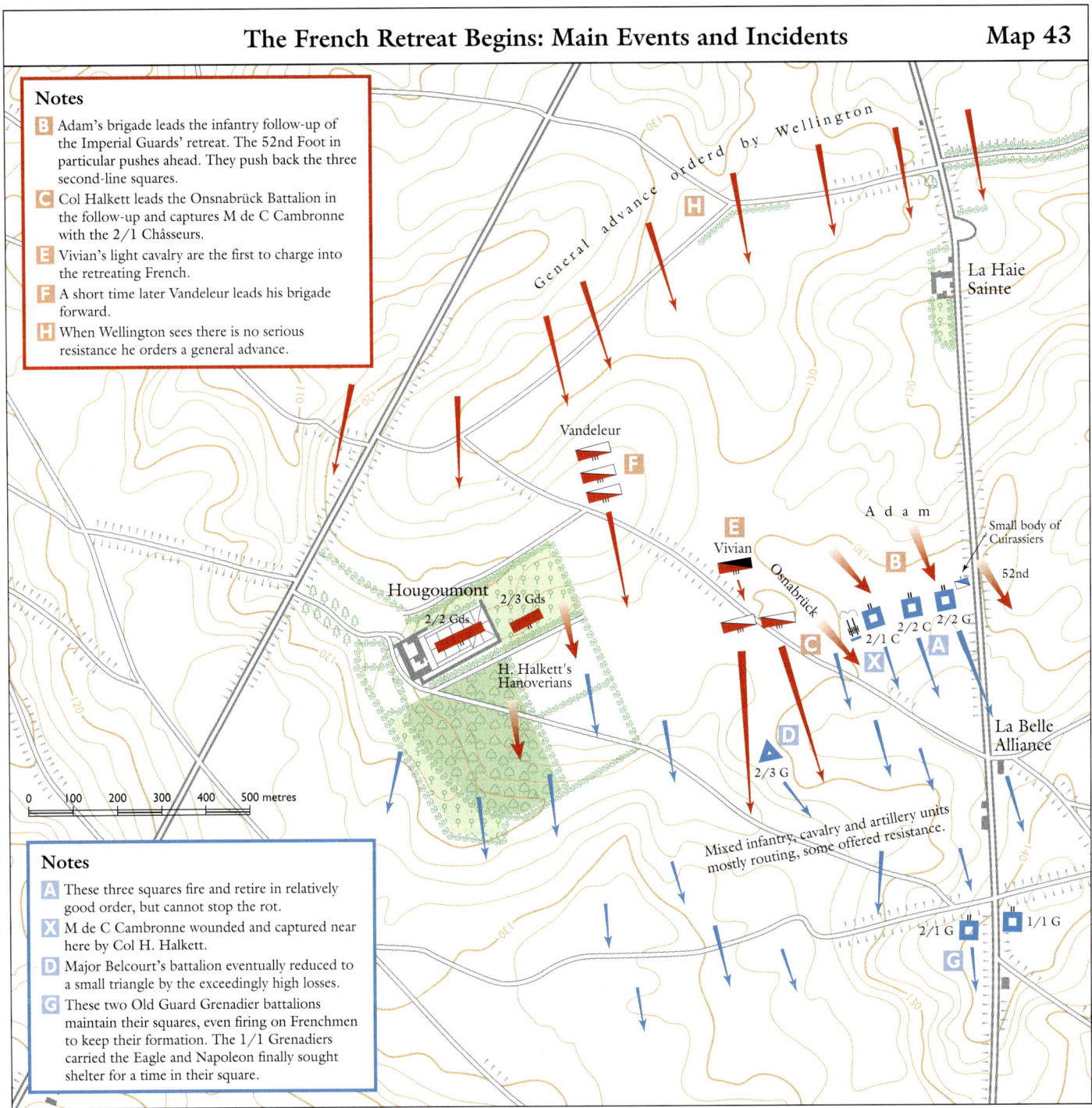

Notes

B Adam's brigade leads the infantry follow-up of the Imperial Guards' retreat. The 52nd Foot in particular pushes ahead. They push back the three second-line squares.

C Col Halkett leads the Onsnabrück Battalion in the follow-up and captures M de C Cambronne with the 2/1 Châsseurs.

E Vivian's light cavalry are the first to charge into the retreating French.

F A short time later Vandeleur leads his brigade forward.

H When Wellington sees there is no serious resistance he orders a general advance.

General advance ordered by Wellington

La Haie Sainte

Vandeleur

Adam

Small body of Cuirassiers

52nd

Vivian

Osnabrück

Hougoumont

2/3 Gds

2/2 Gds

2/1 C   2/2 C   2/2 G

H. Halkett's Hanoverians

La Belle Alliance

2/3 G

Mixed infantry, cavalry and artillery units mostly routing, some offered resistance.

2/1 G   1/1 G

0 100 200 300 400 500 metres

Notes

A These three squares fire and retire in relatively good order, but cannot stop the rot.

X M de C Cambronne wounded and captured near here by Col H. Halkett.

D Major Belcourt's battalion eventually reduced to a small triangle by the exceedingly high losses.

G These two Old Guard Grenadier battalions maintain their squares, even firing on Frenchmen to keep their formation. The 1/1 Grenadiers carried the Eagle and Napoleon finally sought shelter for a time in their square.

---

and bass and snare drums. In their ranks were the 'old grumblers' from Elba, which included the battalion commanders Loubers and Combes. The 1st Battalion protected the Grenadiers' Eagle and, for a while, the Emperor himself. Grouped with them were the Guard Engineers and Marines plus a battery of Guard artillery. Both squares were bursting with dozens of generals, staff officers, musicians and refugee soldiers of all ranks and many regiments. Such was the number packed inside that each square was said to be ten ranks deep.

As the pressure in front increased, and the danger of being cut off by the Prussians from Plancenoit became acute, both battalions withdrew towards Rossomme taking their Emperor and their Eagle with them. Somewhere along the route Napoleon and his immediate entourage (including Generals Drouot and Lobau), escorted by what was left of the duty squadron of Châsseurs à

Cheval, rode on past Rossomme to Le Caillou. There they met with Major Duuring with his 1/1 Châsseurs. This battalion was virtually untouched by the battle since its only action had been against Prussian patrols that had swung south round Plancenoit in an attempt to cut the Genappe road. The Emperor personally questioned Duuring, a Dutchman who had started his service in the Dutch Grenadiers, as to his situation, strength and dispositions. Duuring's final duty was to assist in getting Napoleon away safely to Genappe. He was to follow the Emperor and keep well closed up. Napoleon's last words to this loyal and devoted officer, whose own countrymen were his enemy, were, 'I count on you'.

Napoleon crossed the Sambre at Charleroi at 2.00 a.m. on 19 June. Escorted now by Red Lancers he rode on to Philippeville, en route to Paris, en route to St Helena.

Tactical significance

The Imperial Guard's advance at Waterloo is probably the best-remembered event of the best-remembered battle of the Napoleonic Wars. It has eclipsed even Ney's desperate cavalry charges in the history books. The Emperor's Guard was legendary at Waterloo. Its final attack, although a failure, enhanced that legend. Today numerous re-enactment groups, not only in France but also in Germany, the Netherlands, the United Kingdom and the USA, dress in their uniform and refight their battles. There are several aspects of their march up the slope at Mont St Jean worthy of mention.

•   It was Napoleon's last chance. It was a desperate final throw to save the battle, to save the campaign and to save his throne. By 7.30 p.m. he had eleven battalions of élite infantry uncommitted. His cavalry had been shredded, his artillery was exhausted, but he had managed to push the Prussians out of Plancenoit. If the Prussians reached the Genappe road with his army north of La Belle Alliance, he would be crushed, annihilated. His choice was grim. Either he used these battalions to cover a controlled withdrawal to regroup, to fight again after Grouchy had rejoined, or he used them in a last effort to snatch a victory at the eleventh hour. Almost certainly Napoleon knew that an orderly withdrawal would only postpone defeat. After all, his Guard had never failed him.

•   There is a convincing case that this final attack, even if successful, was too little too late. With more and more Prussians pouring onto the battlefield a successful assault would only delay defeat by

---

'Voilà Grouchy!'

Colonel Octave Levasseur was an ADC to Ney and was present when one of the Emperor's ADCs, Général de Division Dejean, galloped up with the news that Grouchy had arrived with his force. It was a critical moment, just as the Imperial Guard was about to start its attack as a part of a general advance all along the line. He described it thus:

'Monsieur le Maréchal,' he said. '*Vive l'Empereur! Voilà Grouchy!*' The Marshal at once ordered me to go right along the line and announce that Grouchy had arrived. I set off at a gallop, with my hat raised on the point of my sabre, rode down the line shouting: '*Vive l'Empereur! Soldats, voilà Grouchy!*' The sudden shout was taken up by a thousand voices. The exaltation of the troops reached fever pitch and they all shouted: '*En avant! En avant! Vive l'Empereur!*' I had scarcely reached the end of our line when I heard cannon fire behind us. Enthusiasm gave way to a profound silence, to amazement, to anxiety. … The cannonade went on and drew closer. In utter consternation I rode up to the Marshal, who forbade me to go and find out the cause of this panic. I went next to General ———, who said to me: '*Voyez! Ce sont les Prussiens!*' I turned back to look for Marshal Ney, but could not find him.

Dejean was not the only ADC deliberately encouraging false hope, Maréchal de Camp de la Bédoyère had been sent on the same mission.

---

an hour or so. By the time the Guard advanced Blücher had nearly 50,000 men on the field with another 26,000 en route. The two allied armies had joined hands at Papelotte, therefore it was unlikely that Plancenoit would still be in French hands by nightfall so that nothing the Guard did could turn the battle round. To Napoleon, however, it seemed his only hope.

•   The Imperial Guard's attack is often written up as an isolated affair in which the Guard, unsupported, was launched against impossible odds, advancing on their own so that Wellington's line had no difficulty in defeating them. This version does not bear close examination. The Guard advanced as only part (albeit a principal part) of a general advance by what was left of the French army. Except for the troops engaged in defending the right flank and Plancenoit, every French infantry division resumed its attack. Jérôme and Foy continued the struggle for Hougoumont, Bachelu's division advanced on the Guard's left and Donzelot's on its right. East of the Genappe road Quiot, Marcognet and Pégot's brigade from Durutte's division tramped wearily back up towards the ridge. These divisions had been decimated (some at least twice) and they were exhausted, with their morale badly eroded by hours of tactical defeats and retreats. Despite this, they made one last effort for their Emperor. When the (false) news was passed that Grouchy had arrived, cries of '*Vive l'Empereur!*' were heard again as the French infantry all along the line stepped out once more.

•   French guns played a key role in this last attack. Guns were dispersed between the Guard battalions, the 'Grand Battery' continued

---

Wellington and Blücher Meet

Tradition has it that the two victorious commanders met at or near La Belle Alliance after the battle. According to Major-General Constant-Rebecque, who was present at the time, it was not far from Le Caillou. According to another witness, Lieutenant Jackson of the Royal Staff Corps, the meeting took place within a few metres of the main Genappe road about 200–300 metres from, and to the south of, La Belle Alliance. Writing in the *United Service Magazine* in 1847 Jackson recalled:

Just before he [Wellington] reached La Belle Alliance, the outlines of a numerous party on horseback, surrounded by crowds of infantry, could be made out, though it was dark, approaching the road from the direction of Papelotte and La Haye. When first observed the party was about fifty yards from the road, and, on seeing it, the Duke, aware perhaps that it was Marshal Blücher and his Staff, turned aside to meet the brave old Prussian. I was very close to the two heroes during their short conference, which may have lasted

about ten minutes; but it was too dark for me to distinguish old Blücher's features. It is a remarkable circumstance that this meeting should have taken place within two or three hundred yards of La Belle Alliance; and most probably Blücher did express a wish for the battle to bear that name ['the fine alliance'], as we have been told. It must have been quite half-past nine when these distinguished men shook hands and parted. The Duke regained the *chaussée*, and proceeded, as before, at a walk.

Captain Francis von Blücher, the old Field-Marshal's son, was serving on his staff and wrote to his mother that, 'Father Blücher embraced Wellington in so hearty a manner, that every one present said it was the most touching scene that could be imagined'. Blücher was also supposed to have greeted the Duke with the words '*Mein lieber kamerad, quelle affaire!*' ('My dear friend, what a business!'). Wellington was later to claim, jokingly, that the last two words were the only French words that Blücher knew.

to fire and horse artillery guns were dragged up the slope to positions from which they could support the infantry. These cannons were magnificently served by depleted detachments and bone weary gunners. It was their fire, as it had done throughout the battle, which frightened the Allies. During the Imperial Guard's advance, even as they retired, it was the French artillery that did the real damage, causing heavy loss to Colin Halkett's and Adam's brigades in particular.

• What Napoleon lacked for his final fling was cavalry. But at 7.30 p.m. he had none left. All those superb regiments of cuirassiers, châsseurs and dragoons had been squandered in two hours of reinforcing failure on the ridge during the late afternoon. To repeat young Macready's remark, 'Fifty cuirassiers would have annihilated our brigade'. Wellington's infantry had mostly formed into line to give the maximum firepower to defeat an infantry attack, but several battalions became decidedly shaky (see below) at the crucial moment when the Guard reached the ridge. At that point they were highly vulnerable to cavalry – one regiment at the right place (coming up behind the Guard) would probably have been enough to punch a hole, cause panic and tip the balance in favour of the French, at least on that part of the field. A small detachment of cuirassiers did accompany the second line of squares but they were too weak and timid to do anything. The cavalry that did follow up behind the Guard, and there were some, did so at a distance. They did not have the numbers, the morale or the leadership to exploit opportunities.

• All Wellington had to do was hang on. He had pulled in troops from both flanks to reinforce the crucial central part of his line. Blücher had arrived. With every minute that passed the Duke's position improved. If he could roll back the Guard, Wellington, with his Prussian allies, could be reasonably certain to win the battle, the campaign and the Napoleonic Wars. All he had to do was hold on for thirty minutes. In the event it was, as he was to say of the battle itself, 'a close run thing'. As the Guard approached, the Brunswick battalions might well have broken had he not personally ridden up to steady them. Kruse's Nassauers drove back Donzelot's men, advanced, panicked and retired in some confusion. The four battalions of Colin Halkett's brigade suffered heavily from French cannons when they made a short advance to push back the Grenadiers. They too rushed back to the ridgeline, for a short time becoming hopelessly entangled and confused. Even the British Guards under Maitland faltered briefly at this critical time. Enemy threatening their right flank, a misunderstood order was enough to send even these élite troops scurrying back from whence they had come. If all, even any, of these opportunities had been exploited by a fresh regiment of cavalry, the Imperial Guard's attack could have had a very different outcome.

Forces engaged

Although it is not possible to give precise figures for all the units of the Imperial Guard, or other French formations, engaged in this final attack, an estimate can be made. A similar approximation can be provided for the Anglo-Allied formations involved in repelling the attack. The figures given below take account of the approximate casualties received at Ligny or Quatre-Bras, as well as those sustained at Waterloo prior to 7.30 p.m. The French units shown are only those west of the Genappe road that were used or available to support the Guard's assault. The Anglo-Allied units were those deployed in the front line to meet the initial attack from the Genappe road west to north of Hougoumont. These all rank figures are rounded up or down to the nearest twenty-five.

French
Imperial Guard

• Assault battalions. Provided by five battalions of the Middle Guard.

1/3 Grenadiers (Guilleman)	500
4th Grenadiers (Lafargue)	500 (this regiment only raised one battalion)
1/3 Châsseurs (Cardinal)	500
2/3 Châsseurs (Angelet)	500
4th Châsseurs (Agnès)	850 (losses at Ligny had forced two battalions to combine)
Total in actual assault	2,850

The average strength of these battalions was 570.

• Supporting battalions in second line during the advance. Provided by three battalions from the Old Guard.

2/2 Grenadiers (Golzio)	500
2/2 Châsseurs (Mompez)	575
2/1 Châsseurs (Lamouret)	625
Total in support	1,700

The average strength of these battalions was 567.

• Battalions held back in reserve on the battlefield, not committed to the attack. Provided by one battalion from the Middle and two from the Old Guard.

2/3 Grenadiers (Belcourt)	550 (positioned between La Haie Sainte and Hougoumont)
1/1 Grenadiers (Loubers)	625 (positioned south of La Belle Alliance)
2/1 Grenadiers (Combes)	625 (positioned south of La Belle Alliance)
Total in reserve	1,800

The average strength of these battalions was 600.

Napoleon had available a total of around 6,350 Imperial Guard infantry in eleven battalions (six Middle Guard and five Old Guard). He deployed 45 per cent in the assault, 28 per cent in support and 27 per cent in reserve. In open square, in three ranks, the frontage of each battalion was between 30–35 metres.

Other infantry

French infantry west of the Genappe road, not involved at Hougoumont, and known to have advanced in support of the Guard was as follows:

2nd Infantry Division (Donzelot)	3,000
5th Infantry Division (Bachelu)	3,600
Total (at least)	6,600

Artillery

It is impossible to calculate the number of artillery batteries used to support this final advance. One horse battery certainly accompanied the assault battalions. There were guns with the supporting battalions and the reserve, and one battery (possibly 12-pounders) was with the two Grenadier battalions of the Old Guard south of La Belle Alliance. The artillery inflicted considerable loss on the Anglo-Allied units on the ridge as guns were brought forward with, and just behind, the advancing infantry. A fair estimate would be eight batteries available in support with, allowing for losses, about fifty pieces of ordnance.

Cavalry

If the entire Guard and heavy cavalry had not been frittered away and largely destroyed, demoralized or exhausted during the late afternoon, the Emperor would have been able to call on about 9000 horsemen (Lefèbvre-Desnouëttes, Guyot, Milhaud and Kellerman). As it was he could only count on a few squadrons to move forward behind the infantry. None of these were in a position to exploit the confusion in some of Wellington's battalions during the attack. Some cuirassiers accompanied the second line of the Imperial Guard. It is doubtful if more than 2000 cavalry supported, in a half-hearted fashion, this final advance.

Anglo-Allied
Infantry
• Those formations that actually engaged the Imperial Guard's five assault battalions were:

5th British Infantry Brigade (Colin Halkett)	1,500 (2/30 with 2/73, 33rd with 2/69)
1st British Infantry (Guards) Brigade (Maitland)	1,400 (2/1 and 3/1 Guards)
3rd British Infantry Brigade (Adam)	2,600 (1/52, 71st, 2/95, two companies 3/95)
Total	5,500

• A number of battalions of KGL, Brunswick and Nassau troops were deployed in or near the front line immediately west of the 'Elm Tree' crossroads. It is a matter of dispute as to whether the Brunswick or Nassau units engaged the Imperial Guard or Donzelot's infantry or a mixture of both – it was probably the latter. These units were certainly involved in repelling the overall French advance. They were:

2nd KGL Brigade (Ompteda, although he was dead by this time)	800 (this brigade had suffered heavy losses in or around La Haie Sainte)
Nassau Reserve Contingent (Kruse)	2,000 (three battalions of 1st Nassau)
Brunswick Contingent	1,200 (this allows for two of the seven battalions being on or near the ridge)
Total	4,000

Wellington had some 9,500 infantry deployed along a front of about 1,100 metres. The frontage actually attacked by the Imperial Guard (five battalions of 2,850 men) was some 500 metres. About 2,900 British infantrymen in a much more suitable formation (line) to develop musket fire occupied this frontage.

• The front line was supported by substantial reserves of infantry immediately in rear of the ridge, although the quality of some was suspect. These included the 7000 men in Chassé's 3rd Netherlands Infantry Division.

Artillery
Like the French, the Anglo-Allied artillery had endured a long, hard day. Losses had occurred and some guns were disabled. By this time the Duke had brought up batteries from the rear (Bull, Mercer, Sinclair and Bolton) and others from the flanks (Webber-Smith, Rogers and Ross). Chassé sent forward Krahmer's battery at the critical moment. At least twelve batteries would have been able to bring fire to bear on some of the attackers as they approached. The rate of fire would have been slowed by fatigue, and shortages of ammunition meant that it is unlikely that more than sixty guns or howitzers defended this 1,100-metre section of the ridge.

Cavalry
Wellington's position with cavalry was vastly superior to the French. Some had been badly mauled (Household and Union Brigades), some were less than 100 per cent dependable (Brunswick, Netherlands). Others, although they had taken casualties and been in action (Grant, Dornberg), were still reliable. And there were two fresh brigades (Vivian and Vandeleur) brought across from the right flank. Wellington had at least 7000 horsemen in immediate reserve west of the Genappe road.

Imperial Guard infantry casualties
While it is impossible to be precise about the number of casualties suffered by the Imperial Guard at Waterloo, and specifically in their final attack, it is possible to draw some general conclusions from the available figures. The approximate numbers present with

Chaos at Charleroi – Paymaster Peyrusse Loses the Emperor's Gold

The only bridge in Charleroi became a fearful bottleneck during the desperate flight of the French Army. It was some 40 metres long and 9 metres wide, and the approach from the north was excessively steep down a street appropriately named 'Rue de la Montagne'. Some cuirassiers were knocked into the river and drowned in the crush to get over. In the process a sentry box by the bridge was overturned, wagons that came careering down the street were unable to stop in time and crashed, further obstructing access. Several drivers were crushed. Sacks of flour and rice, casks of brandy or wine and hundreds of loaves were scattered on the pavement. Fugitives on foot clambered over the wreckage, not forgetting to skewer the bread on their bayonets or to slake their thirst from holes smashed in the wine barrels. The blockage was complete.

When the Emperor's paymaster, Peyrusse, arrived from Le Caillou with the treasury wagon the street was blocked for 100 metres from the bridge. This was the same adventurous official who had saved much of Napoleon's cash after the first abdication, had served him loyally on Elba and marched all the way to Paris with him on his return. Yet again he was responsible for saving the

money. Peyrusse saw the impossibility of getting the six-horse wagon any further. He made a bold, if somewhat trusting decision. The wagon was opened and the bags of coins divided up amongst his men and the soldiers of the escort. Each man got as much as he could carry and Peyrusse noted down his name and the number of bags of 20,000 francs entrusted to each. All these men were to make their own way over the river and meet again at an agreed spot on the other side. In the midst of these proceedings shots were fired nearby and the yell went up, 'The Prussians! Save yourselves!' Peyrusse's men were scattered or overwhelmed by a rush of fugitives who, with boot and bayonet, seized most of the bags of gold. The entire fortune was plundered.

The rest of the convoy of wagons had been halted, making the entire street impassable to vehicles. Towards the rear Hugues-Bernard Maret, the Duke of Bussano and Napoleon's Secretary of State, ordered all the important cabinet papers torn to shreds. As he wrote a week later, '... they were all torn up one after the other and thrown in the mud in such a way that the enemy would not have been able even to pick up the bits'.

───────── **Chaos at Genappe – Napoleon Loses his Carriage and Other Valuables** ─────────

A number of stories have circulated as to how the Emperor's carriage was taken. That given by Lieutenant Golz of the Brandenburg Uhlans has a ring of authenticity about it:

> It was already quite dark when we reached Genappe. The gate was blocked with guns and wagons, but was not manned. … Half the squadron dismounted, the passage was soon free and the pursuit continued. Meanwhile the moon had come out. All along the high street of the town, which seemed to be the only one it had, stood six carriages. Each of the six was harnessed to six or eight good horses, but there was nobody in sight. To get through, the uhlans had to force themselves around the carriages and no doubt several of the troopers of the squadron took the opportunity to help themselves to some of the

contents. However, because of the great hurry, they could not spend long there even though it would have been well worth their while. This was, after all, the Imperial baggage, and Napoleon's own carriage was among them. The following cavalry took their share, but the bulk of the prizes fell into the hands of the pursuing infantry, the Fusilier Battalion of the 15th Regiment [a unit that suffered heavy loss in Plancenoit].

Major von Keller of the Fus/15th did indeed find the Emperor's belongings. Napoleon's medals and a set of diamonds were found in the carriage. The diamonds were later presented to King Frederick William of Prussia and were incorporated into the crown jewels. The King thanked the regiment and awarded Keller the Pour le Merite with oak leaves.

---

the Guard at the start of the battle are known, as is the strength of the various regiments at their musters 23–26 June. These statistics, obtained from the French Army Historical Service at Château Vincennes, are quoted by Scott Bowden in his book *Armies at Waterloo*. The all rank figures are given below:

Old Guard	18 June	26 June	% loss
1st Grenadiers	1,280	644	50
2nd Grenadiers	1,090	374	66
1st Châsseurs	1,307	588	55
2nd Châsseurs	1,163	375	68
Total	4,840	1,981	59
Middle Guard			
3rd Grenadiers	1,164	201	84
4th Grenadiers	520	100	83
3rd Châsseurs	1,602	165	85
4th Châsseurs	841	244	71
Total	4,127	710	82
Young Guard			
1st Voltigeurs	1,219	196	84
3rd Voltigeurs	967	146	87
1st Tirailleurs	1,109	92	92
3rd Tirailleurs	988	164	84
Total	4,283	598	86
Overall totals	13,250	3,289	75

The Guard were in action at Ligny where the 4th Châsseurs suffered severely enough for the two battalions to fight as one at Waterloo. Undoubtedly all lost men during the retreat from the battlefield, but the Guard, being an élite, highly disciplined formation, probably less than most. The following tentative conclusions can be made from the figures:

• The Old Guard suffered the least. This is not surprising as, apart from two battalions committed to Plancenoit in the evening, the other six were, as usual, kept in reserve and only saw serious action at the end. The 1/1 Châsseurs were left out of the battle altogether at Le Caillou. Interestingly, the two regiments with very high losses (2nd Grenadiers and 2nd Châsseurs), both with casualties topping two-thirds, were those sent into the struggle for Plancenoit and provided two out of the three battalions that advanced as supports in the final attack on the ridge. Overall the Old Guard suffered less than half the losses of the Middle and Young Guards.

• The Middle Guard suffered crippling losses. These were the battalions that made the final assault, or in the case of the 2/3 Grenadiers,

were cut down from a square to a triangle covering the retreat. Not only did the Middle Guard mount the slope under heavy cannon fire, then get driven off by devastating musket volleys at close range, but they had the furthest to retreat and were caught by Wellington's cavalry.

• The Young Guard had the most horrendous losses of the three divisions. This was largely because they spent all their time in action at Waterloo in the defence of Plancenoit. Fighting in this village was particularly bloody and prolonged. There was little let up as the Prussians poured more and more men into the close quarter street fighting. The struggle was ferocious, each side knowing that to hold Plancenoit was crucial to the outcome of the battle. By 26 June the 1st Tirailleurs had virtually ceased to exist, with casualties amounting to 92 per cent, the highest for any unit of comparable size in the French Army. That only some 600 men out of nearly 4,300 paraded a week after the battle speaks for itself.

• Napoleon's Guard lost 75 per cent of its strength, most of the losses occurring at Waterloo. They marched into history with their superb reputation considerably enhanced.

The Battlefield the Next Day

Assistant-Commissary-General Tupper Carey, after first taking the wrong fork at Mont St Jean village, rode down the main Brussels–Genappe road on 19 June, and has left a detailed account of what he saw:

> Our march was very slow of course, and we passed through Waterloo, now a busy scene, the medical officers being fully occupied in collecting and attending to the wounded. … It was dreadful to see the numbers of the killed, both men and horses on each side of the road. Many bodies were stripped of their clothes. As we descended down towards La Haye Sainte, the scene of carnage was still more developed. All round the Haye Sainte and on the Chaussee leading to the French position, the dead were innumerable, French and English intermixed. Those who had fallen in the road had been trampled on by horses and wheels of artillery, into a mass of blood, flesh and clothes, hardly to be distinguished one from the other. In the hollow between the two armies on each side of the road, there lay piles of dead Frenchmen and horses, among whom were many of the Imperial Guard. Their large bearskin caps, which they had thrown away in the struggle, strewed the ground. To add to the numbers were many dead cuirassiers, still with their cuirasses on. … With the exception of a few parties wandering in the quest of wounded men, as well as plunder, all was quiet as a churchyard.

Myths and Controversies

Recoil'd in common rout and fear,
Lancer and Guard and Cuirassier,
Horseman and foot – a mingled host,
Their leaders fall'n, their standards lost.

Sir Walter Scott

General

Because Waterloo has gone down as perhaps the most famous battle in history, and is certainly the most written about, countless myths and controversies have arisen. The two greatest generals of the age faced each other for the first time in twenty years of war. The future history of Europe hung on the result. Hundreds of questions have been raised, hundreds of opinions given, but very few definite answers have been forthcoming. Could, or should, Napoleon have won? Was it Napoleon's fault, or Ney's or Soult's or Grouchy's that the French lost so decisively? Could Wellington have won without the arrival of Blücher and his Prussians? Was it really the Prussians that won the battle? Opinions will always differ but arguments will continue (which is why the battle is so fascinating) and the controversies remain. Many, perhaps most, of these debates centre on strategic matters, on what happened during the three days prior to Waterloo. Why was Wellington so slow to react to the French crossing the border? Why did Napoleon fail to win decisively at Ligny? Why was Blücher allowed to withdraw to fight again at Waterloo? Why did Ney fail to hold, and Napoleon fail to attack, Wellington in his exposed position at Quatre-Bras on 17 June? Why did Grouchy not march to the sound of the guns on 18 June? All these have been discussed ad nauseam in scores of books, so it is not the intention of this writer to go over them yet again.

This book is primarily concerned with the events and the men on the battlefield. Therefore this section will examine some of the myths and controversies that have arisen concerning the actual fighting at Waterloo. They have been selected at random, some are well known, others less so. The list of those discussed is anything but exhaustive. Myths are those events that have come by many to be regarded as fact (and have frequently been repeated as such) but about which there is serious doubt as to their veracity. Often they are events that have been embellished by writers from national prejudice to cover up faults, mistakes or protect regimental pride. This work will attempt to set out the myth and then produce facts or arguments to show how the truth has perhaps been obscured, and arrive at a more likely conclusion. Controversies are more concerned with events about which there is genuine disagreement as to what happened or why. Both sides will be examined in an endeavour to come to some conclusion.

Myths

THE DEPLOYMENT AND PERFORMANCE OF BIJLANDT'S BRIGADE (Maps 12 & 27, pp. 158 & 348)

The Myth

Bijlandt commanded a brigade of five battalions (four Dutch and one Belgian): something under 3000 men at Waterloo. This was at least 600 short of its original strength due to losses at Quatre-Bras. It had fought well at the earlier battle, with the 5th Dutch Militia retaking Gemioncourt Farm twice and resisting several cavalry charges. This battalion paid a high price: 41 per cent casualties. The 27th Dutch Jaeger also lost heavily, dropping from over 800 to around 550. This unit was sent to Nivelles on the evening of 16 June to recover. Its appearance – straggling along the road – did not impress Captain Mercer of the British RHA who mistook them all for deserters.

During the night of 17/18 June the brigade had been posted in line on outpost duty on the forward slope of the Mont St Jean ridge, some 300 metres east of the 'Elm Tree' crossroads. There, like the rest of the army, it had spent a wet, miserable, sleepless night. It maintained picquets down the slope. To its right rear was Kempt's brigade, to its left Pack's, both belonging to Picton's 5th British Division. Bijlandt's own division (2nd Netherlands under Perponcher-Sedlnitzky) was the most scattered formation in Wellington's army, with a battalion in Hougoumont, Bijlandt in the centre and Saxe-Weimar's brigade spread as far east as Frichermont. During Sunday morning this brigade remained on the forward slope despite all other formations taking up positions on the reverse slope – a normal Wellingtonian practice to conceal his men from view and protect them from artillery fire. Virtually all the French could see were Bijlandt and the Anglo-Allied guns deployed along the crest – they had to be able to see to shoot. Bijlandt had four battalions standing in line on the forward slope and the very weak 5th Dutch Militia in reserve behind the hedge on the ridge. This was the situation about noon.

According to some historians, this brigade was still in this exposed position when the French 'Grand Battery' opened fire about 1.00 p.m. These writers claim that the brigade was subjected to the full weight of this bombardment, the only unit in the army to do so, suffering grievously as a result. After some time the brigade allegedly fled ignominiously to the rear, leaving a huge hole in the Anglo-Allied line. The Netherlanders were sent on their way to jeers and possibly a few shots from the British lying down behind the ridge. A few remained or were rallied but the majority did not stay to face the coming assault by d'Erlon's corps. One author does have them staying to receive the French infantry but fleeing well before bayonets were crossed. David Chandler in *Waterloo: The Hundred Days* states, '... the unfortunate Dutch and Belgian troops of Bylandt, in their blue uniforms with orange facings, suffered grievously from the fire of the massed guns'. And later, '... the exposed position of Bylandt must have been an oversight'. Siborne, in his *History of the War in France and Belgium 1815*, who claims they were dreadfully shaken by the bombardment, has this to say of their performance when d'Erlon's infantry attacked:

> ... the Dutch-Belgians, who had already evinced a considerable degree of unsteadiness, began firing in their turn, but with very little effect: immediately after which they commenced a hurried retreat, not partially and promiscuously, but collectively and simultaneously – so much so that the movement carried with it the appearance of its having resulted from a word of command.

There was an attempt to rally them on the ridge but this failed. Siborne continues:

> ... though they [Byleveld's battery and the 5th Militia] seemed to stem the torrent for a moment, they were quickly swept away by its accumulating force. As they rushed passed the British columns, hissings hootings, and execrations, were instantly heaped upon them; and one portion, in its eagerness to get away, nearly ran over the grenadier company of the 28th British regiment, the men of which were so enraged that it was with difficulty they could be prevented from firing on the fugitives.

Jack Weller in his *Wellington at Waterloo* follows Siborne's line. Referring to Nassau and Brunswick troops, he states, 'They were ... far superior, for instance, to Bylandt's and D'Aubreme's Dutch-Belgians who either ran away before the enemy was within effective range, or were seized by panic without even seeing the French.'

Until comparatively recently this was the myth – that Bijlandt's brigade was the only unit exposed to the full fury of the French bombardment and that it ran away either while under artillery fire or when the enemy infantry advanced. The implication being that they were useless troops.

The Last Waterloo Banquet

This was held on 18 June 1852 at Apsley House, Wellington's London residence. The Duke had only three months to live. These banquets (for surviving officers) had been a regular anniversary feature since the battle. They were sumptuous occasions attracting large crowds to applaud arriving guests. Prince Albert attended, together with eighty-four veterans from the military aristocracy – men who had fought as fit young subalterns came as decrepit generals. The lowest rank of officers attending was colonel. Present were General Maitland, General Hew Halkett, Lieutenant-General Scovell, Wellington's decoder from those distant days in the Peninsula, and Major-General Harry Smith whose wife was the young girl he rescued from Badajoz forty years before. The Guards' band played as the Duke, walking with Prince Albert, led the way into the Waterloo Gallery. A dazzling display of gleaming gold and silver, highlighted by huge vases of fresh flowers, awaited. Dinner was served on Dresden china, the dessert on dishes of solid gold. It was interspersed with countless toasts, martial music and a succession of ancient generals staggering to their feet to propose yet another toast – that to the Duke was drunk three times as the band played, 'See the Conquering Hero Comes'.

By way of a footnote, the last British survivor of the battle was Private Morris Shea formerly of the 2/73 Foot, a battalion that had barely fifty men unwounded at the close of the action. He died in February 1892 at the age of ninety-seven.

Comments

There are several powerful reasons why the above deployment was a myth and the poor behaviour almost certainly exaggerated:

• The first is it presupposes a high degree of professional incompetence by several senior commanders. Wellington had given orders for all formations to deploy behind the ridge before the 'Grand Battery' opened fire. Many units were lying down and cavalry regiments had dismounted. Only the artillery (and some skirmishers) were on or slightly forward of the crest. It made no military sense whatsoever to leave Bijlandt's men totally exposed on the forward slope – the only unit in the entire army to be so, and for no good reason. While the Duke may have been too busy to notice, it was blatantly obvious to the divisional, brigade and battalion commanders. Similarly, if the Duke's order had not for some reason reached Bijlandt, it is difficult to accept that no senior officer queried their exposed position.

• If these men had been standing in the open only 500 metres from the 'Grand Battery' when it opened fire with canister and round shot, Bijlandt's brigade would quickly have ceased to exist. This was not the case, as will be seen below. These battalions were able to put up some reasonable resistance to the French infantry assault from the ridge, which would have been impossible had the French guns pounded them on the forward slope. In addition, had these men been in line along the forward slope they would have covered some 500–750 metres of front. This would have prevented Allied guns behind them from firing when it is known that they did fire, inflicting considerable damage on the advancing French.

• Lieutenant-General Perponcher-Sedlnitzky, the divisional commander, queried the situation with Wellington before midday and received authority to pull his brigade back. As his chief of staff, Colonel van Zuylen van Nyevelt, later reported:

> At twelve o'clock the whole of the first brigade (Bijlandt) and the artillery of the right wing moved further back, in order not to hinder the evolutions of the English guns placed in their rear, and also to be less exposed to the [artillery] fire of the enemy. Crossing the sunken road, the corps [brigade] formed itself on the northern side of the road in battle array as before, supported on its right and left by the English and Scottish troops, the guns in line with those of the English.

At 11.30 a.m. the brigade was in front of the ridge but by shortly after noon they had pulled back. Only skirmishers and some guns remained on the forward slope.

• At around 2.00 p.m. these Dutch-Belgians engaged the advancing infantry of Bourgeois' brigade and Donzelot's division with musket fire at close range from the hedge line. Lieutenant Scheltens of the 7th Belgian Infantry stated:

> ... our battalion opened fire as soon as our skirmishers had come in. The French column imprudently halted and began to deploy. We were at such close quarters that Captain Henry l'Olvier, commanding our grenadier company, was struck on the arm by a musket ball, of which the wad, or paper cartridge, remained smoking in the cloth of his tunic.

Watching from the second line with the 92nd Highlanders was Lieutenant James Hope. He also described the unequal struggle:

> ... the Belgians, assailed with terrible fury, returned the fire of the enemy for some time with great spirit. ... [then they] partially retired from the hedge. At the entreaty of their officers, the greater part of them returned to their posts, but it was merely to satisfy their curiosity, for they almost immediately again retired without firing a shot. The officers exerted themselves to the utmost to keep their men at their duty, but their efforts were fruitless.

• The French fire did indeed become too much for most of Bijlandt's men. As Donzelot pushed forward through the hedge, over the road, the Dutch and Belgian troops (with the exception of the 7th Belgian Line) fell back in some haste and disorder. Colonel van Zuylen van Nyevelt again:

> Having approached us to within fifty paces, not a shot had been fired, but now the impatience of the soldiers could no longer be restrained, and they greeted the enemy with a double row, which caused the firing to be meagre and badly kept up whilst the downfall of some files made an opening to the enemy, through which he forced his way with his columns... . The enemy had now succeeded in passing our first line, and had arrived on the plain [crossed the crest of the ridge]. The second line [Pack's and Kempt's brigades] made ready to advance against him...

• The retreat of the bulk of Bijlandt's battalions is confirmed by the testimony of the Netherlands chief of staff, Major-General Constant-Rebecque. He stated that 'the first brigade ... received the first shock and was cut up'. Constant-Rebecque spent some time attempting to rally these battalions.

Conclusions

The most likely sequence of events is:
• Bijlandt's brigade was initially drawn up in line on the forward slope.
• At around noon, before the French 'Grand Battery' started its bombardment, the brigade was withdrawn to behind the hedge line on the ridge, probably on the instigation of the divisional commander, Perponcher-Sedlnitzky.
• These battalions resisted the assault of d'Erlon's columns for several minutes. There was a firefight on the ridge but the weight of the attack was too much for all except one of these weakened units and they retired in some disorder as the French pushed over the crest. Their departure was the subject of a barrage of disparaging comments from the British battalions they passed.
• Their officers strove to keep their men in the line and were successful with some, although the majority retired. They were rallied at the rear by the Netherlands' chief of staff, but took no further active part in the battle.

THAT THE BUILDINGS AND WALLED GARDEN AT HOUGOUMONT WERE DEFENDED SOLELY BY THE BRITISH GUARDS (Maps 21-25, pp. 337-341)

The myth

The view that the British Guards were wholly responsible for the successful defence of the buildings and garden at Hougoumont.

Comments

This myth has arisen, not so much with serious students of the battle, but through the more casual reader or visitor to the battlefield. Great emphasis is placed in many accounts of the fight for this farm on the role played by the British Guards. They did eventually play the dominant role in its defence but they were never the only defenders. This misunderstanding is certainly compounded, if not caused, by the numerous plaques commemorating the actions of the British Guards in Hougoumont. Five plaques are dedicated to Guards' units or individuals, one to the Royal Wagon Train and two to the French. There is nothing to show others played an important role.

Although the Light Company of each of the four Guards' battalions were posted to Hougoumont on the night of 17/18 June, and spent the hours of darkness frantically preparing the place for defence, no guardsmen were in either the buildings or garden at the start of the battle. When Wellington sent the 1/2 Nassau battalion to reinforce Hougoumont early on the Sunday morning, these six strong companies (each almost 150 all ranks) effectively took over the defence of the whole strongpoint. In particular they were the only troops garrisoning the buildings and formal garden. The Grenadier Company of the 1/2 Nassau took over the buildings, another company the garden and two were posted in the Great Orchard. Final defensive preparations had been facilitated by the arrival on the previous evening of the pioneer section of the 2nd Light Battalion, KGL (to the detriment of the defences at La Haie Sainte).

When the 1/2 Nassau arrived, the light companies of the 2/1 and 3/1 Guards under Lord Saltoun withdrew (temporarily) from the Great Orchard. When Reille's guns opened fire and Prince Jérôme's division advanced to attack, the light companies of the 2nd Coldstream Guards and 2/3 Guards had taken up positions immediately west and south-west of the buildings, outside the walls. It was from these vantage points that they fought off the initial attack when it penetrated the wood.

The total garrison of the entire Hougoumont strongpoint (i.e. including the orchard and wood) at 11.30 that morning was nearly 1,300 all ranks. Of these, only about 200 (15 per cent) were British guardsmen. It was not for about another two hours that British outnumbered German troops in the buildings and garden. This occurred with the arrival of most of the remaining companies of the 2nd Coldstream Guards. Nevertheless, it is true to say that throughout the struggle for Hougoumont the Nassau troops always made up a substantial proportion of the defenders.

Conclusion

While the British Guards, in particular the 2nd Coldstream and 2/3 Guards, deserve most of the credit for defending the buildings and garden at Hougoumont, they did not do so without considerable assistance from the 1/2 Nassau. During the initial French assault the buildings and garden were garrisoned entirely by Germans. Only about two hours into the battle did the British outnumber their allies at Hougoumont.

THAT D'ERLON'S CORPS WAS DESTROYED BY PICTON'S
DIVISION AND THE UNION BRIGADE (Maps 26-28, pp. 344-53)

The myth
The myth has arisen that the French I Corps of four divisions
(almost 20,000 men) was destroyed when it attacked the left of
Wellington's line at the outset of the battle.

Comments
The impression given in many accounts of the recoil of this attack
and the charge by the Union Brigade is that d'Erlon's corps was
utterly routed, fled in complete panic and lost thousands of prisoners and was thus destroyed as a fighting force. Defeated – yes;
destroyed – no. Some examples of how this repulse of the French
has been described follow:
• Hamilton-Williams in *Waterloo New Perspectives* – 'The Royals
slashed and stabbed into Durutte's brigade with as much terrible
effect as the Greys had on Marcognet's division. Men threw themselves to the ground to avoid being cut down. Panic ensued and the
whole formation broke, the soldiers fleeing left and right.'
• Lieutenant Shelton of the 28th Foot – 'The column that was
charged by the Royals was broken and the greater part taken prisoner.'
• A British officer – 'The solid mass [of French infantry] I had seen
twenty minutes before was there no more, and had now become a
defenceless crowd. French officers were brought up from the hollow in great numbers, delivering up their swords.'
• Lieutenant Winchester – '... they could not prevent the Greys
destroying the column in under three minutes. One could hardly
believe, had he not witnessed it, that such a complete destruction
could have been effected in so short a time.'
• Private Louis Canler, French 28th Ligne in Bourgeois' brigade
– 'The 1st Division not having time to form square, was unable to
withstand this charge [by the Royal Dragoons] and was broken. A
real carnage then ensued.'

• Houssaye in his *1815: Waterloo* – 'It was a harrowing sight to
see the English breaking through and slaughtering these fine divisions as if they were flocks of sheep. ... The columns were,
divided, scattered, and hurled down to the foot of the slopes by
the swords of the dragoons.'
• Jac Weller in *Wellington at Waterloo* – 'These men [the Union
Brigade] not only completely broke Donzelot's Division, but also
smashed Marcognet's; ... the carnage was awful; ... Two eagles
were taken and upwards of 3,000 prisoners actually secured; many
others surrendered and then escaped because there were insufficient men to guard them.'
• Finally, it is hard to beat the lofty patriotism and purple prose of
Siborne in his *History of the War in France and Belgium 1815* –
'Behold at once the glorious spectacle spread out before you! The dragoons are in the midst of the enemy columns – the furious impetuosity
of their onslaught overcomes all resistance – the terror stricken masses,
paralyzed by this sudden apparition of cavalry amongst them ... . Their
[the Union Brigade's] triumph admits of no restraint...'.

Reading these accounts one would automatically assume that
d'Erlon's corps was finished, dead, out of the battle, incapable of
further fighting. This would be far from the truth. A more accurate assessment of the damage inflicted by Picton's division and
the Union Brigade needs to take account of:
• The fact that the corps was able to rally so quickly and resume
active operations. In particular it resumed the attacks on La Haie
Sainte, which continued throughout the afternoon.
• In the east Durutte's division resumed the struggle for
Papelotte, La Haie and the village of Smohain. These places were
taken by French troops during the afternoon.
• D'Erlon's corps succeeded in capturing La Haie Sainte at
around 6.30 p.m. after a prolonged and costly struggle. The final
attack was conducted by Donzelot's division, led by the 13th
Légère Regiment, a formation that supposedly had been com-
pletely broken hours earlier.

The Trial of Maréchal de Camp Charles-Angelique de la Bédoyère

Bédoyère was twenty-nine when he was put on trial for 'Treason,
Rebellion and Military Seduction' after Waterloo. He had gone
over to Napoleon with the 7th Ligne at Grenoble. He was
rewarded with promotion and the plum appointment as an ADC to
the Emperor. On 16 June Napoleon had sent him with the crucial
order to summon d'Erlon's corps to the Ligny battlefield. D'Erlon
was to spend several fruitless hours marching between Quatre-Bras
and Ligny without firing a shot at either. Bédoyère was also used by
Napoleon at Waterloo as one of the officers taking the false message
that Grouchy had arrived on the right flank to bolster flagging
morale at the start of the French final attack.

Part of the evidence put forward against him was that on 7
March at Grenoble he had a heated argument with the District
Commander, General Marchand, about whether the troops
should go over to Napoleon:

> About three o'clock he [Bédoyère] gave orders [to the 7th
> Ligne] to march forward, and was scarcely out of the town
> when he drew his sword and exclaimed '*Vivre l'Empereur*.' He
> caused a chest to be searched, from which he took a gilt eagle,
> which he placed at the end of a branch of willow, and the same
> evening entered Grenoble in the suit of Buonaparte.

Bédoyère never denied his actions. The prosecutor called for the

death sentence. When Bédoyère spoke in his own defence it was
not to contest what he had done, although he did deny
strenuously that he had any dealings with Napoleon while he had
been on Elba. He finished his speech with the words:

> ... [all] will see again, I hope, a great nation in the French,
> united around their king. Perhaps I shall not be called upon to
> enjoy that sight; but I have shed my blood for my country, and
> I love to persuade myself that my death, preceded by the
> acknowledgement of my error, may be of some use; that my
> memory will not be held in horror; and that when my son shall
> have reached the age at which he shall be able to serve his
> country, that country will not reproach him with his name.

On 26 August 1815 Bédoyère, accompanied by a priest, was taken
to the place of execution. He knelt in prayer. He stood up and
refused to have a blindfold. Pointing at his chest he cried out to the
firing party, 'Above all things do not miss me!' His last wish was
fulfilled. At about the same time that Bédoyère was being shot his
distraught mother was at the Court of the Tuileries trying to see the
King to beg for his life. She was not allowed in his presence. Justice
had been done in great haste and on the cheap. Like Ney's widow,
so Bédoyère's was billed for the cost of the trial. Included was the
sum of three francs each for the soldiers in the firing party!

• Pégot's (of Durutte's division) brigade was brought across from the right flank in the evening to support the attacks in the centre around La Haie Sainte. Evidently Brue's weak brigade (half of Durutte's division) was considered capable of holding its own around Papelotte.

• The whole corps advanced again as part of the French general advance to support the Imperial Guard's attack in the late evening.

• While the corps as a whole may have been defeated and pushed back in confusion by the Union Brigade, not all formations were equally affected. Colonel Charlet's brigade became embroiled in the attack on La Haie Sainte from the start and was not charged by the Union Brigade. Pégot's brigade never reached the ridge and was able to conduct a fairly dignified withdrawal to conform with the other formations' rush for the rear. Half of Durutte's division (Brue's brigade) was deliberately left out of the main attack altogether. Thus of the four divisions in the corps, only two-and-a-half actually assaulted Wellington's positions on the ridge and felt the full weight of the British heavy cavalry sabres.

• The quotations above would lead the reader to believe that these divisions suffered horrendous losses, that their morale had gone and that they were surrendering (officers included) in droves. In fact most of them quickly recovered their morale. All these units were able to fight effectively again. Their recovery from this setback was due to the leadership of the officers, plus the fact that casualties had not been quite so catastrophic as these accounts appear to indicate.

Consider the following: when the corps mustered about a week later it had shrunk from almost 17,000 infantrymen to about 4,500 – a loss of 12,500, or 73 per cent. But the great majority of these losses had occurred during events other than the first main French attack of the battle. They had lost men around Papelotte and La Haie. They lost considerable numbers attacking and eventually taking La Haie Sainte; they lost more during the final, abortive general advance. They lost heavily in the debacle of the rush to escape the battlefield at the end; and they lost many more due to desertions during the days following the French defeat. Finally, it is a well-established fact that cavalry seldom inflict crippling losses with their swords. Cannons and muskets would have caused most of the casualties – the British cavalry probably doing better at forcing surrenders rather than killing people. It is therefore reasonable to suggest that d'Erlon's corps lost between 3000–4000 all ranks (18–24 per cent) during that first assault.

Conclusions

• D'Erlon's corps was undoubtedly repulsed with severe but not crippling losses when it attacked Wellington's line shortly before 2.00 p.m.

• Only two-and-a-half out of the four divisions actually attacked the ridge.

• Most of the casualties were unlikely to have been inflicted by the Union Brigade.

• The corps was able to recover quite quickly and participate effectively in further fighting.

• The great majority of its losses at Waterloo occurred after the first attack and in the final retreat.

CONTROVERSIES

THAT THE PRUSSIANS WON WATERLOO

The controversy

The argument, that has come to the fore again recently with the publication of Peter Hofschröer's book *1815 The Waterloo Campaign – The German Victory*, is that Wellington would have lost Waterloo had it not been for the arrival of the Prussians.

Comments

British writers in particular have long either refuted the idea, or glossed over the possibility, that Wellington on his own would not have won. The best that is conceded is a stalemate. Tenacity, courage, superior tactics, a line always beat a column, skilful use of the reverse slope, and that there was little difference in numbers between the French and Anglo-Allied armies have all been cited in combination as reasons why Wellington would at least have held on. After all, it is a well-established military maxim that an attacker needs a superiority of 3:1 to dig a determined defender out of a good position. And the Duke certainly had a good position.

The argument continues: Napoleon had lost his touch, was sick even, had virtually handed over command to Ney who, with or without the Prussians, made a series of ill co-ordinated, piecemeal frontal attacks, first with infantry alone, then with cavalry alone. The French high command allowed some 14,000 infantry to be sucked into a day-long effort to take Hougoumont, defended by a fraction of that number. Such tactics, such generalship would never have taken the ridge.

Those who consider that the Prussians won the battle for the Allies make the following points.

• Their sighting at around 1.00 p.m. caused Napoleon to switch 7000 infantry men, 3,500 cavalrymen and twenty-eight guns (Lobau's VI Corps) to the extreme right flank before any attack had been made on Wellington's main position. The battle had seven hours to run and a major part of his reserve had already been committed outside the critical area of operations. In other words, the Emperor's strength had been reduced to some 66,800, less than Wellington's army, before a shot (discounting Hougoumont) had been fired.

• As the Prussians closed in on and assaulted Plancenoit behind the French centre right, so more men were diverted from Napoleon's reserve to deal with the threat. In all, another ten infantry battalions from the Imperial Guard were needed to hold off the Prussians. Therefore, in total, Blücher's intervention stripped Napoleon of twenty-five battalions, twenty cavalry squadrons and around forty-four guns that should have been available elsewhere. This represented 23 per cent of his infantry strength.

• With these troops in reserve, used to support attacks, exploit opportunities and concentrate yet more pressure on the Anglo-Allied centre, surely it would have cracked – so the argument goes.

• To be specific, supposing Lobau had been available to follow up d'Erlon's corps attack as was intended, perhaps it would have tipped the scales. Three of d'Erlon's divisions reached the ridge, or nearly so, and at least one crossed the road. They were tumbled back by cavalry, but if Domon's and Subervie's squadrons had been in support of or between the infantry divisions to counter the Allies' horsemen, the attack could have had a different ending.

• Later, when the French finally took La Haie Sainte, brought up guns and caused serious problems in Wellington's centre, when Ney was yelling for infantry support, suppose there was not a Prussian in sight. With both Lobau and the entire Imperial Guard available, surely this window of opportunity would have been flung wide open.

• Even supposing in these circumstances, with no threat to the French right, the battle had continued into the late evening and a final attack was necessary, it would have been far stronger. Discounting Lobau, virtually the entire Imperial Guard, all twenty-one battalions, would have been available. As it was, the Guard's assault with five came perilously near to succeeding for a few minutes – several British battalions got into a confusing tangle, while even Maitland's Guards scrambled back to the ridge in a decidedly unguardsman-like manner on the approach of the 4th Châsseurs' square.

Conclusions

It would seem, on balance, that if the Prussians had not put in an appearance so early, Napoleon should have won Waterloo. Whether he would or not depended on the generalship of the Emperor and Ney. They would have had the means, but whether they would have seized the opportunities will never be known. Certainly, even with the Prussian presence, there were several occasions when, as Wellington himself said, 'it was a close-run thing'. Perhaps the final word should be that of a British cavalry general, Sir Hussy Vivian. In his opinion, 'We were greatly indebted to the Prussians, and it was their coming on the right and rear of Napoleon that gave us the victory at Waterloo.'

COULD THE FRENCH HAVE WON WATERLOO (EVEN AFTER THE PRUSSIAN ARRIVAL)?

The controversy

This controversy is clearly linked with the previous one, but it has been suggested that a tactical victory at Waterloo was a possibility even after the presence of the Prussians had been detected. The case in favour of this outcome rests on a series of 'ifs'. Only the purely tactical 'ifs' are considered here – the strategic ones (involving the actions of Grouchy and the battles at Ligny and Quatre-Bras) need a book to themselves:

• If Napoleon had started the battle much earlier, as he originally intended (see below), he would have been able to use Lobau's corps to support d'Erlon's attack before his right was threatened. Undoubtedly if this attack had been launched two hours earlier and had succeeded (it was against Wellington's weakest flank), then Waterloo would probably have had a different ending.

• If the French had not wasted so much time and manpower trying to take Hougoumont, these soldiers would have been available to clinch a victory elsewhere. A brigade was sufficient to keep the Hougoumont garrison busy. That would have meant at least another 8,500 men for action at more critical times and places.

• If Lobau, when sent to block the Prussians, had marched further east and disputed the Bois de Paris, or even the Lasne defile, then the Prussians would never have reached the battlefield before dark, if at all (see below).

• If the major French attacks had been properly co-ordinated and supported, they would have had a good chance of succeeding. In other words, if d'Erlon's attack had been supported by more cavalry, if the massed cavalry attacks had been less massive and had infantry and more artillery backing, and if Ney and Napoleon had conducted an all arms battle, then the chances of winning would have been better.

• If the French cavalry had spiked the Duke's guns after the first massed cavalry attack, the biggest killer of Frenchmen would have been all but eliminated for the remainder of the battle.

Comments

If all the 'ifs' listed above had been fulfilled Napoleon would probably have won at Waterloo, despite Blücher's march from Wavre (he would not have arrived in time to influence the outcome). However, this is tantamount to asking the impossible. The absolute essential for a French victory was for the Prussians not to arrive. As soon as they debouched from the Bois de Paris the pressure they applied to the French was going to get greater and greater. Whether Lobau could have done more to keep them away is discussed below, as is the possibility of an earlier start to the battle.

The criticism regarding the wasted effort and manpower at Hougoumont is entirely justified. It was never Napoleon's intention to take the place but neither he, Ney nor Reille had the courage to limit the attacks. The 'if' concerning the need for better battlefield all arms co-operation is probably only a half-justified condemnation of the French handling of their forces. Specifically:
• D'Erlon's advance was preceded by at least thirty minutes of sustained artillery fire from eighty guns. They continued to fire over the heads of the advancing infantry for as long as they could. It was a major example of co-operation between guns and infantry – that it was not as effective as was hoped was not the fault of the French gunners. It was not possible for d'Erlon to take forward any of his corps artillery as they were all part of the 'Grand Battery'.
• D'Erlon could have done with some more cavalry support as his divisions arrived on the ridge, but there was cavalry (Dubois) on the left flank and Jacquinot moved forward to a more suitable position on the right.
• The lack of effective use of artillery to breach the walls or doors at Hougoumont has already been noted and was certainly a tactical error, albeit a comparatively minor one. The French use (on Napoleon's orders) of incendiary carcasses on the buildings produced good results.
• After the fall of La Haie Sainte guns were brought up to within 200 metres of the Anglo-Allied positions and fired with great effect. Many British survivors (such as Captain Mercer) testify with feeling as to the losses they caused.
• Perhaps the most serious failure in respect of not using all arms in combination was during the continuous cavalry attacks of the afternoon. Artillery was used to pound the Allies' positions while the cavalry recuperated (or was replaced by yet more horsemen) between attacks, but there was never any infantry available. If the French had forced Wellington's infantry to form squares by cavalry attacks and had brought up guns and infantry, it could have swung the balance in their favour. What was needed were less horsemen not more – to make room for guns and footsoldiers.
• With the final assault by the Imperial Guard an attempt was made to make it a general advance. A horse artillery battery placed its guns between the advancing squares and proved how effective such tactics could be. D'Erlon's infantry was galvanized to march forward yet again with some degree of enthusiasm – which quickly evaporated when it was realized that the gunfire on the right was Blücher's rather than Grouchy's. Of cavalry, however, there was little sign. The remaining squadrons were an exhausted shadow of the magnificent regiments that had advanced four hours earlier.

Conclusion

Apart from Ney's handling of the cavalry, the French did make an effort to use at least two of the arms in combination. Nevertheless, better tactical handling of itself would not have affected the outcome of the battle unless the Prussians failed to arrive.

LOBAU'S ROLE AND PERFORMANCE ON THE EASTERN FLANK (Map 35, p. 379)

The controversy

If only Lobau had not sat down and waited for the Prussians but had pushed on through the Bois de Paris to the Lasne valley and disputed Bülow's progress there, the Prussians would never have arrived on the battlefield in time to prevent a French victory.

Comments

• Even if Lobau had kept the Prussians away from the battlefield entirely, it would not necessarily have ensured Wellington's defeat. However, it would have enhanced Napoleon's chances considerably. He would not have had the running sore of Plancenoit, so the entire Young Guard Division would have been available to him. Indeed, all the twenty-one battalions of the Imperial Guard (12,600 men) would have provided a most powerful reserve of fresh troops for use to exploit opportunities.

• There is no doubt that the Prussian advance from Wavre was slow. When their leading brigade debouched from the Bois de Paris to begin its attack, Blücher's rearmost columns were barely clear of Wavre some 10 to 12 kilometres to the rear. There were long delays as the troops struggled to cross the Lasne River and drag themselves up the slippery slopes into and through the Bois de Paris. As they did so their only opposition came from Marbot's three squadrons of hussars. There can be little doubt that had the Lasne defile or even the Bois de Paris been seriously contested, no worthwhile numbers of Prussians would have reached the battlefield before dark.

• Napoleon first became aware of the Prussian threat shortly after 1.00 p.m. Within fifteen minutes he knew from the Prussian prisoner that it was Bülow's corps. He despatched first the cavalry and, a few minutes later, the remainder of Lobau's corps to block this unexpected threat. By 1.30 p.m. some 7000 infantry, 3,500 cavalry and twenty-eight guns were marching east. On the Emperor's orders Soult wrote a message to Grouchy timed 1.00 p.m. Although happy with Grouchy's stated intention to move on Wavre, he was told to 'manoeuvre therefore to join our right'. An important postscript reads:

> P.S. – A letter which has just been intercepted states that General Bülow is about to attack our right flank. We believe that we notice this corps now on the heights of S. Lambert. So do not lose a moment in drawing near to us, and effecting a junction with us, in order to crush Bülow whom you will catch in the very act of concentrating [with Wellington].

The significance of this in terms of Grouchy's response (it would arrive too late for him to reach the Waterloo battlefield much before dark) is outside the scope of this book. Its relevance here is that Napoleon, who had always dismissed the possibility of Prussian interference, now realized it was going to happen. The captured Prussian prisoner led him to think it might be only one corps, although he now knew Blücher had spent the night around Wavre.

• Some critics have suggested that Napoleon was premature in sending Lobau's entire corps to block the Prussians at this stage. It is claimed that there was still plenty of time to beat Wellington before Bülow could arrive if he used Lobau to support d'Erlon's attack. The argument goes that once the Prussians saw Wellington being overwhelmed or forced to retire, they would themselves

have held back. There is some merit in this contention. The Prussian advance was hesitant, their formations could only arrive piecemeal and it would be another four hours after Lobau moved off before Bülow was in a position to attack effectively. With the advantage of hindsight it is easy to see how a commander could have done better. Perhaps the Emperor was too cautious – we will never know.

• It is uncertain exactly what orders were given to Lobau before he moved off. Was he told to go to a specific place? Was he told to await the Prussian arrival before engaging them? Was he to conduct an aggressive or more passive defence of the right flank? Were these things left to his own discretion? Was he told of the possibility of Grouchy's arrival, and if so, was he to wait until Grouchy's guns could be heard before taking the offensive? Lobau was an extremely experienced general, certainly a cut above most senior French commanders present that day. In the event he handled the fighting withdrawal back to Plancenoit with considerable skill against ever worsening odds.

• Perhaps the crux of this issue is whether it was actually possible for Lobau to seriously dispute the Prussians' passage through the Lasne defile or the Bois de Paris. In other words, could he have got there in time? It is a question of time and distance.

• Assuming Lobau started his march at 1.30 p.m., he had some 2,700 metres to reach the position he actually took up. Moving along a road, as he was able to do, this should not have taken much more than an hour – his cavalry would have got there earlier. So he would be deploying between 2.30 p.m. and 3.00 p.m. At this time Bülow's leading units were negotiating the Lasne defile. Lobau then had about a two-hour wait for the Prussian infantry to advance from the western edge of the Bois de Paris.

• If Lobau had marched into the Bois de Paris he would have to cover about 3,700 metres from his starting point. He would therefore have needed about another forty minutes. So he might have expected to be moving into the Paris Wood at around 3.15 p.m. By this time the Prussians were starting to enter the eastern side of the wood. Discounting cavalry patrols from both sides, the first serious clash between the opposing infantry would probably have occurred in the wood.

• It is obvious from these estimates that Lobau would have had insufficient time to reach the Lasne defile, at least another 1000 metres east, before the bulk of Bülow's corps had crossed.

Conclusions

It will always be arguable that Napoleon would have done better by not sending Lobau to the east immediately on spotting the Prussian advance. He played safe, something he would probably not have done in his earlier days. In addition, despite Bülow's surprise arrival in the distance, the Emperor's confidence in victory was seemingly not dented.

If Lobau had, from the outset of his march, been determined to oppose the Prussians as far east as possible, then he could probably have done so in the Bois de Paris, but not in the Lasne defile. Fighting in the wood would have favoured the French – such fighting always favours the defender as it gives him cover, concealment and confuses the attacker, who is usually unaware of the strength of the opposition. In the difficult circumstances of the Prussian advance that afternoon, had they additionally met stiff infantry resistance in the wood, the advance would have been stalled for a considerable time.

D'ERLON'S ATTACK FORMATION (Diagram p. 195 and Maps 27, p. 348)

The controversy

The argument revolves around why the attack formation of divisional columns, with battalions formed up in three rank lines, one behind the other, was adopted, and whether it contributed to the attack's failure. It is an important question as the repulse of this attack abruptly ended all French hopes of a quick or inexpensive victory.

Comments

• First the reader needs to be clear as to the actual formation adopted, and by which formations – see the diagram on p. 195. Most authorities agree that the divisions of Donzelot (nine battalions) and Marcognet (eight battalions) were formed up with all their battalions in three rank lines, one behind the other. With Quiot's division on the left, only one brigade (Bourgeois, four battalions) attacked the ridge, while the other was committed to taking La Haie Sainte. Similarly, on the extreme right only Pégot's brigade (four battalions) advanced on the ridge, the other being held in reserve or committed to attacking the Papelotte area. Both Bourgeois and Pégot probably adopted the same formation but, while their frontage would have been the same as the other divisions, their depth would have been halved. The divisional blocks in particular must have been an impressive sight, closely resembling an ancient Greek phalanx.

• Discounting the two flank brigades that had other objectives, some 13,000 infantrymen were involved in the main attack. It is important to know how much ground (frontage) these large divisional (and brigade) blocks covered and relate this to actual distances on the ground. First, it has been reliably established (from Anglo-Allied witnesses) that, as was normal practice, the French deployed a dense line of skirmishers ahead of the advance. This could have meant using the leading battalion from each division (something over 2000 men) or, and this is more likely, the voltigeur company from every battalion (twenty-five). This would have produced slightly more – about 2,250 – trained skirmishers. It would also reduce the average strength of each battalion from around 540 to around 460. With 460 men in three ranks there would be between 140–150 files depending on the number of officers and supernumeraries. So the average frontage of each battalion or each brigade or each division would have been about 110–120 metres. However, before they formed into these huge blocks each battalion had to weave its way through the mass of wagons, caissons and guns deployed in front of the corps. Having negotiated the 'Grand Battery', the two divisions

and two brigades (all having an equal frontage) formed up covering some 1,100 metres with perhaps 200 metres between each formation. During the advance in echelon the overall frontage narrowed, so that as they approached, the objective distances between formations had shrunk to about 100 metres.

• Some historians have suggested this formation was a mistake. They maintain that the usual order would have been 'colonne de battaillons par division', meaning each battalion formed its own column on a two-division frontage – in this case the word 'division' meaning half a company. If the order had been 'colonne de divisions par battaillon' then they would have advanced, as they did, in the phalanx type blocks. This is a possibility but unlikely. It assumes a considerable degree of incompetence on the part of staff officers, ADCs and commanders. Perhaps one brigade or division might have got things confused, but not all. The balance of probability must be that divisional commanders had the right order, understood it and complied.

• This formation was unusual, but not unique, and has been the subject of considerable criticism. It was much less manoeuvrable than battalion columns, slower, with increased difficulties in maintaining dressing (alignment) over the muddy fields of high-standing crops. It was also highly vulnerable to artillery fire by either canister or round shot – a well-aimed projectile cutting a swath through the ranks like a ball in a bowling alley. Certainly Captain Duthilt of the 45th Ligne leading Marcognet's divisional column did not think much of it:

> [We] had to advance like the others in deployed battalions, with only four paces between one and the next – a strange formation and one which was to cost us dear, since we were unable to form square as a defence against cavalry attacks, while the enemy's artillery could plough our formations to a depth of twenty ranks. To whom the 1st Corps owed this unfortunate formation, which proved to be one cause, maybe even the cause of our failure, nobody knows. … The four columns moved off down the slope, with ported arms and in serried ranks. We were to mount the opposite slope where the English held the ridge and from where their batteries were blasting us. No doubt the distance involved was not great [about 600 metres], and an average person on foot would have taken no more than five or six minutes to cover the ground; but the soft rain-sodden earth and the tall rye slowed up our progress considerably. As a result the English gunners had plenty of time in which to work destruction upon us.

Some Civilian Survivors

The newspaper the *Morning Post* carried an article on 27 March, 1899. It read:

> In the village of Rolvenden, in the Weald of Kent, there is living an old woman named Moon, who was present at the battles of Quatre Bras and Waterloo. Her father, a colour-sergeant of the 3rd Battalion the Rifle Brigade, served throughout the Peninsular War, and took part in the battles of Badajoz, Salamanca and other conflicts. He died of wounds received at Waterloo some months after the battle and before he had received his pension. Mrs. Moon was born in the Peninsula, her mother doing work for the forces when operating there. Though Mrs. Moon is now infirm, her intellect is clear and her memory good.

Mrs Moon died in October 1903. She was four years old at the time of the battle and rode in a wagon over the field on the evening of 18 June 1815. Another brief note appeared in Notes and Queries dated 5th December 1903:

> Elizabeth Watkins, of Norwich, born 31st January 1810 at Beaminster, near Bridport. Her father, one Daniel Gale, was pressed into the King's service just before Waterloo. Gale's wife and child followed him to Brussels and were in the women's camp near the field of Waterloo. The child remembers cutting up lint – saw many dead, and some stirring incidents of the battle.

Interestingly, to walk 600 metres in six minutes is a fair estimate and confirms that the divisions formed up after passing through the 'Grand Battery', otherwise the distance would have been 1000 metres – requiring well over six minutes to cover in normal circumstances. In the event, the 600 metres took between fifteen and twenty minutes to cover.

• Duthilt raised the question, but did not know the answer, as to who ordered this formation. He might also have added, why? It was a decision taken at the top of the French high command, excluding Napoleon (as it is unlikely he concerned himself with such details as it was not his job – he told his senior commanders what to do rather than how to do it). There is certainly no mention of it in his 11.00 a.m. order. It seems likely that Ney and the corps commanders conferred, sometime before noon, on how best to carry out the attack. This meeting probably involved Soult, Reille, d'Erlon, Lobau and Drouot. Of these, Soult, Reille and d'Erlon had considerable Peninsula experience of the problem of attacking a British force, most of which was hidden on the reverse slope of a ridge. As all understood, an attacking battalion column wanted maximum firepower when they met the enemy. To achieve this they needed to deploy into line at precisely the right moment. This was no easy matter for commanding officers if all they could see as they neared the crest were enemy skirmishers. What was on the other side of the hill? If there was cavalry and you deployed too early, you risked being cut to pieces; if there was a line of infantry and you deployed too late, you risked being shot to pieces. On countless occasions in Spain and Portugal French commanders had got it wrong and been caught in column or trying to deploy by close range musket volleys.

It was likely that they opted for a compromise at Waterloo. They would sacrifice flexibility and speed of movement. In exchange they would use a formation that was headed by a battalion already deployed in line with over 400 muskets able to fire. Each formation would also retain the weight of a column to smash through the enemy position. There would be no question of further deployment at the last moment, as every battalion was already in line and there was no room to deploy further (nor were they trained to do so from such a formation). Cavalry remained a threat but should be possible to deal with if these massive columns halted and the rear battalion turned about and the men on the flanks faced outwards; it was really a different version of a closed square. With cannon fire the generals may have reasoned, with some justification, that this formation was no more vulnerable than battalion columns.

Conclusions

There is no doubt that these huge columns were used and that they were vulnerable to artillery fire. That they were used was almost certainly a conscious decision of the high command to accept the disadvantages in order to have battalions already in line, backed by the weight of a column, when they closed with the enemy. Their slowness exposed them as a vulnerable target to artillery fire for longer than had they been in smaller, more mobile formations. Cavalry did not attack them until they had reached or crossed the ridge, so this gamble had paid off. However, by then they had been badly cut up by gunfire, they had lost formation and were confused. Despite all this, they had gained their objective, and with support by cavalry might have retained it. The adoption of the phalanx formation was risky and may have contributed to the failure of the attack, but not necessarily more so than attacking in battalion columns that had failed so often before.

THE TIMING OF THE START OF THE BATTLE

The controversy

There has always been the contention that if the French had opened the battle earlier then they might have snatched a victory before the Prussians could make their presence felt. The controversy revolves around why Napoleon waited so long – the assault on Hougoumont started about 11.30 a.m. and d'Erlon's attack (the main attack with which the Emperor intended to secure the Mont St Jean crossroads) stepped off two hours later.

Comments

• There can be little doubt that if the battle had started around 11.00 a.m. and Lobau's VI Corps had been available, the chances of the French succeeding would have been dramatically increased. As discussed earlier in this book, late at night on 17 June the Emperor had every intention of starting his attack early – very early. Initially it was around 6.00 a.m., then 9.00 a.m. and finally the 11.00 a.m. orders envisaged the main advance on Mont St Jean starting soon after 1.00 p.m.

• These series of postponements did not appear to worry the Emperor. There is no evidence to suggest that he was annoyed at the delays. He was in a confident mood, dismissing Reille's caution as to the strength of Wellington's position. He was absolutely sure he would win, late start or no late start. This over-confidence was based primarily on the fact that he was sure in his own mind that the Prussians could not intervene. His complacency led him to neglect to send out cavalry – Marbot's 7th Hussars – until about 10.00 a.m. Earlier, more wide ranging patrols would have revealed the true situation with regard to the Prussian movements.

• Many writers attribute the delays to the need for the ground to dry out. It is claimed that a wait was necessary so that artillery could be deployed and to facilitate cross-country movement by cavalry. The rain had been torrential and prolonged. There is no doubt that the ground was saturated, mud was ankle deep or more in many areas, pools of water had formed in hollows and to plod over the fields through the high crops was a slow and exhausting undertaking. For soldiers to run was almost impossible, for horses even to trot was tiring, while dragging guns or wagons was punishing. Napoleon's artillery commander pleaded for time for the ground to dry. The problem with this argument is that for the ground to dry out appreciably would require hot summer sunshine for several hours. The weather was not obliging. Clouds predominated after the rain stopped early in the morning. To delay the attack from 9.00 a.m. to 11.00 a.m., or even to 1.00 p.m., was never going to make that much difference to the state of the ground without a hot sun. Napoleon and anybody else in the French Army who gave it a moment's thought was surely well aware of this.

• The actual cause of the postponements was due to the army being late in assembling. Like the troops of all the armies, the French had had a rotten night. They had been strung out and scattered in sodden bivouacs up to 12 kilometres from the battlefield. Many units had dispersed in the hunt for wood, warmth, shelter and food. The French equivalent of the Provost-Marshal had resigned as he was unable to control the indiscipline of so many troops. Units had been slow to assemble, slow to start their march and had been further slowed by the state of the tracks and the fact that there was only one main road for the entire army. Foy's division had been ordered to parade at 3.30 a.m. in Genappe, only 8 kilometres from the battlefield, in anticipation of an early start to the conflict. Had it marched off at 4.00 a.m. it could reasonably have been expected to be deploying by 6.00–6.30 a.m. However, conditions were far from reasonable, so Foy and many other formations started late and arrived late. When Napoleon dictated his orders for the battle, which Soult timed at 11.00 a.m., his army was still far from ready. A fact acknowledged by the start of the action being timed for after 1.00 p.m. In the event, Reille's corps began its supposedly diversionary attack on Hougoumont before the arrival of the Middle and Old Guards. Even Durutte's division was still plodding into position after Reille's attack had gone in.

Conclusions

The state of the ground was only marginally responsible for the late start of the battle. Historians, particularly French historians, have exaggerated the need for the ground to dry out in order to excuse the delays. If any worthwhile drying was to occur, several hours of summer sun were required, which, to all at Waterloo that morning, did not look likely. Napoleon had wanted to start early but was prevented from doing so by the late arrival of so many formations. He showed no real concern about the postponements as he was over-confident and had convinced himself the Prussians were no longer in the equation for that Sunday.

WELLINGTON'S ORDERS TO HIS ARTILLERY

The controversy

Wellington's orders to his artillery at Waterloo contained three possibly controversial features. They were:
1. To remove the RHA batteries (except one) from their cavalry brigades and to use them as positional artillery
2. To instruct them not to indulge in counter-battery fire
3. That if pressed closely, particularly by cavalry, the gunners were to abandon their cannons to seek shelter in the nearest infantry square

Comments

• Taking the RHA guns from the cavalry formations and giving them static roles alongside the foot artillery was unusual. It meant that if mounted formations were deployed forward or to the flanks of a position, given a specific task to delay the enemy or act as a screen, they must do so without mobile artillery support. Horse artillery was created in order to keep up with, and quickly support, cavalry operations. They expected to come into and out of action quickly. Foot artillery was intended to be more static as it was only expected to keep up with and support the infantry. Wellington knew he was going to fight a purely defensive action at Waterloo. He had no intention of sending his cavalry on any wide flanking or semi-independent manoeuvres; what he required was the maximum number of guns along his front. There they would remain, with a few minor adjustments of position, throughout the long hours of the battle. As the Duke had foreseen, this was where he needed every possible gun.

• It was (and still is) very tempting to shoot back at somebody who is shooting at you. For much of the battle the only worthwhile target that the French gunners could see was the Anglo-Allied artillery deployed on the forward slope. Wellington's gunners had instructions to reserve their fire for softer targets – for infantry and cavalry. It must have been frustrating not to be able to concentrate fire on the 'Grand Battery' so prominently

deployed and firing continuously from about 700 metres away. No doubt some Allied guns succumbed to the temptation. Certainly Mercer let fly at some of Piré's guns early in the battle – and quickly regretted his action. The Duke had given his instructions in order to conserve ammunition for the assaults he knew would come. It was far from easy to put cannons out of action with long range gunfire. The target was small and required a direct hit by a cannon ball. A lot of accurate shooting was necessary. Better to ensure artillery fire was directed at humans and horses where its effects would be bloody and possibly decisive.

• Wellington's third order to his artillery was the most controversial, the most risky. To tell gunners to abandon their guns when under close attack was like telling infantry to abandon their Colours. In fact the artillery carried no Colours, their guns were regarded as Colours. To lose their ordnance was (and remains) the greatest disgrace for artillery of any nation. To cut and run was against all normal artillery training, yet this is what Wellington ordered. However, in really dire circumstances (as gunners were too few to expect to emerge victorious from hand-to-hand combat) if a detachment was forced to leave its guns, they were trained to take all tools for firing with them (particularly rammers). This aimed to ensure that the guns could not be immediately used against nearby units.

There were two potentially battle-losing risks involved. The first was that once the detachments had run back for shelter there was no guarantee that some (or all) of the men would not keep on running. Officers and NCOs could lose control of their men. There was also no guarantee that once the threat was over that all the detachment would return. The second danger was that such action was equivalent to handing over the guns to the enemy. At Waterloo the French cavalry captured virtually all the Duke's guns in the front line at about 4.00 p.m. This was repeated several times over the next hour and a half. Wellington had taken a gamble that the French horsemen would not, or could not, spike or drag away his guns. Had they done so it would possibly have put the outcome of the battle in doubt, despite the Prussians' arrival. As discussed earlier, a little initiative on the part of some French officers or NCOs, the opening of some axle boxes to use Allied spikes and tools, the smashing of wheels or the dragging of guns down the slope would have cost the Anglo-Allied Army dear. One sergeant in Major Rogers' battery, which was overrun by Bourgeois' infantry early in the afternoon, did what his training told him to do if he had to abandon his gun to the enemy: he spiked it. A number of historians have implied that he did something stupid or even cowardly – an unfair allegation for an NCO carrying out a normal procedure. The fact that no other gunner did it would seem to indicate that they were acting on orders merely to grab their tools and run – an order that had not got through to our unknown sergeant.

Conclusions

Wellington's decisions to use all his guns, horse and foot, as guns of position and to forbid firing in the counter-battery role were proved sound. Indeed, it was the artillery that inflicted the highest proportion of casualties on the French precisely because he had given these orders. The real risk was in allowing the detachments to abandon their guns. He was relying on the gunners returning after the danger had passed and that there would be guns to return to. This gamble came off due to the incompetence of the French cavalry commanders – but perhaps the Duke knew his enemy almost as well as he did his own men.

THE AMMUNITION SUPPLY TO LA HAIE SAINTE

The controversy

The primary reason that La Haie Sainte fell to the French has invariably been ascribed to the garrison running out of ammunition. The controversy revolves around why this happened, despite five urgent requests from Baring for replenishment.

Comments

• Not all accounts have made it clear that it was rifle ammunition for his Baker rifles that Baring was requesting. Neither is it made clear as to the numbers of rifles as distinct from muskets there were in the garrison. Baring's battalion (the original defenders) was a seriously depleted unit with no more than 400 rifles. Each man carried sixty rounds, so at the outset Baring had around 24,000 rounds. Between 3.00 p.m. and 4.00 p.m. La Haie Sainte received about 170 (two companies) of rifle-armed reinforcements from the 1st Light Battalion, KGL. They would have started the battle with sixty rounds each and most would have had about this amount when sent to the farm. The total number of riflemen with Baring at this time was around 570. So approximately 34,200 rifle cartridges would have been taken into La Haie Sainte by mid-afternoon. But even before this Baring had started to request more ammunition. If the rifles had been fired at the rate of two shots a minute, the ammunition would only have lasted half an hour. As the fighting went on for over four hours, the rate of fire was far less than this. Considerable efforts were made to conserve it, while all dead or wounded had their pouches emptied. By 6.00 p.m. the surviving riflemen were virtually all out of ammunition. So in the four hours from, say, 2.00 p.m. they had fired off about 34,000 rounds. Averaged out, this gives a rate of fire over the period by the riflemen of 142 shots a minute – not much considering at any one time perhaps 500 riflemen were theoretically available to fire (discounting dead and wounded).

• The reason the ammunition lasted as long as it did was that the rate of fire was so slow. This was only partly due to deliberate conservation. The other more important reason, never previously discussed, was the simple fact that the average defender had so few opportunities to fire once he was inside the farm compound. There were no platforms behind the walls as at Hougoumont, there were no windows looking outwards towards the enemy, and the only loopholes were the two or three in the wall facing the orchard. The defenders were forced to fire through open doorways, some perhaps from the roofs of buildings and from the roof of the pigpens. In other words, many defenders could not get into a reasonable position from which to shoot. They waited their turn, or replaced casualties. This lack of opportunity (until the French forced their way in at the end) was a key factor in enabling the ammunition to last as long as it did.

• However, for the last two hours or so before the farm fell at 6.30 p.m. all the reinforcements had been musket-armed troops. The first to arrive were about eighty-five men from the Light Company of the 5th KGL. They were followed shortly afterwards by 150 soldiers in the 1/2 Nassau from the Hougoumont area. Assuming they had previously been replenished at least once during the battle, it is reasonable to expect them to have had about forty rounds in their pouches – another 9,400 cartridges. Over the final two hours these would have permitted an average rate of musket fire of about seventy-eight shots a minute – a far lower rate than for the rifles. Put another way, had the musketeers been able to maintain two shots a minute for ninety minutes they would have needed over 42,000 rounds. But like their rifle-armed comrades, even if they had had an unlimited supply they would have been unable to use it due to the restricted number of firing positions.

These somewhat confusing statistics have been included to show not only why the defenders of La Haie Sainte were desperately short of ammunition by the end (both rifle and musket) but, equally importantly, show that had there not been so few positions from which the defenders could fire on the French, La Haie Sainte might have fallen earlier.

It must have been desperately frustrating for Baring to keep sending back messengers for ammunition only to receive nothing. There was no explanation, nobody among the reinforcements could tell him. It was inconceivable that none of his requests had got through, indeed as more and more troops arrived it would seem men were being sent instead of ammunition. It has been suggested that he might have obtained rifle ammunition for the 1/95 Rifles in the sandpit just north of the farm, on the other side of the road. Perhaps he could, we shall never know, but it is possible also they too were short. But what Baring needed was not a few soldiers with stuffed pouches but full casks, which in turn meant an ammunition wagon such as the one that delivered to Hougoumont.

• The main field ammunition park had been established (according to Craan's map) about 400 metres south-west of the Mont St Jean crossroads, on the north of the road (track) leading to Merbraine (Map 12). It was 1,600 metres by the Genappe road (the obvious and direct route) to La Haie Sainte. Captain James Shaw (afterwards General Sir James Shaw-Kennedy) was an assistant-quartermaster-general with the 3rd Division, of which Baring's battalion

---

Napoleon's 'Grumblers' Fade Away

Almost three months after Waterloo the remnants of the 1st Regiment of Foot Grenadiers of the Imperial Guard paraded for disbandment. The scene is best described in the words of the Guard's historian, Henry Lachouque:

> On 11 September Old Man Roguet, with death in his soul, reviewed the 1st Grenadiers for the last time. 'Without a murmur', according to the Inspector [the officer charged with disbanding the regiment], General Petit, and Major Combes and Loubers, 23 officers, 95 NCOs, 24 sappers and 707 grenadiers listened impassively as seventeen drummers beat 'To the Colours'; then their flag was delivered to the Inspector. Tears were rolling down the mustaches of the grenadiers. For three-quarters of them life was over.

For fifteen or more years the Imperial Guard had been masters of Europe. After Waterloo, disbanded and disgruntled, they were scattered about France and beyond. Some had no talents beyond the manual of arms, but all belonged to an élite company, a brotherhood. Most found a home where they could put away their uniform and hang their medals under a portrait of their Emperor. Old men sat to tell tales, to relive their glories. Toasts were drunk to 'the other one' or 'his Guard'. They never forgot 'him'. When he died on St Helena many refused to believe it. A rumour said he had landed at Ostend. 'Where are you going?' asked the wife of a Belgian veteran when he pulled on his grenadier's greatcoat. 'To him!' was the instant response.

In 1845 there was a dinner for former officers. Fifteen years later survivors received from 'his' nephew the St Helena Medal, while trumpeters of the old horse châsseurs saluted with the fanfare, 'To the Emperor' at the foot of 'his' column.

was a part. He was an officer with wide Peninsula experience. It was part of his responsibility to oversee the ammunition supply to units in the 3rd Division. He later wrote:

> Much has been said of Baring's having sent repeatedly for ammunition, and that none was sent to him. This matter has certainly been grossly mismanaged. The arrangement for the brigades getting their spare ammunition was, that each brigade should communicate with the guard over the ammunition, and order forward what was wanted. How the brigade failed to do this has not been explained, as so many of its superior officers fell in action.

In other words, it was up to brigades to go to the park and ask for it. A wagon would then be sent forward. It is certain that Baring repeatedly sent messengers back to (presumably) the brigade where they would have sought out the brigade major or any officer. The brigade commander and his staff were assuredly well aware that La Haie Sainte needed resupplying, not only by some of Baring's messengers getting through, but also by military common-sense, as the garrison was almost surrounded and under persistent attack. Other units in the brigade and division were replenished, so why not Baring?

• Major Heise of the 2nd Light Battalion, KGL who was an ADC to the divisional commander, Lieutenant-General Alten, offers a plausible explanation. He stated that the cart with the ammunition was overturned on the Genappe road during the confusion when the Cumberland Hussars bolted from the battlefield.

• It does not appear to be recorded whether or not there were separate carts for rifle ammunition, or whether they were merely separate casks of cartridges on the same wagon as a lot of musket ammunition. If the latter was the case then that for Baring may have got diverted to other units. If the former then an accident or delay to one wagon could have caused the failure. Assistant-Commissary Richard Henegan, the officer commanding the Field Train, has made the comment that possibly all the rifle ammunition had already been issued. The truth is that there is a multitude of reasons.

• However, all these explanations assume the need for a cart taking the ammunition – something that the circumstances at the farm made virtually impossible. Once the farm was more or less surrounded, while it might be possible for reinforcements to fight their way in or individuals to slip through, a horse-drawn cart might have found it too perilous, if not impossible, to approach. As at Hougoumont, a cart would have to enter through the main gate. At La Haie Sainte this entailed driving down the main road between the cuttings exposed to heavy fire, with Frenchmen a few metres from the gate. Even if they reached the gate, it was heavily barricaded from the inside and could not be opened without difficulty and at the risk of the attackers rushing in. Finally, the road was itself blocked by a barricade just north of the sandpit. The only way ammunition could have been got into the farm compound was through the kitchen garden at the rear and thence through the passage in the farmhouse. In other words it would have to have been manhandled in.

• Captain Shaw, when a general with plenty of hindsight, nevertheless made the very valid point that once Baring knew he was to defend the farm early that Sunday morning he should have stocked up with ammunition before the battle started. He had at least six hours in which to do so. As Shaw-Kennedy wrote, 'What were 60 rounds per man for the defence of such a post?'

Conclusions
The following conclusions can be drawn from this incident:
• The lack of ammunition, both rifle and, at the end, musket, contributed to the fall of La Haie Sainte.
• Baring should take some of the blame for not ensuring that he had reserve stocks before the fighting started. This was a matter of common sense for any commander ordered to defend a post, not military expertise.
• Staff at brigade headquarters almost certainly knew of the desperate shortage of ammunition at the farm, and equally surely tried to get the ammunition. They failed for some reason and probably sent troops instead.
• Whether or not the wagon was overturned (Heise specifically says it was) will never be known. Nevertheless, had a wagon been sent it would have had virtually insuperable problems in getting into the farm.
• That the meagre stocks of ammunition of both types lasted as long as they did was due, in part at least, to the fact that only a comparatively small percentage of the defenders of the buildings could actually see to shoot at any one time.

THE TAKING OF THE EAGLE OF THE FRENCH 105TH LIGNE
The controversy
The argument revolves around whether Captain Alexander Kennedy Clark 1st (Royal) Dragoons (later Lieutenant-General Sir Alexander Clark-Kennedy) or Corporal Francis Stiles (later Ensign Stiles 6th West India Regiment) of the same regiment captured the Eagle of the 105th Ligne. Until modern times the controversy has continued, with the officers of the Royal Dragoons and its successor regiments claiming it was Captain Clark, with the sergeants favouring Corporal Stiles.

Comments
• The 105th Ligne headed the column of Bourgeois' brigade when it attacked Picton's division as part of d'Erlon's corps advance shortly before 2.00 p.m. The Eagle was carried by the 1/105 under Chef de Bataillon Coste. The 1st (Royal) Dragoons captured it after they charged the French column and pushed it back some 200 metres down the forward slope of the ridge. Captain Clark was wounded twice after the Eagle was taken and spent two months in Brussels recovering. A week after the events he wrote to his sister, stating: 'I had the honour to stab the standard bearer of the 45th Battalion of Infantry and take the Eagle which is now in London. It is a very handsome blue silk flag with a large gilt Eagle on top of the pole with its wings spread.'

There are two errors in this statement. The most obvious being that it was the 105th Regiment's Eagle not the 45th (taken by Sergeant Ewart of the Scots Greys) that had been captured. As Clark had only touched the Eagle briefly in the confusion of the mêlée, had been wounded and later forced to leave the field, this mistake is understandable. More difficult to explain is Clark's mistaking a tricolour flag surmounted by an Eagle for one which he claimed to be a blue flag. Five days after the battle Colonel Clifton (then acting brigade commander) wrote to the acting cavalry commander, Colonel Felton Hervey, in the following terms:

> I have particularly to mention my entire satisfaction with the conduct of Brevet Lieutenant-Colonel Dorville, as well as of Brigade Major Radclyffe and Captain Clark, the latter's conduct contributing to a great degree to the capture of the Eagle. The above mentioned officers I beg to recommend to His Grace for promotion.

Waterloo Awards

The British government was exceptionally generous in rewarding all who fought at Waterloo although, as was the custom, the higher your rank the more you got. The thanks of both Houses of Parliament were given to Wellington and to the officers and men; a national monument was to be erected in honour of the victory. Memorials to Sir Thomas Picton and Sir William Ponsonby were to be placed in St Paul's Cathedral. All general officers were decorated, no less than 121 lieutenant-colonels and majors were made Companions of the Military Order of the Bath (CB), fifty-two majors were promoted lieutenant-colonel, and thirty-seven captains to major – all within eleven days.

The battle honour 'WATERLOO' was awarded to twenty British cavalry regiments (including four KGL), thirty-four infantry regiments (including eight KGL), the Royal Artillery, Royal Engineers, Royal Wagon Train, Royal Staff Corps and the German (KGL) Artillery. The British battalions posted at Hal (2/35, 1/54, 2/59 and 1/91) did not qualify.

Ensigns in the Foot Guards were ranked as 'Ensigns and Lieutenants' and the 1st Foot Guards was renamed the Grenadier Guards in the erroneous belief that they had defeated the French Grenadiers of the Imperial Guard. Disability pensions for officers would increase with promotions and not be tied to the rank held at the time of injury. An example of an officer to benefit under this regulation is Captain (Army rank major) John Parker RHA, who lost a leg at Waterloo serving in Lieutenant-Colonel Ross's troop, but who subsequently rose to be a major-general. Subaltern officers who participated were granted two years extra seniority plus an extra shilling a day after five years' service. Every NCO, trumpeter, drummer and private was to be shown on the muster rolls and pay lists as a 'Waterloo Man' and could count an extra two years' service towards pay and pension. Two years after the battle prize money was paid to all participants. The amounts were:

Commander-in-chief	£61,000
Generals	£1,275 10 11
Colonels and field officers	£433 2 5
Captains	£90 7 4
Subalterns	£34 14 9
Sergeants	£19 4 4
Corporals, drummers, privates	£2 11 4

At this stage it seems Clifton was not entirely convinced that Clark had actually captured the Eagle himself. It is worth noting that of the three officers recommended for promotion, Clark was the only one not to receive it – much to his disgust.

• By July 1815 Clark was still recovering and becoming increasingly anxious that his deeds at Waterloo had been overlooked (he was unaware of Clifton's letter to Hervey). His worry was that he had not received any brevet promotion and that his absence from his regiment was resulting in his being forgotten by the authorities. He wrote to Colonel Dorville, who had received brevet rank for his taking command of the regiment at Waterloo after Colonel Clifton had replaced the wounded acting brigade commander. It was a blatant, almost pathetic plea for promotion based on his claim to have captured an Eagle:

It is a terrible blow to me to be absent at this moment. If I was able to be on the spot, it is possible I might succeed in procuring brevet rank but as it is, I have no person sufficiently interested in my progress in the army to exert themselves on my behalf. I give you my solemn word of honour that I do not believe the standard bearer was touched by anyone until I reined up my horse and ran my sword through his right side above the kidneys, when he fell more than half down and I could touch part of the silk cord but could not hold it … . If you can do me a good turn I shall be grateful. But you will also do me a favour if you will give me your opinion on this business. If you think I have no claim, please tell me and I shall be obliged to you for your candour.

• Dorville obviously felt Clark had a point since he took the matter to Colonel Clifton (the commanding officer of the 1st (Royal) Dragoons at the start of the battle). Clifton instructed Lieutenant-Colonel Charles Radclyffe (the brigade major at Waterloo and a renowned swordsman who took a musket ball in the knee during the battle) to investigate. He submitted statements from Clark and Privates Anderson and Wilson, both of whom had been closely involved in the struggle. Clark stated:

… I perceived a little to my left an enemy's Eagle with which the bearer was making away with the intention of carrying it off to the rear. I immediately rode to the place calling out to secure the colour and at the instant I reached the spot ran my sword into the officer's right side who carried the Eagle. He staggered and fell forward. But I do not think at this time reached the ground on account of the pressure of his companions. I called out a second time, 'Secure the Colour! It belongs to me!' This was addressed to some of the men close behind me at the time. The officer was in the act of falling and as he fell with the Eagle a little towards the left, I was not able to catch the standard so as to hold it. Corporal Stiles and some other men rushed to my assistance and the Eagle was secured, it falling across his horse's neck, as he came up on my left, before it reached the ground. I immediately ordered the corporal to carry it to the rear and I remained though wounded, in charge of my squadron.

According to Radclyffe, Anderson's statement was to the effect that:

Anderson was to the left of Captain Clark when he stabbed the officer. He and the officer fell and the eagle fell across the heads of his and Captain Clark's horses and against that of Corporal Stiles. Captain Clark called out twice together 'Secure the Colour.' Corporal Stiles seized it and carried off the Eagle to the rear. He [Anderson] was wounded soon after and rode part of the way from the field with the corporal.

Wilson's description of events, as stated by Radclyffe, was that:

Wilson was about to quit the field when he heard Captain Clark call out to secure the colour and turned about to assist in taking it. He was a horse's length to the right of Captain Clark when he stabbed the officer who carried it. The Colour and Eagle fell against the neck of Corporal Stiles' horse who snatched it up and galloped off to the rear. A man of the Greys, I believe a sergeant [this was Ewart] who took another and he [Wilson] saw them both [Stiles and Ewart] on the road to Brussels.

• About a year after the battle Colonel Clifton was still struggling to get to the bottom of this issue. He sent for Corporal Stiles. During the interview he made it plain that Stiles needed some witnesses as to what happened if his claim to have taken the Eagle was to be substantiated. Stiles wrote to his former troop commander at Waterloo, Lieutenant George Gunning, as he claimed that it was Gunning who had ordered him to attack the Eagle. He dated his letter 31 July 1816 at Ipswich Barracks:

> Sir,
> This day Colonel Clifton did send for me about the taking of the Eagle and Colour. He asked me if I had any person who saw me take the Eagle; I told him you see me. I believe as the officer of the French was making away with it. I belonged to your troop, at the time and you gave me orders to charge him, which I did and took it from him. When I stated it to him this day, he wants to know the particulars about it and me to write to you for you to state to him how it was. I would thank you to write to the Colonel, as you were the nearest officer to me that day. Sir, by doing so you would much oblige.
> Your most obedient humble servant,
> Francis Stiles
> Sergeant in Royal Dragoons

Interestingly, Stiles was somewhat coy about his recent promotion; when he wrote this letter he had been an ensign since April. Whether or not Gunning replied is not known.

• During the next twenty-three years a thoroughly disgruntled and frustrated Clark was to submit his statement to higher authority no less than ten times. It certainly reached Wellington. He made it to major in 1825 and lieutenant-colonel in 1830. The following year he applied for the Order of the Bath, submitting his statement or Memorial, as he now called it, to support his claim. It was not granted. Clark did eventually get the promotion he craved, making it to lieutenant-general in 1860. He died four years later.

• Corporal Stiles claimed that he took the Eagle after being given an order to attack it by his troop commander, Lieutenant Gunning. Gunning's version of events has never materialized. However, like Sergeant Ewart, Stiles was promoted, first to sergeant and then to ensign. Performing an exceptionally gallant action in combat was one way for a soldier or NCO to receive a commission. It had to be recommended by the commander-in-chief in the field and be referred to Horse Guards for the final agreement of the Prince Regent to bestow the commission. In this case Wellington approved Stiles's recommendation, which presumably had originated with his unit or brigade. This presupposes that a number of senior officers considered that he captured, or at least played a major part in the capture, of the Eagle. Colonel Clifton's comment on Clark's conduct a week after the battle bears repeating: 'contributing to a great degree to the capture of the Eagle'.

• An interesting aside on this issue concerns a Lieutenant Charles Bridges of the 1st (Royal) Dragoons. His name does not appear in Dalton's *Waterloo Roll Call* as he never received the Waterloo Medal, although he was certainly present on the field with his regiment when it charged Bourgeois' brigade. He features in this incident as at some stage Stiles handed the Eagle to Bridges, if only briefly, for safe custody. However, this officer's conduct at Waterloo almost brought him in front of a court martial for cowardice. Colonel Clifton held an unofficial regimental meeting of officers at Major Dorville's house to enquire into Bridges' conduct. Why had he left the regiment before or during the charge? Bridges made no attempt to deny he had done so, excusing himself by saying his saddle had turned and then that his horse had bolted. Nobody believed him. His choice was resignation or face arrest and court martial. He chose the former, although he did not leave the regiment until December 1816.

Conclusions

The most likely conclusion is that Captain Clark, Corporal Stiles and probably several other soldiers all contributed to the capture of this Eagle. There is strong evidence to suggest that Clark killed the French officer carrying the Eagle, but was unable to get hold of it himself at that moment. It would seem Stiles grabbed the Eagle as it fell across his horse and rode to the rear with it – possibly on orders from Clark. It is strange there is no record of Lieutenant Gunning's views on the matter. Stiles was directly rewarded for its capture but Clark was not. There may be some injustice here but Wellington had approved Stiles's promotion for his actions and Clark's repeated and prolonged protestations, coupled with demands for recognition, can have done little to endear him with the authorities – although he made it to the top in the end.

GENERAL CAMBRONNE'S WORDS
The controversy

Cambronne was with the square of the 2/1 Châsseurs of the Imperial Guard as they retreated slowly and under heavy attacks towards La Belle Alliance after the Guard's repulse. By the time they neared the farm they had been reduced to less than 200 men. According to most accounts the remnants were called on to surrender. Cambronne was supposed to have shouted back either '*Merde!*' ('Shit!') or the more heroically polite '*La Garde meurt, elle ne se rend pas!*' ('The Guard dies, but does not surrender!')

Comments

• It is an established fact that Cambronne was captured by Colonel Hew Halkett personally (see p. 399) during the general advance in which his brigade led the way. All authorities agree that Cambronne had suffered a head wound, probably by a spent musket ball, at about the time of his capture. The wound was slight and did not prevent Cambronne from attempting to escape capture.

• Cambronne was very much the rough spoken, hard as nails ex-ranker – a soldier's soldier. For this reason perhaps '*Merde!*' is the more likely in the circumstances, the modern English equivalent being 'F*** off!' Of course he could have said both – the shorter followed by the longer.

• The controversy over what he said, if anything, grew after the battle. Cambronne initially did not deny the short expletive but later in England when he was to marry into a wealthy English society family, began to refute such vulgarity and emphasize the politer version. His alleged response was later immortalized by Victor Hugo in his writings, while the words '*La Garde meurt, elle ne se rend pas!*' is inscribed on his tomb at Nantes.

• Some recent authors have claimed that because he was wounded and captured he could not have said these words. This does not necessarily follow as he could have responded to a call to surrender before his capture. A letter to *The Times* dated 18 June 1932 makes amusing reading. It was sent in by the great-great-grandson of Colonel Hew Halkett. It reads in part:

Napoleon's Carriage

The Emperor lost his famous campaign carriage in the chaos and confusion of the stampede to get away. It was captured and plundered at Genappe. On 19 June the Commissariat officer Tupper Carey passed it surrounded by Prussians 'scraping and sifting the ground, in consequence of a report that some diamonds had fallen from their settings in the night scramble'.

In the field Napoleon used this large green carriage as a mobile command post. It had strength, stability, manoeuvrability and was weather-proofed. Inside considerable ingenuity had ensured that the needs of a commander on campaign were met. One seat across the back was partially partitioned so that two persons could work without being thrown around. Opposite this was a lockable cabinet with a leaf, which could be pulled out to make a writing desk, and contained several drawers for files, despatches and a map case. Other cupboards contained writing materials, books, telescopes, food, drinks and toilet necessities; a silver chronometer hung on one wall. Napoleon's seat could be converted into a bed, and at night the interior was lit by a large suspended lantern. His camp bed was under the driver's seat; spare clothes and bedding were in the boot. The carriage was designed so that the Emperor and his chief of staff (usually Berthier, but Soult at Waterloo) could travel together and work on the move. Riding outside would be a duty equerry on the right, with a senior officer of the Guard cavalry on the left. Messages could be handed through the window, maps consulted, orders written and ADCs summoned to deliver them – all without stopping. This carriage ended up in Madame Tussauds in London but was later destroyed by a fire in 1925.

... there is in our possession a singularly unflattering French print of the gentleman in question [Cambronne] in uniform, with the bare record of his capture at Waterloo by 'le Colonel Hugh Halkett.' Underneath however, stands a naked sword encircled by a laurel wreath and the following pointed description:
'La Garde meurt, elle ne se rend pas.'
'Cambronne se rend, il ne meurt pas.'
('The Guard dies, it does not surrender. Cambronne surrenders, he does not die'.)

Conclusions

There can never be a definitive ending to this controversy. If you believe he was wounded and captured before he had a chance to say anything then that is the end of the matter. If you do not subscribe to this view then it is certainly possible, even likely, that Cambronne would have responded in an emphatic and soldierly way to be asked to surrender. If he said anything, the odds must surely be on '*Merde!*', with perhaps the longer phrase following. An old gentleman living in Plancenoit had no doubts – he named his house '*Le mot de Cambronne*' ('The word of Cambronne').

THE IMPERIAL GUARD'S FORMATION FOR THEIR FINAL ATTACK (Maps 39–43, pp. 392–400)

The controversy

This argument revolves around whether the Guard advanced and attacked Wellington's line in columns or squares.

Comments

• British witnesses are almost unanimous in claiming the Imperial Guard battalions attacked in columns. A sample is given below:

Ensign Macready, 30th Foot – 'Our regiment and the 73rd were in line four deep behind the hedge, and the enemy's columns two or three hundred yards from them...'.

Ensign Batty, 1st Foot Guards is quoted by one of Wellington's ADCs, Lieutenant Cathcart, as saying there were two columns of twelve battalions.

Lord Edward Somerset, commanding the Household Brigade – 'The advance of the Enemy upon this part of the position was in heavy Columns of Infantry, with crowds of Tirailleurs in their front...'.

Lieutenant Pringle, Royal Artillery – 'The enemy advanced in heavy close column ... the Column waving, at each successive discharge, like standing corn blown by the wind.'

Lieutenant Sharpin, Royal Artillery – '... we saw the French bonnets just above the high corn [it is odd it had not been flattened by then], and within forty or fifty yards of our Guns. I believe they were in close Columns of Grand Divisions...'.

Lieutenant Wilson, Royal Artillery – 'I could see the French advancing, apparently against the right, in heavy masses of close columns.'

Major-General Maitland, commanding the 1st (Guards) Infantry Brigade – 'The force employed by the Enemy in this service consisted of two strong Columns of Infantry...'.

Lord Saltoun, 1st Foot Guards – '... and we advanced against the second Column of the Imperial Guards...'.

Lieutenant and Captain Davis, 1st Foot Guards – '... and the French Guards, whose attack was made in column...'.

Ensign Dirom, 1st Foot Guards – 'The Imperial Guard advanced in close Column with ported arms...'.

And then two who were not so sure:

Captain Rudyard, Royal Artillery – 'The French advanced in masses of Infantry...'.

Lieutenant Gawler, 52nd Foot – 'I cannot describe positively from my own observation the formation of the Enemy, for, ... the smoke was very dense...'. However, he goes on to accept other people's opinion that it was in two columns.

• There is a problem with the supposition by many British witnesses that the French attacked in two columns. It is certain that the French battalions hit Wellington's line over a frontage of some 700 metres – at least from the 30/73 in the east to the right of the 2/1 Guards in the west. Two columns could not have covered this distance and at the same time been engaged by six British battalions in line and then two more on their left (western) flank. We know the assault was actually made by five separate battalions.

• According to Général de Division Petit, who wrote an account of the Guard's advance no later than 1820, there is no doubt that the battalions of the Guard all attacked in square, probably as a precaution against cavalry. Petit was commanding the two battalions of the 1st Grenadiers à Pied. He watched the Guard form up, saw them advance and later consulted with many survivors. He states: 'They [the Guard] passed along the left of the [Genappe] road where they were formed in squares by battalion with the exception of the two 4th Regiments which, in view of their small effectives formed but one square each. ... they were, as has been said, in squares, but all drawn up close to one another. ... The troops advanced in this way at the pas de charge ... and by musketry which crashed into our squares...'.

• It is relevant to point out that the British accounts were all written some twenty years after the event. Only one acknowledged the obvious difficulty of seeing clearly in the smoke – something that surely applied to all. Previous experience of the French before Waterloo was that they attacked in columns; a square with a frontage of about 35 metres with men inside (supernumerary officers, regimental staff, drummers, etc.) could give the impression of a column advancing.

Conclusions

I am firmly of the opinion that the Guard advanced in battalion squares. It is certainly possible that, through the smoke and confusion, the squares resembled columns, which is what the Allies would have been expecting. By the time they arrived at the crest they had been badly mauled by artillery fire, so undoubtedly their formation had become somewhat ragged. There is no good reason to disbelieve General Petit when he states they advanced in squares. Why would he say they were in squares if they were in columns? Surely we must give such an experienced officer who was there, watching it all happen, the credit of knowing the difference between the two.

The Waterloo Subscription and His Majesty's Royal Bounty

The British government set up a fund called the 'Waterloo Subscription' from which to pay annuities for life or limited periods to widows, disabled officers and soldiers, dependent children, relatives and orphans of those who fought at the battle. The public was asked to contribute. The response was excellent. By May 1817 the fund had received some £518,288. Of this, some £190,000 had been disbursed as one off payments, donations or annuities.

In addition there were substantial payments made in the form of annual allowances from a fund entitled His Majesty's Royal Bounty. Such payments were made to widows, parents and children of officers who fell during the campaign, and were in addition to any pension entitlement. Examples make rather sad reading:

Kennedy, Mary, £40. Mother of Lieutenant Kennedy, of the 79th Foot, who was killed in action at Waterloo.

Robertson, Jane, £25; Robertson, Jane, £25, Robertson, Elizabeth, £25 – Mother and sisters of the late Lieutenant John Robertson, of the 9th Foot, who died of wounds received at San Sebastian; and of Ensign Alexander Robertson, of the Royals, who was killed at Waterloo; in consideration of their distressed circumstances.

Meyer, Margaret Caroline, £150 – Widow of Lieutenant-Colonel Lewis Meyer, of the 3rd Hussars, King's German Legion, who died of wounds received at the battle of Waterloo.

Von Wurmb, Louise Fredericke Ernestine Wilelmine, £50 – Widow of Captain Ernest Christian Charles Von Wurmb, of the 5th Line battalion, King's German Legion, who was killed in the battle of Waterloo.

Buckley, Mary, £60 – Widow of the late Captain William Buckley, of the 18th Foot [incorrect, he was serving with the 1/3 Foot], who was killed at Waterloo [wrong again, it was Quatre-Bras] on the 16th June, 1815; she being left with four infant children in distressed circumstances [the last child was born three weeks after her husband's death].

EPILOGUE

After Waterloo

THE FATE OF THE COMMANDERS

The boast of heraldry, the pomp of power,
And all that beauty, all that wealth e'er gave,
Await alike the inevitable hour.
The paths of glory lead but to the grave.

Thomas Gray

Wellington

The Duke made an enormous amount of money from his military victories. His share of the prize money for Waterloo (£61,000) was but a fraction of his overall financial gain. For his victory on 18 June 1815, which finally brought to a close the Napoleonic Wars, a grateful Parliament voted to award him the huge sum of £200,000. But even this pales, almost to insignificance, when compared with the £500,000 awarded for winning the Peninsular War. To the victor go the spoils. He was to have another thirty-seven years to enjoy them, during which time he was to become commander-in-chief of the British Army, Prime Minister and a field-marshal in seven countries' armies – Britain, Austria, Portugal, Spain (captain-general), Hanover, Prussia and the Netherlands.

Wellington was placed in command of the international Army of Occupation of France after the fall of Paris and the re-establishment of the monarchy. One of his first acts was to reject the passionate appeals of Ney's wife to intervene to stop his execution. France was to be occupied by foreign troops for five years, although in fact it was only to last for three. Although initially the Duke enjoyed considerable popularity in France, it did not last. He was soon blamed for any untoward incident. People do not readily accept foreign troops for long; antagonism becomes hatred, confrontations unavoidable. Wellington was quickly seen for what he was: the cold, autocratic commander of a conquering army. He was the target of two assassination attempts. The first occurred in June 1816 and involved an abortive attempt to blow up the Duke's house with a barrel of gunpowder in the cellar – reminiscent of Guy Fawkes. The second, eighteen months later, took the form of the would-be assassin firing a pistol through the window of the Duke's carriage.

In October Wellington returned to England to become the Master-General of the Ordnance and take his place in the Cabinet. It was on his recommendation and insistence that the Waterloo Medal was instituted and awarded to all ranks – a complete break with precedence as medals previously had only been for officers, and senior officers at that. It was a time in England of distressing conditions for most people. Rebellion was in the wind. Mass meetings were held, reform was demanded of the corrupt system of franchise and the repeal of the Corn Laws. There was no police force so such duties devolved on the army. In August 1819 over 50,000 people assembled at a protest meeting at St Peter's Field near Manchester. The military dispersed the crowds, killing six and injuring many more. Ironically, this incident has been known ever since as the 'Battle of Peterloo'.

A year later a radical called Arthur Thistlewood (a former army officer) concocted a plot that became known as the Cato Street conspiracy. It involved a plan to attack a dinner party to be attended by cabinet ministers, including Wellington. It failed and six gang members were sentenced to death, including Thistlewood. On the gallows he was said to have prayed, 'Oh God – if there be a God – save my soul – if I have a soul!'

With the death of the Duke of York in 1827 Wellington was appointed commander-in-chief. After the death of Canning he was persuaded to become Prime Minister in early 1828. He had not wanted the post (he had previously claimed it would be 'an act of madness' for him to take it) but accepted when pressed by the King. He was Prime Minister in turbulent times. There was an ever-increasing clamour for Catholic emancipation. Wellington, initially opposed, supported the bill in Parliament, despite opposition from the King and members of his own party. He was convinced that failure to get the bill passed would have led to civil war. His change of heart provoked an exchange of increasingly acrimonious letters in the *Standard* newspaper between the Earl of Winchelsea, who accused the Duke of 'carrying on his insidious designs for the infringement of our liberties, and the introduction of Popery in every department of the State'. It ended with Wellington demanding 'satisfaction' – a duel. On 21 March 1829 the Duke and the Earl squared off with pistols on Battersea Fields. Both deliberately fired wide and Winchelsea, after some 'arm twisting', apologized.

As soon as Catholic emancipation was carried, the demand for parliamentary reform and extension of the franchise agitated the country from end to end. Wellington, seemingly oblivious to the strength of public feeling, declared against any parliamentary reform whatever. This declaration led to the immediate fall of his government. The new government brought in the Reform Bill. Wellington's continued opposition led to him being booed and hooted at by a mob on the anniversary of Waterloo. At this stage in his life his biographer Herbert Maxwell, in the book *Life of Wellington*, best describes his extreme unpopularity:

> From the pinnacle of fame and popularity he had been lowered to the depths of odium. Coarse reproach and bloodthirsty menace were yelled at him from the very throats which, only a few years before, had ached with unceasing cheers. His matchless services to King and Country were forgotten: for many months he had continued to receive warnings of the danger in which he went of his life; warnings which he put aside lightly enough, although causing the ground-floor windows of Apsley House to be protected by iron shutters, organising a complete system of domestic defence, and, when travelling, carrying loaded firearms in his carriage.

The Reform Bill was eventually passed in June 1832 and Wellington spent two years in opposition. In 1834 Wellington served briefly again in Sir Robert Peel's Cabinet as Foreign Secretary. Again in 1841 he was back in government, but only in his capacity of commander-in-chief. In 1846 he retired from active public life.

Death came peacefully, at Walmer Castle on 14 September 1852. He was eighty-three. There was a lying-in-state at the castle but the funeral did not take place for over two months – there was much work to be done on the preparations. Queen Victoria insisted he be interred in St Paul's Cathedral. The first task was to design the funeral car. Six wheels supported the solid bronze carriage, which was 27 feet long, 11 feet wide and 17 feet high. The sides were covered in gilt carvings and the emblazoned names of the Duke's victories, while the whole was decorated with arms and banners. The bier was to be 6 feet high and 4 feet wide, covered in black velvet. The coffin, covered in crimson velvet, was placed on the bier with the Duke's hat and sword on the lid. The body was contained inside four separate coffins. The inner one, containing his body was of pine, made by the carpenter at Walmer Castle. This was placed in a lead coffin which, in turn, was put inside one of English oak. The outer coffin was of highly polished Spanish mahogany. Twelve black horses, draped in black, under the charge of sergeants from the Royal Artillery were to be used to haul the car.

In the late afternoon of 10 November the Duke's body was transferred to London by rail from Deal station. The escort from the castle to the station was provided by 150 men from the Rifle Brigade. It was met in London by a troop of the 1st Life Guards who escorted the coffin to Chelsea Hospital for a further period of lying-in-state. The Queen paid her respects on 11 November. On 18 November London was not to see another performance like it until the Queen's diamond jubilee at the end of the century. Some 10,000 troops under the command of Major-General the Duke of Cambridge escorted the funeral car. Every regiment in the army was represented. The Royal Horse Artillery was commanded by Colonel Whinyates, the son of the commander of the Rocket Troop at Waterloo. In the centre of this seemingly endless procession was the enormous car itself, the twelve horses being led slowly along behind a Grenadier Guards' band playing the 'Dead March' from Handel's *Saul*. Immediately behind were members of the Duke's family, followed by one of his horses with boots reversed in the stirrups. Then the Royal family and finally the other half of the marching troops. They moved slowly, solemnly, to the monotonous thump of the bass drums. One and a half million people lined the route. Up towards Constitution Hill, through the arch at Hyde Park Corner, past Apsley House, along Piccadilly, down St James's Street to Pall Mall, Trafalgar Square, the Strand and under Temple Bar to St Paul's Cathedral. The two-mile journey took four hours. Britain's foremost soldier was finally laid to rest alongside her foremost sailor.

Blücher

There was little left of Blücher's career, or indeed life, after Waterloo. His troops had the primary responsibility for pursuit after the battle. His army attacked Paris from the south while Wellington's advanced on the north. Blücher remained in Paris for some months but his age and infirmities compelled him to retire to his Silesian estates and residence at Kreiblowitz, where he died on 12 September 1819, aged seventy-seven. The qualities that made him a successful general were his patriotism, his hatred of the French, combined with his courage, determination and the ability to inspire the loyalty of his soldiers. He was the perfect 'Sergeant-Major General' – exactly right for the situation of the Prussians in the Waterloo campaign.

Napoleon

After his defeat the Emperor rode due south escorted by a dozen Red Lancers of the Guard. Riding with him were Soult, Bertrand and Drouot. They passed through Genappe before halting briefly at Quatre-Bras. Napoleon had hoped to be able to utilize Girard's division that had been left at Fleurus as a rear guard, but it never arrived. He rode on, reaching Charleroi by 5.00 a.m. and Philippville by 9.00 a.m. on 19 June. They had covered just under 60 kilometres in twelve hours.

Meanwhile Grouchy had proceeded to defeat the Prussians at Wavre, only to learn to his horror at 10.30 a.m. on 19 June that Napoleon had been routed. Grouchy was then only 17 kilometres from Brussels. Although the shock induced him to tears, he quickly recovered and conducted a skilful withdrawal – forever regarded as an excellent example of generalship.

Napoleon arrived in Paris on 21 June exhausted but determined to gather together an army of some 200,000 from the depots, the remnants of the Armée du Nord and border garrisons. However, he started by making a political blunder. Instead of dissolving the Chamber of Peers and Deputies and ruling by decree, Napoleon allowed the Chamber to meet. Treachery by political enemies, including Fouche, and opposition by Ney to further resistance, resulted in the Emperor abdicating on 23 June in favour of his son. This condition was ignored. A provisional government was set up under Fouche. When Napoleon appealed to Maréchal Davout (Minister of War and commander-in-chief of the new provisional government) to give him command of the army to attack Wellington and Blücher, who were once again separated and vulnerable, he was refused. Davout told him to leave Paris or he would be arrested. Napoleon was later to say, 'If I had hanged just two men, Talleyrand and Fouche, I would still be on the throne today.' Paris fell to the armies of Wellington and Blücher on 3 July, after some sharp fighting the day before. Louis XVIII arrived five days later.

On 29 June Napoleon left Paris for Rochefort on the west coast. Could he escape by sea? For almost a month after Waterloo, and despite the close blockade of French ports by over thirty British warships, strenuous efforts were made to get him away. Two French frigates at Rochefort were alerted for the purpose. However, when Napoleon arrived at the port it became obvious that the obstacles to French ships breaking the blockade were almost insurmountable. Several wild proposals were mooted, including Napoleon's being shut up in a barrel with holes for breathing and placed in a neutral ship. He would have none of it. He had a horror of being taken captive by his enemies (particularly the Prussians). His preference was to surrender with honour, and place himself under the protection of his adversaries. In truth the idea of life in America as an ordinary citizen had little appeal. When his brother Joseph arrived in Rochefort Napoleon was on the islet of Aix in the centre of the Basque Roads. Joseph nobly offered to remain on Aix and impersonate Napoleon while he attempted to make a break, but Napoleon declined the offer. Joseph departed and succeeded in getting to America by ship.

On 15 July Napoleon surrendered to Captain Maitland on board the 74-gun warship HMS *Bellerophon* that had fought at Trafalgar, saying, 'I come to throw myself on the protection of your Prince and your laws'. English breakfast was served, which Napoleon did not enjoy. From that time until his death six years later he regarded himself not as a prisoner of England but as a guest. Although the *Bellerophon* sailed first to England, Napoleon was not allowed ashore. The British Prime Minister, Lord Liverpool, had proposed St Helena as his only possible destination.

At Torbay and then in Portsmouth harbour his close proximity caused great excitement. Crowds of sightseers clambered into small boats to catch a glimpse of the man who had straddled Europe for more than a generation. Napoleon encouraged their curiosity by appearing on deck frequently and doffing his hat to any well-dressed woman he saw. At Plymouth frigates positioned themselves on either side of the *Bellerophon* and put out guard boats, which rammed the tourist craft, capsizing one and drowning an occupant. Volleys were fired in the air but the crush grew worse. On 30 July about 1000 craft bobbed and jostled around the warships. Seamen on the *Bellerophon* erected a large blackboard on which Napoleon's activities were chalked up: 'At breakfast', 'In his cabin', 'Dictating to his officers' or 'Coming on deck' were some of the brief but informative bulletins posted.

He was transported to St Helena on HMS *Northumberland*. The officers were somewhat startled by his eating habits, which coupled with his sedentary lifestyle on the island may have hastened his end. He ate every dish using his fingers instead of a fork:

'At dinner he ate heartily of every dish, his fork remaining useless, while his fingers were busily employed.' He seemed to enjoy the rich dishes and never touched vegetables. At meal times on St Helena he ate fast, masticated little, and never refused creamy pastries. He arrived on the island on 27 October 1815.

Napoleon spent almost six years on St Helena, but only the first two months were reasonably happy. At the beginning he was staying at a place called The Briars, which was temporary accommodation while his permanent residence, Longwood House, was put in order. He did not like Longwood and for virtually all his time on the island he was at loggerheads with the governor, Sir Hudson Lowe (the man Wellington had rejected as his quartermaster-general for the Waterloo campaign), who arrived in April 1816. After a meeting at which Napoleon lost his temper the two did not meet again (on Napoleon's insistence) during the remaining years of his life. Napoleon was continuously writing to complain vehemently about the injustices inflicted on him – his grievances. For much of the time he was dictating his memoirs, seeking to justify, excuse his failures and putting the most creditable gloss possible on his own actions. They do not make for accurate history in many respects.

When Napoleon died in his fifty-second year he had been sick for at least two years. His symptoms were plain to see: his features were pale and sweaty and his huge belly rested on fat thighs. His last seven weeks were spent suffering a painful, lingering death from what was thought until recently to have been cancer. His long illness had not been helped by a succession of incompetent doctors who diagnosed liver disease, hepatitis and various stomach disorders aggravated by the climate.

When Napoleon had requested a French doctor, priest and cook, the doctor engaged was a semiqualified Corsican named Francesco Antommarchi. He had been the assistant of a prominent anatomist in Florence, in which capacity he had spent much of his time dissecting corpses rather than practising on the living. He was, however, a competent anatomist who later wrote a book on the subject. Among the remedies tried on the unfortunate patient by a number of medical men were bleeding, the application of blisters and emetics. In late March 1821 Napoleon complained of a pain in the abdomen 'like the cutting of a knife'. Antommarchi induced him to take doses of tartar emetic, which induced violent vomiting. His suffering was considerable and he refused to continue the ordeal. The emetic was then disguised in lemonade. Napoleon viewed the glass with suspicion and demanded that Count Montholon drink it. Montholon was instantly sick, prompting Napoleon to turn furiously on Antommarchi calling him an 'assassin'. He had lost all confidence in medicines, exclaiming on one occasion, 'I do not wish to have two diseases, one due to nature and the other to medicine'.

Napoleon's Grievances

Napoleon's stay on St Helena was an unhappy one for him. The differences between himself and the governor, Sir Hudson Lowe, were never reconciled and as the years passed he fought a losing battle with poor health and pain. He compiled a list of ten grievances against the British Government. The struggle to get them accepted or alleviated was endless and monotonously unsuccessful. They were:

1 His detention – he objected to being treated as a prisoner of war.
2 The place of detention – he objected to the isolation.
3 The climate – he claimed it was unhealthy.
4 Longwood House – he claimed it was inadequate.
5 Sir Hudson Lowe – the two were incompatible.
6 His title – he wished to be called the Emperor Napoleon not 'General Bonaparte'.
7 Limits – he objected to the restrictions on movement beyond certain limits without a British escort.
8 Visitors – there was conflict with the issue of passes allowing visitors to Longwood.
9 Correspondence – he demanded freedom of correspondence. When not granted he resorted to sending secret letters to Europe via obliging ships' captains.
10 Provisions – he objected to budgetary restrictions being imposed on his staff and food.

The 1995 publication of Dr Ben Weider's and toxicologist Sten Forshufvud's book *Assassination at St Helena Revisited* sets out to prove that Napoleon died as a result of arsenic poisoning over a long period of time, not of cancer. Their evidence is compelling. People who die of cancer do not die fat, but Napoleon was supposedly grossly overweight at the time of his death. When his body was exhumed seventeen years after burial it was in a remarkably good state of preservation. The authors attribute this to the arsenic in the body preserving it, explaining that biologists have long known of its preservative properties in preparing museum specimens of birds and other small animals.

A sample of Napoleon's hair was submitted to the Federal Bureau of Investigation's top expert for testing for arsenic. The result was positive. Traces of arsenic, twenty to thirty times normal levels and fully consistent with poisoning, were confirmed. The authors contend that the arsenic (administered in wine) was not intended to kill quickly but rather to break down Napoleon's health gradually. Shortly before his death he was given calomel to relieve his constipation and orgeat to relieve his thirst (both symptoms of chronic arsenic intoxication). These combined in the stomach, creating mercury cyanide that brought on his actual death. The authors point the finger at Count Montholon as the assassin. By no means do all modern medical professionals accept this idea, pointing instead to the clear findings of the autopsy which revealed considerable cancerous growth in the stomach. Napoleon's father had died of cancer before he was forty-five, and his son always had a dread that he would die the same way. Perhaps it was a combination of both.

Napoleon realized he was dying. At the end he was delirious much of the time, but in a period of near normality he declared: 'When I am dead each one of you will have the sweet consolation of returning to Europe. You will see your relations and your friends; as for me, I shall rejoin my comrades in the Elysian Fields ... [they] will come to meet me; they will talk of what we have done together. ... We will talk of our wars with Scipio, Hannibal. Caesar, Frederick. There will be pleasure in that.'

On the evening of 5 May, shortly after the sunset gun had fired, his time finally came. His mouth fell and his eyes opened; the shallow breathing stopped. He was covered with the cloak he wore at Marengo, a crucifix upon it; by his side they placed his sword. He was buried four days later among willow trees close to a place called Hutt's Gate, near the centre of the island in an area known as Geranium Valley. Napoleon had chosen the spot himself. It was peaceful. The water from the nearby brook had been brought every day to Longwood for him to drink. He was dressed in his favourite uniform of the Châsseurs à Cheval of the Imperial Guard, with his decorations, white breeches, long boots and spurs. Twelve grenadiers of the 20th Foot (East Devon) carried the coffin to the funeral carriage. The procession was a third of a mile long. Behind the carriage came his horse 'Sheikh', then his personal household, midshipmen of the squadron, naval and army officers, members of the island council, the commandant, the admiral, the governor, the French commissioner, followed by units of the garrison, arms reversed. The troops were headed by the St Helena Volunteers, followed by the St Helena Regiment, St Helena Artillery, the 66th Foot (Berkshire), Royal Marines, the 20th Foot (East Devon) and the Royal Artillery. Twenty-four grenadiers from every unit present bore the coffin from the carriage to the graveside, where his Marengo cloak and sword were removed. Three volleys of musketry were fired, followed by a 33-gun salute. The noise was deafening. Then there was the booming of the minute guns from the ships in the harbour.

When the grave was filled in, the site was covered by a large cement slab. There was no name on the slab; Napoleon's companions had wanted the name 'Napoleon' but Sir Hudson Lowe insisted on 'Napoleon Bonaparte' – so in the end there was nothing. A metal fence later surrounded the area.

Twenty-five years after his defeat at Waterloo Napoleon got his wish – he was taken home to France and interred at Les Invalides. On 5 December 1840 the surviving 'Grumblers' of the Imperial Guard shook out their moth-eaten greatcoats and, bent and shuffling, formed behind 'his' hearse for the final parade. Veterans came from Belgium and the Rhineland to march again down the Champs Elysées, under the Tricolour, under the Eagles. As the sixteen black horses drawing the funeral car moved slowly along, guns crashed, crowds cheered and memories flooded back.

Napoleon's Post-Mortem

Antommarchi was given the honour of cutting up Napoleon's body in front of six doctors, all agog to discover the cause of death. Lieutenant-Colonel Sir Thomas Reade recorded the proceedings:

> During the first part of the operation nothing appeared to arrest the attention of the medical gentlemen except the extraordinary quantity of fat which covered almost every part of the interior, under the chest, but particularly about the heart, which was literally enveloped in fat.... . They found the stomach had adhered to the left side of the liver, in consequence of the stomach being very much diseased. The medical gentlemen immediately and unanimously expressed their conviction 'that the diseased state of the stomach was the sole cause of his death'. The stomach was taken out and exhibited to me. Two-thirds of it appeared in a horrible state covered with cancerous substances...

Reade ordered Assistant-Surgeon Rutledge to remain in the room all night and not to let the body, heart or stomach (these latter having been put in a vase) out of his sight – Antommarchi wanted to take the stomach to Europe to prove death could not be attributed to him.

The next day a plaster cast was taken of Napoleon's head. Lieutenant Darroch of the 20th Foot wrote to his mother, 'I went in once again when they were taking the cast of the head, but the stench was so horrible that I could not remain.'

BIBLIOGRAPHY

Barthorp, Michael, *Wellington's Generals*, Osprey, London, 1978

Beamish, N.L., *History of the King's German Legion*, London, 1837

Becke, A.F., *Napoleon and Waterloo Vol. 2*, Kegan Paul, Trench, Trubner & Co. Ltd, London, 1914

Belloc, Hilaire, *Six British Battles*, Arrowsmith, Bristol, 1931

Blanco, R.L., *Wellington's Surgeon-General Sir James McGrigor*, Durham, North Carolina, 1974

Bourrienne, de Fauvelet, *Memoirs of Napoleon Bonaparte Vol. 4*, Charles Scribners and Sons, London, 1891

Bowden, Scott, *Armies at Waterloo*, Empire Games Press, Arlington, Texas, 1983

Boyd, D., *The Royal Engineers*, 1975

Brack, Antoine F. de, *Avant-Postes de Cavalerie Legere*, Broese, Breda, 1824

Brett-James, Antony, *The Hundred Days*, Macmillan & Co. Ltd, London, 1964

Bukhari, Emir, *Napoleon's Cavalry*, Osprey, London, 1979

— *French Napoleonic Line Infantry*, Almark Publishing Co. Ltd, New Malden, 1973

Caldwell, George and Cooper, Robert, *Rifles at Waterloo*, Bugle Horn Publications, London, 1995

Cantlie, Lieutenant-General Sir Neil, *A History of the Army Medical Department Vol. 1*, Churchill Livingston, London, 1974

Chalfont, Lord (Ed.), *Waterloo, Battle of Three Armies*, Sidgwick and Jackson, London, 1979

Chandler, David, *Waterloo: The Hundred Days*, Osprey, London, 1980

— *The Campaigns of Napoleon*, Weidenfeld & Nicolson Ltd, London, 1966

— *Dictionary of the Napoleonic Wars*, Arms and Armour, London, 1979

Chesney, Charles C., *Waterloo Lectures*, Longmans, Green and Co., London, 1907

Coignet, Captain, *The Note-Books of Captain Coignet*, Peter Davies, London, 1928

Connolly, T.W.J., *History of the Royal Sappers and Miners Vol. 1*, London, 1857

Dalton, Charles, *Waterloo Roll Call*, Eyre and Spottiswoode, London, 1904

De Bas, Colonel F., and de Wommerson, Le Comte J. de T'Serclaes, *La Campagne de 1815*, Brussels, 1908

Elting, John R., *Swords Around a Throne*, Weidenfeld and Nicolson Ltd, London, 1988

Evrard, E. (Ed.), *Medic: Evolution du Service de Sante Militaire*, Brussels, 1997

Fortescue, J.W., *History of the British Army Vol. 10*, Macmillan & Co. Ltd, London, 1920

Gardner, Dorsey, *Quatre Bras, Ligny and Waterloo*, Kegan Paul, Trench & Co., London, 1882

Gaulle, General Charles de, *France and her Army*, Hutchinson & Co., London, 1945

Gleig, Rev. G.R., *Battle of Waterloo*, John Murray, London, 1849

Glover, Michael, *Wellington's Army*, David and Charles, London, 1977

Gronow, R.H., *The Reminiscences and Recollections of Captain Gronow*, 2 volume edition, J.C. Nimmo, London, 1889

Hamilton, Sir F.W., *The Origin and History of the 1st or Grenadier Guards*, London, 1874

Hamilton-Williams, D., *Waterloo, New Perspectives*, Arms and Armour, London, 1993

Haythornthwaite, Philip J., *Uniforms of Waterloo*, Arms and Armour, London, 1996

— *Die Hard*, Cassell, London, 1996

— *Weapons and Equipment of the Napoleonic Wars*, Blandford Press, Poole, 1979

— *Napoleon's Specialist Troops*, Osprey, Oxford, 1988

— *Napoleon's Light Infantry*, Osprey, London, 1983

— *Wellington's Specialist Troops*, Osprey, London, 1988

— *The Napoleonic Source Book*, Guild Publishing, London, 1990

Head, Michael, *French Napoleonic Artillery*, Almark Publishing, New Malden, 1973

— *Foot Regiments of the Imperial Guard*, Almark Publishing, London, 1973

Hofschroer, Peter, *1815: The Waterloo Campaign – Wellington, his German Allies and the Battles of Ligny and Quatre Bras*, Greenhill Books, 1997

— *1815: The Waterloo Campaign – The German Victory*, Greenhill Books, London, 1999

Horricks, Raymond, *In Flight with the Eagle*, D.J. Costello (Publishers) Ltd, Tunbridge Wells, 1988

Houssaye, Henry, *1815: Waterloo*, Adam and Black, London, 1900

Hughes, Major-General B.P., *Firepower*, Purnell Book Services, London, 1974

Keegan, John, *The Face of Battle*, Jonathan Cape, London, 1976

Kennedy, Sir James Shaw, *Notes on the Battle of Waterloo*, London, 1865

Kincaid, Captain J., *Adventures in the Rifle Brigade, in the Peninsula, France and the Netherlands from 1808–1815*, London, 1830

Lachouque, Henry, and Brown, Anne S., *The Anatomy of Glory*, Arms and Armour, London, 1978

Lachouque, Henry, *Waterloo*, Arms and Armour, London, 1972

Linck, Tony, *Napoleon's Generals: The Waterloo Campaign*, Emperor's Press, Chicago, 1994

Longford, Elizabeth, *Wellington: The Years of the Sword*, World Books, London, 1971

Mackinnon, Daniel, *History of the Coldstream Guards*, London, 1835

Maxwell, Herbert, *The Life of Wellington*, Sampson, Low, Marston and Co., London, 1907

Mercer, Cavalie, *Journal of the Waterloo Campaign*, Peter Davies Ltd, London, 1927

Nafziger, George, *Imperial Bayonets*, Greenhill Books, 1995

Nash, David, *The Prussian Army 1808–1815*, Allmark Publishing, London, 1972

Navez, Louis, *Le Champ de Bataille et le Pays de Waterloo en 1815*, Brussels, 1908

A Near Observer, *Additional Particulars to the Battle of Waterloo*, John Booth, London, 1817

Nofi, Albert A., *The Waterloo Campaign*, Combined Publishing USA, 1993

Nosworthy, Brent, *Battle Tactics of Napoleon and his Enemies*, Constable, London, 1995

Oman, C.W.C., *Wellington's Army*, Edward Arnold, London, 1912

Paget, Julian, and Saunders, Derek, *Hougoumont*, Leo Cooper, London, 1992

Park, S.J. & Nafziger, G.F., *The British Military 1803–1815*, Rafm Co. Inc., Cambridge, Ontario, Canada, 1983

Pawley, Ronald, *The Red Lancers*, Crowood Press, Marlborough, 1998

Pivka, Otto von, *The Black Brunswickers*, Osprey, Reading, 1973

— *The King's German Legion*, Osprey, Reading, 1974

Priesdorf, von, *Soldatisches Fuhrertum*, Germany, 1930

Rothenberg, Gunther E., *The Art of Warfare in the Age of Napoleon*, Batsford, London, 1977

Siborne, Major-General H.T. (Ed.), *Waterloo Letters*, Cassell and Co. Ltd, London, 1891

Siborne, W., *History of the War in France and Belgium 1815*, T & W Boone, London, 1848

Speeckaert, Georgs, Patrick and Baecker, Isabelle, *Les 135 Vestiges et Monuments Commemoratifs des Combat de 1815 en Belgique*, Belgium, 1990

Uffindell, Andrew and Corum, Michael, *On the Fields of Glory*, Greenhill Books, London, 1996

Ward, S.G.P., *Wellington's Headquarters*, Oxford University Press, London, 1957

Waterloo Memoirs, 1817

Weller, Jac, *Wellington at Waterloo*, Greenhill Books, London, 1992

Wise, Terence, *Artillery Equipments of the Napoleonic Wars*, Osprey, Oxford, 1979

Wood, General Sir Evelyn, *Cavalry in the Waterloo Campaign*, Pall Mall Press, London, 1897

Young, Peter, *Blucher's Army*, Osprey, Reading, 1973

Periodicals and Papers

Abbot, Major P.E. Royal Artillery (Ed.), 'A Waterloo Letter: The Royal Artillery and its casualties', *Society of Army Historical Research Journal*, 1964

Carey, Tupper, 'Reminiscences of a Commissariat Officer', *The Cornhill Magazine*, Vol.VI, 1899

Churchill, General Horace, 'Letters describing Waterloo and the removal of Napoleon's body from St. Helena', *The Army Quarterly*, July 1935

Clay, Private Matthew, 'Adventures at Hougoumont', *Household Brigade Magazine*, 1958

Collins, Major R.M., 'The 12th Light Dragoons at Waterloo', *Tradition Magazine*, No. 17, 1960

Daniel, John, Edgecumbe, Journal of an Officer in the Commissariat Department of the Army, 1820

Elmer, R. and Lepage, Alison, 'Napoleon's Willow', *The Waterloo Journal* Vol.20, December 1998

Elucidation of Several Parts of His Majesty's Regulations for the Formations and Movements of Cavalry 1808, Home Guards

Gawler, Lieutenant-Colonel George, 'The Crisis of Waterloo', *United Service Magazine*, Part 2, 1936

Gerke, Lucien, 'Another Look at Historic Waterloo', *The Waterloo Journal*, Vol. 19, December 1997

— 'The Grave of Lord Uxbridge's Leg', *The Waterloo Journal*, August 1981

Glover, Gareth, 'Mercer's Troop at Waterloo', *The Waterloo Journal*, Vol.22, April 2000

Greenshields, Dr. Thomas, *The 42nd Royal Highland Regiment at Quatre Bras and Waterloo: An analysis of the Soldier's Discharge Documents*, 1997

Griffiths, Captain F.A. Royal Artillery, *The Artillerist's Manual and British Soldier's Compendium*, Woolwich, 1847

Hillingford, Robert A., 'Incident at Waterloo', *The Waterloo Journal*, Vol.18, December 1996

Kronenberger, Luke, 'The Royal Netherlands Army During the 1815 Campaign', *The Waterloo Journal*, Vol.21, April 1999

Macready, Major Edward, 'Correspondence on Waterloo', *United Service Magazine*, Vol.1, 1845

— 'Comments on Captain Siborne's History of the Waterloo Campaign', *United Service Magazine*, Vol.1, 1844; Vol.2, 1845; Vol.3, 1852

Marshal-Cornwall, Sir James, 'Article on British Artillery at Waterloo', *Tradition Magazine*, No.20, 1960

Moore Smith, G.C. (Ed.), 'General Petit's Account of the Waterloo Campaign', *The English Historical Review*, Vol.18, 1903

'Operations of Picton's Division by an Officer of the Division', *United Service Journal*, Part 2, 1841

Ridgley, Paul, 'Wellington's Funeral', *The Waterloo Journal*, Vol.21, December 1999

Staff Officer, 'Recollections of Waterloo', *United Service Magazine*, Vol.3, 1847

Tennant, R. J., 'The Royal Sappers and Miners', *Tradition Magazine*, No.64

Waterloo Medal Roll, Naval and Military Press, Dallington, 1992

Waters, Lieutenant-Colonel J., Assistant-Adjutant General, *The Morning State: Strength of the British Army on the morning of the Battle of Waterloo 18th June, 1815*, Dispatches of Field-Marshal The Duke of Wellington, Vol.12, 1838

Wellington, *The Dispatches of Field-Marshal the Duke of Wellington during his various Campaigns Vol. 12*, compiled by Lieutenant-Colonel Gurwood, 1838

The Battle of Waterloo – Timechart

Time (*Estimated*)	Anglo-Allied	French	Prussian
6.00 a.m.	Wellington leaves Waterloo for the battlefield. Army in position at Mont St Jean.	En route from Genappe area to La Belle Alliance. Many units still in bivouac.	IV Corps under Bülow starts to move through Wavre en route to the battlefield.
7.00–8.00 a.m.	Wellington inspects position, visits Hougoumont and orders its reinforcement by 1/2 Nassau.	Napoleon at breakfast at Le Caillou. Conference with Soult, Ney, Reille and Jérôme. Confident of victory, he dismisses cautionary advice.	Delay and confusion getting through Wavre due to congestion and fire. Only IV Corps on the move.
8.30–9.00 a.m.	Army takes up final deployment positions.	Napoleon rides forward to La Belle Alliance for a final look at Wellington's position. He is accompanied by staff and the civilian guide Decoster.	Leading units of IV Corps clear Wavre and begin the march west.
9.00–9.30 a.m.		Napoleon, at the front, sends his Imperial Guard engineer commander, General Haxo, to check on any Anglo-Allies' fortifications. His report is negative.	On the march.
9.30–10.00 a.m.	1/2 Nassau under Captain Büsgen arrive at Hougoumont to reinforce the Guard's Light Companies. Wellington meets and halts Lord Saltoun as he withdraws with the Light Companies of 2/1 and 3/1 Guards to the main position after handing over to the 1/2 Nassau.	Napoleon rides back to Rossomme Farm area.	On the march to Lasne River defile. Blücher writes to his liaison officer, Muffling, at Wellington's HQ to say he is marching west to join Wellington and attack the French. Leading elements of IV Corps about half way between Wavre and Chapelle St Robert. They are followed by II Corps (Pirch I) and I Corps (Ziethen).
10.00–10.45 a.m.	1/2 Nassau takes over the defence of Hougoumont buildings, garden, orchard and wood. Colonel Macdonnell with Light Companies of 2nd (Coldstream) and 2/3 Guards move to kitchen garden area west of buildings. Wellington informed via the 10th Hussars that a Prussian patrol has confirmed that Blücher is marching to join him.	Napoleon at Rossomme sends message to Grouchy, sends 7th Hussars to reconnoitre the eastern flank. Dictates his attack order, which Soult times at 11.00 a.m. This envisages an advance by d'Erlon's corps supported by Reille to seize the Mont St Jean crossroads preparatory to a march on Brussels.	
11.00–noon	Army deployment complete except for Lambert's brigade.	Napoleon rides north to La Belle Alliance and reviews his troops as they arrive and move into their forming-up positions. At about 11.00 a.m. Napoleon has second thoughts as to the plan of attack. Ney makes a pencilled note on Soult's 11.00 a.m. orders that the attack will now begin on the left, i.e. with Reille's diversionary attack on Hougoumont.	Losthin's brigade of IV Corps is approaching Chapelle St Robert. Prussian advance is slow due to the mud and congestion. Blücher leaves Wavre and rides along the southern route, encouraging the struggling columns to greater efforts. The Prussians hear the shots of the battle as Reille's guns open fire at 11.20 a.m.
11.20 a.m.–12.20 p.m.	Defend Hougoumont Wood and orchard. By shortly after midday the Nassauers and Hanoverians are driven from the wood and orchard. Bull's Troop of howitzers brought up to fire on Hougoumont Wood. Lord Saltoun with the two Light Companies of 2/1 and 3/1 Guards sent back to retake the Great Orchard at Hougoumont.	Bauduin's 1st Brigade from Prince Jérôme's 6th Division attacks and takes Hougoumont Wood and orchard. The Middle and Old Guards have yet to reach Rossomme. Durutte's 4th Division is still marching into its deployment area. Napoleon gives orders for the expansion of the 'Grand Battery', its task and location. Noon to 12.30 p.m. Napoleon rides back to Rossomme.	
12.30–1.15 p.m.	Bijlandt's Netherlands brigade withdrawn from forward slope to the main position on the ridge. Macdonnell's two companies withdraw inside the château compound at Hougoumont. Sergeant Fraser wounds but spares Colonel Cubiéres near the west wall of Hougoumont. At about 1.15 p.m. three companies followed by another four from the 2nd (Coldstream) Guards drive French from the north of Hougoumont, and reinforce the garrison.	Jérôme launches his 2nd Brigade (Soye) into the attack on Hougoumont. Cubiéres, now commanding the 1st Brigade, attacks round the western side of the château. He is wounded. S/Lieutenant Legros with 30 men succeed in forcing entry through the north gate at Hougoumont. They are trapped inside and all killed (except a drummer) after the gates are shut. French deployment completed. All Imperial Guard grouped north of Rossomme.	Leading units of IV Corps reach Chapelle St Lambert. Blücher arrives at the front of the column and orders a halt to allow further reconnaissance and for trailing units to catch up.

TIME (*Estimated*)	ANGLO-ALLIED	FRENCH	PRUSSIAN
1.00–1.15 p.m.		1.00 p.m. 'Grand Battery' opens fire. Napoleon sights the Prussians near Chapelle St Robert and sends message to Grouchy. The cavalry of Domon's and Subervie's divisions (VI Corps) are sent east to delay the Prussians. At 1.15 p.m. a captured Prussian confirms Bülow's corps is approaching. Napoleon orders the remainder of VI Corps (Lobau) east to block the Prussians.	
1.15–2.15 p.m.	Two companies 2/3 Guards sent to assist Saltoun holding Great Orchard. By this time some 2,600 men are defending Hougoumont and the Great Orchard. The Lüneberg Battalion from Kielmannsegge's Hanoverian brigade almost destroyed by French cuirassiers when attempting to reinforce La Haie Sainte. Bijlandt's Netherlands brigade retreats after offering some resistance on the ridge. Three companies of 1/95 Rifles withdraw from sandpit area. La Haie Sainte isolated. Uxbridge launches the Household and Union Brigades against d'Erlon's corps.	Foy commits his 1st Brigade (Tissot) from his 9th Division to the assault on the Great Orchard at Hougoumont. By 2.15 p.m. his 2nd Brigade is sent in. At this stage 24 battalions (12,700 men) have been drawn into the attempt to take the château. 1.30 p.m. 'Grand Battery's' main bombardment ends and d'Erlon's corps advances to attack Wellington's left. IV Corps starts its march to face the Prussian threat in the east. Colonel Charlet's brigade of Quiot's 1st Division attacks and surrounds La Haie Sainte. Shortly before 2.00 p.m. Dubois' cuirassiers scatter a Hanoverian battalion west of La Haie Sainte. D'Erlon's divisions reach the Anglo-Allied position on the ridge. By 2.00 p.m. Domon's and Subervie's cavalry is arriving to the east of the French position to delay the Prussians. Napoleon has moved forward to his battlefield command post south of La Belle Alliance.	IV Corps remains halted to allow its rearmost units to close up. Ziethen's I Corps begins its march along the northern Rixensart–Grenval–Ohain route to link up with Wellington's left flank. Prussian cavalry is scouting ahead in the Lasne valley and Bois de Paris.
2.15–3.00 p.m.	Defence of Hougoumont continues. 2/3 Guards under Hepburn retake Great Orchard. Saltoun's two companies withdrawn to the ridge. Household Brigade scatters Dubois' cuirassiers west of La Haie Sainte. Union Brigade drives d'Erlon's divisions back in disorder. Sergeant Ewart captures the Eagle of the French 45th Regiment; Captain Clark/Corporal Stiles take the Eagle of the 105th Regiment. Some 2000 prisoners taken. Union Brigade plus some of the Household Brigade charge out of control up to the 'Grand Battery' inflicting heavy losses among the gunners but no guns spiked or destroyed. These British heavy cavalry are scattered by a well-timed French cavalry counterattack from the south and east. Artillery batteries west of crossroads break up Bachelu's attempt to join the assault on Hougoumont. Defence on La Haie Sainte continues.	D'Erlon's corps is driven back in disorder by Wellington's heavy cavalry. 'Grand Battery' temporarily put out of action by Union Brigade. Napoleon launches eleven squadrons of cuirassiers (Travers and Farine) plus five of lancers and three of châsseurs (Jacquinot) in counterattack against Union Brigade, inflicting heavy losses. Union Brigade commander (Ponsonby) killed. About 3.00 p.m. Bachelu's 5th Division from Reille's corps is ordered to attack Hougoumont. His 2nd Brigade (Campi) advances diagonally across the front to assault from the south-east. Driven back by intense artillery fire from the ridge.	The leading brigades of IV Corps (Losthin and Hiller) negotiate the Lasne defile. Progress is slow.
3.00–4.00 p.m.	The buildings in Hougoumont are set on fire. Ammunition is replenished by a daring dash by a Royal Wagon Train driver. La Haie Sainte reinforced by two companies of the 1st Light battalion KGL and one company 5th KGL. Requests for ammunition unanswered. 1/95 Rifles reoccupy the sandpit. Wellington strengthens his centre by summoning Chassé's Netherlands Division from Braine l'Alleud. Three Brunswick battalions moved into the front line.	A renewed strong assault made on La Haie Sainte by Quiot's battalions. The farm and garden virtually surrounded but the French are unable to penetrate the buildings. D'Erlon's corps regroups. Infantrymen replace the 'Grand Battery' casualties, the battery reorganizes and comes into action again. Shortly before 4.00 p.m. Ney mistakes troop adjustments on the ridge, together with wounded moving to the rear, as a more general wavering of Wellington's army. He orders a cavalry assault.	At around 3.30 p.m. the first serious clash occurs between the Prussians, led by Count Schwerin's 1st Cavalry, Brigade and French cavalry on the eastern edge of the Bois de Paris. Schwerin becomes probably the first Prussian to be killed in the battle. The leading infantry units of Bülow's corps enter the Bois de Paris.

TIME (Estimated)	ANGLO-ALLIED	FRENCH	PRUSSIAN
4.00–5.00 p.m.	All infantry battalions in the first and second line west of the Brussels–Nivelles road form square. Wellington's guns take a fearful toll on the attacking cavalry. The infantry squares drive off successive waves of cavalry. The Allies' cavalry brigades in reserve are used to counterattack the French horsemen that penetrate between the squares.	Ney leads forward ten regiments of cavalry, eight of cuirassiers plus the Imperial Guard Châsseurs and the Red Lancers. The attack is preceded by a heavy artillery bombardment. Despite severe losses, the attacks are repeated again and again but no square is destroyed. Lobau's VI Corps engages the Prussians as they debouch from the Bois de Paris. Attacks continue on Hougoumont and La Haie Sainte. Pégot's brigade from Durutte's division is brought across to support the attacks in the centre.	At around 4.30 p.m. Bülow's corps deployed west of the Bois de Paris with Losthin's brigade north and Hiller's south of the track to Plancenoit. It is the start of the Prussians advance to capture the village.
5.00–6.00 p.m.	Wellington pushes forward Adam's brigade onto the forward slope north-east of Hougoumont, partly to stiffen the morale of the Brunswick squares. Despite being heavily reinforced, the French cavalry make no impression on the squares, although their guns inflict considerable damage in the intervals between attacks. 150 men from the 1/2 Nassau reinforce La Haie Sainte.	Ney reinforces failure by doubling the number of cavalry. Kellerman's division and Guyot's heavy cavalry of the Guard advance to renew the assault – but without success. Just before 6.00 p.m. the 13th Légère launches a powerful attack on La Haie Sainte. Lobau's VI Corps is slowly pushed back to Plancenoit. The defence of the village is initially in the hands of Simmer's 19th Infantry Division.	By 5.30 p.m. the whole of IV Corps is in action against Lobau. The heavily outnumbered French are pushed back to Plancenoit. By 6.00 p.m. Ziethen's leading brigade (Steinmetz) has reached Ohain.
6.00–6.30 p.m.	The struggle for Hougoumont continues. The French hold the wood, the orchard has changed hands several times but the buildings remain firmly in the possession of the British Guards and Nassauers. The continued defence of La Haie Sainte becomes impossible, mainly due to an acute shortage of rifle ammunition. By 6.30 p.m. the farm has fallen to the French.	Plancenoit is lost to the Prussians and Napoleon is compelled to send the Young Guard Division of eight battalions to retake it.	The 16th Brigade (Hiller) with the 15th Brigade (Losthin) attacking north of the village launches the first all out assault on Plancenoit. The Prussians succeed in driving the French out. The fighting around the church is particularly intense.
6.30–7.30 p.m.	The loss of La Haie Sainte is a serious blow to Wellington. French artillery causes heavy losses. An ill-timed counterattack by the 5th Line Battalion KGL to retake La Haie Sainte fails, with the battalion being badly cut up by cuirassiers and the death of the brigade commander, Ompteda. The Cumberland Hussars refuse to advance and then disappear along the road to Brussels.	By about 6.45 p.m. the Young Guard succeeds in driving the Prussians out of Plancenoit, thus temporarily holding back the threat to the French rear. Heavily reinforced Prussians are able to retake the village, compelling Napoleon to send first one battalion of the Old Guard in, and then a second to reinforce the defenders. By 7.30 p.m. the village is once again in French hands.	The Young Guard drives the Prussians from Plancenoit. Heavily reinforced, Bülow again attacks and takes the village after desperate close quarter fighting. But they again lose the village when counterattacked by two battalions of the Old Guard. Ziethen's I Corps arriving on the Ohain road is nearly diverted south by Blücher; the leading brigade links up with Wellington's eastern flank.
7.30–8.30 p.m.	By this time Wellington has reorganized and reinforced his centre with Chassé's Netherlands Infantry Division and Vivian and Vandeleur's cavalry brigades from the flanks. Hew Halkett's Hanoverians and Du Platt's KGL brigade have moved forward to support Hougoumont, which is still holding out. Adam's brigade is pulled back from the forward slope to just behind the ridge. Despite some confusion in Colin Halkett's and Maitland's brigades, the four-deep lines roll back the Guard. Their defeat is clinched by a well-timed flank attack by the 52nd Foot from Adam's brigade.	Napoleon prepares for his final effort – an attack by the Imperial Guard as part of a general advance. Five battalions of the Middle Guard form the main assault, supported by three from the Old Guard. The erroneous message that Grouchy has arrived is passed to the other formations to boost morale. Shortly after 7.30 p.m. the Guard starts its advance west of the Genappe road in squares. Napoleon himself rides up the road as far as La Haie Sainte orchard, where he hands over to Ney. The Guard suffers severely from artillery fire during its advance. There are few cavalry able to support the attack. The five leading battalions are thrown back from the ridge by Colin Halkett's, Maitland's and Adam's brigades deployed in line. By 8.30 p.m. the French rout had started.	At about 8.00 p.m. the 5th Infantry Brigade (Tippelskirch) from II Corps (Pirch I) spearheads a final assault on Plancenoit. Within about half an hour the French are driven out of the village for the last time.
8.30–10.00 p.m.	Wellington signals a general advance. The follow up of the retreating Imperial Guard is led by Hew Halkett's Hanoverian brigade and Vivian's light cavalry. Wellington meets Blücher south of La Belle Alliance.	The rush to the rear is in full flow. The Old Guard squares retire slowly and steadily. General Cambronne is captured. Napoleon initially seeks shelter in the square of the 1/1 Grenadiers.	The Prussians take over the pursuit of the fleeing French. They murder many wounded French and ravage and destroy French property as they advance into France. Blücher meets Wellington south of La Belle Alliance.

INDEX